GENERAL STUDIES IN ENGLISH
SOUTHERN ILLINOIS UNIVERSITY

THE ART OF
DRAMA

GENERAL STUDIES IN ENGLISH
SOUTHERN ILLINOIS UNIVERSITY

THE ART OF
DRAMA

R. F. DIETRICH
University of South Florida

WILLIAM E. CARPENTER
University of Delaware

KEVIN KERRANE
University of Delaware

HOLT, RINEHART AND WINSTON, INC.
NEW YORK CHICAGO SAN FRANCISCO ATLANTA DALLAS

For Linn, Melinda, and Sheila

PREFACE

This anthology contains plays that are excellent in themselves, but we had additional reasons for choosing them and for doing this anthology.

Perhaps the most important consideration was our belief, apparently shared by many, that an anthology should provide stimulation for the instructor without usurping his function as a teacher. Nearly every modern anthology has such an abundance of critical apparatus that the instructor finds himself either fighting the text or being replaced by it. Our text avoids both problems by reserving almost all the critical material for an instructor's manual, which the instructor may use as he pleases. The manual contains material that we hope will stimulate fresh thinking about the plays, but, at the same time, will allow the instructor to approach his students without a barrier of preconceived opinion.

Our selection of plays was made on the following bases: we sought, overall, to choose plays that are representative of important types and periods so that the instructor would be able to present a balanced view of drama; we tried as well to include some of the less anthologized plays for the sake of freshness and variety; where translations were involved, we selected the very best available; we deliberately included both *Oedipus Rex* and *Antigone* as a unique feature of our text because we believe that not only are these the two greatest Greek plays but also that they are best taught in tandem; so, too, we included both *Antony and Cleopatra* and *Caesar and Cleopatra* because they are taught remarkably well together; and, finally, many of our plays were chosen because they have been made into films that are readily available to colleges.

In short, we hope you will find this anthology both useful and enjoyable.

Newark, Delaware   R. F. D.
JANUARY 1969   W. E. C.
                                                                    K. K.

Publisher's note: The eight modern plays of this book are also published separately as *The Art of Modern Drama.*

CONTENTS

THE ART OF
DRAMA

TO THE STUDENT

Fiction and Drama. Suppose that you are a budding writer with a "story to tell," and that you wish to render it through the medium of prose fiction. The story will deal primarily with how a young man has been deeply changed by his experience of war, how this change coincides with his passage from adolescence to mature manhood, and how he is no longer capable of living a "simple" civilian life.

Assume you decide, in order to lend immediacy to your story, to make the Vietnam war your main character's experience. But, in order to focus on his conflicts in civilian life, you put the war itself in the background, beginning your narrative with the day after his return home. To emphasize the universal applicability of your theme, you decide to make your main character an "average" young man, relatively unsophisticated. You make his home a small town, and you decide to intensify his conflicts by setting this town in the South, as part of a "traditional" society. Once you have arrived at this decision, you see an extra advantage in it—hot, steamy weather, which can mirror a mood of depression, and which can also provoke people to fits of temper. Your story takes place in midsummer.

Finally, after arriving at other strategic decisions about the pattern of events which will take place in the story, you write a draft of its opening paragraphs:

> Men go to war, and they return. But they are different men.
>
> It was a hot southern day in late June, the morning after Bobby Joe's return. He stepped out of the house warily, feeling slightly improper without his uniform. The smothering Louisiana heat depressed him. He could see that it was starting to drizzle; but the rain would be a light one, and would only add to the burden of the heat.
>
> He walked down the front steps. Suddenly a baseball kicked up dust at his feet and rolled past him, hitting the steps. Bobby Joe retrieved it, then looked up to see a gangly boy loping toward the yard, wearing a catcher's mitt. It was Little Davy Chapman—but not so little now. "God, that kid sure has grown in two years!" Bobby Joe thought. "He's almost big enough for a uniform." After shouting hello, Bobby Joe signaled to Davy that he wanted to pitch the ball to him, and he pegged back a curve, the way he used to in high school. The ball broke neatly and popped into the mitt, but Bobby Joe felt vaguely that something was wrong. He turned toward the street, thinking uneasily of the day before him. Familiar faces asking silly questions: "How were things in Vietnam?" "Hey, how are them Oriental chicks, Bobby Joe?"
>
> He dreaded the thought of conversation with his friends, but still he needed to see them. He started walking up the street, toward Jamie's house. When he came to the middle of the block he began to run.

These opening paragraphs, written especially for this purpose, illustrate explicitly the options open to you as a writer of fiction. You are free to make a thematic statement: "Men go to war, and they return. But they are not the same men." You can inform the reader directly of the story's setting and describe the weather objectively. You are free to add exposition, so that the reader quickly learns that Bobby Joe has just come home from the military, and that he has not seen Davy Chapman for two years. Most important, you have the option of providing *subjective* information: what the central character is thinking, feeling, and experiencing. You can *tell* the reader that Bobby Joe feels "improper" without his uniform; that the heat "depresses" him; that as he looks at Davy Chapman, he "thinks" about how quickly things can change; that he feels strangely uneasy after throwing the ball; and, finally, that he experiences mixed emotions as he thinks about seeing his friends once again.

Now suppose that you had the job of rendering your story in the medium of *drama*—through actors, on a stage, before a live audience. How much of the opening "scene" of your fictional version could be acted out? Very little—for what you could *tell* to the reader of fiction, you must now *show* to the audience of drama. The dramatist makes plays, not for a reader, but for spectators. Or perhaps a better way of stating this obvious fact is that a playwright writes speeches for actors and instructions about sets, costumes, or movements for directors, who, in turn, render the material for the spectators. (This is not to say that plays should not be read, a point that will be dealt with later.)

Your freedom to dramatize your story is inhibited most obviously by the physical limitations of the stage. The sets might suggest a "house" and a "yard," but Bobby Joe's movements will be confined. It would be impossible, for example, to show him walking "to the middle of the block." And what about that baseball? How could it "kick up dust"? Would it not be impractical for the actor to throw the ball within the confines of a normal stage? And who in the audience will be able to see that it is a "curve"? Furthermore, how can the audience be made so specifically aware of the weather? Bobby Joe can react to the heat, of course; he might be wearing light clothes (shorts, perhaps), and he might fan himself. But there will not be much room here for nuance, and it will be difficult to call the audience's attention to such details as the impending rain, unless a character on stage *mentions* it aloud or extensive use is made of special effects such as thunder and lightning.

More serious difficulties await you. How will exposition be provided? The theatre program might tell the audience that the setting of the action is in Rayville, Louisiana, and that the time is "the present." But how can the audience be made aware, seeing Bobby Joe in civilian clothes, that he had been wearing a uniform until the day before? Or that he has not seen Davy Chapman for two years? Or that he pitched baseball in high school? Again, these details will become known only when a character *talks* about them (and has reason or motivation to do so).

Even more important, how can you give the audience a clear impression of Bobby Joe's thoughts and emotions? Stage directions might call for the actor to *step warily out of the house,* and they might provide him with pantomimic gestures for expressing his indecision near the end of the scene. But enlightening as the actor's gestures may be, they represent a less analytical "language" than that which is available to the writer of fiction. (And they will almost certainly depend more on the actor's use of his body rather than his face—which cannot be caught in "closeup," and which the people in the back rows might not even be able to see clearly.) Once again, your "dramatic" solution would have to involve dialogue, and you would have to take special pains to make this dialogue believable. Only rarely in real life do people reveal their innermost thoughts and

feelings aloud. This happens far more often in drama (and it has every right to),
but when it does there should be some dramatic "occasion" for it. You cannot
write the scene so that Bobby Joe, after throwing the ball to Davy Chapman, then
says, "I feel vaguely that something is wrong," and then begins to describe to
Davy the mixed emotions he feels about seeing his friends.

At this point, it should be clear just how much the dramatic medium *limits*
the freedom of the writer, creating barriers between him and his audience, and
pushing him towards "objective" presentation. But it would be a mistake to
think that this objectivity is ever total. The dramatic audience, even more than
the audience at a movie, is aware that what it is seeing is *"artificial"*: that the
performers are acting out episodes conceived, selected, and arranged by a dramatist—episodes which have their own internal coherence, but which are nevertheless "unreal." Usually, theatrical "props" are far more suggestive than realistic; they, like other details in a drama, are meant to convey an impression. The
audience of a drama undergoes a "willing suspension of disbelief"; but they do
not undergo an illusion that commands total "belief."

Moreover, the great tradition of drama has been nonrealistic. Dramatists have
always taken liberties with the supposed "objectivity" of the action onstage, using
accepted conventions of performance in order to "tell" as well as "show" things
to the audience. Greek drama used a "chorus," a group of actors who might
represent characters (for example, the Theban citizens in *Oedipus Rex*), but
who also interrupted the action with chanted odes—filling in the story, commenting directly on events and motives, and guiding the audience's emotions
(sometimes by expressing the emotions the dramatist wanted the audience to
experience). Elizabethan drama used the "soliloquy" and the "aside"—conventions whereby an actor on stage speaks his thoughts aloud to himself when alone,
or speaks them to the audience in the presence of other actors who are not
supposed to be able to hear him. These conventions are occasionally revived in
modern dramas, and some contemporary plays use "narrators"—as in *The
Glass Menagerie* or *A View from the Bridge*—who speak directly to the audience,
and who are also characters in the dramatic action. And these—the chorus, soliloquy, aside, and narrator—are not the final limitations. Imaginative dramatists,
feeling cramped by the traditional conventions of the stage, continually expand
the medium of drama.

It does seem safe to suggest, however, that even the most inventive of dramatists
will always be faced with the task of rendering scenes "objectively." And even
with the freedom that *all* the conventions can give, you would still have a difficult
time writing your fictional opening as a dramatic scene. It is likely, in fact, that
you would have to rethink the *whole* story in dramatic terms to make that first
scene work. (You might use the time-tested device of delaying the appearance
of your main character, allowing other people who have reason to do so—for
example, Bobby Joe's mother and father—to talk about him.) "But why bother?"
you might ask. Is drama merely a secondary form of art, doing crudely and without credibility what prose fiction (and even the movies) can do better? The
answer is that the dramatist, like every other artist, renounces in order to gain.
The medium of drama presents the writer with inherent difficulties, but it offers
"compensations" not available in any other form of art.

Above all, the drama offers a sense of immediacy. The opening paragraphs of
your story about Bobby Joe are (except for the thematic statement) in the past
tense—the tense most natural to fiction. By contrast, a drama exists, even in
written form, in the present tense; the action is always happening "now." No
matter how well we know a play, no matter how many times we have seen or
read it before, its action always pulls us forward, commanding our active attention.

This leads to the second "compensation" of drama: the demands that it makes upon its audience. The more trivial forms of storytelling (for example, the fiction in love-story magazines) are those which force their readers into a passive role by "telling" them everything, making no requirements on the imagination or intellect. In fact, one of the drawbacks to the opening paragraphs of the story about Bobby Joe is that they lack subtlety; the reader can afford to be passive, since he is being hit over the head with the main point from the very beginning. The difference between enjoying fiction of this kind and enjoying a more subtle work like Hemingway's "The Big Two-Hearted River" (also a story about a young man's return from war) is, in one sense, the difference between enjoying checkers and enjoying chess.

Similarly, the medium of drama—with its apparent "objectivity"—forces our imagination and intellect to probe below the surface, to fill in gaps. When we hear two characters conversing at the beginning of a play, a part of our mind should be interpolating the motives of each character for saying what he does; another should be deducing the situation as it existed before the play began; another should grasp certain repeated ideas, phrases, or foreshadowing (for example, "blindness" in *Oedipus Rex*), and think, "Something may come of this." In addition, the "point" of a drama is almost always something we arrive at by seeing a number of characters react to a problem in different ways, each illuminating one aspect of the problem—rather than having the author *tell* us "the whole truth."

Aristotle, in his seminal work of dramatic criticism, the *Poetics* (about 340 B.C.), claimed that other forms of storytelling (for example, the epic) aspire to the condition of drama. The same point has been made in modern times—by Henry James, in speaking about prose fiction, and by T. S. Eliot, in speaking of poetry. These three critics all seem to have had in mind a concept of the superior subtlety of objective presentation. They may also have been thinking of the immense possibilities for irony within the dramatic mode. In a "dramatic monologue" (like Eliot's "The Love Song of J. Alfred Prufrock") the poet himself remains in the background. The speaker addresses another character, or perhaps talks to himself; he is unaware of being "overheard" by an audience. Invariably, there is a discrepancy between what we think of him and what he thinks of himself. The result is that a character unwittingly stands revealed. And if we judge him negatively, the effect is all the stronger because he has damned himself with his own words; the author has "told" us nothing. Ballads are another kind of poetry (significantly, a storytelling form) that exploit the resources of dramatic irony. In "Sir Patrick Spence," for example, the anonymous medieval balladeer has arranged his narrative so that things are suggested rather than stated directly. In the first three stanzas we see the king deciding to send Sir Patrick Spence, an expert sailor, on a dangerous mission; he notifies him in a letter. Here are stanzas four through seven:

> The first line that Sir Patrick red,
>   A loud lauch lauced he;
> The next line that Sir Patrick red,
>   The teir blinded his ee.
>
> "O wha is this has don this deid,
>   This ill deid don to me,
> To send me out this time o' the yeir,
>   To sail upon the se!
>
> "Mak haste, mak haste, my mirry men all,
>   Our guid schip sails the morne."
> "O say na sae, my master deir,
>   For I feir a deadlie storme.

"Late late yestreen I saw the new moone,
　Wi' the auld moone in hir arme,
And I feir, I feir my deir master,
　That we will cum to harme."

The poet does not probe Sir Patrick Spence's motives and emotions, but we are intensely aware of them. In stanza five, Sir Patrick stands alone, bewailing his fate; in stanza six he addresses his men with a confident tone, as though nothing were wrong. Our imagination fills in the "gap" between these two stanzas; we can attribute a complex personality to Sir Patrick, even though the poet has not "described" him from the inside. In addition, when a sailor (unidentified) voices a fearful warning, we know, although he does not, that Sir Patrick is aware of the danger but has chosen to go anyway. This ballad, like many other ballads, jumps without transition from one situation to another, usually concentrating on what is most "dramatic," and, like many ballads, it tends toward a direct transcription of dialogue.

Needless to say, the possibilities for irony inherent in the dramatic monologue and the ballad are multiplied many times in the medium of drama itself. It is worth remarking, however, that irony in a dramatic production can also be more intense, because we are aware *as a group* of something which a character on stage does not know. The appeal of a play to a "group mind" is probably the most difficult to discuss of all the qualities of drama. Many scholars are agreed that drama had its origins in primitive rituals, in which a community or tribe, intensely aware of itself as a group, "imitated" events that they wished to take place (for example, the coming of spring, or a successful hunt). Later, at the Theatre of Dionysus in Athens, the ancient Greeks produced (and attended) plays as part of a collective religious festival. There may be less sense of a religious rite in Elizabethan drama, and even less in modern drama—but the fact remains that plays continue to address themselves to the group spirit. Consider for a moment the experience of watching a play (say, Molière's *The Misanthrope*) as the only person in the audience. Not only would you tend to laugh less at the humor, but you would also be more immediately aware of the props *as props,* the costumes *as costumes,* and the dialogue *as dialogue.* It would become more difficult, in short, to suspend your disbelief. A willing suspension of disbelief seems somehow to thrive upon a *group* will; collectively we sustain the conventions which make dramas "playable."

Reading Plays: The Stage in The Mind. The previous discussion raises the whole question of the difference between *seeing* a play and *reading* it. This textbook is a collection of plays meant to be "taught" in a classroom. But is it possible to do this? Are you, the student, being forced to consider second-rate realities? In a sense, yes. Certainly you will understand any play in this book better if you see a production of it—even a poor production—for the exigencies of stage presentation are such that you are bound to "experience" the play more fully, becoming aware of options in the text that you had not seen before. We should remember, however, that both the actors and the director began as "readers." In fact, the play exists in the form of words before the performance and after, and we can experience what is most essential in it as we read. But in order for any play to "come alive" when we read it, we must willingly allow our imaginations to work, to participate actively in the play, to visualize, and by so doing, to discover a way for the language on the printed page to "play" on the physical stage. Reading dramas requires great concentration, but it yields worthwhile rewards and distinct pleasures. The mind delights in building its own stage, making its own costumes and sets, choosing the perfect actors for every part, and directing the play exactly as it wants. (If, for example, Paul Newman is your perfect Hamlet, so be it.) But the mind does not have to imagine the events in the play as "staged" events with actors, costumes, and props; it may instead visualize the scenes as reality, things happening to real people in real environments. Either way, the good reader experiences the play by visualizing it. Obviously there is no "one right way" a play should be performed or imagined; quite the contrary, one great appeal of drama is that it lends itself to almost endless possibilities of presentation—with different actors, different sets, different direction. So, as you read a work, experiment with the possibilities, always keeping your imaginative eye on the words of the author.

Plays can be read quickly, so we suggest that each be read at least twice. The first reading should reveal, in broad terms, "what happens" in the play. *Drama* comes from a Greek verb *dran* meaning *to act* or *to do;* this action answers the question, What happens? Action arises from all the elements of the drama, but particularly from characters in conflict; therefore, try to comprehend the central conflict of the work, for all drama depends on conflict to show us the true nature of the central character (protagonist) and his opponent (the antagonist). From conflicts spring the excitement that we expect from great plays, as well as the resolutions which make us feel, This should be. So, as you read, look for dramatic moments, confrontation scenes between protagonist and antagonist or between other characters, any scenes in which a character makes important revelations about himself, and scenes in which expectations—a character's or the audience's—are reversed. (When a character's expectations are reversed, the result is often ironic; when the audience's expectations are reversed, the dramatic result can be a shock of recognition, a clarification of the play's major themes.)

If the first reading answers the question *what* happens, the second explores the questions of *why* and *how* it happens. A second reading will show *why* the situations in the plot are arranged as they are; *why* the characters behave as they do (motivation); *how* the characters speak and *why* the author wishes them to speak that way; *how* minor characters and incidents relate to the major themes of the play; and a host of other similar *how-why* questions. In answering these questions it is useful to examine the first scene very closely, almost line for line, because this scene usually provides very important exposition, suggests the play's mood and atmosphere, establishes the nature of the central conflict, and introduces through its language, imagery fundamental to the play's themes. Also, examine the stage directions—something the spectator at a play cannot do —because directions are often significantly revelatory of the author's ideas and his conception of the play. (An excellent example is Tennessee Williams' *The Glass Menagerie,* in which the stage directions support and help explain the patterns of imagery in the work, and through them the mood and theme it presents.) The second reading, then, should reveal nuances of the play's architecture and theme.

In *As You Like It* Shakespeare wrote about the stage and the nature of man:

> All the world's a stage
> And all the men and women merely players;
> They have their exits and their entrances;
> And one man in his time plays many parts.

Consider this idea in another way: the drama is a "world" in itself, an imaginary one that may or may not be a mirror image of the world we live in. (Interestingly enough, Shakespeare's theater was called the Globe.) The audience's acceptance of this world on the stage, which is governed by a set of rules or conventions, constitutes the dramatic illusion, and, although we know that this world is not literally real, we also know that it has a special imaginative reality. Each dramatist creates his make-believe "play" world, arranges his material so that from the work emerges meaning, significance, and pleasure. By way of explanation, consider for a moment the ghost in *Hamlet:* Shakespeare does not examine the question of whether ghosts exist; he merely states that, for his dramatic purpose, in the world of Elsinore, where Hamlet lives, one ghost does indeed exist. This ghost makes the point that Elsinore and Hamlet are haunted by the past—Elsinore by the horrors of regicide, and Hamlet by the demands of vengeance. In Molière's *The Misanthrope,* to use an example from your text, the characters speak in couplets; thus, in his excellent translation, Richard Wilbur has retained this convention of dialogue. Obviously seventeenth-century Parisians did not speak in rhyme, but rhymed dialogue was a convention of classical French drama, and this dialogue aids Molière in creating a world preoccupied with polished manners, elegant conversation, and sparkling wit— a stage world that simultaneously mirrors and criticizes the fashionable society of his day. In *The Glass Menagerie,* Tennessee Williams uses the convention of a narrator who talks directly to the audience and then steps back into the action of the play as a central character. This device gives Williams both the immediacy of drama and the interpretive quality of fiction, an excellent combination for his "memory play," a work that achieves its emotional impact by showing both the narrator's memory and its effects on him.

Quite clearly, then, the ghost in *Hamlet,* the rhymed dialogue in *The Misanthrope,* and the narrator in *The Glass Menagerie* contribute meaningfully to the total dramatic worlds presented in these plays. Why emphasize this obvious point? Because, as students of the drama, we must understand *how* an author creates his dramatic world and then *why* he does so; only then can we experience the full force and meaning of the play as it relates to the world we inhabit.

In this volume we have presented thirteen great plays. Each contains a brilliantly conceived world inhabited by endlessly fascinating people. As you read these plays, we hope you will begin to explore and understand more about the nature of drama and about human nature.

SOPHOCLES
[496–406 B.C.]

Sophocles was born in a district of Athens known as Colonus, commemorated as a "sacred place" in his last play, *Oedipus at Colonus*. His father was wealthy enough to secure him a good Athenian education, which included training in music and gymnastics. It is possible that Sophocles later studied the art of tragedy under Aeschylus. By 468 B.C., Sophocles had become accomplished in that art: his first production (no longer extant) won first prize at the Athenian dramatic festival. In the course of his career Sophocles wrote about 120 plays, of which seven have survived, and he won 24 first prizes, more than any other playwright. Strangely enough, Sophocles' masterpiece, *Oedipus Rex,* won only second prize the year it was produced (about 430 B.C.).

Sophocles' long life coincided with one of the greatest "Golden Ages" in Western civilization, and his plays are imbued with the full force of Athenian culture at its height. Among his contemporaries were not only Aeschylus, but also the playwrights Euripides and Aristophanes, the philosopher Socrates, the artist and sculptor Phidias (who supervised the construction of the Parthenon), the political leader Pericles, and the historian Herodotus. Sophocles was a well-known public figure in his own right, having served as a civil official on several occasions. When he died in 406 B.C.—two years before Athens capitulated in the war against Sparta and began its cultural decline—he was mourned as a national hero.

Sophocles' innovation in breaking away from the Aeschylean tradition of continuous trilogies was to conceive of each play as a coherent whole rather than as part of a larger structure. This is particularly true of his three "Theban plays": *Antigone* (441 B.C.), *Oedipus Rex* (430 B.C.), and *Oedipus at Colonus* (produced posthumously in 401 B.C.). At different points in his career Sophocles detached separate elements from the traditional body of legends surrounding "the house of Laïos"; though there are correlations among the three plays, each is a logical unity in itself. This is one reason why Aristotle—in his seminal work, *The Poetics* (about 340 B.C.)—was so lavish in his praise of Sophocles' sense of plot. Sophocles scrupulously avoided such "external" and "accidental" intrusions as the *deus ex machina* (where a god suddenly appears on stage to provide a contrived solution), preferring a rigorous, "probable," and *internal* development of the action.

OEDIPUS REX

SOPHOCLES
Translated by Dudley Fitts and Robert Fitzgerald

PERSONS REPRESENTED

OEDIPUS

A PRIEST

CREON

TEIRESIAS

CHORUS OF THEBAN ELDERS

IOCASTE

MESSENGER

SHEPHERD OF LAÏOS

SECOND MESSENGER

CHORAGOS (*leader of the* CHORUS)

THE SCENE   *Before the palace of Oedipus, King of Thebes. A central door and two lateral doors open onto a platform which runs the length of the façade. On the platform, right and left, are altars; and three steps lead down into the "orchestra," or chorus-ground. At the beginning of the action these steps are crowded by suppliants who have brought branches and chaplets of olive leaves and who lie in various attitudes of despair.* OEDIPUS *enters.*

PROLOGUE

OEDIPUS   My children, generations of the living
          In the line of Kadmos, nursed at his ancient hearth:
          Why have you strewn yourselves before these altars
          In supplication, with your boughs and garlands?
          The breath of incense rises from the city   [5
          With a sound of prayer and lamentation.
                                        Children,
          I would not have you speak through messengers,
          And therefore I have come myself to hear you—
          I, Oedipus, who bear the famous name.   [10
          [*To a* PRIEST]
          You, there, since you are eldest in the company,
          Speak for them all, tell me what preys upon you,
          Whether you come in dread, or crave some blessing:
          Tell me, and never doubt that I will help you
          In every way I can; I should be heartless   [15
          Were I not moved to find you suppliant here.
PRIEST   Great Oedipus, O powerful King of Thebes!
          You see how all the ages of our people
          Cling to your altar steps: here are boys
          Who can barely stand alone, and here are priests   [20
          By weight of age, as I am a priest of God,
          And young men chosen from those yet unmarried;
          As for the others, all that multitude,
          They wait with olive chaplets in the squares,
          At the two shrines of Pallas, and where Apollo   [25
          Speaks in the glowing embers.
                                        Your own eyes
          Must tell you: Thebes is in her extremity
          And can not lift her head from the surge of death.
          A rust consumes the buds and fruits of the earth;   [30
          The herds are sick; children die unborn,
          And labor is vain. The god of plague and pyre
          Raids like detestable lightning through the city,
          And all the house of Kadmos is laid waste,
          All emptied, and all darkened: Death alone   [35
          Battens upon the misery of Thebes.

          You are not one of the immortal gods, we know;
          Yet we have come to you to make our prayer
          As to the man of all men best in adversity
          And wisest in the ways of God. You saved us   [40
          From the Sphinx, that flinty singer, and the tribute
          We paid to her so long; yet you were never
          Better informed than we, nor could we teach you:
          It was some god breathed in you to set us free.

          Therefore, O mighty King, we turn to you: [45
          Find us our safety, find us a remedy,
          Whether by counsel of the gods or men.
          A king of wisdom tested in the past

Can act in a time of troubles, and act well.
Noblest of men, restore   [50
Life to your city! Think how all men call you
Liberator for your triumph long ago;
Ah, when your years of kingship are remembered,
Let them not say *We rose, but later fell*—
Keep the State from going down in the storm!   [55
Once, years ago, with happy augury,
You brought us fortune; be the same again!
No man questions your power to rule the land:
But rule over men, not over a dead city!
Ships are only hulls, citadels are nothing,   [60
When no life moves in the empty passageways.
OEDIPUS   Poor children! You may be sure I know
All that you longed for in your coming here.
I know that you are deathly sick; and yet,
Sick as you are, not one is as sick as I.   [65
Each of you suffers in himself alone
His anguish, not another's; but my spirit
Groans for the city, for myself, for you.

I was not sleeping, you are not waking me.
No, I have been in tears for a long while   [70
And in my restless thought walked many ways.
In all my search, I found one helpful course,
And that I have taken: I have sent Creon,
Son of Menoikeus, brother of the Queen,
To Delphi, Apollo's place of revelation,   [75
To learn there, if he can,
What act or pledge of mine may save the city.
I have counted the days, and now, this very day,
I am troubled, for he has overstayed his time.
What is he doing? He has been gone too long.   [80
Yet whenever he comes back, I should do ill
To scant whatever hint the god may give.
PRIEST   It is a timely promise. At this instant
They tell me Creon is here.
OEDIPUS   O Lord Apollo!   [85
May his news be fair as his face is radiant!
PRIEST   It could not be otherwise: he is crowned with bay,
The chaplet is thick with berries.
OEDIPUS   We shall soon know;
He is near enough to hear us now.   [90
[*Enter* CREON.]
                            O Prince:
Brother: son of Menoikeus:
What answer do you bring us from the god?
CREON   It is favorable. I can tell you, great afflictions
Will turn out well, if they are taken well.   [95
OEDIPUS   What was the oracle? These vague words
Leave me still hanging between hope and fear.
CREON   Is it your pleasure to hear me with all these
Gathered around us? I am prepared to speak,
But should we not go in?   [100

OEDIPUS   Let them all hear it.
    It is for them I suffer, more than for myself.
CREON   Then I will tell you what I heard at Delphi.

    In plain words
    The god commands us to expel from the land of Thebes   [*105*
    An old defilement that it seems we shelter.
    It is a deathly thing, beyond expiation.
    We must not let it feed upon us longer.
OEDIPUS   What defilement? How shall we rid ourselves of it?
CREON   By exile or death, blood for blood. It was   [*110*
    Murder that brought the plague-wind on the city.
OEDIPUS   Murder of whom? Surely the god has named him?
CREON   My lord: long ago Laïos was our king,
    Before you came to govern us.
OEDIPUS   I know;   [*115*
    I learned of him from others; I never saw him.
CREON   He was murdered; and Apollo commands us now
    To take revenge upon whoever killed him.
OEDIPUS   Upon whom? Where are they? Where shall we find a clue
    To solve that crime, after so many years?   [*120*
CREON   Here in this land, he said.
                          If we make enquiry,
    We may touch things that otherwise escape us.
OEDIPUS   Tell me: Was Laïos murdered in his house,
    Or in the fields, or in some foreign country?   [*125*
CREON   He said he planned to make a pilgrimage.
    He did not come home again.
OEDIPUS   And was there no one,
    No witness, no companion, to tell what happened?
CREON   They were all killed but one, and he got away   [*130*
    So frightened that he could remember one thing only.
OEDIPUS   What was that one thing? One may be the key
    To everything, if we resolve to use it.
CREON   He said that a band of highwaymen attacked them,
    Outnumbered them, and overwhelmed the King.   [*135*
OEDIPUS   Strange, that a highwayman should be so daring—
    Unless some faction here bribed him to do it.
CREON   We thought of that. But after Laïos' death
    New troubles arose and we had no avenger.
OEDIPUS   What troubles could prevent your hunting down the killers?   [*140*
CREON   The riddling Sphinx's song
    Made us deaf to all mysteries but her own.
OEDIPUS   Then once more I must bring what is dark to light.
    It is most fitting that Apollo shows,
    As you do, this compunction for the dead.   [*145*
    You shall see how I stand by you, as I should,
    To avenge the city and the city's god,
    And not as though it were for some distant friend,
    But for my own sake, to be rid of evil.
    Whoever killed King Laïos might—who knows?—   [*150*
    Decide at any moment to kill me as well.
    By avenging the murdered king I protect myself.
    Come, then, my children: leave the altar steps,

Lift up your olive boughs!
                    One of you go   [155
And summon the people of Kadmos to gather here.
I will do all that I can; you may tell them that.
[*Exit a* PAGE.]
So, with the help of God,
We shall be saved—or else indeed we are lost.
PRIEST   Let us rise, children. It was for this we came,   [160
And now the King has promised it himself.
Phoibos has sent us an oracle; may he descend
Himself to save us and drive out the plague.

[*Exeunt* OEDIPUS *and* CREON *into the palace by the central door. The* PRIEST
and the SUPPLIANTS *disperse R and L. After a short pause the* CHORUS *enters
the orchestra.*]

PARODOS

CHORUS   What is God singing in his profound   (STROPHE 1)
     Delphi of gold and shadow?
     What oracle for Thebes, the sunwhipped city?
     Fear unjoints me, the roots of my heart tremble.
     Now I remember, O Healer, your power, and wonder;   [5
     Will you send doom like a sudden cloud, or weave it
     Like nightfall of the past?
     Speak, speak to us, issue of holy sound:
     Dearest to our expectancy: be tender!

                                                (ANTISTROPHE 1)
     Let me pray to Athenê, the immortal daughter of Zeus,   [10
     And to Artemis her sister
     Who keeps her famous throne in the market ring,
     And to Apollo, bowman at the far butts of heaven—

     O gods, descend! Like three streams leap against
     The fires of our grief, the fires of darkness;   [15
     Be swift to bring us rest!

     As in the old time from the brilliant house
     Of air you stepped to save us, come again!

     Now our afflictions have no end,   (STROPHE 2)
     Now all our stricken host lies down   [20
     And no man fights off death with his mind;

     The noble plowland bears no grain,
     And groaning mothers can not bear—

     See, how our lives like birds take wing,
     Like sparks that fly when a fire soars,   [25
     To the shore of the god of evening.

The plague burns on, it is pitiless,   (ANTISTROPHE 2)
Though pallid children laden with death
Lie unwept in the stony ways,

And old gray women by every path   [*30*
Flock to the strand about the altars

There to strike their breasts and cry
Worship of Phoibos in wailing prayers:
Be kind, God's golden child!

There are no swords in this attack by fire,   (STROPHE 3)   [*35*
No shields, but we are ringed with cries.
Send the besieger plunging from our homes
Into the vast sea-room of the Atlantic
Or into the waves that foam eastward of Thrace—
For the day ravages what the night spares—   [*40*

Destroy our enemy, lord of the thunder!
Let him be riven by lightning from heaven!

Phoibos Apollo, stretch the sun's bowstring,   (ANTISTROPHE 3)
That golden cord, until it sing for us,
Flashing arrows in heaven!   [*45*

            Artemis, Huntress,
Race with flaring lights upon our mountains!

O scarlet god, O golden-banded brow,
O Theban Bacchos in a storm of Maenads,
[*Enter* OEDIPUS, *C.*]
Whirl upon Death, that all the Undying hate!   [*50*
Come with blinding cressets, come in joy!

SCENE I

OEDIPUS   Is this your prayer? It may be answered. Come,
     Listen to me, act as the crisis demands,
     And you shall have relief from all these evils.

     Until now I was a stranger to this tale,
     As I had been a stranger to the crime.   [*5*
     Could I track down the murderer without a clue?
     But now, friends,
     As one who became a citizen after the murder,
     I make this proclamation to all Thebans:
     If any man knows by whose hand Laïos, son of Labdakos,   [*10*
     Met his death, I direct that man to tell me everything,
     No matter what he fears for having so long withheld it.
     Let it stand as promised that no further trouble
     Will come to him, but he may leave the land in safety.

Moreover: If anyone knows the murderer to be foreign,   [15
Let him not keep silent: he shall have his reward from me.
However, if he does conceal it; if any man
Fearing for his friend or for himself disobeys this edict,
Hear what I propose to do:

I solemnly forbid the people of this country,   [20
Where power and throne are mine, ever to receive that man
Or speak to him, no matter who he is, or let him
Join in sacrifice, lustration, or in prayer.
I decree that he be driven from every house,
Being, as he is, corruption itself to us: the Delphic   [25
Voice of Zeus has pronounced this revelation.
Thus I associate myself with the oracle
And take the side of the murdered king.

As for the criminal, I pray to God—
Whether it be a lurking thief, or one of a number—   [30
I pray that that man's life be consumed in evil and wretchedness.
And as for me, this curse applies no less
If it should turn out that the culprit is my guest here,
Sharing my hearth.
                    You have heard the penalty.   [35
I lay it on you now to attend to this
For my sake, for Apollo's, for the sick
Sterile city that heaven has abandoned.
Suppose the oracle had given you no command:
Should this defilement go uncleansed for ever?   [40
You should have found the murderer: your king,
A noble king, had been destroyed!
                    Now I,
Having the power that he held before me,
Having his bed, begetting children there   [45
Upon his wife, as he would have, had he lived—
Their son would have been my children's brother,
If Laïos had had luck in fatherhood!
(But surely ill luck rushed upon his reign) —
I say I take the son's part, just as though   [50
I were his son, to press the fight for him
And see it won! I'll find the hand that brought
Death to Labdakos' and Polydoros' child,
Heir of Kadmos' and Agenor's line.
And as for those who fail me,   [55
May the gods deny them the fruit of the earth,
Fruit of the womb, and may they rot utterly!
Let them be wretched as we are wretched, and worse!

For you, for loyal Thebans, and for all
Who find my actions right, I pray the favor   [60
Of justice, and of all the immortal gods.
CHORAGOS   Since I am under oath, my lord, I swear
    I did not do the murder, I can not name
    The murderer. Might not the oracle
    That has ordained the search tell where to find him?   [65

OEDIPUS   An honest question. But no man in the world
Can make the gods do more than the gods will.
CHORAGOS   There is one last expedient—
OEDIPUS   Tell me what it is.
Though it seem slight, you must not hold it back.   [*70*
CHORAGOS   A lord clairvoyant to the lord Apollo,
As we all know, is the skilled Teiresias.
One might learn much about this from him, Oedipus.
OEDIPUS   I am not wasting time:
Creon spoke of this, and I have sent for him—   [*75*
Twice, in fact; it is strange that he is not here.
CHORAGOS   The other matter—that old report—seems useless.
OEDIPUS   Tell me. I am interested in all reports.
CHORAGOS   The King was said to have been killed by highwaymen.
OEDIPUS   I know. But we have no witnesses to that.   [*80*
CHORAGOS   If the killer can feel a particle of dread,
Your curse will bring him out of hiding!
OEDIPUS   No.
The man who dared that act will fear no curse.

[*Enter the blind seer* TEIRESIAS, *led by a* PAGE.]

CHORAGOS   But there is one man who may detect the criminal.   [*85*
This is Teiresias, this is the holy prophet
In whom, alone of all men, truth was born.
OEDIPUS   Teiresias: seer: student of mysteries,
Of all that's taught and all that no man tells,
Secrets of Heaven and secrets of the earth: [*90*
Blind though you are, you know the city lies
Sick with plague; and from this plague, my lord,
We find that you alone can guard or save us.

Possibly you did not hear the messengers?
Apollo, when we sent to him,   [*95*
Sent us back word that this great pestilence
Would lift, but only if we established clearly
The identity of those who murdered Laïos.
They must be killed or exiled.
                              Can you use   [*100*
Birdflight or any art of divination
To purify yourself, and Thebes, and me
From this contagion? We are in your hands.
There is no fairer duty
Than that of helping others in distress.   [*105*
TEIRESIAS   How dreadful knowledge of the truth can be
When there's no help in truth! I knew this well,
But did not act on it: else I should not have come.
OEDIPUS   What is troubling you? Why are your eyes so cold?
TEIRESIAS   Let me go home. Bear your own fate, and I'll   [*110*
Bear mine. It is better so: trust what I say.
OEDIPUS   What you say is ungracious and unhelpful
To your native country. Do not refuse to speak.
TEIRESIAS   When it comes to speech, your own is neither temperate
Nor opportune. I wish to be more prudent.   [*115*
OEDIPUS   In God's name, we all beg you—

TEIRESIAS　　　　　　　　　　　　You are all ignorant.
　　No; I will never tell you what I know.
　　Now it is my misery; then, it would be yours.
OEDIPUS　What! You do know something, and will not tell us?　　　[*120*
　　You would betray us all and wreck the State?
TEIRESIAS　I do not intend to torture myself, or you.
　　Why persist in asking? You will not persuade me.
OEDIPUS　What a wicked old man you are! You'd try a stone's
　　Patience! Out with it! Have you no feeling at all?　　　[*125*
TEIRESIAS　You call me unfeeling. If you could only see
　　The nature of your own feelings . . .
OEDIPUS　　　　　　　　　　　Why,
　　Who would not feel as I do? Who could endure
　　Your arrogance toward the city?　　　[*130*
TEIRESIAS　　　　　　　　　　What does it matter!
　　Whether I speak or not, it is bound to come.
OEDIPUS　Then, if "it" is bound to come, you are bound to tell me.
TEIRESIAS　No, I will not go on. Rage as you please.
OEDIPUS　Rage? Why not!　　　[*135*
　　　　　　　　　　And I'll tell you what I think:
　　You planned it, you had it done, you all but
　　Killed him with your own hands: if you had eyes,
　　I'd say the crime was yours, and yours alone.
TEIRESIAS　So? I charge you, then,　　　[*140*
　　Abide by the proclamation you have made:
　　From this day forth
　　Never speak again to these men or to me;
　　You yourself are the pollution of this country.
OEDIPUS　You dare say that! Can you possibly think you have　　　[*145*
　　Some way of going free, after such insolence?
TEIRESIAS　I have gone free. It is the truth sustains me.
OEDIPUS　Who taught you shamelessness? It was not your craft.
TEIRESIAS　You did. You made me speak. I did not want to.
OEDIPUS　Speak what? Let me hear it again more clearly.　　　[*150*
TEIRESIAS　Was it not clear before? Are you tempting me?
OEDIPUS　I did not understand it. Say it again.
TEIRESIAS　I say that you are the murderer whom you seek.
OEDIPUS　Now twice you have spat out infamy. You'll pay for it!
TEIRESIAS　Would you care for more? Do you wish to be really angry?　　　[*155*
OEDIPUS　Say what you will. Whatever you say is worthless.
TEIRESIAS　I say you live in hideous shame with those
　　Most dear to you. You can not see the evil.
OEDIPUS　It seems you can go on mouthing like this for ever.
TEIRESIAS　I can, if there is power in truth.　　　[*160*
OEDIPUS　　　　　　　　　　There is:
　　But not for you, not for you,
　　You sightless, witless, senseless, mad old man!
TEIRESIAS　You are the madman. There is no one here
　　Who will not curse you soon, as you curse me.　　　[*165*
OEDIPUS　You child of endless night! You can not hurt me
　　Or any other man who sees the sun.
TEIRESIAS　True: it is not from me your fate will come.
　　That lies within Apollo's competence,
　　As it is his concern.　　　[*170*

OEDIPUS   Tell me:
 Are you speaking for Creon, or for yourself?
TEIRESIAS   Creon is no threat. You weave your own doom.
OEDIPUS   Wealth, power, craft of statesmanship!
 Kingly position, everywhere admired!   [*175*
 What savage envy is stored up against these,
 If Creon, whom I trusted, Creon my friend,
 For this great office which the city once
 Put in my hands unsought—if for this power
 Creon desires in secret to destroy me!   [*180*

 He has bought this decrepit fortune-teller, this
 Collector of dirty pennies, this prophet fraud—
 Why, he is no more clairvoyant than I am!
         Tell us:
 Has your mystic mummery ever approached the truth?   [*185*
 When that hellcat the Sphinx was performing here,
 What help were you to these people?
 Her magic was not for the first man who came along:
 It demanded a real exorcist. Your birds—
 What good were they? or the gods, for the matter of that?   [*190*
 But I came by,
 Oedipus, the simple man, who knows nothing—
 I thought it out for myself, no birds helped me!
 And this is the man you think you can destroy,
 That you may be close to Creon when he's king!   [*195*
 Well, you and your friend Creon, it seems to me,
 Will suffer most. If you were not an old man,
 You would have paid already for your plot.
CHORAGOS   We can not see that his words or yours
 Have been spoken except in anger, Oedipus,   [*200*
 And of anger we have no need. How can God's will
 Be accomplished best? That is what most concerns us.
TEIRESIAS   You are a king. But where argument's concerned
 I am your man, as much a king as you.
 I am not your servant, but Apollo's.   [*205*
 I have no need of Creon to speak for me.

 Listen to me. You mock my blindness, do you?
 But I say that you, with both your eyes, are blind:
 You can not see the wretchedness of your life,
 Nor in whose house you live, no, nor with whom.   [*210*
 Who are your father and mother? Can you tell me?
 You do not even know the blind wrongs
 That you have done them, on earth and in the world below.
 But the double lash of your parents' curse will whip you
 Out of this land some day, with only night   [*215*
 Upon your precious eyes.
 Your cries then—where will they not be heard?
 What fastness of Kithairon will not echo them?
 And that bridal-descant of yours—you'll know it then,
 The song they sang when you came here to Thebes   [*220*
 And found your misguided berthing.

All this, and more, that you can not guess at now,
Will bring you to yourself among your children.

Be angry, then. Curse Creon. Curse my words.
I tell you, no man that walks upon the earth   [225
Shall be rooted out more horribly than you.
OEDIPUS   Am I to bear this from him?—Damnation
Take you! Out of this place! Out of my sight!
TEIRESIAS   I would not have come at all if you had not asked me.
OEDIPUS   Could I have told that you'd talk nonsense, that   [230
You'd come here to make a fool of yourself, and of me?
TEIRESIAS   A fool? Your parents thought me sane enough.
OEDIPUS   My parents again!—Wait: who were my parents?
TEIRESIAS   This day will give you a father, and break your heart.
OEDIPUS   Your infantile riddles! Your damned abracadabra!   [235
TEIRESIAS   You were a great man once at solving riddles.
OEDIPUS   Mock me with that if you like; you will find it true.
TEIRESIAS   It was true enough. It brought about your ruin.
OEDIPUS   But if it saved this town?
TEIRESIAS   (*To the* PAGE)
                         Boy, give me your hand.   [240
OEDIPUS   Yes, boy; lead him away.
                         —While you are here
We can do nothing. Go; leave us in peace.
TEIRESIAS   I will go when I have said what I have to say.
How can you hurt me? And I tell you again: [245
The man you have been looking for all this time,
The damned man, the murderer of Laïos,
That man is in Thebes. To your mind he is foreignborn,
But it will soon be shown that he is a Theban,
A revelation that will fail to please.   [250
                         A blind man,
Who has his eyes now; a penniless man, who is rich now;
And he will go tapping the strange earth with his staff;
To the children with whom he lives now he will be
Brother and father—the very same; to her   [255
Who bore him, son and husband—the very same
Who came to his father's bed, wet with his father's blood.
Enough. Go think that over.

If later you find error in what I have said,
You may say that I have no skill in prophecy.   [260
[*Exit* TEIRESIAS, *led by his* PAGE. OEDIPUS *goes into the palace.*]

ODE I

CHORUS   The Delphic stone of prophecies   (STROPHE 1)
          Remembers ancient regicide
          And a still bloody hand.
          That killer's hour of flight has come.
          He must be stronger than riderless   [5

Coursers of untiring wind,
For the son of Zeus armed with his father's thunder
Leaps in lightning after him;
And the Furies follow him, the sad Furies.

Holy Parnassos' peak of snow   (ANTISTROPHE 1)   [*10*
Flashes and blinds that secret man,
That all shall hunt him down:
Though he may roam the forest shade
Like a bull gone wild from pasture
To rage through glooms of stone.   [*15*
Doom comes down on him; flight will not avail him;
For the world's heart calls him desolate,
And the immortal Furies follow, for ever follow.

But now a wilder thing is heard   (STROPHE 2)
From the old man skilled at hearing Fate in the wingbeat of a bird.   [*20*
Bewildered as a blown bird, my soul hovers and can not find
Foothold in this debate, or any reason or rest of mind.
But no man ever brought—none can bring
Proof of strife between Thebes' royal house,
Labdakos' line, and the son of Polybos;   [*25*
And never until now has any man brought word
Of Laïos' dark death staining Oedipus the King.

Divine Zeus and Apollo hold   (ANTISTROPHE 2)
Perfect intelligence alone of all tales ever told;
And well though this diviner works, he works in his own night;   [*30*
No man can judge that rough unknown or trust in second sight,
For wisdom changes hands among the wise.
Shall I believe my great lord criminal
At a raging word that a blind old man let fall?
I saw him, when the carrion woman faced him of old,   [*35*
Prove his heroic mind! These evil words are lies.

SCENE II

CREON   Men of Thebes:
    I am told that heavy accusations
    Have been brought against me by King Oedipus.

    I am not the kind of man to bear this tamely.

    If in these present difficulties   [*5*
    He holds me accountable for any harm to him
    Through anything I have said or done—why, then,
    I do not value life in this dishonor.
    It is not as though this rumor touched upon
    Some private indiscretion. The matter is grave.   [*10*
    The fact is that I am being called disloyal
    To the State, to my fellow citizens, to my friends.
CHORAGOS   He may have spoken in anger, not from his mind.
CREON   But did you not hear him say I was the one
    Who seduced the old prophet into lying?   [*15*

CHORAGOS   The thing was said; I do not know how seriously.
CREON   But you were watching him! Were his eyes steady?
    Did he look like a man in his right mind?
CHORAGOS   I do not know.
    I can not judge the behavior of great men.   [20
    But here is the King himself.
    [*Enter* OEDIPUS.]
OEDIPUS   So you dared come back.
    Why? How brazen of you to come to my house,
    You murderer!
                Do you think I do not know   [25
    That you plotted to kill me, plotted to steal my throne?
    Tell me, in God's name: am I coward, a fool,
    That you should dream you could accomplish this?
    A fool who could not see your slippery game?
    A coward, not to fight back when I saw it?   [30
    You are the fool, Creon, are you not? hoping
    Without support or friends to get a throne?
    Thrones may be won or bought: you could do neither.
CREON   Now listen to me. You have talked; let me talk, too.
    You can not judge unless you know the facts.   [35
OEDIPUS   You speak well: there is one fact; but I find it hard
    To learn from the deadliest enemy I have.
CREON   That above all I must dispute with you.
OEDIPUS   That above all I will not hear you deny.
CREON   If you think there is anything good in being stubborn   [40
    Against all reason, then I say you are wrong.
OEDIPUS   If you think a man can sin against his own kind
    And not be punished for it, I say you are mad.
CREON   I agree. But tell me: what have I done to you?
OEDIPUS   You advised me to send for that wizard, did you not?   [45
CREON   I did. I should do it again.
OEDIPUS   Very well. Now tell me:
    How long has it been since Laïos—
CREON   What of Laïos?
OEDIPUS   Since he vanished in that onset by the road?   [50
CREON   It was long ago, a long time.
OEDIPUS   And this prophet,
    Was he practicing here then?
CREON   He was; and with honor, as now.
OEDIPUS   Did he speak of me at that time?   [55
CREON   He never did;
    At least, not when I was present.
OEDIPUS   But . . . the enquiry?
    I suppose you held one?
CREON   We did, but we learned nothing.   [60
OEDIPUS   Why did the prophet not speak against me then?
CREON   I do not know; and I am the kind of man
    Who holds his tongue when he has no facts to go on.
OEDIPUS   There's one fact that you know, and you could tell it.
CREON   What fact is that? If I know it, you shall have it.   [65
OEDIPUS   If he were not involved with you, he could not say
    That it was I who murdered Laïos.
CREON   If he says that, you are the one that knows it!—
    But now it is my turn to question you.

OEDIPUS   Put your questions. I am no murderer.   [*70*

CREON   First, then: You married my sister?

            I married your sister.

CREON   And you rule the kingdom equally with her?

OEDIPUS   Everything that she wants she has from me.

CREON   And I am the third, equal to both of you?   [*75*

OEDIPUS   That is why I call you a bad friend.

CREON   No. Reason it out, as I have done.

  Think of this first: Would any sane man prefer

  Power, with all a king's anxieties,

  To that same power and the grace of sleep?   [*80*

  Certainly not I.

  I have never longed for the king's power—only his rights.

  Would any wise man differ from me in this?

  As matters stand, I have my way in everything

  With your consent, and no responsibilities.   [*85*

  If I were king, I should be a slave to policy.

  How could I desire a scepter more

  Than what is now mine—untroubled influence?

  No, I have not gone mad; I need no honors,

  Except those with the perquisites I have now.   [*90*

  I am welcome everywhere; every man salutes me,

  And those who want your favor seek my ear,

  Since I know how to manage what they ask.

  Should I exchange this ease for that anxiety?

  Besides, no sober mind is treasonable.   [*95*

  I hate anarchy

  And never would deal with any man who likes it.

  Test what I have said. Go to the priestess

  At Delphi, ask if I quoted her correctly.

  And as for this other thing: if I am found   [*100*

  Guilty of treason with Teiresias,

  Then sentence me to death! You have my word

  It is a sentence I should cast my vote for—

  But not without evidence!

        You do wrong   [*105*

  When you take good men for bad, bad men for good.

  A true friend thrown aside—why, life itself

  Is not more precious!

      In time you will know this well:

  For time, and time alone, will show the just man,   [*110*

  Though scoundrels are discovered in a day.

CHORAGOS   This is well said, and a prudent man would ponder it.

  Judgments too quickly formed are dangerous.

OEDIPUS   But is he not quick in his duplicity?

  And shall I not be quick to parry him?   [*115*

  Would you have me stand still, hold my peace, and let

  This man win everything, through my inaction?

CREON   And you want—what is it, then? To banish me?

OEDIPUS   No, not exile. It is your death I want,

  So that all the world may see what treason means.   [*120*

CREON   You will persist, then? You will not believe me?
OEDIPUS   How can I believe you?
CREON   Then you are a fool.
OEDIPUS   To save myself?
CREON   In justice, think of me.   [125
OEDIPUS   You are evil incarnate.
CREON   But suppose that you are wrong?
OEDIPUS   Still I must rule.
CREON   But not if you rule badly.
OEDIPUS   O city, city!   [130
CREON   It is my city, too!
CHORAGOS   Now, my lords, be still. I see the Queen,
    Iocastê, coming from her palace chambers;
    And it is time she came, for the sake of you both.
    This dreadful quarrel can be resolved through her.   [135
    [Enter IOCASTE.]
IOCASTE   Poor foolish men, what wicked din is this?
    With Thebes sick to death, is it not shameful
    That you should rake some private quarrel up?
    [To OEDIPUS:]
    Come into the house.
                            —And you, Creon, go now: [140
    Let us have no more of this tumult over nothing.
CREON   Nothing? No, sister: what your husband plans for me
    Is one of two great evils: exile or death.
OEDIPUS   He is right.
                    Why, woman I have caught him squarely   [145
    Plotting against my life.
CREON   No! Let me die
    Accurst if ever I have wished you harm!
IOCASTE   Ah, believe it, Oedipus!
    In the name of the gods, respect this oath of his   [150
    For my sake, for the sake of these people here!

                                                            (STROPHE 1)
CHORAGOS   Open your mind to her, my lord. Be ruled by her, I beg
    you!
OEDIPUS   What would you have me do?
CHORAGOS   Respect Creon's word. He has never spoken like a fool,   [155
    And now he has sworn an oath.
OEDIPUS   You know what you ask?
CHORAGOS   I do.
OEDIPUS   Speak on, then.
CHORAGOS   A friend so sworn should not be baited so,   [160
    In blind malice, and without final proof.
OEDIPUS   You are aware, I hope, that what you say
    Means death for me, or exile at the least.
CHORAGOS   No, I swear by Helios, first in Heaven   (STROPHE 2)
        May I die friendless and accurst,   [165
    The worst of deaths, if ever I meant that!

                It is the withering fields
                    That hurt my sick heart:
                Must we bear all these ills,
                    And now your bad blood as well?   [170

OEDIPUS   Then let him go. And let me die, if I must,
Or be driven by him in shame from the land of Thebes.
It is your unhappiness, and not his talk,
That touches me.
As for him—   [*175*
Wherever he is, I will hate him as long as I live.
CREON   Ugly in yielding, as you were ugly in rage!
Natures like yours chiefly torment themselves.
OEDIPUS   Can you not go? Can you not leave me?
CREON   I can.   [*180*
You do not know me; but the city knows me,
And in its eyes I am just, if not in yours.
[*Exit* CREON.]

(ANTISTROPHE 1)

CHORAGOS   Lady Iocastê, did you not ask the King to go to his cham-
bers?
IOCASTE   First tell me what has happened.   [*185*
CHORAGOS   There was suspicion without evidence; yet it rankled
As even false charges will.
IOCASTE   On both sides?
CHORAGOS   On both.
IOCASTE   But what was said?   [*190*
CHORAGOS   Oh let it rest, let it be done with!
Have we not suffered enough?
OEDIPUS   You see to what your decency has brought you:
You have made difficulties where my heart saw none.

(ANTISTROPHE 2)

CHORAGOS   Oedipus, it is not once only I have told you—   [*195*
You must know I should count myself unwise
To the point of madness, should I now forsake you—

You, under whose hand,
In the storm of another time,
Our dear land sailed out free.   [*200*
But now stand fast at the helm!

IOCASTE   In God's name, Oedipus, inform your wife as well:
Why are you so set in this hard anger?
OEDIPUS   I will tell you, for none of these men deserves
My confidence as you do. It is Creon's work,   [*205*
His treachery, his plotting against me.
IOCASTE   Go on, if you can make this clear to me.
OEDIPUS   He charges me with the murder of Laïos.
IOCASTE   Has he some knowledge? Or does he speak from hearsay?
OEDIPUS   He would not commit himself to such a charge,   [*210*
But he has brought in that damnable soothsayer
To tell his story.
IOCASTE   Set your mind at rest.
If it is a question of soothsayers, I tell you
That you will find no man whose craft gives knowledge   [*215*
Of the unknowable.
Here is my proof:

An oracle was reported to Laïos once
(I will not say from Phoibos himself, but from

His appointed ministers, at any rate) [*220*
That his doom would be death at the hands of his own son—
His son, born of his flesh and of mine!

Now, you remember the story: Laïos was killed
By marauding strangers where three highways meet;
But his child had not been three days in this world [*225*
Before the King had pierced the baby's ankles

And left him to die on a lonely mountainside.
Thus, Apollo never caused that child
To kill his father, and it was not Laïos' fate
To die at the hands of his son, as he had feared. [*230*
This is what prophets and prophecies are worth!
Have no dread of them.
              It is God himself
Who can show us what he wills, in his own way.
OEDIPUS How strange a shadowy memory crossed my mind, [*235*
    Just now while you were speaking; it chilled my heart.
IOCASTE What do you mean? What memory do you speak of?
OEDIPUS If I understand you, Laïos was killed
At a place where three roads meet.
IOCASTE   So it was said; [*240*
    We have no later story.
OEDIPUS   Where did it happen?
IOCASTE Phokis, it is called: at a place where the Theban Way
    Divides into the roads towards Delphi and Daulia.
OEDIPUS When?
IOCASTE   We had the news not long before you came [*245*
    And proved the right to your succession here.
OEDIPUS Ah, what net has God been weaving for me?
IOCASTE Oedipus! Why does this trouble you?
OEDIPUS   Do not ask me yet. [*250*
    First, tell me how Laïos looked, and tell me
    How old he was.
IOCASTE   He was tall, his hair just touched
    With white; his form was not unlike your own.
OEDIPUS I think that I myself may be accurst [*255*
    By my own ignorant edict.
IOCASTE   You speak strangely.
    It makes me tremble to look at you, my King.
OEDIPUS I am not sure that the blind man can not see.
    But I should know better if you were to tell me— [*260*
IOCASTE Anything—though I dread to hear you ask it.
OEDIPUS Was the King lightly escorted, or did he ride
    With a large company, as a ruler should?
IOCASTE There were five men with him in all: one was a herald;
    And a single chariot, which he was driving. [*265*
OEDIPUS Alas, that makes it plain enough!
                  But who—
    Who told you how it happened?
IOCASTE   A household servant,
    The only one to escape. [*270*

OEDIPUS   And is he still
    A servant of ours?
IOCASTE   No; for when he came back at last
    And found you enthroned in the place of the dead king,
    He came to me, touched my hand with his, and begged   [275
    That I would send him away to the frontier district
    Where only the shepherds go—
    As far away from the city as I could send him.
    I granted his prayer; for although the man was a slave,
    He had earned more than this favor at my hands.   [280
OEDIPUS   Can he be called back quickly?
IOCASTE   Easily.
    But why?
OEDIPUS   I have taken too much upon myself
    Without enquiry; therefore I wish to consult him.   [285
IOCASTE   Then he shall come.
                            But am I not one also
    To whom you might confide these fears of yours?
OEDIPUS   That is your right; it will not be denied you,
    Now least of all; for I have reached a pitch   [290
    Of wild foreboding. Is there anyone
    To whom I should sooner speak?
    Polybos of Corinth is my father.
    My mother is a Dorian: Meropê.
    I grew up chief among the men of Corinth   [295
    Until a strange thing happened—
    Not worth my passion, it may be, but strange.

    At a feast, a drunken man maundering in his cups
    Cries out that I am not my father's son!

    I contained myself that night, though I felt anger   [300
    And a sinking heart. The next day I visited
    My father and mother, and questioned them. They stormed,
    Calling it all the slanderous rant of a fool;
    And this relieved me. Yet the suspicion
    Remained always aching in my mind;   [305
    I knew there was talk; I could not rest;
    And finally, saying nothing to my parents,
    I went to the shrine at Delphi.
    The god dismissed my question without reply;
    He spoke of other things.   [310
                            Some were clear,
    Full of wretchedness, dreadful, unbearable:
    As, that I should lie with my own mother, breed
    Children from whom all men would turn their eyes;
    And that I should be my father's murderer.   [315

    I heard all this, and fled. And from that day
    Corinth to me was only in the stars
    Descending in that quarter of the sky,
    As I wandered farther and farther on my way
    To a land where I should never see the evil   [320
    Sung by the oracle. And I came to this country

Where, so you say, King Laïos was killed.
I will tell you all that happened there, my lady.
There were three highways
Coming together at a place I passed;   [*325*
And there a herald came towards me, and a chariot
Drawn by horses, with a man such as you describe
Seated in it. The groom leading the horses
Forced me off the road at his lord's command;
But as this charioteer lurched over towards me   [*330*
I struck him in my rage. The old man saw me
And brought his double goad down upon my head
As I came abreast.

              He was paid back, and more!
Swinging my club in this right hand I knocked him   [*335*
Out of his car, and he rolled on the ground.

                        I killed him.
I killed them all.
Now if that stranger and Laïos were—kin,
Where is a man more miserable than I?   [*340*
More hated by the gods? Citizen and alien alike
Must never shelter me or speak to me—
I must be shunned by all.

                And I myself
Pronounced this malediction upon myself!   [*345*
Think if it: I have touched you with these hands,
These hands that killed your husband. What defilement!
Am I all evil, then? It must be so,
Since I must flee from Thebes, yet never again
See my own countrymen, my own country,   [*350*
For fear of joining my mother in marriage
And killing Polybos, my father.

                Ah,
If I was created so, born to this fate,
Who could deny the savagery of God?   [*355*

O holy majesty of heavenly powers!
May I never see that day! Never!
Rather let me vanish from the race of men
Than know the abomination destined me!
CHORAGOS We too, my lord, have felt dismay at this.   [*360*
    But there is hope: you have yet to hear the shepherd.
OEDIPUS Indeed, I fear no other hope is left me.
IOCASTE What do you hope from him when he comes?
OEDIPUS   This much:
    If his account of the murder tallies with yours,   [*365*
    Then I am cleared.
IOCASTE   What was it that I said
    Of such importance?
OEDIPUS   Why, "marauders," you said,
    Killed the King, according to this man's story.   [*370*
    If he maintains that still, if there were several,
    Clearly the guilt is not mine: I was alone.
    But if he says one man, singlehanded, did it,
    Then the evidence all points to me.

IOCASTE   You may be sure that he said there were several;   [*375*
          And can he call back that story now? He cán not.
          The whole city heard it as plainly as I.
          But suppose he alters some detail of it:
          He can not ever show that Laïos' death
          Fulfilled the oracle: for Apollo said   [*380*
          My child was doomed to kill him; and my child—
          Poor baby!—it was my child that died first.
          No. From now on, where oracles are concerned,
          I would not waste a second thought on any.
OEDIPUS   You may be right.   [*385*
                        But come: let someone go
          For the shepherd at once. This matter must be settled.
IOCASTE   I will send for him.
          I would not wish to cross you in anything,
          And surely not in this.—Let us go in.   [*390*
          [*Exeunt into the palace.*]

ODE II

CHORUS   Let me be reverent in the ways of right,   (STROPHE 1)
         Lowly the paths I journey on;
         Let all my words and actions keep
         The laws of the pure universe
         From highest Heaven handed down.   [*5*
         For Heaven is their bright nurse,
         Those generations of the realms of light;
         Ah, never of mortal kind were they begot,
         Nor are they slaves of memory, lost in sleep:
         Their Father is greater than Time, and ages not.   [*10*

         The tyrant is a child of Pride   (ANTISTROPHE 1)
         Who drinks from his great sickening cup
         Recklessness and vanity,
         Until from his high crest headlong
         He plummets to the dust of hope.   [*15*
         That strong man is not strong.
         But let no fair ambition be denied;
         May God protect the wrestler for the State
         In government, in comely policy,
         Who will fear God, and on His ordinance wait.   [*20*

         Haughtiness and the high hand of disdain   (STROPHE 2)
         Tempt and outrage God's holy law;
         And any mortal who dares hold
         No immortal Power in awe
         Will be caught up in a net of pain: [*25*
         The price for which his levity is sold.
         Let each man take due earnings, then,
         And keep his hands from holy things,
         And from blasphemy stand apart—

Else the crackling blast of heaven   [*30*
Blows on his head, and on his desperate heart;
Though fools will honor impious men,
In their cities no tragic poet sings.

Shall we lose faith in Delphi's obscurities,   (ANTISTROPHE 2)
We who have heard the world's core   [*35*
Discredited, and the sacred wood
Of Zeus at Elis praised no more?
The deeds and the strange prophecies
Must make a pattern yet to be understood.
Zeus, if indeed you are lord of all,   [*40*
Throned in light over night and day,
Mirror this in your endless mind:
Our masters call the oracle
Words on the wind, and the Delphic vision blind!
Their hearts no longer know Apollo,   [*45*
And reverence for the gods has died away.

SCENE III

[*Enter* IOCASTE.]
IOCASTE   Princes of Thebes, it has occurred to me
     To visit the altars of the gods, bearing
     These branches as a suppliant, and this incense.
     Our King is not himself: his noble soul
     Is overwrought with fantasies of dread,   [*5*
     Else he would consider
     The new prophecies in the light of the old.
     He will listen to any voice that speaks disaster,
     And my advice goes for nothing.
[*She approaches the altar,* R.]
                         To you, then, Apollo,   [*10*
     Lycean lord, since you are nearest, I turn in prayer.
     Receive these offerings, and grant us deliverance
     From defilement. Our hearts are heavy with fear
     When we see our leader distracted, as helpless sailors
     Are terrified by the confusion of their helmsman.   [*15*
[*Enter* MESSENGER.]
MESSENGER   Friends, no doubt you can direct me:
     Where shall I find the house of Oedipus,
     Or, better still, where is the King himself?
CHORAGOS   It is this very place, stranger; he is inside.
     This is his wife and mother of his children.   [*20*
MESSENGER   I wish her happiness in a happy house,
     Blest in all the fulfillment of her marriage.
IOCASTE   I wish as much for you: your courtesy
     Deserves a like good fortune. But now, tell me:
     Why have you come? What have you to say to us?   [*25*
MESSENGER   Good news, my lady, for your house and your husband.
IOCASTE   What news? Who sent you here?

MESSENGER   I am from Corinth.
    The news I bring ought to mean joy for you,
    Though it may be you will find some grief in it.   [30
IOCASTE   What is it? How can it touch us in both ways?
MESSENGER   The people of Corinth, they say,
    Intend to call Oedipus to be their king.
IOCASTE   But old Polybos—is he not reigning still?
MESSENGER   No. Death holds him in his sepulchre.   [35
IOCASTE   What are you saying? Polybos is dead?
MESSENGER   If I am not telling the truth, may I die myself.
IOCASTE   [*To a* MAIDSERVANT]   Go in, go quickly; tell this to your master.

    O riddlers of God's will, where are you now!   [40
    This was the man whom Oedipus, long ago,
    Feared so, fled so, in dread of destroying him—
    But it was another fate by which he died.
    [*Enter* OEDIPUS, C.]
OEDIPUS   Dearest Iocastê, why have you sent for me?
IOCASTE   Listen to what this man says, and then tell me   [45
    What has become of the solemn prophecies.
OEDIPUS   Who is this man? What is his news for me?
IOCASTE   He has come from Corinth to announce your father's death!
OEDIPUS   Is it true, stranger? Tell me in your own words.
MESSENGER   I can not say it more clearly: the King is dead.   [50
OEDIPUS   Was it by treason? Or by an attack of illness?
MESSENGER   A little thing brings old men to their rest.
OEDIPUS   It was sickness, then?
MESSENGER   Yes, and his many years.
OEDIPUS   Ah!   [55
    Why should a man respect the Pythian hearth, or
    Give heed to the birds that jangle above his head?
    They prophesied that I should kill Polybos,
    Kill my own father; but he is dead and buried,
    And I am here—I never touched him, never,   [60
    Unless he died of grief for my departure,
    And thus, in a sense, through me. No. Polybos
    Has packed the oracles off with him underground.
    They are empty words.
IOCASTE   Had I not told you so?   [65
OEDIPUS   You had; it was my faint heart that betrayed me.
IOCASTE   From now on never think of those things again.
OEDIPUS   And yet—must I not fear my mother's bed?
IOCASTE   Why should anyone in this world be afraid,
    Since Fate rules us and nothing can be foreseen?   [70
    A man should live only for the present day.

    Have no more fear of sleeping with your mother:
    How many men, in dreams, have lain with their mothers!
    No reasonable man is troubled by such things.
OEDIPUS   That is true; only—   [75
    If only my mother were not still alive!
    But she is alive. I can not help my dread.
IOCASTE   Yet this news of your father's death is wonderful.

OEDIPUS   Wonderful. But I fear the living woman.
MESSENGER   Tell me, who is this woman that you fear?   [80
OEDIPUS   It is Meropê, man; the wife of King Polybos.
MESSENGER   Meropê? Why should you be afraid of her?
OEDIPUS   An oracle of the gods, a dreadful saying.
MESSENGER   Can you tell me about it or are you sworn to silence?
OEDIPUS   I can tell you, and I will.   [85
    Apollo said through his prophet that I was the man
    Who should marry his own mother, shed his father's blood
    With his own hands. And so, for all these years
    I have kept clear of Corinth, and no harm has come—
    Though it would have been sweet to see my parents again.   [90
MESSENGER   And is this the fear that drove you out of Corinth?
OEDIPUS   Would you have me kill my father?
MESSENGER   As for that
    You must be reassured by the news I gave you.
OEDIPUS   If you could reassure me, I would reward you.   [95
MESSENGER   I had that in mind, I will confess: I thought
    I could count on you when you returned to Corinth.
OEDIPUS   No: I will never go near my parents again.
MESSENGER   Ah, son, you still do not know what you are doing—
OEDIPUS   What do you mean? In the name of God tell me!   [100
MESSENGER   —If these are your reasons for not going home.
OEDIPUS   I tell you, I fear the oracle may come true.
MESSENGER   And guilt may come upon you through your parents?
OEDIPUS   That is the dread that is always in my heart.
MESSENGER   Can you not see that all your fears are groundless?   [105
OEDIPUS   How can you say that? They are my parents, surely?
MESSENGER   Polybos was not your father.
OEDIPUS   Not my father?
MESSENGER   No more your father than the man speaking to you.
OEDIPUS   But you are nothing to me!   [110
MESSENGER   Neither was he.
OEDIPUS   Then why did he call me son?
MESSENGER   I will tell you:
    Long ago he had you from my hands, as a gift.
OEDIPUS   Then how could he love me so, if I was not his?   [115
MESSENGER   He had no children, and his heart turned to you.
OEDIPUS   What of you? Did you buy me? Did you find me by chance?
MESSENGER   I came upon you in the crooked pass of Kithairon.
OEDIPUS   And what were you doing there?
MESSENGER   Tending my flocks.   [120
OEDIPUS   A wandering shepherd?
MESSENGER   But your savior, son, that day.
OEDIPUS   From what did you save me?
MESSENGER   Your ankles should tell you that.
OEDIPUS   Ah, stranger, why do you speak of that childhood pain?   [125
MESSENGER   I cut the bonds that tied your ankles together.
OEDIPUS   I have had the mark as long as I can remember.
MESSENGER   That was why you were given the name you bear.
OEDIPUS   God! Was it my father or my mother who did it?
    Tell me!   [130
MESSENGER   I do not know. The man who gave you to me
    Can tell you better than I.

OEDIPUS   It was not you that found me, but another?

MESSENGER   It was another shepherd gave you to me.

OEDIPUS   Who was he? Can you tell me who he was?   [*135*

MESSENGER   I think he was said to be one of Laïos' people.

OEDIPUS   You mean the Laïos who was king here years ago?

MESSENGER   Yes; King Laïos; and the man was one of his herdsmen.

OEDIPUS   Is he still alive? Can I see him?

MESSENGER   These men here   [*140*
    Know best about such things.

OEDIPUS   Does anyone here
    Know this shepherd that he is talking about?
    Have you seen him in the fields, or in the town?
    If you have, tell me. It is time things were made plain.   [*145*

CHORAGOS   I think the man he means is that same shepherd
    You have already asked to see. Iocastê perhaps
    Could tell you something.

OEDIPUS   Do you know anything
    About him, Lady? Is he the man we have summoned?   [*150*
    Is that the man this shepherd means?

IOCASTE   Why think of him?
    Forget this herdsman. Forget it all.
    This talk is a waste of time.

OEDIPUS   How can you say that,   [*155*
    When the clues to my true birth are in my hands?

IOCASTE   For God's love, let us have no more questioning!
    Is your life nothing to you?
    My own is pain enough for me to bear.

OEDIPUS   You need not worry. Suppose my mother a slave,   [*160*
    And born of slaves: no baseness can touch you.

IOCASTE   Listen to me, I beg you: do not do this thing!

OEDIPUS   I will not listen; the truth must be made known.

IOCASTE   Everything that I say is for your own good!

OEDIPUS   My own good   [*165*
    Snaps my patience, then; I want none of it.

IOCASTE   You are fatally wrong! May you never learn who you are!

OEDIPUS   Go, one of you, and bring the shepherd here.
    Let us leave this woman to brag of her royal name.

IOCASTE   Ah, miserable!   [*170*
    That is the only word I have for you now.
    That is the only word I can ever have.
    [*Exit into the palace.*]

CHORAGOS   Why has she left us, Oedipus? Why has she gone
    In such a passion of sorrow? I fear this silence:
    Something dreadful may come of it.   [*175*

OEDIPUS   Let it come!
    However base my birth, I must know about it.
    The Queen, like a woman, is perhaps ashamed
    To think of my low origin. But I
    Am a child of Luck; I can not be dishonored.   [*180*
    Luck is my mother; the passing months, my brothers,
    Have seen me rich and poor.
                  If this is so,
    How could I wish that I were someone else?
    How could I not be glad to know my birth?   [*185*

ODE III

CHORUS   If ever the coming time were known   (STROPHE)
  To my heart's pondering,
  Kithairon, now by Heaven I see the torches
  At the festival of the next full moon,
  And see the dance, and hear the choir sing   [5
  A grace to your gentle shade:
  Mountain where Oedipus was found,
  O mountain guard of a noble race!
  May the god who heals us lend his aid,
  And let that glory come to pass   [10
  For our king's cradling-ground.

  Of the nymphs that flower beyond the years,   (ANTISTROPHE)
  Who bore you, royal child,
  To Pan of the hills or the timberline Apollo,
  Cold in delight where the upland clears,   [15
  Or Hermês for whom Kyllenê's heights are piled?
  Or flushed as evening cloud,
  Great Dionysos, roamer of mountains,
  He—was it he who found you there,
  And caught you up in his own proud   [20
  Arms from the sweet god-ravisher ·
  Who laughed by the Muses' fountains?

SCENE IV

OEDIPUS   Sirs: though I do not know the man,
  I think I see him coming, this shepherd we want:
  He is old, like our friend here, and the men
  Bringing him seem to be servants of my house.
  But you can tell, if you have ever seen him.   [5
  [*Enter* SHEPHERD *escorted by servants.*]
CHORAGOS   I know him, he was Laïos' man. You can trust him.
OEDIPUS   Tell me first, you from Corinth: is this the shepherd
  We were discussing?
MESSENGER   This is the very man.
OEDIPUS   [*To* SHEPHERD]   Come here. No, look at me. You must   [10
  answer
  Everything I ask.—You belonged to Laïos?
SHEPHERD   Yes: born his slave, brought up in his house.
OEDIPUS   Tell me: what kind of work did you do for him?
SHEPHERD   I was a shepherd of his, most of my life.   [15
OEDIPUS   Where mainly did you go for pasturage?
SHEPHERD   Sometimes Kithairon, sometimes the hills near-by.
OEDIPUS   Do you remember ever seeing this man out there?
SHEPHERD   What would he be doing there? This man?
OEDIPUS   This man standing here. Have you ever seen him before?   [20
SHEPHERD   No. At least, not to my recollection.

MESSENGER   And that is not strange, my lord. But I'll refresh
  His memory: he must remember when we two
  Spent three whole seasons together, March to September,
  On Kithairon or thereabouts. He had two flocks;   [25
  I had one. Each autumn I'd drive mine home
  And he would go back with his to Laïos' sheepfold.—
  Is this not true, just as I have described it?
SHEPHERD   True, yes; but it was all so long ago.
MESSENGER   Well, then: do you remember, back in those days [30
  That you gave me a baby boy to bring up as my own?
SHEPHERD   What if I did? What are you trying to say?
MESSENGER   King Oedipus was once that little child.
SHEPHERD   Damn you, hold your tongue!
OEDIPUS   No more of that! [35
  It is your tongue needs watching, not this man's.
SHEPHERD   My King, my Master, what is it I have done wrong?
OEDIPUS   You have not answered his question about the boy.
SHEPHERD   He does not know . . . He is only making trouble . . .
OEDIPUS   Come, speak plainly, or it will go hard with you. [40
SHEPHERD   In God's name, do not torture an old man!
OEDIPUS   Come here, one of you; bind his arms behind him.
SHEPHERD   Unhappy king! What more do you wish to learn?
OEDIPUS   Did you give this man the child he speaks of?
SHEPHERD   I did. [45
  And I would to God I had died that very day.
OEDIPUS   You will die now unless you speak the truth.
SHEPHERD   Yet if I speak the truth, I am worse than dead.
OEDIPUS   Very well; since you insist upon delaying—
SHEPHERD   No! I have told you already that I gave him the boy. [50
OEDIPUS   Where did you get him? From your house? From somewhere
  else?
SHEPHERD   Not from mine, no. A man gave him to me.
OEDIPUS   Is that man here? Do you know whose slave he was?
SHEPHERD   For God's love, my King, do not ask me any more! [55
OEDIPUS   You are a dead man if I have to ask you again.
SHEPHERD   Then . . . Then the child was from the palace of Laïos.
OEDIPUS   A slave child? or a child of his own line?
SHEPHERD   Ah, I am on the brink of dreadful speech!
OEDIPUS   And I of dreadful hearing. Yet I must hear. [60
SHEPHERD   If you must be told, then . . .
          They said it was Laïos' child,
  But it is your wife who can tell you about that.
OEDIPUS   My wife!—Did she give it to you?
SHEPHERD   My lord, she did. [65
OEDIPUS   Do you know why?
SHEPHERD   I was told to get rid of it.
OEDIPUS   An unspeakable mother!
SHEPHERD   There had been prophecies . . .
OEDIPUS   Tell me. [70
SHEPHERD   It was said that the boy would kill his own father.
OEDIPUS   Then why did you give him over to this old man?
SHEPHERD   I pitied the baby, my King,
  And I thought that this man would take him far away
  To his own country. [75
       He saved him—but for what a fate!

For if you are what this man says you are,
No man living is more wretched than Oedipus.
OEDIPUS   Ah God!
It was true!   [*80*
                    All the prophecies!
                              —Now,
O Light, may I look on you for the last time!
I, Oedipus,
Oedipus, damned in his birth, in his marriage damned,   [*85*
Damned in the blood he shed with his own hand!
[*He rushes into the palace.*]

ODE IV

CHORUS   Alas for the seed of men.   (STROPHE 1)

What measure shall I give these generations
That breathe on the void and are void
And exist and do not exist?

Who bears more weight of joy   [*5*
Than mass of sunlight shifting in images,
Or who shall make his thought stay on
That down time drifts away?

Your splendor is all fallen.

O naked brow of wrath and tears,   [*10*
O change of Oedipus!
I who saw your days call no man blest—
Your great days like ghósts góne.

That mind was a strong bow.   (ANTISTROPHE 1)

Deep, how deep you drew it then, hard archer,   [*15*
At a dim fearful range,
And brought dear glory down!

You overcame the stranger—
The virgin with her hooking lion claws—
And though death sang, stood like a tower   [*20*
To make pale Thebes take heart.

Fortress against our sorrow!

Divine king, giver of laws,
Majestic Oedipus!
No prince in Thebes had ever such renown,   [*25*
No prince won such grace of power.

And now of all men ever known   (STROPHE 2)
Most pitiful is this man's story:

His fortunes are most changed, his state
Fallen to a low slave's   [30
Ground under bitter fate.

O Oedipus, most royal one!
The great door that expelled you to the light
Gave at night—ah, gave night to your glory:
As to the father, to the fathering son.   [35

All understood too late.

How could that queen whom Laïos won,
The garden that he harrowed at his height,
Be silent when that act was done?

But all eyes fail before time's eye,   (ANTISTROPHE 2)   [40
All actions come to justice there.
Though never willed, though far down the deep past,
Your bed, your dread sirings,
Are brought to book at last.
Child by Laïos doomed to die,   [45
Then doomed to lose that fortunate little death,
Would God you never took breath in this air
That with my wailing lips I take to cry:

For I weep the world's outcast.

I was blind, and now I can tell why: [50
Asleep, for you had given ease of breath
To Thebes, while the false years went by.

EXODOS

[*Enter, from the palace,* SECOND MESSENGER.]
SECOND MESSENGER   Elders of Thebes, most honored in his land,
    What horrors are yours to see and hear, what weight
    Of sorrow to be endured, if, true to your birth,
    You venerate the line of Labdakos!
    I think neither Istros nor Phasis, those great rivers,   [5
    Could purify this place of the corruption
    It shelters now, or soon must bring to light—
    Evil not done unconsciously, but willed.

    The greatest griefs are those we cause ourselves.
CHORAGOS   Surely, friend, we have grief enough already;   [10
    What new sorrow do you mean?
SECOND MESSENGER   The Queen is dead.
CHORAGOS   Iocastê? Dead? But at whose hand?
SECOND MESSENGER   Her own.
    The full horror of what happened you can not know,   [15
    For you did not see it; but I, who did, will tell you
    As clearly as I can how she met her death.

When she had left us,
In passionate silence, passing through the court,
She ran to her apartment in the house,   [*20*
Her hair clutched by the fingers of both hands.
She closed the doors behind her; then, by that bed
Where long ago the fatal son was conceived—
That son who should bring about his father's death—
We heard her call upon Laïos, dead so many years,   [*25*
And heard her wail for the double fruit of her marriage,
A husband by her husband, children by her child.

Exactly how she died I do not know:
For Oedipus burst in moaning and would not let us
Keep vigil to the end: it was by him   [*30*
As he stormed about the room that our eyes were caught.
From one to another of us he went, begging a sword,
Cursing the wife who was not his wife, the mother
Whose womb had carried his own children and himself.
I do not know: it was none of us aided him,   [*35*
But surely one of the gods was in control!
For with a dreadful cry
He hurled his weight, as though wrenched out of himself,
At the twin doors: the bolts gave, and he rushed in.
And there we saw her hanging, her body swaying   [*40*
From the cruel cord she had noosed about her neck.
A great sob broke from him, heartbreaking to hear,
As he loosed the rope and lowered her to the ground.

I would blot out from my mind what happened next!
For the King ripped from her own gown the golden brooches [*45*
That were her ornament, and raised them, and plunged them down
Straight into his own eyeballs, crying, "No more,
No more shall you look on the misery about me,
The horrors of my own doing! Too long you have known
The faces of those whom I should never have seen,   [*50*
Too long been blind to those for whom I was searching!
From this hour, go in darkness!" And as he spoke,
He struck at his eyes—not once, but many times;
And the blood spattered his beard,
Bursting from his ruined sockets like red hail.   [*55*

So from the unhappiness of two this evil has sprung,
A curse on the man and woman alike. The old
Happiness of the house of Labdakos
Was happiness enough: where is it today?
It is all wailing and ruin, disgrace, death—all   [*60*
The misery of mankind that has a name—
And it is wholly and for ever theirs.
CHORAGOS   Is he in agony still? Is there no rest for him?
SECOND MESSENGER   He is calling for someone to lead him to the gates
So that all the children of Kadmos may look upon   [*65*
His father's murderer, his mother's—no,
I can not say it!
                And then he will leave Thebes,

Self-exiled, in order that the curse
Which he himself pronounced may depart from the house.   [70
He is weak, and there is none to lead him,
So terrible is his suffering.
                              But you will see:
Look, the doors are opening; in a moment
You will see a thing that would crush a heart of stone.   [75
[*The central door is opened;* OEDIPUS, *blinded, is led in.*]
CHORAGOS   Dreadful indeed for men to see.
       Never have my own eyes
       Looked on a sight so full of fear.

       Oedipus!
       What madness came upon you, what daemon   [80
       Leaped on your life with heavier
       Punishment than a mortal man can bear?
       No: I can not even
       Look at you, poor ruined one.
       And I would speak, question, ponder,   [85
       If I were able. No.
       You make me shudder.
OEDIPUS   God.   God.
       Is there a sorrow greater?
       Where shall I find harbor in this world?   [90
       My voice is hurled far on a dark wind.
       What has God done to me?
CHORAGOS   Too terrible to think of, or to see.

OEDIPUS   O cloud of night,   (STROPHE 1)
       Never to be turned away: night coming on,   [95
       I can not tell how: night like a shroud!

       My fair winds brought me here.
                              Oh God. Again
       The pain of the spikes where I had sight,
       The flooding pain   [100
       Of memory, never to be gouged out.
CHORAGOS   This is not strange.
       You suffer it all twice over, remorse in pain,
       Pain in remorse.

OEDIPUS   Ah dear friend   (ANTISTROPHE 1)   [105
       Are you faithful even yet, you alone?
       Are you still standing near me, will you stay here,
       Patient, to care for the blind?
                              The blind man!
       Yet even blind I know who it is attends me,   [110
       By the voice's tone—
       Though my new darkness hide the comforter.
CHORAGOS   Oh fearful act!
       What god was it drove you to rake black
       Night across your eyes?   [115

OEDIPUS   Apollo. Apollo. Dear   (STROPHE 2)
       Children, the god was Apollo.

He brought my sick, sick fate upon me.
But the blinding hand was my own!
How could I bear to see   [*120*
When all my sight was horror everywhere?
CHORAGOS   Everywhere; that is true.
OEDIPUS   And now what is left?
Images? Love? A greeting even,
Sweet to the senses? Is there anything?   [*125*
Ah, no, friends: lead me away.
Lead me away from Thebes.
                       Lead the great wreck
And hell of Oedipus, whom the gods hate.
CHORAGOS   Your fate is clear, you are not blind to that.   [*130*
Would God you had never found it out!

OEDIPUS   Death take the man who unbound   (ANTISTROPHE 2)
My feet on that hillside
And delivered me from death to life! What life?
If only I had died,   [*135*
This weight of monstrous doom
Could not have dragged me and my darlings down.
CHORAGOS   I would have wished the same.
OEDIPUS   Oh never to have come here
With my father's blood upon me! Never   [*140*
To have been the man they call his mother's husband!
Oh accurst! Oh child of evil,
To have entered that wretched bed—
                   the selfsame one!   [*145*
More primal than sin itself, this fell to me.
CHORAGOS   I do not know how I can answer you.
You were better dead than alive and blind.
OEDIPUS   Do not counsel me any more. This punishment
That I have laid upon myself is just.   [*150*
If I had eyes,
I do not know how I could bear the sight
Of my father, when I came to the house of Death,
Or my mother: for I have sinned against them both
So vilely that I could not make my peace   [*155*
By strangling my own life.
                Or do you think my children,
Born as they were born, would be sweet to my eyes?
Ah never, never! Nor this town with its high walls,
Nor the holy images of the gods.   [*160*
              For I,
Thrice miserable!—Oedipus, noblest of all the line
Of Kadmos, have condemned myself to enjoy
These things no more, by my own malediction
Expelling that man whom the gods declared   [*165*
To be a defilement in the house of Laïos.
After exposing the rankness of my own guilt,
How could I look men frankly in the eyes?
No, I swear it,
If I could have stifled my hearing at its source,   [*170*
I would have done it and made all this body

A tight cell of misery, blank to light and sound:
So I should have been safe in a dark agony
Beyond all recollection.
                                   Ah Kithairon!   [*175*
Why did you shelter me? When I was cast upon you,
Why did I not die? Then I should never
Have shown the world my execrable birth.
Ah Polybos! Corinth, city that I believed
The ancient seat of my ancestors: how fair   [*180*
I seemed, your child! And all the while this evil
Was cancerous within me!
                                         For I am sick
In my daily life, sick in my origin.

O three roads, dark ravine, woodland and way   [*185*
Where three roads met: you, drinking my father's blood,
My own blood, spilled by my own hand: can you remember
The unspeakable things I did there, and the things
I went on from there to do?
                                       O marriage, marriage!   [*190*
The act that engendered me, and again the act
Performed by the son in the same bed—
                                                Ah, the net
Of incest, mingling fathers, brothers, sons,
With brides, wives, mothers: the last evil   [*195*
That can be known by men: no tongue can say
How evil!
                 No. For the love of God, conceal me
Somewhere far from Thebes; or kill me; or hurl me
Into the sea, away from men's eyes for ever.   [*200*

Come, lead me. You need not fear to touch me.
Of all men, I alone can bear this guilt.
[*Enter* CREON.]
CHORAGOS   We are not the ones to decide; but Creon here
      May fitly judge of what you ask. He only
      Is left to protect the city in your place.   [*205*
OEDIPUS   Alas, how can I speak to him? What right have I
      To beg his courtesy whom I have deeply wronged?
CREON   I have not come to mock you, Oedipus,
      Or to reproach you, either.
      [*To* ATTENDANTS]   —You, standing there: [*210*
      If you have lost all respect for man's dignity,
      At least respect the flame of Lord Helios:
      Do not allow this pollution to show itself
      Openly here, an affront to the earth
      And Heaven's rain and the light of day. No, take him   [*215*
      Into the house as quickly as you can.
      For it is proper
      That only the close kindred see his grief.
OEDIPUS   I pray you in God's name, since your courtesy
      Ignores my dark expectation, visiting   [*220*
      With mercy this man of all men most execrable:
      Give me what I ask—for your good, not for mine.

CREON   And what is it that you would have me do?
OEDIPUS   Drive me out of this country as quickly as may be
    To a place where no human voice can ever greet me.   [225
CREON   I should have done that before now—only,
    God's will had not been wholly revealed to me.
OEDIPUS   But his command is plain: the parricide
    Must be destroyed. I am that evil man.
CREON   That is the sense of it, yes; but as things are,   [230
    We had best discover clearly what is to be done.
OEDIPUS   You would learn more about a man like me?
CREON   You are ready now to listen to the god.
OEDIPUS   I will listen. But it is to you
    That I must turn for help. I beg you, hear me.   [235

The woman in there—
Give her whatever funeral you think proper:
She is your sister.
                    —But let me go, Creon!
Let me purge my father's Thebes of the pollution   [240
Of my living here, and go out to the wild hills,
To Kithairon, that has won such fame with me,
The tomb my mother and father appointed for me,
And let me die there, as they willed I should.
And yet I know   [245
Death will not ever come to me through sickness
Or in any natural way: I have been preserved
For some unthinkable fate. But let that be.
As for my sons, you need not care for them.
They are men, they will find some way to live.   [250
But my poor daughters, who have shared my table,
Who never before have been parted from their father—
Take care of them, Creon; do this for me.
And will you let me touch them with my hands
A last time, and let us weep together?   [255
Be kind, my lord,
Great prince, be kind!
                    Could I but touch them,
They would be mine again, as when I had my eyes.
[Enter ANTIGONE and ISMENE, attended.]
Ah, God!   [260
Is it my dearest children I hear weeping?
Has Creon pitied me and sent my daughters?
CREON   Yes, Oedipus: I knew that they were dear to you
    In the old days, and know you must love them still.
OEDIPUS   May God bless you for this—and be a friendlier   [265
    Guardian to you than he has been to me!

Children, where are you?
Come quickly to my hands: they are your brother's—
Hands that have brought your father's once clear eyes
To this way of seeing—   [270
                    Ah dearest ones,
I had neither sight nor knowledge then, your father
By the woman who was the source of his own life!

And I weep for you—having no strength to see you—,
I weep for you when I think of the bitterness   [275
That men will visit upon you all your lives.
What homes, what festivals can you attend
Without being forced to depart again in tears?
And when you come to marriageable age,
Where is the man, my daughters, who would dare   [280
Risk the bane that lies on all my children?
Is there any evil wanting? Your father killed
His father; sowed the womb of her who bore him;
Engendered you at the fount of his own existence!
That is what they will say of you.   [285
                                        Then, whom
Can you ever marry? There are no bridegrooms for you,
And your lives must wither away in sterile dreaming.
O Creon, son of Menoikeus!
You are the only father my daughters have,   [290
Since we, their parents, are both of us gone for ever.
They are your own blood: you will not let them
Fall into beggary and loneliness;
You will keep them from the miseries that are mine!
Take pity on them; see, they are only children,   [295
Friendless except for you. Promise me this,
Great Prince, and give me your hand in token of it.
[CREON *clasps his right hand.*]
Children:
I could say much, if you could understand me,
But as it is, I have only this prayer for you: [300
Live where you can, be as happy as you can—
Happier, please God, than God has made your father!
CREON   Enough. You have wept enough. Now go within.
OEDIPUS   I must; but it is hard.
CREON   Time eases all things.   [305
OEDIPUS   But you must promise—
CREON   Say what you desire.
OEDIPUS   Send me from Thebes!
CREON   God grant that I may!
OEDIPUS   But since God hates me . . .   [310
CREON   No, he will grant your wish.
OEDIPUS   You promise?
CREON   I can not speak beyond my knowledge.
OEDIPUS   Then lead me in.
CREON   Come now, and leave your children.   [315
OEDIPUS   No! Do not take them from me!
CREON   Think no longer
That you are in command here, but rather think
How, when you were, you served your own destruction.
[*Exeunt into the house all but the* CHORUS; *the* CHORAGOS *chants directly
to the audience.*]
CHORAGOS   Men of Thebes: look upon Oedipus.   [320

This is the king who solved the famous riddle
And towered up, most powerful of men.
No mortal eyes but looked on him with envy,

Yet in the end ruin swept over him.

Let every man in mankind's frailty   [*325*
Consider his last day; and let none
Presume on his good fortune until he find
Life, at his death, a memory without pain.

ANTIGONE

SOPHOCLES
Translated by Dudley Fitts and Robert Fitzgerald

THE CHARACTERS REPRESENTED

ANTIGONE	TEIRESIAS
ISMENE	A SENTRY
EURYDICE	A MESSENGER
CREON	CHORUS
HAIMON	CHORAGOS *(leader of chorus)*

SCENE *Before the palace of Creon, King of Thebes. A central double door, and two lateral doors. A platform extends the length of the façade, and from this platform three steps lead down into the orchestra, or chorus-ground. Time: dawn of the day after the repulse of the Argive army from the assault on Thebes.*

PROLOGUE

[ANTIGONE *and* ISMENE *enter from the central door of the palace.*]
ANTIGONE   Ismenê, dear sister,
You would think that we had already suffered enough
For the curse on Oedipus:
I cannot imagine any grief
That you and I have not gone through. And now—   [*5*
Have they told you of the new decree of our King Creon?
ISMENE   I have heard nothing: I know
That two sisters lost two brothers, a double death
In a single hour; and I know that the Argive army
Fled in the night; but beyond this, nothing.   [*10*
ANTIGONE   I thought so. And that is why I wanted you
To come out here with me. There is something we must do.
ISMENE   Why do you speak so strangely?
ANTIGONE   Listen, Ismenê:
Creon buried our brother Eteoclês   [*15*
With military honours, gave him a soldier's funeral,
And it was right that he should; but Polyneicês,
Who fought as bravely and died as miserably,—
They say that Creon has sworn
No one shall bury him, no one mourn for him,   [*20*
But his body must lie in the fields, a sweet treasure
For carrion birds to find as they search for food.
That is what they say, and our good Creon is coming here
To announce it publicly; and the penalty—
Stoning to death in the public square!   [*25*
                              There it is,
And now you can prove what you are:
A true sister, or a traitor to your family.
ISMENE   Antigonê, you are mad! What could I possibly do?
ANTIGONE   You must decide whether you will help me or not.   [*30*
ISMENE   I do not understand you. Help you in what?
ANTIGONE   Ismenê, I am going to bury him. Will you come?
ISMENE   Bury him! You have just said the new law forbids it.
ANTIGONE   He is my brother. And he is your brother, too.
ISMENE   But think of the danger! Think what Creon will do!   [*35*
ANTIGONE   Creon is not strong enough to stand in my way.
ISMENE   Ah sister!
Oedipus died, everyone hating him
For what his own search brought to light, his eyes
Ripped out by his own hand; and Iocastê died,   [*40*
His mother and wife at once: she twisted the cords
That strangled her life; and our two brothers died,
Each killed by the other's sword. And we are left:
But oh, Antigonê,
Think how much more terrible than these   [*45*
Our own death would be if we should go against Creon
And do what he has forbidden! We are only women,
We cannot fight with men, Antigonê!
The law is strong, we must give in to the law
In this thing, and in worse. I beg the Dead   [*50*
To forgive me, but I am helpless: I must yield

To those in authority. And I think it is dangerous business
To be always meddling.
ANTIGONE   If that is what you think,
I should not want you, even if you asked to come.   [55
You have made your choice, you can be what you want to be.
But I will bury him; and if I must die,
I say that this crime is holy: I shall lie down
With him in death, and I shall be as dear
To him as he to me.   [60
                    It is the dead,
Not the living, who make the longest demands:
We die for ever . . .
                    You may do as you like,
Since apparently the laws of the gods mean nothing to you.   [65
ISMENE   They mean a great deal to me; but I have no strength
To break laws that were made for the public good.
ANTIGONE   That must be your excuse, I suppose. But as for me,
I will bury the brother I love.
ISMENE   Antigonê,   [70
I am so afraid for you!
ANTIGONE   You need not be:
You have yourself to consider, after all.
ISMENE   But no one must hear of this, you must tell no one!
I will keep it a secret, I promise!   [75
ANTIGONE   Oh tell it! Tell everyone!
Think how they'll hate you when it all comes out
If they learn that you knew about it all the time!
ISMENE   So fiery! You should be cold with fear.
ANTIGONE   Perhaps. But I am doing only what I must.   [80
ISMENE   But can you do it? I say that you cannot.
ANTIGONE   Very well: when my strength gives out, I shall do no more.
ISMENE   Impossible things should not be tried at all.
ANTIGONE   Go away, Ismenê:
I shall be hating you soon, and the dead will too,   [85
For your words are hateful. Leave me my foolish plan:
I am not afraid of the danger; if it means death,
It will not be the worst of deaths—death without honour.
ISMENE   Go then, if you feel that you must.
You are unwise,   [90
But a loyal friend indeed to those who love you.
[*Exit into the palace.* ANTIGONE *goes off, left. Enter the* CHORUS.]

PARODOS

CHORUS   Now the long blade of the sun, lying   (STROPHE 1)
    Level east to west, touches with glory
    Thebes of the Seven Gates. Open, unlidded
    Eye of golden day! O marching light
    Across the eddy and rush of Dircê's stream,[1]   [5
    Striking the white shields of the enemy

---

1. *Dircê's stream*, a spring named for Dircê, wife of a king of Thebes. Dircê was cruel to Antiope, whose sons (sired by Zeus) killed Dircê and cast her body into the spring.

Thrown headlong backward from the blaze of morning!
CHORAGOS   Polyneicês their commander
    Roused them with windy phrases,
    He the wild eagle screaming   [*10*
    Insults above our land,
    His wings their shields of snow,
    His crest their marshalled helms.
CHORUS   Against our seven gates in a yawning ring   (ANTISTROPHE 1)
    The famished spears came onward in the night;   [*15*
    But before his jaws were sated with our blood,
    Or pinefire took the garland of our towers,
    He was thrown back; and as he turned, great Thebes—
    No tender victim for his noisy power—
    Rose like a dragon behind him, shouting war.   [*20*
CHORAGOS   For God hates utterly
    The bray of bragging tongues;
    And when he beheld their smiling,
    Their swagger of golden helms,
    The frown of his thunder blasted   [*25*
    Their first man from our walls.
CHORUS   We heard his shout of triumph high in the air   (STROPHE 2)
    Turn to a scream; far out in a flaming arc
    He fell with his windy torch, and the earth struck him.
    And others storming in fury no less than his   [*30*
    Found shock of death in the dusty joy of battle.
CHORAGOS   Seven captains at seven gates
    Yielded their clanging arms to the god
    That bends the battle-line and breaks it.
    These two only, brothers in blood,   [*35*
    Face to face in matchless rage,
    Mirroring each the other's death,
    Clashed in long combat.
CHORUS   But now in the beautiful morning of victory   (ANTISTROPHE 2)
    Let Thebes of the many chariots sing for joy!   [*40*
    With hearts for dancing we'll take leave of war:
    Our temples shall be sweet with hymns of praise,
    And the long night shall echo with our chorus.

Scene I

CHORAGOS   But now at last our new King is coming:
    Creon of Thebes, Menoikeus' son.
    In this auspicious dawn of his reign
    What are the new complexities
    That shifting Fate has woven for him?   [*5*
    What is his counsel? Why has he summoned
    The old men to hear him?
    [*Enter* CREON *from the palace, center. He addresses the* CHORUS *from the top step.*]
CREON   Gentlemen: I have the honour to inform you that our Ship of State, which recent storms have threatened to destroy, has come safely to harbour at last, guided by the merciful wisdom of Heaven. I have summoned you [*10* here this morning because I know that I can depend upon you: your devotion to King Laïos was absolute; you never hesitated in your duty

to our late ruler Oedipus; and when Oedipus died, your loyalty was
transferred to his children. Unfortunately, as you know, his two sons, the
princes Eteoclês and Polyneicês, have killed each other in battle; and I,   [*1*
as the next in blood, have succeeded to the full power of the throne.

I am aware, of course, that no Ruler can expect complete loyalty from
his subjects until he has been tested in office. Nevertheless, I say to you at
the very outset that I have nothing but contempt for the kind of Governor
who is afraid, for whatever reason, to follow the course that he knows is   [*2*
best for the State; and as for the man who sets private friendship above the
public welfare,—I have no use for him, either. I call God to witness that
if I saw my country headed for ruin, I should not be afraid to speak out
plainly; and I need hardly remind you that I would never have any dealings with an enemy of the people. No one values friendship more highly   [*2*
than I; but we must remember that friends made at the risk of wrecking
our Ship are not real friends at all.

These are my principles, at any rate, and that is why I have made the
following decision concerning the sons of Oedipus: Eteoclês, who died as
a man should die, fighting for his country, is to be buried with full mili-   [*3*
tary honours, with all the ceremony that is usual when the greatest heroes
die; but his brother Polyneicês, who broke his exile to come back with fire
and sword against his native city and the shrines of his fathers' gods, whose
one idea was to spill the blood of his blood and sell his own people into
slavery—Polyneicês, I say, is to have no burial: no man is to touch him   [*3*
or say the least prayer for him; he shall lie on the plain, unburied; and
the birds and the scavenging dogs can do with him whatever they like.

This is my command, and you can see the wisdom behind it. As long as
I am King, no traitor is going to be honoured with the loyal man. But
whoever shows by word and deed that he is on the side of the State,—he   [*4*
shall have my respect while he is living, and my reverence when he is dead.
CHORAGOS   If that is your will, Creon son of Menoikeus,
   You have the right to enforce it: we are yours.
CREON   That is my will. Take care that you do your part.
CHORAGOS   We are old men: let the younger ones carry it out.   [*4.*
CREON   I do not mean that: the sentries have been appointed.
CHORAGOS   Then what is it that you would have us do?
CREON   You will give no support to whoever breaks this law.
CHORAGOS   Only a crazy man is in love with death!
CREON   And death it is; yet money talks, and the wisest   [*5*
   Have sometimes been known to count a few coins too many.
   [*Enter* SENTRY *from left.*]
SENTRY   I'll not say that I'm out of breath from running, King, because every
   time I stopped to think about what I have to tell you, I felt like going
   back. And all the time a voice kept saying, "You fool, don't you know   [*5.*
   you're walking straight into trouble?"; and then another voice: "Yes, but
   if you let somebody else get the news to Creon first, it will be even worse
   than that for you!" But good sense won out, at least I hope it was good
   sense, and here I am with a story that makes no sense at all; but I'll tell
   it anyhow, because, as they say, what's going to happen's going to happen,   [*6c*
   and—
CREON   Come to the point. What have you to say?
SENTRY   I did not do it. I did not see who did it. You must not punish me for
   what someone else has done.
CREON   A comprehensive defence! More effective, perhaps,
   If I knew its purpose. Come: what is it?   [*6*
SENTRY   A dreadful thing . . . I don't know how to put it—

CREON   Out with it!
SENTRY   Well, then;
   The dead man—
          Polyneicês—   [*70*
[Pause. The SENTRY *is overcome, fumbles for words,* CREON *waits impassively.]*
          out there—
               someone,—
   New dust on the slimy flesh!
[Pause. No sign from CREON.]
   Someone has given it burial that way, and
   Gone . . .   [*75*
[Long pause. CREON *finally speaks with deadly control.]*
CREON   And the man who dared do this?
SENTRY   I swear I
   Do not know! You must believe me!
              Listen:
   The ground was dry, not a sign of digging, no,   [*80*
   Not a wheeltrack in the dust, no trace of anyone.
   It was when they relieved us this morning: and one of them,
   The corporal, pointed to it.
             There it was,
   The strangest—   [*85*
       Look:
   The body, just mounded over with light dust: you see?
   Not buried really, but as if they'd covered it
   Just enough for the ghost's peace. And no sign
   Of dogs or any wild animal that had been there.   [*90*
   And then what a scene there was! Every man of us
   Accusing the other: we all proved the other man did it,
   We all had proof that we could not have done it.
   We were ready to take hot iron in our hands,
   Walk through fire, swear by all the gods,   [*95*
*   It was not I!*
*   I do not know who it was, but it was not I!*
*[*CREON's *rage has been mounting steadily, but the* SENTRY *is too intent upon
his story to notice it.]*
   And then, when this came to nothing, someone said
   A thing that silenced us and made us stare
   Down at the ground: you had to be told the news,   [*100*
   And one of us had to do it! We threw the dice,
   And the bad luck fell to me. So here I am,
   No happier to be here than you are to have me:
   Nobody likes the man who brings bad news.
CHORAGOS   I have been wondering, King: can it be that the gods have   [*105*
      done this?
CREON   *[Furiously]*   Stop!
   Must you doddering wrecks
   Go out of your heads entirely? "The gods!"
   Intolerable!   [*110*
   The gods favour this corpse? Why? How had he served them?
   Tried to loot their temples, burn their images,
   Yes, and the whole State, and its laws with it!
   Is it your senile opinion that the gods love to honour bad men?
   A pious thought!—   [*115*
          No, from the very beginning

There have been those who have whispered together,
Stiff-necked anarchists, putting their heads together,
Scheming against me in alleys. These are the men,
And they have bribed my own guard to do this thing.   [*120*
Money!
[*Sententiously*]   There's nothing in the world so demoralising as money.
Down go your cities,
Homes gone, men gone, honest hearts corrupted,
Crookedness of all kinds, and all for money!   [*125*
                    [*To* SENTRY]   But you—!
I swear by God and by the throne of God,
The man who has done this thing shall pay for it!
Find that man, bring him here to me, or your death
Will be the least of your problems: I'll string you up   [*130*
Alive, and there will be certain ways to make you
Discover your employer before you die;
And the process may teach you a lesson you seem to have missed:
The dearest profit is sometimes all too dear:
That depends on the source. Do you understand me?   [*135*
A fortune won is often misfortune.
SENTRY   King, may I speak?
CREON   Your very voice distresses me.
SENTRY   Are you sure that it is my voice, and not your conscience?
CREON   By God, he wants to analyze me now!   [*140*
SENTRY   It is not what I say, but what has been done, that hurts you.
CREON   You talk too much.
SENTRY   Maybe; but I've done nothing.
CREON   Sold your soul for some silver: that's all you've done.
SENTRY   How dreadful it is when the right judge judges wrong!   [*145*
CREON   Your figures of speech
May entertain you now; but unless you bring me the man,
You will get little profit from them in the end.
                            [*Exit* CREON *into the palace.*]
SENTRY   "Bring me the man"—!
I'd like nothing better than bringing him the man!   [*150*
But bring him or not, you have seen the last of me here.
At any rate, I am safe!   [*Exit* SENTRY.]

ODE I

CHORUS   Numberless are the world's wonders, but none   (STROPHE 1)
        More wonderful than man; the stormgrey sea
        Yields to his prows, the huge crests bear him high;
        Earth, holy and inexhaustible, is graven
        With shining furrows where his plows have gone   [*5*
        Year after year, the timeless labour of stallions.

        The lightboned birds and beasts that cling to cover,   (ANTISTROPHE 1)
        The lithe fish lighting their reaches of dim water,
        All are taken, tamed in the net of his mind;
        The lion on the hill, the wild horse windy-maned,
        Resign to him; and his blunt yoke has broken   [*10*
        The sultry shoulders of the mountain bull.

Words also, and thought as rapid as air,   (STROPHE 2)
He fashions to his good use; statecraft is his,
And his the skill that deflects the arrows of snow,   [*15*
The spears of winter rain: from every wind
He has made himself secure—from all but one:
In the late wind of death he cannot stand.

O clear intelligence, force beyond all measure!   (ANTISTROPHE 2)
O fate of man, working both good and evil!   [*20*
When the laws are kept, how proudly his city stands!
When the laws are broken, what of his city then?
Never may the anárchic man find rest at my hearth,
Never be it said that my thoughts are his thoughts.

Scene II

[*Re-enter* SENTRY *leading* ANTIGONE.]
CHORAGOS   What does this mean? Surely this captive woman
   Is the Princess, Antigonê. Why should she be taken?
SENTRY   Here is the one who did it! We caught her
   In the very act of burying him.—Where is Creon?
CHORAGOS   Just coming from the house.   [*5*
   [*Enter* CREON, *center.*]
CREON   What has happened?
   Why have you come back so soon?
SENTRY   [*Expansively*]   O King,
   A man should never be too sure of anything:
   I would have sworn   [*10*
   That you'd not see me here again: your anger
   Frightened me so, and the things you threatened me with;
   But how could I tell then
   That I'd be able to solve the case so soon?
   No dice-throwing this time: I was only too glad to come!   [*15*
   Here is this woman. She is the guilty one:
   We found her trying to bury him.
   Take her, then; question her; judge her as you will.
   I am through with the whole thing now, and glád óf it.
CREON   But this is Antigonê! Why have you brought her here?   [*20*
SENTRY   She was burying him, I tell you!
CREON   [*Severely*]   Is this the truth?
SENTRY   I saw her with my own eyes. Can I say more?
CREON   The details: come, tell me quickly!
SENTRY   It was like this: [*25*
   After those terrible threats of yours, King,
   We went back and brushed the dust away from the body.
   The flesh was soft by now, and stinking,
   So we sat on a hill to windward and kept guard.
   No napping this time! We kept each other awake.   [*30*
   But nothing happened until the white round sun
   Whirled in the centre of the round sky over us:
   Then, suddenly,
   A storm of dust roared up from the earth, and the sky
   Went out, the plain vanished with all its trees   [*35*
   In the stinging dark. We closed our eyes and endured it.

The whirlwind lasted a long time, but it passed;
And then we looked, and there was Antigonê!
I have seen
A mother bird come back to a stripped nest, heard   [45
Her crying bitterly a broken note or two
For the young ones stolen. Just so, when this girl
Found the bare corpse, and all her love's work wasted,
She wept, and cried on heaven to damn the hands
That had done this thing.   [50
                          And then she brought more dust
And sprinkled wine three times for her brother's ghost.
We ran and took her at once. She was not afraid,
Not even when we charged her with what she had done.
She denied nothing.   [55
                     And this was a comfort to me,
And some uneasiness: for it is a good thing
To escape from death, but it is no great pleasure
To bring death to a friend.
                           Yet I always say   [60
There is nothing so comfortable as your own safe skin!
CREON   [Slowly, dangerously]   And you, Antigonê,
You with your head hanging—do you confess this thing?
ANTIGONE   I do. I deny nothing.
CREON   [To SENTRY]   You may go.   [65
                                              [Exit SENTRY.]

[To ANTIGONE]   Tell me, tell me briefly:
Had you heard my proclamation touching this matter?
ANTIGONE   It was public. Could I help hearing it?
CREON   And yet you dared defy the law.
ANTIGONE   I dared.   [70
It was not God's proclamation. That final Justice
That rules the world below makes no such laws.
Your edict, King, was strong,
But all your strength is weakness itself against
The immortal unrecorded laws of God.   [75
They are not merely now: they were, and shall be,
Operative for ever, beyond man utterly.
I knew I must die, even without your decree:
I am only mortal. And if I must die
Now, before it is my time to die,   [80
Surely this is no hardship: can anyone
Living, as I live, with evil all about me,
Think Death less than a friend? This death of mine
Is of no importance; but if I had left my brother
Lying in death unburied, I should have suffered.   [85
Now I do not.
              You smile at me. Ah Creon,
Think me a fool, if you like; but it may well be
That a fool convicts me of folly.
CHORAGOS   Like father, like daughter: both headstrong, deaf to reason!   [90
She has never learned to yield.
CREON   She has much to learn.
The inflexible heart breaks first, the toughest iron
Cracks first, and the wildest horses bend their necks
At the pull of the smallest curb.   [95

                     Pride? In a slave?
This girl is guilty of a double insolence,
Breaking the given laws and boasting of it.
Who is the man here,
She or I, if this crime goes unpunished?   [*100*
Sister's child, or more than sister's child,
Or closer yet in blood—she and her sister
Win bitter death for this!
                [*To Servants*]   Go, some of you,
Arrest Ismenê. I accuse her equally.   [*105*
Bring her: you will find her sniffling in the house there.
Her mind's a traitor: crimes kept in the dark
Cry for light, and the guardian brain shudders;
But how much worse than this
Is brazen boasting of barefaced anarchy!   [*110*
ANTIGONE   Creon, what more do you want than my death?
CREON   Nothing.
That gives me everything.
ANTIGONE   Then I beg you: kill me.
This talking is a great weariness: your words   [*115*
Are distasteful to me, and I am sure that mine
Seem so to you. And yet they should not seem so:
I should have praise and honour for what I have done.
All these men here would praise me
Were their lips not frozen shut with fear of you.   [*120*
[*Bitterly*]   Ah the good fortune of kings,
Licensed to say and do whatever they please!
CREON   You are alone here in that opinion.
ANTIGONE   No, they are with me. But they keep their tongues in leash.
CREON   Maybe. But you are guilty, and they are not.   [*125*
ANTIGONE   There is no guilt in reverence for the dead.
CREON   But Eteoclês—was he not your brother too?
ANTIGONE   My brother too.
CREON   And you insult his memory?
ANTIGONE   [*Softly*]   The dead man would not say that I insult it.   [*130*
CREON   He would: for you honour a traitor as much as him.
ANTIGONE   His own brother, traitor or not, and equal in blood.
CREON   He made war on his country. Eteoclês defended it.
ANTIGONE   Nevertheless, there are honours due all the dead.
CREON   But not the same for the wicked as for the just.   [*135*
ANTIGONE   Ah Creon, Creon,
Which of us can say what the gods hold wicked?
CREON   An enemy is an enemy, even dead.
ANTIGONE   It is my nature to join in love, not hate.
CREON   [*Finally losing patience*]   Go join them, then; if you must have   [*140*
    your love,
Find it in hell!
CHORAGOS   But see, Ismenê comes:
    [*Enter* ISMENE, *guarded.*]
Those tears are sisterly, the cloud
That shadows her eyes rains down gentle sorrow.   [*145*
CREON   You too, Ismenê,
Snake in my ordered house, sucking my blood
Stealthily—and all the time I never knew
That these two sisters were aiming at my throne!

Ismenê,   [*150*

Do you confess your share in this crime, or deny it?
Answer me.

ISMENE   Yes, if she will let me say so. I am guilty.

ANTIGONE   [*Coldly*]   No, Ismenê. You have no right to say so.
You would not help me, and I will not have you help me.   [*155*

ISMENE   But now I know what you meant; and I am here
To join you, to take my share of punishment.

ANTIGONE   The dead man and the gods who rule the dead
Know whose act this was. Words are not friends.

ISMENE   Do you refuse me, Antigonê? I want to die with you: [*160*
I too have a duty that I must discharge to the dead.

ANTIGONE   You shall not lessen my death by sharing it.

ISMENE   What do I care for life when you are dead?

ANTIGONE   Ask Creon. You're always hanging on his opinions.

ISMENE   You are laughing at me. Why, Antigonê?   [*165*

ANTIGONE   It's a joyless laughter, Ismene.

ISMENE   But can I do nothing?

ANTIGONE   Yes. Save yourself. I shall not envy you.
There are those who will praise you; I shall have honour, too.

ISMENE   But we are equally guilty!   [*170*

ANTIGONE   No more, Ismenê.
You are alive, but I belong to Death.

CREON   [*To the* CHORUS]   'Gentlemen, I beg you to observe these girls:
One has just now lost her mind; the other,
It seems, has never had a mind at all.   [*175*

ISMENE   Grief teaches the steadiest minds to waver, King.

CREON   Yours certainly did, when you assumed guilt with the guilty!

ISMENE   But how could I go on living without her?

CREON   You are.
She is already dead.   [*180*

ISMENE   But your own son's bride!

CREON   There are places enough for him to push his plow.
I want no wicked women for my sons!

ISMENE   O dearest Haimon, how your father wrongs you!

CREON   I've had enough of your childish talk of marriage!   [*185*

CHORAGOS   Do you really intend to steal this girl from your son?

CREON   No; Death will do that for me.

CHORAGOS   Then she must die?

CREON   [*Ironically*]   You dazzle me.
                         —But enough of this talk!   [*190*
[*To* GUARDS]   You, there, take them away and guard them well:
For they are but women, and even brave men run
When they see Death coming.   [*Exeunt* ISMENE, ANTIGONE, and GUARDS.]

ODE II

(STROPHE 1)

CHORUS   Fortunate is the man who has never tasted God's vengeance!
Where once the anger of heaven has struck, that house is shaken
For ever: damnation rises behind each child
Like a wave cresting out of the black northeast,

When the long darkness under sea roars up   [5
And bursts drumming death upon the windwhipped sand.

(ANTISTROPHE 1)

I have seen this gathering sorrow from time long past
Loom upon Oedipus' children: generation from generation
Takes the compulsive rage of the enemy god.
So lately this last flower of Oedipus' line   [10
Drank the sunlight! but now a passionate word
And a handful of dust have closed up all its beauty.

    What mortal arrogance   (STROPHE 2)
    Transcends the wrath of Zeus?
Sleep canot lull him, nor the effortless long months   [15
Of the timeless gods: but he is young for ever,
And his house is the shining day of high Olympos.
        All that is and shall be,
        And all the past, is his.
No pride on earth is free of the curse of heaven.   [20

    The straying dreams of men   (ANTISTROPHE 2)
    May bring them ghosts of joy:
But as they drowse, the waking embers burn them;
Or they walk with fíxed éyes, as blind men walk.
But the ancient wisdom speaks for our own time: [25

        Fate works most for woe
        With Folly's fairest show.

Man's little pleasure is the spring of sorrow.

Scene III

CHORAGOS   But here is Haimon, King, the last of all your sons.
    Is it grief for Antigonê that brings him here,
    And bitterness at being robbed of his bride?
    [*Enter* HAIMON.]
CREON   We shall soon see, and no need of diviners.
                                            —Son,
    You have heard my final judgment on that girl: [5
    Have you come here hating me, or have you come
    With deference and with love, whatever I do?
HAIMON   I am your son, father. You are my guide.
    You make things clear for me, and I obey you.
    No marriage means more to me than your continuing wisdom.   [10
CREON   Good. That is the way to behave: subordinate
    Everything else, my son, to your father's will.
    This is what a man prays for, that he may get
    Sons attentive and dutiful in his house,
    Each one hating his father's enemies,   [15
    Honouring his father's friends. But if his sons
    Fail him, if they turn out unprofitably,
    What has he fathered but trouble for himself
    And amusement for the malicious?
                            So you are right   [20
    Not to lose your head over this woman.

Your pleasure with her would soon grow cold, Haimon,
And then you'd have a hellcat in bed and elsewhere.
Let her find her husband in Hell!
Of all the people in this city, only she   [25
Has had contempt for my law and broken it.
Do you want me to show myself weak before the people?
Or to break my sworn word? No, and I will not.
The woman dies.
I suppose she'll plead "family ties." Well, let her.   [30
If I permit my own family to rebel,
How shall I earn the world's obedience?
Show me the man who keeps his house in hand,
He's fit for public authority.
                          I'll have no dealings   [35
With law-breakers, critics of the government:
Whoever is chosen to govern should be obeyed—
Must be obeyed, in all things, great and small,
Just and unjust! O Haimon,
The man who knows how to obey, and that man only,   [40
Knows how to give commands when the time comes.
You can depend on him, no matter how fast
The spears come: he's a good soldier, he'll stick it out.
Anarchy, anarchy! Show me a greater evil!
This is why cities tumble and the great houses rain down,   [45
This is what scatters armies!
No, no: good lives are made so by discipline.
We keep the laws then, and the lawmakers,
And no woman shall seduce us. If we must lose,
Let's lose to a man, at least! Is a woman stronger than we?   . [50
CHORAGOS   Unless time has rusted my wits,
What you say, King, is said with point and dignity.
HAIMON   [*Boyishly earnest*]   Father:
Reason is God's crowning gift to man, and you are right
To warn me against losing mine. I cannot say—   [55
I hope that I shall never want to say!—that you
Have reasoned badly. Yet there are other men
Who can reason, too; and their opinions might be helpful.
You are not in a position to know everything
That people say or do, or what they feel: [60
Your temper terrifies them—everyone
Will tell you only what you like to hear.
But I, at any rate, can listen; and I have heard them
Muttering and whispering in the dark about this girl.
They say no woman has ever, so unreasonably,   [65
Died so shameful a death for a generous act:
"She covered her brother's body. Is this indecent?
She kept him from dogs and vultures. Is this a crime?
Death?—She should have all the honour that we can give her!"
This is the way they talk out there in the city.   [70
You must believe me:
Nothing is closer to me than your happiness.
What could be closer? Must not any son
Value his father's fortune as his father does his?
I beg you, do not be unchangeable: [75

Do not believe that you alone can be right.
The man who thinks that,
The man who maintains that only he has the power
To reason correctly, the gift to speak, the soul—
A man like that, when you know him, turns out empty.   [*80*
It is not reason never to yield to reason!
In flood time you can see how some trees bend,
And because they bend, even their twigs are safe,
While stubborn trees are torn up, roots and all.
And the same thing happens in sailing: [*85*
Make your sheet fast, never slacken,—and over you go,
Head over heels and under: and there's your voyage.
Forget you are angry! Let yourself be moved!
I know I am young; but please let me say this:
The ideal condition   [*90*
Would be, I admit, that men should be right by instinct;
But since we are all too likely to go astray,
The reasonable thing is to learn from those who can teach.
CHORAGOS   You will do well to listen to him, King,
If what he says is sensible. And you, Haimon,   [*95*
Must listen to your father.—Both speak well.
CREON   You consider it right for a man of my years and experience
To go to school to a boy?
HAIMON   It is not right
If I am wrong. But if I am young, and right,   [*100*
What does my age matter?
CREON   You think it right to stand up for an anarchist?
HAIMON   Not at all. I pay no respect to criminals.
CREON   Then she is not a criminal?
HAIMON   The City would deny it, to a man.   [*105*
CREON   And the City proposes to teach me how to rule?
HAIMON   Ah. Who is it that's talking like a boy now?
CREON   My voice is the one voice giving orders in this City!
HAIMON   It is no City if it takes orders from one voice.
CREON   The State is the King!   [*110*
HAIMON   Yes, if the State is a desert.

                                                            [*Pause.*]

CREON   This boy, it seems, has sold out to a woman.
HAIMON   If you are a woman: my concern is only for you.
CREON   So? Your "concern"! In a public brawl with your father!
HAIMON   How about you, in a public brawl with justice?   [*115*
CREON   With justice, when all that I do is within my rights?
HAIMON   You have no right to trample on God's right.
CREON   [*Completely out of control*]   Fool, adolescent fool! Taken in by a
    woman!
HAIMON   You'll never see me taken in by anything vile.   [*120*
CREON   Every word you say is for her!
HAIMON   [*Quietly, darkly*]   And for you.
    And for me. And for the gods under the earth.
CREON   You'll never marry her while she lives.
HAIMON   Then she must die.—But her death will cause another.   [*125*
CREON   Another?
    Have you lost your senses? Is this an open threat?
HAIMON   There is no threat in speaking to emptiness.

CREON   I swear you'll regret this superior tone of yours!
You are the empty one!   [*130*
HAIMON   If you were not my father,
I'd say you were perverse.
CREON   You girlstruck fool, don't play at words with me!
HAIMON   I am sorry. You prefer silence.
CREON   Now, by God—!   [*135*
I swear, by all the gods in heaven above us,
You'll watch it, I swear you shall!
        [*To the Servants*]   Bring her out!
Bring the woman out! Let her die before his eyes!
Here, this instant, with her bridegroom beside her!   [*140*
HAIMON   Not here, no; she will not die here, King.
And you will never see my face again.
Go on raving as long as you've a friend to endure you.   [*Exit* HAIMON.]
CHORAGOS   Gone, gone.
Creon, a young man in a rage is dangerous!   [*145*
CREON   Let him do, or dream to do, more than a man can.
He shall not save these girls from death.
CHORAGOS   These girls?
You have sentenced them both?
CREON   No, you are right.   [*150*
I will not kill the one whose hands are clean.
CHORAGOS   But Antigonê?
CREON   [*Somberly*]   I will carry her far away
Out there in the wilderness, and lock her
Living in a vault of stone, She shall have food,   [*155*
As the custom is, to absolve the State of her death.
And there let her pray to the gods of hell:
They are her only gods:
Perhaps they will show her an escape from death,
Or she may learn,   [*160*
                    though late,
That piety shown the dead is pity in vain.   [*Exit* CREON.]

ODE III

CHORUS   Love, unconquerable   (STROPHE)
Waster of rich men, keeper
Of warm lights and all-night vigil
In the soft face of a girl:
Sea-wanderer, forest-visitor!   [*5*
Even the pure Immortals cannot escape you,
And mortal man, in his one day's dusk,
Trembles before your glory.

Surely you swerve upon ruin   (ANTISTROPHE)
The just man's consenting heart,   [*10*
As here you have made bright anger
Strike between father and son—
And none has conquered but Love!

A girl's glánce wórking the will of heaven:
Pleasure to her alone who mocks us,   [*15*
Merciless Aphroditê.

Scene IV

[*As* ANTIGONE *enters guarded.*]
CHORAGOS   But I can no longer stand in awe of this,
    Nor, seeing what I see, keep back my tears.
    Here is Antigonê, passing to that chamber
    Where all find sleep at last.
ANTIGONE   Look upon me, friends, and pity me   (STROPHE 1)   [*5*
    Turning back at the night's edge to say
    Goodbye to the sun that shines for me no longer;
    Now sleepy Death
    Summons me down to Acheron, that cold shore:
    There is no bridesong there, nor any music.   [*10*
CHORUS   Yet not unpraised, not without a kind of honour,
    You walk at last into the underworld;
    Untouched by sickness, broken by no sword.
    What woman has ever found your way to death?
ANTIGONE   How often I have heard the story of Niobê, (ANTISTROPHE 1)   [*15*
    Tantalos' wretched daughter, how the stone
    Clung fast about her, ivy-close: and they say
    The rain falls endlessly
    And sifting soft snow; her tears are never done.
    I feel the loneliness of her death in mine.   [*20*
CHORUS   But she was born of heaven, and you
    Are woman, woman-born. If her death is yours,
    A mortal woman's, is this not for you
    Glory in our world and in the world beyond?
ANTIGONE   You laugh at me. Ah, friends, friends,   (STROPHE 2)   [*25*
    Can you not wait until I am dead? O Thebes,
    O men many-charioted, in love with Fortune,
    Dear springs of Dircê, sacred Theban grove,
    Be witnesses for me, denied all pity,
    Unjustly judged! and think a word of love   [*30*
    For her whose path turns
    Under dark earth, where there are no more tears.
CHORUS   You have passed beyond human daring and come at last
    Into a place of stone where Justice sits.
    I cannot tell   [*35*
    What shape of your father's guilt appears in this.
ANTIGONE   You have touched it at last: that bridal bed   (ANTISTROPHE 2)
    Unspeakable, horror of son and mother mingling:
    Their crime, infection of all our family!
    O Oedipus, father and brother!   [*40*
    Your marriage strikes from the grave to murder mine.
    I have been a stranger here in my own land:
    All my life
    The blasphemy of my birth has followed me.
CHORUS   Reverence is a virtue, but strength   [*45*
    Lives in established law: that must prevail.

You have made your choice,
Your death is the doing of your conscious hand.

ANTIGONE   Then let me go, since all your words are bitter,   (EPODE)
And the very light of the sun is cold to me.   [50
Lead me to my vigil, where I must have
Neither love nor lamentation; no song, but silence.
[CREON *interrupts impatiently.*]

CREON   If dirges and planned lamentations could put off death,
Men would be singing for ever.
[*To the Servants*]   Take her, go!   [55
You know your orders: take her to the vault
And leave her alone there. And if she lives or dies,
That's her affair, not ours: our hands are clean.

ANTIGONE   O tomb, vaulted bride-bed in eternal rock,
Soon I shall be with my own again   [60
Where Persephonê welcomes the thin ghosts underground:
And I shall see my father again, and you, mother,
And dearest Polyneicês—
                    dearest indeed
To me, since it was my hand   [65
That washed him clean and poured the ritual wine:
And my reward is death before my time!
And yet, as men's hearts know, I have done no wrong,
I have not sinned before God. Or if I have,
I shall know the truth in death. But if the guilt   [70
Lies upon Creon who judged me, then, I pray,
May his punishment equal my own.

CHORAGOS   O passionate heart,
Unyielding, tormented still by the same winds!

CREON   Her guards shall have good cause to regret their delaying.   [75

ANTIGONE   Ah! That voice is like the voice of death!

CREON   I can give you no reason to think you are mistaken.

ANTIGONE   Thebes, and you my fathers' gods,
And rulers of Thebes, you see me now, the last
Unhappy daughter of a line of kings,   [80
Your kings, led away to death. You will remember
What things I suffer, and at what men's hands,
Because I would not transgress the laws of heaven.
[*To the Guards, simply*]   Come: let us wait no longer.

                              [*Exit* ANTIGONE, *left, guarded.*]

ODE IV

CHORUS   All Danaê's beauty was locked away   (STROPHE 1)
In a brazen cell where the sunlight could not come:
A small room, still as any grave, enclosed her.
Yet she was a princess too,
And Zeus in a rain of gold poured love upon her.   [5
O child, child,
No power in wealth or war
Or tough sea-blackened ships

Can prevail against untiring Destiny!

And Dryas' son [2] also, that furious king,   (ANTISTROPHE 1)   [*10*
Bore the god's prisoning anger for his pride:
Sealed up by Dionysos in deaf stone,
His madness died among echoes.
So at the last he learned what dreadful power
His tongue had mocked: [*15*
For he had profaned the revels,
And fired the wrath of the nine
Implacable Sisters that love the sound of the flute.

And old men tell a half-remembered tale [3]   (STROPHE 2)
Of horror done where a dark ledge splits the sea   [*20*
And a double surf beats on the gréy shóres:
How a king's new woman, sick
With hatred for the queen he had imprisoned,
Ripped out his two sons' eyes with her bloody hands
While grinning Arês watched the shuttle plunge   [*25*
Four times: four blind wounds crying for revenge,
Crying, tears and blood mingled.—Piteously born,   (ANTISTROPHE 2)
Those sons whose mother was of heavenly birth!
Her father was the god of the North Wind
And she was cradled by gales,   [*30*
She raced with young colts on the glittering hills
And walked untrammeled in the open light:
But in her marriage deathless Fate found means
To build a tomb like yours for all her joy.

Scene V

[*Enter blind* TEIRESIAS, *led by a boy. The opening speeches of* TEIRESIAS
should be in singsong contrast to the realistic lines of CREON.]

TEIRESIAS   This is the way the blind man comes, Princes, Princes,
    Lock-step, two heads lit by the eyes of one.
CREON   What new thing have you to tell us, old Teiresias?
TEIRESIAS   I have much to tell you: listen to the prophet, Creon.
CREON   I am not aware that I have ever failed to listen.   [*5*
TEIRESIAS   Then you have done wisely, King. and ruled well.
CREON   I admit my debt to you. But what have you to say?
TEIRESIAS   This, Creon: you stand once more on the edge of fate.
CREON   What do you mean? Your words are a kind of dread.
TEIRESIAS   Listen, Creon: [*10*
    I was sitting in my chair of augury, at the place
    Where the birds gather about me. They were all a-chatter,
    As is their habit, when suddenly I heard

---

2. *Dryas' son,* Lykurgos, a king of Thrace who insulted Dionysos. Lykurgos was imprisoned in a rocky cave by Dionysos and later struck blind by Zeus.
3. *a half-remembered tale,* a reference to the story of Cleopatra, Phineus, and
Eidothea (Idaea). Cleopatra, daughter of the North Wind, and Phineus, a king, had
two sons. After Cleopatra's death, Phineus married Eidothea, who accused the sons of
improper advances to her. Phineus imprisoned them in a cave and had them blinded.
In Sophocles' version, Eidothea rips out the sons' eyes.

A strange note in their jangling, a scream, a
Whirring fury; I knew that they were fighting,   [15
Tearing each other, dying
In a whirlwind of wings clashing. And I was afraid.
I began the rites of burnt-offering at the altar,
But Hephaistos failed me: instead of bright flame,
There was only the sputtering slime of the fat thigh-flesh   [20
Melting: the entrails dissolved in grey smoke,
The bare bone burst from the welter. And no blaze!
This was a sign from heaven. My boy described it,
Seeing for me as I see for others.
I tell you, Creon, you yourself have brought   [25
This new calamity upon us. Our hearths and altars
Are stained with the corruption of dogs and carrion birds
That glut themselves on the corpse of Oedipus' son.
The gods are deaf when we pray to them, their fire
Recoils from our offering, their birds of omen   [30
Have no cry of comfort, for they are gorged
With the thick blood of the dead.
                                    O my son,
These are no trifles! Think: all men make mistakes,
But a good man yields when he knows his course is wrong,   [35
And repairs the evil. The only crime is pride.
Give in to the dead man, then: do not fight with a corpse—
What glory is it to kill a man who is dead?
Think, I beg you:
It is for your own good that I speak as I do.   [40
You should be able to yield for your own good.
CREON   It seems that prophets have made me their especial province.
All my life long
I have been a kind of butt for the dull arrows
Of doddering fortune-tellers!   [45
                                    No, Teiresias:
If your birds—if the great eagles of God himself
Should carry him stinking bit by bit to heaven,
I would not yield. I am not afraid of pollution:
No man can defile the gods.   [50
                                    Do what you will,
Go into business, make money, speculate
In India gold or that synthetic gold from Sardis,
Get rich otherwise than by my consent to bury him.
Teiresias, it is a sorry thing when a wise man
Sells his wisdom, lets out his words for hire!
TEIRESIAS   Ah Creon! Is there no man left in the world—
CREON   To do what?—Come, let's have the aphorism!
TEIRESIAS   No man who knows that wisdom outweighs any wealth?
CREON   As surely as bribes are baser than any baseness.   [60
TEIRESIAS   You are sick, Creon! You are deathly sick!
CREON   As you say: it is not my place to challenge a prophet.
TEIRESIAS   Yet you have said my prophecy is for sale.
CREON   The generation of prophets has always loved gold.
TEIRESIAS   The generation of kings has always loved brass.   [65
CREON   You forget yourself! You are speaking to your King.

TEIRESIAS I know it. You are a king because of me.
CREON You have a certain skill; but you have sold out.
TEIRESIAS King, you will drive me to words that—
CREON   Say them, say them!   [70
  Only remember: I will not pay you for them.
TEIRESIAS No, you will find them too costly.
CREON   No doubt. Speak:
  Whatever you say, you will not change my will.
TEIRESIAS Then take this, and take it to heart!   [75
  The time is not far off when you shall pay back
  Corpse for corpse, flesh of your own flesh.
  You have thrust the child of this world into living night,
  You have kept from the gods below the child that is theirs:
  The one in a grave before her death, the other,   [80
  Dead, denied the grave. This is your crime:
  And the Furies and the dark gods of Hell
  Are swift with terrible punishment for you.
  Do you want to buy me now, Creon?
                              Not many days,   [85
  And your house will be full of men and women weeping,
  And curses will be hurled at you from far
  Cities grieving for sons unburied, left to rot
  Before the walls of Thebes.
  These are my arrows, Creon: they are all for you.   [90
  [*To Boy*] But come, child: lead me home.
  Let him waste his fine anger upon younger men.
  Maybe he will learn at last
  To control a wiser tongue in a better head.   [*Exit* TEIRESIAS.]
CHORAGOS The old man is gone, King, but his words   [95
  Remain to plague us. I am old, too,
  But I cannot remember that he was ever false.
CREON That is true. . . . It troubles me.
  Oh it is hard to give in! but it is worse
  To risk everything for stubborn pride.   [100
CHORAGOS Creon: take my advice.
CREON   What shall I do?
CHORAGOS Go quickly: free Antigonê from her vault
  And build a tomb for the body of Polyneicês.
CREON You would have me do this?   [105
CHORAGOS   Creon, yes!
  And it must be done at once: God moves
  Swiftly to cancel the folly of stubborn men.
CREON It is hard to deny the heart! But I
  Will do it: I will not fight with destiny.   [110
CHORAGOS You must go yourself, you cannot leave it to others.
CREON I will go.
              —Bring axes, servants:
  Come with me to the tomb. I buried her, I
  Will set her free.   [115
              Oh quickly!
  My mind misgives—
  The laws of the gods are mighty, and a man must serve them
  To the last day of his life!   [*Exit* CREON.]

PÆAN

CHORAGOS God of many names	(STROPHE 1)

CHORUS   O Iacchos [4]
                                   son
   of Cadmeian Sémelê
                        O born of the Thunder!   [5
      Guardian of the West
                     Regent
      of Eleusis' plain
                     O Prince of mænad Thebes
      and the Dragon Field by rippling Ismenos: [10
CHORAGOS   God of many names   (ANTISTROPHE 1)
CHORUS   the flame of torches
      flares on our hills
                     the nymphs of Iacchos
      dance at the spring of Castalia: [15
      from the vine-close mountain
                        come ah come in ivy:
      Evohé evohé! sings through the streets of Thebes.
CHORAGOS   God of many names   (STROPHE 2)
CHORUS   Iacchos of Thebes   [20
      heavenly Child
                     of Sémelê bride of the Thunderer!
      The shadow of plague is upon us:
                              come
      with clement feet   [25
                     oh come from Parnasos
      down the long slopes
                     across the lamenting water.
CHORAGOS   Iô Fire! Chorister of the throbbing stars!   (ANTISTROPHE 2)
      O purest among the voices of the night!   [30
      Thou son of God, blaze for us!
CHORUS   Come with choric rapture of circling Mænads
      Who cry *Iô Iacche!*
                     God of many names!

EXODOS

   [*Enter* MESSENGER, *left.*]
MESSENGER   Men of the line of Cadmos, you who live
      Near Amphion's citadel:
                     I cannot say
   Of any condition of human life "This is fixed,
   This is clearly good, or bad." Fate raises up,   [5
   And Fate casts down the happy and unhappy alike:

---

4. *Iacchos,* another name for Dionysos; actually a minor deity associated with the Eleusinian mysteries and linked to Dionysos probably because the name sounds like Bacchus.

No man can foretell his Fate.
                                   Take the case of Creon:
Creon was happy once, as I count happiness:
Victorious in battle, sole governor of the land,   [*10*
Fortunate father of children nobly born.
And now it has all gone from him! Who can say
That a man is still alive when his life's joy fails?
He is a walking dead man. Grant him rich,
Let him live like a king in his great house: [*15*
If his pleasure is gone, I would not give
So much as the shadow of smoke for all he owns.
CHORAGOS   Your words hint at sorrow: what is your news for us?
MESSENGER   They are dead. The living are guilty of their death.
CHORAGOS   Who is guilty? Who is dead? Speak!   [*20*
MESSENGER   Haimon.
Haimon is dead; and the hand that killed him
Is his own hand.
CHORAGOS   His father's? or his own?
MESSENGER   His own, driven mad by the murder his father had done. [*25*
CHORAGOS   Teiresias, Teiresias, how clearly you saw it all!
MESSENGER   This is my news: you must draw what conclusions you can
        from it.
CHORAGOS   But look: Eurydicê, our Queen:
Has she overheard us?   [*30*
[*Enter* EURYDICE *from the palace, center.*]
EURYDICE   I have heard something, friends:
As I was unlocking the gate of Pallas' shrine,
For I needed her help today, I heard a voice
Telling of some new sorrow. And I fainted
There at the temple with all my maidens about me.   [*35*
But speak again: whatever it is, I can bear it:
Grief and I are no strangers.
MESSENGER   Dearest Lady,
I will tell you plainly all that I have seen.
I shall not try to comfort you: what is the use,   [*40*
Since comfort could lie only in what is not true?
The truth is always best.
                           I went with Creon
To the outer plain where Polyneicês was lying,
No friend to pity him, his body shredded by dogs.   [*45*
We made our prayers in that place to Hecatê
And Pluto, that they would be merciful. And we bathed
The corpse with holy water, and we brought
Fresh-broken branches to burn what was left of it,
And upon the urn we heaped up a towering barrow   [*50*
Of the earth of his own land.
                              When we were done, we ran
To the vault where Antigonê lay on her couch of stone.
One of the servants had gone ahead,
And while he was yet far off he heard a voice   [*55*
Grieving within the chamber, and he came back
And told Creon. And as the King went closer,
The air was full of wailing, the words lost,
And he begged us to make all haste. "Am I a prophet?"

He said, weeping, "And must I walk this road,   [*60*
The saddest of all that I have gone before?
My son's voice calls me on. Oh quickly, quickly!
Look through the crevice there, and tell me
If it is Haimon, or some deception of the gods!"
We obeyed; and in the cavern's farthest corner   [*65*
We saw her lying:
She had made a noose of her fine linen veil
And hanged herself. Haimon lay beside her,
His arms about her waist, lamenting her,
His love lost under ground, crying out   [*70*
That his father had stolen her away from him.
When Creon saw him the tears rushed to his eyes
And he called to him: "What have you done, child? Speak to me.
What are you thinking that makes your eyes so strange?
O my son, my son, I come to you on my knees!"   [*75*
But Haimon spat in his face. He said not a word,
Staring—
                   And suddenly drew his sword
And lunged. Creon shrank back, the blade missed; and the boy,
Desperate against himself, drove it half its length   [*80*
Into his own side, and fell. And as he died
He gathered Antigonê close in his arms again,
Choking, his blood bright red on her white cheek.
And now he lies dead with the dead, and she is his
At last, his bride in the houses of the dead.   [*85*
                                      [*Exit* EURYDICE *into the palace.*]
CHORAGOS   She has left us without a word. What can this mean?
MESSENGER   It troubles me, too; yet she knows what is best,
      Her grief is too great for public lamentation,
      And doubtless she has gone to her chamber to weep
      For her dead son, leading her maidens in his dirge.   [*90*
CHORAGOS   It may be so: but I fear this deep silence.
                                                          [*Pause.*]

MESSENGER   I will see what she is doing. I will go in.
                                      [*Exit* MESSENGER *into the palace.*]
      Enter CREON *with attendants, bearing* HAIMON's *body.*]
CHORAGOS   But here is the King himself: oh look at him,
      Bearing his own damnation in his arms.
CREON   Nothing you say can touch me any more.   [*95*
      My own blind heart has brought me
      From darkness to final darkness. Here you see
      The father murdering, the murdered son—
      And all my civic wisdom!
      Haimon my son, so young, so young to die,   [*100*
      I was the fool, not you; and you died for me.
CHORAGOS   That is the truth; but you were late in learning it.
CREON   This truth is hard to bear. Surely a god
      Has crushed me beneath the hugest weight of heaven,
      And driven me headlong a barbaric way   [*105*
      To trample out the thing I held most dear.
      The pains that men will take to come to pain!
      [*Enter* MESSENGER *from the palace.*]
MESSENGER   The burden you carry in your hands is heavy,

But it is not all: you will find more in your house.

CREON   What burden worse than this shall I find there?   [*110*

MESSENGER   The Queen is dead.

CREON   O port of death, deaf world,
  Is there no pity for me? And you, Angel of evil,
  I was dead, and your words are death again.
  Is it true, boy? Can it be true?   [*115*
  Is my wife dead? Has death bred death?

MESSENGER   You can see for yourself.

  [*The doors are opened, and the body of* EURYDICE *is disclosed within.*]

CREON   Oh pity!
  All true, all true, and more than I can bear!
  O my wife, my son!   [*120*

MESSENGER   She stood before the altar, and her heart
  Welcomed the knife her own hand guided,
  And a great cry burst from her lips for Megareus dead,
  And for Haimon dead, her sons; and her last breath
  Was a curse for their father, the murderer of her sons.   [*125*
  And she fell, and the dark flowed in through her closing eyes.

CREON   O God, I am sick with fear.
  Are there no swords here? Has no one a blow for me?

MESSENGER   Her curse is upon you for the deaths of both.

CREON   It is right that it should be. I alone am guilty.   [*130*
  I know it, and I say it. Lead me in,
  Quickly, friends.
  I have neither life nor substance. Lead me in.

CHORAGOS   You are right, if there can be right in so much wrong.
  The briefest way is best in a world of sorrow.   [*135*

CREON   Let it come,
  Let death come quickly, and be kind to me.
  I would not ever see the sun again.

CHORAGOS   All that will come when it will; but we, meanwhile.
  Have much to do. Leave the future to itself.   [*140*

CREON   All my heart was in that prayer!

CHORAGOS   Then do not pray any more: the sky is deaf.

CREON   Lead me away. I have been rash and foolish.
  I have killed my son and my wife.
  I look for comfort; my comfort lies here dead.   [*145*
  Whatever my hands have touched has come to nothing.
  Fate has brought all my pride to a thought of dust.

  [*As* CREON *is being led into the house, the* CHORAGOS *advances and speaks
  directly to the audience.*]

CHORAGOS   There is no happiness where there is no wisdom;
  No wisdom but in submission to the gods.
  Big words are always punished,   [*150*
  And proud men in old age learn to be wise.

WILLIAM SHAKESPEARE
[1564–1616]

Few facts are available about the life of Shakespeare, although there is more than sufficient evidence to disprove the occasional contentions that his plays were written by "someone else" (for example, Christopher Marlowe or Francis Bacon). Shakespeare was born in Stratford-on-Avon (about 75 miles northwest of London). There, he was married in 1582 to Anne Hathaway, who later bore him three children. It was to Stratford that he returned near the end of his life after a successful theatrical career in London, and, with his new wealth, acquired a coat of arms, an estate, and the status of a country squire.

Sometime prior to 1590, Shakespeare came to London and began his theatrical career. Within a few years he was recognized as an accomplished playwright in the forms of chronicle-play (*Henry VI*), comedy (*The Comedy of Errors*), and tragedy (*Titus Andronicus*).

In 1594, Shakespeare became associated with the "Lord Chamberlain's Company" as both writer and producer. It is about this time that he seems to have made a great creative leap forward. From this point until the turn of the century, the development of Shakespeare's art can be traced in his histories, comedies, and tragedies. The histories (for example, *Richard II*) began to explore the theme of kingship in subtle detail, and to portray chief characters not as melodramatic types but as complex beings. Similarly, in the comedies (for example, *As You Like It*) Shakespeare, in treating the vicissitudes of romantic love, moved from farcical types to fully conceived characters involved in situations of social and moral relevance. And in his tragedies (for example, *Julius Caesar*) he came to rely far less on external conflict and physical gore than on internal conflict and metaphysical questioning of evil.

In 1599, Shakespeare's company built the Globe Theatre, the playhouse in which the dramas of Shakespeare's mature genius were performed. In this last period he wrote such "problem plays" or "dark comedies" as *Troilus and Cressida* and *Measure for Measure,* such philosophical comedies as *The Winter's Tale* and *The Tempest,* and the great tragedies for which he is best known— *Hamlet, Othello, King Lear,* and *Macbeth.* Culminating the period of the great tragedies is *Antony and Cleopatra* (1606–1607), in which Shakespeare returned to Plutarch's *Lives*—the source for his earlier Roman plays—and invested this famous love story with his profound tragic vision.

The Tragedy of

ANTONY
AND
CLEOPATRA

WILLIAM SHAKESPEARE

DRAMATIS PERSONÆ.

MARK ANTONY,
OCTAVIUS CÆSAR, } *Triumvirs*
M. ÆMILIUS LEPIDUS,
SEXTUS POMPEIUS.

DOMITIUS ENOBARBUS,
VENTIDIUS,
EROS,
SCARUS, } *friends to* AN-
DERCETAS, TONY
DEMETRIUS,
PHILO,

CANIDIUS, *Lieutenant-General to* AN-TONY

MÆCENAS,
AGRIPPA,
DOLABELLA,
PROCULEIUS, } *friends to* CÆSAR
THYREUS,
GALLUS,

TAURUS, *Lieutenant-General to* CÆSAR
MENAS,
MENECRATES, } *friends to* POMPEY
VARRIUS,

SILIUS, *an Officer in the army of* VENTIDIUS

EUPHRONIUS, *an Ambassador from* ANTONY *to* CÆSAR

ALEXAS,
MARDIAN,
SELEUCUS, } *attendants on* CLEOPATRA
DIOMEDES,

A Soothsayer
A Clown
CLEOPATRA, *Queen of Egypt*
OCTAVIA, *sister to* CÆSAR *and wife to* ANTONY

Reprinted by permission of the publisher from *Antony and Cleopatra,* edited by George Lyman Kittredge, revised by Irving Ribner (Waltham, Massachusetts: Blaisdell Publishing Company, A Division of Ginn and Co., 1967).

CHARMIAN, ⎫ *ladies attending on* CLE-   *Officers, Soldiers, Messengers, Attend-*
IRAS,   ⎭ OPATRA   *ants*

SCENE   *In several parts of the Roman empire.*

ACT ONE

Scene I

[*Alexandria. A room in* CLEOPATRA'S *Palace.*]

[*Enter* DEMETRIUS *and* PHILO.]
PHILO   Nay, but this dotage of our general's
O'erflows the measure. Those his goodly eyes
That o'er the files and musters of the war
Have glow'd like plated Mars, now bend, now turn
The office and devotion of their view   [
Upon a tawny front. His captain's heart,
Which in the scuffles of great fights hath burst
The buckles on his breast, reneges all temper
And is become the bellows and the fan
To cool a gypsy's lust.
[*Flourish. Enter* ANTONY, CLEOPATRA, *her* LADIES, *the* TRAIN, *with* EUNUCHS
fanning her.]
                            Look where they come!   [*1*
Take but good note, and you shall see in him
The triple pillar of the world transform'd
Into a strumpet's fool. Behold and see.
CLEOPATRA   If it be love indeed, tell me how much.
ANTONY   There's beggary in the love that can be reckon'd.   [*1,*
CLEOPATRA   I'll set a bourn how far to be belov'd.
ANTONY   Then must thou needs find out new heaven, new earth.
[*Enter a* MESSENGER.]
MESSENGER   News, my good lord, from Rome.

Note: In the following footnotes [K] identifies Kittredge's glosses, F¹ refers to the
Folio of 1623 and F² refers to the Folio of 1632.
   I.I. 2 *o'erflows the measure* is so great that it cannot be measured.   3 *files and
musters* military ranks (the words are synonymous) .   4 *plated* wearing armour.   5 *The
office . . . their view* all their looks, as if they had no other duty to which to devote
themselves [K].   6 *tawny front* Cleopatra is imagined as a dark Egyptian, though in fact
she was of Greek descent [K].   *tawny* dark, literally a yellowish brown.   *front* forehead,
brow.   8 *reneges* rejects, renounces.   *temper* moderation, self-restraint.   10 *To cool* by
his amorous sighs, which seem to come from the heart [K].   *gypsy's* The gypsies were
thought to have come from Egypt. Their name is a shortened form of "Egyptian" [K].
"Gypsy" was common Elizabethan slang for "whore."   12 *The triple pillar of the world*
one of the three pillars on whom the world rests. The other two Triumvirs were
Octavius Cæsar and Lepidus [K].   13 *fool* dupe. Not here used in the sense of "buffoon"
[K].   15 *There's beggary . . . reckon'd* they are only beggars in love who have so little
of it that it can be measured—my love exceeds all bounds.   16 *set a bourn* propose a
boundary or limit.   17 *find out* discover.
   18 *Grates* annoys. The subject is "news from Rome." Antony expects nothing

ANTONY   Grates me! The sum.
CLEOPATRA   Nay, hear them, Antony.
    Fulvia perchance is angry; or who knows   [20
    If the scarce-bearded Cæsar have not sent
    His pow'rful mandate to you: "Do this, or this;
    Take in that kingdom, and enfranchise that.
    Perform't, or else we damn thee."
ANTONY   How, my love?
CLEOPATRA   Perchance? Nay, and most like: [25
    You must not stay here longer; your dismission
    Is come from Cæsar; therefore hear it, Antony.
    Where's Fulvia's process? Cæsar's I would say—both?
    Call in the messengers. As I am Egypt's Queen,
    Thou blushest, Antony, and that blood of thine   [30
    Is Cæsar's homager! Else so thy cheek pays shame
    When shrill-tongu'd Fulvia scolds. The messengers!
ANTONY   Let Rome in Tiber melt and the wide arch
    Of the rang'd empire fall! Here is my space.
    Kingdoms are clay; our dungy earth alike   [35
    Feeds beast as man. The nobleness of life
    Is to do thus [*embracing*]; when such a mutual pair
    And such a twain can do't, in which I bind,
    On pain of punishment, the world to weet
    We stand up peerless.
CLEOPATRA   Excellent falsehood!   [40
    Why did he marry Fulvia, and not love her?
    I'll seem the fool I am not. Antony
    Will be himself.
ANTONY   But stirr'd by Cleopatra.
    Now for the love of Love and her soft hours,

---

but vexatious tidings from that quarter [K]. *The sum* tell me briefly the sum and
substance of the news [K].

    20 *Fulvia* Antony's wife, whom he married about 44 B.C. and who died in 40 B.C.
Fulvia was notorious for her earlier debaucheries, her masculine energy, and her
savage temper. She was passionately fond of her wayward husband and jealous accordingly. Cleopatra takes delight in suggesting that Antony is henpecked [K].
21 *scarce-bearded* At this time (40 B.C.) Antony was about forty-three years old,
Octavius twenty-three [K]. 22 *mandate* command. 23 *Take in* occupy, take possession
of. *enfranchise* liberate. 24 *we* Cleopatra makes Octavius use the "royal we" (instead of "I"), as if he were a king and Antony his subject [K]. *damn* condemn.
26 *dismission* dismissal, recall. 28 *process* written document (containing instructions
or orders); summons [K]. 30–1 *that blood . . . homager* by rising to your cheek
in a blush of shame, your blood does homage to Cæsar; for such a blush is a
confession that what I have said about his authority over you is true [K]. 31 *Else* The
only other explanation for his blush, Cleopatra says tauntingly, is that he remembers
some of Fulvia's reproaches and feels that he deserves them [K]. 34 *rang'd* (a) well-
ordered [K] (b) wide-ranging. Probably both meanings are included. *my space* all
the space that I wish to control; empire enough for me [K]. 37 *thus* The stage
direction ("embracing") was inserted by Pope. Some critics reject this obvious
interpretation as undignified. See, however, III.II.62–4, where Antony and Cæsar embrace at parting [K]. 38–40 *in which . . . peerless* and in this respect (our love) I
put the world under bonds to acknowledge that you and I have no equals [K]. *to weet*
to know. 42 *seem the fool I am not* pretend to be foolish enough to believe you. 43
himself i.e. a deceiver, as he has always been (both to Fulvia and to me) [K]. *stirr'd*
inspired and animated in all his actions. Antony accepts the word "himself" but
rejects the sense which Cleopatra has given it. He declares that he will be "his own
great self," that Cleopatra shall be his inspiration to mighty deeds [K].

Let's not confound the time with conference harsh.   [4
There's not a minute of our lives should stretch
Without some pleasure now. What sport to-night?
CLEOPATRA   Hear the ambassadors.
ANTONY   Fie, wrangling queen!
Whom every thing becomes—to chide, to laugh,
To weep; whose every passion fully strives   [5
To make itself, in thee, fair and admir'd!
No messenger but thine, and all alone
To-night we'll wander through the streets and note
The qualities of people. Come, my queen;
Last night you did desire it.—Speak not to us.   [5
[*Exeunt* (ANTONY *and* CLEOPATRA) *with the* TRAIN.]
DEMETRIUS   Is Cæsar with Antonius priz'd so slight?
PHILO   Sir, sometimes when he is not Antony
He comes too short of that great property
Which still should go with Antony.
DEMETRIUS   I am full sorry   [6
That he approves the common liar, who
Thus speaks of him at Rome; but I will hope
Of better deeds to-morrow. Rest you happy!   [*Exeunt.*]

Scene II

[*Alexandria. Another room in* CLEOPATRA'S *Palace.*]

[*Enter a* SOOTHSAYER, CHARMIAN, IRAS, *and* ALEXAS.]
CHARMIAN   Lord Alexas, sweet Alexas, most anything Alexas, almost most ab-
solute Alexas, where's the soothsayer that you prais'd so to th' Queen? O
that I knew this husband which, you say, must charge his horns with
garlands!
ALEXAS   Soothsayer!   [?
SOOTHSAYER   Your will?
CHARMIAN   Is this the man? Is't you, sir, that know things?
SOOTHSAYER   In nature's infinite book of secrecy

---

45 *confound* waste.   *conference harsh* unpleasant conversation.   46 *should   stretch*
that should pass. The word "stretch" suggests tedium [K].   50 *whose* F²; F¹: "who."
passion emotional mood [K].   52 *No messenger but thine* I will hear not messages but
those that come from thee.   53 *wander through the streets* A favourite pastime of
Antony and Cleopatra was to roam about the streets in disguise after dark, amusing
themselves with the humours of the populace [K].   54 *qualities* characteristics.
58–9 *that great . . . Antony* that great personality which should always be associated
with the name of Antony [K].   60 *approves . . . liar* proves (by his conduct) that
common Fame or Rumour, though a notorious liar, tells the truth in this instance [K].
62 *Rest you happy* God keep you fortunate.
I.II.   1 *most anything* Charmian pretends that she cannot think of an adjective
good enough to express her admiration [K].   2 *absolute* perfect.   3 *this   husband*
Alexas has been telling Charmian that the Soothsayer will reveal who her husband
shall be [K].   *charge* load. A cuckold (husband of an unfaithful wife) was jestingly
said to grow horns on his forehead. Alexas, it appears, has been declaring that Charmian's future husband will meet this fate, but that he will be so thoroughly deluded
by her as to wear his horns proudly and even to hang garlands upon them. There
is a clear allusion to the ancient practice of decorating with garlands the ox that was
led to the sacrifice [K] (THEOBALD; F¹: "change." The reading has been much disputed) .

A little I can read.
ALEXAS   Show him your hand.
[*Enter* ENOBARBUS.]
ENOBARBUS   Bring in the banquet quickly; wine enough   [*10*
  Cleopatra's health to drink.
CHARMIAN   Good sir, give me good fortune.
SOOTHSAYER   I make not, but foresee.
CHARMIAN   Pray then, foresee me one.
SOOTHSAYER   You shall be yet far fairer than you are.   [*15*
CHARMIAN   He means in flesh.
IRAS   No, you shall paint when you are old.
CHARMIAN   Wrinkles forbid!
ALEXAS   Vex not his prescience; be attentive.
CHARMIAN   Hush!   [*20*
SOOTHSAYER   You shall be more beloving than beloved.
CHARMIAN   I had rather heat my liver with drinking.
ALEXAS   Nay, hear him.
CHARMIAN   Good now, some excellent fortune! Let me be married to three
  kings in a forenoon and widow them all. Let me have a child at fifty,   [*25*
  to whom Herod of Jewry may do homage. Find me to marry me with
  Octavius Cæsar, and companion me with my mistress.
SOOTHSAYER   You shall outlive the lady whom you serve.
CHARMIAN   O excellent! I love long life better than figs.
SOOTHSAYER   You have seen and prov'd a fairer former fortune   [*30*
  Than that which is to approach.
CHARMIAN   Then belike my children shall have no names. Prithee, how many
  boys and wenches must I have?
SOOTHSAYER   If every of your wishes had a womb,
  And fertile every wish, a million.   [*35*
CHARMIAN   Out, fool! I forgive thee for a witch.
ALEXAS   You think none but your sheets are privy to your wishes.
CHARMIAN   Nay, come, tell Iras hers.
ALEXAS   We'll know all our fortunes.
ENOBARBUS   Mine, and most of our fortunes, to-night, shall be—drunk to   [*40*
  bed.
IRAS   There's a palm presages chastity, if nothing else.
CHARMIAN   E'en as the o'erflowing Nilus presageth famine.
IRAS   Go, you wild bedfellow, you cannot soothsay.
CHARMIAN   Nay, if an oily palm be not a fruitful prognostication, I cannot   [*45*
  scratch mine ear. Prithee tell her but a workyday fortune.

---

9 *your hand* so that he may read the palm.   10 *banquet* light dessert.   15 *fairer* (a)
more beautiful (b) more fortunate.   16 *in flesh* To be "fair in flesh" is to be plump.
17 *paint* use cosmetics.   19 *prescience* foreknowledge (a mock title of respect, like
"his lordship").   22 *heat . . . drinking* She would rather heat her liver, the supposed
seat of the passion of love, by drinking than by love.   26 *Herod of Jewry* Herod the
Great, King of Judea, was traditionally regarded as a proud and ferocious tyrant, and
such is the character in which he appears in the old religious plays [K].   27 *companion . . . mistress* As the wife of Octavius she would be comparable in rank to her
mistress, Cleopatra, whom she regards as married to Antony, a fellow Triumvir.
30 *prov'd* experienced.   32 *belike* perhaps.   *have no names* be illegitimate.   33 *wenches*
girls.   35 *fertile* THEOBALD; F¹: "foretell."   36 *I forgive . . . witch* I absolve you from
the sin of witchcraft (for you are no true prophet).   37 *are privy* to have private
knowledge of.   42 *a palm* Iras holds out her hand for the Soothsayer to read the lines
in her palm [K].   44 *wild* wanton, licentious.   45 *oily palm* A moist or sweaty palm was

SOOTHSAYER   Your fortunes are alike.

IRAS   But how, but how? Give me particulars.

SOOTHSAYER   I have said.

IRAS   Am I not an inch of fortune better than she?   [5

CHARMIAN   Well, if you were but an inch of fortune better than I,
where would you choose it?

IRAS   Not in my husband's nose.

CHARMIAN   Our worser thoughts heavens mend! Alexas—come, his fortune, his
fortune! O, let him marry a woman that cannot go, sweet Isis, I beseech   [5
thee! and let her die too, and give him a worse! and let worse follow worse
till the worst of all follow him laughing to his grave, fiftyfold a cuckold!
Good Isis, hear me this prayer, though thou deny me a matter of more
weight; good Isis, I beseech thee!

IRAS   Amen. Dear goddess, hear that prayer of the people! For, as it is a heart- [6
breaking to see a handsome man loose-wiv'd, so it is a deadly sorrow to behold a foul knave uncuckolded. Therefore, dear Isis, keep decorum, and
fortune him accordingly!

CHARMIAN   Amen.

ALEXAS   Lo now, if it lay in their hands to make me a cuckold, they would   [6
make themselves whores but they'ld do't!

ENOBARBUS   Hush! Here comes Antony.

[Enter CLEOPATRA.]

CHARMIAN   Not he! the Queen.

CLEOPATRA   Saw you my lord?

ENOBARBUS   No, lady.

CLEOPATRA   Was he not here?

CHARMIAN   No, madam.

CLEOPATRA   He was dispos'd to mirth; but on the sudden   [7
A Roman thought hath struck him. Enobarbus!

ENOBARBUS   Madam?

CLEOPATRA   Seek him, and bring him hither. Where's Alexas?

ALEXAS   Here at your service. My lord approaches.

[Enter ANTONY *with a* MESSENGER *(and* ATTENDANTS) .]

CLEOPATRA   We will not look upon him. Go with us.   [7
[Exeunt (CLEOPATRA, ENOBARBUS *and the rest)* .]

MESSENGER   Fulvia thy wife first came into the field.

ANTONY   Against my brother Lucius?

MESSENGER   Ay.
But soon that war had end, and the time's state
Made friends of them, jointing their force 'gainst Cæsar,   [8
Whose better issue in the war from Italy
Upon the first encounter drave them.

ANTONY   Well, what worst?

---

believed to indicate a lecherous disposition.   *fruitful prognostication* prophetic indication of fertility.   46 *workyday* ordinary (as opposed to holiday) .

55 *cannot go* (a) cannot walk (b) cannot bear children.   *Isis* the Egyptian goddess of the earth, the moon, and fertility.   60 *of the people* Iras pretends that the
whole nation joins in this prayer [K].   61 *loose-wiv'd* married to a loose (unfaithful)
wife.   62 *foul knave* ugly fellow.   *keep decorum* act properly, as a goddess should.
68 *Saw you* F²; F¹: "Saue you."   71 *A Roman thought* (a) thought of Rome (b) such
a thought as a virtuous Roman might have.   76 *Fulvia . . . field* The messages with
regard to the war waged by Lucius Antonius and Fulvia and the conquest achieved by
Labienus reached Antony at Alexandria. The news of Fulvia's death came after Antony

MESSENGER   The nature of bad news infects the teller.
ANTONY   When it concerns the fool or coward. On!
    Things that are past are done with me. 'Tis thus: [*85*
    Who tells me true, though in his tale lie death,
    I hear him as he flatter'd.
MESSENGER   Labienus
    (This is stiff news) hath with his Parthian force
    Extended Asia from Euphrates,
    His conquering banner shook from Syria   [*90*
    To Lydia and to Ionia,
    Whilst—
ANTONY   Antony, thou wouldst say.
MESSENGER   O, my lord!
ANTONY   Speak to me home. Mince not the general tongue.
    Name Cleopatra as she is call'd in Rome.
    Rail thou in Fulvia's phrase, and taunt my faults   [*95*
    With such full license as both truth and malice
    Have power to utter. O, then we bring forth weeds
    When our quick minds lie still, and our ills told us
    Is as our earing. Fare thee well awhile.
MESSENGER   At your noble pleasure. [*Exit.*]   [*100*
ANTONY   From Sicyon, ho, the news! Speak there!
1. ATTENDANT   The man from Sicyon—is there such an one?
2. ATTENDANT   He stays upon your will.
ANTONY   Let him appear.
    These strong Egyptian fetters I must break
    Or lose myself in dotage.
    [*Enter another* MESSENGER, *with a letter.*]
                What are you?   [*105*
MESSENGER   Fulvia thy wife is dead.
ANTONY   Where died she?
MESSENGER   In Sicyon.
    Her length of sickness, with what else more serious
    Importeth thee to know, this bears.   [*Gives the letter.*]
ANTONY   Forbear me.

---

had left Egypt for a campaign against the Parthians. Shakespeare condenses history with dramatic efficiency [K]. 79 *the time's state* the condition of the times; the political situation, which forced Fulvia and Lucius to make common cause against Octavius Cæsar [K]. 81 *issue* success. 82 *drave* drove.

    83 *infects the teller* and thus makes him seem hateful [K]. 87 *as* as though. *Labienus* Quintus Labienus, having been sent by Brutus and Cassius to enlist the aid of Parthia in their cause, was now overrunning the eastern dependencies of the Roman Empire with the aid of a Parthian army under Pacorus, the son of King Orodes. He was at last defeated by Ventidius, whom Antony sent against him. 89 *Extended* seized upon, taken quick possession of. An "extent" was a summary legal process for the seizure of property [K]. 93 *home* without reserve, to the point. *Mince . . . tongue* do not soften what is being generally said. 96 *license* freedom. 98 *quick* lively, fertile. *minds* WARBURTON; F¹: "windes." *still* idle (like a fallow field) . Our minds, like the earth, must always bring forth something. When they lie untilled, they produce weeds [K]. 98-9 *our ills . . . earing* to have our faults told us is like a ploughing for us. The figure comes from destroying the weeds in a field or garden by "ploughing them under" [K]. To "ear" is to "plough." 101 *Sicyon* a town in the Peloponnesus, where Antony had left Fulvia in 40 B.C. [K]. *ho* DYCE; F¹: "how." 103 *stays upon your will* awaits your pleasure. 109 *Importeth* concerns. *Forbear me* leave me.

[*Exit* MESSENGER.]
There's a great spirit gone! Thus did I desire it.   [*11*
What our contempts doth often hurl from us,
We wish it ours again. The present pleasure,
By revolution low'ring, does become
The opposite of itself. She's good, being gone;
The hand could pluck her back that shov'd her on.   [*11*
I must from this enchanting queen break off.
Ten thousand harms more than the ills I know
My idleness doth hatch. How now, Enobarbus!
[*Enter* ENOBARBUS.]
ENOBARBUS   What's your pleasure, sir?
ANTONY   I must with haste from hence.   [*12*
ENOBARBUS   Why, then we kill all our women. We see how mortal an unkind-
ness is to them. If they suffer our departure, death's the word.
ANTONY   I must be gone.
ENOBARBUS   Under a compelling occasion let women die. It were pity to cast
them away for nothing, though, between them and a great cause, they should [*12*
be esteemed nothing. Cleopatra, catching but the least noise of this, dies
instantly. I have seen her die twenty times upon far poorer moment. I do
think there is mettle in death, which commits some loving act upon her,
she hath such a celerity in dying.
ANTONY   She is cunning past man's thought.   [*13*
ENOBARBUS   Alack, sir, no! Her passions are made of nothing but the finest
part of pure love. We cannot call her winds and waters sighs and tears.
They are greater storms and tempests than almanacs can report. This cannot
be cunning in her; if it be, she makes a show'r of rain as well as Jove.
ANTONY   Would I had never seen her!   [*13*
ENOBARBUS   O, sir, you had then left unseen a wonderful piece of work, which
not to have been blest withal would have discredited your travel.
ANTONY   Fulvia is dead.
ENOBARBUS   Sir?
ANTONY   Fulvia is dead.   [*14*
ENOBARBUS   Fulvia?
ANTONY   Dead.
ENOBARBUS   Why, sir, give the gods a thankful sacrifice. When it pleaseth their
deities to take the wife of a man from him, it shows to man the tailors of
the earth; comforting therein, that when old robes are worn out, there are [*14*
members to make new. If there were no more women but Fulvia, then had

---

111 *doth* An old plural form (F¹; F², K: "do"). 113 *By revolution* as by a turn of
the wheel. Our feelings never remain constant: pleasure turns to pain and pain to
pleasure. The figure is suggested by the Wheel of Fortune [K]. 115 *could* would if it
could. 116 *enchanting queen* Cleopatra, whom the Romans believed to have witchlike
powers of seduction. 118 *idleness* folly, dotage. 124 *compelling occasion* ROWE; F¹:
"compelling an occasion." 126 *noise* rumour. 127 *upon . . . moment* on a far less
momentous occasion; for a far less weighty cause [K]. 128 *mettle* vigour. 128-9 *which
commits . . . dying* The image is of Cleopatra rushing to embrace Death as a lover; it
foreshadows her final suicide. 134 *Jove* Jupiter Pluvius, the rain god of the Romans.
The point of the sarcasm lies in the double meaning of "cunning" ("skill" and "crafti-
ness") and in the verb "makes." If her tears are not the genuine effect of natural feeling, they are "made" or "artificial," and her skill in rain making is equal to Jupiter's
[K]. 136-7 *which not . . . travel* not to have been blessed with a view of which, would
have been a disgrace to you as an intelligent traveller and sightseer [K]. 144-5 *it shows*

you indeed a cut, and the case to be lamented. This grief is crown'd with
consolation; your old smock brings forth a new petticoat; and indeed the
tears live in an onion that should water this sorrow.

ANTONY The business she hath broached in the state [*150*
Cannot endure my absence.

ENOBARBUS And the business you have broach'd here cannot be without you;
especially that of Cleopatra's, which wholly depends on your abode.

ANTONY No more light answers. Let our officers
Have notice what we purpose. I shall break [*155*
The cause of our expedience to the Queen
And get her leave to part. For not alone
The death of Fulvia, with more urgent touches,
Do strongly speak to us, but the letters too
Of many our contriving friends in Rome [*160*
Petition us at home. Sextus Pompeius
Hath given the dare to Cæsar and commands
The empire of the sea. Our slippery people,
Whose love is never link'd to the deserver
Till his deserts are past, begin to throw [*165*
Pompey the Great and all his dignities
Upon his son; who, high in name and power,
Higher than both in blood and life, stands up
For the main soldier; whose quality, going on,
The sides o' th' world may danger. Much is breeding [*170*
Which, like the courser's hair, hath yet but life
And not a serpent's poison. Say, our pleasure,
To such whose place is under us, requires
Our quick remove from hence.

ENOBARBUS I shall do't. [*Exeunt.*] [*175*

. . . *of the earth* it exhibits them (the gods) to men in the capacity of repairers of
loss and damage. Enobarbus explains his curious metaphor in what follows [K].
147 *cut* blow, injury. *case* (a) situation (b) sheathe, in a common bawdy sense.
148 *old smock . . . petticoat* The point is that he is able to change his old wife
for a new one. 149 *the tears . . . sorrow* an onion will cause you to weep all the tears
necessary for Fulvia's death (since you have no real cause for sorrow) . 150 *broached*
set abroach, set in motion. The figure is from "broaching a cask" of liquor. Antony
refers to the civil war Fulvia has started [K]. 152 *business . . . broached* Enobarbus
puns on "business" in the sense of "sexual intercourse" and on "broached" as "opened
for use." 153 *your abode* your remaining here [K]. 154 *light* frivolous, licentious
(referring to Enobarbus' bawdy quibbling) . 155 *break* reveal. 156 *expedience* hasty
departure. 157 *leave* POPE; F¹: "loue." *part* depart. 158 *touches* motives. 160 *many
our contriving friends* many friends of mine who are making plans in my interest [K].
161 *Petition us at home* beg me to come home. *Sextus Pompeius* the younger son of
Pompey the Great. He had possession of Sicily and was master of the sea. Peace was
made between him and the Triumvirs in 39 B.C., but hostilities soon broke out afresh.
In 36 B.C. he was defeated, and in the next year he was put to death [K]. 162 *Hath*
F²; F¹: "Haue." 165 *throw* transfer. 168 *blood and life* spirit and energy. 168–9 *stands
. . . soldier* takes his position as the great soldier of the world [K]. 169–70 *whose
quality . . . danger* and his (aspiring) nature, as he continues to advance in power,
may endanger the whole body of our worldwide empire [K]. 171 *the courser's hair*
Horsehairs, falling into stagnant water, were thought to come to life as worms or small
serpents [K]. 173 *whose place . . . requires* F²; F¹: "whose places under us, requires."
174 *remove* departure.

Scene III

[*Alexandria. Another room in* CLEOPATRA's *Palace.*]

[*Enter* CLEOPATRA, CHARMIAN, ALEXAS, *and* IRAS.]

CLEOPATRA   Where is he?

CHARMIAN   I did not see him since.

CLEOPATRA   See where he is, who's with him, what he does.
I did not send you. If you find him sad,
Say I am dancing; if in mirth, report
That I am sudden sick. Quick, and return!

[*Exit* ALEXAS.]

CHARMIAN   Madam, methinks, if you did love him dearly,
You do not hold the method to enforce
The like from him.

CLEOPATRA   What should I do, I do not?

CHARMIAN   In each thing give him way, cross him in nothing.

CLEOPATRA   Thou teachest like a fool. The way to lose him!

CHARMIAN   Tempt him not so too far; I wish, forbear.
In time we hate that which we often fear.

[*Enter* ANTONY.]

But here comes Antony.

CLEOPATRA   I am sick and sullen.

ANTONY   I am sorry to give breathing to my purpose—

CLEOPATRA   Help me away, dear Charmian! I shall fall.
It cannot be thus long; the sides of nature
Will not sustain it.

ANTONY   Now, my dearest queen—

CLEOPATRA   Pray you stand farther from me.

ANTONY   What's the matter?

CLEOPATRA   I know by that same eye there's some good news.
What, says the married woman you may go?
Would she had never given you leave to come!
Let her not say 'tis I that keep you here.
I have no power upon you; hers you are.

ANTONY   The gods best know—

CLEOPATRA   O, never was there queen
So mightily betray'd! Yet at the first
I saw the treasons planted.

ANTONY   Cleopatra—

CLEOPATRA   Why should I think you can be mine, and true,
Though you in swearing shake the throned gods,
Who have been false to Fulvia? Riotous madness,
To be entangled with those mouth-made vows
Which break themselves in swearing!

ANTONY   Most sweet queen—

I.III. 3 *sad* in a serious frame of mind—not sorrowful [K]. 8 *The like* the same feeling. *I do not* that I am not doing. 11 *Tempt* try, test. *I wish, forbear* I wish, indeed, you would give up tempting him altogether [K]. 13 *sullen* in low spirits. 14 *breathing* utterance. 16 *the sides of nature* my natural bodily strength [K]. 20 *married woman* Fulvia, your wife. 21 *leave* permission. She taunts Antony with being a henpecked husband. 28 *shake the throned gods* make the gods tremble on their thrones (by your tremendous oaths) [K]. 30 *with* by. *mouth-made* composed only of speech and thus having no real substance.

CLEOPATRA   Nay, pray you seek no colour for your going,
    But bid farewell, and go. When you su'd staying,
    Then was the time for words. No going then!
    Eternity was in our lips and eyes,   [*35*
    Bliss in our brows' bent, none our parts so poor
    But was a race of heaven. They are so still,
    Or thou, the greatest soldier of the world,
    Art turn'd the greatest liar.
ANTONY   How now, lady?
CLEOPATRA   I would I had thy inches! Thou shouldst know   [*40*
    There were a heart in Egypt.
ANTONY   Hear me, Queen.
    The strong necessity of time commands
    Our services awhile; but my full heart
    Remains in use with you. Our Italy
    Shines o'er with civil swords. Sextus Pompeius   [*45*
    Makes his approaches to the port of Rome.
    Equality of two domestic powers
    Breed scrupulous faction. The hated, grown to strength,
    Are newly grown to love. The condemn'd Pompey,
    Rich in his father's honour, creeps apace   [*50*
    Into the hearts of such as have not thriv'd
    Upon the present state, whose numbers threaten;
    And quietness, grown sick of rest, would purge
    By any desperate change. My more particular,
    And that which most with you should safe my going,   [*55*
    Is Fulvia's death.
CLEOPATRA   Though age from folly could not give me freedom,
    It does from childishness. Can Fulvia die?
ANTONY   She's dead, my queen.
    Look here, and at thy sovereign leisure read   [*60*
    The garboils she awak'd. At the last, best,
    See when and where she died.
CLEOPATRA   O most false love!
    Where be the sacred vials thou shouldst fill
    With sorrowful water? Now I see, I see,

---

32 *colour* pretext.   33 *su'd staying* begged my permission to remain.   35 *Eternity* immortal pleasures [K].   36 *Bliss* the joy of heaven [K].   *our brows' bent* the arch of my eyebrows.   *none our parts* no feature or quality of mine [K].   37 *a race of heaven* (a) godlike, of divine origine (b) of heavenly flavour. "Race" is a term used to describe the quality or flavour of wine.   41 *a heart* courage, ability to repay injuries. *Egypt* the Queen of Egypt.   44 *Remains in use* remains, as it were, on deposit with you—for you to make use of as you will; you have the "usufruct" of my whole heart [K].   46 *port of Rome* Ostia, at the mouth of the Tiber [K].   47–8 *Equality . . . faction* the fact that Pompey's resources and those of the Triumvirs are so evenly balanced breeds party divisions among the Romans on small points of disagreement [K].   48–9 *The hated . . . love* those who were hated, having grown strong, are beginning to be loved.   52 *Upon* under the rule of.   52 *whose* Pompey is the antecedent.   53–4 *And quietness . . . change* That peace (quietness) caused the body politic to become diseased and had to be cured by periodic bloodletting (desperate change) was a commonplace of Renaissance political theory.   54 *more particular* more personal reason.   55 *with you . . . going* ought to make my departure safe from your point of view [K].   61 *garboils* tumults, disturbances.   63 *sacred vials* The Romans sometimes placed bottles of tears in the funeral urns of their loved ones.

In Fulvia's death, how mine receiv'd shall be.   [6
ANTONY   Quarrel no more, but be prepar'd to know
    The purposes I bear; which are, or cease,
    As you shall give the advice. By the fire
    That quickens Nilus' slime, I go from hence
    Thy soldier, servant, making peace or war   [7
    As thou affects.
CLEOPATRA   Cut my lace, Charmian, come!
    But let it be. I am quickly ill, and well—
    So Antony loves.
ANTONY   My precious queen, forbear,
    And give true evidence to his love, which stands
    An honourable trial.
CLEOPATRA   So Fulvia told me.   [7
    I prithee turn aside and weep for her;
    Then bid adieu to me, and say the tears
    Belong to Egypt. Good now, play one scene
    Of excellent dissembling, and let it look
    Like perfect honour.
ANTONY   You'll heat my blood. No more!   [8
CLEOPATRA   You can do better yet; but this is meetly.
ANTONY   Now by my sword—
CLEOPATRA   And target. Still he mends;
    But this is not the best. Look, prithee, Charmian,
    How this Herculean Roman does become
    The carriage of his chafe.   [8
ANTONY   I'll leave you, lady.
CLEOPATRA   Courteous lord, one word.
    Sir, you and I must part—but that's not it.
    Sir, you and I have lov'd—but there's not it.
    That you know well. Something it is I would—
    O, my oblivion is a very Antony,   [9
    And I am all forgotten!
ANTONY   But that your royalty

---

67 *bear* bring, have to tell you. 67 *are* continue to exist. 68 *advice* instructions.
69 *quickens* vivifies, wakes to life and fertility. Antony swears by the sun [K]. *Nilus'*
slime The mud left by the Nile when it recedes after flooding is exceedingly fertile
[K]. 71 *affects* desirest (F¹; F², K: "affects") . *lace* the lacing of my stays. Cleopatra pretends to be fainting, but quickly recovers [K]. 72 *well* well again. 73 *So Antony loves*
Antony's love is as changeable as my feelings of health and sickness. Some editors take
"so" as meaning "provided that," but Cleopatra is not yet ready to admit that Antony
really loves her [K]. 73 *forbear* cease this kind of talk, refrain [K]. 74 *which* who.
75 *So Fulvia told me* Cleopatra tauntingly suggests that Fulvia would be good authority
on the subject of Antony's faithfulness in love [K]. 78 *Egypt* the Queen of Egypt. *Good*
Often thus used as a vocative noun [K]. 81 *meetly* fitly, well acted [K]. 82 *by my sword*
F²; F¹: "by sword." *target* shield, buckler. *Still he mends* he continues to improve (in
his acting) . 84 *Herculean Roman* Antony was considered to be a descendent of Hercules. 84–5 *become . . . chafe* becomingly plays the role of an angry man (specifically
of Hercules) . 89 *would* wished to say. 90 *oblivion* utter forgetfulness. *a very Antony*
As if the word "Antony" were a synonym for forgetfulness in the highest degree
[K]. 91 *I am all forgotten* (a) I have completely forgotten what I meant to say
[K] (b) I have been forgotten, abandoned, by Antony. 91–3 *But that . . . idleness itself*
were it not that you hold rule over your absurdities (in speech and manner) in such a
way as to make them serviceable to yourself, I should regard you as absurdity person-
ified. "Idleness" is common in the sense of "foolishness" in thought, language, or con-

Holds idleness your subject, I should take you
For idleness itself.
CLEOPATRA   'Tis sweating labour
To bear such idleness to near the heart
As Cleopatra this. But, sir, forgive me;   [*95*
Since my becomings kill me when they do not
Eye well to you. Your honour calls you hence;
Therefore be deaf to my unpitied folly,
And all the gods go with you! Upon your sword
Sit laurel victory, and smooth success   [*100*
Be strew'd before your feet!
ANTONY   Let us go. Come.
Our separation so abides and flies
That thou, residing here, goes yet with me,
And I, hence fleeting, here remain with thee.
Away!   [*Exeunt.*]   [*105*

Scene IV

[*Rome.* CÆSAR'S *house.*]

[*Enter* OCTAVIUS (*Cæsar*), *reading a letter*, LEPIDUS, *and their* TRAIN.]
CÆSAR   You may see, Lepidus, and henceforth know
It is not Cæsar's natural vice to hate
Our great competitor. From Alexandria
This is the news: he fishes, drinks, and wastes
The lamps of night in revel; is not more manlike   [*5*
Than Cleopatra, nor the queen of Ptolemy
More womanly than he; hardly gave audience, or
Vouchsaf'd to think he had partners. You shall find there
A man who is the abstract of all faults
That all men follow.
LEPIDUS   I must not think there are   [*10*
Evils enow to darken all his goodness.
His faults, in him, seem as the spots of heaven,
More fiery by night's blackness; hereditary

duct. Antony implies that even folly is charming in Cleopatra, and that she knows it
and practices it accordingly [K].
    93 *sweating labour* the labour of childbirth. She compares her passion and grief
(what Antony calls "idleness") to the pain of a woman in childbirth. 96 *becomings*
attractive qualities. 97 *Eye well to you* seem beautiful in your eyes [K]. 101 *strew'd*
like flowers or laurel branches in the path of a triumphant general [K]. 102 *so abides
and flies* unites itself into the opposites of staying and going: although he goes he is
still with her, and although she stays she remains with him. 103 *goes* F¹; CAPELL, K:
"go'st."
    I.IV. 2 *vice* fault—in a general sense, not limited as in modern usage. 3 *Our*
SINGER; F¹: "One." *competitor* partner, colleague. 4 *fishes* Plutarch speaks of fishing
as one of the childish pastimes with which Antony wasted his time in Egypt. 6
Ptolemy Cleopatra was the widow of Ptolemy XII, King of Egypt [K]. 7 *gave audience*
to the ambassadors from Rome. 9 *who is . . . faults* who includes in his single self
all human faults, as the abstract of a document gives a summary of its contents [K].
abstract F²; F¹: "abstracts." 11 *Evils enow* faults enough. 12–13 *His faults . . . blackness* his faults, as the stars seem more bright against the dark night, seem to stand out

Rather than purchas'd; what he cannot change
Than what he chooses.   [⌐

CÆSAR   You are too indulgent. Let us grant it is not
Amiss to tumble on the bed of Ptolemy,
To give a kingdom for a mirth, to sit
And keep the turn of tippling with a slave,
To reel the streets at noon, and stand the buffet   [⌐
With knaves that smell of sweat. Say this becomes him
(As his composure must be rare indeed
Whom these things cannot blemish), yet must Antony
No way excuse his foils when we do bear
So great weight in his lightness. If he fill'd   [⌐
His vacancy with his voluptuousness,
Full surfeits and the dryness of his bones
Call on him for't! But to confound such time
That drums him from his sport and speaks as loud
As his own state and ours—'tis to be chid   [⌐
As we rate boys who, being mature in knowledge,
Pawn their experience to their present pleasure
And so rebel to judgment.
            [*Enter a* MESSENGER.]
LEPIDUS   Here's more news.
MESSENGER   Thy biddings have been done, and every hour,
Most noble Cæsar, shalt thou have report   [⌐
How 'tis abroad. Pompey is strong at sea,
And it appears he is belov'd of those
That only have fear'd Cæsar. To the ports
The discontents repair, and men's reports
Give him much wrong'd.
CÆSAR   I should have known no less.   [⌐
It hath been taught us from the primal state
That he which is was wish'd until he were;
And the ebb'd man, ne'er lov'd till ne'er worth love,
Comes dear'd by being lack'd. This common body,
Like to a vagabond flag upon the stream,   [⌐
Goes to and back, lackeying the varying tide,
To rot itself with motion.

more in the present dark political situation.   14 *purchas'd* acquired.   18 *for a mirth* as a reward for the invention of some novel amusement [K].   19 *keep the turn of tippling* drink healths, turn and turn about [K].   20–1 *stand . . . knaves* deign to engage in fisticuffs with low fellows [K].   *smell* F²; F¹: "smels."   22 *his composure* the man's composition or make-up.   24 *foils* disgraceful traits or acts—those that thwart or defeat his good qualities [K].   24–5 *when we . . . lightness* when we are so strongly affected by his frivolous conduct.   26 *vacancy* spare time.   27 *Full surfeits* fits of indigestion.   *dryness of his bones* a supposed symptom of syphilis.   28 *Call on him* take him to task, be his punishment.   28 *confound* waste.   29 *drums* calls as with the sound of the drum (which summons him to arms) [K].   30 *his own state* his own greatness; the maintenance of his own authority as a ruler of the world [K].   31 *rate* scold.   *mature in knowledge* old enough to know better [K].   32 *Pawn . . . pleasure* risk suffering what their experience has taught them must be the consequence of pleasure, merely for the sake of enjoying themselves at the moment [K].   33 *rebel to judgment* revolt against common sense [K].   39 *discontents* discontented persons.   40 *Give* give out, declare.   41 *from . . . state* ever since government began.   44 *Comes dear'd* becomes beloved.   *dear'd* THEOBALD; F¹: "fear."   44 *common body* common people.   45 *flag* a common species of iris.   46 *lackeying* following closely, like a lackey

MESSENGER   Cæsar, I bring thee word
   Menecrates and Menas, famous pirates,
   Make the sea serve them, which they ear and wound
   With keels of every kind. Many hot inroads   [*50*
   They make in Italy; the borders maritime
   Lack blood to think on't, and flush youth revolt.
   No vessel can peep forth but 'tis as soon
   Taken as seen; for Pompey's name strikes more
   Than could his war resisted.
CÆSAR   Antony,   [*55*
   Leave thy lascivious wassails. When thou once
   Was beaten from Modena, where thou slew'st
   Hirtius and Pansa, consuls, at thy heel
   Did famine follow; whom thou fought'st against
   (Though daintily brought up) with patience more   [*60*
   Than savages could suffer. Thou didst drink
   The stale of horses and the gilded puddle
   Which beasts would cough at. Thy palate then did deign
   The roughest berry on the rudest hedge.
   Yea, like the stag when snow the pasture sheets,   [*65*
   The barks of trees thou browsed. On the Alps
   It is reported thou didst eat strange flesh,
   Which some did die to look on. And all this
   (It wounds thine honour that I speak it now)
   Was borne so like a soldier that thy cheek   [*70*
   So much as lank'd not.
LEPIDUS   It is pity of him.
CÆSAR   Let his shames quickly
   Drive him to Rome. 'Tis time we twain
   Did show ourselves i'th' field; and to that end
   Assemble we immediate council. Pompey   [*75*
   Thrives in our idleness.
LEPIDUS   To-morrow, Cæsar,
   I shall be furnish'd to inform you rightly
   Both what by sea and land I can be able
   To front this present time.
CÆSAR   Till which encounter,
   It is my business too. Farewell.   [*80*
LEPIDUS   Farewell, my lord. What you shall know meantime
   Of stirs abroad, I shall beseech you, sir,
   To let me be partaker.
CÆSAR   Doubt not, sir;
   I knew it for my bond.   [*Exeunt.*]

---

who, without will of his own, attends his master everywhere [K] (THEOBALD; F¹: "lacking").   47 *motion* mere motion as opposed to intelligent action [K].

   49 *Make* F⁴; F¹: "Makes." *ear* plough.   52 *Lack blood* turn pale.   *flush* full-blooded,
spirited.   *revolt* to join the pirates.   54–5 *strikes more . . . resisted* is more effective
than his forces would be if opposed in battle.   56 *wassails* revels.   57 *Was* F¹; STEEVENS,
K: "Wast."   *Modena* In 43 B.C. the consuls Hirtius and Pansa were sent to drive Antony (who had been pronounced a public enemy by the Senate) out of Italy. Antony
was defeated at Modena, but both consuls fell in the battle. Antony fled across the
Alps [K].   60–1 *with patience . . . suffer* with greater fortitude than the endurance
which even savages could show [K].   62 *stale* urine.   *gilded* covered with yellow scum
[K].   63 *deign* not disdain.   66 *browsed* F¹; F², K: "browsed'st."   71 *lank'd not* did not

Scene V

[*Alexandria. A room in* CLEOPATRA'S *Palace.*]

[*Enter* CLEOPATRA, CHARMIAN, IRAS, *and* MARDIAN.]

CLEOPATRA   Charmian!

CHARMIAN   Madam?

CLEOPATRA   Ha, ha!
   Give me to drink mandragora.

CHARMIAN   Why, madam?

CLEOPATRA   That I might sleep out this great gap of time   [
   My Antony is away.

CHARMIAN   You think of him too much.

CLEOPATRA   O, 'tis treason!

CHARMIAN   Madam, I trust, not so.

CLEOPATRA   Thou, eunuch Mardian!

MARDIAN   What's your Highness' pleasure?

CLEOPATRA   Not now to hear thee sing. I take no pleasure
   In aught an eunuch has. 'Tis well for thee   [
   That, being unseminar'd, thy freer thoughts
   May not fly forth of Egypt. Hast thou affections?

MARDIAN   Yes, gracious madam.

CLEOPATRA   Indeed?

MARDIAN   Not in deed, madam; for I can do nothing   [
   But what indeed is honest to be done.
   Yet have I fierce affections, and think
   What Venus did with Mars.

CLEOPATRA   O Charmian!
   Where think'st thou he is now? Stands he, or sits he?
   Or does he walk? or is he on his horse?   [
   O happy horse, to bear the weight of Antony!
   Do bravely, horse! for wot'st thou whom thou mov'st?
   The demi-Atlas of this earth, the arm
   And burgonet of men. He's speaking now,
   Or murmuring "Where's my serpent of old Nile?"   [
   For so he calls me. Now I feed myself
   With most delicious poison. Think on me,
   That am with Phœbus' amorous pinches black
   And wrinkled deep in time? Broad-fronted Cæsar,
   When thou wast here above the ground, I was   [
   A morsel for a monarch; and great Pompey
   Would stand and make his eyes grow in my brow;

---

grow thin.   75 *we* F²; F¹: "me."   78 *can be able* can muster in the way of forces [K].
79 *front* cope with.   *present time* immediate crisis.   *encounter* meeting.   84 *knew* already knew (before you reminded me).   *bond* bounden duty.

   I.v.   4 *mandragora* mandrake, used in sleeping potions.   11 *unseminar'd* emascu-
lated.   12 *affections* natural feelings, passions.   16 *honest* chaste.   22 *Do bravely* act
finely; display thy proud spirit in action [K].   *wot'st* do you know.   23 *demi-Atlas*
Atlas bore the globe on his shoulders; Antony bears half of it (for Lepidus does not.
count) [K].   *arm* armour.   24 *burgonet* a kind of helmet.   28 *with . . . black* tanned
by the loving glances of Phœbus, the sun god; the sun is her lover.   29 *Cæsar* Julius
Cæsar, who had been her lover.   31 *great Pompey* Gnæus Pompey, the son of Pompey
the Great, had been Cleopatra's lover; Shakespeare seems to have confused father and
son here.

There would he anchor his aspect, and die
With looking on his life.
[*Enter* ALEXAS.]
ALEXAS   Sovereign of Egypt, hail!
CLEOPATRA   How much unlike art thou Mark Antony!   [*35*
Yet, coming from him, that great med'cine hath
With his tinct gilded thee.
How goes it with my brave Mark Antony?
ALEXAS   Last thing he did, dear Queen,
He kiss'd—the last of many doubled kisses—   [*40*
This orient pearl. His speech sticks in my heart.
CLEOPATRA   Mine ear must pluck it thence.
ALEXAS   "Good friend," quoth he,
"Say the firm Roman to great Egypt sends
This treasure of an oyster; at whose foot,
To mend the petty present, I will piece   [*45*
Her opulent throne with kingdoms. All the East,
Say thou, shall call her mistress." So he nodded,
And soberly did mount an arm-gaunt steed,
Who neigh'd so high that what I would have spoke
Was beastly dumb'd by him.
CLEOPATRA   What, was he sad or merry?   [*50*
ALEXAS   Like to the time o' th' year between the extremes
Of hot and cold. He was nor sad nor merry.
CLEOPATRA   O well-divided disposition! Note him,
Note him, good Charmian; 'tis the man; but note him!
He was not sad, for he would shine on those   [*55*
That make their looks by his; he was not merry,
Which seem'd to tell them his remembrance lay
In Egypt with his joy; but between both.
O heavenly mingle! Be'st thou sad or merry,
The violence of either thee becomes,   [*60*
So does it no man else.—Met'st thou my posts?
ALEXAS   Ay, madam, twenty several messengers.
Why do you send so thick?
CLEOPATRA   Who's born that day
When I forget to send to Antony
Shall die a beggar. Ink and paper, Charmian.   [*65*
Welcome, my good Alexas. Did I, Charmian,
Ever love Cæsar so?
CHARMIAN   O that brave Cæsar!

---

33 *anchor his aspect* fix his gaze.   34 *his life* all that he lived for.   36 *that great . . . gilded thee* the mere fact that you come from Antony has made you look to me a little like him—has "gilded" you, though not transformed you into "gold." The "great medicine" is the "elixir" or transmuting powder (the so-called "philosopher's stone" of the alchemists), which was thought to turn the baser metals into gold [K]. 38 *brave* splendid, glorious. A general word of commendation in Elizabethan English— not referring exclusively to valour [K].   41 *orient* lustrous.   43 *firm* constant.   45 *piece* piece out—add kingdoms to her throne so as to make it opulent [K].   48 *arm-gaunt* trained down by hard service in armour [K].   50 *beastly dumb'd by him* drowned (rendered inaudible) by the beast's voice (literally, in beast's fashion) [K].   *dumb'd* THEOBALD; F¹: "dumbe."   53 *disposition* mood.   54 *the man* the very man—the real Antony.   55 *would* wished to.   61 *man* F²; F¹: "mans."   *posts* special messengers, riding posthaste.   63 *thick* in quick succession.   65 *Shall die a beggar* for that day shall be

CLEOPATRA   Be chok'd with such another emphasis!
Say "the brave Antony."
CHARMIAN   The valiant Cæsar!
CLEOPATRA   By Isis, I will give thee bloody teeth   [
If thou with Cæsar paragon again
My man of men!
CHARMIAN   By your most gracious pardon,
I sing but after you.
CLEOPATRA   My salad days,
When I was green in judgment, cold in blood,   [
To say as I said then. But come, away!
Get me ink and paper.
He shall have every day a several greeting,
Or I'll unpeople Egypt.   [*Exeunt.*]

ACT TWO

Scene 1

[*Messina.* POMPEY's *house.*]

[*Enter* POMPEY, MENECRATES, *and* MENAS, *in warlike
manner.*]
POMPEY   If the great gods be just, they shall assist
The deeds of justest men.
MENECRATES   Know, worthy Pompey,
That what they do delay, they not deny.
POMPEY   While we are suitors to their throne, decays   [
The thing we sue for.
MENECRATES   We, ignorant of ourselves,
Beg often our own harms, which the wise pow'rs
Deny us for our good. So find we profit
By losing of our prayers.
POMPEY   I shall do well.
The people love me, and the sea is mine;
My powers are crescent, and my auguring hope   [
Says it will come to th' full. Mark Antony
In Egypt sits at dinner, and will make
No wars without doors. Cæsar gets money where
He loses hearts. Lepidus flatters both,
Of both is flatter'd; but he neither loves,   [
Nor either cares for him.
MENAS   Cæsar and Lepidus
Are in the field; a mighty strength they carry.

---

accursed. Cleopatra means to say that no such day shall ever dawn [K].   67 *Cæsar*
Julius Cæsar.   67 *brave* splendid.
      68 *emphasis* intensity of feeling or expression.   71 *paragon* compare, equalize.
73 *salad days* green youth.
      II.i.   2 *worthy* noble.   4–5 *While . . . sue for* while we pray to the Gods, the thing
for which we are praying steadily loses its value.   8 *losing of our prayers* praying in
vain.   10 *powers* troops. *crescent* increasing.   11 *it* the crescent moon (of my for-

POMPEY   Where have you this? 'Tis false.
MENAS   From Silvius, sir.
POMPEY   He dreams. I know they are in Rome together,
    Looking for Antony. But all the charms of love,   [20
    Salt Cleopatra, soften thy wan'd lip!
    Let witchcraft join with beauty, lust with both!
    Tie up the libertine in a field of feasts,
    Keep his brain fuming. Epicurean cooks
    Sharpen with cloyless sauce his appetite,   [25
    That sleep and feeding may prorogue his honour
    Even till a Lethe'd dulness!
    [Enter VARRIUS.]
                                  How now, Varrius?
VARRIUS   This is most certain that I shall deliver:
    Mark Antony is every hour in Rome
    Expected. Since he went from Egypt 'tis   [30
    A space for farther travel.
POMPEY   I could have given less matter
    A better ear. Menas, I did not think
    This amorous surfeiter would have donn'd his helm
    For such a petty war. His soldiership
    Is twice the other twain. But let us rear   [35
    The higher our opinion, that our stirring
    Can from the lap of Egypt's widow pluck
    The ne'er-lust-wearied Antony.
MENAS   I cannot hope
    Cæsar and Antony shall well greet together.
    His wife that's dead did trespasses to Cæsar;   [40
    His brother warr'd upon him; although, I think,
    Not mov'd by Antony.
POMPEY   I know not, Menas,
    How lesser enmities may give way to greater.
    Were't not that we stand up against them all,
    'Twere pregnant they should square between themselves,   [45
    For they have entertained cause enough
    To draw their swords; but how the fear of us
    May cement their divisions and bind up
    The petty difference we yet not know.
    Be't as our gods will have't! It only stands   [50
    Our lives upon to use our strongest hands.
    Come, Menas. [Exeunt.]

---

tunes) [K]. 13 without doors out of doors.
    21 Salt lascivious. wan'd ageing, withered. 23 Tie . . . of feasts The reference is
probably to an animal being staked in a pasture, although the meaning of the expression is uncertain. 24 fuming The fumes of wine were thought to rise from the
stomach into the brain and thus to cause drunkenness [K]. 25 cloyless which never
cloys the taste. 26–7 may prorogue . . . dulness may postpone all thought of his
honour until he sinks into apathy and forgetfulness, as if he had drunk of the river
Lethe [K]. 28 deliver report. 30–1 'tis . . . travel time enough has elapsed for even a
longer journey [K]. 33 surfeiter indulger to excess. 35–6 rear . . . our opinion raise
our estimate of our own worth. 38 hope expect. The word was often used of disagree-
able expectation as well as of that which is pleasant [K]. 39 greet agree, commune
amicably. 41 His brother Lucius Antonius, who, with Antony's wife, Fulvia, had made
war upon Octavius [K]. warr'd F²; F¹: "wan'd." 42 mov'd urged on. 45 pregnant very

Scene II

[*Rome. The house of* LEPIDUS.]

[*Enter* ENOBARBUS *and* LEPIDUS.]

LEPIDUS   Good Enobarbus, 'tis a worthy deed,
And shall become you well, to entreat your captain
To soft and gentle speech.

ENOBARBUS   I shall entreat him
To answer like himself. If Cæsar move him,
Let Antony look over Cæsar's head
And speak as loud as Mars. By Jupiter,
Were I the wearer of Antonius' beard,
I would not shave't to-day!

LEPIDUS   'Tis not a time
For private stomaching.

ENOBARBUS   Every time
Serves for the matter that is then born in't.

LEPIDUS   But small to greater matters must give way.

ENOBARBUS   Not if the small come first.

LEPIDUS   Your speech is passion;
But pray you stir no embers up. Here comes
The noble Antony.

[*Enter* ANTONY *and* VENTIDIUS.]

ENOBARBUS   And yonder, Cæsar.

[*Enter* CÆSAR, MÆCENAS, *and* AGRIPPA.]

ANTONY   If we compose well here, to Parthia.
Hark, Ventidius.

CÆSAR   I do not know,
Mæcenas. Ask Agrippa.

LEPIDUS   Noble friends,
That which combin'd us was most great, and let not
A leaner action rend us. What's amiss,
May it be gently heard. When we debate
Our trivial difference loud, we do commit
Murder in healing wounds. Then, noble partners,
The rather for I earnestly beseech,
Touch you the sourest points with sweetest terms,
Nor curstness grow to th' matter.

ANTONY   'Tis spoken well.

<hr>

probable, obviously to be expected [K]. *square* quarrel. 46 *entertained* received.
50-1 *stands . . . hands* concerns our lives—i.e. our lives depend upon our using our
utmost strength [K].
II.II. 4 *like himself* in a way that shall be worthy of his own greatness [K]. 8
I would not shav't (a) I would go to the conference with my beard untrimmed, as a
sign of defiant lack of ceremony [K] (b) I would dare him to pluck it. 9 *stomaching*
taking offence, resentment. 15 *compose* come to a friendly agreement. Antony enters
in conversation with Ventidius; Cæsar is conversing with Mæcenas. They take no notice
of each other until Lepidus, anxious for his own sake to keep the peace, addresses
them both together [K]. 19 *What's* whatever is. 22 *in healing wounds* in the very
attempt to heal our differences. The figure is that of a surgeon who kills his wounded
patient by rough treatment [K]. 23 *The rather . . . beseech* and all the more because
I earnestly beg you to do so [K]. 25 *Nor curstness . . . matter* and let not angry speech
and manner associate itself with the subjects we discuss [K].

Were we before our armies, and to fight,
I should do thus. [*Flourish.*]
CÆSAR Welcome to Rome.
ANTONY   Thank you.
CÆSAR   Sit.
ANTONY   Sit, sir.
CÆSAR   Nay then.
  [*They sit.*]
ANTONY I learn you take things ill which are not so,
Or being, concern you not.
CÆSAR   I must be laugh'd at   [*30*
If, or for nothing or a little, I
Should say myself offended, and with you
Chiefly i' th' world; more laugh'd at that I should
Once name you derogately when to sound your name
It not concern'd me.
ANTONY   My being in Egypt, Cæsar,   [*35*
What was't to you?
CÆSAR No more than my residing here at Rome ·
Might be to you in Egypt. Yet if you there
Did practise on my state, your being in Egypt
Might be my question.
ANTONY   How intend you? practis'd?   [*40*
CÆSAR You may be pleas'd to catch at mine intent
By what did here befall me. Your wife and brother
Made wars upon me, and their contestation
Was theme for you; you were the word of war.
ANTONY You do mistake your business. My brother never   [*45*
Did urge me in his act. I did inquire it
And have my learning from some true reports
That drew their swords with you. Did he not rather
Discredit my authority with yours,
And make the wars alike against my stomach,   [*50*
Having alike your cause? Of this my letters
Before did satisfy you. If you'll patch a quarrel,
As matter whole you have not to make it with,
It must not be with this.
CÆSAR   You praise yourself

---

27 *thus* Antony makes some courteous gesture [K]. 28 *Nay then* well then—since you insist. And so Octavius takes his seat while Antony remains (for a moment) standing [K]. 30 *being* being ill—objectionable. 31 *or for* either for. 34 *name you derogately* speak disparagingly of you. 39 *practise on my state* plot against my power or government [K]. 40 *question* concern, business. *How* what. *intend* mean. 41 *catch at mine intent* grasp my meaning. 43 *their contestation* the strife they began. 44 *Was theme for you* concerned you. *you were . . . war* in your name the war was waged. 45 *You do . . . business* you are mistaken as to the matter you are speaking of [K]. 46 *urge me* use my name—claim to be fighting in my cause. 47 *true reports* trustworthy informants. 49 *Discredit . . . yours* Antony argues that the war undertaken by Lucius Antonius was really a rebellion against the authority of the Triumvirs in general—or rather, against that of the only two Triumvirs who counted for anything: he ignores Lepidus [K]. 50 *stomach* inclination. 51 *Having . . . cause* having as much reason as you had to be displeased with him [K]. 52 *satisfy you* inform you fully. *patch a quarrel* make up a cause for quarrel out of shreds and patches [K]. 53 *As matter . . . with* as (you must do if you wish to quarrel with me, for) you have no

By laying defects of judgment to me; but   [
You patch'd up your excuses.
ANTONY   Not so, not so!
I know you could not lack, I am certain on't,
Very necessity of this thought, that I,
Your partner in the cause 'gainst which he fought,
Could not with graceful eyes attend those wars   [
Which fronted mine own peace. As for my wife,
I would you had her spirit in such another!
The third o' th' world is yours, which with a snaffle
You may pace easy, but not such a wife.
ENOBARBUS   Would we had all such wives, that the men might go to wars   [
with the women!
ANTONY   So much uncurbable, her garboils, Cæsar,
Made out of her impatience,—which not wanted
Shrewdness of policy too,—I grieving grant
Did you too much disquiet. For that you must   [
But say I could not help it.
CÆSAR   I wrote to you
When rioting in Alexandria. You
Did pocket up my letters, and with taunts
Did gibe my missive out of audience.
ANTONY   Sir,
He fell upon me ere admitted. Then   [
Three kings I had newly feasted, and did want
Of what I was i' th' morning; but next day
I told him of myself, which was as much
As to have ask'd him pardon. Let this fellow
Be nothing of our strife. If we contend,   [
Out of our question wipe him.
CÆSAR   You have broken
The article of your oath, which you shall never
Have tongue to charge me with.
LEPIDUS   Soft, Cæsar!
ANTONY   No,
Lepidus; let him speak.
The honour is sacred which he talks on now,   [
Supposing that I lack'd it. But on, Cæsar.
The article of my oath—

---

substantial material to make a quarrel out of [K]. *you have not* CAPELL; F¹: "you
haue."

56 *You patch'd* Cæsar's language, particularly in retorting Antony's own word
("patch"), is coldly insulting: but Antony keeps his temper admirably [K]. 60 *graceful* favouring. *attend* behold. 61 *fronted* opposed. 63 *snaffle* bridle bit. 64 *pace
easy* cause to move at an easy pacing gait [K]. 66 *with* along with, by the side of. The
speech of Enobarbus is doubtless an "aside" [K]. 67 *garboils* tumults, disturbances.
68 *impatience* at my absence in Egypt [K]. 69 *Shrewdness of policy* since these disturbances might force Antony to return from Egypt [K]. 71 *I wrote* Cæsar seems to accept Antony's defence on the first count and passes on to a second ground of complaint
[K]. 74 *missive* messenger. 76–7 *did want . . . morning* was not quite so much master
of myself as I had been earlier in the day [K]. 78 *told him of myself* explained to
him what my condition had been [K]. 82 *article of your oath* particular agreement
which you swore to fulfill [K]. 83 *Soft* go slowly, be careful. Lepidus wishes to keep
the peace [K]. 85 *honour* He means specifically the obligation to keep his oath, which

CÆSAR To lend me arms and aid when I requir'd them,
The which you both denied.
ANTONY   Neglected rather;
And then when poisoned hours had bound me up   [*90*
From mine own knowledge. As nearly as I may,
I'll play the penitent to you; but mine honesty
Shall not make poor my greatness, nor my power
Work without it. Truth is, that Fulvia,
To have me out of Egypt, made wars here,   [*95*
For which myself, the ignorant motive, do
So far ask pardon as befits mine honour
To stoop in such a case.
LEPIDUS   'Tis noble spoken.
MÆCENAS If it might please you to enforce no further
The griefs between ye—to forget them quite   [*100*
Were to remember that the present need
Speaks to atone you.
LEPIDUS   Worthily spoken, Mæcenas.
ENOBARBUS Or, if you borrow one another's love for the instant, you may,
when you hear no more words of Pompey, return it again. You shall
have time to wrangle in when you have nothing else to do. [*105*
ANTONY Thou art a soldier only. Speak no more.
ENOBARBUS That truth should be silent I had almost forgot.
ANTONY You wrong this presence; therefore speak no more.
ENOBARBUS Go to, then! your considerate stone.
CÆSAR I do not much dislike the matter, but   [*110*
The manner of his speech; for 't cannot be
We shall remain in friendship, our conditions
So diff'ring in their acts. Yet if I knew
What hoop should hold us staunch, from edge to edge
O' th' world I would pursue it.
AGRIPPA   Give me leave, Cæsar.   [*115*
CÆSAR Speak, Agrippa.
AGRIPPA Thou has a sister by the mother's side,
Admir'd Octavia. Great Mark Antony
Is now a widower.
CÆSAR   Say not so, Agrippa.
If Cleopatra heard you, your reproof   [*120*
Were well deserv'd of rashness.
ANTONY I am not married, Cæsar. Let me hear
Agrippa further speak.

Cæsar is questioning. 86 *Supposing . . . it* if I have failed in it (the point of honour).
88 *requir'd* requested. 90–1 *bound me . . . own knowledge* so paralyzed me that
I no longer realized what I was doing. 92–4 *mine honesty . . . without it* my wish to
act honourably (which prompts me to apologize) shall not induce me to sacrifice my
dignity; nor, on the other hand, shall my power lead me to ignore my duty to act
honourably. Antony is ready to apologize, as his feeling of what is honourable prompts;
but he will not apologize in any humiliating way [K]. 96 *motive* moving cause. 99 *enforce* insist on, emphasize. 100 *griefs* grievances. 102 *atone* reconcile. 106 *a soldier
only* merely a soldier—not a statesman. 108 *wrong this presence* insult the dignity of
the great personages who are present [K]. 109 *considerate stone* "Dumb as a stone"
was an old proverbial comparison. Enobarbus means that—out of consideration for
Antony's wishes—he will hold his tongue [K]. Being "considerate" however, he continues to "consider" or "think" in spite of his silence. 112 *conditions* characters, dis-

AGRIPPA   To hold you in perpetual amity,   [12
  To make you brothers, and to knit your hearts
  With an unslipping knot, take Antony
  Octavia to his wife; whose beauty claims
  No worse a husband than the best of men;
  Whose virtue and whose general graces speak   [13
  That which none else can utter. By this marriage
  All little jealousies, which now seem great,
  And all great fears, which now import their dangers,
  Would then be nothing. Truths would be tales,
  Where now half-tales be truths. Her love to both   [1
  Would each to other, and all loves to both,
  Draw after her. Pardon what I have spoke;
  For 'tis a studied, not a present thought,
  By duty ruminated.
ANTONY   Will Cæsar speak?
CÆSAR   Not till he hears how Antony is touch'd
  With what is spoke already.
ANTONY   What power is in Agrippa,   [14
  If I would say "Agrippa, be it so,"
  To make this good?
CÆSAR   The power of Cæsar, and
  His power unto Octavia.
ANTONY   May I never
  To this good purpose, that so fairly shows,
  Dream of impediment! Let me have thy hand.   [1
  Further this act of grace; and from this hour
  The heart of brothers govern in our loves
  And sway our great designs!
CÆSAR   There is my hand.
  A sister I bequeath you, whom no brother
  Did ever love so dearly. Let her live   [1
  To join our kingdoms and our hearts; and never
  Fly off our loves again!
LEPIDUS.   Happily, amen!
ANTONY   I did not think to draw my sword 'gainst Pompey;
  For he hath laid strange courtesies and great
  Of late upon me. I must thank him only,   [1
  Lest my remembrance suffer ill report;
  At heel of that, defy him.
LEPIDUS   Time calls upon's.
  Of us must Pompey presently be sought,
  Or else he seeks out us.

---

positions.   114 *staunch* free from leaks. The image is that of a wine barrel.   119 *not so* ROWE; F¹: "not say."   120 *reproof* HANMER; F¹: "proofe."   121 *of rashness* because of your rashness in speaking thus [K].

  129 *graces* fine qualities.   129–30 *speak . . . utter* speak for themselves; nobody can describe them adequately [K].   131 *jealousies* suspicions, misunderstandings.   132 *import their dangers* bring their several dangers with them [K].   134 *Where . . . truths* whereas now mere vague reports are accepted as true [K].   137 *present* spur of the moment.   139 *touch'd* affected.   144 *so fairly shows* looks so promising.   146 *grace* reconciliation.   148 *sway* control, rule.   149 *bequeath* bestow upon.   151–2 *never . . . loves again* may our love for each other never be estranged again. "Fly off" is an idiom for sudden alienation [K].   154 *strange* rare, remarkable.   156 *remembrance* memory of favours received.   158 *presently* immediately, without delay.

ANTONY   Where lies he?
CÆSAR   About the Mount Misenum.   [*160*
ANTONY   What is his strength by land?
CÆSAR   Great and increasing; but by sea
He is an absolute master.
ANTONY   So is the fame.
Would we had spoke together! Haste we for it.
Yet, ere we put ourselves in arms, dispatch we   [*165*
The business we have talk'd of.
CÆSAR   With most gladness;
And do invite you to my sister's view,
Whither straight I'll lead you.
ANTONY   Let us, Lepidus,
Not lack your company.
LEPIDUS   Noble Antony,
Not sickness should detain me.   [*170*
[*Flourish. Exeunt. Manent* ENOBARBUS, AGRIPPA, MÆCENAS.]
MÆCENAS   Welcome from Egypt, sir.
ENOBARBUS   Half the heart of Cæsar, worthy Mæcenas! My honourable friend,
Agrippa!
AGRIPPA   Good Enobarbus!
MÆCENAS   We have cause to be glad that matters are so well digested. You   [*175*
stay'd well by't in Egypt.
ENOBARBUS   Ay, sir; we did sleep day out of countenance and made the night
light with drinking.
MÆCENAS   Eight wild boars roasted whole at a breakfast, and but twelve persons
there. Is this true?   [*180*
ENOBARBUS   This was but as a fly by an eagle. We had much more monstrous
matter of feast, which worthily deserved noting.
MÆCENAS   She's a most triumphant lady, if report be square to her.
ENOBARBUS   When she first met Mark Antony, she purs'd up his heart, upon
the river of Cydnus.   [*185*
AGRIPPA   There she appear'd indeed; or my reporter devis'd well for her.
ENOBARBUS   I will tell you.
The barge she sat in, like a burnish'd throne,
Burn'd on the water. The poop was beaten gold;
Purple the sails, and so perfumed that   [*190*
The winds were lovesick with them; the oars were silver,
Which to the tune of flutes kept stroke, and made
The water which they beat to follow faster,
As amorous of their strokes. For her own person,
It beggar'd all description. She did lie   [*195*
In her pavilion, cloth-of-gold of tissue,

---

163 *fame* common report.   164 *spoke together* had the preliminary conference by
which a battle was always preceded. This is the usual explanation, but it has been
suggested that "we" may refer to Antony and Cæsar and that Antony is regretting their
failure to come to terms earlier.   168 *straight* at once.   172 *Half the heart* Mæcenas
and Agrippa were equally favoured by Octavius [ĸ].   175 *digested* settled.   176 *stay'd
well by't* kept at it (your revelling) without tiring.   177 *out of countenance*
Enobarbus humorously suggests that the daytime was abashed by such disregard of it
[ĸ].   179 *Eight wild boars* This extravagant feasting is reported by Plutarch, who had
heard of it from his own grandfather.   181 *by* in comparison with.   183 *triumphant*
magnificent—from "triumph" in the sense of "a splendid show" [ĸ].   *square* just.   184
purs'd up put in her purse; made it her own property [ĸ].   186 *appear'd indeed* made

O'erpicturing that Venus where we see
The fancy outwork nature. On each side her
Stood pretty dimpled boys, like smiling Cupids,
With divers-colour'd fans, whose wind did seem   [20
To glow the delicate cheeks which they did cool,
And what they undid did.

AGRIPPA   O, rare for Antony!

ENOBARBUS   Her gentlewomen, like the Nereides,
So many mermaids, tended her i' th' eyes,
And made their bends adornings. At the helm   [20
A seeming mermaid steers. The silken tackle
Swell with the touches of those flower-soft hands
That yarely frame the office. From the barge
A strange invisible perfume hits the sense
Of the adjacent wharfs. The city cast   [21
Her people out upon her; and Antony,
Enthron'd i' th' market place, did sit alone,
Whistling to th' air; which, but for vacancy,
Had gone to gaze on Cleopatra too,
And made a gap in nature.

AGRIPPA   Rare Egyptian!   [21

ENOBARBUS   Upon her landing, Antony sent to her,
Invited her to supper. She replied,
It should be better he became her guest;
Which she entreated. Our courteous Antony,
Whom ne'er the word of "no" woman heard speak,   [22
Being barber'd ten times o'er, goes to the feast,
And for his ordinary pays his heart
For what his eyes eat only.

AGRIPPA   Royal wench!
She made great Cæsar lay his sword to bed.
He plough'd her, and she cropp'd.

ENOBARBUS   I saw her once   [22
Hop forty paces through the public street;
And having lost her breath, she spoke, and panted,
That she did make defect perfection
And, breathless, pow'r breathe forth.

MÆCENAS   Now Antony must leave her utterly.   [23

---

a truly magnificent appearance [K].   186 *devis'd* invented.   196 *cloth-of-gold of tissue*
a kind of cloth interwoven with gold threads.

197 *that Venus* Shakespeare may have in mind a specific portrait of Venus rising
from the sea, a common theme of Renaissance painting.   198 *The fancy* the painter's
imagination [K].   201 *To glow* to make glow (ROWE; F¹: "To gloue").   202 *what they
undid did* what the fans cooled, the wind heated up again.   203 *Nereides* sea nymphs.
204 *tended . . . eyes* watched and obeyed her every look [K].   205 *made their bends
adornings* they were so graceful that, as they bent their bodies in submissive attendance, every such inclination was an adornment to Cleopatra—the central figure in the
tableau [K].   206 *seeming mermaid* attendant dressed as a mermaid.   *tackle* rigging,
including the sails.   208 *yarely frame the office* do their duty (in handling the ropes)
nimbly and skillfully [K].   209 *hits* reaches.   210 *cast* as if in one mass [K].   213 *but
for vacancy* but for the fact that this would have made a vacuum (which "nature ab-
hors") [K].   222 *ordinary* a dinner or other meal at the public table of a tavern.
Enobarbus has now descended to his usual tone of humorous satire [K].   223 *eat* ate.
Antony could not eat any supper, but sat feasting his eyes on Cleopatra. Yet he pur-
chased the supper at the price of his heart [K].   225 *cropp'd* bore fruit—Julius Cæsar's

ENOBARBUS   Never! He will not.
    Age cannot wither her nor custom stale
    Her infinite variety. Other women cloy
    The appetites they feed, but she makes hungry
    Where most she satisfies; for vilest things   [*235*
    Become themselves in her, that the holy priests
    Bless her when she is riggish.
MÆCENAS   If beauty, wisdom, modesty, can settle
    The heart of Antony, Octavia is
    A blessed lottery to him.
AGRIPPA   Let us go.   [*240*
    Good Enobarbus, make yourself my guest
    Whilst you abide here.
ENOBARBUS   Humbly, sir, I thank you.
    [*Exeunt.*]

Scene III

    [Rome. CÆSAR's *house.*]

    [*Enter* ANTONY, CÆSAR, OCTAVIA *between them.*]
ANTONY   The world and my great office will sometimes
    Divide me from your bosom.
OCTAVIA   All which time
    Before the gods my knees shall bow my prayers
    To them for you.
ANTONY   Good night, sir. My Octavia,
    Read not my blemishes in the world's report.   [*5*
    I have not kept my square; but that to come
    Shall all be done by th' rule. Good night, dear lady.
OCTAVIA   Good night, sir.
CÆSAR   Good night. [*Exit (with* OCTAVIA*).*]
    [*Enter* SOOTHSAYER.]
ANTONY   Now, sirrah, you do wish yourself in Egypt?   [*10*
SOOTHSAYER   Would I had never come from thence, nor you thither!
ANTONY   If you can, your reason!
SOOTHSAYER   I see it in my motion, have it not in my tongue.
    But yet hie you to Egypt again.
ANTONY   Say to me,
    Whose fortunes shall rise higher, Cæsar's or mine?   [*15*
SOOTHSAYER   Cæsar's.
    Therefore, O Antony, stay not by his side!
    Thy demon, that thy spirit which keeps thee, is
    Noble, courageous, high, unmatchable,
    Where Cæsar's is not; but near him thy angel   [*20*

---

son, Cæsarion. 228 *defect* her defective, panting utterance [K]. 229 *breathe* did
breathe. 232 *stale* make stale. 236 *Become themselves* make themselves becoming.
237 *riggish* wanton, lewd. "Rig" is a common term for "strumpet." 240 *lottery* prize
(as in a game in which one casts lots) ; gift of fortune [K].

    II.III. 2 *Divide* separate. 5 *Read* interpret. 6 *kept my square* lived a well-reg-
ulated life [K]. 8 *Good-night, sir* F²; F¹ adds the line to Antony's preceding speech.
13 *motion* mind. 18 *demon* guardian angel. *keeps* guards, protects. 20 *Where Cæsar's
is not* everywhere except in the presence of Cæsar's demon [K].

Becomes a fear, as being o'erpow'r'd. Therefore
Make space enough between you.
ANTONY   Speak this no more.
SOOTHSAYER   To none but thee; no more but when to thee.
If thou dost play with him at any game,
Thou art sure to lose; and of that natural luck   [2
He beats thee 'gainst the odds. Thy lustre thickens
When he shines by. I say again, thy spirit
Is all afraid to govern thee near him;
But he away, 'tis noble.
ANTONY   Get thee gone.
Say to Ventidius I would speak with him.   [3
[*Exit* (SOOTHSAYER).]
He shall to Parthia.—Be it art or hap,
He hath spoken true. The very dice obey him,
And in our sports my better cunning faints
Under his chance. If we draw lots, he speeds;
His cocks do win the battle still of mine   [3.
When it is all to naught, and his quails ever
Beat mine, inhoop'd, at odds. I will to Egypt;
And though I make this marriage for my peace,
I' th' East my pleasure lies.
[*Enter* VENTIDIUS.]
                        O, come, Ventidius,
You must to Parthia. Your commission's ready;   [4
Follow me, and receive't.   [*Exeunt.*]

Scene IV

[*Rome. A street.*]

[*Enter* LEPIDUS, MÆCENAS, *and* AGRIPPA.]
LEPIDUS   Trouble yourselves no further. Pray you, hasten
Your generals after.
AGRIPPA   Sir, Mark Antony
Will e'en but kiss Octavia, and we'll follow.
LEPIDUS   Till I shall see you in your soldier's dress,
Which will become you both, farewell.
MÆCENAS   We shall,   [
As I conceive the journey, be at th' Mount
Before you, Lepidus.
LEPIDUS   Your way is shorter;
My purposes do draw me much about.

---

21 *a fear* a timorous creature (thus unable to protect you). 25 *and of* and because of. 26 *thickens* is dimmed, obscured. 27 *by* nearby. 29 *away, 'tis* POPE; F¹:
"alway, 'tis." 31 *art* prophetic art. *hap* chance. 33 *better cunning* superior skill.
34 *speeds* prospers. 35 *still* always. Cockfighting was a popular sport in Shakespeare's
England. 36 *when . . . naught* when the odds are everything to nothing in my
favour [K]. *quails* Quail fighting was common among the Romans. 37 *inhoop'd*
encircled by a hoop. This was sometimes the practice in English cockfighting [K]. 40
commission as commander in Parthia.
II.IV. 1 *Trouble yourselves* by escorting me. Lepidus dismisses them courteously
[K]. 6 *at th' Mount* at Mount Misenum (POPE; F¹: "at Mount"). 8 *much about* by a
very roundabout way.

You'll win two days upon me.
BOTH   Sir, good success!
LEPIDUS   Farewell.   [*Exeunt.*]   [*10*

Scene v

[*Alexandria.* CLEOPATRA's *Palace.*]

[*Enter* CLEOPATRA, CHARMIAN, IRAS, *and* ALEXAS.]
CLEOPATRA   Give me some music! music, moody food
Of us that trade in love.
OMNES   The music, ho!
[*Enter* MARDIAN *the* EUNUCH.]
CLEOPATRA   Let it alone! Let's to billiards. Come, Charmian.
CHARMIAN   My arm is sore; best play with Mardian.
CLEOPATRA   As well a woman with an eunuch play'd   [*5*
As with a woman. Come, you'll play with me, sir?
MARDIAN   As well as I can, madam.
CLEOPATRA   And when good will is show'd, though 't come too short,
The actor may plead pardon. I'll none now.
Give me mine angle! we'll to th' river. There,   [*10*
My music playing far off, I will betray
Tawny-finn'd fishes. My bended hook shall pierce
Their slimy jaws; and as I draw them up,
I'll think them every one an Antony,
And say, "Ah, ha! y'are caught!"
CHARMIAN   'Twas merry when   [*15*
You wager'd on your angling, when your diver
Did hang a salt fish on his hook, which he
With fervency drew up.
CLEOPATRA   That time? O times!
I laugh'd him out of patience; and that night
I laugh'd him into patience; and next morn   [*20*
Ere the ninth hour I drunk him to his bed,
Then put my tires and mantles on him, whilst
I wore his sword Philippan.
[*Enter a* MESSENGER.]
                        O, from Italy!
Ram thou thy fruitful tidings in mine ears,
That long time have been barren.
MESSENGER   Madam, madam—   [*25*
CLEOPATRA   Antony's dead! If thou say so, villain,
Thou kill'st thy mistress; but well and free,
If thou so yield him, there is gold, and here
My bluest veins to kiss—a hand that kings

II.v. 1 *moody* pensive, melancholy. 8 *come too short* is inadequate for the purpose. 10 *angle* fishing tackle. 12 *tawny-finn'd* THEOBALD; F¹: "Tawny fine." 15–18
'Twas merry . . . drew up This episode is reported in Plutarch. 17 *salt* dried. 22
tires headdresses. Cleopatra recalls how she acted the part of Omphale, to whom Hercules (Antony's supposed ancestor) had been at one time enslaved. Hercules wore Omphale's clothes, while she attired herself in his lion-skin robe and carried his club [K].
23 *sword Philippan* the sword which he wielded at the great victory over Brutus and

Have lipp'd, and trembled kissing.   [3•

MESSENGER   First, madam, he is well.
CLEOPATRA   Why, there's more gold.
But, sirrah, mark, we use
To say the dead are well. Bring it to that,
The gold I give thee will I melt and pour
Down thy ill-uttering throat.   [3

MESSENGER   Good madam, hear me.
CLEOPATRA   Well, go to, I will.
But there's no goodness in thy face. If Antony
Be free and healthful, why so tart a favour
To trumpet such good tidings? If not well,
Thou shouldst come like a Fury crown'd with snakes,   [4
Not like a formal man.

MESSENGER   Will't please you hear me?
CLEOPATRA   I have a mind to strike thee ere thou speak'st.
Yet, if thou say Antony lives, is well,
Or friends with Cæsar or not captive to him,
I'll set thee in a shower of gold and hail   [4
Rich pearls upon thee.

MESSENGER   Madam, he's well.
CLEOPATRA   Well said.
MESSENGER   And friends with Cæsar.
CLEOPATRA   Th'art an honest man.
MESSENGER   Cæsar and he are greater friends than ever.
CLEOPATRA   Make thee a fortune from me!
MESSENGER   But yet, madam—
CLEOPATRA   I do not like "but yet." It does allay   [5
The good precedence. Fie upon "but yet"!
"But yet" is as a jailer to bring forth
Some monstrous malefactor. Prithee, friend,
Pour out the pack of matter to mine ear,
The good and bad together. He's friends with Cæsar;   [5
In state of health thou say'st; and thou say'st free.

MESSENGER   Free, madam? No; I made no such report.
He's bound unto Octavia.
CLEOPATRA   For what good turn?
MESSENGER   For the best turn i' th' bed.
CLEOPATRA   I am pale, Charmian.
MESSENGER   Madam, he's married to Octavia.   [6•
CLEOPATRA   The most infectious pestilence upon thee!
[*Strikes him down.*]
MESSENGER   Good madam, patience.

Cassius at Philippi (42 B.C.) [K].   27 *free* not a captive.

32 *use* are accustomed.   33 *well* in blessed state, in heaven. This equivocal use of
"well" was common in breaking bad news [K]. *Bring it to that* explain that your
meaning is that [K]. 38 *why so tart* why so gloomy (CAPELL; F¹: "so tart"). *favour*
countenance. 40 *like* in the shape of. 41 *formal* normally shaped, of normal human
figure [K]. 43 *is well* TYRWHITT; F¹: "'tis well." 47 *honest* honourable, *worthy*. 50–1
allay . . . precedence alloys the good report that precedes; reduces its favourable character as alloy lessens the purity of gold [K]. 54 *pack* She thinks of the messenger with
his news as a peddler with a pack. 58 *good turn* Cleopatra (perhaps with intentional
blindness) understands "bound" in the sense of "obliged," and asks what favour
Octavia has done Antony. The messenger, embarrassed by his message, and at his

CLEOPATRA   What say you?   [*Strikes him.*]
                                                  Hence,
Horrible villain! or I'll spurn thine eyes
Like balls before me. I'll unhair thy head!
[*She hales him up and down.*]
Thou shalt be whipp'd with wire and stew'd in brine,   [*65*
Smarting in ling'ring pickle.
MESSENGER   Gracious madam,
I that do bring the news made not the match.
CLEOPATRA   Say 'tis not so, a province I will give thee
And make thy fortunes proud. The blow thou hadst
Shall make thy peace for moving me to rage;   [*70*
And I will boot thee with what gift beside
Thy modesty can beg.
MESSENGER   He's married, madam.
CLEOPATRA   Rogue, thou hast liv'd too long.   [*Draws a knife.*]
MESSENGER   Nay, then I'll run.
What mean you, madam? I have made no fault.   [*Exit.*]
CHARMIAN   Good madam, keep yourself within yourself.   [*75*
The man is innocent.
CLEOPATRA   Some innocents scape not the thunderbolt.
Melt Egypt into Nile! and kindly creatures
Turn all to serpents! Call the slave again.
Though I am mad, I will not bite him. Call!   [*80*
CHARMIAN   He is afeard to come.
CLEOPATRA   I will not hurt him.
These hands do lack nobility, that they strike
A meaner than myself; since I myself
Have given myself the cause.
[*Enter the* MESSENGER *again.*]
                              Come hither, sir.
Though it be honest, it is never good   [*85*
To bring bad news. Give to a gracious message
An host of tongues, but let ill tidings tell
Themselves when they be felt.
MESSENGER   I have done my duty.
CLEOPATRA   Is he married?
I cannot hate thee worser than I do   [*90*
If thou again say yes.
MESSENGER   He's married, madam.
CLEOPATRA   The gods confound thee! Dost thou hold there still?
MESSENGER   Should I lie, madam?
CLEOPATRA   O, I would thou didst,
So half my Egypt were submerg'd and made

---

wit's end how to break the news, blurts out his tidings in the form of a course jest [K].
63 *spurn* kick. 64 s.d. *hales* drags (by the hair). 66 *ling'ring pickle* pickling
solution (brine) in which you will last a long time. 71 *boot thee* make thee amends.
72 *modesty* moderation. Cleopatra means that any gift that he can beg, however great,
will seem moderate to her [K]. 75 *keep yourself . . . yourself* keep control of yourself
—as opposed to being "beside yourself." 83 *A meaner* one of lower social rank. 83–4
I myself . . . cause I myself am to blame for the fact that the news of Antony's marriage
is bad news. If I had never loved him ,the report would have been indifferent to me
[K]. 86 *gracious* pleasing. 92 *confound* destroy. 94 *So* even if. She would give half
Egypt to have the report prove false [K].

A cistern for scal'd snakes! Go get thee hence!　　　　　[9?
Hadst thou Narcissus in thy face, to me
Thou wouldst appear most ugly. He is married?
MESSENGER　I crave your Highness' pardon.
CLEOPATRA　　　　　　　　　　　　He is married?
MESSENGER　Take no offence that I would not offend you.
To punish me for what you make me do　　　　　　　[10(
Seems much unequal. He's married to Octavia.
CLEOPATRA　O, that his fault should make a knave of thee,
That art not what th' art sure of! Get thee hence.
The merchandise which thou hast brought from Rome
Are all too dear for me. Lie they upon thy hand,　　　[10?
And be undone by 'em!　[*Exit* MESSENGER.]
CHARMIAN　　　　　　　Good your Highness, patience.
CLEOPATRA　In praising Antony I have disprais'd Cæsar.
CHARMIAN　Many times, madam.
CLEOPATRA　　　　　　　　　I am paid for't now.
Lead me from hence,
I faint. O Iras, Charmian! 'Tis no matter.　　　　　　[11(
Go to the fellow, good Alexas. Bid him
Report the feature of Octavia, her years,
Her inclinations; let him not leave out
The colour of her hair. Bring me word quickly.
[*Exit* ALEXAS.]
Let him for ever go!—let him not!—Charmian,　　　　[11?
Though he be painted one way like a Gorgon,
The other way's a Mars.—[*To* MARDIAN] Bid you Alexas
Bring me word how tall she is.—Pity me, Charmian,
But do not speak to me. Lead me to my chamber.
[*Exeunt.*]

Scene VI

[*Near Misenum.*]

[*Flourish. Enter* POMPEY (*and*) MENAS *at one door, with Drum and Trum-pet: at another,* CÆSAR, LEPIDUS, ANTONY, ENOBARBUS, MÆCENAS, AGRIPPA, *with* SOLDIERS *marching.*]
POMPEY　Your hostages I have, so have you mine;
And we shall talk before we fight.
CÆSAR　　　　　　　　　　　Most meet
That first we come to words; and therefore have we
Our written purposes before us sent;
Which if thou hast considered, let us know　　　　　　[.
If 'twill tie up thy discontented sword

---

96 *Narcissus* a youth so beautiful that he fell in love with his own face when he saw it reflected in the water [K]. 99 *Take no . . . offend you* do not be offended at my hesitating to answer—it is because I do not wish to offend you [K]. 101 *much un-equal* very unjust. 103 *That art . . . sure of* who art not really hateful, as is the certain news you bring. 105 *dear* expensive. The language is that of commerce. *Lie . . . hand* let them lie unsold. 106 *undone* financially ruined. 112 *Report the feature* describe the appearance—her beauty, *years* age. 113 *inclinations* disposition. 117 *way's* way he is. II.VI. 2 *meet* fitting, proper.

And carry back to Sicily much tall youth
That else must perish here.
POMPEY   To you all three,
The senators alone of this great world,
Chief factors for the gods: I do not know   [*10*
Wherefore my father should revengers want,
Having a son and friends, since Julius Cæsar,
Who at Philippi the good Brutus ghosted,
There saw you labouring for him. What was't
That mov'd pale Cassius to conspire? and what   [*15*
Made the all-honour'd honest Roman, Brutus,
With the arm'd rest, courtiers of beauteous freedom,
To drench the Capitol, but that they would
Have one man but a man? And that is it
Hath made me rig my navy, at whose burden   [*20*
The anger'd ocean foams; with which I meant
To scourge th' ingratitude that despiteful Rome
Cast on my noble father.
CÆSAR   Take your time.
ANTONY   Thou canst not fear us, Pompey, with thy sails.
We'll speak with thee at sea. At land thou know'st   [*25*
How much we do o'ercount thee.
POMPEY   At land indeed
Thou dost o'ercount me of my father's house!
But since the cuckoo builds not for himself,
Remain in't as thou mayst.
LEPIDUS   Be pleas'd to tell us
(For this is from the present) how you take   [*30*
The offers we have sent you.
CÆSAR   There's the point.
ANTONY   Which do not be entreated to, but weigh
What it is worth embrac'd.
CÆSAR   And what may follow,
To try a larger fortune.
POMPEY   You have made me offer
Of Sicily, Sardinia; and I must   [*35*
Rid all the sea of pirates; then, to send
Measures of wheat to Rome; this 'greed upon,
To part with unhack'd edges and bear back
Our targes undinted.

---

7 *tall* valiant. 10 *factors* agents. 11 *Wherefore* why. 13 *ghosted* haunted as a
ghost. 16 *Made the* F²; F¹: "Made." 16 *honest* honourable. 24 *fear* frighten. 25
speak with meet with in battle. 26 *o'ercount* outnumber. 27 *o'ercount . . . house*
Pompey catches up the word ("o'ercount") and turns it to the sense of "get the better
of me in accounting," "overreach," "cheat." Antony had possession of the mansion of
Pompey the Great in Rome. This had been confiscated by the government, and Antony
had bought it at "open sale," but when the authorities called for the purchase price,
he had refused payment [K]. 28 *the cuckoo* The cuckoo builds no nest, but lays its
eggs in other birds' nests [K]. 29 *as thou may'st* as long as thou canst (with an implied
threat) [K]. 30 *from the present* foreign to the business that now concerns us [K].
33 *embrac'd* if accepted. 34 *To try . . . fortune* if you try the fortune of war in the
attempt to get more than we have offered [K]. 36 *to send* I am to send. 38 *with unhack'd edges* without hacking each other's swords (in battle). 39 *targes* shields.

OMNES   That's our offer.
POMPEY   Know then
   I came before you here a man prepar'd   [4
   To take this offer; but Mark Antony
   Put me to some impatience. Though I lose
   The praise of it by telling, you must know,
   When Cæsar and your brother were at blows,
   Your mother came to Sicily and did find   [4
   Her welcome friendly.
ANTONY   I have heard it, Pompey,
   And am well studied for a liberal thanks,
   Which I do owe you.
POMPEY   Let me have your hand.
   I did not think, sir, to have met you here.
ANTONY   The beds i' th' East are soft; and thanks to you,   [5
   That call'd me timelier than my purpose hither;
   For I have gain'd by 't.
CÆSAR   Since I saw you last
   There is a change upon you.
POMPEY   Well, I know not
   What counts harsh fortune casts upon my face;
   But in my bosom shall she never come   [5
   To make my heart her vassal.
LEPIDUS   Well met here.
POMPEY   I hope so, Lepidus. Thus we are agreed.
   I crave our composition may be written,
   And seal'd between us.
CÆSAR   That's the next to do.
POMPEY   We'll feast each other ere we part, and let's   [6
   Draw lots who shall begin.
ANTONY   That will I, Pompey.
POMPEY   No, Antony, take the lot;
   But, first or last, your fine Egyptian cookery
   Shall have the fame. I have heard that Julius Cæsar
   Grew fat with feasting there.
ANTONY   You have heard much.   [6
POMPEY   I have fair meanings, sir.
ANTONY   And fair words to them.
POMPEY   Then so much have I heard;
   And I have heard Apollodorus carried—
ENOBARBUS   No more of that! He did so.
POMPEY   What, I pray you?
ENOBARBUS   A certain queen to Cæsar in a mattress.   [7
POMPEY   I know thee now. How far'st thou, soldier?

---

    44 *your brother* Lucius Antonius.   47 *am well . . . thanks* am fully prepared to thank you liberally [K]. The kind reception of Antony's mother by Sextus Pompeius is reported by Plutarch.   51 *timelier* earlier.   54 *What counts . . . my face* what lines harsh Fortune has scored upon my face as records of her dealings with me. The figure is from "casting accounts" by means of marks or "scores" upon a tally stick [K].   58 *composition* agreement, compact.   64 *have the fame* have a chance to do justice to its reputation [K].   66 *meanings* MALONE; F¹: "meaning."   68 *Apollodorus* Plutarch reports that Cleopatra was brought to Julius Cæsar in Alexandria tied up in a mattress on the back of her Sicilian servant, Apollodorus, as a means of entering the court without

ENOBARBUS   Well;
    And well am like to do, for I perceive
    Four feasts are toward.
POMPEY   Let me shake thy hand.
    I never hated thee. I have seen thee fight
    When I have envied thy behaviour.
ENOBARBUS   Sir,   [75
    I never lov'd you much; but I ha' prais'd ye
    When you have well deserv'd ten times as much
    As I have said you did.
POMPEY   Enjoy thy plainness;
    It nothing ill becomes thee.
    Aboard my galley I invite you all.   [80
    Will you lead, lords?
ALL   Show us the way, sir.
POMPEY   Come.
    [*Exeunt. Manent* ENOBARBUS *and* MENAS.]
MENAS [*aside*] Thy father, Pompey, would ne'er have made this treaty.—
    You and I have known, sir.
ENOBARBUS At sea, I think.
MENAS We have, sir.   [85
ENOBARBUS You have done well by water.
MENAS And you by land.
ENOBARBUS I will praise any man that will praise me; though it cannot be denied
    what I have done by land.
MENAS Nor what I have done by water.   [90
ENOBARBUS Yes, something you can deny for your own safety. You have been
    a great thief by sea.
MENAS And you by land.
ENOBARBUS There I deny my land service. But give my your hand,
    Menas. If our eyes had authority, here they might take two thieves   [95
    kissing.
MENAS All men's faces are true, whatsome'er their hands are.
ENOBARBUS But there is never a fair woman has a true face.
MENAS No slander. They steal hearts.
ENOBARBUS We came hither to fight with you.   [100
MENAS For my part, I am sorry it is turn'd to a drinking. Pompey doth this
    day laugh away his fortune.
ENOBARBUS If he do, sure he cannot weep't back again.
MENAS Y'have said, sir. We look'd not for Mark Antony here. Pray you, is he
    married to Cleopatra?   [105
ENOBARBUS Cæsar's sister is call'd Octavia.
MENAS True, sir. She was the wife of Caius Marcellus.
ENOBARBUS But she is now the wife of Marcus Antonius.
MENAS Pray ye, sir?
ENOBARBUS 'Tis true.   [110
MENAS Then is Cæsar and he for ever knit together.

---

being recognized by the people.
    73 *toward* about to begin. 79 *Enjoy thy plainness* make free use of thy straight-
forward manner of speech. 83 *have known* have been acquainted with each other [K].
95 *authority* to make arrests (like a constable). 95 *take* arrest. 95 *two thieves* your
hand and mine. 97 *true* honest. 104 *Y'have said* you have told the truth; you have
hit the mark [K]. 104 *look'd not for* did not expect. 109 *Pray ye, sir* A phrase of surprised incredulity, meaning literally "Pray repeat that, for I didn't quite catch it" [K].

ENOBARBUS If I were bound to divine of this unity, I would not prophesy so.
MENAS I think the policy of that purpose made more in the marriage than the love of the parties.
ENOBARBUS I think so too. But you shall find the band that seems to tie their [1 friendship together will be the very strangler of their amity. Octavia is of a holy, cold, and still conversation.
MENAS Who would not have his wife so?
ENOBARBUS Not he that himself is not so; which is Mark Antony. He will to his Egyptian dish again. Then shall the sighs of Octavia blow the fire up [1 in Cæsar, and, as I said before, that which is the strength of their amity shall prove the immediate author of their variance. Antony will use his affection where it is. He married but his occasion here.
MENAS And thus it may be. Come, sir, will you aboard? I have a health for you. [1
ENOBARBUS I shall take it, sir. We have us'd our throats in Egypt.
MENAS Come, let's away. [*Exeunt.*]

Scene VII

[*On board* POMPEY's *galley, off Misenum.*]

[*Music plays. Enter two or three* SERVANTS, *with a banquet.*]
1. SERVANT Here they'll be, man. Some o' their plants are ill-rooted already; the least wind i' the' world will blow them down.
2. SERVANT Lepidus is high-colour'd.
1. SERVANT They have made him drink alms-drink.
2. SERVANT As they pinch one another by the disposition, he cries out ["No more!" reconciles them to his entreaty and himself to th' drink.
1. SERVANT But it raises the greater war between him and his discretion.
2. SERVANT Why, this it is to have a name in great men's fellowship. I had as lief have a reed that will do me no service as a partisan I could not heave.
1. SERVANT To be call'd into a huge sphere and not to be seen to move in't, [1 are the holes where eyes should be, which pitifully disaster the cheeks.
[*A sennet sounded. Enter* CÆSAR, ANTONY, POMPEY, LEPIDUS, AGRIPPA, MÆCENAS, ENOBARBUS, MENAS, *with other* CAPTAINS.]
ANTONY [*to* CÆSAR] Thus do they, sir; they take the flow o' th' Nile By certain scales i' th' pyramid. They know

---

112 *If I were . . . unity* if I were under obligation to interpret the future of this compact [K]. 113 *policy of that purpose* political expediency of that arrangement. *made more in* had more effect in; had a greater share in [K]. 115 *band* bond. 117 *conversation* demeanour, behaviour. 122–3 *use his . . . it is* will continue loving where he now loves (i.e. in Egypt). "Affection" was a stronger word then than it is today; it often meant "passion" or "deep feeling" [K]. 123 *his occasion* the requirements of his situation. Antony's marriage, Enobarbus means, was brought about by the necessities of the moment [K].
II.vii. s.d. *banquet* light dessert served after a meal. 1 *plants* A pun on the two meanings—(a) soles of the feet (b) young trees [K]. 3 *high-colour'd* flushed (with drink). 4 *made him drink alms-drink* induced him to drink more than his share. In accordance with the old theory and practice of drinking bouts, it was each man's duty to drain his cup whenever anyone had drunk to him. To relieve a man of this duty by drinking in his place was to "drink alms-drink." In the present passage the meaning is that the others have (as a practical joke) tricked Lepidus into drinking more than his share by pledging him frequently [K]. 5 *pinch . . . disposition* taunt and tease one another according to each's nature. 9 *lief* F¹, K: "live," a variant form. *partisan* a kind of spear. *heave* lift. 10–11 *To be call'd . . . cheeks* to be called (as Lepidus

By th' height, the lowness, or the mean, if dearth
Or foison follow. The higher Nilus swells,   [*15*
The more it promises. As it ebbs, the seedsman
Upon the slime and ooze scatters his grain,
And shortly comes to harvest.
LEPIDUS   Y'have strange serpents there.
ANTONY   Ay, Lepidus.   [*20*
LEPIDUS   Your serpent of Egypt is bred now of your mud by the operation of
your sun; so is your crocodile.
ANTONY   They are so.
POMPEY   Sit—and some wine! A health to Lepidus!
LEPIDUS   I am not so well as I should be, but I'll ne'er out.   [*25*
ENOBARBUS   Not till you have slept. I fear me you'll be in till then.
LEPIDUS   Nay, certainly, I have heard the Ptolemies' pyramises are very goodly
things. Without contradiction I have heard that.
MENAS   [*aside to* POMPEY] Pompey, a word.
POMPEY   [*aside to* MENAS]   Say in mine ear. What is't?
MENAS   [*aside to* POMPEY] Forsake thy seat, I do beseech thee, Captain,   [*30*
And hear me speak a word.
POMPEY   [*aside to* MENAS]   Forbear me till anon.
[*Whispers in's ear.*]
This wine for Lepidus!
LEPIDUS   What manner o' thing is your crocodile?
ANTONY   It is shap'd, sir, like itself, and it is as broad as it hath breadth. It is
just so high as it is, and moves with it own organs. It lives by that which   [*35*
nourisheth it, and the elements once out of it, it transmigrates.
LEPIDUS   What colour is it of?
ANTONY   Of it own colour too.
LEPIDUS   'Tis a strange serpent.
ANTONY   'Tis so. And the tears of it are wet.   [*40*
CÆSAR   Will this description satisfy him?
ANTONY   With the health that Pompey gives him; else he is a very epicure.
POMPEY   [*aside to* MENAS] Go hang, sir, hang! Tell me of that? Away!
Do as I bid you.—Where's this cup I call'd for?
MENAS   [*aside to* POMPEY] If for the sake of merit thou wilt hear me,   [*45*
Rise from thy stool.

---

has been) to a great position in life ("a huge sphere" of action), and then to have obviously no real power in that position (as is the case with him), is, as it were, to have "eye-holes without eyes," which give a pitiful appearance of misfortune to the cheeks [K].   13 *scales i'th' pyramid* As they enter, Antony is talking to Cæsar. He has mentioned some pyramid or obelisk used for measuring the rise and fall of the Nile. There seems to have been some confusion in Elizabethan usage between "obelisk" and "pyramid" [K].

15 *foison* plenty, abundance. Used especially of good harvests [K].   21–2 *bred now . . . your sun* That living matter could be produced by the operation of the sun upon the earth (equivocal generation or abiogenesis) was very commonly believed in Shakespeare's day.   24 *A health to Lepidus* Pompey is keeping up the practical joke of making Lepidus drink alms-drink [K].   25 *ne'er out* never give up.   27 *pyramises* "Pyramis" as a singular was common. Lepidus gives it a drunken plural form. The usual plural was "pyramides" [K].   *goodly* handsome. A ridiculously inadequate adjective to apply to pyramids. It fits the drunken condition of the speaker [K].   32 *Forbear me* let me alone. Pompey is too intent on the trick they are playing on Lepidus to listen to Menas [K].   36 *transmigrates* Antony probably means merely "it passes from life to death"; but his phrase designedly suggests the doctrine of the transmigration of souls [K].   In Egypt actually transmigration of souls was believed in and the crocodile

POMPEY [*aside to* MENAS] I think th'art mad.
    [*Rises and walks aside.*]
                                       The matter?
MENAS I have ever held my cap off to thy fortunes.
POMPEY Thou hast serv'd me with much faith. What's else to say?—
    Be jolly, lords.
ANTONY   These quicksands, Lepidus,   [⸱
    Keep off them, for you sink.
MENAS Wilt thou be lord of all the world?
POMPEY   What say'st thou?
MENAS Wilt thou be lord of the whole world? That's twice.
POMPEY How should that be?
MENAS   But entertain it,
    And though thou think me poor, I am the man   [⸱
    Will give thee all the world.
POMPEY   Hast thou drunk well?
MENAS No, Pompey, I have kept me from the cup.
    Thou art, if thou dar'st be, the earthly Jove.
    Whate'er the ocean pales, or sky inclips,
    Is thine, if thou wilt ha't.
POMPEY   Show me which way.   [⸱
MENAS These three world-sharers, these competitors,
    Are in thy vessel. Let me cut the cable;
    And when we are put off, fall to their throats.
    All there is thine.
POMPEY   Ah, this thou shouldst have done,
    And not have spoke on't! In me 'tis villainy;   [⸱
    In thee 't had been good service. Thou must know,
    'Tis not my profit that does lead mine honour;
    Mine honour, it. Repent that e'er thy tongue
    Hath so betray'd thine act. Being done unknown,
    I should have found it afterwards well done,   [⸱
    But must condemn it now. Desist, and drink.
MENAS [*aside*] For this,
    I'll never follow thy pall'd fortunes more.
    Who seeks, and will not take when once 'tis offer'd,
    Shall never find it more.
POMPEY   This health to Lepidus!   [⸱
ANTONY Bear him ashore. I'll pledge it for him, Pompey.
ENOBARBUS Here's to thee, Menas!
MENAS   Enobarbus, welcome!
POMPEY Fill till the cup be hid.
ENOBARBUS There's a strong fellow, Menas.
    [*Points to the* SERVANT *who carries off* LEPIDUS.]
MENAS Why?   [⸱
ENOBARBUS 'A bears the third part of the world, man; see'st not?

---

was a subject of special worship, but it is difficult to understand how Shakespeare could have known these things. 42 *epicure* atheist. 45 *merit* my deserts, past services.
    48 *held my cap off to* shown deference to, been devoted to. 50 *quicksands* Pompey sees that Lepidus is about to drink again [K]. 54 *But entertain it* only accept my offer [K]. 58 *pales* encloses. *inclips* embraces, encircles. 61 *competitors* partners. 73 *pall'd* enfeebled, impaired. Pompey's fortunes, Menas thinks, begin to wane at the instant of his refusal, since he has rejected such an opportunity as Fortune, the fickle goddess, offers but once in a lifetime [K]. 76 *I'll pledge it for him* Antony is now taking an

MENAS The third part, then, is drunk. Would it were all,
  That it might go on wheels!
ENOBARBUS Drink thou. Increase the reels.
MENAS Come.   [*85*
POMPEY This is not yet an Alexandrian feast.
ANTONY It ripens towards it. Strike the vessels, ho!
  Here's to Cæsar!
CÆSAR   I could well forbear't.
  It's monstrous labour when I wash my brain
  And it grows fouler.
ANTONY   Be a child o' th' time.   [*90*
CÆSAR Possess it; I'll make answer.
  But I had rather fast from all four days
  Than drink so much in one.
ENOBARBUS [*to* ANTONY]   Ha, my brave emperor!
  Shall we dance now the Egyptian Bacchanals
  And celebrate our drink?
POMPEY   Let's ha't, good soldier.   [*95*
ANTONY Come, let's all take hands
  Till that the conquering wine hath steep'd our sense
  In soft and delicate Lethe.
ENOBARBUS   All take hands.
  Make battery to our ears with the loud music.
  The while I'll place you; then the boy shall sing.   [*100*
  The holding every man shall bear as loud
  As his strong sides can volley.
  [*Music plays.* ENOBARBUS *places them hand in hand.*]

                 THE SONG
      Come, thou monarch of the vine,
      Plumpy Bacchus with pink eyne!
      In thy fats our cares be drown'd,   [*105*
      With thy grapes our hairs be crown'd.
      Cup us till the world go round,
      Cup us till the world go round!

CÆSAR What would you more? Pompey, good night. Good
      brother,   [*110*
  Let me request you off. Our graver business
  Frowns at this levity. Gentle lords, let's part;
  You see we have burnt our cheeks. Strong Enobarb
  Is weaker than the wine, and mine own tongue
  Splits what it speaks. The wild disguise hath almost [*115*

"alms-drink." 81 *'A* he.
  82–83 *Would . . . wheels* would that the whole world were drunk, that the saying "The world runs on wheels" might be fulfilled. This saying was common in the sense "All goes well" [K]. 82 *then, is drunk* ROWE; F¹: "then he is drunk." 84 *Increase the reels* for every man who staggers makes one more toward the "whole world's reeling" [K]. 86 *Alexandrian* such as Antony was accustomed to in Egypt. 87 *Strike the vessels* broach the wine casks. Antony forgets that he is not the host [K]. 88 *I could well forbear't* I should be pleased to refrain from drinking in response [K]. 89 *monstrous* abnormal, unnatural. 90 *grows* F²; F¹: "grow." 91 *Possess it* drink it off. 98 *Lethe* forgetfulness. 99 *Make battery to* assault. 101 *The holding* the burden, the refrain—in this case, the repeated last line of the song [K]. *bear* THEOBALD; F¹: "beate." 104 *pink eyne* half-shut eyes. 105 *fats* vats (an old form). 111 *off* to come away. 115 *splits* stutters. 115–16 *The wild disguise . . . us all* this wild guising (play-

Antick'd us all. What needs more words? Good night.
Good Antony, your hand.
POMPEY   I'll try you on the shore.
ANTONY   And shall, sir. —Give 's your hand.
POMPEY   O Antony,
You have my father's house—but what? We are friends!
Come, down into the boat.
ENOBARBUS   Take heed you fall not.   [1
[*Exeunt all but* ENOBARBUS *and* MENAS.]
Menas, I'll not on shore.
MENAS   No, to my cabin.
These drums! these trumpets, flutes! what!
Let Neptune hear we bid a loud farewell
To these great fellows. Sound and be hang'd, sound out!
[*Sound a flourish, with drums.*]
ENOBARBUS   Hoo! says 'a. There's my cap.   [1
MENAS   Hoo! Noble Captain, come.   [*Exeunt.*]

ACT THREE

Scene 1

[*A plain in Syria.*]

[*Enter* VENTIDIUS *as it were in triumph, (with* SILIUS *and other* ROMANS, OF-
FICERS, *and* SOLDIERS;) *the dead body of* PACORUS *borne before him.*]
VENTIDIUS   Now, darting Parthia, art thou struck, and now
Pleas'd fortune does of Marcus Crassus' death
Make me revenger. Bear the King's son's body
Before our army. Thy Pacorus, Orodes,
Pays this for Marcus Crassus.
SILIUS   Noble Ventidius,   [
Whilst yet with Parthian blood thy sword is warm,
The fugitive Parthians follow. Spur through Media,
Mesopotamia, and the shelters whither
The routed fly. So thy grand captain, Antony,
Shall set thee on triumphant chariots and   [
Put garlands on thy head.

---

acting in the dance) has almost turned us all into fantastic mummers [K].
    117 *try you* try your strength in another drinking bout [K]. 119 *You have my
father's house* Pompey is slightly maudlin. His mind reverts to his pet grievance (see
II.VI.27)—Antony's seizure of the mansion of Pompey the Great; but he adds, senti-
mentally—"What of that? We're friends" [K]. 125 *Hoo* Enobarbus gives the Triumvirs
and Pompey a parting shout, throwing his cap up in the air. Menas repeats the shout
and then invites Enobarbus to his cabin [K].
    III.I. This scene cannot be fitted into any historical time scheme. Ventidius was
sent against the Parthians at the end of II.III. [K]. 1 *darting* The Parthians were
famous for their tactic of shooting arrows backwards while riding swiftly away in
seeming retreat. *struck* defeated. The Parthians who have so often struck others
with their arrows have now fittingly been struck themselves (F¹, [K]: "stroke," an
Elizabethan spelling variant). 2 *Marcus Crassus* A Roman general killed by the
Parthians after a disastrous campaign against them. In vengeance Ventidius has
now killed Pacorus, son of Orodes, King of Parthia.

VENTIDIUS   O Silius, Silius,
    I have done enough. A lower place, note well,
    May make too great an act. For learn this, Silius:
    Better to leave undone than by our deed
    Acquire too high a fame when him we serve's away.   [*15*
    Cæsar and Antony have ever won
    More in their officer than person. Sossius,
    One of my place in Syria, his lieutenant,
    For quick accumulation of renown,
    Which he achiev'd by th' minute, lost his favour.   [*20*
    Who does i' th' wars more than his captain can
    Becomes his captain's captain; and ambition,
    The soldier's virtue, rather makes choice of loss
    Than gain which darkens him.
    I could do more to do Antonius good,   [*25*
    But 'twould offend him; and in his offence
    Should my performance perish.
SILIUS   Thou hast, Ventidius, that
    Without the which a soldier and his sword
    Grants scarce distinction. Thou wilt write to Antony?
VENTIDIUS   I'll humbly signify what in his name,   [*30*
    That magical word of war, we have effected;
    How with his banners and his well-paid ranks
    The ne'er-yet-beaten horse of Parthia
    We have jaded out o' th' field.
SILIUS   Where is he now?
VENTIDIUS   He purposeth to Athens; whither, with what haste   [*35*
    The weight we must convey with 's will permit,
    We shall appear before him. —On, there! Pass along!
    [*Exeunt.*]

Scene II

[*Rome.* CÆSAR'S *house.*]

[*Enter* AGRIPPA *at one door,* ENOBARBUS *at another.*]
AGRIPPA   What, are the brothers parted?
ENOBARBUS   They have dispatch'd with Pompey; he is gone;
    The other three are sealing. Octavia weeps

---

12 *A lower place* one in a subordinate position. 13 *make too great an act* perform
a deed too great for his own good. Plutarch reports that Ventidius feared to achieve too
great a victory over the Parthians lest by doing so he incur Antony's displeasure. 17
More . . . person more by the exploits of their officers than by their own deeds [κ].
Sossius one of Antony's lieutenants who did good service in Syria, as Plutarch reports.
20 *by th' minute* continually. *lost his favour* This is Shakespeare's addition to Plutarch's account. 24 *darkens* throws into the shade. *him* the commander-in-chief.
27–9 *Thou hast . . . distinction* Silius means that Ventidius has wisdom, discretion—
which is "the better part of valour." Without such wisdom, he says, "to be a soldier
and wield a sword hardly confers any distinction at all" [κ]. 33 *horse* cavalry. 34
jaded out o' th' field driven out of the field like wornout nags. "Jade" was the common word for a wretched horse [κ]. 36 *with 's* with us.

III.II. 1 *brothers* brothers-in-law—Cæsar and Antony. 2 *dispatch'd* completed
their business. 3 *sealing* putting their seals to the new agreement.

To part from Rome; Cæsar is sad; and Lepidus
Since Pompey's feast, as Menas says, is troubled
With the green-sickness.

AGRIPPA   'Tis a noble Lepidus.

ENOBARBUS   A very fine one. O, how he loves Cæsar!

AGRIPPA   Nay, but how dearly he adores Mark Antony!

ENOBARBUS   Cæsar? Why, he's the Jupiter of men.

AGRIPPA   What's Antony? The god of Jupiter.

ENOBARBUS   Spake you of Cæsar? Hoo! the nonpareil!

AGRIPPA   O Antony! O thou Arabian bird!

ENOBARBUS   Would you praise Cæsar, say "Cæsar"—go no further.

AGRIPPA   Indeed he plied them both with excellent praises.

ENOBARBUS   But he loves Cæsar best. Yet he loves Antony!
Hoo! hearts, tongues, figures, scribes, bards, poets, cannot
Think, speak, cast, write, sing, number—hoo!—
His love to Antony. But as for Cæsar,
Kneel down, kneel down, and wonder!

AGRIPPA   Both he loves.

ENOBARBUS   They are his shards, and he their beetle. [*Trumpet
within.*] So—
This is to horse. Adieu, noble Agrippa.

AGRIPPA   Good fortune, worthy soldier, and farewell!
[*Enter* CÆSAR, ANTONY, LEPIDUS, *and* OCTAVIA.]

ANTONY   No further, sir.

CÆSAR   You take from me a great part of myself;
Use me well in't. Sister, prove such a wife
As my thoughts make thee, and as my farthest band
Shall pass on thy approof. Most noble Antony,
Let not the piece of virtue which is set
Betwixt us as the cement of our love
To keep it builded, be the ram to batter
The fortress of it; for better might we
Have lov'd without this mean, if on both parts
This be not cherish'd.

ANTONY   Make me not offended
In your distrust.

CÆSAR   I have said.

ANTONY   You shall not find,
Though you be therein curious, the least cause
For what you seem to fear. So the gods keep you

[
[*1*
[*1*
[2
[2,
[3(
[35

---

6 *greensickness* a form of anemia common to love-sick young girls. Lepidus is being compared to such a mere girl in his relations to Cæsar and Antony.   12 *Arabian bird* the phœnix, of which there is never more than one specimen in the world at any one time [K].   16 *figures* numbers (HANMER; F¹: "Figure")   20 *They . . . beetle* Enobarbus sums up Lepidus's love as pure self-interest. "Without Cæsar and Antony he would be like a beetle without wings." "Shard" is, literally, "potsherd," "a fragment of pottery." The shining wing cases of the beetle (commonly supposed to be the wings) were so called from their resemblance to such glazed fragments [K].   23 *No further, sir* Antony politely protests against Cæsar's taking the trouble to escort him farther on his way [K].   26–7 *as my . . . thy approof* and as I am ready to give my bond to any amount (pledge to the utmost) ,that thou wilt prove thyself [K].   *band* bond.   28 *piece of virtue* the masterpiece of woman's excellence [K].   30 *ram* battering ram.   32 *mean* intermediary person.   34 *In your distrust* by your lack of confidence (in me) .   35 *therein curious* minutely careful in looking for such causes of offence [K].

And make the hearts of Romans serve your ends!
We will here part.
CÆSAR   Farewell, my dearest sister, fare thee well.
The elements be kind to thee and make   [40
Thy spirits all of comfort! Fare thee well.
OCTAVIA   My noble brother!
ANTONY   The April's in her eyes. It is love's spring,
And these the showers to bring it on. Be cheerful.
OCTAVIA   Sir, look well to my husband's house; and—
CÆSAR   What,   [45
Octavia?
OCTAVIA   I'll tell you in your ear.
ANTONY   Her tongue will not obey her heart, nor can
Her heart inform her tongue—the swan's down-feather
That stands upon the swell at full of tide,
And neither way inclines.   [50
ENOBARBUS   [aside to AGRIPPA] Will Cæsar weep?
AGRIPPA   [aside to ENOBARBUS]   He has a cloud in's face.
ENOBARBUS   [aside to AGRIPPA] He were the worse for that, were he a
horse;
So is he, being a man.
AGRIPPA   [aside to ENOBARBUS] Why, Enobarbus,
When Antony found Julius Cæsar dead,
He cried almost to roaring; and he wept   [55
When at Philippi he found Brutus slain.
ENOBARBUS   [aside to AGRIPPA] That year indeed he was troubled
with a rheum.
What willingly he did confound he wail'd,
Believe 't, till I wept too.
CÆSAR   No, sweet Octavia,
You shall hear from me still. The time shall not   [60
Outgo my thinking on you.
ANTONY   Come, sir, come.
I'll wrestle with you in my strength of love.
Look, here I have you; thus I let you go,
And give you to the gods.
CÆSAR   Adieu, be happy!

---

40 *The elements* Since the world, with all there is in it—including human life—
was thought to be composed of the four elements, Cæsar's words amount to a wish that
"all the forces of nature and all the circumstances of life may combine to treat Octavia
kindly and thus may keep her always in happiness." Such a wish includes a hope that
she may have a safe and comfortable journey by land and sea [K]. Some think that he
is merely wishing her good weather on her voyage. 43 *love's spring* the springtime of
her love [K]. 44 *bring it on* make her love for me increase—as April showers bring
on the flowers of spring [K]. 47–50 *Her tongue . . . inclines* Antony means that
Octavia's tongue cannot express her conflicting emotions, and that her heart is too
full to allow her tongue utterance. Her state of feeling is so delicately balanced
between sorrow at parting with her brother and a desire to accompany her husband
that it is like a "swan's down-feather" on the water when the tide is at the pause
between flood and ebb [K]. *at full* F²; F¹: "at the full." 52 *horse* Horses without face
markings (clouds) were believed to be ill-tempered. 57 *rheum* head cold (which
causes the eyes to run). 58 *confound* destroy 59 *wept* THEOBALD; F¹: "weepe." 60
still continually. Octavia has whispered in Cæsar's ear, begging him not to forget her
[K]. 62 *wrestle with you* Antony hugs Cæsar to his breast [K].

LEPIDUS   Let all the number of the stars give light
   To thy fair way!
CÆSAR   Farewell, farewell!   [*Kisses* OCTAVIA.]   [6
ANTONY   Farewell!
   [*Trumpets sound. Exeunt.*]

Scene III

[*Alexandria.* CLEOPATRA's *Palace.*]

[*Enter* CLEOPATRA, CHARMIAN, IRAS, *and* ALEXAS.]
CLEOPATRA   Where is the fellow?
ALEXAS   Half afeard to come.
CLEOPATRA   Go to, go to!
   [*Enter the* MESSENGER, *as before.*]
                    Come hither, sir.
ALEXAS   Good Majesty,
   Herod of Jewry dare not look upon you
   But when you are well pleas'd.
CLEOPATRA   That Herod's head
   I'll have! But how, when Antony is gone   [.
   Through whom I might command it? Come thou near.
MESSENGER   Most gracious Majesty!
CLEOPATRA   Didst thou behold Octavia?
MESSENGER   Ay, dread Queen.
CLEOPATRA   Where?   [1(
MESSENGER   Madam, in Rome.
   I look'd her in the face, and saw her led
   Between her brother and Mark Antony.
CLEOPATRA   Is she as tall as me?
MESSENGER   She is not, madam.
CLEOPATRA   Didst hear her speak? Is she shrill-tongu'd or low?   [1!
MESSENGER   Madam, I heard her speak. She is low-voic'd.
CLEOPATRA   That's not so good! He cannot like her long.
CHARMIAN   Like her? O Isis! 'tis impossible.
CLEOPATRA   I think so, Charmian. Dull of tongue, and dwarfish!
   What majesty is in her gait? Remember,   [2(
   If e'er thou look'st on majesty.
MESSENGER   She creeps!
   Her motion and her station are as one.
   She shows a body rather than a life,
   A statue than a breather.
CLEOPATRA   Is this certain?
MESSENGER   Or I have no observance.
CHARMIAN   Three in Egypt   [2!
   Cannot make better note.
CLEOPATRA   He's very knowing;
   I do perceive't. There's nothing in her yet.
   The fellow has good judgment.

III.III. 3 *Herod of Jewry* a traditional symbol of ferocity.   4 *But* except.   17 *not
so good* unfavourable (for Octavia) . Cleopatra takes "low-voic'd" as indicating a lack
of vitality and thus a defect.   21 *look'st* F¹; POPE, K: "look'dst."   *She creeps* The
messenger has learned his lesson, and he describes Octavia's gait in terms that are
sure to please Cleopatra [K].   22 *station* manner of standing.   23 *shows* appears to be.

CHARMIAN   Excellent.
CLEOPATRA Guess at her years, I prithee.
MESSENGER   Madam,
  She was a widow—
CLEOPATRA   Widow? Charmian, hark!   [*30*
MESSENGER And I do think she's thirty.
CLEOPATRA Bear'st thou her face in mind? Is't long or round?
MESSENGER Round even to faultiness.
CLEOPATRA For the most part, too, they are foolish that are so.
  Her hair, what colour?   [*35*
MESSENGER Brown, madam; and her forehead
  As low as she would wish it.
CLEOPATRA   There's gold for thee.
  Thou must not take my former sharpness ill.
  I will employ thee back again; I find thee
  Most fit for business. Go, make thee ready;   [*40*
  Our letters are prepar'd. [*Exit* MESSENGER.]
CHARMIAN   A proper man.
CLEOPATRA Indeed he is so. I repent me much
  That so I harried him. Why, methinks, by him,
  This creature 's no such thing.
CHARMIAN   Nothing, madam.
CLEOPATRA The man hath seen some majesty, and should know.   [*45*
CHARMIAN Hath he seen majesty? Isis else defend,
  And serving you so long!
CLEOPATRA I have one thing more to ask him yet, good Charmian.
  But 'tis no matter. Thou shalt bring him to me
  Where I will write. All may be well enough.   [*50*
CHARMIAN I warrant you, madam. [*Exeunt.*]

Scene IV

  [*Athens.* ANTONY's *house.*]

  [*Enter* ANTONY *and* OCTAVIA.]
ANTONY Nay, nay, Octavia; not only that—
  That were excusable, that and thousands more
  Of semblable import—but he hath wag'd
  New wars 'gainst Pompey; made his will, and read it
  To public ear;   [*5*
  Spoke scantly of me: when perforce he could not
  But pay me terms of honour, cold and sickly

---

31 *thirty* Cleopatra herself was thirty-eight at the time. 34 *foolish* In the old pseudo science of physiognomy, round-faced persons were believed to be foolish, long-faced persons wise. 36 *Brown* Blondes were far more highly prized than brunettes in Shakespeare's England. 37 *As low . . . it* quite as low as she could wish it, if not lower. High foreheads were regarded as a beauty in the Elizabethan time [K]. 41 *proper* handsome. 43 *harried* mistreated. 44 *no such thing* nothing very remarkable [K]. 46 *defend* forbid.
  III.IV. 1 *Nay, nay* Antony enters in the midst of a conversation with Octavia. He has been finding fault with Cæsar and she has been excusing him [K]. 3 *semblable* similar. 4 *made his will and read it* Shakespeare here departs from Plutarch, who records that it was Antony's will which Cæsar read to the Senate. 6 *scantly* slightingly.
  8 *vented* uttered. *them* ROWE; F¹: "then." 9 *hint* occasion, opportunity. *took't*

He vented them, most narrow measure lent me;
When the best hint was given him, he not took't,
Or did it from his teeth.
OCTAVIA   O, my good lord,   [*1*
Believe not all; or if you must believe,
Stomach not all. A more unhappy lady,
If this division chance, ne'er stood between,
Praying for both parts.
The good gods will mock me presently   [*1*
When I shall pray "O, bless my lord and husband!"
Undo that prayer by crying out as loud
"O, bless my brother!" Husband win, win brother,
Prays, and destroys the prayer; no midway
'Twixt these extremes at all.
ANTONY   Gentle Octavia,   [*2*
Let your best love draw to that point which seeks
Best to preserve it. If I lose mine honour,
I lose myself. Better I were not yours
Than yours so branchless. But, as you requested,
Yourself shall go between 's. The mean time, lady,   [*2*
I'll raise the preparation of a war
Shall stain your brother. Make your soonest haste;
So your desires are yours.
OCTAVIA   Thanks to my lord.
The Jove of power make me most weak, most weak,
Your reconciler! Wars 'twixt you twain would be   [*3*
As if the world should cleave, and that slain men
Should solder up the rift.
ANTONY   When it appears to you where this begins,
Turn your displeasure that way, for our faults
Can never be so equal that your love   [*3*
Can equally move with them. Provide your going;
Choose your own company, and command what cost
Your heart has mind to.   [*Exeunt.*]

Scene v

[*Athens. Another room in* ANTONY's *house.*]

[*Enter* ENOBARBUS *and* EROS, (*meeting*) .]
ENOBARBUS   How now, friend Eros?
EROS   There's strange news come, sir.
ENOBARBUS   What, man?

THEOBALD; F¹: "look't." 10 *from his teeth* grudgingly—not from his heart [K]. 12
Stomach resent. 15 *presently* immediately. 24 *yours* F²; F¹: "your." *branchless* pruned
(with honour loped off like branches of a tree) . 25 *go between's* serve as mediator
between us. 27 *stain* eclipse (your brother's preparations for war) . 31 *that* as if.
32 *solder* POPE; F¹: "soader." *rift* Octavia emphasizes the slaughter by saying that men
enough would be slain to fill the chasm between the two halves of the rent world [K].
33 *where this begins* which of us two (Cæsar or I) began it—gave the first offence [K].
34–6 *our faults . . . with them* our faults cannot be so equal that your love for each
of us will continue in equal measure. 38 *has* F²; F¹: "he's."

EROS   Cæsar and Lepidus have made wars upon Pompey.

ENOBARBUS   This is old. What is the success?   [5

EROS   Cæsar, having made use of him in the wars 'gainst Pompey, presently
    denied him rivality, would not let him partake in the glory of the action;
    and not resting here, accuses him of letters he had formerly wrote to
    Pompey; upon his own appeal, seizes him. So the poor third is up till
    death enlarge his confine.   [10

ENOBARBUS   Then, world, thou hast a pair of chaps, no more;
    And throw between them all the food thou hast,
    They'll grind the one the other. Where's Antony?

EROS   He's walking in the garden thus, and spurns
    The rush that lies before him; cries "Fool Lepidus!"   [15
    And threats the throat of that his officer
    That murd'red Pompey.

ENOBARBUS   Our great navy 's rigg'd.

EROS   For Italy and Cæsar. More, Domitius:
    My lord desires you presently. My news
    I might have told hereafter.   [20

ENOBARBUS   'Twill be naught;
    But let it be. Bring me to Antony.

EROS   Come, sir.   [*Exeunt.*]

Scene VI

[*Rome.* CÆSAR's *house.*]

[*Enter* AGRIPPA, MÆCENAS, *and* CÆSAR.]

CÆSAR   Contemning Rome, he has done all this and more
    In Alexandria. Here's the manner of't:
    I' th' market place on a tribunal silver'd
    Cleopatra and himself in chairs of gold
    Were publicly enthron'd. At the feet sat   [5
    Cæsarion, whom they call my father's son,
    And all the unlawful issue that their lust
    Since then hath made between them. Unto her
    He gave the stablishment of Egypt; made her
    Of lower Syria, Cyprus, Lydia,   [10
    Absolute queen.

MÆCENAS   This in the public eye?

CÆSAR   I' th' common show-place, where they exercise.
    His sons he there proclaim'd the kings of kings:

III.v. 5 *success* sequel, outcome. 6 *presently* immediately—as soon as Pompey was
defeated. 7 *rivality* partnership. 8 *resting here* stopping with this. 9 *his* Cæsar's.
appeal accusation. *up* in prison. 10 *enlarge his confine* free him. 12 *world* HANMER;
F¹: "would." *chaps* chops, jaws. 13 *the one the other* CAPELL; F¹: "the other." 14 *thus*
Emphatic and accompanied by imitative action [K]. 16 *that his officer* that officer of
his. 17 *murd'red Pompey* According to Plutarch, Sextus Pompeius was murdered on
Antony's order by his lieutenant, Titus.
    III.vi. Between this scene and Scene v time enough had elapsed for Octavia to
travel from Athens to Rome [K]. 1 *Contemning Rome* holding Rome in contempt.
6 *Cæsarion* Cleopatra's son by Julius Cæsar. *my father's* Octavius was adopted as a
son by Julius Cæsar in his will and changed his name to C. Julius Cæsar Octavianus
[K]. 9 *stablishment* government, rule. 12 *exercise* perform military drill. 13 *he there*

Great Media, Parthia, and Armenia
He gave to Alexander; to Ptolemy he assign'd
Syria, Cilicia, and Phœnicia. She
In th' habiliments of the goddess Isis
That day appear'd; and oft before gave audience,
As 'tis reported, so.

MÆCENAS   Let Rome be thus
Inform'd.

AGRIPPA   Who, queasy with his insolence
Already, will their good thoughts call from him.

CÆSAR   The people knows it, and have now receiv'd
His accusations.

AGRIPPA   Who does he accuse?

CÆSAR   Cæsar; and that, having in Sicily
Sextus Pompeius spoil'd, we had not rated him
His part o' th' isle. Then does he say he lent me
Some shipping unrestor'd. Lastly, he frets
That Lepidus of the triumvirate
Should be depos'd; and, being, that we detain
All his revenue.

AGRIPPA   Sir, this should be answer'd.

CÆSAR   'Tis done already, and the messenger gone.
I have told him Lepidus was grown too cruel.
That he his high authority abus'd
And did deserve his change. For what I have conquer'd,
I grant him part; but then in his Armenia,
And other of his conquer'd kingdoms, I
Demand the like.

MÆCENAS   He'll never yield to that.

CÆSAR   Nor must not then be yielded to in this.

[*Enter* OCTAVIA *with her* TRAIN.]

OCTAVIA   Hail, Cæsar, and my lord! hail, most dear Cæsar!

CÆSAR   That ever I should call thee castaway!

OCTAVIA   You have not call'd me so, nor have you cause.

CÆSAR   Why have you stol'n upon us thus? You come not
Like Cæsar's sister. The wife of Antony
Should have an army for an usher, and
The neighs of horse to tell of her approach
Long ere she did appear. The trees by th' way
Should have borne men, and expectation fainted,
Longing for what it had not. Nay, the dust
Should have ascended to the roof of heaven,
Rais'd by your populous troops. But you are come
A market-maid to Rome, and have prevented
The ostentation of our love, which, left unshown,

[*1*

[*2*

[*2*

[*3*

[*3*

[*4*

[*4*

[*5*

JOHNSON; F¹: "hither."

17 *habiliments* costume. *Isis* the Egyptian moon goddess. 20 *queasy* nauseated.
22 *knows* The singular verb with a collective subject is common in Elizabethan
English (F¹; F³, K: "know"). 25 *spoil'd* despoiled (of his territory). *rated him* assigned to him (in due proportion) [K]. 29 *being* being deposed. 34 *For* as for. 43 *Like* in the guise of—i.e. with fitting pomp and ceremony [K]. 47 *borne men* been filled with men (waiting to see her procession pass by). 51 *prevented* forestalled. 52 *ostentation* fitting display. 52-3 *left unshown . . . unlov'd* love which does not show itself is often no better than no love at all [K].

Is often left unlov'd. We should have met you
By sea and land, supplying every stage
With an augmented greeting.

OCTAVIA   Good my lord,   [55
To come thus was I not constrain'd, but did it
On my free will. My lord, Mark Antony,
Hearing that you prepar'd for war, acquainted
My grieved ear withal; whereon I begg'd
His pardon for return.

CÆSAR   Which soon he granted,   [60
Being an abstract 'tween his lust and him.

OCTAVIA   Do not say so, my lord.

CÆSAR   I have eyes upon him,
And his affairs come to me on the wind.
Where is he now?

OCTAVIA   My lord, in Athens.

CÆSAR   No, my most wronged sister. Cleopatra   [65
Hath nodded him to her. He hath given his empire
Up to a whore, who now are levying
The kings o' th' earth for war. He hath assembled
Bocchus, the king of Libya; Archelaus,
Of Cappadocia; Philadelphos, king   [70
Of Paphlagonia; the Thracian king, Adallas;
King Malchus of Arabia; King of Pont;
Herod of Jewry; Mithridates, king
Of Comagene; Polemon and Amyntas,
The kings of Mede and Lycaonia, with a   [75
More larger list of sceptres.

OCTAVIA   Ay me most wretched,
That have my heart parted betwixt two friends
That does afflict each other!

CÆSAR   Welcome hither.
Your letters did withhold our breaking forth,
Till we perceiv'd both how you were wrong led   [80
And we in negligent danger. Cheer your heart!
Be you not troubled with the time, which drives
O'er your content these strong necessities;
But let determin'd things to destiny
Hold unbewail'd their way. Welcome to Rome,   [85
Nothing more dear to me! You are abus'd
Beyond the mark of thought; and the high gods,
To do you justice, makes his ministers

---

53 *should* This does not imply duty, but what would actually have occurred if Octavia had not come so privately [K]. 59 *withal* with that fact. *whereon* because of which. 60 *pardon for* permission to. 61 *Being an abstract . . . and him* since your return to Rome shortened the distance between his lust and him; made it easier for him to go back to Cleopatra [K] (F¹; Some editors read "obstruct," quite unnecessarily). 66 *nodded* beckoned with a mere nod. 67 *who* and they (Antony and Cleopatra) [K]. 72 *Malchus* F¹: "Mauchus." 78 *does* A common Elizabethan form (F¹; F²; K: "do"). 78 *afflict* clash with, attack. 80 *wrong led* F¹; CAPELL, K: "wrong'd." Although the emendation makes for a smoother line, it is impossible to justify on textual grounds. Some editors have suggested "wrangl'd" in the sense of "mistreated." 81 *negligent danger* danger from inaction. 83 *content* happiness. 84 *determin'd* predestined. *to destiny* to their destined conclusion. 87 *mark* range, possibility. 88 *makes his* F¹; CAPELL,

Of us and those that love you. Best of comfort,
And ever welcome to us!
AGRIPPA   Welcome, lady.   [
MÆCENAS Welcome, dear madam.
Each heart in Rome does love and pity you.
Only th' adulterous Antony, most large
In his abominations, turns you off   [
And gives his potent regiment to a trull
That noises it against us.
OCTAVIA   Is it so, sir?
CÆSAR Most certain. Sister, welcome. Pray you
Be ever known to patience. My dear'st sister!   [*Exeunt.*]

Scene VII

[ANTONY's *camp, near Actium.*]

[*Enter* CLEOPATRA *and* ENOBARBUS.]
CLEOPATRA I will be even with thee, doubt it not.
ENOBARBUS But why, why, why?
CLEOPATRA Thou hast forspoke my being in these wars,
And say'st it is not fit.
ENOBARBUS   Well, is it, is it?
CLEOPATRA Is't not denounc'd against us? Why should not we   [
Be there in person?
ENOBARBUS [*aside*]   Well, I could reply:
If we should serve with horse and mares together,
The horse were merely lost; the mares would bear
A soldier and his horse.
CLEOPATRA   What is't you say?
ENOBARBUS Your presence needs must puzzle Antony;   [
Take from his heart, take from his brain, from 's time,
What should not then be spar'd. He is already
Traduc'd for levity; and 'tis said in Rome
That Photinus an eunuch and your maids
Manage this war.
CLEOPATRA   Sink Rome, and their tongues rot   [
That speak against us! A charge we bear i' th' war
And, as the president of my kingdom, will
Appear there for a man. Speak not against it.
I will not stay behind!
[*Enter* ANTONY *and* CANIDIUS.]
ENOBARBUS   Nay, I have done.
Here comes the Emperor.

K: "make them." For "high gods" (a collective equivalent to "God") to take a singular
verb is common Elizabethan English. *ministers* agents, servants.
  93 *large* free, unrestrained—with a suggestion of "licentious" [K]. 95 *his potent
regiment* his powerful rule; all his great authority [K]. *trull* harlot. 96 *noises it*
makes a noise, is clamorous. 98 *Be . . . patience* be always calm.
  III.VII. 3 *forspoke* spoken against. 5 *denounc'd* proclaimed, declared. The Senate
and people of Rome declared war against Cleopatra in 32 B.C. [K]. 8 *merely* utterly.
8–9 *mares would . . . his horse* A ribald jest is doubtless intended, although its precise
terms are not clear. "Bear" is often used in the sense of "support the male." 10 *puzzle*
paralyze. A very strong word [K]. 16 *charge* responsibility.

ANTONY   Is it not strange, Canidius,   [*20*
    That from Tarentum and Brundusium
    He could so quickly cut the Ionian sea
    And take in Toryne?—You have heard on't, sweet?
CLEOPATRA   Celerity is never more admir'd
    Than by the negligent,
ANTONY   A good rebuke,   [*25*
    Which might have well becom'd the best of men
    To taunt at slackness. Canidius, we
    Will fight with him by sea.
CLEOPATRA   By sea? What else?
CANIDIUS   Why will my lord do so?
ANTONY   For that he dares us to 't.
ENOBARBUS   So hath my lord dar'd him to single fight.   [*30*
CANIDIUS   Ay, and to wage this battle at Pharsalia,
    Where Cæsar fought with Pompey. But these offers,
    Which serve not for his vantage, he shakes off;
    And so should you.
ENOBARBUS   Your ships are not well mann'd;
    Your mariners are muleters, reapers, people   [*35*
    Ingross'd by swift impress. In Cæsar's fleet
    Are those that often have 'gainst Pompey fought;
    Their ships are yare; yours, heavy. No disgrace
    Shall fall you for refusing him at sea,
    Being prepar'd for land.
ANTONY   By sea, by sea!   [*40*
ENOBARBUS   Most worthy sir, you therein throw away
    The absolute soldiership you have by land;
    Distract your army, which doth most consist
    Of war-mark'd footmen; leave unexecuted
    Your own renowned knowledge; quite forgo   [*45*
    The way which promises assurance, and
    Give up yourself merely to chance and hazard
    From firm security.
ANTONY   I'll fight at sea.
CLEOPATRA   I have sixty sails, Cæsar none better.
ANTONY   Our overplus of shipping will we burn,   [*50*
    And with the rest full-mann'd, from th' head of Actium
    Beat the approaching Cæsar. But if we fail,
    We then can do 't at land.
    [*Enter a* MESSENGER.]
                 Thy business?
MESSENGER   The news is true, my lord. He is descried;
    Cæsar has taken Toryne.   [*55*
ANTONY   Can he be there in person? 'Tis impossible;
    Strange that his power should be! Canidius,

---

23 *take in* capture. 29 *For that* because. 35 *muleters* muleteers, mule drivers (the Elizabethan form of the word). 36 *Ingross'd* gathered in large quantities (and thus not very carefully selected). *impress* impressment, forced enlistment. 38 *yare* light, and easy to handle. 39 *you* to you. 41 *worthy* honourable. 42 *absolute soldiership* perfect generalship; skill in land tactics [K]. 43 *Distract* divide. 44 *leave unexecuted* allow no opportunity for the use of. 47 *merely* entirely, absolutely. 50 *overplus of* surplus, excess. 51 *head* headland, promontory. *Actium* on the coast of Epirus. The battle was fought in 31 B.C. [K] (F²; F¹: "Action"). 57 *power* troops.

Our nineteen legions thou shalt hold by land
And our twelve thousand horse. We'll to our ship.
Away, my Thetis!
[*Enter a* SOLDIER.]
                              How now, worthy soldier?   [
SOLDIER O noble Emperor, do not fight by sea!
  Trust not to rotten planks. Do you misdoubt
  This sword and these my wounds? Let the Egyptians
  And the Phœnicians go a-ducking. We
  Have us'd to conquer standing on the earth   [
  And fighting foot to foot.
ANTONY   Well, well. Away!
[*Exeunt* ANTONY, CLEOPATRA, *and* ENOBARBUS.]
SOLDIER By Hercules, I think I am i' th' right.
CANIDIUS Soldier, thou art; but his whole action grows
  Not in the power on't. So our leader's led,
  And we are women's men.
SOLDIER   You keep by land   [
  The legions and the horse whole, do you not?
CANIDIUS Marcus Octavius, Marcus Justeius,
  Publicola, and Cælius are for sea;
  But we keep whole by land. This speed of Cæsar's
  Carries beyond belief.
SOLDIER   While he was yet in Rome,   [
  His power went out in such distractions as
  Beguil'd all spies.
CANIDIUS   Who's his lieutenant, hear you?
SOLDIER They say, one Taurus.
CANIDIUS   Well I know the man.
[*Enter a* MESSENGER.]
MESSENGER The Emperor calls Canidius.
CANIDIUS With news the time's with labour and throws forth   [
  Each minute some. [*Exeunt.*]

Scene VIII

[*A plain near Actium.*]

[*Enter* CÆSAR, *with his* ARMY, *marching.*]
CÆSAR Taurus!
TAURUS My lord?

---

60 *Thetis* a sea goddess. Perhaps Antony so calls Cleopatra because she is urging him to fight by sea. 64 *a-ducking* a-diving. 65 *Have us'd* are accustomed. 68–9 *his whole . . . power on't* his whole course of action is proceeding in such a way as not to exercise its best powers—i.e. not in the way in which it would naturally accomplish most. Antony's rejection of the soldier's advice is but a symptom of the general perversity or infatuation which governs his whole conduct [K]. 69 *leader's led* THEOBALD; F¹: "leaders leade." 70 *men* servants. 75 *Carries* carries on; makes headway [K]. 76 *His power . . . distractions* his forces were split up and sent out in so many separate detachments. 80 *throws forth* gives birth to (F¹: THEOBALD, K: "throes forth"). The metaphor of childbirth is perfectly clear without the emendation; the two words, however, were usually spelled identically in Shakespeare's day.

CÆSAR Strike not by land; keep whole; provoke not battle
Till we have done at sea. Do not exceed
The prescript of this scroll. Our fortune lies   [5
Upon this jump. [*Exeunt.*]

Scene IX

[*Another part of the plain.*]

[*Enter* ANTONY *and* ENOBARBUS.]
ANTONY Set we our squadrons on yond side o' th' hill
In eye of Cæsar's battle; from which place
We may the number of the ships behold,
And so proceed accordingly. [*Exeunt.*]

Scene X

[*Another part of the plain.*]

[CANIDIUS *marcheth with his land army one way over the stage, and* TAURUS, *the* LIEUTENANT *of* CÆSAR, *the other way. After their going in, is heard the noise of a sea-fight. Alarum. Enter* ENOBARBUS.]
ENOBARBUS Naught, naught, all naught! I can behold no longer.
Th' Antoniad, the Egyptian admiral,
With all their sixty, fly and turn the rudder.
To see't mine eyes are blasted.
[*Enter* SCARUS.]
SCARUS   Gods and goddesses,
All the whole synod of them!
ENOBARBUS   What's thy passion?   [5
SCARUS The greater cantle of the world is lost
With very ignorance. We have kiss'd away
Kingdoms and provinces.
ENOBARBUS   How appears the fight?
SCARUS On our side like the token'd pestilence
Where death is sure. Yon ribaudred nag of Egypt   [10
(Whom leprosy o'ertake!) i' th' midst o' th' fight,
When vantage like a pair of twins appear'd,
Both as the same, or rather ours the elder,—
The breese upon her, like a cow in June,—
Hoist sails, and flies.   [15
ENOBARBUS That I beheld.
Mine eyes did sicken at the sight and could not
Endure a further view.

III.VIII. 4 *exceed* depart from. 5 *prescript* prescription, written orders. 6 *jump* hazard.
III.IX. 1 *squadrons* troops, land forces. 2 *battle* embattled army.
III.X. 2 *admiral* flagship. 5 *synod* assembly (almost always used of the gods). *passion* cause of excitement. 6 *cantle* segment, slice, portion [K]. 7 *With very* by absolute. 9 *token'd pestilence* the plague when spots on the skin (called "God's tokens") have begun to appear. 10 *ribaudred nag* foul, wanton jade (F¹; STEEVENS, K: "ribald-rid nag"). Although many emendations have been proposed, none really improves upon the F¹ reading, whose meaning is quite clear. 14 *breese* a stinging gadfly (with a quibble on "breeze").

SCARUS   She once being loof'd,
   The noble ruin of her magic, Antony,
   Claps on his sea-wing, and (like a doting mallard)
   Leaving the fight in height, flies after her.
   I never saw an action of such shame.
   Experience, manhood, honour, ne'er before
   Did violate so itself.
ENOBARBUS   Alack, alack!
   [*Enter* CANIDIUS.]
CANIDIUS   Our fortune on the sea is out of breath
   And sinks most lamentably. Had our general
   Been what he knew himself, it had gone well.
   O, he has given example for our flight
   Most grossly by his own!
ENOBARBUS   Ay, are you thereabouts?
   Why then, good night indeed.
CANIDIUS   Toward Peloponnesus are they fled.
SCARUS   'Tis easy to't; and there I will attend
   What further comes.
CANIDIUS   To Cæsar will I render
   My legions and my horse. Six kings already
   Show me the way of yielding.
ENOBARBUS   I'll yet follow
   The wounded chance of Antony, though my reason
   Sits in the wind against me.   [*Exeunt.*]

Scene XI

   [*Alexandria.* CLEOPATRA'S *palace.*]

   [*Enter* ANTONY *with* ATTENDANTS.]
ANTONY   Hark! the land bids me tread no more upon't!
   It is asham'd to bear me! Friends, come hither.
   I am so lated in the world that I
   Have lost my way for ever. I have a ship
   Laden with gold. Take that; divide it. Fly,
   And make your peace with Cæsar.
OMNES   Fly? Not we!
ANTONY   I have fled myself, and have instructed cowards
   To run and show their shoulders. Friends, be gone.
   I have myself resolv'd upon a course
   Which has no need of you. Be gone.
   My treasure's in the harbour. Take it! O,
   I follow'd that I blush to look upon.
   My very hairs do mutiny; for the white
   Reprove the brown for rashness, and they them

---

18 *being loof'd* having made ready to sail. To "luff" is to bring the head of a boat into the wind.   20 *mallard* wild male duck.   27 *Been . . . himself* been true to his own generalship and valour [K].   28 *he* F²; F¹: "his."   29 *are you thereabouts* is that what you are thinking about?   32 *attend* await.   33 *render* surrender.   36 *wounded chance* broken fortunes.   37 *Sits . . . me* prompts me to do otherwise.
   III.XI. 3 *lated* belated—out late, like a traveller after nightfall who cannot see his way.   12 *that* what.   13 *mutiny* rise against each other. He was too old to act hastily and too young to be a coward and a dotard [K].   14 *rashness* hasty.

For fear and doting. Friends, be gone. You shall   [15
Have letters from me to some friends that will
Sweep your way for you. Pray you look not sad
Nor make replies of loathness. Take the hint
Which my despair proclaims. Let that be left
Which leaves itself. To the seaside straightway!   [20
I will possess you of that ship and treasure.
Leave me, I pray, a little; pray you now!
Nay, do so; for indeed I have lost command;
Therefore I pray you. I'll see you by and by. *[Sits down.]*
[Enter CLEOPATRA *led by* CHARMIAN *and* IRAS, (EROS *following*) .]*
EROS Nay, gentle madam, to him! comfort him!   [25
IRAS Do, most dear Queen
CHARMIAN Do? Why, what else?
CLEOPATRA Let me sit down. O Juno!
ANTONY No, no, no, no, no!
EROS See you here, sir?   [30
ANTONY O fie, fie, fie!
CHARMIAN Madam!
IRAS Madam, O good Empress!
EROS Sir, sir!
ANTONY Yes, my lord, yes! He at Philippi kept   [35
His sword e'en like a dancer, while I struck
The lean and wrinkled Cassius; and 'twas I
That the mad Brutus ended. He alone
Dealt on lieutenantry and no practice had
In the brave squares of war. Yet now—No matter.   [40
CLEOPATRA Ah, stand by!
EROS The Queen, my lord, the Queen!
IRAS Go to him, madam, speak to him.
He is unqualitied with very shame.
CLEOPATRA Well then, sustain me. O!   [45
EROS Most noble sir, arise. The Queen approaches.
Her head's declin'd, and death will seize her, but
Your comfort makes the rescue.
ANTONY I have offended reputation—
A most unnoble swerving.
EROS   Sir, the Queen.   [50

---

inconsiderate conduct—not temerity or foolhardiness [K].
   17 *Sweep your way* make easy your approach to Cæsar's favour [K]. 18 *of loathness*
indicating reluctance. *hint* opportunity, occasion. 19 *Let that* CAPELL; F¹: "Let them."
20 *leaves itself* is no longer true to its own nature. 21 *possess you of* put you in
possession of. 23 *lost command* lost my ability to order you to do what I ask.
35 *Yes . . . yes* Antony inattentively replies to Eros, and then turns aside immediately to his own bitter thoughts [K]. 36 *like a dancer* Antony means that
Cæsar, throughout the Battle of Philippi, wore his sword as if he had been at a
ball—in its sheath—so that it might just as well have been a dress rapier, and not
a soldier's weapon at all [K]. 38 *the mad Brutus* Though Antony had spoken a
noble and appreciative valediction over Brutus' body at the end of JULIUS CÆSAR,
he regarded him as an unbalanced enthusiast [K]. Antony is not to be taken
literally here since Brutus, of course, committed suicide. *He* Octavius Cæsar.
39 *Dealt on lieutenantry* depended altogether on the service of his lieutenants
instead of fighting in person [K]. 40 *brave* magnificent. *squares* squadrons.
44 *unqualitied* deprived of his essential quality; not himself. 47 *seize* F²; F¹: "cease."

ANTONY   O, whither hast thou led me, Egypt? See
How I convey my shame out of thine eyes
By looking back what I have left behind
Stroy'd in dishonour.
CLEOPATRA   O my lord, my lord,
Forgive my fearful sails! I little thought
You would have followed.
ANTONY   Egypt, thou knew'st too well
My heart was to thy rudder tied by th' strings,
And thou shouldst tow me after. O'er my spirit
Thy full supremacy thou knew'st, and that
Thy beck might from the bidding of the gods
Command me.
CLEOPATRA   O, my pardon!
ANTONY   Now I must
To the young man send humble treaties, dodge
And palter in the shifts of lowness, who
With half the bulk o' th' world play'd as I pleas'd,
Making and marring fortunes. You did know
How much you were my conqueror, and that
My sword, made weak by my affection, would
Obey it on all cause.
CLEOPATRA   Pardon, pardon!
ANTONY   Fall not a tear, I say. One of them rates
All that is won and lost. Give me a kiss.
Even this repays me. We sent our schoolmaster.
Is 'a come back? Love, I am full of lead.
Some wine, within there, and our viands! Fortune knows
We scorn her most when most she offers blows.
[*Exeunt.*]

Scene XII

[CÆSAR's *camp in Egypt.*]

[*Enter* CÆSAR, AGRIPPA, DOLABELLA, (THYREUS,) *with others.*]
CÆSAR   Let him appear that's come from Antony.
Know you him?
DOLABELLA   Cæsar, 'tis his schoolmaster.
An argument that he is pluck'd, when hither
He sends so poor a pinion of his wing,

---

but unless.

53 *By looking back* by looking back at. Antony keeps his face averted, that Cleopatra may not see the shame that is in it. Thus he is, as it were, looking backward at his past achievements, which now lie in dishonoured ruins behind him [K]. 54 *Stroy'd* destroyed. 55 *fearful* frightened. 57 *th' strings* the heartstrings. 58 *shouldst* would certainly. *tow* ROWE; F¹: "stowe." 59 *Thy* THEOBALD; F¹: "The." 60 *beck* a mere beckoning gesture [K]. 62 *young man* Octavius. *treaties* entreaties, offers to negotiate for peace. 63 *palter* equivocate. *shifts of lowness* the pitiful evasions that poor humble creatures use [K]. 69 *Fall* let fall. *rates* equals in value. 71 *schoolmaster* Euphronius, the tutor of Antony and Cleopatra's children [K]. 72 *full of lead* heavy, sorrowful.
III.XII. 3 *argument* indication.

Which had superfluous kings for messengers   [*5*
Not many moons gone by.
[*Enter* (EUPHRONIUS,) AMBASSADOR *from* ANTONY.]
CÆSAR   Approach and speak.
AMBASSADOR   Such as I am, I come from Antony.
   I was of late as petty to his ends
   As is the morn-dew on the myrtle leaf
   To his grand sea.
CÆSAR   Be't so. Declare thine office.   [*10*
AMBASSADOR   Lord of his fortunes he salutes thee, and
   Requires to live in Egypt; which not granted,
   He lessens his requests and to thee sues
   To let him breathe between the heavens and earth,
   A private man in Athens. This for him.   [*15*
   Next, Cleopatra does confess thy greatness,
   Submits her to thy might, and of thee craves
   The circle of the Ptolemies for her heirs,
   Now hazarded to thy grace.
CÆSAR   For Antony,
   I have no ears to his request. The Queen   [*20*
   Of audience nor desire shall fail, so she
   From Egypt drive her all-disgraced friend
   Or take his life there. This if she perform,
   She shall not sue unheard. So to them both.
AMBASSADOR   Fortune pursue thee!
CÆSAR   Bring him through the bands.   [*25*
   [*Exit* AMBASSADOR.]
   [*To* THYREUS] To try thy eloquence now 'tis time. Dispatch.
   From Antony win Cleopatra. Promise,
   And in our name, what she requires; add more,
   From thine invention, offers. Women are not
   In their best fortunes strong, but want will perjure   [*30*
   The ne'er-touch'd Vestal. Try thy cunning, Thyreus.
   Make thine own edict for thy pains, which we
   Will answer as a law.
THYREUS   Cæsar, I go.
CÆSAR   Observe how Antony becomes his flaw,
   And what thou think'st his very action speaks   [*35*
   In every power that moves.
THYREUS   Cæsar, I shall.   *Exeunt.*

---

5 *Which* who.   8 *petty to his ends* unimportant in his affairs.   11 *Lord* as lord.
12 *Requires* requests, asks leave that he may.   13 *lessens* F²; F¹: "Lessons," which has
been defended by some editors as meaning "disciplines."   16 *confess* acknowledge.
18 *circle* crown.   19 *hazarded to thy grace* exposed to the hazard of thy mercy—i.e.
lost, but for the chance that thou wilt be merciful [K].   21 *audience* a hearing. *so*
provided that.   22 *friend* lover.   24 *So to them* thus reply to them.   25 *Bring him*
escort him safely. *bands* of troops.   28 *what she requires* whatever she requests.
30–1 *perjure . . . Vestal* make an immaculate Vestal virgin break her vows [K].   31 *cunning* skill.   32–3 *Make thine . . . as a law* if you succeed, make your own decree as to
the reward for your efforts, and I will conform as if it were a law [K].   34 *becomes
his flaw* adapts himself to his disaster; accepts what has happened to him.   36 *In
every . . . moves* in every bodily function that has to do with motion—i.e. (in effect),
in every motion that he makes [K].

Scene XIII

[*Alexandria.* CLEOPATRA's *Palace.*]

[*Enter* CLEOPATRA, ENOBARBUS, CHARMIAN, *and* IRAS.]

CLEOPATRA   What shall we do, Enobarbus?

ENOBARBUS   Think, and die.

CLEOPATRA   Is Antony or we in fault for this?

ENOBARBUS   Antony only, that would make his will
Lord of his reason. What though you fled
From that great face of war whose several ranges   [
Frighted each other? Why should he follow?
The itch of his affection should not then
Have nick'd his captainship, at such a point,
When half to half the world oppos'd, he being
The meered question. 'Twas a shame no less   [1
Than was his loss, to course your flying flags
And leave his navy gazing.

CLEOPATRA   Prithee peace!

[*Enter the* AMBASSADOR (EUPHRONIUS) *with* ANTONY.]

ANTONY   Is that his answer?

AMBASSADOR   Ay, my lord.

ANTONY   The Queen shall then have courtesy, so she   [1
Will yield us up.

AMBASSADOR   He says so.

ANTONY   Let her know't.
To the boy Cæsar send this grizzled head,
And he will fill thy wishes to the brim
With principalities.

CLEOPATRA   That head, my lord?

ANTONY   To him again! Tell him he wears the rose   [2
Of youth upon him; from which the world should note
Something particular. His coin, ships, legions
May be a coward's, whose ministers would prevail
Under the service of a child as soon
As i' th' command of Cæsar. I dare him therefore   [2
To lay his gay comparisons apart

III.xiii.   1 *Think* brood despondently. *die* of melancholy.   2 *we* I.   3–4 *would
. . . reason* insisted on making his desire the ruler over his reason. "Will" was a
regular mild synonym for "lust" [K].   5 *ranges* ranged squadron; squadrons drawn up
in battle array [K].   7 *affection* passion.   8 *nick'd his captainship* made a fool of his
generalship; turned it into folly. The hair of fools (jesters) was cut in nicks or notches
on the forehead to add to their grotesque appearance [K]. A "nick" also is a winning
throw at dice, and thus "to nick" may mean "to cheat" or to "curtail."   10 *meered
question* A "mere" or "meer" is a boundary, and "meered" (found only here) seems
to mean "bounded," "limited." Antony was "the limited or appointed (i.e. exclusive)
question" of the whole war, since it was waged to determine his fate [K]. The
meaning, however, has been much disputed.   11 *course* chase, pursue.   15 *so* provided
that.   17 *grizzled* used of dark hair mingled with white [K].   22 *Something particular*
something of his own; some personal achievement or exploit [K].   26 *gay comparisons*
fine caparisons or equipments. "His gay comparisons" might mean "those fine things
in whose possession he contrasts so sharply with me"; but Shakespeare probably wrote
"caparisons" ("trappings") —a scornful word for the outfit of "coin, ships, legions,"

And answer me declin'd, sword against sword,
Ourselves alone. I'll write it. Follow me.
[*Exeunt* ANTONY *and* AMBASSADOR.]
ENOBARBUS   [*aside*] Yes, like enough high-battled Cæsar will
Unstate his happiness and be stag'd to th' show   [*30*
Against a sworder! I see men's judgments are
A parcel of their fortunes, and things outward
Do draw the inward quality after them
To suffer all alike. That he should dream,
Knowing all measures, the full Cæsar will   [*35*
Answer his emptiness! Cæsar, thou hast subdu'd
His judgment too.
[*Enter a* SERVANT.]
SERVANT   A messenger from Cæsar.
CLEOPATRA   What, no more ceremony? See, my women!
Against the blown rose may they stop their nose
That kneel'd unto the buds. Admit him, sir.   [*40*
[*Exit* SERVANT.]
ENOBARBUS   [*aside*] Mine honesty and I begin to square.
The loyalty well held to fools does make
Our faith mere folly. Yet he that can endure
To follow with allegiance a fall'n lord
Does conquer him that did his master conquer   [*45*
And earns a place i' th' story.
[*Enter* THYREUS.]
CLEOPATRA   Cæsar's will?
THYREUS   Hear it apart.
CLEOPATRA   None but friends. Say boldly.
THYREUS   So haply are they friends to Antony.
ENOBARBUS   He needs as many, sir, as Cæsar has,
Or needs not us. If Cæsar please, our master   [*50*
Will leap to be his friend. For us, you know
Whose he is we are, and that is Cæsar's.
THYREUS   So.
Thus then, thou most renown'd: Cæsar entreats
Not to consider in what case thou stand'st
Further than he is Cæsar.

---

which Antony has just mentioned [K].
27 *answer me declin'd* meet me on equal terms in my fallen fortunes—by reducing himself to the same level, man to man [K]. 29 *high-battled* blessed with full and victorious battalions [K]. 30 *Unstate his happiness* strip himself of the splendid advantages which fortune has given him [K]. *stag'd to th' show* shown upon a stage for a public spectacle [K]. 31 *sworder* gladiator. Prize fights with swords were common London shows in Elizabethan times and later [K]. 32 *parcel* part. A man's judgment, Enobarbus reflects, is so closely connected with his fortunes that, when his fortunes sink, his judgment fails [K]. 33 *inward quality* mind and character. 34 *To suffer all alike* so that they all (both the external circumstances and "the inward quality") decline in the same degree [K]. 35 *Knowing all measures* despite the fact that he has had experience of prosperity as well as adversity [K]. 35-6 *the full . . . emptiness* that Cæsar, who abounds in power and resources, will lay them aside and thus meet Antony's destitution on equal terms [K]. 39 *blown* overblown—and so beginning to fall to pieces in decay [K]. 41 *honesty* sense of honour. *square* quarrel. 47 *apart* in private. 48 *haply* very likely, probably. 54-5 *Not to consider . . . Cæsar* not to be troubled about your state of fortune, but to remember that your conqueror is Cæsar, who will treat

CLEOPATRA   Go on. Right royal!   [.
THYREUS   He knows that you embrace not Antony
    As you did love, but as you fear'd him.
CLEOPATRA   O!
THYREUS   The scars upon your honour, therefore, he
    Does pity, as constrained blemishes,
    Not as deserv'd.
CLEOPATRA   He is a god, and knows   [•
    What is most right. Mine honour was not yielded,
    But conquer'd merely.
ENOBARBUS   [*aside*] To be sure of that,
    I will ask Antony. Sir, sir, thou art so leaky
    That we must leave thee to thy sinking, for
    Thy dearest quit thee.   [*Exit.*]
THYREUS   Shall I say to Cæsar   [•
    What you require of him? For he partly begs
    To be desir'd to give. It much would please him
    That of his fortunes you should make a staff
    To lean upon. But it would warm his spirits
    To hear from me you had left Antony   [;
    And put yourself under his shroud,
    The universal landlord.
CLEOPATRA   What's your name?
THYREUS   My name is Thyreus.
CLEOPATRA   Most kind messenger,
    Say to great Cæsar this: in deputation   [;
    I kiss his conqu'ring hand. Tell him I am prompt
    To lay my crown at's feet, and there to kneel.
    Tell him, from his all-obeying breath I hear
    The doom of Egypt.
THYREUS   'Tis your noblest course.
    Wisdom and fortune combating together,   [ε
    If that the former dare but what it can,
    No chance may shake it. Give me grace to lay
    My duty on your hand.
CLEOPATRA   Your Cæsar's father oft,
    When he hath mus'd of taking kingdoms in,
    Bestow'd his lips on that unworthy place
    As it rain'd kisses.

---

you nobly, in accordance with his nature. This is what Thyreus means Cleopatra to understand, but he speaks with such equivocation that he actually promises nothing whatever [K]. *Cæsar* F²; F¹: "Cæsars."   57 *O* Cleopatra's exclamation is meant to convey to Thyreus not only eager acceptance of Cæsar's theory of her union with Antony, but also gratified surprise that Cæsar should have shown so sympathetic an understanding of the case. All this she expresses in plain terms in her next speech [K].   61–2 *not yielded . . . merely* not voluntarily surrendered, but overcome by out-and-out force [K].   66 *require* request.   71–2 *under his . . . landlord* under the protection of him, the ruler of the world [K]. 74 *in deputation* by deputy—i.e. making use of you as my agent in this act of submission [K] (WARBURTON; F¹: "in disputation").   77 *all-obeying breath* words which all men must obey [K].   78 *doom of* judgment upon—not condemnation of. *Egypt* the Queen of Egypt.   79–81 *Wisdom and fortune . . . shake it* when a person sees that fortune is adverse, then, if he runs no risks beyond what he knows he is able to accomplish, no fortune—however adverse—can dislodge him from his position of security [K]. A truism of Stoic philosophy.   81 *Give me grace* grant me the favour.   83 *taking*

[*Enter* ANTONY *and* ENOBARBUS.]

ANTONY   Favours, by Jove that thunders!   [*85*
What art thou, fellow?

THYREUS   One that but performs
The bidding of the fullest man, and worthiest
To have command obey'd.

ENOBARBUS   [*aside*] You will be whipp'd.

ANTONY Approach there!—Ah, you kite!—Now, gods and devils!
Authority melts from me. Of late, when I cried "Ho!"   [*90*
Like boys unto a muss, kings would start forth
And cry "Your will?" Have you no ears? I am
Antony yet.
[*Enter* SERVANTS.]
              Take hence this Jack and whip him.

ENOBARBUS [*aside*] 'Tis better playing with a lion's whelp
Than with an old one dying.

ANTONY   Moon and stars!   [*95*
Whip him. Were't twenty of the greatest tributaries
That do acknowledge Cæsar, should I find them
So saucy with the hand of she here—what's her name
Since she was Cleopatra? Whip him, fellows,
Till like a boy you see him cringe his face   [*100*
And whine aloud for mercy. Take him hence.

THYREUS Mark Antony—

ANTONY   Tug him away. Being whipp'd,
Bring him again. This Jack of Cæsar's shall
Bear us an errand to him.
[*Exeunt* (SERVANTS) *with* THYREUS.]
You were half blasted ere I knew you. Ha!   [*105*
Have I my pillow left unpress'd in Rome,
Forborne the geting of a lawful race,
And by a gem of women, to be abus'd
By one that looks on feeders?

CLEOPATRA   Good my lord—

ANTONY You have been a boggler ever.   [*110*
But when we in our viciousness grow hard
(O misery on't!) the wise gods seel our eyes,
In our own filth drop our clear judgments, make us
Adore our errors, laugh at's while we strut
To our confusion.

CLEOPATRA   O, is't come to this?   [*115*

ANTONY I found you as a morsel cold upon

---

kingdoms in conquering kingdoms. 85 *As it* as if it.
    89 *kite* This word, as the name of an ignoble bird of prey, was often applied to a wanton [K]. 91 *a muss* a scramble for nuts, etc., thrown on the ground [K]. 93 *Jack* fellow. 100 *cringe* wrinkle up (in pain) . 103 *This Jack* POPE; F¹: "the Jack." 107 *getting of a lawful race* begetting of legitimate children. Shakespeare here departs from Plutarch, who mentions the children of Antony and Octavia. 108 *abus'd* betrayed. 109 *feeders* servants. 110 *boggler* waverer, shifty person. To "boggle" is to "dodge" or "evade." 111–15 *But when . . . confusion* In this splendid passage Antony expresses the old Greek doctrine of infatuation or "atë." When a man imagines himself superior to humanity, the gods let him go on in his mad folly until he accomplishes his own ruin [K]. 112 *seel* close up—as the eyes of falcons were sewn with thread for training purposes. 115 *confusion* destruction, ruin.

Dead Cæsar's trencher. Nay, you were a fragment
Of Gneius Pompey's, besides what hotter hours,
Unregist'red in vulgar fame, you have
Luxuriously pick'd out: for I am sure,   [*12*
Though you can guess what temperance should be,
You know not what it is.
CLEOPATRA   Wherefore is this?
ANTONY   To let a fellow that will take rewards,
And say "God quit you!" be familiar with
My playfellow, your hand, this kingly seal   [*12*
And plighter of high hearts! O that I were
Upon the hill of Basan to outroar
The horned herd! for I have savage cause,
And to proclaim it civilly were like
A halter'd neck which does the hangman thank   [*13*
For being yare about him.
[*Enter a* SERVANT *with* THYREUS.]
                                    Is he whipp'd?
SERVANT   Soundly, my lord.
ANTONY   Cried he? and begg'd 'a pardon?
SERVANT   He did ask favour.
ANTONY   If that thy father live, let him repent
Thou wast not made his daughter; and be thou sorry   [*13*
To follow Cæsar in his triumph, since
Thou hast been whipp'd for following him. Henceforth
The white hand of a lady fever thee!
Shake thou to look on't! Get thee back to Cæsar;
Tell him thy entertainment. Look thou say   [*14*
He makes me angry with him; for he seems
Proud and disdainful, harping on what I am,
Not what he knew I was. He makes me angry;
And at this time most easy 'tis to do't,
When my good stars that were my former guides   [*14*
Have empty left their orbs and shot their fires
Into th' abysm of hell. If he mislike
My speech and what is done, tell him he has
Hipparchus, my enfranched bondman, whom
He may at pleasure whip or hang or torture,   [*15*
As he shall like, to quit me. Urge it thou.
Hence with thy stripes, be gone!   [*Exit* THYREUS.]
CLEOPATRA   Have you done yet?

---

117 *trencher* a wooden dish. *fragment* bit of leftover food. 119 *vulgar fame* common report. 120 *Luxuriously* lasciviously. 121 *temperance* sexual continence. 124 *God quit you* The reply of a beggar receiving alms. *quit* repay. 127 *hill of Basan* The roaring of the bulls of Basan is described in PSALMS, XXII, 12–13. Antony thinks of himself as chief of these horned animals—and thus as chief of the many lovers made cuckolds by Cleopatra. 128 *savage cause* cause enough to run wild [K]. 130 *A halter'd neck* one about to be hanged. 131 *yare* quick and adroit. 138 *fever thee* make thee shiver (with fright). 140 *entertainment* manner of reception, treatment. 146 *orbs* spheres. The heavenly bodies were thought to be set in hollow spheres, concentric with the earth [K]. 147 *hell* the great void below this universe [K]. 149 *enfranched* enfranchised, freed. He had, according to Plutarch, earlier deserted Antony for Cæsar; Antony is thus not condemning an entirely innocent man. 151 *quit* repay. *Urge*

ANTONY   Alack, our terrene moon
   Is now eclips'd, and it portends alone
   The fall of Antony!
CLEOPATRA   I must stay his time.   [*155*
ANTONY   To flatter Cæsar, would you mingle eyes
   With one that ties his points?
CLEOPATRA   Not know me yet?
ANTONY   Cold-hearted toward me?
CLEOPATRA   Ah, dear, if I be so,
   From my cold heart let heaven engender hail,
   And poison it in the source, and the first stone   [*160*
   Drop in my neck; as it determines, so
   Dissolve my life! The next Cæsarion smite!
   Till by degrees the memory of my womb,
   Together with my brave Egyptians all,
   By the discandying of this pelleted storm,   [*165*
   Lie graveless, till the flies and gnats of Nile
   Have buried them for prey!
ANTONY   I am satisfied.
   Cæsar sits down in Alexandria, where
   I will oppose his fate. Our force by land
   Hath nobly held; our sever'd navy too   [*170*
   Have knit again, and fleet, threat'ning most sea-like.
   Where hast thou been, my heart? Dost thou hear, lady?
   If from the field I shall return once more
   To kiss these lips, I will appear in blood.
   I and my sword will earn our chronicle.   [*175*
   There's hope in't yet.
CLEOPATRA   That's my brave lord!
ANTONY   I will be treble-sinewed, hearted, breath'd,
   And fight maliciously. For when mine hours
   Were nice and lucky, men did ransom lives   [*180*
   Of me for jests; but now I'll set my teeth
   And send to darkness all that stop me. Come,
   Let's have one other gaudy night. Call to me
   All my sad captains; fill our bowls once more.
   Let's mock the midnight bell.

---

mention.
   153 *terrene moon* Cleopatra, our earthly moon goddess, the Isis of this earth
[K]. 155 *stay his time* be patient until his fit of fury is over. 157 *one . . . points*
his valet. The double (jacket) of the Elizabethans was attached to the hose
(breeches) by means of "points"—laces or strings with metal tags [K]. 161 *determines*
comes to an end, melts. 162 *smite* ROWE; F¹: "smile." 163 *memory* memorials—
i.e. all my children [K]. 164 *brave* noble. 165 *discandying* melting (THEOBALD;
F¹: "discandering"). 165 *pelleted* made up of pellets, hailstones. 167 *for prey* by
devouring them. 169 *I will oppose his fate* Even if it is Cæsar's destiny, as Antony
half believes, to destroy him and reign supreme, Antony will oppose that destiny under
arms [K]. 171 *fleet* are afloat 172 *my heart* my courage. He is not addressing Cleopatra. 175 *earn our chronicle* win a place in history [K]. 177 *brave* fine, noble. This
is the usual meaning in Shakespeare [K]. 179 *maliciously* fiercely, savagely [K].
180 *nice* pampered. "Nice" refers literally to that condition of Antony's fortunes when
he was a "nice critic" of pleasures and could appreciate trifling gratifications if they
happened to suit his taste. Then, he was easygoing and liberal; now he will be a savage
and "fight maliciously" [K]. The meaning of the word has been much debated. 183

CLEOPATRA   It is my birthday.   [1
   I had thought t' have held it poor; but since my lord
   Is Antony again, I will be Cleopatra.
ANTONY We will yet do well.
CLEOPATRA Call all his noble captains to my lord.
ANTONY Do so, we'll speak to them; and to-night I'll force   [1
   The wine peep through their scars. Come on, my queen,
   There's sap in't yet! The next time I do fight,
   I'll make Death love me; for I will contend
   Even with his pestilent scythe.
   [*Exeunt (all but* ENOBARBUS)*.*]
ENOBARBUS Now he'll outstare the lightning. To be furious   [1
   Is to be frighted out of fear, and in that mood
   The dove will peck the estridge. I see still
   A diminution in our captain's brain
   Restores his heart. When valour preys on reason,
   It eats the sword it fights with. I will seek   [20
   Some way to leave him. [*Exit.*]

ACT FOUR

Scene 1

[CÆSAR's *camp before Alexandria.*]

[*Enter* CÆSAR, AGRIPPA, *and* MÆCENAS, *with his* ARMY; CÆSAR *reading a letter.*]
CÆSAR He calls me boy, and chides as he had power
   To beat me out of Egypt. My messenger
   He hath whipp'd with rods; dares me to personal combat,
   Cæsar to Antony. Let the old ruffian know
   I have many other ways to die, meantime   [
   Laugh at his challenge.
MÆCENAS   Cæsar must think,
   When one so great begins to rage, he's hunted
   Even to falling. Give him no breath, but now
   Make boot of his distraction. Never anger
   Made good guard for itself.
CÆSAR   Let our best heads   [1
   Know that to-morrow the last of many battles

---

gaudy night night of joyous revel [K]. 184 *sad* sober, serious.
   186 *poor* without festivity. 192 *sap in't* life in us. 193–4 *I will contend . . . scythe*
I will slay as many men as Death himself mows down with the scythe of the plague [K].
195 *outstare the lightning* meet the lightning eye to eye and stare it out of countenance
[K]. *furious* frenzied. 197 *estridge* goshawk (a species of hawk). *still* Enobarbus
continues his despairing reflections on Antony's loss of judgment from lines 29–37. In
this frenzy of desperate valour he sees only further evidence that Antony's wisdom is
failing with his fortunes. To his mind, then, Antony is doomed; he is merely "strutting
to his confusion" (lines 114–15) [K]. 199 *heart* courage. *preys on* ROWE; F¹: "prayes
in."
   IV.I. 5 *I have . . . to die* This reply is not an admission on Cæsar's part that he
should certainly be killed if he fought with Antony. It merely presupposes the actual
risk of death in such a duel and scornfully declines to take that risk [K]. 8 *Give him*

We mean to fight. Within our files there are,
Of those that serv'd Mark Antony but late,
Enough to fetch him in. See it done;
And feast the army. We have store to do't,   [*15*
And they have earn'd the waste. Poor Antony!   [*Exeunt.*]

Scene II

[*Alexandria.* CLEOPATRA's *Palace.*]

[*Enter* ANTONY, CLEOPATRA, ENOBARBUS, CHARMIAN, IRAS, ALEXAS, *with others.*]
ANTONY   He will not fight with me, Domitius?
ENOBARBUS   No.
ANTONY   Why should he not?
ENOBARBUS   He thinks, being twenty times of better fortune,
   He is twenty men to one.
ANTONY   To-morrow, soldier,
   By sea and land I'll fight. Or I will live,   [*5*
   Or bathe my dying honour in the blood
   Shall make it live again. Woo't thou fight well?
ENOBARBUS   I'll strike, and cry "Take all!"
ANTONY   Well said. Come on.
   Call forth my household servants. Let's to-night
   Be bounteous at our meal.
   [*Enter three or four* SERVITORS.]
                           Give me thy hand,   [*10*
   Thou hast been rightly honest. So hast thou;
   And thou, and thou, and thou. You have serv'd me well,
   And kings have been your fellows.
CLEOPATRA   [*aside to* ENOBARBUS]   What means this?
ENOBARBUS   [*aside to* CLEOPATRA] 'Tis one of those odd tricks which
                  sorrow shoots
   Out of the mind.
ANTONY   And thou art honest too.   [*15*
   I wish I could be made so many men,
   And all of you clapp'd up together in
   An Antony, that I might do you service
   So good as you have done.
OMNES   The gods forbid!
ANTONY   Well, my good fellows, wait on me to-night.   [*20*
   Scant not my cups, and make as much of me

---

no breath give him no time to rest and recover his sanity.   9 *Make boot* take advantage.
12 *files* military units.   15 *store* abundance.   16 *Poor Antony* An expression rather of
pity and regret than of scorn [K].
   IV.II.   5 *Or* either.   6 *bathe . . . blood* Bathing in warm blood was actually believed to cure certain diseases.   7 *Woo't* wilt thou.   8 *Take all* The cry of the
gambler when he throws down his last stake: "Here is my all! Take it if you can
win it!" Hence used proverbially as an exclamation of desperate challenge or of utter
defiance [K].   14–15 *odd tricks . . . mind* random actions that sorrow produces by the
spasmodic working of the mind [K].   16 *be made so many men* be divided up so as to
equal you in number [K].   19 *The gods forbid* A passionate rejection of the idea that

    As when mine empire was your fellow too
    And suffer'd my command.
CLEOPATRA   [*aside to* ENOBARBUS] What does he mean?
ENOBARBUS   [*aside to* CLEOPATRA] To make his followers weep.
ANTONY   Tend me to-night.
    May be it is the period of your duty.   [2
    Haply you shall not see me more; or if,
    A mangled shadow. Perchance to-morrow
    You'll serve another master. I look on you
    As one that takes his leave. Mine honest friends,
    I turn you not away; but, like a master   [3
    Married to your good service, stay till death.
    Tend me to-night two hours, I ask no more,
    And the gods yield you for't!
ENOBARBUS   What mean you, sir,
    To give them this discomfort? Look, they weep,
    And I, an ass, am onion-ey'd. For shame!   [3
    Transform us not to women.
ANTONY   Ho, ho, ho!
    Now the witch take me if I meant it thus!
    Grace grow where those drops fall! My hearty friends,
    You take me in too dolorous a sense;
    For I spake to you for your comfort, did desire you [4
    To burn this night with torches. Know, my hearts,
    I hope well of to-morrow, and will lead you
    Where rather I'll expect victorious life
    Than death and honour. Let's to supper come,
    And drown consideration. [*Exeunt.*]   [4

Scene III

    [*Alexandria. Before* CLEOPATRA's *Palace.*]

    [*Enter a* COMPANY *of* SOLDIERS.]
1. SOLDIER   Brother, good night. To-morrow is the day.
2. SOLDIER   It will determine one way. Fare you well.
    Heard you of nothing strange about the streets?
1. SOLDIER   Nothing. What news?
2. SOLDIER   Belike 'tis but a rumour. Good night to you.   [
1. SOLDIER   Well, sir, good night.
    [*They meet other* SOLDIERS.]
2. SOLDIER   Soldiers, have careful watch.
3. SOLDIER   And you. Good night, good night.
    [*They place themselves in every corner of the stage.*]
4. SOLDIER   Here we. And if to-morrow

Antony should serve them. He is their master—let him ever remain so [K].

    23 *suffer'd* submitted to. 25 *period* end. 26 *Haply* perhaps. 31 *stay till death* I remain your master until my death releases you from your service [K]. 33 *yield* repay, reward. 35 *onion-ey'd* tearful. 37 *the witch take me* may I be bewitched, *take* bewitch. 38 *Grace* virtue, goodness. Tears like these, that express a sound and faithful nature, should cause a crop of such virtues to spring from the earth [K]. There is a glance also at "rue" known as the "herb of grace." *hearty* kindhearted. 40 *for your comfort* to encourage you. "Comfort" originally meant to "support" [K].

    IV.III. 2 *determine one way* settle the question one way or the other [K]. 5 *Belike* very likely. 8 *Here we* here is our post.

Our navy thrive, I have an absolute hope
Our landmen will stand up.
3. SOLDIER   'Tis a brave army,   [*10*
And full of purpose.
[*Music of the hautboys is under the stage.*]
2. SOLDIER   Peace! What noise?
1. SOLDIER   List, list!
2. SOLDIER   Hark!
1. SOLDIER   Music i' th' air.
3. SOLDIER   Under the earth.
4. SOLDIER   It signs well, does it not?
3. SOLDIER   No.
1. SOLDIER   Peace, I say!
What should this mean?
2. SOLDIER   'Tis the god Hercules, whom Antony lov'd,   [*15*
Now leaves him.
1. SOLDIER   Walk. Let's see if other watchmen
Do hear what we do.
2. SOLDIER   How now, masters?
OMNES   (*speak together*)   How now?
How now? Do you hear this?
1. SOLDIER   Ay. Is't not strange?
3. SOLDIER   Do you hear, masters? Do you hear?
1. SOLDIER   Follow the noise so far as we have quarter.   [*20*
Let's see how it will give off.
OMNES   Content. 'Tis strange.   [*Exeunt.*]

Scene IV

[*Alexandria.* CLEOPATRA's *Palace.*]

[*Enter* ANTONY *and* CLEOPATRA, (CHARMIAN, IRAS,) *with others.*]
ANTONY   Eros! mine armour, Eros!
CLEOPATRA   Sleep a little.
ANTONY   No, my chuck. Eros! Come, mine armour, Eros!
[*Enter* EROS (*with armour*).]
Come, good fellow, put thine iron on.
If fortune be not ours to-day, it is
Because we brave her. Come.
CLEOPATRA   Nay, I'll help too.   [*5*
What's this for?
ANTONY   Ah, let be, let be! Thou art
The armourer of my heart. False, false! This, this!

---

10 *brave* fine, gallant. 13 *signs well* is a favorable omen. 15–16 *Hercules . . . leaves him* Shakespeare here departs from Plutarch, who records among the signs and wonders before the battle of Actium that Bacchanalian revelers departed from the city of Alexandria to the sound of strange music by night and that a statue of Bacchus was thrown down by a great wind in Athens. Plutarch says that Antony was descended from the god Hercules, but that it was Bacchus whom he followed in his manner of life. 20 *noise* music. *as we have quarter* as the limits of our post extend [K]. 21 *give off* end.
    IV.IV. 2 *chuck* A term of endearment (literally "chick") which was used of either sex. 3 *thine iron* the armour (of mine) you have there (F¹; HANMER, K: "mine iron"). 5 *help too* CAPELL; F¹: "helpe, too, Anthony." 6–7 *Ah, let . . . this* CAPELL; F¹ gives to

CLEOPATRA   Sooth, la, I'll help. Thus it must be.
ANTONY   Well, well.
   We shall thrive now. Seest thou, my good fellow?
   Go put on thy defences.
EROS   Briefly, sir.   [*1*
CLEOPATRA   Is not this buckled well?
ANTONY   Rarely, rarely!
   He that unbuckles this, till we do please
   To daff't for our repose, shall hear a storm.
   Thou fumblest, Eros, and my queen's a squire
   More tight at this than thou. Dispatch. O love,   [*1*
   That thou couldst see my wars to-day, and knew'st
   The royal occupation! Thou shouldst see
   A workman in't.
   [*Enter an armed* SOLDIER.]
          Good morrow to thee! Welcome.
   Thou look'st like him that knows a warlike charge.
   To business that we love we rise betime   [*20*
   And go to't with delight.
SOLDIER   A thousand, sir,
   Early though't be, have on their riveted trim
   And at the port expect you.
   [*Shout. Trumpets. Flourish. Enter* CAPTAINS *and* SOLDIERS.]
CAPTAIN   The morn is fair. Good morrow, General.
ALL   Good morrow, General.
ANTONY   'Tis well blown, lads.   [*2*
   This morning, like the spirit of a youth
   That means to be of note, begins betimes.
   So, so. Come, give me that! This way. Well said.
   Fare thee well, dame, whate'er becomes of me.
   This is a soldier's kiss. Rebukable   [*3*
   And worthy shameful check it were to stand
   On more mechanic compliment. I'll leave thee
   Now like a man of steel. You that will fight,
   Follow me close; I'll bring you to't. Adieu.
   [*Exeunt* (ANTONY, EROS, CAPTAINS, *and* SOLDIERS) .]
CHARMIAN   Please you retire to your chamber?
CLEOPATRA   Lead me.   [*3*
   He goes forth gallantly. That he and Cæsar might
   Determine this great war in single fight!
   Then Antony—but now—Well, on!   [*Exeunt.*]

Cleopatra.   *False* wrong. Cleopatra is putting on the wrong piece of armour [K].
   8 *Sooth* in truth. 10 *Briefly* in a moment. 13 *daff't* doff it, put it off. 14 *squire*
To arm the knight was a traditional duty of the squire. 15 *tight* adroit, skillful.
16–17 *knew'st . . . occupation* wert a judge of warfare, which is the trade of kings
[K]. 19 *charge* duty, business—not onset [K]. 20 *betime* early. 22 *trim* dress—armour.
23 *port* gate. 25 *'Tis well blown* the morning blossoms well. The "fair morn" of
which the Captain has spoken augurs a fair day—fair both in weather and in our
fortunes. What follows shows that this is the meaning, though some editors insist on
referring "well blown" to the flourish of trumpets [K]. 28 *that* that piece of armour.
The arming is still going on. *Well said* well done. The arming is now finished [K].
31 *check* reproof. *stand* insist. 32 *more mechanic compliment* further words of ceremony, such as common people might think necessary [K]. 33 *like* in the guise of.

Scene v

[*Alexandria.* ANTONY'S *camp.*]

[*Trumpets sound. Enter* ANTONY *and* EROS. *(a* SOLDIER *meeting them)* .]
SOLDIER   The gods make this a happy day to Antony!
ANTONY   Would thou and those thy scars had once prevail'd
To make me fight at land!
SOLDIER   Hadst thou done so,
The kings that have revolted and the soldier
That has this morning left thee would have still   [5
Followed thy heels.
ANTONY   Who's gone this morning?
SOLDIER   Who?
One ever near thee. Call for Enobarbus.
He shall not hear thee, or from Cæsar's camp
Say "I am none of thine."
ANTONY   What sayest thou?
SOLDIER   Sir,
He is with Cæsar.
EROS   Sir, his chests and treasure   [10
He has not with him.
ANTONY   Is he gone?
SOLDIER   Most certain.
ANTONY   Go, Eros, send his treasure after. Do it;
Detain no jot, I charge thee. Write to him
(I will subscribe) gentle adieus and greetings.
Say that I wish he never find more cause   [15
To change a master. O, my fortunes have
Corrupted honest men! Dispatch. Enobarbus!   [*Exeunt.*]

Scene vi

[*Alexandria.* CÆSAR'S *camp.*]

[*Flourish. Enter* AGRIPPA, CÆSAR, *with* ENOBARBUS, *and* DOLABELLA.]
CÆSAR   Go forth, Agrippa, and begin the fight.
Our will is Antony be took alive.
Make it so known.
AGRIPPA   Cæsar, I shall.   [*Exit.*]
CÆSAR   The time of universal peace is near.
Prove this a prosp'rous day, the three-nook'd world   [5
Shall bear the olive freely.
[*Enter a* MESSENGER.]
MESSENGER   Antony
Is come into the field.
CÆSAR   Go charge Agrippa
Plant those that have revolted in the vant,

IV.v. 1 *The gods . . . Antony* THEOBALD; F¹ gives to Eros. *happy* lucky. 3–6 *Hadst . . . heels* THEOBALD; F¹ gives to Eros.
IV.vi. 6 *Prove this* if this prove. *three-nook'd world* The three nooks or corners (interior angles) of the world are Europe, Asia, and Africa. The ancient world made a rough triangle, with the apex towards the south [K]. 7 *bear* bring forth. *olive* the emblem of peace and prosperity. 9 *vant* van—a shortened form of "vantward" (F¹; F², K: "van") .

    That Antony may seem to spend his fury   [*10*
    Upon himself
    [*Exeunt (all but* ENOBARBUS) .]
ENOBARBUS   Alexas did revolt and went to Jewry on
    Affairs of Antony; there did dissuade
    Great Herod to incline himself to Cæsar   [*15*
    And leave his master Antony. For this pains
    Cæsar hath hang'd him. Canidius and the rest
    That fell away have entertainment, but
    No honourable trust. I have done ill,
    Of which I do accuse myself so sorely,
    That I will joy no more.
    [*Enter a* SOLDIER *of* CÆSAR'S.]
SOLDIER   Enobarbus, Antony   [*20*
    Hath after thee sent all thy treasure, with
    His bounty overplus. The messenger
    Came on my guard and at thy tent is now
    Unloading of his mules.
ENOBARBUS   I give it you!
SOLDIER   Mock not, Enobarbus.   [*25*
    I tell you true. Best you saf'd the bringer
    Out of the host. I must attend mine office
    Or would have done't myself. Your emperor
    Continues still a Jove.   [*Exit.*]
ENOBARBUS   I am alone the villain of the earth,   [*30*
    And feel I am so most. O Antony,
    Thou mine of bounty, how wouldst thou have paid
    My better service, when my turpitude
    Thou dost so crown with gold! This blows my heart.
    If swift thought break it not, a swifter mean   [*35*
    Shall outstrike thought; but thought will do't, I feel.
    I fight against thee? No! I will go seek
    Some ditch wherein to die; the foul'st best fits
    My latter part of life.   [*Exit.*]

Scene VII

    [*Field of battle between the camps.*]

    [*Alarum. Drums and trumpets. Enter* AGRIPPA *(and others)* .]
AGRIPPA   Retire. We have engag'd ourselves too far.
    Cæsar himself has work, and our oppression
    Exceeds what we expected.   [*Exeunt.*]

---

10 *spend* waste.   11 *himself* his own former soldiers.   13 *dissuade* persuade away from his allegiance [K].   16 *him* Whether this refers to Alexas or Herod is not entirely clear, for Plutarch reports that both were killed by Cæsar.   17 *have entertainment* have been taken into Cæsar's service [K].   20 *no more* F²; F¹: "no mote."   23 *on my guard* while I was on guard.   26 *Best* it were best that. *saf'd* gave safe conduct to.   31 *And . . . most* and am he who feels it most thoroughly.   34 *blows my heart* makes my heart swell to bursting [K].   35 *thought* grief.   36 *Shall outstrike* will surely strike sooner and more effectually than [K].   39 *latter part of* final moments of.
    IV.VII. 1 *engag'd ourselves too far* To "engage" is to "entangle," to "trap." Agrippa means that they have got themselves too deeply involved among the enemy's forces [K].   2 *has work* has all that he can handle himself. *oppression* the crushing weight

[*Alarums. Enter* ANTONY, *and* SCARUS *wounded.*]

SCARUS   O my brave Emperor, this is fought indeed!
Had we done so at first, we had droven them home   [5
With clouts about their heads.

ANTONY   Thou bleed'st apace.

SCARUS   I had a wound here that was like a T,
But now 'tis made an H.
[(*Sound retreat*) *far off.*]

ANTONY   They do retire.

SCARUS   We'll beat 'em into bench-holes. I have yet
Room for six scotches more.   [10
[*Enter* EROS.]

EROS   They are beaten, sir, and our advantage serves
For a fair victory.

SCARUS   Let us score their backs
And snatch 'em up, as we take hares, behind!
'Tis sport to maul a runner.

ANTONY   I will reward thee
Once for thy sprightly comfort, and tenfold   [15
For thy good valour. Come thee on!

SCARUS   I'll halt after.
[*Exeunt.*]

Scene VIII

[*Under the walls of Alexandria.*]

[*Alarum. Enter* ANTONY *again in a march;* SCARUS, *with others.*]

ANTONY   We have beat him to his camp. Run one before
And let the Queen know of our gests. To-morrow,
Before the sun shall see 's, we'll spill the blood
That has to-day escap'd. I thank you all;
For doughty-handed are you, and have fought   [5
Not as you serv'd the cause, but as 't had been
Each man's like mine. You have shown all Hectors.
Enter the city, clip your wives, your friends,
Tell them your feats, whilst they with joyful tears
Wash the congealment from your wounds and kiss   [10
The honour'd gashes whole.
[*Enter* CLEOPATRA (*attended*) .]

                              [*To* SCARUS] Give me thy hand.—
To this great fairy I'll commend thy acts,

---

of the attacks that we have to sustain [K].

   5 *droven* driven. 6 *clouts* cloths, bandages. 8 '*tis made an H* in shape (by an
additional slash) , with a pun: "It has begun to ache." The noun "ache" was pronounced like the name of the letter "H" ("aitch") [K]. 9 *bench-holes* the holes of
privies. 10 *scotches* slashes, wounds. 11–12 *our advantage . . . victory* the advantage
we have already gained may well pass for a brilliant victory [K]. 12 *score* mark. 15
sprightly high-spirited, cheerful. 16 *halt* limp.
   IV.VIII. 2 *gests* exploits (THEOBALD; F¹: "guests") . 5 *doughty-handed* sturdy and
bold in fight [K]. 6 *as* as if. 6–7 *as't had . . . like mine* as if the cause had been as
important to each of you as it is to me. 8 *clip* embrace. 12 *fairy* So called as wielding
magic power, like the Fairy Queen [K].

Make her thanks bless thee. [*To* CLEOPATRA] O thou day o' th' world,
Chain mine arm'd neck! Leap thou, attire and all,
Through proof of harness to my heart, and there   [*1*
Ride on the pants triumphing!
CLEOPATRA   Lord of lords!
O infinite virtue, com'st thou smiling from
The world's great snare uncaught?
ANTONY   My nightingale,
We have beat them to their beds. What, girl! though grey
Do something mingle with our younger brown, yet ha' we   [2
A brain that nourishes our nerves, and can
Get goal for goal of youth. Behold this man.
Commend unto his lips thy favouring hand.—
Kiss it, my warrior!—He hath fought to-day
As if a god in hate of mankind had   [2
Destroyed in such a shape.
CLEOPATRA   I'll give thee, friend,
An armour all of gold. It was a king's.
ANTONY   He has deserv'd it, were it carbuncled
Like holy Phœbus' car. Give me thy hand.
Through Alexandria make a jolly march;   [*3*
Bear our hack'd targets like the men that owe them.
Had our great palace the capacity
To camp this host, we all would sup together
And drink carouses to the next day's fate,
Which promises royal peril. Trumpeters,   [*3*
With brazen din blast you the city's ear;
Make mingle with our rattling tabourines,
That heaven and earth may strike their sounds together,
Applauding our approach.   [*Exeunt.*]

Scene IX

[CÆSAR's *camp.*]

[*Enter a* SENTRY *and his* COMPANY. ENOBARBUS *follows.*]
SENTRY   If we be not reliev'd within this hour,
We must return to th' court of guard. The night
Is shiny, and they say we shall embattle
By th' second hour i' th' morn.
1. WATCH   This last day was
A shrewd one to's.

---

13 *thou day o' th' world* thou who dost give light to the world [K].   15 *proof of harness* armour of proof (which cannot be penetrated).   16 *pants triumphing* He compares his heart to a steed panting after victory.   17 *virtue* valour.   18 *The world's great snare* all the traps and pitfalls of the world at war.   *My* F²; F¹: "Mine."   19 *grey* grey hairs.   20 *something* somewhat.   21 *nerves* sinews.   22 *Get goal . . . youth* hold our own with youth; win a point for every point that youth wins. The reference may be to the sport of tilting at barriers.   23 *Commend* commit, entrust.   *favouring* THEOBALD; F¹: "savouring."   28 *carbuncled* jewelled. The carbuncle was supposed to have light in itself, so that it would shine in the dark [K].   29 *Phœbus' car* the sun god's chariot.   31 *targets* shields.   *owe* own, possess.   34 *carouses* draughts which drain the cup [K].   35 *royal peril* danger of war, the occupation appropriate to kings.   37 *tabourines* small drums.

ENOBARBUS   O, bear me witness, night—   [5
2. WATCH   What man is this?
1. WATCH   Stand close, and list him.
ENOBARBUS   Be witness to me, O thou blessed moon,
     When men revolted shall upon record
     Bear hateful memory, poor Enobarbus did
     Before thy face repent!
SENTRY   Enobarbus?
2. WATCH   Peace!   [10
     Hark further.
ENOBARBUS   O sovereign mistress of true melancholy,
     The poisonous damp of night disponge upon me,
     That life, a very rebel to my will,
     May hang no longer on me! Throw my heart   [15
     Against the flint and hardness of my fault,
     Which, being dried with grief, will break to powder,
     And finish all foul thoughts. O Antony,
     Nobler than my revolt is infamous,
     Forgive me in thine own particular,   [20
     But let the world rank me in register
     A master-leaver and a fugitive!
     O Antony! O Antony!   [*Dies.*]
1. WATCH   Let's speak
     To him.
SENTRY   Let's hear him, for the things he speaks   [25
     May concern Cæsar.
2. WATCH   Let's do so. But he sleeps.
SENTRY   Swoonds rather; for so bad a prayer as his
     Was never yet for sleep.
1. WATCH   Go we to him.
2. WATCH   Awake, sir, awake! Speak to us!
1. WATCH   Hear you, sir?
SENTRY   The hand of death hath raught him.   [*Drums afar off.*]
          Hark! The drums   [30
     Demurely wake the sleepers. Let us bear him
     To th' court of guard. He is of note. Our hour
     Is fully out.
2. WATCH   Come on then.
     He may recover yet.   [*Exeunt (with the body).*]

     IV.IX. 2 *court of guard* place where the guard was mustered.   3 *embattle* draw up
in battle array [K].   5 *shrewd* severe, tough, wicked—as we speak of "a wicked blow."
The literal meaning of "shrewd" is "cursed," but it was often used as we use "plaguy,"
"confounded," and the like [K].   *to's* to us.   6 *list* listen to   8–9 *upon record . . .
memory* in history be remembered with shame.   12 *melancholy* The supposed influence
of the moon in causing melancholia and madness is often mentioned. The old belief
is preserved in our words "lunatic" and "moon-struck" [K].   13 *disponge* The night
air was thought to be saturated with poisonous vapour, like a sponge with moisture
[K].   17 *Which* his heart.   *dried* Sorrow was believed to dry up the blood.   20 *in thine
own particular* in thine own person; so far as my fault concerns thee alone. The world,
however, Enobarbus does not expect or desire to forgive him [K].   21 *in register* in its
record of men's characters [K].   22 *master-leaver* runaway servant. Enobarbus is willing
to be ranked with fugitive slaves and masterless vagabonds. According as it is uttered,
this word will mean either "one who abandons his master" or "a master workman in
the trade of desertion" [K].   30 *raught* reached.   31 *Demurely* with solemn sound. The
drums are heard "afar off," so that their sound is muffled [K].

Scene x

[*Between the two camps.*]

[*Enter* ANTONY *and* SCARUS, *with their* ARMY.]
ANTONY   Their preparation is to-day by sea;
   We please them not by land.
SCARUS   For both, my lord.
ANTONY   I would they'ld fight i' th' fire or i' th' air;
   We'ld fight there too. But this it is, our foot
   Upon the hills adjoining to the city
   Shall stay with us—order for sea is given;
   They have put forth the haven—
   Where their appointment we may best discover
   And look on their endeavor.   [*Exeunt.*]

Scene xi

[*Between the camps.*]

[*Enter* CÆSAR *and his* ARMY.]
CÆSAR   But being charg'd, we will be still by land,
   Which, as I take't, we shall; for his best force
   Is forth to man his galleys. To the vales,
   And hold our best advantage.   [*Exeunt.*]

Scene xii

[*Hill adjoining Alexandria.*]

[*Enter* ANTONY *and* SCARUS.]
ANTONY   Yet they are not join'd. Where yond pine does stand
   I shall discover all. I'll bring thee word
   Straight how 'tis like to go.   [*Exit.*]
SCARUS   Swallows have built
   In Cleopatra's sails their nests. The augurers
   Say they know not, they cannot tell; look grimly
   And dare not speak their knowledge. Antony
   Is valiant, and dejected; and by starts
   His fretted fortunes give him hope and fear
   Of what he has and has not.
   [*Alarum afar off, as at a sea-fight. Enter* ANTONY.]
ANTONY   All is lost!
   This foul Egyptian hath betrayed me!

IV.x. 7 *haven* F¹; ĸ: "haven. Go we up." The punctuation of lines 6 and 7 has been much disputed, and to many editors it has seemed that some words have been omitted from F¹ after "haven." The use of a parenthetical insertion, adopted by most recent editors, makes sense of the F¹ text without the necessity for adding words such as "Go we up" without textual basis.   8 *their appointment* the appearance and array of their ships [ĸ].

IV.xi. 1 *But being charg'd* unless we are attacked.   *still* quiet.   4 *hold . . . advantage* hold such positions as shall best maintain our superiority in land forces [ĸ].

IV.xii. 1 *join'd* in battle.   3 *Straight* straightaway.   4 *augurers* CAPELL; F¹: "Auguries."   8 *fretted* chequered, variegated, constantly shifting.   8–9 *hope and fear . . . has not* hope for what he has not and fear as to what he has; hope for the future and fear

My fleet hath yielded to the foe, and yonder
They cast their caps up and carouse together
Like friends long lost. Triple-turn'd whore! 'tis thou
Hast sold me to this novice, and my heart
Makes only wars on thee. Bid them all fly!   [*15*
For when I am reveng'd upon my charm,
I have done all. Bid them all fly; begone!   [*Exit* SCARUS.]
O sun, thy uprise shall I see no more.
Fortune and Antony part here; even here
Do we shake hands. All come to this? The hearts   [*20*
That spaniel'd me at heels, to whom I gave
Their wishes, do discandy, melt their sweets
On blossoming Cæsar; and this pine is bark'd,
That overtopp'd them all. Betray'd I am.
O this false soul of Egypt! this grave charm—   [*25*
Whose eye beck'd forth my wars and call'd them home,
Whose bosom was my crownet, my chief end—
Like a right gypsy hath at fast and loose
Beguil'd me to the very heart of loss!
What, Eros, Eros!
[*Enter* CLEOPATRA.]
          Ah, thou spell! Avaunt!   [*30*
CLEOPATRA   Why is my lord enrag'd against his love?
ANTONY   Vanish, or I shall give thee thy deserving
And blemish Cæsar's triumph. Let him take thee
And hoist thee up to the shouting plebeians.
Follow his chariot, like the greatest spot   [*35*
Of all thy sex. Most monster-like be shown
For poor'st diminitives, for dolts, and let
Patient Octavia plough thy visage up
With her prepared nails.   [*Exit* CLEOPATRA.]
          'Tis well th'art gone,
If it be well to live; but better 'twere   [*40*
Thou fell'st into my fury, for one death
Might have prevented many. Eros, ho!

---

of the present [K].
    13 *Triple-turn'd* from Pompey to Julius Cæsar, from Cæsar to Antony, and now to Octavius [K].   16 *my charm* this creature who has cast a spell upon me [K].   21 *spaniel'd me* followed me like spaniels—with fawning and flattery (HANMER; F¹: "pannelled") . This is one of the most brilliant and perceptive of eighteenth-century emendations of Shakespeare's text.   22 *discandy* dissolve. Shakespeare often associates flattery with candy and with dogs.   23 *blossoming Cæsar* Cæsar is compared to a flower growing full with greatness.   *bark'd* stripped of bark.   25 *this grave charm* this heavy, benumbing spell; this sorceress whose evil magic has held me under such powerful enchantment that I have lost all sense and wisdom [K].   26 *beck'd* beckoned.   27 *my crownet* since her love for me was the crown of all my efforts [K].   28 *right* true, typical.   *fast and loose* a juggling trick, sometimes used for gambling purposes, in which a girdle or handkerchief was apparently tied in a hard knot but really so adjusted as to come loose at a pull [K].   30 *Avaunt* be gone.   33 *blemish Cæsar's triumph* Cleopatra's death would deprive Cæsar's triumphal procession of its chief trophy [K].   36 *monster-like* The fondness of the Elizabethans for exhibitions of freaks is often mentioned [K].   37 *diminitives* dwarfs, undersized weaklings.   *dolts* idiots (F¹; THIRLBY, K: "doits," meaning "small coins") .   39 *prepared* ready for the purpose.   41–2 *one death . . . many* one death now would have prevented the miseries you are destined to suffer (equal to many deaths) .

The shirt of Nessus is upon me. Teach me,
Alcides, thou mine ancestor, thy rage.
Let me lodge Lichas on the horns o' th' moon   [4
And with those hands that grasp'd the heaviest club
Subdue my worthiest self. The witch shall die.
To the young Roman boy she hath sold me, and I fall
Under this plot. She dies for't. Eros, ho! [*Exit.*]

Scene XIII

[*Alexandria.* CLEOPATRA'S *Palace.*]

[*Enter* CLEOPATRA, CHARMIAN, IRAS, MARDIAN.]
CLEOPATRA   Help me, my women! O, he is more mad
Than Telamon for his shield. The boar of Thessaly
Was never so emboss'd.
CHARMIAN   To th' monument!   [
There lock yourself, and send him word you are dead.
The soul and body rive not more in parting
Than greatness going off.
CLEOPATRA   To th' monument!
Mardian, go tell him I have slain myself.
Say that the last I spoke was "Antony"
And word it, prithee, piteously. Hence, Mardian,
And bring me how he takes my death. To th' monument!   [1
[*Exeunt.*]

Scene XIV

[CLEOPATRA'S *Palace. Another room.*]

[*Enter* ANTONY *and* EROS.]
ANTONY   Eros, thou yet behold'st me?
EROS   Ay, noble lord.
ANTONY   Sometime we see a cloud that's dragonish;
A vapour sometime like a bear or lion,

---

43 *shirt of Nessus* Hercules had killed the centaur Nessus with a poisoned arrow. Nessus, dying, told Deianira to take some of his blood to use as a charmed drug in preserving the love of Hercules for herself. With this blood she anointed a garment for Hercules to wear. The blood poisoned him, and in his agony he went mad, threw Lichas, who had brought him the garment, into the sea, and mounted a funeral pyre on Mount Oeta to burn himself to death; but he was carried to Olympus in a fiery cloud and became immortal. See Ovid, METAMORPHOSES, IX, 117*ff;* Seneca, HERCULES OETAEUS [K]. 44 *Alcides* Hercules.

IV.XIII. 2 *Than Telamon for his shield* than Ajax, son of Telamon, for the loss of the shield of Achilles, which was awarded to Ulysses, his rival for its possession [K]. *boar of Thessaly* the monstrous boar sent by Artemis to ravage Thessaly in retribution for the omission of sacrifices to her. It was killed by Meleager. 3 *emboss'd* enraged, infuriated (a hunting term). *monument* a tomb which Cleopatra, according to Plutarch, had made in preparation for her own death. 5 *rive* rend, tear apart.

IV.XIV. 1 *thou yet behold'st me* The question, which, of course, Eros cannot understand is explained by what follows (in lines 2–14). Antony seems to himself such a faded, shadowlike figure of what he had been, that he wonders if he is still visible

A tower'd citadel, a pendent rock,
A forked mountain, or blue promontory   [5
With trees upon't that nod unto the world
And mock our eyes with air. Thou hast seen these signs;
They are black Vesper's pageants.
EROS   Ay, my lord.
ANTONY   That which is now a horse, even with a thought
The rack dislimns, and makes it indistinct   [10
As water is in water.
EROS   It does, my lord.
ANTONY   My good knave Eros, now thy captain is
Even such a body. Here I am Antony;
Yet cannot hold this visible shape, my knave.
I made these wars for Egypt; and the Queen—   [15
Whose heart I thought I had, for she had mine,
Which, whilst it was mine, had annex'd unto't
A million moe, now lost—she, Eros, has
Pack'd cards with Cæsar and false-play'd my glory
Unto an enemy's triumph.   [20
Nay, weep not, gentle Eros. There is left us
Ourselves to end ourselves.
[*Enter* MARDIAN.]
                            O, thy vile lady!
She has robb'd me of my sword.
MARDIAN   No, Antony.
My mistress lov'd thee and her fortunes mingled
With thine entirely.
ANTONY   Hence, saucy eunuch! Peace!   [25
She hath betray'd me and shall die the death.
MARDIAN   Death of one person can be paid but once,
And that she has discharg'd. What thou wouldst do
Is done unto thy hand. The last she spake
Was, "Antony! most noble Antony!"   [30
Then in the midst a tearing groan did break
The name of Antony; it was divided
Between her heart and lips. She rend'red life,
Thy name so buried in her.
ANTONY   Dead, then?
MARDIAN   Dead.
ANTONY   Unarm, Eros. The long day's task is done,   [35
And we must sleep.   [*To* MARDIAN]   That thou depart'st hence safe

---

and recognizable [K].

    4 *tower'd* ROWE; F¹: "toward."   8 *black Vesper's pageants* the pageants that greet
the approach of evening. The figure comes from the elaborate shows, called pageants,
arranged in the London streets and elsewhere to do honour to great personages on their
entry [K]. 10 *rack* drifting clouds. *dislimns* effaces, paints out (THEOBALD; F¹: "dis-
limes"). 13 *Here* here and now; at this moment [K]. 15 *Egypt* the Queen of Egypt.
18 *moe* more. 19-20 *Pack'd . . . triumph* stacked the cards in collusion with Cæsar and
thus falsely played away my glory (which I had staked on the game) until my enemy
had won it all [K].   *Unto an enemy's triumph* (a) until my enemy had triumphed (b)
into my enemy's trump card. "Trump" is derived from "triumph." 23 *sword* manhood
and ability to fight. 25 *saucy* insolent. 27 *of one* by one. 28. *discharg'd* paid in full.
29 *unto thy hand* for you. 35 *Unarm* F¹; ROWE, K: "unarm me."

Does pay thy labour richly. Go.   [*Exit* MARDIAN.]
                 Off, pluck off!
The sevenfold shield of Ajax cannot keep
The battery from my heart. O, cleave, my sides!
Heart, once be stronger than thy continent,   [4
Crack thy frail case! Apace, Eros, apace.—
No more a soldier. Bruised pieces, go;
You have been nobly borne.—From me awhile.
[*Exit* EROS.]
I will o'ertake thee, Cleopatra, and
Weep for my pardon. So it must be, for now   [4
All length is torture. Since the torch is out,
Lie down, and stray no farther. Now all labour
Mars what it does; yea, very force entangles
Itself with strength. Seal then, and all is done.
Eros!—I come, my queen.—Eros!—Stay for me.   [5
Where souls do couch on flowers, we'll hand in hand
And with our sprightly port make the ghosts gaze.
Dido and her Æneas shall want troops,
And all the haunt be ours.—Come, Eros, Eros!
[*Enter* EROS.]
EROS What would my lord?
ANTONY   Since Cleopatra died   [5
I have liv'd in such dishonour that the gods
Detest my baseness. I, that with my sword
Quarter'd the world and o'er green Neptune's back
With ships made cities, condemn myself to lack
The courage of a woman—less noble mind   [6
Than she which by her death our Cæsar tells
"I am conqueror of myself." Thou art sworn, Eros,
That, when the exigent should come (which now
Is come indeed) when I should see behind me
Th' inevitable prosecution of   [6

---

37 *pay thy labour* thy labour as messenger. Antony implies that the bringer of such evil tidings might well expect death at his hands [K]. 38–9 *sevenfold shield . . . heart* The agitation which makes his heart beat so violently is conceived as something which attacks the heart from without, and against which no armour can protect it. The shield of Ajax was famous in ancient story [K]. 40 *thy continent* that which contains thee. 41 *Apace* quickly. 46 *length* of life. *torch* the light of his life—Cleopatra. 48 *Mars what it does* destroys what it attempts to perform; thus is useless. 48–9 *force . . . strength* the very force of my exertions would cause them to be so entangled with one another as to destroy all effort. 49 *Seal . . . is done* nothing is left to do but to put the seal of death upon my life and deeds. To affix the seal to a document was the final act when all negotiations (like the business of Antony's life) were finished [K]. 50 *Stay* wait. 51 *Where souls . . . flowers* the Elysian fields. 52 *sprightly* (a) high-spirited (b) as spirits—being dead. *port* bearing, behaviour. 53 *want troops* lack hosts of admirers. Actually Dido, according to Virgil's ÆNEID, Book VI, lives in Hades with her husband, Sychæus, where she continually repulses the advances of Æneas, who has repented his desertion of her for the greatness of Rome; Antony, on the contrary, has deserted Rome for Cleopatra. 54 *all the haunt be ours* all the resort shall be to us; we alone shall be the pair of lovers that the ghosts will throng to behold [K]. 56 *such dishonour* He sees his continuing to live after her death as dishonourable. 59 *With ships made cities* His ships were so numerous that they seemed a city upon the waters. 61 *which* who. 63 *exigent* exigency, compelling need. 65 *inevitable prosecution* pursuit from which there is no escape [K].

Disgrace and horror, that, on my command,
Thou then wouldst kill me. Do't; the time is come.
Thou strik'st not me; 'tis Cæsar thou defeat'st.
Put colour in thy cheek.

EROS   The gods withhold me!
Shall I do that which all the Parthian darts,   [*70*
Though enemy, lost aim and could not?

ANTONY   Eros,
Wouldst thou be window'd in great Rome and see
Thy master thus with pleach'd arms, bending down
His corrigible neck, his face subdu'd
To penetrative shame, whilst the wheel'd seat   [*75*
Of fortunate Cæsar, drawn before him, branded
His baseness that ensu'd?

EROS   I would not see't.

ANTONY   Come then; for with a wound I must be cur'd.
Draw that thy honest sword, which thou hast worn
Most useful for thy country.

EROS   O sir, pardon me!   [*80*

ANTONY   When I did make thee free, swor'st thou not then
To do this when I bade thee? Do it at once,
Or thy precedent services are all
But accidents unpurpos'd. Draw, and come.

EROS   Turn from me then that noble countenance   [*85*
Wherein the worship of the whole world lies.

ANTONY   Lo thee! [*Turns from him.*]

EROS   My sword is drawn.

ANTONY   Then let it do at once
The thing why thou hast drawn it.

EROS   My dear master,
My captain, and my emperor, let me say,   [*90*
Before I strike this bloody stroke, farewell.

ANTONY   'Tis said, man; and farewell.

EROS   Farewell, great chief. Shall I strike now?

ANTONY   Now, Eros.

EROS   Why, there then! Thus I do escape the sorrow
Of Antony's death.   [*Kills himself.*]

ANTONY   Thrice nobler than myself!   [*95*
Thou teachest me, O valiant Eros, what
I should, and thou couldst not. My queen and Eros
Have by their brave instruction got upon me
A nobleness in record. But I will be
A bridegroom in my death and run into't   [*100*
As to a lover's bed. Come then; and, Eros,

---

68 *defeat'st* frustratest (by thwarting his triumph).   70 *darts* arrows.   72 *window'd*
positioned at a window to watch the street below.   73 *pleach'd* folded.   74 *corrigible*
submissive, subject to punishment. Antony is describing the typical position of a captive.   74–5 *his face . . . shame* his face brought into complete accordance with the shame
that penetrates him, and so, expressive of shame alone [K].   76–7 *branded . . . ensu'd*
made obvious, as though by a brand, the shame of him who followed (his chariot).
79 *honest* honourable   83 *precedent* former.   86 *the worship . . . world* all that is
worthy of honour in the whole world [K].   89 *why* for which.   98–9 *got upon me . . .
in record* outstripped me in winning a noble name in history [K].

Thy master dies thy scholar. To do thus
[*Falls on his sword.*]
I learn'd of thee. How? not dead? not dead?—
The guard, ho! O, dispatch me!
[*Enter* (DERCETAS *and*) *a* Guard.]
1. GUARD   What's the noise?
ANTONY   I have done my work ill, friends. O, make an end   [10
Of what I have begun.
2. GUARD   The star is fall'n.
1. GUARD   And time is at his period.
ALL   Alas, and woe!
ANTONY   Let him that loves me strike me dead.
1. GUARD   Not I.
2. GUARD   Nor I.
3. GUARD   Nor any one. [*Exeunt* (Guard).]   [11
DERCETAS   Thy death and fortunes bid thy followers fly.
This sword but shown to Cæsar, with this tidings,
Shall enter me with him.
[*Enter* DIOMEDES.]
DIOMEDES   Where's Antony?
DERCETAS   There, Diomed, there.
DIOMEDES   Lives he?
Wilt thou not answer, man? [*Exit* DERCETAS.]   [1
ANTONY   Art thou there, Diomed? Draw thy sword and give me
Sufficing strokes for death.
DIOMEDES   Most absolute lord,
My mistress Cleopatra sent me to thee.
ANTONY   When did she send thee?
DIOMEDES   Now, my lord.
ANTONY   Where is she?
DIOMEDES   Lock'd in her monument. She had a prophesying fear   [1
Of what hath come to pass; for when she saw
(Which never shall be found) you did suspect
She had dispos'd with Cæsar, and that your rage
Would not be purg'd, she sent you word she was dead;
But, fearing since how it might work, hath sent   [1
Me to proclaim the truth; and I am come,
I dread, too late.
ANTONY   Too late, good Diomed. Call my guard, I prithee.
DIOMEDES   What ho! the Emperor's guard! the guard, what ho!
Come, your lord calls!   [1
[*Enter four or five of the Guard of* ANTONY.]
ANTONY   Bear me, good friends, where Cleopatra bides.
'Tis the last service that I shall command you.
1. GUARD   Woe, woe are we, sir, you may not live to wear
All your true followers out.

107 *is at his period* is at its end; has run its course [K]. The end of the world is
upon us. Such comparisons of human disaster to the Day of Judgment are common
in Shakespeare's tragedies. 113 *Shall enter me with him* will be sure to win for me
admission into his service [K]. 122 *found* found to be true. 123 *dispos'd* made arrangements, come to terms. 123-4 *that your rage . . . purg'd* that your insane fury
refused to be pacified (literally, cleared away, as by a purging medicine) [K]. 131
bides abides.
134 *heavy* woeful. 136 *To grace* by honouring (a gerund).

ALL   Most heavy day!
ANTONY   Nay, good my fellows, do not please sharp fate   [*135*
    To grace it with your sorrows. Bid that welcome
    Which comes to punish us, and we punish it,
    Seeming to bear it lightly. Take me up.
    I have led you oft; carry me now, good friends,
    And have my thanks for all. [*Exeunt, bearing* ANTONY.]   [*140*

Scene xv

[*Alexandria. A monument.*]

[*Enter* CLEOPATRA *and her* MAIDS *aloft, with* CHARMIAN *and* IRAS.]
CLEOPATRA   O Charmian, I will never go from hence.
CHARMIAN   Be comforted, dear madam.
CLEOPATRA   No, I will not.
    All strange and terrible events are welcome,
    But comforts we despise. Our size of sorrow,
    Proportion'd to our cause, must be as great   [*5*
    As that which makes it.
    [*Enter* DIOMED (*below*).]
                             How now? Is he dead?
DIOMEDES   His death's upon him, but not dead.
    Look out o' th' other side your monument.
    His guard have brought him thither.
    [*Enter,* (*below,*) ANTONY *and the* GUARD (*bearing him*).]
CLEOPATRA   O sun,
    Burn the great sphere thou mov'st in! Darkling stand   [*10*
    The varying shore o' th' world! O Antony,
    Antony, Antony! Help, Charmian; help, Iras; help!
    Help, friends below! Let's draw him hither.
ANTONY   Peace!
    Not Cæsar's valour hath o'erthrown Antony,
    But Antony's hath triumph'd on itself.   [*15*
CLEOPATRA   So it should be, that none but Antony
    Should conquer Antony; but woe 'tis so!
ANTONY   I am dying, Egypt, dying; only
    I here importune death awhile, until
    Of many thousand kisses the poor last   [*20*
    I lay upon thy lips.

IV.xv. Just how this scene was staged has been the subject of considerable debate. It used to be supposed that "aloft" indicated that the action was performed upon a balcony or "upper stage." More recently it has been suggested that Cleopatra and her maids are on the roof of a wooden structure (a "mansion") placed on the platform stage, having entered through a trap door over which the mansion has been placed. It is more likely, however, that Cleopatra appeared at one of the windows of the tiring house gallery above the stage. Antony, probably in a chair rather than a litter, at line 35*ff*, is lifted to Cleopatra by means of ropes attached to a winch in the theatre superstructure, and the remainder of the scene is staged at the window. 5–6 *as great . . . makes it* as great as Antony, for whose loss I grieve [K]. 10 *sphere* According to the Ptolemaic astronomy, still in vogue in Shakespeare's day, the sun was set in a hollow sphere which revolved about the earth [K]. *Darkling* in darkness. 11 *varying . . . world* The world, with its alternation of night and day, is compared to the shore, which varies in extent and outline as the tide ebbs and flows [K]. 19 *importune death*

CLEOPATRA   I dare not, dear.
Dear my lord, pardon! I dare not,
Lest I be taken. Not th' imperious show
Of the full-fortun'd Cæsar ever shall
Be brooch'd with me! If knife, drugs, serpents have   [2
Edge, sting, or operation, I am safe.
Your wife Octavia, with her modest eyes
And still conclusion, shall acquire no honour
Demuring upon me. But come, come, Antony!
Help me, my women. We must draw thee up.   [3
Assist, good friends.
ANTONY   O, quick, or I am gone.
CLEOPATRA   Here's sport indeed! How heavy weighs my lord!
Our strength is all gone into heaviness:
That makes the weight. Had I great Juno's power,
The strong-wing'd Mercury should fetch thee up   [3
And set thee by Jove's side. Yet come a little!
Wishers were ever fools. O, come, come, come!
[*They heave* ANTONY *aloft to* CLEOPATRA.]
And welcome, welcome! Die when thou hast liv'd!
Quicken with kissing. Had my lips that power,
Thus would I wear them out.
ALL   A heavy sight!   [4
ANTONY   I am dying, Egypt, dying.
Give me some wine, and let me speak a little.
CLEOPATRA   No, let me speak; and let me rail so high
That the false huswife Fortune break her wheel,
Provok'd by my offence.
ANTONY   One word, sweet queen.   [4
Of Cæsar seek your honour, with your safety. O!
CLEOPATRA   They do not go together.
ANTONY   Gentle, hear me.
None about Cæsar trust but Proculeius.
CLEOPATRA   My resolution and my hands I'll trust;
None about Cæsar.   [5
ANTONY   The miserable change now at my end
Lament nor sorrow at; but please your thoughts
In feeding them with those my former fortunes,
Wherein I liv'd the greatest prince o' th' world,
The noblest; and do now not basely die,   [5
Not cowardly put off my helmet to

---

awhile beg death to wait a little while [ᴋ].
   23 *imperious show* imperial triumph. 25 *brooch'd* decorated (as with a brooch).
Cleopatra has not forgotten what Antony said about her being the chief ornament of
Cæsar's triumphal procession (IV.xɪɪ.32–39) [ᴋ]. 28 *still conclusion* calm and reasoning
thoughts [ᴋ]. 29 *Demuring* looking down demurely with an air of innocence. 32 *Here's
sport indeed* Bitter and agonized irony. This feat of drawing her lover up to the
window in her monument reminds Cleopatra of the escapades of their happier days
[ᴋ]. 33 *heaviness* grief (with the obvious pun). 37 *Wishers . . . fools* Alluding to
her impossible wish that she had "great Juno's power" [ᴋ]. 38 *Die when . . . liv'd*
die only when you have lived once more. *when* ꜰ¹; ᴘᴏᴘᴇ, ᴋ: "where." 39 *Quicken
with* come to life by. 40 *heavy* woeful. 44 *huswife* hussy. Fortune is often called a
harlot because of the inconstancy of her favours [ᴋ]. 45 *offence* insulting language.

My countryman—a Roman by a Roman
Valiantly vanquish'd. Now my spirit is going.
I can no more.
CLEOPATRA   Noblest of men, woo't die?
Hast thou no care of me? Shall I abide   [*60*
In this dull world, which in thy absence is
No better than a sty? O, see, my women,   [ANTONY *dies*.]
The crown o' th' earth doth melt. My lord!
O, wither'd is the garland of the war,
The soldier's pole is fall'n! Young boys and girls   [*65*
Are level now with men. The odds is gone,
And there is nothing left remarkable
Beneath the visiting moon.   [*Swoons*.]
CHARMIAN   O, quietness, lady!
IRAS   She's dead too, our sovereign.
CHARMIAN   Lady!
IRAS   Madam!
CHARMIAN   O madam, madam, madam!
IRAS   Royal Egypt!   [*70*
Empress!
CHARMIAN   Peace, peace, Iras!
CLEOPATRA   No more but e'en a woman, and commanded
By such poor passion as the maid that milks
And does the meanest chares. It were for me   [*75*
To throw my sceptre at the injurious gods,
To tell them that this world did equal theirs
Till they had stol'n our jewel. All 's but naught.
Patience is sottish, and impatience does
Become a dog that's mad. Then is it sin   [*80*
To rush into the secret house of death
Ere death dare come to us? How do you, women?
What, what! good cheer! Why, how now, Charmian?
My noble girls! Ah, women, women, look!
Our lamp is spent, it's out! Good sirs, take heart.   [*85*
We'll bury him; and then, what's brave, what's noble,
Let's do it after the high Roman fashion
And make death proud to take us. Come, away!
This case of that huge spirit now is cold.

---

59 *woo't* wilt thou. 63 *crown o' th' earth* highest achievement of which earth
was capable—the greatest man ever born. 64 *garland of the war* the most perfect of all
soldiers. 65 *The soldier's pole* There is no joy for soldiers any more in this world [K].
Shakespeare seems to be thinking of the traditional maypole festivities in which boys
and girls danced about a pole garlanded with flowers. Now that the "pole" has fallen,
there is no centre of joy for young people to look to. 66 *level* equal. *The odds* the
difference; that which distinguished Antony was so immensely superior to all other
men that, now that he is dead, the differences between individuals are too slight to be
noted [K]. 67 *remarkable* worthy of special note [K]. 73 *e'en a woman* merely an
ordinary woman—not an Empress. *e'en* JOHNSON; F¹: "in." 75 *chares* chores, menial
tasks. *It were for me* if I were still a queen, it would befit me [K]. 76 *injurious* un-
justly hostile [K]. 79 *Patience* calm endurance. *sottish* becoming only to a fool (a
sot). 79–80 *does Become* is appropriate to. 85 *Our lamp* the torch that lighted our
lives [K]. *spent* used up. *Good sirs* Cleopatra is still addressing her women. "Sirs"
was sometimes used as a feminine vocative [K]. 86 *brave* fine, splendid. 89 *The case
of* the body which contained.

Ah, women, women! Come; we have no friend
But resolution and the briefest end.
[*Exeunt, bearing off* ANTONY's *body.*]

ACT FIVE

Scene 1

[*Alexandria.* CÆSAR's *camp.*]

[*Enter* CÆSAR, AGRIPPA, DOLABELLA, MÆCENAS, (GALLUS, PROCULEIUS, *and others*), *his* COUNCIL OF WAR.]

CÆSAR   Go to him, Dolabella; bid him yield.
Being so frustrate, tell him he mocks
The pauses that he makes.

DOLABELLA   Cæsar, I shall. [*Exit.*]
[*Enter* DERCETAS, *with the sword of* ANTONY.]

CÆSAR   Wherefore is that? And what art thou that dar'st
Appear thus to us?

DERCETAS   I am call'd Dercetas.
Mark Antony I serv'd, who best was worthy
Best to be serv'd. Whilst he stood up and spoke,
He was my master, and I wore my life
To spend upon his haters. If thou please
To take me to thee, as I was to him
I'll be to Cæsar; if thou pleasest not,
I yield thee up my life.

CÆSAR   What is't thou say'st?

DERCETAS   I say, O Cæsar, Antony is dead.

CÆSAR   The breaking of so great a thing should make
A greater crack. The round world
Should have shook lions into civil streets
And citizens to their dens. The death of Antony
Is not a single doom; in the name lay
A moiety of the world.

DERCETAS   He is dead, Cæsar,
Not by a public minister of justice
Nor by a hired knife; but that self hand
Which writ his honour in the acts it did
Hath, with the courage which the heart did lend it,
Splitted the heart. This is his sword.

V.I. 2 *frustrate* baffled. 2–3 *mocks . . . makes* makes his own hesitation ridiculous. Each fresh delay (to give himself up) is but a mockery of a refusal, since surrender is inevitable [K]. 5 *thus* with a sword drawn and bloody. Cæsar has ample reason to suspect an attempt upon his life. 14 *breaking . . . thing* (a) revelation of so momentous a piece of news (b) destruction of so great a man. 15 *crack* Shakespeare is thinking of the "crack of doom" with which the end of the world was supposedly to be heralded. 16 *shook* as with an earthquake. These are some of the traditional "signs of doom" believed to immediately precede the ending of the world. *civil streets* the streets of cities. 19 *moiety* half. 21 *self* selfsame.
27 *but it is* if it is not. 28–30 *And strange . . . deeds* THEOBALD; F¹: gives both

I robb'd his wound of it. Behold it stain'd [25
With his most noble blood.
CÆSAR   Look you sad, friends?
The gods rebuke me but it is tidings
To wash the eyes of kings!
AGRIPPA   And strange it is
That nature must compel us to lament
Our most persisted deeds.
MÆCENAS   His taints and honours [30
Wag'd equal with him.
AGRIPPA   A rarer spirit never
Did steer humanity; but you gods will give us
Some faults to make us men. Cæsar is touch'd.
MÆCENAS   When such a spacious mirror's set before him,
He needs must see himself.
CÆSAR   O Antony, [35
I have followed thee to this! But we do lanch
Diseases in our bodies. I must perforce
Have shown to thee such a declining day
Or look on thine: we could not stall together
In the whole world. But yet let me lament [40
With tears as sovereign as the blood of hearts
That thou, my brother, my competitor
In top of all design, my mate in empire,
Friend and companion in the front of war,
The arm of mine own body, and the heart [45
Where mine his thoughts did kindle—that our stars,
Unreconciliable, should divide
Our equalness to this. Hear me, good friends—
[*Enter an* EGYPTIAN.]
But I will tell you at some meeter season.
The business of this man looks out of him; [50
We'll hear him what he says. Whence are you?
EGYPTIAN   A poor Egyptian yet. The Queen my mistress,
Confin'd in all she has, her monument,
Of thy intents desires instruction,
That she preparedly may frame herself [55
To th' way she's forced to.
CÆSAR   Bid her have good heart.
She soon shall know of us, by some of ours,
How honourable and how kindly we
Determine for her; for Cæsar cannot live

---

this speech and lines 31–3 to Dolabella. 30 *Our most persisted deeds* the results
we laboured most persistently to accomplish [K]. 31 *Wag'd equal with him* ruled
him in equal measure; were evenly balanced in him. 32 *steer humanity* guide
and govern any man [K]. *will give us* are determined to give us mortals [K]. 36 *I
have . . . to this* this is the result of my pursuit of thee. *lanch* lance (a surgical term).
39–40 *we could not . . . whole world* the world was not large enough for both of us
[K]. *stall* dwell. 41 *sovereign* potent and precious [K]. 42 *competitor* partner. 43 *In
top of all design* in the loftiest enterprises in which men can engage [K]. 46 *his* its.
47–8 *should divide . . . to this* should divide our equal partnership to such an extent
(that one of us must die). 49 *meeter* more fitting. 50 *looks out of him* shows itself
in his eyes [K]. 52 *yet* Emphatic. The messenger implies that, if Cæsar wills it, the
very name of Egyptian will soon cease to exist as that of a distinct nationality [K]. 55

To be ungentle.

EGYPTIAN   So the gods preserve thee!   [*Exit.*]   [6

CÆSAR   Come hither, Proculeius. Go and say
We purpose her no shame. Give her what comforts
The quality of her passion shall require,
Lest, in her greatness, by some mortal stroke
She do defeat us; for her life in Rome   [6
Would be eternal in our triumph. Go,
And with your speediest bring us what she says
And how you find of her.

PROCULEIUS   Cæsar, I shall.   [*Exit.*]

CÆSAR   Gallus, go you along. Where's Dolabella,   [*Exit* GALLUS.]
To second Proculeius?

ALL   Dolabella!   [7

CÆSAR   Let him alone, for I remember now
How he's employ'd. He shall in time be ready.
Go with me to my tent; where you shall see
How hardly I was drawn into this war,
How calm and gentle I proceeded still   [7
In all my writings. Go with me and see
What I can show in this.   [*Exeunt.*]

Scene II

[*Alexandria. The monument.*]

[*Enter* CLEOPATRA, CHARMIAN, IRAS, *and* MARDIAN.]

CLEOPATRA   My desolation does begin to make
A better life. 'Tis paltry to be Cæsar.
Not being Fortune, he's but Fortune's knave,
A minister of her will. And it is great
To do that thing that ends all other deeds,
Which shackles accidents and bolts up change,
Which sleeps, and never palates more the dung,
The beggar's nurse and Cæsar's.

[*Enter* PROCULEIUS.]

PROCULEIUS   Cæsar sends greeting to the Queen of Egypt,
And bids thee study on what fair demands   [1

---

frame herself adapt her course of action [K].   57 *ours* our men.   59 *live* ROWE; F[1]:
"leave."

63 *quality* nature. *passion* grief.   65–6 *her life in Rome . . . triumph* to exhibit
her as a living captive would make my triumphal procession eternally memorable [K].
68 *of* concerning.   76 *writings* dispatches (to Antony) .   V.II. The staging
of this scene has been much debated. Some editors would have
Cleopatra and her followers enter "above," and Proculeius at line 8 enter "below," all
descending only after Cleopatra's capture by Proculeius (or Gallus) and soldiers who
climb a ladder for this purpose at line 35. But there is no reason to doubt that the
entire scene was played upon the platform stage, which was intended to represent a
room inside the monument. Proculeius is admitted into Cleopatra's presence. As a
single emissary, and one whom Antony has urged Cleopatra to trust, there is no reason
why he should not be.   2 *A better life* better, that is, than the life I lived in my prosperity; for now, by acting nobly in disaster, I shall show myself superior to Cæsar [K].
3 *knave* servant.   4 *minister* mere agent.   6 *shackles accidents* fetters every chance (by
making it impossible for anything more to happen to me) [K].   7 *Which sleeps . . .*

Thou mean'st to have him grant thee.
CLEOPATRA   What's thy name?
PROCULEIUS   My name is Proculeius.
CLEOPATRA   Antony
Did tell me of you, bade me trust you; but
I do not greatly care to be deceiv'd,
That have no use for trusting. If your master   [15
Would have a queen his beggar, you must tell him
That majesty, to keep decorum, must
No less beg than a kingdom. If he please
To give me conquer'd Egypt for my son,
He gives me so much of mine own as I   [20
Will kneel to him with thanks.
PROCULEIUS   Be of good cheer;
Y'are fall'n into a princely hand; fear nothing.
Make your full reference freely to my lord,
Who is so full of grace that it flows over
On all that need. Let me report to him   [25
Your sweet dependency, and you shall find
A conqueror that will pray in aid for kindness,
Where he for grace is kneel'd to.
CLEOPATRA   Pray you tell him
I am his fortune's vassal and I send him
The greatness he has got. I hourly learn   [30
A doctrine of obedience, and would gladly
Look him i' th' face.
PROCULEIUS   This I'll report, dear lady.
Have comfort, for I know your plight is pitied
Of him that caus'd it.
    [*Enter* SOLDIERS, *who seize* CLEOPATRA.]
You see how easily she may be surpris'd.   [35
Guard her till Cæsar come.   [*Exit.*]
IRAS   Royal Queen!
CHARMIAN   O Cleopatra! thou art taken, Queen!
CLEOPATRA   Quick, quick, good hands!
    [*Draws a dagger.*]
PROCULEIUS   Hold, worthy lady, hold!
    [*Disarms her.*]
Do not yourself such wrong, who are in this   [40
Reliev'd, but not betray'd.
CLEOPATRA   What, of death too,

Cæsar's for death will give me sleep, and release me forever from all taste of this vile earth, which nourishes beggars as well as Cæsar [K]. 10 *fair demands* requests for favourable terms [K].

14 *care to be deceiv'd* feel anxiety about being deceived; care whether I am deceived in thee or not [K]. 17 *to keep decorum* if it is to observe propriety (by asking nothing unworthy of a queen) [K]. 23 *Make . . . freely* entrust yourself and your fortunes without reserve [K]. 26 *sweet dependency* willing and gracious submission. 27 *pray . . . kindness* ask for help in thinking of kind acts to do. "In" goes with "pray." To "pray in aid" is a law term [K]. 29–30 *I send him . . . has got* I send him, by way of homage, that greatness which he has won by conquering me; I acknowledge that he had subdued my sovereignty and that it now belongs to him [K]. 31 *doctrine* lesson. 34 *Of* by. 35 *You see . . . surpris'd* F[1]; [K], following Plutarch, gives the line to Gallus. *surpris'd* captured. 41 *of death* beguiled (betrayed) of death.

That rids our dogs of languish?

PROCULEIUS   Cleopatra,
Do not abuse my master's bounty by
Th' undoing of yourself. Let the world see
His nobleness well acted, which your death   [4*
Will never let come forth.

CLEOPATRA   Where art thou, death?
Come hither, come! Come, come, and take a queen
Worth many babes and beggars!

PROCULEIUS   O, temperance, lady!

CLEOPATRA   Sir, I will eat no meat; I'll not drink, sir;
If idle talk will once be necessary,   [5*
I'll not sleep neither. This mortal house I'll ruin,
Do Cæsar what he can. Know, sir, that I
Will not wait pinion'd at your master's court
Nor once be chastis'd with the sober eye
Of dull Octavia. Shall they hoist me up   [5.
And show me to the shouting varlotry
Of censuring Rome? Rather a ditch in Egypt
Be gentle grave unto me! Rather on Nilus' mud
Lay me stark-nak'd and let the waterflies
Blow me into abhorring! Rather make   [6*
My country's high pyramides my gibbet
And hang me up in chains!

PROCULEIUS   You do extend
These thoughts of horror further than you shall
Find cause in Cæsar.
    [*Enter* DOLABELLA.]

DOLABELLA   Proculeius,
What thou hast done thy master Cæsar knows,   [6
And he hath sent me for thee. For the Queen,
I'll take her to my guard.

PROCULEIUS   So, Dolabella,
It shall content me best. Be gentle to her.
    [*To* CLEOPATRA] To Cæsar I will speak what you shall please,
If you'll employ me to him.

CLEOPATRA   Say, I would die.   [7*
    [*Exeunt* PROCULEIUS (*and* SOLDIERS).]

DOLABELLA   Most noble Empress, you have heard of me?

CLEOPATRA   I cannot tell.

DOLABELLA   Assuredly you know me.

CLEOPATRA   No matter, sir, what I have heard or known.
You laugh when boys or women tell their dreams;

---

42 *languish* miserable condition caused by disease or injury.   43 *abuse . . . bounty* beguile or cheat my master's generous kindness (by putting it out of his power to exercise it) [K].   44 *undoing* destruction.   46 *come forth* show itself.   48 *Worth . . . beggars* a prize that is more distinguished a victim than a host of the weak creatures that death usually takes [K].   *temperance* control yourself.   50 *If idle . . . necessary* if, for once, I must resort to idle speech rather than to action (parenthetical clause).   53 *wait* attend, as a slave.   *pinion'd* like a bird whose wings have been clipped to prevent it from flying.   56 *varlotry* rabble, mob.   57 *censuring* judging. All Rome will pass judgment on her [K].   60 *Blow me* make me swell up.   61 *pyramides* Accented on the final syllable.   66 *For* as for.   70 *employ me* use my services as a messenger.

Is't not your trick?

DOLABELLA   I understand not, madam.   [75

CLEOPATRA   I dreamt there was an Emperor Antony—
O, such another sleep, that I might see
But such another man!

DOLABELLA   If it might please ye—

CLEOPATRA   His face was as the heav'ns, and therein stuck
A sun and moon, which kept their course and lighted   [80
The little O, the earth.

DOLABELLA   Most sovereign creature—

CLEOPATRA   His legs bestrid the ocean: his rear'd arm
Crested the world. His voice was propertied
As all the tuned spheres, and that to friends;
But when he meant to quail and shake the orb,   [85
He was as rattling thunder. For his bounty,
There was no winter in't; an autumn 'twas
That grew the more by reaping. His delights
Were dolphin-like: they show'd his back above
The element they liv'd in. In his livery   [90
Walk'd crowns and crownets. Realms and islands were
As plates dropp'd from his pocket.

DOLABELLA   Cleopatra—

CLEOPATRA   Think you there was or might be such a man
As this I dreamt of?

DOLABELLA   Gentle madam, no.

CLEOPATRA   You lie, up to the hearing of the gods!   [95
But, if there be or ever were one such,
It's past the size of dreaming. Nature wants stuff
To vie strange forms with fancy; yet, t' imagine
An Antony were nature's piece 'gainst fancy,
Condemning shadows quite.

DOLABELLA   Hear me, good madam.   [100
Your loss is as yourself, great; and you bear it
As answering to the weight. Would I might never
O'ertake pursu'd success but I do feel,
By the rebound of yours, a grief that smites

---

75 *trick* peculiar habit, mannerism. 81 *O, the* STEEVENS; F¹: "o' th'." 83 *Crested* surmounted, dominated (like the raised arm in an heraldic crest) [K]. *was propertied* was of a quality; was as harmonious [K]. 84 *the tuned spheres* the concentric spheres in which (according to the old astronomy) the heavenly bodies are set and which resolve about the earth—the centre of the universe [K]. They make music as they turn, thus echoing the harmony of all creation. 85 *quail* cause to quail, terrify. *the orb* this round earth. 86–8 *For his bounty . . . reaping* as for his generosity, it was inexhaustible—it became the more abundant the more it was exercised [K]. 87 *an autumn 'twas* THEOBALD; F¹: "an Anthony it was." 89–90 *Were dolphin-like . . . liv'd in* as the dolphin shows his back above the water, so Antony rose superior to the pleasures in which he lived [K]. 91 *crownets* coronets (worn by princes, as crowns are worn by kings). Kings and princes were his servants. 92 *plates* silver coins. 95 *up to . . . gods* so loudly that the gods may hear you. 96 *or ever* F²; F¹: "nor ever." 97 *past . . . dreaming* beyond the capability of any dream; no dream can measure up to the reality. 97–100 *Nature . . . quite* Nature lacks material to vie with Imagination in creating wondrous forms; but an Antony (if one could imagine such a man as actually existing) would be Nature's masterpiece in competition with Imagination—a masterpiece that would quite discredit even Imagination's shadowy figures [K]. 102 *answering to* ac-

My very heart at root.
CLEOPATRA   I thank you, sir.   [*10*
Know you what Cæsar means to do with me?
DOLABELLA   I am loth to tell you what I would you knew.
CLEOPATRA   Nay, pray you, sir.
DOLABELLA   Though he be honourable—
CLEOPATRA   He'll lead me, then, in triumph?
DOLABELLA   Madam, he will. I know't.   [*Flourish.*]   [*11*
[*Shout within.*]   "Make way there! Cæsar!"
[*Enter* CÆSAR; PROCULEIUS, GALLUS, MÆCENAS, (SELEUCUS,) *and others of his*
TRAIN.]
CÆSAR   Which is the Queen of Egypt?
DOLABELLA   It is the Emperor, madam.
[CLEOPATRA *kneels.*]
CÆSAR   Arise! You shall not kneel.
I pray you rise. Rise, Egypt.
CLEOPATRA   Sir, the gods   [*11*
Will have it thus. My master and my lord
I must obey.
CÆSAR   Take to you no hard thoughts.
The record of what injuries you did us,
Though written in our flesh, we shall remember
As things but done by chance.
CLEOPATRA   Sole sir o' th' world,   [*12*
I cannot project mine own cause so well
To make it clear; but do confess I have
Been laden with like frailties which before
Have often sham'd our sex.
CÆSAR   Cleopatra, know
We will extenuate rather than enforce.   [*12*
If you apply yourself to our intents,
Which towards you are most gentle, you shall find
A benefit in this change; but if you seek
To lay on me a cruelty by taking
Antony's course, you shall bereave yourself   [*13*
Of my good purposes, and put your children
To that destruction which I'll guard them from
If thereon you rely. I'll take my leave.
CLEOPATRA   And may, through all the world! 'Tis yours, and we,
Your scutcheons and your signs of conquest, shall   [*13*
Hang in what place you please. Here, my good lord.
CÆSAR   You shall advise me in all for Cleopatra.
CLEOPATRA   This is the brief of money, plate, and jewels

cording to.   103 *but I do feel* if I do not feel.   104 *smites* CAPELL; F¹: "suites."
    110 *he will* By thus revealing Cæsar's purpose, Dolabella proves how sincere is the
sympathy he has expressed. He is too deeply moved to play Cæsar's game to the
end [K].   117 *hard thoughts* of me (Cæsar).   121-2 *project . . . it clear* delineate or
explain my own case—my side of the question—well enough to make it clear to you
[K].   125 *extenuate rather than enforce* make light of your offences rather than emphasize them [K].   126 *apply* submit.   *our intents* my purposes.   129-30 *To lay . . . course*
by opposing me, as Antony did, to force me to be cruel [K].   135 *scutcheons* armorial
bearings, hung up as trophies or signs of victory [K].   137 *You shall . . . for Cleopatra*
you shall give me instructions in all things, so far as your own affairs are concerned
[K].   138 *brief* list.

I am possess'd of. 'Tis exactly valued,
Not petty things admitted. Where's Seleucus? [*140*
SELEUCUS Here, madam.
CLEOPATRA This is my treasurer. Let him speak, my lord,
Upon his peril, that I have reserv'd
To myself nothing. Speak the truth, Seleucus.
SELEUCUS Madam, [*145*
I had rather seel my lips than to my peril
Speak that which is not.
CLEOPATRA   What have I kept back?
SELEUCUS Enough to purchase what you have made known.
CÆSAR Nay, blush not, Cleopatra. I approve
Your wisdom in the deed.
CLEOPATRA   See, Cæsar! O, behold, [*150*
How pomp is followed! Mine will now be yours;
And should we shift estates, yours would be mine.
The ingratitude of this Seleucus does
Even make me wild. O slave, of no more trust
Than love that's hir'd! What, goest thou back? Thou shalt [*155*
Go back, I warrant thee; but I'll catch thine eyes,
Though they had wings. Slave, soulless villain, dog!
O rarely base!
CÆSAR   Good Queen, let us entreat you.
CLEOPATRA O Cæsar, what a wounding shame is this,
That thou vouchsafing here to visit me, [*160*
Doing the honour of thy lordiness
To one so meek, that mine own servant should
Parcel the sum of my disgraces by
Addition of his envy! Say, good Cæsar,
That I some lady trifles have reserv'd, [*165*
Immoment toys, things of such dignity
As we greet modern friends withal; and say
Some nobler token I have kept apart
For Livia and Octavia, to induce
Their mediation—must I be unfolded [*170*
With one that I have bred? The gods! It smites me
Beneath the fall I have. [*To* SELEUCUS] Prithee go hence!
Or I shall show the cinders of my spirits
Through th' ashes of my chance. Wert thou a man,
Thou wouldst have mercy on me.
CÆSAR   Forbear, Seleucus. [*175*
[*Exit* SELEUCUS.]
CLEOPATRA Be it known that we, the greatest, are misthought

---

140 *admitted* being allowed me as necessities and therefore omitted from the list
[K]. 146 *seel* sew up (a falconry term) . 151 *How pomp is followed* what faithless followers great personages have [K]. *Mine* my followers. 152 *shift estates* exchange conditions, situations, places in the world [K]. 155 *goest thou back* Seleucus is shrinking
back as Cleopatra advances with uplifted hands [K]. 156 *Go back* get the worst of it
[K]. 163 *Parcel the sum* add an item to the sum total [K]. 164 *envy* malice. 166 *Immoment* of no moment or consequence, valueless. *toys* trinkets. *dignity* value. 167
modern ordinary. *withal* with. 160 *Livia* the wife of Octavius Cæsar. 170 *unfolded*
exposed, betrayed. 171 *With* by. 173–4 *I shall show . . . chance* I shall show some
sparks of my natural spirit, even if my fortunes have been reduced to ashes [K]. 175
Forbear leave us. 176 *misthought* thought ill of, misjudged [K].

For things that others do; and, when we fall,
We answer others' merits in our name,
Are therefore to be pitied.

CÆSAR   Cleopatra,
Not what you have reserv'd, nor what acknowledg'd,   [*18*
Put we i' th' roll of conquest. Still be't yours,
Bestow it at your pleasure; and believe
Cæsar's no merchant, to make prize with you
Of things that merchants sold. Therefore be cheer'd;
Make not your thoughts your prisons. No, dear Queen;   [*18*
For we intend so to dispose you as
Yourself shall give us counsel. Feed and sleep.
Our care and pity is so much upon you
That we remain your friend; and so adieu.

CLEOPATRA   My master and my lord!

CÆSAR   Not so. Adieu.   [*19*
[*Flourish. Exeunt* CÆSAR *and his* TRAIN.]

CLEOPATRA   He words me, girls, he words me, that I should not
Be noble to myself! But hark thee, Charmian.
[*Whispers* CHARMIAN.]

IRAS   Finish, good lady. The bright day is done,
And we are for the dark.

CLEOPATRA   Hie thee again.
I have spoke already, and it is provided.   [*19*
Go put it to the haste.

CHARMIAN   Madam, I will.
[*Enter* DOLABELLA.]

DOLABELLA   Where is the Queen?

CHARMIAN   Behold, sir.   [*Exit.*]

CLEOPATRA   Dolabella!

DOLABELLA   Madam, as thereto sworn, by your command
(Which my love makes religion to obey)
I tell you this: Cæsar through Syria   [*20*
Intends his journey, and within three days
You with your children will he send before.
Make your best use of this. I have perform'd
Your pleasure and my promise.

CLEOPATRA   Dolabella,
I shall remain your debtor.

DOLABELLA   I your servant.   [*20*
Adieu, good Queen; I must attend on Cæsar.

CLEOPATRA   Farewell, and thanks.

---

177 *things that others do* Shifting her ground characteristically, Cleopatra pretends that the omissions in the list of her valuables were made by Seleucus himself with an eye to embezzlement, though she has just admitted her own responsibility for them [K].   178 *We answer . . . in our name* we have to answer for the faults that others have committed in our name [K].   *merits* deserts, either good or bad. 181 *roll of conquest* list of the spoils of victory [K].   182 *Bestow* make use of. 183 *make prize* haggle.   185 *Make not . . . prisons* do not imagine yourself a prisoner. Cæsar implies that the imprisonment that threatens Cleopatra exists in her imagination only [K].   186 *so to dispose you* to make such an arrangement of your affairs [K].   191 *words me* tries to delude me with empty words [K].   192 *be noble* by committing suicide.   195 *it is provided* She has made provisions for the asp.   199 *religion* a religious obligation [K].

[*Exit* (DOLABELLA).]
Now Iras, what think'st thou?

Thou, an Egyptian puppet, shall be shown
In Rome as well as I. Mechanic slaves,
With greasy aprons, rules, and hammers, shall
Uplift us to the view. In their thick breaths,
Rank of gross diet, shall we be enclouded,
And forc'd to drink their vapour. [*210*

IRAS The gods forbid!
CLEOPATRA   Nay, 'tis most certain, Iras. Saucy lictors
Will catch at us like strumpets, and scald rhymers [*215*
Ballad us out o' tune. The quick comedians
Extemporally will stage us and present
Our Alexandrian revels. Antony
Shall be brought drunken forth, and I shall see
Some squeaking Cleopatra boy my greatness [*220*
I' th' posture of a whore.
IRAS O the good gods!
CLEOPATRA   Nay, that's certain.
IRAS   I'll never see't; for I am sure my nails
Are stronger than mine eyes.
CLEOPATRA Why, that's the way
To fool their preparation and to conquer [*225*
Their most absurd intents.
[*Enter* CHARMIAN.]
Now, Charmian!
Show me, my women, like a queen. Go fetch
My best attires. I am again for Cydnus,
To meet Mark Antony. Sirrah Iras, go.
Now, noble Charmian, we'll dispatch indeed; [*230*
And when thou hast done this chare, I'll give thee leave
To play till doomsday.—Bring our crown and all.
[*A noise within.*]

[*Exit* IRAS.]
Wherefore's this noise?
[*Enter a* GUARDSMAN.]
GUARD Here is a rural fellow
That will not be denied your Highness' presence.
He brings you figs. [*235*
CLEOPATRA   Let him come in.
[*Exit* GUARDSMAN.]
What poor an instrument
May do a noble deed! He brings me liberty.

---

208 *puppet* Puppet shows which drew their subjects from contemporary events were very popular in Shakespeare's day. *shall* F¹; F², K: "shalt." 212 *of* because of. 213 *drink* inhale. *vapour* odour. 214 *Saucy* insolent and lascivious. *lictors* Shakespeare seems to equate the lictors (officers) of ancient Rome with the beadles of his own time, whose function it was to whip whores. 215 *scald* scurvy, pitiful—literally, scald-headed [K]. 216 *Ballad us* The ballads or street songs which in Shakespeare's day served to report and comment on remarkable events are often mentioned as adding fresh terrors to misfortune [K] (F²; F¹: "Ballads us"). *quick comedians* quick-witted actors. 220-1 *Some squeaking . . . greatness* some boy actor, with his piping voice, burlesque my majesty [K]. 221 *posture* demeanour. 223 *my nails* F²; F¹: "mine

My resolution's plac'd, and I have nothing
Of woman in me. Now from head to foot
I am marble-constant. Now the fleeting moon   [2
No planet is of mine.
  [*Enter* GUARDSMAN *and* CLOWN *(with basket)* .]
GUARD   This is the man.
CLEOPATRA   Avoid, and leave him.
  [*Exit* GUARDSMAN.]
Hast thou the pretty worm of Nilus there
That kills and pains not?
CLOWN   Truly I have him. But I would not be the party that should desire [2
  you to touch him, for his biting is immortal. Those that do die of it do
  seldom or never recover.
CLEOPATRA   Remember'st thou any that have died on't?
CLOWN   Very many, men and women too. I heard of one of them no longer
  than yesterday; a very honest woman, but something given to lie, as a [2
  woman should not do but in the way of honesty—how she died of the bit-
  ing of it, what pain she felt. Truly, she makes a very good report o' th'
  worm; but he that will believe all that they say shall never be saved by
  half that they do. But this is most falliable, the worm's an odd worm.
CLEOPATRA   Get thee hence; farewell.   [2
CLOWN   I wish you all joy of the worm.
  [*Sets down his basket.*]
CLEOPATRA   Farewell.
CLOWN   You must think this, look you, that the worm will do his kind.
CLEOPATRA   Ay, ay; farewell.
CLOWN   Look you, the worm is not to be trusted but in the keeping of wise [2(
  people; for indeed there is no goodness in the worm.
CLEOPATRA   Take thou no care; it shall be heeded.
CLOWN   Very good. Give it nothing, I pray you, for it is not worth the feeding.
CLEOPATRA   Will it eat me?
CLOWN   You must not think I am so simple but I know the devil himself will [2(
  not eat a woman. I know that a woman is a dish for the gods, if the devil
  dress her not. But truly, these same whoreson devils do the gods great harm
  in their women; for in every ten that they make, the devils mar five.
CLEOPATRA   Well, get thee gone; farewell.
CLOWN   Yes, forsooth, I wish you joy o' th' worm.   [*Exit.*]   [2}
  [*Enter* IRAS *with a robe, crown, etc.*]
CLEOPATRA   Give me my robe, put on my crown. I have
  Immortal longings in me. Now no more
  The juice of Egypt's grape shall moist this lip.
  Yare, yare, good Iras; quick. Methinks I hear
  Antony call. I see him rouse himself   [2}
  To praise my noble act. I hear him mock

Nailes." 227 *Show* display, adorn. 229 *Sirrah* Common in addressing servants [K].
231 *chare* chore, task. 236 *What* how.
   238 *plac'd* fixed, settled. 240 *fleeting moon* a conventional symbol of inconstancy.
241 s.d. *Clown* countryman, rustic. 242 *Avoid* depart. 243 *worm* serpent. 246 *immortal* mortal, deadly (Shakespeare often has his rustics blunder in their speech) .
251 *honesty* chastity (with the obvious quibble involving "lie") . 254 *falliable* The
Clown means "infallible" [K]. 258 *do his kind* act in accordance with its nature.
The simple-minded anxiety of the peasant lest the asp should do someone an
injury gives a touch of vivid reality to the scene. We feel sure that there is a snake in
the basket [K]. 262 *heeded* carefully guarded. 267 *dress* In the culinary sense [K].

The luck of Cæsar, which the gods give men
To excuse their after wrath. Husband, I come!
Now to that name my courage prove my title!
I am fire and air; my other elements   [*280*
I give to baser life. So, have you done?
Come then and take the last warmth of my lips.
Farewell, kind Charmian. Iras, long farewell.
[*Kisses them.* IRAS *falls and dies.*]
Have I the aspic in my lips? Dost fall?
If thou and nature can so gently part,   [*285*
The stroke of death is as a lover's pinch,
Which hurts, and is desir'd. Dost thou lie still?
If thus thou vanishest, thou tell'st the world
It is not worth leave-taking.
CHARMIAN   Dissolve, thick cloud, and rain, that I may say   [*290*
The gods themselves do weep!
CLEOPATRA   This proves me base.
If she first meet the curled Antony,
He'll make demand of her, and spend that kiss
Which is my heaven to have. Come, thou mortal wretch,
[*To an asp, which she applies to her breast.*]
With thy sharp teeth this knot intrinsicate   [*295*
Of life at once untie. Poor venomous fool,
Be angry, and dispatch. O, couldst thou speak,
That I might hear thee call great Cæsar ass
Unpolicied!
CHARMIAN   O Eastern star!
CLEOPATRA   Peace, peace!   [*300*
Dost thou not see my baby at my breast,
That sucks the nurse asleep?
CHARMIAN   O, break! O, break!
CLEOPATRA   As sweet as balm, as soft as air, as gentle—
O Antony! Nay, I will take thee too:
[*Applies another asp to her arm.*]
What should I stay—   [*Dies.*]   [*305*
CHARMIAN   In this wild world? So fare thee well.
Now boast thee, death, in thy possession lies
A lass unparallel'd. Downy windows, close,
And golden Phœbus never be beheld

---

274 *Yare* quickly, nimbly.

277–8 *which the gods . . . wrath* That a man's constant and (as it were) unbridled good fortune makes the gods envious and leads to his sudden downfall is an ancient idea. It persists in a modified form in the feeling that too much good luck is dangerous [K]. 280 *fire and air* Of the four elements these two were considered the lighter and more spiritual, belonging to immortality. *other elements* earth and water, the heavier elements, which remain below. Cleopatra is leaving her mortal body behind and becoming entirely a thing of spirit. 281 *baser life* human life, as distinguished from immortality [K]. 284 *Dost fall* Plutarch records that Cæsar's men found Iras lying dead at Cleopatra's feet. He does not explain her death. Nor does Shakespeare. We are left to infer that she died of grief. There is no warrant for the assumption that she was bitten by the asp [K]. 289 *leave-taking* any ceremony when one departs [K]. 292 *This* the fact that Iras died first [K]. 293 *He'll make . . . kiss* Two explanations are possible: (a) he will inquire about me and for giving him the information give her the kiss that belongs to me (b) he will woo her instead of me and give her the kiss that

Of eyes again so royal! Your crown's awry.
I'll mend it, and then play—   [31
[*Enter the* GUARD, *rustling in.*]
1. GUARD   Where is the Queen?
CHARMIAN   Speak softly, wake her not.
1. GUARD   Cæsar hath sent—
CHARMIAN   Too slow a messenger.
[*Applies an asp.*]
O, come apace, dispatch. I partly feel thee.
1. GUARD   Approach, ho! All's not well. Cæsar's beguil'd.   [31
2. GUARD   There's Dolabella sent from Cæsar. Call him.
1. GUARD   What work is here! Charmian, is this well done?
CHARMIAN   It is well done, and fitting for a princess
Descended of so many royal kings.
Ah, soldier!   [CHARMIAN *dies.*]   [32
[*Enter* DOLABELLA.]
DOLABELLA   How goes it here?
2. GUARD   All dead.
DOLABELLA   Cæsar, thy thoughts
Touch their effects in this. Thyself art coming
To see perform'd the dreaded act which thou
So sought'st to hinder.   [32
[*Shout within.*]   A way there, a way for Cæsar!
[*Enter* CÆSAR *and all his* TRAIN.]
DOLABELLA   O sir, you are too sure an augurer:
That you did fear is done.
CÆSAR   Bravest at the last!
She levell'd at our purposes, and being royal,
Took her own way. The manner of their deaths?
I do not see them bleed.
DOLABELLA   Who was last with them?   [33
1. GUARD   A simple countryman, that brought her figs.
This was his basket.
CÆSAR   Poison'd, then.
1. GUARD   O Cæsar,
This Charmian liv'd but now; she stood and spake.
I found her trimming up the diadem
On her dead mistress. Tremblingly she stood,
And on the sudden dropp'd.   [33
CÆSAR   O noble weakness!
If they had swallow'd poison, 'twould appear
By external swelling; but she looks like sleep,
As she would catch another Antony
In her strong toil of grace.   [34

---

should be mine. 294 *mortal* deadly. 295 *intrinsicate* intricate. This word implies not only (a) that vitality is so closely involved in our bodily frames that death—except by violence—is not a simple matter, but also (b) that life itself is a complicated matter [K]. 298 *Unpolicied* without skill in statecraft or diplomacy (since a mere asp can thwart his best-laid plans) [K]. 305 *What* why. 306 *wild* desert, savage. But the word may be a misprint for "vild," a common form of "vile." 308 *windows* eyelids.   310 *Of* by. *awry* ROWE; F¹: "away." 311 *mend* adjust. *play* play my part. 323–4 *thy thoughts . . . this* what thou didst think would happen is fulfilled in this [K]. 327 *That* what. 328 *Bravest* most magnificent. 329 *levell'd* aimed, guessed. 334 *trim-*

DOLABELLA   Here on her breast
    There is a vent of blood, and something blown;
    The like is on her arm.
1. GUARD   This is an aspic's trail; and these fig leaves
    Have slime upon them, such as th' aspic leaves
    Upon the caves of Nile.   [*345*
CÆSAR   Most probable
    That so she died; for her physician tells me
    She hath pursu'd conclusions infinite
    Of easy ways to die. Take up her bed,
    And bear her women from the monument.
    She shall be buried by Antony.   [*350*
    No grave upon the earth shall clip in it
    A pair so famous. High events as these
    Strike those that make them; and their story is
    No less in pity than his glory which
    Brought them to be lamented. Our army shall   [*355*
    In solemn show attend this funeral,
    And then to Rome. Come, Dolabella, see
    High order in this solemnity.
    [*Exeunt omnes.*]

---

ming up straightening.   339 *As* as if.   340 *toil of grace* snare of beauty.
    342 *vent* discharge. *and something blown* and the spot is somewhat puffed up
[K].   344 *aspic's* asp's.   346 *caves* Apparently Shakespeare imagined the asp as frequent-
ing hollows in the banks of the river [K].   347 *pursu'd conclusions infinite* practised
endless experiments (as reported by Plutarch).   351 *clip* embrace.   353–5 *their story
. . . lamented* the history of such high events causes pity (in the hearers or readers)
no less than it redounds to the glory of him who brought such lamentable things to
pass [K].

MOLIERE
[1622–1673]

Molière, a mordant yet compassionate observer of human absurdity, was born Jean-Baptiste Poquelin, the son of a prosperous upholsterer and interior decorator. After being educated from 1631–1639 by Jesuits at the Collège de Clermont, where he read widely in the works of Plautus and Terence, Jean-Baptiste decided, at the age of twenty-one, to devote his life to the theater. This was a spunky decision since actors had almost no social standing and were generally excommunicated from the Church. He cast his lot with Madeleine Béjart and her family, and together they formed a dramatic company called "L'Illustre Theatre." The company was hardly a success, and Molière (who by this time had changed his name, perhaps to save his family some embarrassment) was actually jailed for his debts. Undiscouraged, he worked hard, learning to be both an actor and a playwright.

The dramatic company left Paris around 1645 and performed in the provinces until 1658, when influential friends encouraged Molière to return to Paris to try his luck at both his arts. On October 24, 1658, performing before the twenty-year-old Louis XIV, Molière proved to be only a passable actor of tragic roles, but when the company performed Molière's own farce, *The Love-Sick Doctor,* as an afterpiece to Corneille's *Nicomède,* all recognized Molière's greatness as a comic writer and as a comic actor. Molière and the company were highly praised by the King and given the right to perform at the Hotel du Petit Bourbon and, later, at the Théatre du Palais Royal, where Molière worked at his arts for the rest of his life.

Molière's great accomplishment was that he raised French comedy to the heights of French tragedy. Such works as *Tartuffe* (1664–1669), *The Doctor in Spite of Himself* (1666), *The Would-Be Gentleman* (1670), *The Learned Ladies* (1672), *The Imaginary Invalid* (1673), and especially *The Misanthrope* (1666) are splendid examples of his comic genius and of his humanity; and in *The Misanthrope,* which examines the problem of the individual and society, Molière wrote one of the most profound comedies of any time.

THE MISANTHROPE

MOLIERE
Translated by Richard Wilbur

CHARACTERS

ALCESTE, *in love with* CELIMENE
PHILINTE, ALCESTE'S *friend*
ORONTE, *in love with* CELIMENE
CELIMENE, ALCESTE'S *beloved*
ELIANTE, CELIMENE'S *cousin*
ARSINOE, *a friend of* CELIMENE'S

ACASTE
CLITANDRE } *marquesses*
BASQUE, CELIMENE'S *servant*
A GUARD *of the Marshalsea*
DUBOIS, ALCESTE'S *valet*

The scene throughout is in Célimène's house at Paris.

ACT ONE

Scene One

[PHILINTE, ALCESTE]
PHILINTE   Now, what's got into you?
ALCESTE   [*Seated*]   Kindly leave me alone.
PHILINTE   Come, come, what is it? This lugubrious tone . . .
ALCESTE   Leave me, I said; you spoil my solitude.

PHILINTE   Oh, listen to me, now, and don't be rude.   [5
ALCESTE   I choose to be rude, Sir, and to be hard of hearing.
PHILINTE   These ugly moods of yours are not endearing;
    Friends though we are, I really must insist . . .
ALCESTE   [*Abruptly rising*] Friends? Friends, you say? Well, cross me off
    your list.
    I've been your friend till now, as you well know;   [10
    But after what I saw a moment ago
    I tell you flatly that our ways must part.
    I wish no place in a dishonest heart.
PHILINTE   Why, what have I done, Alceste? Is this quite just?
ALCESTE   My God, you ought to die of self-disgust.   [15
    I call your conduct inexcusable, Sir,
    And every man of honor will concur.
    I see you almost hug a man to death,
    Exclaim for joy until you're out of breath,
    And supplement these loving demonstrations   [20
    With endless offers, vows, and protestations;
    Then when I ask you "Who was that?", I find
    That you can barely bring his name to mind!
    Once the man's back is turned, you cease to love him,
    And speak with absolute indifference of him!   [25
    By God, I say it's base and scandalous
    To falsify the heart's affections thus;
    If I caught myself behaving in such a way,
    I'd hang myself for shame, without delay.
PHILINTE   It hardly seems a hanging matter to me;   [30
    I hope that you will take it graciously
    If I extend myself a slight reprieve,
    And live a little longer, by your leave.
ALCESTE   How dare you joke about a crime so grave?
PHILINTE   What crime? How else are people to behave?   [35
ALCESTE   I'd have them be sincere, and never part
    With any word that isn't from the heart.
PHILINTE   When someone greets us with a show of pleasure,
    It's but polite to give him equal measure,
    Return his love the best that we know how,   [40

And trade him offer for offer, vow for vow.
ALCESTE   No, no, this formula you'd have me follow,
However fashionable, is false and hollow,
And I despise the frenzied operations
Of all these barterers of protestations,   [*45*
These lavishers of meaningless embraces,
These utterers of obliging commonplaces,
Who court and flatter everyone on earth
And praise the fool no less than the man of worth.
Should you rejoice that someone fondles you,   [*50*
Offers his love and service, swears to be true,
And fills your ears with praises of your name,
When to the first damned fop he'll say the same?
No, no: no self-respecting heart would dream
Of prizing so promiscuous an esteem;   [*55*
However high the praise, there's nothing worse
Than sharing honors with the universe.
Esteem is founded on comparison:
To honor all men is to honor none.
Since you embrace this indiscriminate vice,   [*60*
Your friendship comes at far too cheap a price;
I spurn the easy tribute of a heart
Which will not set the worthy man apart:
I choose, Sir, to be chosen; and in fine,
The friend of mankind is no friend of mine.   [*65*
PHILINTE   But in polite society, custom decrees
That we show certain outward courtesies. . . .
ALCESTE   Ah, no! we should condemn with all our force
Such false and artificial intercourse.
Let men behave like men; let them display   [*70*
Their inmost hearts in everything they say;
Let the heart speak, and let our sentiments
Not mask themselves in silly compliments.
PHILINTE   In certain cases it would be uncouth
And most absurd to speak the naked truth;   [*75*
With all respect for your exalted notions,
It's often best to veil one's true emotions.
Wouldn't the social fabric come undone
If we were wholly frank with everyone?
Suppose you met with someone you couldn't bear;   [*80*
Would you inform him of it then and there?
ALCESTE   Yes.
PHILINTE   Then you'd tell old Emilie it's pathetic
The way she daubs her features with cosmetic
And plays the gay coquette at sixty-four?
ALCESTE   I would.
PHILINTE   And you'd call Dorilas a bore,   [*85*
And tell him every ear at court is lame
From hearing him brag about his noble name?
ALCESTE   Precisely.
PHILINTE   Ah, you're joking.
ALCESTE   *Au contraire:*
In this regard there's none I'd choose to spare.
All are corrupt; there's nothing to be seen   [*90*

In court or town but aggravates my spleen.
I fall into deep gloom and melancholy
When I survey the scene of human folly,
Finding on every hand base flattery,
Injustice, fraud, self-interest, treachery. . . .   [*95*
Ah, it's too much; mankind has grown so base,
I mean to break with the whole human race.

PHILINTE   This philosophic rage is a bit extreme;
You've no idea how comical you seem;
Indeed, we're like those brothers in the play   [*100*
Called *School for Husbands*,[1] one of whom was prey . . .

ALCESTE   Enough, now! None of your stupid similes.

PHILINTE   Then let's have no more tirades, if you please.
The world won't change, whatever you say or do;
And since plain speaking means so much to you,   [*105*
I'll tell you plainly that by being frank
You've earned the reputation of a crank,
And that you're thought ridiculous when you rage
And rant against the manners of the age.

ALCESTE   So much the better; just what I wish to hear.   [*110*
No news could be more grateful to my ear.
All men are so detestable in my eyes,
I should be sorry if they thought me wise.

PHILINTE   Your hatred's very sweeping, is it not?

ALCESTE   Quite right: I hate the whole degraded lot.   [*115*

PHILINTE   Must all poor human creatures be embraced,
Without distinction, by your vast distaste?
Even in these bad times, there are surely a few . . .

ALCESTE   No, I include all men in one dim view:
Some men I hate for being rogues; the others   [*120*
I hate because they treat the rogues like brothers,
And, lacking a virtuous scorn for what is vile,
Receive the villain with a complaisant smile.
Notice how tolerant people choose to be
Toward that bold rascal who's at law with me.   [*125*
His social polish can't conceal his nature;
One sees at once that he's a treacherous creature;
No one could possibly be taken in
By those soft speeches and that sugary grin.
The whole world knows the shady means by which   [*130*
The low-brow's grown so powerful and rich,
And risen to a rank so bright and high
That virtue can but blush, and merit sigh.
Whenever his name comes up in conversation,
None will defend his wretched reputation;   [*135*
Call him knave, liar, scoundrel, and all the rest,
Each head will nod, and no one will protest.
And yet his smirk is seen in every house,
He's greeted everywhere with smiles and bows,
And when there's any honor that can be got   [*140*
By pulling strings, he'll get it, like as not.
My God! It chills my heart to see the ways

---

[1] A popular play by Molière.

Men come to terms with evil nowadays;
Sometimes, I swear, I'm moved to flee and find
Some desert land unfouled by humankind.   [*145*
PHILINTE   Come, let's forget the follies of the times
And pardon mankind for its petty crimes;
Let's have an end of rantings and of railings,
And show some leniency toward human failings.
This world requires a pliant rectitude;   [*150*
Too stern a virtue makes one stiff and rude;
Good sense views all extremes with detestation,
And bids us to be noble in moderation.
The rigid virtues of the ancient days
Are not for us; they jar with all our ways   [*155*
And ask of us too lofty a perfection.
Wise men accept their times without objection,
And there's no greater folly, if you ask me,
Than trying to reform society.
Like you, I see each day a hundred and one   [*160*
Unhandsome deeds that might be better done,
But still, for all the faults that meet my view,
I'm never known to storm and rave like you.
I take men as they are, or let them be,
And teach my soul to bear their frailty;   [*165*
And whether in court or town, whatever the scene,
My phlegm's as philosophic as your spleen.[2]
ALCESTE   This phlegm which you so eloquently commend,
Does nothing ever rile it up, my friend?
Suppose some man you trust should treacherously   [*170*
Conspire to rob you of your property,
And do his best to wreck your reputation?
Wouldn't you feel a certain indignation?
PHILINTE   Why, no. These faults of which you so complain
Are part of human nature, I maintain,   [*175*
And it's no more a matter for disgust
That men are knavish, selfish and unjust,
Than that the vulture dines upon the dead,
And wolves are furious, and apes ill-bred.
ALCESTE   Shall I see myself betrayed, robbed, torn to bits,   [*180*
And not . . . Oh, let's be still and rest our wits.
Enough of reasoning, now. I've had my fill.
PHILINTE   Indeed, you would do well, Sir, to be still.
Rage less at your opponent, and give some thought
To how you'll win this lawsuit that he's brought.   [*185*
ALCESTE   I assure you I'll do nothing of the sort.
PHILINTE   Then who will plead your case before the court?
ALCESTE   Reason and right and justice will plead for me.
PHILINTE   Oh, Lord. What judges do you plan to see?[3]
ALCESTE   Why, none. The justice of my cause is clear.   [*190*
PHILINTE   Of course, man; but there's politics to fear. . . .

---

[2] In Renaissance physiology, four fluids of the body—blood, yellow bile, phlegm, and black bile—determined a person's character. A preponderance of phlegm produced a phlegmatic (apathetic) person; too much spleen, an irascible one.

[3] Influencing judges before a trial was a common and accepted practice.

ALCESTE   No, I refuse to lift a hand. That's flat.
   I'm either right, or wrong.
PHILINTE   Don't count on that.
ALCESTE   No, I'll do nothing.
PHILINTE   Your enemy's influence
   Is great you know . . .
ALCESTE   That makes no difference.   [195
PHILINTE   It will; you'll see.
ALCESTE   Must honor bow to guile?
   If so, I shall be proud to lose the trial.
PHILINTE   Oh, really . . .
ALCESTE   I'll discover by this case
   Whether or not men are sufficiently base
   And impudent and villainous and perverse   [200
   To do me wrong before the universe.
PHILINTE   What a man!
ALCESTE   Oh, I could wish, whatever the cost,
   Just for the beauty of it, that my trial were lost.
PHILINTE   If people heard you talking so, Alceste,
   They'd split their sides. Your name would be a jest.   [205
ALCESTE   So much the worse for jesters.
PHILINTE   May I enquire
   Whether this rectitude you so admire,
   And these hard virtues you're enamored of
   Are qualities of the lady whom you love?
   It much surprises me that you, who seem   [210
   To view mankind with furious disesteem,
   Have yet found something to enchant your eyes
   Amidst a species which you so despise.
   And what is more amazing, I'm afraid,
   Is the most curious choice your heart has made.   [215
   The honest Eliante is fond of you,
   Arsinoé, the prude, admires you too;
   And yet your spirit's been perversely led
   To choose the flighty Célimène instead,
   Whose brittle malice and coquettish ways   [220
   So typify the manners of our days.
   How is it that the traits you most abhor
   Are bearable in this lady you adore?
   Are you so blind with love that you can't find them?
   Or do you contrive, in her case, not to mind them?   [225
ALCESTE   My love for that young widow's not the kind
   That can't perceive defects; no, I'm not blind.
   I see her faults, despite my ardent love,
   And all I see I fervently reprove.
   And yet I'm weak; for all her falsity,   [230
   That woman knows the art of pleasing me,
   And though I never cease complaining of her,
   I swear I cannot manage not to love her.
   Her charm outweighs her faults; I can but aim
   To cleanse her spirit in my love's pure flame.   [235
PHILINTE   That's no small task; I wish you all success.
   You think then that she loves you?
ALCESTE   Heavens, yes!
   I wouldn't love her did she not love me.

PHILINTE   Well, if her taste for you is plain to see,
    Why do these rivals cause you such despair?   [*240*
ALCESTE   True love, Sir, is possessive, and cannot bear
    To share with all the world. I'm here today
    To tell her she must send that mob away.
PHILINTE   If I were you, and had your choice to make,
    Eliante, her cousin, would be the one I'd take;   [*245*
    That honest heart, which cares for you alone,
    Would harmonize far better with your own.
ALCESTE   True, true: each day my reason tells me so;
    But reason doesn't rule in love, you know.
PHILINTE   I fear some bitter sorrow is in store;   [*250*
    This love . . .

Scene Two

[ORONTE, ALCESTE, PHILINTE]
ORONTE   [*To* ALCESTE]   The servants told me at the door
    That Eliante and Célimène were out,
    But when I heard, dear Sir, that you were about,
    I came to say, without exaggeration,
    That I hold you in the vastest admiration,   [*5*
    And that it's always been my dearest desire
    To be the friend of one I so admire.
    I hope to see my love of merit requited,
    And you and I in friendship's bond united.
    I'm sure you won't refuse—if I may be frank—   [*10*
    A friend of my devotedness—and rank.
    [*During this speech of* ORONTE'S, ALCESTE *is abstracted, and seems unaware
    that he is being spoken to. He only breaks off his reverie when* ORONTE *says*]
    It was for you, if you please, that my words were intended.
ALCESTE   For me, Sir?
ORONTE   Yes, for you. You're not offended?
ALCESTE   By no means. But this much surprises me. . . .
    The honor comes most unexpectedly. . . .   [*15*
ORONTE   My high regard should not astonish you;
    The whole world feels the same. It is your due.
ALCESTE   Sir . . .
ORONTE   Why, in all the State there isn't one
    Can match your merits; they shine, Sir, like the sun.
ALCESTE   Sir . . .
ORONTE   You are higher in my estimation   [*20*
    Than all that's most illustrious in the nation.
ALCESTE   Sir . . .
ORONTE   If I lie, may heaven strike me dead!
    To show you that I mean what I have said,
    Permit me, Sir, to embrace you most sincerely,
    And swear that I will prize our friendship dearly.   [*25*
    Give me your hand. And now, Sir, if you choose,
    We'll make our vows.
ALCESTE   Sir . . .
ORONTE   What! You refuse?
ALCESTE   Sir, it's a very great honor you extend:
    But friendship is a sacred thing, my friend;

It would be profanation to bestow [30
The name of friend on one you hardly know.
All parts are better played when well-rehearsed;
Let's put off friendship, and get acquainted first.
We may discover it would be unwise
To try to make our natures harmonize. [35

ORONTE   By heaven! You're sagacious to the core;
This speech has made me admire you even more.
Let time, then, bring us closer day by day;
Meanwhile, I shall be yours in every way.
If, for example, there should be anything [40
You wish at court, I'll mention it to the King.
I have his ear, of course; it's quite well known
That I am much in favor with the throne.
In short, I am your servant. And now, dear friend,
Since you have such fine judgment, I intend [45
To please you, if I can, with a small sonnet
I wrote not long ago. Please comment on it,
And tell me whether I ought to publish it.

ALCESTE   You must excuse me, Sir; I'm hardly fit
To judge such matters.

ORONTE   Why not?

ALCESTE   I am, I fear, [50
Inclined to be unfashionably sincere.

ORONTE   Just what I ask; I'd take no satisfaction
In anything but your sincere reaction.
I beg you not to dream of being kind.

ALCESTE   Since you desire it, Sir, I'll speak my mind. [55

ORONTE   *Sonnet*. It's a sonnet. . . . *Hope* . . . The poem's addressed
To a lady who wakened hopes within my breast.
Hope . . . this is not the pompous sort of thing,
Just modest little verses, with a tender ring.

ALCESTE   Well, we shall see.

ORONTE   *Hope* . . . I'm anxious to hear [60
Whether the style seems properly smooth and clear,
And whether the choice of words is good or bad.

ALCESTE   We'll see, we'll see.

ORONTE   Perhaps I ought to add
That it took me only a quarter-hour to write it.

ALCESTE   The time's irrelevant, Sir: kindly recite it. [65

ORONTE   [*Reading*]

Hope comforts us awhile, 'tis true,
Lulling our cares with careless laughter,
And yet such joy is full of rue,
My Phyllis, if nothing follows after.

PHILINTE   I'm charmed by this already; the style's delightful. [70

ALCESTE   [*Sotto voce to* PHILINTE]   How can you say that? Why, the
thing is frightful.

ORONTE

Your fair face smiled on me awhile,
But was it kindness so to enchant me?
'Twould have been fairer not to smile,
If hope was all you meant to grant me. [75

PHILINTE   What a clever thought! How handsomely you phrase it!
ALCESTE   [*Sotto voce to* PHILINTE]   You know the thing is trash. How
    dare you praise it?
ORONTE

> If it's to be my passion's fate   [*80*
> Thus everlastingly to wait,
> Then death will come to set me free:
> For death is fairer than the fair;
> Phyllis, to hope is to despair
> When one must hope eternally.   [*85*

PHILINTE   The close is exquisite—full of feeling and grace.
ALCESTE   [*Sotto voce, aside*]   Oh, blast the close; you'd better close your
    face
Before you send your lying soul to hell.
PHILINTE   I can't remember a poem I've liked so well.   [*90*
ALCESTE   [*Sotto voce, aside*]   Good Lord!
ORONTE   [*To* PHILINTE]   I fear you're flattering me a bit.
PHILINTE   Oh, no!
ALCESTE   [*Sotto voce, aside*]   What else d'you call it, you hypocrite?
ORONTE   [*To* ALCESTE]   But you, Sir, keep your promise now: don't shrink
    From telling me sincerely what you think.   [*95*
ALCESTE   Sir, these are delicate matters; we all desire
    To be told that we've the true poetic fire.
    But once, to one whose name I shall not mention,
    I said, regarding some verse of his invention,
    That gentlemen should rigorously control   [*100*
    That itch to write which often afflicts the soul;
    That one should curb the heady inclination
    To publicize one's little avocation;
    And that in showing off one's works of art
    One often plays a very clownish part.   [*105*
ORONTE   Are you suggesting in a devious way
    That I ought not . . .
ALCESTE   Oh, that I do not say.
    Further, I told him that no fault is worse
    Than that of writing frigid, lifeless verse,
    And that the merest whisper of such a shame   [*110*
    Suffices to destroy a man's good name.
ORONTE   D'you mean to say my sonnet's dull and trite?
ALCESTE   I don't say that. But I went on to cite
    Numerous cases of once-respected men
    Who came to grief by taking up the pen.   [*115*
ORONTE   And am I like them? Do I write so poorly?
ALCESTE   I don't say that. But I told this person, "Surely
    You're under no necessity to compose;
    Why you should wish to publish, heaven knows.
    There's no excuse for printing tedious rot   [*120*
    Unless one writes for bread, as you do not.
    Resist temptation, then, I beg of you;
    Conceal your pastimes from the public view;
    And don't give up, on any provocation,
    Your present high and courtly reputation,   [*125*

To purchase at a greedy printer's shop
The name of silly author and scribbling fop."
These were the points I tried to make him see.
ORONTE   I sense that they are also aimed at me;
But now—about my sonnet—I'd like to be told . . .   [*130*
ALCESTE   Frankly, that sonnet should be pigeonholed.
You've chosen the worst models to imitate.
The style's unnatural. Let me illustrate:

> Followed by, *'Twould have been fairer not to smile!*
> For example, *Your fair face smiled on me awhile,*   [*135*
> Or this: *such joy is full of rue;*
> Or this: *For death is fairer than the fair;*
> Or, *Phyllis, to hope is to despair*
>   *When one must hope eternally!*

This artificial style, that's all the fashion,   [*140*
Has neither taste, nor honesty, nor passion;
It's nothing but a sort of wordy play,
And nature never spoke in such a way.
What, in this shallow age, is not debased?
Our fathers, though less refined, had better taste;   [*145*
I'd barter all that men admire today
For one old love-song I shall try to say:

> If the King had given me for my own
> Paris, his citadel,
> And I for that must leave alone   [*150*
> Her whom I love so well,
> I'd say then to the Crown,
> Take back your glittering town;
> My darling is more fair, I swear,
> My darling is more fair.   [*155*

The rhyme's not rich, the style is rough and old,
But don't you see that it's the purest gold
Beside the tinsel nonsense now preferred,
And that there's passion in its every word?

> If the King had given me for my own   [*160*
> Paris, his citadel,
> And I for that must leave alone
> Her whom I love so well,
> I'd say then to the Crown,
> Take back your glittering town;   [*165*
> My darling is more fair, I swear,
> My darling is more fair.

There speaks a loving heart. [*To* PHILINTE]   You're laughing, eh?
Laugh on, my precious wit. Whatever you say,
I hold that song's worth all the bibelots   [*170*
That people hail today with ah's and oh's.
ORONTE   And I maintain my sonnet's very good.
ALCESTE   It's not at all surprising that you should.
You have your reasons; permit me to have mine

For thinking that you cannot write a line.   [*175*
ORONTE   Others have praised my sonnet to the skies.
ALCESTE   I lack their art of telling pleasant lies.
ORONTE   You seem to think you've got no end of wit.
ALCESTE   To praise your verse, I'd need still more of it.
ORONTE   I'm not in need of your approval, Sir.   [*180*
ALCESTE   That's good; you couldn't have it if you were.
ORONTE   Come now, I'll lend you the subject of my sonnet;
      I'd like to see you try to improve upon it.
ALCESTE   I might, by chance, write something just as shoddy;
      But then I wouldn't show it to everybody.   [*185*
ORONTE   You're most opinionated and conceited.
ALCESTE   Go find your flatterers, and be better treated.
ORONTE   Look here, my little fellow, pray watch your tone.
ALCESTE   My great big fellow, you'd better watch your own.
PHILINTE   [*Stepping between them*]   Oh, please, please, gentlemen!   [*190*
      This will never do.
ORONTE   The fault is mine, and I leave the field to you.
      I am your servant, Sir, in every way.
ALCESTE   And I, Sir, am your most abject valet.

Scene Three

      [PHILINTE, ALCESTE]
PHILINTE   Well, as you see, sincerity in excess
      Can get you into a very pretty mess;
      Oronte was hungry for appreciation. . . .
ALCESTE   Don't speak to me.
PHILINTE   What?
ALCESTE   No more conversation.
PHILINTE   Really, now . . .
ALCESTE   Leave me alone.
PHILINTE   If I . . .
ALCESTE   Out of my sight!   [5
PHILINTE   But what . . .
ALCESTE   I won't listen.
PHILINTE   But . . .
ALCESTE   Silence!
PHILINTE   Now, is it polite . . .
ALCESTE   By heaven, I've had enough. Don't follow me.
PHILINTE   Ah, you're just joking. I'll keep you company.

ACT TWO

Scene One

      [ALCESTE, CELIMENE]
ALCESTE   Shall I speak plainly, Madam? I confess
      Your conduct gives me infinite distress,
      And my resentment's grown too hot to smother.
      Soon, I foresee, we'll break with one another.

If I said otherwise, I should deceive you; [*5*
Sooner or later, I shall be forced to leave you,
And if I swore that we shall never part,
I should misread the omens of my heart.
CELIMENE   You kindly saw me home, it would appear,
So as to pour invectives in my ear. [*10*
ALCESTE   I've no desire to quarrel. But I deplore
Your inability to shut the door
On all these suitors who beset you so.
There's what annoys me, if you care to know.
CELIMENE   Is it my fault that all these men pursue me? [*15*
Am I to blame if they're attracted to me?
And when they gently beg an audience,
Ought I to take a stick and drive them hence?
ALCESTE   Madam, there's no necessity for a stick;
A less responsive heart would do the trick. [*20*
Of your attractiveness I don't complain;
But those your charms attract, you then detain
By a most melting and receptive manner,
And so enlist their hearts beneath your banner.
It's the agreeable hopes which you excite [*25*
That keep these lovers round you day and night;
Were they less liberally smiled upon,
That sighing troop would very soon be gone.
But tell me, Madam, why it is that lately
This man Clitandre interests you so greatly? [*30*
Because of what high merits do you deem
Him worthy of the honor of your esteem?
Is it that your admiring glances linger
On the splendidly long nail of his little finger?
Or do you share the general deep respect [*35*
For the blond wig he chooses to affect?
Are you in love with his embroidered hose?
Do you adore his ribbons and his bows?
Or is it that this paragon bewitches
Your tasteful eye with his vast German breeches? [*40*
Perhaps his giggle, or his falsetto voice,
Makes him the latest gallant of your choice? [4]
CELIMENE   You're much mistaken to resent him so.
Why I put up with him you surely know:
My lawsuit's very shortly to be tried, [*45*
And I must have his influence on my side.
ALCESTE   Then lose your lawsuit, Madam, or let it drop;
Don't torture me by humoring such a fop.
CELIMENE   You're jealous of the whole world, Sir.
ALCESTE   That's true,
Since the whole world is well-received by you. [*50*
CELIMENE   That my good nature is so unconfined
Should serve to pacify your jealous mind;
Were I to smile on one, and scorn the rest,
Then you might have some cause to be distressed.
ALCESTE   Well, if I mustn't be jealous, tell me, then, [*55*

---

[4] Molière often ridicules the fops found in fashionable society.

Just how I'm better treated than other men.
CELIMENE   You know you have my love. Will that not do?
ALCESTE   What proof have I that what you say is true?
CELIMENE   I would expect, Sir, that my having said it
    Might give the statement a sufficient credit.   [*60*
ALCESTE   But how can I be sure that you don't tell
    The selfsame thing to other men as well?
CELIMENE   What a gallant speech! How flattering to me!
    What a sweet creature you make me out to be!
    Well then, to save you from the pangs of doubt,   [*65*
    All that I've said I hereby cancel out;
    Now, none but yourself shall make a monkey of you:
    Are you content?
ALCESTE   Why, why am I doomed to love you?
    I swear that I shall bless the blissful hour
    When this poor heart's no longer in your power!   [*70*
    I make no secret of it: I've done my best
    To exorcise this passion from my breast;
    But thus far all in vain; it will not go;
    It's for my sins that I must love you so.
CELIMENE   Your love for me is matchless, Sir; that's clear.   [*75*
ALCESTE   Indeed, in all the world it has no peer;
    Words can't describe the nature of my passion,
    And no man ever loved in such a fashion.
CELIMENE   Yes, it's a brand-new fashion, I agree:
    You show your love by castigating me,   [*80*
    And all your speeches are enraged and rude.
    I've never been so furiously wooed.
ALCESTE   Yet you could calm that fury, if you chose.
    Come, shall we bring our quarrels to a close?
    Let's speak with open hearts, then, and begin . . .   [*85*

Scene Two

[CELIMENE, ALCESTE, BASQUE]
CELIMENE   What is it?
BASQUE   Acaste is here.
CELIMENE   Well, send him in.

Scene Three

[CELIMENE, ALCESTE]
ALCESTE   What! Shall we never be alone at all?
    You're always ready to receive a call,
    And you can't bear, for ten ticks of the clock,
    Not to keep open house for all who knock.
CELIMENE   I couldn't refuse him: he'd be most put out.   [*5*
ALCESTE   Surely that's not worth worrying about.
CELIMENE   Acaste would never forgive me if he guessed
    That I consider him a dreadful pest.
ALCESTE   If he's a pest, why bother with him then?
CELIMENE   Heavens! One can't antagonize such men;   [*10*
    Why, they're the chartered gossips of the court,
    And have a say in things of every sort.

One must receive them, and be full of charm;
They're no great help, but they can do you harm,
And though your influence be ever so great, [*15*
They're hardly the best people to alienate.
ALCESTE   I see, dear lady, that you could make a case
For putting up with the whole human race;
These friendships that you calculate so nicely . . .

Scene Four

[ALCESTE, CELIMENE, BASQUE]
BASQUE   Madam, Clitandre is here as well.
ALCESTE   Precisely.
CELIMENE   Where are you going?
ALCESTE   Elsewhere.
CELIMENE   Stay.
ALCESTE   No, no.
CELIMENE   Stay, Sir.
ALCESTE   I can't.
CELIMENE   I wish it.
ALCESTE   No, I must go.
I beg you, Madam, not to press the matter;
You know I have no taste for idle chatter. [*5*
CELIMENE   Stay: I command you.
ALCESTE   No, I cannot stay.
CELIMENE   Very well; you have my leave to go away.

Scene Five

[ELIANTE, PHILINTE, ACASTE, CLITANDRE, ALCESTE, CELIMENE, BASQUE]
ELIANTE   [*To* CELIMENE]   The Marquesses have kindly come to call.
Were they announced?
CELIMENE   Yes. Basque, bring chairs for all.
                   [BASQUE *provides the chairs, and exits*]
[*To* ALCESTE]
You haven't gone?
ALCESTE   No; and I shan't depart
Till you decide who's foremost in your heart.
CELIMENE   Oh, hush.
ALCESTE   It's time to choose; take them, or me. [*5*
CELIMENE   You're mad.
ALCESTE   I'm not, as you shall shortly see.
CELIMENE   Oh?
ALCESTE   You'll decide.
CELIMENE   You're joking now, dear friend.
ALCESTE   No, no; you'll choose; my patience is at an end.
CLITANDRE   Madam, I come from court, where poor Cléonte [*10*
Behaved like a perfect fool, as is his wont.
Has he no friend to counsel him, I wonder,
And teach him less unerringly to blunder?
CELIMENE   It's true, the man's a most accomplished dunce;
His gauche behavior strikes the eye at once; [*15*
And every time one sees him, on my word,
His manner's grown a trifle more absurd.

ACASTE   Speaking of dunces, I've just now conversed
    With old Damon, who's one of the very worst;
    I stood a lifetime in the broiling sun   [20
    Before his dreary monologue was done.
CELIMENE   Oh, he's a wondrous talker, and has the power
    To tell you nothing hour after hour:
    If, by mistake, he ever came to the point,
    The shock would put his jawbone out of joint.   [25
ELIANTE   [*To* PHILINTE]   The conversation takes its usual turn,
    And all our dear friends' ears will shortly burn.
CLITANDRE   Timante's a character, Madam.
CELIMENE   Isn't he, though?
    A man of mystery from top to toe,
    Who moves about in a romantic mist   [30
    On secret missions which do not exist.
    His talk is full of eyebrows and grimaces;
    How tired one gets of his momentous faces;
    He's always whispering something confidential
    Which turns out to be quite inconsequential;   [35
    Nothing's too slight for him to mystify;
    He even whispers when he says "good-by."
ACASTE   Tell us about Géralde.
CELIMENE   That tiresome ass.
    He mixes only with the titled class,
    And fawns on dukes and princes, and is bored   [40
    With anyone who's not at least a lord.
    The man's obsessed with rank, and his discourses
    Are all of hounds and carriages and horses;
    He uses Christian names with all the great,
    And the word Milord, with him, is out of date.   [45
CLITANDRE   He's very taken with Bélise, I hear.
CELIMENE   She is the dreariest company, poor dear.
    Whenever she comes to call, I grope about
    To find some topic which will draw her out,
    But, owing to her dry and faint replies,   [50
    The conversation wilts, and droops, and dies.
    In vain one hopes to animate her face
    By mentioning the ultimate commonplace;
    But sun or shower, even hail or frost
    Are matters she can instantly exhaust.   [55
    Meanwhile her visit, painful though it is,
    Drags on and on through mute eternities,
    And though you ask the time, and yawn, and yawn,
    She sits there like a stone and won't be gone.
ACASTE   Now for Adraste.
CELIMENE   Oh, that conceited elf   [60
    Has a gigantic passion for himself;
    He rails against the court, and cannot bear it
    That none will recognize his hidden merit;
    All honors given to others give offense
    To his imaginary excellence.   [65
CLITANDRE   What about young Cléon? His house, they say,
    Is full of the best society, night and day.
CELIMENE   His cook has made him popular, not he:

It's Cléon's table that people come to see.
ELIANTE   He gives a splendid dinner, you must admit.   [70
CELIMENE   But must he serve himself along with it?
    For my taste, he's a most insipid dish
    Whose presence sours the wine and spoils the fish.
PHILINTE   Damis, his uncle, is admired no end.
    What's your opinion, Madam?
CELIMENE   Why, he's my friend.   [75
PHILINTE   He seems a decent fellow, and rather clever.
CELIMENE   He works too hard at cleverness, however.
    I hate to see him sweat and struggle so
    To fill his conversation with bon mots.
    Since he's decided to become a wit   [80
    His taste's so pure that nothing pleases it;
    He scolds at all the latest books and plays,
    Thinking that wit must never stoop to praise,
    That finding fault's a sign of intellect,
    That all appreciation is abject,   [85
    And that by damning everything in sight
    One shows oneself in a distinguished light.
    He's scornful even of our conversations:
    Their trivial nature sorely tries his patience;
    He folds his arms, and stands above the battle,   [90
    And listens sadly to our childish prattle.
ACASTE   Wonderful, Madam! You've hit him off precisely.
CLITANDRE   No one can sketch a character so nicely.
ALCESTE   How bravely, Sirs, you cut and thrust at all.
    These absent fools, till one by one they fall: [95
    But let one come in sight, and you'll at once
    Embrace the man you lately called a dunce,
    Telling him in a tone sincere and fervent
    How proud you are to be his humble servant.
CLITANDRE   Why pick on us? Madame's been speaking, Sir,   [100
    And you should quarrel, if you must, with her.
ALCESTE   No, no, by God, the fault is yours, because
    You lead her on with laughter and applause,
    And make her think that she's the more delightful
    The more her talk is scandalous and spiteful.   [105
    Oh, she would stoop to malice far, far less
    If no such claque approved her cleverness.
    It's flatterers like you whose foolish praise
    Nourishes all the vices of these days.
PHILINTE   But why protest when someone ridicules   [110
    Those you'd condemn, yourself, as knaves or fools?
CELIMENE   Why, Sir? Because he loves to make a fuss.
    You don't expect him to agree with us,
    When there's an opportunity to express
    His heaven-sent spirit of contrariness?   [115
    What other people think, he can't abide;
    Whatever they say, he's on the other side;
    He lives in deadly terror of agreeing;
    'Twould make him seem an ordinary being.
    Indeed, he's so in love with contradiction,   [120

He'll turn against his most profound conviction
And with a furious eloquence deplore it,
If only someone else is speaking for it.
ALCESTE   Go on, dear lady, mock me as you please;
You have your audience in ecstasies.   [*125*
PHILINTE   But what she says is true: you have a way
Of bridling at whatever people say;
Whether they praise or blame, your angry spirit
Is equally unsatisfied to hear it.
ALCESTE   Men, Sir, are always wrong, and that's the reason   [*130*
That righteous anger's never out of season;
All that I hear in all their conversation
Is flattering praise or reckless condemnation.
CELIMENE   But . . .
ALCESTE   No, no, Madam, I am forced to state
That you have pleasures which I deprecate,   [*135*
And that these others, here, are much to blame
For nourishing the faults which are your shame.
CLITANDRE   I shan't defend myself, Sir; but I vow
I'd thought this lady faultless until now.
ACASTE   I see her charms and graces, which are many;   [*140*
But as for faults, I've never noticed any.
ALCESTE   I see them, Sir; and rather than ignore them,
I strenuously criticize her for them.
The more one loves, the more one should object
To every blemish, every least defect.   [*145*
Were I this lady, I would soon get rid
Of lovers who approved of all I did,
And by their slack indulgence and applause
Endorsed my follies and excused my flaws.
CELIMENE   If all hearts beat according to your measure,   [*150*
The dawn of love would be the end of pleasure;
And love would find its perfect consummation
In ecstasies of rage and reprobation.
ELIANTE   Love, as a rule, affects men otherwise,
And lovers rarely love to criticize.   [*155*
They see their lady as a charming blur,
And find all things commendable in her.
If she has any blemish, fault, or shame,
They will redeem it by a pleasing name.
The pale-faced lady's lily-white, perforce;   [*160*
The swarthy one's a sweet brunette, of course;
The spindly lady has a slender grace;
The fat one has a most majestic pace;
The plain one, with her dress in disarray,
They classify as *beauté négligée;*   [*165*
The hulking one's a goddess in their eyes,
The dwarf, a concentrate of Paradise;
The haughty lady has a noble mind;
The mean one's witty, and the dull one's kind;
The chatterbox has liveliness and verve,   [*170*
The mute one has a virtuous reserve.
So lovers manage, in their passion's cause,

To love their ladies even for their flaws.[5]
ALCESTE   But I will say . . .
CELIMENE   I think it would be nice.
To stroll around the gallery once or twice.   [*175*
What! You're not going, Sirs?
CLITANDRE AND ACASTE   No, Madam, no.
ALCESTE   You seem to be in terror lest they go.
Do what you will, Sirs; leave, or linger on,
But I shan't go till after you are gone.
ACASTE   I'm free to linger, unless I should perceive   [*180*
Madame is tired, and wishes me to leave.
CLITANDRE   And as for me, I needn't go today
Until the hour of the King's *coucher.*
CELIMENE   [*To* ALCESTE]   You're joking, surely?
ALCESTE   Not in the least; we'll see
Whether you'd rather part with them, or me.   [*185*

Scene Six

[ALCESTE, CELIMENE, ELIANTE, ACASTE, PHILINTE, CLITANDRE, BASQUE]
BASQUE   [*To* ALCESTE]   Sir, there's a fellow here who bids me state
That he must see you, and that it can't wait.
ALCESTE   Tell him that I have no such pressing affairs.
BASQUE   It's a long tailcoat that this fellow wears,
With gold all over.   [*5*
CELIMENE   [*To* ALCESTE]   You'd best go down and see.
Or—have him enter.

Scene Seven

[ALCESTE, CELIMENE, ELIANTE, ACASTE, PHILINTE, CLITANDRE, A GUARD *of the
Marshalsea*]
ALCESTE   [*Confronting the* GUARD]   Well, what do you want with me?
Come in, Sir.
GUARD   I've a word, Sir, for your ear.
ALCESTE   Speak it aloud, Sir; I shall strive to hear.
GUARD   The Marshals have instructed me to say
You must report to them without delay.   [*5*
ALCESTE   Who? Me, Sir?
GUARD   Yes, Sir; you.
ALCESTE   But what do they want?
PHILINTE   [*To* ALCESTE]   To scotch your silly quarrel with Oronte.
CELIMENE   [*To* PHILINTE]   What quarrel?
PHILINTE   Oronte and he have fallen out
Over some verse he spoke his mind about;
The Marshals wish to arbitrate the matter.[6]   [*10*
ALCESTE   Never shall I equivocate or flatter!
PHILINTE   You'd best obey their summons; come, let's go.
ALCESTE   How can they mend our quarrel, I'd like to know?

---

[5] See Lucretius, *De Rerum Natura*, Book IV. Molière, who probably translated
Lucretius' poem as a student, included a paraphrase of a passage here.

[6] Although duels were prohibited by law, they still occurred. The Marshals were
supposed to prevent them.

Am I to make a cowardly retraction,
And praise those jingles to his satisfaction?   [*15*
I'll not recant; I've judged that sonnet rightly.
It's bad.
PHILINTE   But you might say so more politely. . . .
ALCESTE   I'll not back down; his verses make me sick.
PHILINTE   If only you could be more politic!
But come, let's go.
ALCESTE   I'll go, but I won't unsay   [*20*
A single word.
PHILINTE   Well, let's be on our way.
ALCESTE   Till I am ordered by my lord the King
To praise that poem, I shall say the thing
Is scandalous, by God, and that the poet
Ought to be hanged for having the nerve to show it.   [*25*
[*To* CLITANDRE *and* ACASTE, *who are laughing*]
By heaven, Sirs, I really didn't know
That I was being humorous.
CELIMENE   Go, Sir, go;
Settle your business.
ALCESTE   I shall, and when I'm through,
I shall return to settle things with you.

ACT THREE

Scene One

[CLITANDRE, ACASTE]
CLITANDRE   Dear Marquess, how contented you appear;
All things delight you, nothing mars your cheer.
Can you, in perfect honesty, declare
That you've a right to be so debonair?
ACASTE   By Jove, when I survey myself, I find   [*5*
No cause whatever for distress of mind.
I'm young and rich; I can in modesty
Lay claim to an exalted pedigree;
And owing to my name and my condition
I shall not want for honors and position.   [*10*
Then as to courage, that most precious trait,
I seem to have it, as was proved of late
Upon the field of honor, where my bearing,
They say, was very cool and rather daring.
I've wit, of course; and taste in such perfection   [*15*
That I can judge without the least reflection,
And at the theater, which is my delight,
Can make or break a play on opening night,
And lead the crowd in hisses or bravos,
And generally be known as one who knows.   [*20*
I'm clever, handsome, gracefully polite;
My waist is small, my teeth are strong and white;

As for my dress, the world's astonished eyes
Assure me that I bear away the prize.
I find myself in favor everywhere,   [*25*
Honored by men, and worshiped by the fair;
And since these things are so, it seems to me
I'm justified in my complacency.
CLITANDRE   Well, if so many ladies hold you dear,
Why do you press a hopeless courtship here?   [*30*
ACASTE   Hopeless, you say? I'm not the sort of fool
That likes his ladies difficult and cool.
Men who are awkward, shy, and peasantish
May pine for heartless beauties, if they wish,
Grovel before them, bear their cruelties,   [*35*
Woo them with tears and sighs and bended knees,
And hope by dogged faithfulness to gain
What their poor merits never could obtain.
For men like me, however, it makes no sense
To love on trust, and foot the whole expense.   [*40*
Whatever any lady's merits be,
I think, thank God, that I'm as choice as she;
That if my heart is kind enough to burn
For her, she owes me something in return;
And that in any proper love affair   [*45*
The partners must invest an equal share.
CLITANDRE   You think, then, that our hostess favors you?
ACASTE   I've reason to believe that that is true.
CLITANDRE   How did you come to such a mad conclusion?
You're blind, dear fellow. This is sheer delusion.   [*50*
ACASTE   All right, then: I'm deluded and I'm blind.
CLITANDRE   Whatever put the notion in your mind?
ACASTE   Delusion.
CLITANDRE   What persuades you that you're right?
ACASTE   I'm blind.
CLITANDRE   But have you any proofs to cite?
ACASTE   I tell you I'm deluded.
CLITANDRE   Have you, then,   [*55*
Received some secret pledge from Célimène?
ACASTE   Oh, no: she scorns me.
CLITANDRE   Tell me the truth, I beg.
ACASTE   She just can't bear me.
CLITANDRE   Ah, don't pull my leg.
Tell me what hope she's given you, I pray.
ACASTE   I'm hopeless, and it's you who win the day.   [*60*
She hates me thoroughly, and I'm so vexed
I mean to hang myself on Tuesday next.
CLITANDRE   Dear Marquess, let us have an armistice
And make a treaty. What do you say to this?
If ever one of us can plainly prove   [*65*
That Célimène encourages his love,
The other must abandon hope, and yield,
And leave him in possession of the field.
ACASTE   Now, there's a bargain that appeals to me;
With all my heart, dear Marquess, I agree.   [*70*
But hush.

Scene Two

[CELIMENE, ACASTE, CLITANDRE]
CELIMENE   Still here?
CLITANDRE   T'was love that stayed our feet.
CELIMENE   I think I heard a carriage in the street.
   Whose is it? D'you know?

Scene Three

[CELIMENE, ACASTE, CLITANDRE, BASQUE]
BASQUE   Arsinoé is here,
   Madame.
CELIMENE   Arsinoé, you say? Oh, dear.
BASQUE   Eliante is entertaining her below.
CELIMENE   What brings the creature here, I'd like to know?   [5
ACASTE   They say she's dreadfully prudish, but in fact
   I think her piety . . .
CELIMENE   It's all an act.
   At heart she's worldly, and her poor success
   In snaring men explains her prudishness.
   It breaks her heart to see the beaux and gallants   [10
   Engrossed by other women's charms and talents,
   And so she's always in a jealous rage
   Against the faulty standards of the age.
   She lets the world believe that she's a prude
   To justify her loveless solitude,   [15
   And strives to put a brand of moral shame
   On all the graces that she cannot claim.
   But still she'd love a lover; and Alceste
   Appears to be the one she'd love the best.
   His visits here are poison to her pride;   [20
   She seems to think I've lured him from her side;
   And everywhere, at court or in the town,
   The spiteful, envious woman runs me down.
   In short, she's just as stupid as can be,
   Vicious and arrogant in the last degree,   [25
   And . . .

Scene Four

[ARSINOE, CELIMENE, CLITANDRE, ACASTE]
CELIMENE   Ah! What happy chance has brought you here?
   I've thought about you ever so much, my dear.
ARSINOE   I've come to tell you something you should know.
CELIMENE   How good of you to think of doing so!
                       [CLITANDRE *and* ACASTE *go out, laughing*]

Scene Five

[ARSINOE, CELIMENE]
ARSINOE   It's just as well those gentlemen didn't tarry.
CELIMENE   Shall we sit down?
ARSINOE   That won't be necessary.

Madam, the flame of friendship ought to burn
Brightest in matters of the most concern,
And as there's nothing which concerns us more   [5
Than honor, I have hastened to your door
To bring you, as your friend, some information
About the status of your reputation.
I visited, last night, some virtuous folk,
And, quite by chance, it was of you they spoke;   [10
There was, I fear, no tendency to praise
Your light behavior and your dashing ways.
The quantity of gentlemen you see
And your by now notorious coquetry
Were both so vehemently criticized   [15
By everyone, that I was much surprised.
Of course, I needn't tell you where I stood;
I came to your defense as best I could,
Assured them you were harmless, and declared
Your soul was absolutely unimpaired.   [20
But there are some things, you must realize,
One can't excuse, however hard one tries,
And I was forced at last into conceding
That your behavior, Madam, is misleading,
That it makes a bad impression, giving rise   [25
To ugly gossip and obscene surmise,
And that if you were more *overtly* good,
You wouldn't be so much misunderstood.
Not that I think you've been unchaste—no! no!
The saints preserve me from a thought so low!   [30
But mere good conscience never did suffice:
One must avoid the outward show of vice.
Madam, you're too intelligent, I'm sure,
To think my motives anything but pure
In offering you this counsel—which I do   [35
Out of a zealous interest in you.
CELIMENE   Madam, I haven't taken you amiss;
I'm very much obliged to you for this;
And I'll at once discharge the obligation
By telling you about *your* reputation.   [40
You've been so friendly as to let me know
What certain people say of me, and so
I mean to follow your benign example
By offering you a somewhat similar sample.
The other day, I went to an affair   [45
And found some most distinguished people there
Discussing piety, both false and true.
The conversation soon came round to you.
Alas! Your prudery and bustling zeal
Appeared to have a very slight appeal.   [50
Your affectation of a grave demeanor,
Your endless talk of virtue and of honor,
The aptitude of your suspicious mind
For finding sin where there is none to find,
Your towering self-esteem, that pitying face   [55

With which you contemplate the human race,
Your sermonizings and your sharp aspersions
On people's pure and innocent diversions—
All these were mentioned, Madam, and, in fact,
Were roundly and concertedly attacked.   [60
"What good," they said, "are all these outward shows,
When everything belies her pious pose?
She prays incessantly; but then, they say,
She beats her maids and cheats them of their pay;
She shows her zeal in every holy place,   [65
But still she's vain enough to paint her face;
She holds that naked statues are immoral,
But with a naked *man* she'd have no quarrel."
Of course, I said to everybody there
That they were being viciously unfair;   [70
But still they were disposed to criticize you,
And all agreed that someone should advise you
To leave the morals of the world alone,
And worry rather more about your own.
They felt that one's self-knowledge should be great   [75
Before one thinks of setting others straight;
That one should learn the art of living well
Before one threatens other men with hell,
And that the Church is best equipped, no doubt,
To guide our souls and root our vices out.   [80
Madam, you're too intelligent, I'm sure,
To think my motives anything but pure
In offering you this counsel—which I do
Out of a zealous interest in you.
ARSINOE   I dared not hope for gratitude, but I   [85
Did not expect so acid a reply;
I judge, since you've been so extremely tart,
That my good counsel pierced you to the heart.
CELIMENE   Far from it, Madam. Indeed, it seems to me
We ought to trade advice more frequently.   [90
One's vision of oneself is so defective
That it would be an excellent corrective.
If you are willing, Madam, let's arrange
Shortly to have another frank exchange
In which we'll tell each other, *entre nous,*   [95
What you've heard tell of me, and I of you.
ARSINOE   Oh, people never censure you, my dear;
It's me they criticize. Or so I hear.
CELIMENE   Madam, I think we either blame or praise
According to our taste and length of days.   [100
There is a time of life for coquetry,
And there's a season, too, for prudery.
When all one's charms are gone, it is, I'm sure,
Good strategy to be devout and pure:
It makes one seem a little less forsaken.   [105
Some day, perhaps, I'll take the road you've taken:
Time brings all things. But I have time aplenty,
And see no cause to be a prude at twenty.

ARSINOE   You give your age in such a gloating tone
    That one would think I was an ancient crone;   [*110*
    We're not so far apart, in sober truth,
    That you can mock me with a boast of youth!
    Madam, you baffle me. I wish I knew
    What moves you to provoke me as you do.
CELIMENE   For my part, Madam, I should like to know   [*115*
    Why you abuse me everywhere you go.
    Is it my fault, dear lady, that your hand
    Is not, alas, in very great demand?
    If men admire me, if they pay me court
    And daily make me offers of the sort   [*120*
    You'd dearly love to have them make to you,
    How can I help it? What would you have me do?
    If what you want is lovers, please feel free
    To take as many as you can from me.
ARSINOE   Oh, come. D'you think the world is losing sleep   [*125*
    Over that flock of lovers which you keep,
    Or that we find it difficult to guess
    What price you pay for their devotedness?
    Surely you don't expect us to suppose
    Mere merit could attract so many beaux?   [*130*
    It's not your virtue that they're dazzled by;
    Nor is it virtuous love for which they sigh.
    You're fooling no one, Madam; the world's not blind;
    There's many a lady heaven has designed
    To call men's noblest, tenderest feelings out,   [*135*
    Who has no lovers dogging her about;
    From which it's plain that lovers nowadays
    Must be acquired in bold and shameless ways,
    And only pay one court for such reward
    As modesty and virtue can't afford.   [*140*
    Then don't be quite so puffed up, if you please,
    About your tawdry little victories;
    Try, if you can, to be a shade less vain,
    And treat the world with somewhat less disdain.
    If one were envious of your amours,   [*145*
    One soon could have a following like yours;
    Lovers are no great trouble to collect
    If one prefers them to one's self-respect.
CELIMENE   Collect them then, my dear; I'd love to see
    You demonstrate that charming theory;   [*150*
    Who knows, you might . . .
ARSINOE   Now, Madam, that will do;
    It's time to end this trying interview.
    My coach is late in coming to your door,
    Or I'd have taken leave of you before.
CELIMENE   Oh, please don't feel that you must rush away;   [*155*
    I'd be delighted, Madam, if you'd stay.
    However, lest my conversation bore you,
    Let me provide some better company for you;
    This gentleman, who comes most apropos,
    Will please you more than I could do, I know.   [*160*

Scene Six

[ALCESTE, CELIMENE, ARSINOE]
CELIMENE   Alceste, I have a little note to write
    Which simply must go out before tonight;
    Please entertain *Madame;* I'm sure that she
    Will overlook my incivility.

Scene Seven

[ALCESTE, ARSINOE]
ARSINOE   Well, Sir, our hostess graciously contrives
    For us to chat until my coach arrives;
    And I shall be forever in her debt
    For granting me this little tête-à-tête.
    We women very rightly give our hearts   [5
    To men of noble character and parts,
    And your especial merits, dear Alceste,
    Have roused the deepest sympathy in my breast.
    Oh, how I wish they had sufficient sense
    At court, to recognize your excellence!   [10
    They wrong you greatly, Sir. How it must hurt you
    Never to be rewarded for your virtue!
ALCESTE   Why, Madam, what cause have I to feel aggrieved?
    What great and brilliant thing have I achieved?
    What service have I rendered to the King   [15
    That I should look to him for anything?
ARSINOE   Not everyone who's honored by the State
    Has done great services. A man must wait
    Till time and fortune offer him the chance.
    Your merit, Sir, is obvious at a glance,   [20
    And . . .
ALCESTE   Ah, forget my merit; I'm not neglected.
    The court, I think, can hardly be expected
    To mine men's souls for merit, and unearth
    Our hidden virtues and our secret worth.
ARSINOE   *Some* virtues, though, are far too bright to hide;   [25
    Yours are acknowledged, Sir, on every side.
    Indeed, I've heard you warmly praised of late
    By persons of considerable weight.
ALCESTE   This fawning age has praise for everyone,
    And all distinctions, Madam, are undone.   [30
    All things have equal honor nowadays,
    And no one should be gratified by praise.
    To be admired, one only need exist,
    And every lackey's on the honors list.
ARSINOE   I only wish, Sir, that you had your eye   [35
    On some position at court, however high;
    You'd only have to hint at such a notion
    For me to set the proper wheels in motion;
    I've certain friendships I'd be glad to use

    To get you any office you might choose.   [*40*
ALCESTE   Madam, I fear that any such ambition
    Is wholly foreign to my disposition.
    The soul God gave me isn't of the sort
    That prospers in the weather of a court.
    It's all too obvious that I don't possess   [*45*
    The virtues necessary for success.
    My one great talent is for speaking plain;
    I've never learned to flatter or to feign;
    And anyone so stupidly sincere
    Had best not seek a courtier's career.   [*50*
    Outside the court, I know, one must dispense
    With honors, privilege, and influence;
    But still one gains the right, foregoing these,
    Not to be tortured by the wish to please.
    One needn't live in dread of snubs and slights,   [*55*
    Nor praise the verse that every idiot writes,
    Nor humor silly Marquesses, nor bestow
    Politic sighs on Madam So-and-So.
ARSINOE   Forget the court, then; let the matter rest.
    But I've another cause to be distressed   [*60*
    About your present situation, Sir.
    It's to your love affair that I refer.
    She whom you love, and who pretends to love you,
    Is, I regret to say, unworthy of you.
ALCESTE   Why, Madam! Can you seriously intend   [*65*
    To make so grave a charge against your friend?
ARSINOE   Alas, I must. I've stood aside too long
    And let that lady do you grievous wrong;
    But now my debt to conscience shall be paid:
    I tell you that your love has been betrayed.   [*70*
ALCESTE   I thank you, Madam; you're extremely kind.
    Such words are soothing to a lover's mind.
ARSINOE   Yes, though she *is* my friend, I say again
    You're very much too good for Célimène.
    She's wantonly misled you from the start.   [*75*
ALCESTE   You may be right; who knows another's heart?
    But ask yourself if it's the part of charity
    To shake my soul with doubts of her sincerity.
ARSINOE   Well, if you'd rather be a dupe than doubt her,
    That's your affair. I'll say no more about her.   [*80*
ALCESTE   Madam, you know that doubt and vague suspicion
    Are painful to a man in my position;
    It's most unkind to worry me this way
    Unless you've some real proof of what you say.
ARSINOE   Sir, say no more: all doubt shall be removed, [*85*
    And all that I've been saying shall be proved.
    You've only to escort me home, and there
    We'll look into the heart of this affair.
    I've ocular evidence which will persuade you
    Beyond a doubt, that Célimène's betrayed you.   [*90*
    Then, if you're saddened by that revelation,
    Perhaps I can provide some consolation.

ACT FOUR

Scene One

[ELIANTE, PHILINTE]

PHILINTE   Madam, he acted like a stubborn child;
I thought they never would be reconciled;
In vain we reasoned, threatened, and appealed;
He stood his ground and simply would not yield.
The Marshals, I feel sure, have never heard   [5
An argument so splendidly absurd.
"No, gentlemen," said he, "I'll not retract.
His verse is bad: extremely bad, in fact.
Surely it does the man no harm to know it.
Does it disgrace him, not to be a poet?   [10
A gentleman may be respected still,
Whether he writes a sonnet well or ill.
That I dislike his verse should not offend him;
In all that touches honor, I commend him;
He's noble, brave, and virtuous—but I fear   [15
He can't in truth be called a sonneteer.
I'll gladly praise his wardrobe; I'll endorse
His dancing, or the way he sits a horse;
But, gentlemen, I cannot praise his rhyme.
In fact, it ought to be a capital crime   [20
For anyone so sadly unendowed
To write a sonnet, and read the thing aloud."
At length he fell into a gentler mood
And, striking a concessive attitude,
He paid Oronte the following courtesies: [25
"Sir, I regret that I'm so hard to please,
And I'm profoundly sorry that your lyric
Failed to provoke me to a panegyric."
After these curious words, the two embraced,
And then the hearing was adjourned—in haste.   [30
ELIANTE   His conduct has been very singular lately;
Still, I confess that I respect him greatly.
The honesty in which he takes such pride
Has—to my mind—its noble, heroic side.
In this false age, such candor seems outrageous;   [35
But I could wish that it were more contagious.
PHILINTE   What most intrigues me in our friend Alceste
Is the grand passion that rages in his breast.
The sullen humors he's compounded of
Should not, I think, dispose his heart to love;   [40
But since they do, it puzzles me still more
That he should choose your cousin to adore.
ELIANTE   It does, indeed, belie the theory
That love is born of gentle sympathy,
And that the tender passion must be based   [45
On sweet accords of temper and of taste.

PHILINTE   Does she return his love, do you suppose?
ELIANTE   Ah, that's a difficult question, Sir. Who knows?
   How can we judge the truth of her devotion?
   Her heart's a stranger to its own emotion.   [*50*
   Sometimes it thinks it loves, when no love's there;
   At other times it loves quite unaware.
PHILINTE   I rather think Alceste is in for more
   Distress and sorrow than he's bargained for;
   Were he of my mind, Madam, his affection   [*55*
   Would turn in quite a different direction,
   And we would see him more responsive to
   The kind regard which he receives from you.
ELIANTE   Sir, I believe in frankness, and I'm inclined,
   In matters of the heart, to speak my mind.   [*60*
   I don't oppose his love for her; indeed,
   I hope with all my heart that he'll succeed,
   And were it in my power, I'd rejoice
   In giving him the lady of his choice.
   But if, as happens frequently enough   [*65*
   In love affairs, he meets with a rebuff—
   If Célimène should grant some rival's suit—
   I'd gladly play the role of substitute;
   Nor would his tender speeches please me less
   Because they'd once been made without success.   [*70*
PHILINTE   Well, Madam, as for me, I don't oppose
   Your hopes in this affair; and heaven knows
   That in my conversations with the man
   I plead your cause as often as I can.
   But if those two should marry, and so remove   [*75*
   All chance that he will offer you his love,
   Then I'll declare my own, and hope to see
   Your gracious favor pass from him to me.
   In short, should you be cheated of Alceste,
   I'd be most happy to be second best.   [*80*
ELIANTE   Philinte, you're teasing.
PHILINTE   Ah, Madam, never fear;
   No words of mine were ever so sincere,
   And I shall live in fretful expectation
   Till I can make a fuller declaration.

Scene Two

[ALCESTE, ELIANTE, PHILINTE]
ALCESTE   Avenge me, Madam! I must have satisfaction,
   Or this great wrong will drive me to distraction!
ELIANTE   Why, what's the matter? What's upset you so?
ALCESTE   Madam, I've had a mortal, mortal blow.
   If Chaos repossessed the universe,   [*5*
   I swear I'd not be shaken any worse.
   I'm ruined. . . . I can say no more. . . . My soul . . .
ELIANTE   Do try, Sir, to regain your self-control.
ALCESTE   Just heaven! Why were so much beauty and grace

Bestowed on one so vicious and so base?   [*10*
ELIANTE   Once more, Sir, tell us. . . . .
ALCESTE   My world has gone to wrack;
   I'm—I'm betrayed; she's stabbed me in the back:
   Yes, Célimène (who would have thought it of her?)
   Is false to me, and has another lover.
ELIANTE   Are you quite certain? Can you prove these things?   [*15*
PHILINTE   Lovers are prey to wild imaginings
   And jealous fancies. No doubt there's some mistake. . . .
ALCESTE   Mind your own business, Sir, for heaven's sake.
   [*To* ELIANTE]
   Madam, I have the proof that you demand
   Here in my pocket, penned by her own hand.   [*20*
   Yes, all the shameful evidence one could want
   Lies in this letter written to Oronte—
   Oronte! whom I felt sure she couldn't love,
   And hardly bothered to be jealous of.
PHILINTE   Still, in a letter, appearances may deceive;   [*25*
   This may not be so bad as you believe.
ALCESTE   Once more I beg you, Sir, to let me be;
   Tend to your own affairs; leave mine to me.
ELIANTE   Compose yourself; this anguish that you feel . . .
ALCESTE   Is something, Madam, you alone can heal.   [*30*
   My outraged heart, beside itself with grief,
   Appeals to you for comfort and relief.
   Avenge me on your cousin, whose unjust
   And faithless nature has deceived my trust;
   Avenge a crime your pure soul must detest.   [*35*
ELIANTE   But how, Sir?
ALCESTE   Madam, this heart within my breast
   Is yours; pray take it; redeem my heart from her,
   And so avenge me on my torturer.
   Let her be punished by the fond emotion,
   The ardent love, the bottomless devotion,   [*40*
   The faithful worship which this heart of mine
   Will offer up to yours as to a shrine.
ELIANTE   You have my sympathy, Sir, in all you suffer;
   Nor do I scorn the noble heart you offer;
   But I suspect you'll soon be mollified,   [*45*
   And this desire for vengeance will subside.
   When some beloved hand has done us wrong
   We thirst for retribution—but not for long;
   However dark the deed that she's committed,
   A lovely culprit's very soon acquitted.   [*50*
   Nothing's so stormy as an injured lover,
   And yet no storm so quickly passes over.
ALCESTE   No, Madam, no—this is no lovers' spat;
   I'll not forgive her; it's gone too far for that;
   My mind's made up; I'll kill myself before   [*55*
   I waste my hopes upon her any more.
   Ah, here she is. My wrath intensifies.
   I shall confront her with her tricks and lies,
   And crush her utterly, and bring you then
   A heart no longer slave to Célimène.   [*60*

Scene Three

[CELIMENE, ALCESTE]

ALCESTE [*Aside*] Sweet heaven, help me to control my passion.

CELIMENE [*Aside*] [*To* ALCESTE] Oh, Lord.
Why stand there staring in that fashion?
And what d'you mean by those dramatic sighs,
And that malignant glitter in your eyes?

ALCESTE I mean that sins which cause the blood to freeze   [5
Look innocent beside your treacheries;
That nothing Hell's or Heaven's wrath could do
Ever produced so bad a thing as you.

CELIMENE Your compliments were always sweet and pretty.

ALCESTE Madam, it's not the moment to be witty.   [10
No, blush and hang your head; you've ample reason,
Since I've the fullest evidence of your treason.
Ah, this is what my sad heart prophesied;
Now all my anxious fears are verified;
My dark suspicion and my gloomy doubt   [15
Divined the truth, and now the truth is out.
For all your trickery, I was not deceived;
It was my bitter stars that I believed.
But don't imagine that you'll go scot-free;
You shan't misuse me with impunity.   [20
I know that love's irrational and blind;
I know the heart's not subject to the mind,
And can't be reasoned into beating faster;
I know each soul is free to choose its master;
Therefore had you but spoken from the heart,   [25
Rejecting my attentions from the start,
I'd have no grievance, or at any rate
I could complain of nothing but my fate.
Ah, but so falsely to encourage me—
That was a treason and a treachery   [30
For which you cannot suffer too severely,
And you shall pay for that behavior dearly.
Yes, now I have no pity, not a shred;
My temper's out of hand; I've lost my head;
Shocked by the knowledge of your double-dealings,   [35
My reason can't restrain my savage feelings;
A righteous wrath deprives me of my senses,
And I won't answer for the consequences.

CELIMENE What does this outburst mean? Will you please explain?
Have you, by any chance, gone quite insane?   [40

ALCESTE Yes, yes, I went insane the day I fell
A victim to your black and fatal spell,
Thinking to meet with some sincerity
Among the treacherous charms that beckoned me.

CELIMENE Pooh. Of what treachery can you complain?   [45

ALCESTE How sly you are, how cleverly you feign!
But you'll not victimize me any more.
Look: here's a document you've seen before.
This evidence, which I acquired today,
Leaves you, I think, without a thing to say.   [50

CELIMENE   Is this what sent you into such a fit?
ALCESTE   You should be blushing at the sight of it.
CELIMENE   Ought I to blush? I truly don't see why.
ALCESTE   Ah, now you're being bold as well as sly;
    Since there's no signature, perhaps you'll claim . . .   [55
CELIMENE   I wrote it, whether or not it bears my name.
ALCESTE   And you can view with equanimity
    This proof of your disloyalty to me!
CELIMENE   Oh, don't be so outrageous and extreme.
ALCESTE   You take this matter lightly, it would seem.   [60
    Was it no wrong to me, no shame to you,
    That you should send Oronte this billet-doux?
CELIMENE   Oronte! Who said it was for him?
ALCESTE   Why, those
    Who brought me this example of your prose.
    But what's the difference? If you wrote the letter   [65
    To someone else, it pleases me no better.
    My grievance and your guilt remain the same.
CELIMENE   But need you rage, and need I blush for shame,
    If this was written to a *woman* friend?
ALCESTE   Ah, Most ingenious. I'm impressed no end;   [70
    And after that incredible evasion
    Your guilt is clear. I need no more persuasion.
    How dare you try so clumsy a deception?
    D'you think I'm wholly wanting in perception?
    Come, come, let's see how brazenly you'll try   [75
    To bolster up so palpable a lie:
    Kindly construe this ardent closing section
    As nothing more than sisterly affection!
    Here, let me read it. Tell me, if you dare to,
    That this is for a woman . . .
CELIMENE   I don't care to.   [80
    What right have you to badger and berate me,
    And so highhandedly interrogate me?
ALCESTE   Now, don't be angry; all I ask of you
    Is that you justify a phrase or two . . .
CELIMENE   No, I shall not. I utterly refuse,   [85
    And you may take those phrases as you choose.
ALCESTE   Just show me how this letter could be meant
    For a woman's eyes, and I shall be content.
CELIMENE   No, no, it's for Oronte; you're perfectly right.
    I welcome his attentions with delight,   [90
    I prize his character and his intellect,
    And everything is just as you suspect.
    Come, do your worst now; give your rage free rein;
    But kindly cease to bicker and complain.
ALCESTE   [*Aside*]   Good God! Could anything be more inhuman?   [95
    Was ever a heart so mangled by a woman?
    When I complain of how she has betrayed me,
    She bridles, and commences to upbraid me!
    She tries my tortured patience to the limit;
    She won't deny her guilt; she glories in it!   [100
    And yet my heart's too faint and cowardly
    To break these chains of passion, and be free,

To scorn her as it should, and rise above
This unrewarded, mad, and bitter love.
[*To* CELIMENE]
Ah, traitress, in how confident a fashion   [*105*
You take advantage of my helpless passion,
And use my weakness for your faithless charms
To make me once again throw down my arms!
But do at least deny this black transgression;
Take back that mocking and perverse confession;   [*110*
Defend this letter and your innocence,
And I, poor fool, will aid in your defense.
Pretend, pretend, that you are just and true,
And I shall make myself believe in you.

CELIMENE   Oh, stop it. Don't be such a jealous dunce,   [*115*
Or I shall leave off loving you at once.
Just why should I *pretend?* What could impel me
To stoop so low as that? And kindly tell me
Why, if I loved another, I shouldn't merely
Inform you of it, simply and sincerely!   [*120*
I've told you where you stand, and that admission
Should altogether clear me of suspicion;
After so generous a guarantee,
What right have you to harbor doubts of me?
Since women are (from natural reticence)   [*125*
Reluctant to declare their sentiments,
And since the honor of our sex requires
That we conceal our amorous desires,
Ought any man for whom such laws are broken
To question what the oracle has spoken?   [*130*
Should he not rather feel an obligation
To trust that most obliging declaration?
Enough, now. Your suspicions quite disgust me;
Why should I love a man who doesn't trust me?
I cannot understand why I continue,   [*135*
Fool that I am, to take an interest in you,
I ought to choose a man less prone to doubt,
And give you something to be vexed about.

ALCESTE   Ah, what a poor enchanted fool I am;
These gentle words, no doubt, were all a sham;   [*140*
But destiny requires me to entrust
My happiness to you, and so I must.
I'll love you to the bitter end, and see
How false and treacherous you dare to be.

CELIMENE   No, you don't really love me as you ought.   [*145*

ALCESTE   I love you more than can be said or thought;
Indeed, I wish you were in such distress
That I might show my deep devotedness.
Yes, I could wish that you were wretchedly poor,
Unloved, uncherished, utterly obscure;   [*150*
That fate had set you down upon the earth
Without possessions, rank, or gentle birth;
Then, by the offer of my heart, I might
Repair the great injustice of your plight;
I'd raise you from the dust, and proudly prove   [*155*

The purity and vastness of my love.
CELIMENE   This is a strange benevolence indeed!
God grant that I may never be in need. . . .
Ah, here's Monsieur Dubois, in quaint disguise.

Scene Four

[CELIMENE, ALCESTE, DUBOIS]
ALCESTE   Well, why this costume? Why those frightened eyes?
What ails you?
DUBOIS   Well, Sir, things are most mysterious.
ALCESTE   What do you mean?
DUBOIS   I fear they're very serious.
ALCESTE   What?
DUBOIS   Shall I speak more loudly?
ALCESTE   Yes; speak out.
DUBOIS   Isn't there someone here, Sir?
ALCESTE   Speak, you lout!   [5
Stop wasting time.
DUBOIS   Sir, we must slip away.
ALCESTE   How's that?
DUBOIS   We must decamp without delay.
ALCESTE   Explain yourself.
DUBOIS   I tell you we must fly.
ALCESTE   What for?
DUBOIS   We mustn't pause to say good-by.
ALCESTE   Now what d'you mean by all of this, you clown?   [*10*
DUBOIS   I mean, Sir, that we've got to leave this town.
ALCESTE   I'll tear you limb from limb and joint from joint
If you don't come more quickly to the point.
DUBOIS   Well, Sir, today a man in a black suit,
Who wore a black and ugly scowl to boot,   [*15*
Left us a document scrawled in such a hand
As even Satan couldn't understand.
It bears upon your lawsuit, I don't doubt;
But all hell's devils couldn't make it out.
ALCESTE   Well, well, go on. What then? I fail to see   [*20*
How this event obliges us to flee.
DUBOIS   Well, Sir: an hour later, hardly more,
A gentleman who's often called before
Came looking for you in an anxious way.
Not finding you, he asked me to convey   [*25*
(Knowing I could be trusted with the same)
The following message. . . . Now, what *was* his name?
ALCESTE   Forget his name, you idiot. What did he say?
DUBOIS   Well, it was one of your friends, Sir, anyway.
He warned you to begone, and he suggested   [*30*
That if you stay, you may well be arrested.
ALCESTE   What? Nothing more specific? Think, man, think!
DUBOIS   No, Sir. He had me bring him pen and ink,
And dashed you off a letter which, I'm sure,
Will render things distinctly less obscure.   [*35*
ALCESTE   Well—let me have it!
CELIMENE   What *is* this all about?

ALCESTE   God knows; but I have hopes of finding out.
        How long am I to wait, you blitherer?
DUBOIS   [*After a protracted search for the letter*]
        I must have left it on your table, Sir.
ALCESTE   I ought to . . .
CELIMENE   No, no, keep your self-control;   [40
        Go find out what's behind his rigmarole.
ALCESTE   It seems that fate, no matter what I do,
        Has sworn that I may not converse with you;
        But, Madam, pray permit your faithful lover
        To try once more before the day is over.   [45

ACT FIVE

Scene One

        [ALCESTE, PHILINTE]
ALCESTE   No, it's too much. My mind's made up, I tell you.
PHILINTE   Why should this blow, however hard, compel you . . .
ALCESTE   No, no, don't waste your breath in argument;
        Nothing you say will alter my intent;
        This age is vile, and I've made up my mind   [5
        To have no further commerce with mankind.
        Did not truth, honor, decency, and the laws
        Oppose my enemy and approve my cause?
        My claims were justified in all men's sight;
        I put my trust in equity and right;   [10
        Yet, to my horror and the world's disgrace,
        Justice is mocked, and I have lost my case!
        A scoundrel whose dishonesty is notorious
        Emerges from another lie victorious!
        Honor and right condone his brazen fraud,   [15
        While rectitude and decency applaud!
        Before his smirking face, the truth stands charmed,
        And virtue conquered, and the law disarmed!
        His crime is sanctioned by a court decree!
        And not content with what he's done to me,   [20
        The dog now seeks to ruin me by stating
        That I composed a book now circulating,
        A book so wholly criminal and vicious
        That even to speak its title is seditious!
        Meanwhile Oronte, my rival, lends his credit   [25
        To the same libelous tale, and helps to spread it!
        Oronte! a man of honor and of rank,
        With whom I've been entirely fair and frank;
        Who sought me out and forced me, willy-nilly,
        To judge some verse I found extremely silly;   [30
        And who, because I properly refused
        To flatter him, or see the truth abused,
        Abets my enemy in a rotten slander!
        There's the reward of honesty and candor!

The man will hate me to the end of time   [*35*
For failing to commend his wretched rhyme!
And not this man alone, but all humanity
Do what they do from interest and vanity;
They prate of honor, truth, and righteousness,
But lie, betray, and swindle nonetheless.   [*40*
Come then: man's villainy is too much to bear;
Let's leave this jungle and this jackal's lair.
Yes! treacherous and savage race of men,
You shall not look upon my face again.

PHILINTE Oh, don't rush into exile prematurely;   [*45*
Things aren't as dreadful as you make them, surely.
It's rather obvious, since you're still at large,
That people don't believe your enemy's charge.
Indeed, his tale's so patently untrue
That it may do more harm to him than you.   [*50*

ALCESTE Nothing could do that scoundrel any harm:
His frank corruption is his greatest charm,
And, far from hurting him, a further shame
Would only serve to magnify his name.

PHILINTE In any case, his bald prevarication   [*55*
Has done no injury to your reputation,
And you may feel secure in that regard.
As for your lawsuit, it should not be hard
To have the case reopened, and contest
This judgment . . .

ALCESTE   No, no, let the verdict rest.   [*60*
Whatever cruel penalty it may bring,
I wouldn't have it changed for anything.
It shows the times' injustice with such clarity
That I shall pass it down to our posterity
As a great proof and signal demonstration   [*65*
Of the black wickedness of this generation.
It may cost twenty thousand francs; but I
Shall pay their twenty thousand, and gain thereby
The right to storm and rage at human evil,
And send the race of mankind to the devil.   [*70*

PHILINTE Listen to me. . . .

ALCESTE   Why? What can you possibly say?
Don't argue, Sir; your labor's thrown away.
Do you propose to offer lame excuses
For men's behavior and the times' abuses?

PHILINTE No, all you say I'll readily concede: [*75*
This is a low, conniving age indeed;
Nothing but trickery prospers nowadays,
And people ought to mend their shabby ways.
Yes, man's a beastly creature; but must we then
Abandon the society of men?   [*80*
Here in the world, each human frailty
Provides occasion for philosophy,
And that is virtue's noblest exercise;
If honesty shone forth from all men's eyes,
If every heart were frank and kind and just,   [*85*
What could our virtues do but gather dust

(Since their employment is to help us bear
The villainies of men without despair) ?
A heart well-armed with virtue can endure. . . .

ALCESTE   Sir, you're a matchless reasoner, to be sure;   [*90*
Your words are fine and full of cogency;
But don't waste time and eloquence on me.
My reason bids me go, for my own good.
My tongue won't lie and flatter as it should;
God knows what frankness it might next commit,   [*95*
And what I'd suffer on account of it.
Pray let me wait for Célimène's return
In peace and quiet. I shall shortly learn,
By her response to what I have in view,
Whether her love for me is feigned or true.   [*100*

PHILINTE   Till then, let's visit Eliante upstairs.

ALCESTE   No, I am too weighed down with somber cares.
Go to her, do; and leave me with my gloom
Here in the darkened corner of this room.

PHILINTE   Why, that's no sort of company, my friend;   [*105*
I'll see if Eliante will not descend.

Scene Two

[CELIMENE, ORONTE, ALCESTE]

ORONTE   Yes, Madam, if you wish me to remain
Your true and ardent lover, you must deign
To give me some more positive assurance.
All this suspense is quite beyond endurance.
If your heart shares the sweet desires of mine,   [*5*
Show me as much by some convincing sign;
And here's the sign I urgently suggest:
That you no longer tolerate Alceste,
But sacrifice him to my love, and sever
All your relations with the man forever.   [*10*

CELIMENE   Why do you suddenly dislike him so?
You praised him to the skies not long ago.

ORONTE   Madam, that's not the point. I'm here to find
Which way your tender feelings are inclined.
Chose, if you please, between Alceste and me,   [*15*
And I shall stay or go accordingly.

ALCESTE   [*Emerging from the corner*]   Yes, Madam, choose; this gentle-
man's demand
Is wholly just, and I support his stand.
I too am true and ardent; I too am here
To ask you that you make your feelings clear.   [*20*
No more delays, now; no equivocation;
The time has come to make your declaration.

ORONTE   Sir, I've no wish in any way to be
An obstacle to your felicity.

ALCESTE   Sir, I've no wish to share her heart with you;   [*25*
That may sound jealous, but at least it's true.

ORONTE   If, weighing us, she leans in your direction . . .

ALCESTE   If she regards you with the least affection . . .

ORONTE   I swear I'll yield her to you there and then.

ALCESTE I swear I'll never see her face again. [*30*
ORONTE Now, Madam, tell us what we've come to hear.
ALCESTE Madam, speak openly and have no fear.
ORONTE Just say which one is to remain your lover.
ALCESTE Just name one name, and it will all be over.
ORONTE What! Is it possible that you're undecided? [*35*
ALCESTE What! Can your feelings possibly be divided?
CELIMENE Enough: this inquisition's gone too far:
    How utterly unreasonable you are!
    Not that I couldn't make the choice with ease;
    My heart has no conflicting sympathies; [*40*
    I know full well which one of you I favor,
    And you'd not see me hesitate or waver.
    But how can you expect me to reveal
    So cruelly and bluntly what I feel?
    I think it altogether too unpleasant [*45*
    To choose between two men when both are present;
    One's heart has means more subtle and more kind
    Of letting its affections be divined,
    Nor need one be uncharitably plain
    To let a lover know he loves in vain. [*50*
ORONTE No, no, speak plainly; I for one can stand it.
    I beg you to be frank.
ALCESTE   And I demand it.
    The simple truth is what I wish to know,
    And there's no need for softening the blow.
    You've made an art of pleasing everyone, [*55*
    But now your days of coquetry are done:
    You have no choice now, Madam, but to choose,
    For I'll know what to think if you refuse;
    I'll take your silence for a clear admission
    That I'm entitled to my worst suspicion. [*60*
ORONTE I thank you for this ultimatum, Sir,
    And I may say I heartily concur.
CELIMENE Really, this foolishness is very wearing:
    Must you be so unjust and overbearing?
    Haven't I told you why I must demur? [*65*
    Ah, here's Eliante; I'll put the case to her.

Scene Three

    [ELIANTE, PHILINTE, CELIMENE, ORONTE, ALCESTE]
CELIMENE Cousin, I'm being persecuted here
    By these two persons, who, it would appear,
    Will not be satisfied till I confess
    Which one I love the more, and which the less,
    And tell the latter to his face that he [*5*
    Is henceforth banished from my company.
    Tell me, has ever such a thing been done?
ELIANTE You'd best not turn to me; I'm not the one
    To back you in a matter of this kind:
    I'm all for those who frankly speak their mind. [*10*
ORONTE Madam, you'll search in vain for a defender.
ALCESTE You're beaten, Madam, and may as well surrender.

ORONTE   Speak, speak, you must; and end this awful strain.
ALCESTE   Or don't, and your position will be plain.
ORONTE   A single word will close this painful scene.   [
ALCESTE   But if you're silent, I'll know what you mean.

Scene Four

[ARSINOE, CELIMENE, ELIANTE, ALCESTE, PHILINTE, ACASTE, CLITANDRE, ORONTE]
ACASTE   [*To* CELIMENE]   Madam, with all due deference, we two
    Have come to pick a little bone with you.
CLITANDRE   [*To* ORONTE *and* ALCESTE]   I'm glad you're present, Sirs; as
        you'll soon learn,
    Our business here is also your concern.
ARSINOE   [*To* CELIMENE]   Madam, I visit you so soon again
    Only because of these two gentlemen,
    Who came to me indignant and aggrieved
    About a crime too base to be believed.
    Knowing your virtue, having such confidence in it,
    I couldn't think you guilty for a minute,   [
    In spite of all their telling evidence;
    And, rising above our little difference,
    I've hastened here in friendship's name to see
    You clear yourself of this great calumny.
ACASTE   Yes, Madam, let us see with what composure   [
    You'll manage to respond to this disclosure.
    You lately sent Clitandre this tender note.
CLITANDRE   And this one, for Acaste, you also wrote.
ACASTE   [*To* ORONTE *and* ALCESTE]   You'll recognize this writing, Sirs, I
        think;
    The lady is so free with pen and ink   [
    That you must know it all too well, I fear.
    But listen: this is something you should hear.

> "How absurd you are to condemn my lightheartedness in society, and
> to accuse me of being happiest in the company of others. Nothing could be
> more unjust; and if you do not come to me instantly and beg pardon   [
> for saying such a thing, I shall never forgive you as long as I live. Our big
> bumbling friend the Viscount . . ."

What a shame that he's not here.

> "Our big bumbling friend the Viscount, whose name stands first in your
> complaint, is hardly a man to my taste; and ever since the day I   [
> watched him spend three-quarters of an hour spitting into a well, so as to
> make circles in the water, I have been unable to think highly of him. As
> for the little Marquess . . ."

In all modesty, gentlemen, that is I.

> "As for the little Marquess, who sat squeezing my hand for such a   [
> long while yesterday, I find him in all respects the most trifling creature
> alive; and the only things of value about him are his cape and his sword.
> As for the man with the green ribbons . . ."

[*To* ALCESTE]
It's your turn now, Sir.

> "As for the man with the green ribbons, he amuses me now and then   [

with his bluntness and his bearish ill-humor; but there are many times indeed when I think him the greatest bore in the world. And as for the sonneteer . . ."

[*To* ORONTE]
Here's your helping.

"And as for the sonneteer, who has taken it into his head to be witty,   [*45*
and insists on being an author in the teeth of opinion, I simply cannot be
bothered to listen to him, and his prose wearies me quite as much as his
poetry. Be assured that I am not always so well-entertained as you suppose;
that I long for your company, more than I dare to say, at all these enter-
tainments to which people drag me; and that the presence of those   [*50*
one loves is the true and perfect seasoning to all one's pleasures."

CLITANDRE   And now for me.

"Clitandre, whom you mention, and who so pesters me with his saccha-
rine speeches, is the last man on earth for whom I could feel any affection.
He is quite mad to suppose that I love him, and so are you, to doubt   [*55*
that you are loved. Do come to your senses; exchange your suppositions
for his; and visit me as often as possible, to help me bear the annoyance of
his unwelcome attentions."

It's a sweet character that these letters show,
And what to call it. Madam, you well know.   [*60*
Enough. We're off to make the world acquainted
With this sublime self-portrait that you've painted.
ACASTE   Madam, I'll make you no farewell oration;
No, you're not worthy of my indignation.
Far choicer hearts than yours, as you'll discover,   [*65*
Would like this little Marquess for a lover.

Scene Five

[CELIMENE, ELIANTE, ARSINOE, ALCESTE, ORONTE, PHILINTE]
ORONTE   So! After all those loving letters you wrote,
You turn on me like this, and cut my throat!
And your dissembling, faithless heart, I find,
Has pledged itself by turns to all mankind!
How blind I've been! But now I clearly see;   [*5*
I thank you, Madam, for enlightening me.
My heart is mine once more, and I'm content;
The loss of it shall be your punishment.
[*To* ALCESTE]
Sir, she is yours; I'll seek no more to stand
Between your wishes and this lady's hand.   [*10*

Scene Six

[CELIMENE, ELIANTE, ARSINOE, ALCESTE, PHILINTE]
ARSINOE   [*To* CELIMENE]   Madam, I'm forced to speak. I'm far too stirred
To keep my counsel, after what I've heard.
I'm shocked and staggered by your want of morals.
It's not my way to mix in others' quarrels;
But really, when this fine and noble spirit,   [*5*
This man of honor and surpassing merit,

Laid down the offering of his heart before you,
How *could* you . . .
ALCESTE   Madam, permit me, I implore you,
   To represent myself in this debate.
   Don't bother, please, to be my advocate.   [*10*
   My heart, in any case, could not afford
   To give your services their due reward;
   And if I chose, for consolation's sake,
   Some other lady, t'would not be you I'd take.
ARSINOE   What makes you think you could, Sir? And how dare you   [*15*
   Imply that I've been trying to ensnare you?
   If you can for a moment entertain
   Such flattering fancies, you're extremely vain.
   I'm not so interested as you suppose
   In Célimène's discarded gigolos.   [*20*
   Get rid of that absurd illusion, do.
   Women like me are not for such as you.
   Stay with this creature, to whom you're so attached;
   I've never seen two people better matched.

Scene Seven

[CELIMENE, ELIANTE, ALCESTE, PHILINTE]
ALCESTE   [*To* CELIMENE]   Well, I've been still throughout this exposé,
   Till everyone but me has said his say.
   Come, have I shown sufficient self-restraint?
   And may I now . . .
CELIMENE   Yes, make your just complaint.
   Reproach me freely, call me what you will;   [*5*
   You've every right to say I've used you ill.
   I've wronged you, I confess it; and in my shame
   I'll make no effort to escape the blame.
   The anger of those others I could despise;
   My guilt toward you I sadly recognize.   [*10*
   Your wrath is wholly justified, I fear;
   I know how culpable I must appear,
   I know all things bespeak my treachery,
   And that, in short, you've grounds for hating me.
   Do so; I give you leave.
ALCESTE   Ah, traitress—how,   [*15*
   How should I cease to love you, even now?
   Though mind and will were passionately bent
   On hating you, my heart would not consent.
   [*To* ELIANTE *and* PHILINTE]
   Be witness to my madness, both of you;
   See what infatuation drives one to;   [*20*
   But wait; my folly's only just begun,
   And I shall prove to you before I'm done
   How strange the human heart is, and how far
   From rational we sorry creatures are.
   [*To* CELIMENE]
   Woman, I'm willing to forget your shame,   [*25*
   And clothe your treacheries in a sweeter name;
   I'll call them youthful errors, instead of crimes,
   And lay the blame on these corrupting times.

My one condition is that you agree
To share my chosen fate, and fly with me   [*30*
To that wild, trackless, solitary place
In which I shall forget the human race.
Only by such a course can you atone
For those atrocious letters; by that alone
Can you remove my present horror of you,   [*35*
And make it possible for me to love you.
CLEIMENE   What! *I* renounce the world at my young age,
And die of boredom in some hermitage?
ALCESTE   Ah, if you really loved me as you ought,
You wouldn't give the world a moment's thought;   [*40*
Must you have me, and all the world beside?
CELIMENE   Alas, at twenty one is terrified
Of solitude. I fear I lack the force
And depth of soul to take so stern a course.
But if my hand in marriage will content you,   [*45*
Why, there's a plan which I might well consent to,
And . . .
ALCESTE   No, I detest you now. I could excuse
Everything else, but since you thus refuse
To love me wholly, as a wife should do,
And see the world in me, as I in you,   [*50*
Go! I reject your hand, and disenthrall
My heart from your enchantments, once for all.

Scene Eight

[ELIANTE, ALCESTE, PHILINTE]
ALCESTE   [*To* ELIANTE]   Madam, your virtuous beauty has no peer;
Of all this world, you only are sincere;
I've long esteemed you highly, as you know;
Permit me ever to esteem you so,
And if I do not now request your hand,   [*5*
Forgive me, Madam, and try to understand.
I feel unworthy of it; I sense that fate
Does not intend me for the married state,
That I should do you wrong by offering you
My shattered heart's unhappy residue,   [*10*
And that in short . . .
ELIANTE   Your argument's well taken:
Nor need you fear that I shall feel forsaken.
Were I to offer him this hand of mine,
Your friend Philinte, I think, would not decline.
PHILINTE   Ah, Madam, that's my heart's most cherished goal,   [*15*
For which I'd gladly give my life and soul.
ALCESTE   [*To* ELIANTE *and* PHILINTE]   May you be true to all you now
         profess,
And so deserve unending happiness.
Meanwhile, betrayed and wronged in everything,
I'll flee this bitter world where vice is king,   [*20*
And seek some spot unpeopled and apart
Where I'll be free to have an honest heart.
PHILINTE   Come, Madam, let's do everything we can
To change the mind of this unhappy man.

HENRIK IBSEN
[1828–1906]

There were two Henrik Ibsens, the one who inspired a social and political revolution under the banner of "Ibsenism," and the one who protested his complete innocence of any revolutionary intentions. That the two Ibsens were the same man is testimony to both the complexity of the man and the misunderstanding that plagued him all his life. The truth seems to be that Ibsen underwent a great change of character. He did indeed begin as the social reformer his disciples took him for, but when disillusionment with his fellow Norwegians forced him inward and away from political and social reform to an examination of man's inner being, his disciples did not notice either the change in Ibsen or the change in his art. But then, neither did Ibsen when he insisted upon the unchanging tenor of his life's work. In 1890 he wrote ingenuously, "I was surprised that I, who had made it my chief life-task to depict human characters and human destinies, should, without conscious or direct intention, have arrived in several matters at the same conclusions as the social democratic moral philosophers had arrived at by scientific processes." This was Ibsen reacting against the simplified view of himself as the great fighting liberal emancipator invented by his disciples. He wished to make it clear that his art was greater than mere political melodrama.

Henrik Ibsen was the product of a frustrated and embittered childhood. When he was eight, his wealthy merchant family lost its fortune, bringing down upon him the full force of all the provincial narrowness and social ostracism of which the small Norwegian town of Skien was capable. He received an inferior education at a poor people's school, and was further disappointed by his parents' lack of sympathy for his artistic ambitions. He was so alienated by his father's indifference and his mother's religious dogmatism that, after leaving home at the age of fifteen, he scarcely bothered to keep up family connections. But the family and its middle class sensibility left its mark on Ibsen. He spent a great deal of his time either flouting middle-class conventions or trying to live up to them. He was considered a revolutionary, but he dressed with unusual care, often revealing the temperament of a conservative banker. He also liked to display the orders of merit that governments and royalty bestowed on him in the days of his international fame, before the scandalous publication of *A Doll's House* and *Ghosts* made his name an anathema to the conventionally pious. The unfavorable public reaction he received in his later years added to the already well-known dourness of his temperament, and pushed him further into himself. It might be said that he emerged only in the great symbolic dramas of his later years.

In his launching of modern drama, Ibsen progressed along the entire range of dramatic production. After an immature excursion into the field of folk and nationalistic drama, he experimented successfully with romantic drama, came into his own with realistic drama, and ended with symbolic drama. His major plays were *Brand* (1866), *Peer Gynt* (1867), *The League of Youth* (1869), *Emperor and Galilean* (1873), *Pillars of Society* (1877), *A Doll's House* (1879), *Ghosts* (1881), *An Enemy of the People* (1882), *The Wild Duck* (1884), *Rosmersholm* (1886), *The Lady from the Sea* (1888), *Hedda Gabler* (1890), *The Master Builder* (1892), *Little Eyolf* (1894), *John Gabriel Borkman* (1896), and *When We Dead Awaken* (1899).

THE WILD DUCK

HENRIK IBSEN
A New Translation by Otto Reinert

CHARACTERS

WERLE, *a manufacturer and merchant*
GREGERS WERLE, *his son*
OLD EKDAL
HJALMAR EKDAL, *his son, a photog-*
rapher
GINA EKDAL, HJALMAR'S *wife*
HEDVIG, *their daughter, fourteen years*
old
MRS. SØRBY, WERLE'S *housekeeper*
RELLING, *a physician*
MOLVIK, *a former student of theology*

GRÅBERG, *a bookkeeper in* WERLE'S
office
PETTERSEN, WERLE'S *servant*
JENSEN, *a hired waiter*
A FLABBY GENTLEMAN
A THIN-HAIRED GENTLEMAN
A NEARSIGHTED GENTLEMAN
SIX OTHER GENTLEMEN, WERLE'S *dinner*
guests
OTHER HIRED WAITERS

SCENE   *The first act takes place at* WERLE'S; *the other four, in*
HJALMAR EKDAL'S *studio.*

ACT I

An expensive-looking and comfortable study in WERLE'S *house; bookcases and upholstered furniture; in the middle of the room a desk with papers and ledgers; lamps with green shades give the room a soft, subdued light. In the rear, open double doors with portieres pulled apart reveal a large, elegant drawing room, brightly illuminated by lamps and candles. Front right, a small door to the office wing. Front left, a fireplace with glowing coals in it. Farther back on the left wall, double doors to the dining room.*

PETTERSEN, WERLE'S *servant, in livery, and the hired waiter* JENSEN, *in black, are setting the study in order for the guests. In the drawing room, two or three other hired waiters are lighting candles, moving chairs, etc. Sounds of conversation and laughter of many people come from the dining room. Someone signals he wishes to make a speech by touching his glass with his knife. Silence follows, a short speech is made, there are noises of approval, then again conversation.*

PETTERSEN [*lights a lamp by the fireplace and puts a shade on it*] Just listen to that, Jensen. There's the old man now, proposing a long toast to Mrs. Sørby.

JENSEN [*moving an armchair*] Do you think it's true what people say, that the two of 'em—y'know—?

PETTERSEN Couldn't say.

JENSEN I bet he used to be quite a goat in the old days.

PETTERSEN Maybe so.

JENSEN They say this dinner is for his son.

PETTERSEN That's right. He came home yesterday.

JENSEN It's the first I've heard Werle has a son.

PETTERSEN He has a son, all right. But he's up at the works at Høydal all the time. He hasn't been home as long as I've been here.

A HIRED WAITER [*in the drawing room doorway*] Pst, Pettersen, there's an old fellow here, says he—

PETTERSEN [*under his breath*] Dammit! Can't have anybody in here now!

[OLD EKDAL *appears from the right in the drawing room. He is dressed in a shabby old coat with a high collar. Wool mittens. He carries a walking stick and a fur cap in his hand. Under his arm a parcel in thick paper. Dirty, reddish brown wig. Small, gray mustache.*]

PETTERSEN [*going towards him*] Good Lord! What are *you* doing here?

EKDAL [*in the doorway*] Got to get into the office, Pettersen.

PETTERSEN The office closed an hour ago, and—

EKDAL They told me that downstairs. But Gråberg is still in there. Be a good boy, Pettersen; let me in this way. [*Points to the small office door.*] Been through here before.

PETTERSEN Oh well, all right. [*Opens the door.*] But see you go out the other way. We're having guests tonight.

EKDAL I know, I know—h'm! Thanks a lot, Pettersen, old boy. Good old friend. Thanks. [*Mutters.*] Ass!

[*He enters the office.* PETTERSEN *closes the door behind him.*]

JENSEN Is he one of them office people, too?

PETTERSEN Oh no. He just does some extra copying for them, when they need it. But he's been a fine enough fellow in his day, old Ekdal has.

JENSEN   You know, he sort of looked like that.

PETTERSEN   Oh yes. He used to be a lieutenant.

JENSEN   I'll be damned! A lieutenant!

PETTERSEN   Yessir: Then he got mixed up in some forest deal or something. They say he pretty near ruined Werle once. The two of 'em were partners—owned the Høydal works together. Oh yes, Ekdal and I are good friends. We've had many a drink together at Madam Eriksen's place, we have.

JENSEN   Didn't look to me like he'd have much to buy people drinks with.

PETERSEN   Good Lord, Jensen. It's my treat, of course. I always say one should be nice to people who've seen better days.

JENSEN   So he went bankrupt?

PETTERSEN   Worse than that. He went to prison.

JENSEN   Prison!

PETTERSEN   Or something.—[Listens.] Shhh. They are getting up from the table. [Servants open the doors to the dining room. MRS. SØRBY appears, in conversation with a couple of the dinner guests. The rest of the company follows in small groups. WERLE is among them. The last to appear are HJALMAR EKDAL and GREGERS WERLE.]

MRS. SØRBY   [to the servant, in passing]   Pettersen, tell them to serve the coffee in the music room, will you?

PETTERSEN   Very well, Mrs. Sørby.
[She and the two guests go into the drawing room and disappear, right. PETTERSEN and JENSEN follow them out.]

A FLABBY GENTLEMAN   [to A THIN-HAIRED one]   Phew! That dinner—It was almost too much for me.

THE THIN-HAIRED GENTLEMAN   Oh, I don't know. With a little bit of good will, it's amazing what one can accomplish in three hours.

THE FLABBY GENTLEMAN   Yes, but afterwards, afterwards, my dear chamberlain!

A THIRD GENTLEMAN   I am told the coffee and liqueurs will be served in the music room.

THE FLABBY GENTLEMAN   Wonderful! Then maybe Mrs. Sørby will play something for us.

THE THIN-HAIRED GENTLEMAN   [in a low voice]   If only she doesn't play us a different tune one of these days.

THE FLABBY GENTLEMAN   Don't worry. Bertha isn't one to let old friends down. [They laugh and enter the drawing room.]

WERLE   [in a low and troubled voice]   I don't think anybody noticed, Gregers.

GREGERS   [looks at him]   Noticed what?

WERLE   You didn't either?

GREGERS   What?

WERLE   We were thirteen at the table.

GREGERS   Really? Were we thirteen?

WERLE   [with a glance at HJALMAR EKDAL]   Usually we are only twelve. [To the other guests] Gentlemen!
[He and the remaining guests, except HJALMAR and GREGERS, leave through the drawing room, rear right.]

HJALMAR   [who has overheard the conversation]   You shouldn't have invited me, Gregers.

GREGERS   Nonsense! This is supposed to be a party for me. Shouldn't I invite my one and only friend?

HJALMAR   But I don't think your father approves. I never come to this house.

GREGERS   So I hear. But I wanted to see you and talk to you.—Well, well,

we two old school fellows have certainly drifted apart. It must be sixteen—
seventeen years since we saw each other.

HJALMAR   Is it really that long?

GREGERS   It is indeed. And how are you? You look fine. You're almost stout.

HJALMAR   Stout is hardly the word, but I suppose I look a little more manly
than I used to.

GREGERS   Yes, you do. Your appearance hasn't suffered any all these years.

HJALMAR   [*gloomily*]   But the inner man—! Believe me, that's a different
story. You know, of course, how utterly everything has collapsed for me
and mine since we last met.

GREGERS   [*in a lower voice*]   How is your father these days?

HJALMAR   I'd just as soon not talk about him. My poor, unfortunate father
lives with me, of course. He has no one else in the whole world to turn to.
But it is so terribly difficult for me to talk about these things. Tell me
rather how you have been—up there at the works.

GREGERS   Lonely—blissfully lonely. I've had all the time in the world to think
over all sort of things.—Here. Let's make ourselves comfortable.
[*He sits down in an armchair near the fireplace and gets* HJALMAR
to take another chair beside him.]

HJALMAR   [*softly*]   All the same, I do want to thank you, Gregers, for inviting
me to your father's table. It proves to me you no longer bear me a grudge.

GREGERS   [*surprised*]   Grudge? What makes you think I ever did?

HJALMAR   You did at first, you know.

GREGERS   When?

HJALMAR   Right after the tragedy. Of course, that was only natural. After all,
your own father only escaped by the skin of his teeth. Oh, that terrible
old business!

GREGERS   And so I bore you a grudge? Who told you that?

HJALMAR   I know you did, Gregers. Your father said so himself.

GREGERS   [*startled*]   Father! Really? H'm. So that's why you've never written—
not a single word.

HJALMAR   Yes.

GREGERS   Not even when you decided to become a photographer?

HJALMAR   Your father thought it would be better if I didn't write about anything at all.

GREGERS   [*looking straight ahead*]   Oh well, maybe he was right, at that.—But
tell me, Hjalmar—do you feel you have adjusted pretty well to your situation?

HJALMAR   [*with a small sigh*]   Oh yes, I think I have. Can't say I haven't, anyway. At first, of course, things seemed very strange. My circumstances were
so completely different. But then, everything had changed. Father's great,
ruinous tragedy—The shame—The disgrace—

GREGERS   [*feelingly*]   Yes, yes. I see.

HJALMAR   Of course there was no way in which I could pursue my studies.
There wasn't a penny left. Rather the opposite; there was debt. Mainly to
your father, I think.

GREGERS   H'm—

HJALMAR   Well—then I thought it best to take the bull by the horns and
make a clean break with the past—you know, all at once. Your father
thought so, too, and since he had been so helpful, and—

GREGERS   Father helped you?

HJALMAR   Yes, surely you know that? Where do you think I got the money
to learn photography and to set up my own studio? Things like that are
expensive, I can tell you.

GREGERS   And father paid for all that?

HJALMAR   Yes, didn't you know? I understood him to say he had written to you about it.

GREGERS   Not a word that it was *he*. He must have forgotten. We only write business letters. So it was father—!

HJALMAR   It certainly was. But he has never wanted people to know that. It was he who made it possible for me to get married, too. Or maybe—maybe you didn't know that, either?

GREGERS   No! How could I? [*Shakes* HJALMAR's *arm*.] My dear Hjalmar, I can't tell you how happy all this makes me—and pains me, too. Perhaps I have been unfair to father. In some respects, anyway. For this shows he has a heart, you know. A kind of conscience—

HJALMAR   Conscience?

GREGERS   Or whatever you want to call it. No, really, I can't tell you how glad I am to hear this about father.—So you are married, Hjalmar. That's more than I ever will be. I trust you find yourself happy as a married man?

HJALMAR   Yes, I certainly do. She is as good and competent a wife as any man could ask for. And she is by no means without culture.

GREGERS   [*a little taken aback*]   No, of course not.

HJALMAR   Life itself is an education, you see. Being with me every day—And then there are a couple of remarkable men we see quite a lot of. I assure you, you'd hardly recognize Gina.

GREGERS   Gina?

HJALMAR   Yes. Surely you remember her name was Gina?

GREGERS   Whose name? I haven't the slightest idea—

HJALMAR   But don't you remember she was here in the house for a while?

GREGERS   [*looks at him*]   Is it Gina Hansen—?

HJALMAR   Of course it is Gina Hansen.

GREGERS   —who kept house for us the last year of mother's illness?

HJALMAR   That's it. But my dear friend, I know for a fact that your father wrote you about my marriage.

GREGERS   [*who has risen*]   Yes, so he did, that's true, but not that—[*paces the floor*]. Wait a minute—Yes, he did—now when I think back. But father always writes such short letters. [*Sits down on the arm of the chair.*] Listen, Hjalmar—this interests me—how did you make Gina's acquaintance—your wife, I mean?

HJALMAR   Quite simply. You remember she didn't stay here very long. Everything was so unsettled during your mother's illness. Gina couldn't take that, so she gave notice and moved out. That was the year before your mother died. Or maybe it was the same year.

GREGERS   It was the same year. I was up at Høydal at the time. Then what happened?

HJALMAR   Well, Gina moved in with her mother, Madam Hansen, an excellent, hardworking woman, who ran a small eating place. And she had a room for rent, too. A nice, comfortable room.

GREGERS   Which you were lucky enough to get?

HJALMAR   Yes. Through your father, in fact. And it was there I really learned to know Gina.

GREGERS   And then you got engaged?

HJALMAR   Yes. It's easy for young people to fall in love, you know. H'm—

GREGERS   [*gets up, walks up and down*]   Tell me—after you'd become engaged, was that when father—I mean, was that when you took up photography?

HJALMAR   That's right. Naturally, I wanted to get married and have a place of my own, the sooner the better. And both your father and I agreed that photography was the best thing I could get into. Gina thought so, too. Oh yes, that was another reason. It so happened that Gina had learned how to retouch.

GREGERS   What a wonderful coincidence.

HJALMAR   [*smiling contentedly*]   Yes, wasn't it? Don't you think it worked out very well?

GREGERS   Remarkably well, I should say. So father has really been a kind of Providence for you, Hjalmar; hasn't he?

HJALMAR   [*moved*]   He did not abandon his old friend's son in his days of need. That's one thing about your father: he does have a heart.

MRS. SØRBY   [*enters on* WERLE'S *arm*]   I don't want to hear another word, my dear sir. You are not to stay in there staring at all those bright lights. It isn't good for you.

WERLE   [*letting go of her arm and moving his hand across his eyes*]   I almost think you are right.

[PETTERSEN *and* JENSEN *enter carrying trays with glasses of punch.*]

MRS. SØRBY   [*to the guests in the drawing room*]   Gentlemen, if you want a glass of punch, you'll have to take the trouble to come in here.

THE FLABBY GENTLEMAN   [*to* MRS. SORBY]   Dear Mrs. Sørby, please tell me it isn't so. You have not withdrawn your cherished permission to smoke?

MRS. SØRBY   Yes, Chamberlain. No smoking here in Mr. Werle's own sanctum.

THE THIN-HAIRED GENTLEMAN   And when did you append these harsh paragraphs to the tobacco regulations, Mrs. Sørby?

MRS. SØRBY   After the last dinner, Chamberlain, when certain persons abused their liberties.

THE THIN-HAIRED GENTLEMAN   And will not even the smallest infraction be tolerated, Mrs. Sørby? Really none at all?

MRS. SØRBY   None whatsoever, Chamberlain.

[*Most of the guests are gathered in the study. The servants are serving punch.*]

WERLE   [*to* HJALMAR, *over by a table*]   Well, Ekdal, what is that you are looking at?

HJALMAR   Oh, just an album, sir.

THE THIN-HAIRED GENTLEMAN   [*moving about*]   Ah yes! Photographs! That's your line, of course.

THE FLABBY GENTLEMAN   [*seated*]   Haven't you brought some of your own along?

HJALMAR   No, I haven't.

THE FLABBY GENTLEMAN   Too bad. Looking at pictures is good for the digestion, you know.

THE THIN-HAIRED GENTLEMAN   And then it would have contributed a mite to the general entertainment.

THE NEARSIGHTED GENTLEMAN   And all contributions are gratefully received.

MRS. SØRBY   The chamberlains think that when one has been invited to dinner, one ought to work for one's food, Mr. Ekdal.

THE FLABBY GENTLEMAN   With a cuisine like this that's only a pleasure.

THE THIN-HAIRED GENTLEMAN   Oh well, if it's a question of the struggle for existence—

MRS. SØRBY   You are so right!

[*They continue their conversation, laughing and joking.*]

GREGERS   [*in a low voice*]   You must join in, Hjalmar.

HJALMAR   [*with a twist of his body*]   What am I to say?

THE FLABBY GENTLEMAN   Don't you believe, sir, that Tokay may be considered relatively beneficial to the stomach?

WERLE [*by the fireplace*] I'll guarantee the Tokay you were served tonight, at any rate. It is one of the very best years. I am sure you noticed that yourself.

THE FLABBY GENTLEMAN Yes, it really was unusually delicate-tasting.

HJALMAR [*hesitantly*] Do the years differ?

THE FLABBY GENTLEMAN [*laughs*] Ah, Mr. Ekdal! Splendid!

WERLE [*with a smile*] I see it is hardly worth while to serve you fine wine.

THE THIN-HAIRED GENTLEMAN Tokay is like photographs, Mr. Ekdal. Both need sunshine. Or isn't that so?

HJALMAR Yes, sunshine has something to do with it.

MRS. SØRBY Just the same with chamberlains. They need sunshine, too—royal sunshine, as the saying goes.

THE THIN-HAIRED GENTLEMAN Ouch! That's a tired old joke, Mrs. Sørby.

THE NEARSIGHTED GENTLEMAN The lady will have her fun—

THE FLABBY GENTLEMAN —and at our expense. [*Wagging his finger.*] Madam Bertha! Madam Bertha!

MRS. SØRBY But it is true that vintages differ widely sometimes. The older the better.

THE NEARSIGHTED GENTLEMAN Do you count me among the older vintages?

MRS. SØRBY Far from it.

THE THIN-HAIRED GENTLEMAN Well, well! But what about me, Mrs. Sørby?

THE FLABBY GENTLEMAN And me? What vintages do we belong to?

MRS. SØRBY I reckon you among the sweet vintages, gentlemen.
[*She sips a glass of punch. The chamberlains laugh and flirt with her.*]

WERLE Mrs. Sørby always finds a way out—when she wants to. But gentlemen, you aren't drinking! Pettersen, please see to it that—! Gregers, let's have a glass together.
[GREGERS *does not move.*]
Won't you join us, Ekdal? I had no opportunity at the table—
[GRÅBERG *comes in through the office door.*]

GRÅBERG Beg your pardon, Mr. Werle, but I can't get out.

WERLE They've locked you in again, eh?

GRÅBERG Yes, they have, sir. And Flakstad has left with the keys.

WERLE That's all right. You just come through here.

GRÅBERG But there is somebody else—

WERLE Doesn't matter. Come on, both of you.
[GRÅBERG *and* OLD EKDAL *enter from the office.*]

WERLE [*involuntarily*] Damn!
[*Laughter and talk among the guests cease.* HJALMAR *gives a start when he sees his father, puts down his glass, and turns away toward the fireplace.*]

EKDAL [*does not look up but makes quick little bows to both sides, as he mutters*] Beg pardon. Came the wrong way. Gate's locked. Gate's locked. Beg pardon. [*He and* GRÅBERG *go out, rear right.*]

WERLE [*between his teeth*] That idiot Gråberg!

GREGERS [*staring, his mouth hanging open, to* HJALMAR] Don't tell me that was—!

THE FLABBY GENTLEMAN What is it? Who was that?

GREGERS Nothing. Just the bookkeeper and somebody else.

THE NEARSIGHTED GENTLEMAN [*to* HJALMAR] Did *you* know that man?

HJALMAR I don't know—I didn't notice—

THE FLABBY GENTLEMAN [*getting up*] What the devil has gotten into everybody? [*He walks over to some other guests, who are talking in low voices.*]

MRS. SØRBY [*Whispers to the servant*] Give him something from the kitchen to take home. Something good.

PETTERSEN [*nods his head*] I'll do that, ma'am. [*Goes out.*]

GREGERS [*shocked, in a low voice to* HJALMAR] Then it really was he?

HJALMAR Yes.

GREGERS And you stood there and denied him!

HJALMAR [*in a fierce whisper*] But how *could* I—?

GREGERS —acknowledge your own father?

HJALMAR [*pained*] Oh, if you had been in my place, maybe—
[*The low conversation among the guests changes to forced gaiety.*]

THE THIN-HAIRED GENTLEMAN [*approaching* HJALMAR *and* GREGERS, *in a friendly mood*] Aha! Reminiscing about university days, gentlemen?—Don't you smoke, Mr. Ekdal? Can I give you a light? Oh that's right. We are not allowed—

HJALMAR Thanks, I don't smoke.

THE FLABBY GENTLEMAN Don't you have a nice little poem you could recite for us, Mr. Ekdal? You used to do that so beautifully.

HJALMAR I am sorry. I don't remember any.

THE FLABBY GENTLEMAN That's a shame. Well, in that case, Balle, what do we do?
[*They both walk into the drawing room.*]

HJALMAR [*gloomily*] Gregers—I am leaving! You see, when a man has felt Fate's crushing blow—Say goodbye to your father for me.

GREGERS Yes, of course. Are you going straight home?

HJALMAR Yes. Why?

GREGERS I thought I might come up and see you a little later.

HJALMAR No, don't do that. Not to my home. My home is a gloomy one, Gregers, particularly after a brilliant banquet such as this. We can meet somewhere in town.

MRS. SØRBY [*has come up to them; in a low voice*] Are you leaving, Ekdal?

HJALMAR Yes.

MRS. SØRBY Say hello to Gina.

HJALMAR Thank you. I'll do that.

MRS. SØRBY Tell her I'll be up to see her one of these days.

HJALMAR Fine. [*To* GREGERS] You stay here. I'll slip out without anybody noticing. [*Drifts off. A little later he goes into the drawing room and out right.*]

MRS. SØRBY [*in a low voice to the servant who has returned*] Well, did you give the old man something?

PETTERSEN Oh yes. A bottle of brandy.

MRS. SØRBY Oh dear. Couldn't you have found something better?

PETTERSEN But Mrs. Sørby, there's nothing he likes better than brandy.

THE FLABBY GENTLEMAN [*in the doorway to the drawing room, with a sheet of music in his hand*] Will you play a duet, Mrs. Sørby?

MRS. SØRBY Yes, gladly.

THE GUESTS Good! Good!
[*She and all the guests go out rear right.* GREGERS *remains standing by the fireplace.* WERLE *is looking for something on the desk and appears to wish to be left alone. Since* GREGERS *does not leave,* WERLE *walks towards the drawing room door.*]

GREGERS Father, do you have a moment?

WERLE [*stops*] What is it?

GREGERS I'd like a word with you.

WERLE Couldn't it wait till we're alone?

GREGERS No, it can't, for maybe we'll never be alone again.

WERLE [*coming closer*] What does that mean?

[*During the following scene, the sound of a piano is faintly heard from the music room.*]

GREGERS   How is it that that family has been allowed to go to ruin so miserably?

WERLE   I suppose you refer to the Ekdals?

GREGERS   Yes, I do mean the Ekdals. Lieutenant Ekdal was once your close friend.

WERLE   Yes, unfortunately. Too close. I have felt that keenly enough for many years. It was his fault that my good name and reputation, too, were—somewhat tarnished.

GREGERS   [*in a low voice*]   Was he the only one who was guilty?

WERLE   Who else, do you mean?

GREGERS   The two of you were together on that big purchase of forest land, weren't you?

WERLE   But it was Ekdal who surveyed the area—surveyed it fraudulently. It was he who felled all that timber on state property. He was responsible for everything that went on up there. I didn't know what he was doing.

GREGERS   I doubt that Lieutenant Ekdal himself knew what he was doing.

WERLE   That may well be. The fact remains that he was convicted and I was not.

GREGERS   Yes, I know there were no proofs.

WERLE   Acquittal is acquittal. Why do you want to bring back that miserable old business that gave me gray hairs before my time? Is that what has been on your mind all these years up there? I can assure you, Gregers, here in town that whole story has been forgotten long ago, as far as *I* am concerned.

GREGERS   But what about that unfortunate family?

WERLE   Well, now, exactly what do you want me to do for those people? When Ekdal got out, he was a broken man, beyond help altogether. Some people go to the bottom as soon as they've got some buckshot in them and never come up again. Believe me, Gregers, I've done all I possibly could do, if I didn't want to put myself in a false light and give people occasion for all sorts of talk and suspicion—

GREGERS   Suspicion? I see.

WERLE   I have given Ekdal copying work to do for the office, and I pay him far, far more than he is worth.

GREGERS   [*without looking at him*]   H'm. I don't doubt that.

WERLE   You are laughing? Don't you think I am telling you the truth? Oh, to be sure, you won't find it in my books. I never enter expenses like that.

GREGERS   [*with a cold smile*]   No, I suppose there are certain expenses that are better not entered.

WERLE   [*puzzled*]   What do you mean?

GREGERS   [*being brave*]   Have you entered what it cost you to let Hjalmar Ekdal learn photography?

WERLE   I? What do you mean—entered?

GREGERS   I know now it was you who paid for it. And I also know it was you who set him up in business—quite comfortably, too.

WERLE   All right! And you still say I have done nothing for the Ekdals! I assure you, Gregers, those people have cost me a pretty penny!

GREGERS   Have you entered those expenses?

WERLE   Why do you ask?

GREGERS   I have my reasons. Listen—at the time you were providing so kindly for your old friend's son, wasn't that just when he was getting married?

WERLE   Damn it, Gregers! How can I remember—! After so many years—!

GREGERS   You wrote me a letter at the time. A business letter, of course. And in a postscript you mentioned very briefly that Hjalmar Ekdal had married one Miss Hansen.

WERLE   That's right. That was her name.

GREGERS   But you did not say anything about Miss Hansen being Gina Hansen, our ex-housekeeper.

WERLE   [*with scornful but forced laughter*] No, to tell the truth, it didn't occur to me that you were particularly interested in our ex-housekeeper.

GREGERS   I wasn't. But—[*Lowers his voice.*] somebody else in this house was.

WERLE   What do you mean? [*Flaring up.*] Don't tell me you're referring to me!

GREGERS   [*in a low but firm voice*] Yes, I am referring to you.

WERLE   And you dare—! You have the audacity—! How can that ingrate, that—photographer fellow—how dare he make accusations like that!

GREGERS   Hjalmar hasn't said a word. I don't think he has the faintest suspicion of anything like this.

WERLE   Then where do you get it from? Who could have said a thing like that?

GREGERS   My poor, unfortunate mother. The last time I saw her.

WERLE   Your mother! I might have thought so! You and she—you always stood together. It was she who first turned you against me.

GREGERS   No, it was all she had to go through, till things became too much for her and she died in sheer misery.

WERLE   Oh, nonsense! She didn't have to go through anything! No more than what others have had to, anyway. There's just no way of getting on with morbid, hysterical people—that's something *I* have had to learn! And here you are, with a suspicion like that—dabbling in old rumors and gossip against your own father. Listen here, Gregers. It really seems to me that at your age you might find something more useful to do.

GREGERS   Yes, it is about time.

WERLE   Then maybe your mind would be more at ease than it seems to be now. What is the point of working away, year in and year out, as just an ordinary clerk up there at Høydal, with not so much as a penny beyond regular wages? It's plain silly!

GREGERS   I wish I could believe that.

WERLE   Not that I don't understand, mind you. You want to be independent, don't want to be obliged to me for anything. But right now there is a chance for you to become independent, to be on your own in everything.

GREGERS   Oh? How so?

WERLE   When I wrote you that I needed you here in town right away—h'm—

GREGERS   Yes, what is it you want of me? I've been waiting to hear all day.

WERLE   I am offering you a partnership in the firm.

GREGERS   I! In your firm? As a partner?

WERLE   Yes. That doesn't mean we have to be together all the time. You could take over the business here in town and I could go up to Høydal.

GREGERS   You would want to do that?

WERLE   Well, you see, Gregers. I can't work as well as I used to. I'll have to save my eyes. They are getting weaker.

GREGERS   You have always had weak eyes.

WERLE   Not as bad as now. Besides—there are other things, too, that may make it advisable for me to live up there—for a while, anyway.

GREGERS   Nothing like this has ever even occurred to me.

WERLE   Look here, Gregers. I know there are many things that stand between us. But after all, we are father and son. It seems to me we ought to be able to come to some sort of understanding.

GREGERS   For appearance's sake, I suppose you mean.

WERLE   Well, that would be something, anyway. Think it over, Gregers.

Wouldn't that be possible? What do you say?

GREGERS   [*looks at him coldly*]   There is something behind this.

WERLE   I don't understand.

GREGERS   You want to use me for something.

WERLE   In a relationship as close as ours I suppose one person can always be of use to the other.

GREGERS   Yes. So they say.

WERLE   I want to have you at home with me for a while. I am a lonely man, Gregers. I have always been lonely, but mostly now, when I am getting older. I need somebody around me.

GREGERS   You have Mrs. Sørby.

WERLE   So I do, and she has become almost indispensable to me. She is bright, she has an even temper, she brings life into the house—and I badly need that.

GREGERS   Well, then, everything is just as you want it.

WERLE   Yes, but I am afraid it won't last. A woman in her circumstances can easily have her position misconstrued in the eyes of the world. I'll almost go so far as to say it does a man no good either.

GREGERS   Oh, I don't know. When a man gives the kind of dinner parties you do he can take quite a few liberties.

WERLE   Yes, but what about *her*, Gregers? I am afraid she will not put up with it much longer. And even if she did, even if she ignored what people are saying and all that sort of thing, out of devotion to me—Do you really think, Gregers, you with your strong sense of justice, do you feel it would be—

GREGERS   [*interrupting*]   Just tell me this: are you going to marry her?

WERLE   What if I did? What then?

GREGERS   That's what I am asking. What then?

WERLE   Would it displease you very much?

GREGERS   No, not at all.

WERLE   Well, you see, I didn't know—I thought perhaps out of regard for your mother—

GREGERS   I am not given to melodramatics.

WERLE   Well, whether you are or not, you have lifted a stone from my heart. I can't tell you how pleased I am that I can count on your support in this matter.

GREGORS   [*looks intently at him*]   Now I see what you want to use me for.

WERLE   Use you for? What an expression!

GREGERS   Let's not be particular in our choice of words—not as long as we're by ourselves, at any rate. [*Laughs.*] So that's it. That's why I had to come to town at all costs. Because of Mrs. Sørby, there are arrangements being made for family life in this house. Touching scene between father and son! That would indeed be something new!

WERLE   I won't have you use that tone!

GREGERS   When were we ever a family here? Never in my memory. But now, of course, there is need for a display of domestic affection. It will look very well to have the son hastening home on wings of filial feeling to attend the aging father's marriage feast. What happens then to all the talk of what the poor, deceased mother had to suffer? It evaporates. Her son takes care of that.

WERLE   Gregers, I don't believe there is anyone you detest as much as me.

GREGERS   [*in a low voice*]   I have seen too much of you.

WERLE   You've seen me with your mother's eyes. [*Lowers his voice a little.*] But don't forget that those eyes were—clouded at times.

GREGERS [*his voice trembles*] I know what you have in mind. But who's to blame for mother's tragic weakness? You and all those—! The last one was that female you palmed off on Hjalmar Ekdal, when you yourself no longer—!

WERLE [*shrugs his shoulders*] Word for word as if I were hearing your mother.

GREGERS [*paying no attention*] —and there he is now, with his great, trusting child's soul in the middle of all this deceit—sharing his roof with a woman like that, unaware that what he calls his home is based on a lie! [*Steps closer to* WERLE.] When I look back upon all you have done, I seem to see a battlefield strewn with mangled human destinies.

WERLE I almost think the gap between us is too wide.

GREGERS [*with a formal bow*] So I have observed. That is why I take my hat and leave.

WERLE You're leaving? The house?

GREGERS Yes. For now at last I see a mission to live for.

WERLE What mission is that?

GREGERS You'd only laugh if I told you.

WERLE A lonely man doesn't laugh so easily, Gregers.

GREGERS [*pointing to the rear*] Look, father. The chamberlains are playing blindman's buff with Mrs. Sørby.—Goodnight and good-bye.

[*He goes out rear right. The sound of people talking, laughing, and playing games can be heard from the drawing room, where the guests are now coming into view.*]

WERLE [*mutters scornfully*] Hah—! The fool! And he says he is not melodramatic!

ACT II

HJALMAR EKDAL'S *studio, a large attic room. To the right, a slanting roof with skylights, half covered by blue cloth. The entrance door from the hallway is in the far right corner; the door to the living room farther forward on the same wall. There are two doors to the left, as well, with an iron stove between them. In the rear, wide, sliding, double doors. The studio is unpretentious but cozy. Between the two doors on the right and a little out from the wall is a sofa with a table and some chairs in front of it. On the table is a lighted lamp with a shade. Near the wall by the stove is an old armchair. Various pieces of photographic equipment here and there in the room. In the rear, to the left of the sliding doors, a shelf with a few books, bottles with chemical solutions, tools, and some other objects. Photographs, brushes, paper, etc., are lying on the table.*

GINA EKDAL *sits by the table, sewing.* HEDVIG *sits on the sofa, reading, her hands shading her eyes, her thumbs in her ears.*

GINA [*glances at* HEDVIG *a few times, as if secretly anxious*] Hedvig!

HEDVIG [*does not hear.*]

GINA [*louder*] Hedvig!

HEDVIG [*takes away her hands and looks up*] Yes, mother?

GINA Hedvig, be a good girl. Don't read any more tonight.

HEDVIG Please, mother, just a little bit longer? Can't I?

GINA No. I want you to put that book away. Your father doesn't like you to read so much. He never reads at night.

HEDVIG [*closing her book*]   Well, father doesn't care much for reading, anyway.
GINA [*puts her sewing aside and picks up a pencil and a small notebook from the table*]   Do you remember how much we spent for the butter today?
HEDVIG One crown and sixty-five øre.
GINA That's right. [*Writes it down.*] We're using an awful lot of butter in this family. Then there was the sausage and the cheese—let me see— [*writing*] —and the ham— [*mumbles figures while adding up*]. Goodness! it does add up—
HEDVIG And the beer.
GINA Right. [*Writes.*] It gets terrible expensive, but it can't be helped.
HEDVIG And you and I didn't need anything hot for supper since father was out.
GINA No, that's right. That helps some. And I did get eight crowns and fifty øre for the pictures.
HEDVIG Was it that much?
GINA Eight-fifty, exactly.
   [*Silence.* GINA *picks up her sewing.* HEDVIG *takes paper and pencil and starts drawing, her left hand shading her eyes.*]
HEDVIG Isn't it nice to think that father is at that big dinner party at Mr. Werle's?
GINA Can't rightly say he's *his* guest. It was the son who invited him. [*After a pause.*] We have nothing to do with the old man.
HEDVIG I can't wait till father comes home. He promised to ask Mrs. Sørby if he could take home something good for me.
GINA Why yes, you can be sure there are plenty of good things in *that* house.
HEDVIG [*still drawing*]   Besides, I think I am a little bit hungry, too.
   [OLD EKDAL *enters right rear, the brown paper parcel under his arm, another parcel in his coat pocket.*]
GINA So late you are today, Grandpa.
EKDAL They'd locked the office. Had to wait for Gråberg. And then I had to go through—h'm—
HEDVIG Did they give you any more copying to do, Grandpa?
EKDAL This whole parcel. Look.
GINA That's nice.
HEDVIG And you've got another one in your pocket.
EKDAL What? Oh never mind. That's nothing. [*Puts his walking stick away in the corner.*] This will keep me busy a long time, Gina. [*Slides one of the double doors half open.*] Shhh! [*Peeks into the attic for a while, then he cautiously slides the door shut. Chuckling.*] They're sound asleep the whole lot of 'em. And she herself's in the basket.
HEDVIG Are you sure she won't be cold in that basket, Grandpa?
EKDAL Cold? With all that straw? Don't you worry about that. [*Goes towards the door left rear.*] There are matches, aren't there?
GINA On the dresser.
   [EKDAL *goes into his room.*]
HEDVIG It's nice that he got all that new work to do.
GINA Yes, poor old thing. It will give him a little spending money.
HEDVIG And he won't be able to stay down at the awful Madam Eriksen's all morning.
GINA No; there's that, too.
HEDVIG Do you think they're still at the table?
GINA Lord knows. Could be.
HEDVIG Just think of all that delicious food. I'm sure he'll be in a good mood when he comes home. Don't you think so, mother?

GINA   Yes, but what if we could tell him we'd rented the room. Wouldn't that be nice?

HEDVIG   But we don't need that tonight.

GINA   Oh yes we do. We could always use the money. The room is no good to us as it is.

HEDVIG   No, I mean that father will be in a good mood tonight, anyway. It's better to have the room for some other time.

GINA   [looking at her]   You like it when you have something nice to tell father when he comes home nights, don't you?

HEDVIG   It makes things more pleasant.

GINA   [reflectively]   Yes, I guess you're right about that.

[OLD EKDAL enters from his room, heads for the kitchen door, left front.]

GINA   [turning half around in her chair]   Do you need anything in the kitchen, Grandpa?

EKDAL   Yes. But don't you get up. [Goes out.]

GINA   I hope he isn't fooling around with the fire out there. [After a while.] Hedvig, go out and see what he's doing.

[OLD EKDAL enters with a pitcher of hot water.]

HEDVIG   Getting hot water, Grandpa?

EKDAL   That's right. Got some writing to do, but the ink's as thick as gruel. H'm—

GINA   But hadn't you better have supper first? It's all ready for you in your room.

EKDAL   Never mind supper, Gina. I tell you I'm busy. I don't want anybody coming in to me. Not anybody. H'm.

[He goes into his room. GINA and HEDVIG look at each other.]

GINA   [in a low voice]   I can't think where he got the money from. Can you?

HEDVIG   From Gråberg, maybe.

GINA   No, it wouldn't be that. Gråberg always gives me the money.

HEDVIG   Maybe he got a bottle on credit.

GINA   Him! Who'd give him credit?

[HJALMAR EKDAL, in overcoat and gray hat, enters right.]

GINA   [throws down her sewing, gets up]   Heavens, Ekdal! Home already?

HEDVIG   [getting up at the same time]   Father? So soon!

HJALMAR   [lays down his hat]   Most of them seemed to be leaving now.

HEDVIG   Already?

HJALMAR   Well, it was a dinner party, you know. [Takes his coat off.]

GINA   Let me help you.

HEDVIG   Me too. [They help him off with his coat. GINA hangs it up in the rear.] Were there many there, father?

HJALMAR   Not too many. About twelve or fourteen at the table.

GINA   Did you get to talk to all of them?

HJALMAR   Oh yes, a little. Though Gregers kept me engaged most of the evening.

GINA   Is he as ugly as he used to be?

HJALMAR   Well—I suppose nobody would call him handsome. Is father back?

HEDVIG   Yes, he is in there writing.

HJALMAR   Did he say anything?

GINA   No. About what?

HJALMAR   He didn't mention—? I thought I heard he'd been with Gråberg. I think I'll go in to him for a moment.

GINA   No, you'd better not.

HJALMAR   Why not? Did he say he didn't want to see me?

GINA   He doesn't want to see anybody.

HEDVIG   [*making signs to her*]   Ahem!

GINA   [*doesn't notice*]   He's gotten himself some hot water.

HJALMAR   Ah! So he is—

GINA   Looks that way.

HJALMAR   Ah yes—my poor old white-haired father. Let him enjoy his little pleasures as best he can.

[OLD EKDAL, *a lighted pipe in his mouth, enters in an old smoking jacket.*]

EKDAL   Home again? Thought it was you I heard talking.

HJALMAR   Yes. I just came back.

EKDAL   Guess you didn't see me, did you?

HJALMAR   No, but they told me you'd gone through, so I thought I'd catch up with you.

EKDAL   H'm. That's good of you, Hjalmar. Who were they—all those people?

HJALMAR   Oh—all sorts. Chamberlain Flor and Chamberlain Balle and Chamberlain Kaspersen and chamberlain this and that. I don't know—

EKDAL   [*nodding his head*]   Hear that, Gina? He's been with nothing but chamberlains all evening.

GINA   Yes, I hear as they've become quite fancy in that house now.

HEDVIG   Did the chamberlains sing, father? Or recite poetry?

HJALMAR   No. They just talked nonsense. They wanted *me* to recite, though, but I didn't want to.

EKDAL   They couldn't get you to, eh?

GINA   Seems to me you might have done that.

HJALMAR   No. I don't see any reason why one has to oblige every Tom, Dick, and Harry all the time. [*Walks up and down.*] At any rate, I won't.

EKDAL   No point in being too obliging, you know. That's Hjalmar for you.

HJALMAR   I don't see why *I* always have to be the one who provides entertainment on the rare occasions when I am out for dinner. Let the others exert themselves for a change. Those fellows go from one big meal to the next, stuffing themselves day in and day out. Let *them* do something for all the food they are getting!

GINA   You didn't tell them that though, did you?

HJALMAR   [*humming a little*]   Well, I don't know about that. They were told a thing or two.

EKDAL   The chamberlains?

HJALMAR   Mmm—[*Casually.*]   Then we had a little controversy over Tokay wine.

EKDAL   Tokay, no less! Say, that's a fine wine!

HJALMAR   [*stops his walking*]   It *may* be a fine wine. But let me tell you: not all the vintages are equally fine. It depends on how much sunshine the grapes get.

GINA   If you don't know everything—!

EKDAL   And they quarreled with that?

HJALMAR   They tried to, but then it was pointed out to them that it was the same way with chamberlains. Not all vintages are equally fine among chamberlains, either—so they were told.

GINA   Goodness! What you don't think of!

EKDAL   Heh-heh! So they got that to put in their pipe.

HJALMAR   Right to their face. That's how they got it.

EKDAL   Gina, d'ye hear that? He gave it to them right to their face!

GINA   Right to their face! Imagine!

HJALMAR   Yes, but I don't want you to talk about it. One doesn't talk about such things. Of course, the whole thing was done in the friendliest possible way. They are all of them pleasant, easy-going people. Why should I hurt them? No!

EKDAL Right to their face, though—

HEDVIG [*ingratiatingly*] It's so nice to see you all dressed up, father. You look very well in tails.

HJALMAR Yes, don't you think so? And it really fits me perfectly. As if it were tailor-made. Possibly a trifle tight in the armpits, that's all. Help me, Hedvig. [*Takes his dinner jacket off.*] I'd rather wear my own coat. Where is it, Gina?

GINA Here it is. [*Helps him on with it.*]

HJALMAR There now! Be sure to have Molvik get his suit back first thing in the morning.

GINA [*putting the clothes away*] I'll take care of it.

HJALMAR [*stretching*] Aaahh. This feels cozier after all. And this kind of loose-fitting, casual wear is really more in keeping with my whole appearance; don't you think so, Hedvig?

HEDVIG Oh yes, father!

HJALMAR Especially when I tie my neckcloth with loose, flying ends—like this? What do you think?

HEDVIG Yes, it goes extremely well with your mustache. And with your curls, too.

HJALMAR I'd hardly call my hair curly. Wavy, rather.

HEDVIG Yes, for the curls are so large.

HJALMAR Waves, really.

HEDVIG [*after a moment, pulling his sleeve*] Father?

HJALMAR What is it?

HEDVIG Oh, you know very well what it is!

HJALMAR I certainly don't.

HEDVIG [*laughing and pleading*] Oh come on, father! Don't tease me!

HJALMAR But what is it?

HEDVIG [*shaking him*] Father! Give it to me! You know, you promised me. Something good to eat.

HJALMAR Oh, dear! I completely forgot!

HEDVIG You are only teasing, father. Shame on you! Where is it?

HJALMAR No, honest, I really did forget. But wait a moment. I have something else for you, Hedvig. [*Goes and searches his coat pockets.*]

HEDVIG [*jumps up and down, clapping her hands*] Oh mother, mother!

GINA See what I mean? If you just give him time—

HJALMAR [*with a piece of paper*] Here it is.

HEDVIG That? But that's just a piece of paper.

HJALMAR It's the menu, Hedvig, the entire menu. Look here. It says "Menu." That means what you get to eat.

HEDVIG Haven't you anything else for me?

HJALMAR I tell you, I forgot all about it. But take my word for it: it's not such a great treat, all that rich food. You just sit down and read the menu, now, and I'll tell you later what the things taste like. Here you are, Hedvig.

HEDVIG [*swallowing her tears*] Thank you.

[*She sits down but doesn't read.* GINA *signals to her.* HJALMAR *notices.*]

HJALMAR [*pacing the floor*] It is really unbelievable all the things a father is supposed to keep in mind. And if he forgets the smallest item—! Long faces right away. Oh well. One gets used to that, too. [*Stops by the stove where* OLD EKDAL *is sitting.*] Have you looked at them tonight, father?

EKDAL I certainly have! She's in the basket!

HJALMAR No! Really? In the basket? She is getting used to it then, I guess.

EKDAL Didn't I tell you she would? But look, Hjalmar, there are still a few things—

HJALMAR —improvements, yes, I know.

EKDAL   They've got to be done.

HJALMAR   Right. Let's talk about it now, father. Come over here to the sofa.

EKDAL   All right. H'm. Guess I want to fill my pipe first, though. Need to clean it, too—h'm—[*Goes into his room.*]

GINA   [*with a smile, to* HJALMAR]   Cleaning his pipe—

HJALMAR   Oh well, Gina—let him. The poor shipwrecked old man.—About those improvements—We'd better get to them tomorrow.

GINA   You won't have time tomorrow, Ekdal.

HEDVIG   [*interrupting*]   Oh, yes, mother.

GINA   For remember those prints you were going to retouch? They came for 'em again today.

HJALMAR   I see. It's those prints again, is it? Well, they'll get done. You can be sure of that. Perhaps there are some new orders come in, too?

GINA   Not a thing, worse luck. Tomorrow I've got only those two portraits I told you about.

HJALMAR   Is that all? Well, if one doesn't exert oneself, what can you expect?

GINA   But what can I do? I advertise in the papers all I can, seems to me.

HJALMAR   The papers, the papers—you see yourself how far that gets us. I suppose there hasn't been anyone to look at the room, either?

GINA   No, not yet.

HJALMAR   Just as I thought. Well, no—if one doesn't *do* anything—One has to make a real effort, Gina!

HEDVIG   [*going to him*]   Shall I get your flute, father?

HJALMAR   No, not the flute. *I* need no pleasures. [*Paces up and down.*] You'll see if I don't work tomorrow! You don't need to worry about *that!* You can be sure I shall work as long as my strength holds out—

GINA   But Ekdal, dear—I didn't mean it that way.

HEDVIG   How about a bottle of beer, father?

HJALMAR   Not at all. I don't need anything—[*Stops.*] Beer? Did you say beer?

HEDVIG   [*brightly*]   Yes, father; lovely, cool beer.

HJALMAR   Oh well—all right—since you insist, I suppose you may bring me a bottle.

GINA   Yes, do that. That'll be nice and cozy.

[HEDVIG *runs towards the kitchen door.*]

HJALMAR   [*by the stove, stops her, looks at her, takes her by the head and presses her to him*]   Hedvig! Hedvig!

HEDVIG   [*happy in tears*]   Oh father! You are so sweet and good!

HJALMAR   No, no, don't say that. There I was—seated at the rich man's table—gorging myself on his ample fare—and I couldn't even remember—

GINA   [*seated by the table*]   Nonsense, Ekdal.

HJALMAR   It is not nonsense. But you must not reckon too strictly. You know I love you, regardless.

HEDVIG   [*throwing her arms around him*]   And we love you, father, so much, so much!

HJALMAR   And if I am unreasonable at times, remember—God forgive me—remember I am a man beset by a host of sorrows. Well, well! [*Drying his eyes.*] No beer at such a moment. Give me my flute.

[HEDVIG *runs to the shelf and fetches it.*]

HJALMAR   Thank you. There now. With my flute in my hand and you two around me—ah!

[HEDVIG *sits down by the table next to* GINA. HJALMAR *walks back and forth, playing a Bohemian folk dance. He plays loudly but in slow tempo and with pronounced sentiment.*]

HJALMAR   [*interrupts his playing, gives his left hand to* GINA, *and says with strong emotion*] Our home may be mean and humble, Gina. But it is our home. And I say to you both: here dwells contentment!

[*He resumes his playing. Presently there is a knock on the door.*]

GINA [*getting up*] Shh, Ekdal. I think somebody's coming.

HJALMAR [*putting the flute back on the shelf*] Yes, yes of course. Somebody would—

[GINA *goes to open the door.*]

GREGERS WERLE [*out in the hall*] I beg your pardon—

GINA [*taking a step back*] Oh!

GREGERS —isn't this where Mr. Ekdal lives, the photographer?

GINA Yes, it is.

HJALMAR [*going to the door*] Gregers! So you did come, after all. Come in.

GREGERS [*entering*] I told you I wanted to see you.

HJALMAR But tonight—? Have you left the party?

GREGERS Both party and home. Good evening, Mrs. Ekdal. I don't know if you recognize me.

GINA Oh yes. Young Mr. Werle isn't hard to recognize.

GREGERS No, for I look like my mother, and you remember her, I am sure.

HJALMAR You have left your home?

GREGERS Yes. I have taken a room at a hotel.

HJALMAR Really?—Well, since you're here, take off your coat and sit down.

GREGERS Thanks. [*Removes his overcoat. He has changed clothes and is now dressed in a plain, gray suit, of somewhat unfashionable cut.*]

HJALMAR Here on the sofa. Make yourself comfortable.

[GREGERS *sits down on the sofa,* HJALMAR *on a chair by the table.*]

GREGERS [*looking around*] So this is your residence, Hjalmar. This is where you live.

HJALMAR This is the studio, as you can see.

GINA It's roomier in here, so this is where we mostly keep ourselves.

HJALMAR The apartment we had before was really nicer than this, but there is one big advantage here: we have plenty of space.

GINA And we have a room across the hallway that we're renting out.

GREGERS [*to* HJALMAR] You have lodgers, too?

HJALMAR No, not yet. These things take time, you see. One has to be on the lookout. [*To* HEDVIG.] What about that beer?

[HEDVIG *nods her head and goes out into the kitchen.*]

GREGERS So that's your daughter.

HJALMAR Yes, that's Hedvig.

GREGERS Your only child, isn't she?

HJALMAR Our only one. Our greatest joy in the world, and [*lowers his voice*] our greatest sorrow, as well.

GREGERS What are you saying!

HJALMAR Yes, Gregers, for there is every probability that she'll lose her sight.

GREGERS Becoming blind!

HJALMAR Yes. So far, there are only early symptoms, and things may be well with her for some time yet. But the doctor has warned us. It is coming, irresistibly.

GREGERS But this is nothing less than a tragedy! How do you account for it?

HJALMAR [*with a sigh*] Heredity, most likely.

GREGERS [*struck*] Heredity?

GINA Ekdal's mother had weak eyes.

HJALMAR That's what father says. I of course don't remember her.

GREGERS Poor child. How does she take it?

HJALMAR Oh, we can't bring ourselves to tell her—I'm sure you can understand that. She suspects nothing. Joyous and carefree, chirping like a little bird, she'll flutter into life's endless night. [*Overcome by emotion.*] Oh Gregers, this is such a terrible burden for me.

[HEDVIG *enters with a tray with beer and glasses. She puts it down on the table.*]

HJALMAR   [*stroking her hair*]   Thanks. Thank you, Hedvig.

HEDVIG   [*puts her arms around his neck and whispers something in his ear.*]

HJALMAR   No. No sandwiches now. [*Looks off.*] That is—unless Gregers wants some?

GREGERS   [*with a gesture of refusal*]   No. No thanks.

HJALMAR   [*still in a melancholic mood*]   Oh well, you might as well bring in some, all the same. A crust, if you have one. And plenty of butter, please.

GREGERS   [*who has followed her with his eyes*]   Otherwise she seems healthy enough.

HJALMAR   Yes, thank God, there is nothing else wrong with her.

GREGERS   I think she is going to look like you, Mrs. Ekdal. How old is she?

GINA   Hedvig is just about fourteen. Her birthday is day after tomorrow.

GREGERS   Quite big for her age, isn't she?

GINA   Yes, she has grown a lot lately.

GREGERS   It's by the children we tell we're growing older ourselves. How long have you two been married now?

GINA   We've been married for—let's see—fifteen years, pretty near.

GREGERS   Just imagine! Has it really been that long?

GINA   [*taking notice, looks at him*]   It certainly has.

HJALMAR   That's right. Fifteen years, less a few months. [*Changing topic.*] Those must have been long years for you up there at the works, Gregers.

GREGERS   They were long while they lasted. Now afterwards I hardly know where they went.

[OLD EKDAL *enters from his room, without his pipe, but with his old-fashioned lieutenant's cap on his head. His walk is a trifle unsteady.*]

EKDAL   I'm ready for you now, Hjalmar. Let's talk about this—h'm—What was it again?

HJALMAR   [*going towards him*]   Father, there's someone here. Gregers Werle. I don't know if you remember him?

EKDAL   [*looks at* GREGERS, *who has stood up*]   Werle? That's the son, isn't it? What does he want from me?

HJALMAR   Nothing. He has come to see me.

EKDAL   Then there's nothing wrong?

HJALMAR   Of course not.

EKDAL   [*swinging one arm back and forth*]   Not that I am scared, mind you, but—

GREGERS   [*goes up to him*]   I just wanted to bring you greetings from your old hunting grounds, Lieutenant Ekdal.

EKDAL   Hunting grounds?

GREGERS   Yes, the woods up around the Høydal works.

EKDAL   Oh yes, up there. Yes, I used to know that country quite well in the old days.

GREGERS   You were quite a hunter then, weren't you?

EKDAL   Could be. Maybe I was. You're looking at my get-up. I don't ask anybody's permission to wear it in the house. Just as long as I don't go outside—

[HEDVIG *brings a plate with open-faced sandwiches, which she puts down on the table.*]

HJALMAR   You sit down, father, and have a glass of beer. Help yourself, Gregers.

[EKDAL *mutters something and shuffles over to the sofa.* GREGERS *sits down on a chair next to him;* HJALMAR *is on the other side of* GREGERS. GINA *sits some distance from the table, sewing.* HEDVIG *is standing by her father.*]

GREGERS Do you remember, Lieutenant Ekdal, when Hjalmar and I used to come up and visit you summers and Christmas?

EKDAL You did? No; can't say as I do. But it's true I used to be a good hunter, if I do say so myself. I've killed bears, too. Nine of 'em.

GREGERS [*looks at him with compassion*] And now your hunting days are over.

EKDAL Oh—I wouldn't say that. I still go hunting once in a while. Well, yes, not in the old way, of course. For you see, the woods—the woods—the woods—! [*Drinks.*] Nice-looking woods up there now?

GREGERS Not as in your time. They have cut a great deal.

EKDAL Cut? [*In a lower voice and as if afraid.*] That's risky business, that is. It has consequences. The woods are vengeful.

HJALMAR [*filling his glass*] Here, father. Have some more.

GREGERS How can a man like you—such an outdoors man as you used to be— how can you stand living here in the middle of a musty city, within four walls?

EKDAL [*chuckles, glancing at* HJALMAR] Oh, it's not so bad here. Not bad at all.

GREGERS But surely—all the things your soul grew used to up there—? The cool, invigorating breezes? The free life in woods and mountains, among beasts and birds—?

EKDAL [*smiling*] Hjalmar, shall we show it to him?

HJALMAR [*quickly, a little embarrassed*] Oh no, father. Not tonight.

GREGERS What is it he wants to show me?

HJALMAR Oh, it's just—something. You can see it some other time.

GREGERS [*continues addressing* OLD EKDAL] You see, this is what I had in mind, Lieutenant. Why don't you come up to Høydal with me? I'll probably be going back shortly. I'm sure you could get some copying work to do up there as well. For down here you can't have a thing to cheer you up and keep you occupied.

EKDAL [*looks at him in astonishment*] Don't *I* have—!

GREGERS Yes, of course, you have Hjalmar. But then he has his own family. And a man like you, who have always loved the outdoors—

EKDAL [*striking the table*] Hjalmar, he *shall* see it!

HJALMAR But father, do you really think so? It's dark and—

EKDAL Nonsense. There's a moon. [*Getting up.*] I say he's got to see it. Let me out. Come and help me, Hjalmar!

HEDVIG Oh yes, father! Do!

HJALMAR [*getting up*] Oh well, all right.

GREGERS [*to* GINA] What is it?

GINA Oh, don't expect anything much.

[EKDAL *and* HJALMAR *have gone to the rear of the room. Each of them slides one of the double doors back.* HEDVIG *is helping the old man.* GREGERS *remains standing by the sofa.* GINA *keeps on sewing, paying no attention. Through the opened doors can be seen a big, elongated, irregular-shaped attic, with nooks and corners and a couple of chimneys standing free from the wall. Moonlight falls through several skylights, illuminating some parts of the room, while others are in deep shadow.*]

EKDAL [*to* GREGERS] You are welcome to come closer, sir.

GREGERS [*goes up to them*] What is this really?

EKDAL See for yourself. H'm.

HJALMAR [*somewhat embarrassed*] This is all father's, you understand.

GREGERS [*at the door, peering into the attic*] Do you keep chickens, Lieutenant?

EKDAL   Should say we do. They're roosting now. But you ought to see those chickens in daylight!

HEDVIG   And there is—

EKDAL   Hush, don't say anything yet.

GREGERS   And I see you've got pigeons, too.

EKDAL   Could be we have. We've got pigeons, all right! The roosts are up on the rafters, for pigeons like to be up high, you know.

HJALMAR   They aren't all of them just ordinary pigeons.

EKDAL   Ordinary! I should say not! We've got tumblers and even a couple of pouters. But come over here. Do you see that pen over by the wall?

GREGERS   Yes. What do you use that for?

EKDAL   That's where the rabbits are at night.

GREGERS   Oh? You have rabbits, too, do you?

EKDAL   Damn right we have rabbits! He asks if we have rabbits, Hjalmar! H'm. But now we're coming to the *real* thing. Here we are. Move, Hedvig. You stand here and look down—there; that's right. Now, do you see a basket with straw in it?

GREGERS   Yes, I do. And I see a bird.

EKDAL   H'm—A "bird."

GREGERS   Isn't it a duck?

EKDAL   [*offended*]   I'd say it's a duck!

HJALMAR   But what kind of duck, do you think?

HEDVIG   It's not just an ordinary duck.

EKDAL   Hush!

GREGERS   And it's not a muscovy duck, either.

EKDAL   No, Mr.—Werle; it's not a muscovy, for it's a wild duck!

GREGERS   Is it really? A wild duck?

EKDAL   That's what it is. The—"bird," as you called it. A wild duck. It's our wild duck.

HEDVIG   *My* wild duck. For it belongs to me.

GREGERS   And it lives here in the attic? It's thriving?

EKDAL   What's so odd about that? She's got a big pail of water to splash around in.

HJALMAR   Fresh water every other day.

GINA   [*turning to* HJALMAR]   Ekdal, please. I'm freezing.

EKDAL   H'm. All right; let's close up. Just as well not to disturb their night's rest, anyway. Help me Hedvig.

[HJALMAR *and* HEDVIG *slide the double doors shut.*]

EKDAL   You can have a good look at her some other time. [*Sits down in the armchair by the stove.*] I'm telling you, they are strange birds, those wild ducks.

GREGERS   But how did you ever catch it, Lieutenant?

EKDAL   I didn't. There's a certain man in this town we can thank for her.

GREGERS   [*struck by a thought*]   Would that man be my father?

EKDAL   Indeed it is. It's your father, sure enough. H'm.

HJALMAR   Funny you'd guess that, Gregers.

GREGERS   You told me before that you owed a great deal to my father, so I thought that perhaps—

GINA   But we didn't get the duck from Werle himself.

EKDAL   It's Håkon Werle we have to thank for her all the same, Gina. [*To* GREGERS.] He was out in a boat, see, and took a shot at her. But he doesn't see so well, your father doesn't. H'm. Anyway, she was only wounded.

GREGERS   I see. She got some buckshot in her.

HJALMAR   Yes. A little.

HEDVIG   Right under the wing, so she couldn't fly.

GREGERS Then she went to the bottom, I suppose.

EKDAL [*sleepily, his voice muffled*] So it did. Always do that, wild ducks. Dive straight to the bottom—far as they can, sir. Bite themselves fast in the grasses and roots and weeds and all the other damn stuff down there. And never come up again.

GREGERS But, Lieutenant, *your* wild duck did.

EKDAL He had such a wonderfully clever dog, your father. And that dog—it went down and got the duck up.

GREGERS [*to* HJALMAR] And so it came to you?

HJALMAR Not right away. First your father took it home with him, but it didn't seem to get on too well there, and then he told Pettersen to get rid of it.

EKDAL [*half asleep*] H'm—Pettersen—Ass—

HJALMAR That's how we got it, for father knows Pettersen a little, and when he heard about the wild duck, he asked Pettersen to give it to him.

GREGERS And now it seems perfectly contented in there in the attic.

HJALMAR Yes, you would hardly believe how well it gets on. It's becoming fat. I think perhaps it's been in there so long that it has forgotten what wild life is like. And that makes all the difference.

GREGERS I am sure you are right, Hjalmar. The thing to do is never to let it look at sea and sky again.—But I don't think I should stay any longer. I believe your father is asleep.

HJALMAR Oh, as far as that is concerned—

GREGERS Oh yes, one thing more. You said you had a room for rent? A vacant room?

HJALMAR We do. What of it? Do you know anyone who—?

GREGERS Could I get it?

HJALMAR You?

GINA Oh, Mr. Werle, I'm sure *you* don't want to—

GREGERS Couldn't I have it? If I can, I'll move in first thing in the morning.

HJALMAR Yes, indeed, with the greatest pleasure.

GINA No, but Mr. Werle, that's not a room for you.

HJALMAR Gina! How can you say that?

GINA It's not large enough or light enough, and—

GREGERS That doesn't matter, Mrs. Ekdal.

HJALMAR I think it's quite a nice room myself, and decently furnished, too.

GINA But remember those two downstairs.

GREGERS Who are they?

GINA There's one who used to be a private tutor.

HJALMAR Molvik is his name. He studied to be a minister once.

GINA And then there's a doctor, name of Relling.

GREGERS Relling? I know him slightly. He used to practice up at Høydal.

GINA They are a couple of real wild characters those two. Out all hours of the night, and when they come home they aren't always—y'know—

GREGERS One gets used to that sort of thing. I hope I'll be like the wild duck.

GINA H'm. Well, *I* think you ought to sleep on it first.

GREGERS I take it you don't really want me in the house, Mrs. Ekdal.

GINA Good Lord! How can you say a thing like that?

HJALMAR Yes, Gina. It really does seem very odd of you. [*To* GREGERS.] Does this mean you'll be staying in town for a while?

GREGERS [*putting on his overcoat*] Yes, I think I'll stay.

HJALMAR But not with your father? What do you intend to do?

GREGERS If I knew that, Hjalmar, I'd be much better off. But when you're cursed with a name like "Gregers"—and then "Werle" after that—Did you ever hear of an uglier name?

HJALMAR I don't think it's ugly at all.

GREGERS   Ugh! I feel like spitting in the face of anybody with a name like that. But since it's my cross in life to be Gregers Werle, such as I am—

HJALMAR   Ha-ha! If you weren't Gregers Werle, what would you like to be?

GREGERS   If I could choose, I'd like to be a really clever dog.

GINA   A dog!

HEDVIG   [*involuntarily*]   Oh no!

GREGERS   Yes, an exceptionally skillful dog—the kind that goes down to the bottom after wild ducks when they've dived down among the weeds and the grass down there in the mud.

HJALMAR   Honestly, Gregers. This makes no sense whatever.

GREGERS   I suppose it doesn't. But tomorrow morning, then, I'll be moving in. [*To* GINA.] You won't have any trouble with me; I'll do everything myself. [*To* HJALMAR.] The other things we can talk about tomorrow.—Goodnight, Mrs. Ekdal. [*Nods to* HEDVIG.] Goodnight!

GINA   Goodnight, Mr. Werle.

HEDVIG   Goodnight.

HJALMAR   [*who has lighted a candle*]   Wait a moment. I'll see you down. I'm sure it's all dark on the stairs.

[GREGERS *and* HJALMAR *go out through the entrance door, right rear.*]

GINA   [*staring ahead, her sewing lowered in her lap*]   Wasn't it funny all that talk about wanting to be a dog?

HEDVIG   Do you know, mother—I think he really meant something else.

GINA   What would that be?

HEDVIG   No, I couldn't say, but it was just like he had something else in mind all the time.

GINA   You think so? It sure was funny, though.

HJALMAR   [*returning*]   The lamp was still burning. [*Blows out the candle and sits down.*] Ah, at last it's possible to get a bite to eat. [*Starts on the sandwiches.*] Now do you see what I mean, Gina—about seizing the opportunity?

GINA   What opportunity?

HJALMAR   Well—it was lucky, wasn't it, that we got the room rented? And then to somebody like Gregers, a dear old friend.

GINA   Well, I don't know what to say to that.

HEDVIG   Oh mother, you'll see it will be fun.

HJALMAR   I must say you are strange. First you wanted nothing more than to get a lodger; then when we do, you don't like it.

GINA   I know, Ekdal. If only it had been somebody else. What do you think old Werle will say?

HJALMAR   He? It's none of his business.

GINA   But don't you see that something's bound to be wrong between the two of 'em, since the young one is moving out. Sure you know how those two are.

HJALMAR   That may be so, but—

GINA   And maybe Werle will think you are behind it!

HJALMAR   All right! Let him think that. Oh, by all means, Werle has done a great deal for me—I'm the first to admit it. But that doesn't mean I everlastingly have to let him run my life.

GINA   But Ekdal, dear, it could hurt Grandpa. Perhaps he'll lose what little he's making from working for Gråberg.

HJALMAR   I almost wish he would! Is it not humiliating for a man like me to see his gray-haired father treated like dirt? Ah, but soon now the time will be ripe. I feel it. [*Takes another sandwich.*] As sure as I have a mission in life, it shall be accomplished!

HEDVIG   Oh yes, father!

GINA   Shhh! Don't wake him up.

HJALMAR   [*in a lower voice*]   I say it again: I *will* accomplish it! The day will come, when—That's why it's such a good thing we got the room rented out, for that makes me more independent. And that's necessary for a man with a mission in life. [*Over by the armchair, with feeling.*] Poor old white-haired father. Trust your Hjalmar. He has broad enough shoulders—powerful shoulders, at any rate. Some day you'll wake up, and—[*to* GINA.] Or don't you believe that?

GINA   [*getting up*]   Sure I do, but let's first get him to bed.

HJALMAR   Yest, let us

[*They tenderly lift the old man.*]

ACT III

> *The studio. It is morning. Daylight comes in through the skylight, the blue cloth having been pulled aside.*
>
> HJALMAR *sits at the table retouching a photograph. Several other photographs are lying in front of him. After a while,* GINA, *in coat and hat, enters from outside. She is carrying a covered basket.*

HJALMAR   Back already, Gina?

GINA   Yes. I'm in a hurry. [*Puts the basket down on a chair and takes off her coat and hat.*]

HJALMAR   Did you look in at Gregers's?

GINA   I did. It looks real nice in there. He fixed up the place real pretty, soon as he moved in.

HJALMAR   Oh?

GINA   Remember, he was to take care of everything himself? Well, he built a fire in the stove, but he hadn't opened the flue, so the whole room got filled with smoke. Phew! It smelled like—

HJALMAR   Oh dear—

GINA   Then do you know what he does? This really beats everything. He wanted to put out the fire, so he pours the water from the wash basin into the stove. The whole floor is sloppy with filth!

HJALMAR   I am sorry.

GINA   I've got the janitor's wife to clean up after him, pig as he is, but the room can't be lived in till this afternoon.

HJALMAR   Where is he now?

GINA   He said he was going out for a while.

HJALMAR   I went in there for a moment, too—right after you had left.

GINA   He told me. You've asked him for breakfast.

HJALMAR   Just a bit of a late morning meal. It's the first day and all. We can hardly do less. I am sure you have something.

GINA   I'll have to find something, at any rate.

HJALMAR   Be sure it's plenty, though. I think Relling and Molvik are coming, too. I ran into Relling on the stairs just now, and so of course I had to—

GINA   So we are to have those two as well.

HJALMAR   Good heavens, one or two more or less—can that make any difference?

EKDAL   [*opens his door and looks in*]   Listen, Hjalmar—[*Sees* GINA.] Well, never mind.

GINA   Do you want something, Grandpa?

EKDAL   No. It doesn't matter. H'm! [*Goes back inside his room.*]

GINA   [*picking up her basket*]   Make sure he doesn't go out.

HJALMAR   Yes, I will.—Say, Gina—how about some herring salad? I believe Relling and Molvik made a night of it again last night.

GINA   If only they don't get here too soon.

HJALMAR   I'm sure they won't. Just take your time.

GINA   Well, all right. Then you can work some in the meantime.

HJALMAR   I *am* working! I'm working as hard as I can!

GINA   All I mean is you'd have it out of the way for later. [*Goes into the kitchen.*]

[HJALMAR *picks up the photograph and the brush and works for a while—slowly and with evident distaste.*]

EKDAL   [*peeks in, looks around, says in a low voice*]   Pst! Are you busy.

HJALMAR   Yes. I am struggling with these everlasting pictures—

EKDAL   All right, all right. If you're busy, then you're busy. H'm! [*Goes back inside his room. The door remains open.*]

HJALMAR   [*works in silence for a while, puts his brush down, walks over to* EKDAL's *door*]   Are *you* busy, father?

EKDAL   [*grumbling inside his room*]   When *you* are busy, *I* am busy! H'm!

HJALMAR   Oh all right. [*Returns to his work.*]

EKDAL   [*appears in his door again after a while*]   H'm, Hjalmar, listen—I'm not so *terribly* busy, you know.

HJALMAR   I thought you were writing.

EKDAL   Dammit all! Can't that Gråberg wait a day or two? Didn't think it was a matter of life and death.

HJALMAR   Of course not. And you aren't a slave, after all.

EKDAL   And there is this other job in there—

HJALMAR   Just what I was thinking. Do you want to go in there now? Shall I open the door for you?

EKDAL   Good idea.

HJALMAR   [*getting up*]   Then we'd have that job out of the way.

EKDAL   Exactly. It has to be ready for tomorrow, anyway. It *is* tomorrow, isn't it?

HJALMAR   Sure it's tomorrow.

[*They slide the double doors open. The morning sun is shining through the skylight. Some pigeons are flying around; others are cooing on their perches. From farther inside the room the chickens are heard clucking once in a while.*]

HJALMAR   All right, father. Guess you can go ahead.

EKDAL   [*entering the attic*]   Aren't you coming?

HJALMAR   Yes, do you know—I almost think I will. [*Notices* GINA *in the kitchen door.*] I? No, I don't have the time. I have to work. But then there is this thing—

[*He pulls a cord. A curtain comes down from within the attic. Its lower part is made out of a strip of old sailcloth; its upper part is a piece of stretched-out fish net. The attic floor is now no longer visible.*]

HJALMAR   [*returns to the table*]   Now! Maybe I can have peace for a few minutes.

GINA   Is he fooling around in there again?

HJALMAR   Would you rather he went down to Madam Eriksen? [*Sitting down.*] Do you want anything? I thought you said—

GINA   I just wanted to ask you if you think we can set the table in here?

HJALMAR   Yes. There aren't any appointments this early, are there?

GINA   No—only those two sweethearts who want their picture taken.

HJALMAR   Damn! Couldn't they come some other time!

GINA   Goodness, Ekdal, they'll be here after dinner, when you're asleep.

HJALMAR   Oh, in that case it's all right. Yes, let's eat in here.

GINA   Fine. But there's no hurry with the table. You're welcome to use it some more.

HJALMAR   Can't you see I *am* using it?

GINA   Then you'll be all done for afterwards, you know. [*Goes into the kitchen.*] [*Brief silence.*]

EKDAL   [*in the door to the attic, inside the fish net*]   Hjalmar!

HJALMAR   What?

EKDAL   Afraid we'll have to move the pail, after all.

HJALMAR   What else have I been saying all along?

EKDAL   H'm—h'm—h'm! [*Disappears inside again.*]

HJALMAR   [*keeps on working for a moment, glances over towards the attic, half rises, as* HEDVIG *enters from the kitchen. He quickly sits down again*] What do you want?

HEDVIG   Just to be with you, father.

HJALMAR   [*after a short while*]   Seems to me like you're snooping around. Have you been told to watch me, perhaps?

HEDVIG   No, of course not.

HJALMAR   What is mother doing?

HEDVIG   Mother is in the middle of the herring salad. [*Comes over to the table.*] Isn't there any little thing I can help you with, father?

HJALMAR   Oh no. It is better I do it all alone—as long as my strength lasts. There is no need for you to worry about anything, Hedvig, as long as your father is allowed to keep his health.

HEDVIG   Oh father. I won't have you talk that horrid way. [*She walks around a bit, stops by the opening to the inner room and looks in.*]

HJALMAR   What is he doing in there?

HEDVIG   Looks like a new ladder up to the water pail.

HJALMAR   He'll never manage that by himself! And here I am condemned to sit—!

HEDVIG   [*goes to him*]   Give me the brush, father. I can do it.

HJALMAR   I won't hear of it. You'll just be ruining your eyes.

HEDVIG   No, I won't. Give me the brush.

HJALMAR   [*getting up*]   It would only be for a minute or two—

HEDVIG   What possible harm could that do? [*Takes the brush.*] There now. [*Sits down.*] And here is one I can use as model.

HJALMAR   But don't ruin your eyes! Do you hear me? I will not take the responsibility. It's all yours. I'm just telling you.

HEDVIG   [*working*]   Yes, of course.

HJALMAR   You are really very good at it, Hedvig. It will only be for a few minutes, you understand.
[*He slips into the attic by the edge of the curtain.* HEDVIG *keeps on working.* HJALMAR *and* EKDAL *can be heard talking behind the curtain.*]

HJALMAR   [*appearing inside the net*]   Hedvig, please give me the pliers on the shelf. And the chisel. [*Turns around.*] See here, father. Just let me show you what I have in mind first.
[HEDVIG *fetches the tools from the shelf and gives them to him.*]

HJALMAR   Thank you. It was a good thing I went in.

[*He leaves the doorway. Sounds of carpentering and conversation are heard from inside.* HEDVIG *remains watching them. After a while there is a knock on the entrance door. She does not notice.*]

GREGERS   [*bareheaded and coatless, enters, stops near the door*]   H'm!

HEDVIG   [*turns around and walks towards him*]   Good morning! Won't you please come in?

GREGERS   Thank you. [*Looks towards the attic.*] You seem to have workmen in the house.

HEDVIG   Oh no. It's just father and Grandpa. I'll tell them you're here.

GREGERS   Please don't. I'd rather wait a while. [*Sits down on the sofa.*]

HEDVIG   It's such a mess in here—[*Begins removing the photographs.*]

GREGERS   Never mind. Are they pictures you are retouching?

HEDVIG   Yes. It is something I help father with.

GREGERS   I hope you won't let me disturb you.

HEDVIG   I won't.

[*She moves the things more within her reach and resumes work.* GREGERS *watches her in silence.*]

GREGERS   Did the wild duck sleep well last night?

HEDVIG   Yes, thank you. I think so.

GREGERS   [*turning towards the attic*]   In daylight it looks quite different from last night when there was a moon.

HEDVIG   Yes, it varies so. In the morning it looks different than in the afternoon, and when it rains it looks different than when the sun is shining.

GREGERS   You have noticed that?

HEDVIG   Yes, of course.

GREGERS   Do you too spend much time with the wild duck?

HEDVIG   Yes, when I can.

GREGERS   I suppose you don't have much spare time, though. You are going to school, of course?

HEDVIG   Not any more. Father is afraid I'll ruin my eyes.

GREGERS   Then he reads with you himself?

HEDVIG   He has promised to, but he hasn't had the time yet.

GREGERS   But isn't there anyone else who can help you?

HEDVIG   Well, yes, there is Mr. Molvik, but he isn't always—you know—quite—

GREGERS   You mean he is drunk sometimes.

HEDVIG   I think so.

GREGERS   Well, in that case you have time for many things. And in there, I suppose, it's like a world all its own?

HEDVIG   Yes, quite. And there are so many strange things in there.

GREGERS   There are?

HEDVIG   Yes, there are big closets with books in them, and in many of the books there are pictures.

GREGERS   I see.

HEDVIG   And there is an old desk with drawers and drop-down leaves and a big clock with figures that come out. But the clock doesn't run any more.

GREGERS   So time has stopped in there where the wild duck lives?

HEDVIG   Yes. And there are old coloring sets and that sort of thing, and then all the books.

GREGERS   I expect you read the books.

HEDVIG   Yes, whenever I have a chance. But most of them are in English and I can't read that. But I look at the pictures. There is a great, big book that's called "Harrison's History of London." I think it is a hundred years old. There are ever so many pictures in it. In front it shows a picture of Death with an hourglass and a girl. I think that is horrible. But then there are all the pictures of churches and castles and streets and big ships that sail the seas.

GREGERS   Tell me—where do all those strange things come from?

HEDVIG   There was an old sea captain who used to live here. He brought them home. They called him The Flying Dutchman. And that's odd, I think, for he wasn't a Dutchman at all.

GREGERS   No?

HEDVIG   No. But finally he disappeared at sea, and all the things were left here.

GREGERS   Listen—when you sit in there looking at the pictures, don't you ever want to travel and see the real, big world for yourself?

HEDVIG   Oh no. I want to stay here at home always and help father and mother.

GREGERS   With the photographs?

HEDVIG   Not just with that. Best of all I'd like to learn how to engrave pictures like those in the English books.

GREGERS   H'm. And what does your father say to that?

HEDVIG   I don't think father likes the idea very much. He is funny about things like that. You know, he says I ought to learn basket-weaving and straw-plaiting. But I don't think that sounds like much of anything at all.

GREGERS   No, I don't think it does either.

HEDVIG   Though of course father is quite right in saying that if I had learned basket-weaving I could have made the new basket for the wild duck.

GREGERS   That's true. And that really ought to have been your job, you know.

HEDVIG   Yes. Because it is my wild duck.

GREGERS   So I hear.

HEDVIG   Oh yes. I own it. But father and Grandpa get to borrow it as often as they like.

GREGERS   So? And what do they do with it?

HEDVIG   Oh—they take care of it and build things for it and that sort of thing.

GREGERS   I see. For of course the wild duck is the noblest of all the animals in there.

HEDVIG   Yes, she is, for she is a real, wild bird. And then I feel sorrier for her than for any of the others, because she's all alone, poor thing.

GREGERS   No family, like the rabbits.

HEDVIG   No. And the chickens, they have so many they were little chicks together with. But she is all alone, with none of her own near by. And there is the strange thing about the wild duck. Nobody knows her and nobody knows where she is from.

GREGERS   And she has been down to the depths of the sea.

HEDVIG   [glances quickly at him, suppresses a smile, asks]   Why do you say "the depths of the sea"?

GREGERS   What should I say?

HEDVIG   You should say "the sea bottom" or "the bottom of the sea."

GREGERS   Can't I just as well say "the depths of the sea"?

HEDVIG   Yes, but I think it sounds so strange when other people say "the depths of the sea."

GREGERS   Why is that? Tell me.

HEDVIG   No, I won't, for it is so silly.

GREGERS   I don't think so. Please tell me why you smiled.

HEDVIG   It's because every time I think of what's in there—when it comes into my head all of a sudden, I mean—I always feel that the whole room and everything that's in it are the depths of the sea. But that's silly.

GREGERS   Don't say that.

HEDVIG   Yes, for it's just an old attic, you know.

GREGERS   [looking intently at her]   Are you sure?

HEDVIG   [*surprised*]   That it's an attic?

GREGERS   Yes. Are you sure it is?

[HEDVIG *stares at him in silence, her mouth open in astonishment.* GINA *enters from the kitchen with linen, silverware, etc., to set the table.*]

GREGERS   [*getting up*]   I am afraid I am too early for you.

GINA   Oh well. You have to be somewhere. Things are almost ready now, anyway. Clear the table, Hedvig.

[*During the next scene* HEDVIG *clears the table and* GINA *sets it.* GREGERS *seats himself in the armchair and starts leafing through an album of photographs.*]

GREGERS   I understand you know how to retouch, Mrs. Ekdal.

GINA   [*looks at him out of the corner of her eye*]   That's right.

GREGERS   That was fortunate.

GINA   How—fortunate?

GREGERS   I mean since Ekdal is a photographer.

HEDVIG   Mother knows how to take pictures, too.

GINA   Oh yes, I've had to learn *that* business, all right.

GREGERS   Perhaps it is you who are responsible for the daily routine?

GINA   Yes, when Ekdal himself doesn't have the time—

GREGERS   I suppose he busies himself a great deal with his old father?

GINA   Yes, and then it's not for a man like Ekdal to waste his time taking pictures of everybody and his grandmother.

GREGERS   I quite agree, but since he did choose this as his profession, shouldn't he—?

GINA   You know just as well as I do, Mr. Werle, that Ekdal isn't just one of your common, ordinary photographers.

GREGERS   Of course not, but—nevertheless—

[*A shot is heard from the attic.*]

GREGERS   [*jumps up*]   What was that?

GINA   Ugh! There they go, firing away again!

GREGERS   They shoot, too?

HEDVIG   They go hunting.

GREGERS   What? [*Over by the door to the attic.*] Do you go hunting, Hjalmar?

HJALMAR   [*inside the curtain*]   Have you arrived? I didn't know—I've been so busy—[*To* HEDVIG.] And you—not letting us know—! [*Comes into the studio.*]

GREGERS   Do you go shooting in the attic?

HJALMAR   [*showing him a double-barreled pistol*]   Oh, it's only this old thing.

GINA   You and Grandpa are going to have an accident with that pestol of yours one of these days.

HJALMAR   [*irritated*]   I believe I have told you that this kind of firearm is called a pistol.

GINA   I don't see that that makes it any better.

GREGERS   So you have taken up hunting, too, Hjalmar?

HJALMAR   Only a little rabbit hunting now and then. It's mostly for father's sake, you understand.

GINA   Menfolks are strange. They always need something to diverge themselves with.

HJALMAR   [*grimly*]   That's right. We always need something to divert ourselves with.

GINA   That's exactly what I'm saying.

HJALMAR   Oh well—! H'm! [*To* GREGERS.] Well, you see, we're fortunate in that the attic is situated so that nobody can hear the shots.

[*Puts the pistol on the top shelf.*] Don't touch the pistol, Hedvig! Remember, one barrel is loaded!

GREGERS [*peering through the net*]   You have a hunting rifle, too, I see.

HJALMAR   That's father's old gun. It doesn't work any more. There's something wrong with the lock. But it's rather fun to have it around all the same, for we take it apart and clean it once in a while and grease it and put it back together again. It's mostly father, of course, who amuses himself with things like that.

HEDVIG [*standing next to* GREGERS]   Now you can get a good look at the wild duck.

GREGERS   I was just looking at it. One wing is drooping a bit, isn't it?

HJALMAR   Well that's not so strange. She was hit, you know.

GREGERS   And she drags her foot a little. Or doesn't she?

HJALMAR   Perhaps a little bit.

HEDVIG   Yes, for that is the foot the dog seized her by.

HJALMAR   But aside from that she has no other hurt or defect, and that's really quite remarkable when you consider that she has a charge of buckshot in her and has been between the teeth of a dog.

GREGERS [*with a glance at* HEDVIG]   Yes, and been to the depths of the sea—for so long.

HEDVIG [*smiles*]   Yes.

GINA [*busy at the table*]   Oh yes, that precious wild duck. There sure is enough circumstance made over it.

HJALMAR   H'm. Will you be done setting the table soon?

GINA   In a minute. Hedvig, I need your help. [GINA *and* HEDVIG *go into the kitchen.*]

HJALMAR [*in a low voice*]   You had better not watch father. He doesn't like it.

GREGERS [*leaves the attic door.*]

HJALMAR   And I ought to close this before the others arrive. [*Shoos the birds away with his hands.*] Shoo! Shoo—you! [*Raising the curtain and sliding the doors back.*] This arrangement is my own invention. It is really quite amusing to fool around with these things and to fix them when they get broken. And it's absolutely necessary to have something like it, for Gina won't stand for rabbits and chickens in the studio.

GREGERS   No, I suppose not. And perhaps the studio is your wife's department?

HJALMAR   I generally leave the daily run of the business to her. That gives me a chance to retire into the living room and give my thoughts to more important things.

GREGERS   What things, Hjalmar?

HJALMAR   I have been wondering why you haven't asked me that before. Or maybe you haven't heard about the invention?

GREGERS   Invention? No.

HJALMAR   Really? You haven't? Oh well—up there in the woods and wilderness—

GREGERS   So you have invented something!

HJALMAR   Not quite yet, but I am working on it. As you can well imagine, when I decided to devote myself to photography it was not my intent to do nothing but take portraits of all sorts of ordinary people

GREGERS   I suppose not. Your wife just said the same thing.

HJALMAR   I made a pledge to myself that if I were to give my powers to this profession, I would raise it so high that it would become both an art and a science. That is how I decided to make some remarkable invention.

GREGERS   What is it? What does it do?

HJALMAR   Well, Gregers, you must not ask for details just yet. You see, it takes time. And don't think I am driven by vanity. I can truthfully say I am not working for my own sake. Far from it. It is my life's mission that is in my thoughts night and day.

GREGERS   What mission?

HJALMAR   The old man with the silver hair—can you forget him?

GREGERS   Yes, your poor father. But what exactly do you think you can do for him?

HJALMAR   I can resurrect his respect for himself by once again raising the name of Ekdal to fame and honor.

GREGERS   So that is your life's mission.

HJALMAR   Yes. I will rescue that shipwrecked man. For he was shipwrecked the moment the storm broke. During those terrible inquiries he was not himself. The pistol over yonder—the one we use to shoot rabbits with—it has played its part in the tragedy of the Ekdal family.

GREGERS   The pistol? Really?

HJALMAR   When sentence had been pronounced and he was to be confined— he had that pistol in his hand—

GREGERS   He tried to—!

HJALMAR   Yes, but didn't dare. He was a coward. So much of a wreck, so spiritually ruined was he already then. Can you understand it? He, an officer, the killer of nine bears, descended from two lieutenant colonels—I mean one after the other, of course—Can you understand it, Gregers?

GREGERS   I can indeed.

HJALMAR   Not I.—But the pistol came to figure in our family chronicle a second time. When he had begun to wear the garb of gray and sat there behind bolt and bar—oh, those were terrible days for me, believe me. I kept the shades down on both windows. When I looked out, I saw the sun shining as usual. I saw people in the street laughing and talking about nothing. I could not understand it. It seemed to me that all of existence ought to come to a standstill, as during an eclipse of the sun.

GREGERS   I felt that way when mother died.

HJALMAR   In such an hour Hjalmar Ekdal turned the pistol against himself—

GREGERS   You too were thinking of—?

HJALMAR   Yes.

GREGERS   But you did not pull the trigger?

HJALMAR   No. In the decisive moment I won a victory over myself. I remained alive. Take my word for it: it requires courage to go on living in a situation like that.

GREGERS   That depends on how you look at it.

HJALMAR   No, it doesn't. At any rate, it all turned out to be for the best. For soon now I will finish my invention, and when I do, Doctor Relling thinks, as I do myself, that father will be allowed to wear his uniform again. I shall claim that as my only reward.

GREGERS   So it is this business with the uniform that mostly—

HJALMAR   Yes, to be able to wear it again is what he dreams of and longs for. You have no idea how it cuts me to the quick to see him. Whenever we have a little family celebration here, like Gina's and my wedding anniversary or whatever it may be, then the old man appears in his lieutenant's uniform from happier days. But no sooner is there a knock on the door than he scuttles back to his own little room as fast as his old legs will carry him. He doesn't dare to show himself to strangers, you know. A sight like that lacerates a son's heart, Gregers!

GREGERS About when do you think the invention will be ready?

HJALMAR Heavens, you must not ask for details like that. An invention, you see, is something you don't altogether control yourself. It is very largely a matter of inspiration—a sudden idea—and it is next to impossible to tell beforehand when that may come.

GREGERS But it is progressing?

HJALMAR Certainly, it is progressing. It occupies my thoughts every day. It fills me. Every afternoon, after dinner, I shut myself up in the living room to ponder in peace. I just can't be hurried; it won't do any good. That is what Relling says, too.

GREGERS And you don't think that all this business in the attic interferes too much, distracts you from your work?

HJALMAR No, no, no. Quite the contrary. You must not say a thing like that. After all, I cannot everlastingly be pursuing the same exhausting train of thought. I need something else, something to occupy me during the waiting period. The inspiration, the sudden flash of insight, don't you see? —when it comes, it comes.

GREGERS My dear Hjalmar, I almost think there is something of the wild duck in you.

HJALMAR The wild duck? How do you mean?

GREGERS You have plunged down through the sea and got yourself entangled in the grasses on the bottom.

HJALMAR Are you perhaps referring to the well-nigh fatal shot that lodged in father's wing and hit me, too?

GREGERS Not to that so much. I won't say you are crippled. But you are in a poisonous marsh, Hjalmar. You have contracted an insidious disease and gone to the bottom to die in the dark.

HJALMAR I? Die in the dark? Honestly, Gregers. You really shouldn't say such things.

GREGERS Don't you worry. I'll get you up again. For I, too, have got a mission in life. I found it yesterday.

HJALMAR That may well be, but I shall ask you kindly to leave me out of it. I assure you that—aside from my easily explainable melancholia, of course— I am as contented a man as anybody could wish to be.

GREGERS The fact that you are—that is one of the symptoms of the poisoning.

HJALMAR No, really, Gregers. Please don't talk to me any more about disease and poison. I am not used to that sort of talk. In my house we never discuss unpleasant topics.

GREGERS That I can well believe.

HJALMAR No, for it isn't good for me. And there is no marshy air here, as you call it. The roof may be low in the poor photographer's home—I know very well it is—and my lot is lowly. But I am an inventor, and a provider as well. That is what raises me above my humble circumstances.—Ah! Here's lunch!

[GINA *and* HEDVIG *enter with bottles of beer, a decanter of brandy, glasses, and other appurtenances. At the same moment,* RELLING *and* MOLVIK *come through the entrance door. Neither one wears hat or coat.* MOLVIK *is dressed in black.*]

GINA [*putting the things down on the table*] Well, you two arrive just in time.

RELLING Molvik thought he could smell herring salad, and then there was no holding him.—Good morning again, Ekdal.

HJALMAR Gregers, may I introduce you to Mr. Molvik—And Doctor—that's right, you two already know each other, don't you.

GREGERS   Slightly.

RELLING   Oh yes, young Mr. Werle. We used to do some skirmishing up at the Høydal works. I take it you have just moved in?

GREGERS   This morning.

RELLING   Well, Molvik and I live downstairs, so you don't have far to go for doctor and minister if you need them.

GREGERS   Thank you; maybe I shall. We were thirteen at the table yesterday.

HJALMAR   Come now! Please don't start any of that unpleasantness again!

RELLING   Calm down, Ekdal. You are immune.

HJALMAR   I hope so, for my family's sake.—Sit down. Let's eat, drink, and be merry.

GREGERS   Aren't we going to wait for your father?

HJALMAR   No, he'll eat later in his own room. Do sit down!
[*The men seat themselves and begin eating and drinking.* GINA *and* HEDVIG *wait on them.*]

RELLING   Molvik got pretty high last night, Mrs. Ekdal.

GINA   Again?

RELLING   Didn't you hear me bring him home?

GINA   Can't say I did.

RELLING   That's good, for Molvik was awful last night.

GINA   Is that true, Molvik?

MOLVIK   Let us consign last night's events to oblivion. They do not represent my better self.

RELLING   [*to* GREGERS]   It comes over him like an irresistible impulse. Then he has to go out and get drunk. You see, Molvik is demonic.

GREGERS   Demonic?

RELLING   That's right. Molvik is demonic.

GREGERS   H'm.

RELLING   And demonic natures aren't made to follow the straight and narrow path. They have to take off for the fields once in a while.—So you still stick it out up at that filthy old place?

GREGERS   So far.

RELLING   Did you ever collect on that claim you went around presenting?

GREGERS   Claim? [*Looks at him and understands.*] Oh I see.

HJALMAR   Have you been a bill collector, Gregers?

GREGERS   Oh nonsense.

RELLING   Oh yes, he has. He went around to all the cottages up there, trying to collect on something he called "the claim of the ideal."

GREGERS   I was young.

RELLING   You're right. You were very young. And the claim of the ideal—you never collected as long as I was up there.

GREGERS   Not since then, either.

RELLING   In that case, I suppose you have been wise enough to reduce the amount somewhat.

GREGERS   Never when I have to do with a real and genuine human being.

HJALMAR   I think that is reasonable enough.—Some butter, Gina.

RELLING   And a piece of bacon for Molvik.

MOLVIK   Ugh! Not bacon!
[*There is a knock from inside the door to the attic.*]

HJALMAR   Go and open, Hedvig. Father wants to get out.
[HEDVIG *opens the door a little.* OLD EKDAL *enters with the skin of a freshly flayed rabbit.* HEDVIG *closes the door after him.*]

EKDAL   Good morning, gentlemen! Good hunting today. Got me a big one.

HJALMAR   And you skinned it yourself, I see.

EKDAL   Salted it, too. It's nice, tender meat, rabbit is. It's sweet, y'know. Tastes like sugar. Good appetite, gentlemen! [*Goes into his room.*]

MOLVIK   [*getting up*]   Excuse me—I can't—Got to get downstairs—

RELLING   Drink soda water, you idiot!

MOLVIK   Uh—Uh—[*Hurries out, right rear.*]

RELLING   [*to* HJALMAR]   Let us drink to the old hunter.

HJALMAR   [*touching* RELLING'S *glass with his own*]   For the sportsman on the brink of the grave—yes.

RELLING   For the gray-haired—[*Drinks.*] Tell me, is his hair gray or is it white?

HJALMAR   In between, I think. Though I don't think there are many hairs left on his head at all.

RELLING   Oh well. One can live happily with a wig, too. Ah, yes, Ekdal. You are really a very happy man. You have this beautiful ambition of yours to strive for—

HJALMAR   Believe me, I am striving.

RELLING   Then you have your excellent wife, shuffling about in slippered feet with that comfortable waddle of hers, making things nice and pleasant for you.

HJALMAR   Yes, Gina—[*Nods to her.*]—you are a good companion on life's journey.

GINA   Aw, you don't need to sit there and dissectate me!

RELLING   And your Hedvig, Ekdal.

HJALMAR   [*moved*]   Ah yes, the child! The child above all. Hedvig, come to me. [*Stroking her hair.*] What day is tomorrow?

HEDVIG   [*playfully shaking him*]   Oh, stop it, father!

HJALMAR   It's like a knife through my heart, when I consider how little we can do. Just a small celebration here in the attic.

HEDVIG   But that's just the way I like it!

RELLING   You wait till the invention is all done, Hedvig.

HJALMAR   Yes! Then you'll see, Hedvig. I have decided to secure your future. You shall be made comfortable for as long as you live. I will ask for something for you, something or other. That will be the impecunious inventor's sole reward.

HEDVIG   [*whispers, her arms around his neck*]   Oh you good, sweet father!

RELLING   [*to* GREGERS]   Well, now, don't you think it's nice for a change to sit down to a good table in a happy family circle?

HJALMAR   Yes, I really relish these hours at the table.

GREGERS   I, for one, don't like to breathe marsh air.

RELLING   Marsh air?

HJALMAR   Oh, don't start all that again!

GINA   I'll have you know there is no marsh air here, Mr. Werle. The place is aired every single day.

GREGERS   [*leaving the table*]   The stench I have in mind you don't get rid of by opening windows.

HJALMAR   Stench!

GINA   Yes, how do you like that, Ekdal!

RELLING   Begging your pardon—it wouldn't by any chance be you yourself who bring the stench with you from the Høydal mines?

GREGERS   It's just like you to call stench what I bring to this house.

RELLING   [*walks over to* GREGERS]   Listen here, Mr. Werle junior. I strongly suspect that you still carry the claim of the ideal around in your rear pocket.

GREGERS   I carry it in my heart.

RELLING   I don't care where the hell you carry it as long as you don't go bill collecting here while *I* am around.

GREGERS   And if I do so, nevertheless?

RELLING   Then you'll go head first down the stairs. Now you know!

HJALMAR   No, really, Relling—!

GREGERS   Go ahead! Throw me out!

GINA   [*interposing*]   No, we won't have any of that, Relling. But I will say this to you, Mr. Werle, that it seems like you are not the right person to come here and talk about stench after what you did to the stove in your room this morning.

[*There is a knock on the door.*]

HEDVIG   Mother, someone's knocking.

HJALMAR   Oh yes, let's have customers on top of everything else—!

GINA   I'll handle it. [*Opens the door, gives a start, steps back*]: Oh dear!

[WERLE, *in a fur coat, steps inside.*]

WERLE   I beg your pardon, but I am told my son is here.

GINA   [*swallowing hard*]   Yes sir.

HJALMAR   [*closer*]   Sir, wouldn't you like to—?

WERLE   Thanks. I just want a word with my son.

GREGERS   Well. Here I am.

WERLE   I want to talk with you in your room.

GREGERS   In my room—? Oh, all right. [*Is about to leave.*]

GINA   Good Lord, no! That's not a fit place!

WERLE   All right; out here in the hall, then. I want to see you alone.

HJALMAR   You may do that right here, Mr. Werle. Relling, come into the living room with me.

[HJALMAR *and* RELLING *go out, right front.* GINA *takes* HEDVIG *with her into the kitchen, left front.*]

GREGERS   [*after a brief silence*]   Well. We are alone.

WERLE   You dropped some hints last night. And since you have moved in with the Ekdals, I can only assume that you are planning something or other against me.

GREGERS   I plan to open Hjalmar Ekdal's eyes. He is to see his position as it really is. That's all.

WERLE   Is that the life mission you mentioned yesterday?

GREGERS   Yes. You have left me no other.

WERLE   So you feel it is I who have twisted your mind, Gregers?

GREGERS   You have twisted my whole life. I am not thinking of all that with mother. But it is you I can thank for the fact that I am being haunted and driven by a guilty conscience.

WERLE   Ah, I see. So your conscience is ailing.

GREGERS   I should have opposed you the time you were laying traps for Lieutenant Ekdal. I should have warned him, for I suspected how things were going.

WERLE   Yes, in that case you certainly ought to have said something.

GREGERS   I didn't have the courage. I was a coward—frightened. I felt an unspeakable fear of you—both then and for a long, long time afterwards.

WERLE   That fear appears to have left you now.

GREGERS   Yes, fortunately. What has been done to Old Ekdal, both by me and by—others, for that there is no remedy. But Hjalmar I can rescue from the web of lies and deceit in which he is suffocating.

WERLE   Do you think that is a good thing to do?

GREGERS   I am sure it is.

WERLE   I take it you think Mr. Photographer Ekdal is the kind of man who will be grateful for your friendly services?

GREGERS   Yes! He is that kind of man.

WERLE H'm. We'll see.

GREGERS Besides, if I am to continue living, I have to find a way to heal my sick conscience.

WERLE It will never get well. Your conscience has been sickly from the time you were a child. It's hereditary, Gregers. You have it from your mother. The only inheritance she left you.

GREGERS [*with a contemptuous half smile*] I see you still haven't forgotten your disappointment when you found out mother wasn't rich.

WERLE Let's not change the subject. Am I to think, then, that you are firmly resolved to guide Hjalmar Ekdal into the path you consider the right one?

GREGERS Yes. That is my firm intent.

WERLE In that case I could have saved myself coming all the way up here. For then I suppose there is no point in my asking you to move back home again?

GREGERS No.

WERLE And you don't want to join the firm?

GREGERS No.

WERLE Very well. But since I am to marry again, your part of the estate will have to be paid you.

GREGERS [*quickly*] No, I don't want that.

WERLE You don't want it?

GREGERS I dare not, for my conscience's sake.

WERLE [*after a brief pause*] Are you going back up to Høydal?

GREGERS No. I consider myself released from your service.

WERLE But what do you want to do with yourself?

GREGERS Accomplish my mission. Nothing else.

WERLE But afterwards? What are you going to live on?

GREGERS I have saved some of my salary.

WERLE How long do you think that will last?

GREGERS I think it will do for the time I have left.

WERLE What is that supposed to mean?

GREGERS I won't answer any more questions.

WERLE Well, goodbye, Gregers.

GREGERS Goodbye.

[WERLE *leaves.*]

HJALMAR [*looks in*] Did he leave?

GREGERS Yes.

[HJALMAR *and* RELLING *enter from the living room,* GINA *and* HEDVIG *from the kitchen.*]

RELLING Now that was a very successful breakfast.

GREGERS Put on your coat, Hjalmar. I want you to take a long walk with me.

HJALMAR Gladly. What did your father want? Did it have to do with me?

GREGERS Just come. We'll talk. I'll go and get my coat. [*Goes out.*]

GINA You shouldn't go with him, Ekdal.

RELLING No, don't. Stay here.

HJALMAR [*taking his hat and coat*] What! When an old friend feels the need to open his heart for me in private—!

RELLING But goddamit! Can't you see that the fellow is mad, cracked, insane!

GINA Yes, listen to Relling. His mother used to have physicological fits, too.

HJALMAR All the more reason why he needs a friend's alert eyes. [*To* GINA.] Be sure to have dinner ready at the usual time. Goodbye.

[*Goes out.*]

RELLING It's nothing less than a disaster that that man didn't go straight to hell down one of the shafts up at Høydal.

GINA   Heavens—! Why do you say that?

RELLING   [*mutters*]   I have my reasons.

GINA   Do you really think young Werle is crazy?

RELLING   No, unfortunately. He is no madder than most people. He is sick, though.

GINA   What do you think is wrong with him?

RELLING   That I can tell you, Mrs. Ekdal. He suffers from an acute attack of moral integrity.

GINA   Moral integrity?

HEDVIG   Is that a disease?

RELLING   Yes, it is a national disease, but it occurs only sporadically. [*Nods to GINA.*] That was a good meal, thank you. [*Goes out.*]

GINA   [*troubled, walks up and down*]   Ugh! That Gregers Werle—he's always been a weird fish.

HEDVIG   [*by the table, looks at her searchingly*]   I think this is very strange.

ACT IV

The studio. Photographs have just been taken. A cloth-covered camera on a tripod, a couple of chairs, and a small table are standing about in the middle of the floor. Afternoon light. The sun is about to disappear. After a while darkness begins to fall. GINA stands in the open entrance door with a small box and a wet glass plate in her hand. She is talking to someone not in sight.

GINA   Absolutely. When I promise something, I keep it. I'll have the first dozen ready for you on Monday.—Goodbye.

[*Sounds of someone descending the stairs. GINA closes the door, puts the plate inside the box and the box into the camera.*]

HEDVIG   [*enters from the kitchen*]   Did they leave?

GINA   [*putting things in order*]   Yes, thank goodness. I finally got rid of them.

HEDVIG   Can you understand why father isn't back yet?

GINA   You're sure he is not down at Relling's?

HEDVIG   No, he is not there. I just went down the kitchen stairs to ask.

GINA   His food is getting cold and everything.

HEDVIG   Yes. And father who is always so particular about having dinner on time.

GINA   Oh well. You'll see he'll be back soon.

HEDVIG   I wish he'd come. Everything seems so strange.

[*HJALMAR enters from outside.*]

HEDVIG   [*towards him*]   Father! If you knew how we've been waiting for you!

GINA   [*glancing at him*]   You've been gone quite some time.

HJALMAR   [*without looking at her*]   Yes, I suppose I have.

[*He starts taking his coat off. GINA and HEDVIG both go to help him. He turns them away.*]

GINA   Maybe you and Werle had something to eat some place?

HJALMAR   [*hanging up his coat*]   No.

GINA   [*toward the kitchen door*]   I'll get your dinner.

HJALMAR   Never mind. I don't feel like eating now.

HEDVIG   [*coming closer*]   Are you sick, father?

HJALMAR Sick? No, I'm not sick—exactly. We had a strenuous walk, Gregers and I.

GINA You shouldn't do that, Ekdal. You aren't used to it.

HJALMAR H'm. There are many things in life a man has to get used to. [*Paces up and down.*] Anybody here while I've been gone?

GINA Only that engaged couple.

HJALMAR No new appointments?

GINA No, not today.

HEDVIG There will be some tomorrow, father, I am sure.

HJALMAR I hope you are right, for tomorrow I plan to go to work in earnest.

HEDVIG Tomorrow! But don't you remember what day is tomorrow?

HJALMAR That's right. Well, then, the day after tomorrow. From now on I'll do everything myself. I want to assume the entire work load.

GINA Whatever for, Ekdal? That's only making yourself miserable. I'll manage the pictures. You just go on with the invention.

HEDVIG And the wild duck, father. And the chickens and the rabbits and—

HJALMAR Don't ever mention all that junk to me again! Starting tomorrow, I'll never more set foot in the attic.

HEDVIG But father, you promised that tomorrow we're having a celebration—

HJALMAR H'm. That's right. Day after tomorrow then. That damn wild duck. I'd like to wring its neck!

HEDVIG [*with a cry*] The wild duck!

GINA Now I've heard everything!

HEDVIG [*shaking him*] But father—it's *my* wild duck!

HJALMAR That's why I won't do it. I don't have the heart—for your sake, Hedvig. But deep down I feel I ought to do it. I shouldn't harbor under my roof a creature that has been in those hands.

GINA For heaven's sake! Even if Grandpa *did* get it from that awful Pettersen.

HJALMAR [*walking up and down*] There are certain demands—what shall I call them? Let me say ideal demands—certain claims, that a man disregards only at the peril of his soul.

HEDVIG [*following after him*] But think—the wild duck! That poor wild duck!

HJALMAR [*halts*] Didn't I tell you I'll spare it—for your sake? Not a hair on its head will be—h'm. Well, as I said, I'll spare it. After all, there are bigger tasks awaiting me. But you ought to go out for a little walk, Hedvig. The twilight is just right for you.

HEDVIG I don't care to go out now.

HJALMAR Yes, do. Seems to me you are squinting. The fumes in here aren't good for you. The air is close under this roof.

HEDVIG All right. I'll run down the kitchen stairs and walk around a bit. My hat and coat? Oh yes, in my room. Father, please—don't do anything bad to the wild duck while I'm gone!

HJALMAR Not a feather shall be plucked from its head. [*Clutches her to him.*] You and I, Hedvig—we two! Be on your way now.

[HEDVIG *nods goodbye to her parents and goes out through the kitchen door.*]

HJALMAR [*pacing back and forth*] Gina.

GINA Yes?

HJALMAR Starting tomorrow—or let's say the day after tomorrow—I'd like to keep account of the housekeeping expenses myself.

GINA So you want to keep the accounts too, now?

HJALMAR Keep track of what we take in, at any rate.

GINA Lord knows, that's easily done!

HJALMAR One wouldn't think so. It seems to me you make the money go incredibly far. [*Stops and looks at her.*] How do you do it?

GINA   It's because Hedvig and I need so little.

HJALMAR   Is it true that father is overpaid for the copying work he does for Werle?

GINA   I couldn't say about that. I don't know the rates.

HJALMAR   Well, what *does* he get? In round figures.—I want to know.

GINA   It differs. I guess it comes to about what he costs us, plus a little extra in spending money.

HJALMAR   What he costs us! And you haven't told me that!

GINA   No, I couldn't, for you were so happy because he got everything from you.

HJALMAR   And it has really been Werle all the time!

GINA   Oh well. He can afford it.

HJALMAR   Light the lamp!

GINA   [*lighting the lamp*]   And as far as that is concerned, how do we know it is Werle himself? It may be Gråberg—

HJALMAR   Really, Gina. You know that isn't so. Why do you say a thing like that?

GINA   I don't know. I just thought—

HJALMAR   H'm!

GINA   It wasn't me who got Grandpa all that copying to do. It was Bertha, when she took service there.

HJALMAR   It sounds to me like your voice is trembling.

GINA   [*putting the shade on the lamp*]   Does it?

HJALMAR   And your hands are shaking. Aren't they?

GINA   [*firmly*]   You might as well tell me straight, Ekdal. What has he been saying about me?

HJALMAR   Is it true—*can* it be true—that there was some kind of affair between you and Werle while you were in his house?

GINA   That's not so. Not then. He was after me, though. And Mrs. Werle thought there was something going on, and she made a fuss and a big hullaballoo about it, and she beat me and pulled me around—and so I quit.

HJALMAR   But afterwards—!

GINA   Well, then I went to live with mother. And you see—mother—she wasn't all the woman you thought she was, Ekdal. She talked to me about this, that, and the other. For Werle was a widower by that time—

HJALMAR   And then—?

GINA   You might as well know it, I guess. He didn't give up till he had his way.

HJALMAR   [*striking his hands together*]   And this is the mother of my child! How could you keep a thing like this from me?

GINA   Yes, I know it was wrong. I should have told you long ago, I suppose.

HJALMAR   You should have told me right away; that's what you should have. Then I would have known what sort of woman you were.

GINA   But would you have married me, irregardless?

HJALMAR   Of course, I wouldn't!

GINA   I didn't think so, and that's why I didn't dare to tell you. I had come to care for you, you know—a whole lot I cared for you. And I just couldn't see making myself as unhappy as all that—

HJALMAR   [*walking about*]   And this is my Hedvig's mother! And to know that everything I lay my eyes on here [*Kicks a chair.*]—my whole home—I owe to a favored predecessor! Oh, that seducer, that damn Werle!

GINA   Do you regret the fourteen-fifteen years we've had together?

HJALMAR   [*fronting her*]   Tell me if you haven't felt every day and every hour to be one long agony of repentance for that web of deceitful silence you have woven around me, like a spider? Answer me! Haven't you lived here in perpetual torture of guilt and remorse?

GINA Bless you, Ekdal! I've been plenty busy with the house and the pictures—

HJALMAR So you never cast a probing glance at your past?

GINA No, to tell the truth, I had almost forgotten all those old stories.

HJALMAR Oh, this dull, apathetic calm! There is something shocking about it. Not even repentant—!

GINA Just tell me this, Ekdal. What do you think would have become of you if you hadn't got yourself a wife like me?

HJALMAR Like you—!

GINA Yes, for you know I have always been more practical and able to cope with things than you. Of course, I am a couple of years older—

HJALMAR What would have become of me!

GINA For you've got to admit you weren't living exactly right when you first met me.

HJALMAR So you call that living wrong! Oh, what do you know about a man's feelings when he sorrows and despairs—especially a man of my fiery temperament.

GINA No, I guess I don't know. And I don't mean to execrete you for it, either, for you turned into as decent a man as they come as soon as you got a house and a family of your own to take care of. And now we were getting on so nicely here, and Hedvig and I were just thinking that pretty soon we might spend some money on clothes for ourselves.

HJALMAR Yes, in the swamp of deceit!

GINA That that fellow ever poked his nose inside here!

HJALMAR I, too, thought our home a pleasant one. That was a mistake. Where now do I gather the necessary inner resilience to bring my invention into the world of reality? Perhaps it will die with me. If it does, it will be your past, Gina, that has killed it.

GINA [*on the verge of tears*] Please, Ekdal—don't be saying such things! I that have all my days only tried to make things nice and pleasant for you!

HJALMAR I ask—what happens now to the breadwinner's dream? As I reclined in there on the sofa, pondering the invention, it came to me that it was going to drain me of my last drop of vitality. I knew that the day the patent was issued and in my hands—that day would be my—my day of farewell. And then it was my dream that you were to live on as the late inventor's well-to-do widow.

GINA [*wiping her tears*] I won't have you talk that way, Ekdal. May the good Lord never let me live the day when I'm your widow!

HJALMAR Oh what difference does it all make! It is all over now, anyway. Everything!

[GREGERS *cautiously opens the entrance door and peers in.*]

GREGERS May I come in?

HJALMAR Yes, do.

GREGERS [*goes up to them with a beaming, happy face, reaches out his hands to them*] Now, then—you dear people—! [*Looks from one to the other, whispers to* HJALMAR] It hasn't happened yet?

HJALMAR [*loud*] It has happened.

GREGERS It has?

HJALMAR I have lived through the bitterest moment of my life.

GREGERS But also, I trust, its most exalted one.

HJALMAR Anyway, it's done and over with.

GINA May God forgive you, Mr. Werle.

GREGERS [*greatly bewildered*] But I don't understand—!

HJALMAR   What don't you understand?

GREGERS   As crucial a conversation as this—a conversation that is to be the foundation for a whole new way of life—a life, a partnership, in truth and frankness—

HJALMAR   I know. I know it very well.

GREGERS   I was so sure that when I came in here now I would be met with a splendor of revelation shining from both husband and wife. But all I see is this dull, heavy gloom—

GINA   So that's it. [*Removes the lamp shade.*]

GREGERS   You refuse to understand me, Mrs. Ekdal. Well, I suppose you need time. But you, Hjalmar? Surely, you must have felt a higher consecration in this great crisis.

HJALMAR   Of course I did. That is, in a way.

GREGERS   For surely nothing in the world can be compared to finding forgiveness in one's heart for her who has erred and lovingly lifting her up to one's own heights.

HJALMAR   Do you think a man so easily forgets the draught of wormwood I just drained?

GREGERS   An ordinary man, maybe not. But a man like you—!

HJALMAR   Oh, I know. But you must not rush me, Gregers. It takes time.

GREGERS   There is much of the wild duck in you, Hjalmar.

[RELLING *has entered.*]

RELLING   Ah! Here we go with the wild duck again!

HJALMAR   Mr. Werle's crippled prey—yes.

RELLING   Werle? Is it him you're talking about?

HJALMAR   About him—and about ourselves.

RELLING   [*in a low voice, to* GREGERS]   Damn you to hell!

HJALMAR   What are you saying?

RELLING   I am just expressing an ardent wish that this quack here would betake himself home. If he stays around he is likely to ruin both of you.

GREGERS   Those two cannot be ruined, Mr. Relling. Of Hjalmar I need say nothing. Him we know. But she, too, has surely in the depths of her being something reliable, something of integrity—

GINA   [*almost crying*]   Why didn't you leave me alone then?

RELLING   [*to* GREGERS]   Is it impertinent to ask exactly what you want in this house?

GREGERS   I want to lay the foundation for a true marriage.

RELLING   So you don't think the Ekdal's marriage is good enough as it is?

GREGERS   I daresay it is as good a marriage as most, unfortunately. But a true marriage it has yet to become.

HJALMAR   You have never had an eye for the claim of the ideal, Relling!

RELLING   Nonsense, boy!—Begging your pardon, Mr. Werle—how many—roughly—how many true marriages have you observed in your life?

GREGERS   Hardly a single one.

RELLING   Nor have I.

GREGERS   But I have seen a number of the other kind. And I have had occasion to witness what havoc a marriage like that can work in a pair of human beings.

HJALMAR   A man's whole moral foundation may crumble under his feet; that's the terrible thing.

RELLING   Well, I can't say I've ever been exactly married, so I can't judge about that. But I do know this, that the child belongs to marriage too. And you had better leave the child alone.

HJALMAR   Oh, Hedvig! My poor Hedvig!

RELLING   Yes—keep Hedvig out of it, you two! You are grown-ups. In God's name, do whatever fool things you like to your marriage. But I am warning you: be careful what you do to Hedvig. If you're not, there is no telling what may happen to her.

HJALMAR   Happen to her!

RELLING   Yes, she may bring a disaster upon herself—and perhaps on others, too.

GINA   But how can you tell about that, Relling?

HJALMAR   Are you saying there is some immediate danger to her eyes?

RELLING   This has nothing whatever to do with her eyes. Hedvig is in a difficult age. She may do all sorts of crazy things.

GINA   I know—she does already. She's taken to fooling around with the wood-stove in the kitchen. Playing fire, she calls it. Sometimes I'm scared she'll burn the whole house down.

RELLING   There you are. I knew it.

GREGERS   [to RELLING]   But how do you explain a thing like that?

RELLING   [sullenly]   Her voice is changing, sir.

HJALMAR   As long as the child has me—! As long as my head is above the ground! [There is a knock on the door.]

GINA   Shhh, Ekdal. There are people outside. [MRS. SØRBY enters, wearing hat and coat.]

MRS. SØRBY   Good evening!

GINA   [going to her]   Goodness! Is it you, Bertha!

MRS. SØRBY   So it is. Maybe it's inconvenient—?

HJALMAR   Oh by no means! A messenger from that house—!

MRS. SØRBY   [to GINA]   Frankly, I had hoped you'd be without your menfolks this time of day. I've just dropped in to have a word with you about something and say goodbye.

GINA   You're going away?

MRS. SØRBY   Tomorrow morning—to Høydal. Mr. Werle left this afternoon. [Casually, to GREGERS.] He asked me to say hello.

GINA   Imagine—!

HJALMAR   So Mr. Werle has left? And you are going after him?

MRS. SØRBY   Yes. What do you say to that, Ekdal?

HJALMAR   Look out, is all I say.

GREGERS   I can explain. Father and Mrs. Sørby are getting married.

GINA   Oh Bertha! At long last!

RELLING   [his voice trembling a little]   Surely, this cannot be true?

MRS. SØRBY   Yes, my dear Relling, true it is.

RELLING   You want to get married again?

MRS. SØRBY   That's what it amounts to. Werle has got the license. We'll have a quiet little party up at the works.

GREGERS   I suppose I should tender my felicitations like a good stepson.

MRS. SØRBY   Thank you, if you really mean it. I hope this will be for the best for both Werle and myself.

RELLING   I am sure you have every reason to think it will. Mr. Werle never gets drunk—at least not to my knowledge. Nor do I believe he is in the habit of beating up his wife, like the late lamented horse doctor.

MRS. SØRBY   Let Sørby rest quietly in his grave. He had his good sides, too.

RELLING   Mr. Industrialist Werle has better ones, I am sure.

MRS. SØRBY   At least he has not thrown away what is best in himself. The man who does that must take the consequences.

RELLING   Tonight I'll go out with Molvik.

MRS. SØRBY   Don't do that, Relling. Don't—for my sake.

RELLING   There's nothing else to do. [To HJALMAR.] Want to come along?

GINA   No, thank you. Ekdal doesn't go in for excapades like that.

HJALMAR   [angrily, in a half whisper]   For heaven's sake! Keep your mouth shut!

RELLING   Goodbye—Mrs. Werle! [Goes out.]

GREGERS   [to MRS. SØRBY]   It appears that you and Doctor Relling know each other quite well?

MRS. SØRBY   Yes, we've known each other for a good many years. At one time it looked as if we might have made a match of it.

GREGERS   I'm sure it was lucky for you that you didn't.

MRS. SØRBY   You may well say that. But I've always been wary of acting on impulse. A woman can't just throw herself away, you know.

GREGERS   Aren't you afraid I'll let my father know about this old acquaintance-ship?

MRS. SØRBY   Do you really believe I haven't told him myself?

GREGERS   Oh?

MRS. SØRBY   Your father knows every little thing people might say about me with any show of truth at all. I have told him everything. That was the first thing I did when I realized what his intentions were.

GREGERS   It seems to me you are more than usually frank.

MRS. SØRBY   I have always been frank. For us women that's the best policy.

HJALMAR   What do you say to that, Gina?

GINA   Oh, women differ. Some do it one way, others do it different.

MRS. SØRBY   Well, Gina, in my opinion I have followed the wiser course. And Werle hasn't kept back anything either. You see, that's what mainly brought us together. Now he can sit and talk to me as openly as a child. He has never been able to do that before. A healthy, vigorous man like him—all through his youth and all the best years of his life he had his ears drummed full with angry sermons. And very often sermons about sins he hadn't even committed—according to what I have been told.

GINA   That's the truth.

GREGERS   If you ladies want to pursue that topic any further, I had better absent myself.

MRS. SØRBY   You may just as well stay as far as that's concerned. I won't say another word. I just wanted you to know I haven't kept anything back or played him false in any way. Maybe people will say I am a very fortunate woman, and in a way of course that's true. But I don't think I am getting any more than I am giving. I'll certainly never desert him. And I can be of more service and use to him than anybody else, now that he'll soon be helpless.

HJALMAR   Will he be helpless?

GREGERS   [to MRS. SØRBY]   Don't say anything about that here.

MRS. SØRBY   It can't be kept secret any longer, much as he'd like to. He is going blind.

HJALMAR   [struck]   Blind? That's strange. He, too?

GINA   Lots of people go blind.

MRS. SØRBY   And I'm sure you can tell yourself what that must mean to a busi-nessman. Well, I'll try to be his eyes, the best I know how.—But I can't stay any longer. I have so much to do right now.—Oh yes, What I wanted to tell you, Ekdal, is that if Werle can be of any service to you, all you need to do is to get in touch with Gråberg.

GREGERS   That is an offer I am sure Hjalmar Ekdal will decline.

MRS. SØRBY   Really? It seems to me he hasn't always been so—

GINA   Yes, Bertha. Ekdal doesn't need to accept anything more from Mr. Werle.

HJALMAR   [slowly, with weight]   Tell your husband-to-be from me, that in the very near future I intend to go to Mr. Gråberg—

GREGERS   What! You want to do that!

HJALMAR   —I say, go to Mr. Gråberg, and demand an account of the sum I owe his employer. I desire to pay this debt of honor—ha-ha-ha!—let us call it a debt of honor! Enough! I shall pay it all, with five per cent interest.

GINA   But Ekdal—goodness! We don't have that kind of money!

HJALMAR   Be so good as to inform your fiancé that I am working incessantly on my invention. Please tell him that what sustains my mind during this exhausting enterprise is my ambition to free myself from a painful burden of debt. This is why I am an inventor. The entire proceeds from my invention are to be devoted to liberating myself from the obligation to remunerate your husband-to-be for his expenses on behalf of my family.

MRS. SØRBY   Something has happened here.

HJALMAR   Indeed, something has.

MRS. SØRBY   Well, goodbye. I had something else I wanted to talk to you about, Gina, but that will have to wait till some other time. Goodbye.

[HJALMAR and GREGERS return her greeting silently. GINA sees her to the door.]

HJALMAR   Not beyond the threshold, Gina!

[MRS. SØRBY leaves. GINA closes the door.]

HJALMAR   There, now, Gregers. I have that burdensome debt off my chest.

GREGERS   You soon will, at any rate.

HJALMAR   I believe my attitude must be deemed the proper one.

GREGERS   You are the man I have always taken you to be.

HJALMAR   In certain cases it is impossible to disregard the claims of the ideal. As provider for my family, I am bound, of course, to find my course of action difficult and painful. Believe me, it is no joke for a man situated as I am, without means, to assume a debt of many years' standing—a debt, you might say, covered by the sands of oblivion. But never mind. The man in me demands his rights.

GREGERS   [placing his hand on his shoulder]   Dear Hjalmar—wasn't it a good thing that I came?

HJALMAR   Yes.

GREGERS   That your whole situation was made clear to you—wasn't that a good thing?

HJALMAR   [a bit impatiently]   Of course it was. But there is one thing that shocks my sense of justice.

GREGERS   What is that?

HJALMAR   It is this that—But I don't know that I ought to speak so freely about your father—

GREGERS   Don't let that worry you. Say what you want.

HJALMAR   All right. Well, you see, there is something shocking in the notion that now it's he and not I who realizes the true marriage.

GREGERS   How can you say a thing like that!

HJALMAR   Well, it is. For your father and Mrs. Sørby are about to solemnify a union built on full mutual confidence, on complete, unconditional frankness on both sides. They conceal nothing from each other, there are no deceitful silences, there has been declared, if I may put it so, mutual absolution between them.

GREGERS   Well, what of it?

HJALMAR   Well, then—it's all there! All the difficult conditions you yourself said are prerequisites for the building of a true marriage.

GREGERS   But that's in quite a different way, Hjalmar. Surely, you won't compare either yourself or Gina with those two—? Oh I am sure you know what I mean.

HJALMAR   Yet I can't get away from the thought that in all this there is something that offends my sense of justice. It looks exactly as if there were no just order in the universe.

GINA   Ekdal, for God's sake, don't talk like that!

GREGERS   H'm. Let's not get involved in those issues.

HJALMAR   Though, on the other hand, I do in a way discern fate's ruling finger, too. He is going blind.

GINA   We don't know that yet.

HJALMAR   There is no doubt about it. At least, we ought not to doubt it, for in that very fact lies the proof of just retribution. He did once hoodwink a trusting fellow being.

GREGERS   I am afraid he has hoodwinked many.

HJALMAR   And here comes the inexorable, the inscrutable, claiming Werle's own eyes.

GINA   How you talk! I think it's scary.

HJALMAR   It is salutary at times to contemplate the night side of existence.
   [HEDVIG, *dressed for the outside, enters. She is happy, breathless.*]

GINA   Back so soon?

HEDVIG   Yes. I didn't feel like walking any farther. It was a good thing, too, for I met somebody as I was coming in.

HJALMAR   Mrs. Sørby, I suppose.

HEDVIG   Yes.

HJALMAR   [*pacing the floor*]   I hope you have seen her for the last time.
   [*Silence.* HEDVIG, *troubled, looks from one to the other in order to gauge their mood.*]

HEDVIG   [*approaching* HJALMAR, *ingratiatingly*]   Father?

HJALMAR   All right—what is it, Hedvig?

HEDVIG   Mrs. Sørby had something for me.

HJALMAR   [*halts*]   For you?

HEDVIG   Yes. Something for tomorrow.

GINA   Bertha always brings you a little something for your birthday.

HJALMAR   What is it?

HEDVIG   No, you're not to find out now. Mother is to give it to me in the morning, when she brings me breakfast in bed.

HJALMAR   What is all this mystification that I am to be kept in the dark about!

HEDVIG   [*quickly*]   I'll be glad to let you see it, father. It's a big letter. [*Takes the letter out of her coat pocket.*]

HJALMAR   A letter too?

HEDVIG   The letter is all there is. I suppose the other thing will come later. Just think—a letter! I never got a letter before. And it says "Miss" on the outside of it. [*Reads.*] "Miss Hedvig Ekdal." Just think—that's me!

HJALMAR   Let me see that letter.

HEDVIG   Here you are. [*Hands it to him.*]

HJALMAR   It's Werle's handwriting.

GINA   Are you sure, Ekdal?

HJALMAR   See for yourself.

GINA   How would I know?

HJALMAR   Hedvig? May I open the letter? Read it?

HEDVIG   If you like.

GINA   Not tonight, Ekdal. It's supposed to be for tomorrow.

HEDVIG   [*in a low voice*]   Please let him read it! It's bound to be something nice, and then father will be in a good mood, and everything will be pleasant again.

HJALMAR   You say I may open it?

HEDVIG   Yes, please, father. I'd like to know what it is about, too.

HJALMAR   Good. [*Opens the envelope, reads the letter inside. Appears confused.*] What *is* this—?
GINA   What does it say?
HEDVIG   Please, father—tell us!
HJALMAR   Be quiet. [*Reads the letter again. He is pale, but his voice is controlled.*] It is a gift letter, Hedvig.
HEDVIG   Imagine! What is it I get?
HJALMAR   Read for yourself.
[HEDVIG *goes over to the lamp and reads.*]
HJALMAR   [*in a low voice, clenches his fists*]   The eyes, the eyes! And now that letter!
HEDVIG   [*interrupting his reading*]   Seems to me like it's Grandpa who gets it.
HJALMAR   [*taking the letter away from her*]   You, Gina—can you make any sense out of this?
GINA   I don't know a blessed thing about it. Why don't you just tell me?
HJALMAR   Werle writes to Hedvig that her old grandfather no longer needs to trouble himself with the copying work he has been doing, but that he may go to the office every month and draw one hundred crowns—
GREGERS   Aha!
HEDVIG   One hundred crowns, mother! I read that.
GINA   That will be nice for Grandpa.
HJALMAR   —one hundred crowns for as long as he needs it. That means, of course, till he closes his eyes.
GINA   So *he* is all taken care of, poor soul.
HJALMAR   Then it comes. You can't have read that far, Hedvig. After his death, that money will be yours.
HEDVIG   Mine? All of it?
HJALMAR   He writes that the same amount has been set aside for you for the rest of your life. Are you listening, Gina?
GINA   Yes, I hear.
HEDVIG   Just think—all the money I'll be getting! [*Shaking* HJALMAR's *arm.*] Father! Father! But aren't you glad?
HJALMAR   [*going away from her*]   Glad! [*Walking about.*] Oh what vistas, what perspectives, open up before me! It is Hedvig he is so generous to!
GINA   Well, she's the one with the birthday.
HEDVIG   And of course you will get it anyway, father! Don't you know I'll give it all to you and mother?
HJALMAR   To mother, yes! That's just it!
GREGERS   Hjalmar, this is a trap being prepared for you.
HJALMAR   You think this may be another trap?
GREGERS   When he was here this morning, he said, "Hjalmar Ekdal is not the man you think he is."
HJALMAR   Not the man—!
GREGERS   "You just wait and see," he said.
HJALMAR   You were to see me selling myself for money—!
HEDVIG   Mother, what *is* all this?
GINA   Go out and take your wraps off.
[HEDVIG, *about to cry, goes out into the kitchen.*]
GREGERS   Well, Hjalmar—now we shall see who is right—he or I.
HJALMAR   [*slowly tearing the letter in two, putting the pieces down on the table*]   Here is my answer.
GREGERS   Just as I thought.
HJALMAR   [*to* GINA, *who is standing near the stove; in a low voice*]   No more concealment now. If everything was over between you and him when you—

came to care for me, as you call it, then why did he make it possible for us to get married?

GINA   I guess he thought he'd make free of the house.

HJALMAR   Just that? He wasn't worried about a certain possibility?

GINA   I don't know what you're talking about.

HJALMAR   I want to know—if your child has the right to live under my roof.

GINA   [*drawing herself up, her eyes flashing*]   You ask me that!

HJALMAR   Just tell me one thing. Is Hedvig mine or—?—Well?

GINA   [*looks at him with cold defiance*]   I don't know.

HJALMAR   [*with a slight tremble*]   You don't know!

GINA   How can I? A woman like me!

HJALMAR   [*quietly, turning away from her*]   In that case I have nothing more to do in this house.

GREGERS   Think it over, Hjalmar!

HJALMAR   [*putting his overcoat on*]   For a man like me there is nothing to think over.

GREGERS   Yes, there is ever so much to think over. You three must stay together if you are to attain to the sacrificial spirit of sublime forgivingness.

HJALMAR   I don't want to attain it! Never! Never! My hat! [*Takes his hat.*] My house is in ruins about me. [*Bursts out crying.*] Gregers! I have no child!

HEDVIG   [*who has opened the kitchen door*]   Father! What are you saying!

GINA   Oh dear!

HJALMAR   Don't come near me, Hedvig! Go far away from me. I can't stand looking at you. Oh those eyes—! Goodbye. [*Is about to go out.*]

HEDVIG   [*clings to him, cries*]   No! No! Don't leave me!

GINA   Look at the child, Ekdal! Look at the child!

HJALMAR   I will not! I cannot! I must get out—away from all this!
[*He tears himself loose from* HEDVIG *and exits.*]

HEDVIG   [*her eyes desperate*]   He's leaving us, mother! He's leaving us! He'll never come back!

GINA   Just don't cry, Hedvig. Father will be back. You wait.

HEDVIG   [*throws herself sobbing down on the sofa*]   No! No! He'll never come back to us any more!

GREGERS   Do you believe I meant all for the best, Mrs. Ekdal?

GINA   Yes, I suppose you did, but God forgive you all the same.

HEDVIG   [*on the sofa*]   I want to die! What have I done to him, mother? You just have to get him back again!

GINA   Yes, yes, yes; only be quiet. I'll go out and look for him. [*Putting on her coat.*] Perhaps he's gone down to Relling's. But you're not to lie there, bawling like that. Promise?

HEDVIG   [*sobbing convulsively*]   All right, I'll stop, if only father comes home again.

GREGERS   [*to* GINA, *who is leaving*]   But would it not be better to let him fight his agony through by himself?

GINA   He can do that afterwards. First we've got to get the child quieted down. [*Goes out.*]

HEDVIG   [*sitting up, drying her eyes*]   Now you have to tell me what this is all about. Why doesn't father want me any more?

GREGERS   You must not ask that till you're big and grown-up.

HEDVIG   [*sobbing*]   But I just can't stay as miserable as this all the time till I'm grown up.—But I know what it is. Maybe I'm not really father's child.

GREGERS   [*uneasily*]   How could that be?

HEDVIG   Mother might have found me. And now perhaps father has found out about it. I have read about things like that.

GREGERS Well, if it really were so—

HEDVIG I think he could love me just as much, regardless. More, almost. The wild duck is a gift, too, and I love her very, very much.

GREGERS [*glad to turn the conversation*] Oh yes, the wild duck. Let's talk about the wild duck, Hedvig.

HEDVIG That poor wild duck. He can't stand the sight of her, either. Just think, he wants to wring her neck!

GREGERS Oh, I don't think he'll do that.

HEDVIG No, but he said it. And I think that was horrid of father, for I pray for the wild duck every night, that she may be kept safe from death and all that's evil.

GREGERS [*looks at her*] Do you usually say prayers at night?

HEDVIG Yes, I do.

GREGERS Who taught you that?

HEDVIG Myself, for father was terribly sick once and had leeches on his neck, and then he said that death was his dread companion.

GREGERS And—?

HEDVIG So I prayed for him when I went to bed. And I have done so ever since.

GREGERS And now you pray for the wild duck, too?

HEDVIG I thought it was best to mention her as well, for she was so sickly when we first got her.

GREGERS Do you say morning prayers, too?

HEDVIG Of course not.

GREGERS Why is that so of course?

HEDVIG Because it's light in the morning. There's not so much to be afraid of then.

GREGERS And the wild duck you love so much—your father said he'd like to wring her neck?

HEDVIG No, he said it would be better for him if he did, but he was going to spare her for my sake. And that was good of him.

GREGERS [*closer to her*] How would it be if you decided to sacrifice the wild duck for *his* sake?

HEDVIG [*getting up*] The wild duck!

GREGERS What if you willingly gave up the dearest thing in the whole world for him?

HEDVIG Do you think that would help?

GREGERS Try it, Hedvig.

HEDVIG [*softly, with shining eyes*] Yes. I want to.

GREGERS Do you think you have the right kind of strength for doing it?

HEDVIG I shall ask Grandpa to shoot the wild duck for me.

GREGERS Yes, do that. But not a word to your mother about this!

HEDVIG Why not?

GREGERS She doesn't understand us.

HEDVIG The wild duck? I'll try it in the morning!

[GINA *enters from the hall.*]

HEDVIG [*towards her*] Did you find him, mother?

GINA No, but I found out he's got Relling with him.

GREGERS Are you sure?

GINA Yes, the janitor's wife said so. Molvik's with them also.

GREGERS Just now, when his soul so sorely needs to struggle in solitude—!

GINA [*taking off her coat*] Yes, men are funny. God knows where Relling is taking him! I ran over to Madam Eriksen's, but they aren't there.

HEDVIG [*struggling with her tears*] What if he never comes back!

GREGERS   He'll come back. I'll get word to him tomorrow, and then you'll see *how* he comes back. You count on that, Hedvig, and get a good night's sleep. Goodnight. [*Goes out.*]

HEDVIG   [*throws herself sobbing on* GINA's *neck*]   Mother! Mother!

GINA   [*patting her back, sighing*]   Yes, Relling was right. This is what happens when crazy people come around pestering us with the claim of the ordeal.

ACT V

> The studio. Cold, gray morning light. There is wet snow on the big panes of the skylight.
> GINA, aproned, with broom and dust cloth in her hand, enters from the kitchen and goes towards the living room door. HEDVIG hurries in from the outside at the same moment.

GINA   [*stops*]   Well?

HEDVIG   Yes, mother, I almost think he's down at Relling's—

GINA   What did I tell you!

HEDVIG   —for the janitor's wife said she heard Relling bring two others home with him last night.

GINA   I knew it.

HEDVIG   But what good does it do, if he doesn't come up here to us?

GINA   I want to go down and have a talk with him, anyway.

[OLD EKDAL, *in dressing gown and slippers and with his lighted pipe, appears in the door to his room.*]

EKDAL   Eh—Hjalmar—? Isn't Hjalmar here?

GINA   No, he is out, Grandpa.

EKDAL   So early? In this blizzard? Well, I can walk by myself in the morning, I can, if it comes to that.

[*He slides the attic door open.* HEDVIG *helps him. He enters. She closes the door behind him.*]

HEDVIG   [*in a low voice*]   Mother, what do you think will happen when poor Grandpa hears that father has left us?

GINA   Silly! Grandpa mustn't hear anything about it, of course. It was a good thing he wasn't home last night, during all that hullaballoo.

HEDVIG   Yes, but—

[GREGERS *enters.*]

GREGERS   Well? Have you traced him yet?

GINA   They say he's down at Relling's.

GREGERS   At Relling's! Has he really been out with those two?

GINA   It looks like it.

GREGERS   But he is so badly in need of solitude—to find himself in earnest—

GINA   Yes. I should think so, too.

[RELLING *enters.*]

HEDVIG   [*goes towards him*]   Is father with you?

GINA   [*at the same time*]   Is he down there?

RELLING   He certainly is.

HEDVIG   And you haven't told us!

RELLING   I know. I am a big, bad beast. But I had this other big, bad beast to take care of, too—I mean the demonic one. And after that, I just fell asleep —sound asleep—

GINA   What does Ekdal say today?

RELLING   Not a thing.

HEDVIG   Doesn't he say anything at all?

RELLING   Not a blessed word.

GREGERS   I think I understand that.

GINA   But what is he doing?

RELLING   He is on the sofa, snoring.

GINA   Oh. Yes, Ekdal does snore a lot.

HEDVIG   He's asleep? Can he sleep now?

RELLING   It certainly looks that way.

GREGERS   That's reasonable enough, after the spiritual turmoil he's just been through—

GINA   And he isn't used to be out revelling nights, either.

HEDVIG   It may be a good thing that he is sleeping, mother.

GINA   That's what I am thinking. Anyway, we'd better not wake him up too soon. Thank you, Relling. First of all I've got to clean things up a bit and make the place look nice. Come and help me, Hedvig. [*They go into the living room.*]

GREGERS   [*turning to* RELLING]   Can you account for the present spiritual unrest in Hjalmar Ekdal?

RELLING   To tell you the truth, I haven't noticed any spiritual unrest in him.

GREGERS   What? At such a turning point—When his whole life is acquiring a new basis? How can you think that a personality like Hjalmar Ekdal—?

RELLING   Personality? He? If he ever had any tendency to sprout the kind of abnormal growth you call personality, I can assure you that all roots and tendrils were thoroughly extirpated in his boyhood.

GREGERS   That would indeed be strange, considering the loving upbringing he enjoyed.

RELLING   By those two crackpot, hysterical spinster aunts of his, you mean?

GREGERS   Let me tell you that they were women who never forgot the claim of the ideal—though I suppose you'll just be making fun of me again.

RELLING   No, I'm not in the mood. I do know about them, though. He has often enough held forth about "his soul's two mothers." Personally, I don't think he has much to be grateful to them for. Ekdal's misfortune is that he has always been looked upon as a shining light in his own circle.

GREGERS   And you don't think he is that? I mean, when it comes to depth of soul?

RELLING   I have never noticed it. That his father thought so is one thing. The old lieutenant has been an idiot all his days.

GREGERS   He has all his days been a man with a childlike mind. That is what you don't understand.

RELLING   All right. But after dear, sweet Hjalmar had taken up studying— after a fashion—right away he was the light of the future among his friends, too. He was handsome enough, the rascal—red and white, just the way little shop-girls like the fellows. And he had this sentimental temperament and this warm-hearted voice, and he could give such pretty declamations of other people's poetry and other people's thoughts—

GREGERS   [*indignantly*]   Is this Hjalmar Ekdal you are describing?

RELLING   Yes, if you please. For this is what he looks like on the inside, the idol you are prostrating yourself for.

GREGERS   I didn't know I was as blind as all that.

RELLING   Well—not far from it. For you are sick, too, you see.

GREGERS   That is true.

RELLING   Yes it is. And yours is a complicated case. First, there is this pesky integrity fever you're suffering from, and then something worse—you are forever walking around in a delirium of adoration, always looking for something to admire outside of yourself.

GREGERS   Yes, there certainly wouldn't be much point in looking for it within myself.

RELLING   But you are always so hideously wrong about all those big, wonderful flies you see and hear buzzing around you. Once again you have entered a cottage with your claim of the ideal. People here just can't pay.

GREGERS   If this is the way you think of Hjalmar Ekdal, what sort of pleasure can you derive from your constant association with him?

RELLING   Oh well. I am supposed to be a kind of doctor, believe it or not, so the least I can do is to look after the poor patients I share quarters with.

GREGERS   Ah, I see. Hjalmar Ekdal is sick, too?

RELLING   Most people are, worse luck.

GREGERS   And what treatment do you apply in Hjalmar's case?

RELLING   My usual one. I see to it that his vital lie is kept up.

GREGERS   Vital—lie? I am not sure I heard what you said.

RELLING   That's right. I said the vital lie. You see, that's the stimulating principle.

GREGERS   May I ask with what vital lie you have infected Hjalmar?

RELLING   You may not. I never reveal professional secrets to quacks. You are capable of messing him up for me even more than you have. But the method is proven. I have used it with Molvik, too. I have made him demonic. That's the suppurative I have applied to *his* neck.

GREGERS   But *isn't* he demonic?

RELLING   What the hell does it mean—being demonic? It's just some nonsense I thought of to save his life. If I hadn't, the poor, pitiful swine would have succumbed to self-hatred and despair many a year ago. Not to mention the old lieutenant! Though he has found his own cure.

GREGERS   Lieutenant Ekdal? What about him?

RELLING   What do you think? There he is, the old slayer of bears, chasing rabbits in a dark attic. And yet, there isn't a happier hunter alive than that old man when he is playing with all that junk. The four or five dried-out Christmas trees he has saved are the whole big, wild Høydal forest to him. The rooster and the chickens are wild fowl in the tree tops, and the rabbits bouncing about on the floor are bears he's grappling with —the frisky old sportsman.

GREGERS   Ah, yes—that unfortunate old Lieutenant Ekdal. He has certainly had to compromise the ideals of his youth.

RELLING   While I think of it, Mr. Werle—don't use the foreign word "ideals." We have available a good native one: "lies."

GREGERS   You think the two things are related

RELLING   About as closely as typhus and putrid fever.

GREGERS   Doctor Relling! I won't give up till I have rescued Hjalmar from your clutches!

RELLING   That might be his bad luck. Take his vital lie away from the average person, and you take his happiness, too. [*To* HEDVIG, *who enters from the living room.*] Well, now, little duck mother. I am going down to see if papa is still in bed pondering that wonderful invention of his. [*Goes out.*]

GREGERS   [*approaching* HEDVIG]   I can tell from looking at you that it has not yet been accomplished.

HEDVIG   What? Oh, that about the wild duck? No.

GREGERS   Your strength of purpose deserted you, I suppose, when the time for action had come.

HEDVIG   No, it wasn't that. But when I woke up this morning and remembered what we had talked about, it all seemed so strange.

GREGERS   Strange?

HEDVIG   Yes, I don't know—Last night, just at the time—I thought there was something very wonderful about it, but when I had slept and I thought about it again, it didn't seem like anything much.

GREGERS   I see. I could hardly expect you to grow up in this environment without injury to your soul.

HEDVIG   I don't care about that, if only father would come home again.

GREGERS   If only your eyes were opened to what gives life its worth—if only you possessed the true, joyful, brave, sacrificial spirit, then you'd see he'll return. But I still have faith in you, Hedvig. [*Goes out.*]

[HEDVIG *walks around aimlessly. She is about to enter the kitchen, when there is a knock on the inside of the door to the attic.* HEDVIG *opens the doors wide enough for old* EKDAL *to come out. She shuts them again.*]

EKDAL   H'm. Not much fun taking a walk by yourself, y'know.

HEDVIG   Wouldn't you like to go hunting, Grandpa?

EKDAL   It isn't hunting weather today. Too dark. Can hardly see a thing.

HEDVIG   Don't you ever want to shoot something beside rabbits?

EKDAL   Aren't the rabbits good enough, perhaps?

HEDVIG   Yes, but what about the wild duck?

EKDAL   Haw! So you're scared I'll shoot your wild duck? I'll never do that, Hedvig. Never.

HEDVIG   No, for I bet you don't know how. I've heard it's difficult to shoot wild ducks.

EKDAL   Don't know how! Should say I do!

HEDVIG   How would you do it, Grandpa?—I don't mean *my* wild duck, but another one.

EKDAL   Would try to get a shot in just below the breast; that's the best place. And try to shoot *against* the feathers, not *with*.

HEDVIG   Then they die?

EKDAL   Damn right they do—if you shoot right.—Well, better go in and dress up. H'm. Y'know. H'm—[*Goes into his own room.*]

[HEDVIG *waits a moment, glances towards the living room door, stands on tiptoe, takes the double-barreled pistol down from the shelf, looks at it.* GINA, *with broom and dust cloth, enters from the living room.* HEDVIG *quickly puts the pistol back, without* GINA's *noticing.*]

GINA   Don't fool with father's things, Hedvig.

HEDVIG   [*leaving the shelf*]   I just wanted to straighten up some.

GINA   Why don't you go into the kitchen and see if the coffee is keeping hot? I am taking a tray with me when I go down.

[HEDVIG *goes into the kitchen.* GINA *starts putting the studio in order. After a short while, the door to the ouside is hesitantly opened and* HJALMAR *looks in. He is wearing a coat but no hat. He looks unkempt and unwashed. His eyes are dull and lusterless.*]

GINA   [*stands staring at him, still with the broom in her hand*]   Bless you, Ekdal—so you did come back, after all!

HJALMAR   [*enters, answers in a dull voice*]   I return—only to leave.

GINA   Yes, yes, I suppose. But good Lord! how you look!

HJALMAR   Look?

GINA   And your nice winter coat? I'd say that's done for.

HEDVIG   [*in the kitchen door*]   Mother, don't you want me to—[*sees* HJALMAR, *gives a shout of joy and runs towards him.*]   Father! Father!

HJALMAR   [*turning away, with a gesture*]   Go away! Go away! [*To* GINA.]

Get her away from me, I say!

GINA   [in a low voice]   Go into the living room, Hedvig.

[HEDVIG leaves silently.]

HJALMAR   [busy, pulling out the table drawer]   I need my books with me. Where are my books?

GINA   Which books?

HJALMAR   My scientific works, of course—the technical journals I need for my invention.

GINA   [looking on the shelf]   Do you mean these over here, with no covers on them?

HJALMAR   Yes, yes, of course.

GINA   [puts a pile of journals down on the table]   Don't you want me to get Hedvig to cut them open for you?

HJALMAR   No. Nobody needs to cut any pages for me.

[Brief silence.]

GINA   So you are going to leave us, Ekdal?

HJALMAR   [rummaging among the books]   That goes without saying, I should think.

GINA   All right.

HJALMAR   [violently]   For you can hardly expect me to want to stay where my heart is pierced every single hour of the day!

GINA   God forgive you for thinking so bad of me!

HJALMAR   Proof—!

GINA   Seems to me, you're the one who should bring proof.

HJALMAR   After a past like yours? There are certain claims—I might call them the claims of the ideal—

GINA   What about Grandpa? What is he going to do, poor man?

HJALMAR   I know my duty. The helpless one goes with me. I'll go out and make arrangements—H'm [Hesitantly.] Has anybody found my hat on the stairs?

GINA   No. Have you lost your hat?

HJALMAR   I most certainly had it on when I came home last night; there isn't the slightest doubt about that. But now I can't find it.

GINA   Good Lord! Where did you go with those two drunks?

HJALMAR   Oh, don't ask about inessentials. Do you think I'm in a mood for remembering details?

GINA   I only hope you haven't got a cold, Ekdal [Goes into the kitchen.]

HJALMAR   [speaking to himself, in a low voice, angrily, as he empties the drawer]   You're a scoundrel, Relling!—A villain is what you are!— Miserable traitor!—I'd gladly see you assassinated—!

[He puts aside some old letters, discovers the torn gift letter from the day before, picks it up and looks at the two pieces, puts them down quickly as GINA enters.]

GINA   [putting a tray with food down on the table]   Here's a drop of coffee, if you want it. And some salt meat sandwiches.

HJALMAR   [glancing at the tray]   Salt meat? Never under this roof! True it is, I haven't taken solid nourishment for almost twenty-four hours, but that can't be helped.—My notes! My incipient memoirs! Where is my diary— all my important papers! [Opens the door to the living room, but steps back.] If she isn't there, too!

GINA   Heavens, Ekdal. She's got to be somewhere.

HJALMAR   Leave! [He makes room. HEDVIG, scared, enters the studio. With his hand on the door knob; to GINA.] During the last moments I spend in my former home I wish to be spared the sight of intruders—[Enters the living room.]

HEDVIG   [*starts, asks her mother in a low and trembling voice*]   Does that mean
me?

GINA   Stay in the kitchen, Hedvig, or no—go to your own room. [*To* HJALMAR,
as she enters the living room.] Wait a minute, Ekdal. Don't make such a
mess in the dresser. I know where everything is.

HEDVIG   [*remains motionless for a moment, in helpless fright, presses her lips
together not to cry, clenches her hands, whispers*]   The wild duck!
[*She tiptoes over to the shelf and takes the pistol down, opens the doors to
the inner attic, goes inside, closes behind her.* HJALMAR *and* GINA *are heard
talking in the living room.*]

HJALMAR   [*appears with some notebooks and a pile of old papers, which he
puts down on the table*]   The bag obviously won't be enough. There are
thousands of things I need to take with me!

GINA   [*entering with the bag*]   Can't you leave most of it behind for the time
being and just pick up a clean shirt and some underwear?

HJALMAR   Phew—! These exhausting preparations—! [*Takes off his overcoat
and throws it on the sofa.*]

GINA   And there's the coffee getting cold too.

HJALMAR   H'm. [*Without thinking, he takes a sip, and then another one.*]

GINA   [*dusting off the back of chairs*]   How are you ever going to find a large
enough attic for the rabbits?

HJALMAR   You mean I have to drag all those rabbits along, too?

GINA   Grandpa can't do without his rabbits—you know that as well as I do.

HJALMAR   He'll have to get used to that. I shall have to give up higher values
in life than a bunch of rabbits.

GINA   [*dusting off the shelf*]   Shall I put the flute in for you?

HJALMAR   No. No flute for me. But give me my pistol.

GINA   You want that old pestol?

HJALMAR   Yes. My loaded pistol.

GINA   [*looking for it*]   It's gone. He must have taken it inside with him.

HJALMAR   Is he in the attic?

GINA   Sure, he's in the attic.

HJALMAR   H'm. The lonely grayhead—[*He eats a sandwich, empties his cup of
coffee.*]

GINA   If only we hadn't rented that room, you could have moved in there.

HJALMAR   And stay under the same roof as—! Never! Never again!

GINA   But couldn't you stay in the living room for a day or two? There you'd
have everything to yourself.

HJALMAR   Not within these walls!

GINA   How about down at Relling's and Molvik's, then?

HJALMAR   Don't mention their names to me! I get sick just thinking about
them. Oh no—it's out into the wind and the snowdrifts for me—to walk
from house to house seeking shelter for father and myself.

GINA   But you have no hat, Ekdal! You've lost your hat, remember?

HJALMAR   Oh, those two abominations! Rich in nothing but every vice! A hat
must be procured. [*Takes another sandwich.*] Arrangements must be made.
After all, I don't intend to catch my death. [*Looks for something on the
tray.*]

GINA   What are you looking for?

HJALMAR   Butter.

GINA   Just a moment. [*Goes out into the kitchen.*]

HJALMAR   [*shouting after her*]   Oh never mind. Dry bread is good enough
for me.

GINA   [*bringing a plate with butter*]   Here. This is supposed to be freshly
churned.

[*She pours him another cup of coffee. He sits down on the sofa, puts more butter on his bread, eats and drinks in silence.*]

HJALMAR   [*after a pause*]   Could I, without being disturbed by anyone—and I mean *anyone*—stay in the living room for a day or two?

GINA   You certainly can, if you want to.

HJALMAR   You see, I don't know how to get all of father's things moved out on such short notice.

GINA   And there is this, too, that first you'd have to tell him that you don't want to live together with the rest of us any more.

HJALMAR   [*pushing his cup away*]   Yes, yes—that, too. I shall have to go into all those intricate relationships once again, to explain—I must think, I must have air to breathe, I can't bear all the burdens in one single day.

GINA   Of course not. And in such awful weather too—

HJALMAR   [*moving* WERLE's *letter*]   I notice this piece of paper still lying around.

GINA   Well, *I* haven't touched it.

HJALMAR   Not that it concerns *me*—

GINA   I'm sure *I* don't expect to make use of it—

HJALMAR   Nevertheless, I suppose we shouldn't let it get completely lost. In all the fuss of moving, something might easily—

GINA   I'll take care of it, Ekdal.

HJALMAR   For the gift letter belongs to father, first of all. It's his affair whether he wants to make use of it or not.

GINA   [*with a sigh*]   Yes, poor old Grandpa—

HJALMAR   Just to make sure—Is there any glue?

GINA   [*walks over to the shelf*]   Here's a bottle.

HJALMAR   And a brush?

GINA   Here.   [*Brings him both.*]

HJALMAR   [*picks up a pair of scissors*]   Just a strip of paper on the back— [*Cuts and glues.*]   Far be it from me to lay hands on somebody else's property—least of all the property of a poverty-stricken old man.—Well—not on—that other one's, either.—There, now! Leave it to dry for a while. And when it's dry, remove it. I don't want to see that document again— ever!

[GREGERS *enters.*]

GREGERS   [*a little surprised*]   What? So this is where you are, Hjalmar!

HJALMAR   [*quickly gets up*]   Sheer exhaustion drove me to sit down.

GREGERS   And I see you've had breakfast.

HJALMAR   The body, too, makes demands at times.

GREGERS   Well, what have you decided to do?

HJALMAR   For a man like me, there is only one way open. I am in the process of gathering up my most important possessions. Obviously, that takes time.

GINA   [*a trifle impatient*]   Do you want me to make the living room ready for you, or do you want me to pack the bag?

HJALMAR   [*after an irritated glance at* GREGERS]   Pack—and make the room ready.

GINA   [*picking up the bag*]   All right. I'll just put in the shirts and those other things. [*She goes into the living room, closing the door behind her.*]

GREGERS   [*after a short silence*]   I had no idea this would be the end of it. Is it really necessary for you to leave house and home?

HJALMAR   [*paces restlessly up and down*]   What do you want me to do? I am not made to be unhappy, Gregers. I require peace and security and comfort around me.

GREGERS   But you can have all that, Hjalmar. Just try. It seems to me there is a firm foundation to build upon now. Start all over again. And remember, you still have your invention to live for.

HJALMAR Oh don't talk about that invention. It may take a long time yet.

GREGERS So?

HJALMAR Well, yes, for heaven's sake, what do you expect me to invent, anyway? The others have invented most of it already. It's getting more difficult every day.

GREGERS But all the labor you have put into it—?

HJALMAR It was that dissipated Relling who got me started on it.

GREGERS Relling?

HJALMAR Yes, it was he who first called attention to my talent for making some fabulous invention or other in photography.

GREGERS I see. It was Relling—!

HJALMAR Ah—I have been so wonderfully happy about it. Not so much about the invention itself, but because Hedvig believed in it—believed with all the strength and power of a child's soul.—That is, I *thought* she did—fool as I was.

GREGERS Can you really think that Hedvig would be false to you?

HJALMAR I can believe anything now. It is Hedvig who is in the way. She it is who is shutting the sun out of my entire life.

GREGERS Hedvig? You mean Hedvig? How in the world is she going to be an obstacle?

HJALMAR [*without answering*] I have loved that child more than I can ever say. You have no idea how happy I was whenever I came back to my humble dwelling and she rushed towards me with her sweet, squinting eyes. Ha, credulous fool that I was! She was so unspeakably dear to me—and so I lulled myself into the dream that I was equally dear to her.

GREGERS You call that a dream?

HJALMAR How can I tell? I can't get anything out of Gina. Besides, she completely lacks any sense of the ideal aspects of the issue. But to you I can open up, Gregers. It is this terrible doubt—perhaps Hedvig has never really loved me.

GREGERS Maybe you'll receive proof—[*Listens.*] Shh! What's that? The wild duck?

HJALMAR It's just quacking. Father's in the attic.

GREGERS He is! [*Joy lights his face.*] I tell you again, Hjalmar—maybe you will find proof that your poor, misunderstood Hedvig has always loved you!

HJALMAR Pah! What proof could she give? I dare not trust to mere asseverations.

GREGERS Surely, Hedvig doesn't know what deceit is.

HJALMAR Ah, Gregers—that is just what I cannot be certain of. Who knows what Gina and this Mrs. Sørby may have been whispering and scheming? And Hedvig's ears are big enough, believe you me. Maybe that gift letter didn't come as such a surprise to her. It seemed to me I noticed something like that.

GREGERS Good heavens, Hjalmar! What kind of spirit is this that's taken possession of you!

HJALMAR I have had my eyes opened. You just wait. It may turn out that the gift letter was just the beginning. Mrs. Sørby has always been very fond of Hedvig, and now, of course, it's in her power to do anything she likes for the child. They can take her away from me what day and hour they choose.

GREGERS Hedvig will never leave you, Hjalmar. Never.

HJALMAR Don't be too sure. If they beckon her with their arms full—? And I who have loved her so infinitely much! I, whose greatest joy it was to take her tenderly by the hand and lead her, as one leads a frightened child through a dark and deserted room! Now I feel this painful certainty that the poor photographer in his attic has never really meant very much to her. She has only cleverly managed to keep on good terms with him while she bided her time.

GREGERS   You don't believe this, Hjalmar.

HJALMAR   That is just what is so terrible—I don't know what to believe—I'll never be able to find out! But do you really doubt that I am right? Ah, Gregers, you put too much trust in the claim of the ideal! If those others were to come now, with their ample offerings, and called to the child: Leave him; life awaits you here with us—

GREGERS   [quickly]   Yes, what then—?

HJALMAR   If then I were to ask her: Hedvig, are you willing to give your life for me? [Laughs scornfully.] Oh yes—you'd find out soon enough what answer I'd get!

[A pistol shot is heard from within the attic.]

GREGERS   [with a shout of joy]   Hjalmar!

HJALMAR   Must he go shooting today—!

GINA   [enters]   Can't say I like this, Ekdal—Grandpa in there all by himself, banging away.

HJALMAR   I'll take a look—

GREGERS   [agitated, feelingly]   Wait! Do you know what that was?

HJALMAR   Yes, of course, I do.

GREGERS   No, you don't. But I know. It was the proof!

HJALMAR   What proof?

GREGERS   It was a child's sacrifice. She has got your father to shoot the wild duck.

HJALMAR   Shoot the wild duck!

GINA   Heavens—!

HJALMAR   Whatever for?

GREGERS   She wanted to sacrifice to you what she held dearest in the whole world. For then she thought you'd love her again.

HJALMAR   [softly, moved]   Oh that child!

GINA   What she thinks of!

GREGERS   All she wanted was your love, Hjalmar. Without it, life didn't seem possible to her.

GINA   [struggling with tears]   Now, do you see, Ekdal?

HJALMAR   Gina, where is she?

GINA   [sniffling]   Poor thing, She is sitting out in the kitchen, I guess.

HJALMAR   [walks to the kitchen door, flings it open, says]   Hedvig—come! Come to me! [Looks around.] No. She isn't here.

GINA   Then she must be in her own room.

HJALMAR   [offstage]   No, she isn't there, either. [Re-entering the studio.] She must have gone out.

GINA   Yes, for you know you didn't want to see hide nor hair of her in the house.

HJALMAR   If only she'd come back soon—so I can tell her—Now I feel that everything will be all right, Gregers. Now I think we can start life over again.

GREGERS   [quietly]   I knew it. Restitution would come through the child.

[Old EKDAL appears in the door to his room. He is in full uniform and is buckling on his sabre.]

HJALMAR   [surprised]   Father! You're in there!

GINA Do you go shooting in your room, now, Grandpa?

EKDAL [*approaches indignantly*] So you're off hunting by yourself, are you Hjalmar?

HJALMAR [*tense, confused*] You mean it wasn't you who fired that shot in the attic just now?

EKDAL I? Fired? H'm.

GREGERS [*shouts to* HJALMAR] She has shot the wild duck herself!

HJALMAR What *is* this? [*He hurriedly slides the attic doors open, looks in, gives a loud cry.*] Hedvig!

GINA [*runs to the door*] Oh God! What is it?

HJALMAR [*going inside*] She is lying on the floor!

GREGERS Lying—! [*Follows* HJALMAR *inside.*]

GINA [*at the same time*] Hedvig! [*Enters the attic.*] No! No! No!

EKDAL Ho-ho! So *she* has taken to hunting too, now!

[HJALMAR, GINA, *and* GREGERS *drag* HEDVIG *into the studio. Her trailing right hand clasps the pistol tightly.*]

HJALMAR [*beside himself*] The pistol went off! She's hit! Call for help! Help!

GINA [*running out into the hallway, shouts down*] Relling! Relling! Doctor Relling! Hurry up here, fast as you can!

[HJALMAR *and* GREGERS *put* HEDVIG *down on the sofa.*]

EKDAL [*quietly*] The woods avenge themselves.

HJALMAR [*on his knees beside* HEDVIG] She's coming to now. She is coming to. Oh yes, yes, yes—

GINA [*having returned*] Where's she hit? I can't see a thing.

[RELLING *enters hurriedly, followed by* MOLVIK. *The latter is without vest and tie, his tailcoat thrown open.*]

RELLING What's the matter?

GINA They say Hedvig has shot herself.

HJALMAR Come and help us!

RELLING Shot herself! [*He pulls the table back and begins to examine her.*]

HJALMAR [*still on his knees, looking anxiously at* RELLING] It can't be dangerous, can it, Relling? What, Relling? She hardly bleeds at all. It can't possibly be dangerous?

RELLING How did this happen?

HJALMAR Oh, I don't know—

GINA She was going to shoot the wild duck.

RELLING The wild duck?

HJALMAR The pistol must have gone off.

RELLING H'm. I see.

EKDAL The woods avenge themselves. But I'm not afraid. [*Enters the attic and closes the doors behind him.*]

HJALMAR Relling—why don't you say anything?

RELLING The bullet has entered her chest.

HJALMAR Yes, but she's coming to!

RELLING Can't you see that Hedvig is dead?

GINA [*bursts into tears*] Oh, the child, the child—!

GREGERS [*hoarsely*] In the depths of the sea—

HJALMAR [*jumps to his feet*] She must live! I want her to live! For God's sake, Relling—just for a moment—just so I can tell her how unspeakably much I have loved her all the time!

RELLING Her heart has been pierced. Internal hemorrhage. She died instantly.

HJALMAR And I who chased her away from me like an animal! Frightened and lonely she crawled into the attic and died for love of me. [*Sobbing.*]

Never to be able to make up for it! Never to tell her—! [*Shakes his fists upwards.*] You! You above! If thou art at all—! Why hast thou done this unto me?

GINA   Shhh, shhh. You mustn't make such a fuss. We had no right to keep her, I suppose.

MOLVIK   The child is not dead. It sleepeth.

RELLING   Rubbish!

HJALMAR   [*quieting down, walks over to the sofa, looks at* HEDVIG, *his arms crossed*]   There she lies, so stiff and still.

RELLING   [*trying to release the pistol*]   She holds on so tightly, I can't—

GINA   No, no, Relling. Don't break her fingers. Let the pestol be.

HJALMAR   Let her have it with her.

GINA   Yes, let her. But the child isn't going to lie out here for a show. She is going into her own little room, right now. Give me a hand, Ekdal.

[HJALMAR *and* GINA *carry* HEDVIG *between them.*]

HJALMAR   [*carrying*]   Gina, Gina—do you think you can bear this?

GINA   The one has to help the other. Seems to me like now we both have a share in her.

MOLVIK   [*raising his arms, muttering*]   Praise be the Lord, to dust thou returnest, to dust thou returnest—

RELLING   [*whispers*]   Shut up, man! You're drunk.

[HJALMAR *and* GINA *carry* HEDVIG *through the kitchen door.* RELLING *closes the door behind them.* MOLVIK *slinks quietly out into the hall.*]

RELLING   [*goes up to* GREGERS]   Nobody is going to tell me this was an accident.

GREGERS   [*who has remained stunned, moving convulsively*]   Who is to say how this terrible thing happened?

RELLING   There were powder burns on her dress. She must have placed the muzzle against her chest and pulled the trigger.

GREGERS   Hedvig has not died in vain. Did you notice how grief released what is great in him?

RELLING   There is a touch of greatness in most of us when we stand in sorrow by a corpse. How long do you think that will last with him?

GREGERS   As if it won't last and grow throughout the rest of his days!

RELLING   Within a year little Hedvig won't be anything to him but an occasion for spouting pretty sentiments.

GREGERS   And you dare say that about Hjalmar Ekdal!

RELLING   Let's talk about this again when the first grass has withered on her grave. You'll hear all about "the child so early taken from the father's heart." You'll see him wallow in sentimentality and self-admiration and self-pity. You just wait!

GREGERS   If you are right and I am wrong, life isn't worth living.

RELLING   Oh, life would be fairly tolerable if only we'd be spared these blasted bill collectors who come around pestering us paupers with the claim of the ideal.

GREGERS   [*staring ahead*]   In that case I am glad my destiny is what it is.

RELLING   Beg your pardon—what *is* your destiny?

GREGERS   [*about to leave*]   To be the thirteenth man at the table.

RELLING   The hell it is.

GEORGE BERNARD SHAW
[1856–1950]

The "upstart son of a downstart father," George Bernard Shaw was born into an Irish Protestant family in Dublin four years before the American Civil War, and his ashes were scattered on his Ayot St. Lawrence estate in England five years after World War II. This incredible span of time was filled with an equally incredible range of activities. Critic, orator, gadfly, oracle, harlequin, prophet, essayist, novelist, dramatist, pamphleteer, Socialist agitator, pillar of the Fabian Society, successful Labour Party candidate for municipal office, romancer of famous actresses, and perhaps the world's most prolific letter writer, Bernard Shaw amazed the world with his energy and versatile genius. In keeping with his belief that the universe was purposefully driven by a "life force" to achieve higher qualities of life, Shaw wrote: "This is the true joy in life, the being used for a purpose recognized by yourself as a mighty one; the being thoroughly worn out before you are thrown on the scrap heap; the being a force of Nature instead of a feverish selfish little clod of ailments and grievances complaining that the world will not devote itself to making you happy."

The overwhelming success that came to Shaw as a result of his commitment came very slowly and grudgingly at first. Because the overt subjects of his early novels and plays were so controversial—divorce, prostitution, slum landlordism, and so on—they met strong opposition from the establishment, and it was not until the turn of the century, twenty-five years after he had emigrated to London, that people in substantial numbers began coming his way. In the 1880s, Shaw was one of a handful who saw and encouraged the death of the old Victorian order and who sought to prepare for the birth of a new order through a gradual and peaceful enlightening of the establishment. His forensic gifts were ideally suited for one who wished to educate men to change.

Unfortunately, his method for educating people was often misunderstood. Because of his talent for comic impersonation, ironic portrayal, and paradoxical statement, and his belief that "by laughter only can you destroy evil without malice and affirm good fellowship without mawkishness," he was often dismissed as a clown who could not be taken seriously. As Shaw himself explains, "When I first began to promulgate my opinions, I found that they appeared extravagant and even insane. In order to get a hearing, it was necessary for me to attain the footing of a privileged lunatic, with the license of a jester. Fortunately the matter was very easy. I found that I had only to say with perfect simplicity what I seriously meant just as it struck me, to make everybody laugh. My method is to take the utmost trouble to find the right thing to say, and then say it with the utmost levity. And all the time the real joke is that I am in earnest." The necessity to play the jester unfortunately trapped Shaw and considerably lessened his effectiveness as a revolutionary with all those who were unable to appreciate the seriousness of his wit, or the sanity of his method.

As a playwright, Shaw was especially adept at dialectical comedy, although it should be understood that his ultimate interest was not as much in the clash of ideas as in the clash of people who are animated by ideas. He was constantly amused and appalled by the degree to which ordinary people allowed their ideas to determine their behavior or to contradict their character. He seemingly never tired of portraying the obsessed and the hypocritical.

Cæsar and Cleopatra, written in 1898, is one of many Shaw plays that illustrate what Shaw considered to be the final conflict in life—"between the cruel will and the humane will." Chief among the over fifty plays that he wrote are *Widowers' Houses* (1892—his first), *Mrs. Warren's Profession* (1893), *Candida* (1894), *Man and Superman* (1903), *Major Barbara* (1905), *Androcles and the Lion* (1912), *Pygmalion* (1912), *Heartbreak House* (1913), *Back to Methuselah* (1921), *Saint Joan* (1923), *The Apple Cart* (1929), *The Simpleton of the Unexpected Isles* (1935), and *In Good King Charles's Golden Days* (1939).

CÆSAR
AND
CLEOPATRA
A History

GEORGE BERNARD SHAW

PROLOGUE

[*In the doorway of the temple of Ra in Memphis. Deep gloom. An august personage with a hawk's head is mysteriously visible by his own light in the darkness within the temple. He surveys the modern audience with great contempt; and finally speaks the following words to them.*]

Peace! Be silent and hearken unto me, ye quaint little islanders. Give ear, ye men with white paper on your breasts and nothing written thereon (to signify the innocency of your minds). Hear me, ye women who adorn yourselves alluringly and conceal your thoughts from your men, leading them to believe that ye deem them wondrous strong and masterful whilst in truth ye hold them in your hearts as children without judgment. Look upon my hawk's head; and know that I am Ra, who was once in Egypt a mighty god. Ye cannot kneel nor prostrate yourselves; for ye are packed in rows without freedom to move, obstructing one another's vision; neither do any of ye regard it as seemly to do aught until ye see all the rest do so too; wherefore it commonly happens that in great emergencies ye do nothing, though each telleth his fellow that something must be done. I ask you not for worship, but for silence. Let not your men speak nor your women cough; for I am come to draw you back two thousand years over the graves of sixty generations. Ye poor posterity, think not that ye are the first. Other fools before ye have seen the sun rise and set, and the moon change her shape and her hour. As they were so ye are; and yet not so great; for the pyramids my people built stand to this day; whilst the dustheaps on which ye slave, and which ye call empires, scatter in the wind even as ye pile your dead sons' bodies on them to make yet more dust.

Hearken to me then, oh ye compulsorily educated ones. Know that even as there is an old England and a new, and ye stand perplexed between the twain; so in the days when I was worshipped was there an old Rome and a new, and men standing perplexed between them. And the old Rome was poor and little, and greedy and fierce, and evil in many ways; but because its mind was little and its work was simple, it knew its own mind and did its own work; and the gods pitied it and helped it and strengthened it and shielded it; for the gods are patient with littleness. Then the old Rome, like the beggar on horseback, presumed on the favor of the gods, and said, "Lo! there is neither riches nor greatness in our littleness: the road to riches and greatness is through robbery of the poor and slaughter of the weak." So they robbed their own poor until they became great masters of that art, and knew by what laws it could be made to appear seemly and honest. And when they had squeezed their own poor dry, they robbed the poor of other lands, and added those lands to Rome until there came a new Rome, rich and huge. And I, Ra, laughed; for the minds of the Romans remained the same size whilst their dominion spread over the earth.

Now mark me, that ye may understand what ye are presently to see. Whilst the Romans still stood between the old Rome and the new, there arose among them a mighty soldier: Pompey the Great. And the way of the soldier is the way of death; but the way of the gods is the way of life; and so it comes that a god at the end of his way is wise and a soldier at the end of his way is a fool. So Pompey held by the old Rome, in which only soldiers could become great; but the gods turned to the new Rome, in which any man with wit enough could become what he would. And Pompey's friend Julius Cæsar was on the side of the gods; for he saw that Rome had passed beyond the control of the little old Romans. This Cæsar was a great talker and a politician: he bought men with words and with gold, even as ye are bought. And when they would not be satisfied with words and gold, and demanded also the glories of war, Cæsar in his middle age turned his hand to that trade; and they that were against him when he sought their welfare, bowed down before him when he became a slayer and a conqueror; for such is the nature of you mortals. And as for Pompey, the gods grew tired of his triumphs and his airs of being himself a god; for he talked of law and duty and other matters that concerned not a mere human worm. And the gods smiled on Cæsar; for he lived the life they had given him boldly, and was not forever rebuking us for our indecent ways of creation, and hiding our handiwork as a shameful thing. Ye know well what I mean; for this is one of your own sins.

And thus it fell out between the old Rome and the new, that Cæsar said, "Unless I break the law of old Rome, I cannot take my share in ruling her; and the gift of ruling that the gods gave me will perish without fruit." But Pompey said, "The law is above all; and if thou break it thou shalt die." Then said Cæsar, "I will break it: kill me who can." And he broke it. And Pompey went for him, as ye say, with a great army to slay him and uphold the old Rome. So Cæsar fled across the Adriatic sea; for the high gods had a lesson to teach him, which lesson they shall also teach you in due time if ye continue to forget them and to worship that cad among gods, Mammon. Therefore before they raised Cæsar to be master of the world, they were minded to throw him down into the dust, even beneath the feet of Pompey, and blacken his face before the nations. And Pompey they raised higher than ever, he and his laws and his high mind that aped the gods, so that his fall might be the more terrible. And Pompey followed Cæsar, and overcame him with all the majesty of old Rome, and stood over him and over the whole world even as ye stand over it with your fleet that covers thirty miles of the sea. And when Cæsar was brought down to utter nothingness, he made a last stand to die honorably, and did not despair; for he said, "Against me there is Pompey, and the old Rome, and the law and the legions: all all against me; but high above these are the gods; and Pompey is a fool." And the gods laughed and approved; and on the field of Pharsalia the impossible came to pass; the blood and iron ye pin your faith on fell before the spirit of man; for the spirit of man is the will of the gods; and Pompey's power crumbled in his hand, even as the power of imperial Spain crumbled when it was set against your fathers in the days when England was little, and knew her own mind, and had a mind to know instead of a circulation of newspapers. Wherefore look to it, lest some little people whom ye would enslave rise up and become in the hand of God the scourge of your boastings and your injustices and your lusts and stupidities.

And now, would ye know the end of Pompey, or will ye sleep while a god speaks? Heed my words well; for Pompey went where ye are gone, even to Egypt, where there was a Roman occupation even as there was but now a British one. And Cæsar pursued Pompey to Egypt: a Roman fleeing, and a Roman pursuing: dog eating dog. And the Egyptians said, "Lo: these Romans which have lent money to our kings and levied a distraint upon us with their arms, call for ever upon us to be loyal to them by betraying our own country to them. But now behold two Romes! Pompey's Rome and Cæsar's Rome! To which of the twain shall we pretend to be loyal?" So they turned in their perplexity to a soldier that had once served Pompey, and that knew the way of Rome and was full of her lusts. And they said to him, "Lo: in thy country dog eats dog; and both dogs are coming to eat us: what counsel hast thou to give us?" And this soldier, whose name was Lucius Septimius, and whom ye shall presently see before ye, replied, "Ye shall diligently consider which is the bigger dog of the two; and ye shall kill the other dog for his sake and thereby earn his favor." And the Egyptians said, "Thy counsel is expedient; but if we kill a man outside the law we set ourselves in the place of the gods; and this we dare not do. But thou, being a Roman, art accustomed to this kind of killing; for thou hast imperial instincts. Wilt thou therefore kill the lesser dog for us?" And he said, "I will; for I have made my home in Egypt; and I desire consideration and influence among you." And they said, "We knew well thou wouldst not do it for nothing: thou shalt have thy reward." Now when Pompey came, he came alone in a little galley, putting his trust in the law and the constitution. And it was plain to the people of Egypt that Pompey was now but a very small dog. So when he set his foot on the shore he was greeted by his old comrade Lucius Septimius, who welcomed him with one hand and with the other smote off his head, and kept it as it were a pickled cabbage to make a present to Cæsar. And mankind shuddered; but the gods laughed; for Septimius was but a knife that Pompey had sharpened; and when it turned against his own throat they said that Pompey had better have made Septimius a ploughman than so brave and readyhanded a slayer. Therefore again I bid you beware, ye who would all be Pompeys if ye dared; for war is a wolf that may come to your own door.

Are ye impatient with me? Do ye crave for a story of an unchaste woman? Hath the name of Cleopatra tempted ye hither? Ye foolish ones; Cleopatra is as yet but a child that is whipped by her nurse. And what I am about to shew you for the good of your souls is how Cæsar, seeking Pompey in Egypt, found Cleopatra; and how he received that present of a pickled cabbage that was once the head of Pompey; and what things happened between the old Cæsar and the child queen before he left Egypt and battled his way back to Rome to be slain there as Pompey was slain, by men in whom the spirit of Pompey still lived. All this ye shall see; and ye shall marvel, after your ignorant manner, that men twenty centuries ago were already just such as you, and spoke and lived as ye speak and live, no worse and no better, no wiser and no sillier. And the two thousand years that have past are to me, the god Ra, but a moment; nor is this day any other than the day in which Cæsar set foot in the land of my people. And now I leave you; for ye are a dull folk, and instruction is wasted on you; and I had not spoken so much but that it is in the nature of a god to struggle for ever with the dust and the darkness, and to drag from them, by the force of his longing for the divine, more life and more light. Settle ye therefore in your seats and keep silent; for ye are about to hear a man speak, and a great man he was, as ye count greatness. And fear not that I shall speak to you again: the rest of the story must ye learn from them that lived it. Farewell; and do not presume to applaud me. [*The temple vanishes in utter darkness*].

[1912]

AN ALTERNATIVE TO THE PROLOGUE

An October night on the Syrian border of Egypt towards the end of the XXXIII Dynasty, in the year 706 by Roman computation, afterwards reckoned by Christian computation as 48 B.C. A great radiance of silver fire, the dawn of a moonlit night, is rising in the east. The stars and the cloudless sky are our own contemporaries, nineteen and a half centuries younger than we know them; but you would not guess that from their appearance. Below them are two notable drawbacks of civilization: a palace, and soldiers. The palace, an old, low, Syrian building of whitened mud, is not so ugly as Buckingham Palace; and the officers in the courtyard are more highly civilized than modern English officers: for example, they do not dig up the corpses of their dead enemies and mutilate them, as we dug up Cromwell and the Mahdi. They are in two groups: one intent on the gambling of their captain Belzanor, a warrior of fifty, who, with his spear on the ground beside his knee, is stooping to throw dice with a sly-looking young Persian recruit; the other gathered about a guardsman who has just finished telling a naughty story (still current in English barracks) at which they are laughing uproariously. They are about a dozen in number, all highly aristocratic young Egyptian guardsmen, handsomely equipped with weapons and armor, very unEnglish in point of not being ashamed of and uncomfortable in their professional dress; on the contrary, rather ostentatiously and arrogantly warlike, as valuing themselves on their military caste.

Belzanor is a typical veteran, tough and wilful; prompt, capable and crafty where brute force will serve; helpless and boyish when it will not: an active sergeant, an incompetent general, a deplorable dictator. Would, if influentially connected, be employed in the two last capacities by a modern European State on the strength of his success in the first. Is rather to be pitied just now in view of the fact that Julius Cæsar is invading his country. Not knowing this, is intent on his game with the Persian, whom, as a foreigner, he considers quite capable of cheating him.

His subalterns are mostly handsome young fellows whose interest in the game and the story symbolize with tolerable completeness the main interests in life of which they are conscious. Their spears are leaning against the walls, or lying on the ground ready to their hands. The corner of the courtyard forms a triangle of which one side is the front of the palace, with a doorway, the other a wall with a gateway. The storytellers are on the palace side: the gamblers, on the gateway side. Close to the gateway, against the wall, is a stone block' high enough to enable a Nubian sentinel, standing on it, to look over the wall. The yard is lighted by a torch stuck in the wall. As the laughter from the group round the storyteller dies away, the kneeling Persian, winning the throw, snatches up the stake from the ground.

BELZANOR   By Apis, Persian, thy gods are good to thee.

THE PERSIAN   Try yet again, O captain. Double or quits!

BELZANOR   No more. I am not in the vein.

THE SENTINEL   [*poising his javelin as he peers over the wall*]   Stand. Who goes there?

[*They all start, listening. A strange voice replies from without.*]

VOICE   The bearer of evil tidings.

BELZANOR   [*calling to the sentry*]   Pass him.

THE SENTINEL   [*grounding his javelin*]   Draw near, O bearer of evil tidings.

BELZANOR   [*pocketing the dice and picking up his spear*]   Let us receive this man with honor. He bears evil tidings.

[*The guardsmen seize their spears and gather about the gate, leaving a way through for the new comer.*]

PERSIAN   [*rising from his knee*]   Are evil tidings, then, so honorable?

BELZANOR   O barbarous Persian, hear my instruction. In Egypt the bearer of good tidings is sacrificed to the gods as a thank offering; but no god will accept the blood of the messenger of evil. When we have good tidings, we are careful to send them in the mouth of the cheapest slave we can find. Evil tidings are borne by young noblemen who desire to bring themselves into notice. [*They join the rest at the gate*].

THE SENTINEL   Pass, O young captain; and bow the head in the House of the Queen.

VOICE   Go anoint thy javelin with fat of swine, O Blackamoor: for before morning the Romans will make thee eat it to the very butt.

[*The owner of the voice, a fairhaired dandy, dressed in a different fashion from that affected by the guardsmen, but no less extravagantly, comes through the gateway laughing. He is somewhat battlestained; and his left forearm, bandaged, comes through a torn sleeve. In his right hand he carries a Roman sword in its sheath. He swaggers down the courtyard, the Persian on his right, Belzanor on his left, and the guardsmen crowding down behind him.*]

BELZANOR   Who are thou that laughest in the House of Cleopatra the Queen, and in the teeth of Belzanor, the captain of her guard?

THE NEW COMER   I am Bel Affris, descended from the gods.

BELZANOR   [*ceremoniously*]   Hail, cousin!

ALL   [*except the Persian*]   Hail, cousin!

PERSIAN   All the Queen's guards are descended from the gods, O stranger, save myself. I am Persian, and descended from many kings.

BEL AFFRIS   [*to the guardsmen*]   Hail, cousins! [*To the Persian, condescendingly*] Hail, mortal!

BELZANOR   You have been in battle, Bel Affris; and you are a soldier among soldiers. You will not let the Queen's women have the first of your tidings.

BEL AFFRIS   I have no tidings, except that we shall have our throats cut presently, women, soldiers, and all.

PERSIAN   [*to Belzanor*]   I told you so.

THE SENTINEL   [*who has been listening*]   Woe, alas!

BEL AFFRIS   [*calling to him*]   Peace, peace, poor Ethiop: destiny is with the gods who painted thee black. [*To Belzanor*] What has this mortal [*indicating the Persian*] told you?

BELZANOR   He says that the Roman Julius Cæsar, who has landed on our shores with a handful of followers, will make himself master of Egypt. He is afraid of the Roman soldiers. [*The guardsmen laugh with boisterous scorn*]. Peasants, brought up to scare crows and follow the plough! Sons of smiths and millers and tanners! And we nobles, consecrated to arms, descended from the gods!

PERSIAN   Belzanor: the gods are not always good to their poor relations.

BELZANOR   [*hotly, to the Persian*]   Man to man, are we worse than the slaves of Cæsar?

BEL AFFRIS   [*stepping between them*]   Listen, cousin. Man to man, we Egyptians are as gods above the Romans.

THE GUARDSMEN   [*exultantly*]   Aha!

BEL AFFRIS   But this Cæsar does not pit man against man: he throws a legion at you where you are weakest as he throws a stone from a catapult; and that legion is as a man with one head, a thousand arms, and no religion. I have fought against them; and I know.

BELZANOR   [*derisively*]   Were you frightened, cousin?

[*The guardsmen roar with laughter, their eyes sparkling at the wit of their captain.*]

BEL AFFRIS   No, cousin; but I was beaten. They were frightened (perhaps); but they scattered us like chaff.

[*The guardsmen, much damped, utter a growl of contemptuous disgust.*]

BELZANOR   Could you not die?

BEL AFFRIS   No: that was too easy to be worthy of a descendant of the gods. Besides, there was no time: all was over in a moment. The attack came just where we least expected it.

BELZANOR   That shews that the Romans are cowards.

BEL AFFRIS   They care nothing about cowardice, these Romans: they fight to win. The pride and honor of war are nothing to them.

PERSIAN   Tell us the tale of the battle. What befell?

THE GUARDSMEN   [*gathering eagerly round Bel Affris*]   Ay: the tale of the battle.

BEL AFFRIS   Know then, that I am a novice in the guard of the temple of Ra in Memphis, serving neither Cleopatra nor her brother Ptolemy, but only the high gods. We went a journey to inquire of Ptolemy why he had driven Cleopatra into Syria, and how we of Egypt should deal with the Roman Pompey, newly come to our shores after his defeat by Cæsar at Pharsalia. What, think ye, did we learn? Even that Cæsar is coming also in hot pursuit of his foe, and that Ptolemy has slain Pompey, whose severed head he holds in readiness to present to the conqueror. [*Sensation among the guardsmen*]. Nay, more: we found that Cæsar is already come; for we had not made half a day's journey on our way back when we came upon a city rabble flying from his legions, whose landing they had gone out to withstand.

BELZANOR   And ye, the temple guard! did ye not withstand these legions?

BEL AFFRIS   What man could, that we did. But there came the sound of a trumpet whose voice was as the cursing of a black mountain. Then saw we a moving wall of shields coming towards us. You know how the heart burns when you charge a fortified wall; but how if the fortified wall were to charge you?

THE PERSIAN   [*exulting in having told them so*]   Did I not say it?

BEL AFFRIS   When the wall came nigh, it changed into a line of men—common fellows enough, with helmets, leather tunics, and breastplates. Every man of them flung his javelin: the one that came my way drove through my shield as through a papyrus—lo there! [*he points to the bandage on his left arm*] and would have gone through my neck had I not stooped. They were charging at the double then, and were upon us with short swords almost as soon as their javelins. When a man is close to you with such a sword, you can do nothing with our weapons: they are all too long.

THE PERSIAN   What did you do?

BEL AFFRIS   Doubled my fist and smote my Roman on the sharpness of his jaw. He was but mortal after all: he lay down in a stupor; and I took his sword and laid it on. [*Drawing the sword*] Lo! a Roman sword with Roman blood on it!

THE GUARDSMEN   [*approvingly*]   Good! [*They take the sword and hand it round, examining it curiously*].

THE PERSIAN   And your men?

BEL AFFRIS   Fled. Scattered like sheep.

BELZANOR   [*furiously*]   The cowardly slaves! Leaving the descendants of the gods to be butchered!

BEL AFFRIS   [*with acid coolness*]   The descendants of the gods did not stay to be butchered, cousin. The battle was not to the strong; but the race was to the swift. The Romans who have no chariots, sent a cloud of horsemen in pursuit, and slew multitudes. Then our high priest's captain rallied a dozen descendants of the gods and exhorted us to die fighting. I said to myself: surely it is safer to stand than to lose my breath and be stabbed in the back; so I joined our captain and stood. Then the Romans treated us with respect; for no man attacks a lion when the field is full of sheep, except for the pride and honor of war, of which these Romans know nothing. So we escaped with our lives; and I am come to warn you that you must open your gates to Cæsar; for his advance guard is scarce an hour behind me; and not an Egyptian warrior is left standing between you and his legions.

THE SENTINEL   Woe, alas! [*He throws down his javelin and flies into the palace*].

BELZANOR   Nail him to the door, quick! [*The guardsmen rush for him with their spears; but he is too quick for them*]. Now this news will run through the palace like fire through stubble.

BEL AFFRIS   What shall we do to save the women from the Romans?

BELZANOR   Why not kill them?

PERSIAN   Because we should have to pay blood money for some of them. Better let the Romans kill them: it is cheaper.

BELZANOR   [*awestruck at his brain power*]   O subtle one! O serpent!

BEL AFFRIS   But your Queen?

BELZANOR   True: we must carry off Cleopatra.

BEL AFFRIS   Will ye not await her command?

BELZANOR   Command! a girl of sixteen! Not we. At Memphis ye deem her a Queen: here we know better. I will take her on the crupper of my horse. When we soldiers have carried her out of Cæsar's reach, then the priests and the nurses and the rest of them can pretend she is a queen again, and put their commands into her mouth.

PERSIAN   Listen to me, Belzanor.

BELZANOR   Speak, O subtle beyond thy years.

THE PERSIAN   Cleopatra's brother Ptolemy is at war with her. Let us sell her to him.

THE GUARDSMEN   O subtle one! O serpent!

BELZANOR   We dare not. We are descended from the gods; but Cleopatra is descended from the river Nile; and the lands of our fathers will grow no grain if the Nile rises not to water them. Without our father's gifts we should live the lives of dogs.

PERSIAN   It is true: the Queen's guard cannot live on its pay. But hear me further, O ye kinsmen of Osiris.

THE GUARDSMEN   Speak, O subtle one. Hear the serpent begotten!

PERSIAN   Have I heretofore spoken truly to you of Cæsar, when you thought I mocked you?

GUARDSMEN   Truly, truly.

BELZANOR   [*reluctantly admitting it*]   So Bel Affris says.

PERSIAN   Hear more of him, then. This Cæsar is a great lover of women: he makes them his friends and counsellors.

BELZANOR   Faugh! This rule of women will be the ruin of Egypt.

THE PERSIAN   Let it rather be the ruin of Rome! Cæsar grows old now: he is past fifty and full of labors and battles. He is too old for the young women; and the old women are too wise to worship him.

BEL AFFRIS   Take heed, Persian. Cæsar is by this time almost within earshot.

PERSIAN   Cleopatra is not yet a woman: neither is she wise. But she already troubles men's wisdom.

BELZANOR   Ay: that is because she is descended from the river Nile and a black kitten of the sacred White Cat. What then?

PERSIAN   Why, sell her secretly to Ptolemy, and then offer ourselves to Cæsar as volunteers to fight for the overthrow of her brother and the rescue of our Queen, the Great Granddaughter of the Nile.

THE GUARDSMEN   O serpent!

PERSIAN   He will listen to us if we come with her picture in our mouths. He will conquer and kill her brother, and reign in Egypt with Cleopatra for his Queen. And we shall be her guard.

GUARDSMEN   O subtlest of all the serpents! O admiration! O wisdom!

BEL AFFRIS   He will also have arrived before you have done talking, O word spinner.

BELZANOR   That is true. [*An affrighted uproar in the palace interrupts him*]. Quick: the flight has begun: guard the door. [*They rush to the door and form a cordon before it with their spears. A mob of women-servants and nurses surges out. Those in front recoil from the spears, screaming to those behind to keep back. Belzanor's voice dominates the disturbance as he shouts*] Back there. In again, unprofitable cattle.

THE GUARDSMEN   Back, unprofitable cattle.

BELZANOR   Send us out Ftatateeta, the Queen's chief nurse.

THE WOMEN   [*calling into the palace*]   Ftatateeta, Ftatateeta. Come, come. Speak to Belzanor.

A WOMAN   Oh, keep back. You are thrusting me on the spearheads.

[*A huge grim woman, her face covered with a network of tiny wrinkles, and her eyes old, large, and wise; sinewy handed, very tall, very strong; with the mouth of a bloodhound and the jaws of a bulldog, appears on the threshold. She is dressed like a person of consequence in the palace, and confronts the guardsmen insolently.*]

FTATATEETA   Make way for the Queen's chief nurse.

BELZANOR   [*with solemn arrogance*]   Ftatateeta: I am Belzanor, the captain of the Queen's guard, descended from the gods.

FTATATEETA   [*retorting his arrogance with interest*]   Belzanor: I am Ftatateeta, the Queen's chief nurse; and your divine ancestors were proud to be painted on the wall in the pyramids of the kings whom my fathers served.

[*The women laugh triumphantly.*]

BELZANOR   [*with grim humor*]   Ftatateeta: daughter of a long-tongued, swivel-eyed chameleon, the Romans are at hand. [*A cry of terror from the women: they would fly but for the spears*] Not even the descendants of the gods can resist them; for they have each man seven arms, each carrying seven spears. The blood in their veins is boiling quicksilver; and their wives become mothers in three hours, and are slain and eaten the next day.

[*A shudder of horror from the women. Ftatateeta, despising them and scorning the soldiers, pushes her way through the crowd and confronts the spear points undismayed.*]

FTATATEETA   Then fly and save yourselves, O cowardly sons of the cheap clay gods that are sold to fish porters; and leave us to shift for ourselves.

BELZANOR   Not until you have first done our bidding, O terror of manhood. Bring out Cleopatra the Queen to us; and then go whither you will.

FTATATEETA   [*with a derisive laugh*]   Now I know why the gods have taken her out of our hands. [*The guardsmen start and look at one another*]. Know, thou foolish soldier, that the Queen has been missing since an hour past sundown.

BELZANOR   [*furiously*]   Hag: you have hidden her to sell to Cæsar or her brother. [*He grasps her by the left wrist, and drags her, helped by a few of the guard, to the middle of the courtyard, where, as they fling her on her knees, he draws a murderous looking knife*]. Where is she? Where is she? or— [*he threatens to cut her throat*].

FTATATEETA   [*savagely*]   Touch me, dog; and the Nile will not rise on your fields for seven times seven years of famine.

BELZANOR   [*frightened, but desperate*]   I will sacrifice: I will pay. Or stay. [*To the Persian*] You, O subtle one: your father's lands lie far from the Nile. Slay her.

PERSIAN   [*threatening her with his knife*]   Persia has but one god; yet he loves the blood of old women. Where is Cleopatra?

FTATATEETA   Persian: as Osiris lives, I do not know. I chid her for bringing evil days upon us by talking to the sacred cats of the priests, and carrying them in her arms. I told her she would be left alone here when the Romans came as a punishment for her disobedience. And now she is gone—run away— hidden. I speak the truth. I call Osiris to witness—

THE WOMEN   [*protesting officiously*]   She speaks the truth, Belzanor.

BELZANOR   You have frightened the child: she is hiding. Search—quick—into the palace—search every corner.

[*The guards, led by Belzanor, shoulder their way into the palace through the flying crowd of women, who escape through the courtyard gate.*]

FTATATEETA   [*screaming*]   Sacrilege! Men in the Queen's chambers! Sa—[*her voice dies away as the Persian puts his knife to her throat*].

BEL AFFRIS   [*laying a hand on Ftatateeta's left shoulder*]   Forbear her yet a moment, Persian. [*To Ftatateeta, very significantly*] Mother: your gods are asleep or away hunting; and the sword is at your throat. Bring us to where the Queen is hid, and you shall live.

FTATATEETA   [*contemptuously*]   Who shall stay the sword in the hand of a fool, if the high gods put it there? Listen to me, ye young men without understanding. Cleopatra fears me; but she fears the Romans more. There is but one power greater in her eyes than the wrath of the Queen's nurse and the cruelty of Cæsar; and that is the power of the Sphinx that sits in the desert watching the way to the sea. What she would have it know, she tells into the ears of the sacred cats; and on her birthday she sacrifices to it and decks it with poppies. Go ye therefore into the desert and seek Cleopatra in the shadow of the Sphinx; and on your heads see to it that no harm comes to her.

BEL AFFRIS   [*to the Persian*]   May we believe this, O subtle one?

PERSIAN   Which way come the Romans?

BEL AFFRIS   Over the desert, from the sea, by this very Sphinx.

PERSIAN   [*to Ftatateeta*]   O mother of guile! O aspic's tongue! You have made up this tale so that we two may go into the desert and perish on the spears of the Romans. [*Lifting his knife*] Taste death.

FTATATEETA . . Not from thee, baby.

[*She snatches his ankle from under him and flies stooping along the palace wall, vanishing in the darkness within its precinct. Bel Affris roars with laughter as the Persian tumbles. The guardsmen rush out of the palace with Belzanor and a mob of fugitives, mostly carrying bundles*].

PERSIAN   Have you found Cleopatra?

BELZANOR   She is gone. We have searched every corner.

THE NUBIAN SENTINEL   [*appearing at the door of the palace*]   Woe! Alas! Fly, fly!

BELZANOR   What is the matter now?

THE NUBIAN SENTINEL   The sacred white cat has been stolen.

ALL   Woe! woe!

[*General panic. They all fly with cries of consternation. The torch is thrown down and extinguished in the rush. The noise of the fugitives dies away. Darkness and dead silence*].

ACT I

The same darkness into which the temple of Ra and the Syrian palace vanished. The same silence. Suspense. Then the blackness and stillness break softly into silver mist and strange airs as the windswept harp of Memnon plays at the dawning of the moon. It rises full over the desert; and a vast horizon comes into relief, broken by a huge shape which soon reveals itself in the spreading radiance as a Sphinx pedestalled on the sands. The light still clears, until the upraised eyes of the image are distinguished looking straight forward and upward in infinite fearless vigil, and a mass of color between its great paws defines itself as a heap of red poppies on which a girl lies motionless, her silken vest heaving gently and regularly with the breathing of a dreamless sleeper, and her braided hair glittering in a shaft of moonlight like a bird's wing.

Suddenly there comes from afar a vaguely fearful sound (it might be the bellow of a Minotaur softened by great distance) and Memnon's music stops. Silence: then a few faint high-ringing trumpet notes. Then silence again. Then a man comes from the south with stealing steps, ravished by the mystery of the night, all wonder, and halts, lost in contemplation, opposite the left flank of the Sphinx, whose bosom, with its burden, is hidden from him by its massive shoulder.

THE MAN   Hail, Sphinx: salutation from Julius Cæsar! I have wandered in many lands, seeking the lost regions from which my birth into this world exiled me, and the company of creatures such as I myself. I have found flocks and pastures, men and cities, but no other Cæsar, no air native to me, no man kindred to me, none who can do my day's deed, and think my night's thought. In the little world yonder, Sphinx, my place is as high as yours in this great desert; only I wander, and you sit still; I conquer, and you endure;

I work and wonder, you watch and wait; I look up and am dazzled, look down and am darkened, look round and am puzzled, whilst your eyes never turn from looking out—out of the world—to the lost region—the home from which we have strayed. Sphinx, you and I, strangers to the race of men, are no strangers to one another: have I not been conscious of you and of this place since I was born? Rome is a madman's dream: this is my Reality. These starry lamps of yours I have seen from afar in Gaul, in Britain, in Spain, in Thessaly, signalling great secrets to some eternal sentinel below, whose post I never could find. And here at last is their sentinel—an image of the constant and immortal part of my life, silent, full of thoughts, alone in the silver desert. Sphinx, Sphinx: I have climbed mountains at night to hear in the distance the stealthy footfall of the winds that chase your sands in forbidden play—our invisible children, O Sphinx, laughing in whispers. My way hither was the way of destiny; for I am he of whose genius you are the symbol: part brute, part woman, and part god—nothing of man in me at all. Have I read your riddle, Sphinx?

THE GIRL [*who has wakened, and peeped cautiously from her nest to see who is speaking*] Old gentleman.

CÆSAR [*starting violently, and clutching his sword*] Immortal gods!

THE GIRL Old gentleman: dont run away.

CÆSAR [*stupefied*] "Old gentleman: dont run away"!!! This! to Julius Cæsar!

THE GIRL [*urgently*] Old gentleman.

CÆSAR Sphinx: you presume on your centuries. I am younger than you, though your voice is but a girl's voice as yet.

THE GIRL Climb up here, quickly; or the Romans will come and eat you.

CÆSAR [*running forward past the Sphinx's shoulder, and seeing her*] A child at its breast! a divine child!

THE GIRL Come up quickly. You must get up at its side and creep round.

CÆSAR [*amazed*] Who are you?

THE GIRL Cleopatra, Queen of Egypt.

CÆSAR Queen of the Gypsies, you mean.

CLEOPATRA You must not be disrespectful to me, or the Sphinx will let the Romans eat you. Come up. It is quite cosy here.

CÆSAR [*to himself*] What a dream! What a magnificent dream! Only let me not wake, and I will conquer ten continents to pay for dreaming it out to the end.
[*He climbs to the Sphinx's flank, and presently reappears to her on the pedestal, stepping round to its right shoulder*].

CLEOPATRA Take care. Thats right. Now sit down: you may have its other paw. [*She seats herself comfortably on its left paw*]. It is very powerful and will protect us; but [*shivering, and with plaintive loneliness*] it would not take any notice of me or keep me company. I am glad you have come: I was very lonely. Did you happen to see a white cat anywhere?

CÆSAR [*sitting slowly down on the right paw in extreme wonderment*] Have you lost one?

CLEOPATRA Yes: the sacred white cat: is it not dreadful? I brought him here to sacrifice him to the Sphinx; but when we got a little way from the city a black cat called him, and he jumped out of my arms and ran away to it. Do you think that the black cat can have been my great-great-great-grandmother?

CÆSAR [*staring at her*] Your great-great-great-grandmother! Well, why not? Nothing would surprise me on this night of nights.

CLEOPATRA I think it must have been. My great-grandmother's great-grandmother was a black kitten of the sacred white cat; and the river Nile made her his seventh wife. That is why my hair is so wavy. And I always want to be let do as I like, no matter whether it is the will of the gods or not: that is because my blood is made with Nile water.

CÆSAR   What are you doing here at this time of night? Do you live here?

CLEOPATRA   Of course not: I am the Queen; and I shall live in the palace at Alexandria when I have killed my brother, who drove me out of it. When I am old enough I shall do just what I like. I shall be able to poison the slaves and see them wriggle, and pretend to Ftatateeta that she is going to be put into the fiery furnace.

CÆSAR   Hm! Meanwhile why are you not at home and in bed?

CLEOPATRA   Because the Romans are coming to eat us all. You are not at home and in bed either.

CÆSAR   [with conviction]   Yes I am. I live in a tent; and I am now in that tent, fast asleep and dreaming. Do you suppose that I believe you are real, you impossible little dream witch?

CLEOPATRA   [giggling and leaning trustfully towards him]   You are a funny old gentleman. I like you.

CÆSAR   Ah, that spoils the dream. Why dont you dream that I am young?

CLEOPATRA   I wish you were; only I think I should be more afraid of you. I like men, especially young men with round strong arms; but I am afraid of them. You are old and rather thin and stringy; but you have a nice voice; and I like to have somebody to talk to, though I think you are a little mad. It is the moon that makes you talk to yourself in that silly way.

CÆSAR   What! you heard that, did you? I was saying my prayers to the great Sphinx.

CLEOPATRA   But this isnt the great Sphinx.

CÆSAR   [much disappointed, looking up at the statue]   What!

CLEOPATRA   This is only a dear little kitten of a Sphinx. Why, the great Sphinx is so big that it has a temple between its paws. This is my pet Sphinx. Tell me: do you think the Romans have any sorcerers who could take us away from the Sphinx by magic?

CÆSAR   Why? Are you afraid of the Romans?

CLEOPATRA   [very seriously]   Oh, they would eat us if they caught us. They are barbarians. Their chief is called Julius Cæsar. His father was a tiger and his mother a burning mountain; and his nose is like an elephant's trunk. [Cæsar involuntarily rubs his nose]. They all have long noses, and ivory tusks, and little tails, and seven arms with a hundred arrows in each; and they live on human flesh.

CÆSAR   Would you like me to shew you a real Roman?

CLEOPATRA   [terrified]   No. You are frightening me.

CÆSAR   No matter: this is only a dream—

CLEOPATRA   [excitedly]   It is not a dream: it is not a dream. See, see. [She plucks a pin from her hair and jabs it repeatedly into his arm].

CÆSAR   Ffff—Stop. [Wrathfully] How dare you?

CLEOPATRA   [abashed]   You said you were dreaming. [Whimpering] I only wanted to shew you—

CÆSAR   [gently]   Come, come: dont cry. A queen mustnt cry. [He rubs his arm, wondering at the reality of the smart]. Am I awake? [He strikes his hand against the Sphinx to test its solidity. It feels so real that he begins to be alarmed, and says perplexedly] Yes. I— [quite panicstricken] no: impossible: madness, madness! [Desperately] Back to camp—to camp. [He rises to spring down from the pedestal].

CLEOPATRA   [flinging her arms in terror round him]   No: you shant leave me. No, no, no: dont go. I'm afraid—afraid of the Romans.

CÆSAR [*as the conviction that he is really awake forces itself on him*] Cleopatra: can you see my face well?

CLEOPATRA Yes. It is so white in the moonlight.

CÆSAR Are you sure it is the moonlight that makes me look whiter than an Egyptian? [*Grimly*] Do you notice that I have a rather long nose?

CLEOPATRA [*recoiling, paralysed by a terrible suspicion*] Oh!

CÆSAR It is a Roman nose, Cleopatra.

CLEOPATRA Ah! [*With a piercing scream she springs up; darts round the left shoulder of the Sphinx; scrambles down to the sand; and falls on her knees in frantic supplication, shrieking*] Bite him in two, Sphinx: bite him in two. I meant to sacrifice the white cat—I did indeed—I [*Cæsar, who has slipped down from the pedestal, touches her on the shoulder*]—Ah! [*She buries her head in her arms*].

CÆSAR Cleopatra: shall I teach you a way to prevent Cæsar from eating you?

CLEOPATRA [*clinging to him piteously*] Oh do, do, do. I will steal Ftatateeta's jewels and give them to you. I will make the river Nile water your lands twice a year.

CÆSAR Peace, peace, my child. Your gods are afraid of the Romans: you see the Sphinx dare not bite me, nor prevent me carrying you off to Julius Cæsar.

CLEOPATRA [*in pleading murmurings*] You wont, you wont. You said you wouldnt.

CÆSAR Cæsar never eats women.

CLEOPATRA [*springing up full of hope*] What!

CÆSAR [*impressively*] But he eats girls [*she relapses*] and cats. Now you are a silly little girl; and you are descended from the black kitten. You are both a girl and a cat.

CLEOPATRA [*trembling*] And will he eat me?

CÆSAR Yes; unless you make him believe that you are a woman.

CLEOPATRA Oh, you must get a sorcerer to make a woman of me. Are you a sorcerer?

CÆSAR Perhaps. But it will take a long time; and this very night you must stand face to face with Cæsar in the palace of your fathers.

CLEOPATRA No, no. I darent.

CÆSAR Whatever dread may be in your soul—however terrible Cæsar may be to you—you must confront him as a brave woman and a great queen; and you must feel no fear. If your hand shakes: if your voice quavers; then— night and death! [*She moans*]. But if he thinks you worthy to rule, he will set you on the throne by his side and make you the real ruler of Egypt.

CLEOPATRA [*despairingly*] No: he will find me out: he will find me out.

CÆSAR [*rather mournfully*] He is easily deceived by women. Their eyes dazzle him; and he sees them not as they are, but as he wishes them to appear to him.

CLEOPATRA [*hopefully*] Then we will cheat him. I will put on Ftatateeta's head-dress; and he will think me quite an old woman.

CÆSAR If you do that he will eat you at one mouthful.

CLEOPATRA But I will give him a cake with my magic opal and seven hairs of the white cat baked in it; and—

CÆSAR [*abruptly*] Pah! you are a little fool. He will eat your cake and you too. [*He turns contemptuously from her*].

CLEOPATRA [*running after him and clinging to him*] Oh please, please! I will do whatever you tell me. I will be good. I will be your slave.
[*Again the terrible bellowing note sounds across the desert, now closer at hand. It is the bucina, the Roman war trumpet*].

CÆSAR Hark!

CLEOPATRA   [*trembling*]   What was that?

CÆSAR   Cæsar's voice.

CLEOPATRA   [*pulling at his hand*]   Let us run away. Come. Oh, come.

CÆSAR   You are safe with me until you stand on your throne to receive Cæsar. Now lead me thither.

CLEOPATRA   [*only too glad to get away*]   I will, I will. [*Again the bucina*]. Oh come, come, come: the gods are angry. Do you feel the earth shaking?

CÆSAR   It is the tread of Cæsar's legions.

CLEOPATRA   [*drawing him away*]   This way, quickly. And let us look for the white cat as we go. It is he that has turned you into a Roman.

CÆSAR   Incorrigible, oh, incorrigible! Away!

[*He follows her, the bucina sounding louder as they steal across the desert. The moonlight wanes: the horizon again shews black against the sky, broken only by the fantastic silhouette of the Sphinx. The sky itself vanishes in darkness, from which there is no relief until the gleam of a distant torch falls on great Egyptian pillars supporting the roof of a majestic corridor. At the further end of this corridor a Nubian slave appears carrying the torch. Cæsar, still led by Cleopatra, follows him. They come down the corridor, Cæsar peering keenly about at the strange architecture, and at the pillar shadows between which, as the passing torch makes them hurry noiselessly backwards, figures of men with wings and hawk's heads, and vast black marble cats, seem to flit in and out of ambush. Further along, the wall turns a corner and makes a spacious transept in which Cæsar sees, on his right, a throne, and behind the throne a door. On each side of the throne is a slender pillar with a lamp on it*].*

CÆSAR   What place is this?

CLEOPATRA   This is where I sit on the throne when I am allowed to wear my crown and robes. [*The slave holds his torch to shew the throne*].

CÆSAR   Order the slave to light the lamps.

CLEOPATRA   [*shyly*]   Do you think I may?

CÆSAR   Of course. You are the Queen. [*She hesitates.*] Go on.

CLEOPATRA   [*timidly, to the slave*]   Light all the lamps.

FTATATEETA   [*suddenly coming from behind the throne*]   Stop. [*The slave stops. She turns sternly to Cleopatra, who quails like a naughty child*]. Who is this you have with you; and how dare you order the lamps to be lighted without my permission? [*Cleopatra is dumb with apprehension*].

CÆSAR   Who is she?

CLEOPATRA   Ftatateeta.

FTATATEETA   [*arrogantly*]   Chief nurse to—

CÆSAR   [*cutting her short*]   I speak to the Queen. Be silent. [*To Cleopatra*] Is this how your servants know their places? Send her away; and do you [*to the slave*] do as the Queen has bidden. [*The slave lights the lamps. Meanwhile Cleopatra stands hesitating, afraid of Ftatateeta*]. You are the Queen: send her away.

CLEOPATRA   [*cajoling*]   Ftatateeta, dear: you must go away—just for a little.

CÆSAR   You are not commanding her to go away: you are begging her. You are no Queen. You will be eaten. Farewell. [*He turns to go*].

CLEOPATRA   [*clutching him*]   No, no, no. Dont leave me.

CÆSAR   A Roman does not stay with queens who are afraid of their slaves.

CLEOPATRA   I am not afraid. Indeed I am not afraid.

FTATATEETA   We shall see who is afraid here. [*Menacingly*] Cleopatra—

CÆSAR   On your knees, woman: am I also a child that you dare trifle with me? [*He points to the floor at Cleopatra's feet. Ftatateeta, half cowed, half savage, hesitates. Cæsar calls to the Nubian*] Slave. [*The Nubian comes to him*] Can you cut off a head? [*The Nubian nods and grins ecstatically, showing all his teeth. Cæsar takes his sword by the scabbard, ready to offer the hilt to the Nubian, and turns again to Ftatateeta, repeating his gesture*]. Have you remembered yourself, mistress?

> *Ftatateeta, crushed, kneels before Cleopatra, who can hardly believe her eyes.*

FTATATEETA [*hoarsely*] O Queen, forget not thy servant in the days of thy greatness.

CLEOPATRA [*blazing with excitement*] Go. Begone. Go away. [*Ftatateeta rises with stooped head, and moves backwards towards the door. Cleopatra watches her submission eagerly, almost clapping her hands, which are trembling. Suddenly she cries*] Give me something to beat her with.

[*She snatches a snake-skin from the throne and dashes after Ftatateeta, whirling it like a scourge in the air. Cæsar makes a bound and manages to catch her and hold her while Ftatateeta escapes*].

CÆSAR You scratch, kitten, do you?

CLEOPATRA [*breaking from him*] I will beat somebody. I will beat him. [*She attacks the slave.*] There, there, there! [*The slave flies for his life up the corridor and vanishes. She throws the snake-skin away and jumps on the step of the throne with her arms waving, crying*] I am a real Queen at last—a real, real Queen! Cleopatra the Queen! [*Cæsar shakes his head dubiously, the advantage of the change seeming open to question from the point of view of the general welfare of Egypt. She turns and looks at him exultantly. Then she jumps down from the steps, runs to him, and flings her arms round him rapturously, crying*] Oh, I love you for making me a Queen.

CÆSAR But queens love only kings.

CLEOPATRA I will make all the men I love kings. I will make you a king. I will have many young kings, with round, strong arms; and when I am tired of them I will whip them to death; but you shall always be my king: my nice, kind, wise, good old king.

CÆSAR Oh, my wrinkles, my wrinkles! And my child's heart! You will be the most dangerous of all Cæsar's conquests.

CLEOPATRA [*appalled*] Cæsar! I forgot Cæsar. [*Anxiously*] You will tell him that I am a Queen, will you not?—a real Queen. Listen! [*stealthily coaxing him*]: let us run away and hide until Cæsar is gone.

CÆSAR If you fear Cæsar, you are no true queen; and though you were to hide beneath a pyramid, he would go straight to it and lift it with one hand. And then—! [*he chops his teeth together*].

CLEOPATRA [*trembling*] Oh!

CÆSAR Be afraid if you dare. [*The note of the bucina resounds again in the distance. She moans with fear. Cæsar exults in it, exclaiming*] Aha! Cæsar approaches the throne of Cleopatra. Come: take your place. [*He takes her hand and leads her to the throne. She is too downcast to speak*]. Ho, there, Teetatota. How do you call your slaves?

CLEOPATRA [*spiritlessly, as she sinks on the throne and cowers there, shaking*] Clap your hands.

[*He claps his hands. Ftatateeta returns.*]

CÆSAR Bring the Queen's robes, and her crown, and her women; and prepare her.

CLEOPATRA [*eagerly—recovering herself a little*] Yes, the crown, Ftatateeta: I shall wear the crown.

FTATATEETA For whom must the Queen put on her state?

CÆSAR For a citizen of Rome. A king of kings, Totateeta.

CLEOPATRA [*stamping at her*] How dare you ask questions? Go and do as you are told. [*Ftatateeta goes out with a grim smile. Cleopatra goes on eagerly, to Cæsar*] Cæsar will know that I am a Queen when he sees my crown and robes, will he not?

CÆSAR   No. How shall he know that you are not a slave dressed up in the Queen's ornaments?

CLEOPATRA   You must tell him.

CÆSAR   He will not ask me. He will know Cleopatra by her pride, her courage, her majesty, and her beauty. [*She looks very doubtful*] Are you trembling?

CLEOPATRA   [*shivering with dread*] No, I—I—[*in a very sickly voice*] No.
[*Ftatateeta and three women come in with the regalia.*]

FTATATEETA   Of all the Queen's women, these three alone are left. The rest are fled. [*They begin to deck Cleopatra, who submits, pale and motionless*].

CÆSAR   Good, good. Three are enough. Poor Cæsar generally has to dress himself.

FTATATEETA   [*contemptuously*]   The queen of Egypt is not a Roman barbarian. [*To Cleopatra*] Be brave, my nursling. Hold up your head before this stranger.

CÆSAR   [*admiring Cleopatra, and placing the crown on her head*]   Is it sweet or bitter to be a Queen, Cleopatra?

CLEOPATRA   Bitter.

CÆSAR   Cast out fear; and you will conquer Cæsar. Tota: are the Romans at hand?

FTATATEETA   They are at hand; and the guard has fled.

THE WOMEN   [*wailing subduedly*]   Woe to us!
[*The Nubian comes running down the hall.*]

NUBIAN   The Romans are in the courtyard.
[*He bolts through the door. With a shriek, the women fly after him. Ftatateeta's jaw expresses savage resolution: she does not budge. Cleopatra can hardly restrain herself from following them. Cæsar grips her wrist, and looks steadfastly at her. She stands like a martyr*].

CÆSAR   The Queen must face Cæsar alone. Answer "So be it."

CLEOPATRA   [*white*]   So be it.

CÆSAR   [*releasing her*]   Good.
[*A tramp and tumult of armed men is heard. Cleopatra's terror increases. The bucina sounds close at hand, followed by a formidable clangor of trumpets. This is too much for Cleopatra: she utters a cry and darts towards the door. Ftatateeta stops her ruthlessly.*]

FTATATEETA   You are my nursling. You have said "So be it"; and if you die for it, you must make the Queen's word good.
[*She hands Cleopatra to Cæsar, who takes her back, almost beside herself with apprehension, to the throne*].

CÆSAR   Now, if you quail—! [*He seats himself on the throne*].
[*She stands on the step, all but unconscious, waiting for death. The Roman soldiers troop in tumultuously through the corridor, headed by their ensign with his eagle, and their bucinator, a burly fellow with his instrument coiled round his body, its brazen bell shaped like the head of a howling wolf. When they reach the transept, they stare in amazement at the throne; dress into ordered rank opposite; draw their swords and lift them in the air with a shout of* Hail, Cæsar. *Cleopatra turns and stares wildly at Cæsar; grasps the situation; and, with a great sob of relief, falls into his arms.*]

ACT II

Alexandria. A hall on the first floor of the Palace, ending in a loggia approached by two steps. Through the arches of the loggia the Mediterranean can be seen, bright in the morning sun. The clean lofty walls, painted with a procession of the Egyptian theocracy, presented in profile as flat ornament, and the absence of mirrors, sham perspectives, stuffy upholstery and textiles, make the place handsome, wholesome, simple and cool, or, as a rich English manufacturer would express it, poor, bare, ridiculous and unhomely. For Tottenham Court Road civilization is to this Egyptian civilization as glass bead and tattoo civilization is to Tottenham Court Road.

The young king Ptolemy Dionysus (aged ten) is at the top of the steps, on his way in through the loggia, led by his guardian Pothinus, who has him by the hand. The court is assembled to receive him. It is made up of men and women (some of the women being officials) of various complexions and races, mostly Egyptian; some of them, comparatively fair, from lower Egypt, some, much darker, from upper Egypt; with a few Greeks and Jews. Prominent in a group on Ptolemy's right hand is Theodotus, Ptolemy's tutor. Another group, on Ptolemy's left, is headed by Achillas, the general of Ptolemy's troops. Theodotus is a little old man, whose features are as cramped and wizened as his limbs, except his tall straight forehead, which occupies more space than all the rest of his face. He maintains an air of magpie keenness and profundity, listening to what the others say with the sarcastic vigilance of a philosopher listening to the exercises of his disciples. Achillas is a tall handsome man of thirty-five, with a fine black beard curled like the coat of a poodle. Apparently not a clever man, but distinguished and dignified. Pothinus is a vigorous man of fifty, a eunuch, passionate, energetic and quick witted, but of common mind and character; impatient and unable to control his temper. He has fine tawny hair, like fur. Ptolemy, the King, looks much older than an English boy of ten; but he has the childish air, the habit of being in leading strings, the mixture of impotence and petulance, the appearance of being excessively washed, combed and dressed by other hands, which is exhibited by court-bred princes of all ages.

All receive the King with reverences. He comes down the steps to a chair of state which stands a little to his right, the only seat in the hall. Taking his place before it, he looks nervously for instructions to Pothinus, who places himself at his left hand.

POTHINUS   The king of Egypt has a word to speak.

THEODOTUS   [in a squeak which he makes impressive by sheer self-opinionativeness]   Peace for the King's word!

PTOLEMY   [without any vocal inflexions: he is evidently repeating a lesson]   Take notice of this all of you. I am the first-born son of Auletes the Flute Blower who was your King. My sister Berenice drove him from his throne and reigned in his stead but—but—[he hesitates]—

POTHINUS   [*stealthily prompting*]—but the gods would not suffer—

PTOLEMY   Yes—the gods would not suffer—not suffer—[*He stops; then, crest-fallen*] I forgot what the gods would not suffer.

THEODOTUS   Let Pothinus, the King's guardian, speak for the King.

POTHINUS   [*suppressing his impatience with difficulty*]   The King wished to say that the gods would not suffer the impiety of his sister to go un-punished.

PTOLEMY   [*hastily*]   Yes: I remember the rest of it. [*He resumes his monotone*]. Therefore the gods sent a stranger one Mark Antony a Roman captain of horsemen across the sands of the desert and he set my father again upon the throne. And my father took Berenice my sister and struck her head off. And now that my father is dead yet another of his daughters my sister Cleopatra would snatch the kingdom from me and reign in my place. But the gods would not suffer—[*Pothinus coughs admonitorily*]—the gods—the gods would not suffer—

POTHINUS   [*prompting*]—will not maintain—

PTOLEMY   Oh yes—will not maintain such iniquity they will give her head to the axe even as her sister's. But with the help of the witch Ftatateeta she hath cast a spell on the Roman Julius Cæsar to make him uphold her false pretence to rule in Egypt. Take notice then that I will not suffer—that I will not suffer—[*pettishly, to Pothinus*] What is it that I will not suffer?

POTHINUS   [*suddenly exploding with all the force and emphasis of political passion*]   The King will not suffer a foreigner to take from him the throne of our Egypt. [*A shout of applause*]. Tell the King, Achillas, how many soldiers and horsemen follow the Roman?

THEODOTUS   Let the King's general speak!

ACHILLAS   But two Roman legions, O King. Three thousand soldiers and scarce a thousand horsemen.

[*The court breaks into derisive laughter; and a great chattering begins, amid which Rufio, a Roman officer, appears in the loggia. He is a burly, black-bearded man of middle age, very blunt, prompt and rough, with small clear eyes, and plump nose and cheeks, which, however, like the rest of his flesh, are in ironhard condition.*]

RUFIO   [*from the steps*]   Peace, ho! [*The laughter and chatter cease abruptly*]. Cæsar approaches.

THEODOTUS   [*with much presence of mind*]   The King permits the Roman commander to enter!

[*Cæsar, plainly dressed, but wearing an oak wreath to conceal his baldness, enters from the loggia, attended by Britannus, his secretary, a Briton, about forty, tall, solemn, and already slightly bald, with a heavy, drooping, hazel-colored moustache trained so as to lose its ends in a pair of trim whiskers. He is carefully dressed in blue, with portfolio, inkhorn, and reed pen at his girdle. His serious air and sense of the importance of the business in hand is in marked contrast to the kindly interest of Cæsar, who looks at the scene, which is new to him, with the frank curiosity of a child, and then turns to the king's chair: Britannus and Rufio posting themselves near the steps at the other side.*]

CÆSAR   [*looking at Pothinus and Ptolemy*]   Which is the King? the man or the boy?

POTHINUS   I am Pothinus, the guardian of my lord the King.

CÆSAR   [*patting Ptolemy kindly on the shoulder*]   So you are the King. Dull work at your age, eh? [*To Pothinus*] Your servant, Pothinus. [*He turns away unconcernedly and comes slowly along the middle of the hall, looking from side to side at the courtiers until he reaches Achillas*]. And this gentleman?

THEODOTUS Achillas, the King's general.

CÆSAR [*to Achillas, very friendly*] A general, eh? I am a general myself. But I began too old, too old. Health and many victories, Achillas!

ACHILLAS As the gods will, Cæsar.

CÆSAR [*turning to Theodotus*] And you, sir, are—?

THEODOTUS Theodotus, the King's tutor.

CÆSAR You teach men how to be kings, Theodotus. That is very clever of you. [*Looking at the gods on the walls as he turns away from Theodotus and goes up again to Pothinus*] And this place?

POTHINUS The council chamber of the chancellors of the King's treasury, Cæsar.

CÆSAR Ah! that reminds me. I want some money.

POTHINUS The King's treasury is poor, Cæsar.

CÆSAR Yes: I notice that there is but one chair in it.

RUFIO [*shouting gruffly*] Bring a chair there, some of you, for Cæsar.

PTOLEMY [*rising shyly to offer his chair*] Cæsar—

CÆSAR [*kindly*] No, no, my boy: that is your chair of state. Sit down. [*He makes Ptolemy sit down again. Meanwhile Rufio, looking about him, sees in the nearest corner an image of the god Ra, represented as a seated man with the head of a hawk. Before the image is a bronze tripod, about as large as a three-legged stool, with a stick of incense burning on it. Rufio, with Roman resourcefulness and indifference to foreign superstitions, promptly seizes the tripod; shakes off the incense; blows away the ash; and dumps it down behind Cæsar, nearly in the middle of the hall.*]

RUFIO Sit on that, Cæsar. [*A shiver runs through the court, followed by a hissing whisper of* Sacrilege!]

CÆSAR [*seating himself*] Now, Pothinus, to business. I am badly in want of money.

BRITANNUS [*disapproving of these informal expressions*] My master would say that there is a lawful debt due to Rome by Egypt, contracted by the King's deceased father to the Triumvirate; and that it is Cæsar's duty to his country to require immediate payment.

CÆSAR [*blandly*] Ah, I forgot. I have not made my companions known here. Pothinus: this is Britannus, my secretary. He is an islander from the western end of the world, a day's voyage from Gaul. [*Britannus bows stiffly*]. This gentleman is Rufio, my comrade in arms. [*Rufio nods*]. Pothinus: I want 1,600 talents. [*The courtiers, appalled, murmur loudly, and Theodotus and Achillas appeal mutely to one another against so monstrous a demand.*]

POTHINUS [*aghast*] Forty million sesterces! Impossible. There is not so much money in the King's treasury.

CÆSAR [*encouragingly*] Only sixteen hundred talents, Pothinus. Why count it in sesterces? A sestertius is only worth a loaf of bread.

POTHINUS And a talent is worth a racehorse. I say it is impossible. We have been at strife here, because the King's sister Cleopatra falsely claims his throne. The King's taxes have not been collected for a whole year.

CÆSAR Yes they have, Pothinus. My officers have been collecting them all morning. [*Renewed whisper and sensation, not without some stifled laughter, among the courtiers*].

RUFIO [*bluntly*] You must pay, Pothinus. Why waste words? You are getting off cheaply enough.

POTHINUS [*bitterly*] Is it possible that Cæsar, the conqueror of the world, has time to occupy himself with such a trifle as our taxes?

CÆSAR My friend: taxes are the chief business of a conqueror of the world.

POTHINUS Then take warning, Cæsar. This day, the treasures of the temple and the gold of the King's treasury shall be sent to the mint to be melted down for our ransom in the sight of the people. They shall see us sitting under bare walls and drinking from wooden cups. And their wrath be on your head, Cæsar, if you force us to this sacrilege!

CÆSAR Do not fear, Pothinus: the people know how well wine tastes in wooden cups. In return for your bounty, I will settle this dispute about the throne for you, if you will. What say you?

POTHINUS If I say no, will that hinder you?

RUFIO [*defiantly*] No.

CÆSAR You say the matter has been at issue for a year, Pothinus. May I have ten minutes at it?

POTHINUS You will do your pleasure, doubtless.

CÆSAR Good! But first, let us have Cleopatra here.

THEODOTUS She is not in Alexandria: she is fled into Syria.

CÆSAR I think not. [*To Rufio*] Call Totateeta.

RUFIO [*calling*] Ho there, Teetatota.

[*Ftatateeta enters the loggia, and stands arrogantly at the top of the steps.*]

FTATATEETA Who pronounces the name of Ftatateeta, the Queen's chief nurse?

CÆSAR Nobody can pronounce it, Tota, except yourself. Where is your mistress?

[*Cleopatra, who is hiding behind Ftatateeta, peeps out at them, laughing. Cæsar rises.*]

CÆSAR Will the Queen favor us with her presence for a moment?

CLEOPATRA [*pushing Ftatateeta aside and standing haughtily on the brink of the steps*] Am I to behave like a Queen?

CÆSAR Yes.

[*Cleopatra immediately comes down to the chair of state; seizes Ptolemy; drags him out of his seat; then takes his place in the chair. Ftatateeta seats herself on the step of the loggia, and sits there, watching the scene with sibylline intensity.*]

PTOLEMY [*mortified, and struggling with his tears*] Cæsar: this is how she treats me always. If I am king why is she allowed to take everything from me?

CLEOPATRA You are not to be King, you little cry-baby. You are to be eaten by the Romans.

CÆSAR [*touched by Ptolemy's distress*] Come here, my boy, and stand by me. [*Ptolemy goes over to Cæsar, who, resuming his seat on the tripod, takes the boy's hand to encourage him. Cleopatra, furiously jealous, rises and glares at them.*]

CLEOPATRA [*with flaming cheeks*] Take your throne: I dont want it. [*She flings away from the chair, and approaches Ptolemy, who shrinks from her*]. Go this instant and sit down in your place.

CÆSAR Go, Ptolemy. Always take a throne when it is offered to you.

RUFIO I hope you will have the good sense to follow your own advice when we return to Rome, Cæsar.

[*Ptolemy slowly goes back to the throne, giving Cleopatra a wide berth, in evident fear of her hands. She takes his place beside Cæsar.*]

CÆSAR Pothinus—

CLEOPATRA [*interrupting him*] Are you not going to speak to me?

CÆSAR Be quiet. Open your mouth again before I give you leave; and you shall be eaten.

CLEOPATRA   I am not afraid. A queen must not be afraid. Eat my husband there, if you like: he is afraid.

CÆSAR   [*starting*]   Your husband! What do you mean?

CLEOPATRA   [*pointing to Ptolemy*]   That little thing.

[*The two Romans and the Briton stare at one another in amazement.*]

THEODOTUS   Cæsar: you are a stranger here, and not conversant with our laws. The kings and queens of Egypt may not marry except with their own royal blood. Ptolemy and Cleopatra are born king and consort just as they are born brother and sister.

BRITANNUS   [*shocked*]   Cæsar: this is not proper.

THEODOTUS   [*outraged*]   How!

CÆSAR   [*recovering his self-possession*]   Pardon him, Theodotus: he is a barbarian, and thinks that the customs of his tribe and island are the laws of nature.

BRITANNUS   On the contrary, Cæsar, it is these Egyptians who are barbarians; and you do wrong to encourage them. I say it is a scandal.

CÆSAR   Scandal or not, my friend, it opens the gate of peace. [*He addresses Pothinus seriously*]. Pothinus: hear what I propose.

RUFIO   Hear Cæsar there.

CÆSAR   Ptolemy and Cleopatra shall reign jointly in Egypt.

ACHILLAS   What of the King's younger brother and Cleopatra's younger sister?

RUFIO   [*explaining*]   There is another little Ptolemy, Cæsar: so they tell me.

CÆSAR   Well, the little Ptolemy can marry the other sister; and we will make them both a present of Cyprus.

POTHINUS   [*impatiently*]   Cyprus is of no use to anybody.

CÆSAR   No matter: you shall have it for the sake of peace.

BRITANNUS   [*unconsciously anticipating a later statesman*]   Peace with honor, Pothinus.

POTHINUS   [*mutinously*]   Cæsar: be honest. The money you demand is the price of our freedom. Take it; and leave us to settle our own affairs.

THE BOLDER COURTIERS   [*encouraged by Pothinus's tone and Cæsar's quietness*]   Yes, yes. Egypt for the Egyptians!

[*The conference now becomes an altercation, the Egyptians becoming more and more heated. Cæsar remains unruffled; but Rufio grows fiercer and doggeder, and Britannus haughtily indignant.*]

RUFIO   [*contemptuously*]   Egypt for the Egyptians! Do you forget that there is a Roman army of occupation here, left by Aulus Gabinius when he set up your toy king for you?

ACHILLAS   [*suddenly asserting himself*]   And now under my command. *I* am the Roman general here, Cæsar.

CÆSAR   [*tickled by the humor of the situation*]   And also the Egyptian general, eh?

POTHINUS   [*triumphantly*]   That is so, Cæsar.

CÆSAR   [*to Achillas*]   So you can make war on the Egyptians in the name of Rome, and on the Romans—on me, if necessary—in the name of Egypt?

ACHILLAS   That is so, Cæsar.

CÆSAR   And which side are you on at present, if I may presume to ask, general?

ACHILLAS   On the side of the right and of the gods.

CÆSAR   Hm! How many men have you?

ACHILLAS   That will appear when I take the field.

RUFIO   [*truculently*]   Are your men Romans? If not, it matters not how many there are, provided you are no stronger than 500 to ten.

POTHINUS   It is useless to try to bluff us, Rufio. Cæsar has been defeated before and may be defeated again. A few weeks ago Cæsar was flying for his life before Pompey: a few months hence he may be flying for his life before Cato and Juba of Numidia, the African King.

ACHILLAS [*following up Pothinus's speech menacingly*] What can you do with 4,000 men?

THEODOTUS [*following up Achillas's speech with a raucous squeak*] And without money? Away with you.

ALL THE COURTIERS [*shouting fiercely and crowding towards Cæsar*] Away with you. Egypt for the Egyptians! Begone.

[*Rufio bites his beard, too angry to speak. Cæsar sits as comfortably as if he were at breakfast, and the cat were clamoring for a piece of Finnan-haddie.*]

CLEOPATRA Why do you let them talk to you like that, Cæsar? Are you afraid?

CÆSAR Why, my dear, what they say is quite true.

CLEOPATRA But if you go away, I shall not be Queen.

CÆSAR I shall not go away until you are Queen.

POTHINUS Achillas: if you are not a fool, you will take that girl whilst she is under your hand.

RUFIO [*daring them*] Why not take Cæsar as well, Achillas?

POTHINUS [*retorting the defiance with interest*] Well said, Rufio. Why not?

RUFIO Try, Achillas. [*Calling*] Guard there.

[*The loggia immediately fills with Cæsar's soldiers, who stand, sword in hand, at the top of the steps, waiting the word to charge from their centurion, who carries a cudgel. For a moment the Egyptians face them proudly: then they retire sullenly to their former places.*]

BRITANNUS You are Cæsar's prisoners, all of you.

CÆSAR [*benevolently*] Oh no, no, no. By no means. Cæsar's guests, gentlemen.

CLEOPATRA Wont you cut their heads off?

CÆSAR What! Cut off your brother's head?

CLEOPATRA Why not? He would cut off mine, if he got the chance. Wouldnt you, Ptolemy?

PTOLEMY [*pale and obstinate*] I would. I will, too, when I grow up.

[*Cleopatra is rent by a struggle between her newly-acquired dignity as a queen, and a strong impulse to put out her tongue at him. She takes no part in the scene which follows, but watches it with curiosity and wonder, fidgeting with the restlessness of a child, and sitting down on Cæsar's tripod when he rises.*]

POTHINUS Cæsar: if you attempt to detain us—

RUFIO He will succeed, Egyptian: make up your mind to that. We hold the palace, the beach, and the eastern harbor. The road to Rome is open; and you shall travel it if Cæsar chooses.

CÆSAR [*courteously*] I could do no less, Pothinus, to secure the retreat of my own soldiers. I am accountable for every life among them. But you are free to go. So are all here, and in the palace.

RUFIO [*aghast at this clemency*] What! Renegades and all?

CÆSAR [*softening the expression*] Roman army of occupation and all, Rufio.

POTHINUS [*bewildered*] But—but—but—

CÆSAR Well, my friend?

POTHINUS You are turning us out of our own palace into the streets; and you tell us with a grand air that we are free to go! It is for you to go.

CÆSAR Your friends are in the street, Pothinus. You will be safer there.

POTHINUS This is a trick. I am the king's guardian: I refuse to stir. I stand on my right here. Where is your right?

CÆSAR It is in Rufio's scabbard, Pothinus. I may not be able to keep it there if you wait too long.

[*Sensation.*]

POTHINUS [*bitterly*] And this is Roman justice!

THEODOTUS But not Roman gratitude, I hope.

CÆSAR Gratitude! Am I in your debt for any service, gentlemen?

THEODOTUS Is Cæsar's life of so little account to him that he forgets that we have saved it?

CÆSAR My life! Is that all?

THEODOTUS Your life. Your laurels. Your future.

POTHINUS It is true. I can call a witness to prove that but for us, the Roman army of occupation, led by the greatest soldier in the world, would now have Cæsar at its mercy. [*Calling through the loggia*] Ho, there, Lucius Septimius [*Cæsar starts, deeply moved*]: if my voice can reach you, come forth and testify before Cæsar.

CÆSAR [*shrinking*] No, no.

THEODOTUS Yes, I say. Let the military tribune bear witness.

[*Lucius Septimius, a clean shaven, trim athlete of about 40, with symmetrical features, resolute mouth, and handsome, thin Roman nose, in the dress of a Roman officer, comes in through the loggia and confronts Cæsar, who hides his face with his robe for a moment; then, mastering himself, drops it, and confronts the tribune with dignity.*]

POTHINUS Bear witness, Lucius Septimius. Cæsar came hither in pursuit of his foe. Did we shelter his foe?

LUCIUS As Pompey's foot touched the Egyptian shore, his head fell by the stroke of my sword.

THEODOTUS [*with viperish relish*] Under the eyes of his wife and child! Remember that, Cæsar! They saw it from the ship he had just left. We have given you a full and sweet measure of vengeance.

CÆSAR [*with horror*] Vengeance!

POTHINUS Our first gift to you, as your galley came into the roadstead, was the head of your rival for the empire of the world. Bear witness, Lucius Septimius: is it not so?

LUCIUS It is so. With this hand, that slew Pompey, I placed his head at the feet of Cæsar.

CÆSAR Murderer! So would you have slain Cæsar, had Pompey been victorious at Pharsalia.

LUCIUS Woe to the vanquished, Cæsar! When I served Pompey, I slew as good men as he, only because he conquered them. His turn came at last.

THEODOTUS [*flatteringly*] The deed was not yours, Cæsar, but ours—nay, mine; for it was done by my counsel. Thanks to us, you keep your reputation for clemency, and have your vengeance too.

CÆSAR Vengeance! Vengeance!! Oh, if I could stoop to vengeance, what would I not exact from you as the price of this murdered man's blood? [*They shrink back, appalled and disconcerted*]. Was he not my son-in-law, my ancient friend, for 20 years the master of great Rome, for 30 years the compeller of victory? Did not I, as a Roman, share his glory? Was the Fate that forced us to fight for the mastery of the world, of our making? Am I Julius Cæsar, or am I a wolf, that you fling to me the grey head of the old soldier, the laurelled conqueror, the mighty Roman, treacherously struck down by this callous ruffian, and then claim my gratitude for it! [*To Lucius Septimius*] Begone: you fill me with horror.

LUCIUS [*cold and undaunted*] Pshaw! You have seen severed heads before, Cæsar, and severed right hands too, I think; some thousands of them, in Gaul, after you vanquished Vercingetorix. Did you spare him, with all your clemency? Was that vengeance?

CÆSAR No, by the gods! would that it had been! Vengeance at least is human.

No, I say: those severed right hands, and the brave Vercingetorix basely strangled in a vault beneath the Capitol were [*with shuddering satire*] a wise severity, a necessary protection to the commonwealth, a duty of statesmanship—follies and fictions ten times bloodier than honest vengeance! What a fool was I then! To think that men's lives should be at the mercy of such fools! [*Humbly*] Lucius Septimius, pardon me: why should the slayer of Vercingetorix rebuke the slayer of Pompey? You are free to go with the rest. Or stay if you will: I will find a place for you in my service.

LUCIUS   The odds are against you, Cæsar. I go. [*He turns to go out through the loggia*].

RUFIO   [*full of wrath at seeing his prey escaping*]   That means that he is a Republican.

LUCIUS   [*turning defiantly on the loggia steps*]   And what are you?

RUFIO   A Cæsarian, like all Cæsar's soldiers.

CÆSAR   [*courteously*]   Lucius: believe me, Cæsar is no Cæsarian. Were Rome a true republic, then were Cæsar the first of Republicans. But you have made your choice. Farewell.

LUCIUS   Farewell. Come, Achillas, whilst there is yet time.

[*Cæsar, seeing that Rufio's temper threatens to get the worse of him, puts his hand on his shoulder and brings him down the hall out of harm's way, Britannus accompanying them and posting himself on Cæsar's right hand. This movement brings the three in a little group to the place occupied by Achillas, who moves haughtily away and joins Theodotus on the other side. Lucius Septimius goes out through the soldiers in the loggia. Pothinus, Theodotus and Achillas follow him with the courtiers, very mistrustful of the soldiers, who close up in their rear and go out after them, keeping them moving without much ceremony. The King is left in his chair, piteous, obstinate, with twitching face and fingers. During these movements Rufio maintains an energetic grumbling, as follows:—*]

RUFIO   [*as Lucius departs*]   Do you suppose he would let us go if he had our heads in his hands?

CÆSAR   I have no right to suppose that his ways are any baser than mine.

RUFIO   Psha!

CÆSAR   Rufio: if I take Lucius Septimius for my model, and become exactly like him, ceasing to be Cæsar, will you serve me still?

BRITANNUS   Cæsar: this is not good sense. Your duty to Rome demands that her enemies should be prevented from doing further mischief. [*Cæsar, whose delight in the moral eye-to-business of his British secretary is inexhaustible, smiles indulgently*].

RUFIO   It is no use talking to him, Britannus: you may save your breath to cool your porridge. But mark this, Cæsar. Clemency is very well for you; but what is it for your soldiers, who have to fight tomorrow the men you spared yesterday? You may give what orders you please; but I tell you that your next victory will be a massacre, thanks to your clemency. *I*, for one, will take no prisoners. I will kill my enemies in the field; and then you can preach as much clemency as you please: I shall never have to fight them again. And now, with your leave, I will see these gentry off the premises. [*He turns to go*].

CÆSAR   [*turning also and seeing Ptolemy*]   What! have they left the boy alone! Oh shame, shame!

RUFIO   [*taking Ptolemy's hand and making him rise*]   Come, your majesty!

PTOLEMY   [*to Cæsar, drawing away his hand from Rufio*]   Is he turning me out of my palace?

RUFIO [*grimly*] You are welcome to stay if you wish.

CÆSAR [*kindly*] Go, my boy. I will not harm you; but you will be safer away, among your friends. Here you are in the lion's mouth.

PTOLEMY [*turning to go*] It is not the lion I fear, but [*looking at Rufio*] the jackal. [*He goes out through the loggia*].

CÆSAR [*laughing approvingly*] Brave boy!

CLEOPATRA [*jealous of Cæsar's approbation, calling after Ptolemy*] Little silly. You think that very clever.

CÆSAR Britannus: attend the King. Give him in charge to that Pothinus fellow. [*Britannus goes out after Ptolemy*].

RUFIO [*pointing to Cleopatra*] And this piece of goods? What is to be done with her? However, I suppose I may leave that to you. [*He goes out through the loggia*].

CLEOPATRA [*flushing suddenly and turning on Cæsar*] Did you mean me to go with the rest?

CÆSAR [*a little preoccupied, goes with a sigh to Ptolemy's chair, whilst she waits for his answer with red cheeks and clenched fists*] You are free to do just as you please, Cleopatra.

CLEOPATRA Then you do not care whether I stay or not?

CÆSAR [*smiling*] Of course I had rather you stayed.

CLEOPATRA Much, much rather?

CÆSAR [*nodding*] Much, much rather.

CLEOPATRA Then I consent to stay, because I am asked. But I do not want to, mind.

CÆSAR That is quite understood. [*Calling*] Totateeta.

[*Ftatateeta, still seated, turns her eyes on him with a sinister expression, but does not move.*]

CLEOPATRA [*with a splutter of laughter*] Her name is not Totateeta: it is Ftatateeta. [*Calling*] Ftatateeta. [*Ftatateeta instantly rises and comes to Cleopatra*].

CÆSAR [*stumbling over the name*] Tfatafeeta will forgive the erring tongue of a Roman. Tota: the Queen will hold her state here in Alexandria. Engage women to attend upon her; and do all that is needful.

FTATATEETA Am I then the mistress of the Queen's household?

CLEOPATRA [*sharply*] No: *I* am the mistress of the Queen's household. Go and do as you are told, or I will have you thrown into the Nile this very afternoon, to poison the poor crocodiles.

CÆSAR [*shocked*] Oh no, no.

CLEOPATRA Oh yes, yes. You are very sentimental, Cæsar; but you are clever; and if you do as I tell you, you will soon learn to govern.

[*Cæsar, quite dumbfounded by this impertinence, turns in his chair and stares at her. Ftatateeta, smiling grimly, and shewing a splendid set of teeth, goes, leaving them alone together.*]

CÆSAR Cleopatra: I really think I must eat you, after all.

CLEOPATRA [*kneeling beside him and looking at him with eager interest, half real, half affected to shew how intelligent she is*] You must not talk to me now as if I were a child.

CÆSAR You have been growing up since the sphinx introduced us the other night; and you think you know more than I do already.

CLEOPATRA [*taken down, and anxious to justify herself*] No: that would be very silly of me: of course I know that. But—[*suddenly*] are you angry with me?

CÆSAR No.

CLEOPATRA [*only half believing him*] Then why are you so thoughtful?

CÆSAR   [*rising*]   I have work to do, Cleopatra.

CLEOPATRA   [*drawing back*]   Work!   [*Offended*]   You are tired of talking to me; and that is your excuse to get away from me.

CÆSAR   [*sitting down again to appease her*]   Well, well: another minute. But then—work!

CLEOPATRA   Work! what nonsense! You must remember that you are a king now: I have made you one. Kings dont work.

CÆSAR   Oh! Who told you that, little kitten? Eh?

CLEOPATRA   My father was King of Egypt; and he never worked. But he was a great king, and cut off my sister's head because she rebelled against him and took the throne from him.

CÆSAR   Well; and how did he get his throne back again?

CLEOPATRA   [*eagerly, her eyes lighting up*]   I will tell you. A beautiful young man, with strong round arms, came over the desert with many horsemen, and slew my sister's husband and gave my father back his throne. [*Wistfully*] I was only twelve then. Oh, I wish he would come again, now that I am queen. I would make him my husband.

CÆSAR   It might be managed, perhaps; for it was I who sent that beautiful young man to help your father.

CLEOPATRA   [*enraptured*]   You know him!

CÆSAR   [*nodding*]   I do.

CLEOPATRA   Has he come with you? [*Cæsar shakes his head: she is cruelly disappointed*]. Oh, I wish he had, I wish he had. If only I were a little older; so that he might not think me a mere kitten, as you do! But perhaps that is because you are old. He is many many years younger than you, is he not?

CÆSAR   [*as if swallowing a pill*]   He is somewhat younger.

CLEOPATRA   Would he be my husband, do you think, if I asked him?

CÆSAR   Very likely.

CLEOPATRA   But I should not like to ask him. Could you not persuade him to ask me—without knowing that I wanted him to?

CÆSAR   [*touched by her innocence of the beautiful young man's character*] My poor child!

CLEOPATRA   Why do you say that as if you were sorry for me? Does he love anyone else?

CÆSAR   I am afraid so.

CLEOPATRA   [*tearfully*]   Then I shall not be his first love.

CÆSAR   Not quite the first. He is greatly admired by women.

CLEOPATRA   I wish I could be the first. But if he loves me, I will make him kill all the rest. Tell me: is he still beautiful? Do his strong round arms shine in the sun like marble?

CÆSAR   He is in excellent condition—considering how much he eats and drinks.

CLEOPATRA   Oh, you must not say common, earthly things about him; for I love him. He is a god.

CÆSAR   He is a great captain of horsemen, and swifter of foot than any other Roman.

CLEOPATRA   What is his real name?

CÆSAR   [*puzzled*]   His real name?

CLEOPATRA   Yes, I always call him Horus, because Horus is the most beautiful of our gods. But I want to know his real name.

CÆSAR   His name is Mark Antony.

CLEOPATRA   [*musically*]   Mark Antony, Mark Antony, Mark Antony! What a beautiful name! [*She throws her arms round Cæsar's neck*]. Oh, how I love you for sending him to help my father! Did you love my father very much?

CÆSAR   No, my child; but your father, as you say, never worked. I always work.

So when he lost his crown he had to promise me 16,000 talents to get it back for him.

CLEOPATRA   Did he ever pay you?

CÆSAR   Not in full.

CLEOPATRA   He was quite right: it was too dear. The whole world is not worth 16,000 talents.

CÆSAR   That is perhaps true, Cleopatra. Those Egyptians who work paid as much of it as he could drag from them. The rest is still due. But as I most likely shall not get it, I must go back to my work. So you must run away for a little and send my secretary to me.

CLEOPATRA   [coaxing]   No: I want to stay and hear you talk about Mark Antony.

CÆSAR   But if I do not get to work, Pothinus and the rest of them will cut us off from the harbor; and then the way from Rome will be blocked.

CLEOPATRA   No matter: I dont want you to go back to Rome.

CÆSAR   But you want Mark Antony to come from it.

CLEOPATRA   [springing up]   Oh yes, yes, yes: I forgot. Go quickly and work, Cæsar; and keep the way over the sea open for my Mark Antony. [She runs out through the loggia, kissing her hand to Mark Antony across the sea].

CÆSAR   [going briskly up the middle of the hall to the loggia steps]   Ho, Britannus. [He is startled by the entry of a wounded Roman soldier, who confronts him from the upper step]. What now?

SOLDIER   [pointing to his bandaged head]   This, Cæsar; and two of my comrades killed in the market place.

CÆSAR   [quiet, but attending]   Ay. Why?

SOLDIER   There is an army come to Alexandria, calling itself the Roman army.

CÆSAR   The Roman army of occupation. Ay?

SOLDIER   Commanded by one Achillas.

CÆSAR   Well?

SOLDIER   The citizens rose against us when the army entered the gates. I was with two others in the market place when the news came. They set upon us. I cut my way out; and here I am.

CÆSAR   Good. I am glad to see you alive. [Rufio enters the loggia hastily, passing behind the soldier to look out through one of the arches at the quay beneath]. Rufio: we are besieged.

RUFIO   What! Already?

CÆSAR   Now or tomorrow: what does it matter? We shall be besieged. [Britannus runs in.]

BRITANNUS   Cæsar—

CÆSAR   [anticipating him]   Yes: I know. [Rufio and Britannus come down the hall from the loggia at opposite sides, past Cæsar, who waits for a moment near the step to say to the soldier] Comrade: give the word to turn out on the beach and stand by the boats. Get your wound attended to. Go. [The soldier hurries out. Cæsar comes down the hall between Rufio and Britannus] Rufio: we have some ships in the west harbor. Burn them.

RUFIO   [staring]   Burn them!!

CÆSAR   Take every boat we have in the east harbor, and seize the Pharos—that island with the lighthouse. Leave half our men behind to hold the beach and the quay outside this palace: that is the way home.

RUFIO   [disapproving strongly]   Are we to give up the city?

CÆSAR   We have not got it, Rufio. This palace we have; and—what is that building next door?

RUFIO   The theatre.

CÆSAR   We will have that too: it commands the strand. For the rest, Egypt for the Egyptians!

RUFIO   Well, you know best, I suppose. Is that all?

CÆSAR   That is all. Are those ships burnt yet?

RUFIO   Be easy: I shall waste no more time. [*He runs out*].

BRITANNUS   Cæsar: Pothinus demands speech of you. In my opinion he needs a lesson. His manner is most insolent.

CÆSAR   Where is he?

BRITANNUS   He waits without.

CÆSAR   Ho there! admit Pothinus.

[*Pothinus appears in the loggia, and comes down the hall very haughtily to Cæsar's left hand.*]

CÆSAR   Well, Pothinus?

POTHINUS   I have brought you our ultimatum, Cæsar.

CÆSAR   Ultimatum! The door was open: you should have gone out through it before you declared war. You are my prisoner now. [*He goes to the chair and loosens his toga*].

POTHINUS   [*scornfully*]   I your prisoner! Do you know that you are in Alexandria, and that King Ptolemy, with an army outnumbering your little troop a hundred to one, is in possession of Alexandria?

CÆSAR   [*unconcernedly taking off his toga and throwing it on the chair*]   Well, my friend, get out if you can. And tell your friends not to kill any more Romans in the market place. Otherwise my soldiers, who do not share my celebrated clemency, will probably kill you. Britannus: pass the word to the guard; and fetch my armor. [*Britannus runs out. Rufio returns*]. Well?

RUFIO   [*pointing from the loggia to a cloud of smoke drifting over the harbor*]   See there! [*Pothinus runs eagerly up the steps to look out*].

CÆSAR   What, ablaze already! Impossible!

RUFIO   Yes, five good ships, and a barge laden with oil grappled to each. But it is not my doing: the Egyptians have saved me the trouble. They have captured the west harbor.

CÆSAR   [*anxiously*]   And the east harbor? The lighthouse, Rufio?

RUFIO   [*with a sudden splutter of raging ill usage, coming down to Cæsar and scolding him*]   Can I embark a legion in five minutes? The first cohort is already on the beach. We can do no more. If you want faster work, come and do it yourself.

CÆSAR   [*soothing him*]   Good, good. Patience, Rufio, patience.

RUFIO   Patience! Who is impatient here, you or I? Would I be here, if I could not oversee them from that balcony?

CÆSAR   Forgive me, Rufio; and [*anxiously*] hurry them as much as—

[*He is interrupted by an outcry as of an old man in the extremity of misfortune. It draws near rapidly; and Theodotus rushes in, tearing his hair, and squeaking the most lamentable exclamations. Rufio steps back to stare at him, amazed at his frantic condition. Pothinus turns to listen.*]

THEODOTUS   [*on the steps, with uplifted arms*]   Horror unspeakable! Woe, alas! Help!

RUFIO   What now?

CÆSAR   [*frowning*]   Who is slain?

THEODOTUS   Slain! Oh, worse than the death of ten thousand men! Loss irreparable to mankind!

RUFIO   What has happened, man?

THEODOTUS   [*rushing down the hall between them*]   The fire has spread from your ships. The first of the seven wonders of the world perishes. The library of Alexandria is in flames.

RUFIO   Psha! [*Quite relieved, he goes up to the loggia and watches the prepara-tions of the troops on the beach*].

CÆSAR   Is that all?

THEODOTUS   [*unable to believe his senses*]   All! Cæsar: will you go down to posterity as a barbarous soldier too ignorant to know the value of books?

CÆSAR   Theodotus: I am an author myself; and I tell you it is better that the Egyptians should live their lives than dream them away with the help of books.

THEODOTUS   [*kneeling, with genuine literary emotion: the passion of the pedant*] Cæsar: once in ten generations of men, the world gains an immortal book.

CÆSAR   [*inflexible*]   If it did not flatter mankind, the common executioner would burn it.

THEODOTUS   Without history, death will lay you beside your meanest soldier.

CÆSAR   Death will do that in any case. I ask no better grave.

THEODOTUS   What is burning there is the memory of mankind.

CÆSAR   A shameful memory. Let it burn.

THEODOTUS   [*wildly*]   Will you destroy the past?

CÆSAR   Ay, and build the future with its ruins. [*Theodotus, in despair, strikes himself on the temples with his fists*]. But harken, Theodotus, teacher of kings: you who valued Pompey's head no more than a shepherd values an onion, and who now kneel to me, with tears in your old eyes, to plead for a few sheepskins scrawled with errors. I cannot spare you a man or a bucket of water just now; but you shall pass freely out of the palace. Now, away with you to Achillas; and borrow his legions to put out the fire. [*He hurries him to the steps*].

POTHINUS   [*significantly*]   You understand, Theodotus: I remain a prisoner.

THEODOTUS   A prisoner!

CÆSAR   Will you stay to talk whilst the memory of mankind is burning? [*Calling through the loggia*] Ho there! Pass Theodotus out. [*To Theodotus*] Away with you.

THEODOTUS   [*To Pothinus*]   I must go to save the library. [*He hurries out*].

CÆSAR   Follow him to the gate, Pothinus. Bid him urge your people to kill no more of my soldiers, for your sake.

POTHINUS   My life will cost you dear if you take it, Cæsar.
[*He goes out after Theodotus. Rufio, absorbed in watching the embarkation, does not notice the departure of the two Egyptians.*]

RUFIO   [*shouting from the loggia to the beach*]   All ready, there?

A CENTURION   [*from below*]   All ready. We wait for Cæsar.

CÆSAR   Tell them Cæsar is coming—the rogues! [*Calling*] Britannicus. [*This magniloquent version of his secretary's name is one of Cæsar's jokes. In later years it would have meant, quite seriously and officially, Conqueror of Britain*].

RUFIO   [*calling down*]   Push off, all except the longboat. Stand by it to embark, Cæsar's guard there. [*He leaves the balcony and comes down into the hall*]. Where are those Egyptians? Is this more clemency? Have you let them go?

CÆSAR   [*chuckling*]   I have let Theodotus go to save the library. We must respect literature, Rufio.

RUFIO   [*raging*]   Folly on folly's head! I believe if you could bring back all the dead of Spain, Gaul, and Thessaly to life, you would do it that we might have the trouble of fighting them over again.

CÆSAR   Might not the gods destroy the world if their only thought were to be at peace next year? [*Rufio, out of all patience, turns away in anger. Cæsar suddenly grips his sleeve, and adds slyly in his ear*] Besides, my friend:

every Egyptian we imprison means imprisoning two Roman soldiers to guard him. Eh?

RUFIO   Agh! I might have known there was some fox's trick behind your fine talking. [*He gets away from Cæsar with an ill-humored shrug, and goes to the balcony for another look at the preparations; finally goes out*].

CÆSAR   Is Britannus asleep? I sent him for my armor an hour ago. [*Calling*] Britannicus, thou British islander. Britannicus!

[*Cleopatra runs in through the loggia with Cæsar's helmet and sword, snatched from Britannus, who follows her with a cuirass and greaves. They come down to Cæsar, she to his left hand, Britannus to his right.*]

CLEOPATRA   I am going to dress you, Cæsar. Sit down. [*He obeys*]. These Roman helmets are so becoming! [*She takes off his wreath*]. Oh! [*She bursts out laughing at him*].

CÆSAR   What are you laughing at?

CLEOPATRA   Youre bald [*beginning with a big B, and ending with a splutter*].

CÆSAR   [*almost annoyed*]   Cleopatra! [*He rises, for the convenience of Britannus, who puts the cuirass on him*].

CLEOPATRA   So that is why you wear the wreath—to hide it.

BRITANNUS   Peace, Egyptian: they are the bays of the conqueror. [*He buckles the cuirass*].

CLEOPATRA   Peace, thou: islander! [*To Cæsar*] You should rub your head with strong spirits of sugar, Cæsar. That will make it grow.

CÆSAR   [*with a wry face*]   Cleopatra: do you like to be reminded that you are very young?

CLEOPATRA   [*pouting*]   No.

CÆSAR   [*sitting down again, and setting out his leg for Britannus, who kneels to put on his greaves*]. Neither do I like to be reminded that I am—middle aged. Let me give you ten of my superfluous years. That will make you 26, and leave me only—no matter. Is it a bargain?

CLEOPATRA   Agreed. 26, mind. [*She puts the helmet on him*]. Oh! How nice! You look only about 50 in it!

BRITANNUS   [*looking up severely at Cleopatra*]   You must not speak in this manner to Cæsar.

CLEOPATRA   Is it true that when Cæsar caught you on that island, you were painted all over blue?

BRITANNUS   Blue is the color worn by all Britons of good standing. In war we stain our bodies blue; so that though our enemies may strip us of our clothes and our lives, they cannot strip us of our respectability. [*He rises*].

CLEOPATRA   [*with Cæsar's sword*]   Let me hang this on. Now you look splendid. Have they made any statues of you in Rome?

CÆSAR   Yes, many statues.

CLEOPATRA   You must send for one and give it to me.

RUFIO   [*coming back into the loggia, more impatient than ever*]   Now Cæsar: have you done talking? The moment your foot is aboard there will be no holding our men back: the boats will race one another for the lighthouse.

CÆSAR   [*drawing his sword and trying the edge*]   Is this well set today, Britannicus? At Pharsalia it was as blunt as a barrel-hoop.

BRITANNUS   It will split one of the Egyptian's hairs today, Cæsar. I have set it myself.

CLEOPATRA   [*suddenly throwing her arms in terror round Cæsar*]   Oh, you are not really going into battle to be killed?

CÆSAR   No, Cleopatra. No man goes to battle to be killed.

CLEOPATRA   But they do get killed. My sister's husband was killed in battle. You must not go. Let him go [*pointing to Rufio. They all laugh at her*].

Oh please, please dont go. What will happen to me if you never come back?

CÆSAR [*gravely*] Are you afraid?

CLEOPATRA [*shrinking*] No.

CÆSAR [*with quiet authority*] Go to the balcony; and you shall see us take the Pharos. You must learn to look on battles. Go. [*She goes, downcast, and looks out from the balcony*]. That is well. Now, Rufio. March.

CLEOPATRA [*suddenly clapping her hands*] Oh, you will not be able to go!

CÆSAR Why? What now?

CLEOPATRA They are drying up the harbor with buckets—a multitude of soldiers—over there [*pointing out across the sea to her left*]—they are dipping up the water.

RUFIO [*hastening to look*] It is true. The Egyptian army! Crawling over the edge of the west harbor like locusts. [*With sudden anger he strides down to Cæsar*]. This is your accursed clemency, Cæsar. Theodotus has brought them.

CÆSAR [*delighted at his own cleverness*] I meant him to, Rufio. They have come to put out the fire. The library will keep them busy whilst we seize the lighthouse. Eh?

[*He rushes out buoyantly through the loggia, followed by Britannus*].

RUFIO [*disgustedly*] More foxing! Agh! [*He rushes off. A shout from the soldiers announces the appearance of Cæsar below*].

CENTURION [*below*] All aboard. Give way there. [*Another shout*].

CLEOPATRA [*waving her scarf through the loggia arch*] Goodbye, goodbye, dear Cæsar. Come back safe. Goodbye!

ACT III

> The edge of the quay in front of the palace, looking out west over the east harbor of Alexandria to Pharos island, just to the end of which, and connected with it by a narrow mole, is the famous lighthouse, a gigantic square tower of white marble diminishing in size storey by storey to the top, on which stands a cresset beacon. The island is joined to the main land by the Heptastadium, a great mole or causeway five miles long bounding the harbor on the south.
>
> In the middle of the quay a Roman sentinel stands on guard, pilum in hand, looking out to the lighthouse with strained attention, his left hand shading his eyes. The pilum is a stout wooden shaft 4½ feet long, with an iron spit about three feet long fixed in it. The sentinel is so absorbed that he does not notice the approach from the north end of the quay of four Egyptian market porters carrying rolls of carpet, preceded by Ftatateeta and Apollodorus the Sicilian. Apollodorus is a dashing young man of about 24, handsome and debonair, dressed with deliberate æstheticism in the most delicate purples and dove greys, with ornaments of bronze, oxydized silver, and stones of jade and agate. His sword, designed as carefully as a medieval cross, has a blued blade shewing through an openwork scabbard of purple leather and filigree. The porters, conducted by Ftatateeta, pass along the quay behind the sentinel to the steps of the

palace, where they put down their bales and squat on the ground. Apollodorus does not pass along with them: he halts, amused by the preoccupation of the sentinel.

APOLLODORUS   [*calling to the sentinel*]   Who goes there, eh?

SENTINEL   [*starting violently and turning with his pilum at the charge, revealing himself as a small, wiry, sandy-haired, conscientious young man with an elderly face*]   Whats this? Stand. Who are you?

APOLLODORUS   I am Apollodorus the Sicilian. Why, man, what are you dreaming of? Since I came through the lines beyond the theatre there, I have brought my caravan past three sentinels, all so busy staring at the lighthouse that not one of them challenged me. Is this Roman discipline?

SENTINEL   We are not here to watch the land but the sea. Cæsar has just landed on the Pharos. [*Looking at Ftatateeta*] What have you here? Who is this piece of Egyptian crockery?

FTATATEETA   Apollodorus: rebuke this Roman dog; and bid him bridle his tongue in the presence of Ftatateeta, the mistress of the Queen's household.

APOLLODORUS   My friend: this is a great lady, who stands high with Cæsar.

SENTINEL   [*not at all impressed, pointing to the carpets*]   And what is all this truck?

APOLLODORUS   Carpets for the furnishing of the Queen's apartments in the palace. I have picked them from the best carpets in the world; and the Queen shall choose the best of my choosing.

SENTINEL   So you are the carpet merchant?

APOLLODORUS   [*hurt*]   My friend: I am a patrician.

SENTINEL   A patrician! A patrician keeping a shop instead of following arms!

APOLLODORUS   I do not keep a shop. Mine is a temple of the arts. I am a worshipper of beauty. My calling is to choose beautiful things for beautiful queens. My motto is Art for Art's sake.

SENTINEL   That is not the password.

APOLLODORUS   It is a universal password.

SENTINEL   I know nothing about universal passwords. Either give me the password for the day or get back to your shop.

[*Ftatateeta, roused by his hostile tone, steals towards the edge of the quay with the step of a panther, and gets behind him.*]

APOLLODORUS   How if I do neither?

SENTINEL   Then I will drive this pilum through you.

APOLLODORUS   At your service, my friend.

[*He draws his sword, and springs to his guard with unruffled grace*].

FTATATEETA   [*suddenly seizing the sentinel's arms from behind*]   Thrust your knife into the dog's throat, Apollodorus.

[*The chivalrous Apollodorus laughingly shakes his head; breaks ground away from the sentinel towards the palace; and lowers his point*].

SENTINEL   [*struggling vainly*]   Curse on you! Let me go. Help ho!

FTATATEETA   [*lifting him from the ground*]   Stab the little Roman reptile. Spit him on your sword.

[*A couple of Roman soldiers, with a centurion, come running along the edge of the quay from the north end. They rescue their comrade, and throw off Ftatateeta, who is sent reeling away on the left hand of the sentinel.*]

CENTURION   [*an unattractive man of fifty, short in his speech and manners, with a vinewood cudgel in his hand*]   How now? What is all this?

FTATATEETA   [*to Apollodorus*]   Why did you not stab him? There was time!

APOLLODORUS   Centurion: I am here by order of the Queen to—

CENTURION   [*interrupting him*]   The Queen! Yes, yes: [*to the sentinel*] pass him in. Pass all these bazaar people in to the Queen, with their goods. But mind you pass no one out that you have not passed in—not even the Queen herself.

SENTINEL   This old woman is dangerous: she is as strong as three men. She wanted the merchant to stab me.

APOLLODORUS   Centurion: I am not a merchant. I am a patrician and a votary of art.

CENTURION   Is the woman your wife?

APOLLODORUS   [*horrified*]   No, no! [*Correcting himself politely*] Not that the lady is not a striking figure in her own way. But [*emphatically*] she is not my wife.

FTATATEETA   [*to the centurion*]   Roman: I am Ftatateeta, the mistress of the Queen's household.

CENTURION   Keep your hands off our men, mistress; or I will have you pitched into the harbor, though you were as strong as ten men. [*To his men*] To your posts: march!

[*He returns with his men the way they came*].

FTATATEETA   [*looking malignantly after him*]   We shall see whom Isis loves best: her servant Ftatateeta or a dog of a Roman.

SENTINEL   [*to Apollodorus, with a wave of his pilum towards the palace*]   Pass in there; and keep your distance. [*Turning to Ftatateeta*] Come within a yard of me, you old crocodile; and I will give you this [*the pilum*] in your jaws.

CLEOPATRA   [*calling from the palace*]   Ftatateeta, Ftatateeta.

FTATATEETA   [*looking up, scandalized*]   Go from the window, go from the window. There are men here.

CLEOPATRA   I am coming down.

FTATATEETA   [*distracted*]   No, no. What are you dreaming of? O ye gods, ye gods! Apollodorus: bid your men pick up your bales; and in with me quickly.

APOLLODORUS   Obey the mistress of the Queen's household.

FTATATEETA   [*impatiently, as the porters stoop to lift the bales*]   Quick, quick: she will be out upon us. [*Cleopatra comes from the palace and runs across the quay to Ftatateeta*]. Oh that ever I was born!

CLEOPATRA   [*eagerly*]   Ftatateeta: I have thought of something. I want a boat—at once.

FTATATEETA   A boat! No, no: you cannot. Apollodorus: speak to the Queen.

APOLLODORUS   [*gallantly*]   Beautiful queen: I am Apollodorus the Sicilian, your servant, from the bazaar. I have brought you the three most beautiful Persian carpets in the world to choose from.

CLEOPATRA   I have no time for carpets today. Get me a boat.

FTATATEETA   What whim is this? You cannot go on the water except in the royal barge.

APOLLODORUS   Royalty, Ftatateeta, lies not in the barge but in the Queen. [*To Cleopatra*] The touch of your majesty's foot on the gunwale of the meanest boat in the harbor will make it royal. [*He turns to the harbor and calls seaward*] Ho there, boatman! Pull in to the steps.

CLEOPATRA   Apollodorus: you are my perfect knight; and I will always buy my carpets through you. [*Apollodorus bows joyously. An oar appears above the quay; and the boatman, a bullet-headed, vivacious, grinning fellow, burnt almost black by the sun, comes up a flight of steps from the water on the sentinel's right, oar in hand, and waits at the top*]. Can you row, Apollodorus?

APOLLODORUS   My oars shall be your majesty's wings. Whither shall I row my Queen?

CLEOPATRA   To the lighthouse. Come. [*She makes for the steps*].

SENTINEL   [*opposing her with his pilum at the charge*]   Stand. You cannot pass.

CLEOPATRA   [*flushing angrily*]   How dare you? Do you know that I am the Queen?

SENTINEL   I have my orders. You cannot pass.

CLEOPATRA   I will make Cæsar have you killed if you do not obey me.

SENTINEL   He will do worse to me if I disobey my officer. Stand back.

CLEOPATRA   Ftatateeta: strangle him.

SENTINEL   [*alarmed—looking apprehensively at Ftatateeta, and brandishing his pilum*]   Keep off, there.

CLEOPATRA   [*running to Apollodorus*]   Apollodorus: make your slaves help us.

APOLLODORUS   I shall not need their help, lady. [*He draws his sword*]. Now, soldier: choose which weapon you will defend yourself with. Shall it be sword against pilum, or sword against sword?

SENTINEL   Roman against Sicilian, curse you. Take that. [*He hurls his pilum at Apollodorus, who drops expertly on one knee. The pilum passes whizzing over his head and falls harmless. Apollodorus, with a cry of triumph, springs up and attacks the sentinel, who draws his sword and defends himself, crying*] Ho there, guard. Help!

[*Cleopatra, half frightened, half delighted, takes refuge near the palace, where the porters are squatting among the bales. The boatman, alarmed, hurries down the steps out of harm's way, but stops, with his head just visible above the edge of the quay, to watch the fight. The sentinel is handicapped by his fear of an attack in the rear from Ftatateeta. His swordsmanship, which is of rough and ready sort, is heavily taxed, as he has occasionally to strike at her to keep her off between a blow and a guard with Apollodorus. The centurion returns with several soldiers. Apollodorus springs back towards Cleopatra as this reinforcement confronts him.*]

CENTURION   [*coming to the sentinel's right hand*]   What is this? What now?

SENTINEL   [*panting*]   I could do well enough by myself if it werent for the old woman. Keep her off me: that is all the help I need.

CENTURION   Make your report, soldier. What has happened?

FTATATEETA   Centurion: he would have slain the Queen.

SENTINEL   [*bluntly*]   I would, sooner than let her pass. She wanted to take boat, and go—so she said—to the lighthouse. I stopped her, as I was ordered to; and she set this fellow on me.

[*He goes to pick up his pilum and returns to his place with it*].

CENTURION   [*turning to Cleopatra*]   Cleopatra: I am loth to offend you; but without Cæsar's express order we dare not let you pass beyond the Roman lines.

APOLLODORUS   Well, Centurion; and has not the lighthouse been within the Roman lines since Cæsar landed there?

CLEOPATRA   Yes, yes. Answer that, if you can.

CENTURION   [*to Apollodorus*]   As for you, Apollodorus, you may thank the gods that you are not nailed to the palace door with a pilum for your meddling.

APOLLODORUS   [*urbanely*]   My military friend, I was not born to be slain by so ugly a weapon. When I fall, it will be [*holding up his sword*] by this white queen of arms, the only weapon fit for an artist. And now that you are convinced that we do not want to go beyond the lines, let me finish killing your sentinel and depart with the Queen.

CENTURION   [*as the sentinel makes an angry demonstration*]   Peace there, Cleopatra: I must abide by my orders, and not by the subtleties of this Sicilian. You must withdraw into the palace and examine your carpets there.

CLEOPATRA [*pouting*] I will not: I am the Queen. Cæsar does not speak to me as you do. Have Cæsar's centurions changed manners with his scullions?

CENTURION [*sulkily*] I do my duty. That is enough for me.

APOLLODORUS Majesty: when a stupid man is doing something he is ashamed of, he always declares that it is his duty.

CENTURION [*angry*] Apollodorus—

APOLLODORUS [*interrupting him with defiant elegance*] I will make amends for that insult with my sword at fitting time and place. Who says artist, says duellist. [*To Cleopatra*] Hear my counsel, star of the east. Until word comes to these soldiers from Cæsar himself, you are a prisoner. Let me go to him with a message from you, and a present; and before the sun has stooped half way to the arms of the sea, I will bring you back Cæsar's order of release.

CENTURION [*sneering at him*] And you will sell the Queen the present, no doubt.

APOLLODORUS Centurion: the Queen shall have from me, without payment, as the unforced tribute of Sicilian taste to Egyptian beauty, the richest of these carpets for her present to Cæsar.

CLEOPATRA [*exultantly, to the centurion*] Now you see what an ignorant common creature you are!

CENTURION [*curtly*] Well, a fool and his wares are soon parted. [*He turns to his men*] Two more men to this post here; and see that no one leaves the palace but this man and his merchandize. If he draws his sword again inside the lines, kill him. To your posts. March.

[*He goes out, leaving two auxiliary sentinels with the other.*]

APOLLODORUS [*with polite goodfellowship*] My friends: will you not enter the palace and bury our quarrel in a bowl of wine? [*He takes out his purse, jingling the coins in it*]. The Queen has presents for you all.

SENTINEL [*very sulky*] You heard our orders. Get about your business.

FIRST AUXILIARY Yes: you ought to know better. Off with you.

SECOND AUXILIARY [*looking longingly at the purse—this sentinel is a hooknosed man, unlike his comrade, who is squab faced*] Do not tantalize a poor man.

APOLLODORUS [*to Cleopatra*] Pearl of Queens: the centurion is at hand; and the Roman soldier is incorruptible when his officer is looking. I must carry your word to Cæsar.

CLEOPATRA [*who has been meditating among the carpets*] Are these carpets very heavy?

APOLLODORUS It matters not how heavy. There are plenty of porters.

CLEOPATRA How do they put the carpets into boats? Do they throw them down?

APOLLODORUS Not into small boats, majesty. It would sink them.

CLEOPATRA Not into that man's boat, for instance? [*pointing to the boatman*].

APOLLODORUS No. Too small.

CLEOPATRA But you can take a carpet to Cæsar in it if I send one?

APOLLODORUS Assuredly.

CLEOPATRA And you will have it carried gently down the steps and take great care of it?

APOLLODORUS Depend on me.

CLEOPATRA Great, great care?

APOLLODORUS More than of my own body.

CLEOPATRA You will promise me not to let the porters drop it or throw it about?

APOLLODORUS Place the most delicate glass goblet in the palace in the heart of the roll, Queen; and if it be broken, my head shall pay for it.

CLEOPATRA Good. Come, Ftatateeta. [*Ftatateeta comes to her. Apollodorus offers to squire them into the palace*]. No, Apollodorus, you must not come. I will choose a carpet for myself. You must wait here. [*She runs into the palace*].

APOLLODORUS [*to the porters*] Follow this lady [*indicating Ftatateeta*] and obey her.

[*The porters rise and take up their bales.*]

FTATATEETA [*addressing the porters as if they were vermin*] This way. And take your shoes off before you put your feet on those stairs.

[*She goes in, followed by the porters with the carpets. Meanwhile Apollodorus goes to the edge of the quay and looks out over the harbor. The sentinels keep their eyes on him malignantly.*]

APOLLODORUS [*addressing the sentinel*] My friend—

SENTINEL [*rudely*] Silence there.

FIRST AUXILIARY Shut your muzzle, you.

SECOND AUXILIARY [*in a half whisper, glancing apprehensively towards the north end of the quay*] Cant you wait a bit?

APOLLODORUS Patience, worthy three-headed donkey. [*They mutter ferociously; but he is not at all intimidated*]. Listen: were you set here to watch me, or to watch the Egyptians?

SENTINEL We know our duty.

APOLLODORUS Then why dont you do it? There is something going on over there [*pointing southwestward to the mole*].

SENTINEL [*sulkily*] I do not need to be told what to do by the like of you.

APOLLODORUS Blockhead. [*He begins shouting*] Ho there, Centurion. Hoiho!

SENTINEL Curse your meddling. [*Shouting*] Hoiho! Alarm! Alarm!

FIRST AND SECOND AUXILIARIES Alarm! alarm! Hoiho!

[*The Centurion comes running in with his guard.*]

CENTURION What now? Has the old woman attacked you again? [*Seeing Apollodorus*] Are you here still?

APOLLODORUS [*pointing as before*] See there. The Egyptians are moving. They are going to recapture the Pharos. They will attack by sea and land: by land along the great mole; by sea from the west harbor. Stir yourselves, my military friends: the hunt is up. [*A clangor of trumpets from several points along the quay*]. Aha! I told you so.

CENTURION [*quickly*] The two extra men pass the alarm to the south posts. One man keep guard here. The rest with me—quick.

[*The two auxiliary sentinels run off to the south. The centurion and his guard run off northward; and immediately afterwards the bucina sounds. The four porters come from the palace carrying a carpet, followed by Ftatateeta.*]

SENTINEL [*handling his pilum apprehensively*] You again!

[*The porters stop*].

FTATATEETA Peace, Roman fellow: you are now singlehanded. Apollodorus: this carpet is Cleopatra's present to Cæsar. It has rolled up in it ten precious goblets of the thinnest Iberian crystal, and a hundred eggs of the sacred blue pigeon. On your honor, let not one of them be broken.

APOLLODORUS On my head be it! [*To the porters*] Into the boat with them carefully.

[*The porters carry the carpet to the steps.*]

FIRST PORTER [*looking down at the boat*] Beware what you do, sir. Those eggs of which the lady speaks must weigh more than a pound apiece. This boat is too small for such a load.

BOATMAN [*excitedly rushing up the steps*] Oh thou injurious porter! Oh thou unnatural son of a she-camel! [*To Apollodorus*] My boat, sir, hath often carried five men. Shall it not carry your lordship and a bale of pigeon's eggs? [*To the porter*] Thou mangey dromedary, the gods shall punish thee for this envious wickedness.

FIRST PORTER [*stolidly*] I cannot quit this bale now to beat these; but another day I will lie in wait for thee.

APOLLODORUS [*going between them*] Peace there. If the boat were but a single plank, I would get to Cæsar on it.

FTATATEETA [*anxiously*] In the name of the gods, Apollodorus, run no risks with that bale.

APOLLODORUS Fear not, thou venerable grotesque: I guess its great worth. [*To the porters*] Down with it, I say; and gently; or ye shall eat nothing but stick for ten days.

[*The boatman goes down the steps, followed by the porters with the bale: Ftatateeta and Apollodorus watching from the edge.*]

APOLLODORUS Gently, my sons, my children—[*with sudden alarm*] gently, ye dogs. Lay it level in the stern—so—tis well.

FTATATEETA [*screaming down at one of the porters*] Do not step on it, do not step on it. Oh thou brute beast!

FIRST PORTER [*ascending*] Be not excited, mistress: all is well.

FTATATEETA [*panting*] All well! Oh, thou hast given my heart a turn! [*She clutches her side, gasping*].

[*The four porters have now come up and are waiting at the stairhead to be paid.*]

APOLLODORUS Here, ye hungry ones. [*He gives money to the first porter, who holds it in his hand to shew to the others. They crowd greedily to see how much it is, quite prepared, after the Eastern fashion, to protest to heaven against their patron's stinginess. But his liberality overpowers them*].

FIRST PORTER O bounteous prince!

SECOND PORTER O lord of the bazaar!

THIRD PORTER O favored of the gods!

FOURTH PORTER O father to all the porters of the market.

SENTINEL [*enviously, threatening them fiercely with his pilum*] Hence, dogs: off. Out of this. [*They fly before him northward along the quay*].

APOLLODORUS Farewell, Ftatateeta. I shall be at the lighthouse before the Egyptians. [*He descends the steps*].

FTATATEETA The gods speed thee and protect my nursling!

[*The sentry returns from chasing the porters and looks down at the boat, standing near the stairhead lest Ftatateeta should attempt to escape.*]

APOLLODORUS [*from beneath, as the boat moves off*] Farewell, valiant pilum pitcher.

SENTINEL Farewell, shopkeeper.

APOLLODORUS Ha, ha! Pull, thou brave boatman, pull. Soho-o-o-o-o! [*He begins to sing in barcarolle measure to the rhythm of the oars*]

> My heart, my heart, spread out thy wings:
> Shake off thy heavy load of love—

Give me the oars, O son of a snail.

SENTINEL [*threatening Ftatateeta*] Now mistress: back to your henhouse. In with you.

FTATATEETA [*falling on her knees and stretching her hands over the waters*] Gods of the seas, bear her safely to the shore!

SENTINEL Bear who safely? What do you mean?

FTATATEETA [*looking darkly at him*] Gods of Egypt and of Vengeance, let this Roman fool be beaten like a dog by his captain for suffering her to be taken over the waters.

SENTINEL Accursed one: is she then in the boat? [*He calls over the sea*] Hoiho, there, boatman! Hoiho!

APOLLODORUS [*singing in the distance*]

> My heart, my heart, be whole and free:
> Love is thine only enemy.

[*Meanwhile Rufio, the morning's fighting done, sits munching dates on a faggot of brushwood outside the door of the lighthouse, which towers gigantic to the clouds on his left. His helmet, full of dates, is between his knees; and a leathern bottle of wine is by his side. Behind him the great stone pedestal of the lighthouse is shut in from the open sea by a low stone parapet, with a couple of steps in the middle to the broad coping. A huge chain with a hook hangs down from the lighthouse crane above his head. Faggots like the one he sits on lie beneath it ready to be drawn up to feed the beacon. Cæsar is standing on the step at the parapet looking out anxiously, evidently ill at ease. Britannus comes out of the lighthouse door.*]

RUFIO Well, my British islander. Have you been up to the top?

BRITANNUS I have. I reckon it at 200 feet high.

RUFIO Anybody up there?

BRITANNUS One elderly Tyrian to work the crane; and his son, a well conducted youth of 14.

RUFIO [*looking at the chain*] What! An old man and a boy work that! Twenty men, you mean.

BRITANNUS Two only, I assure you. They have counterweights, and a machine with boiling water in it which I do not understand: it is not of British design. They use it to haul up barrels of oil and faggots to burn in the brazier on the roof.

RUFIO But—

BRITANNUS Excuse me: I came down because there are messengers coming along the mole to us from the island. I must see what their business is. [*He hurries out past the lighthouse*].

CÆSAR [*coming away from the parapet, shivering and out of sorts*] Rufio: this has been a mad expedition. We shall be beaten. I wish I knew how our men are getting on with that barricade across the great mole.

RUFIO [*angrily*] Must I leave my food and go starving to bring you a report?

CÆSAR [*soothing him nervously*] No, Rufio, no. Eat, my son, eat. [*He takes another turn, Rufio chewing dates meanwhile*]. The Egyptians cannot be such fools as not to storm the barricade and swoop down on us here before it is finished. It is the first time I have ever run an avoidable risk. I should not have come to Egypt.

RUFIO An hour ago you were all for victory.

CÆSAR [*apologetically*] Yes: I was a fool—rash, Rufio—boyish.

RUFIO Boyish! Not a bit of it. Here [*offering him a handful of dates*].

CÆSAR What are these for?

RUFIO To eat. Thats whats the matter with you. When a man comes to your age, he runs down before his midday meal. Eat and drink; and then have another look at our chances.

CÆSAR [*taking the dates*] My age! [*He shakes his head and bites a date*]. Yes, Rufio: I am an old man—worn out now—true, quite true. [*He gives way to melancholy contemplation, and eats another date*]. Achillas is still in his prime: Ptolemy is a boy. [*He eats another date, and plucks up a little*]. Well, every dog has his day; and I have had mine: I cannot complain. [*With sudden cheerfulness*] These dates are not bad, Rufio. [*Britannus returns, greatly excited, with a leathern bag. Cæsar is himself again in a moment*]. What now?

BRITANNUS   [*triumphantly*]   Our brave Rhodian mariners have captured a treasure. There! [*He throws the bag down at Cæsar's feet*]. Our enemies are delivered into our hands.

CÆSAR   In that bag?

BRITANNUS   Wait till you hear, Cæsar. This bag contains all the letters which have passed between Pompey's party and the army of occupation here.

CÆSAR   Well?

BRITTANUS   [*impatient of Cæsar's slowness to grasp the situation*]   Well, we shall now know who your foes are. The name of every man who has plotted against you since you crossed the Rubicon may be in these papers, for all we know.

CÆSAR   Put them in the fire.

BRITANNUS   Put them—[*he gasps*]!!!!

CÆSAR   In the fire. Would you have me waste the next three years of my life of proscribing and condemning men who will be my friends when I have proved that my friendship is worth more than Pompey's was—than Cato's is. O incorrigible British islander: am I a bull dog, to seek quarrels merely to shew how stubborn my jaws are?

BRITANNUS   But your honor—the honor of Rome—

CÆSAR   I do not make human sacrifices to my honor, as your Druids do. Since you will not burn these, at least I can drown them. [*He picks up the bag and throws it over the parapet into the sea*].

BRITANNUS   Cæsar: this is mere eccentricity. Are traitors to be allowed to go free for the sake of a paradox?

RUFIO   [*rising*]   Cæsar: when the islander has finished preaching, call me again. I am going to have a look at the boiling water machine. [*He goes into the lighthouse*].

BRITANNUS   [*with genuine feeling*]   O Cæsar, my great master, if I could but persuade you to regard life seriously, as men do in my country!

CÆSAR   Do they truly do so, Britannus?

BRITANNUS   Have you not been there? Have you not seen them? What Briton speaks as you do in your moments of levity? What Briton neglects to attend the services at the sacred grove? What Briton wears clothes of many colors as you do, instead of plain blue, as all solid, well esteemed men should? These are moral questions with us.

CÆSAR   Well, well, my friend: some day I shall settle down and have a blue toga, perhaps. Meanwhile, I must get on as best I can in my flippant Roman way. [*Apollodorus comes past the lighthouse*]. What now?

BRITANNUS   [*turning quickly, and challenging the stranger with official haughtiness*]   What is this? Who are you? How did you come here?

APOLLODORUS   Calm yourself, my friend: I am not going to eat you. I have come by boat, from Alexandria, with precious gifts for Cæsar.

CÆSAR   From Alexandria!

BRITANNUS   [*severely*]   This is Cæsar, sir.

RUFIO   [*appearing at the lighthouse door*]   Whats the matter now?

APOLLODORUS   Hail, great Cæsar! I am Apollodorus the Sicilian, an artist.

BRITANNUS   An artist! Why have they admitted this vagabond?

CÆSAR   Peace, man. Apollodorus is a famous patrician amateur.

BRITANNUS   [*disconcerted*]   I crave the gentleman's pardon. [*To Cæsar*] I understood him to say that he was a professional.

[Somewhat out of countenance, he allows Apollodorus to approach Cæsar, changing places with him. Rufio, after looking Apollodorus up and down with marked disparagement, goes to the other side of the platform].

CÆSAR   You are welcome, Apollodorus. What is your business?

APOLLODORUS   First, to deliver to you a present from the Queen of Queens.

CÆSAR   Who is that?

APOLLODORUS   Cleopatra of Egypt.

CÆSAR   *[taking him into his confidence in his most winning manner]* Apollodorus: this is no time for playing with presents. Pray you, go back to the Queen, and tell her that if all goes well I shall return to the palace this evening.

APOLLODORUS   Cæsar: I cannot return. As I approached the lighthouse, some fool threw a great leathern bag into the sea. It broke the nose of my boat; and I had hardly time to get myself and my charge to the shore before the poor little cockleshell sank.

CÆSAR   I am sorry, Apollodorus. The fool shall be rebuked. Well, well: what have you brought me? The Queen will be hurt if I do not look at it.

RUFIO   Have we time to waste on this trumpery? The Queen is only a child.

CÆSAR   Just so: that is why we must not disappoint her. What is the present, Apollodorus?

APOLLODORUS   Cæsar: it is a Persian carpet—a beauty! And in it are—so I am told—pigeons' eggs and crystal goblets and fragile precious things. I dare not for my head have it carried up that narrow ladder from the causeway.

RUFIO   Swing it up by the crane, then. We will send the eggs to the cook; drink our wine from the goblets; and the carpet will make a bed for Cæsar.

APOLLODORUS   The crane! Cæsar: I have sworn to tender this bale of carpet as I tender my own life.

CÆSAR   *[cheerfully]* Then let them swing you up at the same time; and if the chain breaks, you and the pigeons' eggs will perish together.

[He goes to the chain and looks up along it, examining it curiously].

APOLLODORUS   *[to Britannus]* Is Cæsar serious?

BRITANNUS   His manner is frivolous because he is an Italian; but he means what he says.

APOLLODORUS   Serious or not, he spake well. Give me a squad of soldiers to work the crane.

BRITANNUS   Leave the crane to me. Go and await the descent of the chain.

APOLLODORUS   Good. You will presently see me there *[turning to them all and pointing with an eloquent gesture to the sky above the parapet]* rising like the sun with my treasure.

[He goes back the way he came. Britannus goes into the lighthouse.]

RUFIO   *[ill-humoredly]* Are you really going to wait here for this foolery, Cæsar?

CÆSAR   *[backing away from the crane as it gives signs of working]* Why not?

RUFIO   The Egyptians will let you know why not if they have the sense to make a rush from the shore end of the mole before our barricade is finished. And here we are waiting like children to see a carpet full of pigeons' eggs.

[The chain rattles, and is drawn up high enough to clear the parapet. It then swings round out of sight behind the lighthouse.]

CÆSAR   Fear not, my son Rufio. When the first Egyptian takes his first step along the mole, the alarm will sound; and we two will reach the barricade from our end before the Egyptians reach it from their end—we two, Rufio: I, the old man, and you, his biggest boy. And the old man will be there first. So peace; and give me some more dates.

APOLLODORUS   *[from the causeway below]* Soho, haul away. So-ho-o-o-o!

[The chain is drawn up and comes round again from behind the lighthouse.

Apollodorus is swinging in the air with his bale of carpet at the end of it.
He breaks into song as he soars above the parapet]

> Aloft, aloft, behold the blue
> That never shone in woman's eyes

Easy there: stop her. [*He ceases to rise*]. Further round!
[*The chain comes forward above the platform*].
RUFIO   [*calling up*]   Lower away there. [*The chain and its load begin to descend*].
APOLLODORUS   [*calling up*]   Gently—slowly—mind the eggs.
RUFIO   [*calling up*]   Easy there—slowly—slowly.
[*Apollodorus and the bale are deposited safely on the flags in the middle of the platform. Rufio and Cæsar help Apollodorus to cast off the chain from the bale.*]
RUFIO   Haul up.
[*The chain rises clear of their heads with a rattle. Britannus comes from the lighthouse and helps them to uncord the carpet.*]
APOLLODORUS   [*when the cords are loose*]   Stand off, my friends: let Cæsar see.
[*He throws the carpet open*].
RUFIO   Nothing but a heap of shawls. Where are the pigeons' eggs?
APOLLODORUS   Approach, Cæsar; and search for them among the shawls.
RUFIO   [*drawing his sword*]   Ha, treachery! Keep back, Cæsar: I saw the shawl move: there is something alive there.
BRITANNUS   [*drawing his sword*]   It is a serpent.
APOLLODORUS   Dares Cæsar thrust his hand into the sack where the serpent moves?
RUFIO   [*turning on him*]   Treacherous dog—
CÆSAR   Peace. Put up your swords. Apollodorus: your serpent seems to breathe very regularly. [*He thrusts his hand under the shawls and draws out a bare arm*]. This is a pretty little snake.
RUFIO   [*drawing out the other arm*]   Let us have the rest of you.
[*They pull Cleopatra up by the wrists into a sitting position. Britannus, scandalized, sheathes his sword with a drive of protest.*]
CLEOPATRA   [*gasping*]   Oh, I'm smothered. Oh, Cæsar, a man stood on me in the boat; and a great sack of something fell upon me out of the sky; and then the boat sank; and then I was swung up into the air and bumped down.
CÆSAR   [*petting her as she rises and takes refuge on his breast*]   Well, never mind: here you are safe and sound at last.
RUFIO   Ay; and now that she is here, where are we to do with her?
BRITANNUS   She cannot stay here, Cæsar, without the companionship of some matron.
CLEOPATRA   [*jealously, to Cæsar, who is obviously perplexed*]   Arent you glad to see me?
CÆSAR   Yes, yes; I am very glad. But Rufio is very angry; and Britannus is shocked.
CLEOPATRA   [*contemptuously*]   You can have their heads cut off, can you not?
CÆSAR   They would not be so useful with their heads cut off as they are now, my sea bird.
RUFIO   [*to Cleopatra*]   We shall have to go away presently and cut some of your Egyptians' heads off. How will you like being left here with the chance of being captured by that little brother of yours if we are beaten?
CLEOPATRA   But you mustnt leave me alone. Cæsar: you will not leave me alone, will you?

RUFIO   What! not when the trumpet sounds and all our lives depend on Cæsar's being at the barricade before the Egyptians reach it? Eh?

CLEOPATRA   Let them lose their lives: they are only soldiers.

CÆSAR   [*gravely*]   Cleopatra: when that trumpet sounds, we must take every man his life in his hand, and throw it in the face of Death. And of my soldiers who have trusted me there is not one whose hand I shall not hold more sacred than your head. [*Cleopatra is overwhelmed. Her eyes fill with tears*]. Apollodorus: you must take her back to the palace.

APOLLODORUS   Am I a dolphin, Cæsar, to cross the seas with young ladies on my back? My boat is sunk: all yours are either at the barricade or have returned to the city. I will hail one if I can: that is all I can do. [*He goes back to the causeway*].

CLEOPATRA   [*struggling with her tears*]   It does not matter. I will not go back. Nobody cares for me.

CÆSAR   Cleopatra—

CLEOPATRA   You want me to be killed.

CÆSAR   [*still more gravely*]   My poor child: your life matters little here to anyone but yourself.

[*She gives way altogether at this, casting herself down on the faggots weeping. Suddenly a great tumult is heard in the distance, bucinas and trumpets sounding through a storm of shouting. Britannus rushes to the parapet and looks along the mole. Cæsar and Rufio turn to one another with quick intelligence*].

CÆSAR   Come, Rufio.

CLEOPATRA   [*scrambling to her knees and clinging to him*].   No no. Do not leave me, Cæsar. [*He snatches his skirt from her clutch*]. Oh!

BRITANNUS   [*from the parapet*]   Cæsar: we are cut off. The Egyptians have landed from the west harbor between us and the barricade!!!

RUFIO   [*running to see*]   Curses! It is true. We are caught like rats in a trap.

CÆSAR   [*ruthfully*]   Rufio, Rufio: my men at the barricade are between the sea party and the shore party. I have murdered them.

RUFIO   [*coming back from the parapet to Cæsar's right hand*]   Ay: that comes of fooling with this girl here.

APOLLODORUS   [*coming up quickly from the causeway*]   Look over the parapet, Cæsar.

CÆSAR   We have looked, my friend. We must defend ourselves here.

APOLLODORUS   I have thrown the ladder into the sea. They cannot get in without it.

RUFIO   Ay; and we cannot get out. Have you thought of that?

APOLLODORUS   Not get out! Why not? You have ships in the east harbor.

BRITANNUS   [*hopefully, at the parapet*]   The Rhodian galleys are standing in towards us already. [*Cæsar quickly joins Britannus at the parapet*].

RUFIO   [*to Apollodorus, impatiently*]   And by what road are we to walk to the galleys, pray?

APOLLODORUS   [*with gay, defiant rhetoric*]   By the road that leads everywhere— the diamond path of the sun and moon. Have you never seen the child's shadow play of The Broken Bridge? "Ducks and geese with ease get over"— eh? [*He throws away his cloak and cap, and binds his sword on his back*].

RUFIO   What are you talking about?

APOLLODORUS   I will shew you. [*Calling to Britannus*] How far off is the nearest galley?

BRITANNUS   Fifty fathom.

CÆSAR   No, no: they are further off than they seem in this clear air to your British eyes. Nearly quarter of a mile, Apollodorus.

APOLLODORUS   Good. Defend yourselves here until I send you a boat from that galley.

RUFIO   Have you wings, perhaps?

APOLLODORUS   Water wings, soldier. Behold!

[*He runs up the steps between Cæsar and Britannus to the coping of the parapet; springs into the air; and plunges head foremost into the sea.*]

CÆSAR   [*like a schoolboy—wildly excited*]   Bravo, bravo! [*Throwing off his cloak*] By Jupiter, I will do that too.

RUFIO   [*seizing him*]   You are mad. You shall not.

CÆSAR   Why not? Can I not swim as well as he?

RUFIO   [*frantic*]   Can an old fool dive and swim like a young one? He is twenty-five and you are fifty.

CÆSAR   [*breaking loose from Rufio*]   Old!!!

BRITANNUS   [*shocked*]   Rufio: you forget yourself.

CÆSAR   I will race you to the galley for a week's pay, father Rufio.

CLEOPATRA   But me! me!! me!!! what is to become of me?

CÆSAR   I will carry you on my back to the galley like a dolphin. Rufio: when you see me rise to the surface, throw her in: I will answer for her. And then in with you after her, both of you.

CLEOPATRA   No, no, NO. I shall be drowned.

BRITANNUS   Cæsar: I am a man and a Briton, not a fish. I must have a boat. I cannot swim.

CLEOPATRA   Neither can I.

CÆSAR   [*to Britannus*]   Stay here, then, alone, until I recapture the lighthouse: I will not forget you. Now, Rufio.

RUFIO   You have made up your mind to this folly?

CÆSAR   The Egyptians have made it up for me. What else is there to do? And mind where you jump: I do not want to get your fourteen stone in the small of my back as I come up. [*He runs up the steps and stands on the coping*].

BRITANNUS   [*anxiously*]   One last word, Cæsar. Do not let yourself be seen in the fashionable part of Alexandria until you have changed your clothes.

CÆSAR   [*calling over the sea*]   Ho, Apollodorus: [*he points skyward and quotes the barcarolle*]

The white upon the blue above—

APOLLODORUS   [*swimming in the distance*]

Is purple on the green below—

CÆSAR   [*exultantly*]   Aha! [*He plunges into the sea*].

CLEOPATRA   [*running excitedly to the steps*]   Oh, let me see. He will be drowned [*Rufio seizes her*]—Ah—ah—ah—ah! [*He pitches her screaming into the sea. Rufio and Britannus roar with laughter*].

RUFIO   [*looking down after her*].   He has got her. [*To Britannus*] Hold the fort, Briton. Cæsar will not forget you. [*He springs off*].

BRITANNUS   [*running to the steps to watch them as they swim*]   All safe, Rufio?

RUFIO   [*swimming*]   All safe.

CÆSAR   [*swimming further off*]   Take refuge up there by the beacon; and pile the fuel on the trap door, Britannus.

BRITANNUS   [*calling in reply*]   I will first do so, and then commend myself to my country's gods. [*A sound of cheering from the sea. Britannus gives full vent to his excitement*]. The boat has reached him: Hip, hip, hip, hurrah!

ACT IV

Cleopatra's sousing in the east harbor of Alexandria was in October 48 B.C. In March 47 she is passing the afternoon in her boudoir in the palace, among a bevy of her ladies, listening to a slave girl who is playing the harp in the middle of the room. The harpist's master, an old musician, with a lined face, prominent brows, white beard, moustache and eyebrows twisted and horned at the ends, and a consciously keen and pretentious expression, is squatting on the floor close to her on her right, watching her performance. Ftatateeta is in attendance near the door, in front of a group of female slaves. Except the harp player all are seated: Cleopatra in a chair opposite the door on the other side of the room; the rest on the ground. Cleopatra's ladies are all young, the most conspicuous being Charmian and Iras, her favorites. Charmian is a hatchet faced, terra cotta colored little goblin, swift in her movements, and neatly finished at the hands and feet. Iras is a plump, goodnatured creature, rather fatuous, with a profusion of red hair, and a tendency to giggle on the slightest provocation.

CLEOPATRA   Can I—

FTATATEETA   [*insolently, to the player*]   Peace, thou! The Queen speaks. [*The player stops*].

CLEOPATRA   [*to the old musician*]   I want to learn to play the harp with my own hands. Cæsar loves music. Can you teach me?

MUSICIAN   Assuredly I and no one else can teach the queen. Have I not discovered the lost method of the ancient Egyptians, who could make a pyramid tremble by touching a bass string? All the other teachers are quacks: I have exposed them repeatedly.

CLEOPATRA   Good: you shall teach me. How long will it take?

MUSICIAN   Not very long: only four years. Your Majesty must first become proficient in the philosophy of Pythagoras.

CLEOPATRA   Has she [*indicating the slave*] become proficient in the philosophy of Pythagoras?

MUSICIAN   Oh, she is but a slave. She learns as a dog learns.

CLEOPATRA   Well, then, I will learn as a dog learns; for she plays better than you. You shall give me a lesson every day for a fortnight. [*The musician hastily scrambles to his feet and bows profoundly*]. After that, whenever I strike a false note you shall be flogged; and if I strike so many that there is not time to flog you, you shall be thrown into the Nile to feed the crocodiles. Give the girl a piece of gold; and send them away.

MUSICIAN   [*much taken aback*]   But true art will not be thus forced.

FTATATEETA   [*pushing him out*]   What is this? Answering the Queen, forsooth. Out with you.

[*He is pushed out by Ftatateeta, the girl following with her harp, amid the laughter of the ladies and slaves.*]

CLEOPATRA   Now, can any of you amuse me? Have you any stories or any news?

IRAS   Ftatateeta—

CLEOPATRA   Oh, Ftatateeta, Ftatateeta, always Ftatateeta. Some new tale to set me against her.

IRAS   No: this time Ftatateeta has been virtuous. [*All the ladies laugh—not the slaves*]. Pothinus has been trying to bribe her to let him speak with you.

CLEOPATRA   [*wrathfully*]   Ha! you all sell audiences with me, as if I saw whom you please, and not whom I please. I should like to know how much of her gold piece that harp girl will have to give up before she leaves the palace.

IRAS   We can easily find out that for you.

[*The ladies laugh.*]

CLEOPATRA   [*frowning*]   You laugh; but take care, take care. I will find out some day how to make myself served as Cæsar is served.

CHARMIAN   Old hooknose! [*They laugh again*].

CLEOPATRA   [*revolted*]   Silence. Charmian: do not you be a silly little Egyptian fool. Do you know why I allow you all to chatter impertinently just as you please, instead of treating you as Ftatateeta would treat you if she were Queen?

CHARMIAN   Because you try to imitate Cæsar in everything; and he lets everybody say what they please to him.

CLEOPATRA   No; but because I asked him one day why he did so; and he said "Let your women talk; and you will learn something from them." What have I to learn from them? I said. "What they are," said he; and oh! you should have seen his eye as he said it. You would have curled up, you shallow things. [*They laugh. She turns fiercely on Iras*]. At whom are you laughing—at me or at Cæsar?

IRAS   At Cæsar.

CLEOPATRA   If you were not a fool, you would laugh at me; and if you were not a coward you would not be afraid to tell me so. [*Ftatateeta returns*]. Ftatateeta: they tell me that Pothinus has offered you a bribe to admit him to my presence.

FTATATEETA   [*protesting*]   Now by my father's gods—

CLEOPATRA   [*cutting her short despotically*]   Have I not told you not to deny things? You would spend the day calling your father's gods to witness to your virtues if I let you. Go take the bribe; and bring in Pothinus. [*Ftatateeta is about to reply*]. Dont answer me. Go.

[*Ftatateeta goes out; and Cleopatra rises and begins to prowl to and fro between her chair and the door, meditating. All rise and stand.*]

IRAS   [*as she reluctantly rises*]   Heigho! I wish Cæsar were back in Rome.

CLEOPATRA   [*threateningly*]   It will be a bad day for you all when he goes. Oh, if I were not ashamed to let him see that I am as cruel at heart as my father, I would make you repent that speech! Why do you wish him away?

CHARMIAN   He makes you so terribly prosy and serious and learned and philosophical. It is worse than being religious, at our ages. [*The ladies laugh*].

CLEOPATRA   Cease that endless cackling, will you. Hold your tongues.

CHARMIAN   [*with mock resignation*]   Well, well: we must try to live up to Cæsar.

[*They laugh again. Cleopatra rages silently as she continues to prowl to and fro. Ftatateeta comes back with Pothinus, who halts on the threshold.*]

FTATATEETA   [*at the door*]   Pothinus craves the ear of the—

CLEOPATRA   There, there: that will do: let him come in. [*She resumes her seat. All sit down except Pothinus, who advances to the middle of the room. Ftatateeta takes her former place*]. Well, Pothinus: what is the latest news from your rebel friends?

POTHINUS   [*haughtily*]   I am no friend of rebellion. And a prisoner does not receive news.

CLEOPATRA   You are no more a prisoner than I am—than Cæsar is. These six months we have been besieged in this palace by my subjects. You are allowed to walk on the beach among the soldiers. Can I go further myself, or can Cæsar?

POTHINUS   You are but a child, Cleopatra, and do not understand these matters. [*The ladies laugh. Cleopatra looks inscrutably at him.*]

CHARMIAN   I see you do not know the latest news, Pothinus.

POTHINUS   What is that?

CHARMIAN   That Cleopatra is no longer a child. Shall I tell you how to grow much older, and much, much wiser in one day?

POTHINUS   I should prefer to grow wiser without growing older.

CHARMIAN   Well, go up to the top of the lighthouse; and get somebody to take you by the hair and throw you into the sea. [*The ladies laugh*].

CLEOPATRA   She is right, Pothinus: you will come to the shore with much conceit washed out of you. [*The ladies laugh. Cleopatra rises impatiently*]. Begone, all of you. I will speak with Pothinus alone. Drive them out, Ftatateeta. [*They run out laughing. Ftatateeta shuts the door on them*]. What are you waiting for?

FTATATEETA   It is not meet that the Queen remain alone with—

CLEOPATRA   [*interrupting her*]   Ftatateeta: must I sacrifice you to your father's gods to teach you that *I* am Queen of Egypt, and not you?

FTATATEETA   [*indignantly*]   You are like the rest of them. You want to be what these Romans call a New Woman. [*She goes out, banging the door*].

CLEOPATRA   [*sitting down again*]   Now, Pothinus: why did you bribe Ftatateeta to bring you hither?

POTHINUS   [*studying her gravely*]   Cleopatra: what they tell me is true. You are changed.

CLEOPATRA   Do you speak with Cæsar every day for six months: and you will be changed.

POTHINUS   It is the common talk that you are infatuated with this old man?

CLEOPATRA   Infatuated? What does that mean? Made foolish, is it not? Oh no: I wish I were.

POTHINUS   You wish you were made foolish! How so?

CLEOPATRA   When I was foolish, I did what I liked, except when Ftatateeta beat me; and even then I cheated her and did it by stealth. Now that Cæsar has made me wise, it is no use my liking or disliking: I do what must be done, and have no time to attend to myself. That is not happiness; but it is greatness. If Cæsar were gone, I think I could govern the Egyptians; for what Cæsar is to me, I am to the fools around me.

POTHINUS   [*looking hard at her*]   Cleopatra: this may be the vanity of youth.

CLEOPATRA   No, no: it is not that I am so clever, but that the others are so stupid.

POTHINUS   [*musingly*]   Truly, that is the great secret.

CLEOPATRA   Well, now tell me what you came to say?

POTHINUS   [*embarrassed*]   I! Nothing.

CLEOPATRA   Nothing!

POTHINUS   At least—to beg for my liberty: that is all.

CLEOPATRA   For that you would have knelt to Cæsar. No, Pothinus: you came with some plan that depended on Cleopatra being a little nursery kitten. Now that Cleopatra is a Queen, the plan is upset.

POTHINUS   [*bowing his head submissively*]   It is so.

CLEOPATRA   [*exultant*]   Aha!

POTHINUS   [*raising his eyes keenly to hers*]   Is Cleopatra then indeed a Queen, and no longer Cæsar's prisoner and slave?

CLEOPATRA   Pothinus: we are all Cæsar's slaves—all we in this land of Egypt—whether we will or no. And she who is wise enough to know this will reign when Cæsar departs.

POTHINUS   You harp on Cæsar's departure.

CLEOPATRA   What if I do?

POTHINUS   Does he not love you?

CLEOPATRA   Love me! Pothinus: Cæsar loves no one. Who are those we love. Only those whom we do not hate: all people are strangers and enemies to us except those we love. But it is not so with Cæsar. He has no hatred in him: he makes friends with everyone as he does with dogs and children. His kindness to me is a wonder: neither mother, father, nor nurse have ever taken so much care for me, or thrown open their thoughts to me so freely.

POTHINUS   Well: is not this love?

CLEOPATRA   What! when he will do as much for the first girl he meets on his way back to Rome? Ask his slave, Britannus: he has been just as good to him. Nay, ask his very horse! His kindness is not for anything in me: it is in his own nature.

POTHINUS   But how can you be sure that he does not love you as men love women?

CLEOPATRA   Because I cannot make him jealous. I have tried.

POTHINUS   Hm! Perhaps I should have asked, then, do you love him?

CLEOPATRA   Can one love a god? Besides, I love another Roman: one whom I saw long before Cæsar—no god, but a man—one who can love and hate— one whom I can hurt and who would hurt me.

POTHINUS   Does Cæsar know this?

CLEOPATRA   Yes.

POTHINUS   And he is not angry?

CLEOPATRA   He promises to send him to Egypt to please me!

POTHINUS   I do not understand this man.

CLEOPATRA   [*with superb contempt*]   You understand Cæsar! How could you? [*Proudly*] I do—by instinct.

POTHINUS   [*deferentially, after a moment's thought*]   Your Majesty caused me to be admitted today. What message has the Queen for me?

CLEOPATRA   This. You think that by making my brother king, you will rule in Egypt because you are his guardian and he is a little silly.

POTHINUS   The Queen is pleased to say so.

CLEOPATRA   The Queen is pleased to say this also. That Cæsar will eat up you, and Achillas, and my brother, as a cat eats up mice; and that he will put on this land of Egypt as a shepherd puts on his garment. And when he has done that, he will return to Rome, and leave Cleopatra here as his viceroy.

POTHINUS   [*breaking out wrathfully*]   That he shall never do. We have a thousand men to his ten; and we will drive him and his beggarly legions into the sea.

CLEOPATRA   [*with scorn, getting up to go*]   You rant like any common fellow. Go, then, and marshal your thousands; and make haste; for Mithridates of Pergamos is at hand with reinforcements for Cæsar. Cæsar has held you at bay with two legions: we shall see what he will do with twenty.

POTHINUS   Cleopatra—

CLEOPATRA   Enough, enough: Cæsar has spoiled me for talking to weak things like you. [*She goes out. Pothinus, with a gesture of rage, is following, when Ftatateeta enters and stops him.*]

POTHINUS   Let me go forth from this hateful place.

FTATATEETA   What angers you?

POTHINUS   The curse of all the gods of Egypt be upon her! She sold her country to the Roman, that she may buy it back from him with her kisses.

FTATATEETA   Fool: did she not tell you that she would have Cæsar gone?

POTHINUS   You listened?

FTATATEETA   I took care that some honest woman should be at hand whilst you were with her.

POTHINUS   Now by the gods—

FTATATEETA   Enough of your gods! Cæsar's gods are all powerful here. It is no use you coming to Cleopatra: you are only an Egyptian. She will not listen to any of her own race: she treats us all as children.

POTHINUS   May she perish for it!

FTATATEETA   [*balefully*]   May your tongue wither for that wish! Go! send for Lucius Septimius, the slayer of Pompey. He is a Roman: may be she will listen to him. Begone!

POTHINUS   [*darkly*]   I know to whom I must go now.

FTATATEETA   [*suspiciously*]   To whom, then?

POTHINUS   To a greater Roman than Lucius. And mark this, mistress. You thought, before Cæsar came, that Egypt should presently be ruled by you and your crew in the name of Cleopatra. I set myself against it—

FTATATEETA   [*interrupting him—wrangling*]   Ay; that it might be ruled by you and your crew in the name of Ptolemy.

POTHINUS   Better me, or even you, than a woman with a Roman heart; and that is what Cleopatra is now become. Whilst I live, she shall never rule. So guide yourself accordingly. [*He goes out*].

[*It is by this time drawing on to dinner time. The table is laid on the roof of the palace; and thither Rufio is now climbing, ushered by a majestic palace official, wand of office in hand, and followed by a slave carrying an inlaid stool. After many stairs they emerge at last into a massive colonnade on the roof. Light curtains are drawn between the columns on the north and east to soften the westering sun. The official leads Rufio to one of these shaded sections. A cord for pulling the curtains apart hangs down between the pillars.*]

THE OFFICIAL   [*bowing*]   The Roman commander will await Cæsar here.

[*The slave sets down the stool near the southernmost column, and slips out through the curtains.*]

RUFIO   [*sitting down, a little blown*]   Pouf! That was a climb. How high have we come?

THE OFFICIAL   We are on the palace roof, O Beloved of Victory!

RUFIO   Good! the Beloved of Victory has no more stairs to get up.

[*A second official enters from the opposite end, walking backwards.*]

THE SECOND OFFICIAL   Cæsar approaches.

[*Cæsar, fresh from the bath, clad in a new tunic of purple silk, comes in, beaming and festive, followed by two slaves carrying a light couch, which is hardly more than an elaborately designed bench. They place it near the northmost of the two curtained columns. When this is done they slip out through the curtains; and the two officials, formally bowing, follow them. Rufio rises to receive Cæsar.*]

CÆSAR   [*coming over to him*]   Why, Rufio! [*Surveying his dress with an air of admiring astonishment*]   A new baldrick! A new golden pommel to your sword! And you have had your hair cut! But not your beard—? impossible! [*He sniffs at Rufio's beard*].   Yes, perfumed, by Jupiter Olympus!

RUFIO   [*growling*]   Well: is it to please myself?

CÆSAR   [*affectionately*]   No, my son Rufio, but to please me—to celebrate my birthday.

RUFIO   [*contemptuously*]   Your birthday! You always have a birthday when there is a pretty girl to be flattered or an ambassador to be conciliated. We had seven of them in ten months last year.

CÆSAR   [*contritely*]   It is true, Rufio! I shall never break myself of these petty deceits.

RUFIO   Who is to dine with us—besides Cleopatra?

CÆSAR   Apollodorus the Sicilian.

RUFIO   That popinjay!

CÆSAR   Come! the popinjay is an amusing dog—tells a story; sings a song; and saves us the trouble of flattering the Queen. What does she care for old politicans and camp-fed bears like us? No, Apollodorus is good company, Rufio, good company.

RUFIO   Well, he can swim a bit and fence a bit: he might be worse, if he only knew how to hold his tongue.

CÆSAR   The gods forbid he should ever learn! Oh, this military life! this tedious, brutal life of action! That is the worst of us Romans: we are mere doers and drudgers: a swarm of bees turned into men. Give me a good talker—one with wit and imagination enough to live without continually doing something!

RUFIO   Ay! a nice time he would have of it with you when dinner was over! Have you noticed that I am before my time?

CÆSAR   Aha! I thought that meant something. What is it?

RUFIO   Can we be overheard here?

CÆSAR   Our privacy invites eavesdropping. I can remedy that. [*He claps his hands twice. The curtains are drawn, revealing the roof garden with a banqueting table set across in the middle for four persons, one at each end, and two side by side. The side next Cæsar and Rufio is blocked with golden wine vessels and basins. A gorgeous major-domo is superintending the laying of the table by a staff of slaves. The colonnade goes round the garden at both sides to the further end, where a gap in it, like a great gateway, leaves the view open to the sky beyond the western edge of the roof, except in the middle, where a life size image of Ra, seated on a huge plinth, towers up, with hawk head and crown of asp and disk. His altar, which stands at his feet, is a single white stone.*] Now everybody can see us, nobody will think of listening to us. [*He sits down on the bench left by the two slaves*].

RUFIO   [*sitting down on his stool*]   Pothinus wants to speak to you. I advise you to see him: there is some plotting going on here among the women.

CÆSAR   Who is Pothinus?

RUFIO   The fellow with hair like squirrel's fur—the little King's bear leader, whom you kept prisoner.

CÆSAR   [*annoyed*]   And has he not escaped?

RUFIO   No.

CÆSAR   [*rising imperiously*]   Why not? You have been guarding this man instead of watching the enemy. Have I not told you always to let prisoners escape unless there are special orders to the contrary? Are there not enough mouths to be fed without him?

RUFIO   Yes; and if you would have a little sense and let me cut his throat, you would save his rations. Anyhow he wont escape. Three sentries have told him they would put a pilum through him if they saw him again. What more can they do? He prefers to stay and spy on us. So would I if I had to do with generals subject to fits of clemency.

CÆSAR   [*resuming his seat, argued down*]   Hm! And so he wants to see me.

RUFIO   Ay. I have brought him with me. He is waiting there [*jerking his thumb over his shoulder*] under guard.

CÆSAR   And you want me to see him?

RUFIO   [*obstinately*]   I dont want anything. I daresay you will do what you like. Dont put it on to me.

CÆSAR [*with an air of doing it expressly to indulge Rufio*]   Well, well: let us have him.

RUFIO [*calling*]   Ho there, guard! Release your man and send him up. [*Beckoning*]. Come along!
[*Pothinus enters and stops mistrustfully between the two, looking from one to the other.*]

CÆSAR [*graciously*]   Ah, Pothinus! You are welcome. And what is the news this afternoon?

POTHINUS   Cæsar: I come to warn you of a danger, and to make you an offer.

CÆSAR   Never mind the danger. Make the offer.

RUFIO   Never mind the offer. Whats the danger?

POTHINUS   Cæsar: you think that Cleopatra is devoted to you.

CÆSAR [*gravely*]   My friend: I already know what I think. Come to your offer.

POTHINUS   I will deal plainly. I know not by what strange gods you have been enabled to defend a palace and a few yards of beach against a city and an army. Since we cut you off from Lake Mareotis, and you dug wells in the salt sea sand and brought up buckets of fresh water from them, we have known that your gods are irresistible, and that you are a worker of miracles. I no longer threaten you—

RUFIO [*sarcastically*]   Very handsome of you, indeed.

POTHINUS   So be it: you are the master. Our gods sent the north west winds to keep you in our hands; but you have been too strong for them.

CÆSAR [*gently urging him to come to the point*]   Yes, yes, my friend. But what then?

RUFIO   Spit it out, man. What have you to say?

POTHINUS   I have to say that you have a traitress in your camp. Cleopatra—

THE MAJOR-DOMO [*at the table, announcing*]   The Queen! [*Cæsar and Rufio rise*].

RUFIO [*aside to Pothinus*]   You should have spat it out sooner, you fool. Now it is too late.
[*Cleopatra, in gorgeous raiment, enters in state through the gap in the colonnade, and comes down past the image of Ra and past the table to Cæsar. Her retinue, headed by Ftatateeta, joins the staff at the table. Cæsar gives Cleopatra his seat, which she takes.*]

CLEOPATRA [*quickly, seeing Pothinus*]   What is he doing here?

CÆSAR [*seating himself beside her, in the most amiable of tempers*]   Just going to tell me something about you. You shall hear it. Proceed, Pothinus.

POTHINUS [*disconcerted*]   Cæsar—[*he stammers*]

CÆSAR   Well, out with it.

POTHINUS   What I have to say is for your ear, not for the Queen's.

CLEOPATRA [*with subdued ferocity*]   There are means of making you speak. Take care.

POTHINUS [*defiantly*]   Cæsar does not employ those means.

CÆSAR   My friend: when a man has anything to tell in this world, the difficulty is not to make him tell it, but to prevent him from telling it too often. Let me celebrate my birthday by setting you free. Farewell: we shall not meet again.

CLEOPATRA [*angrily*]   Cæsar: this mercy is foolish.

POTHINUS [*to Cæsar*]   Will you not give me a private audience? Your life may depend on it. [*Cæsar rises loftily*].

RUFIO [*aside to Pothinus*]   Ass! Now we shall have some heroics.

CÆSAR [*oratorically*]   Pothinus—

RUFIO [*interrupting him*]   Cæsar: the dinner will spoil if you begin preaching your favorite sermon about life and death.

CLEOPATRA [*priggishly*]   Peace, Rufio. I desire to hear Cæsar.

RUFIO [*bluntly*] Your Majesty has heard it before. You repeated it to Apollodorus last week; and he thought it was all your own. [*Cæsar's dignity collapses. Much tickled, he sits down again and looks roguishly at Cleopatra, who is furious. Rufio calls as before*] Ho there, guard! Pass the prisoner out. He is released. [*To Pothinus*] Now off with you. You have lost your chance.

POTHINUS [*his temper overcoming his prudence*] I will speak.

CÆSAR [*to Cleopatra*] You see. Torture would not have wrung a word from him.

POTHINUS Cæsar: you have taught Cleopatra the arts by which the Romans govern the world.

CÆSAR Alas! they cannot even govern themselves. What then?

POTHINUS What then? Are you so besotted with her beauty that you do not see that she is impatient to reign in Egypt alone, and that her heart is set on your departure?

CLEOPATRA [*rising*] Liar!

CÆSAR [*shocked*] What! Protestations! Contradictions!

CLEOPATRA [*ashamed, but trembling with suppressed rage*] No. I do not deign to contradict. Let him talk. [*She sits down again*].

POTHINUS From her own lips I have heard it. You are to be her catspaw: you are to tear the crown from her brother's head and set it on her own, delivering us all into her hand—delivering yourself also. And then Cæsar can return to Rome, or depart through the gate of death, which is nearer and surer.

CÆSAR [*calmly*] Well, my friend; and is not this very natural?

POTHINUS [*astonished*] Natural! Then you do not resent treachery?

CÆSAR Resent! O thou foolish Egyptian, what have I to do with resentment? Do I resent the wind when it chills me, or the night when it makes me stumble in darkness? Shall I resent youth when it turns from age, and ambition when it turns from servitude? To tell me such a story as this is but to tell me that the sun will rise tomorrow.

CLEOPATRA [*unable to contain herself*] But it is false—false. I swear it.

CÆSAR It is true, though you swore it a thousand times, and believed all you swore. [*She is convulsed with emotion. To screen her, he rises and takes Pothinus to Rufio, saying*] Come, Rufio: let us see Pothinus past the guard. I have a word to say to him. [*Aside to them*] We must give the Queen a moment to recover herself. [*Aloud*] Come. [*He takes Pothinus and Rufio out with him, conversing with them meanwhile*]. Tell your friends, Pothinus, that they must not think I am opposed to a reasonable settlement of the country's affairs—[*They pass out of hearing*].

CLEOPATRA [*in a stifled whisper*] Ftatateeta, Ftatateeta.

FTATATEETA [*hurrying to her from the table and petting her*] Peace, child: be comforted—

CLEOPATRA [*interrupting her*] Can they hear us?

FTATATEETA No, dear heart, no.

CLEOPATRA Listen to me. If he leaves the Palace alive, never see my face again.

FTATATEETA He? Poth—

CLEOPATRA [*striking her on the mouth*] Strike his life out as I strike his name from your lips. Dash him down from the wall. Break him on the stones. Kill, kill, kill him.

FTATATEETA [*shewing all her teeth*] The dog shall perish.

CLEOPATRA Fail in this, and you go out from before me for ever.

FTATATEETA [*resolutely*] So be it. You shall not see my face until his eyes are darkened.

[*Cæsar comes back, with Apollodorus, exquisitely dressed, and Rufio.*]

CLEOPATRA [*to Ftatateeta*] Come soon—soon. [*Ftatateeta turns her meaning eyes for a moment on her mistress; then goes grimly away past Ra and out. Cleopatra runs like a gazelle to Cæsar*] So you have come back to me, Cæsar. [*Caressingly*] I thought you were angry. Welcome, Apollodorus. [*She gives him her hand to kiss, with her other arm about Cæsar*].

APOLLODORUS Cleopatra grows more womanly beautiful from week to week.

CLEOPATRA Truth, Apollodorus?

APOLLODORUS Far, far short of the truth! Friend Rufio threw a pearl into the sea: Cæsar fished up a diamond.

CÆSAR Cæsar fished up a touch of rheumatism, my friend. Come: to dinner! to dinner! [*They move towards the table*].

CLEOPATRA [*skipping like a young fawn*] Yes, to dinner. I have ordered such a dinner for you, Cæsar!

CÆSAR Ay? What are we to have?

CLEOPATRA Peacocks' brains.

CÆSAR [*as if his mouth watered*] Peacocks' brains, Apollodorus!

APOLLODORUS Not for me. I prefer nightingales' tongues. [*He goes to one of the two covers set side by side*].

CLEOPATRA Roast boar, Rufio!

RUFIO [*gluttonously*] Good! [*He goes to the seat next Apollodorus, on his left*].

CÆSAR [*looking at his seat, which is at the end of the table, to Ra's left hand*] What has become of my leathern cushion?

CLEOPATRA [*at the opposite end*] I have got new ones for you.

THE MAJOR-DOMO These cushions, Cæsar, are of Maltese gauze, stuffed with rose leaves.

CÆSAR Rose leaves! Am I a caterpillar? [*He throws the cushions away and seats himself on the leather mattress underneath*].

CLEOPATRA What a shame! My new cushions!

THE MAJOR-DOMO [*at Cæsar's elbow*] What shall we serve to whet Cæsar's appetite?

CÆSAR What have you got?

THE MAJOR-DOMO Sea hedgehogs, black and white sea acorns, sea nettles, beccaficoes, purple shellfish—

CÆSAR Any oysters?

THE MAJOR-DOMO Assuredly.

CÆSAR British oysters?

THE MAJOR-DOMO [*assenting*] British oysters, Cæsar.

CÆSAR Oysters, then. [*The Major-Domo signs to a slave at each order; and the slave goes out to execute it*]. I have been in Britain—that western land of romance—the last piece of earth on the edge of the ocean that surrounds the world. I went there in search of its famous pearls. The British pearl was a fable; but in searching for it I found the British oyster.

APOLLODORUS All posterity will bless you for it. [*To the Major-Domo*] Sea hedgehogs for me.

RUFIO Is there nothing solid to begin with?

THE MAJOR-DOMO Fieldfares with asparagus—

CLEOPATRA [*interrupting*] Fattened fowls! have some fattened fowls, Rufio.

RUFIO Ay, that will do.

CLEOPATRA [*greedily*] Fieldfares for me.

THE MAJOR-DOMO Cæsar will deign to choose his wine? Sicilian, Lesbian, Chian—

RUFIO [*contemptuously*] All Greek.

APOLLODORUS Who would drink Roman wine when he could get Greek. Try the Lesbian, Cæsar.

CÆSAR   Bring me my barley water.

RUFIO   [*with intense disgust*]   Ugh! Bring me my Falernian.

[*The Falernian is presently brought to him*].

CLEOPATRA   [*pouting*]   It is waste of time giving you dinners, Cæsar. My scullions would not condescend to your diet.

CÆSAR   [*relenting*]   Well, well: let us try the Lesbian. [*The Major-Domo fills Cæsar's goblet; then Cleopatra's and Apollodorus's*]. But when I return to Rome, I will make laws against these extravagances. I will even get the laws carried out.

CLEOPATRA   [*coaxingly*]   Never mind. Today you are to be like other people: idle, luxurious, and kind.

[*She stretches her hand to him along the table*].

CÆSAR   Well, for once I will sacrifice my comfort—[*kissing her hand*] there! [*He takes a draught of wine*]. Now are you satisfied?

CLEOPATRA   And you no longer believe that I long for your departure for Rome?

CÆSAR   I no longer believe anything. My brains are asleep. Besides, who knows whether I shall return to Rome?

RUFIO   [*alarmed*]   How? Eh? What?

CÆSAR   What has Rome to shew me that I have not seen already? One year of Rome is like another, except that I grow older, whilst the crowd in the Appian Way is always the same age.

APOLLODORUS   It is no better here in Egypt. The old men, when they are tired of life, say "We have seen everything except the source of the Nile."

CÆSAR   [*his imagination catching fire*]   And why not see that? Cleopatra: will you come with me and track the flood to its cradle in the heart of the regions of mystery? Shall we leave Rome behind us—Rome, that has achieved greatness only to learn how greatness destroys nations of men who are not great! Shall I make you a new kingdom, and build you a holy city there in the great unknown?

CLEOPATRA   [*rapturously*]   Yes, yes. You shall.

RUFIO   Ay: now he will conquer Africa with two legions before we come to the roast boar.

APOLLODORUS   Come: no scoffing. This is a noble scheme: in it Cæsar is no longer merely the conquering soldier, but the creative poet-artist. Let us name the holy city, and consecrate it with Lesbian wine.

CÆSAR   Cleopatra shall name it herself.

CLEOPATRA   It shall be called Cæsar's Gift to his Beloved.

APOLLODORUS   No, no. Something vaster than that—something universal, like the starry firmament.

CÆSAR   [*prosaically*]   Why not simply The Cradle of the Nile?

CLEOPATRA   No: the Nile is my ancestor; and he is a god. Oh! I have thought of something. The Nile shall name it himself. Let us call upon him. [*To the Major-Domo*] Send for him. [*The three men stare at one another; but the Major-Domo goes out as if he had received the most matter-of-fact order*]. And [*to the retinue*] away with you all.

[*The retinue withdraws, making obeisance. A priest enters, carrying a miniature sphinx with a tiny tripod before it. A morsel of incense is smoking in the tripod. The priest comes to the table and places the image in the middle of it. The light begins to change to the magenta purple of the Egyptian sunset, as if the god had brought a strange colored shadow with him. The three men are determined not to be impressed; but they feel curious in spite of themselves.*]

CÆSAR   What hocus-pocus is this?

CLEOPATRA You shall see. And it is not hocus-pocus. To do it properly, we should kill something to please him; but perhaps he will answer Cæsar without that if we spill some wine to him.

APOLLODORUS [*turning his head to look up over his shoulder at Ra*] Why not appeal to our hawkheaded friend here?

CLEOPATRA [*nervously*] Sh! He will hear you and be angry.

RUFIO [*phlegmatically*] The source of the Nile is out of his district, I expect.

CLEOPATRA No: I will have my city named by nobody but my dear little sphinx, because it was in its arms that Cæsar found me asleep. [*She languishes at Cæsar then turns curtly to the priest*]. Go. I am a priestess, and have power to take your charge from you. [*The priest makes a reverence and goes out*]. Now let us call on the Nile all together. Perhaps he will rap on the table.

CÆSAR What! table rapping! Are such superstitions still believed in this year 707 of the Republic?

CLEOPATRA It is no superstition: our priests learn lots of things from the tables. Is it not so, Apollodorus?

APOLLODORUS Yes: I profess myself a converted man. When Cleopatra is priestess, Apollodorus is a devotee. Propose the conjuration.

CLEOPATRA You must say with me "Send us thy voice, Father Nile."

ALL FOUR [*holding their glasses together before the idol*] Send us thy voice, Father Nile.

[*The death cry of a man in mortal terror and agony answers them. Appalled, the men set down their glasses, and listen. Silence. The purple deepens in the sky. Cæsar, glancing at Cleopatra, catches her pouring out her wine before the god, with gleaming eyes, and mute assurances of gratitude and worship. Apollodorus springs up and runs to the edge of the roof to peer down and listen.*]

CÆSAR [*looking piercingly at Cleopatra*] What was that?

CLEOPATRA [*petulantly*] Nothing. They are beating some slave.

CÆSAR Nothing.

RUFIO A man with a knife in him, I'll swear.

CÆSAR [*rising*] A murder!

APOLLODORUS [*at the back, waving his hand for silence*] S-sh! Silence. Did you hear that?

CÆSAR Another cry?

APOLLODORUS [*returning to the table*] No, a thud. Something fell on the beach, I think.

RUFIO [*grimly, as he rises*] Something with bones in it, eh?

CÆSAR [*shuddering*] Hush, hush, Rufio.

[*He leaves the table and returns to the colonnade: Rufio following at his left elbow, and Apollodorus at the other side*].

CLEOPATRA [*still in her place at the table*] Will you leave me, Cæsar? Apollodorus: are you going?

APOLLODORUS Faith, dearest Queen, my appetite is gone.

CÆSAR Go down to the courtyard, Apollodorus; and find out what has happened.

[*Apollodorus nods and goes out, making for the staircase by which Rufio ascended.*]

CLEOPATRA Your soldiers have killed somebody, perhaps. What does it matter?

[*The murmur of a crowd rises from the beach below. Cæsar and Rufio look at one another.*]

CÆSAR This must be seen to.

[*He is about to follow Apollodorus when Rufio stops him with a hand on his arm as Ftatateeta comes back by the far end of the roof, with dragging*

*steps, a drowsy satiety in her eyes and in the corners of the bloodhound lips.
For a moment Cæsar suspects that she is drunk with wine. Not so Rufio:
he knows well the red vintage that has inebriated her*].

RUFIO [*in a low tone*] There is some mischief between these two.

FTATATEETA The Queen looks again on the face of her servant.

[*Cleopatra looks at her for a moment with an exultant reflection of her
murderous expression. Then she flings her arms round her; kisses her repeatedly and savagely; and tears off her jewels and heaps them on her. The
two men turn from the spectacle to look at one another. Ftatateeta drags
herself sleepily to the altar; kneels before Ra; and remains there in prayer.
Cæsar goes to Cleopatra, leaving Rufio in the colonnade.*]

CÆSAR [*with searching earnestness*] Cleopatra: what has happened?

CLEOPATRA [*in mortal dread of him, but with her utmost cajolery*] Nothing,
dearest Cæsar. [*With sickly sweetness, her voice almost failing*] Nothing. I
am innocent. [*She approaches him affectionately*] Dear Cæsar: are you angry
with me? Why do you look at me so? I have been here with you all the
time. How can I know what has happened?

CÆSAR [*reflectively*] That is true.

CLEOPATRA [*greatly relieved, trying to caress him*] Of course it is true. [*He
does not respond to the caress*] You know it is true, Rufio.

[*The murmur without suddenly swells to a roar and subsides.*]

RUFIO I shall know presently. [*He makes for the altar in the burly trot that
serves him for a stride, and touches Ftatateeta on the shoulder*]. Now,
mistress: I shall want you. [*He orders her, with a gesture, to go before him*].

FTATATEETA [*rising and glowering at him*] My place is with the Queen.

CLEOPATRA She has done no harm, Rufio.

CÆSAR [*to Rufio*] Let her stay.

RUFIO [*sitting down on the altar*] Very well. Then my place is here too; and
you can see what is the matter for yourself. The city is in a pretty uproar,
it seems.

CÆSAR [*with grave displeasure*] Rufio: there is a time for obedience.

RUFIO And there is a time for obstinacy. [*He folds his arms doggedly*].

CÆSAR [*to Cleopatra*] Send her away.

CLEOPATRA [*whining in her eagerness to propitiate him*] Yes, I will. I will do
whatever you ask me, Cæsar, always, because I love you. Ftatateeta: go
away.

FTATATEETA The Queen's word is my will. I shall be at hand for the Queen's
call. [*She goes out past Ra, as she came*].

RUFIO [*following her*] Remember, Cæsar, your bodyguard is also within call.
[*He follows her out*].

[*Cleopatra, presuming upon Cæsar's submission to Rufio, leaves the table
and sits down on the bench in the colonnade.*]

CLEOPATRA Why do you allow Rufio to treat you so? You should teach him his
place.

CÆSAR Teach him to be my enemy, and to hide his thoughts from me as you
are now hiding yours?

CLEOPATRA [*her fears returning*] Why do you say that, Cæsar? Indeed, indeed,
I am not hiding anything. You are wrong to treat me like this. [*She stifles
a sob*]. I am only a child; and you turn into stone because you think some
one has been killed. I cannot bear it. [*She purposely breaks down and
weeps. He looks at her with profound sadness and complete coldness. She
looks up to see what effect she is producing. Seeing that he is unmoved,
she sits up, pretending to struggle with her emotion and to put it bravely
away*]. But there: I know you hate tears: you shall not be troubled with

them. I know you are not angry, but only sad; only I am so silly, I cannot help being hurt when you speak coldly. Of course you are quite right: it is dreadful to think of anyone being killed or even hurt; and I hope nothing really serious has—[*her voice dies away under his contemptuous penetration*].

CÆSAR   What has frightened you into this? What have you done? [*A trumpet sounds on the beach below*]. Aha! that sounds like the answer.

CLEOPATRA   [*sinking back trembling on the bench and covering her face with her hands*]   I have not betrayed you, Cæsar: I swear it.

CÆSAR   I know that. I have not trusted you. [*He turns from her, and is about to go out when Apollodorus and Britannus drag in Lucius Septimius to him. Rufio follows. Cæsar shudders*]. Again, Pompey's murderer!

RUFIO   The town has gone mad, I think. They are for tearing the palace down and driving us into the sea straight away. We laid hold of this renegade in clearing them out of the courtyard.

CÆSAR   Release him. [*They let go his arms*]. What has offended the citizens, Lucius Septimius?

LUCIUS   What did you expect, Cæsar? Pothinus was a favorite of theirs.

CÆSAR   What has happened to Pothinus? I set him free, here, not half an hour ago. Did they not pass him out?

LUCIUS   Ay, through the gallery arch sixty feet above ground, with three inches of steel in his ribs. He is as dead as Pompey. We are quits now, as to killing —you and I.

CÆSAR   [*shocked*]   Assassinated!—our prisoner, our guest! [*He turns reproachfully on Rufio*] Rufio—

RUFIO   [*emphatically—anticipating the question*]   Whoever did it was a wise man and a friend of yours [*Cleopatra is greatly emboldened*]; but none of us had a hand in it. So it is no use to frown at me. [*Cæsar turns and looks at Cleopatra*].

CLEOPATRA   [*violently—rising*]   He was slain by order of the Queen of Egypt. I am not Julius Cæsar the dreamer, who allows every slave to insult him. Rufio has said I did well: now the others shall judge me too. [*She turns to the others*]. This Pothinus sought to make me conspire with him to betray Cæsar to Achillas and Ptolemy. I refused; and he cursed me and came privily to Cæsar to accuse me of his own treachery. I caught him in the act; and he insulted me—me, the Queen! to my face. Cæsar would not avenge me: he spoke him fair and set him free. Was I right to avenge myself? Speak, Lucius.

LUCIUS   I do not gainsay it. But you will get little thanks from Cæsar for it.

CLEOPATRA   Speak, Apollodorus. Was I wrong?

APOLLODORUS   I have only one word of blame, most beautiful. You should have called upon me, your knight; and in a fair duel I should have slain the slanderer.

CLEOPATRA   [*passionately*]   I will be judged by your very slave, Cæsar. Britannus: speak. Was I wrong?

BRITANNUS   Were treachery, falsehood, and disloyalty left unpunished, society must become like an arena full of wild beasts, tearing one another to pieces. Cæsar is in the wrong.

CÆSAR   [*with quiet bitterness*]   And so the verdict is against me, it seems.

CLEOPATRA   [*vehemently*]   Listen to me, Cæsar. If one man in all Alexandria can be found to say that I did wrong, I swear to have myself crucified on the door of the palace by my own slaves.

CÆSAR   If one man in all the world can be found, now or forever, to know that you did wrong, that man will have either to conquer the world as I have, or be crucified by it [*The uproar in the streets again reaches them*]. Do you hear? These knockers at your gate are also believers in vengeance and in stabbing. You have slain their leader: it is right that they shall slay you. If you doubt it, ask your four counsellors here. And then in the name of that right [*he emphasizes the word with great scorn*] shall I not slay them for murdering their Queen, and be slain in my turn by their countrymen as the invader of their fatherland? Can Rome do less then than slay these slayers, too, to shew the world how Rome avenges her sons and her honor. And so, to the end of history, murder shall breed murder, always in the name of right and honor and peace, until the gods are tired of blood and create a race that can understand. [*Fierce uproar. Cleopatra becomes white with terror*]. Hearken, you who must not be insulted. Go near enough to catch their words: you will find them bitterer than the tongue of Pothinus. [*Loftily, wrapping himself up in an impenetrable dignity*] Let the Queen of Egypt now give her orders for vengeance, and take her measures for defence; for she has renounced Cæsar. [*He turns to go*].

CLEOPATRA [*terrified, running to him and falling on her knees*] You will not desert me, Cæsar. You will defend the palace.

CÆSAR You have taken the powers of life and death upon you. I am only a dreamer.

CLEOPATRA But they will kill me.

CÆSAR And why not?

CLEOPATRA In pity—

CÆSAR Pity! What! has it come to this so suddenly, that nothing can save you now but pity? Did it save Pothinus?

[*She rises, wringing her hands, and goes back to the bench in despair. Apollodorus shews his sympathy with her by quietly posting himself behind the bench. The sky has by this time become the most vivid purple, and soon begins to change to a glowing pale orange, against which the colonnade and the great image shew darklier and darklier.*]

RUFIO Cæsar: enough of preaching. The enemy is at the gate.

CÆSAR [*turning on him and giving way to his wrath*] Ay; and what has held him baffled at the gate all these months? Was it my folly, as you deem it, or your wisdom? In this Egyptian Red Sea of blood, whose hand has held all your heads above the waves? [*Turning on Cleopatra*] And yet, when Cæsar says to such an one, "Friend, go free," you, clinging for your little life to my sword, dare steal out and stab him in the back? And you, soldiers and gentlemen, and honest servants as you forget that you are, applaud this assassination, and say "Cæsar is in the wrong." By the gods, I am tempted to open my hand and let you all sink into the flood.

CLEOPATRA [*with a ray of cunning hope*] But, Cæsar, if you do, you will perish yourself.

[*Cæsar's eyes blaze.*]

RUFIO [*greatly alarmed*] Now, by great Jove, you filthy little Egyptian rat, that is the very word to make him walk out alone into the city and leave us here to be cut to pieces. [*Desperately, to Cæsar*] Will you desert us because we are a parcel of fools? I mean no harm by killing: I do it as a cat, by instinct. We are all dogs at your heels; but we have served you faithfully.

CÆSAR [*relenting*] Alas, Rufio, my son, my son: as dogs we are like to perish now in the streets.

APOLLODORUS [*at his post behind Cleopatra's seat*] Cæsar: what you say has an Olympian ring in it: it must be right; for it is fine art. But I am still on the side of Cleopatra. If we must die, she shall not want the devotion of a man's heart nor the strength of a man's arm.

CLEOPATRA [*sobbing*]   But I dont want to die.

CÆSAR [*sadly*]   Oh, ignoble, ignoble!

LUCIUS [*coming forward between Cæsar and Cleopatra*]   Hearken to me, Cæsar. It may be ignoble; but I also mean to live as long as I can.

CÆSAR   Well, my friend, you are likely to outlive Cæsar. Is it any magic of mine, think you, that has kept your army and this whole city at bay for so long? Yesterday, what quarrel had they with me that they should risk their lives against me? But today we have flung them down their hero, murdered; and now every man of them is set upon clearing out this nest of assassins—for such we are and no more. Take courage then; and sharpen your sword. Pompey's head has fallen; and Cæsar's head is ripe.

APOLLODORUS   Does Cæsar despair?

CÆSAR [*with infinite pride*]   He who has never hoped can never despair. Cæsar, in good or bad fortune, looks his fate in the face.

LUCIUS   Look it in the face, then; and it will smile as it always has on Cæsar.

CÆSAR [*with involuntary haughtiness*]   Do you presume to encourage me?

LUCIUS   I offer you my services. I will change sides if you will have me.

CÆSAR [*suddenly coming down to earth again, and looking sharply at him, divining that there is something behind the offer*]   What! At this point?

LUCIUS [*firmly*]   At this point.

RUFIO   Do you suppose Cæsar is mad, to trust you?

LUCIUS   I do not ask him to trust me until he is victorious. I ask for my life, and for a command in Cæsar's army. And since Cæsar is a fair dealer, I will pay in advance.

CÆSAR   Pay! How?

LUCIUS   With a piece of good news for you.

[*Cæsar divines the news in a flash.*]

RUFIO   What news?

CÆSAR [*with an elate and buoyant energy which makes Cleopatra sit up and stare*]   What news! What news, did you say, my son Rufio? The relief has arrived: what other news remains for us? Is it not so, Lucius Septimius? Mithridates of Pergamos is on the march.

LUCIUS   He has taken Pelusium.

CÆSAR [*delighted*]   Lucius Septimius: you are henceforth my officer. Rufio: the Egyptians must have sent every soldier from the city to prevent Mithridates crossing the Nile. There is nothing in the streets now but mob—mob!

LUCIUS   It is so. Mithridates is marching by the great road to Memphis to cross above the Delta. Achillas will fight him there.

CÆSAR [*all audacity*]   Achillas shall fight Cæsar there. See, Rufio. [*He runs to the table; snatches a napkin; and draws a plan on it with his finger dipped in wine, whilst Rufio and Lucius Septimius crowd about him to watch, all looking closely, for the light is now almost gone*]. Here is the palace [*pointing to his plan*]: here is the theatre. You [*to Rufio*] take twenty men and pretend to go by that street [*pointing it out*]; and whilst they are stoning you, out go the cohorts by this and this. My streets are right, are they, Lucius?

LUCIUS   Ay, that is the fig market—

CÆSAR [*too much excited to listen to him*]   I saw them the day we arrived. Good! [*He throws the napkin on the table, and comes down again into the colonnade*]. Away, Britannus: tell Petronius that within an hour half our forces must take ship for the western lake. See to my horse and armor. [*Britannus runs out*] With the rest, *I* shall march round the lake and up the Nile to meet Mithridates. Away, Lucius; and give the word. [*Lucius hurries out after Britannus*]. Apollodorus: lend me your sword and your right arm for this campaign.

APOLLODORUS Ay, and my heart and life to boot.

CÆSAR [*grasping his hand*] I accept both. [*Mighty handshake*]. Are you ready for work?

APOLLODORUS Ready for Art—the Art of War [*he rushes out after Lucius, totally forgetting Cleopatra*].

RUFIO Come! this is something like business.

CÆSAR [*buoyantly*] Is it not, my only son? [*He claps his hands. The slaves hurry in to the table*]. No more of this mawkish revelling: away with all this stuff: shut it out of my sight and be off with you. [*The slaves begin to remove the table; and the curtains are drawn, shutting in the colonnade*]. You understand about the streets, Rufio?

RUFIO Ay, I think I do. I will get through them, at all events.

[*The bucina sounds busily in the courtyard beneath.*]

CÆSAR Come, then: we must talk to the troops and hearten them. You down to the beach: I to the courtyard. [*He makes for the staircase*].

CLEOPATRA [*rising from her seat, where she has been quite neglected all this time, and stretching out her hands timidly to him*] Cæsar.

CÆSAR [*turning*] Eh?

CLEOPATRA Have you forgotten me?

CÆSAR [*indulgently*] I am busy now, my child, busy. When I return your affairs shall be settled. Farewell; and be good and patient.

[*He goes, preoccupied and quite indifferent. She stands with clenched fists, in speechless rage and humiliation.*]

RUFIO That game is played and lost, Cleopatra. The woman always gets the worst of it.

CLEOPATRA [*haughtily*] Go. Follow your master.

RUFIO [*in her ear, with rough familiarity*] A word first. Tell your executioner that if Pothinus had been properly killed—in the throat—he would not have called out. Your man bungled his work.

CLEOPATRA [*enigmatically*] How do you know it was a man?

RUFIO [*startled, and puzzled*] It was not you: you were with us when it happened. [*She turns her back scornfully on him. He shakes his head, and draws the curtains to go out. It is now a magnificent moonlit night. The table has been removed. Ftatateeta is seen in the light of the moon and stars, again in prayer before the white altar-stone of Ra. Rufio starts; closes the curtains again softly; and says in a low voice to Cleopatra*] Was it she? with her own hand?

CLEOPATRA [*threateningly*] Whoever it was, let my enemies beware of her. Look to it, Rufio, you who dare make the Queen of Egypt a fool before Cæsar.

RUFIO [*looking grimly at her*] I will look to it, Cleopatra.

[*He nods in confirmation of the promise, and slips out through the curtains, loosening his sword in its sheath as he goes*].

ROMAN SOLDIERS [*in the courtyard below*] Hail, Cæsar! Hail, hail!

[*Cleopatra listens. The bucina sounds again, followed by several trumpets.*]

CLEOPATRA [*wringing her hands and calling*] Ftatateeta. Ftatateeta. It is dark; and I am alone. Come to me. [*Silence*] Ftatateeta. [*Louder*] Ftatateeta. [*Silence. In a panic she snatches the cord and pulls the curtains apart*]. [*Ftatateeta is lying dead on the altar of Ra, with her throat cut. Her blood deluges the white stone.*]

ACT V

*High noon. Festival and military pageant on the esplanade be-
fore the palace. In the east harbor Cæsar's galley, so gorgeously
decorated that it seems to be rigged with flowers, is alongside
the quay, close to the steps Apollodorus descended when he em-
barked with the carpet. A Roman guard is posted there in charge
of a gangway, whence a red floorcloth is laid down the middle of
the esplanade, turning off to the north opposite the central gate
in the palace front, which shuts in the esplanade on the south
side. The broad steps of the gate, crowded with Cleopatra's ladies,
all in their gayest attire, are like a flower garden. The façade is
lined by her guard, officered by the same gallants to whom Bel
Affris announced the coming of Cæsar six months before in the
old palace on the Syrian border. The north side is lined by Roman soldiers, with the townsfolk on tiptoe behind them, peering
over their heads at the cleared esplanade, in which the officers
stroll about, chatting. Among these are Belzanor and the Persian;
also the centurion, vinewood cudgel in hand, battle worn, thick-
booted, and much outshone, both socially and decoratively, by
the Egyptian officers.*
*Apollodorus makes his way through the townsfolk and calls to
the officers from behind the Roman line.*

APOLLODORUS   Hullo! May I pass?

CENTURION   Pass Apollodorus the Sicilian there!
  [*The soldiers let him through*].

BELZANOR   Is Cæsar at hand?

APOLLODORUS   Not yet. He is still in the market place. I could not stand any
  more of the roaring of the soldiers! After half an hour of the enthusiasm
  of an army, one feels the need of a little sea air.

PERSIAN   Tell us the news. Hath he slain the priests?

APOLLODORUS   Not he. They met him in the market place with ashes on their
  heads and their gods in their hands. They placed the gods at his feet. The
  only one that was worth looking at was Apis: a miracle of gold and ivory
  work. By my advice he offered the chief priest two talents for it.

BELZANOR   [*appalled*]   Apis the all-knowing for two talents! What said the
  chief Priest?

APOLLODORUS   He invoked the mercy of Apis, and asked for five.

BELZANOR   There will be famine and tempest in the land for this.

PERSIAN   Pooh! Why did not Apis cause Cæsar to be vanquished by Achillas?
  Any fresh news from the war, Apollodorus?

APOLLODORUS   The little King Ptolemy was drowned.

BELZANOR   Drowned! How?

APOLLODORUS   With the rest of them. Cæsar attacked them from three sides at
  once and swept them into the Nile. Ptolemy's barge sank.

BELZANOR   A marvellous man, this Cæsar! Will he come soon, think you?

APOLLODORUS   He was settling the Jewish question when I left.
  [*A flourish of trumpets from the north, and commotion among the townsfolk, announces the approach of Cæsar.*]

PERSIAN   He has made short work of them. Here he comes.
  [*He hurries to his post in front of the Egyptian lines*].

BELZANOR   [*following him*]   Ho there! Cæsar comes.
[*The soldiers stand at attention, and dress their lines. Apollodorus goes to the Egyptian line.*]

CENTURION   [*hurrying to the gangway guard*]   Attention there! Cæsar comes.
[*Cæsar arrives in state with Rufio: Britannus following. The soldiers receive him with enthusiastic shouting.*]

CÆSAR   I see my ship awaits me. The hour of Cæsar's farewell to Egypt has arrived. And now, Rufio, what remains to be done before I go?

RUFIO   [*at his left hand*]   You have not yet appointed a Roman governor for this province.

CÆSAR   [*looking whimsically at him, but speaking with perfect gravity*]   What say you to Mithridates of Pergamos, my reliever and rescuer, the great son of Eupator?

RUFIO   Why, that you will want him elsewhere. Do you forget that you have some three or four armies to conquer on your way home?

CÆSAR   Indeed! Well, what say you to yourself?

RUFIO   [*incredulously*]   I! I a governor! What are you dreaming of? Do you not know that I am only the son of a freedman?

CÆSAR   [*affectionately*]   Has not Cæsar called you his son? [*Calling to the whole assembly*] Peace awhile there; and hear me.

THE ROMAN SOLDIERS   Hear Cæsar.

CÆSAR   Hear the service, quality, rank and name of the Roman governor. By service, Cæsar's shield; by quality, Cæsar's friend; by rank, a Roman soldier. [*The Roman soldiers give a triumphant shout*]. By name, Rufio. [*They shout again*].

RUFIO   [*kissing Cæsar's hand*]   Ay: I am Cæsar's shield; but of what use shall I be when I am no longer on Cæsar's arm? Well, no matter—[*He becomes husky, and turns away to recover himself*].

CÆSAR   Where is that British Islander of mine?

BRITANNUS   [*coming forward on Cæsar's right hand*]   Here, Cæsar.

CÆSAR   Who bade you, pray, thrust yourself into the battle of the Delta, uttering the barbarous cries of your native land, and affirming yourself a match for any four of the Egyptians, to whom you applied unseemly epithets?

BRITANNUS   Cæsar: I ask you to excuse the language that escaped me in the heat of the moment.

CÆSAR   And how did you, who cannot swim, cross the canal with us when we stormed the camp?

BRITANNUS   Cæsar: I clung to the tail of your horse.

CÆSAR   These are not the deeds of a slave, Britannicus, but of a free man.

BRITANNUS   Cæsar: I was born free.

CÆSAR   But they call you Cæsar's slave.

BRITANNUS   Only as Cæsar's slave have I found real freedom.

CÆSAR   [*moved*]   Well said. Ungrateful that I am, I was about to set you free; but now I will not part from you for a million talents.
[*He claps him friendly on the shoulder. Britannus, gratified, but a trifle shamefaced, takes his hand and kisses it sheepishly*].

BELZANOR   [*to the Persian*]   This Roman knows how to make men serve him.

PERSIAN   Ay: men too humble to become dangerous rivals to him.

BELZANOR   O subtle one! O cynic!

CÆSAR   [*seeing Apollodorus in the Egyptian corner, and calling to him*]   Apollodorus: I leave the art of Egypt in your charge. Remember: Rome loves art and will encourage it ungrudgingly.

APOLLODORUS   I understand, Cæsar. Rome will produce no art itself; but it will buy up and take away whatever the other nations produce.

CÆSAR   What! Rome produce no art! Is peace not an art? is war not an art? is government not an art? is civilization not an art? All these we give you in exchange for a few ornaments. You will have the best of the bargain. [*Turning to Rufio*] And now, what else have I to do before I embark? [*Trying to recollect*] There is something I cannot remember: what can it be? Well, well: it must remain undone: we must not waste this favorable wind. Farewell, Rufio.

RUFIO   Cæsar: I am loth to let you go to Rome without your shield. There are too many daggers there.

CÆSAR   It matters not: I shall finish my life's work on my way back; and then I shall have lived long enough. Besides: I have always disliked the idea of dying: I had rather be killed. Farewell.

RUFIO   [*with a sigh, raising his hands and giving Cæsar up as incorrigible*] Farewell. [*They shake hands*].

CÆSAR   [*waving his hand to Apollodorus*] Farewell, Apollodorus, and my friends, all of you. Aboard!

[*The gangway is run out from the quay to the ship. As Cæsar moves towards it, Cleopatra, cold and tragic, cunningly dressed in black, without ornaments or decoration of any kind, and thus making a striking figure among the brilliantly dressed bevy of ladies as she passes through it, comes from the palace and stands on the steps. Cæsar does not see her until she speaks.*]

CLEOPATRA   Has Cleopatra no part in this leavetaking?

CÆSAR   [*enlightened*] Ah, I knew there was something. [*To Rufio*] How could you let me forget her, Rufio? [*Hastening to her*] Had I gone without seeing you, I should never have forgiven myself. [*He takes her hands, and brings her into the middle of the esplanade. She submits stonily*]. Is this mourning for me?

CLEOPATRA   No.

CÆSAR   [*remorsefully*] Ah, that was thoughtless of me! It is for your brother.

CLEOPATRA   No.

CÆSAR   For whom, then?

CLEOPATRA   Ask the Roman governor whom you have left us.

CÆSAR   Rufio?

CLEOPATRA   Yes: Rufio. [*She points at him with deadly scorn*]. He who is to rule here in Cæsar's name, in Cæsar's way, according to Cæsar's boasted laws of life.

CÆSAR   [*dubiously*] He is to rule as he can, Cleopatra. He has taken the work upon him, and will do it in his own way.

CLEOPATRA   Not in your way, then?

CÆSAR   [*puzzled*] What do you mean by my way?

CLEOPATRA   Without punishment. Without revenge. Without judgment.

CÆSAR   [*approvingly*] Ay: that is the right way, the great way, the only possible way in the end. [*To Rufio*] Believe it, Rufio, if you can.

RUFIO   Why, I believe it, Cæsar. You have convinced me of it long ago. But look you. You are sailing for Numidia today. Now tell me: if you meet a hungry lion there, you will not punish it for wanting to eat you?

CÆSAR   [*wondering what he is driving at*] No.

RUFIO   Nor revenge upon it the blood of those it has already eaten.

CÆSAR   No.

RUFIO   Nor judge it for its guiltiness.

CÆSAR   No.

RUFIO   What, then, will you do to save your life from it?

CÆSAR   [*promptly*] Kill it, man, without malice, just as it would kill me. What does this parable of the lion mean?

RUFIO Why, Cleopatra had a tigress that killed men at her bidding. I thought she might bid it kill you some day. Well, had I not been Cæsar's pupil, what pious things might I not have done to that tigress! I might have punished it. I might have revenged Pothinus on it.

CÆSAR [*interjects*] Pothinus!

RUFIO [*continuing*] I might have judged it. But I put all these follies behind me; and, without malice, only cut its throat. And that is why Cleopatra comes to you in mourning.

CLEOPATRA [*vehemently*] He has shed the blood of my servant Ftatateeta. On your head be it as upon his, Cæsar, if you hold him free of it.

CÆSAR [*energetically*] On my head be it, then; for it was well done. Rufio: had you set yourself in the seat of the judge, and with hateful ceremonies and appeals to the gods handed that woman over to some hired executioner to be slain before the people in the name of justice, never again would I have touched your hand without a shudder. But this was natural slaying: I feel no horror at it.

[*Rufio, satisfied, nods at Cleopatra, mutely inviting her to mark that.*]

CLEOPATRA [*pettish and childish in her impotence*] No: not when a Roman slays an Egyptian. All the world will now see how unjust and corrupt Cæsar is.

CÆSAR [*taking her hands coaxingly*] Come: do not be angry with me. I am sorry for that poor Totateeta. [*She laughs in spite of herself*]. Aha! you are laughing. Does that mean reconciliation?

CLEOPATRA [*angry with herself for laughing*] No, no, NO!! But it is so ridiculous to hear you call her Totateeta.

CÆSAR What! As much a child as ever, Cleopatra! Have I not made a woman of you after all?

CLEOPATRA Oh, it is you who are a great baby: you make me seem silly because you will not behave seriously. But you have treated me badly; and I do not forgive you.

CÆSAR Bid me farewell.

CLEOPATRA I will not.

CÆSAR [*coaxing*] I will send you a beautiful present from Rome.

CLEOPATRA [*proudly*] Beauty from Rome to Egypt indeed! What can Rome give me that Egypt cannot give me?

APOLLODORUS That is true, Cæsar. If the present is to be really beautiful, I shall have to buy it for you in Alexandria.

CÆSAR You are forgetting the treasures for which Rome is most famous, my friend. You cannot buy them in Alexandria.

APOLLODORUS What are they, Cæsar?

CÆSAR Her sons. Come, Cleopatra: forgive me and bid me farewell; and I will send you a man, Roman from head to heel and Roman of the noblest; not old and ripe for the knife; not lean in the arms and cold in the heart; not hiding a bald head under his conqueror's laurels; not stooped with the weight of the world on his shoulders; but brisk and fresh, strong and young, hoping in the morning, fighting in the day, and revelling in the evening. Will you take such an one in exchange for Cæsar?

CLEOPATRA [*palpitating*] His name, his name?

CÆSAR Shall it be Mark Antony? [*She throws herself into his arms*].

RUFIO You are a bad hand at a bargain, mistress, if you will swop Cæsar for Antony.

CÆSAR So now you are satisfied.

CLEOPATRA You will not forget.

CÆSAR I will not forget. Farewell: I do not think we shall meet again. Farewell.

[*He kisses her on the forehead. She is much affected and begins to sniff. He embarks*].

THE ROMAN SOLDIERS [*as he sets his foot on the gangway*] Hail, Cæsar; and farewell!

[*He reaches the ship and returns Rufio's wave of the hand.*]

APOLLODORUS [*to Cleopatra*] No tears, dearest Queen: they stab your servant to the heart. He will return some day.

CLEOPATRA I hope not. But I cant help crying, all the same.

[*She waves her handkerchief to Cæsar; and the ship begins to move*].

THE ROMAN SOLDIERS [*drawing their swords and raising them in the air*] Hail, Cæsar!

NOTES TO CÆSAR AND CLEOPATRA

Cleopatra's Cure for Baldness

For the sake of conciseness in a hurried situation I have made Cleopatra recommend rum. This, I am afraid, is an anachronism: the only real one in the play. To balance it, I give a couple of the remedies she actually believed in. They are quoted by Galen from Cleopatra's book on Cosmetic.

"For bald patches, powder red sulphuret of arsenic and take it up with oak gum, as much as it will bear. Put on a rag and apply, having soaped the place well first. I have mixed the above with a foam of nitre, and it worked well."

Several other receipts follow, ending with: "The following is the best of all, acting for fallen hairs, when applied with oil or pomatum; acts for falling off of eyelashes or for people getting bald all over. It is wonderful. Of domestic mice burnt, one part; of vine rag burnt, one part; of horse's teeth burnt, one part; of bear's grease one; of deer's marrow one; of reed bark one. To be pounded when dry, and mixed with plenty of honey til it gets the consistency of honey; then the bear's grease and marrow to be mixed (when melted), the medicine to be put in a brass flask, and the bald part rubbed til it sprouts."

Concerning these ingredients, my fellow-dramatist Gilbert Murray, who, as a Professor of Greek, has applied to classical antiquity the methods of high scholarship (my own method is pure divination), writes to me as follows: "Some of this I dont understand, and possibly Galen did not, as he quotes your heroine's own language. Foam of nitre is, I think, something like soapsuds. Reed bark is an odd expression. It might mean the outside membrane of a reed: I do not know what it ought to be called. In the burnt mice receipt I take it that you first mixed the solid powders with honey, and then added the grease. I expect Cleopatra preferred it because in most of the others you have to lacerate the skin, prick it, or rub it till it bleeds. I do not know what vine rag is. I translate literally."

Apparent Anachronisms

The only way to write a play which shall convey to the general public an impression of antiquity is to make the characters speak blank verse and abstain from reference to steam, telegraphy, or any of the material conditions of their existence. The more ignorant men are, the more convinced are they that their little parish and their little chapel is an apex to which civilization and philosophy has painfully struggled up the pyramid of time from a desert of savagery. Savagery, they think, became barbarism; barbarism became ancient civilization; ancient civilization became Pauline Christianity; Pauline Christianity became Roman Catholicism; Roman Catholicism became the Dark Ages; and the Dark Ages were finally enlightened by the Protestant instincts of the English race. The whole process is summed up as Progress with a capital P. And any elderly gentleman of Progressive temperament will testify that the improvement since he was a boy is enormous.

Now if we count the generations of Progressive elderly gentlemen since, say, Plato, and add together the successive enormous improvements to which each of them has testified, it will strike us at once as an unaccountable fact that the world, instead of having been improved in 67 generations out of all recognition, presents, on the whole, a rather less dignified appearance in Ibsen's Enemy of the People than in Plato's Republic. And in truth, the period of time covered by history is far too short to allow of any perceptible progress in the popular sense of Evolution of the Human Species. The notion that there has been any such Progress since Cæsar's time (less than 20 centuries) is too absurd for discussion. All the savagery, barbarism, dark ages and the rest of it of which we have any record as existing in the past, exists at the present moment. A British carpenter or stonemason may point out that he gets twice as much money for his labor as his father did in the same trade, and that his suburban house, with its bath, its cottage piano, its drawing room suite, and its album of photographs, would have shamed the plainness of his grandmother's. But the descendants of feudal barons, living in squalid lodgings on a salary of fifteen shillings a week instead of in castles on princely revenues, do not congratulate the world on the change. Such changes, in fact, are not to the point. It has been known, as far back as our records go, that man running wild in the woods is different from man kennelled in a city slum; that a dog seems to understand a shepherd better than a hewer of wood and drawer of water can understand an astronomer; and that breeding, gentle nurture, and luxurious food and shelter will produce a kind of man with whom the common laborer is socially incompatible. The same thing is true of horses and dogs. Now there is clearly room for great changes in the world by increasing the percentage of individuals who are carefully bred and gently nurtured, even to finally making the most of every man and woman born. But that possibility existed in the days of the Hittites as much as it does today. It does not give the slightest real support to the common assumption that the civilized contemporaries of the Hittites were unlike their civilized descendants today.

This would appear the tritest commonplace if it were not that the ordinary citizen's ignorance of the past combines with his idealization of the present to mislead and flatter him. Our latest book on the new railway across Asia describes the dulness of the Siberian farmer and the vulgar pursepride of the Siberian man of business without the least consciousness that the string of contemptuous instances given might have been saved by writing simply "Farmers and provincial plutocrats in Siberia are exactly what they are in England." The latest professor descanting on the civilization of the Western Empire in the fifth century feels bound to assume, in the teeth of his own researches, that the Christian was one sort of animal and the Pagan another. It might as well be assumed as indeed it generally is assumed by implication, that a murder committed with a poisoned arrow is different from a murder committed with a Mauser rifle. All such notions are illusions. Go back to the first syllable of recorded time, and there you will find your Christian and your Pagan, your yokel and your poet, helot and hero, Don Quixote and Sancho, Tamino and Papageno, Newton and bushman unable to count eleven, all alive and contemporaneous, and all convinced that they are the heirs of all the ages and the privileged recipients of THE truth (all others damnable heresies) , just as you have them today, flourishing in countries each of which is the bravest and best that ever sprang at Heaven's command from out the azure main.

Again, there is the illusion of "increased command over Nature," meaning that cotton is cheap and that ten miles of country road on a bicycle have replaced four on foot. But even if man's increased command over Nature included any increased command over himself (the only sort of command relevant to his evolution into a higher being) , the fact remains that it is only by running away from the increased command over Nature to country places where Nature is still in primitive command over Man that he can recover from the effects of the smoke, the stench, the foul air, the overcrowding, the racket, the ugliness, the dirt which the cheap cotton costs us. If manufacturing activity means Progress, the town must be more advanced than the country; and the field laborers and village artisans of today must be much less changed from servants of Job than the proletariat of modern London from the proletariat of Cæsar's Rome. Yet the cockney proletarian is so inferior to the village laborer that it is only by steady recruiting from the country that London is kept alive. This does not seem as if the change since Job's time were Progress in the popular sense: quite the reverse. The common stock of discoveries in physics has accumulated a little: that is all.

One more illustration. Is the Englishman prepared to admit that the American is his superior as a human being? I ask this question because the scarcity of labor in America relatively to the demand for it has led to a development of machinery there, and a consequent "increase of command over Nature" which makes many of our English methods appear almost medieval to the up-to-date Chicagoan. This means that the American has an advantage over the Englishman of exactly the same nature that the Englishman has over the contemporaries of Cicero. Is the Englishman prepared to draw the same conclusion in both cases? I think not. The American, of course, will draw it cheerfully; but I must then ask him whether, since a modern negro has a greater "command over Nature" than Washington had, we are also to accept the conclusion, involved in his former one, that humanity has progressed from Washington to the *fin de siècle* negro.

Finally, I would point out that if life is crowned by its success and devotion in industrial organization and ingenuity, we had better worship the ant and the bee (as moralists urge us to do in our childhood) , and humble ourselves before the arrogance of the birds of Aristophanes.

My reason then for ignoring the popular conception of Progress in Cæsar and Cleopatra is that there is no reason to suppose that any Progress has taken place since their time. But even if I shared the popular delusion, I do not see that I could have made any essential difference in the play. I can only imitate humanity as I know it. Nobody knows whether Shakespear thought that ancient Athenian joiners, weavers, or bellows menders were any different from Elizabethan ones; but it is quite certain that he could not have made them so, unless, indeed, he had played the literary man and made Quince say, not "Is all our company here?" but "Bottom: was not that Socrates that passed us at the Piræus with Glaucon and Polemarchus on his way to the house of Kephalus?" And so on.

Cleopatra

Cleopatra was only sixteen when Cæsar went to Egypt; but in Egypt sixteen is a riper age than it is in England. The childishness I have ascribed to her, as far as it is childishness of character and not lack of experience, is not a matter of years. It may be observed in our own climate at the present day in many women of fifty. It is a mistake to suppose that the difference between wisdom and folly has anything to do with the difference between physical age and physical youth. Some women are younger at seventy than most women at seventeen.

It must be borne in mind, too, that Cleopatra was a queen, and was therefore not the typical Greek-cultured, educated Egyptian lady of her time. To represent her by any such type would be as absurd as to represent George IV by a type founded on the attainments of Sir Isaac Newton. It is true that an ordinarily well educated Alexandrian girl of her time would no more have believed bogey stories about the Romans than the daughter of a modern Oxford professor would believe them about the Germans (though, by the way, it is possible to talk great nonsense at Oxford about foreigners when we are at war with them). But I do not feel bound to believe that Cleopatra was well educated. Her father, the illustrious Flute Blower, was not at all a parent of the Oxford professor type. And Cleopatra was a chip of the old block.

Britannus

I find among those who have read this play in manuscript a strong conviction that an ancient Briton could not possibly have been like a modern one. I see no reason to adopt this curious view. It is true that the Roman and Norman conquests must have for a time disturbed the normal British type produced by the climate. But Britannus, born before these events, represents the unadulterated Briton who fought Cæsar and impressed Roman observers much as we should expect the ancestors of Mr Podsnap to impress the cultivated Italians of their time.

I am told that it is not scientific to treat national character as a product of climate. This only shews the wide difference between common knowledge and the intellectual game called science. We have men of exactly the same stock, and speaking the same language, growing in Great Britain, in Ireland, and in America. The result is three of the most distinctly marked nationalities under the sun. Racial characteristics are quite another matter. The difference between a Jew and a Gentile has nothing to do with the difference between an Englishman and a German. The characteristics of Britannus are local characteristics, not race characteristics. In an ancient Briton they would, I take it, be exaggerated, since modern Britain, disforested, drained, urbanified and consequently cosmopolized, is presumably less characteristically British than Cæsar's Britain.

And again I ask does anyone who, in the light of a competent knowledge of his own age, has studied history from contemporary documents, believe that 67 generations of promiscuous marriage have made any appreciable difference in the human fauna of these isles? Certainly I do not.

Julius Cæsar

As to Cæsar himself, I have purposely avoided the usual anachronism of going to Cæsar's books, and concluding that the style is the man. That is only true of authors who have the specific literary genius, and have practised long enough to attain complete self-expression in letters. It is not true even on these conditions in an age when literature is conceived as a game of style, and not as a vehicle of self-expression by the author. Now Cæsar was an amateur stylist writing books of travel and campaign histories in a style so impersonal that the authenticity of the later volumes is disputed. They reveal some of his qualities just as the Voyage of a Naturalist Round the World reveals some of Darwin's, without expressing his private personality. An Englishman reading them would say that Cæsar was a man of great common sense and good taste, meaning thereby a man without originality or moral courage.

In exhibiting Cæsar as a much more various person than the historian of the Gallic wars, I hope I have not been too much imposed on by the dramatic illusion to which all great men owe part of their reputation and some of the whole of it. I admit that reputations gained in war are specially questionable. Able civilians taking up the profession of arms, like Cæsar and Cromwell, in middle age, have snatched all its laurels from opponent commanders bred to it, apparently because capable persons engaged in military pursuits are so scarce that the existence of two of them at the same time in the same hemisphere is extremely rare. The capacity of any conqueror is therefore more likely than not to be an illusion produced by the incapacity of his adversary. At all events, Cæsar might have won his battles without being wiser than Charles XII or Nelson or Joan of Arc, who were, like most modern "self-made" millionaires, half-witted geniuses, enjoying the worship accorded by all races to certain forms of insanity. But Cæsar's victories were only advertisements for an eminence that would never have become popular without them. Cæsar is greater off the battle field than on it. Nelson off his quarterdeck was so quaintly out of the question that when his head was injured at the battle of the Nile, and his conduct became for some years openly scandalous, the difference was not important enough to be noticed. It may, however, be said that peace hath her illusory reputations no less than war. And it is certainly true that in civil life mere capacity for work—the power of killing a dozen secretaries under you, so to speak, as a life-or-death courier kills horses— enables men with common ideas and superstitions to distance all competitors in the strife of political ambition. It was this power of work that astonished Cicero as the most prodigious of Cæsar's gifts, as it astonished later observers in Napoleon before it wore him out. How if Cæsar were nothing but a Nelson and a Gladstone combined! a prodigy of vitality without any special quality of mind! nay, with ideas that were worn out before he was born, as Nelson's and Gladstone's were! I have considered that possibility too, and rejected it. I cannot cite all the stories about Cæsar which seem to me to shew that he was genuinely original; but let me at least point out that I have been careful to attribute nothing but originality to him. Originality gives a man an air of frankness, generosity, and magnanimity by enabling him to estimate the value of truth, money, or success in any particular instance quite independently of convention and moral generalization. He therefore will not, in the ordinary Treasury bench fashion, tell a lie which everybody knows to be a lie (and consequently expects him as a matter of good taste to tell.) His lies are not found out: they pass for candors. He understands the paradox of money, and gives it away when he can get most for it: in other words, when its value is least, which is just when a common man tries hardest to get it. He knows that the real moment of success is not the moment apparent to the crowd. Hence, in order to produce an impression of complete disinterestedness and magnanimity, he has only to act with entire selfishness; and this is perhaps the only sense in which a man can be said to be *naturally* great. It is in this sense that I have represented Cæsar as great. Having virtue, he has no need of goodness. He is neither forgiving, frank, nor generous, because a man who is too great to resent has nothing to forgive; a man who says things that other people are afraid to say need be no more frank than Bismarck was; and there is no generosity in giving things you do not want to people of whom you intend to make use. This distinction between virtue and goodness is not understood in England: hence the poverty of our drama in heroes. Our stage attempts at them are mere goody-goodies. Goodness, in its popular British sense of self-denial, implies that man is vicious by nature, and that supreme goodness is supreme martyrdom. Not sharing that pious opinion, I have not given countenance to it in any of my plays. In this I follow the precedent of the ancient myths, which represent the hero as vanquishing his enemies, not in fair fight, but with enchanted sword, superequine horse and magical invulnerability, the possession of which, from the vulgar moralistic point of view, robs his exploits of any merit whatever.

As to Cæsar's sense of humor, there is no more reason to assume that he lacked it than to assume that he was deaf or blind. It is said that on the occasion of his assassination by a conspiracy of moralists (it is always your moralist who makes assassination a duty, on the scaffold or off it), he defended himself until the good Brutus struck him, when he exclaimed "What! you too, Brutus!" and disdained further fight. If this be true, he must have been an incorrigible comedian. But even if we waive this story, or accept the traditional sentimental interpretation of it, there is still abundant evidence of his lightheartedness and adventurousness. Indeed it is clear from his whole history that what has been called his ambition was an instinct for exploration. He had much more of Columbus and Franklin in him than of Henry V.

However, nobody need deny Cæsar a share, at least, of the qualities I have attributed to him. All men, much more Julius Cæsars, possess all qualities in some degree. The really interesting question is whether I am right in assuming that the way to produce an impression of greatness is by exhibiting a man, not as mortifying his nature by doing his duty, in the manner which our system of putting little men into great positions (not having enough great men in our influential families to go round) forces us to inculcate, but as simply doing what he naturally wants to do. For this raises the question whether our world has not been wrong in its moral theory for the last 2,500 years or so. It must be a constant puzzle to many of us that the Christian era, so excellent in its intentions, should have been practically such a very discreditable episode in the history of the race. I doubt if this is altogether due to the vulgar and sanguinary sensationalism of our religious legends, with their substitution of gross physical torments and public executions for the passion of humanity. Islam, substituting voluptuousness for torment (a merely superficial difference, it is true) has done no better. It may have been the failure of Christianity to emancipate itself from expiatory theories of moral responsibility, guilt, innocence, reward, punishment, and the rest of it, that baffled its intention of changing the world. But these are bound up in all philosophies of creation as opposed to cosmism. They may therefore be regarded as the price we pay for popular religion.

ANTON CHEKHOV
[1860–1904]

The son of an ex-serf, Anton Chekhov began his writing career with short, realistic tales of the common life that he had experienced among the country and town folk of Czarist Russia. Though he sometimes practiced medicine among the peasantry, his stories sold well enough for him to refrain from the medical practice he had qualified for. He led a relatively quiet life, highlighted by his travels, literary successes, and friendships with famous people. He was known and admired by such opposite temperaments as Tolstoi and Gorki, both of whom perceived in Chekhov a simplicity and gentleness that struck them as almost a kind of saintliness. Gorki, for instance, wrote that "in Anton Chekhov's presence everyone involuntarily felt in himself a desire to be simple, more truthful, more one's self."

Whether Chekhov's quietly merry and retiring temperament was the result of delicate health (he had contracted tuberculosis while studying at the University of Moscow) or of a delicate spirituality, it is surprising that this least dramatic of men should have become a dramatist. He at first professed a disdain for everything theatrical, but wound up married to the theater in more ways than one. Two years before his death, he married the Moscow Art Theatre's ablest actress, Olga Knipper, who often remained in Moscow while Chekhov worked on *The Cherry Orchard* in the country, their marriage largely carried on by correspondence.

The Cherry Orchard, Chekhov's last play, was produced by the famous Stanislavsky in Moscow in 1904. When the strong-minded Stanislavsky played his sprightly comedy as a slow-moving tragedy, Chekhov characteristically said little to Stanislavsky in person, though he grumbled persistently in letters to his wife and friends. *The Cherry Orchard* is a remarkable play for many reasons, one being that it is the play of a man who possessed such strength and health of mind that he could write a gay comedy celebrating life's absurdity even as he knew he was dying.

The Cherry Orchard was preceded by a few minor plays and a trio of major plays—*The Sea Gull* (1896), *Uncle Vanya* (1899), and *The Three Sisters* (1901) —that combine with *The Cherry Orchard* to form an imposing quartet of dramatic achievement.

THE
CHERRY ORCHARD
A Comedy in Four Acts

ANTON CHEKHOV

Translated by Robert Corrigan

CAST

LYUBOV ANDREYEVNA RANEVSKY, *owner of the cherry orchard*
ANYA, *her daughter, age 17*
VARYA, *her adopted daughter, age 24*
LEONID ANDREYEVICH GAEV, *Lyubov's brother*
YERMOLAY ALEXEYEVICH LOPAHIN, *a business man*
PYOTR SERGEYEVICH TROFIMOV, *a student*
BORIS BORISOVICH SEMYONOV-PISHCHIK, *a landowner*

CHARLOTTA IVANOVNA, *a governess*
SEMYON PANTALEYEVICH EPIHODOV, *a clerk on the Ranevsky estate*
DUNYASHA, *a maid*
FEERS, *an old servant, age 87*
YASHA, *a young servant*
A TRAMP
THE STATION MASTER
A POST-OFFICE CLERK
GUESTS *and* SERVANTS

The action takes place on the estate of Madame Ranevsky.

From *Six Plays of Chekhov* edited and translated by Robert W. Corrigan. Rinehart Edition. Copyright © 1962 by Robert W. Corrigan. Reprinted by permission of Holt, Rinehart and Winston, Inc.

ACT I

A room which used to be the children's room and is still called the nursery. Several doors, one leading into ANYA's *room. It is early in the morning and the sun is rising. It is early in May, but there is a morning frost. The windows are closed but through them can be seen the blossoming cherry trees. Enter* DUNYASHA, *carrying a candle, and* LOPAHIN *with a book in his hand.*

LOPAHIN   The train's arrived, thank God. What time is it?

DUNYASHA   It's nearly two. [*Blows out the candle.*] It's daylight already.

LOPAHIN   The train must have been at least two hours late. [*Yawns and stretches.*] And what a fool I am! I make a special trip out here to meet them at the station, and then I fall asleep. . . . Just sat down in the chair and dropped off. What a nuisance. Why didn't you wake me up?

DUNYASHA   I thought you'd gone. [*Listens.*] I think they're coming.

LOPAHIN   [*Also listens.*]   No . . . I should've been there to help them with their luggage and other things . . . [*Pause.*] Lyubov Andreyevna has been abroad for five years. I wonder what she's like now. She used to be such a kind and good person. So easy to get along with and always considerate. Why, I remember when I was fifteen, my father—he had a store in town then—hit me in the face and it made my nose bleed. . . . We'd come out here for something or other, and he was drunk. Oh, I remember it as if it happened yesterday. . . . She was so young and beautiful . . . Lyubov Andreyevna brought me into this very room—the nursery, and she fixed my nose and she said to me, "Don't cry, little peasant, it'll be better by the time you get married.". . . [*Pause.*] "Little peasant". . . She was right, my father was a peasant. And look at me now—going about in a white waistcoat and brown shoes, like a crown in peacock's feathers. Oh, I am rich all right, I've got lots of money, but when you think about it, I'm still just a peasant. [*Turning over pages of the book.*] Here, I've been reading this book, and couldn't understand a word of it. Fell asleep reading it. [*Pause.*]

DUNYASHA   The dogs have been awake all night: they know their mistress is coming.

LOPAHIN   Why, what's the matter with you, Dunyasha?

DUNYASHA   My hands are shaking. I think I'm going to faint.

LOPAHIN   You've become too delicate and refined, Dunyasha. You get yourself all dressed up like a lady, and you fix your hair like one, too. You shouldn't do that, you know. You must remember your place.

[*Enter* EPIHODOV *with a bouquet of flowers; he wears a jacket and brightly polished high boots which squeak loudly. As he enters he drops the flowers.*]

EPIHODOV   [*Picks up the flowers.*]   The gardener sent these. He says they're to go in the dining room. [*Hands the flowers to* DUNYASHA.]

LOPAHIN   And bring me some kvass.

DUNYASHA   All right.

EPIHODOV   It's chilly outside this morning, three degrees of frost, and here the cherry trees are all in bloom. I can't say much for this climate of ours, you know. [*Sighs.*] No, I really can't. It doesn't contribute to—well, you know, things . . . And what do you think, Yermolay Alexeyevich, the day before yesterday I bought myself a pair of boots and they squeak so much . . . well, I mean to say, they're impossible. . . . What can I use to fix them?

LOPAHIN   Oh, be quiet! And don't bother me!

EPIHODOV   Every day something unpleasant happens to me. But I don't complain; I'm used to it, why I even laugh. [*Enter* DUNYASHA: *she serves* LOPAHIN *with kvass.*] Well, I have to be going. [*Bumps into a chair which falls over.*] There, you see! [*Triumphantly.*] You can see for yourself what I mean, you see . . . so to speak . . . It's absolutely amazing! [*Goes out.*]

DUNYASHA   I must tell you a secret, Yermolay Alexeyevich. Epihodov proposed to me.

LOPAHIN   Really!

DUNYASHA   I don't know what to do. . . . He's a quiet man, but then sometimes he starts talking, and then you can't understand a word he says. It sounds nice, and he says it with so much feeling, but it doesn't make any sense. I think I like him a little, and he's madly in love with me. But the poor man, he's sort of unlucky! Do you know, something unpleasant seems to happen to him every day. That's why they tease him and call him "two-and-twenty misfortunes."

LOPAHIN   [*Listens.*]   I think I hear them coming. . . .

DUNYASHA   Coming! . . . Oh, what's the matter with me. . . . I feel cold all over.

LOPAHIN   Yes, they're really coming! Let's go and meet them at the door. I wonder if she'll recognize me? We haven't seen each other for five years.

DUNYASHA   [*Agitated.*]   I'm going to faint . . . Oh, I'm going to faint! . . .
[*The sound of two carriages driving up to the house can be heard.* LOPAHIN *and* DUNYASHA *hurry out. The stage is empty. Then there are sounds of people arriving in the next room.* FEERS, *who has gone to meet the train, enters the room leaning on a cane. He crosses the stage as rapidly as he can. He is dressed in an old-fashioned livery coat and a top hat and is muttering to himself, though it is impossible to make out what he is saying. The noises off-stage become louder.*]

VOICE   [*Off-stage.*]   Let's go through here.
[*Enter* LYUBOV ANDREYEVNA, ANYA, *and* CHARLOTTA IVANOVNA, *leading a small dog, all in traveling clothes,* VARYA, *wearing an overcoat and a kerchief over her head,* GAEV, SEMYONOV-PISHCHIK, LOPAHIN, DUNYASHA, *carrying a bundle and parasol, and other servants with luggage.*]

ANYA   Let's go through here. Do you remember what room this is, Mamma?

LYUBOV   [*Joyfully, through her tears.*]   The nursery!

VARYA   How cold it is! My hands are numb. [*To* LYUBOV.] Your rooms are the same as always, Mamma dear, the white one, and the lavender one.

LYUBOV   The nursery, my dear, beautiful room! . . . I used to sleep here when I was little. [*Cries.*] And here I am again, like a little child . . . [*She kisses her brother, then* VARYA, *then her brother again.*] And Varya hasn't changed a bit, looking like a nun. And I recognized Dunyasha, too. [*Kisses* DUNYASHA.]

GAEV   The train was two hours late. Just think of it! Such efficiency!

CHARLOTTA   [*To* PISHCHIK.]   And my dog eats nuts, too.

PISHCHIK   [*Astonished.*]   Think of that!
[*They all go out except* ANYA *and* DUNYASHA.]

DUNYASHA   We've waited and waited for you . . . [*Helps* ANYA *to take off her hat and coat.*]

ANYA   I haven't slept for four nights . . . I'm freezing.

DUNYASHA   It was Lent when you left, and it was snowing and freezing; but it's spring now. Darling! [*She laughs and kisses her.*] Oh, how I've missed you! I could hardly stand it. My pet, my precious . . . But I must tell you . . . I can't wait another minute . . .

ANYA   [*Without enthusiasm.*]   What time is it? . . .

DUNYASHA   Epihodov, the clerk, proposed to me right after Easter.

ANYA   You never talk about anything else . . . [*Tidies her hair.*] I've lost all my hairpins. . . . [*She's so tired she can hardly keep on her feet.*]

DUNYASHA   I really don't know what to think. He loves me . . . he loves me very much!

ANYA   [*Looking through the door into her room, tenderly.*]   My own room, my own windows, just as if I'd never left them! I'm home again! Tomorrow I'm going to get up and run right to the garden! Oh, if only I could fall asleep! I couldn't sleep all the way back, I've been so worried.

DUNYASHA   Pyotr Sergeyevich came the day before yesterday.

ANYA   [*Joyfully.*]   Petya!

DUNYASHA   We put him in the bathhouse, he's probably asleep now. He said he didn't want to inconvenience you. [*Looks at her watch.*] I should have gotten him up, but Varya told me not to. "Don't you dare get him up," she said.

[*Enter* VARYA *with a bunch of keys at her waist.*]

VARYA   Dunyasha, get some coffee, and hurry! Mamma wants some.

DUNYASHA   I'll get it right away. [*Goes out.*]

VARYA   Thank God, you're back! You're home again. [*Embracing her.*] My little darling's come home! How are you, my precious?

ANYA   If you only knew what I've had to put up with!

VARYA   I can just imagine . . .

ANYA   You remember, I left just before Easter and it was cold then. And Charlotta never stopped talking the whole time, talking and those silly tricks of hers. Why did you make me take Charlotta?

VARYA   But you couldn't go all alone, darling. At seventeen!

ANYA   When we got to Paris it was cold and snowing. My French was terrible. Mamma was living on the fifth floor, and the place was filled with people —some French ladies, and an old priest with a little book, and the room was full of cigarette smoke. It was so unpleasant. All of a sudden I felt so sorry for Mamma that I put my arms around her neck and hugged her and wouldn't let go I was so upset. Later Mamma cried and was very kind.

VARYA   [*Tearfully.*]   I can't stand to hear it! . . .

ANYA   She had already sold her villa at Mentone, and she had nothing left, not a thing. And I didn't have any money left either, not a penny. In fact, I barely had enough to get to Paris. And Mamma didn't understand it at all. On the way, we'd eat at the best restaurants and she'd order the most expensive dishes and tip the waiters a rouble each. Charlotta's the same way. And Yasha expected a full-course dinner for himself; it was horrible. You know, Yasha is Mamma's valet, now, we brought him with us.

VARYA   Yes, I've seen the scoundrel.

ANYA   Well, how's everything here? Have you paid the interest on the mortgage?

VARYA   With what?

ANYA   Oh dear! Oh dear!

VARYA   The time runs out in August, and then it will be up for sale.

ANYA   Oh dear!

LOPAHIN   [*Puts his head through the door and moos like a cow.*]   Moo-o. . . . [*Disappears.*]

VARYA   [*Tearfully.*]   I'd like to hit him . . . [*Clenches her fist.*]

ANYA   [*Her arms round* VARYA, *dropping her voice.*] Varya, has he proposed to you? [VARYA *shakes her head.*] But he loves you. . . . Why don't you talk to him, what are you waiting for?

VARYA   Nothing will come of it. He's too busy to have time to think of me . . . He doesn't notice me at all. It's easier when he isn't around, it makes me miserable just to see him. Everybody talks of our wedding and congratulates me, but in fact there's nothing to it; it's all a dream. [*In a different tone.*] You've got a new pin, it looks like a bee.

ANYA   [*Sadly.*]   Mamma bought it for me. [*She goes into her room and then with childlike gaiety.*] Did you know that in Paris I went up in a balloon?

VARYA   My darling's home again! My precious one's home. [DUNYASHA *returns with a coffeepot and prepares coffee. Standing by* ANYA'S *door.*] You know, all day long, as I go about the house doing my work, I'm always dreaming. If only we could marry you to some rich man, I'd be more at peace. Then they could go away; first I'd go to the cloisters, and then I'd go on a pilgrimage to Kiev, and then Moscow . . . I'd spend my life just walking from one holy place to another. On and on. Oh, what a wonderful life that would be!

ANYA   The birds are singing in the garden. What time is it?

VARYA   It must be nearly three. Time you went to bed, darling. [*Goes into* ANYA'S *room.*] Oh, what a wonderful life!

[*Enter* YASHA, *with a blanket and a small bag.*]

YASHA   [*Crossing the stage, in an affectedly genteel voice.*]   May I go through here?

DUNYASHA   My, how you've changed since you've been abroad, Yasha. I hardly recognized you.

YASHA   Hm! And who are you?

DUNYASHA   When you went away, I was no bigger than this . . . [*Shows her height from the floor.*] I'm Dunyasha, Fyodor's daughter. You don't remember me!

YASHA   Hm! You're quite a little peach! [*Looks around and embraces her; she screams and drops a saucer.* YASHA *goes out quickly.*]

VARYA   [*In the doorway, crossly.*]   What's happening in here?

DUNYASHA   [*Tearfully.*]   I've broken a saucer.

VARYA   That's good luck.

ANYA   [*Coming out of her room.*]   We ought to warn Mamma that Petya's here.

VARYA   I gave strict orders not to wake him up.

ANYA   [*Pensively.*]   Six years ago father died, and then a month later Grisha was drowned in the river. He was such a beautiful little boy—and only seven! Mamma couldn't stand it so she went away . . . and never looked back. [*Shivers.*] How well I understand her! If she only knew! [*Pause.*] And, Petya was Grisha's tutor, he might remind her . . .

[*Enter* FEERS, *wearing a jacket and a white waistcoat.*]

FEERS   [*Goes over and is busy with the samovar.*]   The mistress will have her coffee in here. [*Puts on white gloves.*] Is it ready? [*To* DUNYASHA, *severely.*] Where's the cream?

DUNYASHA   Oh, I forgot! [*Goes out quickly.*]

FEERS   [*Fussing around the coffeepot.*]   That girl's hopeless. . . . [*Mutters.*] They've come from Paris . . . Years ago the master used to go to Paris . . . Used to go by carriage . . . [*Laughs.*]

VARYA   Feers, what are you laughing at?

FEERS   What would you like? [*Happily.*] The mistress has come home! Home at last! I don't mind if I die now . . . [*Weeps with joy.*]

[*Enter* LYUBOV, LOPAHIN, GAEV *and* SEMYONOV-PISHCHIK, *the latter in a long peasant coat of fine cloth and full trousers tucked inside high boots.* GAEV, *as he comes in, moves his arms and body as if he were playing billiards.*]

LYUBOV   How does it go now? Let me think . . . The red off the side and into the middle pocket!

GAEV   That's right! Then I put the white into the corner pocket! . . . Years ago we used to sleep in this room, and now I'm fifty-one, strange as it may seem.

LOPAHIN   Yes, time flies.

GAEV   What?

LOAPHIN   Time flies, I say.

GAEV   This place smells of patchouli . . .

ANYA   I'm going to bed. Goodnight, Mamma. [*Kisses her.*]

LYUBOV   My precious child! [*Kisses her hands.*] Are you glad you're home? I still can't get used to it.

ANYA   Goodnight, Uncle.

GAEV   [*Kisses her face and hands.*]   God bless you. You're so much like your mother! [*To his sister.*] You looked exactly like her at her age, Lyuba.

ANYA   [*Shakes hands with* LOPAHIN *and* PISHCHIK, *goes out and shuts the door after her.*]

LYUBOV   She's very tired.

PISHCHIK   It's been a long trip for her.

VARYA   [*To* LOPAHIN *and* PISHCHIK.]   Well, gentlemen? It's nearly three o'clock, time to say good-bye.

LYUBOV   [*Laughs.*]   You haven't changed a bit, Varya. [*Draws* VARYA *to her and kisses her.*] Let me have some coffee, then we'll all turn in. [FEERS *places a cushion under her feet.*] Thank you, my dear. I've got into the habit of drinking coffee. I drink it day and night. Thank you, my dear old friend. [*Kisses* FEERS.]

VARYA   I'd better see if they brought all the luggage in. [*Goes out.*]

LYUBOV   Is it really me sitting here? [*Laughing.*] I'd like to dance and wave my arms about. [*Covering her face with her hands.*] But am I just dreaming? God, how I love it here—my own country! Oh, I love it so much, I could hardly see anything from the train, I was crying so hard. [*Through tears.*] Here, but I must drink my coffee. Thank you, Feers, thank you, my dear old friend. I'm so glad you're still alive.

FEERS   The day before yesterday.

GAEV   He doesn't hear very well.

LOPAHIN   I've got to leave for Kharkov a little after four. What a nuisance! It's so good just to see you, and I want to talk with you . . . You look as lovely as ever.

PISHCHIK   [*Breathing heavily.*] Prettier. In her fancy Parisian clothes . . . She's simply ravishing!

LOPAHIN   Your brother here—Leonid Andreyevich—says that I'm nothing but a hick from the country, a tight-fisted peasant, but it doesn't bother me. Let him say what he likes. All I want is that you trust me as you always have. Merciful God! My father was your father's serf, and your grandfather's, too, but you've done so much for me that I've forgotten all that. I love you as if you were my own sister . . . more than that even.

LYUBOV   I just can't sit still, I can't for the life of me! [*She jumps up and walks about in great excitement.*] I'm so happy, it's too much for me. It's all right, you can laugh at me. I know I'm being silly . . . My wonderful old bookcase! [*Kisses bookcase.*] And my little table!

GAEV   You know, the old Nurse died while you were away.

LYUBOV   [*Sits down and drinks coffee.*] Yes, you wrote to me about it. May she rest in peace.

GAEV   Anastasy died, too. And Petrushka quit and is working in town for the chief of police. [*Takes a box of gumdrops out of his pocket and puts one in his mouth.*]

PISHCHIK   My daughter, Dashenka, sends you her greetings.

LOPAHIN I feel like telling you some good news, something to cheer you up. [*Looks at his watch.*] I'll have to leave in a minute, so there's not much time to talk. But briefly it's this. As you know, the cherry orchard is going to be sold to pay your debts. They've set August 22nd as the date for the auction, but you can sleep in peace and not worry about it; there's a way out. Here's my plan, so please pay close attention. Your estate is only twenty miles from town, and the railroad is close by. Now, if the cherry orchard and the land along the river were subdivided and leased for the building of summer cottages, you'd have a yearly income of at least twenty-five thousand roubles.

GAEV Such nonsense!

LYUBOV I'm afraid I don't quite understand, Yermolay Alexeyevich.

LOPAHIN You'd divide the land into one acre lots and rent them for at least twenty-five roubles a year. I'll bet you, that if you advertise it now there won't be a lot left by the fall; they'll be snapped up almost at once. You see, you're saved! And really, I must congratulate you; it's a perfect setup. The location is marvelous and the river's deep enough for swimming. Of course, the land will have to be cleared and cleaned up a bit. For instance, all those old buildings will have to be torn down . . . And this house, too . . . but then it's not really good for anything any more. . . . And then, the old cherry orchard will have to be cut down . . .

LYUBOV Cut down? My good man, forgive me, but you don't seem to understand. If there's one thing that's interesting and really valuable in this whole part of the country, it's our cherry orchard.

LOPAHIN The only valuable thing about it is that it's very large. It only produces a crop every other year and then who wants to buy it?

GAEV Why, this orchard is even mentioned in the Encyclopedia.

LOPAHIN [*Looking at his watch.*] If you don't decide now, and do something about it before August, the cherry orchard as well as the estate will be auctioned off. So make up your minds! There's no other way out, I promise you. There's no other way.

FEERS In the old days, forty or fifty years ago, the cherries were dried, preserved, pickled, made into jam, and sometimes. . . .

GAEV Be quiet, Feers.

FEERS And sometimes, whole wagon-loads of dried cherries were shipped to Moscow and Kharkov. We used to make a lot of money on them then! And the dried cherries used to be soft, juicy, sweet, and very good . . . They knew how to do it then . . . they had a way of cooking them . . .

LYUBOV And where is that recipe now?

FEERS They've forgotten it. Nobody can remember it.

PISHCHIK [*To* LYUBOV.] What's it like in Paris. Did you eat frogs?

LYUBOV I ate crocodiles.

PISHCHIK Well, will you imagine that!

LOPAHIN Until recently only rich people and peasants lived in the country, but now lots of people come out for the summer. Almost every town, even the small ones, is surrounded with summer places. And probably within the next twenty years there'll be more and more of these people. Right now, all they do is sit on the porch and drink tea, but later on they might begin to grow a few things, and then your cherry orchard would be full of life again . . . rich and prosperous.

GAEV [*Indignantly.*] Such a lot of nonsense!

[*Enter* VARYA *and* YASHA.]

VARYA There were two telegrams for you, Mamma dear. [*Takes out the keys and opens the old bookcase, making a great deal of noise.*] Here they are.

LYUBOV They're from Paris. [*Tears them up without reading them.*] I'm through with Paris.

GAEV Do you know, Lyuba, how old this bookcase is? Last week I pulled out the bottom drawer, and I found the date it was made burned in the wood. Just think, it's exactly a hundred years old. What do you think of that, eh? We ought to celebrate its anniversary. I know it's an inanimate object, but still—it's a bookcase!

PISHCHIK [*Astonished.*] A hundred years! Can you imagine that!

GAEV Yes . . . That's quite something [*Feeling round the bookcase with his hands.*] Dear, most honored bookcase! I salute you! For one hundred years you have served the highest ideals of goodness and justice. For one hundred years you have made us aware of the need for creative work; several generations of our family have had their courage sustained and their faith in a brighter future fortified by your silent call; you have fostered in us the ideals of public service and social consciousness. [*Pause.*]

LOPAHIN Yes . . .

LYUBOV You haven't changed a bit, Leonid.

GAEV [*Slightly embarrassed.*] I shoot it off the corner into the middle pocket! . . .

LOPAHIN [*Looks at his watch.*] Well, I've got to go.

YASHA [*Brings medicine to* LYUBOV.] Would you like to take your pills now; it's time.

PISHCHIK You shouldn't take medicine, my dear . . . they don't do you any good . . . or harm either. Let me have them. [*Takes the box from her, pours the pills into the palm of his hand, blows on them, puts them all into his mouth and drinks them down with kvass.*] There!

LYUBOV [*Alarmed.*] You're out of your mind!

PISHCHIK I took all the pills.

LOPAHIN What a stomach! [*All laugh.*]

FEERS His honor was here during Holy Week, and he ate half a bucket of pickles. [*Mutters.*]

LYUBOV What's he saying?

VARYA He's been muttering like that for three years now. We're used to it.

YASHA It's his age. . . .

[CHARLOTTA IVANOVNA, *very thin, and tightly laced in a white dress, with a lorgnette at her waist, passes across the stage.*]

LOPAHIN Excuse me, Charlotta Ivanovna, for not greeting you. I didn't have a chance. [*Tries to kiss her hand.*]

CHARLOTTA [*Withdrawing her hand.*] If I let you kiss my hand, then you'd want to kiss my elbow next, and then my shoulder.

LOPAHIN This just isn't my lucky day. [*All laugh.*] Charlotta Ivanovna, do a trick for us.

CHARLOTTA Not now. I want to go to bed. [*Goes out.*]

LOPAHIN I'll be back in three weeks. [*Kisses* LYUBOV's *hand.*] It's time I'm going so I'll say good-bye. [*To* GAEV.] Au revoir. [*Embraces* PISHCHIK.] Au revoir. [*Shakes hands with* VARYA, *then with* FEERS *and* YASHA.] I don't want to go, really. [*To* LYUBOV.] Think over the idea of the summer cottages and if you decide anything, let me know, and I'll get you a loan of at least fifty thousand. So think it over seriously.

VARYA [*Crossly.*] Won't you ever go?

LOPAHIN I'm going, I'm going. [*Goes out.*]

GAEV What a boor! I beg your pardon . . . Varya's going to marry him, he's Varya's fiancé.

VARYA Please don't talk like that, Uncle.

LYUBOV Well, Varya, I'd be delighted. He's a good man.

PISHCHIK He's a man . . . you have to say that . . . a most worthy fellow . . . My Dashenka says so too . . . she says all sorts of things. . . . [*He drops asleep and snores, but wakes up again at once.*] By the way, my dear, will you lend me two hundred and forty roubles? I've got to pay the interest on the mortgage tomorrow . . .

VARYA [*In alarm.*] We haven't got it, really we haven't!

LYUBOV It's true, I haven't got a thing.

PISHCHIK It'll turn up. [*Laughs.*] I never lose hope. There are times when I think everything's lost, I'm ruined, and then—suddenly!—a railroad is built across my land, and they pay me for it! Something's bound to happen, if not today, then tomorrow, or the next day. Perhaps Dashenka will win two thousand—she's got a lottery ticket.

LYUBOV Well, we've finished our coffee; now we can go to bed.

FEERS [*Brushing* GAEV, *admonishing him.*] You've got on the trousers again! What am I going to do with you?

VARYA [*In a low voice.*] Anya's asleep. [*Quietly opens a window.*] The sun's rising and see how wonderful the trees are! And the air smells so fragrant! The birds are beginning to sing.

GAEV [*Coming to the window.*] The orchard is all white. You haven't forgotten, Lyuba? How straight that lane is . . . just like a ribbon. And how it shines on moonlight nights. Do you remember? You haven't forgotten, have you?

LYUBOV [*Looks through the window at the orchard.*] Oh, my childhood, my innocent childhood! I used to sleep here, and I'd look out at the orchard and every morning when I woke up I was so happy. The orchard was exactly the same, nothing's changed. [*Laughs happily.*] All, all white! Oh, my orchard! After the dark, gloomy autumn and the cold winter, you are young again and full of joy; the angels have not deserted you! If only this burden could be taken from me, if only I could forget my past!

GAEV Yes, and now the orchard's going to be sold to pay our debts, how strange it all is.

LYUBOV Look, there's Mother walking through the orchard . . . dressed all in white! [*Laughs happily.*] It is Mother!

GAEV Where?

VARYA Oh, please, Mamma dear!

LYUBOV You're right, it's no one, I only imagined it. Over there, you see, on the right, by the path that goes to the arbor, there's a small white tree that's bending so it looks just like a woman.

[*Enter* TROFIMOV. *He is dressed in a shabby student's uniform, and wears glasses.*]

What a wonderful orchard! Masses of white blossoms, the blue sky . . .

TROFIMOV Lyubov Andreyevna! [*She turns to him.*] I'll just say hello and leave at once. [*Kisses her hand warmly.*] They told me to wait until morning, but I couldn't wait any longer. [LYUBOV *looks at him, puzzled.*]

VARYA [*Through tears.*] This is Petya Trofimov.

TROFIMOV Petya Trofimov, I was Grisha's tutor. Have I changed that much? [LYUBOV *puts her arms round him and weeps quietly.*]

GAEV [*Embarrassed.*] Now, now, Lyuba . . .

VARYA [*Weeps.*] Didn't I tell you to wait until tomorrow, Petya?

LYUBOV My Grisha . . . my little boy . . . Oh, Grisha . . . my son . . .

VARYA Don't cry, Mamma darling. There's nothing we can do, it was God's will.

TROFIMOV [*Gently, with emotion.*] Don't, don't . . . please.

LYUBOV   [*Weeping quietly.*]   My little boy was lost . . . drowned . . . Why? Why, my friend? [*More quietly.*] Anya's asleep in there, and here I'm crying and making a scene. But tell me, Petya, what's happened to your good looks? You've aged so.

TROFIMOV   A peasant woman on the train called me "that moth-eaten man."

LYUBOV   You used to be such an attractive boy, a typical young student. But now your hair is thin and you wear glasses. Are you still a student? [*She walks to the door.*]

TROFIMOV   I expect I'll be a student as long as I live.

LYUBOV   [*Kisses her brother, then* VARYA.]   Well, go to bed now. You have aged, too, Leonid.

PISHCHIK   [*Following her.*]   Yes, I suppose it's time to get to bed. Oh, my gout! I'd better spend the night here, and in the morning, Lyubov Andreyevna, my dear, I'd like to borrow the two hundred and forty roubles.

GAEV   Don't you ever stop?

PISHCHIK   Just two hundred and forty roubles . . . To pay the interest on my mortgage.

LYUBOV   I haven't any money, my friend.

PISHCHIK   Oh, I'll pay you back, my dear. It's not much, after all.

LYUBOV   Oh, all right. Leonid will give it to you. You give him the money, Leonid.

GAEV   Why, of course; glad to. As much as he wants!

LYUBOV   What else can we do? He needs it. He'll pay it back.

[LYUBOV, TROFIMOV, PISHCHIK *and* FEERS *go out.* GAEV, VARYA *and* YASHA *remain.*]

GAEV   My sister hasn't lost her habit of throwing money away. [*To* YASHA.] Get out of the way, you smell like a barnyard.

YASHA   [*With a sneer.*]   And you haven't changed either, have you Leonid Andreyevich?

GAEV   What's that? [*To* VARYA.] What did he say?

VARYA   [*To* YASHA.]   Your mother came out from town yesterday to see you, and she's been waiting out in the servant's quarters ever since.

YASHA   I wish she wouldn't bother me.

VARYA   Oh, you ought to be ashamed of yourself.

YASHA   What's she in such a hurry for? She could have come tomorrow. [YASHA *goes out.*]

VARYA   Mamma hasn't changed a bit. She'd give away everything we had, if she could.

GAEV   Yes . . . You know, when many things are prescribed to cure a disease, that means it's incurable. I've been wracking my brains to find an answer, and I've come up with several solutions, plenty of them—which means there aren't any. It would be wonderful if we could inherit some money, or if our Anya were to marry some very rich man, or if one of us went to Yaroslavl and tried our luck with our old aunt, the Countess. You know she's very rich.

VARYA   [*Weeping.*]   If only God would help us.

GAEV   Oh, stop blubbering! The Countess is very rich, but she doesn't like us . . . To begin with, my sister married a lawyer, and not a nobleman . . . [ANYA *appears in the doorway.*] She married a commoner . . . and since then no one can say she's behaved in the most virtuous way possible. She's good, kind, and lovable, and I love her very much, but no matter how much you may allow for extenuating circumstances, you've got to admit that her morals have not been beyond reproach. You can sense it in everything she does . . .

VARYA   [*In a whisper.*]   Anya's standing in the doorway.

GAEV   What? [*A pause.*] Isn't that strange, something's gotten into my right eye . . . I'm having a terrible time seeing. and last Thursday, when I was in the District Court . . . [ANYA *comes in.*]

VARYA   Anya, why aren't you asleep?

ANYA   I don't feel like sleeping. I just can't.

GAEV   My dear little girl! [*Kisses* ANYA's *face and hands.*] My child! [*Tearfully.*] You're not just my niece, you're an angel, my whole world. Please believe me, believe . . .

ANYA   I believe you, Uncle. Everyone loves you, respects you . . . but, dear Uncle, you shouldn't talk so much, just try to keep quiet. What were you saying just now about mother, about your own sister? What made you say that?

GAEV   Yes, yes! [*He takes her hand and puts it over his face.*] You're quite right, it was a horrible thing to say! My God! My God! And that speech I made to the bookcase . . . so stupid! As soon as I finished it, I realized how stupid it was.

VARYA   It's true, Uncle dear, you oughtn't to talk so much. Just keep quiet, that's all.

ANYA   If you keep quiet, you'll find life is more peaceful.

GAEV   I'll be quiet. [*Kisses* ANYA's *and* VARYA's *hands.*] I'll be quiet. But I must tell you something about all this business, it's important. Last Thursday I went to the District Court, and I got talking with some friends, and from what they said it looks as if it might be possible to get a second mortgage so we can pay the interest to the bank.

VARYA   If only God would help us!

GAEV   I'm going again on Tuesday to talk with them some more. [*To* VARYA.] Oh, stop crying. [*To* ANYA.] Your mother's going to talk with Lopahin, and he certainly won't refuse her. And after you've had a little rest, you can go to Yaroslavl to see your grandmother, the Countess. You see, we'll attack the problem from three sides, and—it's as good as solved! We'll pay the interest, I'm sure of it. [*He eats a gumdrop.*] On my honor, on anything you like, I swear the estate'll not be sold! [*Excited.*] I'll bet my happiness on it! Here's my hand, you can call me a worthless liar if I allow the auction to take place. I swear it with all my soul!

ANYA   [*Calmer, with an air of happiness.*] How good you are, Uncle, and how sensible! [*Embracing him.*] I'm not afraid anymore. I feel so happy and at peace.

[*Enter* FEERS.]

FEERS   [*Reproachfully.*] Leonid Andreyevich, aren't you ashamed of yourself? When are you going to bed?

GAEV   In a minute. Now you go away, Feers. I can get ready for bed myself. Come along, children, time for bed. We'll talk about it some more tomorrow, you must go to bed now. [*Kisses* ANYA *and* VARYA.] You know, I'm a man of the 'eighties. People don't think much of that period these days, but still I can say that I've suffered a great deal in my lifetime because of my convictions. There's a reason why the peasants love me. You have to know the peasants! You have to know . . .

ANYA   You're beginning again, Uncle!

VARYA   Yes, you'd better keep quiet, Uncle dear.

FEERS   [*Sternly.*] Leonid Andreyevich!

GAEV   I'm coming, I'm coming! Go to bed now! Bank the white into the side pocket. There's a shot for you . . . [*Goes out;* FEERS *hobbles after him.*]

ANYA   I feel better now, although I don't want to go to Yaroslavl. I don't like the Countess at all, but then, thanks to Uncle, we really don't have to worry at all. [*She sits down.*]

VARYA   I've got to get some sleep. I'm going. Oh, by the way, we had a terrible scene while you were gone. You know, there are only a few old servants left out in the servants' quarters: just Yefmushka, Polya, Yevstignay, and Karp. Well, they let some tramp sleep out there, and at first I didn't say anything about it. But then later, I heard people saying that I had given orders to feed them nothing but beans. Because I was stingy, you see . . . Yevstignay was the cause of it all. "Well," I think to myself, "if that's how things are, just you wait!" So I called Yevstignay in. [*Yawns.*] So he came. "What's all this, Yevstignay," I said to him, "you're such a fool." [*She walks up to* ANYA.] Anichka! [*A pause.*] She's asleep! . . . [*Takes her arm.*] Let's go to bed! Come! [*Leads her away.*] My darling's fallen asleep! Come . . . [*They go towards the door. The sound of a shepherd's pipe is heard from far away, beyond the orchard.* TROFIMOV *crosses the stage, but, seeing* VARYA *and* ANYA, *stops.*] Sh-sh! She's asleep . . . asleep . . . Come along, come along.

ANYA   [*Softly, half-asleep.*]   I'm so tired. . . . I can hear the bells ringing all the time . . . Uncle . . . dear . . . Mamma and Uncle. . . .

VARYA   Come, darling, come. . . . [*They go into* ANYA's *room.*]

TROFIMOV   [*Deeply moved.*]   Oh, Anya . . . my sunshine! My spring!

CURTAIN

ACT II

An old abandoned chapel in a field. Beside it are a well, an old bench, and some tombstones. A road leads to the Ranevsky estate. On one side a row of poplars casts a shadow; at that point the cherry orchard begins. In the distance, a line of telegraph poles can be seen, and beyond them, on the horizon, is the outline of a large town, visible only in very clear weather. It's nearly sunset. CHARLOTTA, YASHA *and* DUNYASHA *are sitting on the bench;* EPIHODOV *is standing near by, playing a guitar; everyone is lost in thought.* CHARLOTTA *is wearing an old hunting cap; she has taken a shotgun off her shoulder and is adjusting the buckle on the strap.*

CHARLOTTA   [*Thoughtfully.*]   I don't know how old I am. For you see, I haven't got a passport . . . but I keep pretending that I'm still very young. When I was a little girl, my father and mother traveled from fair to fair giving performances—oh, very good ones. And I used to do the *"salto-mortale"* and all sorts of other tricks, too. When Papa and Mamma died, a German lady took me to live with her and sent me to school. So when I grew up I became a governess. But where I come from and who I am, I don't know. Who my parents were—perhaps they weren't even married—I don't know. [*Taking a cucumber from her pocket and beginning to eat it.*] I don't know anything. [*Pause.*] I'm longing to talk to someone, but there isn't anybody. I haven't anybody . . .

EPIHODOV   [*Plays the guitar and sings.*]   "What care I for the noisy world? . . . What care I for friends and foes?" How pleasant it is to play the mandolin!

DUNYASHA   That's a guitar, not a mandolin. [*She looks at herself in a little mirror and powders her face.*]

EPIHODOV   To a man who's madly in love this is a mandolin. [*Sings quietly.*] "If only my heart were warmed by the fire of love requited." . . . [YASHA *joins in.*]

CHARLOTTA   How dreadfully these people sing! . . . Ach! Like a bunch of jackals.

DUNYASHA   [*To* YASHA.] You're so lucky to have been abroad!

YASHA   Of course I am. Naturally. [*Yawns, then lights a cigar.*]

EPIHODOV   Stands to reason. Abroad everything's reached its maturity . . . I mean to say, everything's been going on for such a long time.

YASHA   Obviously.

EPIHODOV   Now, I'm a cultured man, I read all kinds of extraordinary books, you know, but somehow I can't seem to figure out where I'm going, what it is I really want, I mean to say—whether to live or to shoot myself. Nevertheless, I always carry a revolver on me. Here it is. [*Shows the revolver.*]

CHARLOTTA   That's finished, so now I'm going. [*Slips the strap of the gun over her shoulder.*] Yes, Epihodov, you are a very clever man, and frightening, too; the women must be wild about you! Brr! [*Walks off.*] All these clever people are so stupid, I haven't anyone to talk to. I'm so lonely, always alone, I have nobody and . . . and who I am and what I'm here for, nobody knows . . . [*Wanders out.*]

EPIHODOV   Frankly, and I want to keep to the point, I have to admit that Fate, so to speak, treats me absolutely without mercy, like a small ship is buffeted by the storm, as it were. I mean to say, suppose I'm mistaken, then why for instance should I wake up this morning and suddenly see a gigantic spider sitting on my chest? Like this . . . [*Showing the size with both hands.*] Or if I pick up a jug to have a drink of kvass, there's sure to be something horrible, like a cockroach, inside it. [*Pause.*] Have you read Buckle? [*Pause.*] May I trouble you for a moment, Dunyasha? I'd like to speak with you.

DUNYASHA   Well, go ahead.

EPIHODOV   I'd very much like to speak with you alone. [*Sighs.*]

DUNYASHA   [*Embarrassed.*] Oh, all right . . . But first bring me my little cape . . . It's hanging by the cupboard. It's getting terribly chilly . . .

EPIHODOV   Very well, I'll get it. . . . Now I know what to do with my revolver. [*Takes his guitar and goes off playing it.*]

YASHA   Two-and-twenty misfortunes! Just between you and me, he's a stupid fool. [*Yawns.*]

DUNYASHA   I hope to God he doesn't shoot himself. [*Pause.*] He makes me so nervous and I'm always worrying about him. I came to live here when I was still a little girl. Now I no longer know how to live a simple life, and my hands are as white . . . as white as a lady's. I've become such a delicate and sensitive creature. I'm afraid of everything . . . so frightened. If you deceive me, Yasha, I don't know what will happen to my nerves.

YASHA   [*Kisses her.*] You sweet little peach! Just remember, a girl must always control herself. Personally I think nothing is worse than a girl who doesn't behave herself.

DUNYASHA   I love you so much, so passionately! You're so intelligent, you can talk about anything. [*Pause.*]

YASHA   [*Yawns.*] Yes, I suppose so . . . In my opinion, it's like this: if a girl loves someone it means she's immoral. [*Pause.*] I enjoy smoking a cigar in the fresh air . . . [*Listens.*] Someone's coming. It's the ladies and gentlemen.

. . . [DUNYASHA *impulsively embraces him.*] Go to the house now, as though you'd been swimming down at the river. No, this way or they'll see you. I wouldn't want them to think I was interested in you.

DUNYASHA   [*Coughing softly.*]   That cigar has given me such a headache . . . [*Goes out.*]

[YASHA *remains sitting by the shrine. Enter* LYUBOV, GAEV *and* LOPAHIN.]

LOPAHIN   You've got to make up your minds once and for all; there's no time to lose. After all, it's a simple matter. Will you lease your land for the cottages, or won't you? You can answer in one word: yes or no? Just one word!

LYUBOV   Who's been smoking such wretched cigars? [*Sits down.*]

GAEV   How very convenient everything is with the railroad nearby. [*Sits down.*] Well, here we are—we've been to town, had lunch and we're home already. I put the red into the middle pocket! I'd like to go in . . . just for one game. . . .

LYUBOV   You've got lots of time.

LOPAHIN   Just one word! [*Beseechingly.*] Please give me an answer!

GAEV   [*Yawns.*]   What did you say?

LYUBOV   [*Looking into her purse.*]   Yesterday I had lots of money, but today there's practically none left. My poor Varya feeds us all milk soups to economize; the old servants in the kitchen have nothing but dried peas, and here I am wasting money senselessly, I just don't understand it. . . . [*She drops her purse, scattering gold coins.*] Now I've dropped it again. . . . [*Annoyed.*]

YASHA   Allow me, madam, I'll pick them right up. [*Picks up the money.*]

LYUBOV   Thank you, Yasha . . . And why did we go out for lunch today? And that restaurant of yours . . . the food was vile, the music ghastly, and the tablecloths smelled of soap. And Leonid, why do you drink so much? And eat so much? And talk so much? Today at the restaurant you were at it again, and it was all so pointless. About the seventies, and the decadents. And to whom? Really, talking to the waiters about the decadents!

LOPAHIN   Yes, that's too much.

GAEV   [*Waving his hand.*]   I know I'm hopeless. [*To* YASHA, *irritably.*] Why are you always bustling about in front of me?

YASHA   [*Laughs.*]   The minute you open your mouth I start laughing.

GAEV   [*To his sister.*]   Either he goes, or I do. . . .

LYUBOV   Get along, Yasha, you'd better leave us now.

YASHA   [*Hands the purse to* LYUBOV.]   I'm going. [*He can hardly restrain his laughter.*] Right this minute. . . . [*Goes out.*]

LOPAHIN   You know, that rich merchant Deriganov is thinking of buying your estate. They say he's coming to the auction himself.

LYUBOV   Where did you hear that?

LOPAHIN   That's what they say in town.

GAEV   Our Aunt in Yaroslavl has promised to send us some money, but when and how much we don't know.

LOPAHIN   How much will she send? A hundred thousand? Two hundred?

LYUBOV   Well, hardly . . . Ten or fifteen thousand, perhaps. And we should be thankful for that.

LOPAHIN   Forgive me for saying it, but really, in my whole life I've never met such unrealistic, unbusinesslike, queer people as you. You're told in plain language that your estate's going to be sold, and you don't seem to understand it at all.

LYUBOV   But what are we to do? Please, tell us.

LOPAHIN   I keep on telling you. Every day I tell you the same thing. You must lease the cherry orchard and the rest of the land for summer cottages, and you must do it now, as quickly as possible. It's almost time for the auction. Please, try to understand! Once you definitely decide to lease it for the cottages, you'll be able to borrow as much money as you like, and you'll be saved.

LYUBOV Summer cottages and vacationers! Forgive me, but it's so vulgar.

GAEV I agree with you entirely.

LOPAHIN Honestly, I'm going to burst into tears, or scream, or faint. I can't stand it any more! It's more than I can take! [*To* GAEV.] And you're an old woman!

GAEV What did you say?

LOPAHIN I said, you're an old woman!

LYUBOV [*Alarmed.*] No, don't go, please stay. I beg you! Perhaps we can think of something.

LOPAHIN What's there to think of?

LYUBOV Please don't go! I feel so much more cheerful when you're here. [*Pause.*] I keep expecting something horrible to happen . . . as though the house were going to collapse on top of us.

GAEV [*In deep thought.*] I bank it off the cushions, and then into the middle pocket. . . .

LYUBOV We've sinned too much. . . .

LOPAHIN Sinned! What sins have you . . .

GAEV [*Putting a gumdrop into his mouth.*] They say I've eaten up my fortune in gumdrops. [*Laughs.*]

LYUBOV Oh, my sins! Look at the way I've always wasted money. It's madness. And then I married a man who had nothing but debts. And he was a terrible drinker . . . Champagne killed him! And then, as if I hadn't enough misery, I fell in love with someone else. We went off together, and just at that time—it was my first punishment, a blow that broke my heart—my little boy was drowned right here in this river . . . so I went abroad. I went away for good, never to return, never to see this river again . . . I just shut my eyes and ran away in a frenzy of grief, but *he* . . . he followed me. It was so cruel and brutal of him! I bought a villa near Mentone because he fell ill there, and for three years, day and night, I never had any rest. He was very sick, and he completely exhausted me; my soul dried up completely. Then, last year when the villa had to be sold to pay the debts, I went to Paris, and there he robbed me of everything I had and left me for another woman. . . . I tried to poison myself. . . . It was all so stupid, so shameful! And then suddenly I felt an urge to come back to Russia, to my own country, to my little girl . . . [*Dries her tears.*] Oh, Lord, Lord, be merciful, forgive my sins! Don't punish me any more! [*Takes a telegram out of her pocket.*] This came from Paris today. He's asking my forgiveness, he's begging me to return. [*Tears up the telegram.*] Sounds like music somewhere. [*Listens.*]

GAEV That's our famous Jewish orchestra. Don't you remember, four violins, a flute, and a bass?

LYUBOV Are they still playing? Sometime we should have a dance and they could play for us.

LOPAHIN [*Listens.*] I can't hear anything . . . [*Sings quietly.*] "And the Germans, if you pay, will turn Russians into Frenchmen, so they say" . . . [*Laughs.*] I saw a wonderful play last night. It was so funny.

LYUBOV It probably wasn't funny at all. Instead of going to plays, you should take a good look at yourself. Just think how dull your life is, and how much nonsense you talk!

LOPAHIN That's true, I admit it! Our lives are stupid . . . [*Pause.*] My father was a peasant, an idiot. He knew nothing and he taught me nothing. He only beat me when he was drunk, and always with a stick. And as a matter of fact, I'm just as much an idiot myself. I don't know anything and my handwriting's awful. I'm ashamed for people to see it—it's like a pig's.

LYUBOV   You ought to get married, my friend.

LOPAHIN   Yes . . . That's true.

LYUBOV   You ought to marry our Varya. She's a fine girl.

LOPAHIN   Yes.

LYUBOV   She comes from simple people, and she works hard all day long without stopping. But the main thing is she loves you, and you've liked her for a long time yourself.

LOPAHIN   Well. . . . I think it's a fine idea . . . She's a nice girl. [*Pause.*]

GAEV   I've been offered a job at the bank. Six thousand a year. Did I tell you?

LYUBOV   Yes, you did. You'd better stay where you are.

[FEERS *enters, bringing an overcoat.*]

FEERS   [*To* GAEV.]   Please put it on, sir, you might catch cold.

GAEV   [*Puts on the overcoat.*]   Oh, you *are* a nuisance.

FEERS   You must stop this! You went off this morning without letting me know. [*Looks him over.*]

LYUBOV   How you've aged, Feers!

FEERS   What can I do for you, Madam?

LOPAHIN   She says you've aged a lot.

FEERS   I've lived for a long time. They were planning to marry me before your father was born. [*Laughs.*] Why, I was already head butler at the time of the emancipation, but I wouldn't take my freedom, I stayed on with the master and mistress. . . . [*Pause.*] I remember everyone was happy at the time, but what they were happy about, they didn't know themselves.

LOPAHIN   That was the good life all right! All the peasants were flogged!

FEERS   [*Not having heard him.*]   That's right! The peasants belonged to their masters, and the masters belonged to the peasants; but now everything's all confused, and people don't know what to make of it.

GAEV   Be quiet, Feers. Tomorrow I've got to go to town. I've been promised an introduction to some general or other who might lend us some money for the mortgage.

LOPAHIN   Nothing will come of it. And how would you pay the interest, anyway?

LYUBOV   He's talking nonsense again. There aren't any generals.

[*Enter* TROFIMOV, ANYA *and* VARYA.]

GAEV   Here come the children.

ANYA   There's Mamma.

LYUBOV   Come here, my dears. Oh, my darling children. . . . [*Embraces* ANYA *and* VARYA.] If you only knew how much I love you! Here now, sit down beside me. [*All sit down.*]

LOPAHIN   Our perennial student is always with the girls.

TROFIMOV   It's none of your business.

LOPAHIN   He'll soon be fifty, and he's still a student.

TROFIMOV   Oh, stop your stupid jokes.

LOPAHIN   What's bothering you? My, you *are* a strange fellow!

TROFIMOV   Why do you keep pestering me?

LOPAHIN   [*Laughs.*]   Just let me ask you one question: what's your opinion of me?

TROFIMOV   My opinion of you, Yermolay Alexeyevich, is this: you're a rich man, and soon you'll be a millionaire. For the same reason that wild beasts are

THE CHERRY ORCHARD 357

necessary to maintain nature's economic laws, you are necessary, too—each of you devours everything that gets in his way.

[*Everybody laughs.*]

VARYA You'd better talk about the planets, Petya.

LYUBOV No, let's go on with the conversation we had yesterday.

TROFIMOV What was that?

GAEV About pride.

TROFIMOV We talked for a long time yesterday, but we didn't agree on anything. The proud man, the way you use the word, has some mysterious quality about him. Perhaps you're right in a way, but if we look at it simply, without trying to be too subtle, you have to ask yourself why should we be proud at all? Why be proud when you realize that Man, as a species, is poorly constructed physiologically, and is usually coarse, stupid, and profoundly unhappy, too? We ought to put an end to such vanity and just go to work. That's right, we ought to work.

GAEV You'll die just the same, no matter what you do.

TROFIMOV Who knows? And anyway, what does it mean—to die? It could be that man has a hundred senses, and when he dies only the five that are known perish, while the other ninety-five go on living.

LYUBOV How clever you are, Petya!

LOPAHIN [*Ironically.*] Oh, very clever!

TROFIMOV Humanity is continually advancing, is continually seeking to perfect its powers. Someday all the things which we can't understand now, will be made clear. But if this is to happen, we've got to work, work with all our might to help those who are searching for truth. Up until now, here in Russia only a few have begun to work. Nearly all of the intelligentsia that I know have no commitment, they don't do anything, and are as yet incapable of work. They call themselves "the intelligentsia," but they still run roughshod over their servants, and they treat the peasants like animals, they study without achieving anything, they read only childish drivel, and they don't do a thing. As for their knowledge of science, it's only jargon, and they have no appreciation of art either. They are all so serious, and they go about with solemn looks on their faces; they philosophize and talk about important matters; and yet before our very eyes our workers are poorly fed, they live in the worst kind of squalor, sleeping not on beds, but on the floor thirty to forty in a room—with roaches, odors, dampness, and depravity everywhere. It's perfectly clear that all our moralizing is intended to deceive not only ourselves, but others as well. Tell me, where are the nursery schools we're always talking about, where are the libraries? We only write about them in novels, but in actuality there aren't any. There's nothing but dirt, vulgarity, and decadent Orientalism. . . . I'm afraid of those serious faces, I don't like them; I'm afraid of serious talk. It would be better if we'd just keep quiet.

LOPAHIN Well, let me tell you that *I'm* up before five every morning, and I work from morning till night. I always have money, my own and other people's, and I have lots of opportunities to see what the people around me are like. You only have to start doing something to realize how few honest, decent people there are. Sometimes, when I can't sleep, I start thinking about it. God's given us immense forests, and wide-open fields, and unlimited horizons—living in such a world we ought to be giants!

LYUBOV But why do you want giants? They're all right in fairy tales, anywhere else they're terrifying.

[EPIHODOV *crosses the stage in the background, playing his guitar.*]

LYUBOV   [*Pensively.*]   There goes Epihodov. . . .
ANYA   [*Pensively.*]   There goes Epihodov. . . .
GAEV   The sun's gone down, my friends.
TROFIMOV   Yes.
GAEV   [*In a subdued voice, as if reciting a poem.*]   Oh, glorious Nature, shining with eternal light, so beautiful, yet so indifferent to our fate . . . you, whom we call Mother, the wellspring of Life and Death, you live and you destroy. . . .
VARYA   [*Imploringly.*]   Uncle, please!
ANYA   You're doing it again, Uncle!
TROFIMOV   You'd better bank the red into middle pocket.
GAEV   All right, I'll keep quiet.
    [*They all sit deep in thought; the only thing that can be heard is the muttering of* FEERS. *Suddenly there is a sound in the distance, as if out of the sky, like the sound of a harp string breaking, gradually and sadly dying away.*]
LYUBOV   What was that?
LOPAHIN   I don't know. Sounded like a cable broke in one of the mines. But it must've been a long way off.
GAEV   Perhaps it was a bird . . . a heron, maybe.
TROFIMOV   Or an owl. . . .
LYUBOV   [*Shudders.*]   Whatever it was, it sounded unpleasant . . . [*A pause.*]
FEERS   It was the same way before the disaster: the owl hooted and the samovar was humming.
GAEV   What disaster?
FEERS   Before they freed us. [*A pause.*]
LYUBOV   We'd better get started, my friends. It's getting dark and we should get home. [*To* ANYA.] You're crying, my darling! What's wrong? [*She embraces her.*]
ANYA   Nothing, Mamma. It's nothing.
TROFIMOV   Someone's coming.
    [*Enter* A TRAMP *in a battered white hunting cap and an overcoat; he's slightly drunk.*]
TRAMP   Excuse me, but can I get to the station through here?
GAEV   Yes, just follow the road.
TRAMP   Much obliged to you, sir. [*Coughs.*] It's a beautiful day today. [*Declaiming.*] "Oh, my brother, my suffering brother! . . . Come to the Volga, whose groans . . ." [*To* VARYA.] Mademoiselle, could a poor starving Russian trouble you for just enough to . . . [VARYA *cries out, frightened.*]
LOPAHIN   [*Angrily.*]   Really, this is too much!
LYUBOV   [*At a loss what to do.*]   Here, take this . . . here you are. [*Looks in her purse.*] I haven't any silver . . . but that's all right, here's a gold one. . . .
TRAMP   Thank you very much! [*Goes off. Laughter.*]
VARYA   [*Frightened.*]   I'm going. . . . I'm going . . . Oh, Mamma, you know there's not even enough to eat in the house, and you gave him all that!
LYUBOV   Well, what can you do with a silly woman like me? I'll give you everything I've got as soon as we get home. Yermolay Alexeyevich, you'll lend me some more, won't you?
LOPAHIN   Why of course I will.
LYUBOV   Come, it's time to go now. By the way, Varya, we've just about arranged your marriage. Congratulations!
VARYA   [*Through her tears.*]   Don't joke about things like that, Mother!

LOPAHIN Go to a nunnery, Okhmelia! . . .
GAEV Look at how my hands are trembling. I haven't had a game for so long.
LOPAHIN Okhmelia, nymph, remember me in your prayers!
LYUBOV Come along, everybody. It's almost supper time.
VARYA That man frightened me so. My heart's still pounding.
LOPAHIN My friends, just one thing, please just a word: the cherry orchard's to be sold on the 22nd of August. Remember that! Think of what. . . .
[*All go out except* TROFIMOV *and* ANYA.]
ANYA [*Laughs.*] We can thank the tramp for a chance to be alone! He frightened Varya so.
TROFIMOV Varya's afraid—she's afraid we might fall in love—so she follows us about all day long. She's so narrow-minded, she can't understand that we're above falling in love. To free ourselves of all that's petty and ephemeral, all that prevents us from being free and happy, that's the whole aim and meaning of our life. Forward! We march forward irresistibly towards that bright star shining there in the distance! Forward! Don't fall behind, friends!
ANYA [*Raising her hands.*] How beautifully you talk! [*A pause.*] It's wonderful here today.
TROFIMOV Yes, the weather's marvelous.
ANYA What have you done to me, Petya? Why don't I love the cherry orchard like I used to? I used to love it so very much I used to think that there wasn't a better place in all the world than our orchard.
TROFIMOV The whole of Russia is our orchard. The earth is great and beautiful and there are many wonderful places in it. [*A pause.*] Just think, Anya: Your grandfather, and your great grandfather, and all your ancestors were serf owners—they owned living souls. Don't you see human beings staring at you from every tree in the orchard, from every leaf and every trunk? Don't you hear their voices? . . . They owned living souls—and it has made you all different persons, those who came before you, and you who are living now, so that your mother, your uncle and you yourself don't even notice that you're living on credit, at the expense of other people, people you don't admit any further than your kitchen. We're at least two hundred years behind the times; we have no real values, no sense of our past, we just philosophize and complain of how depressed we feel, and drink vodka. Yet it's obvious that if we're ever to live in the present, we must first atone for our past and make a clean break with it, and we can only atone for it by suffering, by extraordinary, unceasing work. You've got to understand that, Anya.
ANYA The house we live in hasn't really been ours for a long time. I'll leave it, I promise you.
TROFIMOV Yes, leave it, and throw away the keys. Be free as the wind.
ANYA [*In rapture.*] How beautifully you say things.
TROFIMOV You must believe me, Anya, you must. I'm not thirty yet, I'm young, and I'm still a student, but I've suffered so much already. As soon as winter comes, I'll be hungry and sick and nervous, poor as a beggar. Fate has driven me everywhere! And yet, my soul is always—every moment of every day and every night—it's always full of such marvelous hopes and visions. I have a premonition of happiness, Anya, I can sense it's coming. . . .
ANYA [*Pensively.*] The moon's coming up.
[EPIHODOV *is heard playing the same melancholy tune on his guitar. The moon comes up. Somewhere near the poplars* VARYA *is looking for* ANYA *and calling.*]
VARYA [*Off-stage.*] Anya! Where are you?

TROFIMOV   Yes, the moon is rising. [*A pause.*] There it is—happiness—it's coming nearer and nearer. Already, I can hear its footsteps. And if we never see it, if we never know it, what does it matter? Others will see it!

[VARYA's *voice.*]   Anya! Where are you?

TROFIMOV   It's Varya again! [*Angrily.*] It's disgusting!

ANYA   Well? Let's go to the river. It's lovely there.

TROFIMOV   Yes, let's. [TROFIMOV *and* ANYA *go out.*]

[VARYA's *voice.*]   Anya! Anya!

CURTAIN

ACT III

> *The drawing room separated by an arch from the ballroom. The same Jewish orchestra that was mentioned in Act II, is playing off-stage. The chandelier is lighted. It is evening. In the ballroom they are dancing the Grand-rond.* SEMYONOV-PISHCHIK *is heard calling:* "Promenade à une paire!" *Then they all enter the drawing room.* PISHCHIK *and* CHARLOTTA IVANOVNA *are the first couple, followed by* TROFIMOV *and* LYUBOV, ANYA *and a* POST-OFFICE CLERK, VARYA *and* THE STATION MASTER, *etc.* VARYA *is crying softly and wipes away her tears as she dances.* DUNYASHA *is in the last couple.* PISHCHIK *shouts:* "Grand rond balancez!" *and* "Les cavaliers à genoux et remerciez vos dames!" FEERS, *wearing a dress coat, crosses the room with soda water on a tray.* PISHCHIK *and* TROFIMOV *come back into the drawing room.*

PISHCHIK   I've got this high blood-pressure—I've had two strokes already, you know—and it makes dancing hard word for me; but, as they say, if you're one of a pack, you wag your tail, whether you bark or not. Actually I'm as strong as a horse. My dear father—may he rest in peace—had a little joke. He used to say that the ancient line of Semyonov-Pishchik was descended from the very same horse that Caligula made a member of the Senate. [*Sitting down.*] But my trouble is, I haven't any money. A starving dog can think of nothing but food . . . [*Starts to snore, but wakes up almost at once.*] That's just like me—I can't think of anything but money . . .

TROFIMOV   You know, you're right, there *is* something horsy about you.

PISHCHIK   Well, a horse is a fine animal, you can sell a horse. . . .

[*The sound of someone playing billiards is heard in the next room.* VARYA *appears under the arch to the ballroom.*]

TROFIMOV   [*Teasing her.*]   Madame Lopahin! Madame Lopahin!

VARYA   [*Angrily.*]   The "moth-eaten man!"

TROFIMOV   Yes, I am a moth-eaten man, and I'm proud of it.

VARYA   [*Thinking bitterly.*]   Now we've hired an orchestra—but how are we going to pay for it? [*Goes out.*]

TROFIMOV   [*To* PISHCHIK.]   If all the energy you've spent during your life looking for money to pay the interest on your debts had been used for something useful, you'd have probably turned the world upside down by now.

PISHCHIK   The philosopher Nietzsche, the greatest, the most famous—a man of the greatest intelligence, in fact—says its quite all right to counterfeit.

TROFIMOV   Oh, you've read Nietzsche?

PISHCHIK Of course not, Dashenka told me. But right now I'm in such an impossible position that I could forge a few notes. The day after tomorrow I've got to pay 310 roubles. I've borrowed 130 already. . . . [*Feels in his pockets, in alarm.*] The money's gone! I've lost the money. [*Tearfully.*] Where's the money? [*Joyfully.*] Oh, here it is, inside the lining! I'm so upset, I'm sweating all over! . . . [*Enter* LYUBOV *and* CHARLOTTA.]

LYUBOV [*Humming the "Lezginka."*] What's taking Leonid so long? What's he doing in town? [*To* DUNYASHA.] Dunyasha, offer the musicians some tea.

TROFIMOV The auction was probably postponed.

LYUBOV The orchestra came at the wrong time, and the party started at the wrong time . . . Oh, well . . . never mind . . . [*She sits down and hums quietly.*]

CHARLOTTA [*Hands a deck of cards to* PISHCHIK.] Here's a deck of cards—think of any card.

PISHCHIK I've thought of one.

CHARLOTTA Now shuffle the deck. That's right. Now give it to me, my dear Monsieur Pishchik. "*Ein, zwei, drei!*" Why look! There it is, in your coat pocket.

PISHCHIK [*Takes the card out of his coat pocket.*] The eight of spades, that's right! [*In astonishment.*] Isn't that amazing!

CHARLOTTA [*Holding the deck of cards on the palm of her hand, to* TROFIMOV.] Quickly, which card's on the top?

TROFIMOV Well . . . ahh . . . the queen of spades.

CHARLOTTA You're right, here it is! Now, which card?

PISHCHIK The ace of hearts.

CHARLOTTA Right again! [*She claps her hand over the pack of cards, which disappears.*] What beautiful weather we're having today!

[*A woman's voice, as if coming from underneath the floor, answers her.*]

VOICE Oh yes, indeed, the weather's perfectly marvelous!

CHARLOTTA [*Addressing the voice.*] How charming you are! I'm fond of you!

VOICE And I like you very much, too.

STATION MASTER [*Applauding.*] Bravo, Madame ventriloquist! Bravo!

PISHCHIK [*Astonished.*] Isn't that amazing! Charlotta Ivanovna, you're absolutely wonderful! I'm completely in love with you!

CHARLOTTA [*Shrugging her shoulders.*] In love? What do you know about love? "*Guter Mensch, aber schlechter Musikant.*"

TROFIMOV [*Slaps* PISHCHIK *on the shoulder.*] He's just an old horse, he is!

CHARLOTTA Your attention please! Here's one more trick. [*She takes a shawl from a chair.*] Now there's this very nice shawl . . . [*Shakes it out.*] Who'd like to buy it?

PISHCHIK [*Amazed.*] Imagine that!

CHARLOTTA "*Ein, zwei, drei!*"

[*She lifts up the shawl and* ANYA *is standing behind it;* ANYA *curtsies, runs to her mother, gives her a hug, and runs back to the ballroom. Everybody's delighted.*]

LYUBOV [*Clapping.*] Bravo, bravo!

CHARLOTTA Once more. "*Ein, zwei, drei!*"

[*Lifts the shawl again; behind it is* VARYA, *who bows.*]

PISHCHIK [*Amazed.*] Isn't that amazing!

CHARLOTTA It's all over!

[*She throws the shawl over* PISHCHIK, *curtsies, and runs into the ballroom.*]

PISHCHIK [*Going after her.*] You little rascal! . . . Have you ever seen anything like her? What a girl . . . [*Goes out.*]

LYUBOV Leonid's still not here. I can't understand what's keeping him all this time in town. Anyway, by now everything's been settled; either the estate's been sold or the auction didn't take place. Why does he wait so long to let us know?

VARYA   [*Trying to comfort her.*]   Uncle's bought it, I'm sure he did.

TROFIMOV   [*Sarcastically.*]   Why of course he did!

VARYA   Our great-aunt sent him power of attorney to buy it in her name, and transfer the mortgage to her. She's done it for Anya's sake . . . God will look after us, I'm sure of it—Uncle will buy the estate.

LYUBOV   Your great-aunt sent us fifteen thousand to buy the estate in her name —she doesn't trust us—but that's not enough to even pay the interest. [*She covers her face with her hands.*] My fate is being decided today, my fate. . . .

TROFIMOV   [*To* VARYA, *teasingly.*]   Madame Lopahin!

VARYA   [*Crossly.*]   The perpetual student! Why, you've been thrown out of the University twice already!

LYUBOV   But why get so cross, Varya? He's only teasing you about Lopahin, there's no harm in that, is there? If you want to, why don't you marry him; he's a fine man, and he's interesting, too. Of course, if you don't want to, don't. No one's trying to force you, darling.

VARYA   I'm very serious about this. Mother . . . and I want to be frank with you . . . he's a good man and I like him.

LYUBOV   Then marry him. What are you waiting for? I don't understand you at all.

VARYA   But, Mother, I can't propose to him myself, can I? It's been two years now since everybody began talking to me about him, and everybody's talking, but he doesn't say a word, or when he does, he just jokes with me. I understand, of course. He's getting rich and his mind's busy with other things, and he hasn't any time for me. If only I had some money, even a little, just a hundred roubles, I'd leave everything and go away, the farther the better. I'd go into a convent.

TROFIMOV   How beautiful!

VARYA   [*To* TROFIMOV.]   Of course, a student like you has to be so intelligent! [*Quietly and tearfully.*] How ugly you've become, Petya, how much older you look! [*To* LYUBOV, *her tearfulness gone.*] The only thing I can't stand, Mother, is not having any work to do. I've got to stay busy.
[*Enter* YASHA.]

YASHA   [*With difficulty restraining his laughter.*]   Epihodov's broken a cue! . . . [*Goes out.*]

VARYA   But what's Epihodov doing here? Who let him play billiards? I don't understand these people. . . . [*Goes out.*]

LYUBOV   Please don't tease her, Petya. Don't you see she's upset already?

TROFIMOV   Oh, she's such a busy-body—always sticking her nose into other people's business. She hasn't left Anya and me alone all summer. She's afraid we might fall in love. What difference should it make to her? Besides, I didn't give her any reason to think so. I don't believe in such trivialities. We're above love!

LYUBOV   And I suppose I'm below love. [*Uneasily.*] Why isn't Leonid back? If only I knew whether the estate's been sold or not. It's such an incredible calamity that for some reason I don't know what to think, I feel so helpless. I think I'm going to scream this very minute . . . I'll do something silly. Help me, Petya. Talk to me, say something!

TROFIMOV   What difference does it make whether the estate's sold today or not? It was gone a long time ago. You can't turn back, the path's lost. You mustn't worry, and above all you mustn't deceive yourself. For once in your life you must look the truth straight in the face.

LYUBOV What truth? *You* know what truth is and what it isn't, but I've lost
such visionary powers. I don't see anything. You're able to solve all your
problems so decisively—but, tell me, my dear boy, isn't that because you're
young, because life is still hidden from your young eyes, because you can't
believe anything horrible will ever happen to you and you don't expect it
to? Oh, yes, you're more courageous and honest and serious than we are,
but put yourself in our position, try to be generous—if only a little bit—
and have pity on me. I was born here, you know, and my father and mother
lived here, and my grandfather, too, and I love this house—I can't conceive
of life without the cherry orchard, and if it really has to be sold, then sell
me with it . . . [*Embraces* TROFIMOV, *kisses him on the forehead.*] You know,
my little boy was drowned here. . . . [*Weeps.*] Have pity on me, my dear,
kind friend.

TROFIMOV You know that I sympathize with you from the bottom of my heart.

LYUBOV But you should say it differently . . . differently. [*Takes out her handkerchief and a telegram falls on to the floor.*] There's so much on my mind
today, you can't imagine. It's so noisy around here that my soul trembles
with every sound, and I'm shaking all over—yet I can't go to my room because the silence of being alone frightens me. . . . Don't blame me, Petya.
. . . I love you as if you were my own son. I'd gladly let Anya marry you,
honestly I would, but, my dear boy, you must study, you've got to graduate.
You don't do anything, Fate tosses you from one place to another—it's so
strange—Well, it is, isn't it? Isn't it? And you should do something about
your beard, make it grow somehow. . . . [*Laughs.*] You look so funny!

TROFIMOV [*Picks up the telegram.*] I don't care how I look. That's so superficial.

LYUBOV This telegram's from Paris. I get one every day . . . Yesterday, today.
That beast is sick again, and everything's going wrong for him. . . . He
wants me to forgive him, he begs me to return, and, really, I suppose I
should go to Paris and stay with him for awhile. You're looking very stern,
Petya, but what am I to do, my dear boy, what am I to do? He's sick, and
lonely, and unhappy, and who'll take care of him, who'll stop him from
making a fool of himself, and give him his medicine at the right time? And
anyway, why should I hide it, or keep quiet about it? I love him; yes, I love
him. I do, I do. . . . He's a stone around my neck, and I'm sinking to the
bottom with him—but I love him and I can't live without him. [*She presses*
TROFIMOV's *hand.*] Don't think I'm evil, Petya, don't say anything, please
don't. . . .

TROFIMOV [*With strong emotion.*] Please—forgive my frankness, but that
man's swindling you!

LYUBOV No, no, no, you mustn't talk like that. . . .
[*Puts her hands over her ears.*]

TROFIMOV But he's a scoundrel, and you're the only one who doesn't know it!
He's a despicable, worthless scoundrel. . . .

LYUBOV [*Angry, but in control of herself.*] You're twenty-six or twenty-seven
years old, but you're talking like a schoolboy!

TROFIMOV Say whatever you want!

LYUBOV You should be a man at your age, you ought to understand what it
means to be in love. And you should be in love. . . . Tell me, why haven't
you fallen in love! [*Angrily.*] Yes, yes! Oh, you're not so "pure," your purity
is a perversion, you're nothing but a ridiculous prude, a freak. . . .

TROFIMOV [*Horrified.*] What is she saying?

LYUBOV "I'm above love!" You're not above love, you're useless, as Feers would
say. Imagine not having a mistress at your age! . . .

TROFIMOV   [*Horrified.*]   This is terrible! What's she saying? [*Goes quickly towards the ballroom, clutching his head between his hands.*] This is dreadful. . . . I can't stand it, I'm going. . . . [*Goes out, but returns at once.*] Everything's over between us!
[*Goes out through the door into the hall.*]

LYUBOV   [*Calls after him.*]   Petya, wait! You funny boy, I was only joking! Petya!
[*Someone can be heard running quickly downstairs and suddenly falling down with a crash.* ANYA *and* VARYA *scream, and then begin laughing.*] What's happened?
[ANYA *runs in.*]

ANYA   [*Laughing.*]   Petya fell down the stairs. [*Runs out.*]

LYUBOV   What a strange boy he is!
[*The* STATION MASTER *stands in the middle of the ballroom and begins to recite "The Sinner" by Alexey Tolstoy. The others listen to him, but he's hardly had time to recite more than a little bit when a waltz is played, and he stops. Everyone dances.* TROFIMOV, ANYA, VARYA *come in from the hall.*] Poor Petya . . . there, my dear boy . . . Please forgive me . . . Come, let's dance . . . [*She dances with* PETYA. ANYA *and* VARYA *dance. Enter* FEERS, *then* YASHA. FEERS *leans on his cane by the side door.* YASHA *looks at the dancers from the drawing room.*]

YASHA   How are you, old boy?

FEERS   Not too well . . . We used to have generals, barons, and admirals at our parties . . . long ago, but now we send for the post-office clerk and the station master, and even they don't want to come it seems. I seem to be getting weaker somehow . . . My old master, the mistress' grandfather, used to make everyone take sealing wax no matter what was wrong with them. I've been taking it every day for the last twenty years, maybe even longer. Perhaps that's why I'm still alive.

YASHA   How you bore me, old man! [*Yawns.*] Why don't you just go away and die . . . It's about time.

FEERS   Eh, you! . . . You're useless . . . [*Mutters.*]
[TROFIMOV *and* LYUBOV *dancing, come into the drawing room.*]

LYUBOV   Thank you. I think I'll sit down for a bit. [*Sits down.*] I'm tired.
[*Enter* ANYA.]

ANYA   [*Agitated.*]   There's a man in the kitchen who's been saying that the cherry orchard was sold today.

LYUBOV   Sold? To whom?

ANYA   He didn't say. He's gone.
[*She and* TROFIMOV *dance into the ballroom.*]

YASHA   There was some old man gossiping there. A stranger.

FEERS   Leonid Andreyevich isn't back yet, he hasn't come yet. And he's only got his light overcoat on; he'll probably catch a cold. Oh, these youngsters!

LYUBOV   I've got to know, or I think I'll die. Yasha, go and find out who bought it.

YASHA   But the old guy went away a long time ago. [*Laughs.*]

LYUBOV   [*With a touch of annoyance.*]   What are you laughing at? What's so humorous?

YASHA   Epihodov's so funny—he's so stupid. Two-and-twenty misfortunes!

LYUBOV   Feers, if the estate's sold, where will you go?

FEERS   I'll go wherever you tell me to go.

LYUBOV   Why are you looking like that? Aren't you well? You ought to be in bed.

FEERS   Yes . . . [*With a faint smile.*] But if I went to bed, who'd take care of the guests and keep things going? There's no one in the house but me.

YASHA [*To* LYUBOV.] Lyubov Andreyevna! I want to ask you something! If you go back to Paris, will you please take me with you? I couldn't stand staying here. [*Looking round and speaking in a low voice.*] I don't have to say it, you can see for yourself how uncivilized everything is here. The people are immoral, it's frightfully dull, and the food is terrible. And then there's that Feers walking about the place and muttering all sorts of stupid things. Take me with you, please!

[*Enter* PISHCHIK.]

PISHCHIK May I have this dance, beautiful lady . . . [LYUBOV *gets up to dance.*] I'll have that 180 roubles from you yet, you enchantress . . . Yes, I will . . . [*Dances.*] Just 180 roubles, that's all . . .

[*They go into the ballroom.*]

YASHA [*Sings quietly.*] "Don't you understand the passion in my soul? . . . [*In the ballroom a woman in a grey top hat and check trousers starts jumping and throwing her arms about; shouts of:* "Bravo, Charlotta Ivanovna!"]

DUNYASHA [*Stops to powder her face.*] Anya told me to dance: there are so many men and not enough ladies; but I get so dizzy from dancing and it makes my heart beat so fast. Feers Nikolayevich, the post-office clerk said something to me just now that completely took my breath away.

[*The music stops.*]

FEERS What did he say?

DUNYASHA You're like a flower, he said.

YASHA [*Yawns.*] What ignorance! . . .

[*Goes out.*]

DUNYASHA Like a flower . . . I'm so sensitive, I love it when people say beautiful things to me.

FEERS You'll be having your head turned if you're not careful.

[*Enter* EPIHODOV.]

EPIHODOV Avdotya Fyodorovna, you act as if you don't want to see me . . . as if I were some kind of insect. [*Sighs.*] Such is life!

DUNYASHA What do you want?

EPIHODOV But then, you may be right. [*Sighs.*] Of course, if one looks at it from a certain point of view—if I may so express myself, and please excuse my frankness, you've driven me into such a state . . . Oh, I know what my fate is; every day some misfortune's sure to happen to me, but I've long since been accustomed to that, so I look at life with a smile. You gave me your word, and though I . . .

DUNYASHA Please, let's talk later, just let me alone now. I'm lost in a dream. [*Plays with her fan.*]

EPIHODOV Some misfortune happens to me every day, but I—how should I put it—I just smile, I even laugh.

[VARYA *enters from the ballroom.*]

VARYA Are you still here, Semyon? Your manners are abominable, really! [*To* DUNYASHA.] You'd better go now, Dunyasha. [*To* EPIHODOV.] First you play billiards and break a cue, and now you're going about the drawing room, like one of the guests.

EPIHODOV Permit me to inform you, but you have no right to attack me like this.

VARYA I'm not attacking, I'm telling you. You just wander from one place to another, instead of doing your work. We've hired a clerk, but why no one knows.

EPIHODOV [*Offended.*] Whether I work, wander, eat, or play billiards, the only people who are entitled to judge my actions are those who are older than me and have some idea of what they're talking about.

VARYA How dare you say that to me? [*Beside herself in anger.*] You dare to say

that? Are you suggesting that I don't know what I'm talking about? Get out
of here! Right now!

EPIHODOV   [*Cowed.*]   I wish you'd express yourself more delicately. ✸

VARYA   [*Beside herself.*]   Get out this minute! Get out! [*He goes to the door,
she follows him.*] Two-and-twenty misfortunes! Get out of here! I don't
want ever to see you again!

EPIHODOV   [*Goes out; his voice is heard from outside the door.*]   I'm going to
complain.

VARYA   Oh, you're coming back, are you? [*She seizes the stick which* FEERS *left
by the door.*] Well, come along, come in . . . I'll show you! So, you're coming
back . . . are you? There, take that . . .
    [*Swings the stick, and at that moment* LOPAHIN *comes in.*]

LOPAHIN   [*Whom the stick did not, in fact, touch.*]   Thank you very much!

VARYA   [*Angry and ironically.*]   I'm sorry!

LOPAHIN   Don't mention it. I'm much obliged to you for the kind reception.

VARYA   That's quite all right. [*Walks away and then looks around and asks
gently.*] I haven't hurt you, have I?

LOPAHIN   No, not at all. . . . But there's going to be a huge bump, though.

VOICES   [*In the ballroom.*]   Lopahin's here! Yermolay Alexeyevich!

PISHCHIK   There he is! You can see him, do you hear him? . . . [*Embraces*
LOPAHIN.] You smell of cognac, my good fellow! . . . Well we're having a
party here, too.
    [*Enter* LYUBOV.]

LYUBOV   It's you, Yermolay Alexeyevich? What's taken you to long? Where's
Leonid?

LOPAHIN   Leonid Andreyevich's here, he'll be along in a minute.

LYUBOV   [*Agitated.*]   Well, what happened? Was there an auction? Tell me!

LOPAHIN   [*Embarrassed, afraid of betraying his joy.*]   The auction was over by
four o'clock . . . We missed our train and had to wait until nine-thirty.
[*Sighs heavily.*] Ugh! I feel a little dizzy . . .
    [*Enter* GAEV; *he carries packages in his right hand and wipes away his tears
with his left.*]

LYUBOV   Leonid, what happened? Leonid? [*Impatiently, with tears.*] Tell me
quickly, for God's sake! . . .

GAEV   [*Doesn't answer, but waves his hand. To* FEERS, *crying.*] Here, take these
    . . . it's some anchovies and Kerch herrings . . . I haven't eaten all day . . .
What I've been through!
    [*Through the open door leading to the ballroom a game of billards can be
heard and* YASHA's *voice is heard.*]

YASHA   Seven and eighteen.

GAEV   [*His expression changes and he stops crying.*]   I'm very tired. Come, Feers,
I want to change my things.
    [*Goes out through the ballroom, followed by* FEERS.]

PISHCHIK   Well, what happened at the auction? Come on, tell us!

LYUBOV   Has the cherry orchard been sold?

LOPAHIN   It has.

LYUBOV   Who bought it?

LOPAHIN   I did.
    [*A pause.* LYUBOV *is overcome; only the fact that she is standing beside a
table and a chair keeps her from falling.* VARYA *takes the keys from her belt,
throws them on the floor in the middle of the room and goes out.*]
    I bought it. Wait a moment, ladies and gentlemen, please. I'm so mixed
up, I don't quite know what to say . . . [*Laughs.*] When we got to the auction, Deriganov was already there. Leonid had only fifteen thousand roubles,

and immediately Deriganov bid thirty thousand over and above the mortgage. I saw how things were, so I stepped in and raised it to forty. He bid forty-five, I went to fifty-five; he kept on raising five thousand and I raised it ten thousand. Well, finally it ended—I bid ninety thousand over and above the mortgage, and it went to me. The cherry orchard's mine now! All right, tell me I'm drunk, tell me I'm crazy and that I'm just imagining all this. . . . [*Stamps his feet.*] Don't laugh at me! If only my father and grandfather could rise from their graves and see all that's happened . . . how their Yermolay, their ignorant, beaten Yermolay, the little boy that ran around in his bare feet in the winter . . . if only they could see that he's bought this estate, the most beautiful place in the world! Yes, he's bought the very estate where his father and grandfather were slaves and where they weren't even admitted to the kitchen! I must be asleep, I'm dreaming, it only seems to be true . . . it's all just my imagination, my imagination must be confused . . . [*Picks up the keys, smiling gently.*] She threw these down because she wanted to show that she's not the mistress here anymore. [*Jingles the keys.*] Well, never mind. [*The orchestra is heard tuning up.*] Hey there! you musicians, play something for us! I want some music! My friends, come along and soon you'll see Yermolay Lopahin take an axe to the cherry orchard, you'll see the trees come crashing to the ground! We're going to build hundreds of summer cottages, and our children and our grandchildren will see a whole new world growing up here . . . So play, let's have some music!
[*The band plays.* LYUBOV *has sunk into a chair and is crying bitterly. Reproachfully.*]
Why, why didn't you listen to me? My poor, dear lady, you'll never get it back now. [*With tears.*] Oh, if only all this could be over soon, if only we could change this unhappy and disjointed life of ours somehow!
PISHCHIK   [*Taking his arm, in a low voice.*] She's crying. Come into the ballroom, let her be by herself . . . Come on . . .
[*Takes his arm and leads him away to the ballroom.*]
LOPAHIN   What's the matter! Where's the music? Come on, play! Play! Everything will be as *I* want it now. [*Ironically.*] Here comes the new owner, here comes the owner of the cherry orchard! [*He tips over a little table accidentally and nearly upsets the candelabra.*] Don't worry about it, I can pay for everything!
[*Goes out with* PISHCHIK. *There is no one left in the ballroom or drawing room, but* LYUBOV, *who sits huddled up in a chair, crying bitterly. The orchestra continues to play quietly.* ANYA *and* TROFIMOV *enter quickly;* ANYA *goes up to her mother and kneels beside her,* TROFIMOV *remains at the entrance to the ballroom.*]
ANYA   Mamma! . . . Mamma, you're crying. Dear, kind, good Mamma, my precious one, I love you! God bless you, Mamma! The cherry orchard's sold, that's true, it's gone, but don't cry, Mamma, you still have your life ahead of you, you still have your good, innocent heart. You must come with me, Mamma, away from here! We'll plant a new orchard, even more wonderful than this one—and when you see it, you'll understand everything, and your heart will be filled with joy, like the sun in the evening; and then you'll smile again, Mamma! Come, dearest one, come with me! . . .

CURTAIN

ACT IV

> *The same setting as for Act I. There are no pictures on the walls, or curtains at the windows; most of the furniture is gone and the few remaining pieces are stacked in a corner, as if for sale. There is a sense of desolation. Beside the door, suitcases and other luggage have been piled together. The voices of* VARYA *and* ANYA *can be heard through the door on the left, which is open.* LOPAHIN *stands waiting;* YASHA *is holding a tray with glasses of champagne. In the hall* EPIHODOV *is tying up a large box. Off-stage there is a low hum of voices; the peasants have called to say good-bye.* GAEV's *voice from off-stage.*

GAEV   Thank you, friends, thank you.

YASHA   The peasants have come to say good-bye. In my opinion, Yermolay Alexeyevich, they're good people, but they don't know much.
   [*The hum subsides.* LYUBOV *and* GAEV *enter from the hall;* LYUBOV *is not crying but her face is pale and it quivers. She is unable to speak.*]

GAEV   You gave them everything you had, Lyuba. You shouldn't have done that. You really shouldn't.

LYUBOV   I couldn't help it! I couldn't help it! [*Both go out.*]

LOPAHIN   [*Calls after them through the door.*] Please, have some champagne, please do! Just a little glass before you go. I didn't think to bring some from town, and at the station I could find only this one bottle. Please have some. [*A pause.*] You don't want any, my friends? [*Walks away from the door.*] If I'd known that, I wouldn't have brought it. . . . Well, then I won't have any either. [YASHA *carefully puts the tray on a chair.*] Have a drink, Yasha, nobody else wants any.

YASHA   To the travelers! And to those staying behind. [*Drinks.*] This champagne isn't the real thing, believe me.

LOPAHIN   What do you mean, eight roubles a bottle. [*A pause.*] God, it's cold in here.

YASHA   The stoves weren't lit today. What difference does it make since we're leaving? [*Laughs.*]

LOPAHIN   Why are you laughing?

YASHA   Because I feel good.

LOPAHIN   It's October already, but it's still sunny and clear, just like summer. Good building weather. [*Looks at his watch, then at the door.*] Ladies and gentlemen, the train leaves in forty-seven minutes. We've got to start in twenty minutes. So hurry up.
   [TROFIMOV, *wearing an overcoat, comes in from outdoors.*]

TROFIMOV   It's time we get started. The horses are ready. God knows where my goloshes are, they've disappeared. [*Calls through the door.*] Anya, my goloshes aren't here; I can't find them.

LOPAHIN   I've got to go to Kharkov. I'm taking the same train. I'll be spending the winter in Kharkov: I've stayed around here too long, and it drives me crazy having nothing to do. I can't be without work: I just don't know what to do with my hands; they hang there, as if they didn't belong to me.

TROFIMOV   We'll be gone soon, then you can start making money again.

LOPAHIN   Have a drink.

TROFIMOV   No, thanks.

LOPAHIN   So, you're going to Moscow?

TROFIMOV   Yes, I'll go with them to town, and then, tomorrow I'll leave for Moscow.

LOPAHIN   I suppose the professors are waiting for you to come before they begin classes.

TROFIMOV   That's none of your business.

LOPAHIN   How many years have you been studying at the university?

TROFIMOV   Can't you say something new for a change, that's getting pretty old. [*Looks for his goloshes.*] By the way, since we probably won't see each other again, let me give you a bit of advice, as we say good-bye: stop waving your arms! Try to get rid of that habit of making wide, sweeping gestures. And another thing, all this talk about building estates, these calculations about summer tourists that are going to buy property, all these predictions—they're all sweeping gestures, too. . . . You know, in spite of everything, I like you. You've got beautiful delicate fingers, like an artist's, you've a fine, sensitive soul. . . .

LOPAHIN   [*Embraces him.*]   Good-bye, my friend. Thanks for everything. I can give you some money for your trip, if you need it.

TROFIMOV   What for? I don't need it.

LOPAHIN   But you haven't got any!

TROFIMOV   Yes, I have, thank you. I got some money for a translation. Here it is, in my pocket. [*Anxiously.*] But I can't find my goloshes.

VARYA   [*From the other room.*]   Here, take the nasty things!
   [*She throws a pair of rubber goloshes into the room.*]

TROFIMOV   What are you so angry about, Varya? Hm . . . but these aren't my goloshes!

LOPAHIN   I sowed three thousand acres of poppies last spring, and I've made forty thousand on it. And when they were in bloom, what a picture it was! What I mean to say is that I've made the forty thousand, so now I can lend you some money. Why be so stuck up? So I'm a peasant . . . I speak right out.

TROFIMOV   Your father was a peasant, mine was a druggist. What's that got to do with it? [LOPAHIN *takes out his wallet.*] Forget it, put it away . . . Even if you offered me two hundred thousand, I wouldn't take it. I'm a free man. And all that you rich men—and poor men too—all that you value so highly doesn't have the slightest power over me—it's all just so much fluff floating about in the air. I'm strong and I'm proud! I can get along without you, I can pass you by. Humanity is advancing towards the highest truth, the greatest happiness that it's possible to achieve on earth, and I'm one of the avant-garde!

LOPAHIN   Will you get there?

TROFIMOV   Yes. [*A pause.*] I'll get there myself, or show others the way to get there.
   [*The sound of an axe hitting a tree is heard in the distance.*]

LOPAHIN   Well, my friend, it's time to go. Good-bye. We show off in front of one another, and all the time life is slipping by. When I work all day long, without resting, I'm happier and sometimes I even think I know why I exist. But how many people there are in Russia, my friend, who exist for no reason at all. But, never mind, it doesn't matter. They say Leonid Andreyevich has a job at the bank, at six thousand a year. That won't last long; he's too lazy. . . .

ANYA   [*In the doorway.*]   Mamma begs you not to let them cut down the orchard until we've left.

TROFIMOV   Really, haven't you got any tact?
   [*Goes out through the hall.*]

LOPAHIN   All right, I'll take care of it. . . . These people!
   [*Follows* TROFIMOV.]

ANYA   Has Feers been taken to the hospital?

YASHA   I told them to take him this morning. He's gone, I think.

ANYA   [*To* EPIHODOV, *who passes through the ballroom.*] Semyon Pantaleye-vich, will you please find out whether Feers has been taken to the hospital?

YASHA   [*Offended.*]   I told Yegor this morning. Why ask a dozen times?

EPIHODOV   That old Feers—frankly speaking, I mean—he's beyond repair, it's time he joined his ancestors. As for me, I can only envy him. [*He places a suitcase on top of a cardboard hatbox and squashes it.*] There you are, you see! . . . I might have known it!
    [*Goes out.*]

YASHA   [*Sardonically.*]   Two-and-twenty misfortunes!

VARYA   [*From behind the door.*]   Has Feers been taken to the hospital?

ANYA   Yes.

VARYA   Why wasn't the letter to the doctor taken then?

ANYA   I'll send someone after them with it . . .
    [*Goes out.*]

VARYA   [*From the adjoining room.*]   Where's Yasha? Tell him his mother is here and wants to say good-bye to him.

YASHA   [*Waves his hand.*]   This is too much! I'll lose my patience.
    [*While the foregoing action has been taking place,* DUNYASHA *has been busy with the luggage; now that* YASHA *is alone, she comes up to him.*]

DUNYASHA   If only you'd look at me just once, Yasha! You're going . . . you're leaving me! . . . [*She cries and throws her arms round his neck.*]

YASHA   What are you crying for? [*Drinks champagne.*] In a week I'll be in Paris again. Tomorrow we'll get on the train—and off we'll go—gone! I can't believe it. *"Vive la France!"* I can't stand it here and could never live here—nothing ever happens. I've seen enough of all this ignorance. I've had enough of it. [*Drinks.*] What are you crying for? Behave yourself properly, then you won't cry.

DUNYASHA   [*Looking into a handmirror and powdering her nose.*]   Please, write to me from Paris. You know how much I've loved you, Yasha. Oh, I've loved you so much! I'm very sensitive, Yasha!

YASHA   Sshh, someone's coming. [*Pretends to be busy with a suitcase, humming quietly.*]
    [*Enter* LYUBOV ANDREYEVNA, GAEV, ANYA *and* CHARLOTTA IVANOVNA.]

GAEV   We've got to leave soon. There isn't much time left. [*Looks at* YASHA.] What a smell! Who's been eating herring?

LYUBOV   We'll have to leave in the carriage in ten minutes. [*Looks about the room.*] Good-bye, dear house, the home of our fathers. Winter will pass and spring will come again, and then you won't be here any more, you'll be torn down. How much these walls have seen! [*Kisses her daughter passionately.*] My little treasure, how radiant you look, your eyes are shining like diamonds. Are you glad? Very glad?

ANYA   Oh, yes, very glad, Mamma! Our new life is just beginning!

GAEV   [*Gaily.*]   Really, everything's all right now. Before the cherry orchard was sold we were all worried and upset, but as soon as things were settled once and for all, we all calmed down and even felt quite cheerful. I'm working in a bank now, a real financier. . . . The red into the side pocket . . . And say what you like, Lyuba, you're looking much better. No doubt about it.

LYUBOV   Yes, that's true, my nerves are better. [*Someone helps her on with her hat and coat.*] I'm sleeping better, too. Take out my things, Yasha, it's time. [*To* ANYA.] My little darling, we'll be seeing each other again soon. I'm going to Paris—I'll live on the money which your Grandmother sent us to buy

the estate—God bless Grandmamma!—but that money won't last very long
either.

ANYA You'll come back soon, Mamma . . . won't you? I'll study and pass my
exams and then I'll work and help you. We'll read together, Mamma . . .
all sort of things . . . won't we? [*She kisses her mother's hands.*] We'll read
during the long autumn evenings. We'll read lots of books, and a new
wonderful world will open up before us . . . [*Dreamily.*] Mamma, come back
soon . . .

LYUBOV I'll come back, my precious. [*Embraces her.*]

[*Enter* LOPAHIN. CHARLOTTA *quietly sings to herself.*]

GAEV Happy Charlotta! She's singing.

CHARLOTTA [*Picks up a bundle that looks like a baby in a blanket.*] Bye-bye,
little baby. [*A sound like a baby crying is heard.*] Hush, be quiet, my
darling, be a good little boy. [*The "crying" continues.*] Oh, my baby, you
poor thing! [*Throws the bundle down.*] Are you going to find me another
job? If you don't mind, I've got to have one.

LOPAHIN We'll find you one, Charlotta Ivanovna, don't worry.

GAEV Everybody's leaving us, Varya's going away . . . all of a sudden nobody
wants us.

CHARLOTTA There's no place for me to live in town. I'll have to go. [*Hums.*]
Oh, well, what do I care. [*Enter* PISHCHIK.]

LOPAHIN Look what's here!

PISHCHIK [*Gasping for breath.*] Oohhh, let me get my breath . . . I'm worn
out . . . My good friends. . . . Give me some water . . .

GAEV I suppose you want to borrow some money? I'm going . . . Excuse me . . .
[*Goes out.*]

PISHCHIK I haven't seen you for a long time . . . my beautiful lady . . . [*To*
LOPAHIN.] You're here, too . . . glad to see you . . . you're a man of great
intelligence . . . here . . . take this . . . [*Gives money to* LOPAHIN.] Four
hundred roubles . . . I still owe you eight hundred and forty. . . .

LOPAHIN [*Shrugging his shoulders in amazement.*] It's like a dream. . . .
Where did you get it?

PISHCHIK Wait a minute . . . I'm so hot . . . A most extraordinary thing happened. Some Englishman came along and discovered some kind of white clay
on my land. . . . [*To* LYUBOV.] Here's four hundred for you also, my dear
. . . enchantress . . . [*Gives her the money.*] You'll get the rest later. [*Takes
a drink of water.*] A young man on the train was just telling me that some
great philosopher advises people to jump off roofs. You just jump off, he
says, and that settles the whole problem. [*Amazed at what he has just said.*]
Imagine that! More water, please

LOPAHIN What Englishmen?

PISHCHIK I leased the land to them for twenty-four years. . . . And now you
must excuse me, I'm in a hurry and have to get on. I'm going to Znoikov's,
then to Kardamonov's . . . I owe them all money. [*Drinks.*] Your health.
I'll come again on Thursday . . .

LYUBOV We're just leaving for town, and tomorrow I'm going abroad.

PISHCHIK What's that? [*In agitation.*] Why to town? Oh, I see . . . this furniture
and the suitcases. . . . Well, never mind . . . [*Tearfully.*] What difference
does it make. . . . These Englishmen, you know, they're very intelligent . . .
Never mind. . . . I wish you all the best, God bless you. Never mind, everything comes to an end eventually. [*Kisses* LYUBOV'*s hand.*] And when you
hear that my end has come, just think of a horse, and say: "There used to
be a man like that once . . . his name was Semyonov-Pishchik—God bless
him!" Wonderful weather we're having. Yes . . . [*Goes out embarrassed,*

but returns at once and stands in the doorway.] Dashenka sends her greetings. [*Goes out.*]

LYUBOV   Well, we can get started now. I'm leaving with two worries on my mind. One is Feers—he's sick. [*Glances at her watch.*] We've still got five minutes. . . .

ANYA   Mamma, Feers has been taken to the hospital. Yasha sent him this morning.

LYUBOV   The other is Varya. She's used to getting up early and working, and now, with nothing to do, she's like a fish out of water. She's gotten so thin and pale, and she cries a lot, the poor dear. [*A pause.*] You know very well, Yermolay Alexeyevich, that I've been hoping you two would get married . . . and everything pointed to it. [*Whispers to* ANYA *and motions to* CHARLOTTA, *and they both go out.*] She loves you, and you're fond of her, too . . . I just don't know, I don't know why you seem to avoid each other. I don't understand it.

LOPAHIN   Neither do I, I admit it. The whole thing's so strange. . . . If there's still time, I'm ready to. . . . Let's settle it at once—and get it over with! Without you here, I don't feel I'll ever propose to her.

LYUBOV   That's an excellent idea! You won't need more than a minute. I'll call her at once.

LOPAHIN   And there's champagne here, too, we'll celebrate. [*Looks at the glasses.*] They're empty, someone's drunk it all. [YASHA *coughs.*] They must have poured it down.

LYUBOV   [*With animation.*] Oh, I'm so glad. I'll call her, and we'll leave you alone. Yasha, "allez!" [*Through the door.*] Varya, come here for a minute, leave what you're doing and come here! Varya! [*Goes out with* YASHA.]

LOPAHIN   [*Looking at his watch.*] Yes. . . .

[*A pause. Whispering and suppressed laughter are heard behind the door, then* VARYA *comes in and starts fussing with the luggage. At last she says:*]

VARYA   That's strange, I can't find it. . . .

LOPAHIN   What are you looking for?

VARYA   I packed it myself, and I can't remember . . . [*A pause.*]

LOPAHIN   Where are you going to now, Varvara Mihailovna?

VARYA   I? To the Rogulins. I've taken a job as their housekeeper.

LOPAHIN   That's in Yashnevo, isn't it? Almost seventy miles from here. [*A pause.*] So this is the end of life in this house. . . .

VARYA   [*Still fussing with the luggage.*] Where could it be? Perhaps I put it in the trunk? Yes, life in this house has come to an end . . . there won't be any more. . . .

LOPAHIN   And I'm going to Kharkov. . . . On the next train. I've got a lot of work to do there. I'm leaving Epihodov here. . . . I've hired him.

VARYA   Really! . . .

LOPAHIN   Remember, last year at this time it was snowing already, but now it's still so bright and sunny. Though it's cold . . . Three degrees of frost.

VARYA   I haven't looked. [*A pause.*] Besides, our thermometer's broken. . . .

[*A pause. A voice is heard from outside the door.*]

VOICE   Yermolay Alexeyevich!

LOPAHIN   [*As if he had been waiting for it.*] I'm coming! Right away! [*Goes out quickly.*]

[VARYA *sits on the floor, with her head on a bundle of clothes, crying quietly. The door opens,* LYUBOV *enters hesitantly.*]

LYUBOV   Well? [*A pause.*] We must be going.

VARYA   [*Stops crying and wipes her eyes.*] Yes, Mamma, it's time we got started. I'll just have time to get to the Rogulins today, if we don't miss the train.

LYUBOV   [*Calls through the door.*] Anya, put your things on. [*Enter* ANYA, *fol-*

lowed by GAEV *and* CHARLOTTA. GAEV *wears a heavy overcoat with a hood. Servants and coachmen come into the room.* EPIHODOV *is picking up the luggage.*] Now we can begin our journey!

ANYA   [*Joyfully.*]   Our journey!

GAEV   My friends, my dear, beloved friends! As I leave this house forever, how can I be silent, how can I refrain from expressing to you, as I say good-bye for the last time, the feelings which now overwhelm me. . . .

ANYA   [*Begging.*]   Uncle!

VARYA   Uncle, please don't!

GAEV   [*Downcast.*]   I put the red into the corner and then . . . I'll keep quiet. [*Enter* TROFIMOV *and* LOPAHIN.]

TROFIMOV   Well, ladies and gentlemen, it's time we get started.

LOPAHIN   Epihodov, my coat!

LYUBOV   I'll just stay for one more minute. It seems as if I'd never seen the walls and ceilings of this house before, and now I look at them with such longing, such love. . . .

GAEV   I remember when I was six—it was Trinity Sunday . . . I was sitting here at this window watching father on his way to church. . . .

LYUBOV   Have they taken everything out?

LOPAHIN   It looks like it. [*To* EPIHODOV, *as he puts on his coat.*] Be sure to take care of everything, Epihodov.

EPIHODOV   [*In a husky voice.*]   Don't worry, Yermolay Alexeyevich!

LOPAHIN   What is wrong with your voice?

EPIHODOV   I just had some water, and it went down the wrong throat.

YASHA   [*With contempt.*]   What a fool!

LYUBOV   After we leave, there won't be a soul here. . . .

LOPAHIN   Not until spring. [VARYA *pulls an umbrella from a bundle of clothes;* LOPAHIN *pretends to be afraid.*] What are you doing that for? . . . I didn't mean to. . . .

TROFIMOV   Ladies and gentlemen, hurry up, it's time. The train will be here soon.

VARYA   Petya, here are your goloshes beside the suitcase. [*Tearfully.*] How dirty and old they are! . . .

TROFIMOV   [*Puts them on.*]   Hurry up, ladies and gentlemen!

GAEV   [*Greatly embarrassed, afraid of breaking into tears.*] The train, the station . . . The red off the white into the middle pocket. . . .

LYUBOV   Let us go!

LOPAHIN   Are we all here? No one left? [*Locks the door on the left.*] There are some things stored in there, best to keep it locked up. Come along!

ANYA   Good-bye, old house! Good-bye, old life!

TROFIMOV   Welcome to the new life! . . . [*Goes out with* ANYA.] [VARYA *looks around the room and goes out slowly.* YASHA *and* CHARLOTTA, *with her little dog, follow.*]

LOPAHIN   And so, until the spring. Come, my friends. . . . *Au revoir!* [*Goes out.*] [LYUBOV *and* GAEV *alone. They seem to have been waiting for this moment, and now they embrace each other and cry quietly, with restraint, so as not to be heard.*]

GAEV   [*In despair.*]   Sister, my sister. . . .

LYUBOV   Oh, my orchard, my beloved, my beautiful orchard! My life, my youth, my happiness . . . good-bye! . . . Good-bye!

ANYA   [*Off-stage, calling gaily.*]   Mamma! . . .

TROFIMOV   [*Off-stage, gaily and excitedly.*]   Yoo-hoo! . . .

LYUBOV   Just one last time—to look at these walls, these windows. . . . Mother loved to walk in this room. . . .

GAEV   Sister, my sister . . .

ANYA   [*Off-stage.*]   Mamma!

TROFIMOV   [*Off-stage.*]   Yoo-hoo!

LYUBOV   We're coming . . . [*They go out.*]

[*The stage is empty. The sound of doors being locked and then of carriages driving off. Silence. In the stillness the dull sounds of an axe striking on a tree can be heard. They sound mournful and sad. Footsteps are heard and from the door on the right* FEERS *enters. He is dressed, as usual, in a coat and white waistcoat, and is wearing slippers. He is ill.*]

FEERS   [*Walks up to the middle door and tries the handle.*]   Locked. They've gone . . . [*Sits down on a sofa.*] They've forgotten me. Never mind. . . . I'll sit here for a bit. I don't suppose Leonid Andreyevich put on his fur coat, he probably wore his light one. [*Sighs, preoccupied.*] I didn't take care of it . . . These young people! . . . [*Mutters something unintelligible.*] My life's slipped by as if I'd never lived. . . . [*Lies down.*] I'll lie down a bit. You haven't got any strength left, nothing's left, nothing. . . . Oh, you . . . you old good-for-nothing! . . . [*Lies, motionless.*]

[*A distant sound that seems to come out of the sky, like a breaking harp, slowly and sadly dying away. Then all is silent, except for the sound of an axe striking a tree in the orchard far away.*]

CURTAIN

LUIGI PIRANDELLO
[1867–1936]

Luigi Pirandello, son of a mine owner, was born in Agrigento, Sicily. Because of the family's wealth, he could pursue a fine education at the universities in Rome and Bonn, writing a doctoral dissertation at Bonn on his native dialect. His parents negotiated his marriage to a girl Pirandello had never seen before, and he settled down to the leisurely life of a "man of letters." Then hardships befell him and forced his life to take new directions: first, his father suffered financial misfortunes, which placed upon Pirandello the burden of supporting his wife; second, his wife went mad after a few years, and Pirandello chose to live with her rather than to put her in an institution.

Before he became a playwright, Pirandello had established a reputation as a major novelist, short-story writer, poet, and critic. When he turned his attention to the drama, he proved to be a prolific playwright and an exceedingly influential force in the modern theater. He loved the theater, and in 1925, in Rome, he established his own company, which he took on tours to Europe and America.

Along with Ibsen, Shaw, and others, Pirandello is generally classified as an intellectual dramatist—one who makes his audience think. What he repeatedly asks his audience to think about are the conflicts between illusion and reality, life and art, and the problem of identity. Probably no writer has ever been more obsessed by this problem of individual personality than Pirandello. While exploring this mystery, he also explored the possibilities for expanding the limits of dramatic form. His genius and freshness of thought led him to produce such excitingly original works as *Henry IV* (1922), *Each in His Own Way* (1924), *Tonight We Improvise* (1930), and *Six Characters in Search of an Author* (1921, revised 1925). G. B. Shaw called *Six Characters* "the most original dramatic production of any people in any age." Certainly few plays raise so many questions about the nature of the dramatic illusion; yet, perhaps no play celebrates more the power of drama to create an intense reality. In 1934, Pirandello received the Nobel Prize for literature.

SIX CHARACTERS
IN SEARCH
OF AN AUTHOR
A Comedy in the Making

LUIGI PIRANDELLO
Translated by Edward Storer

CHARACTERS OF THE COMEDY IN THE MAKING

THE FATHER	THE SON
THE MOTHER	MADAME PACE
THE STEPDAUGHTER	THE BOY ⎱ *These two do*
	THE CHILD ⎰ *not speak*

ACTORS OF THE COMPANY

THE MANAGER	OTHER ACTORS AND ACTRESSES
LEADING LADY	PROPERTY MAN
LEADING MAN	PROMPTER
SECOND LADY LEAD	MACHINIST
L'INGENUE	MANAGER'S SECRETARY
JUVENILE LEAD	DOORKEEPER
	SCENE SHIFTERS

Daytime: The Stage of a Theater

ACT I

N. B. *The Comedy is without acts or scenes. The performance is interrupted once, without the curtain being lowered, when the* MANAGER *and the chief characters withdraw to arrange the scenario. A second interruption of the action takes place when, by mistake, the stage hands let the curtain down.*

The spectators will find the curtain raised and the stage as it usually is during the daytime. It will be half dark, and empty, so that from the beginning the public may have the impression of an impromptu performance.

PROMPTER's *box and a small table and chair for the* MANAGER.

Two other small tables and several chairs scattered about as during rehearsals.

The ACTORS *and* ACTRESSES *of the company enter from the back of the stage:*

First one, then another, then two together: nine or ten in all. They are about to rehearse a Pirandello play: Mixing It Up. *Some of the company move off towards their dressing rooms. The* PROMPTER *who has the "book" under his arm, is waiting for the* MANAGER *in order to begin the rehearsal.*

The ACTORS *and* ACTRESSES, *some standing, some sitting, chat and smoke. One perhaps reads a paper; another cons his part.*

Finally, the MANAGER *enters and goes to the table prepared for him. His* SECRETARY *brings him his mail, through which he glances. The* PROMPTER *takes his seat, turns on a light, and opens the "book."*

THE MANAGER [*throwing a letter down on the table*]   I can't see. [*To* PROPERTY MAN.] Let's have a little light, please!

PROPERTY MAN   Yes sir, yes, at once. [*A light comes down on to the stage.*]

THE MANAGER [*clapping his hands*]   Come along! Come along! Second act of *Mixing It Up.* [*Sits down.*]

[*The* ACTORS *and* ACTRESSES *go from the front of the stage to the wings, all except the three who are to begin the rehearsal.*]

THE PROMPTER [*reading the "book"*]   "Leo Gala's house. A curious room serving a dining-room and study."

THE MANAGER [*to* PROPERTY MAN]   Fix up the old red room.

PROPERTY MAN [*noting it down*]   Red set. All right!

THE PROMPTER [*continuing to read from the "book"*]   "Table already laid and writing desk with books and papers. Bookshelves. Exit rear to Leo's bedroom. Exit left to kitchen. Principal exit to right."

THE MANAGER [*energetically*]   Well, you understand: The principal exit over there; here the kitchen. [*Turning to* ACTOR *who is to play the part of Socrates.*] You make your entrances and exits here. [*To* PROPERTY MAN.] The baize doors at the rear, and curtains.

PROPERTY MAN [*noting it down*]   Right-o!

PROMPTER [*reading as before*]   "When the curtain rises, Leo Gala, dressed in cook's cap and apron is busy beating an egg in a cup. Philip, also dressed as a cook, is beating another egg. Guido Venanzi is seated and listening."

LEADING MAN   [*to* MANAGER]   Excuse me, but must I absolutely wear a cook's cap?

THE MANAGER   [*annoyed*]   I imagine so. It says so there anyway. [*Pointing to the "book."*]

LEADING MAN   But it's ridiculous!

THE MANAGER   Ridiculous? Ridiculous? Is it my fault if France won't send us any more good comedies, and we are reduced to putting on Pirandello's works, where nobody understands anything, and where the author plays the fool with us all? [*The* ACTORS *grin. The* MANAGER *goes to* LEADING MAN *and shouts.*] Yes sir, you put on the cook's cap and beat eggs. Do you suppose that with all this egg-beating business you are on an ordinary stage? Get that out of your head. You represent the shell of the eggs you are beating! [*Laughter and comments among the* ACTORS.] Silence! and listen to my explanations, please! [*To* LEADING MAN.] "The empty form of reason without the fullness of instinct, which is blind"—You stand for reason, your wife is instinct. It's a mixing up of the parts, according to which you who act your own part become the puppet of yourself. Do you understand?

LEADING MAN   I'm hanged if I do.

THE MANAGER   Neither do I. But let's get on with it. It's sure to be a glorious failure anyway. [*Confidentially.*] But I say, please face three-quarters. Otherwise, what with the abstruseness of the dialogue, and the public that won't be able to hear you, the whole thing will go to hell. Come on! come on!

PROMPTER   Pardon sir, may I get into my box? There's a bit of a draught.

THE MANAGER   Yes, yes, of course!

[*At this point, the* DOORKEEPER *has entered from the stage door and advances towards the* MANAGER's *table, taking off his braided cap. During this manœuver, the* SIX CHARACTERS *enter, and stop by the door at back of stage, so that when the* DOORKEEPER *is about to announce their coming to the* MANAGER, *they are already on the stage. A tenuous light surrounds them, almost as if irradiated by them—the faint breath of their fantastic reality. This light will disappear when they come forward towards the* ACTORS. *They preserve, however, something of the dream lightness in which they seem almost suspended; but this does not detract from the essential reality of their forms and expressions.*

He who is known as the FATHER *is a man of about 50: hair, reddish in color, thin at the temples; he is not bald, however; thick moustaches, falling over his still fresh mouth, which often opens in an empty and uncertain smile. He is fattish, pale; with an especially wide forehead. He has blue, oval-shaped eyes, very clear and piercing. Wears light trousers and a dark jacket. He is alternately mellifluous and violent in his manner.*

The MOTHER *seems crushed and terrified as if by an intolerable weight of shame and abasement. She is dressed in modest black and wears a thick widow's veil of crêpe. When she lifts this, she reveals a wax-like face. She always keeps her eyes downcast.*

The STEPDAUGHTER *is dashing, almost impudent, beautiful. She wears mourning too, but with great elegance. She shows contempt for the timid half-frightened manner of the wretched* BOY *(14 years old, and also dressed in black); on the other hand, she displays a lively tenderness for her little sister, the* CHILD *(about four), who is dressed in white, with a black silk sash at the waist.*

The SON *(22) tall, severe in his attitude of contempt for the* FATHER, *supercilious and indifferent to the* MOTHER. *He looks as if he had come on the stage against his will.*]

DOORKEEPER   [*cap in hand*]   Excuse me, sir . . .

THE MANAGER   [*rudely*]   Eh? What is it?

DOORKEEPER   [*timidly*]   These people are asking for you, sir.

THE MANAGER   [*furious*]   I am rehearsing, and you know perfectly well no one's allowed to come in during rehearsals! [*Turning to the* CHARACTERS.] Who are you, please? What do you want?

THE FATHER   [*coming forward a little, followed by the others who seem embarrassed*]   As a matter of fact . . . we have come here in search of an author. . . .

THE MANAGER   [*half angry, half amazed*]   An author? What author?

THE FATHER   Any author, sir.

THE MANAGER   But there's no author here. We are not rehearsing a new piece.

THE STEPDAUGHTER   [*vivaciously*]   So much the better, so much the better! We can be your new piece.

AN ACTOR   [*coming forward from the others*]   Oh, do you hear that?

THE FATHER   [*to* STEPDAUGHTER]   Yes, but if the author isn't here . . . [*to* MANAGER.] . . . unless you would be willing . . .

THE MANAGER   You are trying to be funny.

THE FATHER   No, for Heaven's sake, what are you saying? We bring you a drama, sir.

THE STEPDAUGHTER   We may be your fortune.

THE MANAGER   Will you oblige me by going away? We haven't time to waste with mad people.

THE FATHER   [*mellifluously*]   Oh sir, you know well that life is full of infinite absurdities, which, strangely enough, do not even need to appear plausible, since they are true.

THE MANAGER   What the devil is he talking about?

THE FATHER   I say that to reverse the ordinary process may well be considered a madness: that is, to create credible situations, in order that they may appear true. But permit me to observe that if this be madness, it is the sole *raison d'être* of your profession, gentlemen. [*The* ACTORS *look hurt and perplexed.*]

THE MANAGER   [*getting up and looking at him*]   So our profession seems to you one worthy of madmen then?

THE FATHER   Well, to make seem true that which isn't true . . . without any need . . . for a joke as it were . . . Isn't that your mission, gentlemen: to give life to fantastic characters on the stage?

THE MANAGER   [*interpreting the rising anger of the* COMPANY]   But I would beg you to believe, my dear sir, that the profession of the comedian is a noble one. If today, as things go, the playwrights give us stupid comedies to play and puppets to represent instead of men, remember we are proud to have given life to immortal works here on these very boards! [*The* ACTORS, *satisfied, applaud their* MANAGER.]

THE FATHER   [*interrupting furiously*]   Exactly, perfectly, to living beings more alive than those who breathe and wear clothes: being less real perhaps, but truer! I agree with you entirely. [*The* ACTORS *look at one another in amazement.*]

THE MANAGER   But what do you mean? Before, you said . . .

THE FATHER   No, excuse me, I meant it for you, sir, who were crying out that you had no time to lose with madmen, while no one better than yourself knows that nature uses the instrument of human fantasy in order to pursue her high creative purpose.

THE MANAGER   Very well—but where does all this take us?

THE FATHER   Nowhere! It is merely to show you that one is born to life in many forms, in many shapes, as tree, or as stone, as water, as butterfly, or as woman. So one may also be born a character in a play.

THE MANAGER [*with feigned comic dismay*] So you and these other friends of yours have been born characters?

THE FATHER Exactly, and alive as you see! [MANAGER *and* ACTORS *burst out laughing.*]

THE FATHER [*hurt*] I am sorry you laugh, because we carry in us a drama, as you can guess from this woman here veiled in black.

THE MANAGER [*losing patience at last and almost indignant*] Oh, chuck it! Get away please! Clear out of here! [*To* PROPERTY MAN.] For Heaven's sake, turn them out!

THE FATHER [*resisting*] No, no, look here, we . . .

THE MANAGER [*roaring*] We come here to work, you know.

LEADING ACTOR One cannot let oneself be made such a fool of.

THE FATHER [*determined, coming forward*] I marvel at your incredulity, gentlemen. Are you not accustomed to see the characters created by an author spring to life in yourselves and face each other? Just because there is no "book" [*pointing to the* PROMPTER's *box.*] which contains us, you refuse to believe . . .

THE STEPDAUGHTER [*advances towards* MANAGER, *smiling and coquettish*] Believe me, we are really six most interesting characters, sir; side-tracked however.

THE FATHER Yes, that is the word! [*To* MANAGER *all at once.*] In the sense, that is, that the author who created us alive no longer wished, or was no longer able, materially to put us into a work of art. And this was a real crime, sir; because he who has had the luck to be born a character can laugh even at death. He cannot die. The man, the writer, the instrument of the creation will die, but his creation does not die. And to live for ever, it does not need to have extraordinary gifts or to be able to work wonders. Who was Sancho Panza? Who was Don Abbondio? Yet they live eternally because—live germs as they were—they had the fortune to find a fecundating matrix, a fantasy which could raise and nourish them: make them live for ever!

THE MANAGER That is quite all right. But what do you want here, all of you?

THE FATHER We want to live.

THE MANAGER [*ironically*] For Eternity?

THE FATHER No, sir, only for a moment . . . in you.

AN ACTOR Just listen to him!

LEADING LADY They want to live, in us! . . .

JUVENILE LEAD [*pointing to the* STEPDAUGHTER] I've no objection, as far as that one is concerned!

THE FATHER Look here! Look here! The comedy has to be made. [*To the* MANAGER.] But if you and your actors are willing, we can soon concert it among ourselves.

THE MANAGER [*annoyed*] But what do you want to concert? We don't go in for concerts here. Here we play dramas and comedies!

THE FATHER Exactly! That is just why we have come to you.

THE MANAGER And where is the "book"?

THE FATHER It is in us! [*The* ACTORS *laugh.*] The drama is in us, and we are the drama. We are impatient to play it. Our inner passion drives us on to this.

THE STEPDAUGHTER [*disdainful, alluring, treacherous, full of impudence*] My passion, sir! Ah, if you only knew! My passion for him! [*Points to the* FATHER *and makes a pretence of embracing him. Then she breaks out into a loud laugh.*]

THE FATHER [*angrily*] Behave yourself! And please don't laugh in that fashion.

THE STEPDAUGHTER With your permission, gentlemen, I, who am a two months' orphan, will show you how I can dance and sing. [*Sings and then dances* "Prenez garde à Tchou-Tchin-Tchou."]

> Les chinois sont un peuple malin,
> De Shanghai à Pékin,
> Ils ont mis des écriteaux partout:
> Prenez garde à Tchou-Tchin-Tchou.[1]

ACTORS *and* ACTRESSES Bravo! Well done! Tip-top!

THE MANAGER Silence! This isn't a café concert, you know! [*Turning to the* FATHER *in consternation.*] Is she mad?

THE FATHER Mad? No, she's worse than mad.

THE STEPDAUGHTER [*to* MANAGER] Worse? Worse? Listen! Stage this drama for us at once! Then you will see that at a certain moment I . . . when this little darling here . . . [*Takes the* CHILD *by the hand and leads her to the* MANAGER.] Isn't she a dear? [*Takes her up and kisses her.*] Darling! Darling! [*Puts her down again and adds feelingly.*] Well, when God suddenly takes this dear little child away from that poor mother there; and this imbecile here [*seizing hold of the* BOY *roughly and pushing him forward*] does the stupidest things, like the fool he is, you will see me run away. Yes, gentlemen, I shall be off. But the moment hasn't arrived yet. After what has taken place between him and me [*indicates the* FATHER *with a horrible wink*] I can't remain any longer in this society, to have to witness the anguish of this mother here for that fool . . . [*Indicates the* SON.] Look at him! Look at him! See how indifferent, how frigid he is, because he is the legitimate son. He despises me, despises him [*pointing to the* BOY], despises this baby here; because . . . we are bastards. [*Goes to the* MOTHER *and embraces her.*] And he doesn't want to recognize her as his mother—she who is the common mother of us all. He looks down upon her as if she were only the mother of us three bastards. Wretch!
[*She says all this very rapidly, excitedly. At the word "bastards" she raises her voice, and almost spits out the final "Wretch!"*]

THE MOTHER [*to the* MANAGER, *in anguish*] In the name of these two little children, I beg you . . . [*She grows faint and is about to fall.*] Oh God!

THE FATHER [*coming forward to support her as do some of the* ACTORS] Quick a chair, a chair for this poor widow!

THE ACTORS Is it true? Has she really fainted?

THE MANAGER Quick, a chair! Here!
[*One of the* ACTORS *brings a chair, the others proffer assistance. The* MOTHER *tries to prevent the* FATHER *from lifting the veil which covers her face.*]

THE FATHER Look at her! Look at her!

THE MOTHER No, stop; stop it please!

THE FATHER [*raising her veil*] Let them see you!

THE MOTHER [*rising and covering her face with her hands, in desperation*] I beg you, sir, to prevent this man from carrying out his plan which is loathsome to me.

THE MANAGER [*dumbfounded*] I don't understand at all. What is the situation? Is this lady your wife? [*To the* FATHER.]

---

[1] The Chinese are clever people,
From Shanghai to Peking,
They've put billboards everywhere:
Hearken to Tchou-Tchin-Tchou.
(French ditty)

THE FATHER   Yes, gentlemen: my wife!

THE MANAGER   But how can she be a widow if you are alive? [*The* ACTORS *find relief for their astonishment in a loud laugh.*]

THE FATHER   Don't laugh! Don't laugh like that, for Heaven's sake. Her drama lies just here in this: she has had a lover, a man who ought to be here.

THE MOTHER   [*with a cry*]   No! No!

THE STEPDAUGHTER   Fortunately for her, he is dead. Two months ago as I said. We are in mourning, as you see.

THE FATHER   He isn't here you see, not because he is dead. He isn't here—look at her a moment and you will understand—because her drama isn't a drama of the love of two men for whom she was incapable of feeling anything except possibly a little gratitude—gratitude not for me but for the other. She isn't a woman, she is a mother, and her drama—powerful sir, I assure you—lies, as a matter of fact, all in these four children she has had by two men.

THE MOTHER   I had them? Have you got the courage to say that I wanted them? [*To the* COMPANY.] It was his doing. It was he who gave me that other man, who forced me to go away with him.

THE STEPDAUGHTER   It isn't true.

THE MOTHER   [*startled*]   Not true, isn't it?

THE STEPDAUGHTER   No, it isn't true, it just isn't true.

THE MOTHER   And what can you know about it?

THE STEPDAUGHTER   It isn't true. Don't believe it. [*To* MANAGER.] Do you know why she says so? For that fellow there. [*Indicates the* SON.] She tortures herself, destroys herself on account of the neglect of that son there; and she wants him to believe that if she abandoned him when he was only two years old, it was because he [*indicates the* FATHER] made her do so.

THE MOTHER   [*vigorously*]   He forced me to it, and I call God to witness it. [*To the* MANAGER.] Ask him [*indicates the* FATHER] if it isn't true. Let him speak. You [*to* DAUGHTER] are not in a position to know anything about it.

THE STEPDAUGHTER   I know you lived in peace and happiness with my father while he lived. Can you deny it?

THE MOTHER   No, I don't deny it . . .

THE STEPDAUGHTER   He was always full of affection and kindness for you. [*To the* BOY, *angrily*.] It's true, isn't it? Tell them! Why don't you speak, you little fool?

THE MOTHER   Leave the poor boy alone. Why do you want to make me appear ungrateful, daughter? I don't want to offend your father. I have answered him that I didn't abandon my house and my son through any fault of mine, nor from any wilful passion.

THE FATHER   It is true. It was my doing.

LEADING MAN   [*to the* COMPANY]   What a spectacle!

LEADING LADY   We are the audience this time.

JUVENILE LEAD   For once, in a way.

THE MANAGER   [*beginning to get really interested*]   Let's hear them out. Listen!

THE SON   Oh yes, you're going to hear a fine bit now. He will talk to you of the Demon of Experiment.

THE FATHER   You are a cynical imbecile. I've told you so already a hundred times. [*To the* MANAGER.] He tries to make fun of me on account of this expression which I have found to excuse myself with.

THE SON   [*with disgust*]   Yes, phrases! phrases!

THE FATHER   Phrases! Isn't everyone consoled when faced with a trouble or fact he doesn't understand, by a word, some simple word, which tells us nothing and yet calms us?

THE STEPDAUGHTER   Even in the case of remorse. In fact, especially then.

THE FATHER   Remorse? No, that isn't true. I've done more than use words to quieten the remorse in me.

THE STEPDAUGHTER   Yes, there was a bit of money too. Yes, yes, a bit of money. There were the hundred lire he was about to offer me in payment, gentlemen. . . . [*Sensation of horror among the* ACTORS.]

THE SON   [*to the* STEPDAUGHTER]   This is vile.

THE STEPDAUGHTER   Vile? There they were in a pale blue envelope on a little mahogany table in the back of Madame Pace's shop. You know Madame Pace—one of those ladies who attract poor girls of good family into their ateliers, under the pretext of their selling *robes et manteaux.*[2]

THE SON   And he thinks he has bought the right to tyrannize over us all with those hundred lire he was going to pay; but which, fortunately—note this, gentlemen—he had no chance of paying.

THE STEPDAUGHTER   It was a near thing, though, you know! [*Laughs ironically.*]

THE MOTHER   [*protesting*]   Shame, my daughter, shame!

THE STEPDAUGHTER   Shame indeed! This is my revenge! I am dying to live that scene. . . . The room . . . I see it . . . Here is the window with the mantles exposed, there the divan, the looking-glass, a screen, there in front of the window the little mahogany table with the blue envelope containing one hundred lire. I see it. I see it. I could take hold of it . . . But you, gentlemen, you ought to turn your backs now: I am almost nude, you know. But I don't blush: I leave that to him [*indicating the* FATHER].

THE MANAGER   I don't understand this at all.

THE FATHER   Naturally enough. I would ask you, sir, to exercise your authority a little here, and let me speak before you believe all she is trying to blame me with. Let me explain.

THE STEPDAUGHTER   Ah yes, explain it in your own way.

THE FATHER   But don't you see that the whole trouble lies here. In words, words. Each one of us has within him a whole world of things, each man of us his own special world. And how can we ever come to an understanding if I put in the words I utter the sense and value of things as I see them; while you who listen to me must inevitably translate them according to the conception of things each one of you has within himself. We think we understand each other, but we never really do. Look here! This woman [*indicating the* MOTHER] takes all my pity for her as a specially ferocious form of cruelty.

THE MOTHER   But you drove me away.

THE FATHER   Do you hear her? I drove her away! She believes I really sent her away.

THE MOTHER   You know how to talk, and I don't; but, believe me, sir [*to* MANAGER], after he had married me . . . who knows why? . . . I was a poor insignificant woman . . .

THE FATHER   But, good Heaven! it was just for your humility that I married you. I loved this simplicity in you. [*He stops when he sees she makes signs to contradict him, opens his arms wide in sign of desperation, seeing how hopeless it is to make himself understood.*] You see she denies it. Her mental deafness, believe me, is phenomenal, the limit [*touches his forehead*]: deaf, deaf, mentally deaf! She has plenty of feeling. Oh yes, a good heart for the children; but the brain—deaf, to the point of desperation—!

THE STEPDAUGHTER   Yes, but ask him how his intelligence has helped us.

THE FATHER   If we could see all the evil that may spring from good, what should we do?

---

[2] (French) Dresses and coats.

[*At this point the* LEADING LADY *who is biting her lips with rage at seeing the* LEADING MAN *flirting with the* STEPDAUGHTER, *comes forward and says to the* MANAGER]

LEADING LADY   Excuse me, but are we going to rehearse today?

MANAGER   Of course, of course; but let's hear them out.

JUVENILE LEAD   This is something quite new.

L'INGENUE   Most interesting!

LEADING LADY   Yes, for the people who like that kind of thing. [*Casts a glance at* LEADING MAN.]

THE MANAGER   [*to* FATHER]   You must please explain yourself quite clearly. [*Sits down.*]

THE FATHER   Very well then: listen! I had in my service a poor man, a clerk, a secretary of mine, full of devotion, who became friends with her. [*Indicating the* MOTHER.] They understood one another, were kindred souls in fact, without, however, the least suspicion of any evil existing. They were incapable even of thinking of it.

THE STEPDAUGHTER   So he thought of it—for them!

THE FATHER   That's not true. I meant to do good to them—and to myself, I confess, at the same time. Things had come to the point that I could not say a word to either of them without their making a mute appeal, one to the other, with their eyes. I could see them silently asking each other how I was to be kept in countenance, how I was to be kept quiet. And this, believe me, was just about enough of itself to keep me in a constant rage, to exasperate me beyond measure.

THE MANAGER   And why didn't you send him away then—this secretary of yours?

THE FATHER   Precisely what I did, sir. And then I had to watch this poor woman drifting forlornly about the house like an animal without a master, like an animal one has taken in out of pity.

THE MOTHER   Ah yes! . . .

THE FATHER   [*suddenly turning to the* MOTHER]   It's true about the son anyway, isn't it?

THE MOTHER   He took my son away from me first of all.

THE FATHER   But not from cruelty. I did it so that he should grow up healthy and strong by living in the country.

THE STEPDAUGHTER   [*pointing to him ironically*]   As one can see.

THE FATHER   [*quickly*]   Is it my fault if he has grown up like this? I sent him to a wet nurse in the country, a peasant, as *she* did not seem to me strong enough, though she is of humble origin. That was, anyway, the reason I married her. Unpleasant all this may be, but how can it be helped? My mistake possibly, but there we are! All my life I have had these confounded aspirations towards a certain moral sanity. [*At this point the* STEPDAUGHTER *bursts out into a noisy laugh.*] Oh, stop it! Stop it! I can't stand it.

THE MANAGER   Yes, please stop it, for Heaven's sake.

THE STEPDAUGHTER   But imagine moral sanity from him, if you please—the client of certain ateliers like that of Madame Pace!

THE FATHER   Fool! That is the proof that I am a man! This seeming contradiction, gentlemen, is the strongest proof that I stand here a live man before you. Why, it is just for this very incongruity in my nature that I have had to suffer what I have. I could not live by the side of that woman [*indicating the* MOTHER] any longer; but not so much for the boredom she inspired me with as for the pity I felt for her.

THE MOTHER   And so he turned me out—.

THE FATHER   —well provided for! Yes, I sent her to that man, gentlemen . . . to let her go free of me.

THE MOTHER And to free himself.

THE FATHER Yes, I admit it. It was also a liberation for me. But great evil has come of it. I meant well when I did it; and I did it more for her sake than mine. I swear it. [*Crosses his arms on his chest; then turns suddenly to the* MOTHER.] Did I ever lose sight of you until that other man carried you off to another town, like the angry fool he was? And on account of my pure interest in you . . . my pure interest, I repeat, that had no base motive in it . . . I watched with the tenderest concern the new family that grew up around her. She can bear witness to this. [*Points to the* STEP-DAUGHTER.]

THE STEPDAUGHTER Oh yes, that's true enough. When I was a kiddie, so so high, you know, with plaits over my shoulders and knickers longer than my skirts, I used to see him waiting outside the school for me to come out. He came to see how I was growing up.

THE FATHER This is infamous, shameful!

THE STEPDAUGHTER No. Why?

THE FATHER Infamous! Infamous! [*Then excitedly to* MANAGER, *explaining.*] After she [*indicating* MOTHER] went away, my house seemed suddenly empty. She was my incubus, but she filled my house. I was like a dazed fly alone in the empty rooms. This boy here [*indicating the* SON] was educated away from home, and when he came back, he seemed to me to be no more mine. With no mother to stand between him and me, he grew up entirely for himself, on his own, apart, with no tie of intellect or affection binding him to me. And then—strange but true—I was driven, by curiosity at first and then by some tender sentiment, towards her family, which had come into being through my will. The thought of her began gradually to fill up the emptiness I felt all around me. I wanted to know if she were happy in living out the simple daily duties of life. I wanted to think of her as fortunate and happy because far away from the complicated torments of my spirit. And so, to have proof of this, I used to watch that child coming out of school.

THE STEPDAUGHTER Yes, yes. True. He used to follow me in the street and smiled at me, waved his hand, like this. I would look at him with interest, wondering who he might be. I told my mother, who guessed at once. [*The* MOTHER *agrees with a nod.*] Then she didn't want to send me to school for some days; and when I finally went back, there he was again—looking so ridiculous—with a paper parcel in his hands. He came close to me, caressed me, and drew out a fine straw hat from the parcel, with a bouquet of flowers—all for me!

THE MANAGER A bit discursive this, you know!

THE SON [*contemptuously*] Literature! Literature!

THE FATHER Literature indeed! This is life, this is passion!

THE MANAGER It may be, but it won't act.

THE FATHER I agree. This is only the part leading up. I don't suggest this should be staged. She [*pointing to the* STEPDAUGHTER], as you see, is no longer the flapper with plaits down her back—.

THE STEPDAUGHTER —and the knickers showing below the skirt!

THE FATHER The drama is coming now, sir; something new, complex, most interesting.

THE STEPDAUGHTER As soon as my father died . . .

THE FATHER —there was absolute misery for them. They came back here, un-known to me. Through her stupidity! [*Pointing to the* MOTHER.] It is true she can barely write her own name; but she could anyhow have got her daughter to write to me that they were in need. . . .

THE MOTHER   And how was I to divine all this sentiment in him?

THE FATHER   That is exactly your mistake, never to have guessed any of my sentiments.

THE MOTHER   After so many years apart, and all that had happened . . .

THE FATHER   Was it my fault if that fellow carried you away? It happened quite suddenly; for after he had obtained some job or other, I could find no trace of them; and so, not unnaturally, my interest in them dwindled. But the drama culminated unforeseen and violent on their return, when I was impelled by my miserable flesh that still lives . . . Ah! what misery, what wretchedness is that of the man who is alone and disdains debasing *liaisons!* Not old enough to do without women, and not young enough to go and look for one without shame. Misery? It's worse than misery; it's a horror; for no woman can any longer give him love; and when a man feels this . . . One ought to do without, you say? Yes, yes, I know. Each of us when he appears before his fellows is clothed in a certain dignity. But every man knows what unconfessable things pass within the secrecy of his own heart. One gives way to the temptation, only to rise from it again, afterwards, with a great eagerness to reestablish one's dignity, as if it were a tombstone to place on the grave of one's shame, and a monument to hide and sign the memory of our weaknesses. Everybody's in the same case. Some folks haven't the courage to say certain things, that's all!

THE STEPDAUGHTER   All appear to have the courage to do them though.

THE FATHER   Yes, but in secret. Therefore, you want more courage to say these things. Let a man but speak these things out, and folks at once label him a cynic. But it isn't true. He is like all the others, better indeed, because he isn't afraid to reveal with the light of the intelligence the red shame of human bestiality on which most men close their eyes so as not to see it. Woman—for example, look at her case! She turns tantalizing inviting glances on you. You seize her. No sooner does she feel herself in your grasp than she closes her eyes. It is the sign of her mission, the sign by which she says to man: "Blind yourself, for I am blind."

THE STEPDAUGHTER   Sometimes she can close them no more: when she no longer feels the need of hiding her shame to herself, but dry-eyed and dispassionately, sees only that of the man who has blinded himself without love. Oh, all these intellectual complications make me sick, disgust me—all his philosophy that uncovers the beast in man, and then seeks to save him, excuse him . . . I can't stand it, sir. When a man seeks to "simplify" life bestially, throwing aside every relic of humanity, every chaste aspiration, every pure feeling, all sense of ideality, duty, modesty, shame . . . then nothing is more revolting and nauseous than a certain kind of remorse—crocodiles' tears, that's what it is.

THE MANAGER   Let's come to the point. This is only discussion.

THE FATHER   Very good, sir! But a fact is like a sack which won't stand up when it is empty. In order that it may stand up, one has to put into it the reason and sentiment which have caused it to exist. I couldn't possibly know that after the death of that man, they had decided to return here, that they were in misery, and that she [*pointing to the* MOTHER] had gone to work as a modiste, and at a shop of the type of that of Madame Pace.

THE STEPDAUGHTER   A real high-class modiste, you must know, gentlemen. In appearance, she works for the leaders of the best society; but she arranges matters so that these elegant ladies serve her purpose . . . without prejudice to other ladies who are . . . well . . . only so so.

THE MOTHER   You will believe me, gentlemen, that it never entered my mind that the old hag offered me work because she had her eye on my daughter.

THE STEPDAUGHTER   Poor mamma! Do you know, sir, what that woman did when I brought her back the work my mother had finished? She would point out to me that I had torn one of my frocks, and she would give it back to my mother to mend. It was I who paid for it, always I; while this poor creature here believed she was sacrificing herself for me and these two children here, sitting up at night sewing Madame Pace's robes.

THE MANAGER   And one day you met there . . .

THE STEPDAUGHTER   Him, him. Yes, sir, an old client. There's a scene for you to play! Superb!

THE FATHER   She, the Mother arrived just then . . .

THE STEPDAUGHTER   [*treacherously*]   Almost in time!

THE FATHER   [*crying out*]   No, in time! in time! Fortunately I recognized her . . . in time. And I took them back home with me to my house. You can imagine now her position and mine: she, as you see her; and I who cannot look her in the face.

THE STEPDAUGHTER   Absurd! How can I possibly be expected—after that—to be a modest young miss, a fit person to go with his confounded aspirations for "a solid moral sanity"?

THE FATHER   For the drama lies all in this—in the conscience that I have, that each one of us has. We believe this conscience to be a single thing, but it is many-sided. There is one for this person, and another for that. Diverse consciences. So we have this illusion of being one person for all, of having a personality that is unique in all our acts. But it isn't true. We perceive this when, tragically perhaps, in something we do, we are, as it were, suspended, caught up in the air on a kind of hook. Then we perceive that all of us was not in that act, and that it would be an atrocious injustice to judge us by that action alone, as if all our existence were summed up in that one deed. Now do you understand the perfidy of this girl? She surprised me in a place, where she ought not to have known me, just as I could not exist for her; and she now seeks to attach to me a reality such as I could never suppose I should have to assume for her in a shameful and fleeting moment of my life. I feel this above all else. And the drama, you will see, acquires a tremendous value from this point. Then there is the position of the others . . . his . . . [*indicating the* SON.]

THE SON   [*shrugging his shoulders scornfully*]   Leave me alone! I don't come into this.

THE FATHER   What? You don't come into this?

THE SON   I've got nothing to do with it, and don't want to have; because you know well enough I wasn't made to be mixed up in all this with the rest of you.

THE STEPDAUGHTER   We are only vulgar folk! He is the fine gentleman. You may have noticed, Mr. Manager, that I fix him now and again with a look of scorn while he lowers his eyes—for he knows the evil he has done me.

THE SON   [*scarcely looking at her*]   I?

THE STEPDAUGHTER   You! you! I owe my life on the streets to you. Did you or did you not deny us, with your behavior, I won't say the intimacy of home, but even that mere hospitality which makes guests feel at their ease? We were intruders who had come to disturb the kingdom of your legitimacy. I should like to have you witness, Mr. Manager, certain scenes between him and me. He says I have tyrannized over everyone. But it was just his behavior which made me insist on the reason for which I had come into the house— this reason he calls "vile"—into his house, with my mother who is his mother too. And I came as mistress of the house.

THE SON   It's easy for them to put me always in the wrong. But imagine, gentlemen, the position of a son, whose fate it is to see arrive one day at his home a young woman of impudent bearing, a young woman who inquires for his father, with whom who knows what business she has. This young man has then to witness her return bolder than ever, accompanied by that child there. He is obliged to watch her treat his father in an equivocal and confidential manner. She asks money of him in a way that lets one suppose he must give it her, *must,* do you understand, because he has every obligation to do so.

THE FATHER   But I have, as a matter of fact, this obligation. I owe it to your mother.

THE SON   How should I know? When had I ever seen or heard of her? One day there arrive with her [*indicating* STEPDAUGHTER] that lad and this baby here. I am told: "This is *your* mother too, you know." I divine from her manner [*indicating* STEPDAUGHTER *again*] why it is they have come home. I had rather not say what I feel and think about it. I shouldn't even care to confess to myself. No action can therefore be hoped for from me in this affair. Believe me, Mr. Manager, I am an "unrealized" character, dramatically speaking; and I find myself not at all at ease in their company. Leave me out of it I beg you.

THE FATHER   What? It is just because you are so that . . .

THE SON   How do you know what I am like? When did you ever bother your head about me?

THE FATHER   I admit it. I admit it. But isn't that a situation in itself? This aloofness of yours which is so cruel to me and to your mother, who returns home and sees you almost for the first time grown up, who doesn't recognize you but knows you are her son . . . [*Pointing out the* MOTHER *to the* MANAGER.] See, she's crying!

THE STEPDAUGHTER   [*angrily, stamping her foot*]   Like a fool!

THE FATHER   [*indicating* STEPDAUGHTER]   She can't stand him you know. [*Then referring again to the* SON.] He says he doesn't come into the affair, whereas he is really the hinge of the whole action. Look at that lad who is always clinging to his mother, frightened and humiliated. It is on account of this fellow here. Possibly his situation is the most painful of all. He feels himself a stranger more than the others. The poor little chap feels mortified, humiliated at being brought into a home out of charity as it were. [*In confidence.*] He is the image of his father. Hardly talks at all. Humble and quiet.

THE MANAGER   Oh, we'll cut him out. You've no notion what a nuisance boys are on the stage . . .

THE FATHER   He disappears soon, you know. And the baby too. She is the first to vanish from the scene. The drama consists finally in this: when that mother re-enters my house, her family born outside of it, and shall we say superimposed on the original, ends with the death of the little girl, the tragedy of the boy and the flight of the elder daughter. It cannot go on, because it is foreign to its surroundings. So after much torment, we three remain: I, the mother, that son. Then, owing to the disappearance of that extraneous family, we too find ourselves strange to one another. We find we are living in an atmosphere of mortal desolation which is the revenge, as he [*indicating* SON] scornfully said of the Demon of Experiment, that unfortunately hides in me. Thus, sir, you see when faith is lacking, it becomes impossible to create certain states of happiness, for we lack the necessary humility. Vaingloriously, we try to substitute ourselves for this faith, creating thus for the rest of the world a reality which we believe after this fashion, while, actually, it doesn't exist. For each one of us has his own reality to be respected before God, even when it is harmful to one's very self.

THE MANAGER   There is something in what you say. I assure you all this interests me very much. I begin to think there's the stuff for a drama in all this, and not a bad drama either.

THE STEPDAUGHTER   [*coming forward*]   When you've got a character like me.

THE FATHER   [*shutting her up, all excited to learn the decision of the* MANAGER] You be quiet!

THE MANAGER   [*reflecting, heedless of interruption*]   It's new . . . hem . . . yes . . .

THE FATHER   Absolutely new!

THE MANAGER   You've got a nerve though, I must say, to come here and fling it at me like this . . .

THE FATHER   You will understand, sir, born as we are for the stage . . .

THE MANAGER   Are you amateur actors then?

THE FATHER   No, I say born for the stage, because . . .

THE MANAGER   Oh, nonsense. You're an old hand, you know.

THE FATHER   No sir, no. We act that rôle for which we have been cast, that rôle which we are given in life. And in my own case, passion itself, as usually happens, becomes a trifle theatrical when it is exalted.

THE MANAGER   Well, well, that will do. But you see, without an author . . . I could give you the address of an author if you like.

THE FATHER   No, no. Look here! You must be the author.

THE MANAGER   I? What are you talking about?

THE FATHER   Yes, you! Why not?

THE MANAGER   Because I have never been an author: that's why.

THE FATHER   Then why not turn author now? Everybody does it. You don't want any special qualities. Your task is made much easier by the fact that we are all here alive before you . . .

THE MANAGER   It won't do.

THE FATHER   What? When you see us live our drama . . .

THE MANAGER   Yes, that's all right. But you want someone to write it.

THE FATHER   No, no. Someone to take it down, possibly, while we play it, scene by scene! It will be enough to sketch it out at first, and then try it over.

THE MANAGER   Well . . . I am almost tempted. It's a bit of an idea. One might have a shot at it.

THE FATHER   Of course. You'll see what scenes will come out of it. I can give you one, at once . . .

THE MANAGER   By Jove, it tempts me. I'd like to have a go at it. Let's try it out. Come with me to my office. [*Turning to the* ACTORS.] You are at liberty for a bit, but don't stop out of the theater for long. In a quarter of an hour, twenty minutes, all back here again! [*To the* FATHER.] We'll see what can be done. Who knows if we don't get something really extraordinary out of it?

THE FATHER   There's no doubt about it. They [*indicating the* CHARACTERS] had better come with us too, hadn't they?

THE MANAGER   Yes, yes. Come on! come on! [*Moves away and then turning to the* ACTORS.] Be punctual, please!
[MANAGER *and the* SIX CHARACTERS *cross the stage and go off. The other* ACTORS *remain, looking at one another in astonishment.*]

LEADING MAN   Is he serious? What the devil does he want to do?

JUVENILE LEAD   This is rank madness.

THIRD ACTOR   Does he expect to knock up a drama in five minutes?

JUVENILE LEAD   Like the improvisers!

LEADING LADY   If he thinks I'm going to take part in a joke like this . . .

JUVENILE LEAD   I'm out of it anyway.

FOURTH ACTOR   I should like to know who they are. [*Alludes to* CHARACTERS.]

THIRD ACTOR   What do you suppose? Madmen or rascals!

JUVENILE LEAD   And he takes them seriously!

L'INGENUE   Vanity! He fancies himself as an author now.

LEADING MAN   It's absolutely unheard of. If the stage has come to this . . . well I'm . . .

FIFTH ACTOR   It's rather a joke.

THIRD ACTOR   Well, we'll see what's going to happen next.

[*Thus talking, the* ACTORS *leave the stage; some going out by the little door at the back; others retiring to their dressing-rooms.*
The curtain remains up.
The action of the play is suspended for twenty minutes.]

ACT II

The stage call-bells ring to warn the company that the play is about to begin again.

THE STEPDAUGHTER *comes out of the* MANAGER's *office along with the* CHILD *and the* BOY. *As she comes out of the office, she cries:* Nonsense! Nonsense! Do it yourselves! I'm not going to mix myself up in this mess. [*Turning to the* CHILD *and coming quickly with her on to the stage.*] Come on, Rosetta, let's run!

[*The* BOY *follows them slowly, remaining a little behind and seeming perplexed.*]

THE STEPDAUGHTER   [*stops, bends over the* CHILD *and takes the latter's face between her hands*]   My little darling! You're frightened, aren't you? You don't know where you are, do you? [*Pretending to reply to a question of the* CHILD.] What is the stage? It's a place, baby, you know, where people play at being serious, a place where they act comedies. We've got to act a comedy now, dead serious, you know; and you're in it also, little one. [*Embraces her, pressing the little head to her breast, and rocking the* CHILD *for a moment.*] Oh darling, darling, what a horrid comedy you've got to play! What a wretched part they've found for you! A garden . . . a fountain . . . look . . . just suppose, kiddie, it's here. Where, you say? Why, right here in the middle. It's all pretence you know. That's the trouble, my pet: it's all make-believe here. It's better to imagine it though, because if they fix it up for you, it'll only be painted cardboard, painted cardboard for the rockery, the water, the plants . . . Ah, but I think a baby like this one would sooner have a make-believe fountain than a real one, so she could play with it. What a joke it'll be for the others! But for you, alas! not quite such a joke: you who are real, baby dear, and really play by a real fountain that is big and green and beautiful, with ever so many bamboos around it that are reflected in the water, and a whole lot of little ducks swimming about . . . No, Rosetta, no, your mother doesn't bother about you on account of that wretch of a son there. I'm in the devil of a temper, and as for that lad . . . [*Seizes* BOY *by the arm to force him to take one of his hands out of his pockets.*] What have you got there? What are you hiding? [*Pulls his hand out of his pocket, looks into it and catches the glint of a revolver.*] Ah, where did you get this? [*The* BOY, *very pale in the face, looks at her, but does not answer.*] Idiot! If I'd been in your place, instead of killing myself, I'd have shot one of those two, or both of them: father and son.

[*The* FATHER *enters from the office, all excited from his work. The* MANAGER *follows him.*]

THE FATHER   Come on, come on, dear! Come here for a minute! We've arranged everything. It's all fixed up.

THE MANAGER   [*also excited*]   If you please, young lady, there are one or two points to settle still. Will you come along?

THE STEPDAUGHTER   [*following him towards the office*]   Ouff! what's the good, if you've arranged everything.

[*The* FATHER, MANAGER *and* STEPDAUGHTER *go back into the office again (off) for a moment. At the same time, the* SON, *followed by the* MOTHER, *comes out.*]

THE SON   [*looking at the three entering office*]   Oh this is fine, fine! And to think I can't even get away!

[*The* MOTHER *attempts to look at him, but lowers her eyes immediately when he turns away from her. She then sits down. The* BOY *and the* CHILD *approach her. She casts a glance again at the* SON, *and speaks with humble tones, trying to draw him into conversation.*]

THE MOTHER   And isn't my punishment the worst of all? [*Then seeing from the* SON's *manner that he will not bother himself about her.*] My God! Why are you so cruel? Isn't it enough for one person to support all this torment? Must you then insist on others seeing it also?

THE SON   [*half to himself, meaning the* MOTHER *to hear, however*]   And they want to put it on the stage! If there was at least a reason for it! He thinks he has got at the meaning of it all. Just as if each one of us in every circumstance of life couldn't find his own explanation of it! [*Pauses.*] He complains he was discovered in a place where he ought not to have been seen, in a moment of his life which ought to have remained hidden and kept out of the reach of convention which he has to maintain for other people. And what about my case? Haven't I had to reveal what no son ought ever to reveal: how father and mother live and are man and wife for themselves quite apart from that idea of father and mother which we give them? When this idea is revealed, our life is then linked at one point only to that man and that woman; and as such it should shame them, shouldn't it?

[*The* MOTHER *hides her face in her hands. From the dressing-rooms and the little door at the back of the stage the* ACTORS *and* STAGE MANAGER *return, followed by the* PROPERTY MAN, *and the* PROMPTER. *At the same moment, the* MANAGER *comes out of his office, accompanied by the* FATHER *and the* STEPDAUGHTER.*]

THE MANAGER   Come on, come on, ladies and gentlemen! Heh! you there, machinist!

MACHINIST   Yes sir?

THE MANAGER   Fix up the white parlor with the floral decorations. Two wings and a drop with a door will do. Hurry up!

[*The* MACHINIST *runs off at once to prepare the scene, and arranges it while the* MANAGER *talks with the* STAGE MANAGER, *the* PROPERTY MAN, *and the* PROMPTER *on matters of detail.*]

THE MANAGER   [*to* PROPERTY MAN]   Just have a look, and see if there isn't a sofa or divan in the wardrobe . . .

PROPERTY MAN   There's the green one.

THE STEPDAUGHTER   No, no! Green won't do. It was yellow, ornamented with flowers—very large! and most comfortable!

PROPERTY MAN There isn't one like that.

THE MANAGER It doesn't matter. Use the one we've got.

THE STEPDAUGHTER Doesn't matter? It's most important!

THE MANAGER We're only trying it now. Please don't interfere. [*To* PROPERTY MAN.] See if we've got a shop window—long and narrowish.

THE STEPDAUGHTER And the little table! The little mahogany table for the pale blue envelope!

PROPERTY MAN [*to* MANAGER] There's that little gilt one.

THE MANAGER That'll do fine.

THE FATHER A mirror.

THE STEPDAUGHTER And the screen! We must have a screen. Otherwise how can I manage?

PROPERTY MAN That's all right, Miss. We've got any amount of them.

THE MANAGER [*to the* STEPDAUGHTER] We want some clothes pegs too, don't we?

THE STEPDAUGHTER Yes, several, several!

THE MANAGER See how many we've got and bring them all.

PROPERTY MAN All right!

[*The* PROPERTY MAN *hurries off to obey his orders. While he is putting the things in their places, the* MANAGER *talks to the* PROMPTER *and then with the* CHARACTERS *and the* ACTORS.]

THE MANAGER [*to* PROMPTER] Take your seat. Look here: this is the outline of the scenes, act by act. [*Hands him some sheets of paper.*] And now I'm going to ask you to do something out of the ordinary.

PROMPTER Take it down in shorthand?

THE MANAGER [*pleasantly surprised*] Exactly! Can you do shorthand?

PROMPTER Yes, a little.

MANAGER Good! [*Turning to a stage hand.*] Go and get some paper from my office, plenty, as much as you can find.

[*The* STAGE HAND *goes off, and soon returns with a handful of paper which he gives to the* PROMPTER.]

THE MANAGER [*to* PROMPTER] You follow the scenes as we play them, and try to get the points down, at any rate the most important ones. [*Then addressing the* ACTORS.] Clear the stage, ladies and gentlemen! Come over here [*pointing to the Left*] and listen attentively.

LEADING LADY But, excuse me, we . . .

THE MANAGER [*guessing her thought*] Don't worry! You won't have to improvise.

LEADING MAN What have we to do then?

THE MANAGER Nothing. For the moment you just watch and listen. Everybody will get his part written out afterwards. At present we're going to try the thing as best we can. They're going to act now.

THE FATHER [*as if fallen from the clouds into the confusion of the stage*] We? What do you mean, if you please, by a rehearsal?

THE MANAGER A rehearsal for them. [*Points to the* ACTORS.]

THE FATHER But since we are the characters . . .

THE MANAGER All right: "characters" then, if you insist on calling yourselves such. But here, my dear sir, the characters don't act. Here the actors do the acting. The characters are there, in the "book"—[*pointing towards* PROMPTER'*s box*] when there is a "book"!

THE FATHER I won't contradict you; but excuse me, the actors aren't the characters. They want to be, they pretend to be, don't they? Now if these gentlemen here are fortunate enough to have us alive before them . . .

THE MANAGER Oh this is grand! You want to come before the public yourselves then?

THE FATHER   As we are . . .

THE MANAGER   I can assure you it would be a magnificent spectacle!

LEADING MAN   What's the use of us here anyway then?

THE MANAGER   You're not going to pretend that you can act? It makes me laugh! [*The* ACTORS *laugh.*] There, you see, they are laughing at the notion. But, by the way, I must cast the parts. That won't be difficult. They cast themselves. [*To the* SECOND LADY LEAD.] You play the Mother. [*To the* FATHER.] We must find her a name.

THE FATHER   Amalia, sir.

THE MANAGER   But that is the real name of your wife. We don't want to call her by her real name.

THE FATHER   Why ever not, if it is her name? . . . Still, perhaps, if that lady must . . . [*makes a slight motion of the hand to indicate the* SECOND LADY LEAD]. I see this woman here [*means the* MOTHER] as Amalia. But do as you like. [*Gets more and more confused.*] I don't know what to say to you. Already, I begin to hear my own words ring false, as if they had another sound . . .

THE MANAGER   Don't you worry about it. It'll be our job to find the right tones. And as for her name, if you want her Amalia, Amalia it shall be; and if you don't like it, we'll find another! For the moment though, we'll call the characters in this way: [*to the* JUVENILE LEAD] You are the Son; [*to the* LEADING LADY] You naturally are the Stepdaughter . . .

THE STEPDAUGHTER   [*excitedly*]   What? what? I, that woman there? [*Bursts out laughing.*]

THE MANAGER   [*angry*]   What is there to laugh at?

LEADING LADY   [*indignant*]   Nobody has ever dared to laugh at me. I insist on being treated with respect; otherwise I go away.

THE STEPDAUGHTER   No, no, excuse me . . . I am not laughing at you . . .

THE MANAGER   [*to* STEPDAUGHTER]   You ought to feel honored to be played by . . .

LEADING LADY   [*at once, contemptuously*]   "That woman there" . . .

THE STEPDAUGHTER   But I wasn't speaking of you, you know. I was speaking of myself—whom I can't see at all in you! That is all. I don't know . . . but . . . you . . . aren't in the least like me . . .

THE FATHER   True. Here's the point. Look here, sir, our temperaments, our souls . . .

THE MANAGER   Temperament, soul, be hanged. Do you suppose the spirit of the piece is in you? Nothing of the kind!

THE FATHER   What, haven't we our own temperaments, our own souls?

THE MANAGER   Not at all. Your soul or whatever you like to call it takes shape here. The actors give body and form to it, voice and gesture. And my actors —I may tell you—have given expression to much more lofty material than this little drama of yours, which may or may not hold up on the stage. But if it does, the merit of it, believe me, will be due to my actors.

THE FATHER   I don't dare contradict you, sir; but, believe me, it is a terrible suffering for us who are as we are, with these bodies of ours, these features to see . . .

THE MANAGER   [*cutting him short and out of patience*]   Good heavens! The make-up will remedy all that, man, the make-up . . .

THE FATHER   Maybe. But the voice, the gestures . . .

THE MANAGER   Now, look here! On the stage, you as yourself, cannot exist. The actor here acts you, and that's an end to it!

THE FATHER   I understand. And now I think I see why our author who conceived us as we are, all alive, didn't want to put us on the stage after all. I haven't the least desire to offend your actors. Far from it! But when I think that I am to be acted by . . . I don't know by whom . . .

LEADING MAN [*on his dignity*] By me, if you've no objection!

THE FATHER [*humbly, mellifluously*] Honored, I assure you, sir. [*Bows.*] Still, I must say that try as this gentleman may, with all his good will and wonderful art, to absorb me into himself . . .

LEADING MAN Oh chuck it! "Wonderful art!" Withdraw that, please!

THE FATHER The performance he will give, even doing his best with make-up to look like me . . .

LEADING MAN It will certainly be a bit difficult! [*The* ACTORS *laugh.*]

THE FATHER Exactly! It will be difficult to act me as I really am. The effect will be rather—apart from the make-up—according as to how he supposes I am, as he senses me—if he does sense me—and not as I inside of myself feel myself to be. It seems to me then that account should be taken of this by everyone whose duty it may become to criticize us . . .

THE MANAGER Heavens! The man's starting to think about the critics now! Let them say what they like. It's up to us to put on the play if we can. [*Looking around.*] Come on! come on! Is the stage set? [*To the* ACTORS *and* CHARACTERS.] Stand back—stand back! Let me see, and don't let's lose any more time! [*To the* STEPDAUGHTER.] Is it all right as it is now?

THE STEPDAUGHTER Well, to tell the truth, I don't recognize the scene.

THE MANAGER My dear lady, you can't possibly suppose that we can construct that shop of Madame Pace piece by piece here? [*To the* FATHER.] You said a white room with flowered wall paper, didn't you?

THE FATHER Yes.

THE MANAGER Well then. We've got the furniture right more or less. Bring that little table a bit further forward. [*The stage hands obey the order. To* PROPERTY MAN.] You go and find an envelope, if possible, a pale blue one; and give it to that gentleman. [*Indicates the* FATHER.]

PROPERTY MAN An ordinary envelope?

MANAGER AND FATHER Yes, yes, an ordinary envelope.

PROPERTY MAN At once, sir. [*Exit.*]

THE MANAGER Ready, everyone! First scene—the Young Lady. [*The* LEADING LADY *comes forward.*] No, no, you must wait. I meant her. [*Indicating the* STEPDAUGHTER] You just watch—

THE STEPDAUGHTER [*adding at once*] How I shall play it, how I shall live it! . . .

LEADING LADY [*offended*] I shall live it also, you may be sure, as soon as I begin!

THE MANAGER [*with his hands to his head*] Ladies and gentlemen, if you please! No more useless discussions! Scene I: the young lady with Madame Pace: Oh! [*Looks around as if lost.*] And this Madame Pace, where is she?

THE FATHER She isn't with us, sir.

THE MANAGER Then what the devil's to be done?

THE FATHER But she is alive too.

THE MANAGER Yes, but where is she?

THE FATHER One minute. Let me speak! [*Turning to the* ACTRESSES.] If these ladies would be so good as to give me their hats for a moment . . .

THE ACTRESSES [*half-surprised, half-laughing, in chorus*] What?
Why?
Our hats?
What does he say?

THE MANAGER What are you going to do with the ladies' hats? [*The* ACTORS *laugh.*]

THE FATHER   Oh nothing. I just want to put them on these pegs for a moment. And one of the ladies will be so kind as to take off her mantle . . .

THE ACTORS   Oh, what d'you think of that?

Only the mantle?

He must be mad.

SOME ACTRESSES   But why?

Mantles as well?

THE FATHER   To hang them up here for a moment. Please be so kind, will you?

THE ACTRESSES   [*taking off their hats, one or two also their cloaks, and going to hang them on the racks*]   After all, why not?

There you are!

This is really funny.

We've got to put them on show.

THE FATHER   Exactly; just like that, on show.

THE MANAGER   May we know why?

THE FATHER   I'll tell you. Who knows if, by arranging the stage for her, she does not come here herself, attracted by the very articles of her trade? [*Inviting the* ACTORS *to look towards the exit at back of stage.*] Look! Look!

[*The door at the back of stage opens and* MADAME PACE *enters and takes a few steps forward. She is a fat, oldish woman with puffy oxygenated hair. She is rouged and powdered, dressed with a comical elegance in black silk. Round her waist is a long silver chain from which hangs a pair of scissors. The* STEPDAUGHTER *runs over to her at once amid the stupor of the* ACTORS.]

THE STEPDAUGHTER   [*turning towards her*]   There she is! There she is!

THE FATHER   [*radiant*]   It's she! I said so, didn't I? There she is!

THE MANAGER   [*conquering his surprise, and then becoming indignant*]   What sort of a trick is this?

LEADING MAN   [*almost at the same time*]   What's going to happen next?

JUVENILE LEAD   Where does *she* come from?

L'INGENUE   They've been holding her in reserve, I guess.

LEADING LADY   A vulgar trick!

THE FATHER   [*dominating the protests*]   Excuse me, all of you! Why are you so anxious to destroy in the name of a vulgar, commonplace sense of truth, this reality which comes to birth attracted and formed by the magic of the stage itself, which has indeed more right to live here than you, since it is much truer than you—if you don't mind my saying so? Which is the actress among you who is to play Madame Pace? Well, here is Madame Pace herself. And you will allow, I fancy, that the actress who acts her will be less true than this woman here, who is herself in person. You see my daughter recognized her and went over to her at once. Now you're going to witness the scene.

[*But the scene between the* STEPDAUGHTER *and* MADAME PACE *has already begun despite the protest of the* ACTORS *and the reply of the* FATHER. *It has begun quietly, naturally, in a manner impossible for the stage. So when the* ACTORS, *called to attention by the* FATHER, *turn round and see* MADAME PACE, *who has placed one hand under the* STEPDAUGHTER's *chin to raise her head, they observe her at first with great attention, but hearing her speak in an unintelligible manner their interest begins to wane.*]

THE MANAGER   Well? well?

LEADING MAN   What does she say?

LEADING LADY   One can't hear a word.

JUVENILE LEAD   Louder! Louder please!

THE STEPDAUGHTER   [*leaving* MADAME PACE, *who smiles a Sphinx-like smile, and advancing towards the* ACTORS]   Louder? Louder? What are you talking about? These aren't matters which can be shouted at the top of one's voice. If I have spoken them out loud, it was to shame him and have my revenge. [*Indicates the* FATHER.] But for Madame it's quite a different matter.

THE MANAGER   Indeed? indeed? But here, you know, people have got to make themselves heard, my dear. Even we who are on the stage can't hear you. What will it be when the public's in the theater? And anyway, you can very well speak up now among yourselves, since we shan't be present to listen to you as we are now. You've got to pretend to be alone in a room at the back of a shop where no one can hear you.

[*The* STEPDAUGHTER *coquettishly and with a touch of malice makes a sign of disagreement two or three times with her finger.*]

THE MANAGER   What do you mean by no?

THE STEPDAUGHTER   [*sotto voce, mysteriously*]   There's someone who will hear us if she [*indicating* MADAME PACE] speaks out loud.

THE MANAGER   [*in consternation*]   What? Have you got someone else to spring on us now? [*The* ACTORS *burst out laughing.*]

THE FATHER   No, no sir. She is alluding to me. I've got to be here—there behind that door, in waiting; and Madame Pace knows it. In fact, if you will allow me, I'll go there at once, so I can be quite ready. [*Moves away.*]

THE MANAGER   [*stopping him*]   No! wait! wait! We must observe the conventions of the theater. Before you are ready . . .

THE STEPDAUGHTER   [*interrupting him*]   No, get on with it at once! I'm just dying, I tell you, to act this scene. If he's ready, I'm more than ready.

THE MANAGER   [*shouting*]   But, my dear young lady, first of all, we must have the scene between you and this lady . . . [*Indicates* MADAME PACE.] Do you understand? . . .

THE STEPDAUGHTER   Good Heavens! She's been telling me what you know already: that mamma's work is badly done again, that the material's ruined; and that if I want her to continue to help us in our misery I must be patient . . .

MADAME PACE   [*coming forward with an air of great importance*]   Yes indeed, sir, I no wanta take advantage of her, I no wanta be hard . . .

[*Note:* MADAME PACE *is supposed to talk in a jargon half Italian, half English.*]

THE MANAGER   [*alarmed*]   What? What? she talks like that? [*The* ACTORS *burst out laughing again.*]

THE STEPDAUGHTER   [*also laughing*]   Yes, yes, that's the way she talks, half English, half Italian! Most comical it is!

MADAME PACE   Itta seem not verra polite gentlemen laugha atta me eef I trya best speaka English.

THE MANAGER   *Diamine!*³ Of course! Of course! Let her talk like that! Just what we want. Talk just like that, Madame, if you please! The effect will be certain. Exactly what was wanted to put a little comic relief into the crudity of the situation. Of course she talks like that! Magnificent!

THE STEPDAUGHTER   Magnificent? Certainly! When certain suggestions are made to one in language of that kind, the effect is certain, since it seems almost a joke. One feels inclined to laugh when one hears her talk about an "old signore" "who wanta talka nicely with you." Nice old signore, eh, Madame?

MADAME PACE   Not so old, my dear, not so old! And even if you no lika him, he won't make any scandal!

THE MOTHER   [*jumping up amid the amazement and consternation of the* ACTORS, *who had not been noticing her. They move to restrain her*]   You old devil! You murderess!

---

³ (Italian) The deuce!

THE STEPDAUGHTER [*running over to calm her* MOTHER] Calm yourself, mother, calm yourself! Please don't . . .

THE FATHER [*going to her also at the same time*] Calm yourself! Don't get excited! Sit down now!

THE MOTHER Well then, take that woman away out of my sight!

THE STEPDAUGHTER [*to the* MANAGER] It is impossible for my mother to remain here.

THE FATHER [*to the* MANAGER] They can't be here together. And for this reason, you see: that woman there was not with us when we came . . . If they are on together, the whole thing is given away inevitably, as you see.

THE MANAGER It doesn't matter. This is only a first rough sketch—just to get an idea of the various points of the scene, even confusedly . . . [*Turning to the* MOTHER *and leading her to her chair.*] Come along, my dear lady, sit down now, and let's get on with the scene . . .

[*Meanwhile, the* STEPDAUGHTER, *coming forward again, turns to* MADAME PACE.]

THE STEPDAUGHTER Come on, Madame, come on!

MADAME PACE [*offended*] No, no, *grazie*.[4] I not do anything witha your mother present.

THE STEPDAUGHTER Nonsense! Introduce this "old signore" who wants to talk nicely to me. [*Addressing the company imperiously.*] We've got to do this scene one way or another, haven't we? Come on! [*To* MADAME PACE.] You can go!

MADAME PACE Ah yes! I go'way! I go'way! Certainly! [*Exit furious.*]

THE STEPDAUGHTER [*to the* FATHER] Now you make your entry. No, you needn't go over here. Come here. Let's suppose you've already come in. Like that, yes! I'm here with bowed head, modest like. Come on! Out with your voice! Say "Good morning, Miss" in that peculiar tone, that special tone . . .

THE MANAGER Excuse me, but are you the Manager, or am I? [*To the* FATHER, *who looks undecided and perplexed.*] Get on with it, man! Go down there to the back of the stage. You needn't go off. Then come right forward here. [*The* FATHER *does as he is told, looking troubled and perplexed at first. But as soon as he begins to move, the reality of the action affects him, and he begins to smile and to be more natural. The* ACTORS *watch intently.*]

THE MANAGER [*sotto voce, quickly to the* PROMPTER *in his box*] Ready! ready? Get ready to write now.

THE FATHER [*coming forward and speaking in a different tone*] Good afternoon, Miss!

THE STEPDAUGHTER [*head bowed down slightly, with restrained disgust*] Good afternoon!

THE FATHER [*looks under her hat which partly covers her face. Perceiving she is very young, he makes an exclamation, partly of surprise, partly of fear lest he compromise himself in a risky adventure.*] Ah . . . but . . . ah . . . I say . . . this is not the first time that you have come here, is it?

THE STEPDAUGHTER [*modestly*] No sir.

THE FATHER You've been here before, eh? [*Then seeing her nod agreement.*] More than once? [*Waits for her to answer, looks under her hat, smiles, and then says.*] Well then, there's no need to be so shy, is there? May I take off your hat?

THE STEPDAUGHTER [*anticipating him and with veiled disgust*] No sir . . . I'll do it myself. [*Takes it off quickly.*]

[*The* MOTHER, *who watches the progress of the scene with the* SON *and the*

---

4 (Italian) Thank you (with the implication, as frequently in English, that what is offered is not really desirable).

other two CHILDREN, *who cling to her, is on thorns; and follows with varying expressions of sorrow, indignation, anxiety, and horror the words and
actions of the other two. From time to time she hides her face in her hands
and sobs.*]

THE MOTHER   Oh, my God, my God!

THE FATHER   [*playing his part with a touch of gallantry*]   Give it to me! I'll put
it down. [*Takes hat from her hands.*] But a dear little head like yours ought
to have a smarter hat. Come and help me choose one from the stock, won't
you?

L'INGENUE   [*interrupting*]   I say . . . those are our hats you know.

THE MANAGER   [*furious*]   Silence! silence! Don't try and be funny, if you please
. . . We're playing the scene now I'd have you notice. [*To the* STEP-
DAUGHTER.] Begin again, please!

THE STEPDAUGHTER   [*continuing*]   No thank you, sir.

THE FATHER   Oh, come now. Don't talk like that. You must take it. I shall be
upset if you don't. There are some lovely little hats here; and then—Madame
will be pleased. She expects it, anyway, you know.

THE STEPDAUGHTER   No, no! I couldn't wear it!

THE FATHER   Oh, you're thinking about what they'd say at home if they saw you
come in with a new hat? My dear girl, there's always a way round these little
matters, you know.

THE STEPDAUGHTER   [*all keyed up*]   No, it's not that. I couldn't wear it because
I am . . . as you see . . . you might have noticed . . . [*Showing her black
dress.*]

THE FATHER   . . . in mourning! Of course: I beg your pardon: I'm frightfully
sorry . . .

THE STEPDAUGHTER   [*forcing herself to conquer her indignation and nausea*]
Stop! Stop! It's I who must thank you. There's no need for you to feel
mortified or specially sorry. Don't think any more of what I've said. [*Tries to
smile.*] I must forget that I am dressed so . . .

THE MANAGER   [*interrupting and turning to the* PROMPTER]   Stop a minute!
Stop! Don't write that down. Cut out that last bit. [*Then to the* FATHER *and
the* STEPDAUGHTER.] Fine! It's going fine! [*To the* FATHER *only*.] And now
you can go on as we arranged. [*To the* ACTORS.] Pretty good that scene,
where he offers her the hat, eh?

THE STEPDAUGHTER   The best's coming now. Why can't we go on?

THE MANAGER   Have a little patience! [*To the* ACTORS] Of course, it must be
treated rather lightly.

LEADING MAN   Still, with a bit of go in it!

LEADING LADY   Of course! It's easy enough! [*To the* LEADING MAN.] Shall you and
I try it now?

LEADING MAN   Why, yes! I'll prepare my entrance. [*Exit in order to make his
entrance.*]

THE MANAGER   [*to the* LEADING LADY]   See here! The scene between you and
Madame Pace is finished. I'll have it written out properly after. You remain here . . . oh, where are you going?

LEADING LADY   One minute. I want to put my hat on again. [*Goes over to hat-
rack and puts her hat on her head.*]

THE MANAGER   Good! You stay here with your head bowed down a bit.

THE STEPDAUGHTER   But she isn't dressed in black.

LEADING LADY   But I shall be, and much more effectively than you.

THE MANAGER   [*to* STEPDAUGHTER]   Be quiet please, and watch! You'll be able
to learn something. [*Clapping his hands.*] Come on! come on! Entrance,
please!

[*The door at rear of stage opens, and the* LEADING MAN *enters with the lively manner of an old gallant. The rendering of the scene by the* ACTORS *from the very first words is seen to be quite a different thing, though it has not in any way the air of a parody. Naturally, the* STEPDAUGHTER *and the* FATHER, *not being able to recognize themselves in the* LEADING LADY *and the* LEADING MAN, *who deliver their words in different tones and with a different psychology, express, sometimes with smiles, sometimes with gestures, the impression they receive.*]

LEADING MAN   Good afternoon, Miss . . .

THE FATHER   [*at once unable to contain himself*]   No! no!

[*The* STEPDAUGHTER *noticing the way the* LEADING MAN *enters, bursts out laughing.*]

THE MANAGER   [*furious*]   Silence! And you please just stop that laughing. If we go on like this, we shall never finish.

THE STEPDAUGHTER   Forgive me, sir, but it's natural enough. This lady [*indicating* LEADING LADY] stands there still; but if she is supposed to be me, I can assure you that if I heard anyone say "Good afternoon" in that manner and in that tone, I should burst out laughing as I did.

THE FATHER   Yes, yes, the manner, the tone . . .

THE MANAGER   Nonsense! Rubbish! Stand aside and let me see the action.

LEADING MAN   If I've got to represent an old fellow who's coming into a house of an equivocal character . . .

THE MANAGER   Don't listen to them, for Heaven's sake! Do it again! It goes fine. [*Waiting for the* ACTORS *to begin again.*] Well?

LEADING MAN   Good afternoon, Miss.

LEADING LADY   Good afternoon.

LEADING MAN   [*imitating the gesture of the* FATHER *when he looked under the hat, and then expressing quite clearly first satisfaction and then fear*] Ah, but . . . I say . . . this is not the first time that you have come here, is it?

THE MANAGER   Good, but not quite so heavily. Like this. [*Acts himself.*] "This isn't the first time that you have come here" . . . [*To the* LEADING LADY.] And you say: "No, sir."

LEADING LADY   No, sir.

LEADING MAN   You've been here before, more than once.

THE MANAGER   No, no, stop! Let her nod "yes" first. "You've been here before, eh?" [*The* LEADING LADY *lifts up her head slightly and closes her eyes as though in disgust. Then she inclines her head twice.*]

THE STEPDAUGHTER   [*unable to contain herself*]   Oh my God! [*Puts a hand to her mouth to prevent herself from laughing.*]

THE MANAGER   [*turning round*]   What's the matter?

THE STEPDAUGHTER   Nothing, nothing!

THE MANAGER   [*to* LEADING MAN]   Go on!

LEADING MAN   You've been here before, eh? Well then, there's no need to be so shy, is there? May I take off your hat?

[*The* LEADING MAN *says this last speech in such a tone and with such gestures that the* STEPDAUGHTER, *though she has her hand to her mouth, cannot keep from laughing.*]

LEADING LADY   [*indignant*]   I'm not going to stop here to be made a fool of by that woman there.

LEADING MAN   Neither am I! I'm through with it!

THE MANAGER   [*shouting to* STEPDAUGHTER]   Silence! for once and all, I tell you!

THE STEPDAUGHTER   Forgive me! forgive me!

THE MANAGER   You haven't any manners: that's what it is! You go too far.

THE FATHER   [*endeavoring to intervene*]   Yes, it's true, but excuse her . . .

THE MANAGER   Excuse what? It's absolutely disgusting.

THE FATHER   Yes, sir, but believe me, it has such a strange effect when . . .

THE MANAGER   Strange? Why strange? Where is it strange?

THE FATHER   No, sir; I admire your actors—this gentleman here, this lady; but they are certainly not us!

THE MANAGER   I should hope not. Evidently they cannot be you, if they are actors.

THE FATHER   Just so: actors! Both of them act our parts exceedingly well. But, believe me, it produces quite a different effect on us. They want to be us, but they aren't, all the same.

THE MANAGER   What is it then anyway?

THE FATHER   Something that is . . . that is theirs—and no longer ours . . .

THE MANAGER   But naturally, inevitably. I've told you so already.

THE FATHER   Yes, I understand . . . I understand . . .

THE MANAGER   Well then, let's have no more of it! [*Turning to the* ACTORS.] We'll have the rehearsals by ourselves, afterwards, in the ordinary way. I never could stand rehearsing with the author present. He's never satisfied! [*Turning to the* FATHER *and* STEPDAUGHTER.] Come on! Let's get on with it again; and try and see if you can't keep from laughing.

THE STEPDAUGHTER   Oh, I shan't laugh any more. There's a nice little bit coming for me now: you'll see.

THE MANAGER   Well then: when she says "Don't think any more of what I've said. I must forget, etc.," you [*addressing the* FATHER] come in sharp with "I understand, I understand"; and then you ask her . . .

THE STEPDAUGHTER   [*interrupting*]   What?

THE MANAGER   Why she is in mourning.

THE STEPDAUGHTER   Not at all! See here: when I told him that it was useless for me to be thinking about my wearing mourning, do you know how he answered me? "Ah well," he said, "then let's take off this little frock."

THE MANAGER   Great! Just what we want, to make a riot in the theater!

THE STEPDAUGHTER   But it's the truth!

THE MANAGER   What does that matter? Acting is our business here. Truth up to a certain point, but no further.

THE STEPDAUGHTER   What do you want to do then?

THE MANAGER   You'll see, you'll see! Leave it to me.

THE STEPDAUGHTER   No sir! What you want to do is to piece together a little romantic sentimental scene out of my disgust, out of all the reasons, each more cruel and viler than the other, why I am what I am. He is to ask me why I'm in mourning; and I'm to answer with tears in my eyes, that it is just two months since papa died. No sir, no! He's got to say to me; as he did say: "Well, let's take off this little dress at once." And I; with my two months' mourning in my heart, went there behind that screen, and with these fingers tingling with shame . . .

THE MANAGER   [*running his hands through his hair*]   For Heaven's sake! What are you saying?

THE STEPDAUGHTER   [*crying out excitedly*]   The truth! The truth!

THE MANAGER   It may be. I don't deny it, and I can understand all your horror; but you must surely see that you can't have this kind of thing on the stage. It won't go.

THE STEPDAUGHTER   Not possible, eh? Very well! I'm much obliged to you— but I'm off!

THE MANAGER   Now be reasonable! Don't lose your temper!

THE STEPDAUGHTER   I won't stop here! I won't! I can see you've fixed it all up with him in your office. All this talk about what is possible for the stage . . . I understand! He wants to get at his complicated "cerebral drama," to have his famous remorses and torments acted; but I want to act my part, *my part!*

THE MANAGER   [*annoyed, shaking his shoulders*]   Ah! Just *your* part! But, if you will pardon me, there are other parts than yours: his [*indicating the* FATHER] and hers! [*Indicating the* MOTHER.] On the stage you can't have a character becoming too prominent and overshadowing all the others. The thing is to pack them all into a neat little framework and then act what is actable. I am aware of the fact that everyone has his own interior life which he wants very much to put forward. But the difficulty lies in this fact: to set out just so much as is necessary for the stage, taking the other characters into consideration, and at the same time hint at the unrevealed interior life of each. I am willing to admit, my dear young lady, that from your point of view it would be a fine idea if each character could tell the public all his troubles in a nice monologue or a regular one-hour lecture. [*Good-humoredly.*] You must restrain yourself, my dear, and in your own interest, too; because this fury of yours, this exaggerated disgust you show, may make a bad impression, you know. After you have confessed to me that there were others before him at Madame Pace's and more than once . . .

THE STEPDAUGHTER   [*bowing her head, impressed*]   It's true. But remember those others mean him for me all the same.

THE MANAGER   [*not understanding*]   What? The others? What do you mean?

THE STEPDAUGHTER   For one who has gone wrong, sir, he who was responsible for the first fault is responsible for all that follow. He is responsible for my faults, was, even before I was born. Look at him, and see if it isn't true!

THE MANAGER   Well, well! And does the weight of so much responsibility seem nothing to you? Give him a chance to act it, to get it over!

THE STEPDAUGHTER   How? How can he act all his "noble remorses," all his "moral torments," if you want to spare him the horror of being discovered one day—after he had asked her what he did ask her—in the arms of her, that already fallen woman, that child, sir, that child he used to watch come out of school? [*She is moved.*]

[*The* MOTHER *at this point is overcome with emotion, and breaks out into a fit of crying. All are touched. A long pause.*]

THE STEPDAUGHTER   [*as soon as the* MOTHER *becomes a little quieter, adds resolutely and gravely*]   At present, we are unknown to the public. Tomorrow, you will act us as you wish, treating us in your own manner. But do you really want to see drama, do you want to see it flash out as it really did?

THE MANAGER   Of course! That's just what I do want, so I can use as much of it as is possible.

THE STEPDAUGHTER   Well then, ask that Mother there to leave us.

THE MOTHER   [*changing her low plaint into a sharp cry*]   No! No! Don't permit it, sir, don't permit it!

THE MANAGER   But it's only to try it.

THE MOTHER   I can't bear it. I can't.

THE MANAGER   But since it has happened already . . . I don't understand!

THE MOTHER   It's taking place now. It happens all the time. My torment isn't a pretended one. I live and feel every minute of my torture. Those two children there—have you heard them speak? They can't speak any more. They cling to me to keep my torment actual and vivid for me. But for themselves, they do not exist, they aren't any more. And she [*indicating* STEPDAUGHTER] has run away, she has left me, and is lost. If I now see her here before me, it is only to renew for me the tortures I have suffered for her too.

THE FATHER   The eternal moment! She [*indicating the* STEPDAUGHTER] is here to catch me, fix me, and hold me eternally in the stocks for that one fleeting and shameful moment of my life. She can't give it up! And you, sir, cannot either fairly spare me it.

THE MANAGER   I never said I didn't want to act it. It will form, as a matter of fact, the nucleus of the whole first act right up to her surprise. [*Indicating the* MOTHER.]

THE FATHER   Just so! This is my punishment: the passion in all of us that must culminate in her final cry.

THE STEPDAUGHTER   I can hear it still in my ears. It's driven me mad, that cry!— You can put me on as you like; it doesn't matter. Fully dressed, if you like —provided I have at least the arm bare; because, standing like this [*she goes close to the* FATHER *and leans her head on his breast*] with my head so, and my arms round his neck, I saw a vein pulsing in my arm here; and then, as if that live vein had awakened disgust in me, I closed my eyes like this, and let my head sink on his breast. [*Turning to the* MOTHER.] Cry out, mother! Cry out! [*Buries head in the* FATHER'S *breast, and with her shoulders raised as if to prevent her hearing the cry, adds in tones of intense emotion.*] Cry out as you did then!

THE MOTHER   [*coming forward to separate them*] No! My daughter, my daughter! [*And after having pulled her away from him.*] You brute! you brute! She is my daughter! Don't you see she's my daughter?

THE MANAGER   [*walking backwards toward footlights*] Fine! fine! Damned good! And then, of course—curtain!

THE FATHER   [*going towards him excitedly*] Yes, of course, because that's the way it really happened.

THE MANAGER   [*convinced and pleased*] Oh, yes, no doubt about it. Curtain here, curtain!

[*At the reiterated cry of the* MANAGER, *the* MACHINIST *lets the curtain down, leaving the* MANAGER *and the* FATHER *in front of it before the footlights.*]

THE MANAGER   The darned idiot! I said "curtain" to show the act should end there, and he goes and lets it down in earnest. [*To the* FATHER, *while he pulls the curtain back to go on to the stage again.*] Yes, yes, it's all right. Effect certain! That's the right ending. I'll guarantee the first act at any rate.

ACT III

When the curtain goes up again, it is seen that the stage hands have shifted the bit of scenery used in the last part, and have rigged up instead at the back of the stage a drop, with some trees, and one or two wings. A portion of a fountain basin is visible. The MOTHER *is sitting on the Right with the two children by her side. The* SON *is on the same side, but away from the others. He seems bored, angry, and full of shame. The* FATHER *and the* STEPDAUGHTER *are also seated towards the Right front. On the other side (Left) are the* ACTORS, *much in the positions they occupied before the curtain was lowered. Only the* MANAGER *is standing up in the middle of the stage, with his hand closed over his mouth in the act of meditating.*

THE MANAGER [*shaking his shoulders after a brief pause*] Ah yes: the second act! Leave it to me, leave it all to me as we arranged, and you'll see! It'll go fine!

THE STEPDAUGHTER Our entry into his house [*indicates the* FATHER] in spite of him . . . [*indicates the* SON].

THE MANAGER [*out of patience*] Leave it to me. I tell you!

THE STEPDAUGHTER Do let it be clear, at any rate, that it is in spite of my wishes.

THE MOTHER [*from her corner, shaking her head*] For all the good that's come of it . . .

THE STEPDAUGHTER [*turning towards her quickly*] It doesn't matter. The more harm done us, the more remorse for him.

THE MANAGER [*impatiently*] I understand! Good Heavens! I understand! I'm taking it into account.

THE MOTHER [*supplicatingly*] I beg you, sir, to let it appear quite plain that for conscience' sake I did try in every way . . .

THE STEPDAUGHTER [*interrupting indignantly and continuing for the* MOTHER] . . . to pacify me, to dissuade me from spiting him. [*To* MANAGER.] Do as she wants: satisfy her, because it is true! I enjoy it immensely. Anyhow, as you can see, the meeker she is, the more she tries to get at his heart, the more distant and aloof does he become.

THE MANAGER Are we going to begin this second act or not?

THE STEPDAUGHTER I'm not going to talk any more now. But I must tell you this: you can't have the whole action take place in the garden, as you suggest. It isn't possible!

THE MANAGER Why not?

THE STEPDAUGHTER Because he [*indicates the* SON *again*] is always shut up alone in his room. And then there's all the part of that poor dazed-looking boy there which takes place indoors.

THE MANAGER Maybe! On the other hand, you will understand—we can't change scenes three or four times in one act.

THE LEADING MAN They used to once.

THE MANAGER Yes, when the public was up to the level of that child there.

THE LEADING LADY It makes the illusion easier.

THE FATHER [*irritated*] The illusion! For Heaven's sake, don't say illusion. Please don't use that word, which is particularly painful for us.

THE MANAGER [*astounded*] And why, if you please?

THE FATHER It's painful, cruel, really cruel; and you ought to understand that.

THE MANAGER But why? What ought we to say then? The illusion, I tell you sir, which we've got to create for the audience . . .

THE LEADING MAN With our acting.

THE MANAGER The illusion of a reality.

THE FATHER I understand; but you, perhaps, do not understand us. Forgive me! You see . . . here for you and your actors, the thing is only—and rightly so . . . a kind of game . . .

THE LEADING LADY [*interrupting indignantly*] A game! We're not children here, if you please! We are serious actors.

THE FATHER I don't deny it. What I mean is the game, or play, of your art, which has to give, as the gentleman says, a perfect illusion of reality.

THE MANAGER Precisely——!

THE FATHER Now, if you consider the fact that we [*indicates himself and the other five* CHARACTERS], as we are, have no other reality outside of this illusion . . .

THE MANAGER [*astonished, looking at his* ACTORS, *who are also amazed*] And what does that mean?

THE FATHER   [*after watching them for a moment with a wan smile*] As I say, sir, that which is a game of art for you is our sole reality. [*Brief pause. He goes a step or two nearer the* MANAGER *and adds*] But not only for us, you know, by the way. Just you think it over well. [*Looks him in the eyes.*] Can you tell me who you are?

THE MANAGER   [*perplexed, half smiling*]   What? Who am I? I am myself.

THE FATHER   And if I were to tell you that that isn't true, because you are I? . . .

THE MANAGER   I should say you were mad——! [*The* ACTORS *laugh.*]

THE FATHER   You're quite right to laugh: because we are all making believe here. [*To the* MANAGER.] And you can therefore object that it's only for a joke that that gentleman there [*indicates the* LEADING MAN], who naturally is himself, has to be me, who am on the contrary myself—this thing you see here. You see I've caught you in a trap! [*The* ACTORS *laugh.*]

THE MANAGER   [*annoyed*]   But we've had all this over once before. Do you want to begin again?

THE FATHER   No, no! that wasn't my meaning! In fact, I should like to request you to abandon this game of art [*looking at the* LEADING LADY *as if anticipating her*] which you are accustomed to play here with your actors, and to ask you seriously once again: who are you?

THE MANAGER   [*astonished and irritated, turning to his* ACTORS]   If this fellow here hasn't got a nerve! A man who calls himself a character comes and asks me who I am!

THE FATHER   [*with dignity, but not offended*]   A character, sir, may always ask a man who he is. Because a character has really a life of his own, marked with his especial characteristics; for which reason he is always "somebody." But a man—I'm not speaking of you now—may very well be "nobody."

THE MANAGER   Yes, but you are asking these questions of me, the boss, the manager! Do you understand?

THE FATHER   But only in order to know if you, as you really are now, see yourself as you once were with all the illusions that were yours then, with all the things both inside and outside of you as they seemed to you—as they were then indeed for you. Well, sir, if you think of all those illusions that mean nothing to you now, of all those things which don't even *seem* to you to exist any more, while once they *were* for you, don't you feel that—I won't say these boards—but the very earth under your feet is sinking away from you when you reflect that in the same way this *you* as you feel it today —all this present reality of yours—is fated to seem a mere illusion to you tomorrow?

THE MANAGER   [*without having understood much, but astonished by the specious argument*]   Well, well! And where does all this take us anyway?

THE FATHER   Oh, nowhere! It's only to show you that if we [*indicating the* CHARACTERS] have no other reality beyond illusion, you too must not count overmuch on your reality as you feel it today, since, like that of yesterday, it may prove an illusion for you tomorrow.

THE MANAGER   [*determining to make fun of him*]   Ah, excellent! Then you'll be saying next that you, with this comedy of yours that you brought here to act, are truer and more real than I am.

THE FATHER   [*with the greatest seriousness*]   But of course; without doubt!

THE MANAGER   Ah, really?

THE FATHER   Why, I thought you'd understand that from the beginning.

THE MANAGER   More real than I?

THE FATHER   If your reality can change from one day to another . . .

THE MANAGER   But everyone knows it can change. It is always changing, the same as anyone else's.

THE FATHER [*with a cry*] No, sir, not ours! Look here! That is the very difference! Our reality doesn't change: it can't change! It can't be other than
what it is, because it is already fixed for ever. It's terrible. Ours is an immutable reality which should make you shudder when you approach us if
you are really conscious of the fact that your reality is a mere transitory and
fleeting illusion, taking this form today and that tomorrow, according to the
conditions, according to your will, your sentiments, which in turn are
controlled by an intellect that shows them to you today in one manner and
tomorrow . . . who knows how? . . . Illusions of reality represented in
this fatuous comedy of life that never ends, nor can ever end! Because if
tomorrow it were to end . . . then why, all would be finished.

THE MANAGER Oh for God's sake, will you *at least* finish with this philosophizing and let us try and shape this comedy which you yourself have brought
me here? You argue and philosophize a bit too much, my dear sir. You
know you seem to me almost, almost . . . [*Stops and looks him over from
head to foot.*] Ah, by the way, I think you introduced yourself to me as a—
what shall . . . we say—a "character," created by an author who did not
afterwards care to make a drama of his own creations.

THE FATHER It is the simple truth, sir.

THE MANAGER Nonsense! Cut that out, please! None of us believes it, because
it isn't a thing, as you must recognize yourself, which one can believe seriously. If you want to know, it seems to me you are trying to imitate the
manner of a certain author whom I heartily detest—I warn you—although
I have unfortunately bound myself to put on one of his works. As a matter
of fact, I was just starting to rehearse it, when you arrived. [*Turning to
the* ACTORS.] And this is what we've gained—out of the frying-pan into the
fire!

THE FATHER I don't know to what author you may be alluding, but believe
me I feel what I think; and I seem to be philosophizing only for those who
do not think what they feel, because they blind themselves with their own
sentiment. I know that for many people this self-blinding seems much more
"human"; but the contrary is really true. For man never reasons so much
and becomes so introspective as when he suffers; since he is anxious to get
at the cause of his sufferings, to learn who has produced them, and whether
it is just or unjust that he should have to bear them. On the other hand,
when he is happy, he takes his happiness as it comes and doesn't analyze it,
just as if happiness were his right. The animals suffer without reasoning
about their sufferings. But take the case of a man who suffers and begins
to reason about it. Oh no! it can't be allowed! Let him suffer like an
animal, and then—ah yes, he is "human!"

THE MANAGER Look here! Look here! You're off again, philosophizing worse
than ever.

THE FATHER Because I suffer, sir! I'm not philosophizing: I'm crying aloud the
reason of my sufferings.

THE MANAGER [*makes brusque movement as he is taken with a new idea*] I
should like to know if anyone has ever heard of a character who gets right
out of his part and perorates and speechifies as you do. Have you ever
heard of a case? I haven't.

THE FATHER You have never met such a case, sir, because authors, as a rule,
hide the labor of their creations. When the characters are really alive before their author, the latter does nothing but follow them in their action,
in their words, in the situations which they suggest to him; and he has to
will them the way they will themselves—for there's trouble if he doesn't.
When a character is born, he acquires at once such an independence, even
of his own author, that he can be imagined by everybody even in many

other situations where the author never dreamed of placing him; and so he acquires for himself a meaning which the author never thought of giving him.

THE MANAGER   Yes, yes, I know this.

THE FATHER   What is there then to marvel at in us? Imagine such a misfortune for characters as I have described to you: to be born of an author's fantasy, and be denied life by him; and then answer me if these characters left alive, and yet without life, weren't right in doing what they did do and are doing now, after they have attempted everything in their power to persuade him to give them their stage life. We've all tried him in turn, I, she [indicating the STEPDAUGHTER] and she [indicating the MOTHER].

THE STEPDAUGHTER   It's true. I too have sought to tempt him, many, many times, when he has been sitting at his writing table, feeling a bit melancholy, at the twilight hour. He would sit in his armchair too lazy to switch on the light, and all the shadows that crept into his room were full of our presence coming to tempt him. [As if she saw herself still there by the writing table, and was annoyed by the presence of the ACTORS.] Oh, if you would only go away, go away and leave us alone—mother here with that son of hers—I with that Child—that Boy there always alone—and then I with him—[just hints at the FATHER]—and then I alone, alone . . . in those shadows! [Makes a sudden movement as if in the vision she has of herself illuminating those shadows she wanted to seize hold of herself.] Ah! my life! my life! Oh, what scenes we proposed to him—and I tempted him more than any of the others!

THE FATHER   Maybe. But perhaps it was your fault that he refused to give us life: because you were too insistent, too troublesome.

THE STEPDAUGHTER   Nonsense! Didn't he make me so himself? [Goes close to the MANAGER to tell him as if in confidence.] In my opinion he abandoned us in a fit of depression, of disgust for the ordinary theater as the public knows it and likes it.

THE SON   Exactly what it was, sir; exactly that!

THE FATHER   Not at all! Don't believe it for a minute. Listen to me! You'll be doing quite right to modify, as you suggest, the excesses both of this girl here, who wants to do too much, and of this young man, who won't do anything at all.

THE SON   No, nothing!

THE MANAGER   You too get over the mark occasionally, my dear sir, if I may say so.

THE FATHER   I? When? Where?

THE MANAGER   Always! Continuously! Then there's this insistence of yours in trying to make us believe you are a character. And then too, you must really argue and philosophize less, you know, much less.

THE FATHER   Well, if you want to take away from me the possibility of representing the torment of my spirit which never gives me peace, you will be suppressing me: that's all. Every true man, sir, who is a little above the level of the beasts and plants does not live for the sake of living, without knowing how to live; but he lives so as to give a meaning and a value of his own to life. For me this is *everything*. I cannot give up this, just to represent a mere fact as she [indicating the STEPDAUGHTER] wants. It's all very well for her, since her "vendetta" lies in the "fact." I'm not going to do it. It destroys my *raison d'être*.

THE MANAGER   Your *raison d'être*! Oh, we're going ahead fine! First she starts off, and then you jump in. At this rate, we'll never finish.

THE FATHER   Now, don't be offended. Have it your own way—provided, how-

ever, that within the limits of the parts you assign us each one's sacrifice
isn't too great.

THE MANAGER You've got to understand that you can't go on arguing at your
own pleasure. Drama is action, sir, action and not confounded philosophy.

THE FATHER All right. I'll do just as much arguing and philosophizing as
everybody does when he is considering his own torments.

THE MANAGER If the drama permits! But for Heaven's sake, man, let's get
along and come to the scene.

THE STEPDAUGHTER It seems to me we've got too much action with our coming
into his house. [*Indicating* FATHER.] You said, before, you couldn't change
the scene every five minutes.

THE MANAGER Of course not. What we've got to do is to combine and group
up all the facts in one simultaneous, close-knit action. We can't have it as
you want, with your little brother wandering like a ghost from room to
room, hiding behind doors and meditating a project which—what did you
say it did to him?

THE STEPDAUGHTER Consumes him, sir, wastes him away!

THE MANAGER Well, it may be. And then at the same time, you want the little
girl there to be playing in the garden . . . one in the house, and the other
in the garden: isn't that it?

THE STEPDAUGHTER Yes, in the sun, in the sun! That is my only pleasure: to
see her happy and careless in the garden after the misery and squalor of
the horrible room where we all four slept together. And I had to sleep
with her—I, do you understand?—with my vile contaminated body next to
hers with her folding me fast in her loving little arms. In the garden,
whenever she spied me, she would run to take me by the hand. She didn't
care for the big flowers, only the little ones; and she loved to show me
them and pet me.

THE MANAGER Well then, we'll have it in the garden. Everything shall happen
in the garden; and we'll group the other scenes there. [*Calls a stage hand.*]
Here, a back-cloth with trees and something to do as a fountain basin.
[*Turning around to look at the back of the stage.*] Ah, you've fixed it up.
Good! [*To the* STEPDAUGHTER.] This is just to give an idea, of course. The
boy, instead of hiding behind the doors, will wander about here in the
garden, hiding behind the trees. But it's going to be rather difficult to find
a child to do that scene with you where she shows you the flowers. [*Turning
to the* YOUTH.] Come forward a little, will you please? Let's try it now!
Come along! come along! [*Then seeing him come shyly forward, full of
fear and looking lost.*] It's a nice business, this lad here. What's the matter
with him? We'll have to give him a word or two to say. [*Goes close to
him, puts a hand on his shoulders, and leads him behind one of the trees.*]
Come on! come on! Let me see you a little! Hide here . . . yes, like that.
Try and show your head just a little as if you were looking for someone
. . . [*Goes back to observe the effect, when the* BOY *at once goes through
the action.*] Excellent! fine! [*Turning to the* STEPDAUGHTER.] Suppose the
little girl there were to surprise him as he looks round, and run over to
him, so we could give him a word or two to say?

THE STEPDAUGHTER It's useless to hope he will speak, as long as that fellow
there is here . . . [*Indicates the* SON.] You must send him away first.

THE SON [*jumping up*] Delighted! delighted! I don't ask for anything better.
[*Begins to move away.*]

THE MANAGER [*at once stopping him*] No! No! Where are you going? Wait
a bit!

[*The* MOTHER *gets up alarmed and terrified at the thought that he is really about to go away. Instinctively she lifts her arms to prevent him, without, however, leaving her seat.*]

THE SON [*to* MANAGER *who stops him*] I've got nothing to do with this affair. Let me go please! Let me go!

THE MANAGER What do you mean by saying you've got nothing to do with this?

THE STEPDAUGHTER [*calmly, with irony*] Don't bother to stop him: he won't go away.

THE FATHER He has to act the terrible scene in the garden with his mother.

THE SON [*suddenly resolute and with dignity*] I shall act nothing at all. I've said so from the very beginning. [*To the* MANAGER.] Let me go!

THE STEPDAUGHTER [*going over to the* MANAGER] Allow me? [*Puts down the* MANAGER's *arm, which is restraining the* SON.] Well, go away then, if you want to! [*The* SON *looks at her with contempt and hatred. She laughs and says.*] You see, he can't, he can't go away! He is obliged to stay here, indissolubly bound to the chain. If I, who fly off when that happens which has to happen, because I can't bear him—if I am still here and support that face and expression of his, you can well imagine that he is unable to move. He has to remain here, has to stop with that nice father of his, and that mother whose only son he is. [*Turning to the* MOTHER.] Come on, mother, come along! [*Turning to the* MANAGER *to indicate her.*] You see, she was getting up to keep him back. [*To the* MOTHER, *beckoning her with her hand.*] Come on! come on! [*Then to the* MANAGER.] You can imagine how little she wants to show these actors of yours what she really feels; but so eager is she to get near him that . . . There, you see? She is willing to act her part. [*And in fact, the* MOTHER *approaches him; and as soon as the* STEPDAUGHTER *has finished speaking, opens her arms to signify that she consents.*]

THE SON [*suddenly*] No! no! I can't go away, then I'll stop here; but I repeat: I act nothing!

THE FATHER [*to the* MANAGER *excitedly*] You can force him, sir.

THE SON Nobody can force me.

THE FATHER I can.

THE STEPDAUGHTER Wait a minute, wait . . . First of all, the baby has to go to the fountain . . . [*Runs to take the* CHILD *and leads her to the fountain.*]

THE MANAGER Yes, yes of course; that's it. Both at the same time.

[*The* SECOND LADY LEAD *and the* JUVENILE LEAD *at this point separate themselves from the group of* ACTORS. *One watches the* MOTHER *attentively; the other moves about studying the movements and manner of the* SON, *whom he will have to act.*]

THE SON [*to the* MANAGER] What do you mean by both at the same time? It isn't right. There was no scene between me and her. [*Indicates the* MOTHER.] Ask her how it was!

THE MOTHER Yes, it's true. I had come into his room . . .

THE SON Into my room, do you understand? Nothing to do with the garden.

THE MANAGER It doesn't matter. Haven't I told you we've got to group the action?

THE SON [*observing the* JUVENILE LEAD *studying him*] What do you want?

THE JUVENILE LEAD Nothing! I was just looking at you.

THE SON [*turning towards the* SECOND LADY LEAD] Ah! she's at it too: to re-act her part [*indicating the* MOTHER]!

THE MANAGER Exactly! And it seems to me that you ought to be grateful to them for their interest.

THE SON Yes, but haven't you yet perceived that it isn't possible to live in front of a mirror which not only freezes us with the image of ourselves, but throws our likeness back at us with a horrible grimace?

THE FATHER That is true, absolutely true. You must see that.

THE MANAGER [*to the* SECOND LADY LEAD *and the* JUVENILE LEAD] He's right! Move away from them!

THE SON Do as you like. I'm out of this!

THE MANAGER Be quiet, you, will you? And let me hear your mother! [*To the* MOTHER.] You were saying you had entered . . .

THE MOTHER Yes, into his room, because I couldn't stand it any longer. I went to empty my heart to him of all the anguish that tortures me . . . But as soon as he saw me come in . . .

THE SON Nothing happened! There was no scene. I went away, that's all! I don't care for scenes!

THE MOTHER It's true, true. That's how it was.

THE MANAGER Well, now, we've got to do this bit between you and him. It's indispensable.

THE MOTHER I'm ready . . . when you are ready. If you could only find a chance for me to tell him what I feel here in my heart.

THE FATHER [*going to* SON *in a great rage*] You'll do this for your mother, for your mother, do you understand?

THE SON [*quite determined*] I do nothing!

THE FATHER [*taking hold of him and shaking him*] For God's sake, do as I tell you! Don't you hear your mother asking you for a favor? Haven't you even got the guts to be a son?

THE SON [*taking hold of the* FATHER] No! No! And for God's sake stop it, or else . . . [*General agitation. The* MOTHER, *frightened, tries to separate them.*]

THE MOTHER [*pleading*] Please! please!

THE FATHER [*not leaving hold of the* SON] You've got to obey, do you hear?

THE SON [*almost crying from rage*] What does it mean, this madness you've got? [*They separate.*] Have you no decency, that you insist on showing everyone our shame? I won't do it! I won't! And I stand for the will of our author in this. He didn't want to put us on the stage, after all!

THE MANAGER Man alive! You came here . . .

THE SON [*indicating the* FATHER] *He* did! I didn't!

THE MANAGER Aren't you here now?

THE SON It was his wish, and he dragged us along with him. He's told you not only the things that did happen, but also things that have never happened at all.

THE MANAGER Well, tell me then what did happen. You went out of your room without saying a word?

THE SON Without a word, so as to avoid a scene!

THE MANAGER And then what did you do?

THE SON Nothing . . . walking in the garden . . . [*Hesitates for a moment with expression of gloom.*]

THE MANAGER [*coming closer to him, interested by his extraordinary reserve*] Well, well . . . walking in the garden . . .

THE SON [*exasperated*] Why on earth do you insist? It's horrible! [*The* MOTHER *trembles, sobs, and looks towards the fountain.*]

THE MANAGER [*slowly observing the glance and turning towards the* SON *with increasing apprehension*] The baby?

THE SON There in the fountain . . .

THE FATHER [*pointing with tender pity to the* MOTHER] She was following him at the moment . . .

THE SON   I ran over to her; I was jumping in to drag her out when I saw something that froze my blood . . . the boy there standing stock still, with eyes like a madman's, watching his little drowned sister, in the fountain! [*The* STEPDAUGHTER *bends over the fountain to hide the* CHILD. *She sobs.*] Then . . . [*A revolver shot rings out behind the trees where the* BOY *is hidden.*]

THE MOTHER   [*with a cry of terror runs over in that direction together with several of the* ACTORS *amid general confusion*]   My son! My son! [*Then amid the cries and exclamations one hears her voice.*]   Help! Help!

THE MANAGER   [*pushing the* ACTORS *aside while they lift up the* BOY *and carry him off*]   Is he really wounded?

SOME ACTORS   He's dead! dead!

OTHER ACTORS   No, no, it's only make believe, it's only pretence!

THE FATHER   [*with a terrible cry*]   Pretence? Reality, sir, reality!

THE MANAGER   Pretence? Reality? To hell with it all! Never in my life has such a thing happened to me. I've lost a whole day over these people, a whole day!

CURTAIN

ARTHUR MILLER
[1915-   ]

Throughout his successful career as a dramatist Arthur Miller has probed deeply into the nature of personal guilt, social guilt, and the nexus between the two. Many of Miller's themes are traceable to his Jewish heritage, a heritage of intense moral seriousness about the relationship of the individual to society. It is partly because of his own background, Miller says, that "I couldn't ever write a totally nihilistic work."

Miller was born and raised in New York, the son of a well-to-do Austrian-American father and an American mother. For most of his youth he remained an indifferent student, although he enjoyed reading on his own. He particularly revered Dostoevski's *The Brothers Karamazov,* which first awakened in him the desire to become a writer. After graduating from high school in the midst of the Great Depression, Miller worked at a number of menial jobs in New York for several years. But in 1933 he entered the University of Michigan as a student of journalism. There, under the guidance of Kenneth Rowe, he began his apprenticeship as a playwright. Miller returned to New York after his graduation in 1938, and worked through the war years as a reporter and radio script-writer. The experience of writing half-hour radio plays, he says, sharpened his respect for "the right phrase" and for concentrated dramatic effect: "the economy of words in a good radio play was everything."

Miller's first great success as a playwright came in 1947 with *All My Sons,* the story of a corrupt manufacturer of war materials who is indirectly responsible for the death of his son. The form of this play was the intense realism of the Ibsen tradition, but Miller's later plays generally depend for their full effect on nonrealistic (usually expressionistic) elements. In his masterpiece, *Death of a Salesman* (1949), Miller moves freely from "real" events to the "expression" of events being remembered and imagined by the protagonist (a man worn out by his life-long pursuit of the American dream of "Success," who begins to crack up as he vaguely perceives his spiritual failure). In this play Miller's imaginative stage conception allows the same "set" to serve many purposes, such as the correlation of past and present action. In other plays—*A View from the Bridge* (1955) and *After the Fall* (1963)—Miller makes effective use of a narrator who speaks directly to the audience.

Miller's concern with contemporary social and political issues—reflected in *All My Sons*—has continued to dominate most of his later work. *The Crucible* (1953), a tragedy which deals with the Salem witch trials of the seventeenth century, is an implicit indictment of the McCarthyism of the early 1950's. *After the Fall* (which, unfortunately, was widely interpreted as mere "autobiography," particularly in regard to Miller's marriage to Marilyn Monroe) probes into several areas of social responsibility. The play registers a protest against the arbitrary, destructive power of the House Un-American Activities Committee (at whose hearing Miller himself had earlier refused to testify), and it keeps before the audience's mind the spectre of the six million Jews executed during the Nazi regime.

None of Miller's dramas, however, constitute "social protest" in an abstract sense: all are organized around individual protagonists who are interesting in themselves. *Death of a Salesman* and *A View from the Bridge* present "common men" as protagonists, but each is "common" only in a socio-economic sense, for each is conceived in psychological depth. Miller has argued at length that such characters have the potential of tragic heroism, and that they should not be denied the kind of "respect" usually reserved for the traditional tragic heroes who fall from "high degree."

Miller now lives near Roxbury, Connecticut, where he continues to write for the New York stage. His most recent plays are *Incident at Vichy* (1964) and *The Price* (1968).

A VIEW
FROM THE BRIDGE

ARTHUR MILLER

CHARACTERS

LOUIS	RODOLPHO
MIKE	FIRST IMMIGRATION OFFICER
ALFIERI	SECOND IMMIGRATION OFFICER
EDDIE	MR. LIPARI
CATHERINE	MRS. LIPARI
BEATRICE	TWO "SUBMARINES"
MARCO	NEIGHBORS
TONY	

ACT I

The street and house front of a tenement building. The front is skeletal entirely. The main acting area is the living room-dining room of EDDIE's *apartment. It is a worker's flat, clean, sparse, homely. There is a rocker down front; a round dining table at center, with chairs; and a portable phonograph.*

At back are a bedroom door and an opening to the kitchen; none
of these interiors are seen.
At the right, forestage, a desk. This is MR. ALFIERI'S *law office.*
There is also a telephone booth. This is not used until the last
scenes, so it may be covered or left in view.
A stairway leads up to the apartment, and then farther up to
the next story, which is not seen.
Ramps, representing the street, run upstage and off to right and
left.
As the curtain rises, LOUIS *and* MIKE, *longshoremen, are pitching*
coins against the building at left.
A distant foghorn blows.
Enter ALFIERI, *a lawyer in his fifties turning gray; he is portly,*
good-humored, and thoughtful. The two pitchers nod to him as
he passes. He crosses the stage to his desk, removes his hat, runs
his fingers through his hair, and grinning, speaks to the audience.

ALFIERI   You wouldn't have known it, but something amusing has just happened. You see how uneasily they nod to me? That's because I am a lawyer.
In this neighborhood to meet a lawyer or a priest on the street is unlucky.
We're only thought of in connection with disasters, and they'd rather not
get too close.

I often think that behind that suspicious little nod of theirs lie three
thousand years of distrust. A lawyer means the law, and in Sicily, from
where their fathers came, the law has not been a friendly idea since the
Greeks were beaten.

I am inclined to notice the ruins in things, perhaps because I was born
in Italy. . . . I only came here when I was twenty-five. In those days, Al
Capone, the greatest Carthaginian of all, was learning his trade on these
pavements, and Frankie Yale himself was cut precisely in half by a machine
gun on the corner of Union Street, two blocks away. Oh, there were many
here who were justly shot by unjust men. Justice is very important here.

But this is Red Hook, not Sicily. This is the slum that faces the bay on
the seaward side of Brooklyn Bridge. This is the gullet of New York
swallowing the tonnage of the world. And now we are quite civilized, quite
American. Now we settle for half, and I like it better. I no longer keep a
pistol in my filing cabinet.

And my practice is entirely unromantic.

My wife has warned me, so have my friends; they tell me the people
in this neighborhood lack elegance, glamour. After all, who have I dealt
with in my life? Longshoremen and their wives, and fathers and grand-
fathers, compensation cases, evictions, family squabbles—the petty troubles
of the poor—and yet . . . every few years there is still a case, and as the

parties tell me what the trouble is, the flat air in my office suddenly washes in with the green scent of the sea, the dust in this air is blown away and the thought comes that in some Cæsar's year, in Calabria perhaps or on the cliff at Syracuse, another lawyer, quite differently dressed, heard the same complaint and sat there as powerless as I, and watched it run its bloody course.

[EDDIE *has appeared and has been pitching coins with the men and is highlighted among them. He is forty—a husky, slightly overweight longshoreman.*]

  This one's name was Eddie Carbone, a longshoreman working the docks from Brooklyn Bridge to the breakwater where the open sea begins. [ALFIERI *walks into darkness.*]

EDDIE [*moving up steps into doorway*] Well, I'll see ya, fellas.

[CATHERINE *enters from kitchen, crosses down to window, looks out.*]

LOUIS You workin' tomorrow?

EDDIE Yeah, there's another day yet on that ship. See ya, Louis.

[EDDIE *goes into the house, as light rises in the apartment.*]

[CATHERINE *is waving to* LOUIS *from the window and turns to him.*]

CATHERINE Hi, Eddie!

[EDDIE *is pleased and therefore shy about it; he hangs up his cap and jacket.*]

EDDIE Where you goin' all dressed up?

CATHERINE [*running her hands over her skirt*] I just got it. You like it?

EDDIE Yeah, it's nice. And what happened to your hair?

CATHERINE You like it? I fixed it different. [*Calling to kitchen.*] He's here, B.!

EDDIE Beautiful. Turn around, lemme see in the back. [*She turns for him.*] Oh, if your mother was alive to see you now! She wouldn't believe it.

CATHERINE You like it, huh?

EDDIE You look like one of them girls that went to college. Where you goin'?

CATHERINE [*taking his arm*] Wait'll B. comes in, I'll tell you something. Here, sit down. [*She is walking him to the armchair. Calling offstage.*] Hurry up, will you, B.?

EDDIE [*sitting*] What's goin' on?

CATHERINE I'll get you a beer, all right?

EDDIE Well, tell me what happened. Come over here, talk to me.

CATHERINE I want to wait till B. comes in. [*She sits on her heels beside him.*] Guess how much we paid for the skirt.

EDDIE I think it's too short, ain't it?

CATHERINE [*standing*] No! not when I stand up.

EDDIE Yeah, but you gotta sit down sometimes.

CATHERINE Eddie, it's the style now. [*She walks to show him.*] I mean, if you see me walkin' down the street—

EDDIE Listen, you been givin' me the willies the way you walk down the street, I mean it.

CATHERINE Why?

EDDIE Catherine, I don't want to be a pest, but I'm tellin' you you're walkin' wavy.

CATHERINE I'm walkin' wavy?

EDDIE Now don't aggravate me, Katie, you are walkin' wavy! I don't like the looks they're givin' you in the candy store. And with them new high heels on the sidewalk—clack, clack, clack. The heads are turnin' like windmills.

CATHERINE But those guys look at all the girls, you know that.

EDDIE You ain't "all the girls."

CATHERINE [*almost in tears because he disapproves*] What do you want me to do? You want me to—

EDDIE   Now don't get mad, kid.

CATHERINE   Well, I don't know what you want from me.

EDDIE   Katie, I promised your mother on her deathbed. I'm responsible for you. You're a baby, you don't understand these things. I mean like when you stand here by the window, wavin' outside.

CATHERINE   I was wavin' to Louis!

EDDIE   Listen, I could tell you things about Louis which you wouldn't wave to him no more.

CATHERINE   [*trying to joke him out of his warning*]   Eddie, I wish there was one guy you couldn't tell me things about!

EDDIE   Catherine, do me a favor, will you? You're gettin' to be a big girl now, you gotta keep yourself more, you can't be so friendly, kid. [*Calls.*] Hey, B., what're you doin' in there? [*To* CATHERINE.] Get her in here, will you? I got news for her.

CATHERINE   [*starting out*]   What?

EDDIE   Her cousins landed.

CATHERINE   [*clapping her hands together*]   No! [*She turns instantly and starts for the kitchen.*] B.! Your cousins!

[BEATRICE *enters, wiping her hands with a towel.*]

BEATRICE   [*in the face of* CATHERINE's *shout*]   What?

CATHERINE   Your cousins got in!

BEATRICE   [*astounded, turns to* EDDIE]   What are you talkin' about? Where?

EDDIE   I was just knockin' off work before and Tony Bereli come over to me; he says the ship is in the North River.

BEATRICE   [*her hands are clasped at her breast; she seems half in fear, half in unutterable joy*]   They're all right?

EDDIE   He didn't see them yet, they're still on board. But as soon as they get off he'll meet them. He figures about ten o'clock they'll be here.

BEATRICE   [*sits, almost weak from tension*]   And they'll let them off the ship all right? That's fixed, heh?

EDDIE   Sure, they give them regular seamen papers and they walk off with the crew. Don't worry about it, B., there's nothin' to it. Couple of hours they'll be here.

BEATRICE   What happened? They wasn't supposed to be till next Thursday.

EDDIE   I don't know; they put them on any ship they can get them out on. Maybe the other ship they was supposed to take there was some danger— What you cryin' about?

BEATRICE   [*astounded and afraid*]   I'm—I just—I can't believe it! I didn't even buy a new tablecloth; I was gonna wash the walls—

EDDIE   Listen, they'll think it's a millionaire's house compared to the way they live. Don't worry about the walls. They'll be thankful. [*To* CATHERINE.] Whyn't you run down buy a tablecloth. Go ahead, here. [*He is reaching into his pocket.*]

CATHERINE   There's no stores open now.

EDDIE   [*to* BEATRICE]   You was gonna put a new cover on the chair.

BEATRICE   I know—well, I thought it was gonna be next week! I was gonna clean the walls, I was gonna wax the floors. [*She stands disturbed.*]

CATHERINE   [*pointing upward*]   Maybe Mrs. Dondero upstairs—

BEATRICE   [*of the tablecloth*]   No, hers is worse than this one. [*Suddenly.*] My God, I don't even have nothin' to eat for them! [*She starts for the kitchen.*]

EDDIE   [*reaching out and grabbing her arm*]   Hey, hey! Take it easy.

BEATRICE   No, I'm just nervous, that's all. [*To* CATHERINE.] I'll make the fish.

EDDIE   You're savin' their lives, what're you worryin' about the tablecloth? They probably didn't see a tablecloth in their whole life where they come from.

BEATRICE [*looking into his eyes*] I'm just worried about you, that's all I'm worried.

EDDIE Listen, as long as they know where they're gonna sleep.

BEATRICE I told them in the letters. They're sleepin' on the floor.

EDDIE Beatrice, all I'm worried about is you got such a heart that I'll end up on the floor with you, and they'll be in our bed.

BEATRICE All right, stop it.

EDDIE Because as soon as you see a tired relative, I end up on the floor.

BEATRICE When did you end up on the floor?

EDDIE When your father's house burned down I didn't end up on the floor?

BEATRICE Well, their house burned down!

EDDIE Yeah, but it didn't keep burnin' for two weeks!

BEATRICE All right, look, I'll tell them to go someplace else. [*She starts into the kitchen.*]

EDDIE Now wait a minute. Beatrice! [*She halts. He goes to her.*] I just don't want you bein' pushed around, that's all. You got too big a heart. [*He touches her hand.*] What're you so touchy?

BEATRICE I'm just afraid if it don't turn out good you'll be mad at me.

EDDIE Listen, if everybody keeps his mouth shut, nothin' can happen. They'll pay for their board.

BEATRICE Oh, I told them.

EDDIE Then what the hell. [*Pause. He moves.*] It's an honor, B. I mean it. I was just thinkin' before, comin' home, suppose my father didn't come to this country, and I was starvin' like them over there . . . and I had people in America could keep me a couple of months? The man would be honored to lend me a place to sleep.

BEATRICE [*there are tears in her eyes. She turns to* CATHERINE] You see what he is? [*She turns and grabs* EDDIE's *face in her hands.*] Mmm! You're an angel! God'll bless you. [*He is gratefully smiling.*] You'll see, you'll get a blessing for this!

EDDIE [*laughing*] I'll settle for my own bed.

BEATRICE Go, Baby, set the table.

CATHERINE We didn't tell him about me yet.

BEATRICE Let him eat first, then we'll tell him. Bring everything in. [*She hurries* CATHERINE *out.*]

EDDIE [*sitting at the table*] What's all that about? Where's she goin'?

BEATRICE Noplace. It's very good news, Eddie. I want you to be happy.

EDDIE What's goin' on?
[CATHERINE *enters with plates, forks.*]

BEATRICE She's got a job.
[*Pause.* EDDIE *looks at* CATHERINE, *then back to* BEATRICE.]

EDDIE What job? She's gonna finish school.

CATHERINE Eddie, you won't believe it—

EDDIE No—no, you gonna finish school. What kinda job, what do you mean? All of a sudden you—

CATHERINE Listen a minute, it's wonderful.

EDDIE It's not wonderful. You'll never get nowheres unless you finish school. You can't take no job. Why didn't you ask me before you take a job?

BEATRICE She's askin' you now, she didn't take nothin' yet.

CATHERINE Listen a minute! I came to school this morning and the principal called me out of the class, see? To go to his office.

EDDIE Yeah?

CATHERINE So I went in and he says to me he's got my records, y'know? And there's a company wants a girl right away. It ain't exactly a secretary, it's a stenographer first, but pretty soon you get to be secretary. And he says to me that I'm the best student in the whole class—

BEATRICE You hear that?

EDDIE Well why not? Sure she's the best.

CATHERINE I'm the best student, he says, and if I want, I should take the job and the end of the year he'll let me take the examination and he'll give me the certificate. So I'll save practically a year!

EDDIE [*strangely nervous*] Where's the job? What company?

CATHERINE It's a big plumbing company over Nostrand Avenue.

EDDIE Nostrand Avenue and where?

CATHERINE It's someplace by the Navy Yard.

BEATRICE Fifty dollars a week, Eddie.

EDDIE [*to* CATHERINE, *surprised*] Fifty?

CATHERINE I swear.

[*Pause.*]

EDDIE What about all the stuff you wouldn't learn this year, though?

CATHERINE There's nothin' more to learn, Eddie, I just gotta practice from now on. I know all the symbols and I know the keyboard. I'll just get faster, that's all. And when I'm workin' I'll keep gettin' better and better, you see?

BEATRICE Work is the best practice anyway.

EDDIE That ain't what I wanted, though.

CATHERINE Why! It's a great big company—

EDDIE I don't like that neighborhood over there.

CATHERINE It's a block and half from the subway, he says.

EDDIE Near the Navy Yard plenty can happen in a block and a half. And a plumbin' company! That's one step over the water front. They're practically longshoremen.

BEATRICE Yeah, but she'll be in the office, Eddie.

EDDIE I know she'll be in the office, but that ain't what I had in mind.

BEATRICE Listen, she's gotta go to work sometime.

EDDIE Listen, B., she'll be with a lotta plumbers? And sailors up and down the street? So what did she go to school for?

CATHERINE But it's fifty a week, Eddie.

EDDIE Look, did I ask you for money? I supported you this long I support you a little more. Please, do me a favor, will ya? I want you to be with different kind of people. I want you to be in a nice office. Maybe a lawyer's office someplace in New York in one of them nice buildings. I mean if you're gonna get outa here then get out; don't go practically in the same kind of neighborhood.

[*Pause.* CATHERINE *lowers her eyes.*]

BEATRICE Go, Baby, bring in the supper. [CATHERINE *goes out.*] Think about it a little bit, Eddie. Please. She's crazy to start work. It's not a little shop, it's a big company. Some day she could be a secretary. They picked her out of the whole class. [*He is silent, staring down at the tablecloth, fingering the pattern.*] What are you worried about? She could take care of herself. She'll get out of the subway and be in the office in two minutes.

EDDIE [*somehow sickened*] I know that neighborhood, B., I don't like it.

BEATRICE Listen, if nothin' happened to her in this neighborhood it ain't gonna happen noplace else. [*She turns his face to her.*] Look, you gotta get used to it, she's no baby no more. Tell her to take it. [*He turns his head away.*] You hear me? [*She is angering.*] I don't understand you; she's seventeen years old, you gonna keep her in the house all her life?

EDDIE [*insulted*] What kinda remark is that?

BEATRICE [*with sympathy but insistent force*] Well, I don't understand when it ends. First it was gonna be when she graduated high school, so she graduated high school. Then it was gonna be when she learned stenographer, so she learned stenographer. So what're we gonna wait for now? I mean it, Eddie, sometimes I don't understand you; they picked her out of the whole class, it's an honor for her.

[CATHERINE *enters with food, which she silently sets on the table. After a moment of watching her face,* EDDIE *breaks into a smile, but it almost seems that tears will form in his eyes.*]

EDDIE With your hair that way you look like a madonna, you know that? You're the madonna type. [*She doesn't look at him, but continues ladling out food onto the plates.*] You wanna go to work, heh, Madonna?

CATHERINE [*softly*] Yeah.

EDDIE [*with a sense of her childhood, her babyhood, and the years*] All right, go to work. [*She looks at him, then rushes and hugs him.*] Hey, hey! Take it easy! [*He holds her face away from him to look at her.*] What're you cryin' about? [*He is affected by her, but smiles his emotion away.*]

CATHERINE [*sitting at her place*] I just—[*Bursting out.*] I'm gonna buy all new dishes with my first pay! [*They laugh warmly.*] I mean it. I'll fix up the whole house! I'll buy a rug!

EDDIE And then you'll move away.

CATHERINE No, Eddie!

EDDIE [*grinning*] Why not? That's life. And you'll come visit on Sundays, then once a month, then Christmas and New Year's, finally.

CATHERINE [*grasping his arm to reassure him and to erase the accusation*] No, please!

EDDIE [*smiling but hurt*] I only ask you one thing—don't trust nobody. You got a good aunt but she's got too big a heart, you learned bad from her. Believe me.

BEATRICE Be the way you are, Katie, don't listen to him.

EDDIE [*to* BEATRICE—*strangely and quickly resentful*] You lived in a house all your life, what do you know about it? You never worked in your life.

BEATRICE She likes people. What's wrong with that?

EDDIE Because most people ain't people. She's goin' to work: plumbers; they'll chew her to pieces if she don't watch out. [*To* CATHERINE.] Believe me, Katie, the less you trust, the less you be sorry.

[EDDIE *crosses himself and the women do the same, and they eat.*]

CATHERINE First thing I'll buy is a rug, heh, B.?

BEATRICE I don't mind. [*To* EDDIE.] I smelled coffee all day today. You unloadin' coffee today?

EDDIE Yeah, a Brazil ship.

CATHERINE I smelled it too. It smelled all over the neighborhood.

EDDIE That's one time, boy, to be a longshoreman is a pleasure. I could work coffee ships twenty hours a day. You go down in the hold, y'know? It's like flowers, that smell. We'll bust a bag tomorrow, I'll bring you some.

BEATRICE Just be sure there's no spiders in it, will ya? I mean it. [*She directs this to* CATHERINE, *rolling her eyes upward.*] I still remember that spider coming out of that bag he brung home. I nearly died.

EDDIE You call that a spider? You oughta see what comes outa the bananas sometimes.

BEATRICE Don't talk about it!

EDDIE I seen spiders could stop a Buick.

BEATRICE   [*clapping her hands over her ears*]   All right, shut up!

EDDIE   [*laughing and taking a watch out of his pocket*]   Well, who started with spiders?

BEATRICE   All right, I'm sorry, I didn't mean it. Just don't bring none home again. What time is it?

EDDIE   Quarter nine. [*Puts watch back in his pocket. They continue eating in silence.*]

CATHERINE   He's bringin' them ten o'clock, Tony?

EDDIE   Around, yeah. [*He eats.*]

CATHERINE   Eddie, suppose somebody asks if they're livin' here. [*He looks at her as though already she had divulged something publicly. Defensively.*] I mean if they ask.

EDDIE   Now look, Baby, I can see we're gettin' mixed up again here.

CATHERINE   No, I just mean . . . people'll see them goin' in and out.

EDDIE   I don't care who sees them goin' in and out as long as you don't see them goin' in and out. And this goes for you too, B. You don't see nothin' and you don't know nothin'.

BEATRICE   What do you mean? I understand.

EDDIE   You don't understand; you still think you can talk about this to some-body just a little bit. Now lemme say it once and for all, because you're makin' me nervous again, both of you. I don't care if somebody comes in the house and sees them sleepin' on the floor, it never comes out of your mouth who they are or what they're doin' here.

BEATRICE   Yeah, but my mother'll know—

EDDIE   Sure she'll know, but just don't you be the one who told her, that's all. This is the United States government you're playin' with now, this is the Immigration Bureau. If you said it you knew it, if you didn't say it you didn't know it.

CATHERINE   Yeah, but Eddie, suppose somebody—

EDDIE   I don't care what question it is. You—don't—know—nothin'. They got stool pigeons all over this neighborhood they're payin' them every week for information, and you don't know who they are. It could be your best friend. You hear? [*To* BEATRICE.] Like Vinny Bolzano, remember Vinny?

BEATRICE   Oh, yeah. God forbid.

EDDIE   Tell her about Vinny. [*To* CATHERINE.] You think I'm blowin' steam here? [*To* BEATRICE.] Go ahead, tell her. [*To* CATHERINE.] You was a baby then. There was a family lived next door to her mother, he was about sixteen—

BEATRICE   No, he was no more than fourteen, cause I was to his confirmation in Saint Agnes. But the family had an uncle that they were hidin' in the house, and he snitched to the Immigration.

CATHERINE   The kid snitched?

EDDIE   On his own uncle!

CATHERINE   What, was he crazy?

EDDIE   He was crazy after, I tell you that, boy.

BEATRICE   Oh, it was terrible. He had five brothers and the old father. And they grabbed him in the kitchen and pulled him down the stairs—three flights his head was bouncin' like a coconut. And they spit on him in the street, his own father and his brothers. The whole neighborhood was cryin'.

CATHERINE   Ts! So what happened to him?

BEATRICE   I think he went away. [*To* EDDIE.] I never seen him again, did you?

EDDIE   [*rises during this, taking out his watch*]   Him? You'll never see him no more, a guy do a thing like that? How's he gonna show his face? [*To* CATHERINE, *as he gets up uneasily.*] Just remember, kid, you can quicker get back a million dollars that was stole than a word that you gave away. [*He is standing now, stretching his back.*]

CATHERINE Okay, I won't say a word to nobody, I swear.

EDDIE Gonna rain tomorrow. We'll be slidin' all over the decks. Maybe you oughta put something on for them, they be here soon.

BEATRICE I only got fish, I hate to spoil it if they ate already. I'll wait, it only takes a few minutes; I could broil it.

CATHERINE What happens, Eddie, when that ship pulls out and they ain't on it, though? Don't the captain say nothin'?

EDDIE [*slicing an apple with his pocket knife*] Captain's pieced off, what do you mean?

CATHERINE Even the captain?

EDDIE What's the matter, the captain don't have to live? Captain gets a piece, maybe one of the mates, piece for the guy in Italy who fixed the papers for them, Tony here'll get a little bite. . . .

BEATRICE I just hope they get work here, that's all I hope.

EDDIE Oh, the syndicate'll fix jobs for them; till they pay 'em off they'll get them work every day. It's after the pay-off, then they'll have to scramble like the rest of us.

BEATRICE Well, it be better than they got there.

EDDIE Oh sure, well, listen. So you gonna start Monday, heh, Madonna?

CATHERINE [*embarrassed*] I'm supposed to, yeah.

[EDDIE *is standing facing the two seated women. First* BEATRICE *smiles, then* CATHERINE, *for a powerful emotion is on him, a childish one and a knowing fear, and the tears show in his eyes—and they are shy before the avowal.*]

EDDIE [*sadly smiling, yet somehow proud of her*] Well . . . I hope you have good luck. I wish you the best. You know that, kid.

CATHERINE [*rising, trying to laugh*] You sound like I'm goin' a million miles!

EDDIE I know. I guess I just never figured on one thing.

CATHERINE [*smiling*] What?

EDDIE That you would ever grow up. [*He utters a soundless laugh at himself, feeling his breast pocket of his shirt.*] I left a cigar in my other coat, I think. [*He starts for the bedroom.*]

CATHERINE Stay there! I'll get it for you.

[*She hurries out. There is a slight pause, and* EDDIE *turns to* BEATRICE, *who has been avoiding his gaze.*]

EDDIE What are you mad at me lately?

BEATRICE Who's mad? [*She gets up, clearing the dishes.*] I'm not mad. [*She picks up the dishes and turns to him.*] You're the one is mad. [*She turns and goes into the kitchen as* CATHERINE *enters from the bedroom with a cigar and a pack of matches.*]

CATHERINE Here! I'll light it for you! [*She strikes a match and holds it to his cigar. He puffs. Quietly.*] Don't worry about me, Eddie, heh?

EDDIE Don't burn yourself. [*Just in time she blows out the match.*] You better go in help her with the dishes.

CATHERINE [*turns quickly to the table, and, seeing the table cleared, she says, almost guiltily*] Oh! [*She hurries into the kitchen, and as she exits there.*] I'll do the dishes, B.!

[*Alone,* EDDIE *stands looking toward the kitchen for a moment. Then h* *takes out his watch, glances at it, replaces it in his pocket, sits in the arm chair, and stares at the smoke flowing out of his mouth.*

The lights go down, then come up on ALFIERI, *who has moved onto the forestage.*]

ALFIERI He was as good a man as he had to be in a life that was hard and even. He worked on the piers when there was work, he brought home his pay, and he lived. And toward ten o'clock of that night, after they had eaten, the cousins came.

[*The lights fade on* ALFIERI *and rise on the street. Enter* TONY, *escorting* MARCO *and* RODOLPHO, *each with a valise.* TONY *halts, indicates the house. They stand for a moment looking at it.*]

MARCO [*he is a square-built peasant of thirty-two, suspicious, tender, and quiet-voiced*] Thank you.

TONY You're on your own now. Just be careful, that's all. Ground floor.

MARCO Thank you.

TONY [*indicating the house*] I'll see you on the pier tomorrow. You'll go to work.

[MARCO *nods.* TONY *continues on walking down the street.*]

RODOLPHO This will be the first house I ever walked into in America! Imagine! She said they were poor!

MARCO Ssh! Come. [*They go to door.*]

[MARCO *knocks. The lights rise in the room.* EDDIE *goes and opens the door. Enter* MARCO *and* RODOLPHO, *removing their caps.* BEATRICE *and* CATHERINE *enter from the kitchen. The lights fade in the street.*]

EDDIE You Marco?

MARCO Marco.

EDDIE Come on in! [*He shakes* MARCO's *hand.*]

BEATRICE Here, take the bags!

MARCO [*nods, looks to the women and fixes on* BEATRICE. *Crosses to* BEATRICE] Are you my cousin? [*She nods. He kisses her hand.*]

BEATRICE [*above the table, touching her chest with her hand*] Beatrice. This is my husband, Eddie. [*All nod.*] Catherine, my sister Nancy's daughter. [*The brothers nod.*]

MARCO [*indicating* RODOLPHO] My brother. Rodolpho. [RODOLPHO *nods.* MARCO *comes with a certain formal stiffness to* EDDIE.] I want to tell you now Eddie—when you say go, we will go.

EDDIE Oh, no . . . [*Takes* MARCO's *bag.*]

MARCO I see it's a small house, but soon, maybe, we can have our own house.

EDDIE You're welcome, Marco, we got plenty of room here. Katie, give them supper, heh? [*Exits into bedroom with their bags.*]

CATHERINE Come here, sit down. I'll get you some soup.

MARCO [*as they go to the table*] We ate on the ship. Thank you. [*To* EDDIE, *calling off to bedroom.*] Thank you.

BEATRICE Get some coffee. We'll all have coffee. Come sit down.

[RODOLPHO *and* MARCO *sit, at the table.*]

CATHERINE [*wondrously*] How come he's so dark and you're so light, Rodolpho?

RODOLPHO [*ready to laugh*] I don't know. A thousand years ago, they say, the Danes invaded Sicily.

[BEATRICE *kisses* RODOLPHO. *They laugh as* EDDIE *enters.*]

CATHERINE [*to* BEATRICE] He's practically blond!

EDDIE How's the coffee doin'?

CATHERINE [*brought up*] I'm gettin' it. [*She hurries out to kitchen.*]

EDDIE [*sits on his rocker*] Yiz have a nice trip?

MARCO The ocean is always rough. But we are good sailors.

EDDIE No trouble gettin' here?

MARCO No. The man brought us. Very nice man.

RODOLPHO [*to* EDDIE] He says we start to work tomorrow. Is he honest?

EDDIE   [*laughing*]   No. But as long as you owe them money, they'll get you plenty of work. [*To* MARCO.] Yiz ever work on the piers in Italy?

MARCO   Piers? Ts!—no.

RODOLPHO   [*smiling at the smallness of his town*]   In our town there are no piers, only the beach, and little fishing boats.

BEATRICE   So what kinda work did yiz do?

MARCO   [*shrugging shyly, even embarrassed*]   Whatever there is, anything.

RODOLPHO   Sometimes they build a house, or if they fix the bridge—Marco is a mason and I bring him the cement. [*He laughs.*] In harvest time we work in the fields . . . if there is work. Anything.

EDDIE   Still bad there, heh?

MARCO   Bad, yes.

RODOLPHO   [*laughing*]   It's terrible! We stand around all day in the piazza listening to the fountain like birds. Everybody waits only for the train.

BEATRICE   What's on the train?

RODOLPHO   Nothing. But if there are many passengers and you're lucky you make a few lire to push the taxi up the hill.

[*Enter* CATHERINE; *she listens.*]

BEATRICE   You gotta push a taxi?

RODOLPHO   [*laughing*]   Oh, sure! It's a feature in our town. The horses in our town are skinnier than goats. So if there are too many passengers we help to push the carriages up to the hotel. [*He laughs.*] In our town the horses are only for show.

CATHERINE   Why don't they have automobile taxis?

RODOLPHO   There is one. We push that too. [*They laugh.*] Everything in our town, you gotta push!

BEATRICE   [*to* EDDIE]   How do you like that!

EDDIE   [*to* MARCO]   So what're you wanna do, you gonna stay here in this country or you wanna go back?

MARCO   [*surprised*]   Go back?

EDDIE   Well, you're married, ain't you?

MARCO   Yes. I have three children.

BEATRICE   Three! I thought only one.

MARCO   Oh, no. I have three now. Four years, five years, six years.

BEATRICE   Ah . . . I bet they're cryin' for you already, heh?

MARCO   What can I do? The older one is sick in his chest. My wife—she feeds them from her own mouth. I tell you the truth, if I stay there they will never grow up. They eat the sunshine.

BEATRICE   My God. So how long you want to stay?

MARCO   With your permission, we will stay maybe a—

EDDIE   She don't mean in this house, she means in the country.

MARCO   Oh. Maybe four, five, six years, I think.

RODOLPHO   [*smiling*]   He trusts his wife.

BEATRICE   Yeah, but maybe you'll get enough, you'll be able to go back quicker.

MARCO   I hope. I don't know. [*To* EDDIE.] I understand it's not so good here either.

EDDIE   Oh, you guys'll be all right—till you pay them off, anyway. After that, you'll have to scramble, that's all. But you'll make better here than you could there.

RODOLPHO   How much? We hear all kinds of figures. How much can a man make? We work hard, we'll work all day, all night—

[MARCO *raises a hand to hush him.*]

EDDIE   [*he is coming more and more to address* MARCO *only*]   On the average a whole year? Maybe—well, it's hard to say, see. Sometimes we lay off, there's no ships three four weeks.

MARCO   Three, four weeks!—Ts!

EDDIE   But I think you could probably—thirty, forty a week, over the whole twelve months of the year.

MARCO   [*rises, crosses to* EDDIE]   Dollars.

EDDIE   Sure dollars.

[MARCO *puts an arm round* RODOLPHO *and they laugh.*]

MARCO   If we can stay here a few months, Beatrice—

BEATRICE   Listen, you're welcome, Marco—

MARCO   Because I could send them a little more if I stay here.

BEATRICE   As long as you want, we got plenty a room.

MARCO   [*his eyes are showing tears*]   My wife—[*To* EDDIE.]   My wife—I want to send right away maybe twenty dollars—

EDDIE   You could send them something next week already.

MARCO   [*he is near tears*]   Eduardo . . . [*He goes to* EDDIE, *offering his hand.*]

EDDIE   Don't thank me. Listen, what the hell, it's no skin off me. [*To* CATHER- INE.]   What happened to the coffee?

CATHERINE   I got it on. [*To* RODOLPHO.]   You married too? No.

RODOLPHO   [*rises*]   Oh, no . . .

BEATRICE   [*to* CATHERINE]   I told you he—

CATHERINE   I know, I just thought maybe he got married recently.

RODOLPHO   I have no money to get married. I have a nice face, but no money. [*He laughs.*]

CATHERINE   [*to* BEATRICE]   He's a real blond!

BEATRICE   [*to* RODOLPHO]   You want to stay here too, heh? For good?

RODOLPHO   Me? Yes, forever! Me, I want to be an American. And then I want to go back to Italy when I am rich, and I will buy a motorcycle. [*He smiles.* MARCO *shakes him affectionately.*]

CATHERINE   A motorcycle!

RODOLPHO   With a motorcycle in Italy you will never starve any more.

BEATRICE   I'll get you coffee. [*She exits to the kitchen.*]

EDDIE   What you do with a motorcycle?

MARCO   He dreams, he dreams.

RODOLPHO   [*to* MARCO]   Why? [*To* EDDIE.]   Messages! The rich people in the hotel always need someone who will carry a message. But quickly, and with a great noise. With a blue motorcycle I would station myself in the court- yard of the hotel, and in a little while I would have messages.

MARCO   When you have no wife you have dreams.

EDDIE   Why can't you just walk, or take a trolley or sump'm?

[*Enter* BEATRICE *with coffee.*]

RODOLPHO   Oh, no, the machine, the machine is necessary. A man comes into a great hotel and says, I am a messenger. Who is this man? He disappears walking, there is no noise, nothing. Maybe he will never come back, maybe he will never deliver the message. But a man who rides up on a great machine, this man is responsible, this man exists. He will be given messages. [*He helps* BEATRICE *set out the coffee things.*]   I am also a singer, though.

EDDIE   You mean a regular—?

RODOLPHO   Oh, yes. One night last year Andreola got sick. Baritone. And I took his place in the garden of the hotel. Three arias I sang without a mistake! Thousand-lire notes they threw from the tables, money was falling like a storm in the treasury. It was magnificent. We lived six months on that night, eh, Marco?

[MARCO *nods doubtfully.*]

MARCO   Two months.

[EDDIE *laughs.*]

BEATRICE   Can't you get a job in that place?

RODOLPHO   Andreola got better. He's a baritone, very strong.

[BEATRICE *laughs.*]

MARCO   [*regretfully, to* BEATRICE]   He sang too loud.

RODOLPHO   Why too loud?

MARCO   Too loud. The guests in that hotel are all Englishmen. They don't like too loud.

RODOLPHO   [*to* CATHERINE]   Nobody ever said it was too loud!

MARCO   I say. It was too loud. [*To* BEATRICE.] I knew it as soon as he started to sing. Too loud.

RODOLPHO   Then why did they throw so much money?

MARCO   They paid for your courage. The English like courage. But once is enough.

RODOLPHO   [*to all but* MARCO]   I never heard anybody say it was too loud.

CATHERINE   Did you ever hear of jazz?

RODOLPHO   Oh, sure! I *sing* jazz.

CATHERINE   [*rises*]   You could sing jazz?

RODOLPHO   Oh, I sing Napolidan, jazz, bel canto—I sing "Paper Doll," you like "Paper Doll"?

CATHERINE   Oh, sure, I'm crazy for "Paper Doll." Go ahead, sing it.

RODOLPHO   [*takes his stance after getting a nod of permission from* MARCO, *and with a high tenor voice begins singing*]

> "I'll tell you boys it's tough to be alone,
> And it's tough to love a doll that's not your own.
> I'm through with all of them,
> I'll never fall again,
> Hey, boy, what you gonna do?
> I'm gonna buy a paper doll that I can call my own,
> A doll that other fellows cannot steal.

[EDDIE *rises and moves upstage.*]

> And then those flirty, flirty guys
> With their flirty, flirty eyes
> Will have to flirt with dollies that are real—"

EDDIE   Hey, kid—hey, wait a minute—

CATHERINE   [*enthralled*]   Leave him finish, it's beautiful! [*To* BEATRICE.] He's terrific! It's terrific, Rodolpho.

EDDIE   Look, kid; you don't want to be picked up, do ya?

MARCO   No—no! [*He rises.*]

EDDIE   [*indicating the rest of the building*]   Because we never had no singers here . . . and all of a sudden there's a singer in the house, y'know what I mean?

MARCO   Yes, yes. You'll be quiet, Rodolpho.

EDDIE   [*he is flushed*]   They got guys all over the place, Marco. I mean.

MARCO   Yes. He'll be quiet. [*To* RODOLPHO.] You'll be quiet.

[RODOLPHO *nods.* EDDIE *has risen, with iron control, even a smile. He moves to* CATHERINE.]

EDDIE   What's the high heels for, Garbo?

CATHERINE   I figured for tonight—

EDDIE   Do me a favor, will you? Go ahead.

[*Embarrassed now, angered,* CATHERINE *goes out into the bedroom.* BEATRICE *watches her go and gets up; in passing, she gives* EDDIE *a cold look, restrained only by the strangers, and goes to the table to pour coffee.*]

EDDIE   [*striving to laugh, and to* MARCO, *but directed as much to* BEATRICE]   All actresses they want to be around here.

RODOLPHO   [*happy about it*]   In Italy too! All the girls.

[CATHERINE *emerges from the bedroom in low-heel shoes, comes to the table.* RODOLPHO *is lifting a cup.*]

EDDIE   [*he is sizing up* RODOLPHO, *and there is a concealed suspicion*]   Yeah, heh?

RODOLPHO   Yes! [*Laughs, indicating* CATHERINE.]   Especially when they are so beautiful!

CATHERINE   You like sugar?

RODOLPHO   Sugar? Yes! I like sugar very much!

[EDDIE *is downstage, watching as she pours a spoonful of sugar into his cup, his face puffed with trouble, and the room dies. Lights rise on* ALFIERI.]

ALFIERI   Who can ever know what will be discovered? Eddie Carbone had never expected to have a destiny. A man works, raises his family, goes bowling, eats, gets old, and then he dies. Now, as the weeks passed, there was a future, there was a trouble that would not go away.

[*The lights fade on* ALFIERI, *then rise on* EDDIE *standing at the doorway of the house.* BEATRICE *enters on the street. She sees* EDDIE, *smiles at him. He looks away. She starts to enter the house when* EDDIE *speaks.*]

EDDIE   It's after eight.

BEATRICE   Well, it's a long show at the Paramount.

EDDIE   They must've seen every picture in Brooklyn by now. He's supposed to stay in the house when he ain't working. He ain't supposed to go advertising himself.

BEATRICE   Well that's his trouble, what do you care? If they pick him up they pick him up, that's all. Come in the house.

EDDIE   What happened to the stenography? I don't see her practice no more.

BEATRICE   She'll get back to it. She's excited, Eddie.

EDDIE   She tell you anything?

BEATRICE   [*comes to him, now the subject is opened*]   What's the matter with you? He's a nice kid, what do you want from him?

EDDIE   That's a nice kid? He gives me the heeby-jeebies.

BEATRICE   [*smiling*]   Ah, go on, you're just jealous.

EDDIE   Of *him?* Boy, you don't think much of me.

BEATRICE   I don't understand you. What's so terrible about him?

EDDIE   You mean it's all right with you? That's gonna be her husband?

BEATRICE   Why? He's a nice fella, hard workin', he's a good-lookin' fella.

EDDIE   He sings on the ships, didja know that?

BEATRICE   What do you mean, he sings?

EDDIE   Just what I said, he sings. Right on the deck, all of a sudden, a whole song comes out of his mouth—with motions. You know what they're callin' him now? Paper Doll they're callin' him, Canary. He's like a weird. He comes out on the pier, one-two-three, it's a regular free show.

BEATRICE   Well, he's a kid; he don't know how to behave himself yet.

EDDIE   And with that wacky hair; he's like a chorus girl or sump'm.

BEATRICE   So he's blond, so—

EDDIE   I just hope that's his regular hair, that's all I hope.

BEATRICE   You crazy or sump'm? [*She tries to turn him to her.*]

EDDIE   [*he keeps his head turned away*]   What's so crazy? I don't like his whole way.

BEATRICE   Listen, you never seen a blond guy in your life? What about Whitey Balso?

EDDIE   [*turning ot her victoriously*]   Sure, but Whitey don't sing; he don't do like that on the ships.

BEATRICE   Well, maybe that's the way they do in Italy.

EDDIE   Then why don't his brother sing? Marco goes around like a man; nobody kids Marco. [*He moves from her, halts. She realizes there is a campaign solidified in him.*] I tell you the truth I'm surprised I have to tell you all this. I mean I'm surprised, B.

BEATRICE   [*she goes to him with purpose now*]   Listen, you ain't gonna start nothin' here.

EDDIE   I ain't startin' nothin', but I ain't gonna stand around lookin' at that. For that character I didn't bring her up. I swear, B., I'm surprised at you; I sit there waitin' for you to wake up but everything is great with you.

BEATRICE   No, everything ain't great with me.

EDDIE   No?

BEATRICE   No. But I got other worries.

EDDIE   Yeah. [*He is already weakening.*]

BEATRICE   Yeah, you want me to tell you?

EDDIE   [*in retreat*]   Why? What worries you got?

BEATRICE   When am I gonna be a wife again, Eddie?

EDDIE   I ain't been feelin' good. They bother me since they came.

BEATRICE   It's almost three months you don't feel good; they're only here a couple of weeks. It's three months, Eddie.

EDDIE   I don't know, B. I don't want to talk about it.

BEATRICE   What's the matter, Eddie, you don't like me, heh?

EDDIE   What do you mean, I don't like you? I said I don't feel good, that's all.

BEATRICE   Well, tell me, am I doing something wrong? Talk to me.

EDDIE   [*Pause. He can't speak, then*]   I can't. I can't talk about it.

BEATRICE   Well tell me what—

EDDIE   I got nothin' to say about it!

[*She stands for a moment; he is looking off; she turns to go into the house.*]

EDDIE   I'll be all right, B.; just lay off me, will ya? I'm worried about her.

BEATRICE   The girl is gonna be eighteen years old, it's time already.

EDDIE   B., he's taking her for a ride!

BEATRICE   All right, that's her ride. What're you gonna stand over her till she's forty? Eddie, I want you to cut it out now, you hear me? I don't like it! Now come in the house.

EDDIE   I want to take a walk, I'll be in right away.

BEATRICE   They ain't goin' to come any quicker if you stand in the street. It ain't nice, Eddie.

EDDIE   I'll be in right away. Go ahead. [*He walks off.*]

[*She goes into the house.* EDDIE *glances up the street, sees* LOUIS *and* MIKE *coming, and sits on an iron railing.* LOUIS *and* MIKE *enter.*]

LOUIS   Wanna go bowlin' tonight?

EDDIE   I'm too tired. Goin' to sleep.

LOUIS   How's your two submarines?

EDDIE   They're okay.

LOUIS   I see they're gettin' work allatime.

EDDIE   Oh yeah, they're doin' all right.

MIKE   That's what we oughta do. We oughta leave the country and come in under the water. Then we get work.

EDDIE   You ain't kiddin'.

LOUIS   Well, what the hell. Y'know?

EDDIE   Sure.

LOUIS   [*sits on railing beside* EDDIE]   Believe me, Eddie, you got a lotta credit comin' to you.

EDDIE   Aah, they don't bother me, don't cost me nutt'n.

MIKE   That older one, boy, he's a regular bull. I seen him the other day liftin' coffee bags over the Matson Line. They leave him alone he woulda load the whole ship by himself.

EDDIE   Yeah, he's a strong guy, that guy. Their father was a regular giant, supposed to be.

LOUIS   Yeah, you could see. He's a regular slave.

MIKE   [*grinning*]   That blond one, though—[EDDIE *looks at him.*] He's got a sense of humor. [LOUIS *snickers.*]

EDDIE   [*searchingly*]   Yeah. He's funny—

MIKE   [*starting to laugh*]   Well he ain't exackly funny, but he's always like makin' remarks like, y'know? He comes around, everybody's laughin'. [LOUIS *laughs.*]

EDDIE   [*uncomfortably, grinning*]   Yeah, well . . . he's got a sense of humor.

MIKE   [*laughing*]   Yeah, I mean, he's always makin' like remarks, like, y'know?

EDDIE   Yeah, I know. But he's a kid yet, y'know? He—he's just a kid, that's all.

MIKE   [*getting hysterical with* LOUIS]   I know. You take one look at him— everybody's happy. [LOUIS *laughs.*] I worked one day with him last week over the Moore-MacCormack Line, I'm tellin' you they was all hysterical. [LOUIS *and he explode in laughter.*]

EDDIE   Why? What'd he do?

MIKE   I don't know . . . he was just humorous. You never can remember what he says, y'know? But it's the way he says it. I mean he gives you a look sometimes and you start laughin'!

EDDIE   Yeah. [*Troubled.*] He's got a sense of humor.

MIKE   [*gasping*]   Yeah.

LOUIS   [*rising*]   Well, we see ya, Eddie.

EDDIE   Take it easy.

LOUIS   Yeah. See ya.

MIKE   If you wanna come bowlin' later we're goin' Flatbush Avenue.

[*Laughing, they move to exit, meeting* RODOLPHO *and* CATHERINE *entering on the street. Their laughter rises as they see* RODOLPHO, *who does not understand but joins in.* EDDIE *moves to enter the house as* LOUIS *and* MIKE *exit.* CATHERINE *stops him at the door.*]

CATHERINE   Hey, Eddie—what a picture we saw! Did we laugh!

EDDIE   [*he can't help smiling at sight of her*]   Where'd you go?

CATHERINE   Paramount. It was with those two guys, y'know? That—

EDDIE   Brooklyn Paramount?

CATHERINE   [*with an edge of anger, embarrassed before* RODOLPHO]   Sure, the Brooklyn Paramount. I told you we wasn't goin' to New York.

EDDIE   [*retreating before the threat of her anger*]   All right, I only asked you. [*To* RODOLPHO.] I just don't want her hangin' around Times Square, see? It's full of tramps over there.

RODOLPHO   I would like to go to Broadway once, Eddie. I would like to walk with her once where the theaters are and the opera. Since I was a boy I see pictures of those lights.

EDDIE   [*his little patience waning*]   I want to talk to her a minute, Rodolpho. Go inside, will you?

RODOLPHO   Eddie, we only walk together in the streets. She teaches me.

CATHERINE   You know what he can't get over? That there's no fountains in Brooklyn!

EDDIE [*smiling unwillingly*] Fountains? [RODOLPHO *smiles at his own naïveté.*]

CATHERINE In Italy he says, every town's got fountains, and they meet there. And you know what? They got oranges on the trees where he comes from, and lemons. Imagine—on the trees? I mean it's interesting. But he's crazy for New York.

RODOLPHO [*attempting familiarity*] Eddie, why can't we go once to Broadway—?

EDDIE Look, I gotta tell her something—

RODOLPHO Maybe you can come too. I want to see all those lights. [*He sees no response in* EDDIE's *face. He glances at* CATHERINE.] I'll walk by the river before I go to sleep. [*He walks off down the street.*]

CATHERINE Why don't you talk to him, Eddie? He blesses you, and you don't talk to him hardly.

EDDIE [*enveloping her with his eyes*] I bless you and you don't talk to me. [*He tries to smile.*]

CATHERINE *I* don't talk to you? [*She hits his arm.*] What do you mean?

EDDIE I don't see you no more. I come home you're runnin' around someplace—

CATHERINE Well, he wants to see everything, that's all, so we go. . . . You mad at me?

EDDIE No. [*He moves from her, smiling sadly.*] It's just I used to come home, you was always there. Now, I turn around, you're a big girl. I don't know how to talk to you.

CATHERINE Why?

EDDIE I don't know, you're runnin', you're runnin', Katie. I don't think you listening any more to me.

CATHERINE [*going to him*] Ah, Eddie, sure I am. What's the matter? You don't like him?

[*Slight pause.*]

EDDIE [*turns to her*] *You* like him, Katie?

CATHERINE [*with a blush but holding her ground*] Yeah. I like him.

EDDIE [*his smile goes*] You like him.

CATHERINE [*looking down*] Yeah. [*Now she looks at him for the consequences, smiling but tense. He looks at her like a lost boy.*] What're you got against him? I don't understand. He only blesses you.

EDDIE [*turns away*] He don't bless me, Katie.

CATHERINE He does! You're like a father to him!

EDDIE [*turns to her*] Katie.

CATHERINE What, Eddie?

EDDIE You gonna marry him?

CATHERINE I don't know. We just been . . . goin' around, that's all. [*Turns to him.*] What're you got against him, Eddie? Please, tell me. What?

EDDIE He don't respect you.

CATHERINE Why?

EDDIE Katie . . . if you wasn't an orphan, wouldn't he ask your father's permission before he run around with you like this?

CATHERINE Oh, well, he didn't think you'd mind.

EDDIE He knows I mind, but it don't bother him if I mind, don't you see that?

CATHERINE No, Eddie, he's got all kinds of respect for me. And you too! We walk across the street he takes my arm—he almost bows to me! You got him all wrong, Eddie; I mean it, you—

EDDIE Katie, he's only bowin' to his passport.

CATHERINE His passport!

EDDIE   That's right. He marries you he's got the right to be an American citizen. That's what's goin' on here.
[*She is puzzled and surprised.*]
You understand what I'm tellin' you? The guy is lookin' for his break, that's all he's lookin' for.

CATHERINE   [*pained*]   Oh, no, Eddie, I don't think so.

EDDIE   You don't think so! Katie, you're gonna make me cry here. Is that a workin' man? What does he do with his first money? A snappy new jacket he buys, records, a pointy pair new shoes and his brother's kids are starvin' over there with tuberculosis? That's a hit-and-run guy, baby; he's got bright lights in his head, Broadway. Them guys don't think of nobody but theirself! You marry him and the next time you see him it'll be for divorce!

CATHERINE   [*steps toward him*]   Eddie, he never said a word about his papers or—

EDDIE   You mean he's supposed to tell you that?

CATHERINE   I don't think he's even thinking about it.

EDDIE   What's better for him to think about! He could be picked up any day here and he's back pushin' taxis up the hill!

CATHERINE   No, I don't believe it.

EDDIE   Katie, don't break my heart, listen to me.

CATHERINE   I don't want to hear it.

EDDIE   Katie, listen . . .

CATHERINE   He loves me!

EDDIE   [*with deep alarm*]   Don't say that, for God's sake! This is the oldest racket in the country—

CATHERINE   [*desperately, as though he had made his imprint*]   I don't believe it! [*She rushes to the house.*]

EDDIE   [*following her*]   They been pullin' this since the Immigration Law was put in! They grab a green kid that don't know nothin' and they—

CATHERINE   [*sobbing*]   I don't believe it and I wish to hell you'd stop it!

EDDIE   Katie!
[*They enter the apartment. The lights in the living room have risen and* BEATRICE *is there. She looks past the sobbing* CATHERINE *at* EDDIE, *who, in the presence of his wife, makes an awkward gesture of eroded command, indicating* CATHERINE.]

EDDIE   Why don't you straighten her out?

BEATRICE   [*inwardly angered at his flowing emotion, which in itself alarms her*]   When are you going to leave her alone?

EDDIE   B., the guy is no good!

BEATRICE   [*suddenly, with open fright and fury*]   You going to leave her alone? Or you gonna drive me crazy?
[*He turns, striving to retain his dignity, but nevertheless in guilt walks out of the house, into the street and away.* CATHERINE *starts into a bedoom.*]
Listen, Catherine.
[CATHERINE *halts, turns to her sheepishly.*]
What are you going to do with yourself?

CATHERINE   I don't know.

BEATRICE   Don't tell me you don't know; you're not a baby any more, what are you going to do with yourself?

CATHERINE   He won't listen to me.

BEATRICE   I don't understand this. He's not your father, Catherine. I don't understand what's going on here.

CATHERINE   [*as one who herself is trying to rationalize a buried impulse*]   What am I going to do, just kick him in the face with it?

BEATRICE   Look, honey, you wanna get married, or don't you wanna get married? What are you worried about, Katie?

CATHERINE   [*quietly, trembling*]   I don't know B. It just seems wrong if he's against it so much.

BEATRICE   [*never losing her aroused alarm*]   Sit down, honey, I want to tell you something. Here, sit down. Was there ever any fella he liked for you? There wasn't, was there?

CATHERINE   But he says Rodolpho's just after his papers.

BEATRICE   Look, he'll say anything. What does he care what he says? If it was a prince came here for you it would be no different. You know that, don't you?

CATHERINE   Yeah, I guess.

BEATRICE   So what does that mean?

CATHERINE   [*slowly turns her head to* BEATRICE]   What?

BEATRICE   It means you gotta be your own self more. You still think you're a little girl, honey. But nobody else can make up your mind for you any more, you understand? You gotta give him to understand that he can't give you orders no more.

CATHERINE   Yeah, but how am I going to do that? He thinks I'm a baby.

BEATRICE   Because *you* think you're a baby. I told you fifty times already, you can't act the way you act. You still walk around in front of him in your slip—

CATHERINE   Well I forgot.

BEATRICE   Well you can't do it. Or like you sit on the edge of the bathtub talkin' to him when he's shavin' in his underwear.

CATHERINE   When'd I do that?

BEATRICE   I seen you in there this morning.

CATHERINE   Oh . . . well, I wanted to tell him something and I—

BEATRICE   I know, honey. But if you act like a baby and he be treatin' you like a baby. Like when he comes home sometimes you throw yourself at him like when you was twelve years old.

CATHERINE   Well I like to see him and I'm happy so I—

BEATRICE   Look, I'm not tellin' you what to do honey, but—

CATHERINE   No, you could tell me, B.! Gee, I'm all mixed up. See, I—He looks so sad now and it hurts me.

BEATRICE   Well look Katie, if it's goin' to hurt you so much you're gonna end up an old maid here.

CATHERINE   No!

BEATRICE   I'm tellin' you, I'm not makin' a joke. I tried to tell you a couple of times in the last year or so. That's why I was so happy you were going to go out and get work, you wouldn't be here so much, you'd be a little more independent. I mean it. It's wonderful for a whole family to love each other, but you're a grown woman and you're in the same house with a grown man. So you'll act different now, heh?

CATHERINE   Yeah, I will. I'll remember.

BEATRICE   Because it ain't only up to him, Katie, you understand? I told him the same thing already.

CATHERINE   [*quickly*]   What?

BEATRICE   That he should let you go. But, you see, if only I tell him, he thinks I'm just bawlin' him out, or maybe I'm jealous or somethin', you know?

CATHERINE   [*astonished*]   He said you was jealous?

BEATRICE   No, I'm just sayin' maybe that's what he thinks. [*She reaches over to* CATHERINE's *hand; with a strained smile.*] You think I'm jealous of you, honey?

CATHERINE   No! It's the first I thought of it.

BEATRICE   [*with a quiet sad laugh*]   Well you should have thought of it before . . . but I'm not. We'll be all right. Just give him to understand; you don't have to fight, you're just—You're a woman, that's all, and you got a nice boy, and now the time came when you said good-by. All right?

CATHERINE   [*strangely moved at the prospect*]   All right. . . . If I can.

BEATRICE   Honey . . . you gotta.

[CATHERINE, *sensing now an imperious demand, turns with some fear, with a discovery, to* BEATRICE. *She is at the edge of tears, as though a familiar world had shattered.*]

CATHERINE   Okay.

[*Lights out on them and up on* ALFIERI, *seated behind his desk.*]

ALFIERI   It was at this time that he first came to me. I had represented his father in an accident case some years before, and I was acquainted with the family in a casual way. I remember him now as he walked through my doorway—

[*Enter* EDDIE *down right ramp.*]

His eyes were like tunnels; my first thought was that he had committed a crime.

[EDDIE *sits beside the desk, cap in hand, looking out.*]

But soon I saw it was only a passion that had moved into his body, like a stranger. [ALFIERI *pauses, looks down at his desk, then to* EDDIE *as though he were continuing a conversation with him.*]   I don't quite understand what I can do for you. Is there a question of law somewhere?

EDDIE   That's what I want to ask you.

ALFIERI   Because there's nothing illegal about a girl falling in love with an immigrant.

EDDIE   Yeah, but what about it if the only reason for it is to get his papers?

ALFIERI   First of all you don't know that.

EDDIE   I see it in his eyes; he's laughin' at her and he's laughin' at me.

ALFIERI   Eddie, I'm a lawyer. I can only deal in what's provable. You understand that, don't you? Can you prove that?

EDDIE   *I know what's in his mind, Mr. Alfieri!*

ALFIERI   Eddie, even if you could prove that—

EDDIE   Listen . . . will you listen to me a minute? My father always said you was a smart man. I want you to listen to me.

ALFIERI   I'm only a lawyer, Eddie.

EDDIE   Will you listen a minute? I'm talkin' about the law. Lemme just bring out what I mean. A man, which he comes into the country illegal, don't it stand to reason he's gonna take every penny and put it in the sock? Because they don't know from one day to another, right?

ALFIERI   All right.

EDDIE   He's spendin'. Records he buys now. Shoes. Jackets. Y'understand me? This guy ain't worried. This guy is *here.* So it must be that he's got it all laid out in his mind already—he's stayin'. Right?

ALFIERI   Well? What about it?

EDDIE   All right. [*He glances at* ALFIERI, *then down to the floor.*]   I'm talking to you confidential, ain't I?

ALFIERI   Certainly.

EDDIE   I mean it don't go no place but here. Because I don't like to say this about anybody. Even my wife I didn't exactly say this.

ALFIERI   What is it?

EDDIE   [*takes a breath and glances briefly over each shoulder*]   The guy ain't right, Mr. Alfieri.

ALFIERI   What do you mean?

EDDIE   I mean he ain't right.

ALFIERI   I don't get you.

EDDIE   [*shifts to another position in the chair*]   Dja ever get a look at him?

ALFIERI   Not that I know of, no.

EDDIE   He's a blond guy. Like . . . platinum. You know what I mean?

ALFIERI   No.

EDDIE   I mean if you close the paper fast—you could blow him over.

ALFIERI   Well that doesn't mean—

EDDIE   Wait a minute, I'm tellin' you sump'm. He sings, see. Which is—I mean it's all right, but sometimes he hits a note, see. I turn around. I mean— high. You know what I mean?

ALFIERI   Well, that's a tenor.

EDDIE   I know a tenor, Mr. Alfieri. This ain't no tenor. I mean if you came in the house and you didn't know who was singin', you wouldn't be lookin' for him you be lookin' for her.

ALFIERI   Yes, but that's not—

EDDIE   I'm tellin' you sump'm, wait a minute. Please, Mr. Alfieri. I'm tryin' to bring out my thoughts here. Couple of nights ago my niece brings out a dress which it's too small for her, because she shot up like a light this last year. He takes the dress, lays it on the table, he cuts it up; one-two-three, he makes a new dress. I mean he looked so sweet there, like an angel— you could kiss him he was so sweet.

ALFIERI   Now look, Eddie—

EDDIE   Mr. Alfieri, they're laughin' at him on the piers. I'm ashamed. Paper Doll they call him. Blondie now. His brother thinks it's because he's got a sense of humor, see—which he's got—but that ain't what they're laughin'. Which they're not goin' to come out with it because they know he's my relative, which they have to see me if they make a crack, y'know? But I know what they're laughin' at, and when I think of that guy layin' his hands on her I could—I mean it's eatin' me out, Mr. Alfieri, because I struggled for that girl. And now he comes in my house and—

ALFIERI   Eddie, look—I have my own children. I understand you. But the law is very specific. The law does not . . .

EDDIE   [*with a fuller flow of indignation*]   You mean to tell me that there's no law that a guy which he ain't right can go to work and marry a girl and—?

ALFIERI   You have no recourse in the law, Eddie.

EDDIE   Yeah, but if he ain't right, Mr. Alfieri, you mean to tell me—

ALFIERI   There is nothing you can do, Eddie, believe me.

EDDIE   Nothin'.

ALFIERI   Nothing at all. There's only one legal question here.

EDDIE   What?

ALFIERI   The manner in which they entered the country. But I don't think you want to do anything about that, do you?

EDDIE   You mean—?

ALFIERI   Well, they entered illegally.

EDDIE   Oh, Jesus, no, I wouldn't do nothin' about that, I mean—

ALFIERI   All right, then, let me talk now, eh?

EDDIE   Mr. Alfieri, I can't believe what you tell me. I mean there must be some kinda law which—

ALFIERI   Eddie, I want you to listen to me. [*Pause.*] You know, sometimes God mixes up the people. We all love somebody, the wife, the kids—every man's got somebody that he loves, heh? But sometimes . . . there's too much. You know? There's too much, and it goes where it mustn't. A man works hard, he brings up a child, sometimes it's a niece, sometimes even a daughter, and he never realizes it, but through the years—there is too much love for the daughter, there is too much love for the niece. Do you understand what I'm saying to you?

EDDIE [*sardonically*]   What do you mean, I shouldn't look out for her good?

ALFIERI   Yes, but these things have to end, Eddie, that's all. The child has to grow up and go away, and the man has to learn to forget. Because after all, Eddie—what other way can it end? [*Pause.*] Let her go. That's my advice. You did your job, now it's her life; wish her luck, and let her go. [*Pause.*] Will you do that? Because there's no law, Eddie; make up your mind to it; the law is not interested in this.

EDDIE   You mean to tell me, even if he's a punk? If he's—

ALFIERI   There's nothing you can do.

[EDDIE *stands.*]

EDDIE   Well, all right, thanks. Thanks very much.

ALFIERI   What are you going to do?

EDDIE [*with a helpless but ironic gesture*]   What can I do? I'm a patsy, what can a patsy do? I worked like a dog twenty years so a punk could have her, so that's what I done. I mean, in the worst times, in the worst, when there wasn't a ship comin' in the harbor, I didn't stand around lookin' for relief —I hustled. When there was empty piers in Brooklyn I went to Hoboken, Staten Island, the West Side, Jersey, all over—because I made a promise. I took out of my own mouth to give to her. I took out of my wife's mouth. I walked hungry plenty days in this city! [*It begins to break through.*] And now I gotta sit in my own house and look at a son-of-a-bitch punk like that—which he came out of nowhere! I give him my house to sleep! I take the blankets off my bed for him, and he takes and puts his dirty filthy hands on her like a goddam thief!

ALFIERI [*rising*]   But, Eddie, she's a woman now.

EDDIE   He's stealing from me!

ALFIERI   She wants to get married, Eddie. She can't marry you, can she?

EDDIE [*furiously*]   What're you talkin' about, marry me! I don't know what the hell you're talkin' about!

[*Pause.*]

ALFIERI   I gave you my advice, Eddie. That's it.

[EDDIE *gathers himself. A pause.*]

EDDIE   Well, thanks. Thanks very much. It just—it's breakin' my heart, y'know. I—

ALFIERI   I understand. Put it out of your mind. Can you do that?

EDDIE   I'm—[*He feels the threat of sobs, and with a helpless wave.*] I'll see you around. [*He goes out up the right ramp.*]

ALFIERI [*sits on desk*]   There are times when you want to spread an alarm, but nothing has happened. I knew, I knew then and there—I could have finished the whole story that afternoon. It wasn't as though there was a mystery to unravel. I could see every step coming, step after step, like a dark figure walking down a hall toward a certain door. I knew where he was heading for, I knew where he was going to end. And I sat here many afternoons asking myself why, being an intelligent man, I was so powerless to stop it. I even went to a certain old lady in the neighborhood, a very wise old woman, and I told her, and she only nodded, and said, "Pray for him . . ." And so I—waited here.

[*As lights go out on* ALFIERI, *they rise in the apartment where all are finishing dinner.* BEATRICE *and* CATHERINE *are clearing the table.*]

CATHERINE   You know where they went?

BEATRICE   Where?

CATHERINE   They went to Africa once. On a fishing boat.

[EDDIE *glances at her.*]

It's true, Eddie.

[BEATRICE *exits into the kitchen with dishes.*]

EDDIE   I didn't say nothin'. [*He goes to his rocker, picks up a newspaper.*]

CATHERINE   And I was never even in Staten Island.

EDDIE   [*sitting with the paper*]   You didn't miss nothin'.

[*Pause.* CATHERINE *takes dishes out.*]

How long that take you, Marco—to get to Africa?

MARCO   [*rising*]   Oh . . . two days. We go all over.

RODOLPHO   [*rising*]   Once we went to Yugoslavia.

EDDIE   [*to* MARCO]   They pay all right on them boats?

[BEATRICE *enters. She and* RODOLPHO *stack the remaining dishes.*]

MARCO   If they catch fish they pay all right. [*Sits on a stool.*]

RODOLPHO   They're family boats, though. And nobody in our family owned one. So we only worked when one of the families was sick.

BEATRICE   Y'know, Marco, what I don't understand—there's an ocean full of fish and yiz are all starvin'.

EDDIE   They gotta have boats, nets, you need money.

[CATHERINE *enters.*]

BEATRICE   Yeah, but couldn't they like fish from the beach? You see them down Coney Island—

MARCO   Sardines.

EDDIE   Sure. [*Laughing.*] How you gonna catch sardines on a hook?

BEATRICE   Oh, I didn't know they're sardines. [*To* CATHERINE.] They're sardines!

CATHERINE   Yeah, they follow them all over the ocean, Africa, Yugoslavia . . .

[*She sits and begins to look through a movie magazine.* RODOLPHO *joins her.*]

BEATRICE   [*to* EDDIE]   It's funny, y'know. You never think of it, that sardines are swimming in the ocean! [*She exits to kitchen with dishes.*]

CATHERINE   I know. It's like oranges and lemons on a tree. [*To* EDDIE.] I mean you ever think of oranges and lemons on a tree?

EDDIE   Yeah, I know. It's funny. [*To* MARCO.] I heard that they paint the oranges to make them look orange.

[BEATRICE *enters.*]

MARCO   [*he has been reading a letter*]   Paint?

EDDIE   Yeah, I heard that they grow like green.

MARCO   No, in Italy the oranges are orange.

RODOLPHO   Lemons are green.

EDDIE   [*resenting his instruction*]   I know lemons are green, for Christ's sake, you see them in the store they're green sometimes. I said oranges they paint, I didn't say nothin' about lemons.

BEATRICE   [*sitting; diverting their attention*]   Your wife is gettin' the money all right, Marco?

MARCO   Oh, yes. She bought medicine for my boy.

BEATRICE   That's wonderful. You feel better, heh?

MARCO   Oh, yes! But I'm lonesome.

BEATRICE   I just hope you ain't gonna do like some of them around here. They're here twenty-five years, some men, and they didn't get enough together to go back twice.

MARCO   Oh, I know. We have many families in our town, the children never saw the father. But I will go home. Three, four years, I think.

BEATRICE   Maybe you should keep more here. Because maybe she thinks it comes so easy you'll never get ahead of yourself.

MARCO Oh, no, she saves. I send everything. My wife is very lonesome. [*He smiles shyly.*]

BEATRICE She must be nice. She pretty? I bet, heh?

MARCO [*blushing*] No, but she understand everything.

RODOLPHO Oh, he's got a clever wife!

EDDIE I betcha there's plenty surprises sometimes when those guys get back there, heh?

MARCO Surprises?

EDDIE [*laughing*] I mean, you know—they count the kids and there's a couple extra than when they left?

MARCO No—no . . . The women wait, Eddie. Most. Most. Very few surprises.

RODOLPHO It's more strict in our town.
  [EDDIE *looks at him now.*]
  It's not so free.

EDDIE [*rises, paces up and down*] It ain't so free here either, Rodolpho, like you think. I seen greenhorns sometimes get in trouble that way—they think just because a girl don't go around with a shawl over her head that she ain't strict, y'know? Girl don't have to wear black dress to be strict. Know what I mean?

RODOLPHO Well, I always have respect—

EDDIE I know, but in your town you wouldn't just drag off some girl without permission, I mean. [*He turns.*] You know what I mean, Marco? It ain't that much different here.

MARCO [*cautiously*] Yes.

BEATRICE Well, he didn't exactly drag her off though, Eddie.

EDDIE I know, but I seen some of them get the wrong idea sometimes. [*To* RODOLPHO.] I mean it might be a little more free here but it's just as strict.

RODOLPHO I have respect for her, Eddie. I do anything wrong?

EDDIE Look, kid, I ain't her father, I'm only her uncle—

BEATRICE Well then, be an uncle then.
  [EDDIE *looks at her, aware of her criticizing force.*]
  I *mean.*

MARCO No, Beatrice, if he does wrong you must tell him. [*To* EDDIE.] What does he do wrong?

EDDIE Well, Marco, till he came here she was never out on the street twelve o'clock at night.

MARCO [*to* RODOLPHO] You come home early now.

BEATRICE [*to* CATHERINE] Well, you said the movie ended late, didn't you?

CATHERINE Yeah.

BEATRICE Well, tell him, honey. [*To* EDDIE.] The movie ended late.

EDDIE Look, B., I'm just sayin'—he thinks she always stayed out like that.

MARCO You come home early now, Rodolpho.

RODOLPHO [*embarrassed*] All right, sure. But I can't stay in the house all the time, Eddie.

EDDIE Look, kid, I'm not only talkin' about her. The more you run around like that the more chance you're takin'. [*To* BEATRICE.] I mean suppose he gets hit by a car or something. [*To* MARCO.] Where's his papers, who is he? Know what I mean?

BEATRICE Yeah, but who is he in the daytime, though? It's the same chance in the daytime.

EDDIE [*holding back a voice full of anger*] Yeah, but he don't have to go lookin' for it, Beatrice. If he's here to work, then he should work; if he's here for a good time then he could fool around! [*To* MARCO.] But I understood, Marco, that you was both comin' to make a livin' for your family. You understand me, don't you, Marco? [*He goes to his rocker.*]

MARCO I beg your pardon, Eddie.

EDDIE I mean, that's what I understood in the first place, see.

MARCO Yes. That's why we came.

EDDIE [*sits on his rocker*] Well, that's all I'm askin'.

[EDDIE *reads his paper. There is a pause, an awkwardness. Now* CATHERINE *gets up and puts a record on the phonograph—"Paper Doll."*]

CATHERINE [*flushed with revolt*] You wanna dance, Rodolpho?

[EDDIE *freezes.*]

RODOLPHO [*in deference to* EDDIE] No, I—I'm tired.

BEATRICE Go ahead, dance, Rodolpho.

CATHERINE Ah, come on. They got a beautiful quartet, these guys. Come.

[*She has taken his hand and he stiffly rises, feeling* EDDIE'S *eyes on his back, and they dance.*]

EDDIE [*to* CATHERINE] What's that, a new record?

CATHERINE It's the same one. We bought it the other day.

BEATRICE [*to* EDDIE] They only bought three records. [*She watches them dance;* EDDIE *turns his head away.* MARCO *just sits there, waiting. Now* BEATRICE *turns to* EDDIE.] Must be nice to go all over in one of them fishin' boats. I would like that myself. See all them other countries?

EDDIE Yeah.

BEATRICE [*to* MARCO] But the women don't go along, I bet.

MARCO No, not on the boats. Hard work.

BEATRICE What're you got, a regular kitchen and everything?

MARCO Yes, we eat very good on the boats—especially when Rodolpho comes along; everybody gets fat.

BEATRICE Oh, he cooks?

MARCO Sure, very good cook. Rice, pasta, fish, everything.

[EDDIE *lowers his paper.*]

EDDIE He's a cook, too! [*Looking at* RODOLPHO.] He sings, he cooks . . .

[RODOLPHO *smiles thankfully.*]

BEATRICE Well it's good, he could always make a living.

EDDIE It's wonderful. He sings, he cooks, he could make dresses . . .

CATHERINE They get some high pay, them guys. The head chefs in all the big hotels are men. You read about them.

EDDIE That's what I'm sayin'.

[CATHERINE *and* RODOLPHO *continue dancing.*]

CATHERINE Yeah, well, I mean.

EDDIE [*to* BEATRICE] He's lucky, believe me. [*Slight pause. He looks away, then back to* BEATRICE.] That's why the water front is no place for him. [*They stop dancing.* RODOLPHO *turns off phonograph.*] I mean like me—I can't cook, I can't sing, I can't make dresses, so I'm on the water front. But if I could cook, if I could sing, if I could make dresses, I wouldn't be on the water front. [*He has been unconsciously twisting the newspaper into a tight roll. They are all regarding him now; he senses he is exposing the issue and he is driven on.*] I would be someplace else. I would be like in a dress store. [*He has bent the rolled paper and it suddenly tears in two. He suddenly gets up and pulls his pants up over his belly and goes to* MARCO.] What do you say, Marco, we go to the bouts next Saturday night. You never seen a fight, did you?

MARCO [*uneasily*] Only in the moving pictures.

EDDIE [*going to* RODOLPHO] I'll treat yiz. What do you say, Danish? You wanna come along? I'll buy the tickets.

RODOLPHO Sure. I like to go.

CATHERINE [*goes to* EDDIE; *nervously happy now*] I'll make some coffee, all right?

EDDIE   Go ahead, make some! Make it nice and strong. [*Mystified, she smiles and exits to kitchen. He is weirdly elated, rubbing his fists into his palms. He strides to* MARCO.] You wait, Marco, you see some real fights here. You ever do any boxing?

MARCO   No, I never.

EDDIE   [*to* RODOLPHO]   Betcha you have done some, heh?

RODOLPHO   No.

EDDIE   Well, come on, I'll teach you.

BEATRICE   What's he got to learn that for?

EDDIE   Ya can't tell, one a these days somebody's liable to step on his foot or sump'm. Come on, Rodolpho, I show you a couple a passes. [*He stands below table.*]

BEATRICE   Go ahead, Rodolpho. He's a good boxer, he could teach you.

RODOLPHO   [*embarrassed*]   Well, I don't know how to—[*He moves down to* EDDIE.]

EDDIE   Just put your hands up. Like this, see? That's right. That's very good, keep your left up, because you lead with the left, see, like this. [*He gently moves his left into* RODOLPHO's *face.*] See? Now what you gotta do is you gotta block me, so when I come in like that you—[RODOLPHO *parries his left.*] Hey, that's very good! [RODOLPHO *laughs.*] All right, now come into me. Come on.

RODOLPHO   I don't want to hit you, Eddie.

EDDIE   Don't pity me, come on. Throw it, I'll show you how to block it. [RODOLPHO *jabs at him, laughing. The others join.*] 'At's it. Come on again. For the jaw right here. [RODOLPHO *jabs with more assurance.*] Very good!

BEATRICE   [*to* MARCO]   He's very good!

[EDDIE *crosses directly upstage of* RODOLPHO.]

EDDIE   Sure, he's great! Come on, kid, put sump'm behind it, you can't hurt me. [RODOLPHO, *more seriously, jabs at* EDDIE's *jaw and grazes it.*] Attaboy. [CATHERINE *comes from the kitchen, watches.*]
Now I'm gonna hit you, so block me, see?

CATHERINE   [*with beginning alarm*]   What are they doin'?

[*They are lightly boxing now.*]

BEATRICE   [*she senses only the comradeship in it now*]   He's teachin' him; he's very good!

EDDIE   Sure, he's terrific! Look at him go! [RODOLPHO *lands a blow.*] 'At's it! Now, watch out, here I come, Danish! [*He feints with his left hand and lands with his right. It mildly staggers* RODOLPHO. MARCO *rises.*]

CATHERINE   [*rushing to* RODOLPHO]   Eddie!

EDDIE   Why? I didn't hurt him. Did I hurt you, kid? [*He rubs the back of his hand across his mouth.*]

RODOLPHO   No, no, he didn't hurt me. [*To* EDDIE *with a certain gleam and a smile.*] I was only surprised.

BEATRICE   [*pulling* EDDIE *down into the rocker*]   That's enough, Eddie; he did pretty good, though.

EDDIE   Yeah. [*Rubbing his fists together.*] He could be very good, Marco. I'll teach him again.

[MARCO *nods at him dubiously.*]

RODOLPHO   Dance, Catherine. Come. [*He takes her hand; they go to phonograph and start it. It plays "Paper Doll."*]
[RODOLPHO *takes her in his arms. They dance.* EDDIE *in thought sits in his chair, and* MARCO *takes a chair, places it in front of* EDDIE, *and looks down at it.* BEATRICE *and* EDDIE *watch him.*]

MARCO   Can you lift this chair?

EDDIE   What do you mean?

MARCO   From here. [*He gets on one knee with one hand behind his back, and grasps the bottom on one of the chair legs but does not raise it.*]

EDDIE   Sure, why not? [*He comes to the chair, kneels, grasps the leg, raises the chair one inch, but it leans over to the floor.*] Gee, that's hard, I never knew that. [*He tries again, and again fails.*] It's on an angle, that's why, heh?

MARCO   Here.

[MARCO *kneels, grasps, and with strain slowly raises the chair higher and higher, getting to his feet now.* RODOLPHO *and* CATHERINE *have stopped dancing as* MARCO *raises the chair over his head.*

MARCO *is face to face with* EDDIE, *a strained tension gripping his eyes and jaw, his neck stiff, the chair raised like a weapon over* EDDIE's *head—and he transforms what might appear like a glare of warning into a smile of triumph, and* EDDIE's *grin vanishes as he absorbs his look.*]

CURTAIN

ACT II

[*Light rises on* ALFIERI *at his desk.*]

ALFIERI   On the twenty-third of that December a case of Scotch whisky slipped from a net while being unloaded—as a case of Scotch whisky is inclined to do on the twenty-third of December on Pier Forty-one. There was no snow, but it was cold, his wife was out shopping. Marco was still at work. The boy had not been hired that day; Catherine told me later that this was the first time they had been alone together in the house.

[*Light is rising on* CATHERINE *in the apartment.* RODOLPHO *is watching as she arranges a paper pattern on cloth spread on the table.*]

CATHERINE   You hungry?

RODOLPHO   Not for anything to eat. [*Pause.*] I have nearly three hundred dollars. Catherine?

CATHERINE   I heard you.

RODOLPHO   You don't like to talk about it any more?

CATHERINE   Sure, I don't mind talkin' about it.

RODOLPHO   What worries you, Catherine?

CATHERINE   I been wantin' to ask you about something. Could I?

RODOLPHO   All the answers are in my eyes, Catherine. But you don't look in my eyes lately. You're full of secrets. [*She looks at him. She seems withdrawn.*] What is the question?

CATHERINE   Suppose I wanted to live in Italy.

RODOLPHO   [*smiling at the incongruity*]   You going to marry somebody rich?

CATHERINE   No, I mean live there—you and me.

RODOLPHO   [*his smile vanishing*]   When?

CATHERINE   Well . . . when we get married.

RODOLPHO   [*astonished*]   You want to be an Italian?

CATHERINE   No, but I could live there without being Italian. Americans live there.

RODOLPHO   Forever?

CATHERINE   Yeah.

RODOLPHO   [*crosses to rocker*]   You're fooling.

CATHERINE   No, I mean it.

RODOLPHO   Where do you get such an idea?

CATHERINE   Well, you're always saying it's so beautiful there, with the mountains and the ocean and all the—

RODOLPHO   You're fooling me.

CATHERINE   I mean it.

RODOLPHO   [*goes to her slowly*]   Catherine, if I ever brought you home with no money, no business, nothing, they would call the priest and the doctor and they would say Rodolpho is crazy.

CATHERINE   I know, but I think we would be happier there.

RODOLPHO   Happier! What would you eat? You can't cook the view!

CATHERINE   Maybe you could be a singer, like in Rome or—

RODOLPHO   Rome! Rome is full of singers.

CATHERINE   Well, I could work then.

RODOLPHO   Where?

CATHERINE   God, there must be jobs somewhere!

RODOLPHO   There's nothing! Nothing, nothing, nothing. Now tell me what you're talking about. How can I bring you from a rich country to suffer in a poor country? What are you talking about? [*She searches for words.*] I would be a criminal stealing your face. In two years you would have an old, hungry face. When my brother's babies cry they give them water, water that boiled a bone. Don't you believe that?

CATHERINE   [*quietly*]   I'm afraid of Eddie here.

    [*Slight pause.*]

RODOLPHO   [*steps closer to her*]   We wouldn't live here. Once I am a citizen I could work anywhere and I would find better jobs and we would have a house, Catherine. If I were not afraid to be arrested I would start to be something wonderful here!

CATHERINE   [*steeling herself*]   Tell me something. I mean just tell me, Rodolpho —would you still want to do it if it turned out we had to go live in Italy? I mean just if it turned out that way.

RODOLPHO   This is your question or his question?

CATHERINE   I would like to know, Rodolpho. I mean it.

RODOLPHO   To go there with nothing.

CATHERINE   Yeah.

RODOLPHO   No. [*She looks at him wide-eyed.*] No.

CATHERINE   You wouldn't?

RODOLPHO   No; I will not marry you to live in Italy. I want you to be my wife, and I want to be a citizen. Tell him that, or I will. Yes. [*He moves about angrily.*] And tell him also, and tell yourself, please, that I am not a beggar, and you are not a horse, a gift, a favor for a poor immigrant.

CATHERINE   Well, don't get mad!

RODOLPHO   I am furious! [*Goes to her.*] Do you think I am so desperate? My brother is desperate, not me. You think I would carry on my back the rest of my life a woman I didn't love just to be an American? It's so wonderful? You think we have no tall buildings in Italy? Electric lights? No wide streets? No flags? No automobiles? Only work we don't have. I want to be an American so I can work, that is the only wonder here—work! How can you insult me, Catherine?

CATHERINE   I didn't mean that—

RODOLPHO   My heart dies to look at you. Why are you so afraid of him?

CATHERINE   [*near tears*]   I don't know!

RODOLPHO   Do you trust me, Catherine? You?

CATHERINE   It's only that I—He was good to me, Rodolpho. You don't know him; he was always the sweetest guy to me. Good. He razzes me all the time but he don't mean it. I know. I would—just feel ashamed if I made him sad. 'Cause I always dreamt that when I got married he would be happy at the wedding, and laughin'—and now he's—mad all the time and nasty—[*She is weeping.*] Tell him you'd live in Italy—just tell him, and maybe he would start to trust you a little, see? Because I want him to be happy; I mean—I like him, Rodolpho—and I can't stand it!

RODOLPHO Oh, Catherine—oh, little girl.

CATHERINE I love you, Rodolpho, I love you.

RODOLPHO Then why are you afraid? That he'll spank you?

CATHERINE Don't, don't laugh at me! I've been here all my life. . . . Every day I saw him when he left in the morning and when he came home at night. You think it's so easy to turn around and say to a man he's nothin' to you no more?

RODOLPHO I know, but—

CATHERINE You don't know; nobody knows! I'm not a baby, I know a lot more than people think I know. Beatrice says to be a woman, but—

RODOLPHO Yes.

CATHERINE Then why don't she be a woman? If I was a wife I would make a man happy instead of goin' at him all the time. I can tell a block away when he's blue in his mind and just wants to talk to somebody quiet and nice. . . . I can tell when he's hungry or wants a beer before he even says anything. I know when his feet hurt him, I mean I *know* him and now I'm supposed to turn around and make a stranger out of him? I don't know why I have to do that, I mean.

RODOLPHO Catherine. If I take in my hands a little bird. And she grows and wishes to fly. But I will not let her out of my hands because I love her so much, is that right for me to do? I don't say you must hate him; but anyway you must go, mustn't you? Catherine?

CATHERINE [*softly*] Hold me.

RODOLPHO [*clasping her to him*] Oh, my little girl.

CATHERINE Teach me. [*She is weeping.*] I don't know anything, teach me, Rodolpho, hold me.

RODOLPHO There's nobody here now. Come inside. Come. [*He is leading her toward the bedrooms.*] And don't cry any more.

[*Light rises on the street. In a moment* EDDIE *appears. He is unsteady, drunk. He mounts the stairs. He enters the apartment, looks around, takes out a bottle from one pocket, puts it on the table. Then another bottle from another pocket, and a third from an inside pocket. He sees the pattern and cloth, goes over to it and touches it, and turns toward upstage.*]

EDDIE Beatrice? [*He goes to the open kitchen door and looks in.*] Beatrice? Beatrice?

[CATHERINE *enters from bedroom; under his gaze she adjusts her dress.*]

CATHERINE You got home early.

EDDIE Knocked off for Christmas early. [*Indicating the pattern.*] Rodolpho makin' you a dress?

CATHERINE No. I'm makin' a blouse.

[RODOLPHO *appears in the bedroom doorway.* EDDIE *sees him and his arm jerks slightly in shock.* RODOLPHO *nods to him testingly.*]

RODOLPHO Beatrice went to buy presents for her mother.

[*Pause.*]

EDDIE Pack it up. Go ahead. Get your stuff and get outa here. [CATHERINE *instantly turns and walks toward the bedroom, and* EDDIE *grabs her arm.*] Where you goin'?

CATHERINE [*trembling with fright*] I think I have to get out of here, Eddie.

EDDIE   No, you ain't goin' nowheres, he's the one.

CATHERINE   I think I can't stay here no more. [*She frees her arm, steps back toward the bedroom.*] I'm sorry, Eddie. [*She sees the tears in his eyes.*] Well, don't cry. I'll be around the neighborhood; I'll see you. I just can't stay here no more. You know I can't. [*Her sobs of pity and love for him break her composure.*] Don't you know I can't? You know that, don't you? [*She goes to him.*] Wish me luck. [*She clasps her hands prayerfully.*] Oh, Eddie, don't be like that!

EDDIE   You ain't goin' nowheres.

CATHERINE   Eddie, I'm not gonna be a baby any more! You—
[*He reaches out suddenly, draws her to him, and as she strives to free herself he kisses her on the mouth.*]

RODOLPHO   Don't! [*He pulls on* EDDIE's *arm.*] Stop that! Have respect for her!

EDDIE   [*spun round by* RODOLPHO]   You want something?

RODOLPHO   Yes! She'll be my wife. That is what I want. My wife!

EDDIE   But what're you gonna be?

RODOLPHO   I show you what I be!

CATHERINE   Wait outside; don't argue with him!

EDDIE   Come on, show me! What're you gonna be? Show me!

RODOLPHO   [*with tears of rage*]   Don't say that to me!
[RODOLPHO *flies at him in attack.* EDDIE *pins his arms, laughing, and suddenly kisses him.*]

CATHERINE   Eddie! Let go, ya hear me! I'll kill you! Leggo of him!
[*She tears at* EDDIE's *face and* EDDIE *releases* RODOLPHO. EDDIE *stands there with tears rolling down his face as he laughs mockingly at* RODOLPHO. *She is staring at him in horror.* RODOLPHO *is rigid. They are like animals that have torn at one another and broken up without a decision, each waiting for the other's mood.*]

EDDIE   [*to* CATHERINE]   You see? [*To* RODOLPHO.] I give you till tomorrow, kid. Get outa here. Alone. You hear me? Alone.

CATHERINE   I'm going with him, Eddie. [*She starts toward* RODOLPHO.]

EDDIE   [*indicating* RODOLPHO *with his head*]   Not with that. [*She halts, frightened. He sits, still panting for breath, and they watch him helplessly as he leans toward them over the table.*] Don't make me do nuttin', Catherine. Watch your step, submarine. By rights they oughta throw you back in the water. But I got pity for you. [*He moves unsteadily toward the door, always facing* RODOLPHO.] Just get outa here and don't lay another hand on her unless you wanna go out feet first. [*He goes out of the apartment.*]
[*The lights go down, as they rise on* ALFIERI.]

ALFIERI   On December twenty-seventh I saw him next. I normally go home well before six, but that day I sat around looking out my window at the bay, and when I saw him walking through my doorway, I knew why I had waited. And if I seem to tell this like a dream, it was that way. Several moments arrived in the course of the two talks we had when it occurred to me how—almost transfixed I had come to feel. I had lost my strength somewhere. [EDDIE *enters, removing his cap, sits in the chair, looks thoughtfully out.*] I looked in his eyes more than I listened—in fact, I can hardly remember the conversation. But I will never forget how dark the room became when he looked at me; his eyes were like tunnels. I kept wanting to call the police, but nothing had happened. Nothing at all had really happened. [*He breaks off and looks down at the desk. Then he turns to* EDDIE.] So in other words, he won't leave?

EDDIE   My wife is talkin' about renting a room upstairs for them. An old lady on the top floor is got an empty room.

ALFIERI   What does Marco say?

EDDIE He just sits there. Marco don't say much.

ALFIERI I guess they didn't tell him, heh? What happened?

EDDIE I don't know; Marco don't say much.

ALFIERI What does your wife say?

EDDIE [*unwilling to pursue this*] Nobody's talkin' much in the house. So what about that?

ALFIERI But you didn't prove anything about him. It sounds like he just wasn't strong enough to break your grip.

EDDIE I'm tellin' you I know—he ain't right. Somebody that don't want it can break it. Even a mouse, if you catch a teeny mouse and you hold it in your hand, that mouse can give you the right kind of fight. He didn't give me the right kind of fight, I know it, Mr. Alfieri, the guy ain't right.

ALFIERI What did you do that for, Eddie?

EDDIE To show her what he is! So she would see, once and for all! Her mother'll turn over in the grave! [*He gathers himself almost peremptorily.*] So what do I gotta do now? Tell me what to do.

ALFIERI She actually said she's marrying him?

EDDIE She told me, yeah. So what do I do?

[*Slight pause.*]

ALFIERI This is my last word, Eddie, take it or not, that's your business. Morally and legally you have no rights, you cannot stop it; she is a free agent.

EDDIE [*angering*] Didn't you hear what I told you?

ALFIERI [*with a tougher tone*] I heard what you told me, and I'm telling you what the answer is. I'm not only telling you now, I'm warning you—the law is nature. The law is only a word for what has a right to happen. When the law is wrong it's because it's unnatural, but in this case it is natural and a river will drown you if you buck it now. Let her go. And bless her. [*A phone booth begins to glow on the opposite side of the stage; a faint, lonely blue.* EDDIE *stands up, jaws clenched.*] Somebody had to come for her, Eddie, sooner or later. [EDDIE *starts turning to go and* ALFIERI *rises with new anxiety*.] You won't have a friend in the world, Eddie! Even those who understand will turn against you, even the ones who feel the same will despise you! [EDDIE *moves off.*] Put it out of your mind! Eddie! [*He follows into the darkness, calling desperately.*]

[EDDIE *is gone. The phone is glowing in light now. Light is out on* ALFIERI. EDDIE *has at the same time appeared beside the phone.*]

EDDIE Give me the number of the Immigration Bureau. Thanks. [*He dials.*] I want to report something. Illegal immigrants. Two of them. That's right. Four-forty-one Saxon Street, Brooklyn, yeah. Ground floor. Heh? [*With greater difficulty.*] I'm just around the neighborhood, that's all. Heh?

[*Evidently he is being questioned further, and he slowly hangs up. He leaves the phone just as* LOUIS *and* MIKE *come down the street.*]

LOUIS Go bowlin', Eddie?

EDDIE No, I'm due home.

LOUIS Well, take it easy.

EDDIE I'll see yiz.

[*They leave him, exiting right, and he watches them go. He glances about, then goes up into the house. The lights go on in the apartment.* BEATRICE *is taking down Christmas decorations and packing them in a box.*]

EDDIE Where is everybody? [BEATRICE *does not answer.*] I says where is everybody?

BEATRICE [*looking up at him, wearied with it, and concealing a fear of him*] I decided to move them upstairs with Mrs. Dondero.

EDDIE Oh, they're all moved up there already?

BEATRICE   Yeah.

EDDIE   Where's Catherine? She up there?

BEATRICE   Only to bring pillow cases.

EDDIE   She ain't movin' in with them.

BEATRICE   Look, I'm sick and tired of it. I'm sick and tired of it!

EDDIE   All right, all right, take it easy.

BEATRICE   I don't wanna hear no more about it, you understand? Nothin'!

EDDIE   What're you blowin' off about? Who brought them in here?

BEATRICE   All right, I'm sorry; I wish I'd a drop dead before I told them to come. In the ground I wish I was.

EDDIE   Don't drop dead, just keep in mind who brought them in here, that's all. [*He moves about restlessly.*] I mean I got a couple of rights here. [*He moves, wanting to beat down her evident disapproval of him.*] This is my house here not their house.

BEATRICE   What do you want from me? They're moved out; what do you want now?

EDDIE   I want my respect!

BEATRICE   So I moved them out, what more do you want? You got your house now, you got your respect.

EDDIE   [*he moves about biting his lip*]   I don't like the way you talk to me, Beatrice.

BEATRICE   I'm just tellin' you I done what you want!

EDDIE   I don't like it! The way you talk to me and the way you look at me. This is my house. And she is my niece and I'm responsible for her.

BEATRICE   So that's why you done that to him?

EDDIE   I done what to him?

BEATRICE   What you done to him in front of her; you know what I'm talkin' about. She goes around shakin' all the time, she can't go to sleep! That's what you call responsible for her?

EDDIE   [*quietly*]   The guy ain't right, Beatrice. [*She is silent.*] Did you hear what I said?

BEATRICE   Look, I'm finished with it. That's all. [*She resumes her work.*]

EDDIE   [*helping her to pack the tinsel*]   I'm gonna have it out with you one of these days, Beatrice.

BEATRICE   Nothin' to have out with me, it's all settled. Now we gonna be like it never happened, that's all.

EDDIE   I want my respect, Beatrice, and you know what I'm talkin' about.

BEATRICE   What?

[*Pause.*]

EDDIE   [*finally his resolution hardens*]   What I feel like doin' in the bed and what I don't feel like doin'. I don't want no—

BEATRICE   When'd I say anything about that?

EDDIE   You said, you said, I ain't deaf. I don't want no more conversations about that, Beatrice. I do what I feel like doin' or what I don't feel like doin'.

BEATRICE   Okay.

[*Pause.*]

EDDIE   You used to be different, Beatrice. You had a whole different way.

BEATRICE   *I'm* no different.

EDDIE   You didn't used to jump me all the time about everything. The last year or two I come in the house I don't know what's gonna hit me. It's a shootin' gallery in here and I'm the pigeon.

BEATRICE   Okay, okay.

EDDIE   Don't tell me okay, okay, I'm tellin' you the truth. A wife is supposed to believe the husband. If I tell you that guy ain't right don't tell me he is right.

BEATRICE But how do you know?

EDDIE Because I know. I don't go around makin' accusations. He give me the heeby-jeebies the first minute I seen him. And I don't like you sayin' I don't want her marryin' anybody. I broke my back payin' her stenography lessons so she could go out and meet a better class of people. Would I do that if I didn't want her to get married? Sometimes you talk like I was a crazy man or sump'm.

BEATRICE But she likes him.

EDDIE Beatrice, she's a baby, how is she gonna know what she likes?

BEATRICE Well, you kept her a baby, you wouldn't let her go out. I told you a hundred times.

[*Pause.*]

EDDIE All right. Let her go out, then.

BEATRICE She don't wanna go out now. It's too late, Eddie.

[*Pause.*]

EDDIE Suppose I told her to go out. Suppose I—

BEATRICE They're going to get married next week, Eddie.

EDDIE [*his head jerks around to her*] She said that?

BEATRICE Eddie, if you want my advice, go to her and tell her good luck. I think maybe now that you had it out you learned better.

EDDIE What's the hurry next week?

BEATRICE Well, she's been worried about him bein' picked up; this way he could start to be a citizen. She loves him, Eddie. [*He gets up, moves about uneasily, restlessly.*] Why don't you give her a good word? Because I still think she would like you to be a friend, y'know? [*He is standing, looking at the floor.*] I mean like if you told her you'd go to the wedding.

EDDIE She asked you that?

BEATRICE I know she would like it. I'd like to make a party here for her. I mean there oughta be some kinda send-off. Heh? I mean she'll have trouble enough in her life, let's start it off happy. What do you say? Cause in her heart she still loves you, Eddie. I know it. [*He presses his fingers against his eyes.*] What're you, cryin'? [*She goes to him, holds his face.*] Go . . . whyn't you go tell her you're sorry?

[CATHERINE *is seen on the upper landing of the stairway, and they hear her descending.*]

There . . . she's comin' down. Come on, shake hands with her.

EDDIE [*moving with suppressed suddenness*] No, I can't, I can't talk to her.

BEATRICE Eddie, give her a break; a wedding should be happy!

EDDIE I'm goin', I'm goin' for a walk.

[*He goes upstage for his jacket.* CATHERINE *enters and starts for the bedroom door.*]

BEATRICE Katie? . . . Eddie, don't go, wait a minute. [*She embraces* EDDIE'S *arm with warmth.*] Ask him, Katie. Come on, honey.

EDDIE It's all right, I'm—[*He starts to go and she holds him.*]

BEATRICE No, she wants to ask you. Come on, Katie, ask him. We'll have a party! What're we gonna do, hate each other? Come on!

CATHERINE I'm gonna get married, Eddie. So if you wanna come, the wedding be on Saturday.

[*Pause.*]

EDDIE Okay. I only wanted the best for you, Katie. I hope you know that.

CATHERINE Okay. [*She starts out again.*]

EDDIE Catherine? [*She turns to him.*] I was just tellin' Beatrice . . . if you wanna go out, like . . . I mean I realize maybe I kept you home too much. Because he's the first guy you ever knew, y'know? I mean now that you got a job, you might meet some fellas, and you get a different idea, y'know? I mean you could always come back to him, you're still only kids, the both of yiz. What's the hurry? Maybe you'll get around a little bit, you grow up a little more, maybe you'll see different in a couple of months. I mean you be surprised, it don't have to be him.

CATHERINE   No, we made it up already.

EDDIE   [*with increasing anxiety*]   Katie, wait a minute.

CATHERINE   No, I made up my mind.

EDDIE   But you never knew no other fella, Katie! How could you make up your mind?

CATHERINE   Cause I did. I don't want nobody else.

EDDIE   But, Katie, suppose he gets picked up.

CATHERINE   That's why we gonna do it right away. Soon as we finish the wedding he's goin' right over and start to be a citizen. I made up my mind, Eddie. I'm sorry. [*To* BEATRICE.] Could I take two more pillow cases for the other guys?

BEATRICE   Sure, go ahead. Only don't let her forget where they came from.

[CATHERINE *goes into a bedroom.*]

EDDIE   She's got other boarders up there?

BEATRICE   Yeah, there's two guys that just came over.

EDDIE   What do you mean, came over?

BEATRICE   From Italy. Lipari the butcher—his nephew. They come from Bari, they just got here yesterday. I didn't even know till Marco and Rodolpho moved up there before.

[CATHERINE *enters, going toward exit with two pillow cases.*]

It'll be nice, they could all talk together.

EDDIE   Catherine! [*She halts near the exit door. He takes in* BEATRICE *too.*] What're you, got no brains? You put them up there with two other sub-marines?

CATHERINE   Why?

EDDIE   [*in a driving fright and anger*]   Why! How do you know they're not trackin' these guys? They'll come up for them and find Marco and Rodolpho! Get them out of the house!

BEATRICE   But they been here so long already—

EDDIE   How do you know what enemies Lipari's got? Which they'd love to stab him in the back?

CATHERINE   Well what'll I do with them?

EDDIE   The neighborhood is full of rooms. Can't you stand to live a couple of blocks away from him? Get them out of the house!

CATHERINE   Well maybe tomorrow night I'll—

EDDIE   Not tomorrow, do it now. Catherine, you never mix yourself with some-body else's family! These guys get picked up, Lipari's liable to blame you or me and we got his whole family on our head. They got a temper, that family.

[*Two men in overcoats appear outside, start into the house.*]

CATHERINE   How'm I gonna find a place tonight?

EDDIE   Will you stop arguin' with me and get them out! You think I'm always tryin' to fool you or sump'm? What's the matter with you, don't you believe I could think of your good? Did I ever ask sump'm for myself? You think I got no feelin's? I never told you nothin' in my life that wasn't for your good. Nothin'! And look at the way you talk to me! Like I was an enemy!

Like I—[*A knock on the door. His head swerves. They all stand motionless. Another knock.* EDDIE, *in a whisper, pointing upstage.*] Go up the fire escape, get them out over the back fence.

[CATHERINE *stands motionless, uncomprehending.*]

FIRST OFFICER [*in the hall*] Immigration! Open up in there!

EDDIE Go, go. Hurry up! [*She stands a moment staring at him in a realized horror.*] Well, what're you lookin' at!

FIRST OFFICER Open up!

EDDIE [*calling toward door*] Who's that there?

FIRST OFFICER Immigration, open up.

[EDDIE *turns, looks at* BEATRICE. *She sits. Then he looks at* CATHERINE. *With a sob of fury* CATHERINE *streaks into a bedroom. Knock is repeated.*]

EDDIE All right, take it easy, take it easy. [*He goes and opens the door. The* OFFICER *steps inside.*] What's all this?

FIRST OFFICER Where are they?

[SECOND OFFICER *sweeps past and, glancing about, goes into the kitchen.*]

EDDIE Where's who?

FIRST OFFICER Come on, come on, where are they? [*He hurries into the bed-rooms.*]

EDDIE Who? We got nobody here. [*He looks at* BEATRICE, *who turns her head away. Pugnaciously, furious, he steps toward* BEATRICE.] What's the matter with *you?*

[FIRST OFFICER *enters from the bedroom, calls to the kitchen.*]

FIRST OFFICER Dominick?

[*Enter* SECOND OFFICER *from kitchen.*]

SECOND OFFICER Maybe it's a different apartment.

FIRST OFFICER There's only two more floors up there. I'll take the front, you go up the fire escape. I'll let you in. Watch your step up there.

SECOND OFFICER Okay, right, Charley. [FIRST OFFICER *goes out apartment door and runs up the stairs.*] This is Four-forty-one, isn't it?

EDDIE That's right.

[SECOND OFFICER *goes out into the kitchen.* EDDIE *turns to* BEATRICE. *She looks at him now and sees his terror.*]

BEATRICE [*weakened with fear*] Oh, Jesus, Eddie.

EDDIE What's the matter with *you?*

BEATRICE [*pressing her palms against her face*] Oh, my God, my God.

EDDIE What're you, accusin' me?

BEATRICE [*her final thrust is to turn toward him instead of running from him*] My God, what did you do?

[*Many steps on the outer stair draw his attention. We see the* FIRST OFFICER *descending, with* MARCO, *behind him* RODOLPHO, *and* CATHERINE *and the two strange immigrants, followed by* SECOND OFFICER. BEATRICE *hurries to door.*]

CATHERINE [*backing down stairs, fighting with* FIRST OFFICER; *as they appear on the stairs*] What do yiz want from them? They work, that's all. They're boarders upstairs, they work on the piers.

BEATRICE [*to* FIRST OFFICER] Ah, Mister, what do you want from them, who do they hurt?

CATHERINE [*pointing to* RODOLPHO] They ain't no submarines, he was born in Philadelphia.

FIRST OFFICER Step aside, lady.

CATHERINE What do you mean? You can't just come in a house and—

FIRST OFFICER All right, take it easy. [*To* RODOLPHO.] What street were you born in Philadelphia?

CATHERINE   What do you mean, what street? Could you tell me what street you were born?

FIRST OFFICER   Sure. Four blocks away, One-eleven Union Street. Let's go fellas.

CATHERINE   [*fending him off* RODOLPHO]   No, you can't! Now, get outa here!

FIRST OFFICER   Look, girlie, if they're all right they'll be out tomorrow. If they're illegal they go back where they came from. If you want, get yourself a lawyer, although I'm tellin' you now you're wasting your money. Let's get them in the car, Dom. [*To the men.*] Andiamo, Andiamo, let's go.
[*The men start, but* MARCO *hangs back.*]

BEATRICE   [*from doorway*]   Who're they hurtin', for God's sake, what do you want from them? They're starvin' over there, what do you want! Marco! [MARCO *suddenly breaks from the group and dashes into the room and faces* EDDIE; BEATRICE *and* FIRST OFFICER *rush in as* MARCO *spits into* EDDIE'S *face.* CATHERINE *runs into hallway and throws herself into* RODOLPHO'S *arms.* EDDIE, *with an enraged cry, lunges for* MARCO.]

EDDIE   Oh, you mother's—!
[FIRST OFFICER *quickly intercedes and pushes* EDDIE *from* MARCO, *who stands there accusingly.*]

FIRST OFFICER   [*between them, pushing* EDDIE *from* MARCO]   Cut it out!

EDDIE   [*over the* FIRST OFFICER'S *shoulder, to* MARCO]   I'll kill you for that, you son of a bitch!

FIRST OFFICER   Hey! [*Shakes him.*] Stay in here now, don't come out, don't bother him. You hear me? Don't come out, fella.
[*For an instant there is silence Then* FIRST OFFICER *turns and takes* MARCO'S *arm and then gives a last, informative look at* EDDIE. *As he and* MARCO *are going out into the hall,* EDDIE *erupts.*]

EDDIE   I don't forget that, Marco! You hear what I'm sayin'?
[*Out in the hall,* FIRST OFFICER *and* MARCO *go down the stairs. Now, in the street,* LOUIS, MIKE, *and several neighbors including the butcher,* LIPARI—*a stout, intense, middle-aged man—are gathering around the stoop.* LIPARI, *the butcher, walks over to the two strange men and kisses them. His wife, keening, goes and kisses their hands.* EDDIE *is emerging from the house shouting after* MARCO. BEATRICE *is trying to restrain him.*]

EDDIE   That's the thanks I get? Which I took the blankets off my bed for yiz? You gonna apologize to me, Marco! *Marco!*

FIRST OFFICER   [*in the doorway with* MARCO]   All right, lady, let them go. Get in the car, fellas, it's over there.
[RODOLPHO *is almost carrying the sobbing* CATHERINE *off up the street, left.*]

CATHERINE   He was born in Philadelphia! What do you want from him?

FIRST OFFICER   Step aside, lady, come on now . . .
[*The* SECOND OFFICER *has moved off with the two strange men.* MARCO, *taking advantage of the* FIRST OFFICER'S *being occupied with* CATHERINE, *suddenly frees himself and points back at* EDDIE.]

MARCO   That one! I accuse that one!
[EDDIE *brushes* BEATRICE *aside and rushes out to the stoop.*]

FIRST OFFICER   [*grabbing him and moving him quickly off up the left street*]   Come on!

MARCO   [*as he is taken off, pointing back at* EDDIE]   That one! He killed my children! That one stole the food from my children!
[MARCO *is gone. The crowd has turned to* EDDIE.]

EDDIE   [*to* LIPARI *and wife*]   He's crazy! I give them the blankets off my bed. Six months I kept them like my own brothers!
[LIPARI, *the butcher, turns and starts up left with his arm around his wife.*]

EDDIE   Lipari! [*He follows* LIPARI *up left.*] For Christ's sake, I kept them, I give them the blankets off my bed!

[LIPARI *and wife exit.* EDDIE *turns and starts crossing down right to* LOUIS *and* MIKE.]

EDDIE   Louis! *Louis!*

[LOUIS *barely turns, then walks off and exits down right with* MIKE. *Only* BEATRICE *is left on the stoop.* CATHERINE *now returns, blank-eyed, from off-stage and the car.* EDDIE *calls after* LOUIS *and* MIKE.]

EDDIE   He's gonna take that back. He's gonna take that back or I'll kill him! You hear me? I'll kill him! I'll kill him! [*He exits up street calling.*]

[*There is a pause of darkness before the lights rise, on the reception room of a prison.* MARCO *is seated;* ALFIERI, CATHERINE, *and* RODOLPHO *standing.*]

ALFIERI   I'm waiting, Marco, what do you say?

RODOLPHO   Marco never hurt anybody.

ALFIERI   I can bail you out until your hearing comes up. But I'm not going to do it, you understand me? Unless I have your promise. You're an honorable man, I will believe your promise. Now what do you say?

MARCO   In my country he would be dead now. He would not live this long.

ALFIERI   All right, Rodolpho—you come with me now.

RODOLPHO   No! Please, mister. Marco—promise the man. Please, I want you to watch the wedding. How can I be married and you're in here? Please, you're not going to do anything; you know you're not.

[MARCO *is silent.*]

CATHERINE   [*kneeling left of* MARCO]   Marco, don't you understand? He can't bail you out if you're gonna do something bad. To hell with Eddie. Nobody is gonna talk to him again if he lives to a hundred. Everybody knows you spit in his face, that's enough, isn't it? Give me the satisfaction—I want you at the wedding. You got a wife and kids, Marco. You could be workin' till the hearing comes up, instead of layin' around here.

MARCO   [*to* ALFIERI]   I have no chance?

ALFIERI   [*crosses to behind* MARCO]   No, Marco. You're going back. The hearing is a formality, that's all.

MARCO   But him? There is a chance, eh?

ALFIERI   When she marries him he can start to become an American. They permit that, if the wife is born here.

MARCO   [*looking at* RODOLPHO]   Well—we did something. [*He lays a palm on* RODOLPHO's *arm and* RODOLPHO *covers it.*]

RODOLPHO   Marco, tell the man.

MARCO   [*pulling his hand away*]   What will I tell him? He knows such a promise is dishonorable.

ALFIERI   To promise not to kill is not dishonorable.

MARCO   [*looking at* ALFIERI]   No?

ALFIERI   No.

MARCO   [*gesturing with his head—this is a new idea*]   Then what is done with such a man?

ALFIERI   Nothing. If he obeys the law, he lives. That's all.

MARCO   [*rises, turns to* ALFIERI]   The law? All the law is not in a book.

ALFIERI   Yes. In a book. There is no other law.

MARCO   [*his anger rising*]   He degraded my brother. My blood. He robbed my children, he mocks my work. I work to come here, mister!

ALFIERI   I know, Marco—

MARCO   There is no law for that? Where is the law for that?

ALFIERI   There is none.

MARCO   [*shaking his head, sitting*]   I don't understand this country.

ALFIERI   Well? What is your answer? You have five or six weeks you could work. Or else you sit here. What do you say to me?

MARCO   [*lowers his eyes. It almost seems he is ashamed*]   All right.

ALFIERI   You won't touch him. This is your promise.
   [*Slight pause.*]

MARCO   Maybe he wants to apologize to me.
   [MARCO *is staring away.* ALFIERI *takes one of his hands.*]

ALFIERI   This is not God, Marco. You hear? Only God makes justice.

MARCO   All right.

ALFIERI   [*nodding, not with assurance*]   Good! Catherine, Rodolpho, Marco, let us go.
   [CATHERINE *kisses* RODOLPHO *and* MARCO, *then kisses* ALFIERI'S *hand.*]

CATHERINE   I'll get Beatrice and meet you at the church. [*She leaves quickly.*]
   [MARCO *rises.* RODOLPHO *suddenly embraces him.* MARCO *pats him on the back and* RODOLPHO *exits after* CATHERINE. MARCO *faces* ALFIERI.]

ALFIERI   Only God, Marco.
   [MARCO *turns and walks out.* ALFIERI *with a certain processional tread leaves the stage. The lights dim out.*
      The lights rise in the apartment. EDDIE *is alone in the rocker, rocking back and forth in little surges. Pause. Now* BEATRICE *emerges from a bedroom. She is in her best clothes, wearing a hat.*]

BEATRICE   [*with fear, going to* EDDIE]   I'll be back in about an hour, Eddie. All right?

EDDIE   [*quietly, almost inaudibly, as though drained*]   What, have I been talkin' to myself?

BEATRICE   Eddie, for God's sake, it's her wedding.

EDDIE   Didn't you hear what I told you? You walk out that door to that wedding you ain't comin' back here, Beatrice.

BEATRICE   Why! What do you want?

EDDIE   I want my respect. Didn't you ever hear of that? From my wife?
   [CATHERINE *enters from bedroom.*]

CATHERINE   It's after three; we're supposed to be there already, Beatrice. The priest won't wait.

BEATRICE   Eddie. It's her wedding. There'll be nobody there from her family. For my sister let me go. I'm goin' for my sister.

EDDIE   [*as though hurt*]   Look, I been arguin' with you all day already, Beatrice, and I said what I'm gonna say. He's gonna come here and apologize to me or nobody from this house is goin' into that church today. Now if that's more to you than I am, then go. But don't come back. You be on my side or on their side, that's all.

CATHERINE   [*suddenly*]   Who the hell do you think you are?

BEATRICE   Sssh!

CATHERINE   You got no more right to tell nobody nothin'! Nobody! The rest of your life, nobody!

BEATRICE   Shut up, Katie! [*She turns* CATHERINE *around.*]

CATHERINE   You're gonna come with me!

BEATRICE   I can't Katie, I can't . . .

CATHERINE   How can you listen to him? This rat!

BEATRICE   [*shaking* CATHERINE]   Don't you call him that!

CATHERINE   [*clearing from* BEATRICE]   What're you scared of? He's a rat! He belongs in the sewer!

BEATRICE   Stop it!

CATHERINE [*weeping*] He bites people when they sleep! He comes when no-body's lookin' and poisons decent people. In the garbage he belongs!
[EDDIE *seems about to pick up the table and fling it at her.*]

BEATRICE No, Eddie! Eddie! [*To* CATHERINE.] Then we all belong in the garbage. You, and me too. Don't say that. Whatever happened we all done it, and don't you ever forget it, Catherine. [*She goes to* CATHERINE.] Now go, go to your wedding, Katie, I'll stay home. Go. God bless you, God bless your children.
[*Enter* RODOLPHO.]

RODOLPHO Eddie?

EDDIE Who said you could come in here? Get outa here!

RODOLPHO Marco is coming, Eddie.
[*Pause.* BEATRICE *raises her hands in terror.*]
He's praying in the church. You understand? [*Pause.* RODOLPHO *advances into the room.*] Catherine, I think it is better we go. Come with me.

CATHERINE Eddie, go away, please.

BEATRICE [*quietly*] Eddie. Let's go someplace. Come. You and me.
[*He has not moved.*]
I don't want you to be here when he comes. I'll get your coat.

EDDIE Where? Where am I goin'? This is my house.

BEATRICE [*crying out*] What's the use of it! He's crazy now, you know the way they get, what good is it! You got nothin' against Marco, you always liked Marco!

EDDIE I got nothin' against Marco? Which he called me a rat in front of the whole neighborhood? Which he said I killed his children! Where you been?

RODOLPHO [*quite suddenly, stepping up to* EDDIE] It is my fault, Eddie. Everything. I wish to apologize. It was wrong that I do not ask your permission. I kiss your hand. [*He reaches for* EDDIE's *hand, but* EDDIE *snaps it away from him.*]

BEATRICE Eddie, he's apologizing!

RODOLPHO I have made all our troubles. But you have insult me too. Maybe God understand why you did that to me. Maybe you did not mean to insult me at all—

BEATRICE Listen to him! Eddie, listen what he's tellin' you!

RODOLPHO I think, maybe when Marco comes, if we can tell him we are comrades now, and we have no more argument between us. Then maybe Marco will not—

EDDIE Now, listen—

CATHERINE Eddie, give him a chance!

BEATRICE What do you want! Eddie, what do you want!

EDDIE I want my name! He didn't take my name; he's only a punk. Marco's got my name—[*to* RODOLPHO] and you can run tell him, kid, that he's gonna give it back to me in front of this neighborhood, or we have it out. [*Hoisting up his pants.*] Come on, where is he? Take me to him.

BEATRICE Eddie, listen—

EDDIE I heard enough! Come on, let's go!

BEATRICE Only blood is good? He kissed your hand!

EDDIE What he does don't mean nothin' to nobody! [*To* RODOLPHO.] Come on!

BEATRICE [*barring his way to the stairs*] What's gonna mean somethin'? Eddie, listen to me. Who could give you your name? Listen to me, I love you, I'm talkin' to you, I love you; if Marco'll kiss your hand outside, if he goes on his knees, what is he got to give you? That's not what you want.

EDDIE Don't bother me!

BEATRICE   You want somethin' else, Eddie, and you can never have her!

CATHERINE   [*in horror*]   B.!

EDDIE   [*shocked, horrified, his fists clenching*]   Beatrice!

[MARCO *appears outside, walking toward the door from a distant point.*]

BEATRICE   [*crying out, weeping*]   The truth is not as bad as blood, Eddie! I'm tellin' you the truth—tell her good-by forever!

EDDIE   [*crying out in agony*]   That's what you think of me—that I would have such a thought? [*His fists clench his head as though it will burst.*]

MARCO   [*calling near the door outside*]   Eddie Carbone!

[EDDIE *swerves about; all stand transfixed for an instant. People appear outside.*]

EDDIE   [*as though flinging his challenge*]   Yeah, Marco! Eddie Carbone. Eddie Carbone. Eddie Carbone. [*He goes up the stairs and emerges from the apartment.* RODOLPHO *streaks up and out past him and runs to* MARCO.]

RODOLPHO   No, Marco, please! Eddie, please, he has children! You will kill a family!

BEATRICE   Go in the house! Eddie, go in the house!

EDDIE   [*he gradually comes to address the people*]   Maybe he come to apologize to me. Heh, Marco? For what you said about me in front of the neighborhood? [*He is incensing himself and little bits of laughter even escape him as his eyes are murderous and he cracks his knuckles in his hands with a strange sort of relaxation.*]   He knows that ain't right. To do like that? To a man? Which I put my roof over their head and my food in their mouth? Like in the Bible? Strangers I never seen in my whole life? To come out of the water and grab a girl for a passport? To go and take from your own family like from the stable—and never a word to me? And now accusations in the bargain! [*Directly to* MARCO.]   Wipin' the neighborhood with my name like a dirty rag! I want my name, Marco. [*He is moving now, carefully, toward* MARCO.]   Now gimme my name and we go together to the wedding.

BEATRICE *and* CATHERINE   [*keening*]   Eddie! Eddie, don't! Eddie!

EDDIE   No, Marco knows what's right from wrong. Tell the people, Marco, tell them what a liar you are! [*He has his arms spread and* MARCO *is spreading his.*]   Come on, liar, you know what you done! [*He lunges for* MARCO *as a great hushed shout goes up from the people.*]

[MARCO *strikes* EDDIE *beside the neck.*]

MARCO   Animal! You go on your knees to me!

[EDDIE *goes down with the blow and* MARCO *starts to raise a foot to stomp him when* EDDIE *springs a knife into his hand and* MARCO *steps back.* LOUIS *rushes in toward* EDDIE.]

LOUIS   Eddie, for Christ's sake!

[EDDIE *raises the knife and* LOUIS *halts and steps back.*]

EDDIE   You lied about me, Marco. Now say it. Come on now, say it!

MARCO   Anima-a-a-l!

[EDDIE *lunges with the knife.* MARCO *grabs his arm, turning the blade inward and pressing it home as the women and* LOUIS *and* MIKE *rush in and separate them, and* EDDIE, *the knife still in his hand, falls to his knees before* MARCO. *The two women support him for a moment, calling his name again and again.*]

CATHERINE   Eddie I never meant to do nothing bad to you.

EDDIE   Then why—Oh, B.!

BEATRICE   Yes, yes!

EDDIE   My B.!

[*He dies in her arms, and* BEATRICE *covers him with her body.* ALFIERI, *who is in the crowd, turns out to the audience. The lights have gone down, leaving him in a glow, while behind him the dull prayers of the people and the keening of the women continue.*]

ALFIERI   Most of the time now we settle for half and I like it better. But the truth is holy, and even as I know how wrong he was, and his death useless, I tremble, for I confess that something perversely pure calls to me from his memory—not purely good, but himself purely, for he allowed himself to be wholly known and for that I think I will love him more than all my sensible clients. And yet, it is better to settle for half, it must be! And so I mourn him—I admit it—with a certain . . . alarm.

CURTAIN

TENNESSEE WILLIAMS
[1914–   ]

Born Thomas Lanier Williams, and called "Tennessee" because he was descended from pioneering Tennessee stock, Tennessee Williams grew up in Columbus, Mississippi, as the son of a shoe salesman. His mother, a descendant of Southern aristocracy, along with her father, an Episcopal clergyman with a taste for literature and cocktails, were most responsible for the shaping of the author's mind. From the very first, Tennessee Williams lived in a divided world —the stiflingly unsuccessful world of his father's business contradicting the more cultured and sophisticated world of his grandfather's rectory. It was in that rectory that Williams observed those genteel Southern women whose anguish over the encroachments of a cruder way of life was to inspire a number of his plays.

Biographical details most relevant to *The Glass Menagerie* are to be found in Williams' teen-age sojourn in the city of St. Louis, where his family had moved from Mississippi. In moving to St. Louis where his father was a clerk, Williams experienced a great wrench in his life and learned the hard lesson of shabby gentility. It was in St. Louis, writes Kenneth Tynan, "in a stuffy, back-street apartment, that his world split, amoeba-like, into two irreconcilable halves—the soft, feminine world of the room that he and his sister filled with little glass animals, and the cruel, male world of the alley outside, where cats fought and coupled to a persistent screaming." After a short stay at the University of Missouri, Williams was forced by the depression to take a job in a shoe factory, a job he so detested that after three years he had a heart attack and a complete physical breakdown. Upon recovery, he took a B.A. at the University of Iowa in 1938. Small, local successes with his early literary efforts undoubtedly encouraged him to leave home and break with the future of shabby gentility offered by his father's clerkship and the job at the shoe factory. Then began the long epic of tormented wandering that has been Tennessee Williams' life ever since.

The Glass Menagerie, produced in New York in 1945, was his first success, and remains his most popular play. It was followed by a series of plays most of which have been converted into films, among them being *A Streetcar Named Desire* (1947), *Summer and Smoke* (1948), *The Rose Tattoo* (1950), *Cat on a Hot Tin Roof* (1954), *Orpheus Descending* (1957), *Sweet Bird of Youth* (1959), *Suddenly Last Summer* (1959), and *Night of the Iguana* (1962).

THE
GLASS MENAGERIE

TENNESSEE WILLIAMS

CHARACTERS

AMANDA WINGFIELD, *the mother*
LAURA WINGFIELD, *her daughter*
TOM WINGFIELD, *her son*
JIM O'CONNOR, *the gentleman caller*

SCENE: *An Alley in St. Louis*

PART I. *Preparation for a Gentleman Caller.*
PART II. *The Gentleman calls.*

TIME: *Now and the Past.*

SCENE ONE

> *The Wingfield apartment is in the rear of the building, one of those vast hive-like conglomerations of cellular living-units that flower as warty growths in overcrowded urban centers of lower*

middle-class population and are symptomatic of the impulse of this largest and fundamentally enslaved section of American society to avoid fluidity and differentiation and to exist and function as one interfused mass of automatism.

The apartment faces an alley and is entered by a fire-escape, a structure whose name is a touch of accidental poetic truth, for all of these huge buildings are always burning with the slow and implacable fires of human desperation. The fire-escape is included in the set—that is, the landing of it and steps descending from it.

The scene is memory and is therefore nonrealistic. Memory takes a lot of poetic license. It omits some details; others are exaggerated, according to the emotional value of the articles it touches, for memory is seated predominantly in the heart. The interior is therefore rather dim and poetic.

At the rise of the curtain, the audience is faced with the dark, grim rear wall of the Wingfield tenement. This building, which runs parallel to the footlights, is flanked on both sides by dark, narrow alleys which run into murky canyons of tangled clothes-lines, garbage cans and the sinister lattice-work of neighboring fire-escapes. It is up and down these side alleys that exterior entrances and exits are made, during the play. At the end of TOM'S *opening commentary, the dark tenement wall slowly reveals [by means of a transparency] the interior of the ground floor Wingfield apartment.*

Downstage is the living room, which also serves as a sleeping room for LAURA, *the sofa unfolding to make her bed. Upstage, center, and divided by a wide arch or second proscenium with transparent faded portieres [or second curtain], is the dining room. In an old-fashioned what-not in the living room are seen scores of transparent glass animals. A blown-up photograph of the father hangs on the wall of the living room, facing the audience, to the left of the archway. It is the face of a very handsome young man in a doughboy's First World War cap. He is gallantly smiling, ineluctably smiling, as if to say, "I will be smiling forever."*

The audience hears and sees the opening scene in the dining room through both the transparent fourth wall of the building and the transparent gauze portieres of the dining-room arch. It is during this revealing scene that the fourth wall slowly ascends, out of sight. This transparent exterior wall is not brought down again until the very end of the play, during TOM'S *final speech.*

The narrator is an undisguised convention of the play. He takes whatever license with dramatic convention as is convenient to his purposes.

TOM *enters dressed as a merchant sailor from alley, stage left, and strolls across the front of the stage to the fire-escape. There he stops and lights a cigarette. He addresses the audience.*

TOM   Yes, I have tricks in my pocket, I have things up my sleeve. But I am the opposite of a stage magician. He gives you illusion that has the appearance of truth. I give you truth in the pleasant disguise of illusion. To begin with, I turn back time. I reverse it to that quaint period, the thirties, when the huge middle class of America was matriculating in a school for the blind. Their eyes had failed them, or they had failed their eyes, and so they were having their fingers pressed forcibly down on the fiery Braille alphabet of a dissolving economy. In Spain there was revolution. Here there was only shouting and confusion. In Spain there was Guernica.[1] Here there were disturbances of labor, sometimes pretty violent, in otherwise peaceful cities such as Chicago, Cleveland, Saint Louis . . . This is the social background of the play.

[*MUSIC*]

The play is memory. Being a memory play, it is dimly lighted, it is sentimental, it is not realistic. In memory everything seems to happen to music. That explains the fiddle in the wings. I am the narrator of the play, and also a character in it. The other characters are my mother, Amanda, my sister, Laura, and a gentleman caller who appears in the final scenes. He is the most realistic character in the play, being an emissary from a world of reality that we were somehow set apart from. But since I have a poet's weakness for symbols, I am using this character also as a symbol; he is the long delayed but always expected something that we live for. There is a fifth character in the play who doesn't appear except in this larger-than-life photograph over the mantel. This is our father who left us a long time ago. He was a telephone man who fell in love with long distances; he gave up his job with the telephone company and skipped the light fantastic out of town . . . The last we heard of him was a picture post-card from Mazatlan, on the Pacific coast of Mexico, containing a message of two words—"Hello—Good-bye!" and no address. I think the rest of the play will explain itself. . . .
[AMANDA's *voice becomes audible through the portieres*]

[*LEGEND ON SCREEN:* * *"OÙ SONT LES NEIGES"* [2]]

[*He divides the portieres and enters the upstage area*]

[AMANDA *and* LAURA *are seated at a drop-leaf table. Eating is indicated by gestures without food or utensils.* AMANDA *faces the audience.* TOM *and* LAURA *are seated in profile*]

[*The interior has lit up softly and through the scrim we see* AMANDA *and* LAURA *seated at the table in the upstage area*]
AMANDA [*Calling*] Tom?
TOM Yes, Mother.
AMANDA We can't say grace until you come to the table!
TOM Coming, Mother. [*He bows slightly and withdraws, reappearing a few moments later in his place at the table*]
AMANDA [*To her son*] Honey, don't *push* with your *fingers*. If you have to push with something, the thing to push with is a crust of bread. And chew —chew! Animals have sections in their stomachs which enable them to digest food without mastication, but human beings are supposed to chew their food before they swallow it down. Eat food leisurely, son, and really

---

[1] A town in northern Spain bombed by the Germans in 1937 during the Spanish Civil War and the name of a famous painting by Picasso on the event.
* For playwright's explanation of screen legends see Production Notes following play.
[2] "Where are the Snows [of Yesteryear]," a famous line from a poem by the medieval French poet Villon (1431–1480?) .

enjoy it. A well-cooked meal has lots of delicate flavors that have to be held in the mouth for appreciation. So chew your food and give your salivary glands a chance to function!

[TOM *deliberately lays his imaginary fork down and pushes his chair back from the table*]

TOM   I haven't enjoyed one bite of this dinner because of your constant directions on how to eat it. It's you that make me rush through meals with your hawk-like attention to every bite I take. Sickening—spoils my appetite—all this discussion of animals' secretion—salivary glands—mastication!

AMANDA   [*Lightly*]   Temperament like a Metropolitan star! [*He rises and crosses downstage*] You're not excused from the table.

TOM   I'm getting a cigarette.

AMANDA   You smoke too much.

[LAURA *rises*]

LAURA   I'll bring in the blanc mange.

[*He remains standing with his cigarette by the portieres during the following*]

AMANDA   [*Rising*]   No, sister, no, sister—you be the lady this time and I'll be the darky.

LAURA   I'm already up.

AMANDA   Resume your seat, little sister—I want you to stay fresh and pretty —for gentlemen callers!

LAURA   I'm not expecting any gentlemen callers.

AMANDA   [*Crossing out to kitchenette. Airily*]   Sometimes they come when they are least expected! Why, I remember one Sunday afternoon in Blue Mountain—[*Enters kitchenette*]

TOM   I know what's coming!

LAURA   Yes. But let her tell it.

TOM   Again?

LAURA   She loves to tell it.

[AMANDA *returns with bowl of dessert*]

AMANDA   One Sunday afternoon in Blue Mountain—your mother received— *seventeen!*—gentlemen callers! Why, sometimes there weren't chairs enough to accommodate them all. We had to send the nigger over to bring in folding chairs from the parish house.

TOM   [*Remaining at portieres*]   How did you entertain those gentlemen callers?

AMANDA   I understood the art of conversation!

TOM   I bet you could talk.

AMANDA   Girls in those days *knew* how to talk, I can tell you.

TOM   Yes?

[*IMAGE: AMANDA AS A GIRL ON A PORCH, GREETING CALLERS*]

AMANDA   They knew how to entertain their gentlemen callers. It wasn't enough for a girl to be possessed of a pretty face and a graceful figure— although I wasn't slighted in either respect. She also needed to have a nimble wit and a tongue to meet all occasions.

TOM   What did you talk about?

AMANDA   Things of importance going on in the world! Never anything coarse or common or vulgar. [*She addresses* TOM *as though he were seated in the vacant chair at the table though he remains by portieres. He plays this scene as though he held the book*] My callers were gentlemen—all! Among my callers were some of the most prominent young planters of the Mississippi Delta—planters and sons of planters!

[TOM *motions for music and a spot of light on* AMANDA]

[*Her eyes lift, her face glows, her voice becomes rich and elegiac*]

[*SCREEN LEGEND: "OÙ SONT LES NEIGES"*]

There was young Champ Laughlin who later became vice-president of the Delta Planters Bank. Hadley Stevenson who was drowned in Moon Lake and left his widow one hundred and fifty thousand in Government bonds. There were the Cutrere brothers, Wesley and Bates. Bates was one of my bright particular beaux! He got in a quarrel with that wild Wainwright boy. They shot it out on the floor of Moon Lake Casino. Bates was shot through the stomach. Died in the ambulance on his way to Memphis. His widow was also well-provided for, came into eight or ten thousand acres, that's all. She married him on the rebound—never loved her—carried my picture on him the night he died! And there was that boy that every girl in the Delta had set her cap for! That beautiful, brilliant young Fitzhugh boy from Greene County!

TOM   What did he leave his widow?

AMANDA   He never married! Gracious, you talk as though all of my old admirers had turned up their toes to the daisies!

TOM   Isn't this the first you've mentioned that still survives?

AMANDA   That Fitzhugh boy went North and made a fortune—came to be known as the Wolf of Wall Street! He had the Midas touch, whatever he touched turned to gold! And I could have been Mrs. Duncan J. Fitzhugh, mind you! But—I picked your *father!*

LAURA   [*Rising*]   Mother, let me clear the table.

AMANDA   No, dear, you go in front and study your typewriter chart. Or practice your shorthand a little. Stay fresh and pretty!—It's almost time for our gentlemen callers to start arriving. [*She flounces girlishly toward the kitchenette*] How many do you suppose we're going to entertain this afternoon?

[TOM *throws down the paper and jumps up with a groan*]

LAURA   [*Alone in the dining room*]   I don't believe we're going to receive any, Mother.

AMANDA   [*Reappearing, airily*]   What? No one—not one? You must be joking! [LAURA *nervously echoes her laugh. She slips in a fugitive manner through the half-open portieres and draws them gently behind her. A shaft of very clear light is thrown on her face against the faded tapestry of the curtains. MUSIC: "THE GLASS MENAGERIE" UNDER FAINTLY. Lightly*] Not one gentleman caller? It can't be true! There must be a flood, there must have been a tornado!

LAURA   It isn't a flood, it's not a tornado, Mother. I'm just not popular like you were in Blue Mountain. . . . [TOM *utters another groan.* LAURA *glances at him with a faint, apologetic smile. Her voice catching a little*] Mother's afraid I'm going to be an old maid.

THE SCENE DIMS OUT WITH "GLASS MENAGERIE" MUSIC

SCENE TWO

"Laura, Haven't You Ever Liked Some Boy?"
On the dark stage the screen is lighted with the image of blue roses.
Gradually LAURA'S *figure becomes apparent and the screen goes out.*

The music subsides.

LAURA *is seated in the delicate ivory chair at the small claw-foot table.*

She wears a dress of soft violet material for a kimono—her hair tied back from her forehead with a ribbon.

She is washing and polishing her collection of glass.

AMANDA *appears on the fire-escape steps. At the sound of her ascent, LAURA catches her breath, thrusts the bowl of ornaments away and seats herself stiffly before the diagram of the typewriter keyboard as though it held her spellbound. Something has happened to AMANDA. It is written in her face as she climbs to the landing: a look that is grim and hopeless and a little absurd.*

She has on one of those cheap or imitation velvety-looking cloth coats with imitation fur collar. Her hat is five or six years old, one of those dreadful cloche hats that were worn in the late twenties and she is clasping an enormous black patent-leather pocketbook with nickel clasps and initials. This is her full-dress outfit, the one she usually wears to the D.A.R.

Before entering she looks through the door.

She purses her lips, opens her eyes wide, rolls them upward and shakes her head.

Then she slowly lets herself in the door. Seeing her mother's expression LAURA touches her lips with a nervous gesture.

LAURA   Hello, Mother, I was—[*She makes a nervous gesture toward the chart on the wall.* AMANDA *leans against the shut door and stares at* LAURA *with a martyred look*]

AMANDA   Deception? Deception? [*She slowly removes her hat and gloves, continuing the sweet suffering stare. She lets the hat and gloves fall on the floor—a bit of acting*]

LAURA   [*Shakily*]   How was the D.A.R. meeting? [AMANDA *slowly opens her purse and removes a dainty white handkerchief which she shakes out delicately and delicately touches to her lips and nostrils*] Didn't you go to the D.A.R. meeting, Mother?

AMANDA   [*Faintly, almost inaudibly*]—No.—No. [*Then more forcibly*] I did not have the strength—to go to the D.A.R. In fact, I did not have the courage! I wanted to find a hole in the ground and hide myself in it forever!

[*She crosses slowly to the wall and removes the diagram of the typewriter keyboard. She holds it in front of her for a second, staring at it sweetly and sorrowfully—then bites her lips and tears it in two pieces*]

LAURA   [*Faintly*]   Why did you do that, Mother? [AMANDA *repeats the same procedure with the chart of the Gregg Alphabet*] Why are you—

AMANDA   Why? Why? How old are you, Laura?

LAURA   Mother, you know my age.

AMANDA   I thought that you were an adult; it seems that I was mistaken.

[*She crosses slowly to the sofa and sinks down and stares at* LAURA]

LAURA   Please don't stare at me, Mother.

[AMANDA *closes her eyes and lowers her head. Count ten*]

AMANDA   What are we going to do, what is going to become of us, what is the future?

[*Count ten*]

LAURA   Has something happened, Mother? [AMANDA *draws a long breath and takes out the handkerchief again. Dabbing process*] Mother, has—something happened?

AMANDA   I'll be all right in a minute. I'm just bewildered—[*Count five*]—by life. . . .

LAURA   Mother, I wish that you would tell me what's happened!

AMANDA   As you know, I was supposed to be inducted into my office at the D.A.R. this afternoon. *IMAGE: A SWARM OF TYPEWRITERS.* But I stopped off at Rubicam's Business College to speak to your teachers about your having a cold and ask them what progress they thought you were making down there.

LAURA   Oh. . . .

AMANDA   I went to the typing instructor and introduced myself as your mother. She didn't know who you were. Wingfield, she said. We don't have any such student enrolled at the school! I assured her she did, that you had been going to classes since early in January. "I wonder," she said, "if you could be talking about that terribly shy little girl who dropped out of school after only a few days' attendance?" "No," I said, "Laura, my daughter, has been going to school every day for the past six weeks!" "Excuse me," she said. She took the attendance book out and there was your name, unmistakably printed, and all the dates you were absent until they decided that you had dropped out of school. I still said, "No, there must have been some mistake! There must have been some mix-up in the records!" And she said, "No—I remember her perfectly now. Her hands shook so that she couldn't hit the right keys! The first time we gave a speed-test, she broke down completely—was sick at the stomach and almost had to be carried into the washroom! After that morning she never showed up any more. We phoned the house but never got any answer"—while I was working at Famous and Barr,[3] I suppose, demonstrating those—Oh! I felt so weak I could barely keep on my feet! I had to sit down while they got me a glass of water! Fifty dollars' tuition, all of our plans—my hopes and ambitions for you—just gone up the spout, just gone up the spout like that. [LAURA *draws a long breath and gets awkwardly to her feet. She crosses to the victrola and winds it up*] What are you doing?

LAURA   Oh! [*She releases the handle and returns to her seat*]

AMANDA   Laura, where have you been going when you've gone out pretending that you were going to business college?

LAURA   I've just been going out walking.

AMANDA   That's not true.

LAURA   It is. I just went walking.

AMANDA   Walking? Walking? In winter? Deliberately courting pneumonia in that light coat? Where did you walk to, Laura?

LAURA   All sorts of places—mostly in the park.

AMANDA   Even after you'd started catching that cold?

LAURA   It was the lesser of two evils, Mother. [*IMAGE: WINTER SCENE IN PARK*] I couldn't go back up. I—threw up—on the floor!

AMANDA   From half past seven till after five every day you mean to tell me you walked around in the park, because you wanted to make me think that you were still going to Rubicam's Business College?

LAURA   It wasn't as bad as it sounds. I went inside places to get warmed up.

AMANDA   Inside where?

LAURA   I went in the art museum and the bird-houses at the Zoo. I visited the penguins every day! Sometimes I did without lunch and went to the movies.

---

[3] A St. Louis department store.

Lately I've been spending most of my afternoons in the Jewel-box, that big glass house where they raise the tropical flowers.

AMANDA   You did all this to deceive me, just for deception? [LAURA *looks down*] Why?

LAURA   Mother, when you're disappointed, you get that awful suffering look on your face, like the picture of Jesus' mother in the museum!

AMANDA   Hush!

LAURA   I couldn't face it.

[*Pause. A whisper of strings*]

[LEGEND: "THE CRUST OF HUMILITY"]

AMANDA   [*Hopelessly fingering the huge pocketbook*]   So what are we going to do the rest of our lives? Stay home and watch the parades go by? Amuse ourselves with the glass menagerie, darling? Eternally play those worn-out phonograph records your father left as a painful reminder of him? We won't have a business career—we've given that up because it gave us nervous in-digestion! [*Laughs wearily*] What is there left but dependency all our lives? I know so well what becomes of unmarried women who aren't prepared to occupy a position. I've seen such pitiful cases in the South—barely tolerated spinsters living upon the grudging patronage of sister's husband or brother's wife!—stuck away in some little mouse-trap of a room—encouraged by one in-law to visit another—little birdlike women without any nest—eating the crust of humility all their life! Is that the future that we've mapped out for ourselves? I swear it's the only alternative I can think of! It isn't a very pleasant alternative, is it? Of course—some girls *do marry*. [LAURA *twists her hands nervously*] Haven't you ever liked some boy?

LAURA   Yes. I liked one once. [*Rises*] I came across his picture a while ago.

AMANDA   [*With some interest*]   He gave you his picture?

LAURA   No, it's in the year-book.

AMANDA   [*Disappointed*]   Oh—a high-school boy.

[SCREEN IMAGE: JIM AS HIGH-SCHOOL HERO BEARING A SILVER CUP]

LAURA   Yes. His name was Jim. [LAURA *lifts the heavy annual from the claw-foot table*] Here he is in *The Pirates of Penzance*.[4]

AMANDA   [*Absently*]   The what?

LAURA   The operetta the senior class put on. He had a wonderful voice and we sat across the aisle from each other Mondays, Wednesdays and Fridays in the Aud. Here he is with the silver cup for debating! See his grin?

AMANDA   [*Absently*]   He must have had a jolly disposition.

LAURA   He used to call me—Blue Roses.

[IMAGE: BLUE ROSES]

AMANDA   Why did he call you such a name as that?

LAURA   When I had that attack of pleurosis—he asked me what was the matter when I came back. I said pleurosis—he thought that I said Blue Roses! So that's what he always called me after that. Whenever he saw me, he'd holler, "Hello, Blue Roses!" I didn't care for the girl that he went out with. Emily Meisenbach. Emily was the best-dressed girl at Soldan. She never struck me,

---

[4] An operetta by Gilbert and Sullivan (1879).

though, as being sincere . . . It says in the Personal Section—they're en-
engaged. That's—six years ago! They must be married by now.

AMANDA   Girls that aren't cut out for business careers usually wind up married
to some nice man. [*Gets up with a spark of revival*] Sister, that's what you'll
do!
[LAURA *utters a startled, doubtful laugh. She reaches quickly for a piece of
glass*]

LAURA   But, Mother—

AMANDA   Yes? [*Crossing to photograph*]

LAURA   [*In a tone of frightened apology*]   I'm—crippled!

[IMAGE: SCREEN]

AMANDA   Nonsense! Laura, I've told you never, never to use that word. Why,
you're not crippled, you just have a little defect—hardly noticeable, even!
When people have some slight disadvantage like that, they cultivate other
things to make up for it—develop charm—and vivacity—and—*charm!*
That's all you have to do! [*She turns again to the photograph*] One thing
your father had *plenty of*—was *charm!*
[TOM *motions to the fiddle in the wings*]

THE SCENE FADES OUT WITH MUSIC

SCENE THREE

[LEGEND ON SCREEN: "AFTER THE FIASCO—"]

[TOM *speaks from the fire-escape landing*]

TOM   After the fiasco at Rubicam's Business College, the idea of getting a gentleman caller for Laura began to play a more important part in Mother's
calculations. It became an obsession. Like some archetype of the universal
unconscious, the image of the gentleman caller haunted our small apartment. . . . [*IMAGE: YOUNG MAN AT DOOR WITH FLOWERS*] An
evening at home rarely passed without some allusion to this image, this
spectre, this hope. . . . Even when he wasn't mentioned, his presence hung
in Mother's preoccupied look and in my sister's frightened, apologetic manner—hung like a sentence passed upon the Wingfields! Mother was a woman
of action as well as words. She began to take logical steps in the planned
direction. Late that winter and in the early spring—realizing that extra
money would be needed to properly feather the nest and plume the bird—
she conducted a vigorous campaign on the telephone, roping in subscribers
to one of those magazines for matrons called *The Homemaker's Companion,*
the type of journal that features the serialized sublimations of ladies of
letters who think in terms of delicate cup-like breasts, slim, tapering waists,
rich, creamy thighs, eyes like wood-smoke in autumn, fingers that soothe
and caress like strains of music, bodies as powerful as Etruscan sculpture.

[SCREEN IMAGE: GLAMOR MAGAZINE COVER]

[AMANDA *enters with phone on long extension cord. She is spotted in the
dim stage*]

AMANDA   Ida Scott? This is Amanda Wingfield! We *missed* you at the D.A.R.

last Monday! I said to myself: She's probably suffering with that sinus condition! How is that sinus condition? Horrors! Heaven have mercy!—You're a Christian martyr, yes, that's what you are, a Christian martyr! Well, I just now happened to notice that your subscription to the *Companion*'s about to expire! Yes, it expires with the next issue, honey!—just when that wonderful new serial by Bessie Mae Hopper is getting off to such an exciting start. Oh, honey, it's something that you can't miss! You remember how *Gone With the Wind* [5] took everybody by storm? You simply couldn't go out if you hadn't read it. All everybody *talked* was Scarlett O'Hara. Well, this is a book that critics already compare to *Gone With the Wind*. It's the *Gone With the Wind* of the post-World War generation!—What?—Burning? —Oh, honey, don't let them burn, go take a look in the oven and I'll hold the wire! Heavens—I think she's hung up!

DIM OUT

[LEGEND ON SCREEN: "YOU THINK I'M IN LOVE
WITH CONTINENTAL SHOEMAKERS?"]

[Before the stage is lighted, the violent voices of TOM *and* AMANDA *are heard]*

[They are quarreling behind the portieres. In front of them stands LAURA *with clenched hands and panicky expression]*

[A clear pool of light on her figure throughout this scene]

TOM   What in Christ's name am I—
AMANDA   *[Shrilly]*   Don't you use that—
TOM   Supposed to do!
AMANDA   Expression! Not in my—
TOM   Ohhh!
AMANDA   Presence! Have you gone out of your senses?
TOM   I have, that's true, *driven* out!
AMANDA   What is the matter with you, you—big—big—IDIOT!
TOM   Look—I've got *no thing,* no single thing—
AMANDA   Lower your voice!
TOM   In my life here that I can call my own! Everything is—
AMANDA   Stop that shouting!
TOM   Yesterday you confiscated my books! You had the nerve to—
AMANDA   I took that horrible novel back to the library—yes! That hideous book by that insane Mr. Lawrence.[6] *[TOM laughs wildly]* I cannot control the output of diseased minds or people who cater to them—*[TOM laughs still more wildly]* BUT I WON'T ALLOW SUCH FILTH BROUGHT INTO MY HOUSE! No, no, no, no, no!
TOM   House, house! Who pays rent on it, who makes a slave of himself to—
AMANDA   *[Fairly screeching]*   Don't you DARE to—
TOM   No, no, *I* mustn't say things! *I've* got to just—
AMANDA   Let me tell you—
TOM   I don't want to hear any more! *[He tears the portieres open. The upstage area is lit with a turgid smoky red glow]*
[AMANDA's hair is in metal curlers and she wears a very old bathrobe, much too large for her slight figure, a relic of the faithless Mr. Wingfield]

---

[5] An extremely popular novel by Margaret Mitchell (1936).
[6] D. H. Lawrence (1885–1930), English poet and novelist.

[*An upright typewriter and a wild disarray of manuscripts is on the drop-leaf table. The quarrel was probably precipitated by* AMANDA's *interruption of his creative labor. A chair lying overthrown on the floor*]

[*Their gesticulating shadows are cast on the ceiling by the fiery glow*]

AMANDA   You *will* hear more, you—

TOM   No, I won't hear more, I'm going out!

AMANDA   You come right back in—

TOM   Out, out out! Because I'm—

AMANDA   Come back here, Tom Wingfield! I'm not through talking to you!

TOM   Oh, go—

LAURA   [*Desperately*]—Tom!

AMANDA   You're going to listen, and no more insolence from you! I'm at the end of my patience! [*He comes back toward her*]

TOM   What do you think I'm at? Aren't I suppose to have any patience to reach the end of, Mother? I know, I know. It seems unimportant to you, what I'm *doing*—what I *want* to do—having a little *difference* between them! You don't think that—

AMANDA   I think you've been doing things that you're ashamed of. That's why you act like this. I don't believe that you go every night to the movies. Nobody goes to the movies night after night. Nobody in their right minds goes to the movies as often as you pretend to. People don't go to the movies at nearly midnight, and movies don't let out at two A.M. Come in stumbling. Muttering to yourself like a maniac! You get three hours' sleep and then go to work. Oh, I can picture the way you're doing down there. Moping, doping, because you're in no condition.

TOM   [*Wildly*]   No, I'm in no condition!

AMANDA   What right have you got to jeopardize your job? Jeopardize the security of us all? How do you think we'd manage if you were—

TOM   Listen! You think I'm crazy *about* the *warehouse*? [*He bends fiercely toward her slight figure*] You think I'm in love with the Continental Shoemakers? You think I want to spend fifty-five *years* down there in that—*celotex interior!* with—*fluorescent—tubes!* Look! I'd rather somebody picked up a crowbar and battered out my brains—than go back mornings! I *go!* Every time you come in yelling that God damn *"Rise and Shine!" "Rise and Shine!"* I say to myself, "How *lucky dead* people are!" But I get up. I *go!* For sixty-five dollars a month I give up all that I dream of doing and being *ever!* And you say self—*self's* all I ever think of. Why, listen, if self is what I thought of, Mother, I'd be where he is—GONE! [*Pointing to father's picture*] As far as the system of transportation reaches! [*He starts past her. She grabs his arm*] Don't grab at me, Mother!

AMANDA   Where are you going?

TOM   I'm going to the *movies!*

AMANDA   I don't believe that lie!

TOM   [*Crouching toward her, overtowering her tiny figure. She backs away, gasping*]   I'm going to opium dens! Yes, opium dens, dens of vice and criminals' hang-outs, Mother. I've joined the Hogan gang, I'm a hired assassin, I carry a Tommy gun in a violin case! I run a string of cat-houses in the Valley! They call me Killer, Killer Wingfield, I'm leading a double-life, a simple, honest warehouse worker by day, by night, a dynamic *czar* of the *underworld, Mother*. I go to gambling casinos, I spin away fortunes on the roulette table! I wear a patch over one eye and a false mustache, sometimes I put on green whiskers. On those occasions they call me—*El Diablo!* Oh, I could tell you things to make you sleepless! My enemies plan to dynamite this place. They're going to blow us all sky-high some night! I'll be glad, very happy, and so will you! You'll go up, up on a broomstick, over Blue Mountain with seventeen gentlemen callers! You ugly—babbling old—witch. . . . [*He goes through a series of violent, clumsy movements, seizing his overcoat, lunging to the door, pulling it fiercely open. The women watch him, aghast. His arm catches in the sleeve of the coat as he struggles to pull it on. For a moment he is pinioned by the bulky garment. With an outraged groan he tears the coat off again, splitting the shoulder of it, and hurls it across the room. It strikes against the shelf of* LAURA's *glass collection, there is a tinkle of shattering glass.* LAURA *cries out as if wounded*]

[*MUSIC LEGEND: "THE GLASS MENAGERIE"*]

LAURA [*Shrilly*] My glass!—menagerie. . . . [*She covers her face and turns away*]
[*But* AMANDA *is still stunned and stupefied by the "ugly witch" so that she barely notices this occurrence. Now she recovers her speech*]
AMANDA [*In an awful voice*] I won't speak to you—until you apologize!
[*She crosses through portieres and draws them together behind her.* TOM *is left with* LAURA. LAURA *clings weakly to the mantel with her face averted.* TOM *stares at her stupidly for a moment. Then he crosses to shelf. Drops awkwardly on his knees to collect the fallen glass, glancing at* LAURA *as if he would speak but couldn't*]

"*The Glass Menagerie*" steals in as

THE SCENE DIMS OUT

SCENE FOUR

The interior is dark. Faint light in the alley.
A deep-voiced bell in a church is tolling the hour of five as the scene commences.
TOM *appears at the top of the alley. After each solemn boom of the bell in the tower, he shakes a little noise-maker or rattle as if to express the tiny spasm of man in contrast to the sustained power and dignity of the Almighty. This and the unsteadiness of his advance make it evident that he has been drinking.*
As he climbs the few steps to the fire-escape landing light steals up inside. LAURA *appears in nightdress, observing* TOM's *empty bed in the front room.*
TOM *fishes in his pockets for door key, removing a motley assortment of articles in the search, including a perfect shower of movie-ticket stubs and an empty bottle. At last he finds the key, but just as he is about to insert it, it slips from his fingers. He strikes a match and crouches below the door.*

TOM [*Bitterly*] One crack—and it falls through!
[LAURA *opens the door.*]
LAURA Tom! Tom, what are you doing?
TOM Looking for a door key.
LAURA Where have you been all this time?

TOM   I have been to the movies.

LAURA   All this time at the movies?

TOM   There was a very long program. There was a Garbo picture and a Mickey Mouse and a travelogue and a newsreel and a preview of coming attractions. And there was an organ solo and a collection for the milk-fund—simultaneously—which ended up in a terrible fight between a fat lady and an usher!

LAURA   [*Innocently*]   Did you have to stay through everything?

TOM   Of course! And, oh, I forgot! There was a big stage show! The headliner on this stage show was Malvolio the Magician. He performed wonderful tricks, many of them, such as pouring water back and forth between pitchers. First it turned to wine and then it turned to beer and then it turned to whiskey. I know it was whiskey it finally turned into because he needed somebody to come up out of the audience to help him, and I came up—both shows! It was Kentucky Straight Bourbon. A very generous fellow, he gave souvenirs. [*He pulls from his back pocket a shimmering rainbow-colored scarf*] He gave me this. This is his magic scarf. You can have it, Laura. You wave it over a canary cage and you get a bowl of goldfish. You wave it over the goldfish bowl and they fly away canaries. . . . But the wonderfullest trick of all was the coffin trick. We nailed him into a coffin and he got out of the coffin without removing one nail. [*He has come inside*] There is a trick that would come in handy for me—get me out of this 2 by 4 situation! [*Flops onto bed and starts removing shoes*]

LAURA   Tom—Shhh!

TOM   What're you shushing me for?

LAURA   You'll wake up Mother.

TOM   Goody, goody! Pay 'er back for all those "Rise an' Shines." [*Lies down, groaning*] You know it don't take much intelligence to get yourself into a nailed-up coffin, Laura. But who in hell ever got himself out of one without removing one nail?

[*As if in answer, the father's grinning photograph lights up*]

SCENE DIMS OUT

[*Immediately following: The church bell is heard striking six. At the sixth stroke the alarm clock goes off in* AMANDA's *room, and after a few moments we hear her calling: "Rise and Shine! Rise and Shine! Laura, go tell your brother to rise and shine!"*]

TOM   [*Sitting up slowly*] I'll rise—but I won't shine.

[*The light increases*]

AMANDA   Laura, tell your brother his coffee is ready.

[LAURA *slips into front room*]

LAURA   Tom it's nearly seven. Don't make Mother nervous. [*He stares at her stupidly. Beseechingly*] Tom, speak to Mother this morning. Make up with her, apologize, speak to her!

TOM   She won't to me. It's her that started not speaking.

LAURA   If you just say you're sorry she'll start speaking.

TOM   Her not speaking—is that such a tragedy?

LAURA   Please—please!

AMANDA   [*Calling from kitchenette*]   Laura, are you going to do what I asked you to do, or do I have to get dressed and go out myself?

LAURA   Going, going—soon as I get on my coat! [*She pulls on a shapeless felt hat with nervous, jerky movement, pleadingly glancing at* TOM. *Rushes awkwardly for coat. The coat is one of* AMANDA's, *inaccurately made-over, the sleeves too short for* LAURA] Butter and what else?

AMANDA [*Entering upstage*] Just butter. Tell them to charge it.

LAURA Mother, they make such faces when I do that.

AMANDA Sticks and stones can break our bones, but the expression on Mr. Garfinkel's face won't harm us! Tell your brother his coffee is getting cold.

LAURA [*At door*] Do what I asked you, will you, will you, Tom?

[*He looks sullenly away*]

AMANDA Laura, go now or just don't go at all!

LAURA [*Rushing out*] Going—going! [*A second later she cries out.* TOM *springs up and crosses to door.* AMANDA *rushes anxiously in.* TOM *opens the door*]

TOM Laura?

LAURA I'm all right. I slipped, but I'm all right.

AMANDA [*Peering anxiously after her*] If anyone breaks a leg on those fire-escape steps, the landlord ought to be sued for every cent he possesses! [*She shuts door. Remembers she isn't speaking and returns to other room.*]

[*As* TOM *enters listlessly for his coffee, she turns her back to him and stands rigidly facing the window on the gloomy gray vault of the areaway. Its light on her face with its aged but childish features is cruelly sharp, satirical as a Daumier print*]

[*MUSIC UNDER: "AVE MARIA"*]

[*Tom glances sheepishly but sullenly at her averted figure and slumps at the table. The coffee is scalding hot; he sips it and gasps and spits it back in the cup. At his gasp,* AMANDA *catches her breath and half turns. Then catches herself and turns back to window*]

[*TOM blows on his coffee, glancing sidewise at his mother. She clears her throat.* TOM *clears his. He starts to rise. Sinks back down again, scratches his head, clears his throat again.* AMANDA *coughs.* TOM *raises his cup in both hands to blow on it, his eyes staring over the rim of it at his mother for several moments. Then he slowly sets the cup down and awkwardly and hesitantly rises from the chair*]

TOM [*Hoarsely*] Mother. I—I apologize, Mother. [AMANDA *draws a quick, shuddering breath. Her face works grotesquely. She breaks into childlike tears*] I'm sorry for what I said, for everything that I said, I didn't mean it.

AMANDA [*Sobbingly*] My devotion has made me a witch and so I make myself hateful to my children!

TOM No, you *don't*.

AMANDA I worry so much, don't sleep, it makes me nervous!

TOM [*Gently*] I understand that.

AMANDA I've had to put up a solitary battle all these years. But you're my right-hand bower! Don't fall down, don't fail!

TOM [*Gently*] I try, Mother.

AMANDA [*With great enthusiasm*] Try and you will SUCCEED!

[*The notion makes her breathless*] Why, you—you're just *full* of natural endowments! Both of my children—they're *unusual* children! Don't you think I know it? I'm so—*proud!* Happy and—feel I've—so much to be thankful for but—Promise me one thing, son!

TOM What, Mother?

AMANDA Promise, son, you'll—never be a drunkard!

TOM [*Turns to her grinning*] I will never be a drunkard, Mother.

AMANDA That's what frightened me so, that you'd be drinking! Eat a bowl of Purina!

TOM Just coffee, Mother.

AMANDA Shredded wheat biscuit?

TOM No. No, Mother, just coffee.

AMANDA You can't put in a day's work on an empty stomach. You've got ten minutes—don't gulp! Drinking too-hot liquids makes cancer of the stomach. . . . Put cream in.

TOM No, thank you.

AMANDA To cool it.

TOM No! No, thank you, I want it black.

AMANDA I know, but it's not good for you. We have to do all that we can to build ourselves up. In these trying times we live in, all that we have to cling to is—each other. . . . That's why it's so important to—Tom, I—I sent out your sister so I could discuss something with you. If you hadn't spoken I would have spoken to you. [*Sits down*]

TOM [*Gently*] What is it, Mother, that you want to discuss?

AMANDA *Laura!*

[TOM *puts his cup down slowly*]

[*LEGEND ON SCREEN: "LAURA"*]

[*MUSIC: "THE GLASS MENAGERIE"*]

TOM —Oh.—Laura . . .

AMANDA [*Touching his sleeve*] You know how Laura is. So quiet but—still water runs deep! She notices things and I think she—broods about them. [TOM *looks up*] A few days ago I came in and she was crying.

TOM What about?

AMANDA You.

TOM Me?

AMANDA She has an idea that you're not happy here.

TOM What gave her that idea?

AMANDA What gives her any idea? However, you do act strangely. I—I'm not criticizing, understand *that!* I know your ambitions do not lie in the warehouse, that like everybody in the whole wide world—you've had to—make sacrifices, but—Tom—Tom—life's not easy, it calls for—Spartan endurance! There's so many things in my heart that I cannot describe to you! I've never told you but I—*loved* your father. . . .

TOM [*Gently*] I know that, Mother.

AMANDA And you—when I see you taking after his ways! Staying out late—and—well, you *had* been drinking the night you were in that—terrifying condition! Laura says that you hate the apartment and that you go out nights to get away from it! Is that true, Tom?

TOM No. You say there's so much in your heart that you can't describe to me. That's true of me, too. There's so much in my heart that I can't describe to *you!* So let's respect each other's—

AMANDA But, why—*why,* Tom—are you always so *restless?* Where do you *go* to, nights?

TOM I—go to the movies.

AMANDA Why do you go to the movies so much, Tom?

TOM I go to the movies because—I like adventure. Adventure is something I don't have much of at work, so I go to the movies.

AMANDA But, Tom, you go to the movies *entirely* too *much!*

TOM I like a lot of adventure.

[AMANDA *looks baffled, then hurt. As the familiar inquisition resumes he becomes hard and impatient again.* AMANDA *slips back into her querulous attitude toward him*]

[IMAGE ON SCREEN: SAILING VESSEL WITH JOLLY ROGER]

AMANDA Most young men find adventure in their careers.

TOM Then most young men are not employed in a warehouse.

AMANDA The world is full of young men employed in warehouses and offices and factories.

TOM Do all of them find adventure in their careers?

AMANDA They do or they do without it! Not everybody has a craze for adventure.

TOM Man is by instinct a lover, a hunter, a fighter, and none of those instincts are given much play at the warehouse!

AMANDA Man is by instinct! Don't quote instinct to me! Instinct is something that people have got away from! It belongs to animals! Christian adults don't want it!

TOM What do Christian adults want, then, Mother?

AMANDA Superior things! Things of the mind and the spirit! Only animals have to satisfy instincts! Surely your aims are somewhat higher than theirs! Than monkeys—pigs—

TOM I reckon they're not.

AMANDA You're joking. However, that isn't what I wanted to discuss.

TOM [*rising*] I haven't much time.

AMANDA [*Pushing his shoulders*] Sit down.

TOM You want me to punch in red at the warehouse, Mother?

AMANDA You have five minutes. I want to talk about Laura.

[LEGEND: "PLANS AND PROVISIONS"]

TOM All right! What about Laura?

AMANDA We have to be making plans and provisions for her. She's older than you, two years, and nothing has happened. She just drifts along doing nothing. It frightens me terribly how she just drifts along.

TOM I guess she's the type that people call home-girls.

AMANDA There's no such type, and if there is, it's a pity! That is unless the home is hers, with a husband!

TOM What?

AMANDA Oh, I can see the handwriting on the wall as plain as I see the nose in front of my face! It's terrifying! More and more you remind me of your father! He was out all hours without explanation—Then *left! Good-bye!* And me with the bag to hold. I saw that letter you got from the Merchant Marine. I know what you're dreaming of. I'm not standing here blindfolded. Very well, then. Then *do* it! But not till there's somebody to take your place.

TOM What do you mean?

AMANDA I mean that as soon as Laura has got somebody to take care of her, married, a home of her own, independent—why, then you'll be free to go wherever you please, on land, on sea, whichever way the wind blows you! But until that time you've got to look out for your sister. I don't say me because I'm old and don't matter! I say for your sister because she's young and dependent. I put her in business college—a dismal failure! Frightened her so it made her sick to her stomach. I took her over to the Young People's League at the church. Another fiasco. She spoke to nobody, nobody spoke to her. Now all she does is fool with those pieces of glass and play those wornout records. What kind of a life is that for a girl to lead?

TOM What can I do about it?

AMANDA Overcome selfishness! Self, self, self is all that you ever think of!

[TOM *springs up and crosses to get his coat. It is ugly and bulky. He pulls on a cap with earmuffs*] Where is your muffler? Put your wool muffler on! [*He snatches it angrily from the closet and tosses it around his neck and pulls both ends tight*] Tom! I haven't said what I had in mind to ask you.

TOM   I'm too late to—

AMANDA   [*Catching his arm—very importunately. Then shyly*]   Down at the warehouse, aren't there some—nice young men?

TOM   No!

AMANDA   There *must* be—*some* . . .

TOM   Mother—
   [*Gesture*]

AMANDA   Find out one that's clean-living—doesn't drink and—ask him out for Sister!

TOM   What?

AMANDA   For *Sister!* To *meet!* Get *acquainted!*

TOM   [*Stamping to door*]   Oh, my *go-osh!*

AMANDA   Will you? [*He opens door. Imploringly*] Will you? [*He starts down*] Will you? *Will* you, dear?

TOM   [*Calling back*]   YES!
   [AMANDA *closes the door hesitantly and with a troubled but faintly hopeful expression*]

[*SCREEN IMAGE: GLAMOR MAGAZINE COVER*]

[*Spot* AMANDA *at phone*]

AMANDA   Ella Cartwright? This is Amanda Wingfield! How are you, honey? How is that kidney condition? [*Count five*] Horrors! [*Count five*] You're a Christian martyr, yes, honey, that's what you are, a Christian martyr! Well, I just happened to notice in my little red book that your subscription to the *Companion* has just run out! I knew that you wouldn't want to miss out on the wonderful serial starting in this new issue. It's by Bessie Mae Hopper, the first thing she's written since *Honeymoon for Three.* Wasn't that a strange and interesting story? Well, this one is even lovelier, I believe. It has a sophisticated, society background. It's all about the horsey set on Long Island!

FADE OUT

SCENE FIVE

[*LEGEND ON SCREEN: "ANNUNCIATION." Fade with music.*]

> *It is early dusk of a spring evening. Supper has just been finished in the Wingfield apartment.* AMANDA *and* LAURA *in light-colored dresses are removing dishes from the table, in the upstage area, which is shadowy, their movements formalized almost as a dance or ritual, their moving forms as pale and silent as moths.* TOM, *in white shirt and trousers, rises from the table and crosses toward the fire-escape.*

AMANDA   [*As he passes her*]   Son, will you do me a favor?

TOM   What?

AMANDA   Comb your hair! You look so pretty when your hair is combed! [TOM *slouches on sofa with evening paper. Enormous caption "Franco Triumphs"*] There is only one respect in which I would like you to emulate your father.

TOM   What respect is that?

AMANDA   The care he always took of his appearance. He never allowed himself to look untidy. [*He throws down the paper and crosses to fire-escape*] Where are you going?

TOM   I'm going out to smoke.

AMANDA   You smoke too much. A pack a day at fifteen cents a pack. How much would that amount to in a month? Thirty times fifteen is how much, Tom? Figure it out and you will be astounded at what you could save. Enough to give you a night-school course in accounting at Washington U! Just think what a wonderful thing that would be for you, son!
[TOM *is unmoved by the thought*]

TOM   I'd rather smoke. [*He steps out on landing, letting the screen door slam*]

AMANDA   [*Sharply*] I know! That's the tragedy of it. . . . [*Alone, she turns to look at her husband's picture*]

[*DANCE MUSIC: "ALL THE WORLD IS WAITING FOR THE SUNRISE!"*]

TOM   [*To the audience*]   Across the alley from us was the Paradise Dance Hall. On evenings in spring the windows and doors were open and the music came outdoors. Sometimes the lights were turned out except for a large glass sphere that hung from the ceiling. It would turn slowly about and filter the dusk with delicate rainbow colors. Then the orchestra played a waltz or a tango, something that had a slow and sensuous rhythm. Couples would come outside, to the relative privacy of the alley. You could see them kissing behind ash-pits and telephone poles. This was the compensation for lives that passed like mine, without any change or adventure. Adventure and change were imminent in this year. They were waiting around the corner for all these kids. Suspended in the mist over Berchtesgaden,[7] caught in the folds of Chamberlain's umbrella [8]—In Spain there was Guernica! But here there was only hot swing music and liquor, dance halls, bars, and movies, and sex that hung in the gloom like a chandelier and flooded the world with brief, deceptive rainbows. . . . All the world was waiting for bombardments!
[AMANDA *turns from the picture and comes outside*]

AMANDA   [*Sighing*]   A fire-escape landing's a poor excuse for a porch. [*She spreads a newspaper on a step and sits down, gratefully and demurely as if she were settling into a swing on a Mississippi veranda*] What are you looking at?

TOM   The moon.

AMANDA   Is there a moon this evening?

TOM   It's rising over Garfinkel's Delicatessen.

AMANDA   So it is! A little silver slipper of a moon. Have you made a wish on it yet?

TOM   Um-hum.

AMANDA   What did you wish for?

TOM   That's a secret.

AMANDA   A secret, huh? Well, I won't tell mine either. I will be just as mysterious as you.

---

[7] Hitler's mountain retreat in southern Bavaria.

[8] A popular symbol of Sir Neville Chamberlain, British Prime Minister in the late thirties who was known as an appeaser of Hitler.

TOM   I bet I can guess what yours is.

AMANDA   Is my head so transparent?

TOM   You're not a sphinx.

AMANDA   No, I don't have secrets. I'll tell you what I wished for on the moon. Success and happiness for my precious children! I wish for that whenever there's a moon, and when there isn't a moon, I wish for it, too.

TOM   I thought perhaps you wished for a gentleman caller.

AMANDA   Why do you say that?

TOM   Don't you remember asking me to fetch one?

AMANDA   I remember suggesting that it would be nice for your sister if you brought home some nice young man from the warehouse. I think that I've made that suggestion more than once.

TOM   Yes, you have made it repeatedly.

AMANDA   Well?

TOM   We are going to have one.

AMANDA   *What?*

TOM   A gentleman caller!

THE ANNUNCIATION IS CELEBRATED WITH MUSIC

[AMANDA *rises*]

[*IMAGE ON SCREEN: CALLER WITH BOUQUET*]

AMANDA   You mean you have asked some nice young man to come over?

TOM   Yep. I've asked him to dinner.

AMANDA   You really did?

TOM   I did!

AMANDA   You did, and did he—*accept?*

TOM   He did!

AMANDA   Well, well—well, well! That's—lovely!

TOM   I thought that you would be pleased.

AMANDA   It's definite, then?

TOM   Very definite.

AMANDA   Soon?

TOM   Very soon.

AMANDA   For heaven's sake, stop putting on and tell me some things, will you?

TOM   What things do you want me to tell you?

AMANDA   *Naturally* I would like to know when he's *coming!*

TOM   He's coming tomorrow.

AMANDA   *Tomorrow?*

TOM   Yep. Tomorrow.

AMANDA   But, Tom!

TOM   Yes, Mother?

AMANDA   Tomorrow gives me no time!

TOM   Time for what?

AMANDA   Preparations! Why didn't you phone me at once, as soon as you asked him, the minute that he accepted? Then, don't you see, I could have been getting ready!

TOM   You don't have to make any fuss.

AMANDA   Oh, Tom, Tom, Tom, of course I have to make a fuss! I want things nice, not sloppy! Not thrown together. I'll certainly have to do some fast thinking, won't I?

TOM   I don't see why you have to think at all.

AMANDA   You just don't know. We can't have a gentleman caller in a pigsty! All my wedding silver has to be polished, the monogrammed table linen ought to be laundered! The windows have to be washed and fresh curtains put up. And how about clothes? We have to *wear* something, don't we?

TOM   Mother, this boy is no one to make a fuss over!

AMANDA   Do you realize he's the first young man we've introduced to your sister? It's terrible, dreadful, disgraceful that poor little sister has never received a single gentleman caller! Tom, come inside! [*She opens the screen door*]

TOM   What for?

AMANDA   I want to ask you some things.

TOM   If you're going to make such a fuss, I'll call it off, I'll tell him not to come!

AMANDA   You certainly won't do anything of the kind. Nothing offends people worse than broken engagements. It simply means I'll have to work like a Turk! We won't be brilliant, but we will pass inspection. Come on inside. [TOM *follows, groaning*] Sit down.

TOM   Any particular place you would like me to sit?

AMANDA   Thank heavens I've got that new sofa! I'm also making payments on a floor lamp I'll have sent out! And put the chintz covers on, they'll brighten things up! Of course I'd hoped to have these walls re-papered. . . . What is the young man's name?

TOM   His name is O'Connor.

AMANDA   That, of course, means fish—tomorrow is Friday! I'll have that salmon loaf—with Durkee's dressing! What does he do? He works at the warehouse?

TOM   Of course! How else would I—

AMANDA   Tom, he—doesn't drink?

TOM   Why do you ask me that?

AMANDA   Your father *did!*

TOM   Don't get started on that!

AMANDA   He *does* drink, then?

TOM   Not that I know of!

AMANDA   Make sure, be certain! The last thing I want for my daughter's a boy who drinks!

TOM   Aren't you being a little bit premature? Mr. O'Connor has not yet appeared on the scene!

AMANDA   But will tomorrow. To meet your sister, and what do I know about his character? Nothing! Old maids are better off than wives of drunkards!

TOM   Oh, my God!

AMANDA   Be still!

TOM   [*Leaning forward to whisper*]   Lots of fellows meet girls whom they don't marry!

AMANDA   Oh, talk sensibly, Tom—and don't be sarcastic! [*She has gotten a hairbrush*]

TOM   What are you doing?

AMANDA   I'm brushing that cow-lick down! What is this young man's position at the warehouse?

TOM   [*Submitting grimly to the brush and the interrogation*]   This young man's position is that of a shipping clerk, Mother.

AMANDA   Sounds to me like a fairly responsible job, the sort of a job *you* would be in if you just had more *get-up*. What is his salary? Have you any idea?

TOM   I would judge it to be approximately eighty-five dollars a month.

AMANDA   Well—not princely, but—

TOM   Twenty more than I make.

AMANDA   Yes, how well I know! But for a family man, eighty-five dollars a month is not much more than you can just get by on. . . .

TOM   Yes, but Mr. O'Connor is not a family man.

AMANDA   He might be, mightn't he? Some time in the future?

TOM   I see. Plans and provisions.

AMANDA   You are the only young man that I know of who ignores the fact that the future becomes the present, the present the past, and the past turns into everlasting regret if you don't plan for it!

TOM   I will think that over and see what I can make of it.

AMANDA   Don't be supercilious with your mother! Tell me some more about this —what do you call him?

TOM   James D. O'Connor. The D. is for Delaney.

AMANDA   Irish on *both* sides! *Gracious!* And doesn't drink?

TOM   Shall I call him up and ask him right this minute?

AMANDA   The only way to find out about those things is to make discreet inquiries at the proper moment. When I was a girl in Blue Mountain and it was suspected that a young man drank, the girl whose attentions he had been receiving, if any girl *was,* would sometimes speak to the minister of his church, or rather her father would if her father was living, and sort of feel him out on the young man's character. That is the way such things are discreetly handled to keep a young woman from making a tragic mistake!

TOM   Then how did you happen to make a tragic mistake?

AMANDA   That innocent look of your father's had everyone fooled! He *smiled,* the world was *enchanted!* No girl can do worse than put herself at the mercy of a handsome appearance! I hope that Mr. O'Connor is not too good-looking.

TOM   No, he's not too good-looking. He's covered with freckles and hasn't too much of a nose.

AMANDA   He's not right-down homely, though?

TOM   Not right-down homely. Just medium homely, I'd say.

AMANDA   Character's what to look for in a man.

TOM   That's what I've always said, Mother.

AMANDA   You've never said anything of the kind and I suspect you would never give it a thought.

TOM   Don't be so suspicious of me.

AMANDA   At least I hope he's the type that's up and coming.

TOM   I think he really goes in for self-improvement.

AMANDA   What reason have you to think so?

TOM   He goes to night school.

AMANDA   [*Beaming*]   Splendid! What does he do, I mean study?

TOM   Radio engineering and public speaking!

AMANDA   Then he has visions of being advanced in the world! Any young man who studies public speaking is aiming to have an executive job some day! And radio engineering? A thing for the future! Both of these facts are very illuminating. Those are the sort of things that a mother should know concerning any young man who comes to call on her daughter. Seriously or—not.

TOM   One little warning. He doesn't know about Laura. I didn't let on that we had dark ulterior motives. I just said, why don't you come and have dinner with us? He said okay and that was the whole conversation.

AMANDA   I bet it was! You're eloquent as an oyster. However, he'll know about Laura when he gets here. When he sees how lovely and sweet and pretty she is, he'll thank his lucky stars he was asked to dinner.

TOM   Mother, you mustn't expect too much of Laura.

AMANDA   What do you mean?

TOM   Laura seems all those things to you and me because she's ours and we love her. We don't even notice she's crippled any more.

AMANDA   Don't say crippled! You know that I never allow that word to be used!
TOM   But face facts, Mother. She is and—that's not all—
AMANDA   What do you mean "not all"?
TOM   Laura is very different from other girls.
AMANDA   I think the difference is all to her advantage.
TOM   Not quite all—in the eyes of others—strangers—she's terribly shy and lives in a world of her own and those things make her seem a little peculiar to people outside the house.
AMANDA   Don't say peculiar.
TOM   Face the facts. She is.

THE DANCE-HALL MUSIC CHANGES TO A TANGO THAT HAS A MINOR
AND SOMEWHAT OMINOUS TONE

AMANDA   In what way is she peculiar—may I ask?
TOM   [*Gently*]   She lives in a world of her own—a world of—little glass ornaments, Mother. . . . [*Gets up.* AMANDA *remains holding brush, looking at him, troubled*] She plays old phonograph records and—that's about all—[*He glances at himself in the mirror and crosses to door*]
AMANDA   [*Sharply*]   Where are you going?
TOM   I'm going to the movies. [*Out screen door*]
AMANDA   Not to the movies, every night to the movies! [*Follows quickly to screen door*] I don't believe you always go to the movies! [*He is gone.* AMANDA *looks worriedly after him for a moment. Then vitality and optimism return and she turns from the door. Crossing to portieres*] Laura! Laura! [LAURA *answers from kitchenette*]
LAURA   Yes, Mother.
AMANDA   Let those dishes go and come in front! [LAURA *appears with dish towel. Gaily*] Laura, come here and make a wish on the moon!
LAURA   [*Entering*]   Moon—moon?
AMANDA   A little silver slipper of a moon. Look over your left shoulder, Laura, and make a wish! [LAURA *looks faintly puzzled as if called out of sleep.* AMANDA *seizes her shoulders and turns her at an angle by the door*] No! Now, darling, *wish!*
LAURA   What shall I wish for, Mother?
AMANDA   [*Her voice trembling and her eyes suddenly filling with tears*]   Happiness! Good Fortune!
[*The violin rises and the stage dims out*]

SCENE SIX

[*IMAGE: HIGH SCHOOL HERO*]

TOM   And so the following evening I brought Jim home to dinner. I had known Jim slightly in high school. In high school Jim was a hero. He had tremendous Irish good nature and vitality with the scrubbed and polished look of white chinaware. He seemed to move in a continual spotlight. He was a star in basketball, captain of the debating club, president of the senior class and the glee club and he sang the male lead in the annual light operas. He was always running or bounding, never just walking. He seemed always at the point of defeating the law of gravity. He was shooting with such velocity through his adolescence that you would logically expect him to arrive at nothing short of the White House by the time he was thirty. But Jim apparently ran into more interference after his graduation from Soldan. His speed had definitely slowed. Six years after he left high school he was holding a job that wasn't much better than mine.

[IMAGE: CLERK]

He was the only one at the warehouse with whom I was on friendly terms. I was valuable to him as someone who could remember his former glory, who had seen him win basketball games and the silver cup in debating. He knew of my secret practice of retiring to a cabinet of the washroom to work on poems when business was slack in the warehouse. He called me Shakespeare. And while the other boys in the warehouse regarded me with suspicious hostility, Jim took a humorous attitude toward me. Gradually his attitude affected the others, their hostility wore off and they also began to smile at me as people smile at an oddly fashioned dog who trots across their path at some distance.

I knew that Jim and Laura had known each other at Soldan, and I had heard Laura speak admiringly of his voice. I didn't know if Jim remembered her or not. In high school Laura had been as unobtrusive as Jim had been astonishing. If he did remember Laura, it was not as my sister, for when I asked him to dinner, he grinned and said, "You know, Shakespeare, I never thought of you as having folks!"

He was about to discover that I did. . . .

LIGHT UP STAGE

[*LEGEND ON SCREEN: "THE ACCENT OF A COMING FOOT"*]

[*Friday evening. It is about five o'clock of a late spring evening which comes "scattering poems in the sky"*]

[*A delicate lemony light is in the Wingfield apartment*]

[AMANDA *has worked like a Turk in preparation for the gentleman caller. The results are astonishing. The new floor lamp with its rose-silk shade is in place, a colored paper lantern conceals the broken light fixture in the ceiling, new billowing white curtains are at the windows, chintz covers are on chairs and sofa, a pair of new sofa pillows make their initial appearance*]

[*Open boxes and tissue paper are scattered on the floor*]

[LAURA *stands in the middle with lifted arms while* AMANDA *crouches before her, adjusting the hem of the new dress, devout and ritualistic. The dress is colored and designed by memory. The arrangement of* LAURA's *hair is changed; it is softer and more becoming. A fragile, unearthly prettiness has come out in* LAURA: *she is like a piece of translucent glass touched by light, given a momentary radiance, not actual, not lasting*]

AMANDA   [*Impatiently*]   Why are you trembling?
LAURA   Mother, you've made me so nervous!
AMANDA   How have I made you nervous?
LAURA   By all this fuss! You make it seem so important!
AMANDA   I don't understand you, Laura. You couldn't be satisfied with just

sitting home, and yet whenever I try to arrange something for you, you seem to resist it. [*She gets up*] Now take a look at yourself. No, wait! Wait just a moment—I have an idea!

LAURA What is it now?

[AMANDA *produces two powder puffs which she wraps in handkerchiefs and stuffs in* LAURA'S *bosom*]

LAURA Mother, what are you doing?

AMANDA They call them "Gay Deceivers"!

LAURA I won't wear them!

AMANDA You will!

LAURA Why should I?

AMANDA Because, to be painfully honest, your chest is flat.

LAURA You make it seem like we were setting a trap.

AMANDA All pretty girls are a trap, a pretty trap, and men expect them to be.

[*LEGEND: "A PRETTY TRAP."*] Now look at yourself, young lady. This is the prettiest you will ever be! I've got to fix myself now! You're going to be surprised by your mother's appearance! [*She crosses through portieres, humming gaily*]

[LAURA *moves slowly to the long mirror and stares solemnly at herself*]

[*A wind blows the white curtains inward in a slow, graceful motion and with a faint, sorrowful sighing*]

AMANDA [*Off stage*] It isn't dark enough yet. [*She turns slowly before the mirror with a troubled look.*]

[*LEGEND ON SCREEN: "THIS IS MY SISTER: CELEBRATE HER WITH STRINGS!" MUSIC.*]

AMANDA [*Laughing, off*] I'm going to show you something. I'm going to make a spectacular appearance!

LAURA What is it, Mother?

AMANDA Possess your soul in patience—you will see! Something I've resurrected from that old trunk! Styles haven't changed so terribly much after all. . . . [*She parts the portieres*] Now just look at your mother! [*She wears a girlish frock of yellowed voile with a blue silk sash. She carries a bunch of jonquils —the legend of her youth is nearly revived. Feverishly*] This is the dress in which I led the cotillion. Won the cakewalk twice at Sunset Hill, wore one spring to the Governor's ball in Jackson! See how I sashayed around the ballroom, Laura? [*She raises her skirt and does a mincing step around the room*] I wore it on Sundays for my gentlemen callers! I had it on the day I met your father—I had malaria fever all that spring. The change of climate from East Tennessee to the Delta [9]—weakened resistance—I had a little temperature all the time—not enough to be serious—just enough to make me restless and giddy! Invitations poured in—parties all over the Delta!—"Stay in bed," said Mother, "you have fever!"—but I just wouldn't.—I took quinine but kept on going, going!—Evenings, dances!—Afternoons, long, long rides! Picnics—lovely!—So lovely, that country in May.—All lacy with dogwood, literally flooded with jonquils!—That was the spring I had the craze for jonquils. Jonquils became an absolute obsession. Mother said, "Honey, there's no more room for jonquils." And still I kept on bringing in more jonquils. Whenever, wherever I saw them, I'd say, "Stop! Stop! I see jon-

_____
[9] The rich cotton-growing area of the state of Mississippi.

quils!" I made the young men help me gather the jonquils! It was a joke, Amanda and her jonquils! Finally there were no more vases to hold them, every available space was filled with jonquils. No vases to hold them? All right, I'll hold them myself! And then I—[*She stops in front of the picture.* MUSIC] met your father! Malaria fever and jonquils and then—this—boy. . . . [*She switches on the rose-colored lamp*] I hope they get here before it starts to rain. [*She crosses upstage and places the jonquils in bowl on table*] I gave your brother a little extra change so he and Mr. O'Connor could take the service car home.

LAURA   [*With altered look*]   What did you say his name was?
AMANDA   O'Connor.
LAURA   What is his first name?
AMANDA   I don't remember. Oh, yes, I do. It was—Jim!
[LAURA *sways slightly and catches hold of a chair*]

[*LEGEND ON SCREEN: "NOT JIM!"*]

LAURA   [*Faintly*]   Not—Jim!
AMANDA   Yes, that was it, it was Jim! I've never known a Jim that wasn't nice!

[*MUSIC: OMINOUS*]

LAURA   Are you sure his name is Jim O'Connor?
AMANDA   Yes. Why?
LAURA   Is he the one that Tom used to know in high school?
AMANDA   He didn't say so. I think he just got to know him at the warehouse.
LAURA   There was a Jim O'Connor we both knew in high school—[*Then, with effort*] If that is the one that Tom is bringing to dinner—you'll have to excuse me, I won't come to the table.
AMANDA   What sort of nonsense is this?
LAURA   You asked me once if I'd ever liked a boy. Don't you remember I showed you this boy's picture?
AMANDA   You mean the boy you showed me in the year book?
LAURA   Yes, that boy.
AMANDA   Laura, Laura, were you in love with that boy?
LAURA   I don't know, Mother. All I know is I couldn't sit at the table if it was him!
AMANDA   It won't be him! It isn't the least bit likely. But whether it is or not, you will come to the table. You will not be excused.
LAURA   I'll have to be, Mother.
AMANDA   I don't intend to humor your silliness. Laura. I've had too much from you and your brother, both! So just sit down and compose yourself till they come. Tom has forgotten his key so you'll have to let them in, when they arrive.
LAURA   [*Panicky*]   Oh, Mother—*you* answer the door!
AMANDA   [*Lightly*]   I'll be in the kitchen—busy!
LAURA   Oh, Mother, please answer the door, don't make me do it!
AMANDA   [*Crossing into kitchenette*]   I've got to fix the dressing for the salmon. Fuss, fuss—silliness!—over a gentleman caller!
[*Door swings shut.* LAURA *is left alone*]

[*LEGEND: "TERROR!"*]

[*She utters a low moan and turns off the lamp—sits stiffly on the edge of the sofa, knotting her fingers together*]

[*LEGEND ON SCREEN: "THE OPENING OF A DOOR!"*]

[TOM *and* JIM *appear on the fire-escape steps and climb to landing. Hearing their approach,* LAURA *rises with a panicky gesture. She retreats to the portieres*]

[*The doorbell.* LAURA *catches her breath and touches her throat. Low drums*]

AMANDA   [*Calling*]   Laura, sweetheart! The door!
[LAURA *stares at it without moving*]
JIM   I think we just beat the rain.
TOM   Uh-huh. [*He rings again, nervously.* JIM *whistles and fishes for a cigarette*]
AMANDA   [*Very, very gaily*]   Laura, that is your brother and Mr. O'Connor! Will you let them in, darling?
[LAURA *crosses toward kitchenette door*]
LAURA   [*Breathlessly*]   Mother—you go to the door!
[AMANDA *steps out of kitchenette and stares furiously at* LAURA. *She points imperiously at the door*]
LAURA   Please, please!
AMANDA   [*In a fierce whisper*]   What is the matter with you, you silly thing?
LAURA   [*Desperately*]   Please, you answer it, *please!*
AMANDA   I told you I wasn't going to humor you, Laura. Why have you chosen this moment to lose your mind?
LAURA   Please, please, please, you go!
AMANDA   You'll have to go to the door because I can't!
LAURA   [*Despairingly*]   I can't either!
AMANDA   *Why?*
LAURA   I'm *sick!*
AMANDA   I'm sick, too—of your nonsense! Why can't you and your brother be normal people? Fantastic whims and behavior! [TOM *gives a long ring.*] Preposterous goings on! Can you give me one reason—[*Calls out lyrically*] COMING! JUST ONE SECOND!—why you should be afraid to open a door? Now you answer it, Laura!
LAURA   Oh, oh, oh . . . [*She returns through the portieres. Darts to the victrola and winds it frantically and turns it on*]
AMANDA   Laura Wingfield, you march right to that door!
LAURA   Yes—yes, Mother!
[*A faraway, scratchy rendition of "Dardanella" softens the air and gives her strength to move through it. She slips to the door and draws it cautiously open*]

[TOM *enters with the caller,* JIM O'CONNOR]
TOM   Laura, this is Jim. Jim, this is my sister, Laura.
JIM   [*Stepping inside*]   I didn't know that Shakespeare had a sister!
LAURA   [*Retreating stiff and trembling from the door*]   How—how do you do?
JIM   [*Heartily extending his hand*]   Okay!
[LAURA *touches it hesitantly with hers*]
JIM   Your hand's *cold,* Laura!
LAURA   Yes, well—I've been playing the victrola. . . .
JIM   Must have been playing classical music on it! You ought to play a little hot swing music to warm you up!
LAURA   Excuse me—I haven't finished playing the victrola. . . .

[*She turns awkwardly and hurries into the front room. She pauses a second by the victrola. Then catches her breath and darts through the portieres like a frightened deer*]

JIM   [*Grinning*]   What was the matter?

TOM   Oh—with Laura? Laura is—terribly shy.

JIM   Shy, huh? It's unusual to meet a shy girl nowadays. I don't believe you ever mentioned you had a sister.

TOM   Well, now you know. I have one. Here is the *Post Dispatch*. You want a piece of it?

JIM   Uh-huh.

TOM   What piece? The comics?

JIM   Sports! [*Glances at it*] Ole Dizzy Dean [10] is on his bad behavior.

TOM   [*Disinterest*]   Yeah? [*Lights cigarette and crosses back to fire-escape door*]

JIM   Where are *you* going?

TOM   I'm going out on the terrace.

JIM   [*Goes after him*]   You know, Shakespeare—I'm going to sell you a bill of goods!

TOM   What goods?

JIM   A course I'm taking.

TOM   Huh?

JIM   In public speaking! You and me, we're not the warehouse type.

TOM   Thanks—that's good news. But what has public speaking got to do with it?

JIM   It fits you for—executive positions!

TOM   Awww.

JIM   I tell you it's done a helluva lot for me.

[*IMAGE: EXECUTIVE AT DESK*]

TOM   In what respect?

JIM   In every! Ask yourself what is the difference between you an' me and men in the office down front? Brains?—No!—Ability?—No! Then what? Just one little thing—

TOM   What is that one little thing?

JIM   Primarily it amounts to—social poise! Being able to square up to people and hold your own on any social level!

AMANDA   [*Off stage*]   Tom?

TOM   Yes, Mother?

AMANDA   Is that you and Mr. O'Connor?

TOM   Yes, Mother?

AMANDA   Well, you just make yourselves comfortable in there.

TOM   Yes, Mother.

AMANDA   Ask Mr. O'Connor if he would like to wash his hands.

JIM   Aw, no—no—thank you—I took care of that at the warehouse. Tom—

TOM   Yes?

JIM   Mr. Mendoza was speaking to me about you.

TOM   Favorably?

JIM   What do you think?

TOM   Well—

JIM   You're going to be out of a job if you don't wake up.

TOM   I am waking up—

JIM   You show no signs.

TOM   The signs are interior.

---

[10] A well-known baseball pitcher of the St. Louis Cardinals.

[*IMAGE ON SCREEN: THE SAILING VESSEL WITH
JOLLY ROGER AGAIN*]

TOM   I'm planning to change. [*He leans over the rail speaking with quiet
exhilaration. The incandescent marquees and signs of the first-run movie
houses light his face from across the alley. He looks like a voyager*] I'm
right at the point of committing myself to a future that doesn't include
the warehouse and Mr. Mendoza or even a night-school course in public
speaking.

JIM   What are you gassing about?

TOM   I'm tired of the movies.

JIM   Movies!

TOM   Yes, movies! Look at them—[*A wave toward the marvels of Grand
Avenue*] All of those glamorous people—having adventures—hogging it all,
globbling the whole thing up! You know what happens? People go to the
movies instead of *moving!* Hollywood characters are supposed to have all
the adventures for everybody in America, while everybody in America sits
in a dark room and watches them have them! Yes, until there's a war.
That's when adventure becomes available to the masses! *Everyone's* dish,
not only Gable's! [11] Then the people in the dark room come out of the
dark room to have some adventures themselves—Goody, goody!—It's our
turn now, to go to the South Sea Island—to make a safari—to be exotic,
far-off!—But I'm not patient. I don't want to wait till then. I'm tired of
the *movies* and I am *about* to move!

JIM   [*Incredulously*]   Move?

TOM   Yes.

JIM   When?

TOM   Soon!

JIM   Where? Where?

[*THEME THREE MUSIC SEEMS TO ANSWER THE QUESTION,
WHILE TOM THINKS IT OVER. HE SEARCHES AMONG
HIS POCKETS*]

TOM   I'm starting to boil inside. I know I seem dreamy, but inside—well, I'm
boiling! Whenever I pick up a shoe, I shudder a little thinking how short
life is and what I am doing!—Whatever that means, I know it doesn't
mean shoes—except as something to wear on a traveler's feet! [*Finds
paper*] Look—

JIM   What?

TOM   I'm a member.

JIM   [*Reading*]   The Union of Merchant Seamen.

TOM   I paid my dues this month, instead of the light bill.

JIM   You will regret it when they turn the lights off.

TOM   I won't be here.

JIM   How about your mother?

TOM   I'm like my father. The bastard son of a bastard! See how he grins? And
he's been absent going on sixteen years!

JIM   You're just talking, you drip. How does your mother feel about it?

TOM   Shhh!—Here comes Mother! Mother is not acquainted with my plans!

AMANDA   [*Enters portieres*]   Where are you all?

TOM   On the terrace, Mother.

---

[11] Clark Gable, well-known motion picture actor.

[*They start inside. She advances to them.* TOM *is distinctly shocked at her appearance. Even* JIM *blinks a little. He is making his first contact with girlish Southern vivacity and in spite of the night-school course in public speaking is somewhat thrown off the beam by the unexpected outlay of social charm*]

[*Certain responses are attempted by* JIM *but are swept aside by* AMANDA'S *gay laughter and chatter.* TOM *is embarrassed but after the first shock* JIM *reacts very warmly. Grins and chuckles, is altogether won over*]

[*IMAGE: AMANDA AS A GIRL*]

AMANDA   [*Coyly smiling, shaking her girlish ringlets*]   Well, well, well, so this is Mr. O'Connor. Introductions entirely unnecessary. I've heard so much about you from my boy. I finally said to him, Tom—good gracious! —why don't you bring this paragon to supper? I'd like to meet this nice young man at the warehouse!—Instead of just hearing him sing your praises so much! I don't know why my son is so standoffish—that's not Southern behavior! Let's sit down and—I think we could stand a little more air in here! Tom, leave the door open. I felt a nice fresh breeze a moment ago. Where has it gone to? Mmm, so warm already! And not quite summer, even. We're going to burn up when summer really gets started. However, we're having—we're having a very light supper. I think light things are better fo' this time of year. The same as light clothes are. Light clothes an' light food are what warm weather calls fo'. You know our blood gets so thick during th' winter—it takes a while fo' us to *adjust* ou'selves!—when the season changes . . . It's come so quick this year. I wasn't prepared. All of a sudden—heavens! Already summer!—I ran to the trunk an' pulled out this light dress—Terribly old! Historical almost! But feels so good—so good an' co-ol, y'know. . . .

TOM   Mother—

AMANDA   Yes, honey?

TOM   How about—supper?

AMANDA   Honey, you go ask Sister if supper is ready! You know that Sister is in full charge of supper! Tell her you hungry boys are waiting for it. [*To* JIM] Have you met Laura?

JIM   She—

AMANDA   Let you in? Oh, good, you've met already! It's rare for a girl as sweet an' pretty as Laura to be domestic! But Laura is, thank heavens, not only pretty but also very domestic. I'm not at all. I never was a bit. I never could make a thing but angel-food cake. Well, in the South we had so many servants. Gone, gone, gone. All vestige of gracious living! Gone completely! I wasn't prepared for what the future brought me. All of my gentlemen callers were sons of planters and so of course I assumed that I would be married to one and raise my family on a large piece of land with plenty of servants. But man proposes—and woman accepts the proposal! —To vary that old, old saying a little bit—I married no planter! I married a man who worked for the telephone company!—That gallantly smiling gentleman over there! [*Points to the picture*] A telephone man who—fell in love with long-distance!—Now he travels and I don't even know where! —But what am I going on for about my—tribulations? Tell me yours—I hope you don't have any! Tom?

TOM   [*Returning*]   Yes, Mother?

AMANDA   Is supper nearly ready?

TOM   It looks to me like supper is on the table.

AMANDA   Let me look—[*She rises prettily and looks through portieres*] Oh, lovely!—But where is Sister?

TOM   Laura is not feeling well and she says that she thinks she'd better not come to the table.

AMANDA   What?—Nonsense!—Laura? Oh, Laura!

LAURA   [*Off stage, faintly*]   Yes, Mother.

AMANDA   You really must come to the table. We won't be seated until you come to the table! Come in, Mr. O'Connor. You sit over there, and I'll— Laura? Laura Wingfield! You're keeping us waiting, honey! We can't say grace until you come to the table!

[*The back door is pushed weakly open and* LAURA *comes in. She is obviously quite faint, her lips trembling, her eyes wide and staring. She moves unsteadily toward the table*]

[*LEGEND: "TERROR!"*]

[*Outside a summer storm is coming abruptly. The white curtains billow inward at the windows and there is a sorrowful murmur and deep blue dusk*]

[LAURA *suddenly stumbles—she catches at a chair with a faint moan*]

TOM   Laura!

AMANDA   Laura! [*There is a clap of thunder*] [*LEGEND: "AH!"*] [*Despairingly*] Why, Laura, you *are* sick, darling! Tom, help your sister into the living room, dear! Sit in the living room, Laura—rest on the sofa. Well! [*To the gentleman caller*] Standing over the hot stove made her ill!—I told her that it was just too warm this evening, but—[TOM *comes back in.* LAURA *is on the sofa*] Is Laura all right now?

TOM   Yes.

AMANDA   What *is* that? Rain? A nice cool rain has come up! [*She gives the gentleman caller a frightened look*] I think we may—have grace—now . . . [TOM *looks at her stupidly*] Tom, honey—you say grace!

TOM   Oh . . . "For these and all thy mercies—" [*They bow their heads,* AMANDA *stealing a nervous glance at* JIM. *In the living room* LAURA, *stretched on the sofa, clenches her hand to her lips, to hold back a shuddering sob*] God's Holy Name be praised—

THE SCENE DIMS OUT

SCENE SEVEN

A SOUVENIR.

Half an hour later. Dinner is just being finished in the upstage area which is concealed by the drawn portieres.

As the curtain rises LAURA *is still huddled upon the sofa, her feet drawn under her, her head resting on a pale blue pillow, her eyes wide and mysteriously watchful. The new floor lamp with its shade of rose-colored silk gives a soft, becoming light to her face, bringing out the fragile, unearthly prettiness which usually escapes attention. There is a steady murmur of rain, but it is slackening and stops soon after the scene begins; the air outside becomes pale and luminous as the moon breaks out. A moment after the curtain rises, the lights in both rooms flicker and go out.*

JIM   Hey, there, Mr. Light Bulb!
      [AMANDA *laughs nervously*]

[*LEGEND: "SUSPENSION OF A PUBLIC SERVICE"*]

AMANDA   Where was Moses when the lights went out? Ha-ha. Do you know the answer to that one, Mr. O'Connor?
JIM   No, Ma'am, what's the answer?
AMANDA   In the dark! [JIM *laughs appreciatively*] Everybody sit still. I'll light the candles. Isn't it lucky we have them on the table? Where's a match? Which of you gentlemen can provide a match?
JIM   Here.
AMANDA   Thank you, sir.
JIM   Not at all, Ma'am!
AMANDA   I guess the fuse has burnt out. Mr. O'Connor, can you tell a burnt-out fuse? I know I can't and Tom is a total loss when it comes to mechanics. [*SOUND: GETTING UP: VOICES RECEDE A LITTLE TO KITCHENETTE*] Oh, be careful you don't bump into something. We don't want our gentleman caller to break his neck. Now wouldn't that be a fine howdy-do?
JIM   Ha-ha! Where is the fuse-box?
AMANDA   Right here next to the stove. Can you see anything?
JIM   Just a minute.
AMANDA   Isn't electricity a mysterious thing? Wasn't it Benjamin Franklin who tied a key to a kite? We live in such a mysterious universe, don't we? Some people say that science clears up all the mysteries for us. In my opinion it only creates more! Have you found it yet?
JIM   No, Ma'am. All these fuses look okay to me.
AMANDA   Tom!
TOM   Yes, Mother?
AMANDA   That light bill I gave you several days ago. The one I told you we got the notices about?
TOM   Oh—Yeah.

[*LEGEND: "HA!"*]

AMANDA   You didn't neglect to pay it by any chance?
TOM   Why, I—
AMANDA   Didn't! I might have known it!
JIM   Shakespeare probably wrote a poem on that light bill, Mrs. Wingfield.
AMANDA   I might have known better than to trust him with it! There's such a high price for negligence in this world!
JIM   Maybe the poem will win a ten-dollar prize.
AMANDA   We'll just have to spend the remainder of the evening in the nineteenth century, before Mr. Edison made the Mazda lamp!
JIM   Candlelight is my favorite kind of light.
AMANDA   That shows you're romantic! But that's no excuse for Tom. Well, we got through dinner. Very considerate of them to let us get through

dinner before they plunged us into everlasting darkness, wasn't it, Mr. O'Connor?

JIM   Ha-ha!

AMANDA   Tom, as a penalty for your carelessness you can help me with the dishes.

JIM   Let me give you a hand.

AMANDA   Indeed you will not!

JIM   I ought to be good for something.

AMANDA   Good for something? [*Her tone is rhapsodic*] You? Why, Mr. O'Connor, nobody, *nobody's* given me this much entertainment in years—as you have!

JIM   Aw, now, Mrs. Wingfield!

AMANDA   I'm not exaggerating, not one bit! But Sister is all by her lonesome. You go keep her company in the parlor! I'll give you this lovely old candelabrum that used to be on the altar at the church of the Heavenly Rest. It was melted a little out of shape when the church burnt down. Lightning struck it one spring. Gypsy Jones was holding a revival at the time and he intimated that the church was destroyed because the Episcopalians gave card parties.

JIM   Ha-ha.

AMANDA   And how about you coaxing Sister to drink a little wine? I think it would be good for her! Can you carry both at once?

JIM   Sure. I'm Superman!

AMANDA   Now, Thomas, get into this apron!

[*The door of kitchenette swings closed on* AMANDA's *gay laughter; the flickering light approaches the portieres*]

[LAURA *sits up nervously as he enters. Her speech at first is low and breathless from the almost intolerable strain of being alone with a stranger*]

[*THE LEGEND: "I DON'T SUPPOSE
YOU REMEMBER ME AT ALL!"*]

[*In her first speeches in this scene, before* JIM's *warmth overcomes her paralyzing shyness,* LAURA's *voice is thin and breathless as though she has just run up a steep flight of stairs*]

[JIM's *attitude is gently humorous. In playing this scene it should be stressed that while the incident is apparently unimportant, it is to* LAURA *the climax of her secret life*]

JIM   Hello, there, Laura.

LAURA   [*Faintly*] Hello. [*She clears her throat*]

JIM   How are you feeling now? Better?

LAURA   Yes. Yes, thank you.

JIM   This is for you. A little dandelion wine. [*He extends it toward her with extravagant gallantry*]

LAURA   Thank you.

JIM   Drink it—but don't get drunk! [*He laughs heartily.* LAURA *takes the glass uncertainly; laughs shyly*] Where shall I set the candles?

LAURA   Oh—oh, anywhere . . .

JIM   How about here on the floor? Any objections?

LAURA   No.

JIM   I'll spread a newspaper under to catch the drippings. I like to sit on the floor. Mind if I do?

LAURA   Oh, no.

JIM   Give me a pillow?

LAURA   What?

JIM   A pillow!

LAURA   Oh . . . [Hands him one quickly]

JIM   How about you? Don't you like to sit on the floor?

LAURA   Oh—yes.

JIM   Why don't you, then?

LAURA   I—will.

JIM   Take a pillow! [LAURA does. Sits on the other side of the candelabrum. JIM crosses his legs and smiles engagingly at her] I can't hardly see you sitting way over there.

LAURA   I can—see you.

JIM   I know, but that's not fair, I'm in the limelight. [LAURA moves her pillow closer] Good! Now I can see you! Comfortable?

LAURA   Yes.

JIM   So am I. Comfortable as a cow. Will you have some gum?

LAURA   No, thank you.

JIM   I think that I will indulge, with your permission. [Musingly unwraps it and holds it up] Think of the fortune made by the guy that invented the first piece of chewing gum. Amazing, huh? The Wrigley Building is one of the sights of Chicago.—I saw it summer before last when I went up to the Century of Progress.[12] Did you take in the Century of Progress?

LAURA   No, I didn't.

JIM   Well, it was quite a wonderful exposition. What impressed me most was the Hall of Science. Gives you an idea of what the future will be in America, even more wonderful than the present time is! [Pause. Smiling at her] Your brother tells me you're shy. Is that right, Laura?

LAURA   I—don't know.

JIM   I judge you to be an old-fashioned type of girl. Well, I think that's a pretty good type to be. Hope you don't think I'm being too personal—do you?

LAURA   [Hastily, out of embarrassment]   I believe I will take a piece of gum, if you—don't mind. [Clearing her throat] Mr. O'Connor, have you—kept up with your singing?

JIM   Singing? Me?

LAURA   Yes. I remember what a beautiful voice you had.

JIM   When did you hear me sing?

[VOICE OFF STAGE IN THE PAUSE]

VOICE   [Off stage]

> O blow, ye winds, heigh-ho,
> A-roving I will go!
>   I'm off to my love
>   With a boxing glove—
> Ten thousand miles away!

JIM   You say you've heard me sing?

LAURA   Oh, yes! Yes, very often . . . I—don't suppose you remember me— at all?

JIM   [Smiling doubtfully]   You know I have an idea I've seen you before. I

---

[12] The title given to the theme of the Chicago World's Fair of 1933.

had that idea soon as you opened the door. It seemed almost like I was about to remember your name. But the name that I started to call you—wasn't a name! And so I stopped myself before I said it.

LAURA Wasn't it—Blue Roses?

JIM [*Springs up. Grinning*] Blue Roses! My gosh, yes—Blue Roses! That's what I had on my tongue when you opened the door! Isn't it funny what tricks your memory plays? I didn't connect you with high school somehow or other. But that's where it was; it was high school. I didn't even know you were Shakespeare's sister! Gosh, I'm sorry.

LAURA I didn't expect you to. You—barely knew me!

JIM But we did have a speaking acquaintance, huh?

LAURA Yes, we—spoke to each other.

JIM When did you recognize me?

LAURA Oh, right away!

JIM Soon as I came in the door?

LAURA When I heard your name I thought it was probably you. I knew that Tom used to know you a little in high school. So when you came in the door—Well, then I was—sure.

JIM Why didn't you *say* something, then?

LAURA [*Breathlessly*] I didn't know what to say, I was—too surprised!

JIM For goodness' sakes! You know, this sure is funny!

LAURA Yes! Yes, isn't it, though . . .

JIM Didn't we have a class in something together?

LAURA Yes, we did.

JIM What class was that?

LAURA It was—singing—Chorus!

JIM Aw!

LAURA I sat across the aisle from you in the Aud.

JIM Aw.

LAURA Mondays, Wednesdays and Fridays.

JIM Now I remember—you always came in late.

LAURA Yes, it was so hard for me, getting upstairs. I had that brace on my leg—it clumped so loud!

JIM I never heard any clumping.

LAURA [*Wincing at the recollection*] To me it sounded like—thunder!

JIM Well, well, well, I never even noticed.

LAURA And everybody was seated before I came in. I had to walk in front of all those people. My seat was in the back row. I had to go clumping all the way up the aisle with everyone watching!

JIM You shouldn't have been self-conscious.

LAURA I know, but I was. It was always such a relief when the singing started.

JIM Aw, yes, I've placed you now! I used to call you Blue Roses. How was it that I got started calling you that?

LAURA I was out of school a little while with pleurosis. When I came back you asked me what was the matter. I said I had pleurosis—you thought I said Blue Roses. That's what you always called me after that!

JIM I hope you didn't mind.

LAURA Oh, no—I liked it. You see, I wasn't acquainted with many—people. . . .

JIM As I remember you sort of stuck by yourself.

LAURA I—I—never have had much luck at—making friends.

JIM I don't see why you wouldn't.

LAURA Well, I—started out badly.

JIM You mean being—

LAURA   Yes, it sort of—stood between me—

JIM   You shouldn't have let it!

LAURA   I know, but it did, and—

JIM   You were shy with people!

LAURA   I tried not to be but never could—

JIM   Overcome it?

LAURA   No, I—I never could!

JIM   I guess being shy is something you have to work out of kind of gradually.

LAURA   [*Sorrowfully*]   Yes—I guess it—

JIM   Takes time!

LAURA   Yes—

JIM   People are not so dreadful when you know them. That's what you have to remember! And everybody has problems, not just you, but practically everybody has got some problems. You think of yourself as having the only problems, as being the only one who is disappointed. But just look around you and you will see lots of people as disappointed as you are. For instance, I hoped when I was going to high school that I would be further along at this time, six years later, than I am now—You remember that wonderful write-up I had in the *Torch?*

LAURA   Yes! [*She rises and crosses to table*]

JIM   It said I was bound to succeed in anything I went into! [LAURA *returns with the annual*] Holy Jeez! The *Torch!*
[*He accepts it reverently. They smile across it with mutual wonder.* LAURA *crouches beside him and they begin to turn through it.* LAURA's *shyness is dissolving in his warmth*]

LAURA   Here you are in *Pirates of Penzance!*

JIM   [*Wistfully*]   I sang the baritone lead in that operetta.

LAURA   [*Rapidly*]   So—*beautifully!*

JIM   [*Protesting*]   Aw—

LAURA   Yes, yes—beautifully—beautifully!

JIM   You heard me?

LAURA   All three times!

JIM   No!

LAURA   Yes!

JIM   All three performances?

LAURA   [*Looking down*]   Yes.

JIM   Why?

LAURA   I—wanted to ask you to—autograph my program.

JIM   Why didn't you ask me to?

LAURA   You were always surrounded by your own friends so much that I never had a chance to.

JIM   You should have just—

LAURA   Well, I—thought you might think I was—

JIM   Thought I might think you was—what?

LAURA   Oh—

JIM   [*With reflective relish*]   I was beleaguered by females in those days.

LAURA   You were terribly popular!

JIM   Yeah—

LAURA   You had such a—friendly way—

JIM   I was spoiled in high school.

LAURA   Everybody—liked you!

JIM   Including you?

LAURA   I—yes, I—I did, too—[*She gently closes the book in her lap*]

JIM   Well, well, well!—Give me that program, Laura. [*She hands it to him.*

He signs it with a flourish] There you are—better late than never!

LAURA   Oh, I—what a—surprise!

JIM   My signature isn't worth very much right now. But some day—maybe—it will increase in value! Being disappointed is one thing and being discouraged is something else. I am disappointed but I am not discouraged. I'm twenty-three years old. How old are you?

LAURA   I'll be twenty-four in June.

JIM   That's not old age!

LAURA   No, but—

JIM   You finished high school?

LAURA   [*With difficulty*]   I didn't go back.

JIM   You mean you dropped out?

LAURA   I made bad grades in my final examinations. [*She rises and replaces the book and the program. Her voice strained*] How is—Emily Meisenbach getting along?

JIM   Oh, that kraut-head!

LAURA   Why do you call her that?

JIM   That's what she was.

LAURA   You're not still—going with her?

JIM   I never see her.

LAURA   It said in the Personal Section that you were—engaged!

JIM   I know, but I wasn't impressed by that—propaganda!

LAURA   It wasn't—the truth?

JIM   Only in Emily's optimistic opinion!

LAURA   Oh—

[*LEGEND: "WHAT HAVE YOU DONE SINCE HIGH SCHOOL?"*]

[JIM *lights a cigarette and leans indolently back on his elbows smiling at* LAURA *with a warmth and charm which lights her inwardly with altar candles. She remains by the table and turns in her hands a piece of glass to cover her tumult*]

JIM   [*After several reflective puffs on a cigarette*]   What have you done since high school? [*She seems not to hear him*] Huh? [LAURA *looks up*] I said what have you done since high school, Laura?

LAURA   Nothing much.

JIM   You must have been doing something these six long years.

LAURA   Yes.

JIM   Well, then, such as what?

LAURA   I took a business course at business college—

JIM   How did that work out?

LAURA   Well, not very—well—I had to drop out, it gave me—indigestion— [JIM *laughs gently*]

JIM   What are you doing now?

LAURA   I don't do anything—much. Oh, please don't think I sit around doing nothing! My glass collection takes up a good deal of time. Glass is something you have to take good care of.

JIM   What did you say—about glass?

LAURA   Collection I said—I have one—[*She clears her throat and turns away again, acutely shy*]

JIM   [*Abruptly*]   You know what I judge to be the trouble with you? Inferiority complex! Know what that is? That's what they call it when someone low-rates himself! I understand it because I had it, too. Although my case was not so aggravated as yours seems to be. I had it until I took up public speaking, developed my voice, and learned that I had an aptitude for science. Before that time I never thought of myself as being outstanding in any way whatsoever! Now I've never made a regular study of it, but I have a friend who says I can analyze people better than doctors that make a profession of it. I don't claim that to be necessarily true, but I can sure guess a person's psychology, Laura! [*Takes out his gum*] Excuse me, Laura. I always take it out when the flavor is gone. I'll use this scrap of paper to wrap it in. I know how it is to get it stuck on a shoe. Yep—that's what I judge to be your principal trouble. A lack of confidence in yourself as a person. You don't have the proper amount of faith in yourself. I'm basing that fact on a number of your remarks and also on certain observations I've made. For instance that clumping you thought was so awful in high school. You say that you even dreaded to walk into class. You see what you did? You dropped out of school, you gave up an education because of a clump, which as far as I know was practically non-existent! A little physical defect is what you have. Hardly noticeable even! Magnified thousands of times by imagination! You know what my strong advice to you is? Think of yourself as *superior* in some way?

LAURA   In what way would I think:

JIM   Why, man alive, Laura! Just look about you a little. What do you see? A world full of common people! All of 'em born and all of 'em going to die! Which of them has one-tenth of your good points! Or mine! Or anyone else's, as far as that goes—Gosh! Everybody excels in some one thing. Some in many! [*Unconsciously glances at himself in the mirror*] All you've got to do is discover in *what!* Take me, for instance. [*He adjusts his tie at the mirror*] My interest happens to lie in electro-dynamics. I'm taking a course in radio engineering at night school, Laura, on top of a fairly responsible job at the warehouse. I'm taking that course and studying public speaking.

LAURA   Ohhhh.

JIM   Because I believe in the future of television! [*Turning back to her*] I wish to be ready to go up right along with it. Therefore I'm planning to get in on the ground floor. In fact I've already made the right connections and all that remains is for the industry itself to get under way! Full steam—[*His eyes are starry*] Knowledge—Zzzzzp! Money—Zzzzzp!—Power! That's the cycle democracy is built on! [*His attitude is convincingly dynamic.* LAURA *stares at him, even her shyness eclipsed in her absolute wonder. He suddenly grins*] I guess you think I think a lot of myself!

LAURA   No—o-o-o, I—

JIM   Now how about you? Isn't there something you take more interest in than anything else?

LAURA   Well, I do—as I said—have my—glass collection—

[*A peal of girlish laughter from the kitchen*]

JIM   I'm not right sure I know what you're talking about. What kind of glass is it?

LAURA   Little articles of it, they're ornaments mostly! Most of them are little animals made out of glass, the tiniest little animals in the world. Mother calls them a glass menagerie! Here's an example of one, if you'd like to see it! This one is one of the oldest. It's nearly thirteen. [*MUSIC: "THE GLASS MENAGERIE"*] [*He stretches out his hand*] Oh, be careful—if you breathe, it breaks!

JIM   I'd better not take it. I'm pretty clumsy with things.

LAURA   Go on, I trust you with him! [*Places it in his palm*] There now—you're holding him gently! Hold him over the light, he loves the light! You see how the light shines through him?

JIM   It sure does shine!

LAURA   I shouldn't be partial, but he is my favorite one.

JIM   What kind of a thing is this one supposed to be?

LAURA   Haven't you noticed the single horn on his forehead?

JIM   A unicorn, huh?

LAURA   Mmm-hmmm!

JIM   Unicorns, aren't they extinct in the modern world?

LAURA   I know!

JIM   Poor little fellow, he must feel sort of lonesome.

LAURA   [*Smiling*]   Well, if he does he doesn't complain about it. He stays on a shelf with some horses that don't have horns and all of them seem to get along nicely together.

JIM   How do you know?

LAURA   [*Lightly*]   I haven't heard any arguments among them!

JIM   [*Grinning*]   No arguments, huh? Well, that's a pretty good sign! Where shall I set him?

LAURA   Put him on the table. They all like a change of scenery once in a while!

JIM   [*Stretching*]   Well, well, well, well— Look how big my shadow is when I stretch!

LAURA   Oh, oh, yes—it stretches across the ceiling!

JIM   [*Crossing to door*]   I think it's stopped raining. [*Opens fire-escape door*] Where does the music come from?

LAURA   From the Paradise Dance Hall across the alley.

JIM   How about cutting the rug a little, Miss Wingfield?

LAURA   Oh, I—

JIM   Or is your program filled up? Let me have a look at it. [*Grasps imaginary card*] Why, every dance is taken! I'll just have to scratch some out. [*WALTZ MUSIC: "LA GOLONDRINA"*] Ahhh, a waltz! [*He executes some sweeping turns by himself then holds his arms toward* LAURA]

LAURA   [*Breathlessly*]   I—can't dance!

JIM   There you go, that inferiority stuff!

LAURA   I've never danced in my life!

JIM   Come on, try!

LAURA   Oh, but I'd step on you!

JIM   I'm not made out of glass.

LAURA   How—how—how do we start?

JIM   Just leave it to me. You hold your arms out a little.

LAURA   Like this?

JIM   A little bit higher. Right. Now don't tighten up, that's the main thing about it—relax.

LAURA   [*Laughing breathlessly*]   It's hard not to.

JIM   Okay.

LAURA   I'm afraid you can't budge me.

JIM   What do you bet I can't? [*He swings her into motion*]

LAURA   Goodness, yes, you can!

JIM   Let yourself go, now, Laura, just let yourself go.

LAURA   I'm—

JIM   Come on!

LAURA   Trying!

JIM   Not so stiff—Easy does it!

LAURA   I know but I'm—

JIM   Loosen th' backbone! There now, that's a lot better.

LAURA   Am I?

JIM   Lots, lots better! [*He moves her about the room in a clumsy waltz*]

LAURA   Oh, my!

JIM   Ha-ha!

LAURA   Oh, my goodness!

JIM   Ha-ha-ha! [*They suddenly bump into the table.* JIM *stops*] What did we hit on?

LAURA   Table.

JIM   Did something fall off it? I think—

LAURA   Yes.

JIM   I hope that it wasn't the little glass horse with the horn!

LAURA   Yes.

JIM   Aw, aw, aw. Is it broken?

LAURA   Now it is just like all the other horses.

JIM   It's lost its—

LAURA   Horn! It doesn't matter. Maybe it's a blessing in disguise.

JIM   You'll never forgive me. I bet that that was your favorite piece of glass.

LAURA   I don't have favorites much. It's no tragedy, Freckles. Glass breaks so easily. No matter how careful you are. The traffic jars the shelves and things fall off them.

JIM   Still I'm awfully sorry that I was the cause.

LAURA   [*Smiling*]   I'll just imagine he had an operation. The horn was removed to make him feel less—freakish! [*They both laugh*] Now he will feel more at home with the other horses, the ones that don't have horns . . .

JIM   Ha-ha, that's very funny! [*Suddenly serious*] I'm glad to see that you have a sense of humor. You know—you're—well—very different! Surprisingly different from anyone else I know! [*His voice becomes soft and hesitant with a genuine feeling*] Do you mind me telling you that? [LAURA *is abashed beyond speech*] I mean it in a nice way . . . [LAURA *nods shyly, looking away*] You make me feel sort of—I don't know how to put it! I'm usually pretty good at expressing things, but—This is something that I don't know how to say! [LAURA *touches her throat and clears it—turns the broken unicorn in her hands*] [*Even softer*] Has anyone ever told you that you were pretty? [*PAUSE: MUSIC*] [LAURA *looks up slowly, with wonder, and shakes her head*] Well, you are! In a very different way from anyone else. And all the nicer because of the difference, too. [*His voice becomes low and husky.* LAURA *turns away, nearly faint with the novelty of her emotions*] I wish that you were my sister. I'd teach you to have some confidence in yourself. The different people are not like other people, but being different is nothing to be ashamed of. Because other people are not such wonderful people. They're one hundred times one thousand. You're one times one! They walk all over the earth. You just stay here. They're common as—weeds, but —you—well, you're—*Blue Roses!*

[*IMAGE ON SCREEN: BLUE ROSES*]

MUSIC CHANGES

LAURA   But blue is wrong for—roses . . .

JIM   It's right for you—You're—pretty!

LAURA   In what respect am I pretty?

JIM   In all respects—believe me! Your eyes—your hair—are pretty! Your hands are pretty! [*He catches hold of her hand*] You think I'm making this up because I'm invited to dinner and have to be nice. Oh, I could do that! I could put on an act for you, Laura, and say lots of things without being very sincere. But this time I am. I'm talking to you sincerely. I happened to notice you had this inferiority complex that keeps you from feeling comfortable with people. Somebody needs to build your confidence up and make you proud instead of shy and turning away and—blushing—Somebody ought to—Ought to—*kiss* you, Laura! [*His hand slips slowly up her arm to her shoulder*] [*MUSIC SWELLS TUMULTUOUSLY*] [*He suddenly turns her about and kisses her on the lips*] [*When he releases her* LAURA *sinks on the sofa with a bright, dazed look*] [JIM *backs away and fishes in his pocket for a cigarette*] [*LEGEND ON SCREEN: "SOUVENIR"*] Stumble-john! [*He lights the cigarette, avoiding her look*] [*There is a peal of girlish laughter from* AMANDA *in the kitchen*] [LAURA *slowly raises and opens her hand. It still contains the little broken glass animal. She looks at it with a tender, bewildered expression*] Stumble-john! I shouldn't have done that—That was way off the beam. You don't smoke, do you? [*She looks up, smiling, not hearing the question*] [*He sits beside her a little gingerly. She looks at him speechlessly—waiting*] [*He coughs decorously and moves a little farther aside as he considers the situation and senses her feelings, dimly, with perturbation*] [*Gently*] Would you—care for a—mint? [*She doesn't seem to hear him but her look grows brighter even*] Peppermint—Life Saver? My pocket's a regular drug store—wherever I go . . . [*He pops a mint in his mouth. Then gulps and decides to make a clean breast of it. He speaks slowly and gingerly*] Laura, you know, if I had a sister like you, I'd do the same thing as Tom. I'd bring out fellows and—introduce her to them. The right type of boys of a type to—appreciate her. Only—well—he made a mistake about me. Maybe I've got no call to be saying this. That may not have been the idea in having me over. But what if it was? There's nothing wrong about that. The only trouble is that in my case—I'm not in a situation to—do the right thing. I can't take down your number and say I'll phone. I can't call up next week and—ask for a date. I thought I had better explain the situation in case you misunderstood it and—hurt your feelings. . . . [*Pause*] [*Slowly, very slowly,* LAURA's *look changes, her eyes returning slowly from his to the ornament in her palm*] [AMANDA *utters another gay laugh in the kitchen*]

LAURA   [*Faintly*]   You—won't—call again?

JIM   No, Laura, I can't. [*He rises from the sofa*] As I was just explaining, I've—got strings on me, Laura, I've—been going steady! I go out all the time with a girl named Betty. She's a home-girl like you, and Catholic, and Irish, and in a great many ways we—get along fine. I met her last summer on a moonlight boat trip up the river to Alton, on the *Majestic*. Well—right away from the start it was—love! [*LEGEND: LOVE!*] [LAURA *sways slightly forward and grips the arm of the sofa. He fails to notice, now enrapt in his own comfortable being*] Being in love has made a new man of me! [*Leaning stiffly forward, clutching the arm of the sofa,* LAURA *struggles visibly with her storm. But* JIM *is oblivious, she is a long way off*] The power of love is really pretty tremendous! Love is something that—changes the whole world, Laura! [*The storm abates a little and* LAURA *leans back. He notices her again*] It happened that Betty's aunt took sick, she got a wire and had to go to Centralia. So Tom—when he asked me to dinner—I naturally just accepted the invitation, not knowing that you—that he—that I—[*He stops awkwardly*] Huh—I'm a stumble-john! [*He flops back on the sofa*] [*The holy candles in the altar of* LAURA's *face have been snuffed out. There is a look of almost infinite desolation*] [JIM *glances at her uneasily*] I wish that you would—say something. [*She bites her lip which was trembling and then bravely smiles. She opens her hand again on the broken glass ornament. Then she gently takes his hand and raises it level with her own. She care-*

fully places the unicorn in the palm of his hand, then pushes his fingers closed upon it] What are you—doing that for? You want me to have him?— Laura? *[She nods]* What for?

LAURA   A—souvenir . . .

[She rises unsteadily and crouches beside the victrola to wind it up]

[LEGEND ON SCREEN: "THINGS HAVE A WAY OF TURNING OUT
            SO BADLY!"]

[OR IMAGE: "GENTLEMAN CALLER WAVING GOODBYE!—GAILY"]

[At this moment AMANDA *rushes brightly back in the front room. She bears a pitcher of fruit punch in an old-fashioned cut-glass pitcher and a plate of macaroons. The plate has a gold border and poppies painted on it]*

AMANDA   Well, well, well! Isn't the air delightful after the shower? I've made you children a little liquid refreshment. *[Turns gaily to the gentleman caller]* Jim, do you know that song about lemonade?

> "Lemonade, lemonade
>   Made in the shade and stirred with a spade—
> Good enough for any old maid!"

JIM   *[Uneasily]* Ha-ha! No—I never heard it.

AMANDA   Why, Laura! You look so serious!

JIM   We were having a serious conversation.

AMANDA   Good! Now you're better acquainted!

JIM   *[Uncertainly]* Ha-ha! Yes.

AMANDA   You modern young people are much more serious-minded than my generation. I was so gay as a girl!

JIM   You haven't changed, Mrs. Wingfield.

AMANDA   Tonight I'm rejuvenated! The gaiety of the occasion, Mr. O'Connor! *[She tosses her head with a peal of laughter. Spills lemonade]* Oooo! I'm baptizing myself!

JIM   Here—let me—

AMANDA   *[Setting the pitcher down]* There now. I discovered we had some maraschino cherries. I dumped them in, juice and all!

JIM   You shouldn't have gone to that trouble, Mrs. Wingfield.

AMANDA   Trouble, trouble? Why it was loads of fun! Didn't you hear me cutting up in the kitchen? I bet your ears were burning! I told Tom how outdone with him I was for keeping you to himself so long a time! He should have brought you over much, much sooner! Well, now that you've found your way, I want you to be a very frequent caller! Not just occasional but all the time. Oh, we're going to have a lot of gay times together! I see them coming! Mmm, just breathe that air! So fresh, and the moon's so pretty! I'll skip back out—I know where my place is when young folks are having a—serious conversation!

JIM   Oh, don't go out, Mrs. Wingfield. The fact of the matter is I've got to be going.

AMANDA   Going, now? You're joking! Why, it's only the shank of the evening, Mr. O'Connor!

JIM   Well, you know how it is.

AMANDA   You mean you're a young workingman and have to keep workingmen's hours. We'll let you off early tonight. But only on the condition that next time you stay later. What's the best night for you? Isn't Saturday night the best night for you workingmen?

JIM   I have a couple of time-clocks to punch, Mrs. Wingfield. One at morning, another one at night!

AMANDA   My, but you *are* ambitious! You work at night, too?

JIM   No, Ma'am, not work but—Betty! [*He crosses deliberately to pick up his hat. The band at the Paradise Dance Hall goes into a tender waltz*]

AMANDA   Betty? Betty? Who's—Betty! [*There is an ominous cracking sound in the sky*]

JIM   Oh, just a girl. The girl I go steady with! [*He smiles charmingly. The sky falls*]

[*LEGEND: "THE SKY FALLS"*]

AMANDA   [*A long-drawn exhalation*]   Ohhhh . . . Is it a serious romance, Mr. O'Connor?

JIM   We're going to be married the second Sunday in June.

AMANDA   Ohhhh—how nice! Tom didn't mention that you were engaged to be married.

JIM   The cat's not out of the bag at the warehouse yet. You know how they are. They call you Romeo and stuff like that. [*He stops at the oval mirror to put on his hat. He carefully shapes the brim and the crown to give a discreetly dashing effect*] It's been a wonderful evening, Mrs. Wingfield. I guess this is what they mean by Southern hospitality.

AMANDA   It really wasn't anything at all.

JIM   I hope it don't seem like I'm rushing off. But I promised Betty I'd pick her up at the Wabash depot, an' by the time I get my jalopy down there her train'll be in. Some women are pretty upset if you keep 'em waiting.

AMANDA   Yes, I know— The tyranny of women! [*Extends her hand*] Good-bye, Mr. O'Connor. I wish you luck—and happiness—and success! All three of them, and so does Laura!—Don't you, Laura?

LAURA   Yes!

JIM   [*Taking her hand*]   Good-bye, Laura. I'm certainly going to treasure that souvenir. And don't you forget the good advice I gave you. [*Raises his voice to a cheery shout*] So long, Shakespeare! Thanks again, ladies—Good night!

[*He grins and ducks jauntily out*]

[*Still bravely grimacing,* AMANDA *closes the door on the gentleman caller. Then she turns back to the room with a puzzled expression. She and* LAURA *don't dare to face each other.* LAURA *crouches beside the victrola to wind it*]

AMANDA   [*Faintly*]   Things have a way of turning out so badly. I don't believe that I would play the victrola. Well, well—well—Our gentleman caller was engaged to be married! Tom!

TOM   [*From back*]   Yes, Mother?

AMANDA   Come in here a minute. I want to tell you something awfully funny.

TOM   [*Enters with macaroon and a glass of the lemonade*]   Has the gentleman caller gotten away already?

AMANDA   The gentleman caller has made an early departure. What a wonderful joke you played on us!

TOM   How do you mean?

AMANDA   You didn't mention that he was engaged to be married.

TOM   Jim? Engaged?

AMANDA   That's what he just informed us.

TOM   I'll be jiggered! I didn't know about that.

AMANDA   That seems very peculiar.

TOM   What's peculiar about it?

AMANDA   Didn't you call him your best friend down at the warehouse?

TOM   He is, but how did I know?

AMANDA   It seems extremely peculiar that you wouldn't know your best friend was going to be married!

TOM   The warehouse is where I work, not where I know things about people!

AMANDA   You don't know things anywhere! You live in a dream; you manufacture illusions! [*He crosses to door*] Where are you going?

TOM   I'm going to the movies.

AMANDA   That's right, now that you've had us make such fools of ourselves. The effort, the preparations, all the expense! The new floor lamp, the rugs, the clothes for Laura! All for what? To entertain some other girl's fiancé! Go to the movies, go! Don't think about us, a mother deserted, an unmarried sister who's crippled and has no job! Don't let anything interfere with your selfish pleasure! Just go, go, go—to the movies!

TOM   All right, I will! The more you shout about my selfishness to me the quicker I'll go, and I won't go to the movies!

AMANDA   Go, then! Then go to the moon—you selfish dreamer!

[TOM *smashes his glass on the floor. He plunges out on the fire-escape, slamming the door.* LAURA *screams—cut by door*]

[*Dance-hall music up.* TOM *goes to the rail and grips it desperately, lifting his face in the chill white moonlight penetrating the narrow abyss of the alley*]

[*LEGEND ON SCREEN: "AND SO GOOD-BYE . . ."*]

[TOM's *closing speech is timed with the interior pantomime. The interior scene is played as though viewed through soundproof glass.* AMANDA *appears to be making a comforting speech to* LAURA *who is huddled upon the sofa. Now that we cannot hear the mother's speech, her silliness is gone and she has dignity and tragic beauty.* LAURA's *dark hair hides her face until at the end of the speech she lifts it to smile at her mother.* AMANDA's *gestures are slow and graceful, almost dancelike, as she comforts the daughter. At the end of her speech she glances a moment at the father's picture—then withdraws through the portieres. At close of* TOM's *speech,* LAURA *blows out the candles, ending the play*]

TOM   I didn't go to the moon, I went much further—for time is the longest distance between two places—Not long after that I was fired for writing a poem on the lid of a shoe-box. I left Saint Louis. I descended the steps of this fire-escape for a last time and followed, from then on, in my father's footsteps, attempting to find in motion what was lost in space—I traveled around a great deal. The cities swept about me like dead leaves, leaves that were brightly colored but torn away from the branches. I would have stopped, but I was pursued by something. It always came upon me unawares, taking me altogether by surprise. Perhaps it was a familiar bit of music. Perhaps it was only a piece of transparent glass—Perhaps I am walking along a street at night, in some strange city, before I have found companions. I pass the lighted window of a shop where perfume is sold. The window is filled with pieces of colored glass, tiny transparent bottles in delicate colors, like bits of a shattered rainbow. Then all at once my sister touches my shoulder. I turn around and look into her eyes . . . Oh, Laura, Laura, I tried to leave you behind me, but I am more faithful than I intended to be! I reach for a cigarette, I cross the street, I run into the movies or a bar, I buy a drink, I speak to the nearest stranger—anything that can blow your candles out! [LAURA *bends over the candles*]—for nowadays the world is lit by lightning! Blow out your candles, Laura—and so good-bye. . . .

[*She blows the candles out*]

THE SCENE DISSOLVES

PRODUCTION NOTES

Being a "memory play," *The Glass Menagerie* can be presented with unusual freedom of convention. Because of its considerably delicate or tenuous material, atmospheric touches and subtleties of direction play a particularly important part. Expressionism and all other unconventional techniques in drama have only one valid aim, and that is a closer approach to truth. When a play employs unconventional techniques, it is not, or certainly shouldn't be, trying to escape its responsibility of dealing with reality, or interpreting experience, but is actually or should be attempting to find a closer approach, a more penetrating and vivid expression of things as they are. The straight realistic play with its genuine frigidaire and authentic ice-cubes, its characters that speak exactly as its audience speaks, corresponds to the academic landscape and has the same virtue of a photographic likeness. Everyone should know nowadays the unimportance of the photographic in art: that truth, life, or reality is an organic thing which the poetic imagination can represent or suggest, in essence, only through transformation, through changing into other forms than those which were merely present in appearance.

These remarks are not meant as comments only on this particular play. They have to do with a conception of a new, plastic theatre which must take the place of the exhausted theatre of realistic conventions if the theatre is to resume vitality as a part of our culture.

The Screen Device

There is *only one important difference between the original and acting version of the play* and that is the *omission* in the latter of the device which I tentatively included in my *original* script. This device was the use of a screen on which were projected magic-lantern slides bearing images or titles. I do not regret the omission of this device from the present Broadway production. The extraordinary power of Miss Taylor's [13] performance made it suitable to have the utmost simplicity in the physical production. But I think it may be interesting to some readers to see how this device was conceived. So I am putting it into the published manuscript. These images and legends, projected from behind, were cast on a section of wall between the front-room and dining-room areas, which should be indistinguishable from the rest when not in use.

The purpose of this will probably be apparent. It is to give accent to certain values in each scene. Each scene contains a particular point (or several) which is structurally the most important. In an episodic play, such as this, the basic structure or narrative line may be obscured from the audience; the effect may

---

[13] Who first played the part of Amanda.

seem fragmentary rather than architectural. This may not be the fault of the play so much as a lack of attention in the audience. The legend or image upon the screen will strengthen the effect of what is merely allusion in the writing and allow the primary point to be made more simply and lightly than if the entire responsibility were on the spoken lines. Aside from this structural value, I think the screen will have a definite emotional appeal, less definable but just as important. An imaginative producer or director may invent many other uses for this device than those indicated in the present script. In fact the possibilities of the device seem much larger to me than the instance of this play can possibly utilize.

The Music

Another extra-literary accent in this play is provided by the use of music. A single recurring tune, "The Glass Menagerie," is used to give emotional emphasis to suitable passages. This tune is like circus music, not when you are on the grounds or in the immediate vicinity of the parade, but when you are at some distance and very likely thinking of something else. It seems under those circumstances to continue almost interminably and it weaves in and out of your preoccupied consciousness; then it is the lightest, most delicate music in the world and perhaps the saddest. It expresses the surface vivacity of life with the underlying strain of immutable and inexpressible sorrow. When you look at a piece of delicately spun glass you think of two things: how beautiful it is and how easily it can be broken. Both of those ideas should be woven into the recurring tune, which dips in and out of the play as if it were carried on a wind that changes. It serves as a thread of connection and allusion between the narrator with his separate point in time and space and the subject of his story. Between each episode it returns as reference to the emotion, nostalgia, which is the first condition of the play. It is primarily Laura's music and therefore comes out most clearly when the play focuses upon her and the lovely fragility of glass which is her image.

The Lighting

The lighting in the play is not realistic. In keeping with the atmosphere of memory, the stage is dim. Shafts of light are focused on selected areas or actors, sometimes in contradistinction to what is the apparent center. For instance, in the quarrel scene between Tom and Amanda, in which Laura has no active part, the clearest pool of light is on her figure. This is also true of the supper scene, when her silent figure on the sofa should remain the visual center. The light upon Laura should be distinct from the others, having a peculiar pristine clarity such as light used in early religious portraits of female saints or madonnas. A certain correspondence to light in religious paintings, such as El Greco's, where the figures are radiant in atmosphere that is relatively dusky, could be effectively used throughout the play. (It will also permit a more effective use of the screen.) A free, imaginative use of light can be of enormous value in giving a mobile, plastic quality to plays of a more or less static nature.

T.W.

BERTOLT BRECHT
[1898–1956]

Bertolt Brecht, the son of a factory executive, was born in Augsburg, Bavaria. He was one of countless young Germans whose view of life was changed immeasurably by the experience of the First World War: Brecht's service in a field hospital made him aware of a horrible discrepancy between war itself and the sort of propaganda which justifies it. As a young man, he aimed at a medical career, and he pursued advanced studies at Munich and Berlin before turning to the theater. As a mature playwright, he meant to be a kind of doctor of society itself, prescribing large doses of pacifist and socialist ideology.

During the 1920s Brecht belonged to a group of avant-garde, leftist artists in Berlin. His early plays—such as *In the City's Thickets* (1922) and *One is Another* (1927)—depicted the ironic incongruities of human life in general, and the rat-race of bourgeois life in particular. These plays were radically expressionistic, but Brecht defended them as legitmate departures from the illusionistic "realism" of middle-class dramas portraying middle-class problems with middle-class solutions. In 1928, Brecht collaborated with the brilliant composer Kurt Weill on *The Three-Penny Opera;* this enduringly-successful work was an adaptation of John Gay's eighteenth-century comedy, *The Beggar's Opera,* but Brecht made the play a strikingly contemporary reflection of the confusion—moral, social, and economic—of post-war Germany.

When Hitler came to power in 1933, Brecht was forced to flee Germany. He did not return until 1949 when he became a citizen of East Berlin, professing loyalty to the Communist regime. In the intervening years Brecht lived in Russia, France, Norway, the United States (1941–1947), and Switzerland. Until the end of the Second World War he turned out a steady stream of anti-Nazi poems, plays (*The Private Life of the Master Race,* 1938; *The Fears and Miseries of the Third Reich,* 1944), and direct propaganda. But Brecht often had larger political purposes: *Saint Joan of the Stockyards* (1937) is a direct espousal of Marxism; *Mother Courage* (1941) is an implicit manifesto of pacifism.

Brecht conceived of the stage as a didactic medium. He developed a theory of "epic theater," a theater of "learning," in which the audience is not to be merely entertained or diverted, but moved to social action. Emotions should be frustated so that the audience perceives intellectually the necessity for transforming society; the effect should be one of "alienation" rather than pleasure. This theory has consequences for dramatic production: the atmosphere should be closer to that of the classroom than the "realistic" theater; the play's structure should be disconnected (thus limiting emotional involvement); narrator's songs, pantomimes, and special effects should interrupt the action; the acting should be deliberately artificial.

Paradoxically, Brecht's talent as a dramatist undercuts his own theory: his characteristic voice is that of the poet rather than the propagandist. His grim ironies and brilliant sense of the comic create dramatic situations which involve the audience emotionally—with an interest that extends far beyond the "lesson" of the stage-parable. Moreover, Brecht created many characters who—like Azdak in *The Caucasian Chalk Circle* (1948) —charm us with a personality uniquely their own.

Like Azdak, Brecht was something of an eccentric, and his career in East Berlin (from 1949 until his death in 1956) was not free of occasional conflicts with the Communist authorities. *The Caucasian Chalk Circle* suggests a basis for such conflict, for in the play Brecht the artist and individualist has triumphed over Brecht the ideologist and activist.

THE CAUCASIAN CHALK CIRCLE

BERTOLT BRECHT
Adapted by Eric Bentley

CHARACTERS

OLD MAN *on the right*
PEASANT WOMAN *on the right*
YOUNG PEASANT
A VERY YOUNG WORKER
OLD MAN *on the left*
PEASANT WOMAN *on the left*
AGRICULTURIST KATO
GIRL TRACTORIST
WOUNDED SOLDIER
THE DELEGATE *from the capital*
THE SINGER
GEORGI ABASHWILI, *the Governor*
NATELLA, *the Governor's wife*
MICHAEL, *their son*
SHALVA, *an adjutant*
ARSEN KAZBEKI, *a fat prince*

MESSENGER *from the Capital*
NIKO MIKADZE *and* MIKA LOLADZE, *doctors*
SIMON SHASHAVA, *a soldier*
GRUSHA VASHNADZE, *a kitchen maid*
OLD PEASANT *with the milk*
CORPORAL *and* PRIVATE
PEASANT *and his wife*
LAVRENTI VASHNADZE, *Grusha's brother*
ANIKO, *his wife*
PEASANT WOMAN, *for a while Grusha's mother-in-law*
JUSSUP, *her son*
MONK
AZDAK, *village recorder*
SHAUWA, *a policeman*

GRAND DUKE
DOCTOR
INVALID
LIMPING MAN
BLACKMAILER
LUDOVICA
INNKEEPER, *her father-in-law*

STABLEBOY
POOR OLD PEASANT WOMAN
IRAKLI, *her brother-in-law, a bandit*
THREE WEALTHY FARMERS
ILLO SHUBOLADZE *and* SANDRO OBOLADZE, *lawyers*
OLD MARRIED COUPLE

SOLDIERS, SERVANTS, PEASANTS, BEGGARS, MUSICIANS, MERCHANTS, NOBLES, ARCHITECTS

The time and the place: After a prologue, set in 1945, we move back perhaps 1000 years.

The action of The Caucasian Chalk Circle *centers on Nuka (or Nukha), a town in Azerbaijan. However, the capital referred to in the prologue is not Baku (capital of Soviet Azerbaijan) but Tiflis (or Tbilisi), capital of Georgia. When Azdak, later, refers to "the capital" he means Nuka itself, though whether Nuka was ever capital of Georgia I do not know: in what reading I have done on the subject I have only found Nuka to be the capital of a Nuka Khanate.*

The word "Georgia" has not been used in this English version because of its American associations; instead, the alternative name "Grusinia" (in Russian, Gruziya) has been used.

The reasons for resettling the old Chinese story in Transcaucasia are not far to seek. The play was written when the Soviet chief of state, Joseph Stalin, was a Georgian, as was his favorite poet, cited in the Prologue, Mayakovsky. And surely there is a point in having this story acted out at the place where Europe and Asia meet, a place incomparably rich in legend and history. Here Jason found the Golden Fleece. Here Noah's Ark touched ground. Here the armies of both Genghis Khan and Tamerlane wrought havoc.

—E.B.

PROLOGUE

Summer, 1945.

Among the ruins of a war-ravaged Caucasian village the members of two kolkhoz villages, mostly WOMEN *and* OLDER MEN, *are sitting in a circle, smoking and drinking wine. With them is a* DELEGATE *of the State Reconstruction Commission from Nuka.*

PEASANT WOMAN [*left*] [*pointing*] In those hills over there we stopped three Nazi tanks, but the apple orchard was already destroyed.
OLD MAN [*right*] Our beautiful dairy farm: a ruin.
GIRL TRACTORIST I laid the fire, Comrade.
[*Pause.*]

DELEGATE   Nuka, Azerbaijan S.S.R. Delegation received from the goat-breeding Kolkhoz "Rosa Luxemburg." This is a collective farm which moved eastwards on orders from the authorities at the approach of Hitler's armies. They are now planning to return. Their delegates have looked at the village and the land and found a lot of destruction. [*Delegates on the right nod.*] But the neighboring fruit farm—Kolkhoz [*to the left*] "Galinsk"—proposes to use the former grazing land of Kolkhoz "Rosa Luxemburg" for orchards and vineyards. This land lies in a valley where grass doesn't grow very well. As a delegate of the Reconstruction Commission in Nuka I request that the two Kolkhoz villages decide between themselves whether Kolkhoz "Rosa Luxemburg" shall return or not.

OLD MAN   [*right*]   First of all, I want to protest against the time limit on discussion. We of Kolkhoz "Rosa Luxemburg" have spent three days and three nights getting here. And now discussion is limited to half a day.

WOUNDED SOLDIER   [*left*]   Comrade, we haven't as many villages as we used to have. We haven't as many hands. We haven't as much time.

GIRL TRACTORIST   All pleasures have to be rationed. Tobacco is rationed, and wine. Discussion should be rationed.

OLD MAN   [*right*]   [*sighing*]   Death to the fascists! But I will come to the point and explain why we want our valley back. There are a great many reasons, but I'll begin with one of the simplest. Makinä Abakidze, unpack the goat cheese. [*A peasant woman from right takes from a basket an enormous cheese wrapped in a cloth. Applause and laughter.*] Help yourselves, Comrades, start in!

OLD MAN   [*left*]   [*suspiciously*]   Is this a way of influencing us?

OLD MAN   [*right*]   [*amid laughter*]   How could it be a way of influencing you, Surab, you valley-thief? Everyone knows you'll take the cheese and the valley, too. [*Laughter.*] All I expect from you is an honest answer. Do you like the cheese?

OLD MAN   [*left*]   The answer is: yes.

OLD MAN   [*right*]   Really. [*Bitterly.*]   I ought to have known you know nothing about cheese.

OLD MAN   [*left*]   Why not? When I tell you I like it?

OLD MAN   [*right*]   Because you can't like it. Because it's not what it was in the old days. And why not? Because our goats don't like the new grass as they did the old. Cheese is not cheese because grass is not grass, that's the thing. Please put that in your report.

OLD MAN   [*left*]   But your cheese is excellent.

OLD MAN   [*right*]   It isn't excellent. It's just passable. The new grazing land is no good, whatever the young people may say. One can't live there. It doesn't even smell of morning in the morning. [*Several people laugh.*]

DELEGATE   Don't mind their laughing: they understand you. Comrades, why does one love one's country? Because the bread tastes better there, the air smells better, voices sound stronger, the sky is higher, the ground is easier to walk on. Isn't that so?

OLD MAN   [*right*]   The valley has belonged to us from all eternity.

SOLDIER   [*left*]   What does *that* mean—from all eternity? Nothing belongs to anyone from all eternity. When you were young you didn't even belong to yourself. You belonged to the Kazbeki princes.

OLD MAN   [*right*]   Doesn't it make a difference, though, what kind of trees stand next to the house you are born in? Or what kind of neighbors you have? Doesn't that make a difference? We want to go back just to have you as our neighbors, valley-thieves! Now you can all laugh again.

OLD MAN [*left*] [*laughing*] Then why don't you listen to what your neighbor, Kato Wachtang, our agriculturist, has to say about the valley?

PEASANT WOMAN [*right*] We've not said all we have to say about our valley. By no means. Not all the houses are destroyed. As for the dairy farm, at least the foundation wall is still standing.

DELEGATE You can claim State support—here and there—you know that. I have suggestions here in my pocket.

PEASANT WOMAN [*right*] Comrade Specialist, we haven't come here to haggle. I can't take your cap and hand you another, and say "This one's better." The other one might *be* better, but you *like* yours better.

GIRL TRACTORIST A piece of land is not a cap—not in our country, Comrade.

DELEGATE Don't get mad. It's true we have to consider a piece of land as a tool to produce something useful, but it's also true that we must recognize love for a particular piece of land. As far as I'm concerned, I'd like to find out more exactly what you [*to those on the left*] want to do with the valley.

OTHERS Yes, let Kato speak.

KATO [*rising; she's in military uniform*] Comrades, last winter, while we were fighting in these hills here as Partisans, we discussed how, once the Germans were expelled, we could build up our fruit culture to ten times its original size. I've prepared a plan for an irrigation project. By means of a cofferdam on our mountain lake, 300 hectares of unfertile land can be irrigated. Our Kolkhoz could not only cultivate more fruit, but also have vineyards. The project, however, would pay only if the disputed valley of Kolkhoz "Rosa Luxemburg" were also included. Here are the calculations. [*She hands* DELEGATE *a briefcase.*]

OLD MAN [*right*] Write into the report that our Kolkhoz plans to start a new stud farm.

GIRL TRACTORIST Comrades, the project was conceived during days and nights when we had to take cover in the mountains. We were often without ammunition for our half-dozen rifles. Even finding a pencil was difficult. [*Applause from both sides.*]

OLD MAN [*right*] Our thanks to the Comrades of Kolkhoz "Galinsk" and all those who've defended our country! [*They shake hands and embrace.*]

PEASANT WOMAN [*left*] In doing this our thought was that our soldiers—both your men and our men—should return to a still more productive homeland.

GIRL TRACTORIST As the poet Mayakovsky said: "The home of the Soviet people shall also be the home of Reason!"

[*The delegates excluding the* OLD MAN *have got up, and with the* DELEGATE *specified proceed to study the* AGRICULTURIST's *drawings. Exclamations such as:*] "Why is the altitude of fall 22 meters?"—"This rock will have to be blown up"—"Actually, all they need is cement and dynamite"—"They force the water to come down here, that's clever!"

A VERY YOUNG WORKER [*right*] [*to* OLD MAN, *right*] They're going to irrigate all the fields between the hills, look at that, Aleko!

OLD MAN [*right*] I'm not going to look. I knew the project would be good. I won't have a pistol pointed at me!

DELEGATE But they only want to point a pencil at you! [*Laughter.*]

OLD MAN [*right*] [*gets up gloomily, and walks over to look at the drawings*] These valley-thieves know only too well that we in this country are suckers for machines and projects.

PEASANT WOMAN [*right*] Aleko Bereshwili, you have a weakness for new projects. That's well known.

DELEGATE   What about my report? May I write that you will all support the cession of your old valley in the interests of this project when you get back to your Kolkhoz?

PEASANT WOMAN   [*right*]   I will. What about you, Aleko?

OLD MAN   [*right*]   [*bent over drawings*]   I suggest that you give us copies of the drawings to take along.

PEASANT WOMAN   [*right*]   Then we can sit down and eat. Once he has the drawings and he's ready to discuss them, the matter is settled. I know him. And it will be the same with the rest of us.

[*Delegates laughingly embrace again.*]

OLD MAN   [*left*]   Long live the Kolkhoz "Rosa Luxemburg" and much luck to your horse-breeding project!

PEASANT WOMAN   [*left*]   In honor of the visit of the delegates from Kolkhoz "Rosa Luxemburg" and of the Specialist, the plan is that we all hear a presentation of the Singer Arkadi Tscheidse.

[*Applause.* GIRL TRACTORIST *has gone off to bring the* SINGER.]

PEASANT WOMAN   [*right*]   Comrades, your entertainment had better be good. It's going to cost us a valley.

PEASANT WOMAN   [*left*]   Arkadi Tscheidse knows about our discussion. He's promised to perform something that has a bearing on the problem.

KATO   We wired Tiflis three times. The whole thing nearly fell through at the last minute because his driver had a cold.

PEASANT WOMAN   [*left*]   Arkadi Tscheidse knows 21,000 lines of verse.

OLD MAN   [*left*]   He's hard to get. You and the Planning Commission should persuade him to come north more often, Comrade.

DELEGATE   We are more interested in economics, I'm afraid.

OLD MAN   [*left*]   [*smiling*]   You arrange the redistribution of vines and tractors, why not songs?

[*Enter the* SINGER *Arkadi Tscheidse, led by* GIRL TRACTORIST. *He is a well-built man of simple manners, accompanied by* FOUR MUSICIANS *with their instruments. The artists are greeted with applause.*]

GIRL TRACTORIST   This is the Comrade Specialist, Arkadi.

[*The* SINGER *greets them all.*]

DELEGATE   Honored to make your acquaintance. I heard about your songs when I was a boy at school. Will it be one of the old legends?

SINGER   A very old one. It's called "The Chalk Circle" and comes from the Chinese. But we'll do it, of course, in a changed version. Comrades, it's an honor for me to entertain you after a difficult debate. We hope you will find that the voice of the old poet also sounds well in the shadow of Soviet tractors. It may be a mistake to mix different wines, but old and new wisdom mix admirably. Now I hope we'll get something to eat before the performance begins—it would certainly help.

VOICES   Surely. Everyone into the Club House!

[*While everyone begins to move,* DELEGATE *turns to* GIRL TRACTORIST.]

DELEGATE   I hope it won't take long. I've got to get back tonight.

GIRL TRACTORIST   How long will it last, Arkadi? The Comrade Specialist must get back to Tiflis tonight.

SINGER   [*casually*]   It's actually two stories. An hour or two.

GIRL TRACTORIST   [*confidentially*]   Couldn't you make it shorter?

SINGER   No.

VOICE   Arkadi Tscheidse's performance will take place here in the square after the meal.

[*And they all go happily to eat.*]

1
THE NOBLE CHILD

> *As the lights go up, the* SINGER *is seen sitting on the floor, a black sheepskin cloak round his shoulders, and a little, well-thumbed notebook in his hand. A small group of listeners—the chorus—sits with him. The manner of his recitation makes it clear that he has told his story over and over again. He mechanically fingers the pages, seldom looking at them. With appropriate gestures, he gives the signal for each scene to begin.*

SINGER
> In olden times, in a bloody time,
> There ruled in a Caucasian city—
> Men called it City of the Damned—
> A Governor.
> His name was Georgi Abashwili.
> He was rich as Croesus
> He had a beautiful wife
> He had a healthy baby.
> No other governor in Grusinia
> Had so many horses in his stable
> So many beggars on his doorstep
> So many soldiers in his service
> So many petitioners in his courtyard.
> Georgi Abashwili—how shall I describe him to you?
> He enjoyed his life.
> On the morning of Easter Sunday
> The Governor and his family went to church.
> [*At the left a large doorway, at the right an even larger gateway.* BEGGARS *and* PETITIONERS *pour from the gateway, holding up thin* CHILDREN, *crutches, and petitions. They are followed by* IRONSHIRTS, *and then, expensively dressed, the* GOVERNOR'S FAMILY.]

BEGGARS AND PETITIONERS
> —Mercy! Mercy, Your Grace! The taxes are too high.
> —I lost my leg in the Persian War, where can I get . . .
> —My brother is innocent, Your Grace, a misunderstanding . . .
> —The child is starving in my arms!
> —Our petition is for our son's discharge from the army, our last remaining son!
> —Please, Your Grace, the water inspector takes bribes.
> [*One servant collects the petitions. Another distributes coins from a purse. Soldiers push the crowd back, lashing at them with thick leather whips.*]

SOLDIER   Get back! Clear the church door!
> [*Behind the* GOVERNOR, *his* WIFE, *and the* ADJUTANT, *the* GOVERNOR'S CHILD *is brought through the gateway in an ornate carriage.*]

CROWD
> —The baby!
> —I can't see it, don't shove so hard!
> —God bless the child, Your Grace!

SINGER   [*while the crowd is driven back with whips*]
> For the first time on that Easter Sunday, the people saw the Governor's heir.
>
> Two doctors never moved from the noble child, apple of the Governor's eye.
>
> Even the mighty Prince Kazbeki bows before him at the church door.
> [*The* FAT PRINCE *steps forwards and greets the* FAMILY.]

FAT PRINCE   Happy Easter, Natella Abashwili! What a day! When it was raining last night, I thought to myself, gloomy holidays! But this morning the sky was gay. I love a gay sky, a simple heart, Natella Abashwili. And little Michael is a governor from head to foot! Tititi! [*He tickles the* CHILD.]

GOVERNOR'S WIFE   What do you think, Arsen, at last Georgi has decided to start building the east wing. All those wretched slums are to be torn down to make room for the garden.

FAT PRINCE   Good news after so much bad! What's the latest on the war, Brother Georgi? [*The* GOVERNOR *indicates a lack of interest.*] Strategical retreat, I hear. Well, minor reverses are to be expected. Sometimes things go well, sometimes not. Such is war. Doesn't mean a thing, does it?

GOVERNOR'S WIFE   He's coughing. Georgi, did you hear? [*She speaks sharply to the* DOCTORS, *two dignified men standing close to the little carriage.*] He's coughing!

FIRST DOCTOR   [*to the* SECOND]   May I remind you, Niko Mikadze, that I was against the lukewarm bath? [*To the* GOVERNOR'S WIFE:] There's been a little error over warming the bath water, Your Grace.

SECOND DOCTOR   [*equally polite*]   Mika Loladze, I'm afraid I can't agree with you. The temperature of the bath water was exactly what our great, beloved Mishiko Oboladze prescribed. More likely a slight draft during the night, Your Grace.

GOVERNOR'S WIFE   But do pay more attention to him. He looks feverish, Georgi.

FIRST DOCTOR   [*bending over the* CHILD]   No cause for alarm, Your Grace. The bath water will be warmer. It won't occur again.

SECOND DOCTOR   [*with a venomous glance at the* FIRST]   I won't forget that, my dear Mika Loladze. No cause for concern, Your Grace.

FAT PRINCE   Well, well, well! I always say: "A pain in my liver? Then the doctor gets fifty strokes on the soles of his feet." We live in a decadent age. In the old days one said: "Off with his head!"

GOVERNOR'S WIFE   Let's go into church. Very likely it's the draft here.
> [*The procession of* FAMILY *and* SERVANTS *turns into the doorway. The* FAT PRINCE *follows, but the* GOVERNOR *is kept back by the* ADJUTANT, *a handsome young man. When the crowd of* PETITIONERS *has been driven off, a young dust-stained* RIDER, *his arm in a sling, remains behind.*]

ADJUTANT   [*pointing at the* RIDER, *who steps forward*]   Won't you hear the messenger from the capital, Your Excellency? He arrived this morning. With confidential papers.

GOVERNOR   Not before Service, Shalva. But did you hear Brother Kazbeki wish me a happy Easter? Which is all very well, but I don't believe it did rain last night.

ADJUTANT   [*nodding*]   We must investigate.

GOVERNOR   Yes, at once. Tomorrow.
> [*They pass through the doorway. The* RIDER, *who has waited in vain for an audience, turns sharply round and, muttering a curse, goes off. Only one of the palace guards—*SIMON SHASHAVA—*remains at the door.*]

SINGER

The city is still.
Pigeons strut in the church square.
A soldier of the Palace Guard
Is joking with a kitchen maid
As she comes up from the river with a bundle.

[*A girl*—GRUSHA VASHNADZE—*comes through the gateway with a bundle made of large green leaves under her arm.*]

SIMON   What, the young lady is not in church? Shirking?

GRUSHA   I was dressed to go. But they needed another goose for the banquet. And they asked me to get it. I know about geese.

SIMON   A goose? [*He feigns suspicion.*] I'd like to see that goose. [GRUSHA *does not understand.*] One must be on one's guard with women. "I only went for a fish," they tell you, but it turns out to be something else.

GRUSHA   [*walking resolutely toward him and showing him the goose*]   There! If it isn't a fifteen-pound goose stuffed full of corn, I'll eat the feathers.

SIMON   A queen of a goose! The Governor himself will eat it. So the young lady has been down to the river again?

GRUSHA   Yes, at the poultry farm.

SIMON   Really? At the poultry farm, down by the river . . . not higher up maybe? Near those willows?

GRUSHA   I only go to the willows to wash the linen.

SIMON   [*insinuatingly*]   Exactly.

GRUSHA   Exactly what?

SIMON   [*winking*]   Exactly that.

GRUSHA   Why shouldn't I wash the linen by the willows?

SIMON   [*with exaggerated laughter*]   "Why shouldn't I wash the linen by the willows!" That's good, really good!

GRUSHA   I don't understand the soldier. What's so good about it?

SIMON   [*slyly*]   "If something I know someone learns, she'll grow hot and cold by turns!"

GRUSHA   I don't know what I could learn about those willows.

SIMON   Not even if there was a bush opposite? That one could see everything from? Everything that goes on there when a certain person is—"washing linen"?

GRUSHA   What does go on? Won't the soldier say what he means and have done?

SIMON   Something goes on. Something can be seen.

GRUSHA   Could the soldier mean I dip my toes in the water when it's hot? There's nothing else.

SIMON   There's more. Your toes. And more.

GRUSHA   More what? At most my foot?

SIMON   Your foot. And a little more. [*He laughs heartily.*]

GRUSHA   [*angrily*]   Simon Shashava, you ought to be ashamed of yourself! To sit in a bush on a hot day and wait till a girl comes and dips her legs in the river! And I bet you bring a friend along too! [*She runs off.*]

SIMON   [*shouting after her*]   I didn't bring any friend along!
    [*As the* SINGER *resumes his tale, the* SOLDIER *steps into the doorway as though to listen to the service.*]

SINGER
    The city lies still
    But why are there armed men?
    The Governor's palace is at peace
    But why is it a fortress?

And the Governor returned to his palace
And the fortress was a trap
And the goose was plucked and roasted
But the goose was not eaten this time
And noon was no longer the hour to eat:
Noon was the hour to die.

[*From the doorway at the left the* FAT PRINCE *quickly appears, stands still, looks around. Before the gateway at the right two* IRONSHIRTS *are squatting and playing dice. The* FAT PRINCE *sees them, walks slowly past, making a sign to them. They rise: one goes through the gateway, the other goes off at the right. Muffled voices are heard from various directions in the rear: "To your posts!" The palace is surrounded. The* FAT PRINCE *quickly goes off. Church bells in the distance. Enter, through the doorway, the Governor's family and procession, returning from church.*]

GOVERNOR'S WIFE [*passing the* ADJUTANT] It's impossible to live in such a slum. But Georgi, of course, will only build for his little Michael. Never for me! Michael is all! All for Michael!

[*The procession turns into the gateway. Again the* ADJUTANT *lingers behind. He waits. Enter the wounded* RIDER *from the doorway. Two* IRONSHIRTS *of the Palace Guard have taken up positions by the gateway.*]

ADJUTANT [*to the* RIDER] The Governor does not wish to receive military news before dinner—especially if it's depressing, as I assume. In the afternoon His Excellency will confer with prominent architects. They're coming to dinner too. And here they are! [*Enter three gentlemen through the doorway.*] Go to the kitchen and eat, my friend. [*As the* RIDER *goes, the* ADJUTANT *greets the* ARCHITECTS.] Gentlemen, His Excellency expects you at dinner. He will devote all his time to you and your great new plans. Come!

ONE OF THE ARCHITECTS We marvel that His Excellency intends to build. There are disquieting rumors that the war in Persia has taken a turn for the worse.

ADJUTANT All the more reason to build! There's nothing to those rumors anyway. Persia is a long way off, and the garrison here would let itself be hacked to bits for its Governor. [*Noise from the palace. The shrill scream of a woman. Someone is shouting orders. Dumbfounded, the* ADJUTANT *moves toward the gateway. An* IRONSHIRT *steps out, points his lance at him.*] What's this? Put down that lance, you dog.

ONE OF THE ARCHITECTS It's the Princes! Don't you know the Princes met last night in the capital? And they're against the Grand Duke and his Governors? Gentlemen, we'd better make ourselves scarce. [*They rush off. The* ADJUTANT *remains helplessly behind.*]

ADJUTANT [*furiously to the Palace Guard*] Down with those lances! Don't you see the Governor's life is threatened?

[*The* IRONSHIRTS *of the Palace Guard refuse to obey. They stare coldly and indifferently at the* ADJUTANT *and follow the next events without interest.*]

SINGER
O blindness of the great!
They go their way like gods,
Great over bent backs,
Sure of hired fists,
Trusting in the power
Which has lasted so long.
But long is not forever.

O change from age to age!
Thou hope of the people!
[*Enter the* GOVERNOR, *through the gateway, between two* SOLDIERS *armed to the teeth. He is in chains. His face is gray.*]
Up, great sir, deign to walk upright!
From your palace the eyes of many foes follow you!
And now you don't need an architect, a carpenter will do.
You won't be moving into a new palace
But into a little hole in the ground.
Look about you once more, blind man!
[*The arrested man looks round.*]
Does all you had please you?
Between the Easter Mass and the Easter meal
You are walking to a place whence no one returns.
[*The* GOVERNOR *is led off. A horn sounds an alarm. Noise behind the gateway.*]
When the house of a great one collapses
Many little ones are slain.
Those who had no share in the *good* fortunes of the mighty
Often have a share in their *mis*fortunes.
The plunging wagon
Drags the sweating oxen down with it
Into the abyss.
[*The* SERVANTS *come rushing through the gateway in panic.*]
SERVANTS [*among themselves*]
　—The baskets!
　—Take them all into the third courtyard! Food for five days!
　—The mistress has fainted! Someone must carry her down.
　—She must get away.
　—What about us? We'll be slaughtered like chickens, as always.
　—Goodness, what'll happen? There's bloodshed already in the city, they say.
　—Nonsense, the Governor has just been asked to appear at a Princes' meeting. All very correct. Everything'll be ironed out. I heard this on the best authority . . .
[*The two* DOCTORS *rush into the courtyard.*]
FIRST DOCTOR [*trying to restrain the other*] Niko Mikadze, it is your duty as a doctor to attend Natella Abashwili.
SECOND DOCTOR My duty! It's yours!
FIRST DOCTOR Whose turn is it to look after the child today, Niko Mikadze, yours or mine?
SECOND DOCTOR Do you really think, Mika Loladze, I'm going to stay a minute longer in this accursed house on that little brat's account? [*They start fighting. All one hears is:* "You neglect your duty!" *and* "Duty, my foot!" *Then the* SECOND DOCTOR *knocks the* FIRST *down.*] Go to hell! [*Exit.*]
[*Enter the soldier,* SIMON SHASHAVA. *He searches in the crowd for* GRUSHA.]
SIMON Grusha! There you are at last! What are you going to do?
GRUSHA Nothing. If worst comes to worst, I've a brother in the mountains. How about you?
SIMON Forget about me. [*Formally again*] Grusha Vashnadze, your wish to know my plans fills me with satisfaction. I've been ordered to accompany Madam Abashwili as her guard.
GRUSHA But hasn't the Palace Guard mutinied?

SIMON   [*seriously*]   That's a fact.

GRUSHA   Isn't it dangerous to go with her?

SIMON   In Tiflis, they say: Isn't the stabbing dangerous for the knife?

GRUSHA   You're not a knife, you're a man, Simon Shashava, what has that woman to do with you?

SIMON   That woman has nothing to do with me. I have my orders, and I go.

GRUSHA   The soldier is pigheaded: he is running into danger for nothing—nothing at all. I must get into the third courtyard, I'm in a hurry.

SIMON   Since we're both in a hurry we shouldn't quarrel. You need time for a good quarrel. May I ask if the young lady still has parents?

GRUSHA   No, just a brother.

SIMON   As time is short—my second question is this: Is the young lady as healthy as a fish in water?

GRUSHA   I may have a pain in the right shoulder once in a while. Otherwise I'm strong enough for my job. No one has complained. So far.

SIMON   That's well known. When it's Easter Sunday, and the question arises who'll run for the goose all the same, she'll be the one. My third question is this: Is the young lady impatient? Does she want apples in winter?

GRUSHA   Impatient? No. But if a man goes to war without any reason and then no message comes—that's bad.

SIMON   A message will come. And now my final question . . .

GRUSHA   Simon Shashava, I must get to the third courtyard at once. My answer is yes.

SIMON   [*very embarrassed*]   Haste, they say, is the wind that blows down the scaffolding. But they also say: The rich don't know what haste is. I'm from . . .

GRUSHA   Kutsk . . .

SIMON   The young lady has been inquiring about me? I'm healthy, I have no dependents, I make ten piasters a month, as paymaster twenty piasters, and I'm asking—very sincerely—for your hand.

GRUSHA   Simon Shashava, it suits me well.

SIMON   [*taking from his neck a thin chain with a little cross on it*]   My mother gave me this cross, Grusha Vashnadze. The chain is silver. Please wear it.

GRUSHA   Many thanks, Simon.

SIMON   [*hangs it round her neck*]   It would be better to go to the third courtyard now. Or there'll be difficulties. Anyway, I must harness the horses. The young lady will understand?

GRUSHA   Yes, Simon.

[*They stand undecided.*]

SIMON   I'll just take the mistress to the troops that have stayed loyal. When the war's over, I'll be back. In two weeks. Or three. I hope my intended won't get tired, awaiting my return.

GRUSHA

Simon Shashava, I shall wait for you.
Go calmly into battle, soldier
The bloody battle, the bitter battle
From which not everyone returns:
When you return I shall be there.
I shall be waiting for you under the green elm
I shall be waiting for you under the bare elm
I shall wait until the last soldier has returned
And longer
When you come back from the battle

No boots will stand at my door
The pillow beside mine will be empty
And my mouth will be unkissed.
When you return, when you return
You will be able to say: It is just as it was.

SIMON   I thank you, Grusha Vashnadze. And good-bye!

[*He bows low before her. She does the same before him. Then she runs quickly off without looking round. Enter the* ADJUTANT *from the gateway.*]

ADJUTANT   [*harshly*]   Harness the horses to the carriage! Don't stand there doing nothing, scum!

[SIMON SHASHAVA *stands to attention and goes off. Two* SERVANTS *crowd from the gateway, bent low under huge trunks. Behind them, supported by her women, stumbles* NATELLA ABASHWILI. *She is followed by a* WOMAN *carrying the* CHILD.]

GOVERNOR'S WIFE   I hardly know if my head's still on. Where's Michael? Don't hold him so clumsily. Pile the trunks onto the carriage. No news from the city, Shalva?

ADJUTANT   None. All's quiet so far, but there's not a minute to lose. No room for all those trunks in the carriage. Pick out what you need. [*Exit quickly.*]

GOVERNOR'S WIFE   Only essentials! Quick, open the trunks! I'll tell you what I need. [*The trunks are lowered and opened. She points at some brocade dresses.*] The green one! And, of course, the one with the fur trimming. Where are Niko Mikadze and Mika Loladze? I've suddenly got the most terrible migraine again. It always starts in the temples. [*Enter* GRUSHA.] Taking your time, eh? Go and get the hot water bottles this minute! [GRUSHA *runs off, returns later with hot water bottles; the* GOVERNOR'S WIFE *orders her about by signs.*] Don't tear the sleeves.

A YOUNG WOMAN   Pardon, madam, no harm has come to the dress.

GOVERNOR'S WIFE   Because I stopped you. I've been watching you for a long time. Nothing in your head but making eyes at Shalva Tzereteli. I'll kill you, you bitch! [*She beats the* YOUNG WOMAN.]

ADJUTANT   [*appearing in the gateway*]   Please make haste, Natella Abashwili. Firing has broken out in the city.
[*Exit.*]

GOVERNOR'S WIFE   [*letting go of the* YOUNG WOMAN]   Oh dear, do you think they'll lay hands on us? Why should they? Why? [*She herself begins to rummage in the trunks.*] How's Michael? Asleep?

WOMAN WITH THE CHILD   Yes, madam.

GOVERNOR'S WIFE   Then put him down a moment and get my little saffron-colored boots from the bedroom. I need them for the green dress. [*The* WOMAN *puts down the* CHILD *and goes off.*] Just look how these things have been packed! No love! No understanding! If you don't give them every order yourself . . . At such moments you realize what kind of servants you have! They gorge themselves at your expense, and never a word of gratitude! I'll remember this.

ADJUTANT   [*entering, very excited*]   Natella, you must leave at once!

GOVERNOR'S WIFE   Why? I've got to take this silver dress—it cost a thousand piasters. And that one there, and where's the wine-colored one?

ADJUTANT   [*trying to pull her away*]   Riots have broken out! We must leave at once. Where's the baby?

GOVERNOR'S WIFE   [*calling to the* YOUNG WOMAN *who was holding the baby*]   Maro, get the baby ready! Where on earth are you?

ADJUTANT   [*leaving*]   We'll probably have to leave the carriage behind and go ahead on horseback.

[*The* GOVERNOR'S WIFE *rummages again among her dresses, throws some onto the heap of chosen clothes, then takes them off again. Noises, drums are heard. The* YOUNG WOMAN *who was beaten creeps away. The sky begins to grow red.*]

GOVERNOR'S WIFE [*rummaging desperately*] I simply cannot find the wine-colored dress. Take the whole pile to the carriage. Where's Asja? And why hasn't Maro come back? Have you all gone crazy?

ADJUTANT [*returning*] Quick! Quick!

GOVERNOR'S WIFE [*to the* FIRST WOMAN] Run! Just throw them into the carriage!

ADJUTANT We're not taking the carriage. And if you don't come now, I'll ride off on my own.

GOVERNOR'S WIFE [*as the* FIRST WOMAN *can't carry everything*] Where's that bitch Asja? [*The* ADJUTANT *pulls her away.*] Maro, bring the baby! [*To the* FIRST WOMAN] Go and look for Masha. No, first take the dresses to the carriage. Such nonsense! I wouldn't dream of going on horseback! [*Turning round, she sees the red sky, and starts back rigid. The fire burns. She is pulled out by the* ADJUTANT. *Shaking, the* FIRST WOMAN *follows with the dresses.*]

MARO [*from the doorway with the boots*] Madam! [*She sees the trunks and dresses and runs toward the* CHILD, *picks it up, and holds it a moment.*] They left it behind, the beasts. [*She hands it to* GRUSHA.] Hold it a moment. [*She runs off, following the* GOVERNOR'S WIFE.]
[*Enter* SERVANTS *from the gateway.*]

COOK Well, so they've actually gone. Without the food wagons, and not a minute too early. It's time for us to clear out.

GROOM This'll be an unhealthy neighborhood for quite a while. [*To one of the* WOMEN:] Suliko, take a few blankets and wait for me in the foal stables.

GRUSHA What have they done with the Governor?

GROOM [*gesturing throat cutting*] Ffffft.

A FAT WOMAN [*seeing the gesture and becoming hysterical*] Oh dear, oh dear, oh dear, oh dear! Our master Georgi Abashwili! A picture of health he was, at the morning Mass—and now! Oh, take me away, we've all lost, we must die in sin like our master, Georgi Abashwili!

OTHER WOMAN [*soothing her*] Calm down, Nina! You'll be taken to safety. You've never hurt a fly.

FAT WOMAN [*being led out*] Oh dear, oh dear, oh dear! Quick! Let's all get out before they come, before they come!

A YOUNG WOMAN Nina takes it more to heart than the mistress, that's a fact. They even have to have their weeping done for them.

COOK We'd better get out, all of us.

ANOTHER WOMAN [*glancing back*] That must be the East Gate burning.

YOUNG WOMAN [*seeing the* CHILD *in* GRUSHA's *arms*] The baby! What are you doing with it?

GRUSHA It got left behind.

YOUNG WOMAN She simply left it there. Michael, who was kept out of all the drafts!
[*The* SERVANTS *gather round the* CHILD.]

GRUSHA He's waking up.

GROOM Better put him down, I tell you. I'd rather not think what'd happen to anybody who was found with that baby.

COOK That's right. Once they get started, they'll kill each other off, whole families at a time. Let's go.

[*Exeunt all but* GRUSHA, *with the* CHILD *on her arm, and* TWO WOMEN.]

TWO WOMEN   Didn't you hear? Better put him down.

GRUSHA   The nurse asked me to hold him a moment.

OLDER WOMAN   She's not coming back, you simpleton.

YOUNGER WOMAN   Keep your hands off it.

OLDER WOMAN   [*amiably*]   Grusha, you're a good soul, but you're not very bright, and you know it. I tell you, if he had the plague he couldn't be more dangerous.

GRUSHA   [*stubbornly*]   He hasn't got the plague. He looks at me! He's human!

OLDER WOMAN   Don't look at *him*. You're a fool—the kind that always gets put upon. A person need only say, "Run for the salad, you have the longest legs," and you run. My husband has an ox cart—you can come with us if you hurry! Lord, by now the whole neighborhood must be in flames.

[*Both women leave, sighing. After some hesitation,* GRUSHA *puts the sleeping* CHILD *down, looks at it for a moment, then takes a brocade blanket from the heap of clothes and covers it. Then both women return, dragging bundles.* GRUSHA *starts guiltily away from the* CHILD *and walks a few steps to one side.*]

YOUNGER WOMAN   Haven't you packed anything yet? There isn't much time, you know. The Ironshirts will be here from the barracks.

GRUSHA   Coming!

[*She runs through the doorway. Both women go to the gateway and wait. The sound of horses is heard. They flee screaming. Enter the* FAT PRINCE *with drunken* IRONSHIRTS. *One of them carries the Governor's head on a lance.*]

FAT PRINCE   Here! In the middle! [*One soldier climbs onto the other's back, takes the head, holds it tentatively over the door.*] That's not the middle. Farther to the right. That's it. What I do, my friends, I do well. [*While with hammer and nail, the soldier fastens the head to the wall by its hair:*] This morning at the church door I said to Georgi Abashwili: "I love a gay sky." Actually, I prefer the lightning that comes out of a gay sky. Yes, indeed. It's a pity they took the brat along, though, I need him, urgently.

[*Exit with* IRONSHIRTS *through the gateway. Trampling of horses again. Enter* GRUSHA *through the doorway looking cautiously about her. Clearly she has waited for the* IRONSHIRTS *to go. Carrying a bundle, she walks toward the gateway. At the last moment, she turns to see if the* CHILD *is still there. Catching sight of the head over the doorway, she screams. Horrified, she picks up her bundle again, and is about to leave when the* SINGER *starts to speak. She stands rooted to the spot.*]

SINGER

As she was standing between courtyard and gate,
She heard or she thought she heard a low voice calling.
The child called to her,
Not whining, but calling quite sensibly,
Or so it seemed to her.
"Woman," it said, "help me."
And it went on, not whining, but saying quite sensibly:
"Know, woman, he who hears not a cry for help
But passes by with troubled ears will never hear
The gentle call of a lover nor the blackbird at dawn
Nor the happy sigh of the tired grape-picker as the Angelus rings."

[*She walks a few steps toward the* CHILD *and bends over it.*]

Hearing this she went back for one more look at the child:
Only to sit with him for a moment or two,
Only till someone should come,
His mother, or anyone.
[*Leaning on a trunk, she sits facing the* CHILD.]
Only till she would have to leave, for the danger was too great,
The city was full of flame and crying.
[*The light grows dimmer, as though evening and night were coming on.*]
Fearful is the seductive power of goodness!
[GRUSHA *now settles down to watch over the* CHILD *through the night. Once, she lights a small lamp to look at it. Once, she tucks it in with a coat. From time to time she listens and looks to see whether someone is coming.*]
And she sat with the child a long time,
Till evening came, till night came, till dawn came.
She sat too long, too long she saw
The soft breathing, the small clenched fists,
Till toward morning the seduction was complete
And she rose, and bent down and, sighing, took the child
And carried it away.
[*She does what the* SINGER *says as he describes it.*]
As if it was stolen goods she picked it up.
As if she was a thief she crept away.

2

THE FLIGHT INTO
THE NORTHERN MOUNTAINS

SINGER
When Grusha Vashnadze left the city
On the Grusinian highway
On the way to the Northern Mountains
She sang a song, she bought some milk.

CHORUS
How will this human child escape
The bloodhounds, the trap-setters?
Into the deserted mountains she journeyed
Along the Grusinian highway she journeyed
She sang a song, she bought some milk.
[GRUSHA VASHNADZE *walks on. On her back she carries the* CHILD *in a sack, in one hand is a large stick, in the other a bundle. She sings.*]

THE SONG OF THE FOUR GENERALS

Four generals
Set out for Iran.
With the first one, war did not agree.
The second never won a victory.

For the third the weather never was right.
For the fourth the men would never fight.
Four generals
And not a single man!
Sosso Robakidse
Went marching to Iran
With him the war did so agree
He soon had won a victory.
For him the weather was always right.
For him the men would always fight.
Sosso Robakidse,
He is our man!

[*A peasant's cottage appears.*]

GRUSHA [*to the* CHILD] Noontime is meal time. Now we'll sit hopefully in the grass, while the good Grusha goes and buys a little pitcher of milk. [*She lays the* CHILD *down and knocks at the cottage door. An* OLD MAN *opens it.*] Grandfather, could I have a little pitcher of milk? And a corn cake, maybe?

OLD MAN Milk? We have no milk. The soldiers from the city have our goats. Go to the soldiers if you want milk.

GRUSHA But grandfather, you must have a little pitcher of milk for a baby?

OLD MAN And for a God-bless-you, eh?

GRUSHA Who said anything about a God-bless-you? [*She shows her purse.*] We'll pay like princes. "Head in the clouds, backside in the water." [*The peasant goes off, grumbling, for milk*] How much for the milk?

OLD MAN Three piasters. Milk has gone up.

GRUSHA Three piasters for this little drop? [*Without a word the* OLD MAN *shuts the door in her face.*] Michael, did you hear that? Three piasters! We can't afford it! [*She goes back, sits down again, and gives the* CHILD *her breast.*] Suck. Think of the three piasters. There's nothing there, but you *think* you're drinking, and that's something. [*Shaking her head, she sees that the* CHILD *isn't sucking any more. She gets up, walks back to the door, and knocks again.*] Open, grandfather, we'll pay. [*Softly.*] May lightning strike you! [*When the* OLD MAN *appears:*] I thought it would be half a piaster. But the baby must be fed. How about one piaster for that little drop?

OLD MAN Two.

GRUSHA Don't shut the door again. [*She fishes a long time in her bag.*] Here are two piasters. The milk better be good. I still have two days' journey ahead of me. It's a murderous business you have here—and sinful, too!

OLD MAN Kill the soldiers if you want milk.

GRUSHA [*giving the* CHILD *some milk*] This is an expensive joke. Take a sip, Michael, it's a week's pay. Around here they think we earned our money just sitting on our behinds. Oh, Michael, Michael, you're a nice little load for a girl to take on! [*Uneasy, she gets up, puts the* CHILD *on her back, and walks on. The* OLD MAN, *grumbling, picks up the pitcher and looks after her unmoved.*]

SINGER
As Grusha Vashnadze went northward
The Princes' Ironshirts went after her.

CHORUS
How will the barefoot girl escape the Ironshirts,
The bloodhounds, the trap-setters?

They hunt even by night.
Pursuers never tire.
Butchers sleep little.
[*Two* IRONSHIRTS *are trudging along the highway.*]

CORPORAL You'll never amount to anything, blockhead, your heart's not in it. Your senior officer sees this in little things. Yesterday, when I made the fat gal, yes, you grabbed her husband as I commanded, and you did kick him in the belly, at my request, but did you *enjoy* it, like a loyal Private, or were you just doing your duty? I've kept an eye on you blockhead, you're a hollow reed and a tinkling cymbal, you won't get promoted. [*They walk a while in silence.*] Don't think I've forgotten how insubordinate you are, either. Stop limping! I forbid you to limp! You limp because I sold the horses, and I sold the horses because I'd never have got that price again. You limp to show me you don't like marching. I know you. It won't help. You wait. Sing!

TWO IRONSHIRTS [*singing*]
Sadly to war I went my way
Leaving my loved one at her door.
My friends will keep her honor safe
Till from the war I'm back once more.

CORPORAL Louder!

TWO IRONSHIRTS [*singing*]
When 'neath a headstone I shall be
My love a little earth will bring:
"Here rest the feet that oft would run to me
And here the arms that oft to me would cling."
[*They begin to walk again in silence.*]

CORPORAL A good soldier has his heart and soul in it. When he receives an order, he gets a hard-on, and when he drives his lance into the enemy's guts, he comes. [*He shouts for joy.*] He lets himself be torn to bits for his superior officer, and as he lies dying he takes note that his corporal is nodding approval, and that is reward enough, it's his dearest wish. *You* won't get any nod of approval, but you'll croak all right. Christ, how'm I to get my hands on the Governor's bastard with the help of a fool like you! [*They stay on stage behind.*]

SINGER
When Grusha Vashnadze came to the River Sirra
Flight grew too much for her, the helpless child too heavy.
In the cornfields the rosy dawn
Is cold to the sleepless one, only cold.
The gay clatter of the milk cans in the farmyard where the smoke rises
Is only a threat to the fugitive.
She who carries the child feels its weight and little more.
[GRUSHA *stops in front of a farm. A fat* PEASANT WOMAN *is carrying a milk can through the door.* GRUSHA *waits until she has gone in, then approaches the house cautiously.*]

GRUSHA [*to the* CHILD] Now you've wet yourself again, and you know I've no linen. Michael, this is where we part company. It's far enough from the city. They wouldn't want you *so* much that they'd follow you all *this* way, little good-for-nothing. The peasant woman is kind, and can't you just smell the milk? [*She bends down to lay the* CHILD *on the threshold.*] So farewell, Michael, I'll forget how you kicked me in the back all night to make me walk faster. And you can forget the meager fare—it was meant well. I'd like to have kept you—your nose is so tiny—but it can't be. I'd have shown you your first rabbit, I'd have trained you to keep dry, but now I must turn around. My sweetheart the soldier might be back soon, and suppose he didn't find me? You can't ask that, can you? [*She creeps up to the door and lays the* CHILD *on the threshold. Then, hiding behind a tree, she waits until the* PEASANT WOMAN *opens the door and sees the bundle.*]

PEASANT WOMAN Good heavens, what's this? Husband!

PEASANT What is it? Let me finish my soup.

PEASANT WOMAN [*to the* CHILD] Where's your mother then? Haven't you got one? It's a boy. Fine linen. He's from a good family, you can see that. And they just leave him on our doorstep. Oh, these are times!

PEASANT If they think we're going to feed it, they're wrong. You can take it to the priest in the village. That's the best we can do.

PEASANT WOMAN What'll the priest do with him? He needs a mother. There, he's waking up. Don't you think we could keep him, though?

PEASANT [*shouting*] No!

PEASANT WOMAN I could lay him in the corner by the armchair. All I need is a crib. I can take him into the fields with me. See him laughing? Husband, we have a roof over our heads. We can do it. Not another word out of you! [*She carries the* CHILD *into the house. The* PEASANT *follows protesting.* GRUSHA *steps out from behind the tree, laughs, and hurries off in the opposite direction.*]

SINGER
Why so cheerful, making for home?

CHORUS
Because the child has won new parents with a laugh,
Because I'm rid of the little one, I'm cheerful.

SINGER
And why so sad?

CHORUS
Because I'm single and free, I'm sad
Like someone who's been robbed
Someone who's newly poor.
[*She walks for a short while, then meets the two* IRONSHIRTS *who point their lances at her.*]

CORPORAL Lady, you are running straight into the arms of the Armed Forces. Where are you coming from? And when? Are you having illicit relations with the enemy? Where is he hiding? What movements is he making in your rear? How about the hills? How about the valleys? How are your stockings held in position? [GRUSHA *stands there frightened.*] Don't be scared, we always withdraw, if necessary . . . what, blockhead? I always withdraw. In that respect at least, I can be relied on. Why are you staring like that at my lance? In the field no soldier drops his lance, that's a rule. Learn it by heart, blockhead. Now, lady, where are you headed?

GRUSHA To meet my intended, one Simon Shashava, of the Palace Guard in Nuka.

CORPORAL Simon Shashava? Sure, I know him. He gave me the key so I could look you up once in a while. Blockhead, we are getting to be unpopular. We must make her realize we have honorable intentions. Lady, behind apparent frivolity I conceal a serious nature, so let me tell you officially: I want a child from you. [GRUSHA *utters a little scream.*] Blockhead, she understands me. Uh-huh, isn't it a sweet shock? "Then first I must take the noodles out of the oven, Officer. Then first I must change my torn shirt, Colonel." But away with jokes, away with my lance! We are looking for a baby. A baby from a good family. Have you heard of such a baby, from the city, dressed in fine linen, and suddenly turning up here?

GRUSHA   No, I haven't heard a thing. [*Suddenly she turns round and runs back, panic-stricken. The* IRONSHIRTS *glance at each other, then follow her, cursing.*]

SINGER

Run, kind girl! The killers are coming!
Help the helpless babe, helpless girl!
And so she runs!

CHORUS

In the bloodiest times
There are kind people.

[*As* GRUSHA *rushes into the cottage, the* PEASANT WOMAN *is bending over the* CHILD's *crib.*]

GRUSHA   Hide him. Quick! The Ironshirts are coming! I laid him on your doorstep. But he isn't mine. He's from a good family.

PEASANT WOMAN   Who's coming? What Ironshirts?

GRUSHA   Don't ask questions. The Ironshirts that are looking for it.

PEASANT WOMAN   They've no business in my house. But I must have a little talk with you, it seems.

GRUSHA   Take off the fine linen. It'll give us away.

PEASANT WOMAN   Linen, my foot! In this house I make the decisions! *"You* can't vomit in *my* room!" Why did you abandon it? It's a sin.

GRUSHA   [*looking out of the window*]   Look, they're coming out from behind those trees! I shouldn't have run away, it made them angry. Oh, what shall I do?

PEASANT WOMAN   [*looking out of the window and suddenly starting with fear*] Gracious! Ironshirts!

GRUSHA   They're after the baby.

PEASANT WOMAN   Suppose they come in!

GRUSHA   You mustn't give him to them. Say he's yours.

PEASANT WOMAN   Yes.

GRUSHA   They'll run him through if you hand him over.

PEASANT WOMAN   But suppose they ask for it? The silver for the harvest is in the house.

GRUSHA   If you let them have him, they'll run him through, right here in this room! You've got to say he's yours!

PEASANT WOMAN   Yes. But what if they don't believe me?

GRUSHA   You must be firm.

PEASANT WOMAN   They'll burn the roof over our heads.

GRUSHA   That's why you must say he's yours. His name's Michael. But I shouldn't have told you. [*The* PEASANT WOMAN *nods.*] Don't nod like that. And don't tremble—they'll notice.

PEASANT WOMAN   Yes.

GRUSHA   And stop saying yes, I can't stand it. [*She shakes the* WOMAN.] Don't you have any children?

PEASANT WOMAN   [*muttering*]   He's in the war.

GRUSHA   Then maybe *he's* an Ironshirt? Do you want *him* to run children through with a lance? You'd bawl him out. "No fooling with lances in my house!" you'd shout, "is that what I've reared you for? Wash your neck before you speak to your mother!"

PEASANT WOMAN   That's true, he couldn't get away with anything around here!

GRUSHA   So you'll say he's yours?

PEASANT WOMAN   Yes.

GRUSHA   Look! They're coming!

[*There is a knocking at the door. The women don't answer. Enter* IRON-SHIRTS. *The* PEASANT WOMAN *bows low.*]

CORPORAL   Well, here she is. What did I tell you? What a nose I have! I *smelt* her. Lady, I have a question for you. Why did you run away? What did you think I would do to you? I'll bet it was something unchaste. Confess!

GRUSHA   [*while the* PEASANT WOMAN *bows again and again.*]   I'd left some milk on the stove, and I suddenly remembered it.

CORPORAL   Or maybe you imagined I looked at you unchastely? Like there could be something between us? A carnal glance, know what I mean?

GRUSHA   I didn't see it.

CORPORAL   But it's possible, huh? You admit that much. After all, I might be a pig. I'll be frank with you: I could think of all sorts of things if we were alone. [*To the* PEASANT WOMAN:] Shouldn't you be busy in the yard? Feeding the hens?

PEASANT WOMAN   [*falling suddenly to her knees*]:   Soldier, I didn't know a thing about it. Please don't burn the roof over our heads.

CORPORAL   What are you talking about?

PEASANT WOMAN   I had nothing to do with it. She left it on my doorstep, I swear it!

CORPORAL   [*suddenly seeing the* CHILD *and whistling*]:   Ah, so there's a little something in the crib! Blockhead, I smell a thousand piasters. Take the old girl outside and hold on to her. It looks like I have a little cross-examining to do. [*The* PEASANT WOMAN *lets herself be led out by the* PRIVATE, *without a word.*] So, you've *got* the child I wanted from you! [*He walks toward the crib.*]

GRUSHA   Officer, he's mine. He's not the one you're after.

CORPORAL   I'll just take a look. [*He bends over the crib.*]

[GRUSHA *looks round in despair.*]

GRUSHA   He's mine! He's mine!

CORPORAL   Fine linen!

[GRUSHA *dashes at him to pull him away. He throws her off and again bends over the crib. Again looking round in despair, she sees a log of wood, seizes it, and hits the* CORPORAL *over the head from behind. The* CORPORAL *collapses. She quickly picks up the* CHILD *and rushes off.*]

SINGER

And in her flight from the Ironshirts
After twenty-two days of journeying
At the foot of the Janga-Tau Glacier
Grusha Vashnadze decided to adopt the child.

CHORUS

The helpless girl adopted the helpless child.

[GRUSHA *squats over a half-frozen stream to get the* CHILD *water in the hollow of her hand.*]

GRUSHA

Since no one else will take you, son,
I must take you.
Since no one else will take you, son,
You must take me.
O black day in a lean, lean year,

The trip was long, the milk was dear,
My legs are tired, my feet are sore:
But I wouldn't be without you any more.
I'll throw your silken shirt away
And wrap you in rags and tatters.
I'll wash you, son, and christen you in glacier water.
We'll see it through together.
[*She has taken off the child's fine linen and wrapped it in a rag.*]
SINGER
When Grusha Vashnadze
Pursued by the Ironshirts
Came to the bridge on the glacier
Leading to the villages of the Eastern Slope
She sang the Song of the Rotten Bridge
And risked two lives.
[*A wind has risen. The bridge on the glacier is visible in the dark. One rope is broken and half the bridge is hanging down the abyss.* MERCHANTS, *two men and a woman, stand undecided before the bridge as* GRUSHA *and the* CHILD *arrive. One man is trying to catch the hanging rope with a stick.*]
FIRST MAN   Take your time, young woman. You won't get across here anyway.
GRUSHA   But I *have* to get the baby to the east side. To my brother's place.
MERCHANT WOMAN   Have to? How d'you mean, "have to"? I have to get there, too—because I have to buy carpets in Atum—carpets a woman had to sell because her husband had to die. But can *I* do what I have to? Can she? Andrei's been fishing for that rope for hours. And I ask you, how are we going to fasten it, even if he gets it up?
FIRST MAN   [*listening*]   Hush, I think I hear something.
GRUSHA   The bridge isn't quite rotted through. I think I'll try it.
MERCHANT WOMAN   *I* wouldn't—if the devil himself were after me. It's suicide.
FIRST MAN   [*shouting*]   Hi!
GRUSHA   Don't shout! [*To the* MERCHANT WOMAN] Tell him not to shout.
FIRST MAN   But there's someone down there calling. Maybe they've lost their way.
MERCHANT WOMAN   Why shouldn't he shout? Is there something funny about you? Are they after you?
GRUSHA   All right, I'll tell. The Ironshirts are after me. I knocked one down.
SECOND MAN   Hide our merchandise!
[*The* WOMAN *hides a sack behind a rock.*]
FIRST MAN   Why didn't you say so right away? [*To the others:*] If they catch her they'll make mincemeat out of her!
GRUSHA   Get out of my way. I've got to cross that bridge.
SECOND MAN   You can't. The precipice is two thousand feet deep.
FIRST MAN   Even with the rope it'd be no use. We could hold it up with our hands. But then we'd have to do the same for the Ironshirts.
GRUSHA   Go away.
[*There are calls from the distance*] "Hi, up there!"
MERCHANT WOMAN   They're getting near. But you can't take the child on that bridge. It's sure to break. And look!
[GRUSHA *looks down into the abyss. The* IRONSHIRTS *are heard calling again from below.*]
SECOND MAN   Two thousand feet!
GRUSHA   But those men are worse.
FIRST MAN   You can't do it. Think of the baby. Risk your life but not a child's.

SECOND MAN   With the child she's that much heavier!

MERCHANT WOMAN   Maybe she's *really* got to get across. Give *me* the baby. I'll hide it. Cross the bridge alone!

GRUSHA   I won't. We belong together. [*To the* CHILD] "Live together, die together." [*She sings.*]

THE SONG OF THE ROTTEN BRIDGE

> Deep is the abyss, son,
> I see the weak bridge sway
> But it's not for us, son,
> To choose the way.
>
> The way I know
> Is the one you must tread,
> And all you will eat
> Is my bit of bread.
>
> Of every four pieces
> You shall have three.
> Would that I knew
> How big they will be!

Get out of my way, I'll try it without the rope.

MERCHANT WOMAN   You are tempting God!

[*There are shouts from below.*]

GRUSHA   Please, throw that stick away, or they'll get the rope and follow me. [*Pressing the* CHILD *to her, she steps onto the swaying bridge. The* MERCHANT WOMAN *screams when it looks as though the bridge is about to collapse. But* GRUSHA *walks on and reaches the far side.*]

FIRST MAN   She made it!

MERCHANT WOMAN   [*who has fallen on her knees and begun to pray, angrily*] I still think it was a sin.

[*The* IRONSHIRTS *appear; the* CORPORAL'S *head is bandaged.*]

CORPORAL   Seen a woman with a child?

FIRST MAN   [*while the* SECOND MAN *throws the stick into the abyss*] Yes, there! But the bridge won't carry you!

CORPORAL   You'll pay for this, blockhead!

[GRUSHA, *from the far bank, laughs and shows the* CHILD *to the* IRONSHIRTS. *She walks on. The wind blows.*]

GRUSHA   [*turning to the* CHILD] You mustn't be afraid of the wind. He's a poor thing too. He has to push the clouds along and he gets quite cold doing it. [*Snow starts falling.*] And the snow isn't so bad, either, Michael. It covers the little fir trees so they won't die in winter. Let me sing you a little song. [*She sings.*]

THE SONG OF THE CHILD

> Your father is a bandit
> A harlot the mother who bore you.
> Yet honorable men
> Shall kneel down before you.
> Food to the baby horses
> The tiger's son will take.
> The mothers will get milk
> From the son of the snake.

3

IN THE NORTHERN MOUNTAINS

SINGER

Seven days the sister, Grusha Vashnadze,
Journeyed across the glacier
And down the slopes she journeyed.
"When I enter my brother's house," she thought,
"He will rise and embrace me."
"Is that you, sister?" he will say,
"I have long expected you.
This is my dear wife,
And this is my farm, come to me by marriage,
With eleven horses and thirty-one cows. Sit down.
Sit down with your child at our table and eat."
The brother's house was in a lovely valley.
When the sister came to the brother,
She was ill from walking.
The brother rose from the table.

[*A fat peasant couple rise from the table.* LAVRENTI VASHNADZE *still has a napkin round his neck, as* GRUSHA, *pale and supported by a* SERVANT, *enters with the* CHILD.]

LAVRENTI   Where've *you* come from, Grusha?

GRUSHA   [*feebly*]   Across the Janga-Tu Pass, Lavrenti.

SERVANT   I found her in front of the hay barn. She has a baby with her.

SISTER-IN-LAW   Go and groom the mare.

[*Exit the* SERVANT.]

LAVRENTI   This is my wife Aniko.

SISTER-IN-LAW   I thought you were in service in Nuka.

GRUSHA   [*barely able to stand*]   Yes, I was.

SISTER-IN-LAW   Wasn't it a good job? We were told it was.

GRUSHA   The Governor got killed.

LAVRENTI   Yes, we heard there were riots. Your aunt told us. Remember, Aniko?

SISTER-IN-LAW   Here with us, it's very quiet. City people always want something going on. [*She walks toward the door, calling:*] Sosso, Sosso, don't take the cake out of the oven yet, d'you hear? Where on earth are you? [*Exit, calling.*]

LAVRENTI   [*quietly, quickly*]   Is there a father? [*As she shakes her head*] I thought not. We must think up something. She's religious.

SISTER-IN-LAW   [*returning*]   Those servants! [*To* GRUSHA] You have a child.

GRUSHA   It's mine. [*She collapses.* LAVRENTI *rushes to her assistance.*]

SISTER-IN-LAW   Heavens, she's ill—what are we going to do?

LAVRENTI   [*escorting her to a bench near the stove*]   Sit down, sit. I think it's just weakness. Aniko.

SISTER-IN-LAW   As long as it's not scarlet fever!

LAVRENTI   She'd have spots if it was. It's only weakness. Don't worry, Aniko [*To* GRUSHA:] Better, sitting down?

SISTER-IN-LAW   Is the child hers?

GRUSHA   Yes, mine.

LAVRENTI   She's on her way to her husband.

SISTER-IN-LAW   I see. Your meat's getting cold. [LAVRENTI *sits down and begins to eat.*] Cold food's not good for you, the fat mustn't get cold, you know your stomach's your weak spot. [*To* GRUSHA] If your husband's not in the city, where is he?

LAVRENTI   She got married on the other side of the mountain, she says.

SISTER-IN-LAW   On the other side of the mountain. I see. [*She also sits down to eat.*]

GRUSHA   I think I should lie down somewhere, Lavrenti.

SISTER-IN-LAW   If it's consumption we'll all get it. [*She goes on cross-examining her.*] Has your husband got a farm?

GRUSHA   He's a soldier.

LAVRENTI   But he's coming into a farm—a small one—from his father.

SISTER-IN-LAW   Isn't he in the war? Why not?

GRUSHA   [*with effort*]   Yes, he's in the war.

SISTER-IN-LAW   Then why d'you want to go to the farm?

LAVRENTI   When he comes back from the war, he'll return to his farm.

SISTER-IN-LAW   But you're going there now?

LAVRENTI   Yes, to wait for him.

SISTER-IN-LAW   [*calling shrilly*]   Sosso, the cake!

GRUSHA   [*murmuring feverishly*]   A farm—a soldier—waiting—sit down, eat.

SISTER-IN-LAW   It's scarlet fever.

GRUSHA   [*starting up*]   Yes, he's got a farm!

LAVRENTI   I think it's just weakness, Aniko. Would you look after the cake yourself, dear?

SISTER-IN-LAW   But when will he come back if war's broken out again as people say? [*She waddles off, shouting:*] Sosso! Where on earth are you? Sosso!

LAVRENTI   [*getting up quickly and going to* GRUSHA]   You'll get a bed in a minute. She has a good heart. But wait till after supper.

GRUSHA   [*holding out the* CHILD *to him*]   Take him.

LAVRENTI   [*taking it and looking around*]   But you can't stay here long with the child. She's religious, you see.

GRUSHA *collapses.* LAVRENTI *catches her.*

SINGER
>   The sister was so ill,
>   The cowardly brother had to give her shelter.
>   Summer departed, winter came.
>   The winter was long, the winter was short.
>   People mustn't know anything.
>   Rats mustn't bite.
>   Spring mustn't come.
>   [GRUSHA *sits over the weaving loom in a workroom. She and the* CHILD, *who is squatting on the floor, are wrapped in blankets. She sings.*]
>   [*Enter* LAVRENTI. *He sit down beside his sister.*]

THE SONG OF THE CENTER

>   And the lover started to leave
>   And his betrothed ran pleading after him
>   Pleading and weeping, weeping and teaching:
>   "Dearest mine, dearest mine
>   When you go to war as now you do
>   When you fight the foe as soon you will
>   Don't lead with the front line
>   And don't push with the rear line
>   At the front is red fire
>   In the rear is red smoke
>   Stay in the war's center
>   Stay near the standard bearer

The first always die
The last are also hit
Those in the center come home."

Michael, we must be clever. If we make ourselves as small as cockroaches, the sister-in-law will forget we're in the house, and then we can stay till the snow melts.

[*Enter* LAVRENTI. *He sits down beside his sister.*]

LAVRENTI   Why are you sitting there muffled up like coachmen, you two? Is it too cold in the room?

GRUSHA   [*hastily removing one shawl*]   It's not too cold, Lavrenti.

LAVRENTI   If it's too cold, you shouldn't be sitting here with the child. Aniko would never forgive herself! [*Pause*] I hope our priest didn't question you about the child?

GRUSHA   He did, but I didn't tell him anything.

LAVRENTI   That's good. I wanted to speak to you about Aniko. She has a good heart but she's very, very sensitive. People need only mention our farm and she's worried. She takes everything hard, you see. One time our milk-maid went to church with a hole in her stocking. Ever since, Aniko has worn two pairs of stockings in church. It's the old family in her. [*He listens.*] Are you sure there are no rats around? If there are rats, you couldn't live here. [*There are sounds as of dripping from the roof.*] What's that, dripping?

GRUSHA   It must be a barrel leaking.

LAVRENTI   Yes, it must be a barrel. You've been here six months, haven't you? Was I talking about Aniko? [*They listen again to the snow melting.*] You can't imagine how worried she gets about your soldier-husband. "Suppose he comes back and can't find her!" she says and lies awake. "He can't come before the spring," I tell her. The dear woman! [*The drops begin to fall faster.*] When d'you think he'll come? What do *you* think? [GRUSHA *is silent.*] Not before the spring, you agree? [GRUSHA *is silent.*] You don't believe he'll come at all? [GRUSHA *is silent.*] But when the spring comes and the snow melts here and on the passes, you can't stay on. They may come and look for you. There's already talk of an illegitimate child. [*The "glockenspiel" of the falling drops has grown faster and steadier.*] Grusha, the snow is melting on the roof. Spring is here.

GRUSHA   Yes.

LAVRENTI   [*eagerly*]   I'll tell you what we'll do. You need a place to go, and, because of the child [*he sighs*], you have to have a husband, so people won't talk. Now I've made cautious inquiries to see if we can find you a husband. Grusha, I *have* one. I talked to a peasant woman who has a son. Just the other side of the mountain. A small farm. And she's willing.

GRUSHA   But I *can't* marry! I must wait for Simon Shashava.

LAVRENTI   Of course. That's all been taken care of. You don't need a man in bed—you need a man on paper. And I've found you one. The son of this peasant woman is going to die. Isn't that wonderful? He's at his last gasp. And all in line with our story—a husband from the other side of the mountain! And when you met him he was at the last gasp. So you're a widow. What do you say?

GRUSHA   It's true I could use a document with stamps on it for Michael.

LAVRENTI   Stamps make all the difference. Without something in writing the Shah couldn't prove he's a Shah. And you'll have a place to live.

GRUSHA   How much does the peasant woman want?

LAVRENTI   Four hundred piasters.

GRUSHA Where will you find it?

LAVRENTI [*guiltily*] Aniko's milk money.

GRUSHA No one would know us there. I'll do it.

LAVRENTI [*getting up*] I'll let the peasant woman know.
[*Quick exit.*]

GRUSHA Michael, you make a lot of work. I came by you as the pear tree comes by sparrows. And because a Christian bends down and picks up a crust of bread so nothing will go to waste. Michael, it would have been better had I walked quickly away on that Easter Sunday in Nuka in the second courtyard. Now I *am* a fool.

SINGER
The bridegroom was on his deathbed when the bride arrived.
The bridegroom's mother was waiting at the door, telling her to hurry.
The bride brought a child along.
The witness hid it during the wedding.
[*On one side the bed. Under the mosquito net lies a very sick man.* GRUSHA *is pulled in at a run by her future mother-in-law. They are followed by* LAVRENTI *and the* CHILD.]

MOTHER-IN-LAW Quick! Quick! Or he'll die on us before the wedding. [*To* LAVRENTI] I was never told she had a child already.

LAVRENTI What difference does it make? [*Pointing toward the dying man.*] It can't matter to him—in his condition.

MOTHER-IN-LAW To him? But I'll never survive the shame! We are honest people. [*She begins to weep.*] My Jussup doesn't have to marry a girl with a child!

LAVRENTI All right, make it another two hundred piasters. You'll have it in writing that the farm will go to you: but she'll have the right to live here for two years.

MOTHER-IN-LAW [*drying her tears*] It'll hardly cover the funeral expenses. I hope she'll really lend a hand with the work. And what's happened to the monk? He must have slipped out through the kitchen window. We'll have the whole village on our necks when they hear Jussup's end is come! Oh dear! I'll go get the monk. But he mustn't see the child!

LAVRENTI I'll take care he doesn't. But why only a monk? Why not a priest?

MOTHER-IN-LAW Oh, he's just as good. I only made one mistake: I paid half his fee in advance. Enough to send him to the tavern. I only hope . . .
[*She runs off.*]

LAVRENTI She saved on the priest, the wretch! Hired a cheap monk.

GRUSHA You *will* send Simon Shashava to see me if he turns up after all?

LAVRENTI Yes. [*Pointing at the* SICK PEASANT.] Won't you take a look at him? [GRUSHA, *taking* MICHAEL *to her, shakes her head.*] He's not moving an eyelid. I hope we aren't too late.
[*They listen. On the opposite side enter neighbors who look around and take up positions against the walls, thus forming another wall near the bed, yet leaving an opening so that the bed can be seen. They start murmuring prayers. Enter the* MOTHER-IN-LAW *with a* MONK. *Showing some annoyance and surprise, she bows to the guests.*]

MOTHER-IN-LAW I hope you won't mind waiting a few moments? My son's bride has just arrived from the city. An emergency wedding is about to be celebrated. [*To the* MONK *in the bedroom*] I might have known you couldn't keep your trap shut. [*To* GRUSHA] The wedding can take place at once. Here's the license. Me and the bride's brother [LAVRENTI *tries to hide in the background, after having quietly taken* MICHAEL *back from* GRUSHA. *The* MOTHER-IN-LAW *waves him away.*] are the witnesses.

[GRUSHA *has bowed to the* MONK. *They go to the bed. The* MOTHER-IN-LAW *lifts the mosquito net. The* MONK *starts reeling off the marriage ceremony in Latin. Meanwhile the* MOTHER-IN-LAW *beckons to* LAVRENTI *to get rid of the* CHILD, *but fearing that it will cry he draws its attention to the ceremony.* GRUSHA *glances once at the* CHILD, *and* LAVRENTI *waves the* CHILD's *hand in a greeting.*]

MONK   Are you prepared to be a faithful, obedient, and good wife to this man, and to cleave to him until death you do part?

GRUSHA   [*looking at the* CHILD]   I am.

MONK   [*to the* SICK PEASANT]   Are you prepared to be a good and loving husband to your wife until death you do part? [*As the* SICK PEASANT *does not answer, the* MONK *looks inquiringly around.*]

MOTHER-IN-LAW   Of course he is! Didn't you hear him say yes?

MONK   All right. We declare the marriage contracted! How about extreme unction?

MOTHER-IN-LAW   Nothing doing! The wedding cost quite enough. Now I must take care of the mourners. [*To* LAVRENTI] Did we say seven hundred?

LAVRENTI   Six hundred. [*He pays.*] Now I don't want to sit with the guests and get to know people. So farewell, Grusha, and if my widowed sister comes to visit me, she'll get a welcome from my wife, or I'll show my teeth. [*Nods, gives the* CHILD *to* GRUSHA, *and leaves. The mourners glance after him without interest.*]

MONK   May one ask where this child comes from?

MOTHER-IN-LAW   Is there a child? I don't see a child. And you don't see a child either—you understand? Or it may turn out I saw all sorts of things in the tavern! Now come on.
[*After* GRUSHA *has put the* CHILD *down and told him to be quiet, they move over left;* GRUSHA *is introduced to the neighbors.*]
This is my daughter-in-law. She arrived just in time to find dear Jussup still alive.

ONE WOMAN   He's been ill now a whole year, hasn't he? When our Vassili was drafted he was there to say good-bye.

ANOTHER WOMAN   Such things are terrible for a farm. The corn all ripe and the farmer in bed! It'll really be a blessing if he doesn't suffer too long, I say.

FIRST WOMAN   [*confidentially*]   You know why we thought he'd taken to his bed? Because of the draft! And now his end is come!

MOTHER-IN-LAW   Sit yourselves down, please! And have some cakes!
[*She beckons to* GRUSHA *and both women go into the bedroom, where they pick up the cake pans off the floor. The guests, among them the* MONK, *sit on the floor and begin conversing in subdued voices.*]

ONE PEASANT   [*to whom the* MONK *has handed the bottle which he has taken from his soutane*]   There's a child, you say! How can that have happened to Jussup?

A WOMAN   She was certainly lucky to get herself married, with him so sick!

MOTHER-IN-LAW   They're gossiping already. And wolfing down the funeral cakes at the same time! If he doesn't die today, I'll have to bake some more tomorrow!

GRUSHA   I'll bake them for you.

MOTHER-IN-LAW   Yesterday some horsemen rode by, and I went out to see who it was. When I came in again he was lying there like a corpse! So I sent for you. It can't take much longer. [*She listens.*]

MONK   Dear wedding and funeral guests! Deeply touched, we stand before a bed of death and marriage. The bride gets a veil; the groom, a shroud:

how varied, my children, are the fates of men! Alas! One man dies and has a roof over his head, and the other is married and the flesh turns to dust from which it was made. Amen.

MOTHER-IN-LAW   He's getting his own back. I shouldn't have hired such a cheap one. It's what you'd expect. A more expensive monk would behave himself. In Sura there's one with a real air of sanctity about him, but of course he charges a fortune. A fifty piaster monk like that has no dignity, and as for piety, just fifty piasters' worth and no more! When I came to get him in the tavern he'd just made a speech, and he was shouting: "The war is over, beware of the peace!" We must go in.

GRUSHA   [*giving* MICHAEL *a cake*]   Eat this cake, and keep nice and still, Michael.

[*The two women offer cakes to the guests. The dying man sits up in bed. He puts his head out from under the mosquito net, stares at the two women, then sinks back again. The* MONK *takes two bottles from his soutane and offers them to the peasant beside him. Enter three* MUSICIANS *who are greeted with a sly wink by the* MONK.]

MOTHER-IN-LAW   [*to the* MUSICIANS]   What are you doing here? With instruments?

ONE MUSICIAN   Brother Anastasius here [*pointing at the* MONK] told us there was a wedding on.

MOTHER-IN-LAW   What? You brought them? Three more on my neck! Don't you know there's a dying man in the next room?

MONK   A very tempting assignment for a musician: something that could be either a subdued Wedding March or a spirited Funeral Dance.

MOTHER-IN-LAW   Well, you might as well play. Nobody can stop you eating in any case.

[*The musicians play a potpourri. The women serve cakes.*]

MONK   The trumpet sounds like a whining baby. And you, little drum, what have you got to tell the world?

DRUNKEN PEASANT   [*beside the* MONK, *sings*]
There was a young woman who said:
I thought I'd be happier, wed.
But my husband is old
And remarkably cold
So I sleep with a candle instead.

[*The* MOTHER-IN-LAW *throws the* DRUNKEN PEASANT *out. The music stops. The guests are embarrassed.*]

GUESTS   [*loudly*]
—Have you heard? The Grand Duke is back! But the Princes are against him.
—They say the Shah of Persia has lent him a great army to restore order in Grusinia.
—But how is that possible? The Shah of Persia is the enemy . . .
—The enemy of Grusinia, you donkey, not the enemy of the Grand Duke!
—In any case, the war's over, so our soldiers are coming back.

[GRUSHA *drops a cake pan.* GUESTS *help her pick up the cake.*]

AN OLD WOMAN   [*to* GRUSHA]   Are you feeling bad? It's just excitement about dear Jussup. Sit down and rest a while, my dear. [GRUSHA *staggers.*]

GUESTS   Now everything'll be the way it was. Only the taxes'll go up because now we'll have to pay for the war.

GRUSHA   [*weakly*]   Did someone say the soldiers are back?

A MAN   I did.

GRUSHA   It can't be true.

FIRST MAN [*to a woman*] Show her the shawl. We bought it from a soldier. It's from Persia.

GRUSHA [*looking at the shawl*] They are here. [*She gets up, takes a step, kneels down in prayer, takes the silver cross and chain out of her blouse, and kisses it.*]

MOTHER-IN-LAW [*while the guests silently watch* GRUSHA] What's the matter with you? Aren't you going to look after our guests? What's all this city nonsense got to do with us?

GUESTS [*resuming conversation while* GRUSHA *remains in prayer*]
—You can buy Persian saddles from the soldiers too. Though many want crutches in exchange for them.
—The leaders on one side can win a war, the soldiers on both sides lose it.
—Anyway, the war's over. It's something they can't draft you any more.
[*The dying man sits bolt upright in bed. He listens.*]
—What we need is two weeks of good weather.
—our pear trees are hardly bearing a thing this year.

MOTHER-IN-LAW [*offering cakes*] Have some more cakes and welcome! There are more!
[*The* MOTHER-IN-LAW *goes to the bedroom with the empty cake pans. Unaware of the dying man, she is bending down to pick up another tray when he begins to talk in a hoarse voice.*]

PEASANT How many more cakes are you going to stuff down their throats? D'you think I can shit money?
[*The* MOTHER-IN-LAW *starts, stares at him aghast, while he climbs out from behind the mosquito net.*]

FIRST WOMAN [*talking kindly to* GRUSHA *in the next room*] Has the young wife got someone at the front?

A MAN It's good news that they're on their way home, huh?

PEASANT Don't stare at me like that! Where's this wife you've saddled me with?
[*Receiving no answer, he climbs out of bed and in his nightshirt staggers into the other room. Trembling, she follows him with the cake pan.*]

GUESTS [*seeing him and shrieking*] Good God! Jussup!
[*Everyone leaps up in alarm. The women rush to the door.* GRUSHA, *still on her knees, turns round and stares at the man.*]

PEASANT A funeral supper! You'd enjoy that, wouldn't you? Get out before I throw you out! [*As the guests stampede from the house, gloomily to* GRUSHA] I've upset the apple cart, huh? [*Receiving no answer, he turns round and takes a cake from the pan which his mother is holding.*]

SINGER
O confusion! The wife discovers she has a husband.
By day there's the child, by night there's the husband.
The lover is on his way both day and night.
Husband and wife look at each other.
The bedroom is small.
[*Near the bed the* PEASANT *is sitting in a high wooden bathtub, naked, the* MOTHER-IN-LAW *is pouring water from a pitcher. Opposite,* GRUSHA *cowers with* MICHAEL, *who is playing at mending straw mats.*]

PEASANT [*to his mother*] That's her work, not yours. Where's she hiding out now?

MOTHER-IN-LAW [*calling*] Grusha! The peasant wants you!

GRUSHA [*to* MICHAEL] There are still two holes to mend.

PEASANT [*when* GRUSHA *approaches*] Scrub my back!

GRUSHA Can't the peasant do it himself?

PEASANT "Can't the peasant do it himself?" Get the brush! To hell with you!

Are you the wife here? Or are you a visitor? [*To the* MOTHER-IN-LAW] It's too cold!

MOTHER-IN-LAW   I'll run for hot water.

GRUSHA   Let me go.

PEASANT   You stay here. [*The* MOTHER-IN-LAW *exits.*] Rub harder. And no shirking. You've seen a naked fellow before. That child didn't come out of thin air.

GRUSHA   The child was not conceived in joy, if that's what the peasant means.

PEASANT   [*turning and grinning*] You don't look the type. [GRUSHA *stops scrubbing him, starts back. Enter the* MOTHER-IN-LAW.]

PEASANT   A nice thing you've saddled me with! A simpleton for a wife!

MOTHER-IN-LAW   She just isn't cooperative.

PEASANT   Pour—but go easy! Ow! Go easy, I said. [*To* GRUSHA] Maybe you did something wrong in the city . . . I wouldn't be surprised. Why else should you be here? But I won't talk about that. I've not said a word about the illegitimate object you brought into my house either. But my patience has limits! It's against nature. [*To the* MOTHER-IN-LAW] More! [*To* GRUSHA] And even if your soldier does come back, you're married.

GRUSHA   Yes.

PEASANT   But your soldier won't come back. Don't you believe it.

GRUSHA   No.

PEASANT   You're cheating me. You're my wife and you're not my wife. Where you lie, nothing lies, and yet no other woman can lie there. When I go to work in the morning I'm tired—when I lie down at night I'm awake as the devil. God has given you sex—and what d'you do? I don't have ten piasters to buy myself a woman in the city. Besides, it's a long way. Woman weeds the fields and opens up her legs, that's what our calendar says. D'you hear?

GRUSHA   [*quietly*] Yes. I didn't mean to cheat you out of it.

PEASANT   She didn't mean to cheat me out of it! Pour some more water! [*The* MOTHER-IN-LAW *pours.*] Ow!

SINGER
    As she sat by the stream to wash the linen
    She saw his image in the water
    And his face grew dimmer with the passing moons.
    As she raised herself to wring the linen
    She heard his voice from the murmuring maple
    And his voice grew fainter with the passing moons.
    Evasions and sighs grew more numerous,
    Tears and sweat flowed.
    With the passing moons the child grew up.
    [GRUSHA *sits by a stream, dipping linen into the water. In the rear, a few children are standing.*]

GRUSHA   [*to* MICHAEL] You can play with them, Michael, but don't let them boss you around just because you're the littlest. [MICHAEL *nods and joins the children. They start playing.*]

BIGGEST BOY   Today it's the Heads-Off Game. [*To a* FAT BOY] You're the Prince and you laugh. [*To* MICHAEL] You're the Governor. [*To a* GIRL] You're the Governor's wife and you cry when his head's cut off. And I do the cutting. [*He shows his wooden sword.*] With this. First, they lead the Governor into the yard. The Prince walks in front. The Governor's wife comes last.

    [*They form a procession. The* FAT BOY *is first and laughs. Then comes* MICHAEL, *then the* BIGGEST BOY, *and then the* GIRL, *who weeps.*]

MICHAEL   [*standing still*] Me cut off head!

BIGGEST BOY   That's my job. You're the littlest. The Governor's the easy part. All you do is kneel down and get your head cut off—simple.

MICHAEL   Me want sword!

BIGGEST BOY   It's mine! [*He gives* MICHAEL *a kick.*]

GIRL   [*shouting to* GRUSHA]   He won't play his part!

GRUSHA   [*laughing*]   Even the little duck is a swimmer, they say.

BIGGEST BOY   You can be the Prince if you can laugh. [MICHAEL *shakes his head.*]

FAT BOY   I laugh best. Let him cut off the head just once. Then you do it, then me.

[*Reluctantly, the* BIGGEST BOY *hands* MICHAEL *the wooden sword and kneels down. The* FAT BOY *sits down, slaps his thigh, and laughs with all his might. The* GIRL *weeps loudly.* MICHAEL *swings the big sword and "cuts off" the head. In doing so, he topples over.*]

BIGGEST BOY   Hey! I'll show you how to cut heads off!

[MICHAEL *runs away. The children run after him.* GRUSHA *laughs, following them with her eyes. On looking back, she sees* SIMON SHASHAVA *standing on the opposite bank. He wears a shabby uniform.*]

GRUSHA   Simon!

SIMON   Is that Grusha Vashnadze?

GRUSHA   Simon!

SIMON   [*formally*]   A good morning to the young lady. I hope she is well.

GRUSHA   [*getting up gaily and bowing low*]   A good morning to the soldier. God be thanked he has returned in good health.

SIMON   They found better fish, so they didn't eat me, said the haddock.

GRUSHA   Courage, said the kitchen boy. Good luck, said the hero.

SIMON   How are things here? Was the winter bearable? The neighbor considerate?

GRUSHA   The winter was a trifle rough, the neighbor as usual, Simon.

SIMON   May one ask if a certain person still dips her toes in the water when rinsing the linen?

GRUSHA   The answer is no. Because of the eyes in the bushes.

SIMON   The young lady is speaking of soldiers. Here stands a paymaster.

GRUSHA   A job worth twenty piasters?

SIMON   And lodgings.

GRUSHA   [*with tears in her eyes*]   Behind the barracks under the date trees.

SIMON   Yes, there. A certain person has kept her eyes open.

GRUSHA   She has, Simon.

SIMON   And has not forgotten? [GRUSHA *shakes her head.*] So the door is still on its hinges as they say? [GRUSHA *looks at him in silence and shakes her head again.*] What's this? Is anything not as it should be?

GRUSHA   Simon Shashava, I can never return to Nuka. Something has happened.

SIMON   What can have happened?

GRUSHA   For one thing, I knocked an Ironshirt down.

SIMON   Grusha Vashnadze must have had her reasons for that.

GRUSHA   Simon Shashava, I am no longer called what I used to be called.

SIMON   [*after a pause*]   I do not understand.

GRUSHA   When do women change their names, Simon? Let me explain. Nothing stands between us. Everything is just as it was. You must believe that.

SIMON   Nothing stands between us and yet there's something?

GRUSHA   How can I explain it so fast and with the stream between us? Couldn't you cross the bridge there?

SIMON   Maybe it's no longer necessary.

GRUSHA   It is very necessary. Come over on this side, Simon, Quick!

SIMON   Does the young lady wish to say someone has come too late?

[GRUSHA *looks up at him in despair, her face streaming with tears.* SIMON *stares before him. He picks up a piece of wood and starts cutting it.*]

SINGER

So many words are said, so many left unsaid.

The soldier has come.

Where he comes from, he does not say.

Hear what he thought and did not say:

"The battle began, gray at dawn, grew bloody at noon.

The first man fell in front of me, the second behind me, the third at my side.

I trod on the first, left the second behind, the third was run through by the captain.

One of my brothers died by steel, the other by smoke.

My neck caught fire, my hands froze in my gloves, my toes in my socks.

I fed on aspen buds, I drank maple juice, I slept on stone, in water."

SIMON   I see a cap in the grass. Is there a little one already?

GRUSHA   There is, Simon. There's no keeping *that* from you. But please don't worry, it is not mine.

SIMON   When the wind once starts to blow, they say, it blows through every cranny. The wife need say no more. [GRUSHA *looks into her lap and is silent.*]

SINGER

There was yearning but there was no waiting.

The oath is broken. Neither could say why.

Hear what she thought but did not say:

"While you fought in the battle, soldier,

The bloody battle, the bitter battle

I found a helpless infant

I had not the heart to destroy him

I had to care for a creature that was lost

I had to stoop for breadcrumbs on the floor

I had to break myself for that which was not mine

That which was other people's.

Someone must help!

For the little tree needs water

The lamb loses its way when the shepherd is asleep

And its cry is unheard!"

SIMON   Give me back the cross I gave you. Better still, throw it in the stream. [*He turns to go.*]

GRUSHA   [*getting up*] Simon Shashava, don't go away! He isn't mine! He isn't mine! [*She hears the children calling.*] What's the matter, children?

VOICES   Soldiers! And they're taking Michael away!

[GRUSHA *stands aghast as two* IRONSHIRTS, *with* MICHAEL *between them, come toward her.*]

ONE OF THE IRONSHIRTS   Are you Grusha? [*She nods.*] Is this your child?

GRUSHA   Yes. [SIMON *goes.*] Simon!

IRONSHIRT   We have orders, in the name of the law, to take this child, found in your custody, back to the city. It is suspected that the child is Michael Abashwili, son and heir of the late Governor Georgi Abashwili, and his wife, Natella Abashwili. Here is the document and the seal. [*They lead the* CHILD *away.*]

GRUSHA   [*running after them, shouting*] Leave him here. Please! He's mine!

SINGER
>The Ironshirts took the child, the beloved child.
>The unhappy girl followed them to the city, the dreaded city.
>She who had borne him demanded the child.
>She who had raised him faced trial.
>Who will decide the case?
>To whom will the child be assigned?
>Who will the judge be? A good judge? A bad?
>The city was in flames.
>In the judge's seat sat Azdak.[1]

4
THE STORY OF THE JUDGE

SINGER
>Hear the story of the judge
>How he turned judge, how he passed judgment, what kind of judge he was.
>On that Easter Sunday of the great revolt, when the Grand Duke was over-
>   thrown
>And his Governor Abashwili, father of our child, lost his head
>The Village Scrivener Azdak found a fugitive in the
>   woods and hid him in his hut.

[AZDAK, *in rags and slightly drunk, is helping an old beggar into his cottage.*]

AZDAK Stop snorting, you're not a horse. And it won't do you any good with the police to run like a snotty nose in April. Stand still, I say. [*He catches the* OLD MAN, *who has marched into the cottage as if he'd like to go through the walls.*] Sit down. Feed. Here's a hunk of cheese. [*From under some rags, in a chest, he fishes out some cheese, and the* OLD MAN *greedily begins to eat.*] Haven't eaten in a long time, huh? [*The* OLD MAN *growls.*] Why were you running like that, asshole? The cop wouldn't even have seen you.

OLD MAN Had to! Had to!

AZDAK Blue funk? [*The* OLD MAN *stares, uncomprehending.*] Cold feet? Panic? Don't lick your chops like a Grand Duke. Or an old sow. I can't stand it. We have to accept respectable stinkers as God made them, but not you! I once heard of a senior judge who farted at a public dinner to show an independent spirit! Watching you eat like that gives me the most awful ideas. Why don't you say something? [*Sharply.*] Show me your hand. Can't you hear? [*The* OLD MAN *slowly puts out his hand.*] White! So you're not a beggar at all! A fraud, a walking swindle! And I'm hiding you from the cops like you were an honest man! Why were you running like that if you're a landowner? For that's what you are. Don't deny it! I see it in your guilty face! [*He gets up.*] Get out! [*The* OLD MAN *looks at him uncertainly.*] What are you waiting for, peasant-flogger?

OLD MAN Pursued. Need undivided attention. Make proposition . . .

AZDAK Make what? A proposition? Well, if that isn't the height of insolence. He's making me a proposition! The bitten man scratches his fingers bloody, and the leech that's biting him makes him a proposition! Get out, I tell you!

---

[1] The name Azdak should be accented on the second syllable.—E. B.

OLD MAN Understand point of view! Persuasion! Pay hundred thousand piasters one night! Yes?

AZDAK What, you think you can buy me? For a hundred thousand piasters? Let's say a hundred and fifty thousand. Where are they?

OLD MAN Have not them here. Of course. Will be sent. Hope do not doubt.

AZDAK Doubt very much. Get out!

[*The* OLD MAN *gets up, waddles to the door. A* VOICE *is heard offstage.*]

VOICE Azdak!

[*The* OLD MAN *turns, waddles to the opposite corner, stands still.*]

AZDAK [*calling out*] I'm not in! [*He walks to door.*] So *you're* sniffing around here again, Shauwa?

SHAUWA [*reproachfully*] You caught another rabbit, Azdak. And you'd promised me it wouldn't happen again!

AZDAK [*severely*] Shauwa, don't talk about things you don't understand. The rabbit is a dangerous and destructive beast. It feeds on plants, especially on the species of plants known as weeds. It must therefore be exterminated.

SHAUWA Azdak, don't be so hard on me. I'll lose my job if I don't arrest you. I know you have a good heart.

AZDAK I do not have a good heart! How often must I tell you I'm a man of intellect?

SHAUWA [*slyly*] I know, Azdak. You're a superior person. You say so yourself. I'm just a Christian and an ignoramus. So I ask you: When one of the Prince's rabbits is stolen, and I'm a policeman, what should I do with the offending party?

AZDAK Shauwa, Shauwa, shame on you. You stand and ask me a question, than which nothing could be more seductive. It's like you were a woman—let's say that bad girl Nunowna, and you showed me your thigh—Nunowna's thigh, that would be—and asked me: "What shall I do with my thigh, it itches?" Is she as innocent as she pretends? Of course not. I catch a rabbit, but you catch a man. Man is made in God's image. Not so a rabbit, you know that. I'm a rabbit-eater, but you're a man-eater, Shauwa. And God will pass judgment on you. Shauwa, go home and repent. No, stop, there's something . . . [*He looks at the* OLD MAN *who stands trembling in the corner.*] No, it's nothing. Go home and repent. [*He slams the door behind* SHAUWA.] Now you're surprised, huh? Surprised I didn't hand you over? I couldn't hand over a bedbug to that animal. It goes against the grain. Now don't tremble because of a cop! So old and still so scared? Finish your cheese, but eat it like a poor man, or else they'll still catch you. Must I even explain how a poor man behaves? [*He pushes him down, and then gives him back the cheese.*] That box is the table. Lay your elbows on the table. Now, encircle the cheese on the plate like it might be snatched from you at any moment— what right have you to be safe, huh?—now, hold your knife like an under- sized sickle, and give your cheese a troubled look because, like all beautiful things, it's already fading away. [AZDAK *watches him.*] They're after you, which speaks in your favor, but how can we be sure they're not mistaken about you? In Tiflis one time they hanged a landowner, a Turk, who could prove he quartered his peasants instead of merely cutting them in half, as is the custom, and he squeezed twice the usual amount of taxes out of them, his zeal was above suspicion. And yet they hanged him like a common criminal—because he was a Turk—a thing he couldn't do much about. What injustice! He got onto the gallows by a sheer fluke. In short, I don't trust you.

SINGER
Thus Azdak gave the old beggar a bed,

And learned that old beggar was the old butcher, the Grand Duke himself,
And was ashamed.
He denounced himself and ordered the policeman to
    take him to Nuka, to court, to be judged.

[*In the court of justice three* IRONSHIRTS *sit drinking. From a beam hangs a man in judge's robes. Enter* AZDAK, *in chains, dragging* SHAUWA *behind him.*]

AZDAK [*shouting*] I've helped the Grand Duke, the Grand Thief, the Grand Butcher, to escape! In the name of justice I ask to be severely judged in public trial!

FIRST IRONSHIRT Who's this queer bird?

SHAUWA That's our Village Scrivener, Azdak.

AZDAK I am contemptible! I am a traitor! A branded criminal! Tell them, flatfoot, how I insisted on being tied up and brought to the capital. Because I sheltered the Grand Duke, the Grand Swindler, by mistake. And how I found out afterwards. See the marked man denounce himself! Tell them how I forced you to walk half the night with me to clear the whole thing up.

SHAUWA And all by threats. That wasn't nice of you, Azdak.

AZDAK Shut your mouth, Shauwa. You don't understand. A new age is upon us! It'll go thundering over you. You're finished. The police will be wiped out—poof! Everything will be gone into, everything will be brought into the open. The guilty will give themselves up. Why? They couldn't escape the people in any case. [*To* SHAUWA:] Tell them how I shouted all along Shoemaker Street [*with big gestures, looking at the* IRONSHIRTS] "In my ignorance I let the Grand Swindler escape! So tear me to pieces, brothers!" I wanted to get it in first.

FIRST IRONSHIRT And what did your brothers answer?

SHAUWA They comforted him in Butcher Street, and they laughed themselves sick in Shoemaker Street. That's all.

AZDAK But with you it's different. I can see you're men of iron. Brothers, where's the judge? I must be tried.

FIRST IRONSHIRT [*pointing at the hanged man*] There's the judge. And please stop "brothering" us. It's rather a sore spot this evening.

AZDAK "There's the judge." An answer never heard in Grusinia before. Townsman, where's His Excellency the Governor? [*Pointing to the ground.*] There's His Excellency, stranger. Where's the Chief Tax Collector? Where's the official Recruiting Officer? The Patriarch? The Chief of Police? There, there, there—all there. Brothers, I expected no less of you.

SECOND IRONSHIRT What? *What* was it you expected, funny man?

AZDAK What happened in Persia, brother, what happened in Persia?

SECOND IRONSHIRT What did happen in Persia?

AZDAK Everybody was hanged. Viziers, tax collectors. Everybody. Forty years ago now. My grandfather, a remarkable man by the way, saw it all. For three whole days. Everywhere.

SECOND IRONSHIRT And who ruled when the Vizier was hanged?

AZDAK A peasant ruled when the Vizier was hanged.

SECOND IRONSHIRT And who commanded the army?

AZDAK A soldier, a soldier.

SECOND IRONSHIRT And who paid the wages?

AZDAK A dyer. A dyer paid the wages.

SECOND IRONSHIRT Wasn't it a weaver, maybe?

FIRST IRONSHIRT And why did all this happen, Persian?

AZDAK Why did all this happen? Must there be a special reason? Why do you scratch yourself, brother? War! Too long a war! And no justice! My grandfather brought back a song that tells how it was. I will sing it for you. With my friend the policeman. [*To* SHAUWA] And hold the rope tight. It's very suitable. [*He sings, with* SHAUWA *holding the rope tight around him.*]

THE SONG OF INJUSTICE IN PERSIA

Why don't our sons bleed any more? Why don't our
   daughters weep?
Why do only the slaughterhouse cattle have blood in
   their veins?
Why do only the willows shed tears on Lake Urmia?
The king must have a new province, the peasant must
   give up his savings.
That the roof of the world might be conquered, the
   roof of the cottage is torn down.
Our men are carried to the ends of the earth, so that
   great ones can eat at home.
The soldiers kill each other, the marshals salute each
   other.
They bite the widow's tax money to see if it's good,
   their swords break.
The battle was lost, the helmets were paid for.
Refrain: Is it so? Is it so?

SHAUWA [*refrain*] Yes, yes, yes, yes, yes it's so.
AZDAK Want to hear the rest of it? [*The* FIRST IRONSHIRT *nods.*]
SECOND IRONSHIRT [*to* SHAUWA] Did he teach you that song?
SHAUWA Yes, only my voice isn't very good.
SECOND IRONSHIRT No. [*To* AZDAK] Go on singing.
AZDAK The second verse is about the peace. [*He sings.*]

The offices are packed, the streets overflow with
   officials.
The rivers jump their banks and ravage the fields.
Those who cannot let down their own trousers rule
   countries.
They can't count up to four, but they devour eight
   courses.
The corn farmers, looking round for buyers, see only
   the starving.
The weavers go home from their looms in rags.
Refrain: Is it so? Is it so?

SHAUWA [*refrain*] Yes, yes, yes, yes, yes it's so.
AZDAK

That's why our sons don't bleed any more, that's why
   our daughters don't weep.
That's why only the slaughterhouse cattle have blood
   in their veins,
And only the willows shed tears by Lake Urmia
   toward morning.

FIRST IRONSHIRT Are you going to sing that song here in town?
AZDAK Sure. What's wrong with it?
FIRST IRONSHIRT Have you noticed that the sky's getting red? [*Turning round,* AZDAK *sees the sky red with fire.*] It's the people's quarters on the outskirts of town. The carpet weavers have caught the "Persian Sickness," too. And

they've been asking if Prince Kazbeki isn't eating too many courses. This morning they strung up the city judge. As for us we beat them to pulp. We were paid one hundred piasters per man, you understand?

AZDAK [*after a pause*] I understand. [*He glances shyly round and, creeping away, sits down in a corner, his head in his hands.*]

IRONSHIRTS [*to each other*] If there ever was a troublemaker it's him.

—He must've come to the capital to fish in the troubled waters.

SHAUWA Oh, I don't think he's a really bad character, gentlemen. Steals a few chickens here and there. And maybe a rabbit.

SECOND IRONSHIRT [*approaching* AZDAK] Came to fish in the troubled waters, huh?

AZDAK [*looking up*] I don't know why I came.

SECOND IRONSHIRT Are you in with the carpet weavers maybe? [AZDAK *shakes his head.*] How about that song?

AZDAK From my grandfather. A silly and ignorant man.

SECOND IRONSHIRT Right. And how about the dyer who paid the wages?

AZDAK [*muttering*] That was in Persia.

FIRST IRONSHIRT And this denouncing of yourself? Because your didn't hang the Grand Duke with your own hands?

AZDAK Didn't I tell you I let him run? [*He creeps farther away and sits on the floor.*]

SHAUWA I can swear to that: he let him run.

[*The* IRONSHIRTS *burst out laughing and slap* SHAUWA *on the back.* AZDAK *laughs loudest. They slap* AZDAK *too, and unchain him. They all start drinking as the* FAT PRINCE *enters with a young man.*]

FIRST IRONSHIRT [*to* AZDAK, *pointing at the* FAT PRINCE] There's your "new age" for you! [*More laughter.*]

FAT PRINCE Well, my friends, what is there to laugh about? Permit me a serious word. Yesterday morning the Princes of Grusinia overthrew the warmongering government of the Grand Duke and did away with his Governors. Unfortunately the Grand Duke himself escaped. In this fateful hour our carpet weavers, those eternal troublemakers, had the effrontery to stir up a rebellion and hang the universally loved city judge, our dear Illo Orbeliani. Ts—ts—ts. My friends, we need peace, peace, peace in Grusinia! And justice! So I've brought along my dear nephew Bizergan Kazbeki. He'll be the new judge, hm? A very gifted fellow. What do you say? I want your opinion. Let the people decide!

SECOND IRONSHIRT Does this mean *we* elect the judge?

FAT PRINCE Precisely. Let the people propose some very gifted fellow! Confer among yourselves, my friends. [*The* IRONSHIRTS *confer.*] Don't worry, my little fox. The job's yours. And when we catch the Grand Duke we won't have to kiss this rabble's ass any longer.

IRONSHIRTS [*among themselves*]

—Very funny: they're wetting their pants because they haven't caught the Grand Duke.

When the outlook isn't so bright, they say: "My friends!" and "Let the people decide!"

—Now he even wants justice for Grusinia! But fun is fun as long as it lasts! [*Pointing at* AZDAK.] *He* knows all about justice. Hey, rascal, would you like this nephew fellow to be the judge?

AZDAK Are you asking me? You're not asking *me*?!

FIRST IRONSHIRT Why not? Anything for a laugh!

AZDAK You'd like to test him to the marrow, correct? Have you a criminal on hand? An experienced one? So the candidate can show what he knows?

SECOND IRONSHIRT   Let's see. We do have a couple of doctors downstairs. Let's use them.

AZDAK   Oh, no, that's no good, we can't take real criminals till we're sure the judge will be appointed. He may be dumb, but he must be appointed, or the law is violated. And the law is a sensitive organ. It's like the spleen, you mustn't hit it—that would be fatal. Of course you can hang those two without violating the law, because there was no judge in the vicinity. But judgment, when pronounced, must be pronounced with absolute gravity— it's all such nonsense. Suppose, for instance, a judge jails a woman—let's say she's stolen a corn cake to feed her child—and this judge isn't wearing his robes—or maybe he's scratching himself while passing sentence and half his body is uncovered—a man's thigh *will* itch once in a while—the sentence this judge passes is a disgrace and the law is violated. In short it would be easier for a judge's robe and a judge's hat to pass judgment than for a man with no robe and no hat. If you don't treat it with respect, the law just disappears on you. Now you don't try out a bottle of wine by offering it to a dog; you'd only lose your wine.

FIRST IRONSHIRT   Then what do you suggest, hairsplitter?

AZDAK   I'll be the defendant.

FIRST IRONSHIRT   You? [*He bursts out laughing.*]

FAT PRINCE   What have you decided?

FIRST IRONSHIRT   We've decided to stage a rehearsal. Our friend here will be the defendant. Let the candidate be the judge and sit there.

FAT PRINCE   It isn't customary, but why not? [*To the* NEPHEW] A mere formality, my little fox. What have I taught you? Who got there first—the slow runner or the fast?

NEPHEW   The silent runner, Uncle Arsen.

[*The* NEPHEW *takes the chair. The* IRONSHIRTS *and the* FAT PRINCE *sit on the steps. Enter* AZDAK, *mimicking the gait of the Grand Duke.*]

AZDAK   [*in the Grand Duke's accent*]   Is any here knows me? Am Grand Duke.

IRONSHIRTS
—*What* is he?
—The Grand Duke. He knows him, too.
—Fine. So get on with the trial.

AZDAK   Listen! Am accused instigating war? Ridiculous! Am saying ridiculous! That enough? If not, have brought lawyers. Believe five hundred. [*He points behind him, pretending to be surrounded by lawyers.*] Requisition all available seats for lawyers! [*The* IRONSHIRTS *laugh; the* FAT PRINCE *joins in.*]

NEPHEW   [*to the* IRONSHIRTS]   You really wish me to try this case? I find it rather unusual. From the taste angle, I mean.

FIRST IRONSHIRT   Let's go!

FAT PRINCE   [*smiling*]   Let him have it, my little fox!

NEPHEW   All right. People of Grusinia versus Grand Duke. Defendant, what have you got to say for yourself?

AZDAK   Plenty. Naturally, have read war lost. Only started on the advice of patriots. Like Uncle Arsen Kazbeki. Call Uncle Arsen as witness.

FAT PRINCE   [*to the* IRONSHIRTS, *delightedly*]   What a madcap!

NEPHEW   Motion rejected. One cannot be arraigned for declaring a war, which every ruler has to do once in a while, but only for running a war badly.

AZDAK   Rubbish! Did not run it at all! Had it run! Had it run by Princes! Naturally, they messed it up.

NEPHEW   Do you by any chance deny having been commander-in-chief?

AZDAK   Not at all! Always *was* commander-in-chief. At birth shouted at wet nurse. Was trained drop turds in toilet, grew accustomed to command. Always commanded officials rob my cash box. Officers flog soldiers only on command. Landowners sleep with peasants' wives only on strictest command. Uncle Arsen here grew his belly at *my* command!

IRONSHIRTS [*clapping*] He's good! Long live the Grand Duke!

FAT PRINCE Answer him, my little fox: I'm with you.

NEPHEW I shall answer him according to the dignity of the law. Defendant, preserve the dignity of the law!

AZDAK Agreed. Command you proceed with trial!

NEPHEW It is not your place to command me. You claim that the Princes forced you to declare war. How can you claim, then, that they—er— "messed it up"?

AZDAK Did not send enough people. Embezzled funds. Sent sick horses. During attack, drinking in whorehouse. Call Uncle Arsen as witness.

NEPHEW Are you making the outrageous suggestion that the Princes of this country did not fight?

AZDAK No. Princes fought. Fought for war contracts.

FAT PRINCE [*jumping up*] That's too much! This man talks like a carpet weaver!

AZDAK Really? Told nothing but truth.

FAT PRINCE Hang him! Hang him!

FIRST IRONSHIRT [*pulling the PRINCE down*] Keep quiet! Go on, Excellency!

NEPHEW Quiet! I now render a verdict: You must be hanged! By the neck! Having lost war!

AZDAK Young man, seriously advise not fall publicly into jerky clipped speech. Cannot be watchdog if howl like wolf. Got it? If people realize Princes speak same language as Grand Duke, may hang Grand Duke *and Princes,* huh? By the way, must overrule verdict. Reason? War lost, but not for Princes. Princes won their war. Got 3,863,000 piasters for horses not delivered, 8,240,000 piasters for food supplies not produced. Are therefore victors. War lost only for Grusinia, which is not present in this court.

FAT PRINCE I think that will do, my friends. [*To* AZDAK] You can withdraw, funny man. [*To the* IRONSHIRTS] You may now ratify the new judge's appointment, my friends.

FIRST IRONSHIRT Yes, we can. Take down the judge's gown. [*One* IRONSHIRT *climbs on the back of the other, pulls the gown off the hanged man.*] [*To the* NEPHEW] Now you run away so the right ass can get on the right chair. [*To* AZDAK] Step forward! Go to the judge's seat! Now sit in it! [AZDAK *steps up, bows, and sits down.*] The judge was always a rascal! Now the rascal shall be a judge! [*The judge's gown is placed round his shoulders, the hat on his head.*] And what a judge!

SINGER
And there was civil war in the land.
The mighty were not safe.
And Azdak was made a judge by the Ironshirts.
And Azdak remained a judge for two years.

SINGER AND CHORUS
When the towns were set afire
And rivers of blood rose higher and higher,
Cockroaches crawled out of every crack.
And the court was full of schemers
And the church of foul blasphemers.
In the judge's cassock sat Azdak.

[AZDAK *sits in the judge's chair, peeling an apple.* SHAUWA *is sweeping out the hall. On one side an* INVALID *in a wheelchair. Opposite, a young man accused of blackmail. An* IRONSHIRT *stands guard, holding the Ironshirts' banner.*]

AZDAK   In consideration of the large number of cases, the Court today will hear two cases at a time. Before I open the proceedings, a short announcement—I accept. [*He stretches out his hand. The* BLACKMAILER *is the only one to produce any money. He hands it to* AZDAK.] I reserve the right to punish one of the parties for contempt of court. [*He glances at the* INVALID.] You [*to the* DOCTOR] are a doctor, and you [*to the* INVALID] are bringing a complaint against him. Is the doctor responsible for your condition?

INVALID   Yes. I had a stroke on his account.

AZDAK   That would be professional negligence.

INVALID   Worse than negligence. I gave this man money for his studies. So far, he hasn't paid me back a cent. It was when I heard he was treating a patient free that I had my stroke.

AZDAK   Rightly. [*To a* LIMPING MAN] And what are *you* doing here?

LIMPING MAN   I'm the patient, Your Honor.

AZDAK   He treated your leg for nothing?

LIMPING MAN   The wrong leg! My rheumatism was in the left leg, he operated on the right. That's why I limp.

AZDAK   And you were treated free?

INVALID   A five-hundred-piaster operation free! For nothing! For a God-bless-you! And I paid for this man's studies! [*To the* DOCTOR] Did they teach you to operate free?

DOCTOR   Your Honor, it is the custom to demand the fee before the operation, as the patient is more willing to pay before an operation than after. Which is only human. In the case in question I was convinced, when I started the operation, that my servant had already received the fee. In this I was mistaken.

INVALID   He was mistaken! A good doctor doesn't make mistakes! He examines before he operates!

AZDAK   That's right: [*To* SHAUWA] Public Prosecutor, what's the other case about?

SHAUWA   [*busily sweeping*]   Blackmail.

BLACKMAILER   High Court of Justice, I'm innocent. I only wanted to find out from the landowner concerned if he really *had* raped his niece. He informed me very politely that this was not the case, and gave me the money only so I could pay for my uncle's studies.

AZDAK   Hm. [*To the* DOCTOR] You, on the other hand, can cite no extenuating circumstances for your offense, huh?

DOCTOR   Except that to err is human.

AZDAK   And you are aware that in money matters a good doctor is a highly responsible person? I once heard of a doctor who got a thousand piasters for a sprained finger by remarking that sprains have something to do with blood circulation, which after all a less good doctor might have overlooked, and who, on another occasion made a real gold mine out of a somewhat disordered gall bladder. He treated it with such loving care. You have no excuse, Doctor. The corn merchant Uxu had his son study medicine to get some knowledge of trade, our medical schools are so good. [*To the* BLACKMAILER] What's the landowner's name?

SHAUWA   He doesn't want it mentioned.

AZDAK   In that case I will pass judgment. The Court considers the blackmail proved. And you [*to the* INVALID] are sentenced to a fine of one thousand piasters. If you have a second stroke, the doctor will have to treat you free. Even if he has to amputate. [*To the* LIMPING MAN] As compensation, you will receive a bottle of rubbing alcohol. [*To the* BLACKMAILER] You are sentenced to hand over half the proceeds of your deal to the Public Prosecutor to keep the landowner's name secret. You are advised, moreover, to study medicine—you seem well suited to that calling. [*To the* DOCTOR] You have perpetrated an unpardonable error in the practice of your profession: you are acquitted. Next cases!

SINGER AND CHORUS
Men won't do much for a shilling.
For a pound they may be willing.
For twenty pounds the verdict's in the sack.
As for the many, all too many,
Those who've only got a penny—
They've one single, sole recourse: Azdak.

[*Enter* AZDAK *from the caravansary on the highroad, followed by an old bearded* INNKEEPER. *The judge's chair is carried by a* STABLEMAN *and* SHAUWA. *An* IRONSHIRT, *with a banner, takes up his position.*]

AZDAK   Put me down. Then we'll get some air, maybe even a good stiff breeze from the lemon grove there. It does justice good to be done in the open: the wind blows her skirts up and you can see what she's got. Shauwa, we've been eating too much. These official journeys are exhausting. [*To the* INNKEEPER] It's a question of your daughter-in-law?

INNKEEPER   Your Worship, it's a question of the family honor. I wish to bring an action on behalf of my son, who's away on business on the other side the mountain. This is the offending stableman, and here's my daughter-in-law.

[*Enter the* DAUGHTER-IN-LAW, *a voluptuous wench. She is veiled.*]

AZDAK   [*sitting down*]   I accept. [*Sighing, the* INNKEEPER *hands him some money.*] Good. Now the formalities are disposed of. This is a case of rape?

INNKEEPER   Your Honor, I caught the fellow in the act. Ludovica was in the straw on the stable floor.

AZDAK   Quite right, the stable. Lovely horses! I specially liked the little roan.

INNKEEPER   The first thing I did, of course, was to question Ludovica. On my son's behalf.

AZDAK   [*seriously*]   I said I specially liked the little roan.

INNKEEPER   [*coldly*]   Really? Ludovica confessed the stableman took her against her will.

AZDAK   Take your veil off, Ludovica. [*She does so.*] Ludovica, you please the Court. Tell us how it happened.

LUDOVICA   [*well schooled*]   When I entered the stable to see the new foal the stableman said to me on his own accord: "It's hot today!" and laid his hand on my left breast. I said to him: "Don't do that!" But he continued to handle me indecently, which provoked my anger. Before I realized his sinful intentions, he got much closer. It was all over when my father-in-law entered and accidentally trod on me.

INNKEEPER   [*explaining*]   On my son's behalf.

AZDAK   [*to the* STABLEMAN]   You admit you started it?

STABLEMAN   Yes.

AZDAK   Ludovica, you like to eat sweet things?

LUDOVICA   Yes, sunflower seeds!

AZDAK   You like to lie a long time in the bathtub?

LUDOVICA   Half an hour or so.

AZDAK   Public Prosecutor, drop your knife—there on the ground. [SHAUWA *does so.*] Ludovica, pick up that knife. [LUDOVICA, *swaying her hips, does so.*] See that? [*He points at her.*] The way it moves? The rape is now proven. By eating too much—sweet things, especially—by lying too long in warm water, by laziness and too soft a skin, you have raped that unfortunate man. Think you can run around with a behind like that and get away with it in court? This is a case of intentional assault with a dangerous weapon! You are sentenced to hand over to the Court the little roan which your father liked to ride "on his son's behalf." And now, come with me to the stables, so the Court can inspect the scene of the crime, Ludovica.

SINGER AND CHORUS
> When the sharks the sharks devour
> Little fishes have their hour.
> For a while the load is off their back.
> On Grusinia's highways faring
> Fixed-up scales of justice bearing
> Strode the poor man's magistrate: Azdak.
>
> And he gave to the forsaken
> All that from the rich he'd taken.
> And a bodyguard of roughnecks was Azdak's.
> And our good and evil man, he
> Smiled upon Grusinia's Granny.
> His emblem was a tear in sealing wax.
>
> All mankind should love each other
> But when visiting your brother
> Take an ax along and hold it fast.
> Not in theory but in practice
> Miracles are wrought with axes
> And the age of miracles is not past.

[AZDAK'S *judge's chair is in a tavern. Three rich* FARMERS *stand before* AZDAK. SHAUWA *brings him wine. In a corner stands an* OLD PEASANT WOMAN. *In the open doorway, and outside, stand villagers looking on. An* IRONSHIRT *stands guard with a banner.*]

AZDAK   The Public Prosecutor has the floor.

SHAUWA   It concerns a cow. For five weeks, the defendant has had a cow in her stable, the property of the farmer Suru. She was also found to be in possession of a stolen ham, and a number of cows belonging to Shutoff were killed after he asked the defendant to pay the rent on a piece of land.

FARMERS
> —It's a matter of my ham, Your Honor.
> —It's a matter of my cow, Your Honor.
> —It's a matter of my land, Your Honor.

AZDAK   Well, Granny, what have *you* got to say to all this?

OLD WOMAN   Your Honor, one night toward morning, five weeks ago, there was a knock at my door, and outside stood a bearded man with a cow. "My dear woman," he said, "I am the miracle-working Saint Banditus and because your son has been killed in the war, I bring you this cow as a souvenir. Take good care of it."

FARMERS
> —The robber, Irakli, Your Honor!
> —Her brother-in-law, Your Honor!
> —The cow-thief!

—The incendiary!

—He must be beheaded!

[*Outside, a woman screams. The crowd grows restless, retreats. Enter the* BANDIT *Irakli with a huge ax.*]

BANDIT   A very good evening, dear friends! A glass of vodka!

FARMERS   [*crossing themselves*]   Irakli!

AZDAK   Public Prosecutor, a glass of vodka for our guest. And who are you?

BANDIT   I'm a wandering hermit, Your Honor. Thanks for the gracious gift. [*He empties the glass which* SHAUWA *has brought.*] Another!

AZDAK   I am Azdak. [*He gets up and bows. The* BANDIT *also bows.*] The Court welcomes the foreign hermit. Go on with your story, Granny.

OLD WOMAN   Your Honor, that first night I didn't yet know Saint Banditus could work miracles, it was only the cow. But one night, a few days later, the farmer's servants came to take the cow away again. Then they turned round in front of my door and went off without the cow. And bumps as big as a fist sprouted on their heads. So I knew that Saint Banditus had changed their hearts and turned them into friendly people.

[*The* BANDIT *roars with laughter.*]

FIRST FARMER   I know what changed them.

AZDAK   That's fine. You can tell us later. Continue.

OLD WOMAN   Your Honor, the next one to become a good man was the farmer Shutoff—a devil, as everyone knows. But Saint Banditus arranged it so he let me off the rent on the little piece of land.

SECOND FARMER   Because my cows were killed in the field.

[*The* BANDIT *laughs.*]

OLD WOMAN   [*answering* AZDAK's *sign to continue*]   Then one morning the ham came flying in at my window. It hit me in the small of the back. I'm still lame, Your Honor, look. [*She limps a few steps. The* BANDIT *laughs.*] Your Honor, was there ever a time when a poor old woman could get a ham *without* a miracle?

[*The* BANDIT *starts sobbing.*]

AZDAK   [*rising from his chair*]   Granny, that's a question that strikes straight at the Court's heart. Be so kind as to sit here. [*The* OLD WOMAN, *hesitating, sits in the judge's chair.*]

AZDAK   [*sits on the floor, glass in hand, reciting*]

Granny

We could almost call you Granny Grusinia

The Woebegone

The Bereaved Mother

Whose sons have gone to war.

Receiving the present of a cow

She bursts out crying.

When she is beaten

She remains hopeful.

When she's not beaten

She's surprised.

On us

Who are already damned

May you render a merciful verdict

Granny Grusinia!

[*Bellowing at the* FARMERS]   Admit you don't believe in miracles, you atheists! Each of you is sentenced to pay five hundred piasters! For godlessness! Get out! [*The* FARMERS *slink out.*] And you, Granny, and you [*to

the BANDIT] pious man, empty a pitcher of wine with the Public Prosecutor
and Azdak!

SINGER AND CHORUS

And he broke the rules to save them.
Broken law like bread he gave them,
Brought them to shore upon his crooked back.
At long last the poor and lowly
Had someone who was not too holy
To be bribed by empty hands: Azdak.

For two years it was his pleasure
To give the beasts of prey short measure:
He became a wolf to fight the pack.
From All Hallows to All Hallows
On his chair beside the gallows
Dispensing justice in his fashion sat Azdak.

SINGER

But the era of disorder came to an end.
The Grand Duke returned.
The Governor's wife returned.
A trial was held.
Many died.
The people's quarters burned anew.
And fear seized Azdak.

[AZDAK's *judge's chair stands again in the court of justice.* AZDAK *sits on
the floor, shaving and talking to* SHAUWA. *Noises outside. In the rear the*
FAT PRINCE's *head is carried by on a lance.*]

AZDAK   Shauwa, the days of your slavery are numbered, maybe even the minutes.
For a long time now I have held you in the iron curb of reason, and it has
torn your mouth till it bleeds. I have lashed you with reasonable arguments,
I have manhandled you with logic. You are by nature a weak man, and if
one slyly throws an argument in your path, you *have* to snap it up, you
can't resist. It is your nature to lick the hand of some superior being. But
superior beings can be of very different kinds. And now, with your liberation, you will soon be able to follow your natural inclinations, which are
low. You will be able to follow your infallible instinct, which teaches you
to plant your fat heel on the faces of men. Gone is the era of confusion
and disorder, which I find described in the Song of Chaos. Let us now
sing that song together in memory of those terrible days. Sit down and
don't do violence to the music. Don't be afraid. It sounds all right. And
it has a fine refrain. [*He sings.*]

THE SONG OF CHAOS

Sister, hide your face! Brother, take your knife!
The times are out of joint!
Big men are full of complaint
And small men full of joy.
The city says:
"Let us drive the mighty from our midst!"
Offices are raided. Lists of serfs are destroyed.
They have set Master's nose to the grindstone.
They who lived in the dark have seen the light.

The ebony poor box is broken.
Sesnem ² wood is sawed up for beds.
Who had no bread have full barns.
Who begged for alms of corn now mete it out.

SHAUWA [*refrain*] Oh, oh, oh, oh.
AZDAK [*refrain*]
>Where are you, General, where are you?
>Please, please, please, restore order!

>The nobleman's son can no longer be recognized;
>The lady's child becomes the son of her slave-girl
>The councilors meet in a shed.
>Once, this man was barely allowed to sleep on the wall;
>Now, he stretches his limbs in a bed.
>Once, this man rowed a boat; now, he owns ships.
>Their owner looks for them, but they're his no longer.
>Five men are sent on a journey by their master.
>"Go yourself," they say, "we have arrived."

SHAUWA [*refrain*] Oh, oh, oh, oh.
AZDAK [*refrain*]
Where are you, General, where are you?
Please, please, please, restore order!
Yes, so it might have been, had order been neglected much longer. But now the Grand Duke has returned to the capital, and the Persians have lent him an army to restore order with. The people's quarters are already aflame. Go and get me the big book I always sit on. [SHAUWA *brings the big book from the judge's chair.* AZDAK *opens it.*] This is the Statute Book and I've always used it, as you can testify. Now I'd better look in this book and see what they can do to me. I've let the down-and-outs get away with murder, and I'll have to pay for it. I helped poverty onto its skinny legs, so they'll hang me for drunkenness. I peeped into the rich man's pocket, which is bad taste. And I can't hide anywhere—everybody knows me because I've helped everybody.
SHAUWA Someone's coming!
AZDAK [*in panic, he walks trembling to the chair*] It's the end. And now they'd enjoy seeing what a Great Man I am. I'll deprive them of that pleasure. I'll beg on my knees for mercy. Spittle will slobber down my chin. The fear of death is in me.
[*Enter Natella Abashwili, the* GOVERNOR'S WIFE, *followed by the* ADJUTANT *and an* IRONSHIRT.]
GOVERNOR'S WIFE What sort of a creature is that, Shalva?
AZDAK A willing one, Your Highness, a man ready to oblige.
ADJUTANT Natella Abashwili, wife of the late Governor, has just returned. She is looking for her two-year-old son, Michael. She has been informed that the child was carried off to the mountains by a former servant.
AZDAK The child will be brought back, Your Highness, at your service.
ADJUTANT They say that the person in question is passing it off as her own.

---

² I do not know what kind of wood this is, so I have left the word exactly as it stands in the German original. The song is based on an Egyptian papyrus which Brecht cites as such in his essay, "Five Difficulties in the Writing of the Truth." I should think he must have come across it in Adolf Erman's *Die Literatur der Aegypter*, 1923, p. 130 ff. Erman too gives the word as Sesnem. The same papyrus is quoted in Karl Jaspers' *Man in the Modern Age* (Anchor edition, pp. 18–19) but without the sentence about the Sesnem wood.—E.B.

AZDAK   She will be beheaded, Your Highness, at your service.

ADJUTANT   That is all.

GOVERNOR'S WIFE   [*leaving*]   I don't like that man.

AZDAK   [*following her to door, bowing*]   At your service, Your Highness, it will all be arranged.

5
THE CHALK CIRCLE

SINGER

Hear now the story of the trial
Concerning Governor Abashwili's child
And the determination of the true mother
By the famous test of the Chalk Circle.

[*Law court in Nuka.* IRONSHIRTS *lead* MICHAEL *across stage and out at the back.* IRONSHIRTS *hold* GRUSHA *back with their lances under the gateway until the child has been led through. Then she is admitted. She is accompanied by the former Governor's* COOK. *Distant noises and a fire-red sky.*]

GRUSHA   [*trying to hide*]   He's brave, he can wash himself now.

COOK   You're lucky. It's not a real judge. It's Azdak, a drunk who doesn't know what he's doing. The biggest thieves have got by through him. Because he gets everything mixed up and the rich never offer him big enough bribes, the like of us sometimes do pretty well.

GRUSHA   I *need* luck right now.

COOK   Touch wood. [*She crosses herself.*] I'd better offer up another prayer that the judge may be drunk. [*She prays with motionless lips, while* GRUSHA *looks around, in vain, for the child.*] Why must you hold on to it at any price if it isn't yours? In days like these?

GRUSHA   He's mine. I brought him up.

COOK   Have you never thought what'd happen when she came back?

GRUSHA   At first I thought I'd give him to her. Then I thought she wouldn't come back.

COOK   And even a borrowed coat keeps a man warm, hm? [GRUSHA *nods.*] I'll swear to anything for you. You're a decent girl. [*She sees the soldier* SIMON SHASHAVA *approaching.*] You've done wrong by Simon, though. I've been talking with him. He just can't understand.

GRUSHA   [*unaware of* SIMON'S *presence*]   Right now I can't be bothered whether he understands or not!

COOK   He knows the child isn't yours, but you married and not free "till death you do part"—he can't understand *that.*

[GRUSHA *sees* SIMON *and greets him.*]

SIMON   [*gloomily*]   I wish the lady to know I will swear I am the father of the child.

GRUSHA   [*low*]   Thank you, Simon.

SIMON   At the same time I wish the lady to know my hands are not tied—nor are hers.

COOK   You needn't have said that. You know she's married.

SIMON   And it needs no rubbing in.

[*Enter an* IRONSHIRT.]

IRONSHIRT   Where's the judge? Has anyone seen the judge?

ANOTHER IRONSHIRT [*stepping forward*] The judge isn't here yet. Nothing but a bed and a pitcher in the whole house!
[*Exeunt* IRONSHIRTS.]

COOK I hope nothing has happened to him. With any other judge you'd have as much chance as a chicken has teeth.

GRUSHA [*who has turned away and covered her face*] Stand in front of me. I shouldn't have come to Nuka. If I run into the Ironshirt, the one I hit over the head . . .
[*She screams. An* IRONSHIRT *had stopped and, turning his back, had been listening to her. He now wheels around. It is the* CORPORAL, *and he has a huge scar across his face.*]

IRONSHIRT [*in the gateway*] What's the matter, Shotta? Do you know her?

CORPORAL [*after staring for some time*] No.

IRONSHIRT She's the one who stole the Abashwili child, or so they say. If you know anything about it you can make some money, Shotta.
[*Exit the* CORPORAL, *cursing.*]

COOK Was it him? [GRUSHA *nods.*] I think he'll keep his mouth shut, or he'd be admitting he was after the child.

GRUSHA I'd almost forgotten him.
[*Enter the* GOVERNOR'S WIFE, *followed by the* ADJUTANT *and two* LAWYERS.]

GOVERNOR'S WIFE At least there are no common people here, thank God. I can't stand their smell. It always gives me migraine.

FIRST LAWYER Madam, I must ask you to be careful what you say until we have another judge.

GOVERNOR'S WIFE But I didn't say anything, Illo Shuboladze. I love the people with their simple straightforward minds. It's only that their smell brings on my migraine.

SECOND LAWYER There won't be many spectators. The whole population is sitting at home behind locked doors because of the riots in the people's quarters.

GOVERNOR'S WIFE [*looking at* GRUSHA] Is that the creature?

FIRST LAWYER Please, most gracious Natella Abashwili, abstain from invective until it is certain the Grand Duke has appointed a new judge and we're rid of the present one, who's about the lowest fellow ever seen in judge's gown. Things are all set to move, you see.
[*Enter* IRONSHIRTS *from the courtyard.*]

COOK Her Grace would pull your hair out on the spot if she didn't know Azdak is for the poor. He goes by the face.
[IRONSHIRTS *begin fastening a rope to a beam.* AZDAK, *in chains, is led in, followed by* SHAUWA, *also in chains. The three* FARMERS *bring up the rear.*]

AN IRONSHIRT Trying to run away, were you? [*He strikes* AZDAK.]

ONE FARMER Off with his judge's gown before we string him up!
[IRONSHIRTS *and* FARMERS *tear off Azdak's gown. His torn underwear is visible. Then someone kicks him.*]

AN IRONSHIRT [*pushing him into someone else*] Want a load of justice? Here it is!
[*Accompanied by shouts of* "You take it!" *and* "Let me have him, Brother!" *they throw* AZDAK *back and forth until he collapses. Then he is lifted up and dragged under the noose.*]

GOVERNOR'S WIFE [*who, during this "ballgame," has clapped her hands hysterically*] I disliked that man from the moment I first saw him.

AZDAK [*covered with blood, panting*] I can't see. Give me a rag.

AN IRONSHIRT What is it you want to see?

AZDAK You, you dogs! [*He wipes the blood out of his eyes with his shirt.*] Good morning, dogs! How goes it, dogs! How's the dog world? Does it smell good? Got another boot for me to lick? Are you back at each other's throats, dogs?

[*Accompanied by a* CORPORAL, *a dust-covered* RIDER *enters. He takes some documents from a leather case, looks at them, then interrupts.*]

RIDER Stop! I bring a dispatch from the Grand Duke, containing the latest appointments.

CORPORAL [*bellowing*] Atten—shun!

RIDER Of the new judge it says: "We appoint a man whom we have to thank for saving a life indispensable to the country's welfare—a certain Azdak of Nuka." Which is he?

SHAUWA [*pointing*] That's him, Your Excellency.

CORPORAL [*bellowing*] What's going on here?

AN IRONSHIRT I beg to report that His Honor Azdak was already His Honor Azdak, but on these farmers' denunciation was pronounced the Grand Duke's enemy.

CORPORAL [*pointing at the* FARMERS] March them off! [*They are marched off. They bow all the time.*] See to it that His Honor Azdak is exposed to no more violence.

[*Exeunt* RIDER *and* CORPORAL.]

COOK [*to* SHAUWA] She clapped her hands! I hope he saw it!

FIRST LAWYER It's a catastrophe.

[AZDAK *has fainted. Coming to, he is dressed again in judge's robes. He walks, swaying, toward the* IRONSHIRTS.]

AN IRONSHIRT What does Your Honor desire?

AZDAK Nothing, fellow dogs, or just an occasional boot to lick. [*To* SHAUWA] I pardon you. [*He is unchained.*] Get me some red wine, the sweet kind. [SHAUWA *stumbles off.*] Get out of here, I've got to judge a case. [*Exeunt* IRONSHIRTS. SHAUWA *returns with a pitcher of wine.* AZDAK *gulps it down.*] Something for my backside. [SHAUWA *brings the Statute Book, puts it on the judge's chair.* AZDAK *sits on it.*] I accept.

[*The Prosecutors, among whom a worried council has been held, smile with relief. They whisper.*]

COOK Oh dear!

SIMON A well can't be filled with dew, they say.

LAWYERS [*approaching* AZDAK, *who stands up, expectantly*] A quite ridiculous case, Your Honor. The accused has abducted a child and refuses to hand it over.

AZDAK [*stretching out his hand, glancing at* GRUSHA] A most attractive person. [*He fingers the money, then sits down, satisfied.*] I declare the proceedings open and demand the whole truth. [*To* GRUSHA] Especially from you.

FIRST LAWYER High Court of Justice! Blood, as the popular saying goes, is thicker than water. This old adage . . .

AZDAK [*interrupting*] The Court wants to know the lawyers' fee.

FIRST LAWYER [*surprised*] I beg your pardon? [AZDAK, *smiling, rubs his thumb and index finger.*] Oh, I see. Five hundred piasters, Your Honor, to answer the Court's somewhat unusual question.

AZDAK Did you hear? The question is unusual. I ask it because I listen in quite a different way when I know you're good.

FIRST LAWYER [*bowing*] Thank you, Your Honor. High Court of Justice, of all ties the ties of blood are strongest. Mother and child—is there a more intimate relationship? Can one tear a child from its mother? High Court of Justice, she has conceived it in the holy ecstasies of love. She has carried it in her womb. She has fed it with her blood. She has borne it with pain.

High Court of Justice, it has been observed that the wild tigress, robbed of her young, roams restless through the mountains, shrunk to a shadow. Nature herself . . .

AZDAK [*interrupting, to* GRUSHA] What's your answer to all this and anything else that lawyer might have to say?

GRUSHA He's mine.

AZDAK Is that all? I hope you can prove it. Why should I assign the child to you in any case?

GRUSHA I brought him up like the priest says "according to my best knowledge and conscience." I always found him something to eat. Most of the time he had a roof over his head. And I went to such trouble for him. I had expenses too. I didn't look out for my own comfort. I brought the child up to be friendly with everyone, and from the beginning taught him to work. As well as he could, that is. He's still very little.

FIRST LAWYER Your Honor, it is significant that the girl herself doesn't claim any tie of blood between her and the child.

AZDAK The Court takes note of that.

FIRST LAWYER Thank you, Your Honor. And now permit a woman bowed in sorrow—who has already lost her husband and now has also to fear the loss of her child—to address a few words to you. The gracious Natella Abashwili is . . .

GOVERNOR'S WIFE [*quietly*] A most cruel fate, sir, forces me to describe to you the tortures of a bereaved mother's soul, the anxiety, the sleepless nights, the . . .

SECOND LAWYER [*bursting out*] It's outrageous the way this woman is being treated! Her husband's palace is closed to her! The revenue of her estates is blocked, and she is cold-bloodedly told that it's tied to the heir. She can't do a thing without that child. She can't even pay her lawyer!! [*To the* FIRST LAWYER, *who, desperate about this outburst, makes frantic gestures to keep him from speaking:*] Dear Illo Shuboladze, surely it can be divulged now that the Abashwili estates are at stake?

FIRST LAWYER Please, Honored Sandro Oboladze! We agreed . . . [*To* AZDAK:] Of course it is correct that the trial will also decide if our noble client can take over the Abashwili estates, which are rather extensive. I say "also" advisedly, for in the foreground stands the human tragedy of a mother, as Natella Abashwili very properly explained in the first words of her moving statement. Even if Michael Abashwili were not heir to the estates, he would still be the dearly beloved child of my client.

AZDAK Stop! The Court is touched by the mention of estates. It's a proof of human feeling.

SECOND LAWYER Thanks, Your Honor. Dear Illo Shuboladze, we can prove in any case that the woman who took the child is not the child's mother. Permit me to lay before the Court the bare facts. High Court of Justice, by an unfortunate chain of circumstances, Michael Abashwili was left behind on that Easter Sunday while his mother was making her escape. Grusha, a palace kitchen maid, was seen with the baby . . .

COOK All her mistress was thinking of was what dresses she'd take along!

SECOND LAWYER [*unmoved*] Nearly a year later Grusha turned up in a mountain village with a baby and there entered into the state of matrimony with . . .

AZDAK How'd you get to that mountain village?

GRUSHA On foot, Your Honor. And he was mine.

SIMON I'm the father, Your Honor.

COOK I used to look after it for them, Your Honor. For five piasters.

SECOND LAWYER   This man is engaged to Grusha, High Court of Justice: his testimony is suspect.

AZDAK   Are you the man she married in the mountain village?

SIMON   No, Your Honor, she married a peasant.

AZDAK   [*to* GRUSHA]   Why? [*Pointing at* SIMON.] Is he no good in bed? Tell the truth.

GRUSHA   We didn't get that far. I married because of the baby. So he'd have a roof over his head. [*Pointing at* SIMON.] He was in the war, Your Honor.

AZDAK   And now he wants you back again, huh?

SIMON   I wish to state in evidence . . .

GRUSHA   [*angrily*]   I am no longer free, Your Honor.

AZDAK   And the child, you claim, comes from whoring? [GRUSHA *doesn't answer.*] I'm going to ask you a question: What kind of child is he? A ragged little bastard? Or from a good family?

GRUSHA   [*angrily*]   He's an ordinary child.

AZDAK   I mean—did he have refined features from the beginning?

GRUSHA   He had a nose on his face.

AZDAK   A very significant comment! It has been said of me that I went out one time and sniffed at a rosebush before rendering a verdict—tricks like that are needed nowadays. Well, I'll make it short, and not listen to any more lies. [*To* GRUSHA:] Especially not yours. [*To all the accused*] I can imagine what you've cooked up to cheat me! I know you people. You're swindlers.

GRUSHA   [*suddenly*]   I can understand your wanting to cut it short, now I've seen what you accepted!

AZDAK   Shut up! Did I accept anything from you?

GRUSHA   [*while the* COOK *tries to restrain her*]   I haven't got anything.

AZDAK   True. Quite true. From starvelings I never get a thing. I might just as well starve, myself. You want justice, but do you want to pay for it, hm? When you go to a butcher you know you have to pay, but you people go to a judge as if you were off to a funeral supper.

SIMON   [*loudly*]   When the horse was shod, the horsefly held out its leg, as the saying is.

AZDAK   [*eagerly accepting the challenge*]   Better a treasure in manure than a stone in a mountain stream.

SIMON   A fine day. Let's go fishing, said the angler to the worm.

AZDAK   I'm my own master, said the servant, and cut off his foot.

SIMON   I love you as a father, said the Czar to the peasants, and had the Czarevitch's head chopped off.

AZDAK   A fool's worst enemy is himself.

SIMON   However, a fart has no nose.

AZDAK   Fined ten piasters for indecent language in court! That'll teach you what justice is.

GRUSHA   [*furiously*]   A fine kind of justice! You play fast and loose with us because we don't talk as refined as that crowd with their lawyers.

AZDAK   That's true. You people are too dumb. It's only right you should get it in the neck.

GRUSHA   You want to hand the child over to her, and she wouldn't even know how to keep it dry, she's so "refined"! You know about as much about justice as I do!

AZDAK   There's something in that. I'm an ignorant man. Haven't even a decent pair of pants on under this gown. Look! With me, everything goes on food and drink—I was educated in a convent. Incidentally, I'll fine you ten piasters for contempt of court. And you're a very silly girl, to turn me against you, instead of making eyes at me and wiggling your backside a little to keep me in a good temper. Twenty piasters!

GRUSHA Even if it was thirty, I'd tell you what I think of your justice, you drunken onion! [*Incoherently.*] How dare you talk to me like the cracked Isaiah on the church window? As if you were somebody? For you weren't born to this. You weren't born to rap your own mother on the knuckles if she swipes a little bowl of salt someplace. Aren't you ashamed of yourself when you see how I tremble before you? You've made yourself their servant so no one will take their houses from them—houses they had stolen! Since when have houses belonged to the bedbugs? But you're on the watch, or they couldn't drag our men into their wars! You bribetaker!

[AZDAK *half gets up, starts beaming. With his little hammer he halfheartedly knocks on the table as if to get silence. As* GRUSHA's *scolding continues, he only beats time with his hammer.*]

I've no respect for you. No more than for a thief or a bandit with a knife! You can do what you want. You can take the child away from me, a hundred against one, but I tell you one thing: only extortioners should be chosen for a profession like yours, and men who rape children! As punishment! Yes, let *them* sit in judgment on their fellow creatures. It is worse than to hang from the gallows.

AZDAK [*sitting down*] Now it'll be thirty! And I won't go on squabbling with you—we're not in a tavern. What'd happen to my dignity as a judge? Anyway, I've lost interest in your case. Where's the couple who wanted a divorce? [*To* SHAUWA] Bring 'em in. This case is adjourned for fifteen minutes.

FIRST LAWYER [*to the* GOVERNOR's WIFE] Even without using the rest of the evidence, Madam, we have the verdict in the bag.

COOK [*to* GRUSHA] You've gone and spoiled your chances with him. You won't get the child now.

GOVERNOR's WIFE Shalva, my smelling salts!

[*Enter a very old couple.*]

AZDAK I accept. [*The old couple don't understand.*] I hear you want to be divorced. How long have you been together?

OLD WOMAN Forty years, Your Honor.

AZDAK And why do you want a divorce?

OLD MAN We don't like each other, Your Honor.

AZDAK Since when?

OLD WOMAN Oh, from the very beginning, Your Honor.

AZDAK I'll think about your request and render my verdict when I'm through with the other case. [SHAUWA *leads them back.*] I need the child. [*He beckons* GRUSHA *to him and bends not unkindly toward her.*] I've noticed you have a soft spot for justice. I don't believe he's your child, but if he *were* yours, woman, wouldn't you want him to be rich? You'd only have to say he wasn't yours, and he'd have a palace and many horses in his stable and many beggars on his doorstep and many soldiers in his service and many petitioners in his courtyard, wouldn't he? What do you say—don't you want him to be rich?

[GRUSHA *is silent.*]

SINGER

Hear now what the angry girl thought but did not say:

Had he golden shoes to wear
He'd be cruel as a bear.

Evil would his life disgrace.
He'd laugh in my face.

Carrying a heart of flint
Is too troublesome a stint.
Being powerful and bad
Is hard on a lad.

Then let hunger be his foe!
Hungry men and women, no.
Let him fear the darksome night
But not daylight!

AZDAK   I think I understand you, woman.

GRUSHA   [*suddenly and loudly*]   I won't give him up. I've raised him, and he knows me.

[*Enter* SHAUWA *with the* CHILD.]

GOVERNOR'S WIFE   He's in rags!

GRUSHA   That's not true. But I wasn't given time to put his good shirt on.

GOVERNOR'S WIFE   He must have been in a pigsty.

GRUSHA   [*furiously*]   I'm not a pig, but there are some who are! Where did you leave your baby?

GOVERNOR'S WIFE   I'll show you, you vulgar creature! [*She is about to throw herself on* GRUSHA, *but is restrained by her lawyers.*] She's a criminal, she must be whipped. Immediately!

SECOND LAWYER   [*holding his hand over her mouth*]   Natella Abashwili, you promised . . . Your Honor, the plaintiff's nerves . . .

AZDAK   Plaintiff and defendant! The Court has listened to your case, and has come to no decision as to who the real mother is; therefore, I, the judge, am obliged to *choose* a mother for the child. I'll make a test. Shauwa, get a piece of chalk and draw a circle on the floor. [SHAUWA *does so.*] Now place the child in the center. [SHAUWA *puts* MICHAEL, *who smiles at* GRUSHA, *in the center of the circle.*] Stand near the circle, both of you. [*The* GOVERNOR'S WIFE *and* GRUSHA *step up to the circle.*] Now each of you take the child by one hand. [*They do so.*] The true mother is she who can pull the child out of the circle.

SECOND LAWYER   [*quickly*]   High Court of Justice, I object! The fate of the great Abashwili estates, which are tied to the child, as the heir, should not be made dependent on such a doubtful duel. In addition, my client does not command the strength of this person, who is accustomed to physical work.

AZDAK   She looks pretty well fed to me. Pull! [*The* GOVERNOR'S WIFE *pulls the* CHILD *out of the circle on her side;* GRUSHA *has let go and stands aghast.*] What's the matter with you? You didn't pull.

GRUSHA   I didn't hold on to him.

FIRST LAWYER   [*congratulating the* GOVERNOR'S WIFE]   What did I say! The ties of blood!

GRUSHA   [*running to* AZDAK]   Your Honor, I take back everything I said against you. I ask your forgiveness. But could I keep him till he can speak all the words? He knows a few.

AZDAK   Don't influence the Court. I bet you only know about twenty words yourself. All right, I'll make the test once more, just to be certain. [*The two women take up their positions again.*] Pull! [*Again* GRUSHA *lets go of the* CHILD.]

GRUSHA   [*in despair*]   I brought him up! Shall I also tear him to bits? I can't!

AZDAK [*rising*]   And in this manner the Court has determined the true mother. [*To* GRUSHA:] Take your child and be off. I advise you not to stay in the city with him. [*To the* GOVERNOR'S WIFE:] And you disappear before I fine you for fraud. Your estates fall to the city. They'll be converted into a playground for the children. They need one, and I've decided it'll be called after me: Azdak's Garden.

[*The* GOVERNOR'S WIFE *has fainted and is carried out by the* LAWYERS *and the* ADJUTANT. GRUSHA *stands motionless.* SHAUWA *leads the* CHILD *toward her.*]

Now I'll take off this judge's gown—it's got too hot for me. I'm not cut out for a hero. In token of farewell I invite you all to a little dance in the meadow outside. Oh, I'd almost forgotten something in my excitement . . . to sign the divorce decree.

[*Using the judge's chair as a table, he writes something on a piece of paper, and prepares to leave. Dance music has started.*]

SHAUWA [*having read what is on the paper*]   But that's not right. You've not divorced the old people. You've divorced Grusha!

AZDAK   Divorced the wrong couple? What a pity! And I never retract! If I did, how could we keep order in the land? [*To the old couple:*] I'll invite you to my party instead. You don't mind dancing with each other, do you? [*To* GRUSHA *and* SIMON:] I've got forty piasters coming from you.

SIMON [*pulling out his purse*]   Cheap at the price, Your Honor. And many thanks.

AZDAK [*pocketing the cash*]   I'll be needing this.

GRUSHA [*to* MICHAEL]   So we'd better leave the city tonight, Michael? [*To* SIMON] You like him?

SIMON   With my respects, I like him.

GRUSHA   Now I can tell you: I took him because on that Easter Sunday I got engaged to you. So he's a child of love. Michael, let's dance.

[*She dances with* MICHAEL, SIMON *dances with the* COOK, *the old couple with each other.* AZDAK *stands lost in thought. The dancers soon hide him from view. Occasionally he is seen, but less and less as more couples join the dance.*]

SINGER

And after that evening Azdak vanished and was never seen again.
The people of Grusinia did not forget him but long remembered
The period of his judging as a brief golden age,
Almost an age of justice.

[*All the couples dance off.* AZDAK *has disappeared.*]

But you, you who have listened to the Story of the Chalk Circle,
Take note what men of old concluded:
That what there is shall go to those who are good for it,
Children to the motherly, that they prosper,
Carts to good drivers, that they be driven well,
The valley to the waterers, that it yield fruit.

JOHN OSBORNE
[1929-   ]

Regarded as a leader of England's "angry young men," John Osborne established his place as an important dramatist when his play *Look Back in Anger* was produced in 1956. Although many reviewers thought it a "social outrage" in its harsh criticisms of British social institutions, the play was a spectacular success, running for eighteen months in England, and, when it opened in New York, it won the New York Drama Critics Circle Award as the best foreign play of 1957. Osborne is known as a spokesman both for the post-World War II generation in England and for working class people in rebellion against the status quo and England's ruling classes. Osborne himself comes from a working class family; he remembers his "boyhood in the midst of a brawling, laughing, drinking, moaning" environment provided by his father's pub. After finishing his secondary education and then studying at Belmont College (he did not attend a university), he began acting with repertory companies. While traveling in the provinces with these groups, he learned the crafts of the theater, paying special attention to acting, managing, and writing. Even today, after great success as a playwright, Osborne is a fine actor who often appears in movies and on the stage.

Following *Look Back in Anger,* Osborne wrote *The Entertainer* (1957), which starred Sir Lawrence Olivier, *Epitaph for George Dillon* (1958), *The World of Paul Slickey* (1959), *Luther* (1961), *Inadmissible Evidence* (1964), and *A Patriot for Me* (1965). He also wrote the film versions of *Look Back in Anger, The Entertainer,* and *Tom Jones* (for which he won an Academy Award in 1964). *Luther,* based on the life of Martin Luther, himself an angry man, has captivated American audiences in its Broadway run starring Albert Finney and more recently in a television production starring Robert Shaw. Osborne's *Luther,* along with such plays as Bolt's *A Man for All Seasons* and Anouilh's *Becket,* exemplifies a trend in the modern theater to look to the past for subject matter—particularly for heroic subjects.

LUTHER

JOHN OSBORNE

CAST

KNIGHT	CAJETAN
PRIOR	MILTITZ
MARTIN	LEO
HANS	ECK
LUCAS	KATHERINE
WEINAND	HANS, THE YOUNGER
TETZEL	AUGUSTINIANS, DOMINICANS,
STAUPITZ	HERALD, EMPEROR, PEASANTS, ETC.

ACT ONE

SCENE 1: *The convent of the Augustinian Order of Eremites at Erfurt. 1506*

SCENE 2: *The same. A year later*

SCENE 3: *Two hours later*

ACT TWO

ACT THREE

NOTE: *At the opening of each act, the Knight appears. He grasps a banner and briefly barks the time and place of the scene following at the audience, and then retires.*

ACT ONE

Scene One

The Cloister Chapel of the Eremites of St. Augustine. Erfurt, Thuringia, 1506. MARTIN *is being received into the Order. He is kneeling in front of the* PRIOR *in the presence of the assembled convent.*

PRIOR   Now you must choose one of two ways: either to leave us now, or give up this world, and consecrate and devote yourself entirely to God and our Order. But I must add this: once you have committed yourself, you are not free, for whatever reason, to throw off the yoke of obedience, for you will have accepted it freely, while you were still able to discard it.

[*The habit and hood of the Order are brought in and blessed by the* PRIOR.]

PRIOR   He whom it was your will to dress in the garb of the Order, oh Lord, invest him also with eternal life.

[*He undresses* MARTIN.]

PRIOR   The Lord divest you of the former man and of all his works. The Lord invest you with the new man.

[*The* CHOIR *sings as* MARTIN *is robed in the habit and hood. The long white scapular is thrown over his head and hung down, before and behind; then he kneels again before the* PRIOR, *and, with his hand on the statutes of the Order, swears the oath.*]

MARTIN   I, brother Martin, do make profession and promise obedience to Almighty God, to Mary the Sacred Virgin, and to you, my brother Prior of this cloister, in the name of the Vicar General of the order of Eremites of the holy Bishop of St. Augustine and his successors, to live without property and in chastity according to the Rule of our Venerable Father Augustine until death.

[*The* PRIOR *wishes a prayer over him, and* MARTIN *prostrates himself with arms extended in the form of a cross.*]

PRIOR   Lord Jesus Christ, our leader and our strength, by the fire of humility you have set aside this servant, Martin, from the rest of Mankind. We humbly pray that this fire will also cut him off from carnal intercourse and from the community of those things done on earth by men, through the sanctity shed from heaven upon him, and that you will bestow on him grace to remain yours, and merit eternal life. For it is not he who begins, but he who endures will be saved. Amen.

[*The* CHOIR *sings Veni Creator Spiritus or perhaps Great Father Augustine. A newly lighted taper is put into* MARTIN's *hands, and he is led up the altar steps to be welcomed by the monks with the kiss of peace. Then, in their midst, he marches slowly with them behind the screen and is lost to sight. The procession disappears, and, as the sound of voices dies away, two men are left alone in the congregation. One of them,* HANS, *gets up impatiently and moves down-stage. It is* MARTIN's FATHER, *a stocky man wired throughout with a miner's muscle, lower-middle class, on his way to become a small, primitive capitalist; bewildered, full of pride and resentment. His companion,* LUCAS, *finishes a respectful prayer and joins him.*]

HANS   Well?

LUCAS   Well?

HANS   Don't 'well' me, you feeble old ninny, what do you think?

LUCAS   Think? Of what?

HANS   Yes, think man, think, what do you think, pen and ink, think of all that?

LUCAS   Oh—

HANS   Oh! Of all these monks, of Martin and all the rest of it, what do you think? You've been sitting in this arse-aching congregation all this time, you've been watching, haven't you? What about it?

LUCAS   Yes, well, I must say it's all very impressive.

HANS   Oh, yes?

LUCAS   No getting away from it.

HANS   Impressive?

LUCAS   Deeply. It was moving and oh—

HANS   What?

LUCAS   You must have felt it, surely. You couldn't fail to.

HANS   Impressive! I don't know what impresses me any longer.

LUCAS   Oh, come on—

HANS   Impressive!

LUCAS   Of course it is, and you know it.

HANS   Oh, you—you can afford to be impressed.

LUCAS   It's surely too late for any regrets, or bitterness, Hans. It obviously must be God's will, and there's an end of it.

HANS   That's exactly what it is—an end of it! Very fine for you, my old friend, very fine indeed. You're just losing a son-in-law, and you can take your pick of plenty more of those where he comes from. But what am I losing? I'm losing a son; mark: a son.

LUCAS   How can you say that?

HANS   How can I say it? I do say it, that's how. Two sons to the plague, and now another. God's eyes! Did you see that haircut? Brother Martin!

LUCAS   There isn't a finer order than these people, not the Dominicans or Franciscans—

HANS   Like an egg with a beard.

LUCAS   You said that yourself.

HANS   Oh, I suppose they're Christians under their damned cowls.

LUCAS   There are good, distinguished men in this place, and well you know it.

HANS   Yes—good, distinguished men—

LUCAS   Pious, learned men, men from the University like Martin.

HANS   Learned men! Some of them can't read their own names.

LUCAS   So?

HANS   So! I—I'm a miner. I don't need books. You can't see to read books under the ground. But Martin's a scholar.

LUCAS   He most certainly is.

HANS   A Master of Arts! What's he master of now? Eh? Tell me.

LUCAS   Well, there it is. God's gain is your loss.

HANS   Half these monks do nothing but wash dishes and beg in the streets.

LUCAS   We should be going, I suppose.

HANS   He could have been a man of stature.

LUCAS   And he will, with God's help.

HANS   Don't tell me. He could have been a lawyer.

LUCAS   Well, he won't now.

HANS   No, you're damn right he won't. Of stature. To the Archbishop, or the Duke, or—

LUCAS   Yes.

HANS   Anyone.

LUCAS   Come on.

HANS   Anyone you can think of.

LUCAS   Well, I'm going.

HANS   Brother Martin!

LUCAS   Hans.

HANS   Do you know why? Lucas: Why? What made him do it?

   [*He has ceased to play a role by this time and he asks the question simply as if he expected a short, direct answer.*]

HANS   What made him do it?

   [LUCAS *grasps his forearm.*]

LUCAS   Let's go home.

HANS   Why? That's what I can't understand. Why? Why?

LUCAS   Home. Let's go home.

   [*They go off. The convent bell rings. Some monks are standing at a refectory table. After their prayers, they sit down, and, as they eat in silence, one of the Brothers reads from a lectern. During this short scene,* MARTIN, *wearing a rough apron over his habit, waits on the others.*]

READER
   What are the tools of Good Works?
   First, to love Lord God with all one's heart, all one's soul, and all one's strength. Then, one's neighbour as oneself. Then, not to kill.
   Not to commit adultery
   Not to steal
   Not to covet
   Not to bear false witness
   To honour all men
   To deny yourself, in order to follow Christ
   To chastise the body
   Not to seek soft living
   To love fasting

To clothe the naked
To visit the sick
To bury the dead
To help the afflicted
To console the sorrowing
To prefer nothing to the love of Christ

Not to yield to anger
Not to nurse a grudge
Not to hold guile in your heart
Not to make a feigned peace
To fear the Day of Judgment
To dread Hell
To desire eternal life with all your spiritual longing
To keep death daily before your eyes
To keep constant vigilance over the actions of your life
To know for certain that God sees you everywhere
When evil thoughts come into your heart, to dash them at once on the love
of Christ and to manifest them to your spiritual father
To keep your mouth from evil and depraved talk
Not to love much speaking
Not to speak vain words or such as produce laughter
To listen gladly to holy readings
To apply yourself frequently to prayer
Daily in your prayer, with tears and sighs to confess your past sins to God
Not to fulfil the desires of the flesh
To hate your own will
Behold, these are the tools of the spiritual craft. If we employ these un-
ceasingly day and night, and render account of them on the Day of Judg-
ment, then we shall receive from the Lord in return that reward that He
Himself has promised: Eye hath not seen nor ear heard what God hath
prepared for those that love him. Now this is the workshop in which we
shall diligently execute all these tasks. May God grant that you observe all
these rules cheerfully as lovers of spiritual beauty, spreading around you by
the piety of your deportment the sweet odour of Christ.
[*The convent bell rings. The* MONKS *rise, bow their heads in prayer, and
then move upstage to the steps where they kneel.* MARTIN, *assisted by another Brother, stacks the table and clears it. Presently, they all prostrate
themselves, and, beneath flaming candles, a communal confession begins.*
MARTIN *returns and prostrates himself downstage behind the rest. This
scene throughout is urgent, muted, almost whispered, confidential, secret,
like a prayer.*]

BROTHER   I confess to God, to Blessed Mary and our holy Father Augustine, to
all the saints, and to all present that I have sinned exceedingly in thought,
word and deed by my own fault. Wherefore I pray Holy Mary, all the
saints of God and you all assembled here to pray for me. I confess I did
leave my cell for the Night Office without the Scapular and had to return
for it. Which is a deadly infringement of the first degree of humility, that
of obedience without delay. For this failure to Christ I abjectly seek forgiveness and whatever punishment the Prior and community is pleased
to impose on me.

MARTIN I am a worm and no man, a byword and a laughing stock. Crush out the worminess in me, stamp on me.

BROTHER I confess I have three times made mistakes in the Oratory, in psalm singing and Antiphon.

MARTIN I was fighting a bear in a garden without flowers, leading into a desert. His claws kept making my arms bleed as I tried to open a gate which would take me out. But the gate was no gate at all. It was simply an open frame, and I could have walked through it, but I was covered in my own blood, and I saw a naked woman riding on a goat, and the goat began to drink my blood, and I thought I should faint with the pain and I awoke in my cell, all soaking in the devil's bath.

BROTHER Let Brother Norbert remember also his breakage while working in the kitchen.

BROTHER I remember it, and confess humbly.

BROTHER Let him remember also his greater transgression in not coming at once to the Prior and community to do penance for it, and so increasing his offence.

MARTIN I am alone. I am alone, and against myself.

BROTHER I confess it. I confess it, and beg your prayers that I may undergo the greater punishment for it.

MARTIN How can I justify myself?

BROTHER Take heart, you shall be punished, and severely.

MARTIN How can I be justified?

BROTHER I confess I have failed to rise from my bed speedily enough. I arrived at the Night Office after the Gloria of the 94th Psalm, and though I seemed to amend the shame by not standing in my proper place in the choir, and standing in the place appointed by the Prior for such careless sinners so that they may be seen by all, my fault is too great and I seek punishment.

MARTIN I was among a group of people, men and women, fully clothed. We lay on top of each other in neat rows about seven or eight across. Eventually, the pile was many people deep. Suddenly, I panicked—although I was on top of the pile—and I cried: what about those underneath? Those at the very bottom, and those in between? We all got up in an orderly way, without haste, and when we looked, those at the bottom were not simply flattened by the weight, they were just their clothes, they were just their clothes, neatly pressed and folded on the ground. They were their clothes, neatly pressed and folded on the ground.

BROTHER I did omit to have a candle ready at the Mass.

BROTHER Twice in my sloth, I have omitted to shave, and even excused myself, pretending to believe my skin to be fairer than that of my Brothers, and my beard lighter and my burden also. I have been vain and slothful, and I beg forgiveness and ask penance.

MARTIN If my flesh would leak and dissolve, and I could live as bone, if I were forged bone, plucked bone and brain, warm hair and a bony heart, if I were all bone, I could brandish myself without terror, without any terror at all—I could be indestructible.

BROTHER I did ask for a bath, pretending to myself that it was necessary for my health, but as I lowered my body into the tub, it came to me that it was inordinate desire and that it was my soul that was soiled.

MARTIN My bones fail. My bones fail, my bones are shattered and fall away, my bones fail and all that's left of me is a scraped marrow and a dying jelly.

BROTHER Let Brother Paulinus remember our visit to our near sister house, and lifting his eyes repeatedly at a woman in the town who dropped alms into his bag.

BROTHER I remember, and I beg forgiveness.

BROTHER Then let him remember also that though our dear Father Augustine does not forbid us to see women, he blames us if we should desire them or wish to be the object of their desire. For it is not only by touch and by being affectionate that a man excites disorderly affection in a woman. This can be done also even by looks. You cannot maintain that your mind is pure if you have *wanton* eyes. For a wanton eye is a wanton heart. When people with impure hearts manifest their inclination towards each other through the medium of looks, even though no word is spoken, and when they take pleasure in their desire for each other, the purity of their character has gone even though they may be undefiled by any unchaste act. He who fixes his eyes on a woman and takes pleasure in her glance, must not think that he goes unobserved by his brothers.

MARTIN I confess that I have offended grievously against humility, being sometimes discontented with the meanest and worst of everything, I have not only failed to declare myself to myself lower and lower and of less account than all other men, but I have failed in my most inmost heart to believe it. For many weeks, many weeks it seemed to me, I was put to cleaning the latrines. I did it, and I did it vigorously, not tepidly, with all my poor strength, without whispering or objections to anyone. But although I fulfilled my task, and I did it well, sometimes there were murmurings in my heart. I prayed that it would cease, knowing that God, seeing my murmuring heart, must reject my work, and it was as good as not done. I sought out my master, and he punished me, telling me to fast for two days. I have fasted for three, but, even so, I can't tell if the murmurings are really gone, and I ask for your prayers, and I ask for your prayers that I may be able to go on fulfilling the same task.

BROTHER Let Brother Martin remember all the degrees of humility; and let him go on cleaning the latrines.

[*The convent bell rings. After lying prostrate for a few moments, all the* BROTHERS, *including* MARTIN, *rise and move to the* CHOIR. *The office begins, versicle, antiphon and psalm, and* MARTIN *is lost to sight in the ranks of his fellow* MONKS. *Presently, there is a quiet, violent moaning, just distinguishable amongst the voices. It becomes louder and wilder, the cries more violent, and there is some confusion in* MARTIN's *section of the* CHOIR. *The singing goes on with only a few heads turned. It seems as though the disturbance has subsided.* MARTIN *appears, and staggers between the stalls. Outstretched hands fail to restrain him, and he is visible to all, muscles rigid, breath suspended, then jerking uncontrollably as he is seized in a raging fit. Two* BROTHERS *go to him, but* MARTIN *writhes with such ferocity, that they can scarcely hold him down. He tries to speak, the effort is frantic, and eventually, he is able to roar out a word at a time.*]

MARTIN Not! Me! I am *not!*

[*The attack reaches its height, and he recoils as if he had bitten his tongue and his mouth were full of blood and saliva. Two more* MONKS *come to help, and he almost breaks away from them, but the effort collapses, and they are able to drag him away, as he is about to vomit. The Office continues as if nothing had taken place.*]

[*End of Act One—Scene One*]

ACT ONE

Scene Two

> *A knife, like a butcher's, hanging aloft, the size of a garden fence. The cutting edge of the blade points upwards. Across it hangs the torso of a naked man, his head hanging down. Below it, an enormous round cone, like the inside of a vast barrel, surrounded by darkness. From the upstage entrance, seemingly far, far away, a dark figure appears against the blinding light inside, as it grows brighter. The figure approaches slowly along the floor of the vast cone, and stops as it reaches the downstage opening. It is* MARTIN, *haggard and streaming with sweat.*

MARTIN   I lost the body of a child, a child's body, the eyes of a child; and at the first sound of my own childish voice. I lost the body of a child; and I was afraid, and I went back to find it. But I'm still afraid. I'm afraid, and there's an end of it! But *I* mean . . . [*shouts*] . . . Continually! For instance of the noise the Prior's dog makes on a still evening when he rolls over on his side and licks his teeth. I'm afraid of the darkness, and the hole in it; and I see it sometime of every day! And some days more than once even, and there's no bottom to it, no bottom to my breath, and I can't reach it. Why? Why do you think? There's a bare fist clenched to my bowels and they can't move, and I have to sit sweating in my little monk's house to open them. The lost body of a child, hanging on a mother's tit, and close to the warm, big body of a man, and I can't find it.

[*He steps down, out of the blazing light within the cone, and goes to his cell down* L. *Kneeling by his bed, he starts to try and pray but he soon collapses. From down* R *appear a procession of* MONKS, *carrying various priest's vestments, candles and articles for the altar, for* MARTIN *is about to perform his very first Mass. Heading them is* BROTHER WEINAND. *They pass* MARTIN'S *cell, and, after a few words, they go on, leaving* BROTHER WEINAND *with* MARTIN, *and disappear into what is almost like a small house on the upstage left of the stage: a bagpipe of the period, fat, soft, foolish, and obscene looking.*]

BROTHER WEINAND   Brother Martin! Brother Martin!

MARTIN   Yes.

BROTHER WEINAND   Your father's here.

MARTIN   My father?

BROTHER WEINAND   He asked to see you, but I told him it'd be better to wait until afterwards.

MARTIN   Where is he?

BROTHER WEINAND   He's having breakfast with the Prior.

MARTIN   Is he alone?

BROTHER WEINAND   No, he's got a couple of dozen friends at least, I should say.

MARTIN   Is my mother with him?

BROTHER WEINAND   No.

MARTIN   What did he have to come for? I should have told him not to come.

BROTHER WEINAND   It'd be a strange father who didn't want to be present when his son celebrated his first Mass.

MARTIN   I never thought he'd come. Why didn't he tell me?

BROTHER WEINAND   Well, he's here now, anyway. He's also given twenty guilden to the chapter as a present, so he can't be too displeased with you.

MARTIN   Twenty guilden.

BROTHER WEINAND   Well, are you all prepared?

MARTIN   That's three times what it cost him to send me to the University for a year.

BROTHER WEINAND   You don't look it. Why, you're running all over with sweat again. Are you sick? Are you?

MARTIN   No.

BROTHER WEINAND   Here, let me wipe your face. You haven't much time. You're sure you're not sick?

MARTIN   My bowels won't move, that's all. But that's nothing out of the way.

BROTHER WEINAND   Have you shaved?

MARTIN   Yes. Before I went to confession. Why, do you think I should shave again?

BROTHER WEINAND   No. I don't. A few overlooked little bristles couldn't make much difference, any more than a few imaginary sins. There, that's better.

MARTIN   What do you mean?

BROTHER WEINAND   You were sweating like a pig in a butcher's shop. You know what they say, don't you? Wherever you find a melancholy person, there you'll find a bath running for the devil.

MARTIN   No, no, what did you mean about leaving a few imaginary sins?

BROTHER WEINAND   I mean there are plenty of priests with dirty ears administering the sacraments, but this isn't the time to talk about that. Come on, Martin, you've got nothing to be afraid of.

MARTIN   How do you know?

BROTHER WEINAND   You always talk as if lightning were just about to strike behind you.

MARTIN   Tell me what you meant.

BROTHER WEINAND   I only meant the whole convent knows you're always making up sins you've never committed. That's right—well, isn't it? No sensible confessor will have anything to do with you.

MARTIN   What's the use of all this talk of penitence if I can't feel it.

BROTHER WEINAND   Father Nathin told me he had to punish you only the day before yesterday because you were in some ridiculous state of hysteria, all over some verse in Proverbs or something.

MARTIN   "Know thou the state of thy flocks."

BROTHER WEINAND   And all over the interpretation of one word apparently. When will you ever learn? You must know what you're doing. Some of the brothers laugh quite openly at you, you and your over-stimulated conscience. Which is wrong of them, I know, but you must be able to see why.

MARTIN   It's the single words that trouble me.

BROTHER WEINAND   The moment you've confessed and turned to the altar, you're beckoning for a priest again. Why, every time you break wind they say you rush to a confessor.

MARTIN   Do they say that?

BROTHER WEINAND   It's their favourite joke.

MARTIN   They say that, do they?

BROTHER WEINAND   Martin! You're protected from many of the world's evils in here. You're expected to master them, not be obsessed by them. God bids us hope in His everlasting mercy. Try to remember that.

MARTIN   And you tell me this! What have I gained from coming into this sacred Order? Aren't I still the same? I'm still envious, I'm still impatient, I'm still passionate?

BROTHER WEINAND   How can you ask a question like that?

MARTIN   I do ask it. I'm asking you! What have I gained?

BROTHER WEINAND   In any of this, all we can ever learn is how to die.

MARTIN   That's no answer.

BROTHER WEINAND   It's the only one I can think of at this moment. Come on.

MARTIN   All you teach me in this sacred place is how to doubt—

BROTHER WEINAND   Give you a little praise, and you're pleased for a while, but let a little trial of sin and death come into your day and you crumble, don't you?

MARTIN   But that's all you've taught me, that's really all you've taught me, and all the while I'm living in the Devil's worm-bag.

BROTHER WEINAND   It hurts me to watch you like this, sucking up cares like a leech.

MARTIN   You *will* be there beside me, won't you?

BROTHER WEINAND   Of course, and, if anything at all goes wrong, or if you forget anything, we'll see to it. You'll be all right. But nothing will—you won't make any mistakes.

MARTIN   But what if I do, just one mistake. Just a word, one word—one sin.

BROTHER WEINAND   Martin, kneel down.

MARTIN   Forgive me, Brother Weinand, but the truth is this—

BROTHER WEINAND   Kneel.

[MARTIN *kneels*.]

MARTIN   It's this, just this. All I can feel, all I can feel is God's hatred.

BROTHER WEINAND   Repeat the Apostles' Creed.

MARTIN   He's like a glutton, the way he gorges me, he's a glutton. He gorges me, and then spits me out in lumps.

BROTHER WEINAND   After me. "I believe in God the Father Almighty, maker of Heaven and Earth . . .

MARTIN   I'm a trough, I tell you, and he's swilling about in me. All the time.

BROTHER WEINAND   "And in Jesus Christ, His only Son Our Lord . . .

MARTIN   "And in Jesus Christ, His only Son Our Lord . . .

BROTHER WEINAND   "Who was conceived by the Holy Ghost, born of the Virgin Mary, suffered under Pontius Pilate . . .

MARTIN   [*almost unintelligibly*]   "Was crucified, dead and buried; He descended into Hell; the third day He rose from the dead, He ascended into Heaven, and sitteth on the right hand of God the Father Almighty; from thence He shall come to judge the quick and the dead." And every sunrise sings a song for death.

BROTHER WEINAND   "I believe—"

MARTIN   "I believe—"

BROTHER WEINAND   Go on.

MARTIN   "I believe in the Holy Ghost; the holy Catholic Church; the Communion of Saints; the forgiveness of sins;

BROTHER WEINAND   Again!

MARTIN   "The forgiveness of sins.

BROTHER WEINAND   What was that again?

MARTIN   "I believe in the forgiveness of sins."

BROTHER WEINAND   Do you? Then remember this: St. Bernard says that when we say in the Apostles' Creed "I believe in the forgiveness of sins" each one must believe that *his* sins are forgiven. Well?—

MARTIN   I wish my bowels would open. I'm blocked up like an old crypt.

BROTHER WEINAND   Try to remember, Martin?

MARTIN   Yes, I'll try.

BROTHER WEINAND   Good. Now, you must get yourself ready. Come on, we'd better help you.

[*Some* BROTHERS *appear from out of the bagpipe with the vestments, etc. and help* MARTIN *put them on*.]

MARTIN   How much did you say my father gave to the chapter?

BROTHER WEINAND   Twenty guilden.

MARTIN   That's a lot of money to my father. He's a miner, you know.

BROTHER WEINAND   Yes, he told me.

MARTIN   As tough as you can think of. Where's he sitting?

BROTHER WEINAND   Near the front, I should think. Are you nearly ready?

[*The Convent bell rings. A procession leads out from the bagpipe.*]

MARTIN   Thank you, Brother Weinand.

BROTHER WEINAND   For what? Today would be an ordeal for any kind of man. In a short while, you will be handling, for the first time, the body and blood of Christ. God bless you, my son.

[*He makes the sign of the cross, and the other* BROTHERS *leave.*]

MARTIN   Somewhere, in the body of a child, Satan foresaw in me what I'm suffering now. That's why he prepares open pits for me, and all kinds of tricks to bring me down, so that I keep wondering if I'm the only man living who's baited, and surrounded by dreams, and afraid to move.

BROTHER WEINAND   [*really angry by now*]   You're a fool. You're really a fool. God isn't angry with you. It's you who are angry with Him.

[*He goes out. The* BROTHERS *wait for* MARTIN, *who kneels.*]

MARTIN   Oh, Mary, dear Mary, all I see of Christ is a flame and raging on a rainbow. Pray to your Son, and ask Him to still His anger, for I can't raise my eyes to look at Him. Am I the only one to see all this, and suffer?

[*He rises, joins the procession and disappears off with it. As the Mass is heard to begin offstage, the stage is empty. Then the light within the cone grows increasingly brilliant, and, presently* MARTIN *appears again. He enters through the far entrance of the cone, and advances towards the audience. He is carrying a naked child. Presently, he steps down from the cone, comes downstage, and stands still.*]

MARTIN   And so, the praising ended—and the blasphemy began.

[*He returns, back into the cone, the light fades as the Mass comes to its end.*]

[*End of Act One—Scene Two*]

ACT ONE

Scene Three

> *The Convent refectory. Some monks are sitting at table with* HANS *and* LUCAS. LUCAS *is chatting with the* BROTHERS *eagerly, but* HANS *is brooding. He has drunk a lot of wine in a short time, and his brain is beginning to heat.*

HANS   What about some more of this, eh? Don't think you can get away with it, you know, you old cockchafer. I'm getting me twenty guilden's worth before the day's out. After all, it's a proud day for all of us. That's right, isn't it?

LUCAS   It certainly is.

BROTHER WEINAND   Forgive me, I wasn't looking. Here—

[*He fills* HANS's *glass.*]

HANS   [*trying to be friendly*]   Don't give me that. You monks don't miss much. Got eyes like gimlets and ears like open drains. Tell me—Come on, then, what's your opinion of Brother Martin?

BROTHER WEINAND   He's a good, devout monk.

HANS   Yes. Yes, well, I suppose you can't say much about each other, can you? You're more like a team, in a way. Tell me, Brother—would you say that in this monastery—or, any monastery you like—you were as strong as the weakest member of the team?

BROTHER WEINAND   No, I don't think that's so.

HANS   But wouldn't you say then—I'm not saying this in any criticism, mind, but because I'm just interested, naturally, in the circumstances—but wouldn't you say that one bad monk, say for instance, one really monster sized, roaring great bitch of a monk, if he really got going, really going, couldn't he get his order such a reputation that eventually, it might even have to go into—what do they call it now—liquidation. That's it. Liquidation. Now, you're an educated man, you understand Latin and Greek and Hebrew—

BROTHER WEINAND   Only Latin, I'm afraid, and a very little Greek.

HANS   [*having planted his cue for a quick, innocent boast*]   Oh, really. Martin knows Latin and Greek, and now he's half-way through Hebrew too, they tell me.

BROTHER WEINAND   Martin is a brilliant man. We are not all as gifted as he is.

HANS   No, well, anyway what would be your opinion about this?

BROTHER WEINAND   I think my opinion would be that the Church is bigger than those who are in her.

HANS   Yes, yes, but don't you think it could be discredited by, say, just a few men?

BROTHER WEINAND   Plenty of people have tried, but the Church is still there. Besides, a human voice is small and the world's very large. But the Church reaches out and is heard everywhere.

HANS   Well, what about this chap Erasmus, for instance?

BROTHER WEINAND   [*politely. He knows* HANS *knows nothing about him*]   Yes?

HANS   Erasmus. [*Trying to pass the ball*]   Well, what about him, for instance? What do you think about him?

BROTHER WEINAND   Erasmus is apparently a great scholar, and respected throughout Europe.

HANS   [*resenting being lectured*]   Yes, of course, *I* know who he is, I don't need you to tell me that, what I said was: what do you think about him?

BROTHER WEINAND   Think about him?

HANS   Good God, you won't stand still a minute and let yourself be saddled, will you? Doesn't he criticize the Church or something?

BROTHER WEINAND   He's a scholar, and, I should say, his criticisms could only be profitably argued about by other scholars.

LUCAS   Don't let him get you into an argument. He'll argue about anything, especially if he doesn't know what he's talking about.

HANS   I know what I'm talking about, I was merely asking a question—

LUCAS   Well, you shouldn't be asking questions on a day like today. Just think of it, for a minute, Hans—

HANS   What do you think I'm doing? You soppy old woman!

LUCAS   It's a really "once only" occasion, like a wedding, if you like.

HANS   Or a funeral. By the way, what's happened to the corpse? Eh? Where's Brother Martin?

BROTHER WEINAND   I expect he's still in his cell.

HANS   Well, what's he doing in there?

BROTHER WEINAND   He's perfectly all right, he's a little—disturbed.

HANS   [*pouncing delightedly*]   Disturbed! Disturbed! What's he disturbed about?

BROTHER WEINAND   Celebrating one's first Mass can be a great ordeal for a sensitive spirit.

HANS   Oh, the bread and the wine and all that?

BROTHER WEINAND   Of course; there are a great many things to memorize as well.

LUCAS   Heavens, yes. I don't know how they think of it all.

HANS   I didn't think he made it up as he went along! But doesn't he know we're still here? Hasn't anybody told him we're all waiting for him?

BROTHER WEINAND   He won't be much longer—you'll see. Here, have some more of our wine. He simply wanted to be on his own for a little while before he saw anyone.

HANS   I should have thought he had enough of being on his own by now.

LUCAS   The boy's probably a bit—well, you know, anxious about seeing you again too.

HANS   What's he got to be anxious about?

LUCAS   Well, apart from anything else, it's nearly three years since he last saw you.

HANS   I saw *him*. He didn't see me.

[*Enter* MARTIN.]

LUCAS   There you are, my boy. We were wondering what had happened to you. Come and sit down, there's a good lad. Your father and I have been punishing the convent wine cellar, I'm afraid. Bit early in the day for me, too.

HANS   Speak for yourself, you swirly-eyed old gander. We're not *started* yet, are we?

LUCAS   My dear boy, are you all right? You're so pale.

HANS   He's right though. Brother Martin! Brother Lazarus they ought to call you!

[*He laughs and* MARTIN *smiles at the joke with him.* MARTIN *is cautious,* HANS *too, but manœuvring for position.*]

MARTIN   I'm all right, thank you, Lucas.

HANS   Been sick, have you?

MARTIN   I'm much better now, thank you, father.

HANS   [*relentless*]   Upset tummy, is it? That what it is? Too much fasting I expect. [*Concealing concern*]. You look like death warmed up, all right.

LUCAS   Come and have a little wine. You're allowed that, aren't you? It'll make you feel better.

HANS   I know that milky look. I've seen it too many times. Been sick have you?

LUCAS   Oh, he's looking better already. Drop of wine'll put the colour back in there. You're all right, aren't you, lad?

MARTIN   Yes, what about you—

LUCAS   That's right. Of course he is. He's all right.

HANS   Vomit all over your cell, I expect. [*To* BROTHER WEINAND]. But he'll have to clear that up himself, won't he?

LUCAS   [*to* MARTIN]   Oh, you weren't were you? Poor old lad, well, never mind, no wonder you kept us waiting.

HANS   Can't have his mother coming in and getting down on her knees to mop it all up.

MARTIN   I managed to clean it up all right. How are *you*, father?

HANS   [*feeling an attack, but determined not to lose the initiative*]   Me? Oh, I'm all right. I'm all right, aren't I, Lucas? Nothing ever wrong with me. Your old man's strong enough. But then that's because we've got to be, people like Lucas and me. Because if *we* aren't strong, it won't take any time at all before we're knocked flat on our backs, or flat on our knees, or flat on something or other. Flat on our backs and finished, and we can't afford to be finished because if we're finished, that's it, that's the end, so we just have to stand up to it as best we can. But that's life, isn't it?

MARTIN I'm never sure what people mean when they say that.

LUCAS Your father's doing very well indeed, Martin. He's got his own investment in the mine now, so he's beginning to work for himself if you see what I mean. That's the way things are going everywhere now.

MARTIN [*to* HANS] You must be pleased.

HANS I'm pleased to make money. I'm not pleased to break my back doing it.

MARTIN How's mother?

HANS Nothing wrong there either. Too much work and too many kids for too long, that's all. [*Hiding embarrassment*]. I'm sorry she couldn't come, but it's a rotten journey as you know, and all that, so she sent her love to you. Oh, yes, and there was a pie too. But I was told [*at* BROTHER WEINAND] I couldn't give it to you, but I'd have to give it to the Prior.

MARTIN That's the rule about gifts, father. You must have forgotten?

HANS Well, I hope you get a piece of it anyway. She took a lot of care over it. Oh yes, and then there was Lucas's girl, she asked to be remembered to you.

MARTIN Oh, good. How is she?

HANS Didn't she, Lucas? She asked specially to be remembered to Martin, didn't she?

LUCAS Oh she often talks about you, Martin. Even now. She's married you know.

MARTIN No, I didn't know.

LUCAS Oh, yes, got two children, one boy and a girl.

HANS That's it—two on show on the stall, and now another one coming out from under the counter again—right, Lucas?

LUCAS Yes, oh, she makes a fine mother.

HANS And what's better than that? There's only one way of going 'up you' to Old Nick when he does come for you and that's when you show him your kids. It's the one thing—that is, if you've been lucky, and the plagues kept away from you—you can spring it out from under the counter at him. *That* to you! Then you've done something for yourself forever—forever and ever. Amen. [*Pause*]. Come along, Brother Martin, don't let your guests go without. Poor old Lucas is sitting there with a glass as empty as a nun's womb, aren't you, you thirsty little goosey?

MARTIN Oh, please, I'm sorry.

HANS That's right, and don't forget your old dad. [*Pause*]. Yes, well, as I say, I'm sorry your mother couldn't come, but I don't suppose she'd have enjoyed it much, although I dare say she'd like to have watched her son perform the Holy Office. Isn't a mother supposed to dance with her son after the ceremony? Like Christ danced with *his* mother? Well, I can't see her doing that. I suppose you think *I'm* going to dance with you instead.

MARTIN You're not obliged to, father.

HANS It's like giving a bride away, isn't it?

MARTIN Not unlike.

[*They have been avoiding any direct contact until now, but now they look at each other, and both relax a little.*]

HANS [*encouraged*] God's eyes! Come to think of it, you look like a woman, in all that!

MARTIN [*with affection*] Not any woman you'd want, father.

HANS What do *you* know about it, eh? What do you know about it? [*He laughs but not long*]. Well, Brother Martin.

MARTIN Well? [*Pause*]. Have you had some fish? Or a roast, how about that, that's what you'd like, isn't it?

HANS   Brother Martin, old Brother Martin. Well, Brother Martin, you had a right old time up there by that altar for a bit, didn't you? I wouldn't have been in your shoes, I'll tell you. All those people listening to you, every word you're saying, watching every little tiny movement, watching for one little lousy mistake. I couldn't keep my eyes off it. We all thought you were going to flunk it for one minute there, didn't we, Lucas?

LUCAS   Well, we had a couple of anxious moments—

HANS   Anxious moments! I'll say there were. I thought to myself, "he's going to flunk it, he can't get through it, he's going to flunk it." What was that bit, you know, the worst bit where you stopped and Brother—

MARTIN   Weinand.

HANS   Weinand, yes, and he very kindly helped you up. He was actually holding you up at one point, wasn't he?

MARTIN   Yes.

BROTHER WEINAND   It happens often enough when a young priest celebrates Mass for the first time.

HANS   Looked as though he didn't know if it was Christmas or Wednesday. We thought the whole thing had come to a standstill for a bit, didn't we? Everyone waiting and nothing happening. What was that bit, Martin, what was it?

MARTIN   I don't remember.

HANS   Yes, you know, the bit you really flunked.

MARTIN   [rattling it off]   Receive, oh Holy Father, almighty and eternal God, this spotless host, which I, thine unworthy servant, offer unto thee for my own innumerable sins of commission and omission, and for all here present and all faithful Christians, living and dead, so that it may avail for their salvation and everlasting life. When I entered the monastery, I wanted to speak to God directly, you see. Without any embarrassment, I wanted to speak to him myself, but when it came to it, I dried up—as I always have.

LUCAS   No, you didn't, Martin, it was only for a few moments, besides—

MARTIN   Thanks to Brother Weinand. Father, why do you hate me being here?
    [HANS is outraged at a direct question.]

HANS   Eh? What do you mean? I don't hate you being here.

MARTIN   Try to give me a straight answer if you can, father. I should like you to tell me.

HANS   What are you talking about, Brother Martin, you don't know what you're talking about. You've not had enough wine, that's your trouble.

MARTIN   And don't say I could have been a lawyer.

HANS   Well, so you could have been. You could have been better than that. You could have been a burgomaster, you could have been a magistrate, you could have been a chancellor, you could have been anything! So what! I don't want to talk about it. What's the matter with you! Anyway, I certainly don't want to talk about it in front of complete strangers.

MARTIN   You make me sick.

HANS   Oh, do I? Well, thank you for that, Brother Martin! Thank you for the truth, anyway.

MARTIN   No, it isn't the truth. It isn't the truth at all. You're drinking too much wine—and I'm . . .

HANS   Drinking too much wine! I could drink this convent piss from here till Gabriel's horn—and from all accounts, that'll blow about next Thursday— so what's the difference? [Pause. HANS drinks.] Is this the wine you use? Is it? Well? I'm asking a straight question myself now. Is this the wine you use? [To MARTIN]. Here, have some.
    [MARTIN takes it and drinks.]
    You know what they say?

MARTIN   No, what do they say?

HANS   I'll tell you:

> Bread thou art and wine thou art
> And always shall remain so.

[*Pause*]

MARTIN   My father didn't mean that. He's a very devout man, I know.

[*Some of the* BROTHERS *have got up to leave.*]

MARTIN   [*to* LUCAS]   Brother Weinand will show you over the convent. If you've finished, that is.

LUCAS   Yes, oh yes, I'd like that. Yes, I've had more than enough, thank you. Right, well, let's go, shall we, Brother Weinand? I'll come back for you, shall I. Hans, you'll stay here?

HANS   Just as you like.

LUCAS   [*to* MARTIN]   You're looking a bit better now, lad. Good-bye, my boy, but I'll see you before I go, won't I?

MARTIN   Yes, of course.

[*They all go, leaving* MARTIN *and* HANS *alone together. Pause.*]

HANS   Martin, I didn't mean to embarrass you.

MARTIN   No, it was my fault.

HANS   Not in front of everyone.

MARTIN   I shouldn't have asked you a question like that. It was a shock to see you suddenly, after such a long time. Most of my day's spent in silence you see, except for the Offices; and I enjoy the singing, as you know, but there's not much speaking, except to one's confessor. I'd almost forgotten what your voice sounded like.

HANS   Tell me, son—what made you get all snarled up like that in the Mass?

MARTIN   You're disappointed, aren't you?

HANS   I want to know, that's all. I'm a simple man, Martin, I'm no scholar, but I can understand all right. But you're a learned man, you speak Latin and Greek and Hebrew. You've been trained to remember ever since you were a tiny boy. Men like you don't just forget their words!

MARTIN   I don't understand what happened. I lifted up my head at the host, and, as I was speaking the words, I heard them as if it were the first time, and suddenly—[*pause*] they struck at my life.

HANS   I don't know, I really don't. Perhaps your father and mother are wrong, and God's right, after all. Perhaps. Whatever it is you've got to find, you could only find out by becoming a monk; maybe that's the answer.

MARTIN   But you don't believe that. Do you?

HANS   No; no I don't.

MARTIN   Then say what you mean.

HANS   All right, if that's what you want, I'll say just what I mean. I think a man murders himself in these places.

MARTIN   [*retreating at once*]   I am holy. I kill no one but myself.

HANS   I don't care. I tell you it gives me the creeps. And that's why I couldn't bring your mother, if you want to know.

MARTIN   The Gospels are the only mother I've ever had.

HANS   [*triumphantly*]   And haven't you ever read in the Gospels, don't you know what's written in there? "Thou shalt honour thy father and thy mother."

MARTIN   You're not understanding me, because you don't want to.

HANS   That's fine talk, oh yes, fine, holy talk, but it won't wash, Martin. It won't wash because you can't ever, however you try, you can't ever get away from your body because that's what you live in, and it's all you've got to die in, and you can't get away from the body of your father and your mother! We're bodies, Martin, and so are you, and we're bound together for always. But you're like every man who was ever born into this world, Martin. You'd like to pretend that you made yourself, that it was *you* who made you—and not the body of a woman and another man.

MARTIN   Churches, kings, and fathers—why do they ask so much, and why do they all of them get so much more than they deserve?

HANS   You think so. Well, I think I deserve a little more than you've given me—

MARTIN   I've given you! I don't have to give you! I *am*—that's all I need to give to you. That's your big reward, and that's all you're ever going to get, and it's more than any father's got a right to. You wanted me to learn Latin, to be a Master of Arts, be a lawyer. All you want is me to justify *you*! Well, I can't, and, what's more, I won't. I can't even justify myself. So just stop asking me what have I accomplished, and what have I done for you. I've done all for you I'll ever do, and that's live and wait to die.

HANS   Why do you blame *me* for everything?

MARTIN   I don't blame you. I'm just not grateful, that's all.

HANS   Listen, I'm not a specially good man, I know, but I believe in God and in Jesus Christ, His Son, and the Church will look after me, and I can make some sort of life for myself that has a little joy in it somewhere. But where is your joy? You wrote to me once, when you were at the University, that only Christ could light up the place you live in, but what's the point? What's the point if it turns out the place you're living in is just a hovel? Don't you think it mightn't be better not to see at all?

MARTIN   I'd rather be able to see.

HANS   You'd rather see!

MARTIN   You really are disappointed, aren't you? Go on.

HANS   And why? I see a young man, learned and full of life, my son, abusing his youth with fear and humiliation. You think you're facing up to it in here, but you're not; you're running away, you're running away and you can't help it.

MARTIN   If it's so easy in here, why do you think the rest of the world isn't knocking the gates down to get in?

HANS   Because they haven't given up, that's why.

MARTIN   Well, there it is: you think I've given up.

HANS   Yes, there it is. That damned monk's piss has given me a headache.

MARTIN   I'm sorry.

HANS   Yes, we're all sorry, and a lot of good it does any of us.

MARTIN   I suppose fathers and sons always disappoint each other.

HANS   I worked for you, I went without for you.

MARTIN   Well?

HANS   Well! [*almost anxiously*] And if I beat you fairly often, and pretty hard sometimes I suppose, it wasn't any more than any other boy, was it?

MARTIN   No.

HANS   What do you think it is makes you different? Other men are all right, aren't they? You were stubborn, you were always stubborn, you've always had to resist, haven't you?

MARTIN   You disappointed me too, and not just a few times, but at some time of every day I ever remember hearing or seeing you, but, as you say, maybe that was also no different from any other boy. But I loved you the best. It was always *you* I wanted. I wanted your love more than anyone's, and if anyone was to hold me, I wanted it to be you. Funnily enough, my mother disappointed me the most, and I loved her less, much less. She made a gap which no one else could have filled, but all she could do was make it bigger, bigger and more unbearable.

HANS   I don't know what any of that means; I really don't. I'd better be going, Martin. I think it's best; and I dare say you've got your various duties to perform.

MARTIN   She beat me once for stealing a nut, your wife. I remember it so well, she beat me until the blood came, I was so surprised to see it on my finger-tips; yes, stealing a nut, that's right. But that's not the point. I had corns on my backside already. Always before, when I was beaten for something, the pain seemed outside of me in some way, as if it belonged to the rest of the world, and not only me. But, on that day, for the first time, the pain belonged to me and no one else, it went no further than *my* body, bent between *my* knees and *my* chin.

HANS   You know what, Martin, I think you've always been scared—ever since you could get up off your knees and walk. You've been scared for the good reason that that's what you most like to be. Yes, I'll tell you. I'll tell you what! Like that day, that day when you were coming home from Erfurt, and the thunderstorm broke, and you were so piss-scared, you lay on the ground and cried out to St. Anne because you saw a bit of lightning and thought you'd seen a vision.

MARTIN   I saw it all right.

HANS   And you went and asked her to save you—on condition that you became a monk.

MARTIN   I saw it.

HANS   Did you? So it's still St. Anne is it? I thought you were blaming your mother and me for your damned monkery?

MARTIN   Perhaps I should.

HANS   And perhaps sometime you should have another little think about that heavenly vision that wangled you away into the cloister.

MARTIN   What's that?

HANS   I mean: I hope it really was a vision. I hope it wasn't a delusion and some trick of the devil's. I really hope so, because I can't bear to think of it otherwise. [*Pause*] Good-bye, son. I'm sorry we had to quarrel. It shouldn't have turned out like this at all today.
[*Pause*]

MARTIN   Father—why did you give your consent?

HANS   What, to your monkery, you mean?

MARTIN   Yes. You could have refused, but why didn't you?

HANS   Well, when your two brothers died with the plague . . .

MARTIN   You gave me up for dead, didn't you?

HANS   Good-bye, son. Here—have a glass of holy wine.
[*He goes out.* MARTIN *stands, with the glass in his hand and looks into it. Then he drinks from it slowly, as if for the first time. He sits down at the table and sets the glass before him.*]

MARTIN   But—but what if it isn't true?

CURTAIN

[*End of Act One*]

DECOR NOTE   *After the intense private interior of Act One, with its outer darkness and rich, personal objects, the physical effect from now on should be more intricate, general, less personal; sweeping, concerned with men in time rather than particular man in the unconscious; caricature not portraiture, like the popular woodcuts of the period, like Dürer. Down by the apron in one corner there is now a heavily carved pulpit.*

ACT TWO

Scene One

> *The market place, Jüterbog, 1517. The sound of loud music,*
> *bells as a procession approaches the centre of the market place,*
> *which is covered in the banners of welcoming trade guilds. At*
> *the head of the slow-moving procession, with its lighted tapers*
> *and to the accompaniment of singing, prayers and the smoke*
> *of incense, is carried the Pontiff's bull of grace on a cush-*
> *ion and cloth of gold. Behind this the arms of the Pope and*
> *the Medici. After this, carrying a large red wooden cross, comes*
> *the focus of the procession,* JOHN TETZEL, *Dominican, inquisitor*
> *and most famed and successful indulgence vendor of his day.*
> *He is splendidly equipped to be an ecclesiastical huckster, with*
> *alive, silver hair, the powerfully calculating voice, range and*
> *technique of a trained orator, the terrible, riveting charm of a*
> *dedicated professional able to winkle coppers out of the pockets*
> *of the poor and desperate.*
> *The red cross is taken from* TETZEL *and established prominently*
> *behind him, and, from it are suspended the arms of the Pope.*

TETZEL   Are you wondering who I am, or what I am? Is there anyone here among you, any small child, any cripple, or any sick idiot who hasn't heard of me, and doesn't know why I am here? No? Well, speak up then if there is? What, no one? Do you all know me then? Do you all know who I am? If it's true, it's very good, and just as it should be. Just as it should be, and no more than that! However, however—just in case—just in case, mind, there is one blind, maimed midget among you today who can't hear, I will open his ears and wash them out with sacred soap for him! And, as for the rest of you. I know I can rely on you all to listen patiently while I instruct him. Is that right? Can I go on? I'm asking you, is that right, can I go on? I say "can I go on"?
[*Pause*]
Thank you. And what is there to tell this blind, maimed midget who's down there somewhere among you? No, don't look round for him, you'll only scare him and then he'll lose his one great chance, and it's not likely to come again, or if it does come, maybe it'll be too late. Well, what's the good news on this bright day? What's the information you want? It's this! Who is this friar with his red cross? Who sent him, and what's he here for? Don't try to work it out for yourself because I'm going to tell you now, this very minute. I am John Tetzel, Dominican, inquisitor, sub-commissioner to the Archbishop of Mainz, and what I bring you is indulgences. Indulgences made possible by the red blood of Jesus Christ, and the red cross you see standing up here behind me is the standard of those who carry them. Look at it! Go on, look at it! What else do you see hanging from the red cross? Well, what do they look like? Why, it's the arms of his holiness, because why? Because it's him who sent me here. Yes, my friend, the Pope himself has sent me with indulgences for you! Fine, you say, but what are indulgences? And what are they to me? What are indulgences? They're only the most precious and noble of God's gifts to men, that's all they are! Before God, I tell you I wouldn't swap my privilege at this moment with that of St. Peter in Heaven because I've already saved more souls with my indulgences than he could ever have done with all his

sermons. You think that's bragging, do you? Well, listen a little more carefully, my friend, because this concerns *you!* Just look at it this way. For every mortal sin you commit, the Church says that after confession and contrition, you've got to do penance—either in this life or in purgatory —for seven years. Seven years! Right? Are you with me? Good. Now then, how many mortal sins are committed by you—by you—in a single day? Just think for one moment: in one single day of your life. Do you know the answer? Oh, not so much as one a day. Very well then, how many in a month? How many in six months? How many in a year? And how many in a whole lifetime? Yes, you needn't shuffle your feet—it doesn't bear thinking about, does it? You couldn't even add up all those years without a merchant's clerk to do it for you! Try and add up all the years of torment piling up! What about it? And isn't there anything you can do about this terrible situation you're in? Do you really want to know? Yes! There is something, and that something I have here with me now up here, letters, letters of indulgence. Hold up the letters so that everyone can see them. Is there anyone so small he can't see? Look at them, all properly sealed, an indulgence in every envelope, and one of them can be yours today, now, before it's too late! Come on, come up as close as you like, you won't squash me so easily. Take a good look. There isn't any one sin so big that one of these letters can't remit it. I challenge any one here, any member of this audience, to present me with a sin, anything, any kind of a sin, I don't care what it is, that I can't settle for him with one of these precious little envelopes. Why, if any one had ever offered violence to the blessed Virgin Mary, Mother of God, if he'd only pay up—as long as he paid up all he could—he'd find himself forgiven. You think I'm exaggerating? You do, do you? Well, I'm authorized to go even further than that. Not only am I empowered to give you these letters of pardon for the sins you've already committed, I can give you pardon for those sins you haven't even committed [*pause . . . then slowly*] but, which, however you *intend* to commit! But, you ask—and it's a fair question—but, you ask, why is our Holy Lord prepared to distribute such a rich grace to me? The answer, my friends, is all too simple. It's so that we can restore the ruined church of St. Peter and St. Paul in Rome! So that it won't have its equal anywhere in the world. This great church contains the bodies not only of the holy apostles Peter and Paul, but of a hundred thousand martyrs and no less than forty-six popes! To say nothing of the relics like St. Veronica's handkerchief, the burning bush of Moses and the very rope with which Judas Iscariot hanged himself! But, alas, this fine old building is threatened with destruction, and all these things with it, if a sufficient restoration fund isn't raised, and raised soon. [*With passionate irony*] . . . Will anyone dare to say that the cause is not a good one? [*Pause.*] . . . Very well, and won't you, for as little as one quarter of a florin, my friend, buy yourself one of these letters, so that in the hour of death, the gate through which sinners enter the world of torment shall be closed against you, and the gate leading to the joy of paradise be flung open for you? And, remember this, these letters aren't just for the living but for the dead too. There can't be one amongst you who hasn't at least one dear one who has departed—and to who knows what? Why, these letters are for them too. It isn't even necessary to repent. So don't hold back, come forward, think of your dear ones, think of yourselves! For twelve groats, or whatever it is we think you can afford, you can rescue your father from agony and yourself from certain disaster. And if you only have the coat on your back to call your own, then strip it off, strip it off now so that you too can obtain grace. For remember: As soon as your money rattles in the box and the cash bell rings, the soul flies out of purgatory and sings! So, come on then. Get your money out! What is it then, have your wits flown away with your faith? Listen then, soon, I shall take down the cross, shut the gates of heaven, and put out the brightness of this sun of grace that shines on you here today.

[*He flings a large coin into the open strong box, where it rattles furiously.*] The Lord our God reigns no longer. He has resigned all power to the Pope. In the name of the Father, and of the Son and of the Holy Ghost. Amen.

[*The sound of coins clattering like rain into a great coffer as the light fades.*]

[*End of Act Two—Scene One*]

ACT TWO

Scene Two

> *The Eremite Cloister, Wittenberg. 1517. Seated beneath a single pear tree is* JOHANN VON STAUPITZ, *Vicar General of the Augustinian Order. He is a quiet, gentle-voiced man in late middle age, almost stolidly contemplative. He has profound respect for* MARTIN, *recognizing in him the powerful potential of insight, sensitivity, courage and, also heroics that is quite outside the range of his own endeavour. However, he also understands that a man of his own limitations can offer a great deal to such a young man at this point in his development, and his treatment of* MARTIN *is a successful astringent mixture of sympathy and ridicule. Birds sing as he reads in the shade, and* MARTIN *approaches, prostrating himself.* STAUPITZ *motions him to his feet.*

MARTIN [*looking up*] The birds always seem to fly away the moment I come out here.

STAUPITZ Birds, unfortunately, have no faith.

MARTIN Perhaps it's simply that they don't like me.

STAUPITZ They haven't learned yet that you mean them no harm, that's all.

MARTIN Are you treating me to one of your allegories?

STAUPITZ Well, you recognized it, anyway.

MARTIN I ought to. Ever since I came into the cloister, I've become a craftsman allegory maker myself. Only last week I was lecturing on Galatians Three, verse three, and I allegorized going to the lavatory.

STAUPITZ [*quoting the verse*] "Are ye so foolish, that ye have begun in the spirit, you would now end in the flesh."

MARTIN That's right. But allegories aren't much help in theology—except to decorate a house that's been already built by argument.

STAUPITZ Well, it's a house you've been able to unlock for a great many of us. I never dreamed when I first came here that the University's reputation would ever become what is has, and in such a short time, and it's mostly due to you.

MARTIN [*very deliberately turning the compliment*] If ever a man could get to heaven through monkery, that man would be me.

STAUPITZ I don't mean that. You know quite well what I mean. I'm talking about your scholarship, and what you manage to do with it, not your monkishness as you call it. I've never had any patience with all your mortifications. The only wonder is that you haven't killed yourself with your prayers, and watchings, yes and even your reading too. All these trials and temptations you go through, they're meat and drink to you.

MARTIN [*patient*] Will you ever stop lecturing me about this?

STAUPITZ Of course not, why do you think you come here—to see me in the garden when you could be inside working?

MARTIN Well, if it'll please you, I've so little time, what with my lectures and study, I'm scarcely able to carry out even the basic requirements of the Rule.

STAUPITZ I'm delighted to hear it. Why do you think you've always been obsessed with the Rule? No, I don't want to hear all your troubles again. I'll tell you why: you're obsessed with the Rule because it serves very nicely as a protection for you.

MARTIN What protection?

STAUPITZ You know perfectly well what I mean, Brother Martin, so don't pretend to look innocent. Protection against the demands of your own instincts, that's what. You see, you think you admire authority, and so you do, but unfortunately, you can't submit to it. So, what you do, by your exaggerated attention to the Rule, you make the authority ridiculous. And the reason you do that is because you're determined to substitute that authority with something else—yourself. Oh, come along, Martin, I've been Vicar General too long not to have made that little discovery. Anyway, you shouldn't be too concerned with a failing like that. It also provides the strongest kind of security.

MARTIN Security? I don't feel *that*.

STAUPITZ I dare say, but you've got it all the same, which is more than most of us have.

MARTIN And how have I managed to come by this strange security?

STAUPITZ Quite simply: by demanding an impossible standard of perfection.

MARTIN I don't see what work or merit can come from a heart like mine.

STAUPITZ Oh, my dear, dear friend, I've sworn a thousand times to our holy God to live piously, and have I been able to keep my vows? No, of course I haven't. Now I've given up making solemn promises because I know I'm not able to keep them. If God won't be merciful to me for the love of Christ when I leave this world, then I shan't stand before Him on account of all my vows and good works, I shall perish, that's all.

MARTIN You think I lavish too much attention on my own pain, don't you?

STAUPITZ Well, that's difficult for me to say, Martin. We're very different kinds of men, you and I. Yes, you do lavish attention on yourself, but then a large man is worth the pains he takes. Like St. Paul, some men must say "I die daily."

MARTIN Tell me, Father, have you never felt humiliated to find that you belong to a world that's dying?

STAUPITZ No, I don't think I have.

MARTIN Surely, this must be the last age of time we're living in. There can't be any more left but the black bottom of the bucket.

STAUPITZ Do you mean the Last Judgment?

MARTIN No. I don't mean that. The Last Judgment isn't to come. It's here and now.

STAUPITZ Good. That's a little better, anyway.

MARTIN I'm like a ripe stool in the world's straining anus, and at any moment we're about to let each other go.

STAUPITZ   There's nothing new in the world being damned, dying or without hope. It's always been like that, and it'll stay like it. What's the matter with you? What are you making funny faces for?

MARTIN   It's nothing, Father, just a—a slight discomfort.

STAUPITZ   Slight discomfort? What are you holding your stomach for? Are you in pain?

MARTIN   It's all right. It's gone now.

STAUPITZ   I don't understand you. What's gone now? I've seen you grabbing at yourself like that before. What is it?

MARTIN   I'm—constipated.

STAUPITZ   Constipated? There's always something the matter with you, Brother Martin. If it's not the gripes, insomnia, or faith and works, it's boils or indigestion or some kind of belly-ache you've got. All these severe fasts——

MARTIN   That's what my father says.

STAUPITZ   Your father sounds pretty sensible to me.

MARTIN   He is, and you know, he's a theologian too, I've discovered lately.

STAUPITZ   I thought he was a miner.

MARTIN   So he is, but he made a discovery years and years ago that took me sweat and labour to dig out of the earth for myself.

STAUPITZ   Well, that's no surprise. There's always some chunk of truth buried down away somewhere which lesser men will always reach with less effort.

MARTIN   Anyway, he always knew that works alone don't save any man. Mind you, he never said anything about faith coming first.

STAUPITZ   [*quoting*]   "Oh, well, that's life, and nothing you can do's going to change it."

MARTIN   The same speech.

STAUPITZ   You can't change human nature.

MARTIN   Nor can you.

STAUPITZ   That's right, Martin, and you've demonstrated it only too well in your commentaries on the Gospels and St. Paul. But don't overlook the fact that your father's taken a vow of poverty too, even though it's very different from your own. And he took it the day he told himself, and told *you*, that he was a complete man, or at least, a contented man.

MARTIN   A hog waffling in its own crap is contented.

STAUPITZ   Exactly.

MARTIN   My father, faced with an unfamiliar notion is like a cow staring at a new barn door. Like those who look on the cross and see nothing. All they hear is the priest's forgiveness.

STAUPITZ   One thing I promise you, Martin. You'll never be a spectator. You'll always take part.

MARTIN   How is it you always manage somehow to comfort me?

STAUPITZ   I think some of us are not much more than pretty modest sponges, but we're probably best at quenching big thirsts. How's your tummy?

MARTIN   Better.

STAUPITZ   One mustn't be truly penitent because one anticipates God's forgiveness, but because one already possesses it. You have to sink to the bottom of your black bucket because that's where God judges you, and then look to the wounds of Jesus Christ. You told me once that when you entered the cloister, your father said it was like giving away a bride, and again your father was right. You are a bride and you should hold yourself ready like a woman at conception. And when grace comes and your soul is penetrated by the spirit, you shouldn't pray or exert yourself, but remain passive.

MARTIN   [*smiles*]   That's a hard role.

STAUPITZ [*smiles too*] Too hard for you, I dare say. Did you know the Duke's been complaining to me about you?

MARTIN Why, what have I done?

STAUPITZ Preaching against indulgences again.

MARTIN Oh, that—I was very mild.

STAUPITZ Yes, well I've heard your mildness in the pulpit. When I think some-times of the terror it used to be for you, you used to fall up the steps with fright. Sheer fright! You were too frightened to become a Doctor of The-ology, and you wouldn't be now if I hadn't forced you. "I'm too weak, I'm not strong enough. I shan't live long enough!" Do you remember what I said to you?

MARTIN "Never mind, the Lord still has work in heaven, and there are always vacancies."

STAUPITZ Yes, and the Duke paid all the expenses of your promotion for you. He was very cross when he spoke to me, I may say. He said you even made some reference to the collection of holy relics in the Castle Church, and most of those were paid for by the sale of indulgences, as you know. Did you say anything about them?

MARTIN Well, yes, but not about those in the Castle Church. I did make some point in passing about someone who claimed to have a feather from the wing of the angel Gabriel.

STAUPITZ Oh yes, I heard about him.

MARTIN And the Archbishop of Mainz, who is supposed to have a flame from Moses' burning bush.

STAUPITZ Oh dear, you shouldn't have mentioned that.

MARTIN And I just finished off by saying how does it happen that Christ had twelve apostles and eighteen of them are buried in Germany?

STAUPITZ Well, the Duke says he's coming to your next sermon to hear for himself, so try to keep off the subject, if you possibly can. It's All Saints' Day soon, remember, and all those relics will be out on show for everyone to gawp at. The Duke's a good chap, and he's very proud of his collection, and it doesn't help to be rude about it.

MARTIN I've tried to keep off the subject because I haven't been by any means sure about it. Then I did make a few mild protests in a couple of sermons, as I say.

STAUPITZ Yes, yes, but what did you actually say?

MARTIN That you can't strike bargains with God. There's a Jewish, Turkish, Pelagian heresy if you like.

STAUPITZ Yes, more mildness. Go on.

MARTIN I said, oh it was an evil sanction because only *you* could live *your* life, and only you can die your death. It can't be taken over for you. Am I right?

STAUPITZ [*doubtfully*] Yes, what's difficult to understand is why your sermons are so popular.

MARTIN Well, there are plenty who sit out there stiff with hatred, I can tell you. I can see their faces, and there's no mistaking them. But I wanted to tell you something—

STAUPITZ Yes?

MARTIN About all this. The other day a man was brought to me, a shoemaker. His wife had just died, and I said to him, "What've you done for her?" so he said, "I've buried her and commended her soul to God." "But haven't you had a Mass said for the repose of her soul?" "No," he said, "what's the point? She entered heaven the moment she died." So I asked him, "How do you know that?" And he said, "Well, I've proof. that's why." And out of his pocket he took a letter of indulgence.

STAUPITZ   Ah.

MARTIN   He threw it at me, and said, "And if you still maintain that a Mass is necessary, then my wife's been swindled by our most holy father the Pope. Or, if not by him, then by the priest who sold it to me."

STAUPITZ   Tetzel.

MARTIN   Who else?

STAUPITZ   That old tout!

MARTIN   There's another story going around about him which is obviously true because I've checked it at several sources. It seems that a certain Saxon nobleman had heard Tetzel in Jüterbog. After Tetzel had finished his usual performance, he asked him if he'd repeat what he'd said at one stage, that he—Tetzel I mean—had the power of pardoning sins that men intended to commit. Tetzel was very high and mighty, you know what he's like, and said, "What's the matter, weren't you listening? Of course I can give pardon not only for sins already committed but for sins that men *intend* to commit." "Well, then, that's fine," says this nobleman, "because I'd like to take revenge on one of my enemies. You know, nothing much, I don't want to kill him or anything like that. Just a little slight revenge. Now, if I give you ten guilden, will you give me a letter of indulgence that will justify me—justify me freely and completely?" Well, it seems Tetzel made a few stock objections, but eventually agreed on thirty guilden, and they made a deal. The man went away with his letter of indulgence, and Tetzel set out for the next job, which was Leipzig. Well, half-way between Leipzig and Treblen, in the middle of a wood, he was set on by a band of thugs, and beaten up. While he's lying there on the grass in a pool of his own blood, he looks up and sees that one of them is the Saxon nobleman and that they're making off with his great trunk full of money. So, the moment he's recovered enough, he rushes back to Jüterbog, and takes the nobleman to court. And what does the nobleman do? Takes out the letter of indulgence and shows it to Duke George himself—case dismissed!

STAUPITZ   [*laughing*]   Well, I leave you to handle it. But try and be careful. Remember, *I* agree with all you say, but the moment someone disagrees or objects to what you're saying, *that* will be the moment when you'll suddenly recognize the strength of your belief!

MARTIN   Father, I'm never sure of the words till I hear them out loud.

STAUPITZ   Well, that's probably the meaning of the Word. The Word is me, and I am the Word. Anyway, try and be a little prudent. Look at Erasmus: he never really gets into any serious trouble, but he still manages to make his point.

MARTIN   People like Erasmus get upset because I talk of pigs and Christ in the same breath. I must go. [*Clutches himself unobtrusively.*]

STAUPITZ   Well, you might be right. Erasmus is a fine scholar, but there are too many scholars who think they're better simply because they insinuate in Latin what you'll say in plain German. What's the matter, are you having that trouble again? Good heavens! Martin—just before you go: a man with a strong sword will draw it at some time, even if it's only to turn it on himself. But whatever happens, he can't just let it dangle from his belt. And, another thing, don't forget—you began this affair in the name of Our Lord Jesus Christ. You must do as God commands you, of course, but remember, St. Jerome once wrote about a philosopher who destroyed his own eyes so that it would give him more freedom to study. Take care of your eyes, my son, and do something about those damned bowels!

MARTIN   I will. Who knows? If I break wind in Wittenberg, they might smell
it in Rome.
[*Exit. Church bells.*]

[*End of Act Two—Scene Two*]

ACT TWO

Scene Three

> The steps of the Castle Church, Wittenberg, October 31st,
> 1517. From inside the Church comes the sound of Matins being
> sung. Sitting on the steps is a child, dirty, half-naked and play-
> ing intently by himself. MARTIN enters with a long roll of paper.
> It is his ninety-five theses for disputation against indulgences. As
> he goes up the steps, he stops and watches the child, absorbed
> in his private fantasy. He is absorbed by the child, who doesn't
> notice him at first, but, presently, as soon as the boy becomes
> aware of an intruder, he immediately stops playing and looks
> away distractedly in an attempt to exclude outside attention.
> MARTIN hesitates briefly, then puts out his hand to the child,
> who looks at it gravely and deliberately, then slowly, not rudely,
> but naturally, gets up and skips away sadly out of sight. MARTIN
> watches him, then walks swiftly back down the steps to the
> pulpit and ascends it.

MARTIN   My text is from the Epistle of Paul the Apostle to the Romans, chapter
one, verse seventeen: "For therein is the righteousness of God revealed
from faith to faith."
[*Pause*]
We are living in a dangerous time. You may not think so, but it could be
that this is the most dangerous time since the light first broke upon the
earth. It may not be true, but it's very probably true—but, what's most important is that it's an assumption we are obliged to make. We Christians
seem to be wise outwardly and mad inwardly, and in this Jerusalem we
have built there are blasphemies flourishing that make the Jews no worse
than giggling children. A man is not a good Christian because he understands Greek and Hebrew. Jerome knew five languages, but he's inferior
to Augustine, who knew only one. Of course, Erasmus wouldn't agree with
me, but perhaps one day the Lord will open his eyes for him. But listen!
A man without Christ becomes his own shell. We are content with shells.
Some shells are whole men and some are small trinkets. And, what are the
trinkets? Today is the eve of All Saints, and the holy relics will be on show
to you all; to the hungry ones whose lives are made satisfied by trinkets,
by an imposing procession and the dressings up of all kinds of dismal things.
You'll mumble for magic with lighted candles to St. Anthony for your
erysipelas; to St. Valentine for your epilepsy; to St. Sebastian for the pestilence; to St. Laurentis to protect you from fire, to St. Apollonia if you've
got the toothache, and to St. Louis to stop your beer from going sour. And
tomorrow you'll queue for hours outside the Castle Church so that you
can get a cheap-rate glimpse of St. Jerome's tooth, or four pieces each of
St. Chrysostom and St. Augustine, and six of St. Bernard. The deacons will

have to link hands to hold you back while you struggle to gawp at four hairs from Our Lady's head, at the pieces of her girdle and her veil stained with her Son's blood. You'll sleep outside with the garbage in the streets all night so that you can stuff your eyes like roasting birds on a scrap of swaddling clothes, eleven pieces from the original crib, one wisp of straw from the manger and a gold piece specially minted by three wise men for the occasion. Your emptiness will be frothing over at the sight of a strand of Jesus' beard, at one of the nails driven into His hands, and at the remains of the loaf at the Last Supper. Shells for shells, empty things for empty men. There are some who complain of these things, but they write in Latin for scholars. Who'll speak out in rough German? Someone's got to bell the cat! For you must be made to know that there's no security, there's no security at all, either in indulgences, holy busywork or anywhere in this world. It came to me while I was in my tower, what they call the monk's sweathouse, the jakes, the john or whatever you're pleased to call it. I was struggling with the text I've given you: "For therein is the right-eousness of God revealed, from faith to faith; as it is written, the just shall live by faith." And seated there, my head down, on that privy just as when I was a little boy, I couldn't reach down to my breath for the sickness in my bowels, as I seemed to sense beneath me a large rat, a heavy, wet, plague rat, slashing at my privates with its death's teeth. [*He kneads his knuckles into his abdomen, as if he were suppressing pain. His face runs with sweat.*] I thought of the righteousness of God, and wished his gospel had never been put to paper for men to read; who demanded my love and made it impossible to return it. And I sat in my heap of pain until the words emerged and opened out. "The just shall live by faith." My pain vanished, my bowels flushed and I could get up. I could see the life I'd lost. No man is just because he does just works. The works are just if the man is just. If a man doesn't believe in Christ, not only are his sins mortal, but his good works. This I know; reason is the devil's whore, born of one stinking goat called Aristotle, which believes that good works make a good man. But the truth is that the just shall live by faith alone. I need no more than my sweet redeemer and meditator, Jesus Christ, and I shall praise Him as long as I have voice to sing; and if anyone doesn't care to sing with me, then he can howl on his own. If we are going to be deserted, let's follow the deserted Christ.
[*He murmurs a prayer, descends from the pulpit, then walks up the steps to the Church door, and nails his theses to it. The singing from within grows louder as he walks away.*]

[*End of Act Two—Scene Three*]

ACT TWO

Scene Four

> *The Fugger Palace, Augsburg. October 1518. As a backcloth a satirical contemporary woodcut, showing, for example, the Pope portrayed as an ass playing the bagpipes, or a cardinal dressed up as a court fool. Or perhaps Holbein's cartoon of Luther with the Pope suspended from his nose. However, there is a large area for the director and designer to choose from.*

Seated at a table is THOMAS DE VIO, *known as Cajetan, Cardinal of San Sisto, General of the Dominican Order, as well as its most distinguished theologian, papal legate, Rome's highest representative in Germany. He is about fifty, but youthful, with a shrewd, broad, outlook, quite the opposite of the vulgar bigotry of* TETZEL, *who enters.*

TETZEL He's here.

CAJETAN So I see.

TETZEL What do you mean?

CAJETAN You look so cross. Is Staupitz with him?

TETZEL Yes. At least *he's* polite.

CAJETAN I know Staupitz. He's a straightforward, four-square kind of a man, and probably very unhappy at this moment. From all accounts, he has a deep regard for this monk—which is all to the good from our point of view.

TETZEL He's worried all right, you can see that. These Augustinians, they don't have much fibre.

CAJETAN What about Dr. Luther? What's he got to say for himself?

TETZEL Too much. I said to him if our Lord the Pope were to offer you a good Bishopric and a plenary indulgence for repairing your church, you'd soon start singing a different song.

CAJETAN Dear, oh, dear, and what did he say to that?

TETZEL He asked me—

CAJETAN Well?

TETZEL He asked me how was my mother's syphilis.

CAJETAN It's a fair question in the circumstances. You Germans, you're a crude lot.

TETZEL He's a pig.

CAJETAN I've no doubt. After all, it's what your country's most famous for.

TETZEL That's what I said to him—you're not on your own ground here, you know. These Italians, they're different. They're not just learned, they're subtle, experienced antagonists. You'll get slung in the fire after five minutes.

CAJETAN And?

TETZEL He said, "I've only been to Italy once, and they didn't look very subtle to me. They were lifting their legs on street corners like dogs."

CAJETAN I hope he didn't see any cardinals at it. Knowing some of them as I do, it's not impossible. Well, let's have a look at this foul-mouthed monk of yours.

TETZEL What about Staupitz?

CAJETAN Let him wait in the corridor. It'll help him to worry.

TETZEL Very well, your eminence. I hope he behaves properly. I've spoken to him.

[TETZEL *goes out and returns presently with* MARTIN, *who advances, prostrates himself, his face to the ground before* CAJETAN. CAJETAN *makes a motion and* MARTIN *rises to a kneeling position, where* CAJETAN *studies him.*]

CAJETAN [*courteous*] Please stand up, Dr. Luther. So you're the one they call the excessive doctor. You don't look excessive to me. Do you feel very excessive?

MARTIN [*conscious of being patronized*] It's one of those words which can be used like a harness on a man.

CAJETAN How do you mean?

MARTIN I mean it has very little meaning beyond traducing him.

CAJETAN   Quite. There's never been any doubt in my mind that you've been misinterpreted all round, and, as you say, traduced. Well, what a surprise you are! Here was I expecting to see some doddering old theologian with dust in his ears who could be bullied into a heart attack by Tetzel here in half an hour. And here you are, as gay and sprightly as a young bull. How old are you, my son?

MARTIN   Thirty-four, most worthy father.

CAJETAN   Tetzel, he's a boy—you didn't tell me! And how long have you been wearing your doctor's ring?

MARTIN   Five years—

CAJETAN   So you were only twenty-nine! Well, obviously, everything I've heard about you is true—you must be a very remarkable young man. I wouldn't have believed there was one doctor in the whole of Germany under fifty. Would you, Brother John?

TETZEL   Not as far as I know.

CAJETAN   I'm certain there isn't. What is surprising, frankly, is that they allowed such an honour to be conferred on anyone so young and inexperienced as a man must inevitably be at twenty-nine.
[*He smiles to let his point get home.*]
Your father must be a proud man.

MARTIN   [*irritated*]   Not at all, I should say he was disappointed and constantly apprehensive.

CAJETAN   Really? Well, that's surely one of the legacies of parenthood to offset the incidental pleasures. Now then, to business. I was saying to Tetzel, I don't think this matter need take up very much of our time. But, before we do start, there's just one thing I would like to say, and that is I was sorry you should have decided to ask the Emperor for safe conduct. That was hardly necessary, my son, and it's a little—well, distressing to feel you have such an opinion of us, such a lack of trust in your Mother Church, and in those who have, I can assure you, your dearest interests at heart.

MARTIN   [*out-manœuvred*]   I—

CAJETAN   [*kindly*]   But never mind all that now, that's behind us, and, in the long run, it's unimportant, after all, isn't it? Your Vicar General has come with you, hasn't he?

MARTIN   He's outside.

CAJETAN   I've known Staupitz for years. You have a wonderful friend there.

MARTIN   I know. I—have great love for him.

CAJETAN   And he certainly has for you, I know. Oh my dear, dear son, this is such a ridiculous, unnecessary business for us all to be mixed up in. It's such a tedious, upsetting affair, and what purpose is there in it? Your entire order in Germany has been brought into disgrace. Staupitz is an old man, and he can't honestly be expected to cope. Not now. I have my job to do, and, make no mistake, it isn't all honey for an Italian legate in your country. You know how it is, people are inclined to resent you. Nationalist feeling and all that—which I respect—but it does complicate one's task to the point where this kind of issue thrown in for good measure simply makes the whole operation impossible. You know what I mean? I mean, there's your Duke Frederick, an absolutely fair, honest man, if ever there was one, and one his holiness values and esteems particularly. Well, he instructed me to present him with the Golden Rose of Virtue, so you can see . . . As well as even more indulgences for his Castle Church. But what happens now? Because of all this unpleasantness and the uproar it's caused throughout Germany, the Duke's put in an extremely difficult position about accepting it. Naturally, he wants to do the right thing by every-

one. But he's not going to betray you or anything like that, however much
he's set his heart on that Golden Rose, even after all these years. And, of
course he's perfectly right. I know he has the greatest regard for you and
for some of your ideas—even though, as he's told me—he doesn't agree
with a lot of them. No, I can only respect him for all that. So, you see, my
dear son, what a mess we are in. Now, what are we going to do? Um? The
Duke is unhappy. I am unhappy, his holiness is unhappy, and, you, my
son, you are unhappy.

MARTIN [*formal, as if it were a prepared speech*] Most worthy father, in obedience to the summons of his papal holiness, and in obedience to the orders
of my gracious lord, the Elector of Saxony, I have come before you as a
submissive and dutiful son of the holy Christian church, and acknowledge
that I have published the proposition and theses ascribed to me. I am ready
now to listen most obediently to my indictment, and if I have been wrong,
to submit to your instruction in the truth.

CAJETAN [*impatient*] My son, you have upset all Germany with your dispute
about indulgences. I know you're a very learned doctor of the Holy Scriptures, and that you've already aroused some supporters. However, if you
wish to remain a member of the Church, and to find a gracious father in
the Pope, you'd better listen. I have here, in front of me, three propositions
which, by the command of our holy father, Pope Leo the Tenth, I shall
put to you now. First, you must admit your faults, and retract all your
errors and sermons. Secondly, you must promise to abstain from propagating
your opinions at any time in the future. And, thirdly, you must behave
generally with greater moderation, and avoid anything which might cause
offence or grieve and disturb the Church.

MARTIN May I be allowed to see the Pope's instruction?

CAJETAN No, my dear son, you may not. All you are required to do is confess
your errors, keep a strict watch on your words, and not go back like a dog
to his vomit. Then, once you have done that, I have been authorized by our
most holy father to put everything to rights again.

MARTIN I understand all that. But I'm asking you to tell me where I have
erred.

CAJETAN If you insist. [*Rattling off, very fast.*] Just to begin with, here are
two propositions you have advanced, and which you will have to retract
before anything else. First, the treasure of indulgences does not consist of
the sufferings and torments of our Lord Jesus Christ. Second, the man who
received the holy sacrament must have faith in the grace that is presented
to him. Enough?

MARTIN I rest my case entirely on Holy Scriptures.

CAJETAN The Pope alone has power and authority over all those things.

MARTIN Except Scripture.

CAJETAN Including Scripture. What do you mean?

TETZEL Only the Pope has the right of deciding in matters of Christian faith.
He alone and no one else has the power to interpret the meaning of
Scripture, and to approve or condemn the views of other men, whoever
they are—scholars, councils or the ancient fathers. The Pope's judgement
cannot err, whether it concerns the Christian faith or anything that has
to do with the salvation of the human race.

MARTIN That sounds like your theses.

TETZEL Burned in the market place by your students in Wittenberg—thank
you very much—

MARTIN I assure you, I had nothing to do with that.

CAJETAN Of course. Brother John wasn't suggesting you had.

MARTIN   I can't stop the mouth of the whole world.

TETZEL   Why, your heresy isn't even original. It's no different from Wyclif or Hus.

CAJETAN   True enough, but we mustn't try to deprive the learned doctor of his originality. An original heresy may have been thought of by someone else before you. In fact, I shouldn't think such a thing as an original heresy exists. But it is original so long as it originated in *you*, the virgin heretic.

TETZEL   The time'll come when you'll have to defend yourself before the world, and then every man can judge for himself who's the heretic and schismatic. It'll be clear to everyone, even those drowsy snoring Christians who've never smelled a Bible. They'll find out for themselves that those who scribble books and waste so much paper just for their own pleasure, and are contemptuous and shameless, end up by condemning themselves. People like you always go too far, thank heaven. You play into our hands. I give you a month, Brother Martin, to roast yourself.

MARTIN   You've had your thirty pieces of silver. For the sake of Christ, why don't you betray someone?

CAJETAN   [*to* TETZEL]   Perhaps you should join Staupitz.

TETZEL   Very well, your eminence.

[*He bows and goes out.*]

CAJETAN   In point of fact, he gets eighty guilden a month plus expenses.

MARTIN   What about his vow of poverty?

CAJETAN   Like most brilliant men, my son, you have an innocent spirit. I've also just discovered that he has managed to father two children. So there goes another vow. Bang! But it'll do him no good, I promise you. You've made a hole in that drum for him. I may say there's a lot of bad feelings among the Dominicans about you. I should know—because I'm their General. It's only natural, they're accustomed to having everything their own way. The Franciscans are a grubby, sentimental lot, on the whole, and mercifully ignorant as well. But your people seem to be running alive with scholars and would-be politicians.

MARTIN   I'd no idea that my theses would ever get such publicity.

CAJETAN   Really now!

MARTIN   But it seems they've been printed over and over again, and circulated well, to an extent I'd never dreamed of.

CAJETAN   Oh yes, they've been circulated and talked about wherever men kneel to Christ.

MARTIN   Most holy father, I honour the Holy Roman Church, and I shall go on doing so. I have sought after the truth, and everything I have said I still believe to be right and true and Christian. But I am a man, and I may be deceived, so I am willing to receive instruction where I have been mistaken—

CAJETAN   [*angrily*]   Save your arrogance, my son, there'll be a better place to use it. I can have you sent to Rome and let any of your German princes try to stop me! He'll find himself standing outside the gates of heaven like a leper.

MARTIN   [*stung*]   I repeat, I am here to reply to all the charges you may bring against me—

CAJETAN   No, you're not—

MARTIN   I am ready to submit my theses to the universities of Basle, Freibourg, Louvain or Paris—

CAJETAN   I'm afraid you've not grasped the position. I'm not here to enter into a disputation with you, now or at any other time. The Roman Church is the apex of the world, secular and temporal, and it may constrain with its secular arm any who have once received the faith and gone astray.

Surely I don't have to remind you that it is not bound to use reason to fight and destroy rebels. [*He sighs.*] My son, it's getting late. You must retract. Believe me, I simply want to see this business ended as quickly as possible.

MARTIN Some interests are furthered by finding truth, others by destroying it. I don't care—what pleases or displeases the Pope. He is a man.

CAJETAN [*wearily*] Is that all?

MARTIN He seems a good man, as Popes go. But it's not much for a world that sings out for reformation. I'd say that's a hymn for everyone.

CAJETAN My dear friend, think, think carefully, and see if you can't see some way out of all this. I am more than prepared to reconcile you with the Church, and the sovereign bishop. Retract, my son, the holy father prays for it—

MARTIN But won't you discuss—

CAJETAN Discuss! I've not *discussed* with you, and I don't intend to. If you want a disputation, I dare say Eck will take care of you—

MARTIN John Eck? The Chancellor of Ingolstadt?

CAJETAN I suppose you don't think much of him?

MARTIN He knows theology.

CAJETAN He has a universal reputation in debate.

MARTIN It's understandable. He has a pedestrian style and a judicial restraint and that'll always pass off as wisdom to most men.

CAJETAN You mean he's not original, like you—

MARTIN I'm not an original man, why I'm not even a teacher, and I'm scarcely even a priest. I know Jesus Christ doesn't need my labour or my services.

CAJETAN All right, Martin, I *will* argue with you if you want me to, or, at least, I'll put something to you, because there is something more than your safety or your life involved, something bigger than you and I talking together in this room at this time. Oh, it's fine for someone like you to criticize and start tearing down Christendom, but tell me this, just tell me this: what will you build in its place?

MARTIN A withered arm is best amputated, an infected place is best scoured out, and so you pray for healthy tissue and something sturdy and clean that was crumbling and full of filth.

CAJETAN Can't you see? My son, you'll destroy the perfect unity of the world.

MARTIN Someone always prefers what's withered and infected. But it should be cauterized as honestly as one knows how.

CAJETAN And how honest is that? There's something I'd like to know: suppose you *did* destroy the Pope. What do you think would become of you?

MARTIN I don't know.

CAJETAN Exactly, you wouldn't know what to do because you need him, Martin, you need to hunt him more than he needs his silly wild boar. Well? There have always been Popes, and there always will be, even if they're called something else. They'll have them for people like *you*. You're not a good old revolutionary, my son, you're just a common rebel, a very different animal. You don't fight the Pope because he's too big, but because for your needs he's not big enough.

MARTIN My General's been gossiping—

CAJETAN [*contemptuous*] I don't need Staupitz to explain you to me. Why, some deluded creature might even come to you as a leader of their revolution, but you don't want to break rules, you want to make them. You'd be a master breaker and maker and no one would be able to stand up to you, you'd hope, or ever sufficiently repair the damage you did. I've read some of your sermons on faith. Do you know all they say to me?

MARTIN No.

CAJETAN   They say: I am a man struggling for certainty, struggling insanely like a man in a fit, an animal trapped to the bone with doubt.

[MARTIN *seems about to have a physical struggle with himself.*]

CAJETAN   Don't you see what could happen out of all this? Men could be cast out and left to themselves for ever, helpless and frightened!

MARTIN   Your eminence, forgive me. I'm tired after my journey—I think I might faint soon—

CAJETAN   That's what would become of them without their Mother Church—with all its imperfections, Peter's rock, without it they'd be helpless and unprotected. Allow them their sins, their petty indulgences, my son, they're unimportant to the comfort we receive—

MARTIN   [*somewhat hysterical*]   Comfort! It—doesn't concern me!

CAJETAN   We live in thick darkness, and it grows thicker. How will men find God if they are left to themselves each man abandoned and only known to himself?

MARTIN   They'll have to try.

CAJETAN   I beg of you, my son, I beg of you. Retract.

[*Pause*]

MARTIN   Most holy father, I cannot.

[*Pause*]

CAJETAN   You look ill. You had better go and rest. [*Pause*] Naturally, you will be released from your order.

MARTIN   I—

CAJETAN   Yes?

MARTIN   As you say, your eminence. Will you refer this matter to the Pope for his decision?

CAJETAN   Assuredly. Send in Tetzel.

[MARTIN *prostrates himself, and then kneels.* CAJETAN *is distressed but in control.*]

You know, a time will come when a man will no longer be able to say, "I speak Latin and am a Christian" and go his way in peace. There will come frontiers, frontiers of all kinds—between men—and there'll be no end to them.

[MARTIN *rises and goes out.* TETZEL *returns.*]

TETZEL   Yes?

CAJETAN   No, of course he didn't—that man hates himself. And if he goes to the stake, Tetzel, you can have the pleasure of inscribing it: he could only love others.

[*End of Act Two—Scene Four*]

ACT TWO

Scene Five

A hunting lodge at Magliana in Northern Italy, 1519. Suspended the arms, the brass balls, of the Medici. KARL VON MILTITZ, *a young Chamberlain of the Pope's household is waiting. There are cries off, and sounds of excitement.* POPE LEO THE TENTH *enters with a* HUNTSMAN, *dogs and* DOMINICANS. *He is richly dressed in hunting clothes and long boots. He is indolent, cultured, intelligent, extremely restless, and well able to assimilate*

the essence of anything before anyone else. While he is listening,
he is able to play with a live bird with apparent distraction.
Or shoot at a board with a crossbow. Or generally fidget. MILTITZ
kneels to kiss his toe.

LEO   I should forget it. I've got my boots on. Well? Get on with it. We're missing the good weather.

[*He sits and becomes immediately absorbed in his own play, as it seems.* MILTITZ *has a letter, which he reads.*]

MILTITZ   "To the most blessed father Leo the Tenth, sovereign bishop, Martin Luther, Augustine friar, wishes eternal salvation. I am told that there are vicious reports circulating about me, and that my name is in bad odour with your holiness. I am called a heretic, apostate, traitor and many other insulting names. I cannot understand all this hostility, and I am alarmed by it. But the only basis of my tranquillity remains, as always, a pure and peaceful conscience. Deign to listen to me, most holy father, to me who is like a child.

[LEO *snorts abstractedly.*]

"There have always been, as long as I can remember, complaints and grumbling in the taverns about the avarice of the priests and attacks on the power of the keys. And this has been happening throughout Germany. When I listened to these things my zeal was aroused for the glory of Christ, so I warned not one, but several princes of the Church. But, either they laughed in my face or ignored me. The terror of your name was too much for everyone. It was then I published my disputation, nailing it on the door of the Castle Church here in Wittenberg. And now, most holy father, the whole world has gone up in flames. Tell me what I should do? I cannot retract; but this thing has drawn down hatred on me from all sides, and I don't know where to turn to but to you. I am far too insignificant to appear before the world in a matter as great as this.

[LEO *snaps his fingers to glance at this passage in the letter. He does so and returns it to* MILTITZ *who continues reading.*]

"But in order to quieten my enemies and satisfy my friends I am now addressing myself to you most holy father and speak my mind in the greater safety of the shadow of your wings. All this respect I show to the power of the keys. If I had not behaved properly it would have been impossible for the most serene Lord Frederick, Duke and Elector of Saxony, who shines in your apostolic favour, to have endured me in his University of Wittenberg. Not if I am as dangerous as is made out by my enemies. For this reason, most holy father, I fall at the feet of your holiness, and submit myself to you, with all I have and all that I am. Declare me right or wrong. Take my life, or give it back to me, as you please. I shall acknowledge your voice as the voice of Jesus Christ. If I deserve death, I shall not refuse to die. The earth is God's and all within it. May He be praised through all eternity, and may He uphold you for ever. Amen. Written the day of the Holy Trinity in the year 1518, Martin Luther, Augustine Friar."

[*They wait for* LEO *to finish his playing and give them his full attention. Presently, he gets up and takes the letter from* MILTITZ. *He thinks.*]

LEO   Double faced German bastard! Why can't he say what he means? What else?

MILTITZ   He's said he's willing to be judged by any of the universities of Germany, with the exception of Leipzig, Erfurt and Frankfurt, which he says are not impartial. He says it's impossible for him to appear in Rome in person.

LEO   I'm sure.

MILTITZ   Because his health wouldn't stand up to the rigours of the journey.

LEO   Cunning! Cunning German bastard! What does Staupitz say for him?

MILTITZ   [*reading hastily from another letter*]   "The reverend father, Martin Luther, is the noblest and most distinguished member of our university. For many years, we have watched his talents—"

LEO   Yes, well we know all about that. Write to Cajetan. Take this down. We charge you to summon before you Martin Luther. Invoke for this purpose, the aid of our very dear son in Christ, Maximilian, and all the other princes in Germany, together with all communities, universities, potentates ecclesiastic and secular. And, once you get possession of him, keep him in safe custody, so that he can be brought before us. If, however, he should return to his duty of his own accord and begs forgiveness, we give you the power to receive him into the perfect unity of our Holy Mother the Church. But, should he persist in his obstinacy and you cannot secure him, we authorize you to outlaw him in every part of Germany. To banish and excommunicate him. As well as all prelates, religious orders, universities, counts, and dukes who do not assist in apprehending him. As for the laymen, if they do not immediately obey your orders, declare them infamous, deprived of Christian burial and stripped of anything they may hold either from the apostolic see or from any lord whatsoever. There's a wild pig in our vineyard, and it must be hunted down and shot. Given under the seal of the Fisherman's Ring, etcetera. That's all.

[*He turns quickly and goes out.*]

[*End of Act Two—Scene Five*]

ACT TWO

Scene Six

> *The Elster Gate, Wittenberg. 1520. Evening. A single bell. As a backcloth the bull issued against Luther. Above it a fish-head and bones. The bull is slashed with the reflection of the flames rising round the Elster Gate where the books of canon law, the papal decretals, are burning furiously.* MONKS *come to and fro with more books and documents, and hurl them on the fire.* MARTIN *enters and ascends the pulpit.*

MARTIN   I have been served with a piece of paper. Let me tell you about it. It has come to me from a latrine called Rome, the capital of the devil's own sweet empire. It is called the papal bull and it claims to excommunicate me, Dr. Martin Luther. These lies they rise up from paper like fumes from the bog of Europe; because papal decretals are the devil's excretals. I'll hold it up for you to see properly. You see the signature? Signed beneath the seal of the Fisherman's Ring by one certain midden cock called Leo, an over-indulged jakes' attendant to Satan himself, a glittering worm in excrement, known to you as his holiness the Pope. You may know him as the head of the Church. Which he may still be: like a fish is the head of a cat's dinner; eyes without sight clutched to a stick of sucked bones. God has told me: there can be no dealings between this cat's dinner and me. And, as for this bull, it's going to roast, it's going to roast and so are the balls of the Medici!

[*He descends and casts the bull into the flames. He begins to shake, as if*

he were unable to breathe; as if he were about to have another fit. Shaking,
he kneels.]
Oh, God! Oh, God! Oh, thou my God, my God, help me against the reason
and wisdom of the world. You must—there's only you—to do it. Breathe
into me. Breathe into me, like a lion into the mouth of a stillborn cub. This
cause is not mine but yours. For myself, I've no business to be dealing with
the great lords of this world. I want to be still, in peace, and alone.
Breathe into me, Jesus. I rely on no man, only on you. My God, my God
do you hear me? Are you dead? Are you dead? No, you can't die, you
can only hide yourself, can't you? Lord, I'm afraid. I am a child, the lost
body of a child. I am stillborn. Breathe into me, in the name of Thy Son,
Jesus Christ, who shall be my protector and defender, yes, my mighty
fortress, breathe into me. Give me life, oh Lord. Give me life.
[MARTIN *prays as the deep red light of the flames floods the darkness around*
him.]

[*End of Act Two*]

ACT THREE

Scene One

> *The Diet of Worms, April 18th, 1521. A gold frontcloth, and on*
> *it, in the brightest sunshine of colour, a bold, joyful representa-*
> *tion of this unique gathering of princes, electors, dukes, am-*
> *bassadors, bishops, counts, barons, etc. Perhaps Luther's two-*
> *wheeled wagon which brought him to Worms. The mediaeval*
> *world dressed up for the Renaissance.*
> *Devoid of depth, such scenes are stamped on a brilliant ground*
> *of gold. Movement is frozen, recession in space ignored and*
> *perspective served by the arrangement of figures, or scenes, one*
> *above the other. In this way, landscape is dramatically substituted*
> *by objects in layers. The alternative is to do the opposite, in the*
> *manner of, say, Altdorfer. Well in front of the cloth is a small*
> *rostrum with brass rails sufficient to support one man. If possible,*
> *it would be preferable to have this part of the apron projected*
> *a little into the audience. Anyway, the aim is to achieve the*
> *maximum in physical enlargement of the action, in the sense of*
> *physical participation in the theatre, as if everyone watching*
> *had their chins resting on the sides of a boxing-ring. Also on*
> *the apron, well to the front are several chairs. On one side is*
> *a table with about twenty books on it. The table and books may*
> *also be represented on the gold cloth. The rostrum has a small*
> *crescent of chairs round it. From all corners of the auditorium*
> *comes a fanfare of massed trumpets, and, approaching preferably*
> *from the auditorium up steps to the apron, come a few members*
> *of the Diet audience (who may also be represented on the gold*
> *cloth). Preceded by a* HERALD, *and seating themselves on the*
> *chairs, they should include* THE EMPEROR CHARLES THE FIFTH
> (*in front of the rostrum*), ALEANDER, THE PAPAL NUNCIO; ULRICH
> VON HUTTEN, KNIGHT; THE ARCHBISHOP OF TRIER *and* HIS SECRETARY,

JOHAN VON ECK, *who sit at the table with the books. The trumpets cease, and they wait.* MARTIN *appears from the stage, and ascends the rostrum centre.*

ECK [*rising*]   Martin Luther, you have been brought here by His Imperial Majesty so that you may answer two questions. Do you publicly acknowledge being the author of the books you see here? When I asked you this question yesterday, you agreed immediately that the books were indeed your own. Is that right?

[MARTIN *nods in agreement.*]

When I asked you the second question, you asked if you might be allowed time in which to consider it. Although such time should have been quite unnecessary for an experienced debater and distinguished doctor of theology like yourself, His Imperial Majesty was graciously pleased to grant your request. Well, you have had your time now, a whole day and a night, and so I will repeat the question to you. You have admitted being the author of these books. Do you mean to defend all these books, or will you retract any of them?

[ECK *sits.* MARTIN *speaks quietly, conversationally, hardly raising his voice throughout, and with simplicity.*]

MARTIN   Your serene highness, most illustrious princes and gracious lords, I appear before you by God's mercy, and I beg that you will listen patiently. If, through my ignorance, I have not given anyone his proper title or offended in any way against the etiquette of such a place as this, I ask your pardon in advance for a man who finds it hard to know his way outside the few steps from wall to wall of a monk's cell. We have agreed these books are all mine, and they have all been published rightly in my name. I will reply to your second question. I ask your serene majesty and your gracious lordships to take note that not all my books are of the same kind. For instance, in the first group, I have dealt quite simply with the values of faith and morality, and even my enemies have agreed that all this is quite harmless, and can be read without damaging the most fragile Christian. Even the bull against me, harsh and cruel as it is, admits that some of my books are offensive to no one. Perhaps it's the strange nature of such a questionable compliment, that the bull goes on to condemn these with the rest, which it considers offensive. If I'm to begin withdrawing these books, what should I be doing? I should be condemning those very things my friends and enemies are agreed on. There is a second group of books I have written, and these all attack the power of the keys, which has ravaged Christendom. No one can deny this, the evidence is everywhere and everyone complains of it. And no one has suffered more from this tyranny than the Germans. They have been plundered without mercy. If I were to retract those books now, I should be issuing a licence for more tyranny, and it is too much to ask of me.

I have also written a third kind of book against certain, private, distinguished, and, apparently—highly established—individuals. They are all defenders of Rome and enemies of my religion. In these books, it's possible that I have been more violent than may seem necessary, or, shall I say, tasteful in one who is, after all, a monk. But then, I have never set out to be a saint and I've not been defending my own life, but the teaching of Christ. So you see, again I'm not free to retract, for if I did, the present situation would certainly go on just as before. However, because I am a man and not God, the only way for me to defend what I have written is to employ the same method used by my Saviour. When He was being questioned by Annas, the high priest, about His teaching, and He had been struck in the face by one of the servants, He replied: "If I have spoken lies tell me what the lie is." If the Lord Jesus Himself, who could not err, was willing to listen to the arguments of a servant, how can I refuse to do the same? Therefore, what I ask, by the Mercy of God, is let someone expose my errors in the light of the Gospels. The moment you have done this, I shall ask you to let me be the first to pick up my books and hurl them in the fire.

I think this is a clear answer to your question. I think I understand the danger of my position well enough. You have made it very clear to me. But I can still think of nothing better than the Word of God being the cause of all the dissension among us. For Christ said, "I have not come to bring peace, but a sword. I have come to set a man against his father." We also have to be sure that the reign of this noble, young Prince Charles, so full of promise, should not end in the misery of Europe. We must fear God alone. I commend myself to your most serene majesty and to your lordships, and humbly pray that you will not condemn me as your enemy. That is all.

ECK   [*rising*]   Martin, you have not answered the question put to you. Even if it were true that some of your books are innocuous—a point which, incidentally, we don't concede—we still ask that you cut out these passages which are blasphemous; that you cut out the heresies or whatever could be construed as heresy, and, in fact, that you delete any passage which might be considered hurtful to the Catholic faith. His sacred and imperial majesty is more than prepared to be lenient, and, if you will do these things, he will use his influence with the supreme pontiff to see that the good things in your work are not thrown out with the bad. If, however, you persist in your attitude, there can be no question that all memory of you will be blotted out, and everything you have written, right or wrong, will be forgotten.

You see, Martin, you return to the same place as all other heretics—to Holy Scripture. You demand to be contradicted from Scripture. We can only believe that you must be ill or mad. Do reasons have to be given to anyone who cares to ask a question? Any question? Why, if anyone who questioned the common understanding of the Church on any matter he liked to raise, and had to be answered irrefutably from the Scriptures, there would be nothing certain or decided in Christendom. What would the Jews and Turks and Saracens say if they heard us *debating* whether what we have always believed is true or not? I beg you, Martin, not to believe that you, and you alone, understand the meaning of the Gospels. Don't rate your own opinion so highly, so far beyond that of many other sincere and eminent men. I ask you: don't throw doubt on the most holy, orthodox faith, the faith founded by the most perfect legislator known to us, and spread by His apostles throughout the world, with their blood and miracles. This faith has been defined by sacred councils, and confirmed by the Church. It is your heritage, and we are forbidden to dispute it by the laws of the emperor and the pontiff. Since no amount of argument can lead to a final conclusion, they can only condemn those who refuse to submit to them. The penalties are provided and will be executed. I must, therefore, ask again, I must demand that you answer sincerely, frankly and unambiguously, yes or no: will you or will you not retract your books and the errors contained in them.

MARTIN   Since your serene majesty and your lordships demand a simple answer, you shall have it, without horns and without teeth. Unless I am shown by the testimony of the Scriptures—for I don't believe in popes or councils—unless I am refuted by Scripture and my conscience is captured by God's own word, I cannot and will not recant, since to act against one's conscience is neither safe nor honest. Here I stand; God help me; I can do no more. Amen.

[*End of Act Three—Scene One*]

ACT THREE

Scene Two

> *Wittenberg. 1525. A marching hymn, the sound of cannon and shouts of mutilated men. Smoke, a shattered banner bearing the cross and wooden shoe of the Bundschuh, emblem of the Peasants' Movement. A small chapel altar at one side of the stage opposite the pulpit. Centre is a small handcart, and beside it lies the bloody bulk of a peasant's corpse. Downstage stands* THE KNIGHT, *fatigued, despondent, stained and dirty.*

KNIGHT   There was excitement that day. In Worms—that day I mean. Oh, I don't mean now, not now. A lot's happened since then. There's no excitement like that any more. Not unless murder's your idea of excitement. I tell you, you can't have ever known the kind of thrill that monk set off amongst that collection of all kinds of men gathered together there—those few years ago. We all felt it, every one of us, just without any exception, you couldn't help it, even if you didn't want to, and, believe me, most of those people didn't want to. His scalp looked blotchy and itchy, and you felt sure, just looking at him, his body must be permanently sour and white all over, even whiter than his face and like a millstone to touch. He'd sweated so much by the time he'd finished, I could smell every inch of him even from where I was. But he fizzed like a hot spark in a trail of gunpowder going off in us, that dowdy monk, he went off in us, and nothing could stop it, and it blew up and there was nothing we could do, any of us, that was it. I just felt quite sure, quite certain in my own mind nothing could ever be the same again, just simply that. Something had taken place, something had changed and become something else, an event had occurred in the flesh, in the flesh and the breath—like, even like when the weight of that body slumped on its wooden crotchpiece and the earth grew dark. That's the kind of thing I mean by happen, and this also happened in very likely the same manner to all those of us who stood there, friends and enemies alike. I don't think, no I don't think even if I could speak and write like him, I could begin to give you an idea of what we thought, or what some of us thought, of what we might come to. Obviously, we couldn't have all felt quite the same way, but I wanted to burst my ears with shouting and draw my sword, no, not draw it, I wanted to pluck it as if it were a flower in my blood and plunge it into whatever he would have told me to.

[THE KNIGHT *is lost in his own thoughts, then his eyes catch the body of the peasant. He takes a swipe at the cart.*]

If one could only understand him. He baffles me, I just can't make him out. Anyway, it never worked out. [*To corpse*] Did it, my friend? Not the way we expected anyway, certainly not the way *you* expected, but who'd have ever thought we might end up on different sides, him on one and us on the other. That when the war came between you and them, he'd be there beating the drum for *them* outside the slaughter house, and beating it louder and better than anyone, hollering for *your* blood, cutting you up in your thousands, and hanging you up to drip away into the fire for good. Oh well, I suppose all those various groups were out for their different things, or the same thing really, all out for what we could get, and more than any of us had the right to expect. They were all the same, all those big princes and archbishops, the cut rate nobility and rich layabouts, honourable this and thats scrabbling like boars round a swill bucket for every penny those poor peasants never had. All those great abbots with ther dewlaps dropped and hanging on their necks like goose's eggs, and then those left-over knights, like me for instance, I suppose, left-over men, impoverished, who'd seen better days and were scared and'd stick at nothing to try and make sure they couldn't get any worse. Yes. . . . Not one of them could read the words WAY OUT when it was written up for them, marked out clearly and unmistakably in the pain of too many men. Yes. They say, you know, that the profit motive—and I'm sure you know all about that one—they say that the profit motive was born with the invention of double entry book-keeping in the monasteries. Book-keeping! In the monasteries, and ages before any of us had ever got round to burning them down. But, you know, for men with such a motive, there is only really one entry. The profit is theirs, the loss is someone else's, and usually they don't even bother to write it up.

[*He nudges the corpse with his toe.*]

Well, it was your old loss wasn't it, dead loss, in fact, my friend, you could say his life was more or less a write-off right from the day he was born. Wasn't it? Um? And all the others like him, everywhere, now and after him.

[THE KNIGHT *starts rather weakly to load the body on to the cart.* MARTIN *enters, a book in his hands. They look at each other then* MARTIN *at the* PEASANT. THE KNIGHT *takes his book and glances at it, but he doesn't miss* MARTIN *shrink slightly from the peasant.*]

Another of yours?

[*He hands it back.*]

Do you think it'll sell as well as the others? [*Pause*] I dare say it will. Someone's always going to listen to you. No?

[MARTIN *moves to go, but* THE KNIGHT *stops him.*]

Martin. Just a minute.

[*He turns and places his hand carefully, ritually, on the body in the cart. He smears the blood from it over* MARTIN.]

There we are. That's better.

[MARTIN *makes to move again, but again* THE KNIGHT *stops him.*]

You're all ready now. You even look like a butcher—

MARTIN God is the butcher—

KNIGHT Don't you?

MARTIN Why don't you address your abuse to Him?

KNIGHT Never mind—you're wearing His apron.

[MARTIN *moves to the stairs of the pulpit.*]

It suits you. [*Pause*] Doesn't it? [*Pause*] That day in Worms [*Pause*] you were like a pig under glass weren't you? Do you remember it? I could smell every inch of you even where I was standing. All you've ever managed to do is convert everything into stench and dying and peril, but you could have done it, Martin, and you were the only one who could have ever done it. You could even have brought freedom and order in at one and the same time.

MARTIN There's no such thing as an orderly revolution. Anyway, Christians are called to suffer, not fight.

KNIGHT But weren't we all of us, all of us, without any exceptions to please any old interested parties, weren't we all redeemed by Christ's blood? [*Pointing to the peasant*] Wasn't he included when the Scriptures were being dictated? Or was it just you who was made free, you and the princes you've taken up with, and the rich burghers and—

MARTIN Free? [*Ascends the pulpit steps.*] The princes blame me, you blame me and the peasants blame me—

KNIGHT [*following up the steps*] *You* put the water in the wine didn't you?

MARTIN   When I see chaos, then I see the devil's organ and then I'm afraid. Now, that's enough—

KNIGHT   You're breaking out again—

MARTIN   Go away—

KNIGHT   Aren't you?

[MARTIN *makes a sudden effort to push him back down the steps, but* THE KNIGHT *hangs on firmly.*]

MARTIN   Get back!

KNIGHT   Aren't you, you're breaking out again, you canting pig, I can smell you from here!

MARTIN   He heard the children of Israel, didn't He?

KNIGHT   Up to the ears in revelation, aren't you?

MARTIN   And didn't He deliver them out of the Land of Pharaoh?

KNIGHT   You canting pig, aren't you?

MARTIN   Well? Didn't He?

KNIGHT   Cock's wounds! Don't hold your Bible to my head, piggy, there's enough revelation of my own in there for me, in what I see for myself from here! [*Taps his forehead.*] Hold your gospel against that!

[THE KNIGHT *grabs* MARTIN'S *hand and clamps it to his head.*]

KNIGHT   You're killing the spirit, and you're killing it with the letter. You've been swilling about in the wrong place, Martin, in your own stink and ordure. Go on! You've got your hand on it, that's all the holy spirit there is, and it's all you'll ever get so feel it!

[*They struggle, but* THE KNIGHT *is very weak by now, and* MARTIN *is able to wrench himself away and up into the pulpit.*]

MARTIN   The world was conquered by the Word, the Church is maintained by the Word—

KNIGHT   Word? What Word? Word? That word, whatever that means, is probably just another old relic or indulgence, and you know what you did to those! Why, none of it might be any more than poetry, have you thought of that, Martin. Poetry! Martin, you're a poet, there's no doubt about that in anybody's mind, you're a poet, but do you know what most men believe in, in their hearts—because they don't see in images like you do—they believe in their hearts that Christ was a man as we are, and that He was a prophet and a teacher, and they also believe in their hearts that His supper is a plain meal like their own—if they're lucky enough to get it—a plain meal of bread and wine! A plain meal with no garnish and no word. And *you* helped them to begin to believe it!

MARTIN   [*pause*] Leave me.

KNIGHT   Yes. What's there to stay for? I've been close enough to you for too long. I even smell like you.

MARTIN   [*roaring with pain*]   I smell because of my own argument, I smell because I never stop disputing with Him, and because I expect Him to keep His Word. Now then! If your peasant rebelled against that Word, that was worse than murder because it laid the whole country waste, and who knows now what God will make of us Germans!

KNIGHT   Don't blame God for the Germans, Martin! [*Laughs*] Don't do that! You thrashed about more than anyone on the night they were conceived!

MARTIN   Christ! Hear me! My words pour from Your Body! They deserved their death, these swarming peasants! They kicked against authority, they plundered and bargained and all in Your name! Christ, believe me! [*To* THE KNIGHT] I demanded it, I prayed for it, and I got it! Take that lump away! Now, drag it away with you!

[THE KNIGHT *prepares to trundle off the cart and corpse.*]

KNIGHT   All right, my friend. Stay with your nun then. Marry and stew with your nun. Most of the others have. Stew with her, like a shuddering infant in *her* bed. You think you'll manage?
MARTIN   [*lightly*]   At least my father'll praise me for *that*.
KNIGHT   Your father?
[THE KNIGHT *shrugs, pushes the cart wearily, and goes off.* MARTIN'S *head hangs over the edge of the pulpit.*]
MARTIN   I [*whispering*] trust you. . . . I trust you. . . . You've overcome the world. . . . I trust you. . . . You're all I wish to have . . . ever. . . .
[*Slumped over the pulpit, he seems to be unconscious. Then he makes an effort to recover, as if he had collapsed in the middle of a sermon.*]
I expect you must . . . I'm sure you must remember—Abraham. Abraham was—he was an old man . . . a . . . very old man indeed, in fact, he was a hundred years old, when what was surely, what must have been a miracle happened, to a man of his years—a son was born to him. A son. Isaac he called him. And he loved Isaac. Well, he loved him with such intensity, one can only diminish it by description. But to Abraham his little son was a miraculous thing, a small, incessant . . . animal . . . astonishment. And in the child he sought the father. But, one day, God said to Abraham: Take your little son whom you love so much, kill him, and make a sacrifice of him. And in that moment everything inside Abraham seemed to shrivel once and for all. Because it had seemed to him that God had promised him life through his son. So then he took the boy and prepared to kill him, strapping him down to the wood of the burnt offering just as he had been told to do. And he spoke softly to the boy, and raised the knife over his little naked body, the boy struggling not to flinch or blink his eyes. Never, save in Christ, was there such obedience as in that moment, and, if God had blinked, the boy would have died then, but the Angel intervened, and the boy was released, and Abraham took him up in his arms again. In the teeth of life we seem to die, but God says no—in the teeth of death we live. If He butchers us, He makes us live.
[*Enter* THE KNIGHT, *who stands watching him, the Bundschuh banner in his hands.*]
Heart of my Jesus save me; Heart of my Saviour deliver me; Heart of my Shepherd guard me; Heart of my Master teach me; Heart of my King govern me; Heart of my Friend stay with me.
[*Enter* KATHERINE VON BORA, *his bride, accompanied by two* MONKS. MARTIN *rises from the pulpit and goes towards her. A simple tune is played on a simple instrument. She takes his hand, and they kneel together centre.* THE KNIGHT *watches. Then he smashes the banner he has been holding, and tosses the remains onto the altar.*]

[*End of Act Three—Scene Two*]

ACT THREE

Scene Three

A hymn. The Eremite Cloister. Wittenberg. 1530. The refectory table, and on it two places set, and the remains of two meals. MARTIN *is seated alone. The vigour of a man in his late thirties,*

and at the height of his powers, has settled into the tired pain of
a middle age struggling to rediscover strength.
KATHERINE *enters with a jug of wine. She is a big, pleasant-looking*
girl, almost thirty.

MARTIN   How is he?

KATHERINE   He's all right. He's just coming. Wouldn't let me help him. I think
he's been sick.

MARTIN   Poor old chap. After living all your life in a monastery, one's stomach
doesn't take too easily to your kind of cooking.

KATHERINE   Wasn't it all right?

MARTIN   Oh, it was fine, just too much for an old monk's shrivelled digestion to
chew on, that's all.

KATHERINE   Oh, I see. *You're* all right, aren't you?

MARTIN   Yes, I'm all right, thank you, my dear. [*Smile*] I expect I'll suffer later
though.

KATHERINE   You like your food, so don't make out you don't.

MARTIN   Well, I prefer it to fasting. Did you never hear the story of the soldier
who was fighting in the Holy Crusades? No? Well, he was told by his officer
that if he died in battle, he would dine in Paradise with Christ; and the
soldier ran away. When he came back after the battle, they asked him why
he'd run away. "Didn't you want to dine with Christ?" they said. And he
replied, "No, I'm fasting today."

KATHERINE   I've brought you some more wine.

MARTIN   Thank you.

KATHERINE   Should help you to sleep.

[STAUPITZ *enters, supporting himself with a stick.*]

MARTIN   There you are! I thought you'd fallen down the jakes—right into the
devil's loving arms.

STAUPITZ   I'm so sorry. I was—I was wandering about a bit.

MARTIN   Well, come and sit down. Katie's brought us some more wine.

STAUPITZ   I can't get over being here again. It's so odd. This place was full of
men. And now, now there's only you, you and Katie. It's very, very strange.

KATHERINE   I shouldn't stay up too long, Martin. You didn't sleep well again
last night. I could hear you—hardly breathing all night.

MARTIN   [*amused*]   You could hear me hardly breathing?

KATHERINE   You know what I mean. When you don't sleep, it keeps me awake
too. Good night, Dr. Staupitz.

STAUPITZ   Good night, my dear. Thank you for the dinner. It was excellent.
I'm so sorry I wasn't able to do justice to it.

KATHERINE   That's all right. Martin's always having the same kind of trouble.

STAUPITZ   Yes? Well, he's not changed much then.

MARTIN   Not a bit. Even Katie hasn't managed to shift my bowels for me, have
you?

KATHERINE   And if it's not that, he can't sleep.

MARTIN   Yes, Katie, you've said that already. I've also got gout, piles and bells
in my ears. Dr. Staupitz has had to put up with all my complaints for longer
than you have, isn't that right?

KATHERINE   Well, try not to forget what I said. [*She kisses* MARTIN'S *cheeks.*]

MARTIN   Good night, Katie.

[*She goes out.*]

STAUPITZ   Well, *you've* never been so well looked after.

MARTIN   It's a shame everyone can't marry a nun. They're fine cooks, thrifty
housekeepers, and splendid mothers. Seems to me there are three ways out

of despair. One is faith in Christ, the second is to become enraged by the world and make its nose bleed for it, and the third is the love of a woman. Mind you, they don't all necessarily work—at least, only part of the time. Sometimes, I'm lying awake in the devil's own sweat, and I turn to Katie and touch her. And I say: get me out, Katie, please, Katie, please try and get me out. And sometimes, sometimes she actually drags me out. Poor old Katie, fishing about there in bed with her great, hefty arms, trying to haul me out.

STAUPITZ   She's good.

MARTIN   Wine?

STAUPITZ   Not much. I must go to bed myself.

MARTIN   Help you sleep. You're looking tired.

STAUPITZ   Old. Our old pear tree's in blossom, I see. You've looked after it.

MARTIN   I like to get in a bit in the garden, if I can. I like to think it heals my bones somehow. Anyway, I always feel a bit more pleased with myself afterwards.

STAUPITZ   We'd a few talks under that tree.

MARTIN   Yes.

STAUPITZ   Martin, it's so still. I don't think I'd ever realized how eloquent a monk's silence really was. It was a voice. [*Pause*] It's gone. [*He shakes his head, pause.*] How's your father these days?

MARTIN   Getting old too, but he's well enough.

STAUPITZ   Is he—is he pleased with you?

MARTIN   He was never pleased about anything I ever did. Not when I took my master's degree or when I got to be Dr. Luther. Only when Katie and I were married and she got pregnant. Then he was pleased.

STAUPITZ   Do you remember Brother Weinand?

MARTIN   I ought to. He used to hold my head between my knees when I felt faint in the choir.

STAUPITZ   I wonder what happened to him. [*Pause*] He had the most beautiful singing voice.

MARTIN   My old friend, you're unhappy. I'm sorry. [*Pause*] We monks were really no good to anyone, least of all to ourselves, every one of us rolled up like a louse in the Almighty's overcoat.

STAUPITZ   Yes. Well, you always have a way of putting it. I was always having to give you little lectures about the fanatic way you'd observe the Rule all the time.

MARTIN   Yes, and you talked me out of it, remember? [*Pause*] Father, are *you* pleased with me?

STAUPITZ   Pleased with you? My dear son, I'm not anyone or anything to be pleased with you any more. When we used to talk together underneath that tree you were like a child.

MARTIN   A child.

STAUPITZ   Manhood was something you had to be flung into, my son. You dangled your toe in it longer than most of us could ever bear. But you're not a frightened little monk any more who's come to his prior for praise or blame. Every time you belch now, the world stops what it's doing and listens. Do you know, when I first came to take over this convent, there weren't thirty books published every year. And now, last year it was more like six or seven hundred, and most of those published in Wittenberg too.

MARTIN   The best turn God ever did Himself was giving us a printing press. Sometimes I wonder what He'd have done without it.

STAUPITZ   I heard the other day they're saying the world's going to end in 1532.

MARTIN   It sounds as good a date as any other. Yes—1532. That could easily
be the end of the world. You could write a book about it, and just call it
that—1532.

STAUPITZ   I'm sorry, Martin. I didn't mean to come and see you after all this
time and start criticizing. Forgive me, I'm getting old and a bit silly and
frightened, that meal was just too much for me. It wasn't that I didn't—

MARTIN   Please—I'm sorry too. Don't upset yourself. I'm used to critics, John.
They just help you to keep your muscles from getting slack. All those
hollow cavillers, that subtle clown Erasmus, for instance. He ought to
know better, but all he wants to do is to be able to walk on eggs without
breaking any. As for that mandrill-arsed English baboon Henry, that
leprous son of a bitch never had an idea of his own to jangle on a tombstone, let alone call himself Defender of the Faith.
[*Pause.* STAUPITZ *hasn't responded to his attempt at lightness.*]
Still, one thing for Erasmus, he didn't fool about with all the usual cant
and rubbish about indulgences and the Pope and Purgatory. No, he went
right to the core of it. He's still up to his ears with stuff about morality,
and men being able to save themselves. No one does good, not anyone.
God is true and one. But, and this is what he can't grasp, He's utterly
incomprehensible and beyond the reach of minds. A man's will is like a
horse standing between two riders. If God jumps on its back, it'll go
where God wants it to. But if Satan gets up there, it'll go where he leads it.
And not only that, the horse can't choose its rider. That's left up to them,
to those two. [*Pause*] Why are you accusing me? What have I done?

STAUPITZ   I'm not accusing you, Martin. You know that. A just man is his own
accuser. Because a just man judges as he is.

MARTIN   What's that mean? I'm not just?

STAUPITZ   You try. What else can you do?

MARTIN   You mean those damned peasants, don't you? You think I should
have encouraged them!

STAUPITZ   I don't say that.

MARTIN   Well, what do you say?

STAUPITZ   You needn't have encouraged the princes. They were butchered
and *you* got them to do it. And they had just cause, Martin. They did,
didn't they?

MARTIN   I didn't say they hadn't.

STAUPITZ   Well, then?

MARTIN   Do you remember saying to me, "Remember, brother, you started
this in the name of the Lord Jesus Christ"?

STAUPITZ   Well?

MARTIN   Father, the world can't be ruled with a rosary. They were a mob, a
mob, and if they hadn't been held down and slaughtered, there'd have
been a thousand more tyrants instead of half a dozen. It was a mob, and
because it was a mob it was against Christ. No man can die for another,
or believe for another or answer for another. The moment they try they
become a mob. If we're lucky we can be persuaded in our own mind, and
the most we can hope for is to die each one for himself. Do I have to tell
you what Paul says? You read! "Let every soul be subject unto the highest
powers. For there is no power but of God: the powers that be are or-
dained of God. Whosoever therefore resisteth that power, resisteth the
ordinance of God": that's Paul, Father, and that's Scripture! "And they
that resist shall receive to themselves damnation."

STAUPITZ   Yes, you're probably right.

MARTIN   "Love worketh no ill to his neighbour: therefore love is the fulfilling of the law."

STAUPITZ   Yes, well it seems to be all worked out. I must be tired.

MARTIN   It was worked out for me.

STAUPITZ   I'd better get off to bed.

MARTIN   They're trying to turn me into a fixed star, Father, but I'm a shifting planet. You're leaving me.

STAUPITZ   I'm not leaving you, Martin. I love you. I love you as much as any man has ever loved most women. But we're not two protected monks chattering under a pear tree in a garden any longer. The world's changed. For one thing, you've made a thing called Germany; you've unlaced a language and taught it to the Germans, and the rest of the world will just have to get used to the sound of it. As we once made the body of Christ from bread, you've made the body of Europe, and whatever our pains turn out to be, they'll attack the rest of the world too. You've taken Christ away from the low mumblings and soft voices and jewelled gowns and the tiaras and put Him back where He belongs. In each man's soul. We owe so much to you. All I beg of you is not to be too violent. In spite of everything, of everything you've said and shown us, there *were* men, *some* men who did live holy lives here once. Don't—don't believe you, only you are right.

[STAUPITZ *is close to tears, and* MARTIN *doesn't know what to do.*]

MARTIN   What else can I do? What can I do?

[*He clutches at his abdomen.*]

STAUPITZ   What is it?

MARTIN   Oh, the old trouble, that's all. That's all.

STAUPITZ   Something that's puzzled me, and I've always meant to ask you.

MARTIN   Well?

STAUPITZ   When you were before the Diet in Worms, and they asked you those two questions—why did you ask for that extra day to think over your reply?

MARTIN   Why?

STAUPITZ   You'd known what your answer was going to be for months. Heaven knows, you told me enough times. Why did you wait?

[*Pause*]

MARTIN   I wasn't certain.

STAUPITZ   And were you? Afterwards?

MARTIN   I listened for God's voice, but all I could hear was my own.

STAUPITZ   *Were* you sure?

[*Pause*]

MARTIN   No.

[STAUPITZ *kisses him.*]

STAUPITZ   Thank you, my son. May God bless you. I hope you sleep better. Goodnight.

MARTIN   Goodnight, Father.

[STAUPITZ *goes out, and* MARTIN *is left alone. He drinks his wine.*]

MARTIN   Oh, Lord, I believe. I believe. I do believe. Only help my unbelief.

[*He sits slumped in his chair.* KATHERINE *enters. She is wearing a nightdress, and carries in her arms* HANS, *their young son.*]

KATHERINE   He was crying out in his sleep. Must have been dreaming again. Aren't you coming to bed?

MARTIN   Shan't be long, Katie. Shan't be long.

KATHERINE   All right, but try not to be too long. You look—well, you don't look as well as you should.

[*She turns to go.*]

MARTIN   Give him to me.

KATHERINE   What?

MARTIN   Give him to me.

KATHERINE   What do you mean, what for? He'll get cold down here.

MARTIN   No, he won't. Please, Katie. Let me have him.

KATHERINE   You're a funny man. All right, but only for five minutes. Don't just sit there all night. He's gone back to sleep now. He'll be having another dream if you keep him down here.

MARTIN   Thank you, Katie.

KATHERINE   There! Keep him warm now! He's *your* son.

MARTIN   I will. Don't worry.

KATHERINE   Well, make sure you do. [*Pausing on way out*] Don't be long now, Martin.

MARTIN   Goodnight, Kate.

[*She goes out, leaving* MARTIN *with the sleeping child in his arms.*]

MARTIN   [*softly*]   What was the matter? Was it the devil bothering you? Um? Was he? Old nick? Up you, old nick. Well, don't worry. One day you might even be glad of him. So long as you can show him your little backside. That's right, show him your backside and let him have it. So try not to be afraid. The dark isn't quite as thick as all that. You know, my father had a son, and he'd to learn a hard lesson, which is a human being is a helpless little animal, but he's not created by his father, but by God. It's hard to accept you're anyone's son, and you're not the father of yourself. So, don't have dreams so soon, my son. *They'll* be having *you* soon enough. [*He gets up.*]

You should have seen me at Worms. I was almost like you that day, as if I'd learned to play again, to play, to play out in the world, like a naked child. "I have come to set a man against his father," I said, and they listened to me. Just like a child. Sh! We must go to bed, mustn't we? A little while, and you *shall* see me. Christ said that, my son. I hope that'll be the way of it again. I hope so. Let's just hope so, eh? Eh? Let's just hope so.

[MARTIN *holds the child in his arms, and then walks off slowly*].

The End.

LORRAINE HANSBERRY
[1930–1965]

Lorraine Hansberry, daughter of a prosperous real estate broker, was captivated by the magic of the theater in her high school days in Chicago where, as she says, she began "sort of hanging around little acting groups, and developing the feeling that the theater embraces everything I like all at one time." Her goal was to be a painter, but, after attending the University of Wisconsin, Chicago's Art Institute, and Roosevelt College, she decided she had no talent as an artist, and subsequently moved to New York in 1950. Then a series of menial jobs followed until she married Robert Nemiroff, song writer and music publisher. Miss Hansberry wrote several plays (left unfinished) before completing *A Raisin in the Sun*, the first play written by a Negro woman to be produced on Broadway, and the first play by a Negro to win the New York Drama Critics Circle Award. Although she was committed to the struggle for civil rights, Miss Hansberry tried to write a play about human beings who happened to be Negroes, not a play "about Negroes." Her second and last Broadway play was *The Sign in Sidney Brustein's Window*, produced by her husband in 1964. In this play once again she proved her great commitment to everyday living, or as she put it, to "caring." The history of how this play managed to remain in production despite mixed reviews and poor attendance is one of the exciting stories of the modern theater, and involves such famous people as Steve Allen, Anne Bancroft, James Baldwin, and many others who contributed time and money to keep the play alive. Unfortunately, during the rehearsals and the performances of *The Sign in Sidney Brustein's Window*, Miss Hansberry was in and out of hospitals, until on January 12, 1965, she died of cancer.

A RAISIN
IN THE SUN

LORRAINE HANSBERRY

To Mama: in gratitude for the dream

What happens to a dream deferred?
Does it dry up
Like a raisin in the sun?
Or fester like a sore—
And then run?
Does it stink like rotten meat:
Or crust and sugar over—
Like a syrupy sweet?

Maybe it just sags
Like a heavy load.

Or does it explode?

—Langston Hughes

The action of the play is set in Chicago's Southside, sometime between World War II and the present.

ACT ONE

ACT TWO

ACT THREE

An hour later.

ACT I

Scene One

The YOUNGER living room would be a comfortable and well-ordered room if it were not for a number of indestructible contradictions to this state of being. Its furnishings are typical and undistinguished and their primary feature now is that they have clearly had to accommodate the living of too many people for too many years and—they are tired. Still, we can see that at some time, a time probably no longer remembered by the family (except perhaps for MAMA) the furnishings of this room were actually selected with care and love and even hope—and brought to this apartment and arranged with taste and pride.
That was a long time ago. Now the once loved pattern of the couch upholstery has to fight to show itself from under acres of crocheted doilies and couch covers which have themselves finally come to be more important than the upholstery. And here a table or a chair has been moved to disguise the worn places in the carpet; but the carpet has fought back by showing its weariness, with depressing uniformity, elsewhere on its surface. Weariness has, in fact, won in this room. Everything has been

polished, washed, sat on, used, scrubbed too often. All pre-
tenses but living itself have long since vanished from the very
atmosphere of this room.

Moreover, a section of this room, for it is not really a room
unto itself, though the landlord's lease would make it seem so,
slopes backward to provide a small kitchen area, where the
family prepares the meals that are eaten in the living room
proper, which must also serve as dining room. The single window
that has been provided for these "two" rooms is located in this
kitchen area. The sole natural light the family may enjoy in the
course of a day is only that which fights its way through this
little window.

At left, a door leads to a bedroom which is shared by MAMA *and*
her daughter, BENEATHA. *At right, opposite, is a second room*
(which in the beginning of the life of this apartment was
probably a breakfast room) which serves as a bedroom for
WALTER *and his wife,* RUTH.

Time: Sometime between World War II and the present.
Place: Chicago's Southside.

At Rise: It is morning dark in the living room. TRAVIS *is asleep*
on the make-down bed at center. An alarm clock sounds from
within the bedroom at right, and presently RUTH *enters from*
that room and closes the door behind her. She crosses sleepily
toward the window. As she passes her sleeping son she reaches
down and shakes him a little. At the window she raises the
shade and a dusky Southside morning light comes in feebly.
She fills a pot with water and puts it on to boil. She calls to
the boy, between yawns, in a slightly muffled voice.

RUTH *is about thirty. We can see that she was a pretty girl, even*
exceptionally so, but now it is apparent that life has been little
that she expected, and disappointment has already begun to
hang in her face. In a few years, before thirty-five even, she will
be known among her people as a "settled woman."

She crosses to her son and gives him a good, final, rousing shake.

RUTH   Come on now, boy, it's seven thirty! [*Her son sits up at last, in a stupor*
of sleepiness] I say hurry up, Travis! You ain't the only person in the world
got to use a bathroom! [*The child, a sturdy, handsome little boy of ten or*
eleven, drags himself out of the bed and almost blindly takes his towels
and "today's clothes" from drawers and a closet and goes out to the bath-
room, which is in an outside hall and which is shared by another family or
families on the same floor. RUTH *crosses to the bedroom door at right and*
opens it and calls in to her husband] Walter Lee! . . . It's after seven
thirty! Lemme see you do some waking up in there now! [*She waits*] You
better get up from there, man! It's after seven thirty I tell you. [*She waits*
again] All right, you just go ahead and lay there and next thing you know
Travis be finished and Mr. Johnson'll be in there and you'll be fussing
and cussing round here like a mad man! And be late too! [*She waits, at*
the end of patience] Walter Lee—it's time for you to get up!

[*She waits another second and then starts to go into the bedroom, but is*
apparently satisfied that her husband has begun to get up. She stops, pulls
the door to, and returns to the kitchen area. She wipes her face with a
moist cloth and runs her fingers through her sleep-disheveled hair in a
vain effort and ties an apron around her housecoat. The bedroom door at
right opens and her husband stands in the doorway in his pajamas, which

are rumpled and mismated. He is a lean, intense young man in his middle thirties, inclined to quick nervous movements and erratic speech habits— and always in his voice there is a quality of indictment]

WALTER   Is he out yet?

RUTH   What you mean *out?* He ain't hardly got in there good yet.

WALTER   [*Wandering in, still more oriented to sleep than to a new day*]   Well, what was you doing all that yelling for if I can't even get in there yet? [*Stopping and thinking*] Check coming today?

RUTH   They *said* Saturday and this is just Friday and I hopes to God you ain't going to get up here first thing this morning and start talking to me 'bout no money—'cause I 'bout don't want to hear it.

WALTER   Something the matter with you this morning?

RUTH   No—I'm just sleepy as the devil. What kind of eggs you want?

WALTER   Not scrambled. [RUTH *starts to scramble eggs*] Paper come? [RUTH *points impatiently to the rolled up* Tribune *on the table, and he gets it and spreads it out and vaguely reads the front page*] Set off another bomb yesterday.

RUTH   [*Maximum indifference*]   Did they?

WALTER   [*Looking up*]   What's the matter with you?

RUTH   Ain't nothing the matter with me. And don't keep asking me that this morning.

WALTER   Ain't nobody bothering you. [*Reading the news of the day absently again*] Say Colonel McCormick is sick.

RUTH   [*Affecting tea-party interest*]   Is he now? Poor thing.

WALTER   [*Sighing and looking at his watch*]   Oh, me. [*He waits*] Now what is that boy doing in that bathroom all this time? He just going to have to start getting up earlier. I can't be being late to work on account of him fooling around in there.

RUTH   [*Turning on him*]   Oh, no he ain't going to be getting up no earlier no such thing! It ain't his fault that he can't get to bed no earlier nights 'cause he got a bunch of crazy good-for-nothing clowns sitting up running their mouths in what is supposed to be his bedroom after ten o'clock at night . . .

WALTER   That's what you mad about, ain't it? The things I want to talk about with my friends just couldn't be important in your mind, could they? [*He rises and finds a cigarette in her handbag on the table and crosses to the little window and looks out, smoking and deeply enjoying this first one*]

RUTH   [*Almost matter of factly, a complaint too automatic to deserve emphasis*] Why you always got to smoke before you eat in the morning?

WALTER   [*At the window*]   Just look at 'em down there . . . Running and racing to work . . . [*He turns and faces his wife and watches her a moment at the stove, and then, suddenly*] You look young this morning, baby.

RUTH   [*Indifferently*]   Yeah?

WALTER   Just for a second—stirring them eggs. It's gone now—just for a second it was—you looked real young again. [*Then, drily*] It's gone now—you look like yourself again.

RUTH   Man, if you don't shut up and leave me alone.

WALTER   [*Looking out to the street again*]   First thing a man ought to learn in life is not to make love to no colored woman first thing in the morning. You all some evil people at eight o'clock in the morning. [TRAVIS *appears in the hall doorway, almost fully dressed and quite wide awake now, his towels and pajamas across his shoulders. He opens the door and signals for his father to make the bathroom in a hurry*]

TRAVIS   [*Watching the bathroom*]   Daddy, come on!

[WALTER *gets his bathroom utensils and flies out to the bathroom*]

RUTH   Sit down and have your breakfast, Travis.

TRAVIS   Mama, this is Friday. [*Gleefully*] Check coming tomorrow, huh?

RUTH   You get your mind off money and eat your breakfast.

TRAVIS   [*Eating*]   This is the morning we supposed to bring the fifty cents to school.

RUTH   Well, I ain't got no fifty cents this morning.

TRAVIS   Teacher say we have to.

RUTH   I don't care what teacher say. I ain't got it. Eat your breakfast, Travis.

TRAVIS   I *am* eating.

RUTH   Hush up now and just eat!

[*The boy gives her an exasperated look for her lack of understanding, and eats grudgingly*]

TRAVIS   You think Grandmama would have it?

RUTH   No! And I want you to stop asking your grandmother for money, you hear me?

TRAVIS   [*Outraged*]   Gaaaleee! I don't ask her, she just gimme it sometimes!

RUTH   Travis Willard Younger—I got too much on me this morning to be—

TRAVIS   Maybe Daddy—

RUTH   *Travis!*

[*The boy hushes abruptly. They are both quiet and tense for several seconds*]

TRAVIS   [*Presently*]   Could I maybe go carry some groceries in front of the supermarket for a little while after school then?

RUTH   Just hush, I said. [*Travis jabs his spoon into his cereal bowl viciously, and rests his head in anger upon his fists*] If you through eating, you can get over there and make up your bed.

[*The boy obeys stiffly and crosses the room, almost mechanically, to the bed and more or less carefully folds the covering. He carries the bedding into his mother's room and returns with his books and cap*]

TRAVIS   [*Sulking and standing apart from her unnaturally*]   I'm gone.

RUTH   [*Looking up from the stove to inspect him automatically*]   Come here. [*He crosses to her and she studies his head*] If you don't take this comb and fix this here head, you better! [TRAVIS *puts down his books with a great sigh of oppression, and crosses to the mirror. His mother mutters under her breath about his "slubbornness"*] 'Bout to march out of here with that head looking just like chickens slept in it! I just don't know where you get your slubborn ways . . . And get your jacket, too. Looks chilly out this morning.

TRAVIS   [*With conspicuously brushed hair and jacket*]   I'm gone.

RUTH   Get carfare and milk money—[*Waving one finger*]—and not a single penny for no caps, you hear me?

TRAVIS   [*With sullen politeness*]   Yes'm.

[*He turns in outrage to leave. His mother watches after him as in his frustration he approaches the door almost comically. When she speaks to him, her voice has become a very gentle tease*]

RUTH   [*Mocking; as she thinks he would say it*]   Oh, Mama makes me so mad sometimes, I don't know what to do! [*She waits and continues to his back as he stands stock-still in front of the door*] I wouldn't kiss that woman good-bye for nothing in this world this morning! [*The boy finally turns around and rolls his eyes at her, knowing the mood has changed and he is vindicated; he does not, however, move toward her yet*] Not for nothing in this world! [*She finally laughs aloud at him and holds out her arms to him and we see that it is a way between them, very old and practiced. He crosses to her and allows her to embrace him warmly but keeps his face fixed with masculine rigidity. She holds him back from her presently and looks at him and runs her fingers over the features of his face. With utter gentleness—]* Now—whose little old angry man are you?

TRAVIS *[The masculinity and gruffness start to fade at last]* Aw gaalee—Mama . . .

RUTH *[Mimicking]* Aw—gaaaaalleeeee, Mama! *[She pushes him, with rough playfulness and finality, toward the door]* Get on out of here or you going to be late.

TRAVIS *[In the face of love, new aggresiveness]* Mama, could I *please* go carry groceries?

RUTH Honey, it's starting to get so cold evenings.

WALTER *[Coming in from the bathroom and drawing a make-believe gun from a make-believe holster and shooting at his son]* What is it he wants to do?

RUTH Go carry groceries after school at the supermarket.

WALTER Well, let him go . . .

TRAVIS *[Quickly, to the ally]* I *have* to—she won't gimme the fifty cents . . .

WALTER *[To his wife only]* Why not?

RUTH *[Simply, and with flavor]* 'Cause we don't have it.

WALTER *[To RUTH only]* What you tell the boy things like that for? *[Reaching down into his pants with a rather important gesture]* Here. son—
[He hands the boy the coin, but his eyes are directed to his wife's. TRAVIS takes the money happily]

TRAVIS Thanks, Daddy.
[He starts out. RUTH watches both of them with murder in her eyes. WALTER stands and stares back at her with defiance, and suddenly reaches into his pocket again on an afterthrough]

WALTER *[Without even looking at his son, still staring hard at his wife]* In fact, here's another fifty cents . . . Buy yourself some fruit today—or take a taxicab to school or something!

TRAVIS Whoopee—
[He leaps up and clasps his father around the middle with his legs, and they face each other in mutual appreciation; slowly WALTER LEE peeks around the boy to catch the violent rays from his wife's eyes and draws his head back as if shot]

WALTER You better get down now—and get to school, man.

TRAVIS *[At the door]* O.K. Good-bye.
[He exits]

WALTER *[After him, pointing with pride]* That's *my* boy. *[She looks at him in disgust and turns back to her work]* You know what I was thinking 'bout in the bathroom this morning?

RUTH No.

WALTER How come you always try to be so pleasant!

RUTH What is there to be pleasant 'bout!

WALTER You want to know what I was thinking 'bout in the bathroom or not!

RUTH I know what you thinking 'bout.

WALTER *[Ignoring her]* 'Bout what me and Willy Harris was talking about last night.

RUTH *[Immediately—a refrain]* Willy Harris is a good-for-nothing loud mouth.

WALTER Anybody who talks to me has got to be a good-for-nothing loud mouth, ain't he? And what you know about who is just a good-for-nothing loud mouth? Charlie Atkins was just a "good-for-nothing loud mouth" too, wasn't he! When he wanted me to go in the dry-cleaning business with him. And now—he's grossing a hundred thousand a year. A hundred thousand dollars a year! You still call *him* a loud mouth!

RUTH   [*Bitterly*]   Oh, Walter Lee . . .

[*She folds her head on her arms over the table*]

WALTER   [*Rising and coming to her and standing over her*]   You tired, ain't you? Tired of everything. Me, the boy, the way we live—this beat-up hole —everything. Ain't you? [*She doesn't look up, doesn't answer*] So tired— moaning and groaning all the time, but you wouldn't do nothing to help, would you? You couldn't be on my side that long for nothing, could you?

RUTH   Walter, please leave me alone.

WALTER   A man needs for a woman to back him up . . .

RUTH   Walter—

WALTER   Mama would listen to you. You know she listen to you more than she do me and Bennie. She think more of you. All you have to do is just sit down with her when you drinking your coffee one morning and talking 'bout things like you do and—[*He sits down beside her and demonstrates graphically what he thinks her methods and tone should be*]—you just sip your coffee, see, and say easy like that you been thinking 'bout that deal Walter Lee is so interested in, 'bout the store and all, and sip some more coffee, like what you saying ain't really that important to you—And the next thing you know, she be listening good and asking you questions and when I come home—I can tell her the details. This ain't no fly-by-night proposition, baby. I mean we figured it out, me and Willy and Bobo.

RUTH   [*With a frown*]   Bobo?

WALTER   Yeah. You see, this little liquor store we got in mind cost seventy-five thousand and we figured the initial investment on the place be 'bout thirty thousand, see. That be ten thousand each. Course, there's a couple of hundred you got to pay so's you don't spend your life just waiting for them clowns to let your license get approved—

RUTH   You mean graft?

WALTER   [*Frowning impatiently*]   Don't call it that. See there, that just goes to show you what women understand about the world. Baby, don't *nothing* happen for you in this world 'less you pay *somebody* off!

RUTH   Walter, leave me alone! [*She raises her head and stares at him vigorously —then says, more quietly*] Eat your eggs, they gonna be cold.

WALTER   [*Straightening up from her and looking off*]   That's it. There you are. Man say to his woman: I got me a dream. His woman say: Eat your eggs. [*Sadly, but gaining in power*] Man say: I got to take hold of this here world, baby! And a woman will say: Eat your eggs and go to work. [*Passionately now*] Man say: I got to change my life, I'm choking to death, baby! And his woman say—[*In utter anguish as he brings his fists down on his thighs*]—Your eggs is getting cold!

RUTH   [*Softly*]   Walter, that ain't none of our money.

WALTER   [*Not listening at all or even looking at her*]   This morning, I was lookin' in the mirror and thinking about it . . . I'm thirty-five years old; I been married eleven years and I got a boy who sleeps in the living room —[*Very, very quietly*]—and all I got to give him is stories about how rich white people live . . .

RUTH   Eat your eggs, Walter.

WALTER   *Damn my eggs . . . damn all the eggs that ever was!*

RUTH   Then go to work.

WALTER   [*Looking up at her*]   See—I'm trying to talk to you 'bout myself—

[*Shaking his head with the repetition*]—and all you can say is eat them eggs and go to work.

RUTH   [*Wearily*]   Honey, you never say nothing new. I listen to you every day, every night and every morning, and you never say nothing new. [*Shrugging*] So you would rather *be* Mr. Arnold than be his chauffeur. So— I would *rather* be living in Buckingham Palace.

WALTER   That is just what is wrong with the colored woman in this world . . . Don't understand about building their men up and making 'em feel like they somebody. Like they can do something.

RUTH   [*Drily, but to hurt*]   There *are* colored men who do things.

WALTER   No thanks to the colored woman.

RUTH   Well, being a colored woman, I guess I can't help myself none. [*She rises and gets the ironing board and sets it up and attacks a huge pile of rough-dried clothes, sprinkling them in preparation for the ironing and then rolling them into tight fat balls*]

WALTER   [*Mumbling*]   We one group of men tied to a race of women with small minds. [*His sister* BENEATHA *enters. She is about twenty, as slim and intense as her brother. She is not as pretty as her sister-in-law, but her lean, almost intellectual face has a handsomeness of its own. She wears a bright-red flannel nightie, and her thick hair stands wildly about her head. Her speech is a mixture of many things; it is different from the rest of the family's insofar as education has permeated her sense of English—and perhaps the Midwest rather than the South has finally—at last—won out in her inflection; but not altogether, because over all of it is a soft slurring and transformed use of vowels which is the decided influence of the South-side. She passes through the room without looking at either* RUTH *or* WALTER *and goes to the outside door and looks, a little blindly, out to the bath-room. She sees that it has been lost to the Johnsons. She closes the door with a sleepy vengeance and crosses to the table and sits down a little defeated*]

BENEATHA   I am going to start timing those people.

WALTER   You should get up earlier.

BENEATHA   [*Her face in her hands. She is still fighting the urge to go back to bed*]   Really—would you suggest dawn? Where's the paper?

WALTER   [*Pushing the paper across the table to her as he studies her almost clinically, as though he has never seen her before*]   You a horrible-looking chick at this hour.

BENEATHA   [*Drily*]   Good morning, everybody.

WALTER   [*Senselessly*]   How is school coming?

BENEATHA   [*In the same spirit*]   Lovely. Lovely. And you know, biology is the greatest. [*Looking up at him*] I dissected something that looked just like you yesterday.

WALTER   I just wondered if you've made up your mind and everything.

BENEATHA   [*Gaining in sharpness and impatience*]   And what did I answer yesterday morning—and the day before that?

RUTH   [*From the ironing board, like someone disinterested and old*]   Don't be so nasty, Bennie.

BENEATHA   [*Still to her brother*]   And the day before that and the day before that!

WALTER   [*Defensively*]   I'm interested in you. Something wrong with that? Ain't many girls who decide—

WALTER *and* BENEATHA   [*In unison*]   —"to be a doctor."

[*Silence*]

WALTER Have we figured out yet just exactly how much medical school is going to cost?

RUTH Walter Lee, why don't you leave that girl alone and get out of here to work?

BENEATHA [*Exits to the bathroom and bangs on the door*] Come on out of there, please!

[*She comes back into the room*]

WALTER [*Looking at his sister intently*] You know the check is coming tomorrow.

BENEATHA [*Turning on him with a sharpness all her own*] That money belongs to Mama, Walter, and it's for her to decide how she wants to use it. I don't care if she wants to buy a house or a rocket ship or just nail it up somewhere and look at it. It's hers. Not ours—*hers*.

WALTER [*Bitterly*] Now ain't that fine! You just got your mother's interest at heart, ain't you, girl? You such a nice girl—but if Mama got that money she can always take a few thousand and help you through school too— can't she?

BENEATHA I have never asked anyone around here to do anything for me!

WALTER No! And the line between asking and just accepting when the time comes is big and wide—ain't it!

BENEATHA [*With fury*] What do you want from me, Brother—that I quit school or just drop dead, which!

WALTER I don't want nothing but for you to stop acting holy 'round here. Me and Ruth done made some sacrifices for you—why can't you do something for the family?

RUTH Walter, don't be dragging me in it.

WALTER You are in it—Don't you get up and go work in somebody's kitchen for the last three years to help put clothes on her back?

RUTH Oh, Walter—that's not fair . . .

WALTER It ain't that nobody expects you to get on your knees and say thank you, Brother; thank you, Ruth; thank you, Mama—and thank you, Travis, for wearing the same pair of shoes for two semesters—

BENEATHA [*Dropping to her knees*] Well—I *do*—all right?—thank everybody . . . and forgive me for ever wanting to be anything at all . . . forgive me, forgive me!

RUTH Please stop it! Your mama'll hear you.

WALTER Who the hell told you you had to be a doctor? If you so crazy 'bout messing 'round with sick people—then go be a nurse like other women—or just get married and be quiet . . .

BENEATHA Well—you finally got it said . . . It took you three years but you finally got it said. Walter, give up; leave me alone—it's Mama's money.

WALTER *He was my father, too!*

BENEATHA So what? He was mine, too—and Travis' grandfather—but the insurance money belongs to Mama. Picking on me is not going to make her give it to you to invest in any liquor stores—[*Underbreath, dropping into a chair*]—and I for one say, God bless Mama for that!

WALTER [*To* RUTH] See—did you hear? Did you hear!

RUTH Honey, please go to work.

WALTER Nobody in this house is ever going to understand me.

BENEATHA Because you're a nut.

WALTER Who's a nut?

BENEATHA You—you are a nut. Thee is mad, boy.

WALTER [*Looking at his wife and his sister from the door, very sadly*] The world's most backward race of people, and that's a fact.

BENEATHA [*Turning slowly in her chair*] And then there are all those prophets who would lead us out of the wilderness—[WALTER *slams out of the house*] —into the swamps!

RUTH Bennie, why you always gotta be pickin' on your brother? Can't you be a little sweeter sometimes? [*Door opens.* WALTER *walks in*]

WALTER [*To Ruth*] I need some money for carfare.

RUTH [*Looks at him, then warms; teasing, but tenderly*] Fifty cents? [*She goes to her bag and gets money*] Here, take a taxi.

[WALTER *exits.* MAMA *enters. She is a woman in her early sixties, full-bodied and strong. She is one of those women of a certain grace and beauty who wear it so unobtrusively that it takes a while to notice. Her dark-brown face is surrounded by the total whiteness of her hair, and, being a woman who has adjusted to many things in life and overcome many more, her face is full of strength. She has, we can see, wit and faith of a kind that keep her eyes lit and full of interest and expectancy. She is, in a word, a beautiful woman. Her bearing is perhaps most like the noble bearing of the women of the Hereros of Southwest Africa—rather as if she imagines that as she walks she still bears a basket or a vessel upon her head. Her speech, on the other hand, is as careless as her carriage is precise—she is inclined to slur everything—but her voice is perhaps not so much quiet as simply soft*]

MAMA Who that 'round here slamming doors at this hour?
[*She crosses through the room, goes to the window, opens it, and brings in a feeble little plant growing doggedly in a small pot on the window sill. She feels the dirt and puts it back out*]

RUTH That was Walter Lee. He and Bennie was at it again.

MAMA My children and they tempers. Lord, if this little old plant don't get more sun than it's been getting it ain't never going to see spring again. [*She turns from the window*] What's the matter with you this morning, Ruth? You looks right peaked. You aiming to iron all them things? Leave some for me. I'll get to 'em this afternoon. Bennie honey, it's too drafty for you to be sitting 'round half dressed. Where's your robe?

BENEATHA In the cleaners.

MAMA Well, go get mine and put it on.

BENEATHA I'm not cold, Mama, honest.

MAMA I know—but you so thin . . .

BENEATHA [*Irritably*] Mama, I'm not cold.

MAMA [*Seeing the make-down bed as* TRAVIS *has left it*] Lord have mercy, look at that poor bed. Bless his heart—he tries, don't he?
[*She moves to the bed* TRAVIS *has sloppily made up*]

RUTH No—he don't half try at all 'cause he knows you going to come along behind him and fix everything. That's just how come he don't know how to do nothing right now—you done spoiled that boy so.

MAMA Well—he's a little boy. Ain't supposed to know 'bout housekeeping. My baby, that's what he is. What you fix for his breakfast this morning?

RUTH [*Angrily*] I feed my son, Lena!

MAMA I ain't meddling—[*Underbreath; busy-bodyish*] I just noticed all last week he had cold cereal, and when it starts getting this chilly in the fall a child ought to have some hot grits or something when he goes out in the cold—

RUTH [*Furious*] I gave him hot oats—is that all right!

MAMA   I ain't meddling. [*Pause*] Put a lot of nice butter on it? [RUTH *shoots her an angry look and does not reply*] He likes lots of butter.

RUTH   [*Exasperated*]   Lena—

MAMA   [*To* BENEATHA. MAMA *is inclined to wander conversationally sometimes*] What was you and your brother fussing 'bout this morning?

BENEATHA   It's not important, Mama.

[*She gets up and goes to look out at the bathroom, which is apparently free, and she picks up her towels and rushes out*]

MAMA   What was they fighting about?

RUTH   Now you know as well as I do.

MAMA   [*Shaking her head*]   Brother still worrying hisself sick about that money?

RUTH   You know he is.

MAMA   You had breakfast?

RUTH   Some coffee.

MAMA   Girl, you better start eating and looking after yourself better. You almost thin as Travis.

RUTH   Lena—

MAMA   Un-hunh?

RUTH   What are you going to do with it?

MAMA   Now don't you start, child. It's too early in the morning to be talking about money. It ain't Christian.

RUTH   It's just that he got his heart set on that store—

MAMA   You mean that liquor store that Willy Harris want him to invest in?

RUTH   Yes—

MAMA   We ain't no business people, Ruth. We just plain working folks.

RUTH   Ain't nobody business people till they go into business. Walter Lee say colored people ain't never going to start getting ahead till they start gambling on some different kinds of things in the world—investments and things.

MAMA   What done got into you, girl? Walter Lee done finally sold you on investing.

RUTH   No. Mama, something is happening between Walter and me. I don't know what it is—but he needs something—something I can't give him any more. He needs this chance, Lena.

MAMA   [*Frowning deeply*]   But liquor, honey—

RUTH   Well—like Walter say—I spec people going to always be drinking themselves some liquor.

MAMA   Well—whether they drinks it or not ain't none of my business. But whether I go into business selling it to 'em *is,* and I don't want that on my ledger this late in life. [*Stopping suddenly and studying her daughter-in-law*] Ruth Younger, what's the matter with you today? You look like you could fall over right there.

RUTH   I'm tired.

MAMA   Then you better stay home from work today.

RUTH   I can't stay home. She'd be calling up the agency and screaming at them, "My girl didn't come in today—send me somebody! My girl didn't come in!" Oh, she just have a fit . . .

MAMA   Well, let her have it. I'll just call her up and say you got the flu—

RUTH   [*Laughing*]   Why the flu?

MAMA   'Cause it sounds respectable to 'em. Something white people get, too. They know 'bout the flu. Otherwise they think you been cut up or something when you tell 'em you sick.

RUTH   I got to go in. We need the money.

MAMA Somebody would of thought my children done all but starved to death the way they talk about money here late. Child, we got a great big old check coming tomorrow.

RUTH [*Sincerely, but also self-righteously*] Now that's your money. It ain't got nothing to do with me. We all feel like that—Walter and Bennie and me—even Travis.

MAMA [*Thoughtfully, and suddenly very far away*] Ten thousand dollars—

RUTH Sure is wonderful.

MAMA Ten thousand dollars.

RUTH You know what you should do. Miss Lena? You should take yourself a trip somewhere. To Europe or South America or someplace—

MAMA [*Throwing up her hands at the thought*] Oh, child!

RUTH I'm serious. Just pack up and leave! Go on away and enjoy yourself some. Forget about the family and have yourself a ball for once in your life—

MAMA [*Drily*] You sound like I'm just about ready to die. Who'd go with me? What I look like wandering 'round Europe by myself?

RUTH Shoot—these here rich white women do it all the time. They don't think nothing of packing up they suitcases and piling on one of them big steamships and—swoosh!—they gone, child.

MAMA Something always told me I wasn't no rich white woman.

RUTH Well—what are you going to do with it then?

MAMA I ain't rightly decided. [*Thinking. She speaks now with emphasis*] Some of it got to be put away for Beneatha and her schoolin'—and ain't nothing going to touch that part of it. Nothing. [*She waits several seconds, trying to make up her mind about something, and looks at* RUTH *a little tentatively before going on*] Been thinking that we maybe could meet the notes on a little old two-story somewhere, with a yard where Travis could play in the summertime, if we use part of the insurance for a down payment and everybody kind of pitch in. I could maybe take on a little day work again, few days a week—

RUTH [*Studying her mother-in-law furtively and concentrating on her ironing, anxious to encourage without seeming to*] Well, Lord knows, we've put enough rent into this here rat trap to pay for four houses by now . . .

MAMA [*Looking up at the words "rat trap" and then looking around and leaning back and sighing—in a suddenly reflective mood—*] "Rat trap"—yes, that's all it is. [*Smiling*] I remember just as well the day me and Big Walter moved in here. Hadn't been married but two weeks and wasn't planning on living here no more than a year. [*She shakes her head at the dissolved dream*] We was going to set away, little by little, don't you know, and buy a little place out in Morgan Park. We had even picked out the house. [*Chuckling a little*] Looks right dumpy today. But Lord, child, you should know all the dreams I had 'bout buying that house and fixing it up and making me a little garden in the back—[*She waits and stops smiling*] And didn't none of it happen.

[*Dropping her hands in a futile gesture*]

RUTH [*Keeps her head down, ironing*] Yes, life can be a barrel of disappointments, sometimes.

MAMA Honey, Big Walter would come in here some nights back then and slump down on that couch there and just look at the rug, and look at me and look at the rug and then back at me—and I'd know he was down then . . . really down. [*After a second very long and thoughtful pause; she is seeing back to times that only she can see*] And then, Lord, when I lost that baby—little Claude—I almost thought I was going to lose Big

Walter too. Oh, that man grieved hisself! He was one man to love his children.

RUTH   Ain't nothin' can tear at you like losin' your baby.

MAMA   I guess that's how come that man finally worked hisself to death like he done. Like he was fighting his own war with this here world that took his baby from him.

RUTH   He sure was a fine man, all right. I always liked Mr. Younger.

MAMA   Crazy 'bout his children! God knows there was plenty wrong with Walter Younger—hard-headed, mean, kind of wild with women—plenty wrong with him. But he sure loved his children. Always wanted them to have something—be something. That's where Brother gets all these notions, I reckon. Big Walter used to say, he'd get right wet in the eyes sometimes, lean his head back with the water standing in his eyes and say, "Seem like God didn't see fit to give the black man nothing but dreams—but He did give us children to make them dreams seem worth while." [*She smiles*] He could talk like that, don't you know.

RUTH   Yes, he sure could. He was a good man, Mr. Younger.

MAMA   Yes, a fine man—just couldn't never catch up with his dreams, that's all.

[BENEATHA *comes in, brushing her hair and looking up to the ceiling, where the sound of a vacuum cleaner has started up*]

BENEATHA   What could be so dirty on that woman's rugs that she has to vacuum them every single day?

RUTH   I wish certain young women 'round here who I could name would take inspiration about certain rugs in a certain apartment I could also mention.

BENEATHA   [*Shrugging*] How much cleaning can a house need, for Christ's sakes.

MAMA   [*Not liking the Lord's name used thus*]   Bennie!

RUTH   Just listen to her—just listen!

BENEATHA   Oh, God!

MAMA   If you use the Lord's name just one more time—

BENEATHA   [*A bit of a whine*]   Oh, Mama—

RUTH   Fresh—just fresh as salt, this girl!

BENEATHA   [*Drily*]   Well—if the salt loses its savor—

MAMA   Now that will do. I just ain't going to have you 'round here reciting the scriptures in vain—you hear me?

BENEATHA   How did I manage to get on everybody's wrong side by just walking into a room?

RUTH   If you weren't so fresh—

BENEATHA   Ruth, I'm twenty years old.

MAMA   What time you be home from school today?

BENEATHA   Kind of late. [*With enthusiasm*] Madeline is going to start my guitar lessons today.

[MAMA *and* RUTH *look up with the same expression*]

MAMA   Your *what* kind of lessons?

BENEATHA   Guitar.

RUTH   Oh, Father!

MAMA   How come you done taken it in your mind to learn to play the guitar?

BENEATHA   I just want to, that's all.

MAMA   [*Smiling*] Lord, child, don't you know what to do with yourself? How long it going to be before you get tired of this now—like you got tired of that little play-acting group you joined last year? [*Looking at Ruth*] And what was it the year before that?

RUTH   The horseback-riding club for which she bought that fifty-five-dollar riding habit that's been hanging in the closet ever since!

MAMA   [*To* BENEATHA]   Why you got to flit so from one thing to another, baby?

BENEATHA   [*Sharply*]   I just want to learn to play the guitar. Is there anything wrong with that?

MAMA   Ain't nobody trying to stop you. I just wonders sometimes why you has to flit so from one thing to another all the time. You ain't never done nothing with all that camera equipment you brought home—

BENEATHA   I don't flit! I—I experiment with different forms of expression—

RUTH   Like riding a horse?

BENEATHA   —People have to express themselves one way or another.

MAMA   What is it you want to express?

BENEATHA   [*Angrily*]   Me! [MAMA *and* RUTH *look at each other and burst into raucous laughter*] Don't worry—I don't expect you to understand.

MAMA   [*To change the subject*]   Who you going out with tomorrow night?

BENEATHA   [*With displeasure*]   George Murchison again.

MAMA   [*Pleased*]   Oh—you getting a little sweet on him?

RUTH   You ask me, this child ain't sweet on nobody but herself—[*Underbreath*] Express herself!

[*They laugh*]

BENEATHA   Oh—I like George all right, Mama. I mean I like him enough to go out with him and stuff, but—

RUTH   [*For devilment*]   What does *and stuff* mean?

BENEATHA   Mind your own business.

MAMA   Stop picking at her now, Ruth. [*A thoughtful pause, and then a suspicious sudden look at her daughter as she turns in her chair for emphasis*] What *does* it mean?

BENEATHA   [*Wearily*]   Oh, I just mean I couldn't ever really be serious about George. He's—he's so shallow.

RUTH   Shallow—what do you mean he's shallow? He's *Rich!*

MAMA   Hush, Ruth.

BENEATHA   I know he's rich. He knows he's rich, too.

RUTH   Well—what other qualities a man got to have to satisfy you, little girl?

BENEATHA   You wouldn't even begin to understand. Anybody who married Walter could not possibly understand.

MAMA   [*Outraged*]   What kind of way is that to talk about your brother?

BENEATHA   Brother is a flip—let's face it.

MAMA   [*To* RUTH, *helplessly*]   What's a flip?

RUTH   [*Glad to add kindling*]   She's saying he's crazy.

BENEATHA   Not crazy. Brother isn't really crazy yet—he—he's an elaborate neurotic.

MAMA   Hush your mouth!

BENEATHA   As for George. Well. George looks good—he's got a beautiful car and he takes me to nice places and, as my sister-in-law says, he is probably the richest boy I will ever get to know and I even like him sometimes— but if the Youngers are sitting around waiting to see if their little Bennie is going to tie up the family with the Murchisons, they are wasting their time.

RUTH   You mean you wouldn't marry George Murchison if he asked you someday? That pretty, rich thing? Honey, I knew you was odd—

BENEATHA   No I would not marry him if all I felt for him was what I feel now. Besides, George's family wouldn't really like it.

MAMA   Why not?

BENEATHA   Oh, Mama—The Murchisons are honest-to-God-real-*live*-rich colored people, and the only people in the world who are more snobbish than rich white people are rich colored people. I thought everybody knew that. I've met Mrs. Murchison. She's a scene!

MAMA   You must not dislike people 'cause they well off, honey.

BENEATHA   Why not? It makes just as much sense as disliking people 'cause they are poor, and lots of people do that.

RUTH   [*A wisdom-of-the-ages manner. To* MAMA]   Well, she'll get over some of this—

BENEATHA   Get over it? What are you talking about, Ruth? Listen, I'm going to be a doctor. I'm not worried about who I'm going to marry yet—if I ever get married.

MAMA *and* RUTH   *If!*

MAMA   Now, Bennie—

BENEATHA   Oh, I probably will . . . but first I'm going to be a doctor, and George, for one, still thinks that's pretty funny. I couldn't be bothered with that. I am going to be a doctor and everybody around here better understand that!

MAMA   [*Kindly*]   'Course you going to be a doctor, honey, God willing.

BENEATHA   [*Drily*]   God hasn't got a thing to do with it.

MAMA   Beneatha—that just wasn't necessary.

BENEATHA   Well—neither is God. I get sick of hearing about God.

MAMA   Beneatha!

BENEATHA   I mean it! I'm just tired of hearing about God all the time. What has He got to do with anything? Does he pay tuition?

MAMA   You 'bout to get your fresh little jaw slapped!

RUTH   That's just what she needs, all right!

BENEATHA   Why? Why can't I say what I want to around here, like everybody else?

MAMA   It don't sound nice for a young girl to say things like that—you wasn't brought up that way. Me and your father went to trouble to get you and Brother to church every Sunday.

BENEATHA   Mama, you don't understand. It's all a matter of ideas, and God is just one idea I don't accept. It's not important. I am not going out and be immoral or commit crimes because I don't believe in God. I don't even think about it. It's just that I get tired of Him getting credit for all the things the human race achieves through its own stubborn effort. There simply is no blasted God—there is only man and it is he who makes miracles!

[MAMA *absorbs this speech, studies her daughter and rises slowly and crosses to* BENEATHA *and slaps her powerfully across the face. After, there is only silence and the daughter drops her eyes from her mother's face, and* MAMA *is very tall before her*]

MAMA   Now—you say after me, in my mother's house there is still God. [*There is a long pause and* BENEATHA *stares at the floor wordlessly.* MAMA *repeats the phrase with precision and cool emotion*] In my mother's house there is still God.

BENEATHA   In my mother's house there is still God.

[*A long pause*]

MAMA   [*Walking away from* BENEATHA, *too disturbed for triumphant posture. Stopping and turning back to her daughter*]   There are some ideas we ain't going to have in this house. Not long as I am at the head of this family.

BENEATHA   Yes, ma'am.

[MAMA *walks out of the room*]

RUTH [*Almost gently, with profound understanding*] You think you a woman, Bennie—but you still a little girl. What you did was childish—so you got treated like a child.

BENEATHA I see. [*Quietly*] I also see that everybody thinks it's all right for Mama to be a tyrant. But all the tyranny in the world will never put a God in the heavens!

[*She picks up her books and goes out*]

RUTH [*Goes to* MAMA's *door*] She said she was sorry.

MAMA [*Coming out, going to her plant*] They frightens me, Ruth. My children.

RUTH You got good children, Lena. They just a little off sometimes—but they're good.

MAMA No—there's something come down between me and them that don't let us understand each other and I don't know what it is. One done almost lost his mind thinking 'bout money all the time and the other done commence to talk about things I can't seem to understand in no form or fashion. What is it that's changing, Ruth?

RUTH [*Soothingly, older than her years*] Now . . . you taking it all too seriously. You just got strong-willed children and it takes a strong woman like you to keep 'em in hand.

MAMA [*Looking at her plant and sprinkling a little water on it*] They spirited all right, my children. Got to admit they got spirit—Bennie and Walter. Like this little old plant that ain't never had enough sunshine or nothing —and look at it . . .

[*She has her back to* RUTH, *who has had to stop ironing and lean against something and put the back of her hand to her forehead*]

RUTH [*Trying to keep* MAMA *from noticing*] You . . . sure . . . loves that little old thing, don't you? . . .

MAMA Well, I always wanted me a garden like I used to see sometimes at the back of the houses down home. This plant is close as I ever got to having one. [*She looks out of the window as she replaces the plant*] Lord, ain't nothing as dreary as the view from this window on a dreary day, is there? Why ain't you singing this morning, Ruth? Sing that "No Ways Tired." That song always lifts me up so—[*She turns at last to see that* RUTH *has slipped quietly into a chair, in a state of semiconsciousness*] Ruth! Ruth honey—what's the matter with you . . . Ruth!

CURTAIN

Scene Two

> It is the following morning; a Saturday morning, and house cleaning is in progress at the YOUNGERS. Furniture has been shoved hither and yon and MAMA is giving the kitchen-area walls a washing down. BENEATHA, in dungarees, with a handkerchief tied around her face, is spraying insecticide into the cracks in the walls. As they work, the radio is on and a Southside disk-jockey program is inappropriately filling the house with a rather exotic saxophone blues. TRAVIS, the sole idle one, is leaning on his arms, looking out of the window.

TRAVIS Grandmama, that stuff Bennie is using smells awful. Can I go downstairs, please?

MAMA   Did you get all them chores done already? I ain't seen you doing much.

TRAVIS   Yes'm—finished early. Where did Mama go this morning?

MAMA   [*Looking at* BENEATHA]   She had to go on a little errand.

TRAVIS   Where?

MAMA   To tend to her business.

TRAVIS   Can I go outside then?

MAMA   Oh, I guess so. You better stay right in front of the house, though . . . and keep a good lookout for the postman.

TRAVIS   Yes'm. [*He starts out and decides to give his* AUNT BENEATHA *a good swat on the legs as he passes her*] Leave them poor little old cockroaches alone, they ain't bothering you none.
[*He runs as she swings the spray gun at him both viciously and playfully.* WALTER *enters from the bedroom and goes to the phone*]

MAMA   Look out there, girl, before you be spilling some of that stuff on that child!

TRAVIS   [*Teasing*]   That's right—look out now!
[*He exits*]

BENEATHA   [*Drily*]   I can't imagine that it would hurt him—it has never hurt the roaches.

MAMA   Well, little boys' hides ain't as tough as Southside roaches.

WALTER   [*Into phone*]   Hello—Let me talk to Willy Harris.

MAMA   You better get over there behind the bureau. I seen one marching out of there like Napoleon yesterday.

WALTER   Hello, Willy? It ain't come yet. It'll be here in a few minutes. Did the lawyer give you the papers?

BENEATHA   There's really only one way to get rid of them, Mama—

MAMA   How?

BENEATHA   Set fire to this building.

WALTER   Good. Good. I'll be right over.

BENEATHA   Where did Ruth go, Walter?

WALTER   I don't know.
[*He exits abruptly*]

BENEATHA   Mama, where did Ruth go?

MAMA   [*Looking at her with meaning*]   To the doctor, I think.

BENEATHA   The doctor? What's the matter? [*They exchange glances*] You don't think—

MAMA   [*With her sense of drama*]   Now I ain't saying what I think. But I ain't never been wrong 'bout a woman neither.
[*The phone rings*]

BENEATHA   [*At the phone*]   Hay-lo . . . [*Pause, and a moment of recognition*] Well—when did you get back! . . . And how was it? . . . Of course I've missed you—in my way . . . This morning? No . . . house cleaning and all that and Mama hates it if I let people come over when the house is like this . . . You *have*? Well, that's different . . . What is it—Oh, what the hell, come on over . . . Right, see you then.
[*She hangs up*]

MAMA   [*Who has listened vigorously, as is her habit*]   Who is that you inviting over here with this house looking like this? You ain't got the pride you was born with!

BENEATHA   Asagai doesn't care how houses look, Mama—he's an intellectual.

MAMA   *Who?*

BENEATHA   Asagai—Joseph Asagai. He's an African boy I met on campus. He's been studying in Canada all summer.

MAMA   What's his name?

BENEATHA Asagai, Joseph. Ah-sah-guy . . . He's from Nigeria.

MAMA Oh, that's the little country that was founded by slaves way back . . .

BENEATHA No, Mama—that's Liberia.

MAMA I don't think I never met no African before.

BENEATHA Well, do me a favor and don't ask him a whole lot of ignorant questions about Africans. I mean, do they wear clothes and all that—

MAMA Well, now, I guess if you think we so ignorant 'round here maybe you shouldn't bring your friends here—

BENEATHA It's just that people ask such crazy things. All anyone seems to know about when it comes to Africa is Tarzan—

MAMA [Indignantly] Why should I know anything about Africa?

BENEATHA Why do you give money at church for the missionary work?

MAMA Well, that's to help save people.

BENEATHA You mean save them from heathenism—

MAMA [Innocently] Yes.

BENEATHA I'm afraid they need more salvation from the British and the French.
[RUTH comes in forlornly and pulls off her coat with dejection. They both turn to look at her]

RUTH [Dispiritedly] Well, I guess from all the happy faces—everybody knows.

BENEATHA You pregnant?

MAMA Lord have mercy, I sure hope it's a little old girl. Travis ought to have a sister.
[BENEATHA and RUTH give her a hopeless look for this grandmotherly enthusiasm]

BENEATHA How far along are you?

RUTH Two months.

BENEATHA Did you mean to? I mean did you plan it or was it an accident?

MAMA What do you know about planning or not planning?

BENEATHA Oh, Mama.

RUTH [Wearily] She's twenty years old, Lena.

BENEATHA Did you plan it, Ruth?

RUTH Mind your own business.

BENEATHA It is my business—where is he going to live, on the roof? [There is silence following the remark as the three women react to the sense of it] Gee—I didn't mean that, Ruth, honest. Gee, I don't feel like that at all. I —I think it is wonderful.

RUTH [Dully] Wonderful.

BENEATHA Yes—really.

MAMA [Looking at RUTH, worried] Doctor say everything going to be all right?

RUTH [Far away] Yes—she says everything is going to be fine . . .

MAMA [Immediately suspicious] "She"—What doctor you went to?
[RUTH folds over, near hysteria]

MAMA [Worriedly hovering over RUTH] Ruth honey—what's the matter with you—you sick?
[RUTH has her fists clenched on her thighs and is fighting hard to suppress a scream that seems to be rising in her]

BENEATHA What's the matter with her, Mama?

MAMA [Working her fingers in RUTH's shoulder to relax her] She be all right. Women gets right depressed sometimes when they get her way. [Speaking softly, expertly, rapidly] Now you just relax. That's right . . . just lean back, don't think 'bout nothing at all . . . nothing at all—

RUTH I'm all right . . .
[The glassy-eyed look melts and then she collapses into a fit of heavy sobbing. The bell rings]

BENEATHA   Oh, my God—that must be Asagai.

MAMA   [*To* RUTH]   Come on now, honey. You need to lie down and rest awhile . . . then have some nice hot food.

[*They exit,* RUTH's *weight on her mother-in-law.* BENEATHA, *herself profoundly disturbed, opens the door to admit a rather dramatic-looking young man with a large package*]

ASAGAI   Hello, Alaiyo—

BENEATHA   [*Holding the door open and regarding him with pleasure*]   Hello . . . [*Long pause*] Well—come in. And please excuse everything. My mother was very upset about my letting anyone come here with the place like this.

ASAGAI   [*Coming into the room*]   You look disturbed too . . . Is something wrong?

BENEATHA   [*Still at the door, absently*]   Yes . . . we've all got acute ghetto-itus. [*She smiles and comes toward him, finding a cigarette and sitting*] So—sit down! How was Canada?

ASAGAI   [*A sophisticate*]   Canadian.

BENEATHA   [*Looking at him*]   I'm very glad you are back.

ASAGAI   [*Looking back at her in turn*]   Are you really?

BENEATHA   Yes—very.

ASAGAI   Why—you were quite glad when I went away. What happened?

BENEATHA   You went away.

ASAGAI   Ahhhhhhhh.

BENEATHA   Before—you wanted to be so serious before there was time.

ASAGAI   How much time must there be before one knows what one feels?

BENEATHA   [*Stalling this particular conversation. Her hands pressed together, in a deliberately childish gesture*]   What did you bring me?

ASAGAI   [*Handing her the package*]   Open it and see.

BENEATHA   [*Eagerly opening the package and drawing out some records and the colorful robes of a Nigerian woman*]   Oh, Asagai! . . . You got them for me! . . . How beautiful . . . and the records too! [*She lifts out the robes and runs to the mirror with them and holds the drapery up in front of herself*]

ASAGAI   [*Coming to her at the mirror*]   I shall have to teach you how to drape it properly. [*He flings the material about her for the moment and stands back to look at her*] Ah—Oh-pay-gay-day, oh-gbah-mu-shay. [*A Yoruba exclamation for admiration*] You wear it well . . . very well . . . mutilated hair and all.

BENEATHA   [*Turning suddenly*]   My hair—what's wrong with my hair?

ASAGAI   [*Shrugging*]   Were you born with it like that?

BENEATHA   [*Reaching up to touch it*]   No . . . of course not.

[*She looks back to the mirror, disturbed*]

ASAGAI   [*Smiling*]   How then?

BENEATHA   You know perfectly well how . . . as crinkly as yours . . . that's how.

ASAGAI   And it is ugly to you that way?

BENEATHA   [*Quickly*]   Oh, no—not ugly . . . [*More slowly, apologetically*] But it's so hard to manage when it's, well—raw.

ASAGAI   And so to accommodate that—you mutilate it every week?

BENEATHA   It's not mutilation!

ASAGAI   [*Laughing aloud at her seriousness*]   Oh . . . please! I am only teasing you because you are so very serious about these things. [*He stands back from her and folds his arms across his chest as he watches her pulling at her hair and frowning in the mirror*] Do you remember the first time you met me at school? . . . [*He laughs*] You came up to me and you said—and I thought you were the most serious little thing I had ever seen—you said:

[*He imitates her*] "Mr. Asagai—I want very much to talk with you. About Africa. You see, Mr. Asagai, I am looking for my *identity!*"
[*He laughs*]

BENEATHA   [*Turning to him, not laughing*]   Yes—
[*Her face is quizzical, profoundly disturbed*]

ASAGAI   [*Still teasing and reaching out and taking her face in his hands and turning her profile to him*]   Well . . . it is true that this is not so much a profile of a Hollywood queen as perhaps a queen of the Nile—[*A mock dismissal of the importance of the question*] But what does it matter? Assimilationism is so popular in your country.

BENEATHA   [*Wheeling, passionately, sharply*]   I am not an assimilationist!

ASAGAI   [*The protest hangs in the room for a moment and* ASAGAI *studies her, his laughter fading*]   Such a serious one. [*There is a pause*] So—you like the robes? You must take excellent care of them—they are from my sister's personal wardrobe.

BENEATHA   [*With incredulity*]   You—you sent all the way home—for me?

ASAGAI   [*With charm*]   For you—I would do much more . . . Well, that is what I came for. I must go.

BENEATHA   Will you call me Monday?

ASAGAI   Yes . . . We have a great deal to talk about. I mean about identity and time and all that.

BENEATHA   Time?

ASAGAI   Yes. About how much time one needs to know what one feels.

BENEATHA   You never understood that there is more than one kind of feeling which can exist between a man and a woman—or, at least, there should be.

ASAGAI   [*Shaking his head negatively but gently*]   No. Between a man and a woman there need be only one kind of feeling. I have that for you . . . Now even . . . right this moment . . .

BENEATHA   I know—and by itself—it won't do. I can find that anywhere.

ASAGAI   For a woman it should be enough.

BENEATHA   I know—because that's what it says in all the novels that men write. But it isn't. Go ahead and laugh—but I'm not interested in being someone's little episode in America or—[*With feminine vengeance*]—one of them! [ASAGAI *has burst into laughter again*] That's funny as hell, huh!

ASAGAI   It's just that every American girl I have known has said that to me. White—black—in this you are all the same. And the same speech, too!

BENEATHA   [*Angrily*]   Yuk, yuk, yuk!

ASAGAI   It's how you can be sure that the world's most liberated women are not liberated at all. You all talk about it too much!
[MAMA *enters and is immediately all social charm because of the presence of a guest*]

BENEATHA   Oh—Mama—this is Mr. Asagai.

MAMA   How do you do?

ASAGAI   [*Total politeness to an elder*]   How do you do, Mrs. Younger. Please forgive me for coming at such an outrageous hour on a Saturday.

MAMA   Well, you are quite welcome. I just hope you understand that our house don't always look like this. [*Chatterish*] You must come again. I would love to hear all about—[*Not sure of the name*]—your country. I think it's so sad the way our American Negroes don't know nothing about Africa 'cept Tarzan and all that. And all that money they pour into these churches when they ought to be helping you people over there drive out them French and Englishmen done taken away your land.
[*The mother flashes a slightly superior look at her daughter upon completion of the recitation*]

ASAGAI [*Taken aback by this sudden and acutely unrelated expression of sympathy*] Yes . . . yes . . .

MAMA [*Smiling at him suddenly and relaxing and looking him over*] How many miles is it from here to where you come from?

ASAGAI Many thousands.

MAMA [*Looking at him as she would* WALTER] I bet you don't half look after yourself, being away from your mama either. I spec you better come 'round here from time to time and get yourself some decent homecooked meals . . .

ASAGAI [*Moved*] Thank you. Thank you very much. [*They are all quiet, then—*] Well . . . I must go. I will call you Monday, Alaiyo.

MAMA What's that he call you?

ASAGAI Oh—"Alaiyo." I hope you don't mind. It is what you would call a nickname, I think. It is a Yoruba word. I am a Yoruba.

MAMA [*Looking at* BENEATHA] I—I thought he was from—

ASAGAI [*Understanding*] Nigeria is my country. Yoruba is my tribal origin—

BENEATHA You didn't tell us what Alaiyo means . . . for all I know, you might be calling me Little Idiot or something . . .

ASAGAI Well . . . let me see . . . I do not know how just to explain it . . . The sense of a thing can be so different when it changes languages.

BENEATHA You're evading.

ASAGAI No—really it is difficult . . . [*Thinking*] It means . . . it means One for Whom Bread—Food—Is Not Enough. [*He looks at her*] Is that all right?

BENEATHA [*Understanding, softly*] Thank you.

MAMA [*Looking from one to the other and not understanding any of it*] Well . . . that's nice . . . You must come see us again—Mr.—

ASAGAI Ah-sah-guy . . .

MAMA Yes . . . Do come again.

ASAGAI Good-bye.

[*He exits*]

MAMA [*After him*] Lord, that's a pretty thing just went out here! [*Insinuatingly, to her daughter*] Yes, I guess I see why we done commence to get so interested in Africa 'round here. Missionaries my aunt Jenny!

[*She exits*]

BENEATHA Oh, Mama! . . .

[*She picks up the Nigerian dress and holds it up to her in front of the mirror again. She sets the headdress on haphazardly and then notices her hair again and clutches at it and then replaces the headdress and frowns at herself. Then she starts to wriggle in front of the mirror as she thinks a Nigerian woman might.* TRAVIS *enters and regards her*]

TRAVIS You cracking up?

BENEATHA Shut up.

[*She pulls the headdress off and looks at herself in the mirror and clutches at her hair again and squinches her eyes as if trying to imagine something. Then, suddenly, she gets her raincoat and kerchief and hurriedly prepares for going out*]

MAMA [*Coming back into the room*] She's resting now. Travis, baby, run next door and ask Miss Johnson to please let me have a little kitchen cleanser. This here can is empty as Jacob's kettle.

TRAVIS I just came in.

MAMA Do as you told. [*He exits and she looks at her daughter*] Where you going?

BENEATHA [*Halting at the door*] To become a queen of the Nile!

[*She exits in a breathless blaze of glory.* RUTH *appears in the bedroom doorway*]

MAMA   Who told you to get up?

RUTH   Ain't nothing wrong with me to be lying in no bed for. Where did Bennie go?

MAMA   [*Drumming her fingers*]   Far as I could make out—to Egypt. [RUTH *just looks at her*] What time is it getting to?

RUTH   Ten twenty. And the mailman going to ring that bell this morning just like he done every morning for the last umpteen years.

[TRAVIS *comes in with the cleanser can*]

TRAVIS   She say to tell you that she don't have much.

MAMA   [*Angrily*]   Lord, some people I could name sure is tight-fisted! [*Directing her grandson*] Mark two cans of cleanser down on the list there. If she that hard up for kitchen cleanser, I sure don't want to forget to get her none!

RUTH   Lena—maybe the woman is just short on cleanser—

MAMA   [*Not listening*]—Much baking powder as she done borrowed from me all these years, she could of done gone into the baking business!

[*The bell sounds suddenly and sharply and all three are stunned—serious and silent—mid-speech. In spite of all the other conversations and distractions of the morning, this is what they have been waiting for, even* TRAVIS, *who looks helplessly from his mother to his grandmother.* RUTH *is the first to come to life again*]

RUTH   [*To* TRAVIS]   Get down them steps, boy!

[TRAVIS *snaps to life and flies out to get the mail*]

MAMA   [*Her eyes wide, her hand to her breast*]   You mean it done really come?

RUTH   [*Excited*]   Oh, Miss Lena!

MAMA   [*Collecting herself*]   Well . . . I don't know what we all so excited about 'round here for. We known it was coming for months.

RUTH   That's a whole lot different from having it come and being able to hold it in your hands . . . a piece of paper worth ten thousand dollars . . . [TRAVIS *bursts back into the room. He holds the envelope high above his head, like a little dancer, his face is radiant and he is breathless. He moves to his grandmother with sudden slow ceremony and puts the envelope into her hands. She accepts it, and then merely holds it and looks at it*] Come on! Open it . . . Lord have mercy, I wish Walter Lee was here!

TRAVIS   Open it, Grandmama!

MAMA   [*Staring at it*]   Now you all be quiet. It's just a check.

RUTH   Open it . . .

MAMA   [*Still staring at it*]   Now don't act silly . . . We ain't never been no people to act silly 'bout no money—

RUTH   [*Swiftly*]   We ain't never had none before—*open it!*

[MAMA *finally makes a good strong tear and pulls out the thin blue slice of paper and inspects it closely. The boy and his mother study it raptly over* MAMA'S *shoulders*]

MAMA   Travis! [*She is counting off with doubt*]   Is that the right number of zeros.

TRAVIS   Yes'm . . . ten thousand dollars. Gaalee, Grandmama, you rich.

MAMA   [*She holds the check away from her, still looking at it. Slowly her face sobers into a mask of unhappiness*] Ten thousand dollars. [*She hands it to* RUTH] Put it away somewhere, Ruth. [*She does not look at* RUTH; *her eyes seem to be seeing something somewhere very far off*] Ten thousand dollars they give you. Ten thousand dollars.

TRAVIS   [*To his mother, sincerely*]   What's the matter with Grandmama—don't she want to be rich?

RUTH   [*Distractedly*]   You go on out and play now, baby. [TRAVIS *exits.* MAMA *starts wiping dishes absently, humming intently to herself.* RUTH *turns to her, with kind exasperation*] You've gone and got yourself upset.

MAMA [*Not looking at her*] I spec if it wasn't for you all . . . I would just put that money away or give it to the church or something.

RUTH   Now what kind of talk is that. Mr. Younger would just be plain mad if he could hear you talking foolish like that.

MAMA [*Stopping and staring off*] Yes . . . he sure would. [*Sighing*] We got enough to do with that money, all right. [*She halts then, and turns and looks at her daughter-in-law hard;* RUTH *avoids her eyes and* MAMA *wipes her hands with finality and starts to speak firmly to* RUTH] Where did you go today, girl?

RUTH   To the doctor.

MAMA [*Impatiently*] Now, Ruth . . . you know better than that. Old Doctor Jones is strange enough in his way but there ain't nothing 'bout him make somebody slip and call him "she"—like you done this morning.

RUTH   Well, that's what happened—my tongue slipped.

MAMA   You went to see that woman, didn't you?

RUTH [*Defensively, giving herself away*] What woman you talking about?

MAMA [*Angrily*] That woman who—
   [WALTER *enters in great excitement*]

WALTER   Did it come?

MAMA [*Quietly*] Can't you give people a Christian greeting before you start asking about money?

WALTER [*To Ruth*] Did it come? [RUTH *unfolds the check and lays it quietly before him, watching him intently with thoughts of her own.* WALTER *sits down and grasps it close and counts off the zeros*] Ten thousand dollars— [*He turns suddenly, frantically to his mother and draws some papers out of his breast pocket*] Mama—look. Old Willy Harris put everything on paper—

MAMA   Son—I think you ought to talk to your wife . . . I'll go on out and leave you alone if you want—

WALTER   I can talk to her later—Mama, look—

MAMA   Son—

WALTER   WILL SOMEBODY PLEASE LISTEN TO ME TODAY!

MAMA [*Quietly*] I don't 'low no yellin' in this house, Walter Lee, and you know it—[WALTER *stares at them in frustration and starts to speak several times*] And there ain't going to be no investing in no liquor stores. I don't aim to have to speak on that again.
   [*A long pause*]

WALTER   Oh—so you don't aim to have to speak on that again? So *you* have decided . . . [*Crumpling his papers*] Well, *you* tell that to my boy tonight when you put him to sleep on the living-room couch . . . [*Turning to* MAMA *and speaking directly to her*] Yeah—and tell it to my wife, Mama, tomorrow when she has to go out of here to look after somebody else's kids. And tell it to *me*, Mama, every time we need a new pair of curtains and I have to watch *you* go out and work in somebody's kitchen. Yeah, you tell me then!
   [WALTER *starts out*]

RUTH   Where you going?

WALTER   I'm going out!

RUTH   Where?

WALTER   Just out of this house somewhere—

RUTH [*Getting her coat*] I'll come too.

WALTER   I don't want you to come!

RUTH I got something to talk to you about, Walter.

WALTER That's too bad.

MAMA [*Still quietly*] Walter Lee—[*She waits and he finally turns and looks at her*] Sit down.

WALTER I'm a grown man, Mama.

MAMA Ain't nobody said you wasn't grown. But you still in my house and my presence. And as long as you are—you'll talk to your wife civil. Now sit down.

RUTH [*Suddenly*] Oh, let him go on out and drink himself to death! He makes me sick to my stomach! [*She flings her coat against him*]

WALTER [*Violently*] And you turn mine too, baby! [RUTH *goes into their bedroom and slams the door behind her*] That was my greatest mistake—

MAMA [*Still quietly*] Walter, what is the matter with you?

WALTER Matter with me? Ain't nothing the matter with *me*!

MAMA Yes there is. Something eating you up like a crazy man. Something more than me not giving you this money. The past few years I been watching it happen to you. You get all nervous acting and kind of wild in the eyes—[WALTER *jumps up impatiently at her words*] I said sit there now, I'm talking to you!

WALTER Mama—I don't need no nagging at me today.

MAMA Seem like you getting to a place where you always tied up in some kind of knot about something. But if anybody ask you 'bout it you just yell at 'em and bust out the house and go out and drink somewheres. Walter Lee, people can't live with that. Ruth's a good, patient girl in her way—but you getting to be too much. Boy, don't make the mistake of driving that girl away from you.

WALTER Why—what she do for me?

MAMA She loves you.

WALTER Mama—I'm going out. I want to go off somewhere and be by myself for a while.

MAMA I'm sorry 'bout your liquor store, son. It just wasn't the thing for us to do. That's what I want to tell you about—

WALTER I got to go out, Mama—

[*He rises*]

MAMA It's dangerous, son.

WALTER What's dangerous?

MAMA When a man goes outside his home to look for peace.

WALTER [*Beseechingly*] Then why can't there never be no peace in this house then?

MAMA You done found it in some other house?

WALTER No—there ain't no woman! Why do women always think there's a woman somewhere when a man gets restless. [*Coming to her*] Mama—Mama—I want so many things . . .

MAMA Yes, son—

WALTER I want so many things that they are driving me kind of crazy . . . Mama—look at me.

MAMA I'm looking at you. You a good-looking boy. You got a job, a nice wife, a fine boy and—

WALTER A job. [*Looks at her*] Mama, a job? I open and close car doors all day long. I drive a man around in his limousine and I say, "Yes, sir; no, sir; very good, sir; shall I take the Drive, sir?" Mama, that ain't no kind of job . . . that ain't nothing at all. [*Very quietly*] Mama, I don't know if I can make you understand.

MAMA   Understand what, baby?

WALTER   [*Quietly*] Sometimes it's like I can see the future stretched out in front of me—just plain as day. The future, Mama. Hanging over there at the edge of my days. Just waiting for me—a big, looming blank space —full of *nothing*. Just waiting for *me*. [*Pause*] Mama—sometimes when I'm downtown and I pass them cool, quiet-looking restaurants where them white boys are sitting back and talking 'bout things . . . sitting there turning deals worth millions of dollars . . . sometimes I see guys don't look much older than me—

MAMA   Son—how come you talk so much 'bout money?

WALTER   [*With immense passion*] Because it is life, Mama!

MAMA   [*Quietly*] Oh—[*Very quietly*] So now it's life. Money is life. Once upon a time freedom used to be life—now it's money. I guess the world really do change . . .

WALTER   No—it was always money, Mama. We just didn't know about it.

MAMA   No . . . something has changed. [*She looks at him*] You something new, boy. In my time we was worried about not being lynched and getting to the North if we could and how to stay alive and still have a pinch of dignity too . . . Now here come you and Beneatha—talking 'bout things we ain't never even thought about hardly, me and your daddy. You ain't satisfied or proud of nothing we done. I mean that you had a home; that we kept you out of trouble till you was grown; that you don't have to ride to work on the back of nobody's streetcar—You my children—but how different we done become.

WALTER   You just don't understand, Mama, you just don't understand.

MAMA   Son—do you know your wife is expecting another baby? [WALTER *stands, stunned, and absorbs what his mother has said*] That's what she wanted to talk to you about. [WALTER *sinks down into a chair*] This ain't for me to be telling—but you ought to know. [*She waits*] I think Ruth is thinking 'bout getting rid of that child.

WALTER   [*Slowly understanding*] No—no—Ruth wouldn't do that.

MAMA   When the world gets ugly enough—a woman will do anything for her family. *The part that's already living.*

WALTER   You don't know Ruth, Mama, if you think she would do that.

[RUTH *opens the bedroom door and stands there a little limp*]

RUTH   [*Beaten*] Yes I would too, Walter. [*Pause*] I gave her a five-dollar down payment.

[*There is total silence as the man stares at his wife and the mother stares at her son*]

MAMA   [*Presently*] Well—[*Tightly*] Well—son, I'm waiting to hear you say something . . . I'm waiting to hear how you be your father's son. Be the man he was . . . [*Pause*] Your wife say she going to destroy your child. And I'm waiting to hear you talk like him and say we a people who give children life, not who destroys them—[*She rises*] I'm waiting to see you stand up and look like your daddy and say we done give up one baby to poverty and that we ain't going to give up nary another one . . . I'm waiting.

WALTER   Ruth—

MAMA   If you a son of mine, tell her! (WALTER *turns, looks at her and can say nothing. She continues, bitterly*) You . . . you are a disgrace to your father's memory. Somebody get me my hat.

CURTAIN

ACT II

Scene One

Time: Later the same day.
At rise: RUTH *is ironing again. She has the radio going. Presently*
BENEATHA's *bedroom door opens and* RUTH's *mouth falls and*
she puts down the iron in fascination.

RUTH   What have we got on tonight!
BENEATHA   [*Emerging grandly from the doorway so that we can see her*
thoroughly robed in the costume Asagai brought] You are looking at
what a well-dressed Nigerian woman wears—[*She parades for* RUTH, *her*
hair completely hidden by the headdress; she is coquettishly fanning her-
self with an ornate oriental fan, mistakenly more like Butterfly than any
Nigerian that ever was] Isn't it beautiful? [*She promenades to the radio*
and, with an arrogant flourish, turns off the good loud blues that is playing]
Enough of this assimilationist junk! [RUTH *follows her with her eyes as she*
goes to the phonograph and puts on a record and turns and waits cere-
moniously for the music to come up. Then, with a shout—] OCOMOGO-
SIAY!
[RUTH *jumps. The music comes up, a lovely Nigerian melody.* BENEATHA
listens, enraptured, her eyes far away—"back to the past." She begins to
dance. RUTH *is dumfounded*]
RUTH   What kind of dance is that?
BENEATHA   A folk dance.
RUTH   [*Pearl Bailey*]   What kind of folks do that, honey?
BENEATHA   It's from Nigeria. It's a dance of welcome.
RUTH   Who you welcoming?
BENEATHA   The men back to the village.
RUTH   Where they been?
BENEATHA   How should I know—out hunting or something. Anyway, they
are coming back now . . .
RUTH   Well, that's good.
BENEATHA   [*With the record*]

    Alundi, alundi
    Alundi alunya
    Jop pu a jeepua
    Ang gu sooooooooooo

    Ai yai yae . . .
    Ayehaye—alundi . . .

[WALTER *comes in during this performance; he has obviously been drinking.*
He leans against the door heavily and watches his sister, at first with
distaste. Then his eyes look off—"back to the past"—as he lifts both his
fists to the roof, screaming]
WALTER   YEAH . . . AND ETHIOPIA STRETCH FORTH HER HANDS
AGAIN! . . .

RUTH [*Drily, looking at him*] Yes—and Africa sure is claiming her own to-night. [*She gives them both up and starts ironing again*]

WALTER [*All in a drunken, dramatic shout*] Shut up! . . . I'm digging them drums . . . them drums move me! . . . [*He makes his weaving way to his wife's face and leans in close to her*] In my *heart of hearts*—[*He thumps his chest*]—I am much warrior!

RUTH [*Without even looking up*] In your heart of hearts you are much drunkard.

WALTER [*Coming away from her and starting to wander around the room, shouting*] Me and Jomo . . . [*Intently, in his sister's face. She has stopped dancing to watch him in this unknown mood*] That's my man, Kenyatta. [*Shouting and thumping his chest*] FLAMING SPEAR! HOT DAMN! [*He is suddenly in possession of an imaginary spear and actively spearing enemies all over the room*] OCOMOGOSIAY . . . THE LION IS WAK-ING . . . OWIMOWEH! [*He pulls his shirt open and leaps up on a table and gestures with his spear. The bell rings.* RUTH *goes to answer*]

BENEATHA [*To encourage* WALTER, *thoroughly caught up with this side of him*] OCOMOGOSIAY, FLAMING SPEAR!

WALTER [*On the table, very far gone, his eyes pure glass sheets. He sees what we cannot, that he is a leader of his people, a great chief, a descendant of Chaka, and that the hour to march has come*] Listen, my black brothers—

BENEATHA OCOMOGOSIAY!

WALTER —Do you hear the waters rushing against the shores of the coastlands—

BENEATHA OCOMOGOSIAY!

WALTER —Do you hear the screeching of the cocks in yonder hills beyond where the chiefs meet in council for the coming of the mighty war—

BENEATHA OCOMOGOSIAY!

WALTER —Do you hear the beating of the wings of the birds flying low over the mountains and the low places of our land—

[RUTH *opens the door.* GEORGE MURCHISON *enters*]

BENEATHA OCOMOGOSIAY!

WALTER —Do you hear the singing of the women, singing the war songs of our fathers to the babies in the great houses . . . singing the sweet war songs? OH, DO YOU HEAR, MY BLACK BROTHERS!

BENEATHA [*Completely gone*] We hear you, Flaming Spear—

WALTER Telling us to prepare for the greatness of the time—[*To* GEORGE] Black Brother!

[*He extends his hand for the fraternal clasp*]

GEORGE Black Brother, hell!

RUTH [*Having had enough, and embarrassed for the family*] Beneatha, you got company—what's the matter with you? Walter Lee Younger, get down off that table and stop acting like a fool . . .

[WALTER *comes down off the table suddenly and makes a quick exit to the bathroom*]

RUTH He's had a little to drink . . . I don't know what her excuse is.

GEORGE [*To* BENEATHA] Look honey, we're going *to* the theatre—we're not going to be *in* it . . . so go change, huh?

RUTH You expect this boy to go out with you looking like that?

BENEATHA [*Looking at* GEORGE] That's up to George. If he's ashamed of his heritage—

GEORGE Oh, don't be so proud of yourself, Bennie—just because you look eccentric.

BENEATHA How can something that's natural be eccentric?

GEORGE That's what being eccentric means—being natural. Get dressed.

BENEATHA   I don't like that, George.

RUTH   Why must you and your brother make an argument out of everything people say?

BENEATHA   Because I hate assimilationist Negroes!

RUTH   Will somebody please tell me what assimila-who-ever means!

GEORGE   Oh, it's just a college girl's way of calling people Uncle Toms—but that isn't what it means at all.

RUTH   Well, what does it mean?

BENEATHA   [*Cutting* GEORGE *off and staring at him as she replies to* RUTH] It means someone who is willing to give up his own culture and submerge himself completely in the dominant, and in this case, *oppressive* culture!

GEORGE   Oh, dear, dear, dear! Here we go! A lecture on the African past! On our Great West African Heritage! In one second we will hear all about the great Ashanti empires; the great Songhay civilizations; and the great sculpture of Bénin—and then some poetry in the Bantu—and the whole monologue will end with the word *heritage!* [*Nastily*] Let's face it, baby, your heritage is nothing but a bunch of raggedy-assed spirituals and some grass huts!

BENEATHA   *Grass huts!* [RUTH *crosses to her and forcibly pushes her toward the* bedroom] See there . . . you are standing there in your splendid ignorance talking about people who were the first to smelt iron on the face of the earth! [RUTH *is pushing her through the door*] The Ashanti were performing surgical operations when the English—[RUTH *pulls the door to, with* BENEATHA *on the other side, and smiles graciously at* GEORGE. BENEATHA *opens the door and shouts the end of the sentence defiantly at* GEORGE] —were still tattooing themselves with blue dragons . . . [*She goes back inside*]

RUTH   Have a seat, George. [*They both sit.* RUTH *folds her hands rather primly on her lap, determined to demonstrate the civilization of the family*] Warm, ain't it? I mean for September. [*Pause*] Just like they always say about Chicago weather: If it's too hot or cold for you, just wait a minute and it'll change. [*She smiles happily at this cliché of clichés*] Everybody say it's got to do with them bombs and things they keep setting off. [*Pause*] Would you like a nice cold beer?

GEORGE   No, thank you. I don't care for beer. [*He looks at his watch*] I hope she hurries up.

RUTH   What time is the show?

GEORGE   It's an eight-thirty curtain. That's just Chicago, though. In New York standard curtain time is eight forty.
[*He is rather proud of this knowledge*]

RUTH   [*Properly appreciating it*] You get to New York a lot?

GEORGE   [*Offhand*] Few times a year.

RUTH   Oh—that's nice. I've never been to New York.
[WALTER *enters. We feel he has relieved himself, but the edge of unreality is still with him*]

WALTER   New York ain't got nothing Chicago ain't. Just a bunch of hustling people all squeezed up together—being "Eastern."
[*He turns his face into a screw of displeasure*]

GEORGE   Oh—you've been?

WALTER   *Plenty* of times.

RUTH   [*Shocked at the lie*] Walter Lee Younger!

WALTER   [*Staring her down*] Plenty! [*Pause*] What we got to drink in this house? Why don't you offer this man some refreshment. [*To* GEORGE] They don't know how to entertain people in this house, man.

GEORGE   Thank you—I don't really care for anything.

WALTER   [*Feeling his head; sobriety coming*]   Where's Mama?

RUTH   She ain't come back yet.

WALTER   [*Looking* MURCHISON *over from head to toe, scrutinizing his carefully casual tweed sports jacket over cashmere V-neck sweater over soft eyelet shirt and tie, and soft slacks, finished off with white buckskin shoes*]   Why all you college boys wear them fairyish-looking white shoes?

RUTH   Walter Lee!

[GEORGE MURCHISON *ignores the remark*]

WALTER   [*To* RUTH]   Well, they look crazy as hell—white shoes, cold as it is.

RUTH   [*Crushed*]   You have to excuse him—

WALTER   No he don't! Excuse me for what? What you always excusing me for! I'll excuse myself when I needs to be excused! [*A pause*] They look as funny as them black knee socks Beneatha wears out of here all the time.

RUTH   It's the college *style,* Walter.

WALTER   Style, hell. She looks like she got burnt legs or something!

RUTH   Oh, Walter—

WALTER   [*An irritable mimic*]   Oh, Walter! Oh, Walter! [*To* MURCHISON] How's your old man making out? I understand you all going to buy that big hotel on the Drive? [*He finds a beer in the refrigerator, wanders over to* MURCHISON, *sipping and wiping his lips with the back of his hand, and straddling a chair backwards to talk to the other man*] Shrewd move. Your old man is all right, man. [*Tapping his head and half winking for emphasis*] I mean he knows how to operate. I mean he thinks *big,* you know what I mean, I mean for a *home,* you know? But I think he's kind of running out of ideas now. I'd like to talk to him. Listen, man, I got some plans that could turn this city upside down. I mean I think like he does. *Big.* Invest big, gamble big, hell, lose *big* if you have to, you know what I mean. It's hard to find a man on this whole Southside who understands my kind of thinking—you dig? [*He scrutinizes* MURCHISON *again, drinks his beer, squints his eyes and leans in close, confidential, man to man*] Me and you ought to sit down and talk sometimes, man. Man, I got me some ideas . . .

MURCHISON   [*With boredom*]   Yeah—sometimes we'll have to do that, Walter.

WALTER   [*Understanding the indifference, and offended*]   Yeah—well, when you get the time, man. I know you a busy little boy.

RUTH   Walter, please—

WALTER   [*Bitterly, hurt*]   I know ain't nothing in this world as busy as you colored college boys with your fraternity pins and white shoes . . .

RUTH   [*Covering her face with humiliation*]   Oh, Walter Lee—

WALTER   I see you all all the time—with the books tucked under your arms—going to your [*British A—a mimic*] "clahsses." And for what! What the hell you learning over there? Filling up your heads—[*Counting off on his fingers*]—with the sociology and the psychology—but they teaching you how to be a man? How to take over and run the world? They teaching you how to run a rubber plantation or a steel mill? Naw—just to talk proper and read books and wear white shoes . . .

GEORGE   [*Looking at him with distaste, a little above it all*]   You're all wacked up with bitterness, man.

WALTER   [*Intently, almost quietly, between the teeth, glaring at the boy*]   And you—ain't you bitter, man? Ain't you just about had it yet? Don't you see no stars gleaming that you can't reach out and grab? You happy?—You contented son-of-a-bitch—you happy? You got it made? Bitter? Man,

I'm a volcano. Bitter? Here I am a giant—surrounded by ants! Ants who can't even understand what it is the giant is talking about.

RUTH [*Passionately and suddenly*] Oh, Walter—ain't you with nobody!

WALTER [*Violently*] No! 'Cause ain't nobody with me! Not even my own mother!

RUTH Walter, that's a terrible thing to say!

[BENEATHA *enters, dressed for the evening in a cocktail dress and earrings*]

GEORGE Well—hey, you look great.

BENATHA Let's go, George. See you all later.

RUTH Have a nice time.

GEORGE Thanks. Good night. [*To* WALTER, *sarcastically*] Good night, *Prometheus.*

[BENEATHA *and* GEORGE *exit*]

WALTER [*To* RUTH] Who is Prometheus?

RUTH I don't know. Don't worry about it.

WALTER [*In fury, pointing after* GEORGE] See there—they get to a point where they can't insult you man to man—they got to go talk about something ain't nobody never heard of!

RUTH How do you know it was an insult? [*To humor him*] Maybe Prometheus is a nice fellow.

WALTER Prometheus! I bet there ain't even no such thing! I bet that simple-minded clown—

RUTH Walter—

[*She stops what she is doing and looks at him*]

WALTER [*Yelling*] Don't start!

RUTH Start what?

WALTER Your nagging! Where was I? Who was I with? How much money did I spend?

RUTH [*Plaintively*] Walter Lee—why don't we just try to talk about it . . .

WALTER [*Not listening*] I been out talking with people who understand me. People who care about the things I got on my mind.

RUTH [*Wearily*] I guess that means people like Willy Harris.

WALTER Yes, people like Willy Harris.

RUTH [*With a sudden flash of impatience*] Why don't you all just hurry up and go into the banking business and stop talking about it!

WALTER Why? You want to know why? 'Cause we all tied up in a race of people that don't know how to do nothing but moan, pray and have babies!

[*The line is too bitter even for him and he looks at her and sits down*]

RUTH Oh, Walter . . . [*Softly*] Honey, why can't you stop fighting me?

WALTER [*Without thinking*] Who's fighting you? Who even cares about you?

[*This line begins the retardation of his mood*]

RUTH Well—[*She waits a long time, and then with resignation starts to put away her things*] I guess I might as well go on to bed . . . [*More or less to herself*] I don't know where we lost it . . . but we have . . . [*Then, to him*] I—I'm sorry about this new baby, Walter. I guess maybe I better go on and do what I started . . . I guess I just didn't realize how bad things was with us . . . I guess I just didn't really realize—[*She starts out to the bedroom and stops*] You want some hot milk?

WALTER Hot milk?

RUTH Yes—hot milk.

WALTER Why hot milk?

RUTH 'Cause after all that liquor you come home with you ought to have something hot in your stomach.

WALTER   I don't want no milk.

RUTH   You want some coffee then?

WALTER   No, I don't want no coffee. I don't want nothing hot to drink. [*Almost plaintively*] Why you always trying to give me something to eat?

RUTH   [*Standing and looking at him helplessly*] What else can I give you, Walter Lee Younger?

[*She stands and looks at him and presently turns to go out again. He lifts his head and watches her going away from him in a new mood which began to emerge when he asked her "Who cares about you?"*]

WALTER   It's been rough, ain't it, baby? [*She hears and stops but does not turn around and he continues to her back*] I guess between two people there ain't never as much understood as folks generally thinks there is. I mean like between me and you—[*She turns to face him*] How we gets to the place where we scared to talk softness to each other. [*He waits, thinking hard himself*] Why you think it got to be like that? [*He is thoughtful, almost as a child would be*] Ruth, what is it gets into people ought to be close?

RUTH   I don't know, honey. I think about it a lot.

WALTER   On account of you and me, you mean? The way things are with us. The way something done come down between us.

RUTH   There ain't so much between us, Walter . . . Not when you come to me and try to talk to me. Try to be with me . . . a little even.

WALTER   [*Total honesty*] Sometimes . . . sometimes . . . I don't even know how to try.

RUTH   Walter—

WALTER   Yes?

RUTH   [*Coming to him, gently and with misgiving, but coming to him*] Honey . . . life don't have to be like this. I mean sometimes people can do things so that things are better . . . You remember how we used to talk when Travis was born . . . about the way we were going to live . . . the kind of house . . . [*She is stroking his head*] Well, it's all starting to slip away from us . . .

[MAMA *enters, and* WALTER *jumps up and shouts at her*]

WALTER   Mama, where have you been?

MAMA   My—them steps is longer than they used to be. Whew! [*She sits down and ignores him*] How you feeling this evening, Ruth?

[RUTH *shrugs, disturbed some at having been prematurely interrupted and watching her husband knowingly*]

WALTER   Mama, where have you been all day?

MAMA   [*Still ignoring him and leaning on the table and changing to more comfortable shoes*] Where's Travis?

RUTH   I let him go out earlier and he ain't come back yet. Boy, is he going to get it!

WALTER   Mama!

MAMA   [*As if she has heard him for the first time*] Yes, son?

WALTER   Where did you go this afternoon?

MAMA   I went downtown to tend to some business that I had to tend to.

WALTER   What kind of business?

MAMA   You know better than to question me like a child, Brother.

WALTER   [*Rising and bending over the table*] Where were you, Mama? [*Bringing his fists down and shouting*] Mama, you didn't go do something with that insurance money, something crazy?

[*The front door opens slowly, interrupting him, and* TRAVIS *peeks his head in, less than hopefully*]

TRAVIS [*To his mother*] Mama, I—

RUTH "Mama I" nothing! You're going to get it, boy! Get on in that bedroom and get yourself ready!

TRAVIS But I—

MAMA Why don't you all never let the child explain hisself.

RUTH Keep out of it now, Lena.

[MAMA *clamps her lips together, and* RUTH *advances toward her son menacingly*]

RUTH A thousand times I have told you not to go off like that—

MAMA [*Holding out her arms to her grandson*] Well—at least let me tell him something. I want him to be the first one to hear . . . Come here, Travis. [*The boy obeys, gladly*] Travis—[*She takes him by the shoulder and looks into his face*]—you know that money we got in the mail this morning?

TRAVIS Yes'm—

MAMA Well—what you think your grandmama gone and done with that money?

TRAVIS I don't know, Grandmama.

MAMA [*Putting her finger on his nose for emphasis*] She went out and she bought you a house! [*The explosion comes from* WALTER *at the end of the revelation and he jumps up and turns away from all of them in a fury.* MAMA *continues, to* TRAVIS] You glad about the house? It's going to be yours when you get to be a man.

TRAVIS Yeah—I always wanted to live in a house.

MAMA All right, gimme some sugar then—[TRAVIS *puts his arms around her neck as she watches her son over the boy's shoulder. Then, to* TRAVIS, *after the embrace*] Now when you say your prayers tonight, you thank God and your grandfather—'cause it was him who give you the house—in his way.

RUTH [*Taking the boy from* MAMA *and pushing him toward the bedroom*] Now you get out of here and get ready for your beating.

TRAVIS Aw, Mama—

RUTH Get on in there—[*Closing the door behind him and turning radiantly to her mother-in-law*] So you went and did it!

MAMA [*Quietly, looking at her son with pain*] Yes, I did.

RUTH [*Raising both arms classically*] Praise God! [*Looks at* WALTER *a moment, who says nothing. She crosses rapidly to her husband*] Please, honey—let me be glad . . . you be glad too. [*She has laid her hands on his shoulders, but he shakes himself free of her roughly, without turning to face her*] Oh, Walter . . . a home . . . a home. [*She comes back to* MAMA] Well—where is it? How big is it? How much it going to cost?

MAMA Well—

RUTH When we moving?

MAMA [*Smiling at her*] First of the month.

RUTH [*Throwing back her head with jubilance*] Praise God!

MAMA [*Tentatively, still looking at her son's back turned against her and* RUTH] It's—it's a nice house too . . . [*She cannot help speaking directly to him. An imploring quality in her voice, her manner, makes her almost like a girl now*] Three bedrooms—nice big one for you and Ruth. . . . Me and Beneatha still have to share our room, but Travis have one of his own— and [*With difficulty*] I figure if the—new baby—is a boy, we could get one of them double-decker outfits . . . And there's a yard with a little patch of dirt where I could maybe get to grow me a few flowers . . . And a nice big basement . . .

RUTH Walter honey, be glad—

MAMA [*Still to his back, fingering things on the table*] 'Course I don't want to make it sound fancier than it is . . . It's just a plain little old house—but it's made good and solid—and it will be *ours*. Walter Lee—it makes a difference in a man when he can walk on floors that belong to *him* . . .

RUTH Where is it?

MAMA [*Frightened at this telling*] Well—well—it's out there in Clybourne Park—

[RUTH's *radiance fades abruptly, and* WALTER *finally turns slowly to face his mother with incredulity and hostility*]

RUTH Where?

MAMA [*Matter-of-factly*] Four o six Clybourne Street, Clybourne Park.

RUTH Clybourne Park? Mama, there ain't no colored people living in Clybourne Park.

MAMA [*Almost idiotically*] Well, I guess there's going to be some now.

WALTER [*Bitterly*] So that's the peace and comfort you went out and bought for us today!

MAMA [*Raising her eyes to meet his finally*] Son—I just tried to find the nicest place for the least amount of money for my family.

RUTH [*Trying to recover from the shock*] Well—well—'course I ain't one never been 'fraid of no crackers, mind you—but—well, wasn't there no other houses nowhere?

MAMA Them houses they put up for colored in them areas way out all seem to cost twice as much as other houses. I did the best I could.

RUTH [*Struck senseless with the news, in its various degrees of goodness and trouble, she sits a moment, her fists propping her chin in thought, and then she starts to rise, bringing her fists down with vigor, the radiance spreading from cheek to cheek again*] Well—well!—All I can say is—if this is my time in life—*my time*—to say good-bye—*[And she builds with momentum as she starts to circle the room with an exuberant, almost tearfully happy release]*—to these Goddamned cracking walls!—[*She pounds the walls*]—and these marching roaches!—[*She wipes at an imaginary army of marching roaches*]—and this cramped little closet which ain't now or never was no kitchen! . . . then I say it loud and good, *Hallelujah! and good-bye misery . . . I don't never want to see your ugly face again!* [*She laughs joyously, having practically destroyed the apartment, and flings her arms up and lets them come down happily, slowly, reflectively, over her abdomen, aware for the first time perhaps that the life therein pulses with happiness and not despair*] Lena?

MAMA [*Moved, watching her happiness*] Yes, honey?

RUTH [*Looking off*] Is there—is there a whole lot of sunlight?

MAMA [*Understanding*] Yes, child, there's a whole lot of sunlight.

[*Long pause*]

RUTH [*Collecting herself and going to the door of the room* TRAVIS *is in*] Well —I guess I better see 'bout Travis. [*To* MAMA] Lord, I sure don't feel like whipping nobody today!

[*She exits*]

MAMA [*The mother and son are left alone now and the mother waits a long time, considering deeply, before she speaks*] Son—you—you understand what I done, don't you? [WALTER *is silent and sullen*] I—I just seen my family falling apart today . . . just falling to pieces in front of my eyes . . . We couldn't of gone on like we was today. We was going backwards 'stead of forwards—talking 'bout killing babies and wishing each other was dead . . . When it gets like that in life—you just got to do something different, push on out and do something bigger . . . [*She waits*] I wish you say something, son . . . I wish you'd say how deep inside you you think I done the right thing—

WALTER [*Crossing slowly to his bedroom door and finally turning there and speaking measuredly*] What you need me to say you done right for? *You* the head of this family. You run our lives like you want to. It was your money and you did what you wanted with it. So what you need for me to say it was all right for? [*Bitterly, to hurt her as deeply as he knows is possible*] So you butchered up a dream of mine—you—who always talking 'bout your children's dreams . . .

MAMA Walter Lee—

[*He just closes the door behind him.* MAMA *sits alone, thinking heavily*]

CURTAIN

Scene Two

> Time: Friday night. A few weeks later.
> At rise: Packing crates mark the intention of the family to move. BENEATHA *and* GEORGE *come in, presumably from an evening out again.*

GEORGE O.K. . . . O.K., whatever you say . . . [*They both sit on the couch. He tries to kiss her. She moves away*] Look, we've had a nice evening; let's not spoil it, huh? . . .

[*He again turns her head and tries to nuzzle in and she turns away from him, not with distaste but with momentary lack of interest; in a mood to pursue what they were talking about*]

BENEATHA I'm *trying* to talk to you.

GEORGE We always talk.

BENEATHA Yes—and I love to talk.

GEORGE [*Exasperated; rising*] I know it and I don't mind it sometimes . . . I want you to cut it out, see—The moody stuff, I mean. I don't like it. You're a nice-looking girl . . . all over. That's all you need, honey, forget the atmosphere. Guys aren't going to go for the atmosphere—they're going to go for what they see. Be glad for that. Drop the Garbo routine. It doesn't go with you. As for myself, I want a nice—[*Groping*]—simple [*Thoughtfully*]—sophisticated girl . . . not a poet—O.K.?

[*She rebuffs him again and he starts to leave*]

BENEATHA Why are you angry?

GEORGE Because this is stupid! I don't go out with you to discuss the nature of "quiet desperation" or to hear all about your thoughts—because the world will go on thinking what it thinks regardless—

BENEATHA Then why read books? Why go to school?

GEORGE [*With artificial patience, counting on his fingers*] It's simple. You read books—to learn facts—to get grades—to pass the course—to get a degree. That's all—it has nothing to do with thoughts.

[*A long pause*]

BENEATHA I see. [*A longer pause as she looks at him*] Good night, George.

[GEORGE *looks at her a little oddly, and starts to exit. He meets* MAMA *coming in*]

GEORGE Oh—hello, Mrs. Younger.

MAMA Hello, George, how you feeling?

GEORGE Fine—fine, how are you?

MAMA Oh, a little tired. You know them steps can get you after a day's work. You all have a nice time tonight?

GEORGE   Yes—a fine time. Well, good night.

MAMA   Good night. [*He exits.* MAMA *closes the door behind her*] Hello, honey. What you sitting like that for?

BENEATHA   I'm just sitting.

MAMA   Didn't you have a nice time?

BENEATHA   No.

MAMA   No? What's the matter?

BENEATHA   Mama, George is a fool—honest. [*She rises*]

MAMA   [*Hustling around unloading the packages she has entered with. She stops*]   Is he, baby?

BENEATHA   Yes.

[BENEATHA *makes up* TRAVIS' *bed as she talks*]

MAMA   You sure?

BENEATHA   Yes.

MAMA   Well—I guess you better not waste your time with no fools.

[BENEATHA *looks up at her mother, watching her put groceries in the refrigerator. Finally she gathers up her things and starts into the bedroom. At the door she stops and looks back at her mother*]

BENEATHA   Mama—

MAMA   Yes, baby—

BENEATHA   Thank you.

MAMA   For what?

BENEATHA   For understanding me this time.

[*She exits quickly and the mother stands, smiling a little, looking at the place where* BENEATHA *just stood.* RUTH *enters*]

RUTH   Now don't you fool with any of this stuff, Lena—

MAMA   Oh, I just thought I'd sort a few things out.

[*The phone rings.* RUTH *answers*]

RUTH   [*At the phone*]   Hello—Just a minute. [*Goes to door*] Walter, it's Mrs. Arnold. [*Waits. Goes back to the phone. Tense*] Hello. Yes, this is his wife speaking . . . He's lying down now. Yes . . . well, he'll be in tomorrow. He's been very sick. Yes—I know we should have called, but we were so sure he'd be able to come in today. Yes—yes, I'm very sorry. Yes . . . Thank you very much. [*She hangs up.* WALTER *is standing in the doorway of the bedroom behind her*] That was Mrs. Arnold.

WALTER   [*Indifferently*]   Was it?

RUTH   She said if you don't come in tomorrow that they are getting a new man . . .

WALTER   Ain't that sad—ain't that crying sad.

RUTH   She said Mr. Arnold has had to take a cab for three days . . . Walter, you ain't been to work for three days! [*This is a revelation to her*] Where you been, Walter Lee Younger? [WALTER *looks at her and starts to laugh*] You're going to lose your job.

WALTER   That's right . . .

RUTH   Oh, Walter, and with your mother working like a dog every day—

WALTER   That's sad too—Everything is sad.

MAMA   What you been doing for these three days, son?

WALTER   Mama—you don't know all the things a man what got leisure can find to do in this city . . . What's this—Friday night? Well—Wednesday I borrowed Willy Harris' car and I went for a drive . . . just me and myself and I drove and drove . . . Way out . . . way past South Chicago, and I parked the car and I sat and looked at the steel mills all day long. I just sat in the car and looked at them big black chimneys for hours. Then I drove back and I went to the Green Hat. [*Pause*] And Thursday—Thursday I borrowed the car again and I got in it and I pointed it the other way and I drove the other way—for hours—way, way up to Wisconsin, and I looked at the farms. I just drove and looked at the farms. Then I drove back and I went to the Green Hat. [*Pause*] And today—today I didn't get the car. Today I just walked. All over the Southside. And I looked at the Negroes and they looked at me and finally I just sat down on the curb at Thirty-ninth and South Parkway and I just sat there and watched the Negroes go by. And then I went to the Green Hat. You all sad? You all depressed? And you know where I am going right now—

[RUTH *goes out quietly*]

MAMA   Oh, Big Walter, is this the harvest of our days?

WALTER   You know what I like about the Green Hat? [*He turns the radio on and a steamy, deep blues pours into the room*] I like this little cat they got there who blows a sax . . . He blows. He talks to me. He ain't but 'bout five feet tall and he's got a conked head and his eyes is always closed and he's all music—

MAMA   [*Rising and getting some papers out of her handbag*]   Walter—

WALTER   And there's this other guy who plays the piano . . . and they got a sound. I mean they can work on some music . . . They got the best little combo in the world in the Green Hat . . . You can just sit there and drink and listen to them three men play and you realize that don't nothing matter worth a damn, but just being there—

MAMA   I've helped do it to you, haven't I, son? Walter, I been wrong.

WALTER   Naw—you ain't never been wrong about nothing, Mama.

MAMA   Listen to me, now. I say I been wrong, son. That I been doing to you what the rest of the world been doing to you. [*She stops and he looks up slowly at her and she meets his eyes pleadingly*] Walter—what you ain't never understood is that I ain't got nothing, don't own nothing, ain't never really wanted nothing that wasn't for you. There ain't nothing as precious to me . . . There ain't nothing worth holding on to, money, dreams, nothing else—if it means—if it means it's going to destroy my boy. [*She puts her papers in front of him and he watches her without speaking or moving*] I paid the man thirty-five hundred dollars down on the house. That leaves sixty-five hundred dollars. Monday morning I want you to take this money and take three thousand dollars and put it in a savings account for Beneatha's medical schooling. The rest you put in a checking account —with your name on it. And from now on any penny that come out of it or that go in it is for you to look after. For you to decide. [*She drops her hands a little helplessly*] It ain't much, but it's all I got in the world and I'm putting it in your hands. I'm telling you to be the head of this family from now on like you supposed to be.

WALTER   [*Stares at the money*]   You trust me like that, Mama?

MAMA   I ain't never stop trusting you. Like I ain't never stop loving you.

[*She goes out, and* WALTER *sits looking at the money on the table as the music continues in its idiom, pulsing in the room. Finally, in a decisive gesture, he gets up, and, in mingled joy and desperation, picks up the money. At the same moment,* TRAVIS *enters for bed*]

TRAVIS   What's the matter, Daddy? You drunk?

WALTER   [*Sweetly, more sweetly than we have ever known him*]   No, Daddy ain't drunk. Daddy ain't going to never be drunk again. . . .

TRAVIS   Well, Good night, Daddy.

[*The* FATHER *has come from behind the couch and leans over, embracing his son*]

WALTER   Son, I feel like talking to you tonight.

TRAVIS   About what?

WALTER   Oh, about a lot of things. About you and what kind of man you going to be when you grow up. . . . Son—son, what do you want to be when you grow up?

TRAVIS   A bus driver.

WALTER   [*Laughing a little*]   A what? Man, that ain't nothing to want to be!

TRAVIS   Why not?

WALTER   'Cause, man—it ain't big enough—you know what I mean.

TRAVIS   I don't know then. I can't make up my mind. Sometimes Mama asks me that too. And sometimes when I tell you I just want to be like you— she says she don't want me to be like that and sometimes she says she does. . . .

WALTER   [*Gathering him up in his arms*]   You know what, Travis? In seven years you going to be seventeen years old. And things is going to be very different with us in seven years, Travis. . . . One day when you are seventeen I'll come home—home from my office downtown somewhere—

TRAVIS   You don't work in no office, Daddy.

WALTER   No—but after tonight. After what your daddy gonna do tonight, there's going to be offices—a whole lot of offices. . . .

TRAVIS   What you gonna do tonight, Daddy?

WALTER   You wouldn't understand yet, son, but your daddy's gonna make a transaction . . . a business transaction that's going to change our lives. . . . That's how come one day when you 'bout seventeen years old I'll come home and I'll be pretty tired, you know what I mean, after a day of conferences and secretaries getting things wrong the way they do . . . 'cause an executive's life is hell, man—[*The more he talks the farther away he gets*] And I'll pull the car up on the driveway . . . just a plain black Chrysler, I think, with white walls—no—black tires. More elegant. Rich people don't have to be flashy . . . though I'll have to get something a little sportier for Ruth—maybe a Cadillac convertible to do her shopping in. . . . And I'll come up the steps to the house and the gardener will be clipping away at the hedges and he'll say, "Good evening, Mr. Younger." And I'll say, "Hello, Jefferson, how are you this evening?" And I'll go inside and Ruth will come downstairs and meet me at the door and we'll kiss each other and she'll take my arm and we'll go up to your room to see you sitting on the floor with the catalogues of all the great schools in America around you. . . . All the great schools in the world! And—and I'll say, all right son—it's your seventeenth birthday, what is it you've decided? . . . Just tell me where you want to go to school and you'll *go*. Just tell me, what it is you want to be—and you'll *be* it. . . . Whatever you want to be—Yessir! [*He holds his arms open for* TRAVIS] You just name it, son . . . [TRAVIS *leaps into them*] and I hand you the world!

[WALTER's *voice has risen in pitch and hysterical promise and on the last line he lifts* TRAVIS *high*]

[*Blackout*]

Scene Three

> *Time: Saturday, moving day, one week later.*
> *Before the curtain rises,* RUTH's *voice, a strident, dramatic church alto, cuts through the silence.*
> *It is, in the darkness, a triumphant surge, a penetrating statement*

of expectation: "Oh, Lord, I don't feel no ways tired! Children, oh, glory hallelujah!"

As the curtain rises we see that RUTH *is alone in the living room, finishing up the family's packing. It is moving day. She is nailing crates and tying cartons.* BENEATHA *enters, carrying a guitar case, and watches her exuberant sister-in-law.*

RUTH Hey!

BENEATHA [*Putting away the case*] Hi.

RUTH [*Pointing at a package*] Honey—look in that package there and see what I found on sale this morning at the South Center. [RUTH *gets up and moves to the package and draws out some curtains*] Lookahere—hand-turned hems!

BENEATHA How do you know the window size out there?

RUTH [*Who hadn't thought of that*] Oh—Well, they bound to fit something in the whole house. Anyhow, they was too good a bargain to pass up. [RUTH *slaps her head, suddenly remembering something*] Oh, Bennie—I meant to put a special note on that carton over there. That's your mama's good china and she wants 'em to be very careful with it.

BENEATHA I'll do it.

[BENEATHA *finds a piece of paper and starts to draw large letters on it*]

RUTH You know what I'm going to do soon as I get in that new house?

BENEATHA What?

RUTH Honey—I'm going to run me a tub of water up to here . . . [*With her fingers practically up to her nostrils*] And I'm going to get in it—and I am going to sit . . . and sit . . . and sit in that hot water and the first person who knocks to tell *me* to hurry up and come out—

BENEATHA Gets shot at sunrise.

RUTH [*Laughing happily*] You said it, sister! [*Noticing how large* BENEATHA *is absent-mindedly making the note*] Honey, they ain't going to read that from no airplane.

BENEATHA [*Laughing herself*] I guess I always think things have more emphasis if they are big, somehow.

RUTH [*Looking up at her and smiling*] You and your brother seem to have that as a philosophy of life. Lord, that man—done changed so 'round here. You know—you know what we did last night? Me and Walter Lee?

BENEATHA What?

RUTH [*Smiling to herself*] We went to the movies. [*Looking at* BENEATHA *to see if she understands*] We went to the movies. You know the last time me and Walter went to the movies together?

BENEATHA No.

RUTH Me neither. That's how long it been. [*Smiling again*] But we went last night. The picture wasn't much good, but that didn't seem to matter. We went—and we held hands.

BENEATHA Oh, Lord!

RUTH We held hands—and you know what?

BENEATHA What?

RUTH When we come out of the show it was late and dark and all the stores and things was closed up . . . and it was kind of chilly and there wasn't many people on the streets . . . and we was still holding hands, me and Walter.

BENEATHA You're killing me.

[WALTER *enters with a large package. His happiness is deep in him; he cannot keep still with his new-found exuberance. He is singing and wiggling and snapping his fingers. He puts his package in a corner and puts a phonograph record, which he has brought in with him, on the record player. As the music comes up he dances over to* RUTH *and tries to get her to dance with him. She gives in at last to his raunchiness and in a fit of giggling allows herself to be drawn into his mood and together they deliberately burlesque an old social dance of their youth]*

BENEATHA   *[Regarding them a long time as they dance, then drawing in her breath for a deeply exaggerated comment which she does not particularly mean]*   Talk about—olddddddddddd-fashioneddddddddd—Negroes!

WALTER   *[Stopping momentarily]*   What kind of Negroes?
[He says this in fun. He is not angry with her today, nor with anyone. He starts to dance with his wife again]

BENEATHA   Old-fashioned.

WALTER   *[As he dances with* RUTH*]*   You know, when these *New Negroes* have their convention—*[Pointing at his sister]*—that is going to be the chairman of the Committee on Unending Agitation. *[He goes on dancing, then stops]* Race, race, race! . . . Girl, I do believe you are the first person in the history of the entire human race to successfully brainwash yourself. *[BE-NEATHA breaks up and he goes on dancing. He stops again, enjoying his tease]* Damn, even the N double A C P takes a holiday sometimes! *[BE-NEATHA and* RUTH *laugh. He dances with* RUTH *some more and starts to laugh and stops and pantomimes someone over an operating table]* I can just see that chick someday looking down at some poor cat on an operating table before she starts to slice him, saying . . . *[Pulling his sleeves back maliciously]* "By the way, what are your views on civil rights down there? . . ."
[He laughs at her again and starts to dance happily. The bell sounds]

BENEATHA   Sticks and stones may break my bones but . . . words will never hurt me!
[BENEATHA goes to the door and opens it as WALTER *and* RUTH *go on with the clowning.* BENEATHA *is somewhat surprised to see a quiet-looking middle-aged white man in a business suit holding his hat and a briefcase in his hand and consulting a small piece of paper]*

MAN   Uh—how do you do, miss. I am looking for a Mrs.—*[He looks at the slip of paper]* Mrs. Lena Younger?

BENEATHA   *[Smoothing her hair with slight embarrassment]*   Oh—yes, that's my mother. Excuse me *[She closes the door and turns to quiet the other two]* Ruth! Brother! Somebody's here. *[Then she opens the door. The man casts a curious quick glance at all of them]* Uh—come in please.

MAN   *[Coming in]*   Thank you.

BENEATHA   My mother isn't here just now. Is it business?

MAN   Yes . . . well, of a sort.

WALTER   *[Freely, the Man of the House]*   Have a seat. I'm Mrs. Younger's son. I look after most of her business matters.
[RUTH and BENEATHA exchange amused glances]

MAN   *[Regarding* WALTER*, and sitting]*   Well—My name is Karl Lindner . . .

WALTER   *[Stretching out his hand]*   Walter Younger. This is my wife—*[RUTH nods politely]*—and my sister.

LINDNER   How do you do.

WALTER   *[Amiably, as he sits himself easily on a chair, leaning with interest forward on his knees and looking expectantly into the newcomer's face]* What can we do for you, Mr. Lindner!

LINDNER   *[Some minor shuffling of the hat and briefcase on his knees]*   Well—I am a representative of the Clybourne Park Improvement Association—

WALTER [*Pointing*] Why don't you sit your things on the floor?

LINDNER Oh—yes. Thank you. [*He slides the briefcase and hat under the chair*] And as I was saying—I am from the Clybourne Park Improvement Association and we have had it brought to our attention at the last meeting that you people—or at least your mother—has bought a piece of residential property at—[*He digs for the slip of paper again*]—four o six Clybourne Street. . . .

WALTER That's right. Care for something to drink? Ruth, get Mr. Lindner a beer.

LINDNER [*Upset for some reason*] Oh—no, really. I mean thank you very much, but no thank you.

RUTH [*Innocently*] Some coffee?

LINDNER Thank you, nothing at all.

[BENEATHA *is watching the man carefully*]

LINDNER Well, I don't know how much you folks know about our organization. [*He is a gentle man; thoughtful and somewhat labored in his manner*] It is one of these community organizations set up to look after—oh, you know, things like block upkeep and special projects and we also have what we call our New Neighbors Orientation Committee . . .

BENEATHA [*Drily*] Yes—and what do they do?

LINDNER [*Turning a little to her and then returning the main force to* WALTER] Well—it's what you might call a sort of welcoming committee, I guess. I mean they, we, I'm the chairman of the committee—go around and see the new people who move into the neighborhood and sort of give them the lowdown on the way we do things out in Clybourne Park.

BENEATHA [*With appreciation of the two meanings, which escape* RUTH *and* WALTER] Un-huh.

LINDNER And we also have the category of what the association calls—[*He looks elsewhere*]—uh—special community problems . . .

BENEATHA Yes—and what are some of those?

WALTER Girl, let the man talk.

LINDNER [*With understated relief*] Thank you. I would sort of like to explain this thing in my own way. I mean I want to explain to you in a certain way.

WALTER Go ahead.

LINDNER Yes. Well. I'm going to try to get right to the point. I'm sure we'll all appreciate that in the long run.

BENEATHA Yes.

WALTER Be still now!

LINDNER Well—

RUTH [*Still innocently*] Would you like another chair—you don't look comfortable.

LINDNER [*More frustrated than annoyed*] No, thank you very much. Please. Well—to get right to the point I—[*A great breath, and he is off at last*] I am sure you people must be aware of some of the incidents which have happened in various parts of the city when colored people have moved into certain areas—[BENEATHA *exhales heavily and starts tossing a piece of fruit up and down in the air*] Well—because we have what I think is going to be a unique type of organization in American community life—not only do we deplore that kind of thing—but we are trying to do something about it. [BENEATHA *stops tossing and turns with a new and quizzical interest to the man*] We feel—[*gaining confidence in his mission because of the interest in the faces of the people he is talking to*]—we feel that most of the trouble in this world, when you come right down to it—[*He hits his knee for emphasis*]—most of the trouble exists because people just don't sit down and talk to each other.

RUTH [*Nodding as she might in church, pleased with the remark*] You can say that again, mister.

LINDNER [*More encouraged by such affirmation*] That we don't try hard enough in this world to understand the other fellow's problem. The other guy's point of view.

RUTH Now that's right.

[BENEATHA *and* WALTER *merely watch and listen with genuine interest*]

LINDNER Yes—that's the way we feel out in Clybourne Park. And that's why I was elected to come here this afternoon and talk to you people. Friendly like, you know, the way people should talk to each other and see if we couldn't find some way to work this thing out. As I say, the whole business is a matter of *caring* about the other fellow. Anybody can see that you are a nice family of folks, hard working and honest I'm sure. [BENEATHA *frowns slightly, quizzically, her head tilted regarding him*] Today everybody knows what is means to be on the outside of *something*. And of course, there is always somebody who is out to take the advantage of people who don't always understand.

WALTER What do you mean?

LINDNER Well—you see our community is made up of people who've worked hard as the dickens for years to build up that little community. They're not rich and fancy people; just hard-working, honest people who don't really have much but those little homes and a dream of the kind of community they want to raise their children in. Now, I don't say we are perfect and there is a lot wrong in some of the things they want. But you've got to admit that a man, right or wrong, has the right to want to have the neighborhood he lives in a certain kind of way. And at the moment the overwhelming majority of our people out there feel that people get along better, take more of a common interest in the life of the community, when they share a common background. I want you to believe me when I tell you that race prejudice simply doesn't enter into it. It is a matter of the people of Clybourne Park believing, rightly or wrongly, as I say, that for the happiness of all concerned that our Negro families are happier when they live in their *own* communities.

BENEATHA [*With a grand and bitter gesture*] This, friends, is the Welcoming Committee!

WALTER [*Dumfounded, looking at* LINDNER] Is this what you came marching all the way over here to tell us?

LINDNER Well, now we've been having a fine conversation. I hope you'll hear me all the way through.

WALTER [*Tightly*] Go ahead, man.

LINDNER You see—in the face of all things I have said, we are prepared to make your family a very generous offer . . .

BENEATHA Thirty pieces and not a coin less!

WALTER Yeah?

LINDNER [*Putting on his glasses and drawing a form out of the briefcase*] Our association is prepared, through the collective effort of our people, to buy the house from you at a financial gain to your family.

RUTH Lord have mercy, ain't this the living gall!

WALTER All right, you through?

LINDNER Well, I want to give you the exact terms of the financial arrangement—

WALTER   We don't want to hear no exact terms of no arrangements. I want to know if you got any more to tell us 'bout getting together?

LINDNER   [*Taking off his glasses*]   Well—I don't suppose that you feel . . .

WALTER   Never mind how I feel—you got any more to say 'bout how people ought to sit down and talk to each other? . . . Get out of my house, man. [*He turns his back and walks to the door*]

LINDNER   [*Looking around at the hostile faces and reaching and assembling his hat and briefcase*]   Well—I don't understand why you people are reacting this way. What do you think you are going to gain by moving into a neighborhood where you just aren't wanted and where some elements—well—people can get awful worked up when they feel that their whole way of life and everything they've ever worked for is threatened.

WALTER   Get out.

LINDNER   [*At the door, holding a small card*]   Well—I'm sorry it went like this.

WALTER   Get out.

LINDNER   [*Almost sadly regarding* WALTER]   You just can't force people to change their hearts, son.
[*He turns and put his card on a table and exits.* WALTER *pushes the door to with stinging hatred, and stands looking at it.* RUTH *just sits and* BENEATHA *just stands. They say nothing.* MAMA *and* TRAVIS *enter*]

MAMA   Well—this all the packing got done since I left out of here this morning. I testify before God that my children got all the energy of the dead. What time the moving men due?

BENEATHA   Four o'clock. You had a caller, Mama.
[*She is smiling, teasingly*]

MAMA   Sure enough—who?

BENEATHA   [*Her arms folded saucily*]   The Welcoming Committee.
[WALTER *and* RUTH *giggle*]

MAMA   [*Innocently*]   Who?

BENEATHA   The Welcoming Committee. They said they're sure going to be glad to see you when you get there.

WALTER   [*Devilishly*]   Yeah, they said they can't hardly wait to see your face.
[*Laughter*]

MAMA   [*Sensing their facetiousness*]   What's the matter with you all?

WALTER   Ain't nothing the matter with us. We just telling you 'bout the gentleman who came to see you this afternoon. From the Clybourne Park Improvement Association.

MAMA   What he want?

RUTH   [*In the same mood as* BENEATHA *and* WALTER]   To welcome you, honey.

WALTER   He said they can't hardly wait. He said the one thing they don't have, that they just *dying* to have out there is a fine family of colored people!
[*To* RUTH *and* BENEATHA] Ain't that right!

RUTH *and* BENEATHA   [*Mockingly*]   Yeah! He left his card in case—
[*They indicate the card, and* MAMA *picks it up and throws it on the floor—understanding and looking off as she draws her chair up to the table on which she has put her plant and some sticks and some cord*]

MAMA   Father, give us strength. [*Knowingly—and without fun*] Did he threaten us?

BENEATHA   Oh—Mama—they don't do it like that any more. He talked Brotherhood. He said everybody ought to learn how to sit down and hate each other with good Christian fellowship.
[*She and* WALTER *shake hands to ridicule the remark*]

MAMA   [*Sadly*]   Lord, protect us . . .

RUTH   You should hear the money those folks raised to buy the house from us. All we paid and then some.

BENEATHA   What they think we going to do—eat 'em?

RUTH   No, honey, marry 'em.

MAMA   [*Shaking her head*]   Lord, Lord, Lord . . .

RUTH   Well—that's the way the crackers crumble. Joke.

BENEATHA   [*Laughingly noticing what her mother is doing*]   Mama, what are you doing?

MAMA   Fixing my plant so it won't get hurt none on the way . . .

BENEATHA   Mama, you going to take *that* to the new house?

MAMA   Un-huh—

BENEATHA   That raggedy-looking old thing?

MAMA   [*Stopping and looking at her*]   It expresses *me*.

RUTH   [*With delight, to* BENEATHA]   So there, Miss Thing!

[WALTER *comes to* MAMA *suddenly and bends down behind her and squeezes her in his arms with all his strength. She is overwhelmed by the suddenness of it and, though delighted, her manner is like that of* RUTH *with* TRAVIS]

MAMA   Look out now, boy! You make me mess up my thing here!

WALTER   [*His face lit, he slips down on his knees beside her, his arms still about her*]   Mama . . . you know what it means to climb up in the chariot?

MAMA   [*Gruffly, very happy*]   Get on away from me now . . .

RUTH   [*Near the gift-wrapped package, trying to catch* WALTER's *eye*]   Psst—

WALTER   What the old song say, Mama . . .

RUTH   Walter—Now?

[*She is pointing at the package*]

WALTER   [*Speaking the lines, sweetly, playfully, in his mother's face*]

> *I got wings . . . you got wings . . .*
> *All God's Children got wings . . .*

MAMA   Boy—get out of my face and do some work . . .

WALTER

> *When I get to heaven gonna put on my wings,*
> *Gonna fly all over God's heaven . . .*

BENEATHA   [*Teasingly, from across the room*]   Everybody talking 'bout heaven ain't going there!

WALTER   [*To* RUTH, *who is carrying the box across to them*]   I don't know, you think we ought to give her that . . . Seems to me she ain't been very appreciative around here.

MAMA   [*Eying the box, which is obviously a gift*]   What is that?

WALTER   [*Taking it from* RUTH *and putting it on the table in front of* MAMA]   Well—what you all think? Should we give it to her?

RUTH   Oh—she was pretty good today.

MAMA   I'll good you—

[*She turns her eyes to the box again*]

BENEATHA   Open it, Mama.

[*She stands up, looks at it, turns and looks at all of them, and then presses her hands together and does not open the package*]

WALTER   [*Sweetly*]   Open it, Mama. It's for you. [MAMA *looks in his eyes. It is the first present in her life without its being Christmas. Slowly she opens her package and lifts out, one by one, a brand-new sparkling set of gardening tools.* WALTER *continues, prodding*]   Ruth made up the note—read it . . .

MAMA   [*Picking up the card and adjusting her glasses*]   "To our own Mrs. Miniver—Love from Brother, Ruth and Beneatha." Ain't that lovely . . .

TRAVIS   [*Tugging at his father's sleeve*]   Daddy, can I give her mine now?

WALTER   All right, son. [TRAVIS *flies to get his gift*] Travis didn't want to go in with the rest of us, Mama. He got his own. [*Somewhat amused*] We don't know what it is . . .

TRAVIS   [*Racing back in the room with a large hatbox and putting it in front of his grandmother*]   Here!

MAMA   Lord have mercy, baby. You done gone and bought your grandmother a hat?

TRAVIS   [*Very proud*]   Open it!

[*She does and lifts out an elaborate, but very elaborate, wide gardening hat, and all the adults break up at the sight of it*]

RUTH   Travis, honey, what is that?

TRAVIS   [*Who thinks it is beautiful and appropriate*]   It's a gardening hat! Like the ladies always have on in the magazines when they work in their gardens.

BENEATHA   [*Giggling fiercely*]   Travis—we were trying to make Mama Mrs. Miniver—not Scarlett O'Hara!

MAMA   [*Indignantly*]   What's the matter with you all! This here is a beautiful hat! [*Absurdly*] I always wanted me one just like it!

[*She pops it on her head to prove it to her grandson, and the hat is ludicrous and considerably oversized*]

RUTH   Hot dog! Go, Mama!

WALTER   [*Doubled over with laughter*]   I'm sorry, Mama—but you look like you ready to go out and chop you some cotton sure enough!

[*They all laugh except* MAMA, *out of deference to* TRAVIS' *feelings*]

MAMA   [*Gathering the boy up to her*]   Bless your heart—this is the prettiest hat I ever owned—[WALTER, RUTH *and* BENEATHA *chime in—noisily, festively and insincerely congratulating* TRAVIS *on his gift*] What are we all standing around here for? We ain't finished packin' yet. Bennie, you ain't packed one book.

[*The bell rings*]

BENEATHA   That couldn't be the movers . . . it's not hardly two good yet—

[BENEATHA *goes into her room.* MAMA *starts for door*]

WALTER   [*Turning, stiffening*]   Wait—wait—I'll get it.

[*He stands and looks at the door*]

MAMA   You expecting company, son?

WALTER   [*Just looking at the door*]   Yeah—yeah . . .

[MAMA *looks at* RUTH, *and they exchange innocent and unfrightened glances*]

MAMA   [*Not understanding*]   Well, let them in, son.

BENEATHA   [*From her room*]   We need some more string.

MAMA   Travis—you run to the hardware and get me some string cord.

[MAMA *goes out and* WALTER *turns and looks at* RUTH. TRAVIS *goes to a dish for money*]

RUTH   Why don't you answer the door, man?

WALTER   [*Suddenly bounding across the floor to her*]   'Cause sometimes it hard to let the future begin! [*Stooping down in her face*]

> I got wings! You got wings!
> All Gods children got wings!

[*He crosses to the door and throws it open. Standing there is a very slight little man in a not too prosperous business suit and with haunted frightened*

eyes and a hat pulled down tightly, brim up, around his forehead. TRAVIS
passes between the men and exits. WALTER *leans deep in the man's face,
still in his jubilance*]

> When I get to heaven gonna put on my wings,
> Gonna fly all over God's heaven . . .

[*The little man just stares at him*]

> Heaven—

[*Suddenly he stops and looks past the little man into the empty hallway*]
Where's Willy, man?

BOBO   He ain't with me.

WALTER   [*Not disturbed*]   Oh—come on in. You know my wife.

BOBO   [*Dumbly, taking off his hat*]   Yes—h'you, Miss Ruth.

RUTH   [*Quietly, a mood apart from her husband already, seeing* BOBO]   Hello,
Bobo.

WALTER   You right on time today . . . Right on time. That's the way! [*He
slaps* BOBO *on his back*] Sit down . . . lemme hear.
[RUTH *stands stiffly and quietly in back of them, as though somehow she
senses death, her eyes fixed on her husband*]

BOBO   [*His frightened eyes on the floor, his hat in his hands*]   Could I please
get a drink of water, before I tell you about it, Walter Lee?
[WALTER *does not take his eyes off the man.* RUTH *goes blindly to the tap
and gets a glass of water and brings it to* BOBO]

WALTER   There ain't nothing wrong, is there?

BOBO   Lemme tell you—

WALTER   Man—didn't nothing go wrong?

BOBO   Lemme tell you—Walter Lee. [*Looking at* RUTH *and talking to her more
than to* WALTER] You know how it was. I got to tell you how it was. I mean
first I got to tell you how it was all the way . . . I mean about the money
I put in, Walter Lee . . .

WALTER   [*With taut agitation now*]   What about the money you put in?

BOBO   Well—it wasn't much as we told you—me and Willy—[*He stops*] I'm
sorry, Walter. I got a bad feeling about it. I got a real bad feeling
about it . . .

WALTER   Man, what you telling me about all this for? . . . Tell me what happened in Springfield . . .

BOBO   Springfield.

RUTH   [*Like a dead woman*]   What was supposed to happen in Springfield?

BOBO   [*To her*]   This deal that me and Walter went into with Willy—Me and
Willy was going to go down to Springfield and spread some money 'round
so's we wouldn't have to wait so long for the liquor license . . . That's
what we were going to do. Everybody said that was the way you had to do,
you understand, Miss Ruth?

WALTER   Man—what happened down there?

BOBO   [*A pitiful man, near tears*]   I'm trying to tell you, Walter.

WALTER   [*Screaming at him suddenly*]   THEN TELL ME, GODDAMMIT
. . . WHAT'S THE MATTER WITH YOU?

BOBO   Man . . . I didn't go to no Springfield, yesterday.

WALTER   [*Halted, life hanging in the moment*]   Why not?

BOBO   [*The long way, the hard way to tell*]   'Cause I didn't have no reasons to . . .

WALTER   Man, what are you talking about!

BOBO   I'm talking about the fact that when I got to the train station yesterday morning—eight o'clock like we planned . . . Man—*Willy didn't never show up.*

WALTER   Why . . . where was he . . . where is he?

BOBO   That's what I'm trying to tell you . . . I don't know . . . I waited six hours . . . I called his house . . . and I waited . . . six hours . . . I waited in that train station six hours . . . [*Breaking into tears*] That was all the extra money I had in the world . . . [*Looking up at* WALTER *with the tears running down his face*] Man, *Willy is gone.*

WALTER   Gone, what you mean Willy is gone? Gone where? You mean he went by himself. You mean he went off to Springfield by himself—to take care of getting the license—[*Turns and looks anxiously at* RUTH] You mean maybe he didn't want too many people in on the business down there? [*Looks to* RUTH *again, as before*] You know Willy got his own ways. [*Looks back to* BOBO] Maybe you was late yesterday and he just went on down there without you. Maybe—maybe—he's been callin' you at home tryin' to tell you what happened or something. Maybe—maybe—he just got sick. He's somewhere—he's got to be somewhere. We just got to find him—me and you got to find him. [*Grabs* BOBO *senselessly by the collar and starts to shake him*] We got to!

BOBO   [*In sudden angry, frightened agony*] What's the matter with you, Walter! *When a cat take off with your money he don't leave you no maps!*

WALTER   [*Turning madly, as though he is looking for* WILLY *in the very room*] Willy! . . . Willy . . . don't do it . . . Please don't do it . . . Man, not with that money . . . Man, please, not with that money . . . Oh, God . . . Don't let it be true . . . [*He is wandering around, crying out for* WILLY *and looking for him or perhaps for help from God*] Man . . . I trusted you . . . Man, I put my life in your hands . . . [*He starts to crumple down on the floor as* RUTH *just covers her face in horror.* MAMA *opens the door and comes into the room, with* BENEATHA *behind her*] Man . . . [*He starts to pound the floor with his fists, sobbing wildly*] That money is made out of my father's flesh . . .

BOBO   [*Standing over him helplessly*] I'm sorry, Walter . . . [*Only* WALTER'S *sobs reply.* BOBO *puts on his hat*] I had my life staked on this deal, too . . . [*He exits*]

MAMA   [*To* WALTER] Son—[*She goes to him, bends down to him, talks to his bent head*] Son . . . Is it gone? Son, I gave you sixty-five hundred dollars. Is it gone? All of it? Beneatha's money too?

WALTER   [*Lifting his head slowly*] Mama . . . I never . . . went to the bank at all . . .

MAMA   [*Not wanting to believe him*] You mean . . . your sister's school money . . . you used that too . . . Walter? . . .

WALTER   Yessss! . . . All of it . . . It's all gone . . .

[*There is total silence.* RUTH *stands with her face covered with her hands;* BENEATHA *leans forlornly against a wall, fingering a piece of red ribbon from the mother's gift.* MAMA *stops and looks at her son without recognition and then, quite without thinking about it, starts to beat him senselessly in the face.* BENEATHA *goes to them and stops it*]

BENEATHA   Mama!

[MAMA *stops and looks at both of her children and rises slowly and wanders vaguely, aimlessly away from them*]

MAMA   I seen . . . him . . . night after night . . . come in . . . and look at that rug . . . and then look at me . . . the red showing in his eyes . . .

the veins moving in his head . . . I seen him grow thin and old before he
was forty . . . working and working and working like somebody's old
horse . . . killing himself . . . and you—you give it all away in a day . . .

BENEATHA   Mama—

MAMA   Oh, God . . . [*She looks up to Him*] Look down here—and show me
the strength.

BENEATHA   Mama—

MAMA   [*Folding over*] Strength . . .

BENEATHA   [*Plaintively*] Mama . . .

MAMA   Strength!

CURTAIN

ACT III

> *An hour later.*
> *At curtain, there is a sullen light of gloom in the living room,*
> *gray light not unlike that which began the first scene of Act One.*
> *At left we can see* WALTER *within his room, alone with himself.*
> *He is stretched out on the bed, his shirt out and open, his arms*
> *under his head. He does not smoke, he does not cry out, he*
> *merely lies there, looking up at the ceiling, much as if he were*
> *alone in the world.*
> *In the living room* BENEATHA *sits at the table, still surrounded by*
> *the now almost ominous packing crates. She sits looking off. We*
> *feel that this is a mood struck perhaps an hour before, and it*
> *lingers now, full of the empty sound of profound disappoint-*
> *ment. We see on a line from her brother's bedroom the sameness*
> *of their attitudes. Presently the bell rings and* BENEATHA *rises*
> *without ambition or interest in answering. It is* ASAGAI, *smiling*
> *broadly, striding into the room with energy and happy expecta-*
> *tion and conversation.*

ASAGAI   I came over . . . I had some free time. I thought I might help with
the packing. Ah, I like the look of packing crates! A household in preparation for a journey! It depresses some people . . . but for me . . . it is another feeling. Something full of the flow of life, do you understand? Movement, progress . . . It makes me think of Africa.

BENEATHA   Africa!

ASAGAI   What kind of a mood is this? Have I told you how deeply you move me?

BENEATHA   He gave away the money, Asagai . . .

ASAGAI   Who gave away what money?

BENEATHA   The insurance money. My brother gave it away.

ASAGAI   Gave it away?

BENEATHA   He made an investment! With a man even Travis wouldn't have
trusted.

ASAGAI   And it's gone?

BENEATHA   Gone!

ASAGAI   I'm very sorry . . . And you, now?

BENEATHA   Me? . . . Me? . . . Me I'm nothing . . . Me. When I was very small
. . . we used to take our sleds out in the wintertime and the only hills we
had were the ice-covered stone steps of some houses down the street. And
we used to fill them in with snow and make them smooth and slide down
them all day . . . and it was very dangerous you know . . . far too steep

. . . and sure enough one day a kid named Rufus came down too fast and hit the sidewalk . . . and we saw his face just split open right there in front of us . . . And I remember standing there looking at his bloody open face thinking that was the end of Rufus. But the ambulance came and they took him to the hospital and they fixed the broken bones and they sewed it all up . . . and the next time I saw Rufus he just had a little line down the middle of his face . . . I never got over that . . .

[WALTER *sits up, listening on the bed. Throughout this scene it is important that we feel his reaction at all times, that he visibly respond to the words of his sister and* ASAGAI]

ASAGAI   What?

BENEATHA   That that was what one person could do for another, fix him up— sew up the problem, make him all right again. That was the most marvelous thing in the world . . . I wanted to do that. I always thought it was the one concrete thing in the world that a human being could do. Fix up the sick, you know—and make them whole again. This was truly being God . . .

ASAGAI   You wanted to be God?

BENEATHA   No—I wanted to cure. It used to be so important to me. I wanted to cure. It used to matter. I used to care. I mean about people and how their bodies hurt . . .

ASAGAI   And you've stopped caring?

BENEATHA   Yes—I think so.

ASAGAI   Why?

[WALTER *rises, goes to the door of his room and is about to open it, then stops and stands listening, leaning on the door jamb*]

BENEATHA   Because it doesn't seem deep enough, close enough to what ails mankind—I mean this thing of sewing up bodies or administering drugs. Don't you understand? It was a child's reaction to the world. I thought that doctors had the secret to all the hurts. . . . That's the way a child sees things—or an idealist.

ASAGAI   Children see things very well sometimes—and idealists even better.

BENEATHA   I know that's what you think. Because you are still where I left off— you still care. This is what you see for the world, for Africa. You with the dreams of the future will patch up all Africa—you are going to cure the Great Sore of colonialism with Independence—

ASAGAI   Yes!

BENEATHA   Yes—and you think that one word is the penicillin of the human spirit: "Independence!" But then what?

ASAGAI   That will be the problem for another time. First we must get there.

BENEATHA   And where does it end?

ASAGAI   End? Who even spoke of an end? To life? To living?

BENEATHA   An end to misery!

ASAGAI   [*Smiling*] You sound like a French intellectual.

BENEATHA   No! I sound like a human being who just had her future taken right out of her hands! While I was sleeping in my bed in there, things were happening in this world that directly concerned me—and nobody asked me, consulted me—they just went out and did things—and changed my life. Don't you see there isn't any real progress, Asagai, there is only one large circle that we march in, around and around, each of us with our own little picture—in front of us—our own little mirage that we think is the future.

ASAGAI   That is the mistake.

BENEATHA   What?

ASAGAI   What you just said—about the circle. It isn't a circle—it is simply a long line—as in geometry, you know, one that reaches into infinity. And because we cannot see the end—we also cannot see how it changes. And it is very odd but those who see the changes are called "idealists"—and those who cannot, or refuse to think, they are the "realists." It is very strange, and amusing too, I think.

BENEATHA   You—you are almost religious.

ASAGAI   Yes . . . I think I have the religion of doing what is necessary in the world—and of worshipping man—because he is so marvelous, you see.

BENEATHA   Man is foul! And the human race deserves its misery!

ASAGAI   You see: *you* have become the religious one in the old sense. Already, and after such a small defeat, you are worshipping despair.

BENEATHA   From now on, I worship the truth—and the truth is that people are puny, small and selfish. . . .

ASAGAI   Truth? Why is it that you despairing ones always think that only you have the truth? I never thought to see *you* like that. You! Your brother made a stupid, childish mistake—and you are grateful to him. So that now you can give up the ailing human race on account of it. You talk about what good is struggle; what good is anything? Where are we all going? And why are we bothering?

BENEATHA   *And you cannot answer it!* All your talk and dreams about Africa and Independence. Independence and then what? What about all the crooks and petty thieves and just plain idiots who will come into power to steal and plunder the same as before—only now they will be black and do it in the name of the new Independence— You cannot answer that.

ASAGAI   [*Shouting over her*]   *I live the answer!* [*Pause*] In my village at home it is the exceptional man who can even read a newspaper . . . or who ever *sees* a book at all. I will go home and much of what I will have to say will seem strange to the people of my village . . . But I will teach and work and things will happen, slowly and swiftly. At times it will seem that nothing changes at all . . . and then again . . . the sudden dramatic events which make history leap into the future. And then quiet again. Retrogression even. Guns, murder, revolution. And I even will have moments when I wonder if the quiet was not better than all that death and hatred. But I will look about my village at the illiteracy and disease and ignorance and I will not wonder long. And perhaps . . . perhaps I will be a great man . . . I mean perhaps I will hold on to the substance of truth and find my way always with the right course . . . and perhaps for it I will be butchered in my bed some night by the servants of empire . . .

BENEATHA   *The martyr!*

ASAGAI   . . . or perhaps I shall live to be a very old man, respected and esteemed in my new nation . . . And perhaps I shall hold office and this is what I'm trying to tell you, Alaiyo; perhaps the things I believe now for my country will be wrong and outmoded, and I will not understand and do terrible things to have things my way or merely to keep my power. Don't you see that there will be young men and women, not British soldiers then, but my own black countrymen . . . to step out of the shadows some evening and slit my then useless throat? Don't you see they have always been there . . . that they always will be. And that such a thing as my own death will be an advance? They who might kill me even . . . actually replenish me!

BENEATHA   Oh, Asagai, I know all that.

ASAGAI   Good! Then stop moaning and groaning and tell me what you plan to do.

BENEATHA   Do?

ASAGAI   I have a bit of a suggestion.

BENEATHA   What?

ASAGAI   [*Rather quietly for him*]   That when it is all over—that you come home with me—

BENEATHA   [*Slapping herself on the forehead with exasperation born of misunderstanding*]   Oh—Asagai—at this moment you decide to be romantic!

ASAGAI   [*Quickly understanding the misunderstanding*]   My dear, young creature of the New World—I do not mean across the city—I mean across the ocean; home—to Africa.

BENEATHA   [*Slowly understanding and turning to him with murmured amazement*]   To—to Nigeria?

ASAGAI   Yes! . . . [*Smiling and lifting his arms playfully*]   Three hundred years later the African Prince rose up out of the seas and swept the maiden back across the middle passage over which her ancestors had come—

BENEATHA   [*Unable to play*]   Nigeria?

ASAGAI   Nigeria. Home. [*Coming to her with genuine romantic flippancy*]   I will show you our mountains and our stars; and give you cool drinks from gourds and teach you the old songs and the ways of our people—and, in time, we will pretend that—[*Very softly*]—you have only been away for a day—

[*She turns her back to him, thinking. He swings her around and takes her full in his arms in a long embrace which proceeds to passion*]

BENEATHA   [*Pulling away*]   You're getting me all mixed up—

ASAGAI   Why?

BENEATHA   Too many things—too many things have happened today. I must sit down and think. I don't know what I feel about anything right this minute.

[*She promptly sits down and props her chin on her fist*]

ASAGAI   [*Charmed*]   All right, I shall leave you. No—don't get up. [*Touching her, gently, sweetly*]   Just sit awhile and think . . . Never be afraid to sit awhile and think. [*He goes to door and looks at her*]   How often I have looked at you and said, "Ah—so this is what the New World hath finally wrought . . ."

[*He exits.* BENEATHA *sits on alone. Presently* WALTER *enters from his room and starts to rummage through things, feverishly looking for something. She looks up and turns in her seat*]

BENEATHA   [*Hissingly*]   Yes—just look at what the New World hath wrought! . . . Just look! [*She gestures with bitter disgust*]   There he is! *Monsieur le petit bourgeois noir*—himself! There he is—Symbol of a Rising Class! Entrepreneur! Titan of the system! [*Walter ignores her completely and continues frantically and destructively looking for something and hurling things to floor and tearing things out of their place in his search.* BENEATHA *ignores the eccentricity of his actions and goes on with the monologue of insult*]   Did you dream of yachts on Lake Michigan, Brother? Did you see yourself on that Great Day sitting down at the Conference Table, surrounded by all the mighty bald-headed men in America? All halted, waiting, breathless, waiting for your pronouncements on industry? Waiting for you—Chairman of the Board? [WALTER *finds what he is looking for—a small piece of white paper—and pushes it in his pocket and puts on his coat and rushes out without ever having looked at her. She shouts after him*]   I look at you and I see the final triumph of stupidity in the world!

[*The door slams and she returns to just sitting again.* RUTH *comes quickly out of* MAMA's *room*]

RUTH   Who was that?

BENEATHA   Your husband.

RUTH   Where did he go?

BENEATHA   Who knows—maybe he has an appointment at U. S. Steel.

RUTH   [*Anxiously, with frightened eyes*]   You didn't say nothing bad to him, did you?

BENEATHA   Bad? Say anything bad to him? No—I told him he was a sweet boy and full of dreams and everything is strictly peachy keen, as the ofay kids say!

MAMA *enters from her bedroom. She is lost, vague, trying to catch hold, to make some sense of her former command of the world, but it still eludes her. A sense of waste overwhelms her gait; a measure of apology rides on her shoulders. She goes to her plant, which has remained on the table, looks at it, picks it up and takes it to the window sill and sits it outside, and she stands and looks at it a long moment. Then she closes the window, straightens her body with effort and turns around to her children*]

MAMA   Well—ain't it a mess in here, though? [*A false cheerfulness, a beginning of something*]   I guess we all better stop moping around and get some work done. All this unpacking and everything we got to do. [RUTH *raises her head slowly in response to the sense of the line; and* BENEATHA *in similar manner turns very slowly to look at her mother*] One of you all better call the moving people and tell 'em not to come.

RUTH   Tell 'em not to come?

MAMA   Of course, baby. Ain't no need in 'em coming all the way here and having to go back. They charges for that too. [*She sits down, fingers to her brow, thinking*] Lord, ever since I was a little girl. I always remembers people saying, "Lena—Lena Eggleston, you aims too high all the time. You needs to slow down and see life a little more like it is. Just slow down some." That's what they always used to say down home— "Lord, that Lena Eggleston is a high-minded thing. She'll get her due one day!"

RUTH   No, Lena . . .

MAMA   Me and Big Walter just didn't never learn right.

RUTH   Lena, no! We gotta go. Bennie—tell her . . . [*She rises and crosses to* BENEATHA *with her arms outstretched.* BENEATHA *doesn't respond*] Tell her we can still move . . . the notes ain't but a hundred and twenty-five a month. We got four grown people in this house—we can work . . .

MAMA   [*To herself*]   Just aimed too high all the time—

RUTH   [*Turning and going to* MAMA *fast—the words pouring out with urgency and desperation*] Lena—I'll work . . . I'll work twenty hours a day in all the kitchens in Chicago . . . I'll strap my baby on my back if I have to and scrub all the floors in America and wash all the sheets in America if I have to—but we got to move . . . We got to get out of here . . .

[MAMA *reaches out absently and pats* RUTH's *hand*]

MAMA   No—I sees things differently now. Been thinking 'bout some of the things we could do to fix this place up some. I seen a second-hand bureau over on Maxwell Street just the other day that could fit right there. [*She points to where the new furniture might go.* RUTH *wanders away from her*] Would need some new handles on it and then a little varnish and then it look like something brand-new. And—we can put up them new curtains in the kitchen . . . Why this place be looking fine. Cheer us all up so that we forget trouble ever came . . . [*To Ruth*] And you could get some nice screens to put up in your room round the baby's bassinet . . . [*She looks at both of them, pleadingly*] Sometimes you just got to know when to give up some things . . . and hold on to what you got.

[WALTER *enters from the outside, looking spent and leaning against the door, his coat hanging from him*]

MAMA Where you been, son?

WALTER [*Breathing hard*] Made a call.

MAMA To who, son?

WALTER To The Man.

MAMA What man, baby?

WALTER The Man, Mama. Don't you know who The Man is?

RUTH Walter Lee?

WALTER *The Man.* Like the guys in the streets say—The Man. Captain Boss—Mistuh Charley . . . Old Captain Please Mr. Bossman . . .

BENEATHA [*Suddenly*] Lindner!

WALTER That's right! That's good. I told him to come right over.

BENEATHA [*Fiercely, understanding*] For what? What do you want to see him for!

WALTER [*Looking at his sister*] We going to do business with him.

MAMA What you talking 'bout, son?

WALTER Talking 'bout life, Mama. You all always telling me to see life like it is. Well—I laid in there on my back today . . . and I figured it out. Life just like it is. Who gets and who don't get. [*He sits down with his coat on and laughs*] Mama, you know it's all divided up. Life is. Sure enough. Between the takers and the "tooken." [*He laughs*] I've figured it out finally. [*He looks around at them*] Yeah. Some of us always getting "tooken." [*He laughs*] People like Willy Harris, they don't never get "tooken." And you know why the rest of us do? 'Cause we all mixed up. Mixed up bad. We get to looking 'round for the right and the wrong; and we worry about it and cry about it and stay up nights trying to figure out 'bout the wrong and the right of things all the time . . . And all the time, man, them takers is out there operating, just taking and taking. Willy Harris? Shoot—Willy Harris don't even count. He don't even count in the big scheme of things. But I'll say one thing for old Willy Harris . . . he's taught me something. He's taught me to keep my eye on what counts in this world. Yeah—[*Shouting out a little*] Thanks, Willy!

RUTH What did you call that man for, Walter Lee?

WALTER Called him to tell him to come on over to the show. Gonna put on a show for the man. Just what he wants to see. You see, Mama, the man came here today and he told us that them people out there where you want us to move—well they so upset they willing to pay us not to move out there. [*He laughs again*] And—and oh, Mama—you would of been proud of the way me and Ruth and Bennie acted. We told him to get out . . . Lord have mercy! We told the man to get out. Oh, we was some proud folks this afternoon, yeah. [*He lights a cigarette*] We were still full of that old-time stuff . . .

RUTH [*Coming toward him slowly*] You talking 'bout taking them people's money to keep us from moving in that house?

WALTER I ain't just talking 'bout it, baby—I'm telling you that's what's going to happen.

BENEATHA Oh, God! Where is the bottom! Where is the real honest-to-God bottom so he can't go any farther!

WALTER See—that's the old stuff. You and that boy that was here today. You all want everybody to carry a flag and a spear and sing some marching songs, huh? You wanna spend your life looking into things and trying to find the right and the wrong part, huh? Yeah. You know what's going to happen to that boy someday—he'll find himself sitting in a dungeon, locked in forever

—and the takers will have the key! Forget it, baby! There ain't no causes—
there ain't nothing but taking in this world, and he who takes most is
smartest—and it don't make a damn bit of difference *how*.

MAMA   You making something inside me cry, son. Some awful pain inside me.

WALTER   Don't cry, Mama. Understand. That white man is going to walk in that
door able to write checks for more money than we ever had. It's important
to him and I'm going to help him . . . I'm going to put on the show, Mama.

MAMA   Son—I come from five generations of people who was slaves and share-
croppers—but ain't nobody in my family never let nobody pay 'em no
money that was a way of telling us we wasn't fit to walk the earth. We ain't
never been that poor. [*Raising her eyes and looking at him*] We ain't never
been that dead inside.

BENEATHA   Well—we are dead now. All the talk about dreams and sunlight that
goes on in this house. All dead.

WALTER   What's the matter with you all! I didn't make this world! It was give
to me this way! Hell, yes, I want me some yachts someday! Yes, I want to
hang some real pearls 'round my wife's neck. Ain't she supposed to wear no
pearls? Somebody tell me—tell me, who decides which women is suppose
to wear pearls in this world. I tell you I am a *man*—and I think my wife
should wear some pearls in this world!

[*This last line hangs a good while and* WALTER *begins to move about the
room. The word "Man" has penetrated his consciousness; he mumbles it
to himself repeatedly between strange agitated pauses as he moves about*]

MAMA   Baby, how you going to feel on the inside?

WALTER   Fine! . . . Going to feel fine . . . a man . . .

MAMA   You won't have nothing left then, Walter Lee

WALTER   [*Coming to her*]   I'm going to feel fine, Mama. I'm going to look that
son-of-a-bitch in the eyes and say—[*He falters*]—and say, "All right, Mr.
Lindner—[*He falters even more*]—that's your neighborhood out there. You
got the right to keep it like you want. You got the right to have it like you
want. Just write the check and—the house is yours." And, and I am going
to say—[*His voice almost breaks*] And you—you people just put the money
in my hand and you won't have to live next to this bunch of stinking
niggers! . . . [*He straightens up and moves away from his mother, walking
around the room*] Maybe—maybe I'll just get down on my black knees . . .
[*He does so;* RUTH *and* BENNIE *and* MAMA *watch him in frozen horror*] Captain, Mistuh, Bossman. [*He starts crying*] A-hee-hee-hee! [*Wringing his
hands in profoundly anguished imitation*] Yassssssuh! Great White Father,
just gi' ussen de money, fo' God's sake, and we's ain't gwine come out deh
and dirty up yo' white folks neighborhood . . .

[*He breaks down completely, then gets up and goes into the bedroom*]

BENEATHA   That is not a man. That is nothing but a toothless rat.

MAMA   Yes—death done come in this here house. [*She is nodding, slowly, reflectively*] Done come walking in my house. On the lips of my children. You
what supposed to be my beginning again. You—what supposed to be my
harvest. [*To* BENEATHA] You—you mourning your brother?

BENEATHA   He's no brother of mine.

MAMA   What you say?

BENEATHA   I said that that individual in that room is no brother of mine.

MAMA   That's what I thought you said. You feeling like you better than he is
today? [BENEATHA *does not answer*] Yes? What you tell him a minute ago?
That he wasn't a man? Yes? You give him up for me? You done wrote his
epitaph too—like the rest of the world? Well, who give you the privilege?

BENEATHA   Be on my side for once! You saw what he just did, Mama! You saw him—down on his knees. Wasn't it you who taught me—to despise any man who would do that. Do what he's going to do.

MAMA   Yes—I taught you that. Me and your daddy. But I thought I taught you something else too . . . I thought I taught you to love him.

BENEATHA   Love him? There is nothing left to love.

MAMA   There is always something left to love. And if you ain't learned that, you ain't learned nothing. [*Looking at her*] Have you cried for that boy today? I don't mean for yourself and for the family 'cause we lost the money. I mean for him; what he been through and what it done to him. Child, when do you think is the time to love somebody the most; when they done good and made things easy for everybody? Well then, you ain't through learning—because that ain't the time at all. It's when he's at his lowest and can't believe in hisself 'cause the world done whipped him so. When you starts measuring somebody, measure him right, child, measure him right. Make sure you done taken into account what hills and valleys he come through before he got to wherever he is.

[TRAVIS *bursts into the room at the end of the speech, leaving the door open*]

TRAVIS   Grandmama—the moving men are downstairs! The truck just pulled up.

MAMA   [*Turning and looking at him*]   Are they, baby? They downstairs?

[*She sighs and sits.* LINDNER *appears in the doorway. He peers in and knocks lightly, to gain attention, and comes in. All turn to look at him*]

LINDNER   [*Hat and briefcase in hand*]   Uh—hello . . . [RUTH *crosses mechanically to the bedroom door and opens it and lets it swing open freely and slowly as the lights come up on* WALTER *within, still in his coat, sitting at the far corner of the room. He looks up and out through the room to* LINDNER]

RUTH   He's here.

[*A long minute passes and* WALTER *slowly gets up*]

LINDNER   [*Coming to the table with efficiency, putting his briefcase on the table and starting to unfold papers and unscrew fountain pens*]   Well, I certainly was glad to hear from you people. [WALTER *has begun the trek out of the room, slowly and awkwardly, rather like a small boy, passing the back of his sleeve across his mouth from time to time*] Life can really be so much simpler than people let it be most of the time. Well—with whom do I negotiate? You, Mrs. Younger, or your son here? [MAMA *sits with her hands folded on her lap and her eyes closed as* WALTER *advances.* TRAVIS *goes closer to* LINDNER *and looks at the papers curiously*] Just some official papers, sonny.

RUTH   Travis, you go downstairs.

MAMA   [*Opening her eyes and looking into* WALTER'S]   No. Travis, you stay right here. And you make him understand what you doing, Walter Lee. You teach him good. Like Willy Harris taught you. You show where our five generations done come to. Go ahead, son—

WALTER   [*Looks down into his boy's eyes.* TRAVIS *grins at him merrily and* WALTER *draws him beside him with his arm lightly around his shoulders*] Well, Mr. Lindner. [BENEATHA *turns away*] We called you—[*There is a profound, simple groping quality in his speech*]—because, well, me and my family [*He looks around and shifts from one foot to the other*] Well—we are very plain people . . .

LINDNER   Yes—

WALTER   I mean—I have worked as a chauffeur most of my life—and my wife here, she does domestic work in people's kitchens. So does my mother. I mean—we are plain people . . .

LINDNER   Yes, Mr. Younger—

WALTER   [*Really like a small boy, looking down at his shoes and then up at the man*] And—uh—well, my father, well, he was a laborer most of his life.

LINDNER [*Absolutely confused*] Uh, yes—

WALTER [*Looking down at his toes once again*] My father almost beat a man to death once because this man called him a bad name or something, you know what I mean?

LINDNER No, I'm afraid I don't.

WALTER [*Finally straightening up*] Well, what I mean is that we come from people who had a lot of pride. I mean—we are very proud people. And that's my sister over there and she's going to be a doctor—and we are very proud—

LINDNER Well—I am sure that is very nice, but—

WALTER [*Starting to cry and facing the man eye to eye*] What I am telling you is that we called you over here to tell you that we are very proud and that this is—this is my son, who makes the sixth generation of our family in this country, and that we have all thought about your offer and we have decided to move into our house because my father—my father—he earned it. [MAMA *has her eyes closed and is rocking back and forth as though she were in church, with her head nodding the amen yes*] We don't want to make no trouble for nobody or fight no causes—but we will try to be good neighbors. That's all we got to say. [*He looks the man absolutely in the eyes*] We don't want your money.

[*He turns and walks away from the man*]

LINDNER [*Looking around at all of them*] I take it then that you have decided to occupy.

BENEATHA That's what the man said.

LINDNER [*To* MAMA *in her reverie*] Then I would like to appeal to you, Mrs. Younger. You are older and wiser and understand things better I am sure . . .

MAMA [*Rising*] I am afraid you don't understand. My son said we was going to move and there ain't nothing left for me to say. [*Shaking her head with double meaning*] You know how these young folks is nowadays, mister. Can't do a thing with 'em. Good-bye.

LINDNER [*Folding up his materials*] Well—if you are that final about it . . . There is nothing left for me to say. [*He finishes. He is almost ignored by the family, who are concentrating on* WALTER LEE. *At the door* LINDNER *halts and looks around*] I sure hope you people know what you're doing. [*He shakes his head and exits*]

RUTH [*Looking around and coming to life*] Well, for God's sake—if the moving men are here—LET'S GET THE HELL OUT OF HERE!

MAMA [*Into action*] Ain't it the truth. Look at all this here mess. Ruth, put Travis' good jacket on him . . . Walter Lee, fix your tie and tuck your shirt in, you look just like somebody's hoodlum. Lord have mercy, where is my plant? [*She flies to get it amid the general bustling of the family, who are deliberately trying to ignore the nobility of the past moment*] You all start on down . . . Travis child, don't go empty-handed . . . Ruth, where did I put that box with my skillets in it? I want to be in charge of it myself . . . I'm going to make us the biggest dinner we ever ate tonight . . . Beneatha, what's the matter with them stockings? Pull them things up, girl . . .

[*The family starts to file out as two moving men appear and begin to carry out the heavier pieces of furniture, bumping into the family as they move about*]

BENEATHA Mama, Asagai—asked me to marry him today and go to Africa—

MAMA [*In the middle of her getting-ready activity*] He did? You ain't old enough to marry nobody—[*Seeing the moving men lifting one of her chairs precariously*] Darling, that ain't no bale of cotton, please handle it so we can sit in it again. I had that chair twenty-five years . . .

[*The movers sigh with exasperation and go on with their work*]

BENEATHA [*Girlishly and unreasonably trying to pursue the conversation*] To go to Africa, Mama—be a doctor in Africa . . .

MAMA [*Distracted*] Yes, baby—

WALTER Africa! What he want you to go to Africa for?

BENEATHA To practice there . . .

WALTER Girl, if you don't get all them silly ideas out your head! You better marry yourself a man with some loot . . .

BENEATHA [*Angrily, precisely as in the first scene of the play*] What have you got to do with who I marry!

WALTER Plenty. Now I think George Murchison—

[*He and* BENEATHA *go out yelling at each other vigorously;* BENEATHA *is heard saying that she would not marry* GEORGE MURCHISON *if he were Adam and she were Eve, etc. The anger is loud and real till their voices diminish.* RUTH *stands at the door and turns to* MAMA *and smiles knowingly*]

MAMA [*Fixing her hat at last*] Yeah—they something all right, my children . . .

RUTH Yeah—they're something. Let's go, Lena.

MAMA [*Stalling, starting to look around at the house*] Yes—I'm coming. Ruth—

RUTH Yes?

MAMA [*Quietly, woman to woman*] He finally come into his manhood today, didn't he? Kind of like a rainbow after the rain . . .

RUTH [*Biting her lip lest her own pride explode in front of* MAMA] Yes, Lena. [WALTER'S *voice calls for them raucously*]

MAMA [*Waving* RUTH *out vaguely*] All right, honey—go on down. I be down directly.

[RUTH *hesitates, then exits.* MAMA *stands, at last alone in the living room, her plant on the table before her as the lights start to come down. She looks around at all the walls and ceilings and suddenly, despite herself, while the children call below, a great heaving thing rises in her and she puts her fist to her mouth, takes a final desperate look, pulls her coat about her, pats her hat and goes out. The lights dim down. The door opens and she comes back in, grabs her plant, and goes out for the last time*]

CURTAIN

GLOSSARY

ACTION   In the *Poetics*, Aristotle says that any literary form that tells a story involves the imitation of human action (*praxis*). The term action may be most useful for pointing to the general movement of the story before the dramatist has superimposed all the refinements of PLOT. Action could be, for example, the movement in a tragedy from "happiness" to "misery." Francis Fergusson, in *The Idea of a Theater* (1948), suggests that the action of a drama might be interpreted as a progression of infinitive phrases; in *Oedipus Rex* the action might be construed first in the phrase "to cure the sickness that infects Thebes," and then in "to discover the murderer of Laius," and finally in "to accept the truth." In this sense, the action is interpreted and expressed in different ways by each of the main characters.

AGON   A Greek word meaning "public performance" or "contest." The term agon can refer to a dramatic scene showing the main characters engaged in verbal combat. In *Oedipus Rex,* for example, agon can refer to each of Oedipus' "debates": his encounters with Teiresias, Creon, the Messenger, and the Shepherd. See THOUGHT.

ANTISTROPHE   A turn of thought in the argument of the ode. It is also the second movement in a physical sense: the chorus reverses its line of motion while chanting the antistrophe. See STROPHE.

APOLLO   In Greek mythology, Apollo, a son of Zeus, was the god primarily of "Light"; he was responsible for the passage of the sun through the heavens during the day. By extension, Apollo's power governed "Reason" and "Prophecy" (both symbolized by light). In addition, the Greeks considered Apollo the patron of youth, music, medicine, and archery. Other names for Apollo were Phoebus or Phoibos (literally, "Bright"), Loxias, and The Healer.

APOLLONIAN-DIONYSIAC   Opposed terms used by Friedrich Nietzsche in *The Birth of Tragedy* (1872) to refer, respectively, to the poetic impulse toward rationality and controlled form in a literary work, and the poetic impulse which is essentially irrational (perhaps unconscious) and best defined by its associations with music, intoxication, and ecstasy. The affinities of the Apollonian impulse are with symmetry and formal beauty; the affinities of the Dionysiac impulse are with asymmetry and pure energy. It may be possible to interpret almost any literary work as embodying both the Apollonian and Dionysiac impulses.

ASIDE   Lines spoken by one character which are supposedly not heard by the other characters on stage; a dramatic convention whereby the audience is informed of a character's real thoughts or intentions.

CHARACTER   The word character obviously refers to a personage in a drama. But it also denotes the beliefs, habits of mind, moral choices, and MOTIVATION which distinguish one dramatic personage from another. It is in this latter sense that Aristotle uses the term character (*ethos*) as one of the six QUALITATIVE PARTS of drama. See also CHORUS CHARACTER and STOCK CHARACTER.

CHORUS   In the religious festivals of ancient Greece the "chorus" was a group of men who performed hymns and sacred dances which were often "imitative," that is, celebrating the god in a sort of narrative and pantomime. As ritual evolved into drama, the role of the chorus became less dominant, but it afforded the dramatist many possibilities: providing exposition, commenting on the action, making thematic statements, guiding the emotions and attitudes of the audience, and, most important, expressing "lyrically" the ACTION which the other characters rendered "imitatively." As Aristotle suggested, the chorus should be considered as a "group character."

CHORUS CHARACTER   (*Raisonneur*)   A character who participates in the action of a play, but who also seems to be a spokesman for the dramatist himself. He provides perceptive commentary on the actions of the other characters, and his remarks are usually tinged with irony. In *Antony and Cleopatra,* Enobarbus is a chorus character.

CLIMAX   The point of most intense emotion in a drama, both for the audience and the CHARACTERS.

COMEDY   A play designed to amuse the audience by showing the protagonist moving toward a happy ending, often marriage. Although comedy can deal with serious matters—such as pride, greed, or lust, it seldom condemns evil explicitly. Instead, it ridicules lack of self-knowledge; and the conflict evokes laughter or thoughtful smiles.

COMEDY OF MANNERS   A type of comedy concerned with man in his social context: man as he responds to the manners, mores, and morals of his society. This kind of comedy can satirize characters by revealing their social ineptitudes. Comedies of manners often sparkle with witty dialogue between clever, sophisticated people.

COMPLICATION   Aristotle used the word complication (*desis*) to refer to the progressive "knotting" of the plot—that period of the play from its beginning up to the DENOUEMENT. In Greek drama, the complication may include everything up to the end of the fourth episode (usually the point where DISCOVERY and REVERSAL take place.) In a general sense, for all drama, the complication consists of an intensification of the play's essential conflicts; characters tend to act at cross-purposes, and the protagonist may become more and more stubborn.

CONVENTION   A literary device used by dramatists and accepted by audiences, even though it may be "unrealistic" or "artificial"; examples are SOLILOQUY and ASIDE. In the spirit of the "willing suspension of disbelief" the audience accepts a convention as one of the rules of the game.

CRISIS   The "turning point" of a dramatic structure; usually a decision by the protagonist which determines the direction of action of the play. In a tragedy the crisis is often a demonstration of the protagonist's HAMARTIA. The term crisis, however, is *not* part of Aristotle's theory of plot, and it may be applied less appropriately to a Greek drama than to an Elizabethan or a modern drama in which the action is often represented as taking place over a long period of time (weeks, months, or years). In this sense, a crisis usually falls in the third act of a five-act structure, and the second act of a three-act structure.

DEFINING EVENT   An early point in a dramatic structure when the essential conflict of the play is clarified both for the characters and the audience; then, the COMPLICATION begins. The defining event (or "inciting moment") usually consists of the protagonist being moved to action, or to a statement of commitment, by some force, challenge, or threat. This sometimes occurs when a dramatist, having introduced his main characters separately, assembles them together for the first time.

DENOUEMENT   This French word, like Aristotle's term *lysis,* denotes an "untying"; that part of a plot when conflicts, which have been intensified during the COMPLICATION, are finally resolved.

DISCOVERY   Aristotle's term for that point in the PLOT when the protagonist passes suddenly "from ignorance to knowledge." While Aristotle seems to have conceived of discovery generally as a literal "recognition" of one character by another, the term can also refer to the protagonist's perception of the truth of his situation, the *self*-knowledge he finally achieves. See REVERSAL.

DICTION   The language of a play. See IMAGERY. Diction (*lexis*) is the fourth of Aristotle's six QUALITATIVE PARTS of drama; it can be considered as a stage in the dramatist's composition of a play, his "making of verses"—which is partly delimited by THOUGHT.

DIONYSUS   In Greek mythology, Dionysus, a son of Zeus, was the god of fertility and vegetation, specifically of wine and the grape. The Greek dramas were produced in his honor, under the supervision of his priests, at his temple (the amphitheater) in Athens. In cults honoring Dionysus, male and female votaries (satyrs and maenads) were represented as intoxicated or possessed; they were known as Bacchae or Bacchantes.

EPILOGUE   A speech or poem delivered after the last scene of a play. It may be in the nature of a thematic summary, or a kind of appeal for applause.

EPISODE   In the structure of a Greek drama, the episodes are the sections of action and dialogue that alternate with the choric odes. In modern drama, the term episode can refer to any brief, unified portion of the play, and can often be used interchangeably with the term "scene."

EXODOS   The concluding scene of a Greek drama; the term can also refer to the final chant, or EPILOGUE, of the Greek chorus, delivered as the group moves out of the acting area.

EXPOSITION   The background information necessary for the audience to understand the developing action. Most exposition is given in the opening scenes of a drama. Unless a dramatist uses a convention such as a "narrator," it is difficult to make exposition seem natural and well motivated, for example, when one character passes on "news" to another, or when the audience is able to infer past action from a conversation taking place in the present.

FOIL   Usually a minor character whom the dramatist contrasts with a major character (most often the protagonist), thus "setting off" qualities of personality, and clarifying the play's theme. In *Antigone,* for example, Ismene is a foil to her sister Antigone, particularly in regard to the moral dilemma that the play raises. Similarly, Philinte is a foil to Alceste in *The Misanthrope.*

FORESHADOWING   Clues or hints that prepare the audience for some future action or event. In *Antigone,* Teiresias warns Creon (and the audience) of forthcoming catastrophes. Similarly, in *A View From the Bridge,* the narrator is constantly preparing the audience for Eddie's tragic defeat.

HAMARTIA   Given the essential line of action in tragedy—the passage of an essentially good man from happiness to misery—it is necessary for the dramatist to guide the reaction of the audience, so that it does not become one of disgust, revulsion, or pure shock at the sight of innocent suffering. Aristotle used the term "hamartia" to refer to the dramatist's "assigning" some personal responsibility to the protagonist for his eventual catastrophe—generally an "error of judgment"; hamartia literally means "missing the mark" (as with an arrow). Later critics, however, have preferred another metaphor: the "tragic flaw," an essential chink in the protagonist's moral capability. See HUBRIS. The hamartia usually occurs (or is most fully revealed) at the play's CRISIS.

HUBRIS   (HYBRIS)   Greek word for the overconfidence and excessive pride to which "important" men are susceptible. In most tragedies, the HAMARTIA may be construed as resulting from hubris, or as a form of hubris itself. The dramatist can also develop the tragic protagonist's hubris so as to provide a greater contrast between his good fortune early in the play and his catastrophe at the end.

IMAGE   An aspect of dramatic DICTION whereby words and phrases suggest concrete, physical, or descriptive details such as sounds, odors, colors, and tactile sensations. A good example is *Antony and Cleopatra,* II, ii, 191–197:

> The barge she sat in, like a burnish'd throne,
> Burn'd on the water. The poop was beaten gold;
> Purple the sails, and so perfumed that
> The winds were lovesick with them; the oars were silver,
> Which to the tune of flutes kept stroke, and made
> The water which they beat to follow faster,
> As amorous of their strokes.

IMAGERY   A pattern of figurative language which supports and expands the theme of a literary work. In drama the imagery is usually in speeches made by characters who are, for the moment at least, filled with emotion, and who thus slip easily into the use of metaphors and similes. Such imagery generally gives a physical equivalent for a *state of mind* (for example, "darkness" suggesting ignorance or hopelessness). Most often, imagery "builds" from a literal situation. In *Hamlet,* for example, all of the major characters use images of "poison" —and these images suggest such things as spiritual corruption, lust, slander, and lying; but these images are also tied to the literal fact that Hamlet's father was murdered with poison.

IMITATION   Aristotle's term *(mimesis)* for the "representational" aspect of drama—for example, men on stage, acting out a story by pretending to be other men. Imitation should not be taken as a pejorative term which would deemphasize the dramatist's creativity; it refers directly to the active "making" of a unified work of art with its own internal coherence. The dramatist's act of "imitating" may resolve itself into the successive stages of the six QUALITATIVE PARTS of drama: the "construction" of plot, the "development" of character, and so on.

INCITING MOMENT   (See DEFINING EVENT)

MELODRAMA   Literally, "middle drama"—between TRAGEDY and COMEDY. Melodramas are often pretentiously serious plays which stress plot but not character. The protagonist may become involved in violent, sensational, and thrilling action, but melodrama tends to eschew genuinely human motivations, and generally ends with a kind of "poetic justice."

MOTIVATION   The reasons—moral, psychological, economic, and so on—for a character's behavior; that which causes a character to act.

MUSIC   Aristotle used the term music (*melos*) to refer to the fifth of drama's QUALITATIVE PARTS: the "rhythm" of the speeches, and the rhythm and melody of the choric odes, important for developing the play's "mood" and guiding the audience's emotions. Aristotle's point holds for modern drama as well: the cadence of Shakespearean blank verse, the "clipped" quality of diction in modern realistic drama, the incidental use of music in a play (for example, the chants of the monks in *Luther,* the background music in *The Glass Menagerie*) all add to the emotional effect, and perhaps also to the play's meaning.

NATURALISM   Like REALISM, a revolt against what its exponents felt to be the artificialities of the WELL-MADE PLAY and of romantic drama. Because of its preoccupation with social, psychological, and economic determinism, in its characterization, naturalistic drama often focuses on determining causes. Zola speaks of the "slice of life" style of naturalism, but actually, naturalists selected and arranged their subject matter with great care—particularly in drama, as in Gorky's *The Lower Depths.*

PARODOS   The first of the choric odes in a Greek drama, chanted as the chorus entered the acting area.

PATHOS   Aristotle's term for "scenes of suffering" (usually the protagonist's) in a tragedy. Such scenes are important in the development of the plot. They may serve as an expiation for evil deeds, and may stir the audience to pity. In an expanded sense, the term pathos can refer to the emotion of pity itself, which often dominates the tone of a tragedy at its conclusion, and can be "expressed" in the speeches of the characters, or by a narrator or chorus.

PERIPETY   (See REVERSAL)

PICTURE-FRAME STAGE   Acting area or stage framed by a PROSCENIUM ARCH which divides the players from the audience; the stage does not extend out into the audience, but is recessed into the back wall. Having the audience thus "look into" the scene may add to the illusion of reality.

PLOT   The dramatist's selection and arrangement of incidents in the story he treats. Plot is a principle of unity which governs such questions as where and how to "open" the story; few successful plays try to give the protagonist's life history, from birth to death and, given the nature of the ACTION that the dramatist chooses to develop, there are "appropriate" points by which the story can be limited. Aristotle called plot the "soul" of a drama; it might also be understood as the final form of the action, the progress from initial COMPLICATION to eventual DENOUEMENT. It can include such stages as DISCOVERY, REVERSAL, and PATHOS, and, especially in tragedy, it emphasizes cause-effect relationships.

PROLOGUE   In Greek drama, the section of dialogue and action which precedes the entrance of the chorus in the PARODOS; in modern drama, an introductory speech delivered before the first scene of a play.

PROSCENIUM   Derived from the Greek work *proskienion,* meaning the "space before the scene," the term proscenium refers to the wall separating the stage from the auditorium—as well as the "opening" in that wall, through which the spectator views the play.

PROSCENIUM ARCH   The arch enclosing the opening in the proscenium wall; see PICTURE-FRAME STAGE.

PROTAGONIST   The central character of a drama; literally, its "first contestant." See AGON.

QUALITATIVE PARTS OF DRAMA   According to Aristotle, dramas can be analyzed not only through their *chronological* development, from first scene to last, but also through their *logical* development of six aspects: PLOT, CHARACTER, THOUGHT, DICTION, MUSIC, and SPECTACLE. These might be considered as actual stages of play-writing: in working out the plot, the dramatist is determining the direction of character-development; in developing his characters, he is determining the kind of thought they will express in their speeches; and so on.

RAISONNEUR   (See CHORUS CHARACTER)

REALISM   Realism seeks to represent life and people as they are, or appear to be, through careful attention to details of costume, speech, and setting. As Tennessee Williams notes, realistic drama uses a "genuine frigidaire and authentic ice-cubes" and its characters "speak exactly as its audience speaks." But unlike naturalistic drama, it does not necessarily adhere to a deterministic philosophy.

REVERSAL   (PERIPETY)   Aristotle's term (*peripeteia*) referring to that part of a dramatic structure in which the protagonist's fortunes undergo a sudden and profound change. Insofar as the reversal is also a reversal of the protagonist's expectations, it should be viewed as a principle of *irony*. Aristotle believed that a reversal was best when it coincided with DISCOVERY; such a scheme is admirably carried out in *Oedipus Rex,* at the end of the fourth episode.

SPECTACLE   Aristotle used the word spectacle (*opsis*) to refer to the visual aspect of drama, and the term can be taken to include such elements as sets, props, costumes, and lighting. Aristotle demoted spectacle to last place among the six QUALITATIVE PARTS of drama, and warned the dramatist against excessive reliance on visual effects to carry the play's essential interest.

SOLILOQUY   A dramatic convention whereby a character talks to himself or to no one in particular; in effect, he thinks aloud. Longer and more complex than an ASIDE, a soliloquy reveals a character's inner conflicts, his reactions to an event or situation, or his motivations.

STOCK CHARACTER   A character type readily recognizable because of frequent use in the history of drama (especially in comedies), and because of conformity to type. In *The Misanthrope,* Molière exploits stock characters when he pictures Oronte, Acaste, and Clintandre as perfect fops. See CHARACTER.

STROPHE   The first "movement" of a Greek choric ode, delivered as the chorus moves from right to left in the acting area. See ANTISTROPHE.

THOUGHT   Aristotle's term (*dianoia*) for the "intellectual content" of the characters' speeches. In any drama like the Greek, in which violent physical actions take place off stage and are not presented directly, the ACTION necessarily forms itself around verbal encounters between the main characters; see AGON. Our assessments of the characters are therefore guided to a large extent by how well they argue and the kind of rhetoric they employ. In another sense, however, the term "thought" is often used to refer to the meaning or theme of a play.

TRAGIC FLAW   (See HAMARTIA)

TRAGEDY   A serious play, generally depicting a REVERSAL of fortune—from "happiness" to "misery"—of a man of moral worth (and usually of social stature). Partly through his own error (see HAMARTIA), the protagonist suffers defeat and brings adversity to others. But the "punishment" almost always seems in excess of the "crime"—and thus tragedy is the kind of drama most concerned with such philosophical questions as the meaning of life itself.

TURNING POINT   (See CRISIS)

WELL-MADE PLAY   A carefully plotted, neatly resolved, popular form of drama. The motivation of its characters is plausible but superficial. Originally championed by the French playwright Eugene Scribe (1791–1861), the well-made play is today the essential form of many TV dramas.

INDEX